W9-BEP-740

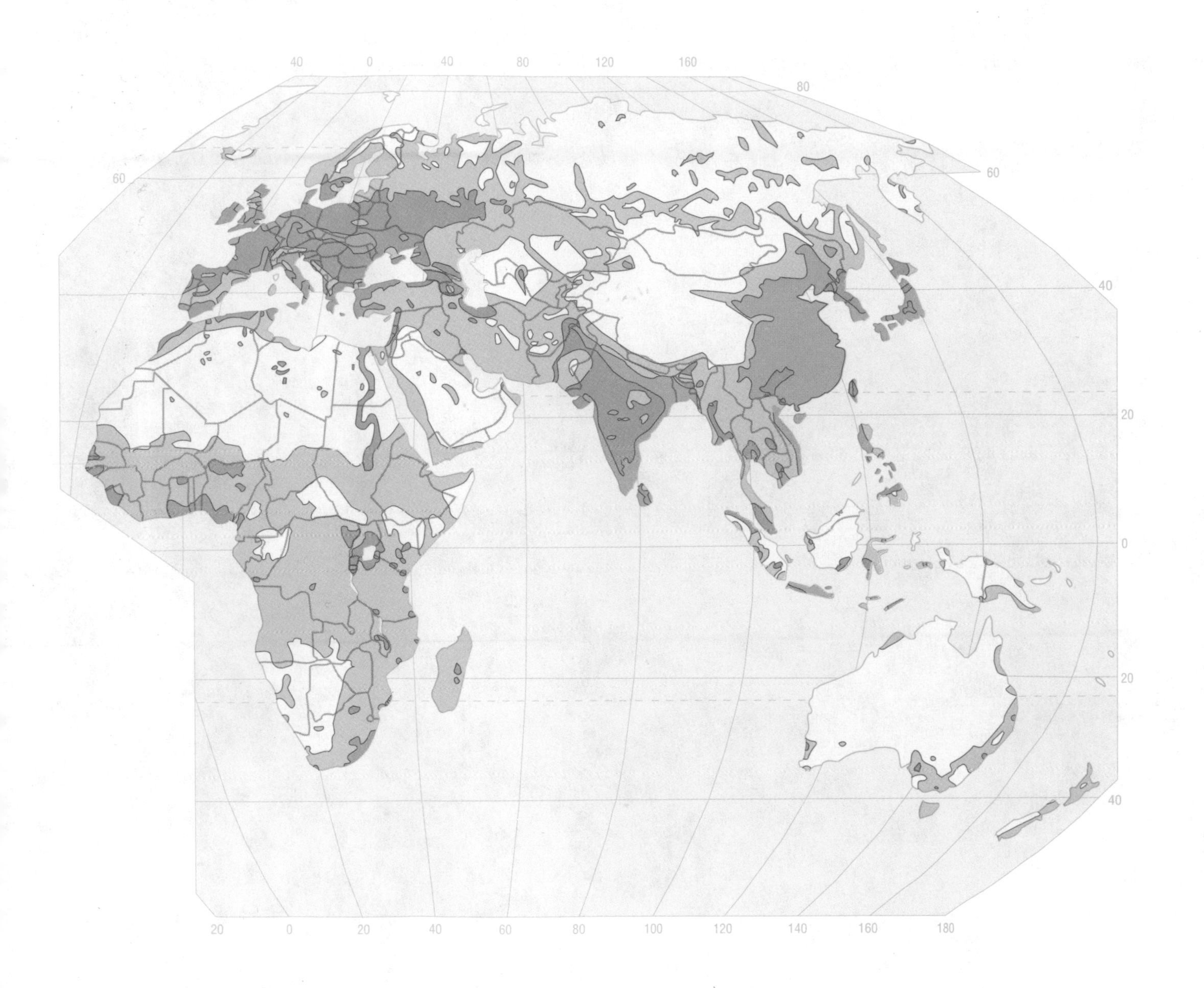
40
0
40
80
120
160
80
60
60
40
20
0
20
40
20
0
20
40
60
80
100
120
140
160
180

The Human Mosaic

The Human Mosaic

A Thematic Introduction to Cultural Geography

7TH EDITION

Terry G. Jordan
University of Texas at Austin

Mona Domosh
Florida Atlantic University

Lester Rowntree
San Jose University

An imprint of Addison Wesley Longman, Inc.

New York • Reading, Massachusetts • Menlo Park, California • Harlow, England
Don Mills, Ontario • Sydney • Mexico City • Madrid • Amsterdam

Executive Editor: Alan McClare
Developmental Editor: Phil Herbst
Project Coordination and Text Design: Ruttle, Shaw & Wetherill, Inc.
Cover Designer: John Callahan
Cover Photograph: Planet Art, The Stock Market
Art Studio/Cartographer: Maryland CartoGraphics
Photo Researcher: Carol Parden
Electronic Production Manager: Angel Gonzalez Jr.
Manufacturing Manager: Willie Lane
Electronic Page Makeup: Ruttle, Shaw & Wetherill, Inc.
Printer and Binder: R. R. Donnelley & Sons Company
Cover Printer: Phoenix Color Corp.

For permission to use copyrighted material, grateful acknowledgment is made to the copyright holders on pp. 537–538, which are hereby made part of this copyright page.

Library of Congress Cataloging-in-Publication Data
Jordan, Terry G.
The human mosaic : a thematic introduction to cultural geography / Terry G. Jordan, Mona Domosh, Lester Rowntree. — 7th ed.
p. cm.
Includes bibliographical references and index.
ISBN 0-673-99822-3
1. Human geography. I. Domosh, Mona, 1957– . II. Rowntree, Lester, 1938– . III. Title.
GF41.J67 1997
304.2--dc20 96-12329
CIP

ISBN 0-673-99822-3

345678910—DOW—999897

Contents

Major World Maps

Preface

The Human Mosaic, Seventh Edition, is built around five themes: **culture region, cultural diffusion, cultural ecology, cultural integration,** and **cultural landscape.** These five themes are introduced and explained in the first chapter and serve as the framework for the topical chapters that follow. The themes are applied to a variety of geographical topics: demography, agriculture, the city, religion, language, ethnicity, politics, industry, folklife, and popular culture. Students are able to relate to one of the five themes at every point in the text. We have found that beginning students learn best when provided with a precise framework, and the five themes provide that framework.

In our classroom experience we have found the thematic framework to be highly successful. Our culture region theme appeals to students' natural human curiosity about the differences among places. The dynamic aspect of culture—particularly relevant to this age of incessant and rapid change—is conveyed through the theme of cultural diffusion. Students acquire an appreciation for how cultural traits spread (or do not spread) from place to place. The topics employed to illustrate the concepts of diffusion include many that college students can quickly relate to—for example, country and western music, football, and migrations. Cultural ecology, also highly relevant in our age, addresses the complicated relationship between cultural and physical environment. Cultural integration permits students to view culture as an interrelated whole, in which one facet acts on and is acted on by other facets, a key to understanding our multicultural society. Last, the theme of cultural landscape heightens students' awareness of the visible expressions of different cultures.

New to the Seventh Edition

Our overriding goal for the seventh edition is to portray accurately the human geography of the world at the close of the century and millennium. We hope that the text will help students become constructive, informed citizens of the twenty-first century.

New and revised features in the seventh edition include:

- Updating of all statistics, with map and table revisions as necessary.
- Introduction of diverse new concepts, including gendered space, ecotheology, cyberspace, postmodernism, regional ethnic sub-

strates, machine space, mythical topography, fertility rate, and militarization of urban space.
- Wholly new sections on class, "race," and gender in the industrial city; cities of the Islamic world; feminist critiques of urban models; sexuality and gentrification; and the decline of public space.
- Thoroughly revised and rewritten sections on agricultural origins and diffusion, desertification, electoral geography, popular music, American sports, Asian migration to North America, and secularization.
- A completely revised Chapter 13 placing the subject of cultural geography in the larger context of academic and applied geography. The issue of jobs for geographers is addressed, including recent information on jobs held by graduates from geography programs across the nation.
- A completely new feature on using the Internet to explore geography. This box coaches students on using the different features of the Net to examine national and international geography department Web sites, bibliographic resources, and archives of data (including aerial photos and remote sensing) useful to geographers.
- More than 50 new figures, including both cartography and photographs.
- New, enhanced maps of world religions, American English dialects, AIDS diffusion, and numerous other topics.
- Updated reading lists at the ends of chapters, reflecting the latest findings and trends in cultural geography.
- Some old boxed readings have been cut from chapters. A few new ones have been added, offering fresh perspectives.

Learning Enhancements

The Human Mosaic, Seventh Edition, offers a variety of special learning devices to motivate and assist students:

- Boxes interspersed throughout the chapter narratives are of two types. Some are essays that elaborate on concepts presented in the chapter, presenting illustrative examples or relating studies of interest to the students. Other boxes are biographical, introducing students to famous personalities who contributed to the rise of the discipline.
- Figure captions are designed to stimulate critical thinking. Many captions ask questions intended to elicit a response or to heighten awareness of geographical facts or issues. Illustrations are included for their instructional value rather than as mere decoration.
- Extensive, updated lists of suggested readings appear at the end of each chapter. Of special value to motivated, interested students, these readings allow them to probe more deeply into cultural geography on their own.
- Key terms are boldfaced in text and immediately defined. These terms are also found in the glossary at the end of the book, which provides students with concise definitions.
- For students' reference, the map on the front endpaper gives the distribution of the religions of the world, and the back endpaper map shows the independent states of the world. A list of all major world maps can be found after the table of contents.

Supplements Package

The following supplementary items are available to accompany the seventh edition of *The Human Mosaic*. This support system includes printed materials, visual aids, and software, all carefully produced to enhance the teaching and learning environment.

- ***Instructor's Manual*** Written by A. Steele Becker of University of Nebraska, this manual includes chapter outlines, chapter overview material, student projects, resource lists, and a guide to integrating the transparency package with the chapter material.
- ***Student Study Guide*** Prepared by Michael Kukral, this study guide contains a chapter overview, study questions, and learning activities for each chapter. It places special emphasis on developing map-reading skills and challenges the student with critical thinking exercises. A highly integrated manual, the *Student Study Guide* supports and enhances the material covered in *The Human Mosaic* and guides the student to a clearer understanding of cultural geography.
- ***Test Package*** Prepared by Barbara Weightman of California State University–Fullerton, this Test Package contains more than 2500 multiple-choice, fill-in, and true-false questions, as well as essay and short-answer exercises that emphasize critical thinking.
- ***TestMaster*** The testbank is available on TestMaster for use with IBM or Macintosh computers.
- ***Transparencies*** Selected by Terry Jordan, the transparency package offers seventy-five full color maps and figures from the text.
- ***Slides*** A collection of one hundred original photographs prepared by Barbara Weightman. The slide package also includes a user's guide which helps to integrate the images with the text.

Acknowledgments

No textbook is ever written single-handedly (or even "triple-handedly"). An introductory text covering a wide range of topics must draw heavily on the research and help of others. In various chapters, we have not hesitated to mention a great many geographers on whose work we have drawn. We apologize for any misinterpretations or oversimplifications of their findings that may have resulted because of our own error or the limited space available.

Numerous geographers have contributed advice, comments, ideas, and assistance as this book moved from outline through draft to publication from the first edition on. We would like to thank particularly those colleagues who offered helpful comments in preparation for the seventh and earlier editions:

Christopher Airess—Ball State University
Nigel Allan—University of California–Davis
Nancy Bain—Ohio University
Cecelia Hudleson—Foothill College
Gregory Jean—Samford University
Michael Kukral—Ohio University
William Laatsch—University of Wisconsin–Green Bay
Ann Legreid—Central Missouri State University
Ronald Lockmann—California State University–Dominiquez Hills
Wayne McKim—Towson State University

Douglas Meyer—Eastern Illinois University
Klaus Meyer-Arendt—Mississippi State University
John Milbauer—Northeastern State University
Don Mitchell—University of Colorado
Brian Osborne—Queen's University
Kenji Oshiro—Wright State University
Robert Rundstrom—University of Oklahoma
Andrew Schoolmaster III—University of North Texas
Philip Wagner—Simon Fraser State University
Barbara Weightman—California State University–Fullerton
David Wilkins—University of Utah
Douglas Wilms—East Carolina State University

Our thanks also go to various members, past and present, of Longman, whose encouragement, skills, and suggestions have created a special working environment and to whom we express our deepest gratitude. In particular, thanks go to Developmental Editor Phil Herbst, whose perceptive and sensitive editing helped smooth the ripples caused by seven editions and three authors; Executive Editor Bonnie Roesch, whose support and assistance during two editions have been essential; and Senior Editor Alan McClare, who provided good counsel and expedited the edition in diverse ways. Bonnie and Alan are due our special thanks for promoting and nurturing geography at Longman. All are professionals in the best sense of the word. Thanks are also due to research assistants Alyson Greiner and Jennifer Helzer, both of whom held the position of Webb Fellow. The beneficial influence of all these people can be detected on every page.

Terry Jordan
Mona Domosh
Lester Rowntree

About the Authors

Terry Jordan is the Walter Prescott Webb Professor in the Department of Geography at the University of Texas at Austin. He earned his PhD at the University of Wisconsin at Madison. A specialist in the cultural and historical geography of the United States, Jordan is particularly interested in the diffusion of Old World culture to North America that helped produce the vivid geographic mosaic evident today. He served as president of the Association of American Geographers in 1987–1988 and earlier received an Honors Award from that organization. He has written on a wide range of American cultural topics, including forest colonization, cattle ranching, folk architecture, and ethnicity. His scholarly books include *The Mountain West: Interpreting the Folk Landscape* (with Jon Kilpinen and Charles Gritzner, 1997), *North American Cattle Ranching Frontiers* (1993), *The American Backwoods Frontier* (with Matti Kaups, 1989), *American Log Buildings* (1985), *Texas Graveyards* (1982), *Trails to Texas: Southern Roots of Western Cattle Ranching* (1981), and *German Seed in Texas Soil* (1966). Having been fascinated with maps and landscapes since childhood, Jordan became a geography major during his college freshman year. For him, the most rewarding aspect of geography has been field research. His only hobby is travel.

Mona Domosh is an associate professor of geography in the College of Liberal Arts at Florida Atlantic University. She earned her PhD at Clark University. Her research and writing concentrate on two general areas: the historical and cultural geography of large American cities, and feminist geography, particularly the intersection of feminist theory and the history of geographic knowledge. Domosh's interest in bringing together these different research agendas has led to her examination of how the symbolic categories of feminine and masculine were used to define and shape the nineteenth-century city. She has written *Invented Cities: The Creation of Landscape in Nineteenth Century New York and Boston* (1996).

Lester Rowntree lives in Berkeley, California, where he is a professor of geography and the director of the Environmental Studies program at San Jose State University. In addition, he is a research associate at the University of California at Berkeley. His PhD (1971) is in geography from the University of Oregon, where he concentrated on both physical and cultural geography to explore the questions and problems of human impact on the environment. Along with teaching, three different research projects currently occupy him: environmental problems and ecological change in the San Francisco bay region; deforestation in southern Mexico; and an interdisciplinary study of prehistory environmental change and human settlement after the last glaciation in the French Pyrenees. Additionally, Rowntree serves on several civic panels and commissions that address environmental problems in the San Francisco bay area. In 1992–1993, he was president of the Association of Pacific Coast Geographers. His hobbies are sailing, windsurfing, rowing, hiking, and mountain biking.

The Human Mosaic

CHAPTER 1

The Nature of Cultural Geography

Geography is the science of place. Its vision is grand, its view panoramic. It sweeps the surface of the Earth, charting the physical, organic and cultural terrains, their areal differentiation, and their ecological dynamics with humankind. Its foremost tool is the map.

Leonard Krishtalka

Carnegie Museum of Natural History

Humans are, by nature, geographers. We possess an awareness of and curiosity about the distinctive character of places and can think territorially or spatially; these attributes encompass the essential geographical qualities and dimensions. As a result, even nongeographers such as Leonard Krishtalka often possess a fundamentally accurate idea of what geography involves. Children, too, possess these qualities of geographers. They create carefully mapped realms in tiny spaces—rooms, backyards, neighborhoods (see box, *Sizing Up the World*). As we grow, our concepts of spatial relationships change constantly, retaining a partially magical quality. Always beyond what we have explored lies the unknown, the mysterious lands that we often populate with our hopes and fears. Places possess an emotional quality and significance that contribute profoundly to our identity as individual human beings—we all must belong some*where* to be complete persons. Geography as an academic discipline is an outgrowth of both our insatiable curiosity about lands other than our own and our need to come to grips with the place-centered element within our souls.

This natural curiosity and intrinsic need were long ago reinforced by pragmatism, by the practical motives of traders and empire builders, who wanted information about the world for the purposes of commerce and conquest. Such a concern for the practical aspects of geography first arose among the ancient Greeks, Romans, Mesopotamians, and Phoenicians, the greatest traders and empire builders of their time. They cataloged factual information on locations, places, and products. Indeed, *geography* is a Greek word meaning literally "to describe the earth." Not content, however, merely to chart and describe the world, these ancient geographers soon began to ask questions about *why* cultures and environments differ from place to place. By the end of the Roman era, geographers had developed theories of a spherical Earth, latitudinal climate zones, environmental influences on humans, and people's role in modifying the Earth.

Centuries later, during Europe's Dark Ages, a newly expanding Arab empire took over academic geography. Muslim scholars, following in the wake of trade and conquest as their Greek and Roman predecessors did, further expanded geographical knowledge. These Arab geographers were great travelers who wandered from China to Spain in search of new knowledge. Although they tended to be even more practical than the Greeks and Romans, they did not entirely ignore the explanatory side of learning. For example, Arab geographers proposed theories about the evolution of mountain ranges.

With the European cultural reawakening known as the Renaissance and the beginning of the Age of Discovery, the center of geographical learning shifted again to Europe. The modern scientific study of geography arose in Germany during the time European power was slowly spreading over much of the globe. In the 1700s, the Germans came to view **geography** as the study of interrelated *spatial* patterns—that is, describing and explaining the differences and similarities between one region and another. If every place on Earth were identical, we would not need geography.

When geographers consider the differences and similarities between places, they want to understand what they see. They first find out exactly what the variation between the areas is by describing differences and similarities as precisely as possible. Then they interpret the

Sizing Up the World: The Maps Children Draw

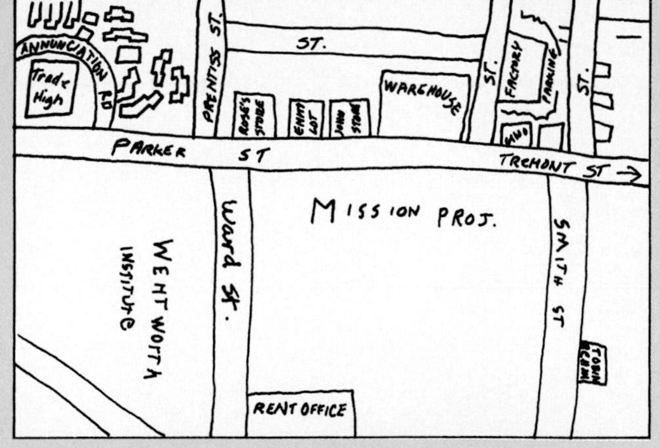

"In the Mission Hill area of Boston, Florence Ladd asked a number of black children to draw a map of their area, and tape-recorded her conversation with them. On Dave's map, the Mission Hill project is where the white children live, and he has drawn it as the largest, completely blank area on his map. From his taped conversation it is clear that he is physically afraid of the area and has never ventured near it. On his map the white residential area is literally *terra incognita,* while all the detail on the map is immediately around his home and school on the other side of Parker Street. Ernest also puts in Parker Street dividing his area from the white Mission [Hill] project, and uses about a quarter of his sheet of paper to emphasize, quite unconsciously, the width of this psychological barrier. Both of these boys going to the local neighborhood schools have never ventured across this barrier to the unknown area beyond."

From Gould, Peter, and Rodney White, *Mental Maps.* Baltimore: Penguin, 1974, pp. 31–33. Maps from Ladd, F. "A Note on 'The World Across the Street.'" *Harvard School of Education Association Bulletin,* 12 (1967): 47–48.

data and decide what forces made these two areas different or alike. This process merely reflects the basic human curiosity that makes us all geographers. No one needs special training to wonder why things are where they are, and that is the geographer's question. Geographers ask What? Where? and Why? This type of analytical geographical research was begun in the nineteenth century by the German geographers Alexander von Humboldt and Carl Ritter (see biographical sketches), who are generally recognized as the founders of modern geography.

Alexander Von Humboldt
1769–1859

Humboldt, a world-famous German scientist, traveled widely and wrote extensively on geographical topics. In 1797, with the permission of the Spanish crown, he sailed to South America. For the next five years, he explored from Mexico to the Andes. Later, at the age of 60, he accepted an invitation from the czar of Russia to explore mineral resources. He traveled by carriage through Siberia, carefully recording and describing the landscape. His interests lay in physical geography—the study of climate, terrain, and vegetation—but Humboldt's writings reveal his belief that humans are part of the ecological system. His main contribution to geography was his attention to cause-and-effect relationships. Most geographies of earlier times merely compiled facts. When Humboldt tried to explain spatial patterns of certain physical phenomena, he found geography useful. Because he brought the prestige and methods of science to geography, he is considered one of the founders of modern geography. Humboldt never held a university position, but he was widely respected as a scholar. His most important geographical publication was ***Cosmos,*** a five-volume work. (For more on Humboldt's life and achievements, see McIntyre, Loren. "Humboldt's Way." ***National Geographic,*** 168 (1985): 318–351.)

What Is Cultural Geography?

As its name implies, **cultural geography** forms one part of the discipline, complementing *physical* geography, the part of the discipline that deals with the natural environment. To understand the scope of cultural geography, we must first agree on the meaning of **culture**.

Social scientists and humanists have suggested many definitions of culture, some broad and some narrow. Furthermore, even within some disciplines not all scholars agree on a common definition. For our purposes, we will define culture as *learned collective human behavior*, as opposed to instinctive, or inborn, behavior. These learned traits form a way of life held in common by a group of people. Learned similarities in speech, behavior, ideology, livelihood, technology, value system, and society bind people together. Culture involves a communication system of acquired beliefs, perceptions, and attitudes that serves to supplement and channel instinctive behavior. In short, as geographer Yi-Fu Tuan has said, culture is the "local, customary way of doing things; geographers write about ways of life."

Cultural geography, then, is the study of spatial variations among cultural groups and the spatial functioning of society. It focuses on describing and analyzing the ways language, religion, economy, government, and other cultural phenomena vary or remain constant from one place to another and on explaining how humans function spatially (Figure 1.1). Cultural geography is, at heart, a celebration of human diversity.

In seeking explanations for spatial cultural diversity, geographers must consider a wide array of causal factors. Some of these involve the

Figure 1.1
Two traditional houses of worship. Geographers seek to learn how and why cultures differ, or are similar, from one place to another. Often those differences and similarities have a visual expression. In what ways are these two structures—one a rural Lutheran church in the treeless tundra of Iceland and the other a Greek Orthodox chapel amid the olive groves of Crete—alike and different?

Carl Ritter
1779–1859

Ritter, a longtime and close associate of Alexander von Humboldt, was a professor of geography at the University of Berlin beginning in 1820. He began his career as a tutor for a wealthy family in Frankfurt. In these comfortable surroundings, he was able to meet other intellectuals and study geography. During the long period he taught in Berlin, his work influenced the thinking of many people, including military leaders. In contrast to Humboldt, his chief concern was cultural geography, the geography of humans. He sought to bring the rigor of science to the study of human geography and believed that laws of human spatial behavior could be discovered. His first book discussed Africa, then a little-known continent, but he is best known for the massive work entitled ***Die Erdkunde*** [***Geography***], which appeared in 19 volumes between 1822 and his death. Ritter is widely regarded as a cofounder, with Humboldt, of the academic discipline of geography.

physical environment—terrain, climate, natural vegetation, wildlife, variations in soil, and the pattern of land and water. We cannot understand culture removed from its physical habitat. For this reason, cultural geography offers not only a spatial perspective but also an ecological one. One of the distinctive attributes of geography is the way it bridges the social and earth sciences, in order to study people in their habitats. For this reason, geographers tend to resist the increasing fragmentation of learning into highly specialized, segregated academic disciplines. We seek an integrative view of humankind in its physical environment, rather than a specialized, fragmented perspective. Mainly for this reason, geography appears less focused than most other disciplines and is more difficult to define.

Geography offers no easy explanations for cultural phenomena, because very complex causal forces are at work. Things are interconnected in very complicated ways. The complexity of the forces that affect culture can be illustrated by an example drawn from agricultural geography: the distribution of wheat cultivation in the world. Looking at Figure 1.2, you can see important wheat cultivation in Australia but not Africa, in the United States but not Brazil, in China but not Southeast Asia. Why does this spatial pattern exist? Partly it results from environmental factors such as climate, terrain, and soils. Some regions have always been too dry for wheat cultivation, others too steep or infertile. Indeed, there is a strong correlation between wheat cultivation and mid-latitude climates, level terrain, and good soil.

Still, do not place a determinant importance on such physical factors. People can modify the effects of climate through irrigation, the use of hothouses, or the development of new, specialized strains of wheat. They can conquer slopes through terracing, and they can make poor soils productive through fertilization. For example, farmers in mountainous parts of Greece wrest an annual harvest of wheat from tiny, terraced plots where soil has been trapped behind hand-built stone retaining walls. Even in the United States, environmental factors alone cannot explain the curious fact that major wheat cultivation is concentrated in the semiarid Great Plains, some distance from states such as Ohio and Illinois, where the climate for growing wheat is better.

The cultural geographer knows that wheat has to survive in a cultural as well as a physical environment. Agricultural patterns cannot be explained by the characteristics of the land and climate alone. Many factors complicate the distribution of wheat, including people's tastes, desires, and traditions. Food preferences and taboos, often backed by religious beliefs, strongly influence the choice of crops to plant. Some cultural groups, such as the Poles, prefer dark bread made from rye flour. Other groups, particularly Native Americans, would rather eat breads made from corn. Obviously, wheat will not "thrive" in such cultural environments. Where wheat bread *is* preferred, people are willing to put great efforts into overcoming hostile physical surroundings. They have even created new strains of wheat, thereby decreasing the environment's influence on distribution. Wheat cultivation can also be encouraged or discouraged by tariffs like those protecting the wheat farmers of Germany and other European Union countries from competition with more efficient American and Canadian producers. In addition, wheat farming is a less profitable use of the land than dairying or fattening livestock. For this and other reasons, wheat is sometimes not grown in the most suitable regions, such as the American Midwest.

This is by no means a complete list of the forces that affect wheat

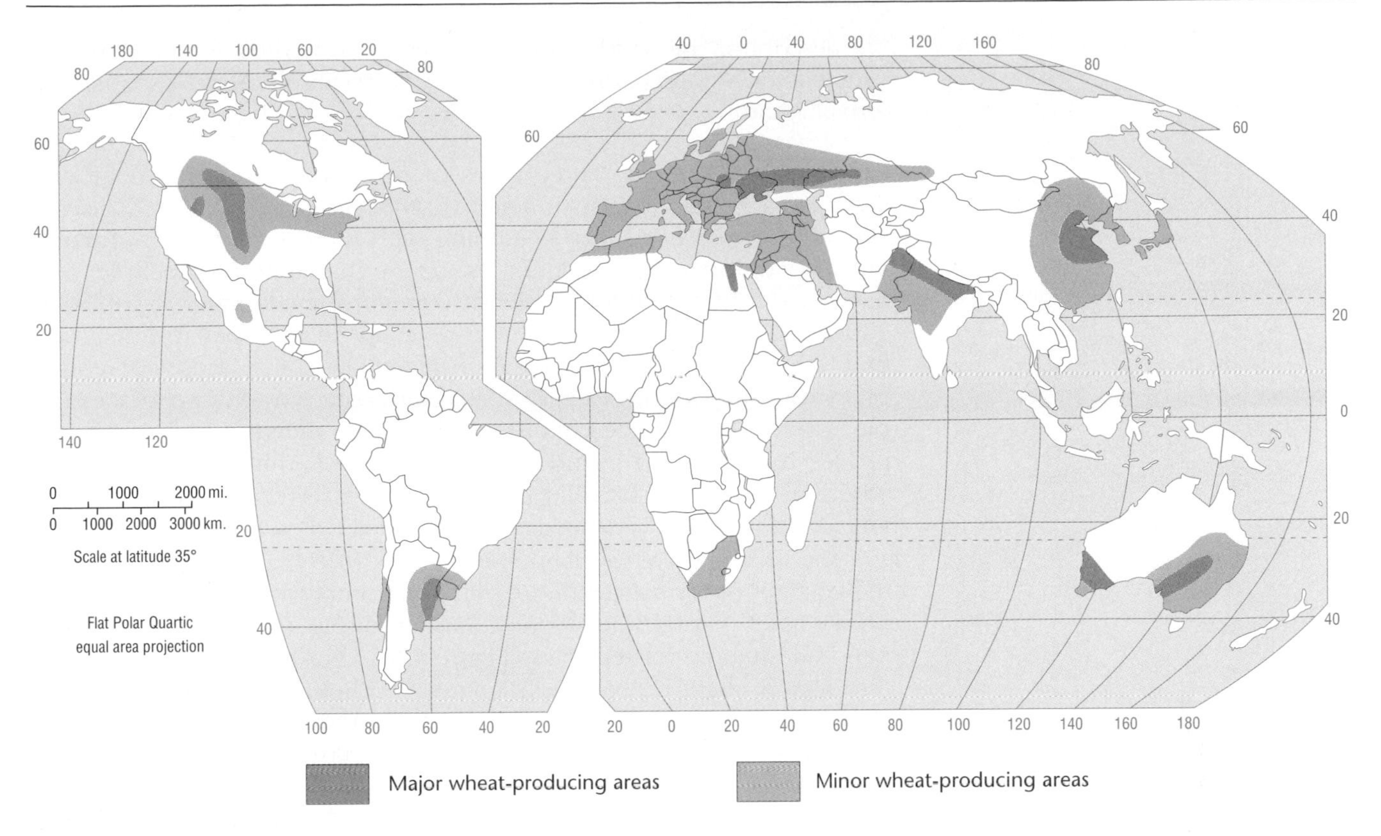

Figure 1.2
Areas of wheat production in the world. These culture regions are based on a single trait—the importance of wheat in the agricultural system.

distribution. It should be clear, though, that the contemporary map of wheat reflects the pushing and pulling of many factors. The distribution of all cultural elements, not only the distribution of wheat, is a result of such constant interplay of diverse causal factors. Cultural geography is the discipline that seeks such explanations.

Themes in Cultural Geography

Our study of cultures is organized around five geographical concepts or themes: *culture region, cultural diffusion, cultural ecology, cultural integration, and cultural landscape.* These themes are stressed throughout the book, giving structure to each chapter.

Culture Region

Places provide the main stuff of geography. How and why are places alike or different? How are they meshed together into functioning spatial networks? How do their inhabitants perceive and identify with them? These are all essential geographical questions. **Region** is the word and concept used by geographers to mean a grouping of like places or the functional union of places to form a spatial unit. A **culture region,** then, is a geographical unit based in *human* traits.

Maps provide an essential tool for describing and revealing regions. If, as is often said, one picture is worth a thousand words, then a well-prepared map is worth at least ten thousand words to the geographer.

No description in words can rival a map's revealing force. Maps are valuable tools particularly because they so concisely portray spatial patterns in culture.

Formal Culture Regions. Three types of regions are recognized by cultural geographers: formal, functional, and vernacular. We will discuss each one of these in turn, beginning with the formal type. A **formal culture region** can be defined as an area inhabited by people who have one or more cultural traits in common. If cultural geography is, above all, a celebration of human diversity in the spatial dimension, then the formal culture region is a depiction of that mosaic. Geographers use this tool to describe spatial differences in culture. For example, a German-language culture region can be drawn on a map of languages, and it would include the area where German is spoken. Or a wheat-farming region could describe the parts of the world where wheat is a major crop (look again at Figure 1.2).

The examples of German speech and wheat cultivation represent the concept of formal culture region at its simplest level. Each is based on a single cultural trait. More commonly, formal culture regions depend on multiple related traits (Figure 1.3). Thus an Inuit (Eskimo) culture region might be based on language, religion, economy, social organization, and type of dwellings. The culture region would reflect the spatial distribution of these five Inuit cultural traits. Districts in which all five of these traits are present would be part of the culture region. A more complex culture, such as that of Europe, can be subdivided into several multitrait regions (Figure 1.4).

Formal culture regions are the geographer's somewhat arbitrary creations. No two cultural traits have the same distribution, and the territorial extent of a culture region depends on what defining traits are used (Figure 1.5). For example, Greeks and Turks differ in language and religion. Culture regions defined on the basis of speech and religious faith would separate these two groups. However, Greeks and Turks hold many other cultural traits in common. Both groups are monotheistic, worshipping a single god. In both groups, male supremacy and patriarchal families are the rule. Certain folk foods, such as shish kebab, are enjoyed in common. Whether Greeks and Turks are

Figure 1.3
A market in the highlands of Papua New Guinea. Various facets of a multitrait formal culture region are apparent here. Agricultural products, marketing, architecture, and clothing all contribute to the region's identity.

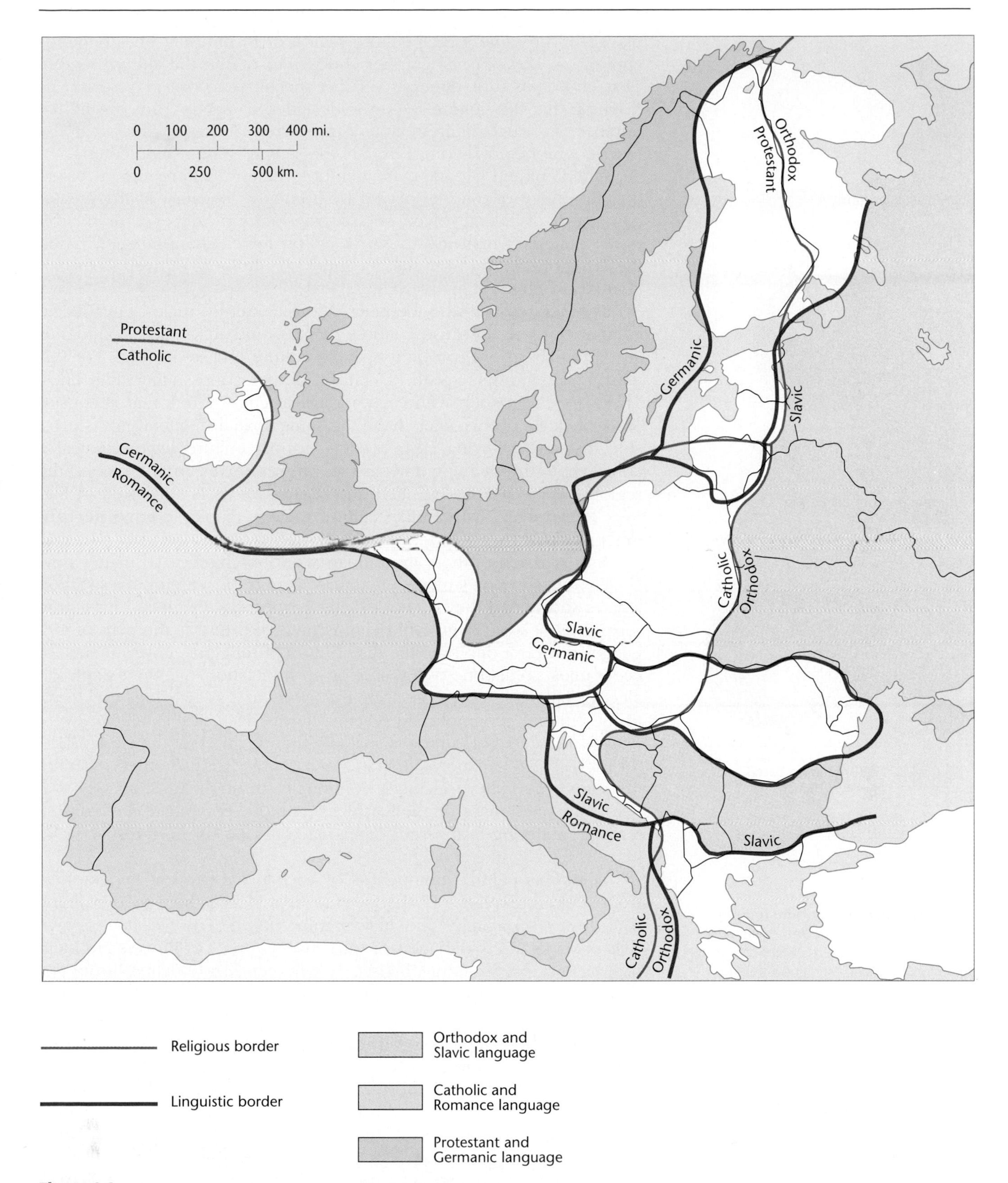

Religious border

Linguistic border

Orthodox and Slavic language

Catholic and Romance language

Protestant and Germanic language

Figure 1.4
Two-trait formal culture regions of Europe. This is based on language and traditional religion. Notice how transitional areas appear between such culture regions even when only two traits are used to define them.

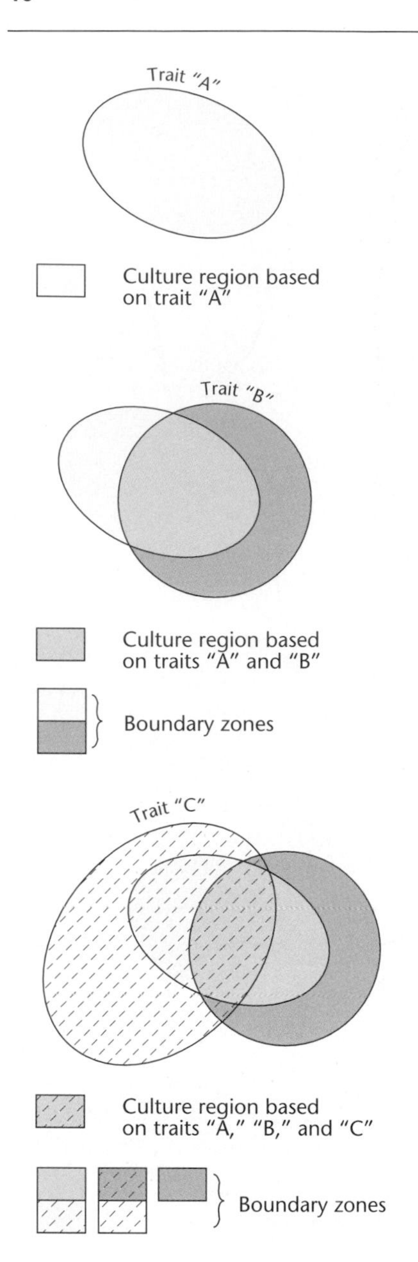

Figure 1.5
Hypothetical formal culture regions based on one, two, and three traits. Notice that no two traits have the same spatial distribution. With each additional trait, the core of the region grows smaller and the boundary zone broader.

placed in the same formal culture region or in different ones depends entirely on how the geographer chooses to define the culture region. That choice in turn depends on the specific purpose of research or teaching that the culture region is designed to serve. Thus an infinite number of formal culture regions can be created. It is unlikely that any two geographers would use exactly the same distinguishing criteria.

Often cultural geographers attempt to delimit culture regions based on the totality of traits displayed by a culture. Because of the greater complexity of traits involved, such regions are typically even more arbitrarily delimited than are those based on fewer characteristics. Often these regions spring from the geographer's intuition, derived from intimate knowledge of an area (Figure 1.6).

The geographer who identifies a formal culture region must locate cultural borders. Because cultures overlap and mix, such boundaries are rarely sharp, even if only a single culture trait is mapped. For this reason, geographers speak of cultural border zones rather than lines. These zones broaden with each additional cultural trait that is considered, because no two traits have the same spatial distribution. As a result, instead of having clear borders, formal culture regions reveal a core, where the defining traits are all present. Away from the core, the regional characteristics weaken and disappear, as is suggested in Figures 1.4 and 1.5. Thus formal culture regions display a **core/periphery** pattern.

In a real sense, then, the human world is chaotic. No matter how closely related two elements of culture seem to be, careful investigation always shows that they do not exactly cover the same area. This is true regardless of what degree of detail is involved. Just as the map of languages does not duplicate the distribution of religions, governments, or economies, so also no two words or pronunciations within a single dialect or language cover precisely the same area. What does this mean to the cultural geographer in practical terms? First, it tells us that every feature and detail of culture is spatially unique and that the explanation for each spatial variation differs in some degree from all others. Second, it means that culture changes continually through an area, and that every inhabited place on the Earth has a unique combination of cultural features, differing from every other place in one or more respects. No place is exactly like another.

Does this cultural uniqueness of each place prevent geographers from seeking explanatory theories? Does it doom them to explaining each locale separately? The answer must be no. The fact that no two hills or rocks, no two planets or stars, no two trees or flowers are identical has not prevented geologists, astronomers, and botanists from formulating theories and explanations based on generalizations.

Functional Culture Regions. A **functional culture region** is different from a formal culture region. The hallmark of the formal type is cultural homogeneity, and the formal culture region is abstract rather than concrete. By contrast, the functional culture region is generally not culturally homogeneous. Instead, it is an area that has been organized to function politically, socially, or economically. A city, an independent state, a precinct, a church diocese or parish, a trade area, a farm, and a Federal Reserve Bank district are all examples of functional regions. Functional culture regions have **nodes,** or central points where the functions are coordinated and directed. Examples of such nodes are city halls, national capitals, precinct voting places, parish churches, factories, and banks. In this sense, functional regions

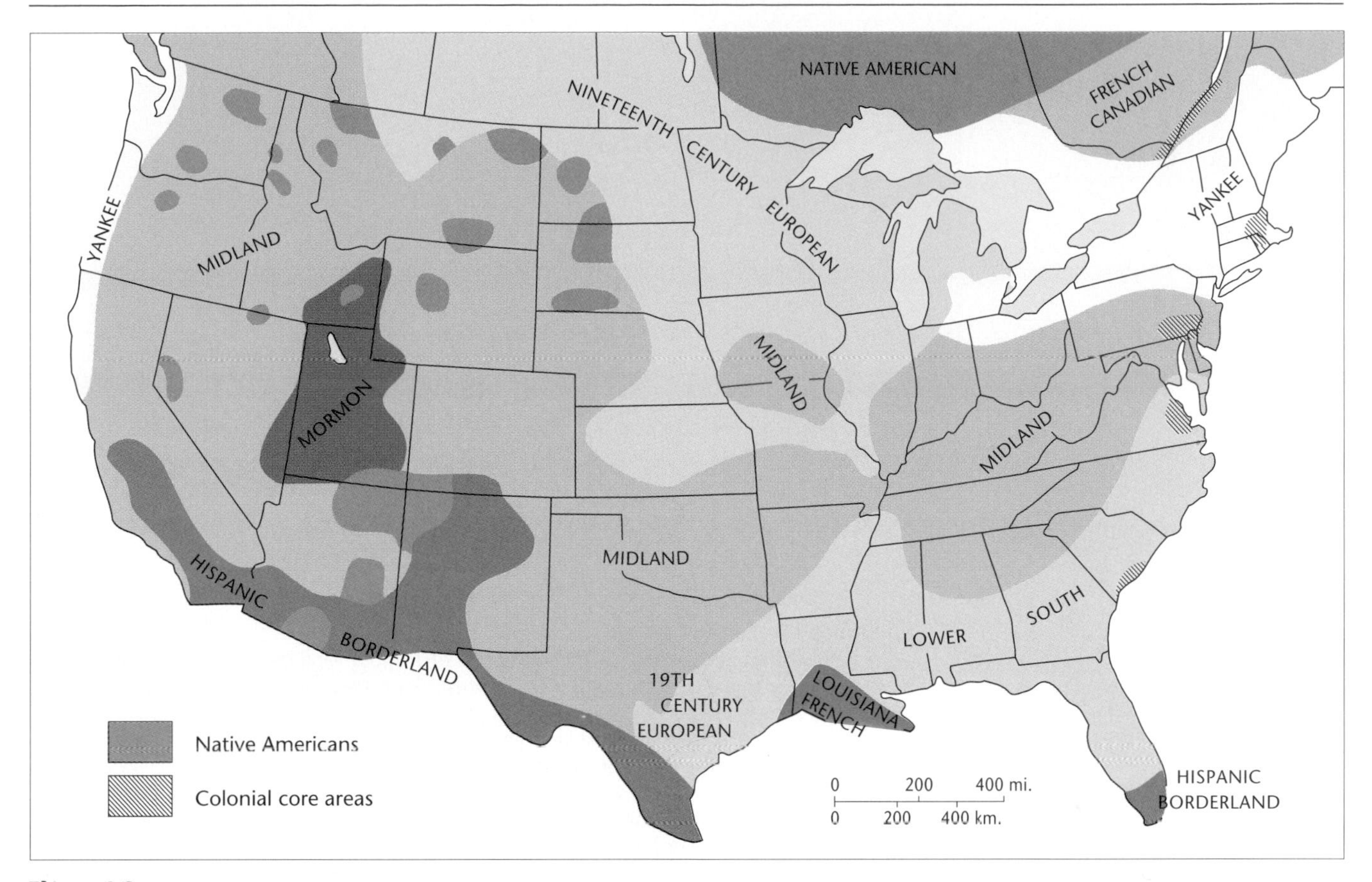

Figure 1.6
Traditional rural formal cultural regions of North America. An attempt was made to consider a totality of traits in drawing the borders, making the delimitation by necessity highly subjective. Really, it is one geographer's intuitive map. The ***Yankee*** region was originally settled by colonists largely from England in the period before American independence. Marginal success in farming caused many colonists to turn to fishing, trading, manufacturing, and lumbering as occupations. In contrast, the ***Midland*** culture area embraced a great variety of ethnic groups. English, Scotch-Irish, Germans, Dutch, Swedes, Finns, Welsh, and other European groups met and mingled here, importing rich and diverse agricultural heritages into a fertile land. The middle-class family farm was instituted here. The result was a farming culture that shaped the face of much of the rural United States from then on. In the ***Lower South,*** British, French, Caribbean, and African traits were combined in a plantation system of agriculture. Large estates, specializing in subtropical cash crops and depending on slave laborers, gave rise to a landed aristocracy that assumed political control of the plantation colonies. The other culture areas on the map also developed uniquely, formed by diverse cultural groups in particular environmental and temporal settings.

also possess a core/periphery configuration, in common with formal culture regions.

Many functional regions have clearly defined borders. A family farm is a functional region that includes all land owned or leased by the farmer (Figure 1.7). Its operation is directed by the farmer, who has organized the land to function as a distinct spatial unit. The node is the farmstead, which contains the home and various structures essential to farming, such as barns, implement sheds, and silos. The borders of this functional region will probably be clearly marked by fences, hedges, or walls. Similarly, each state in the United States and each Canadian province is a functional region, coordinated and directed from a capital and extending government control over a fixed area with clearly defined borders.

Not all functional culture regions have fixed, precise borders, however. A good example is a daily newspaper's circulation area. The node

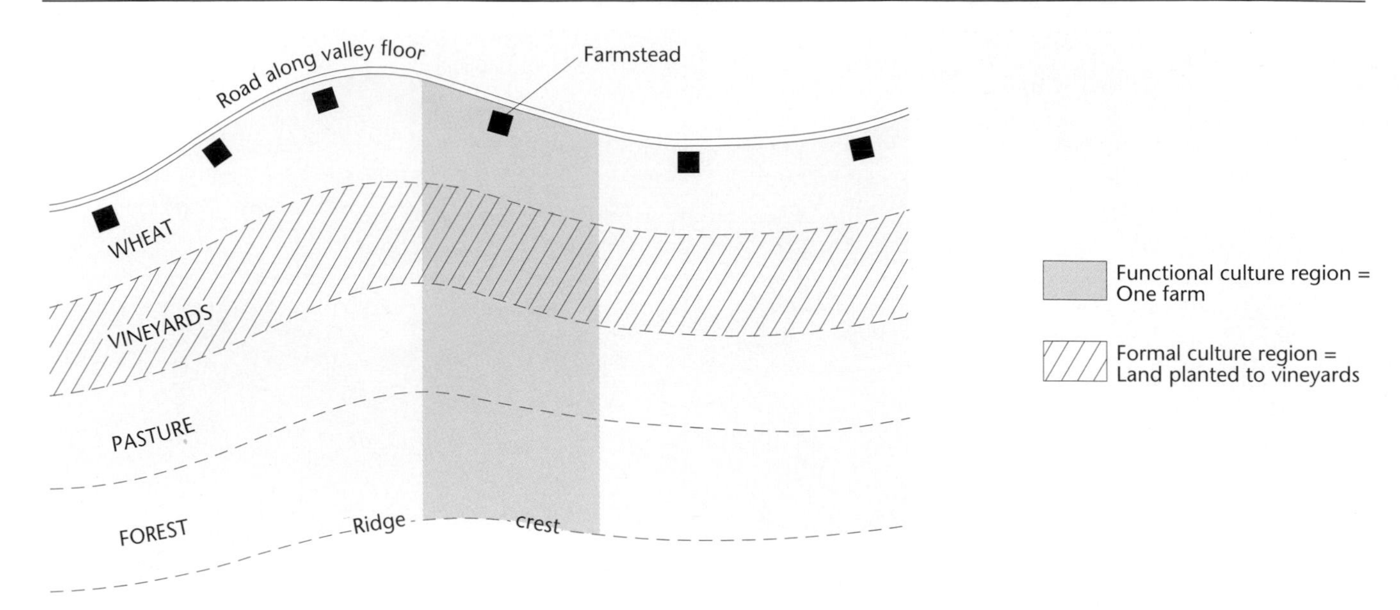

Figure 1.7
A valley filled with farms. Each farm consists of a strip of land reaching from the center of the valley up to the adjacent ridge crest (see map). Farmsteads are at the fronts of the farms, along a road that bisects the valley. On each, the slope of the land becomes steeper as we go away from the road. On the most level land, at the front of each farm, wheat is raised, and with the steadily increasing slope toward the rear of each farm, we encounter vineyards, then pastures, and finally, on the steepest slopes at the rear of the farm, forest. Thus each farm consists of wheat fields, vineyards, pastures, and woodland with increasing distance from the road. Each of these types of land use occupies a continuous strip running lengthwise through the valley. In this situation, both formal and functional culture regions are present. Each farm constitutes a functional culture region, and the strips of wheat, vineyards, pasture, and woodland are each formal culture regions, defined by the homogeneity of land use.

for the paper would be the plant where it is produced. Every morning, trucks move out of the plant to distribute the paper throughout the city. The newspaper may have a sales area extending into the city's suburbs, local bedroom communities, nearby towns, and rural areas. There its sales area overlaps the sales territories of competing newspapers published in other cities. It would be futile to try to define borders for such a process. How would you draw a sales area boundary for the *New York Times?* Its Sunday edition is sold in some quantity even in California, thousands of miles from its node.

The sales areas for manufactured goods present similar problems. Every time you buy a soft drink or a beer, you are part of a functional culture region. Some beer manufacturers have gone nationwide in their marketing, establishing branch breweries in various parts of the country. Schlitz, Budweiser, and Pabst are in this category. Certain others confine sales activity to selected multistate regions, and some, such as Lone Star of Texas, are marketed largely within a single state. Finally, some beers, like Pittsburgh's Iron City brand, are sold in small local areas. Each beer has a unique market area—a functional region—and these often overlap one another. The node for each beer's functional area is the brewery.

Functional culture regions generally do not coincide spatially with formal culture regions, and this disjuncture often creates problems for the functional region. Germany provides an example (Figure 1.8). As an independent state, Germany forms a functional culture region. Language provides a substantial basis for political unity, though the formal culture region of the German language extends beyond the political

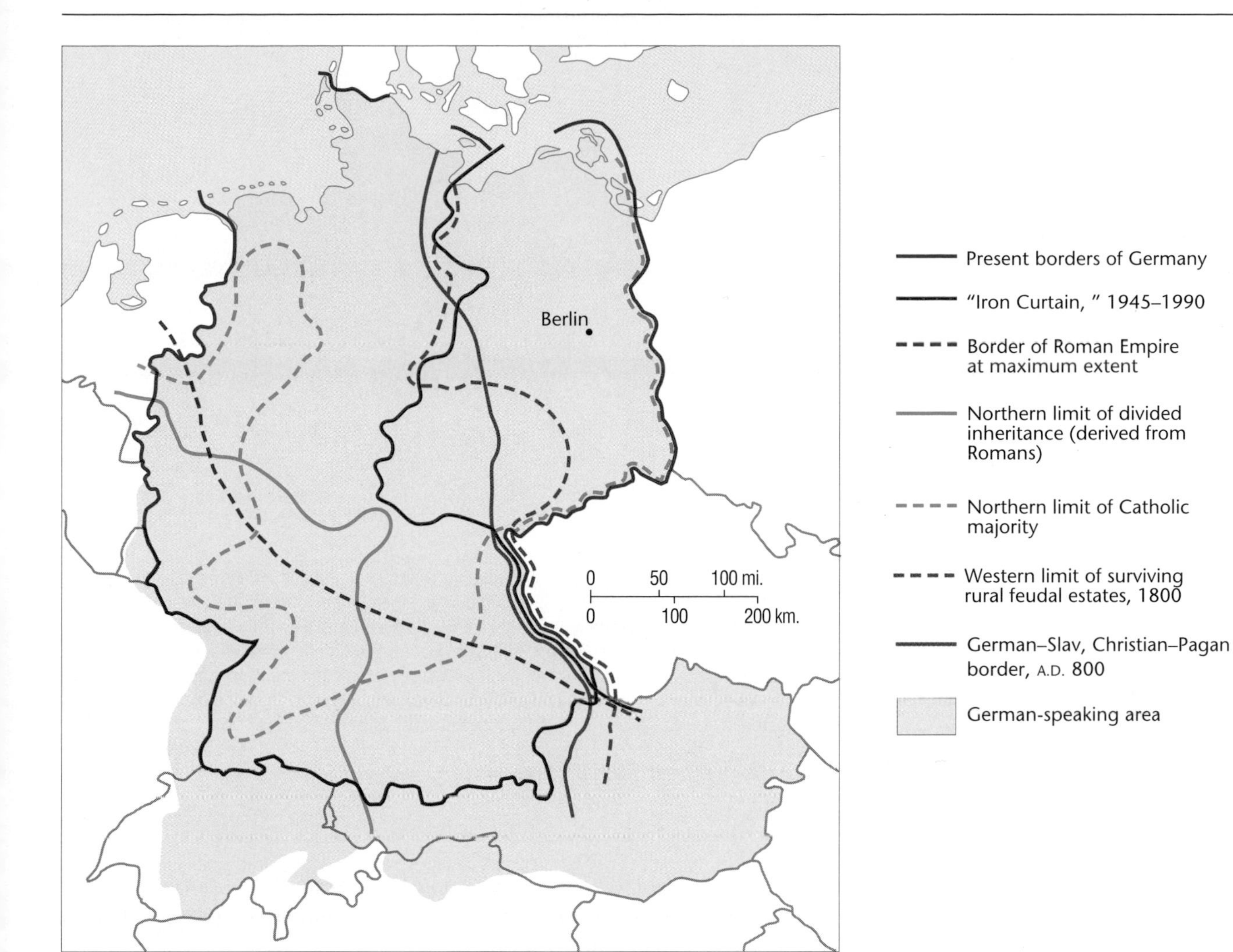

Figure 1.8
East versus west in Germany. As a political unit and functional culture region, Germany must overcome the disruptions caused by numerous formal culture regions that tend to make eastern and western Germany culturally different. Formal and functional culture regions rarely coincide spatially.

borders of Germany and includes part or all of eight other independent states. More important, numerous formal culture regions have borders cutting through German territory, and some of these have endured for millennia, causing differences between eastern and western Germany. These contrasts make the functioning of the German state more difficult and help explain why Germany more often has been politically fragmented than unified.

Vernacular Culture Regions. Geographers recognize a third type of culture region, the **vernacular.** This is a region *perceived* to exist by its inhabitants, as evidenced by the widespread acceptance and use of a special regional name. Figure 1.9 reveals one such popular region in the United States, "Dixie." Some vernacular regions are based on physical environmental features, while others find their basis in economic, political, historical, or promotional aspects. Vernacular regions, like most culture regions, generally lack sharp borders, and the inhabitants of any given area may claim residence in more than one such region. They vary in scale from city neighborhoods to sizable parts of conti-

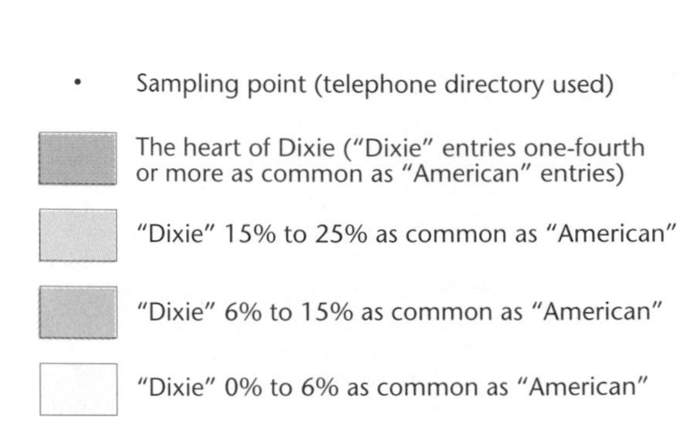

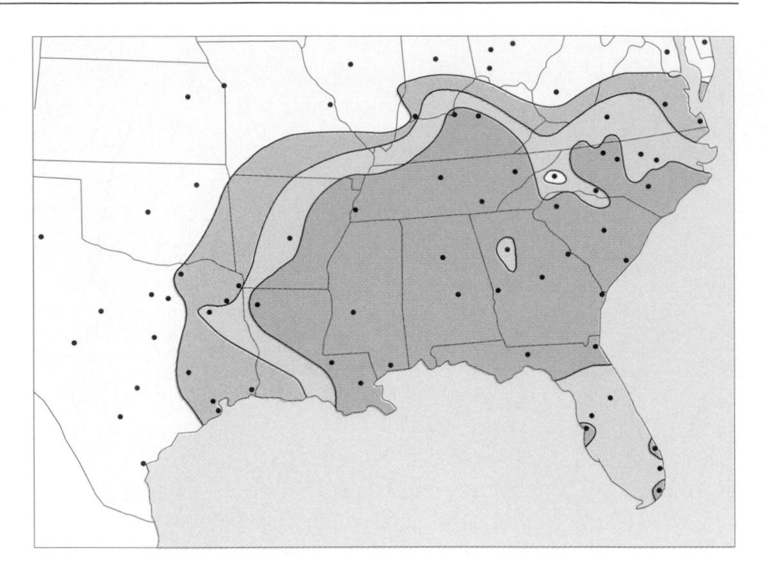

Figure 1.9
Dixie: a vernacular region. "Dixie" is loaded with historical and cultural connotations. The territorial extent of "Dixie" was determined by counting the number of times it appeared in telephone directories as part of the name of business establishments. The total for each city was then divided by the entries for "American," to adjust for the different population sizes of the cities, producing the numbers on the map. The higher the number, the more common the use of "Dixie." Make a count of regional terms in your telephone directory. Does the place where you live lie within a vernacular region such as Dixie? How does the perceived "Dixie" compare to the formal region "Lower South" in Figure 1.6? (After Reed, John Shelton. "The Heart of Dixie: An Essay in Folk Geography." ***Social Forces,*** 54 (1976): 932, with modifications for Texas.)

nents. These perceived regions are often created by publicity campaigns, and their use in the communications media is closely linked to acceptance by the local population.

At a basic level, the vernacular region grows out of people's sense of belonging and regional self-consciousness. By contrast, many formal or functional culture regions lack this attribute and are, as a result, far less potent geographical entities. Self-conscious regional identity can have major political and social ramifications.

Vernacular culture regions, as you can see, are rather different from the functional or formal types. They often lack the organization necessary for functional regions, though often they are centered on a single urban node, and they frequently do not display the cultural homogeneity that characterizes formal regions. They are a type unto themselves, a type rooted in the popular or folk culture, as we will see in Chapter 8.

Cultural Diffusion

Regardless of type, the culture regions of the world evolved through communication and contact among people. In other words, they are the product of **cultural diffusion,** the spatial spread of learned ideas, innovations, and attitudes. As Figure 1.10 shows, each element of culture originates in one or more places and then spreads. Some innovations occur only once, and geographers can sometimes trace a cultural element back to a single place of origin. In other cases, by contrast, **independent invention** occurs. The same or very similar innovation is independently developed at different places by different peoples. The study of cultural diffusion—the origin and spread of ideas and innovations throughout an area—is a very important theme in cultural geography. Through the study of diffusion, the cultural geographer can begin to understand how spatial patterns in culture evolved.

Any culture is the product of almost countless innovations that spread from their points of origin to cover a wider area. Some of these innovations occurred thousands of years ago, others very recently. Some spread widely (see box, *Cultural Diffusion: A 100 Percent American*), while others remained confined to their area of origin.

Geographers, drawing heavily on the research of Torsten Hägerstrand (see biographical sketch), recognize several different kinds of diffusion. Two important types are **expansion diffusion** and **relocation diffusion** (Figure 1.10). In expansion diffusion, ideas spread throughout a population, from area to area, in a snowballing process, so that the total number of knowers and the area of occurrence increase. Relocation diffusion occurs when individuals or groups with a particular idea or practice migrate from one location to another, spreading it to their new homeland. Religions frequently spread this way. An example is the migration of Christianity with European settlers who came to America. Indeed, the entire process of European overseas migration, lasting from about 1500 to 1950, constituted the most important episode of relocation diffusion in all of history.

Expansion diffusion can be further divided into subtypes called hierarchical, contagious, and stimulus diffusion. In **hierarchical diffusion,** ideas leapfrog from one important person to another or from one urban center to another, temporarily bypassing other persons or rural territory. We can see hierarchical diffusion at work in everyday life by observing the acceptance of new modes of dress or hairstyles. By contrast, **contagious diffusion** involves the wavelike spread of ideas, without regard to hierarchies, in the manner of a contagious disease. Sometimes a specific trait is rejected, but the underlying idea is accepted, resulting in **stimulus diffusion.** For example, early Siberian cultures domesticated reindeer only after exposure to the domesticated cattle raised by cultures to their south. The Siberians had no use for cattle, but the idea of domesticated herds appealed to them and they began domesticating reindeer, an animal they had long hunted.

If you throw a rock into a pond and watch the spreading ripples, you can see them become gradually weaker as they move away from the point of impact. In the same way, diffusion becomes weaker as a cultural innovation moves away from its point of origin (diffusion decreases with distance). An innovation will usually be accepted most thoroughly in the areas closest to where it originates. Time is also a factor, because innovations take increasing time to spread outward. Because acceptance decreases with distance, acceptance also decreases with time, producing what geographers call **time-distance decay.** Modern mass media have greatly speeded diffusion, diminishing the impact of time-distance decay.

In addition to the gradual weakening or decay of an innovation through time and distance, barriers tend to retard its spread. **Absorbing barriers** completely halt diffusion, allowing no further progress. For example, for decades television was prevented from entering the Republic of South Africa because the government there outlawed it. The border of the republic thus served as an absorbing barrier to the spread of television. Few absorbing barriers exist in the world. More commonly, barriers are **permeable,** allowing part of the innovation wave to diffuse through but acting to weaken and retard the continued spread. When a school board objects to long hair on boys, the principal of a high school may set a limit on hair length for male students. This

Torsten Hägerstrand
1916–

A native and resident of Sweden, Hägerstrand is professor emeritus of geography at the University of Lund, where he received a doctorate in 1953. His doctoral research was on innovation diffusion, and his findings were published in 1953. His work on diffusion is significant because it is based on models and statistical techniques. As a result, it has been the basis for many theories and has elevated cultural geographers' research on diffusion to a higher, more scientific level. Sweden, and particularly Lund, has become a major center of innovative work in cultural geography. In 1968 Professor Hägerstrand received an Outstanding Achievement Award from the Association of American Geographers, and in 1985 he was awarded an honorary doctor of science degree from Ohio State University. The commendation accompanying the honorary degree noted that "his work on innovation diffusion, carried out in the 1950s and 1960s, continues to be cited as a standard against which current research is measured" and that "this distinguished individual . . . inspired a generation of scholars around the world."

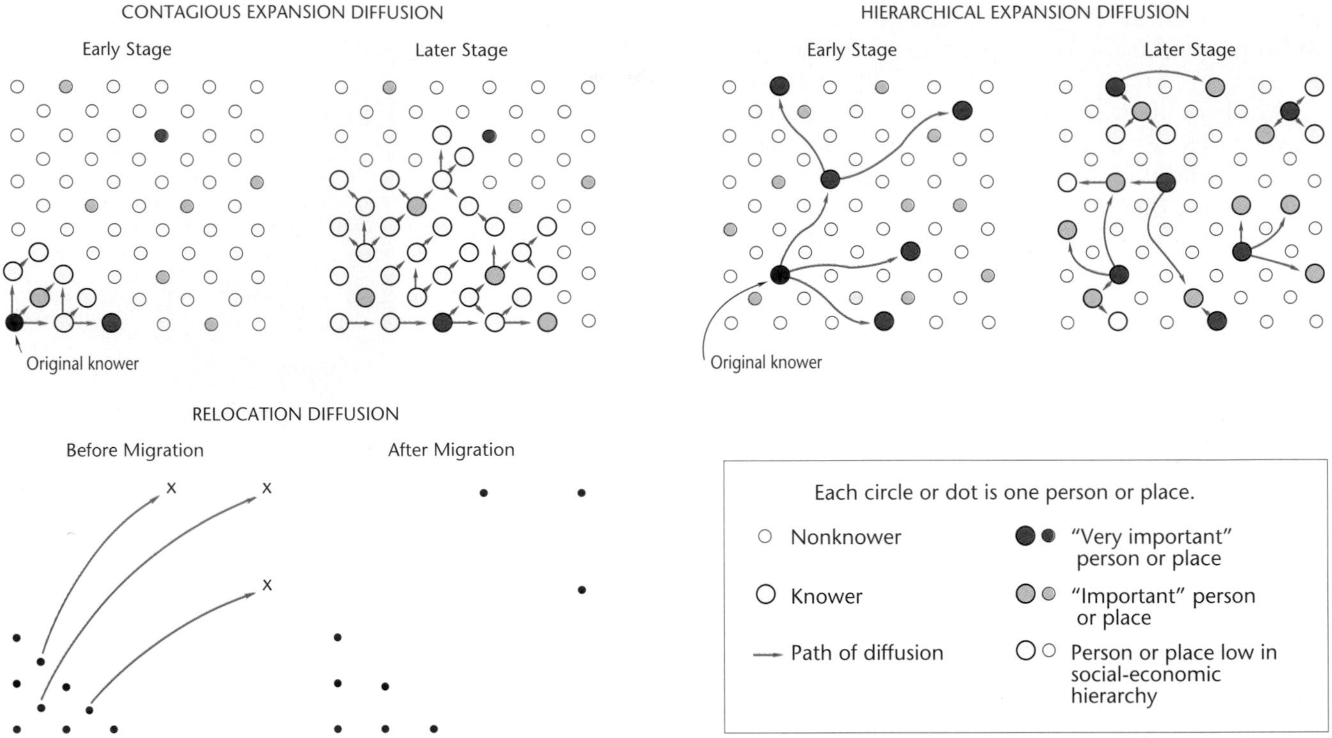
CONTAGIOUS EXPANSION DIFFUSION
Early Stage
Later Stage
Original knower
HIERARCHICAL EXPANSION DIFFUSION
Early Stage
Later Stage
Original knower
RELOCATION DIFFUSION
Before Migration
After Migration
Each circle or dot is one person or place.
Nonknower
Knower
Path of diffusion
"Very important" person or place
"Important" person or place
Person or place low in social-economic hierarchy

Figure 1.10
Types of cultural diffusion. These diagrams are merely suggestive; in reality, spatial diffusion is far more complex. In hierarchical diffusion, different scales can be used, so that, for example, the category "very important person" could be replaced by "large city."

length will likely be longer than the haircuts before the long-hair innovation was introduced, but it will be shorter than the length of the new hairstyle. In this way, the principal and school board act as a permeable barrier to a cultural innovation.

Acceptance of innovations at any given point in space passes through three distinct stages. In the first stage, acceptance takes place at a steady, yet slow, rate, perhaps because the innovation has not yet caught on, the benefits have not been adequately demonstrated, or a

Cultural Diffusion: A 100 Percent American

"Our solid American citizen awakens in a bed built on a pattern that originated in the Near East but that was modified in Northern Europe before it was transmitted to America. He throws back covers made from cotton, domesticated in India; or linen, domesticated in the Near East; or silk, the use of which was discovered in China. All of these materials have been spun and woven by processes invented in the Near East. He slips into his moccasins, invented by the Indians of the Eastern woodlands, and goes to the bathroom, whose fixtures are a mixture of European and American inventions, both of recent date. He takes off his pajamas, a garment invented in India, and washes with soap, invented by the ancient Gauls. He then shaves—a masochistic rite that seems to have been derived from either Sumer or ancient Egypt. . . .

"On his way to breakfast, he stops to buy a paper, paying for it with coins, an ancient Lydian invention. At the restaurant, a whole new series of borrowed elements confronts him. His plate is made of a form of pottery invented in China. His knife is of steel, an alloy first made in southern India; his fork, a medieval Italian invention; and his spoon, a derivative of a Roman original. . . .

"When our friend has finished eating, . . . he reads the news of the day, imprinted in characters invented by the ancient Semites upon a material invented in China by a process invented in Germany. As he absorbs the accounts of foreign trouble, he will, if he is a good, conservative citizen, thank a Hebrew deity in an Indo-European language that he is 100 percent American."

From Linton, Ralph. *The Study of Man: An Introduction.* Copyright © 1936, renewed 1964, 326–327. Adapted by permission of Prentice-Hall, Inc., Englewood Cliffs, NJ.

product is not readily available. Then during the second stage, rapid growth in acceptance occurs, and the trait spreads widely, as with a fashion style or dance fad. Often diffusion on a microscale exhibits what is called the **neighborhood effect,** which means simply that acceptance is usually most rapid in small clusters around an initial adopter (Figure 1.11). Think of a fad that first appeared in your neighborhood one day; a few days later it seemed that everyone you know was doing the same thing. Direct exposure to an innovation is the best advertisement (see box, *Monkey See, Monkey Do*). The third stage of growth shows a slower rate than the second, perhaps because the fad is passing or because an area is already saturated with the innovation.

While all places and communities hypothetically have equal potential for innovation, diffusion normally produces a core/periphery spatial arrangement, the same pattern observed earlier in our discussion of culture regions (Figures 1.4 and 1.5). Recently, Hägerstrand has offered an explanation of how diffusion produces such a regional configuration. While the distribution of innovations can be random, the *overlap* of new ideas and traits as they diffuse through area and time is greatest toward the center and least on the peripheries (Figure 1.12). In this manner, cores develop because of the greater availability of innovations in the central region.

Some other cultural geographers, most notably James Blaut and Richard Ormrod, have sought to modify this Hägerstrandian concept of diffusion. They regard it as too narrow and mechanical, since it does not give enough emphasis to cultural and environmental variables. As a result, "serious difficulties arise whenever efforts are made to generalize the . . . Hägerstrand theory or to apply it in realms and epochs which are culturally distant from the modern Western world." Nondiffusion—the failure of innovations to spread—is more prevalent than diffusion, a condition Hägerstrand's system cannot successfully accommodate.

Similarly, the Hägerstrandian system relies solely on communication and, implicitly, on the assumption that all innovations are beneficial throughout geographical space. In reality, *susceptibility* to an innovation is far more crucial, especially in a world where communications are so rapid and pervasive as to render the friction of distance almost meaningless. In other words, we must evaluate and explain, on a region-by-region or even place-by-place basis, the differing receptiveness to innovations. The inhabitants of two regions will not respond identically to an innovation, and the geographer must seek to understand this spatial variation in receptiveness in order to explain diffusion or the failure to diffuse. Cultural context must not be ignored, and people often "just say no" to an innovation for very good reasons. Within the context of their culture, people must perceive some *advantage* before they will adopt an innovation.

Cultural Ecology

Cultural geographers look on people and nature as interacting. Cultures do not exist in an environmental vacuum, for each human group and the way of life it has developed occupy a piece of the physical earth. The cultural geographer must study the interaction between culture and environment in order to understand spatial variations in culture.

This study is called **cultural ecology.** The word **ecology**, as used here, refers to the two-way relationship between an organism and its physical environment. It comes from two ancient Greek words. *Oikos* means "house" or "habitat"; *logia* means "words" or "teachings." Thus

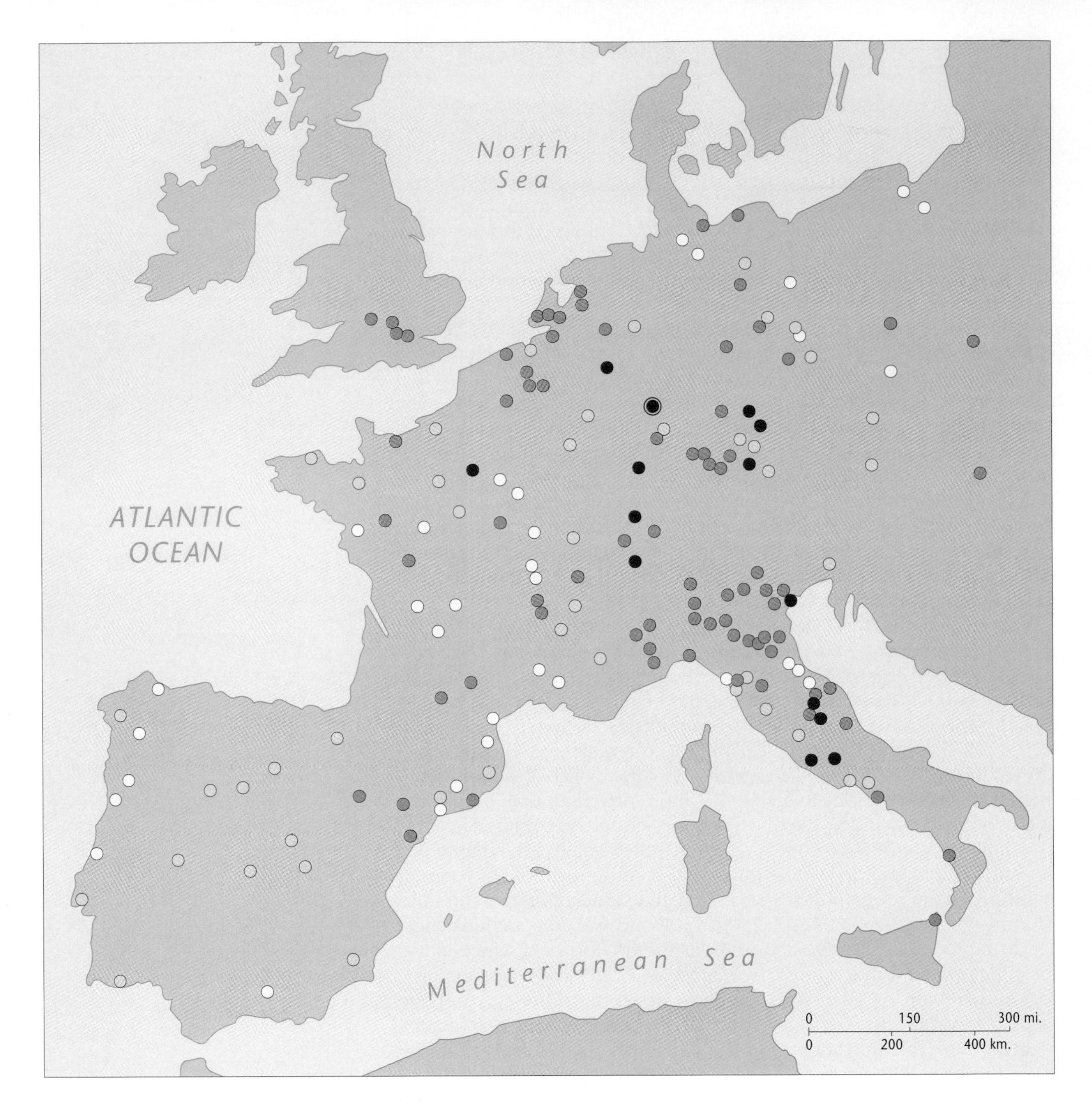

Place of innovation, 1456, Mainz

Printing shops by 1471

By 1480

By 1490

By 1500

Figure 1.11
Early diffusion of the printing press in Europe. Perfected by Johannes Gutenberg at Mainz, Germany, in the 1450s, printing presses using movable type spread rapidly through Europe. By 1500 more than 1000 print shops were operating in the 171 urban places shown. That all of the printing shops were established in cities and towns reveals hierarchical diffusion. Does the pattern shown more strongly suggest ***expansion*** or ***relocation*** diffusion (see Figure 1.10)? Is ***time-distance decay*** evident? The ***neighborhood effect***? The real world is always more complicated than models. (Adapted from Wolff, Philippe. ***Western Languages,*** AD ***100–1500.*** New York: McGraw-Hill, 1971, 222–223.)

Monkey See, Monkey Do

Our understanding of culture and cultural diffusion will be enhanced if we realize that they are natural and occur among other animals. A story from Japan reveals this. Attendants at one seaside wildlife preserve in that country regularly put food out on the beach for an endangered native species of monkeys. The food often gets sandy, making it less appetizing. Attendants observed one monkey rinse the food with sea water before eating. Other monkeys soon copied the practice, carefully washing off the sand, and before long food rinsing became almost universal. "Monkey see, monkey do"—that's diffusion, and we humans have no monopoly on it.

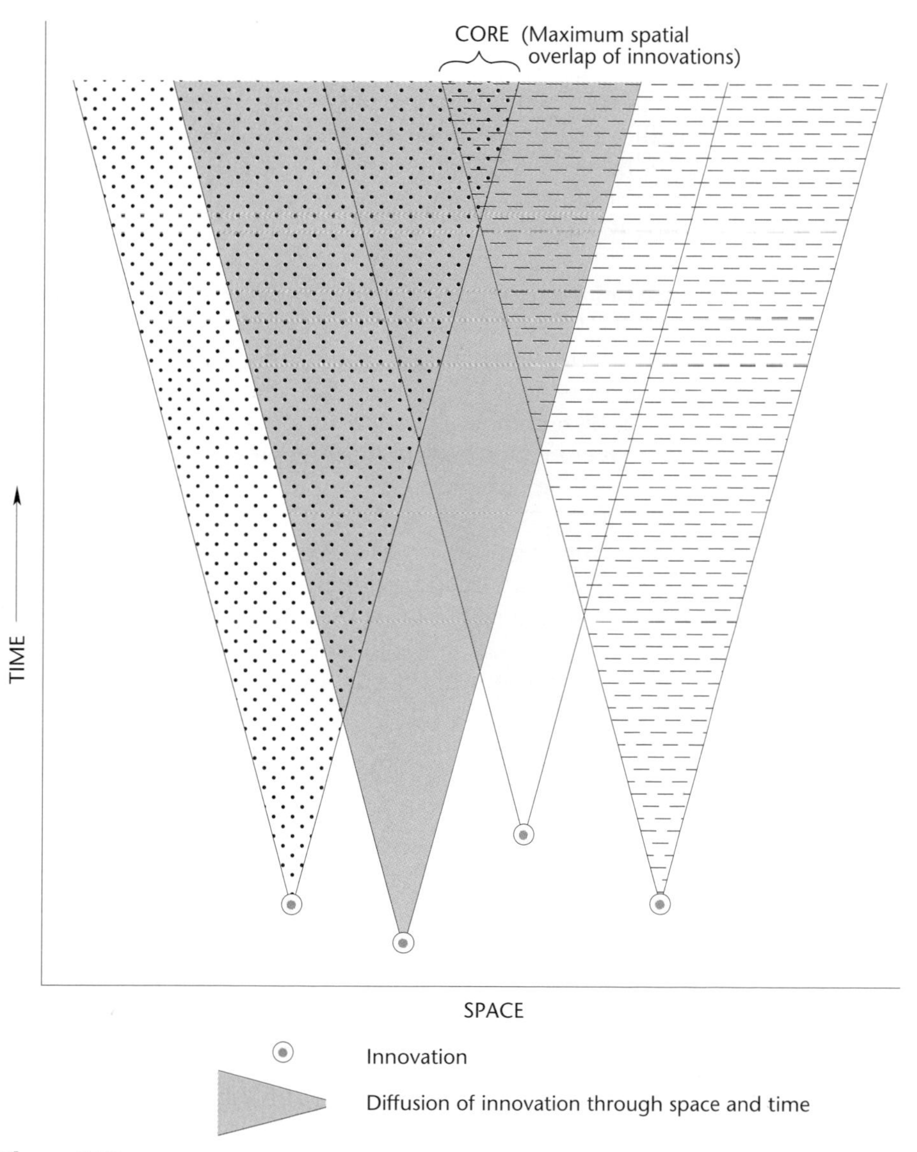

Figure 1.12
Evolution of regional core and periphery from a random distribution of innovations and an equal rate of cultural diffusion in space and time. This scheme was proposed by Torsten Hägerstrand at a symposium on diffusion held at Texas A&M University in 1984.

the Greek *oikologia* could be rendered "teachings about the habitat." Cultural ecology, then, is the study of the cause-and-effect interplay between cultures and the physical environment. An **ecosystem** entails a functioning ecological system in which biological and cultural *Homo sapiens* live and interact with the physical environment.

In sum, we may define cultural ecology as the study of (1) environmental influences on culture and (2) the impact of people, acting through their culture, on the ecosystem. Cultural ecology implies a "two-way street," with people and the environment exerting influence on one another.

The theme of cultural ecology, the meeting ground of cultural and physical geographers, has traditionally provided a focal point for the academic discipline of geography. In fact, some geographers have proposed that geography *is* cultural ecology. They argue that study of the intricate relationships between people and their physical environments constitutes a major academic discipline. While few accept this narrow definition of geography, most will agree that appreciating the complex people-environment relationship is necessary for concerned citizens of the late twentieth century.

Through the years, cultural geographers have developed various perspectives on the interaction between humans and the land. Four schools of thought have developed, which are known as environmental determinism, possibilism, environmental perception, and humans as modifiers of the Earth.

Environmental Determinism. During the first quarter of the twentieth century, many geographers adhered to the doctrine of **environmental determinism.** They believed that the physical environment, especially climate and terrain, provided a dominant force in shaping cultures—that humankind was essentially a passive product of its physical surroundings. Humans were clay to be molded by nature. Similar physical environments produced similar cultures.

For example, determinists believed that peoples of the mountains were predestined by the rugged terrain to be simple, backward, conservative, unimaginative, and freedom loving. Dwellers of the desert were likely to believe in one god, but to live under the rule of tyrants. Temperate climates produced inventiveness, industriousness, and democracy. Coastlands pitted with fjords produced great navigators and fishers.

Determinists overemphasized the role of environment in human affairs. This does not mean that environmental influence is inconsequential or that cultural geographers should not study such influence. Rather, the physical environment is only one of many forces affecting human culture and is rarely the sole determinant of behavior and beliefs.

Possibilism. Since the 1920s, environmental determinism has fallen from favor among cultural geographers. **Possibilism** has taken its place. Possibilists do not ignore the influence of the physical environment, and they realize that the imprint of nature shows in many cultures. However, possibilists stress that cultural heritage is at least as important as the physical environment in affecting human behavior (see box, *The Facts Are Incontestable*).

Possibilists believe that people, rather than their environment, are the primary architects of culture (Figure 1.13). Possibilists claim that any physical environment offers a number of possible ways for a culture to develop. The way of life depends on the choices people make among the possibilities offered by the environment. These choices are guided by cultural heritage. Possibilists, then, see the physical environment as offering opportunities and limitations; people make choices among these in order to satisfy their needs. In short, local traits of culture and economy are the products of culturally based decisions made within the limits of possibilities offered by the environment.

Most possibilists feel that the higher the technological level of a culture, the greater the number of possibilities and the weaker the influences of the physical environment. Technologically advanced cultures, in this view, have achieved near total mastery of the physical surroundings. Geographer Jim Norwine, however, warns that even in these advanced societies "the quantity and quality of human life are still strongly influenced by the natural environment," especially climate. He argues that humankind's control of nature is anything but supreme and perhaps even illusory. An unusually favorable climatic cycle characterized the twentieth century and witnessed the rise of possibilist thought. The current all-time record world population of close to 6 billion and the unprecedentedly high living standard typical of advanced countries may be untenable when a deterioration of the weather regime occurs.

Many possibilist cultural ecologists, particularly those who study traditional rural peoples, employ a somewhat narrower definition of the theme. Their type of cultural ecology is based on the premise that culture is the human method of meeting physical environmental challenges—that culture is an adaptive system. This outlook borrows heavily from the biological sciences, with the assumption that plant and animal adaptations are relevant to the study of humans, that **cultural adaptation** is the essential concept for geographical research. In their view, culture serves to facilitate long-term, successful, nongenetic human adaptation to nature and to environmental change.

Adaptive strategy involves those aspects of culture that serve to provide the necessities of life—food, clothing, shelter, and defense. No

"The Facts Are Incontestable": An Environmental Determinist's and a Possibilist's Views of Creative Genius

An Environmental Determinist's View

"The absence of artistic and poetic development in Switzerland and the Alpine lands [may be ascribed] to the overwhelming aspect of nature there, its majestic sublimity which paralyzes the mind. . . . This position [is reinforced] by the fact that . . . the lower mountains and hill country of Swabia, Franconia and Thuringia, where nature is gentler, stimulating, appealing, and not overpowering, have produced many poets and artists. The facts are incontestable. They reappear in France in the geographical distribution of the awards made by the Paris Salon of 1896. Judged by these awards, the [people of the] rough highlands . . . are singularly lacking in artistic instinct, while art flourishes in all the river lowlands of France. . . . French men of letters, by the distribution of their birthplaces, are essentially products of fluvial valleys and plains, rarely of upland and mountain."

A Possibilist's View

"All [European] patent offices report the Swiss as the foremost inventors. . . . A partial list of books published in different countries showed Switzerland to be far ahead of any other country in this sphere. . . .

"The Swiss themselves attribute much importance in the growth of their industries to the religious persecutions in neighboring countries in the sixteenth and seventeenth centuries—persecutions which drove thousands of intelligent men . . . into Switzerland. The revocation of the Edict of Nantes . . . in 1685 is credited with driving sixty thousand Huguenots from France into Switzerland. They founded the silk industry of Zurich and Bern. It was a Huguenot who founded the watch business at Geneva. . . . Spanish persecution in the Low Countries and Swiss neutrality during the Thirty Years' War added to the human resources of Switzerland."

First selection from Semple, Ellen Churchill. *Influences of Geographic Environment.* Second selection from Jefferson, Mark. "The Geographic Distribution of Inventiveness." *Geographical Review,* 19 (1929): 660–661.

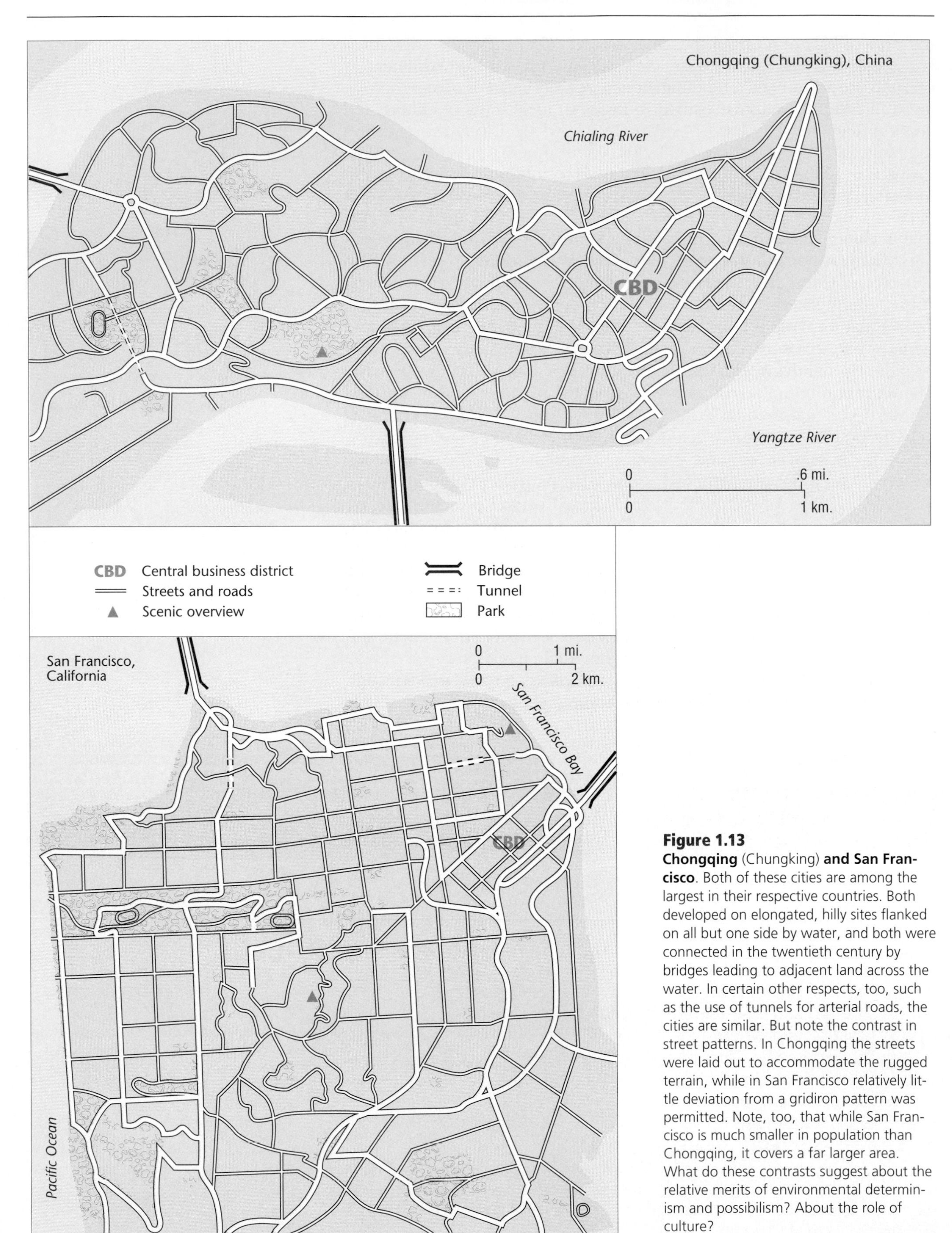

Figure 1.13
Chongqing (Chungking) **and San Francisco**. Both of these cities are among the largest in their respective countries. Both developed on elongated, hilly sites flanked on all but one side by water, and both were connected in the twentieth century by bridges leading to adjacent land across the water. In certain other respects, too, such as the use of tunnels for arterial roads, the cities are similar. But note the contrast in street patterns. In Chongqing the streets were laid out to accommodate the rugged terrain, while in San Francisco relatively little deviation from a gridiron pattern was permitted. Note, too, that while San Francisco is much smaller in population than Chongqing, it covers a far larger area. What do these contrasts suggest about the relative merits of environmental determinism and possibilism? About the role of culture?

two cultures employ the same strategy, even within the same physical environment. Such strategies involve culturally transmitted, or learned, behavior that permits a population to survive in its natural environment. Individual adaptive pathways result from interplay between the unique character of cultures and their physical environments. Culture channels the adaptive strategy by helping to determine what is meaningful as resources in a particular setting, but the individual person exercises considerable decision-making and innovative power.

Environmental Perception. Another very productive approach to the broader theme of cultural ecology focuses on human perception of nature. Each person and cultural group has mental images of the physical environment, shaped by knowledge, ignorance, experience, values, and emotions. To describe such mental images, cultural geographers use the term **environmental perception.** Whereas the possibilist sees humankind as having a choice of different possibilities in a given physical setting, the environmental perceptionist declares that the choices people make will depend more on what they perceive the environment to be than on the actual character of the land. Perception, in turn, is colored by the teachings of culture.

The perceptionist maintains that people cannot perceive their environment with exact accuracy and that decisions are therefore based on distortions of reality. To understand why a cultural group developed as it did in its physical environment, geographers must know not only what the environment is like, but also what the members of the culture think it is like. An excellent example is **geomancy,** an East Asian world view and art. Geomancy, called *feng-shui* in Chinese, is a traditional system of land-use planning dictating that certain environmental settings perceived by the sages to be particularly auspicious should be chosen as the sites for houses, villages, temples, and graves. Particular configurations of terrain, compass directions, textures of soil, and patterns of watercourses are perceived to be more auspicious than others. Belief in geomancy affected the location and morphology of villages and cities in countries such as China and Korea. For more on this particular mode of environmental perception, see Chapter 6.

Some of the most productive research done by geographers in environmental perception has been on the topic of *natural hazards,* such as flooding, hurricanes, volcanic eruptions, earthquakes, insect infestations, and droughts. All cultures react to such hazards and catastrophes, but the reaction varies greatly from one cultural group to another. Some reason that natural disasters and risks are unavoidable acts of the gods, perhaps even divine punishment sent down on them for their shortcomings. Often they seek to cope with the hazards by placating the gods. Others hold government responsible for taking care of them when hazards yield disasters. In Western culture, many groups regard natural hazards as problems that can be solved by technological means. If drought comes, they feel, we should find a way to manipulate the clouds and make it rain. If hurricanes kill and destroy, we should find a technology that will break up these storms.

In virtually all cultures, people knowingly inhabit hazard zones, in particular floodplains, exposed coastal sites, drought-prone regions, and the environs of active volcanoes (Figure 1.14). More Americans than ever now live in areas likely to be devastated by hurricanes along the coast of the Gulf of Mexico and atop earthquake faults in California. How accurately do they perceive the hazard involved? Why have they chosen to live there? How might we minimize the eventual disasters?

Figure 1.14
People often settle in natural hazard areas, exposing themselves to disasters such as volcanic eruptions. What might have led them to perceive their environment in this manner, exposing themselves to risk? This is a volcano in Iceland.

The cultural geographer seeks the answers to such questions and aspires, with other geographers, to mitigate the inevitable disasters through such devices as land-use planning.

The perceptionists' ideas are particularly striking when applied to migrations. They have found that people migrating from one environment to another usually imagine their old and new homelands to be environmentally more similar than is actually the case. For example, American farmers migrating from the humid eastern regions of the United States onto the semiarid Great Plains consistently overestimated the rainfall of their new homeland. Accustomed by the experience of many generations to living and farming in moist climates, they were initially unable to perceive the realities of their new climatic setting. They made decisions based on their experience and had to learn by trial and error that the realities of the Great Plains climate were not what they imagined (see Chapters 3 and 9).

Different cultures treat natural resources quite differently. What to one group is a major resource may be completely worthless or even a nuisance to another. To hunters and gatherers, the principal resources of an area may be wild berries, game animals, and flint deposits from which weapons can be fashioned. An agricultural group occupying the same environment may regard level land, fertile soils, and reliable sources of water as their most valuable resources. An industrial society may cherish the oil, coal, and other minerals buried beneath the land. In this way, people of three cultures perceive the resources of the same environment in different ways.

Humans As Modifiers of the Earth. Many cultural geographers, observing the environmental changes people have wrought, emphasize humans as modifiers of the Earth. This presents yet another facet of cultural ecology. In a sense, this human-as-modifier theme is the opposite of environmental determinism. Whereas the determinists proclaim that nature molds humankind, those cultural geographers who study the human impact on the land assert that humans mold nature (see biographical sketch of George Perkins Marsh).

Even in ancient times, perceptive observers realized that people influenced their environment. Plato, commenting on the soil erosion in the area of Athens around 400 BC, lamented that the once fertile district had been stripped of its soil so that "what now remains compared to what formerly existed is like the skeleton of a sick man, all the fat and soft earth having wasted away, and only the bare framework of the land being left" (Figure 1.15). We now know that even seemingly innocuous behavior, repeated for millennia, centuries, or in some cases for mere decades, can have catastrophic effects on the environment. Plowing fields and grazing livestock can eventually denude regions, as Plato noticed. The use of air conditioners or spray cans apparently has the potential to destroy the planet's very ability to support life. Clearly, access to energy and technology is the key variable that controls the magnitude and speed of environmental alteration. Geographers seek to understand and explain the processes of environmental alteration as they vary from one culture to another and, in applied geography, to propose alternative, less destructive modes of behavior.

Cultural geographers began to concentrate on the human role in changing the face of the Earth long before the present level of ecological consciousness developed. They early learned that different cultural groups have widely different outlooks on humankind's role in changing the Earth. Some, such as those rooted in the Judeo-Christian tradition, tend to regard environmental modification as divinely approved, viewing humans as God's helpers in completing the task of creation. Humans are seen as creatures apart from, and often at war with, nature. Some other groups are much more cautious, taking care not to offend the forces of nature. They see humans as part of nature, meant to be in harmony with their environment (see Chapter 6).

George Perkins Marsh
1801–1882

Some few among us are gifted with the ability to perceive trends and their future consequences long before others do. George Perkins Marsh was such a person. Born to demanding Calvinist parents when America was still very young, when wilderness and open frontier were abundant and parts of his native Vermont still bore the mark of pioneering, Marsh nevertheless came to realize that the physical environment was being drastically altered by people, to the extent that the future of humankind was gravely endangered. At a time when the United States possessed seemingly limitless natural resources and huge expanses of fertile open land for settlement, in an era of almost unbounded optimism and belief in the steady progress of humankind toward a higher and better condition, Marsh intruded with a stern warning of future ecological disaster. His message was most effectively presented in a book, ***Man and Nature; or, Physical Geography as Modified by Human Action,*** published in 1864. Subsequently, after Marsh's death, it made a major impact on the academic discipline of cultural geography in America. It was a geographer who wrote Marsh's biography. (***Source:*** Based on Lowenthal, David. ***George Perkins Marsh, Versatile Vermonter.*** New York: Columbia University Press, 1958.)

Cultural Integration

The relationship between people and the land, the theme of cultural ecology, lies at the heart of traditional geography. However, the explanation of human spatial variations requires consideration of a whole range of cultural factors. The geographer recognizes that all facets of culture are systemically and spatially intertwined, or integrated. In short, cultures are complex wholes rather than series of unrelated traits. They form integrated systems in which the parts fit together causally. All aspects of culture are functionally interdependent on one another. The theme of **cultural integration** addresses this interdependence. The theme of cultural integration reflects the geographer's awareness that the immediate causes of some cultural phenomena are other cultural phenomena. A change in one element of culture requires an accommodating change in others. It is impossible to understand the distribution of one facet of culture without studying the variations in other facets, in order to see how they are interrelated and integrated causally with one another.

For example, religious belief has the potential to influence a group's voting behavior, diet, shopping patterns, type of employment, and social standing. Traditional Hinduism, the majority religion of India, segregates people into social classes called *castes* and specifies what forms of livelihood are appropriate for each. The Mormon faith, among others, forbids the consumption of alcoholic beverages, tobacco, and

Figure 1.15
Human modification of the Earth includes severe soil erosion. The erosion could have been caused by poor farming methods, overgrazing by cattle, or other abuses of the land.

certain other products, thereby influencing both the diet and the shopping patterns of its members. In countless other ways, one facet of a culture influences other facets. The cultural integration theme allows the geographer to examine how these intracultural causal forces help determine variations.

The theme of cultural integration, if improperly used, can lead the geographer to **cultural determinism.** Advocates of this extreme viewpoint, developed in reaction to the earlier environmental determinism, maintain that the physical environment is inconsequential as an influence on culture. Any facet of a culture, they would argue, is shaped entirely by other facets. Cultural integration, for them, offers all the answers for spatial variations. People and culture are the active forces; nature is passive and easily conquered. You should be as wary of cultural determinism as of environmental determinism. Julian Steward, a noted cultural ecologist, warned us long ago of "the fruitless assumption" that all culture comes from culture.

Social Science. Geographers have employed two fundamentally different approaches in studying cultural integration—the social scientific and the humanistic. Those who view cultural geography as a **social science** believe that we should apply the scientific method to the study of people. Emulating physicists and chemists, they devise theories and seek regularities or universal spatial principles that cut across cultural lines to govern all of humankind. Once identified, these principles ideally become the basis for laws of human spatial behavior. *Space* is the word that perhaps best connotes this scientific approach to cultural geography.

These social-scientific geographers derive much of their inspiration from the field of economics, and they tend to believe that economic causal forces are far more powerful in explaining human spatial behavior than any others. As a result, they are often accused of **economic**

determinism and of pursuing a largely acultural analysis. They usually "tune out" cultural variations in their search for explanatory principles, and regard spatial networks, locations, and flows as far more important than areal variation in culture. The social scientists also rely heavily on mathematics and geometry; they approach the task of explanation and law formulation through often-complicated multivariate statistics, equations, and diagrams.

The social scientists face one difficult problem: They have no laboratories in which to test their theories. Unlike physicists and chemists, they cannot run controlled experiments in which certain causal forces are neutralized so that others can be studied. Their response to this deficiency is the technique known as **model** building. Aware that in the real world many causal forces are involved, they set up artificial model situations in order to focus on one or several potential factors. Hägerstrand's diagrams of different types of diffusion and of the evolution of core and periphery patterns are examples of spatial models (Figure 1.10). Note that they are devoid of any reference to cultural traits, a symptom of economic determinism.

Some social-scientific geographers are becoming more sensitive to cultural variables. They have begun devising *culture-specific* models, meant to describe and explain certain facets of spatial behavior within specific cultures. They still seek regularities and spatial principles, but more modestly within the bounds of individual cultures. For example, several geographers proposed a model for Latin American cities, in an effort to stress similarities among them and to understand certain underlying causal forces (Figure 1.16). Obviously, no actual city in Latin America conforms precisely to their uncomplicated geometric plan. Instead, they deliberately generalized and simplified, in order that an urban type could be recognized and studied. The model will look strange to a person living in a city in the United States or Canada, for it describes a very different kind of urban environment, based in another culture.

Humanistic Geography. If the social scientist seeks to level the differences among people in the quest for universal explanations, the **humanistic geographer** celebrates the uniqueness of each region and place. Indeed, **place** becomes the key word connoting the humanistic view, just as *space* identifies the perspective of the social scientist within geography. The humanistic geographer Yi-Fu Tuan even coined the word **topophilia,** literally "love of place," to describe people who exhibit a strong sense of place and the geographers who are attracted to the study of such places and peoples. Edward Relph tells us that "to be human is to have and know your place" in the geographical sense.

Recent decades have witnessed a resurgence of humanistic geography and the decline of the once-ascendant social-scientific approach. Daniel W. Gade beautifully expressed the spirit of the humanistic enterprise in geography, as well as the tension that exists between social scientists and humanists, when he declared that "economic determinism and logical positivism [or the scientific method] have failed to dispel the sense that humanistic understanding of places lies near the heart of the geographical enterprise." Anne Buttimer, one of the leaders of the humanistic revival (see biographical sketch), declared in a similar vein that "there must be more to human geography than the *danse macabre* of materially motivated robots."

Traditional humanists in geography are as concerned about explanation as the social scientists, but they seek to explain unique phenom-

Anne Buttimer
1938–

A leader in the development of a renewed and vital humanistic perspective in geography during the past two decades, Irish-born Professor Buttimer is best known for books such as ***Values in Geography, Experience of Place and Space*** (cowritten with David Seamon), ***The Practice of Geography,*** and ***Geography and the Humanistic Spirit.*** She has beautifully articulated the need for a humanistic presence, a critical and cross-cultural sensitivity in the discipline, which might help us, among other things, to "rediscover wiser ways of dwelling" on the Earth. The emotional significance of ***place*** in human identity and the evolution of Western ideas concerning nature have been her persistent interests. Buttimer feels that humanists should not seek to divide or dominate geography, and she has consistently sought to build bridges to the sciences. "I have always been concerned about the wholeness or integrity of the geographic enterprise." In her view, the humanistic perspective, applied constructively, enhances the holistic nature of the discipline. Much honored, Professor Buttimer holds the position of chair of geography at the University College Dublin. In 1986, she received an award from the Association of American Geographers, and in 1991, she received the Ellen Churchill Semple Award.

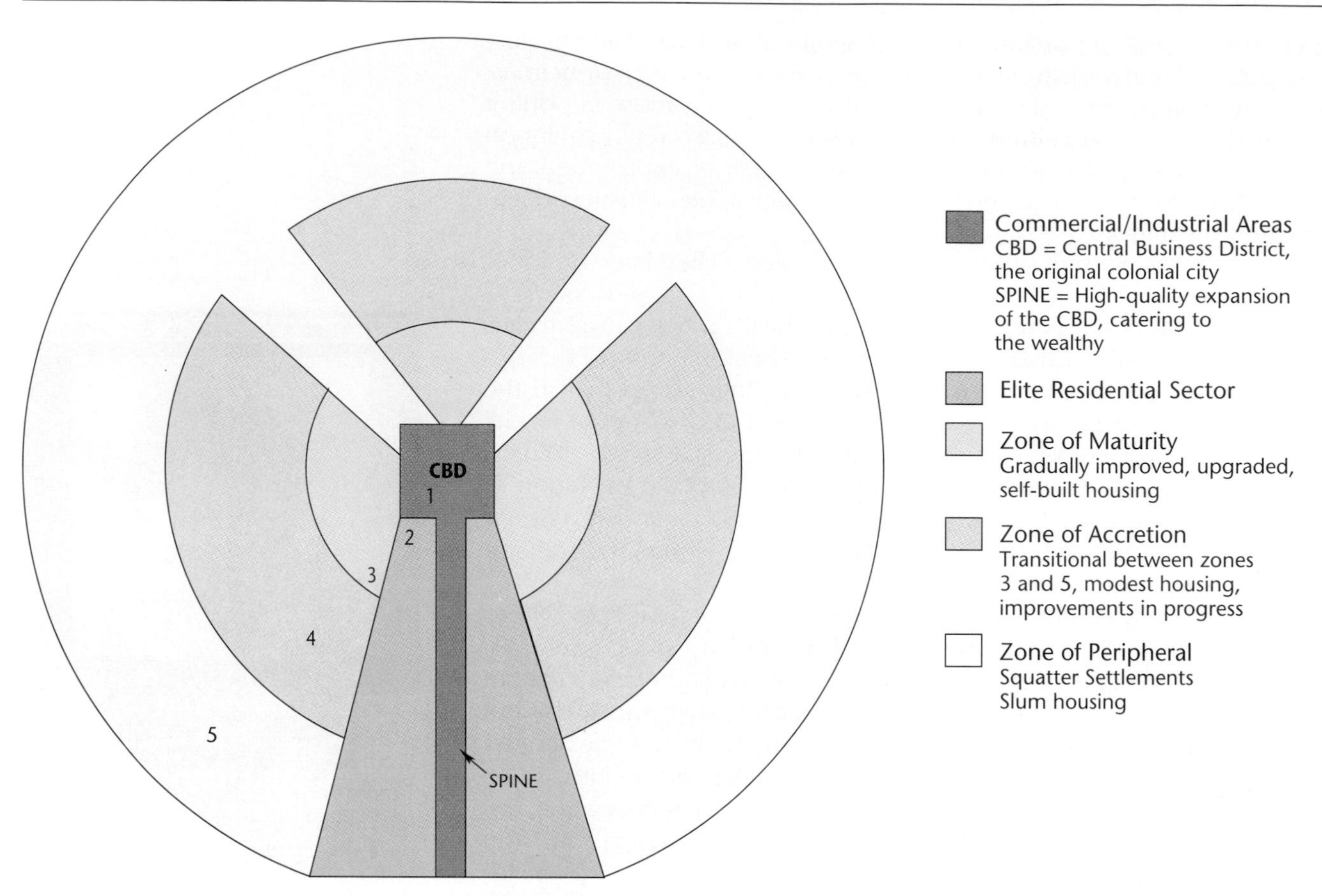

Figure 1.16
A generalized model of the Latin American city. Urban structure differs from one culture to another, and in many ways the cities of Latin America are distinctive, sharing much in common with each other. Geographers Ernst Griffin and Larry Ford developed the model diagramed here to help describe and explain the processes at work shaping the cities of Latin America. In what ways would this model not be applicable to cities in the United States and Canada? (After Griffin, Ernst, and Ford, Larry. "A Model of Latin American City Structure." *Geographical Review,* 70 (1980): 406.)

ena—place and region—rather than seeking universal spatial laws. As the German scholar Heinrich Franke said, "The essence of place derives from a creative force at work over millennia; to comprehend and capture in prose this spirit of place is worth the sweat of the noblest among us." Indeed, most humanists doubt that laws of spatial behavior even exist. They believe in a far more chaotic world than the scientist could tolerate. Humanists reject the use of mathematics, arguing instead that the most essential human beliefs and values cannot be measured.

Some humanists go even further, seeking complete freedom from the structured research methods of science. They regard objectivity in geographical investigation as unattainable, given the subjective quality of the human mind. As geographer Michael Dear put it, "there are no facts or truths about which a common and permanent consensus" can exist, but instead "only degrees of freedom about an interpretation." Such geographers, sometimes called *post-modernists,* are free to create impressionistic and deliberately subjective, nonexplanatory portraits of place, turning cultural geography into art.

The debate between scientists and humanists in cultural geography is both necessary and healthy. The two groups ask different questions about place and space; not surprisingly, they obtain different answers.

The scientist levels diversity through models to seek universal causal forces, while the humanist exalts diversity and strives to understand the unique. Both lines of inquiry yield valuable findings. Here again we can see geography as a bridging discipline, joining the sciences and the humanities—though the resultant internal variety makes the discipline difficult to define. In *The Human Mosaic,* we present both sides of the scientist versus humanist debate, within the theme of cultural integration.

Cultural Landscape

The **cultural landscape** is the visible, material landscape that cultural groups create in inhabiting the Earth. Cultures shape their own landscapes out of the raw materials provided by the Earth. Every inhabited area has a cultural landscape, fashioned from the natural landscape, and each uniquely reflects the culture that created it (Figure 1.17). Landscape mirrors culture, and the cultural geographer can learn much about a group of people by carefully observing the landscape. Indeed, so important is this visual record of cultures that some geographers regard landscape study as geography's central interest.

Why is such importance attached to the cultural landscape? Perhaps part of the answer is that it visually reflects the most basic strivings of humankind: for shelter, food, and clothing. The cultural landscape reflects different attitudes concerning modification of the Earth by people and contains valuable evidence about the origin, spread, and development of cultures, since it usually preserves relict forms of various types. Every cultural landscape is an accumulation of human artifacts, some old and some new.

This potential for interpretive analysis attracts many geographers to study the cultural landscape, for such visible evidence can reveal much

Figure 1.17
Terraced cultural landscape on the island of Bali, Indonesia. In such areas, the artificial landscape made by people overwhelms nature and forms a human mosaic on the land.

about a past long forgotten by the present inhabitants, and about the choices made and changes wrought by a people. The idea that cultural landscapes possess diagnostic interpretive potential was introduced into geography by the German scholar August Meitzen. Long ago, in observing the rural cultural landscape of central Europe, Meitzen wrote that "we walk in every village, in a sense, among the ruins of antiquity." At every step we encounter built landscape features as "readable as hieroglyphics," once we learn to decipher them, that can reveal ancient cultural diffusions, past adaptations to environment, and cultural changes through time. Echoing Meitzen, American geographer Peirce Lewis concluded that "one can read the landscape as we do a book."

Aside from containing relict forms, landscapes also convey revealing messages about the present-day inhabitants and cultures. All humanized landscapes bear cultural meaning. Lewis further proposed that "the cultural landscape is our collective and revealing autobiography, reflecting our tastes, values, aspirations, and fears in tangible forms." Cultural landscapes offer "texts" that geographers read to discover dominant ideas and prevailing practices within a culture. For example, O. F. G. Sitwell and O. S. E. Bilash proposed that "the spatial organization of settlements and the architectural form of buildings and other structures can be interpreted as the expression of the values and beliefs of the people responsible for them." That is, the landscape can serve as a means to study nonmaterial aspects of culture.

The metaphorical and ideological qualities of landscape now receive attention by geographers. Sitwell speculated about the processes creating humanized landscapes. He proposed that three figurative expressions of human worth—three cardinal virtues—are height, durability, and central location. Idioms such as "the high point of my visit," "she's at the peak of her career," "diamonds are forever," and "I love to be in the middle of things" reveal the virtues of height, durability, and centrality. If we apply these expressions of worth to architecture, to buildings, then it follows that centrally located, tall structures built of steel, brick, or stone are the worthiest and most important to the particular culture in question. In medieval Europe, cathedrals and churches best exemplified the three virtues, because they were built of stone on the central square and towered above other structures. A visitor from another land, using Sitwell's method, would correctly conclude that the church dominated and defined medieval culture. What conclusion might the perceptive stranger reach in interpreting the urban landscape shown in Figure 1.18?

Certain other geographers, particularly some of the humanists, are content to study the cultural landscape for its aesthetic value, to obtain highly subjective and personal messages from the textures, colors, and forms of the built environment that help describe the essence of place. Recognizing this diversity of landscape content, Finnish geographer Tarja Keisteri distinguished the factual, concrete, physical, functioning landscape from the experiential, perceived, symbolic, aesthetic landscape, though she noted that the distinction between the two often blurs. In other words, the cultural landscape offers the possibility both for objective, scholarly analysis and for subjective, artistic interpretation. More than that, the landscape is integrally bound to the humanistic geographical concept of place and our personal sense of belonging. As J. B. Jackson suggests, it provides us "with landmarks to reassure us that we are not rootless individuals without identity or place."

Figure 1.18
Folk and popular architecture both reflect culture. The log house, near Ottawa in Canada, is a folk dwelling (see Chapter 7) and stands in sharp contrast to the professional architecture of the New York lower Manhattan skyline.

The physical content of the cultural landscape is both varied and complex. Most geographical studies have focused on three principal aspects of this landscape: settlement forms, land-division patterns, and architecture. In the study of settlement forms, cultural geographers describe and explain the spatial arrangement of buildings, roads, and other features that people construct while inhabiting an area. Land-division patterns reveal the way people have divided the land for economic and social uses. Such patterns vary a great deal from place to place. They range from huge corporate-owned farming complexes to small family-operated farms composed of tens or even hundreds of separate tiny parcels of land; from the fenced, privately owned home lots of American suburbs to the city's public squares. The best way to glimpse settlement and land-division patterns is through an airplane window. Looking down, you can see the multicolored abstract patterns of planted fields, as vivid as any modern painting, and the regular checkerboard or chaotic tangle of urban streets.

Perhaps no other aspect of the human landscape is as readily visible from ground level as the architectural style of a culture. In North American culture, different building styles catch the eye: modest white New England churches and giant urban cathedrals; hand-hewn barns and geodesic domes; wooden one-room schoolhouses and the new windowless school buildings of the urban areas. This architecture provides a vivid record of the resident culture (Figure 1.18). For this reason, cultural geographers have traditionally devoted considerable attention to such structures.

Conclusion

The interests of cultural geographers are, as we have seen, diverse. As Dan Gade has said, geographers investigate "the myriad components that make our planet such a complex place." It might seem to you, confronted by the various themes, subject matter, viewpoints, and methodologies described in this chapter, that cultural geographers run off in all directions, that they lack unity of purpose. What does a geographer studying architecture have in common with a colleague studying the human role in shaping the Earth? What interests do an environmental perceptionist and a student of cultural diffusion share? Why do scholars with such apparently different interests belong in the same academic discipline? Why are they all geographers?

The answer is that regardless of the particular topic the cultural geographer studies, he or she necessarily touches several or all of the five themes we have mentioned. The themes are closely related segments of a whole. Spatial patterns in culture, as revealed by maps of culture regions, are reflected in the cultural landscape, require an ecological interpretation, imply cultural diffusion, and suggest the causal workings of cultural integration.

As an example of how the various themes of cultural geography overlap and intertwine, let us look at one element of architecture—the traditional American log house (Figure 1.18). Once found widely on the American frontier, many log cabins still stand in the mountains of the South and West. They are obviously part of the cultural landscape, and their spatial distribution constitutes a formal culture region that can be mapped.

Geographers studying such houses also need to employ the other themes of cultural geography to gain a complete understanding. They can use the concept of cultural diffusion to learn when and by what routes these techniques diffused and what barriers retarded their diffusion. In this particular case, the geographer would be led back to the ancient prehistory of central Europe. Further, the cultural geographer would need an ecological interpretation of the log house. How does the environment influence the log cabin? Does the use of logs for houses decline as the forests become thinned out? Do log houses differ from one climatic zone to another? Finally, the cultural geographer wants to know how the use of log houses is integrated with other facets of the culture. Did changes in the economy and standard of living lead people to reject log houses? Did changes in technology lead to more elaborate houses? Why was it once almost essential for American presidential candidates to claim birth in a log cabin? Do these humble structures possess a symbolism related to traditional American values and virtues? Why do we so often preserve log cabins as icons in our public parks and squares?

Thus the geographer interested in folk housing is firmly bound by the total fabric of cultural geography, unable to segregate a particular topic such as log houses from the geographical whole. Culture region, cultural landscape, cultural integration, cultural ecology, and cultural diffusion are interwoven.

In this manner, the cultural geographer passes from one theme to another, demonstrating the holistic nature of the discipline. In no small measure, it is this holism, this broad, multithematic approach, that distinguishes the cultural geographer from other students of culture. We believe that, by the end of the course, you will have gained a new perspective on the Earth as the home of humankind. You will agree by then, we feel, that geography is part of any good liberal arts education.

Sources and Suggested Readings

Allen, Barbara, and Thomas J. Schlereth (eds.). *Sense of Place: American Regional Cultures*. Lexington: University Press of Kentucky, 1990.

Birks, H. H., H. J. B. Birks, Peter E. Kaland, and Dagfinn Moe (eds.). *The Cultural Landscape: Past, Present and Future.* Cambridge, UK: Cambridge University Press, 1989.

Blaut, James M. "Two Views of Diffusion." *Annals of the Association of American Geographers,* 67 (1977): 343–349.

Brown, Lawrence A. *Innovation Diffusion: A New Perspective.* New York: Methuen, 1981.

Buttimer, Anne. *Geography and the Human Spirit.* Baltimore: Johns Hopkins University Press, 1993.

Buttimer, Anne (ed.). *The Practice of Geography.* London: Longman, 1983.

Clarkson, J. D. "Ecology and Spatial Analysis." *Annals of the Association of American Geographers,* 60 (1970). 700–716.

Cliff, A. D. and J. K. Ord. *Spatial Processes: Models and Applications.* London: Pion Ltd., 1981.

Denevan, William M. "Adaptation, Variation, and Cultural Geography." *Professional Geographer,* 35 (1983): 399–407.

Domosh, Mona. "A Method for Interpreting Landscape: A Case Study of the New York World Building." *Area,* 21 (1989): 347–355.

Duncan, James S. "The Superorganic in American Cultural Geography." *Annals of the Association of American Geographers,* 70 (1980): 181–198.

Duncan, James S. and David Ley. *Place/Culture/Representation.* London: Routledge, 1993.

Ecumene: A Geographical Journal of Environment, Culture, Meaning (Volume 1 published 1994).

Entrikin, J. Nicholas. *The Characterization of Place.* Worcester, MA: Clark University Press, 1991.

Foote, Kenneth E., et al. (eds.). *Re-Reading Cultural Geography.* Austin: University of Texas Press, 1994.

Gade, Daniel W. "The French Riviera as Elitist Space." *Journal of Cultural Geography,* 3 (1982–1983): 19–28.

Goudie, Andrew. *The Human Impact on the Natural Environment.* Cambridge, MA: M.I.T. Press, 1986.

Gould, Peter, and Rodney White. *Mental Maps,* 2d ed. Winchester, MA: Allen & Unwin, 1986.

Gritzner, Charles F., Jr. "The Scope of Cultural Geography." *Journal of Geography,* 65 (January 1966): 4–11.

Grossman, Larry. "Man-Environment Relationships in Anthropology and Geography." *Annals of the Association of American Geographers,* 67 (1977): 126–144.

Harvey, David. *Explanation in Geography.* New York: St. Martin's Press, 1970.

Holt-Jensen, Arild. *Geography: History and Concepts, a Student's Guide.* New York: Barnes & Noble, 1988.

Jackson, J. B. *Landscapes: Selected Writings of J. B. Jackson.* Ervin H. Zube (ed.). Amherst: University of Massachusetts Press, 1970.

Johnston, R. J., Derek Gregory, and David M. Smith (eds.). *The Dictionary of Human Geography,* 2d ed. Oxford: Basil Blackwell, 1986.

Jordan, Terry G. "The Concept and Method," in Glen E. Lich (ed.), *Regional Studies: The Interplay of Land and People.* College Station: Texas A&M University Press, 1992, pp. 8–24.

Jordan, Terry G. *The European Culture Area,* 3d ed. New York: HarperCollins, 1996.

The Journal of Cultural Geography. The only English-language journal devoted exclusively to cultural geography. Published semiannually by the Department of Geography, Bowling Green State University, OH. Volume 1 was published in 1980.

Journal of Regional Cultures. Published by the Popular Culture Association, Bowling Green State University, OH. Volume I was published in 1983.

Kates, Robert W., and Ian Burton (eds.). *Geography, Resources, and Environment.* 2 vols. Chicago: University of Chicago Press, 1986.

Keisteri, Tarja. "The Study of Changes in Cultural Landscapes." *Fennia,* 168 (1990): 31–115.

Kenzer, Martin S. (ed.). *Applied Geography: Issues, Questions, and Concerns.* Dordrecht, Netherlands: Kluwer Academic Publishers, 1989.

Kniffen, Fred B. "Cultural Diffusion and Landscapes: Selections by Fred B. Kniffen." *Geoscience and Man,* 27 (1990): 1–77.

Landscape. An interdisciplinary journal devoted to the cultural landscape. Cultural geographers regularly contribute articles. Volume I was published in 1951.

Lewis, Peirce. "Learning from Looking: Geographic and Other Writing About the American Cultural Landscape." *American Quarterly,* 35 (1983): 242–261.

Ley, David, and Marwyn S. Samuels. *Humanistic Geography: Prospects and Problems.* Chicago: Maaroufa Press, 1978.

Lowenthal, David, and Martyn J. Bowden. *Geographies of the Mind.* New York: Oxford University Press, 1976.

Mallory, William E., and Paul Simpson-Housley (eds.). *Geography and Literature: A Meeting of the Disciplines.* Syracuse, NY: Syracuse University Press, 1987.

McDonald, James R. "The Region: Its Conception, Design and Limitations." *Annals of the Association of American Geographers,* 56 (1966): 516–528.

Meinig, D. W. "Geography as an Art." *Transactions of the Institute of British Geographers,* 8 (1983): 314–328.

Meinig, D. W. (ed.). *The Interpretation of Ordinary Landscapes: Geographical Essays.* New York: Oxford University Press, 1979.

Morgan, W. B., and R. P. Moss. "Geography and Ecology: The Concept of the Community and Its Relation to Environment." *Annals of the Association of American Geographers,* 55 (1965): 339–350.

Morrill, Richard, Gary L. Gaile, and Grant I. Thrall. *Spatial Diffusion* (Volume 10 in the Scientific Geography Series). Newbury Park, CA: Sage Publications, 1988.

North American Culture. Publication of the North American Culture Society. Department of Geography, Oklahoma State University. Cultural geographers are major contributors to this journal, which focuses on cultural patterns in North America. Volume 1 was published in 1985.

Norton, William. *Explorations in the Understanding of Landscape: A Cultural Geography.* Westport, CT: Greenwood Press, 1989.

Norwine, Jim, and Thomas D. Anderson. *Geography as Human Ecology?* Lanham, MD: University Press of America, 1980.

Ormrod, Richard K. "Adaptation and Cultural Diffusion." *Journal of Geography,* 91 (1992): 258–262.

Ormrod, Richard K. "Local Context and Innovation Diffusion in a Well-Connected World." *Economic Geography,* 66 (1990): 109–122.

Osborne, Brian S. "Fact, Symbol, and Message: Three Approaches to Literary Landscapes." *Canadian Geographer,* 32 (1988): 267–269.

Paasi, Anssi. "The Institutionalization of Regions: A Theoretical Framework for Understanding the Emergence of Regions and the Constitution of Regional Identity." *Fennia,* 164 (1986): 105–146.

Palm, Risa I. *Natural Hazards: An Integrative Framework for Research and Planning.* Baltimore, MD: Johns Hopkins University Press, 1990.

Penning-Rowsell, Edmund C., and David Lowenthal (eds.). *Landscape Meanings and Values.* London: Allen & Unwin, 1986.

Porteous, J. Douglas. *Landscapes of the Mind: Worlds of Sense and Metaphor.* Toronto: University of Toronto Press, 1990.

Progress in Human Geography. A quarterly journal providing critical appraisal of developments and trends in the discipline. Volume 1 was published in 1977.

Relph, Edward. "Post-Modern Geography." *Canadian Geographer,* 35 (1991): 98–105.

Relph, Edward. *Rational Landscapes and Humanistic Geography.* New York: Barnes & Noble, 1981.

Robinson, G. W. S. "The Geographic Region: Form and Function." *Scottish Geographical Magazine,* 69 (1953): 49–58.

Rooney, John F., Jr., Wilbur Zelinsky, Dean R. Louder, et al. (eds.). *This Remarkable Continent: An Atlas of North American Society and Culture.* College Station: Texas A&M University Press, 1982. The first work of its kind, this atlas contains over four hundred maps illustrating the cultural geography of the United States and Canada.

Saarinen, Thomas F. *Perception of Environment.* Resource Paper No. 5. Washington, DC: Association of American Geographers, Commission on College Geography, 1969.

Salter, Christopher L. *The Cultural Landscape.* Belmont, CA: Duxbury Press, 1971.

Sauer, Carl O. "Morphology of Landscape." *University of California Publications in Geography,* 2 (1925): 19–54.

Seager, Joni (ed.). *The State of the Earth Atlas.* New York: Simon & Schuster, 1990. A startling, sobering cartographic portrayal, by a Canadian geographer, of the major ecological problems in the world today.

Simmons, I. G. *Changing the Face of the Earth: Culture, Environment, History.* London: Basil Blackwell, 1989.

Sitwell, O. F. G. "Elements of the Cultural Landscape as Figures of Speech." *Canadian Geographer,* 25 (1981): 167–180.

Sitwell, O. F. G., and Olenka S. E. Bilash. "Analyzing the Cultural Landscape as a Means of Probing the Non-Material Dimensions of Reality." *Canadian Geographer,* 30 (1986): 132–145.

"Special Issue—Landscape History." *Geografiska Annaler,* 70B (1988): 1–237.

Spencer, Joseph E. "The Growth of Cultural Geography." *American Behavioral Scientist,* 22 (1978): 79–92.

Thomas, William L., Jr. (ed.). *Man's Role in Changing the Face of the Earth.* Chicago: University of Chicago Press, 1956.

Tuan, Yi-Fu. "Humanistic Geography." *Annals of the Association of American Geographers,* 66 (1976): 266–276.

Tuan, Yi-Fu. *Topophilia: A Study of Environmental Perception, Attitudes, and Values.* Englewood Cliffs, NJ: Prentice-Hall, 1974.

Turner, B. L. II. "The Specialist-Synthesis Approach to the Revival of Geography: The Case of Cultural Ecology." *Annals of the Association of American Geographers,* 79 (1989): 88–100.

Turner, B. L. II, et al. (eds.). *The Earth as Transformed by Human Action: Global and Regional Changes in the Biosphere over the Past 300 Years.* New York: Cambridge University Press, 1991.

Turner, Frederick. *Spirit of Place: The Making of an American Literary Landscape.* San Francisco: Sierra Club Books, 1989.

Wagner, Philip L. "Cultural Landscapes and Regions: Aspects of Communication." *Geoscience and Man,* 5 (1974): 133–142.

Wagner, Philip L., and Marvin W. Mikesell. *Readings in Cultural Geography.* Chicago: University of Chicago Press, 1962, pp. 1–24.

Wagstaff, J. M. (ed.). *Landscape and Culture: Geographical and Archaeological Perspectives.* London: Basil Blackwell, 1987.

White, Gilbert F. (ed.). *Natural Hazards: Local, National, Global.* New York: Oxford University Press, 1974.

Whole Earth Review. 58 (Spring 1988). Special section on cultural geography, "A Wedding of People and Place," 2–47.

Yapa, Larry S., and Robert C. Mayfield. "Non-Adoption of Innovations: Evidence from Discriminant Analysis." *Economic Geography,* 54 (1978): 145–156.

CHAPTER 2

People on the Land

Population geography is the study of the spatial and ecological aspects of **demography,** the name given to the statistical analysis of human population, including spatial density, fertility, gender, health, age, nutrition, mortality, and migration. At present, about 5.7 billion humans are alive on the Earth, producing an average **population density** of over 100 persons per square mile of land area (40 per square kilometer). The central geographical fact, however, is that people are quite unevenly distributed (Figure 2.1). Population densities range from zero in the uninhabited expanses of Antarctica to countries with over 2000 persons per square mile (775 per sq. km.), such as Bangladesh (Table 2.1). Geographers study these variations in density of people. So basic and important is population distribution that some cultural geographers even regard it as "the essential geographical expression," a worthy focus for the entire academic discipline. Most geographers would at least agree that the uneven spatial distribution of people is vitally important. It provides an appropriate point of departure for our study of cultural geography.

Population geographers do not confine their attention to distribution. They are also interested in the spatial variation of other demographic qualities or characteristics, such as the differences in birthrates, death rates, overpopulation, health, sex ratios, age groups, crime, quality of life, and human mobility.

All these topics receive attention in this chapter, and our study of population geography will make use of the five themes outlined in Chapter 1. Accordingly, we will delimit demographic regions, consider cultural diffusion as it relates to population, probe the ecology of population, investigate the ways that population characteristics are integrated with other cultural patterns, and view the settlement landscapes produced by the differing distribution of people.

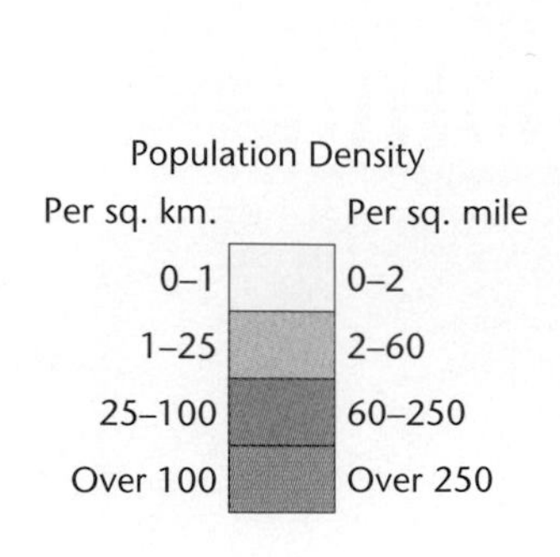

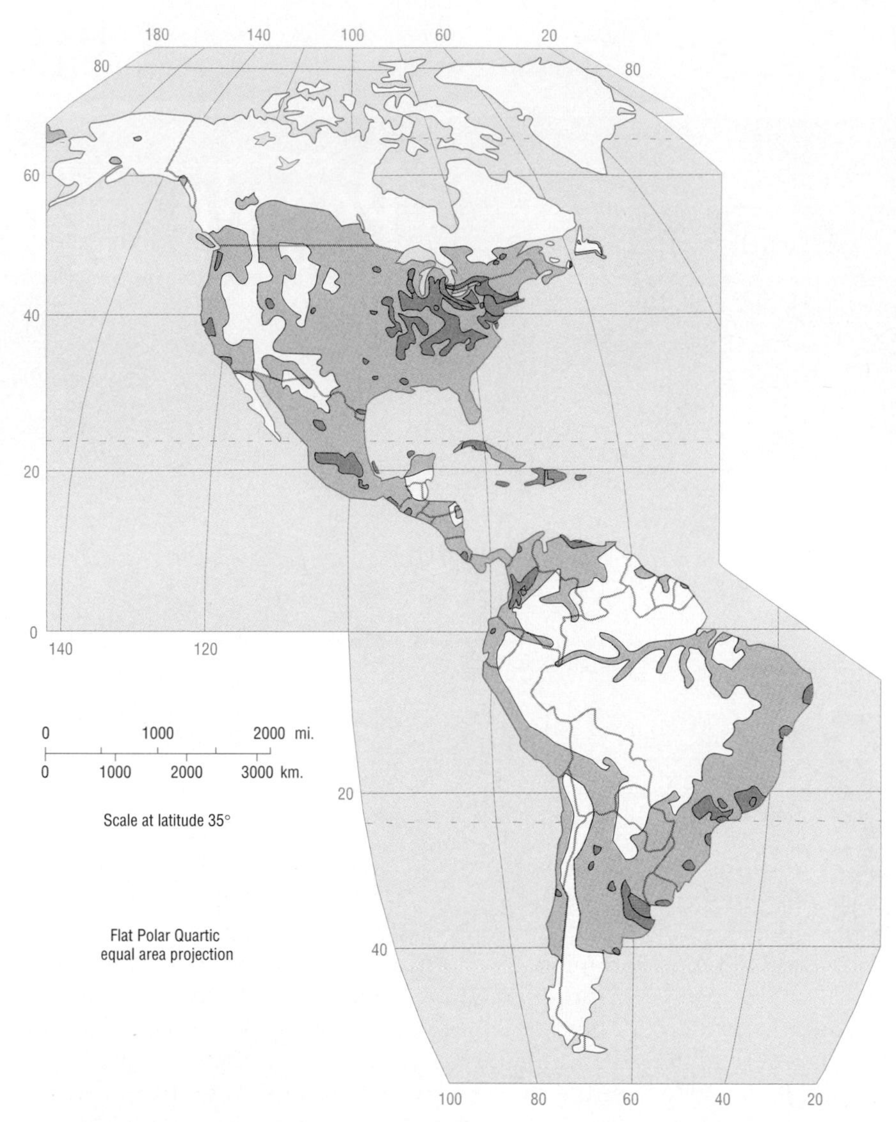

Figure 2.1
Population density in the world. Many causal forces, both physical environmental and cultural, have been at work over the centuries to produce this complicated spatial pattern. It represents the most basic cultural geographical distribution of all. (Sources: Adapted from *Goode's World Atlas.* Chicago: Rand McNally, with modifications based on the *World Population Data Sheet.* Washington, DC: Population Reference Bureau.)

Demographic Regions

The formal regions devised by population geographers can be called **demographic regions.** They prove helpful in describing spatial variations in population density, growth, and characteristics. In this way, geographers learn how demographic and social traits differ from place to place.

Population Distribution

If we consider the distribution of people by continents, we find that 73.5 percent of the human race lives in Eurasia. The continent of North

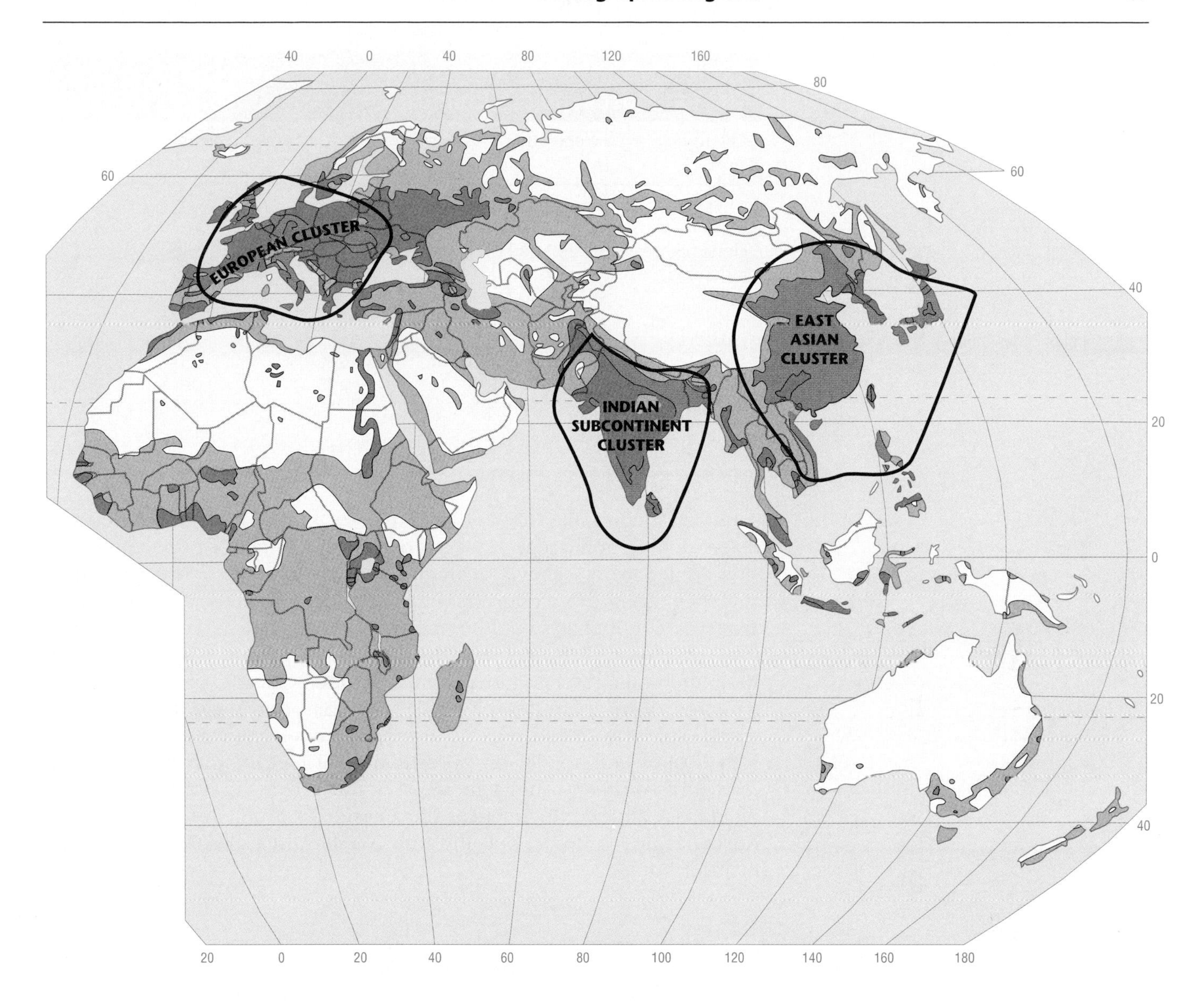

America is home to only 8 percent of all people; Africa to 12.5 percent; South America to 5.5 percent; and Australia and the Pacific Islands to less than one-half of 1 percent. If we consider population distribution by political units, we find that 21 percent of all humans reside in China; 16 percent in India; and only 4.5 percent in the United States (Table 2.1 and Figure 2.2).

We can also divide population distribution into *density* categories such as *thickly settled* areas, which have 250 or more persons per square mile (100 or more per square kilometer); *moderately settled* areas, with 60 to 250 persons per square mile (25 to 100 per sq. km.); *thinly settled* areas, inhabited by 2 to 60 persons per square mile (1 to 25 per sq. km.); and *largely unpopulated* areas, with fewer than 2 per-

TABLE 2.1
The Ten Most Populous Countries

Country	Population	As % of World Total	People per sq. mi. (sq. km.)
China	1,192,000,000	21 %	323 (125)
India	911,600,000	16 %	737 (285)
United States	260,800,000	4.7%	69 (27)
Indonesia	199,700,000	3.6%	265 (102)
Brazil	155,300,000	2.8%	47 (18)
Russia	147,800,000	2.6%	22 (9)
Pakistan	126,400,000	2.3%	372 (144)
Japan	125,000,000	2.2%	857 (331)
Bangladesh	116,600,000	2.1%	2,097 (810)
Nigeria	98,100,000	1.7%	275 (106)

Source: Adapted from *World Population Data Sheet*, Washington, DC: Population Reference Bureau.

sons per square mile (fewer than 1 per sq. km.). These categories represent demographic regions based on the single trait of population density. As Figure 2.1 shows, a fragmented crescent of dense settlement stretches along the western, southern, and eastern edges of the huge Eurasian continent. Two-thirds of the human race is concentrated in this crescent, which contains three main population clusters—eastern Asia, the Indian subcontinent, and Europe. Outside of Eurasia, only scattered districts are densely settled. Despite our image of a crowded world, sparsely settled regions are much more extensive than heavily settled ones and appear on every continent (see box, *Is the World Really Overcrowded?*). Thin settlement characterizes the northern sections of Eurasia and North America, the interior of South America, most of Australia, and a desert belt through North Africa and Arabia into the heart of Eurasia.

Figure 2.2
India ranks second only to China in population size. It lies in the densely settled crescent of peripheral Eurasia. The streets of its towns and cities are often crowded, and overpopulation is perhaps India's greatest problem.

Is the World Really Overcrowded?

Those who fear overpopulation often conjure up the specter of a world in which people are elbow-to-elbow, with no open space left. How crowded is the present world, really? If all of humanity stood in such a crowd, how much area would be covered?

Allowing 4 square feet for each human, the present world population of around 5.5 billion would require about 22 billion square feet, or roughly 790 square miles (2050 square kilometers). This is approximately the size of one typical county in the American Midwest. Amazingly, even at that size, the world population is taxing natural resources to the utmost.

Adapted from Bunge, William W. "The Geography of Human Survival." *Annals of the Association of American Geographers*, 63 (1973): 288.

Although population density allows us to view the distribution of people, it does not tell us anything about standard of living, overpopulation, or underpopulation. Some of the most densely populated areas in the world have the highest standards of living—and even suffer from labor shortages. For example, this has been true of the major industrial areas of Germany and the Netherlands. In certain other cases, regions designated as thinly settled may actually be severely overpopulated, marginal agricultural lands. Although 1000 persons per square mile (400 per square kilometer) is a "dense" population for a farming area, it is "sparse" for an industrial district. In this sense, *physiological density*—the density beyond which people cease to be nutritionally self-sufficient using their traditional adaptive strategy—can be far more useful as an index of overpopulation.

Density, whether absolute or physiological, is a static concept. It conceals the changes that constantly occur, in particular pronounced regional differences in population growth or decline. To gain that dynamic perspective, we need to consider the geography of birthrates and death rates.

Patterns of Natality

Birthrates, measured as the number of births in a year per thousand people, vary greatly from one area to another (Figure 2.3). In many ways, the map of birthrates does not correspond to the map of population density. In fact, the inverse situation occurs in certain areas of the world. Some densely populated areas, such as Europe and China, have low birthrates, while some sparsely settled regions, as for example interior Africa, have high birthrates. In general, high birthrates are concentrated in a belt through the lower latitudes, especially the tropics and subtropics, while mid-latitude and high-latitude countries have low birthrates. Recent data suggest that birthrates are now declining modestly in the Third World.

Another, increasingly popular method of assessing natality is the *fertility rate*, measured as the average number of children born to each woman during her reproductive years. The fertility rate is perhaps more revealing, since it focuses on the female segment of the population and reveals family size. Rates vary markedly from one part of the world to another. In most of Europe, the fertility rate now stands below 2.0, with Spain the lowest at 1.2. Population decline has already set in across wide areas of Europe. Sub-Saharan Africa, by contrast, has a fertility

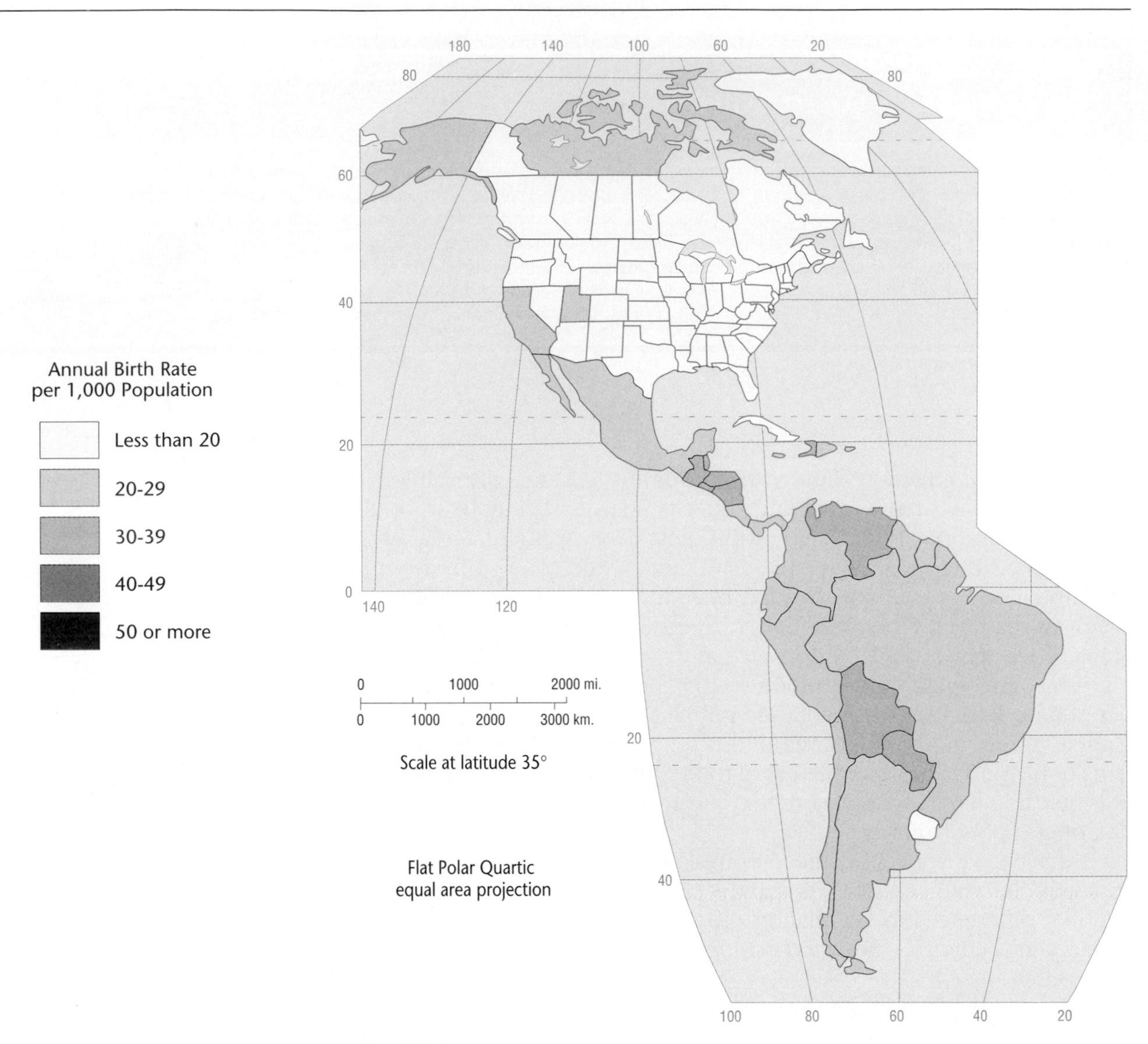

Figure 2.3
The annual birthrate per thousand inhabitants. In general, the highest birthrates occur in the most impoverished, rural nations, while the lowest birthrates are found in urbanized, industrialized countries. (Sources: *World Population Data Sheet.* Washington, DC: Population Reference Bureau; United Nations *Demographic Yearbook*; *Statistical Abstract of the United States.* Washington, DC; *Canada Yearbook*; *Census of Australia*.)

rate of 6.4, led by countries such as Nigeria, Ivory Coast, and Uganda, with a rate of 7.4.

The Geography of Mortality

The global pattern of **death rates,** the number of deaths in a year per thousand people, reveals both similarities to and differences from the map of birthrates. As Figure 2.4 shows, the most striking feature of the mortality map is the concentration of high figures in sub-Saharan Africa, the worst area in the world for life-threatening diseases. By contrast, the American tropics generally have rather low death rates, as is also true of the desert belt across North Africa, the Middle East, and Central

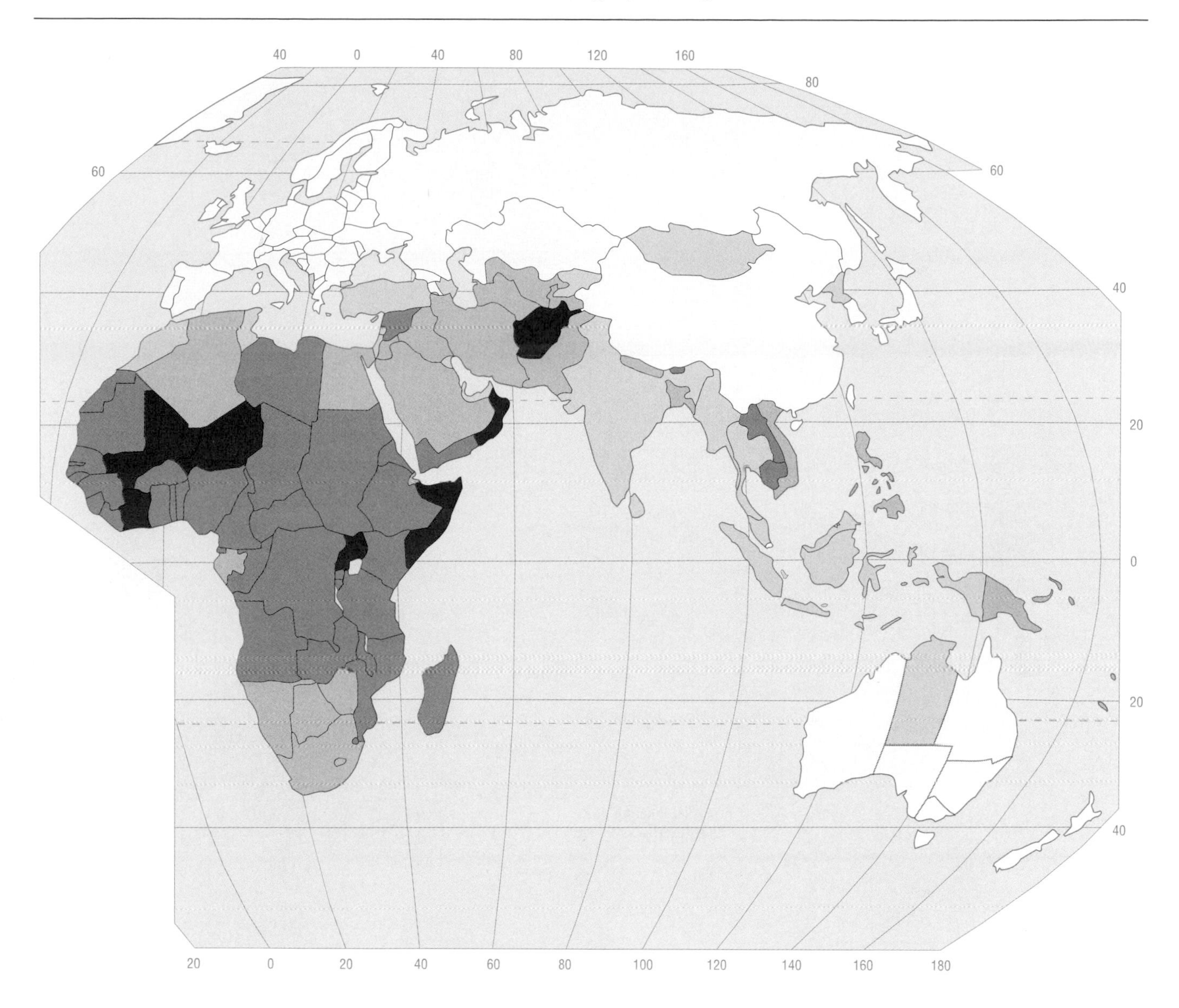

Asia. In these regions, the preponderantly young population depresses the death rate per thousand. Because of its much older population, most of Europe, including Russia, displays a somewhat higher death rate. Australia, Canada, and the United States, which continue to attract mostly young immigrants, have low death rates.

Perhaps the tropical African zone of high mortality is linked to the fact that primates, including human beings, evolved as biological species there. Nature, ever seeking a balance, developed effective diseases to control human population in the region where our species originated. Human migration from Africa occurred so relatively recently and rapidly that on other continents we perhaps temporarily escaped many of the disease and predator controls of our original homeland.

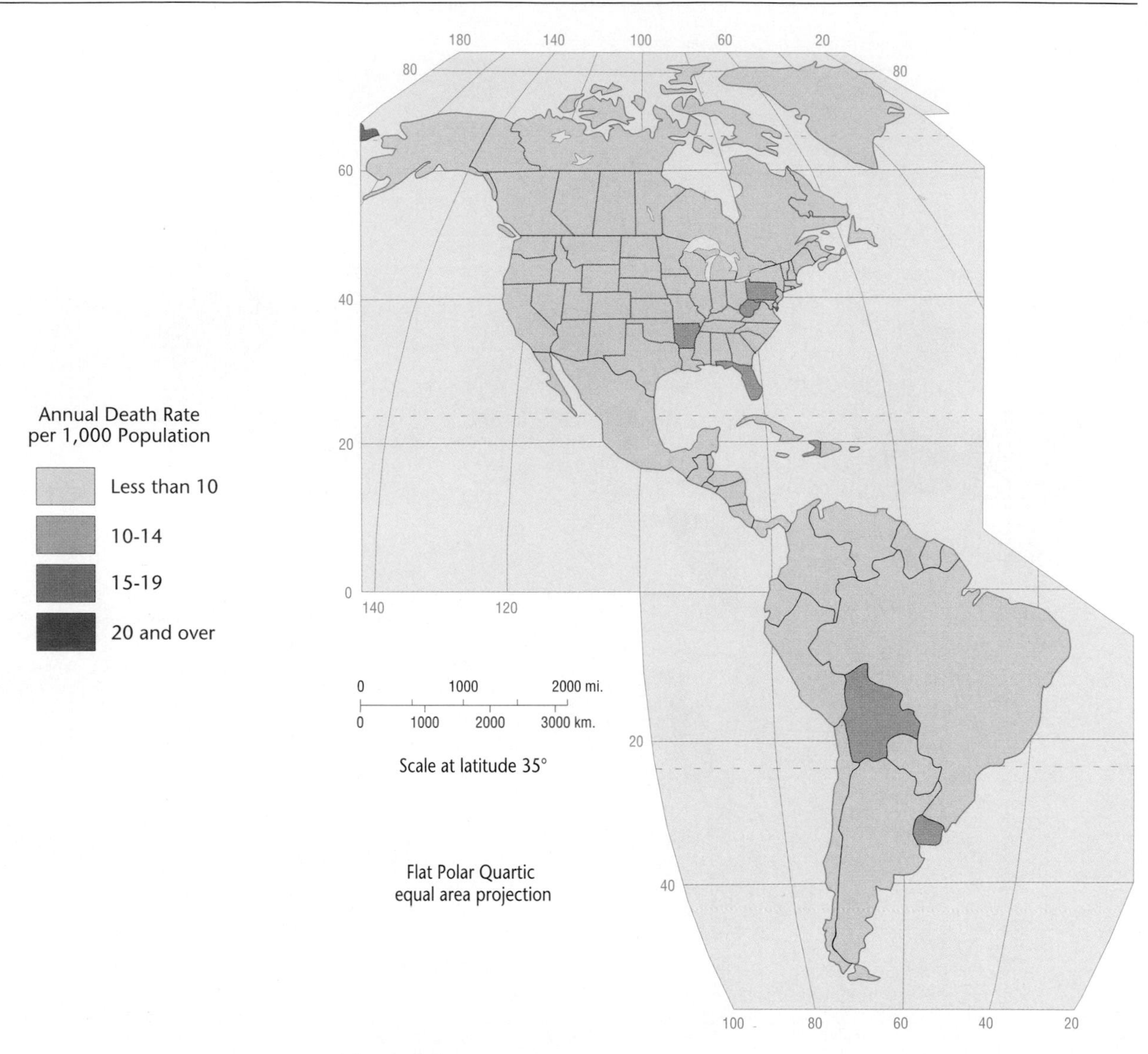

Figure 2.4
The annual death rate per thousand inhabitants. Compare with Figure 2.3, and note that sub-Saharan Africa ranks very high in both birth and death rates. (Sources: Same as for Fig. 2.3.)

Also, shifting climatic patterns imposed a great desert belt between the outward-diffusing human race and our African source, blocking spread of the diseases of the humid tropics. The latest great epidemic to threaten humankind, AIDS, apparently also developed in tropical Africa and shows the highest incidence there (Figure 2.5). Unlike many other fatal diseases of the African tropics, AIDS has a proven ability to take root in temperate lands.

The Population Explosion

When considered together, the spatial contrasts in population density, natality, and mortality reveal one of the epic problems of the modern age: the **population explosion.** The crucial element triggering this ex-

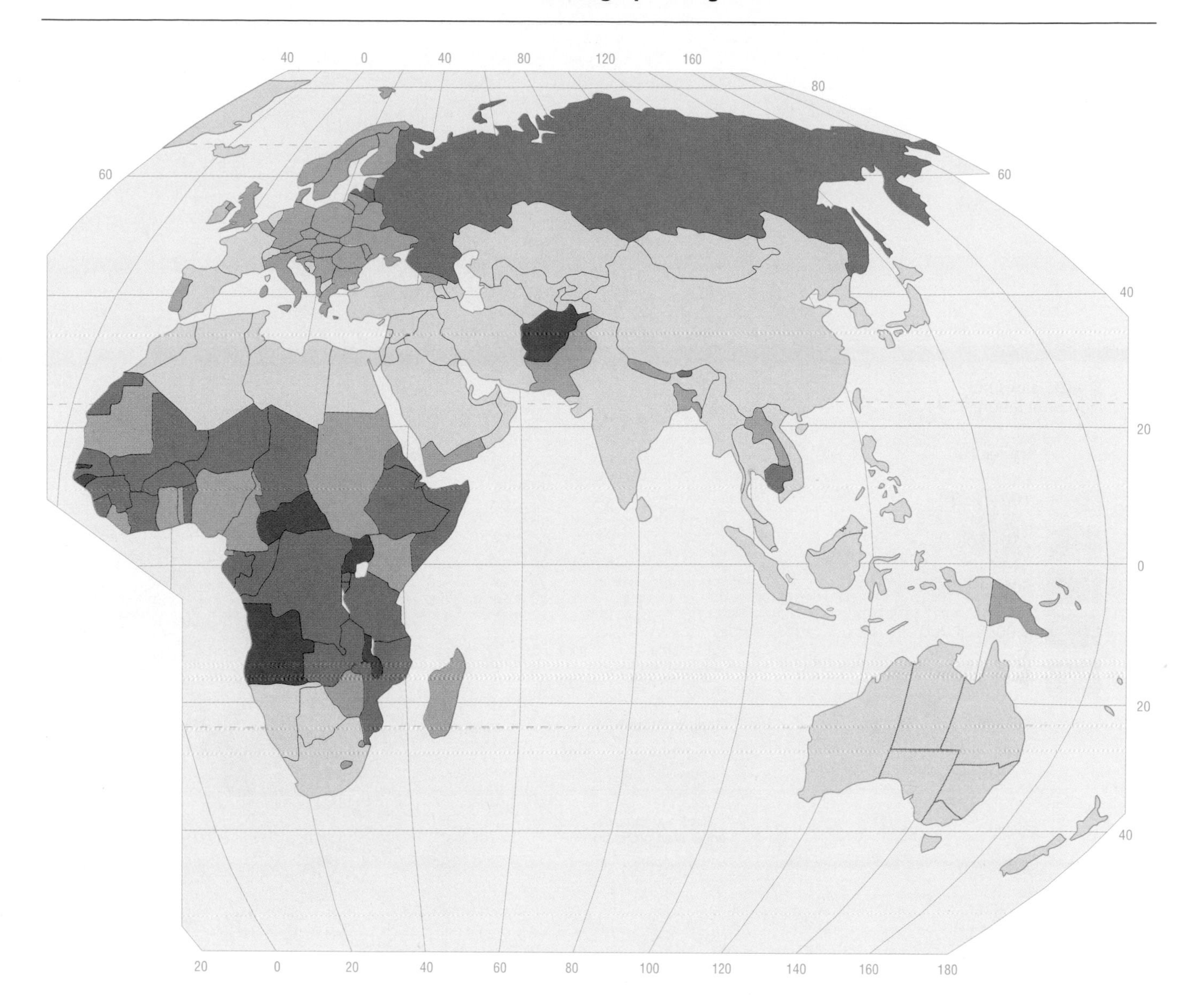

plosion has been a dramatic decrease in the death rate, particularly for infants and children, in most of the world, without an accompanying universal decline in the birthrate. In many traditional cultures, only two or three offspring in a family of six to eight children might live to adulthood, and when improved health conditions allowed more of the children to survive, the cultural norm encouraging large families persisted.

On a global scale, we can easily describe the population crisis. The number of people in the world has been increasing geometrically, doubling in shorter and shorter periods of time. Table 2.2 shows the progression. The overall effect of even a few population doublings is startling. An example of a geometric progression is provided by the legend of the king who was willing to grant any wish to the person who could supply a grain of wheat for the first square of his chessboard, two

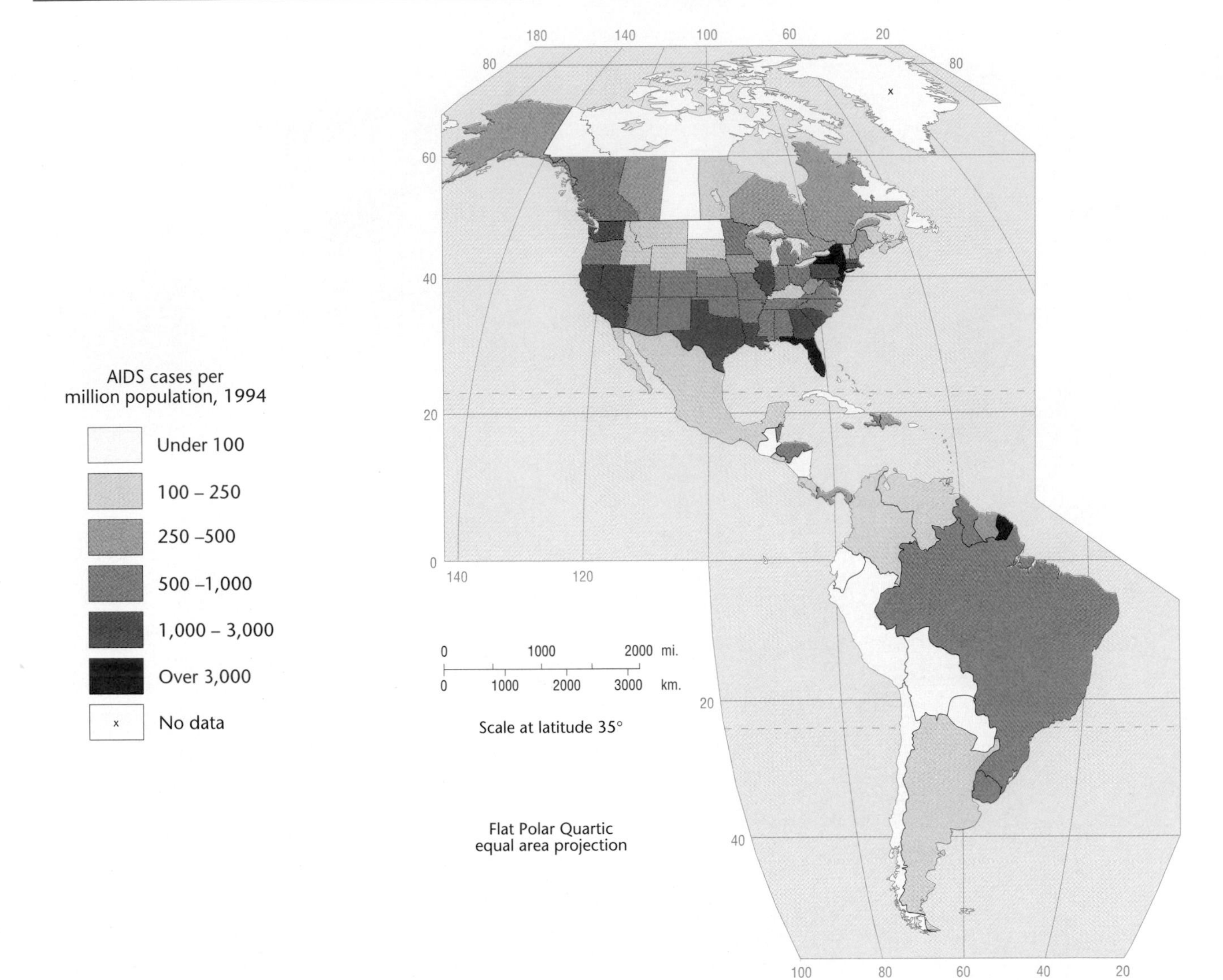

Figure 2.5
The geography of AIDS, shown as documented cumulative cases per million people. The number of cases used in the calculation is the total ever reported, including persons since deceased. HIV-infected persons who do not have symptoms of AIDS are excluded. The quality of data gathering varies widely from one country to another, and is particularly poor in Africa and most of Asia. (Sources: World Health Organization Surveillance Program, Geneva; US Dept. of Health and Human Services, Centers for Disease Control; Government of Canada; Australian government.)

grains for the second square, four for the third, and so on. To cover all 64 squares and win, the candidate would have had to present a cache of wheat many times larger than today's worldwide wheat crop.

Humans reproduced at an extraordinarily modest rate throughout most of history, but about 1700 rapid population growth began. At present, some 100 million more people are born each year than die, and some 170 persons are added to the total world population each *minute*. At the present rate of increase, people double in number every 43 years.

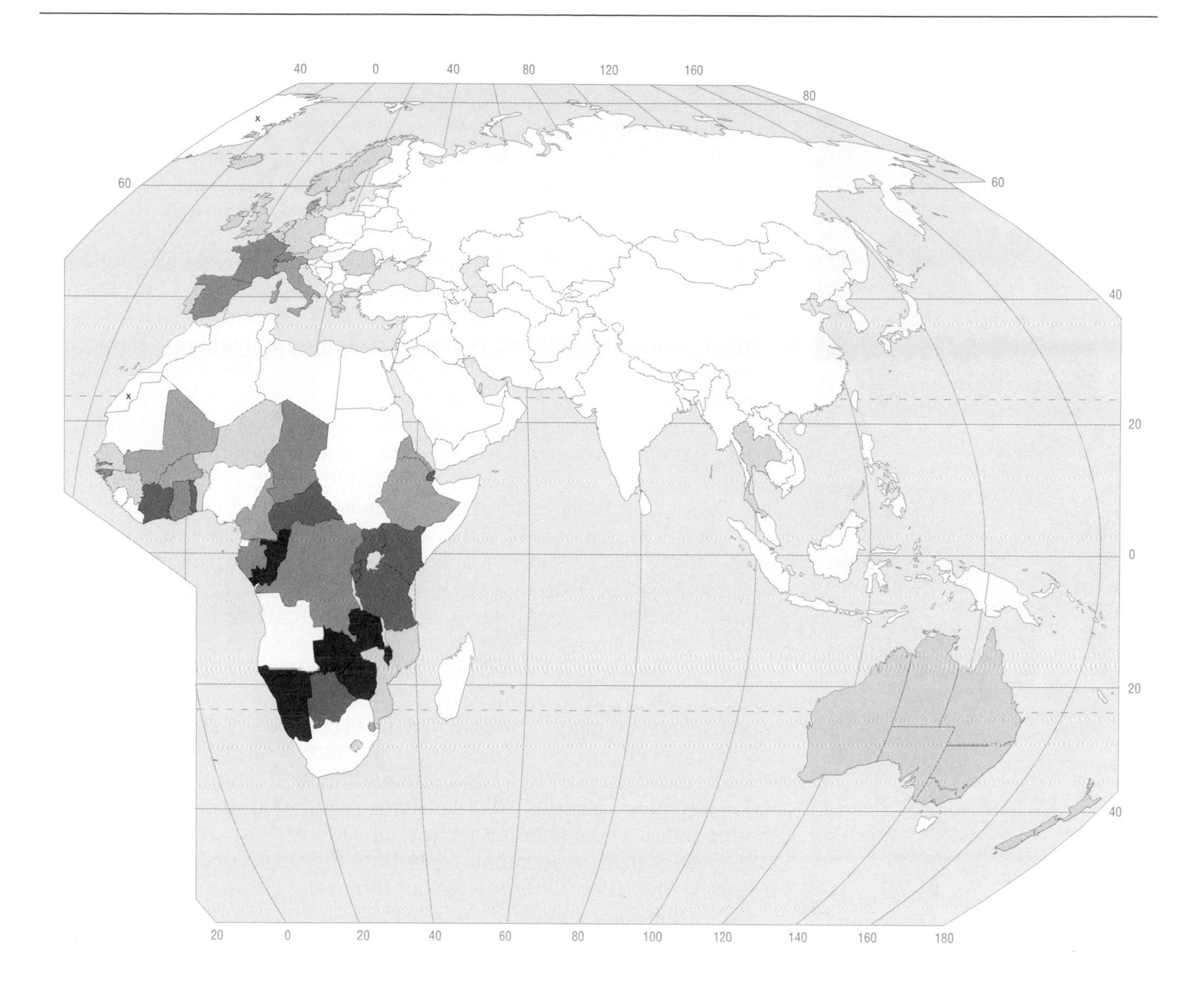

TABLE 2.2
The World Population Growth

Year	World Population	Year	World Population
40,000 BC	1,500,000	1960	3,000,000,000
8,000 BC	10,000,000	1965	3,200,000,000
Birth of Christ	200,000,000	1970	3,610,000,000
1000	275,000,000	1975	4,000,000,000
1300	380,000,000	1980	4,400,000,000
1500	450,000,000	1985	4,850,000,000
1650	500,000,000	1990	5,300,000,000
1750	700,000,000	1995	5,700,000,000
1800	910,000,000	2000 (est.)	6,000,000,000
1850	1,200,000,000	2010 (est.)	7,022,000,000
1900	1,600,000,000	2025 (est.)	8,375,000,000
1950	2,600,000,000		

Thomas R. Malthus
1766–1834

Born in the shire of Surrey, England, Malthus studied theology at Cambridge and became an ordained minister. While still a minister, he began writing his essay on population. Gradually, writing and lecturing became his major interests. In 1805, he was appointed a professor of modern history and political economy at Haileybury College, a position he held until his death. Long before most scholars were concerned with overpopulation, Malthus warned of it. His famous *Essay on the Principles of Population* was published in 1798. Karl Marx, Charles Darwin, and many others read and commented on his work. Malthus rejected most artificial birth-control techniques as theologically unacceptable, approving only delayed marriage and moral restraint. He believed warfare, famine, and disease would solve the problem if people failed to seek a more humane solution. In recent decades, his ideas have received renewed attention as the world experiences a population crisis. (For more on Malthus and his influence, see the books coedited by Dupâquier and Fauve-Chamoux and by Coleman and Schofield in Sources and Suggested Readings.)

Some scholars foresaw long ago that an ever-increasing population would eventually present difficulties. As early as the 1600s, William Petty, who pioneered the science of statistics, predicted that an over-population crisis would develop one thousand years in the future. According to Petty, in the year 2600 there would be one person for each three acres of land. The most famous pioneer observer of population growth, Thomas Malthus (see biographical box), published in 1798 *An Essay on the Principles of Population* (see box, *Excerpts from the Writings of Thomas Malthus*). He believed that the human ability to multiply far exceeds our ability to increase food production. Consequently, Malthus maintained, "a strong and constantly operating check on population" will necessarily act as a natural control on numbers. Malthus regarded famine and war as inevitable because they curb population growth (Figure 2.6). Today, almost two centuries after Malthus penned his warnings, this basic argument is still accepted in many quarters. Geographers, accordingly, have devoted considerable attention to the spatial aspects of food availability and famine, as suggested by the works of Currey and Watts listed in the readings at the end of this chapter.

At the present rate of increase, the world population would, within a relatively few centuries, reach a level where each person had only 1 square foot (less than one-tenth of a square meter) of land area. Obviously, conditions could never become this crowded (see box, *Is the World Really Overcrowded?*). It would be impossible to feed and house such a dense clustering of people. Indeed, some population scholars tend to see the extraordinary rise in human fertility rates at the present time as something of a historic oddity. They expect the world population to level out, perhaps early in the twenty-first century, at somewhere between 8 and 15 billion people. Certain others predict regional demographic collapses—that is, sharp population decline—in the near future, and one may be under way already in parts of eastern Europe. Some feel that demographic stabilization will occur before any catastrophic depletion of resources, but others are convinced that the Earth cannot support many more people without an ecological disaster.

Demographic Transformation

The population explosion is not a worldwide phenomenon. Rather, the problem is confined to underdeveloped and developing countries with a large difference between birth and death rates (Figure 2.7). All industrialized, technologically advanced countries have achieved low fertility rates and nearly stabilized populations, having passed through the **demographic transformation** (Figure 2.8). In preindustrial societies, birth and death rates are both normally high, leading to almost no population growth. With the coming of the industrial era, medical advances and improvements in diet set the stage for a drop in death rates. Human life expectancy in the industrialized countries soared from an average of 35 years in the eighteenth century to 75 years or more at present. The result is population explosion as fertility outruns mortality. Eventually, after a lag, a decline in the birthrate follows the decline in the death rate. Finally, in a *postindustrial* period (see Chapter 12), the demographic transformation produces actual **zero population growth** or decline (Figure 2.8). Many countries fail to pass through the entire demographic transformation, and the population explosion, or stage 2 of the model, becomes prolonged, with potentially catastrophic results.

Excerpts from the Writings of Thomas Malthus

"I think I may fairly make two postulata.

"First, that food is necessary to the existence of man.

"Secondly, that the passion between the sexes is necessary, and will remain nearly in its present state.

". . . Assuming, then, my postulata as granted, I say, that the power of population is indefinitely greater than the power in the earth to produce subsistence for man.

"Population, when unchecked, increases in a geometrical ratio. Subsistence only increases in an arithmetical ratio. A slight acquaintance with numbers will show the immensity of the first power in comparison of the second.

"By that law of our nature which makes food necessary to the life of Man, the effects of these two unequal powers must be kept equal.

"This implies a strong and constantly operating check on population. . . . "

From Malthus, Thomas. *An Essay on the Principles of Population,* chap. 1.

Stages 3 and 4 of the demographic transformation require effective methods of birth control. Traditionally, *infanticide*—the killing of the newborn—served as the principal method in some cultures. *Abortion*, almost as controversial a technique, remains common in some parts of the world (Figure 2.9). Far more common today are various contraceptive devices.

Figure 2.6

War as a device for population control in central Europe, 1618–1648. Thomas Malthus regarded war as inevitable to help control population growth. He would understand this map, which reveals how effective war can be in destroying people. The Thirty Years' War, with its attendant killing, starvation, and disease, drastically reduced the population in some central European provinces. Population density was greatly altered. (After *Westermanns Grosser Atlas Zur Weltgeschichte.* Braunschweig: Georg Westermann, 1956, 107.)

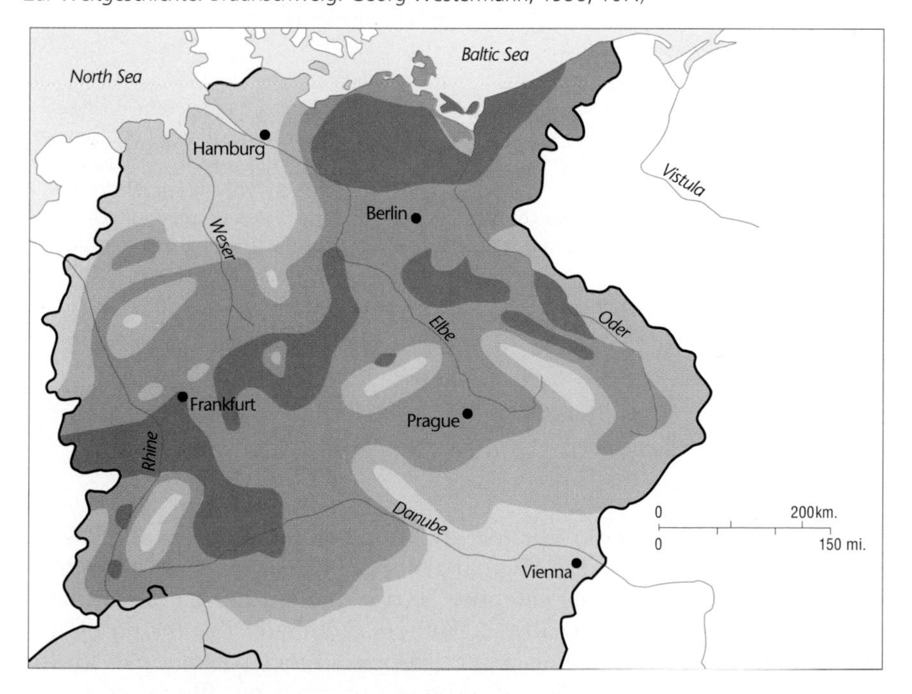

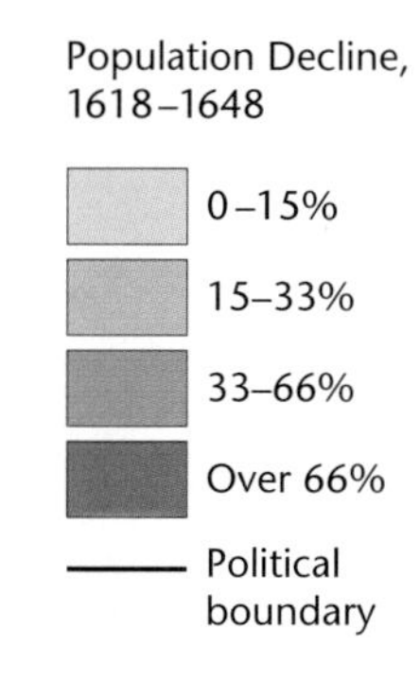

Figure 2.7

The annual natural change of population. The change is calculated as the difference between the number of births and deaths in a year, taken as a percentage of total population. Emigration and immigration are not considered. Note the contrast between tropical areas and the middle and upper latitudes. In several places, countries with very slow increase border areas with extremely high growth. (Source: *World Population Data Sheet.* Washington, DC: Population Reference Bureau; censuses and statistical yearbooks for the United States, Canada, and Australia.)

Age Distributions

Some countries have overwhelmingly young populations, with close to half of their people under 15 years of age. Kenya is such a country, with 49 percent in that age category, as are many other nations in Latin America, Africa, and tropical Asia. Others, generally the countries that industrialized early, have a great preponderance of people in the over-20/under-60 age bracket. A growing number of affluent countries

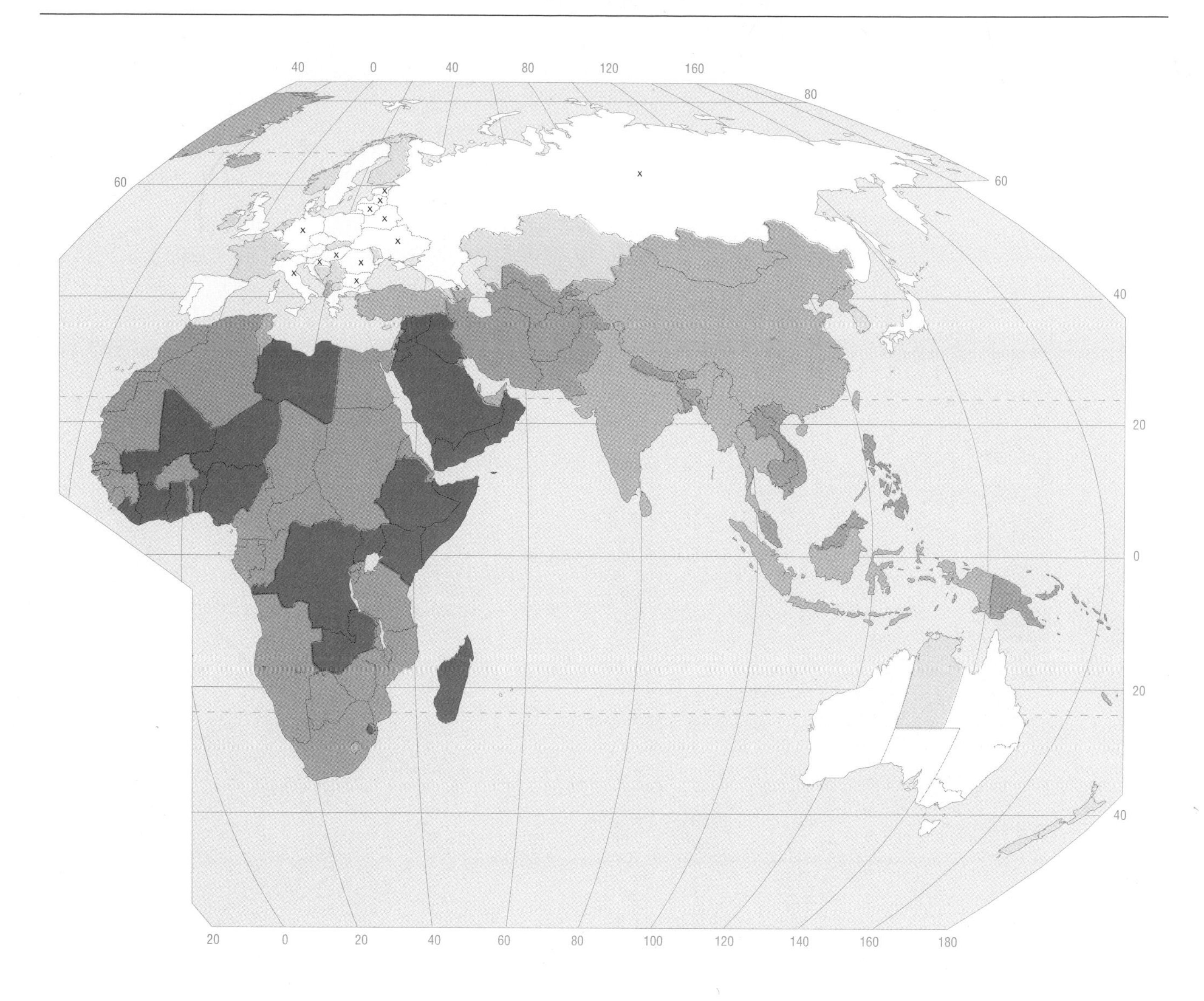

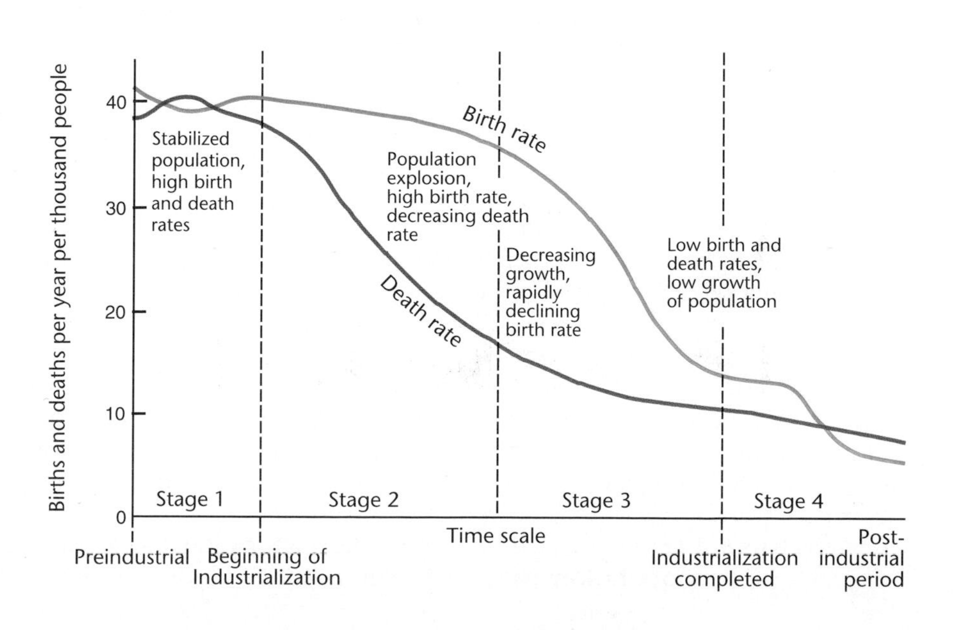

Figure 2.8
The demographic transformation as a graph. The "transformation" occurs in several steps, as the industrialization of a country progresses. Initially, the death rate declines rapidly, causing a population explosion as the gap between the number of births and deaths widens. Then the birthrate begins a sharp decline. The transformation ends when both birth and death rates have reached low levels, by which time the total population is many times greater than at the beginning of the transformation. In the postindustrial phase, population decline eventually begins.

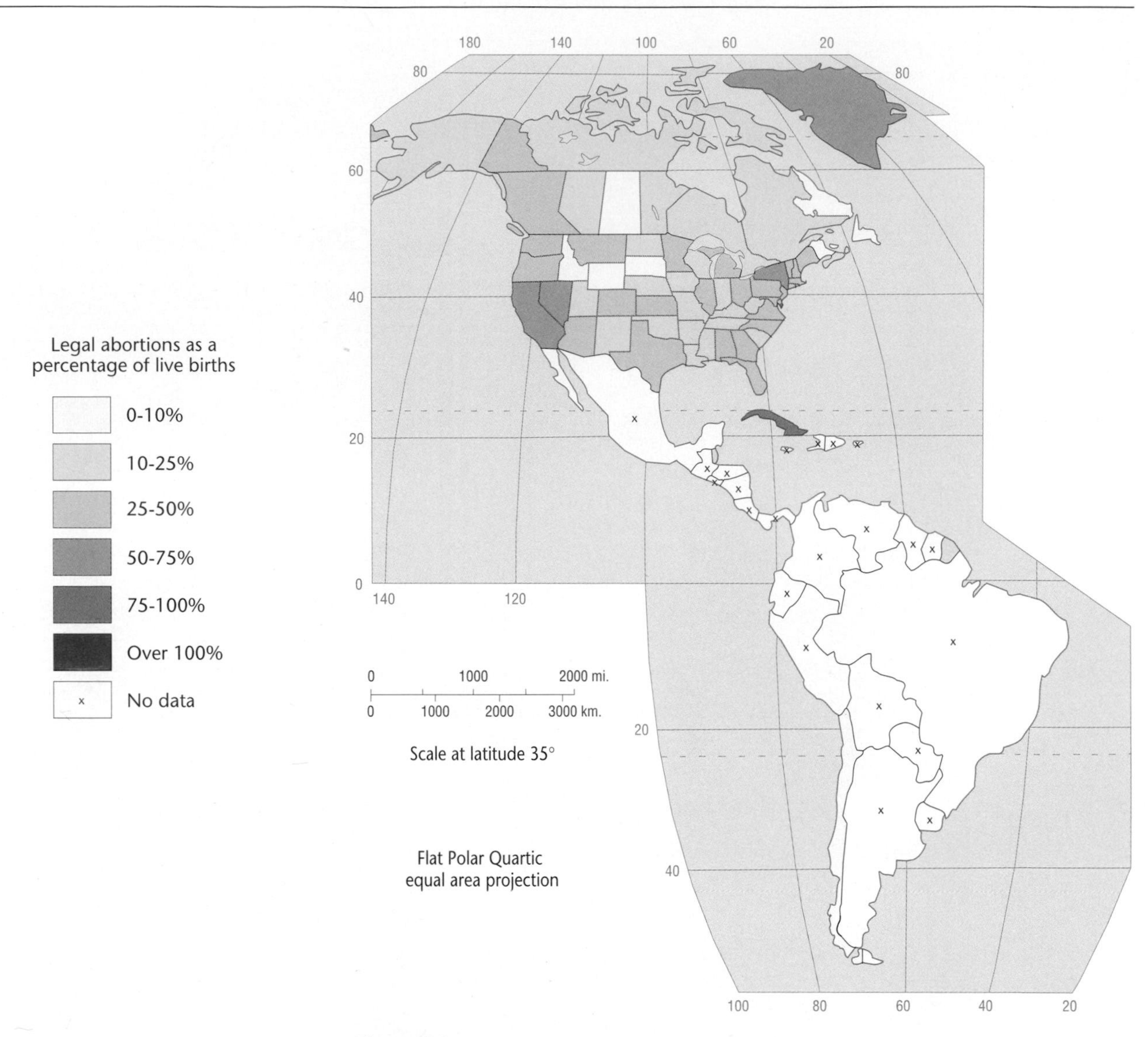

Figure 2.9
Spatial pattern of legal abortion. Why do the highest rates occur in the formerly Communist areas? (Sources: United Nations *Demographic Yearbook*; US Bureau of the Census, *Statistical Abstract of the United States*; *Canada Yearbook*; Australian government. Data are for most recent year avaliable.)

have remarkably aged populations. In Sweden, for example, fully 18 percent of the people have now passed the traditional retirement age of 65, and many other European countries are not far behind. What a contrast emerges when we compare Europe with Africa, Latin America, or parts of Asia, where the average person never even lives to age 65. In Sudan, Gambia, Saudi Arabia, Guatemala, and many other countries, only 2 to 3 percent of the people have reached that age. Very different cultures result in populations that have disproportionate numbers of young or aged people, adding another component to the human mosaic.

A very useful graphic device for comparing such national age characteristics is the **population pyramid** (Figure 2.10). Careful study of

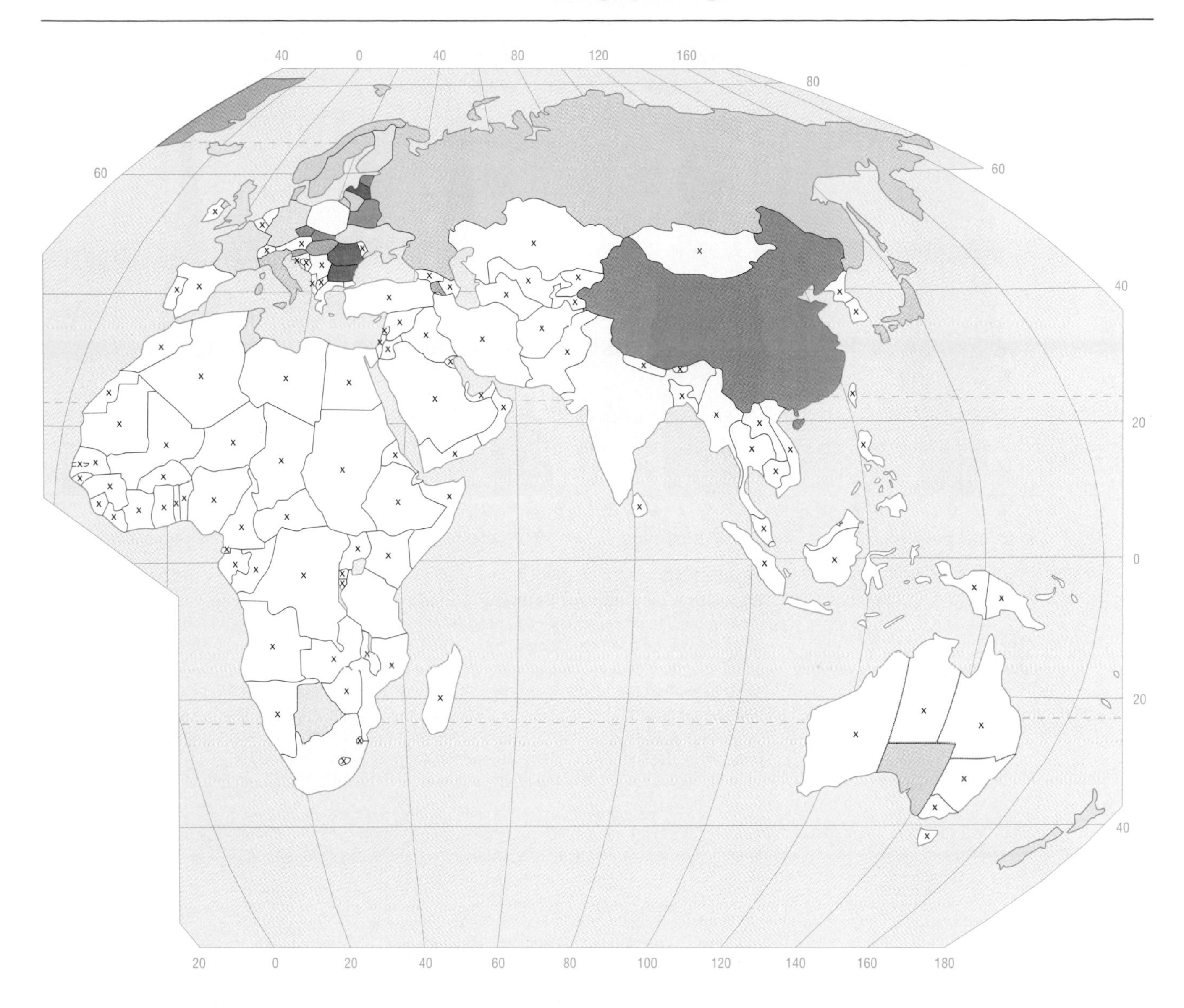

such pyramids not only reveals the past progress of birth control but also allows geographers to predict future population trends. Youth-weighted pyramids, broad at the base, suggest the rapid growth typical of the population explosion. Those excessively narrow at the base represent countries approaching population stability.

Age structure also differs spatially within individual countries. For example, rural populations in the United States and many other countries are usually older than those in urban areas. The flight of young people to the cities has left some rural counties in the United States with populations 45 years or older in median age. Some warm areas of the United States have become retirement havens for the elderly, so that parts of Arizona and Florida have populations far above average in

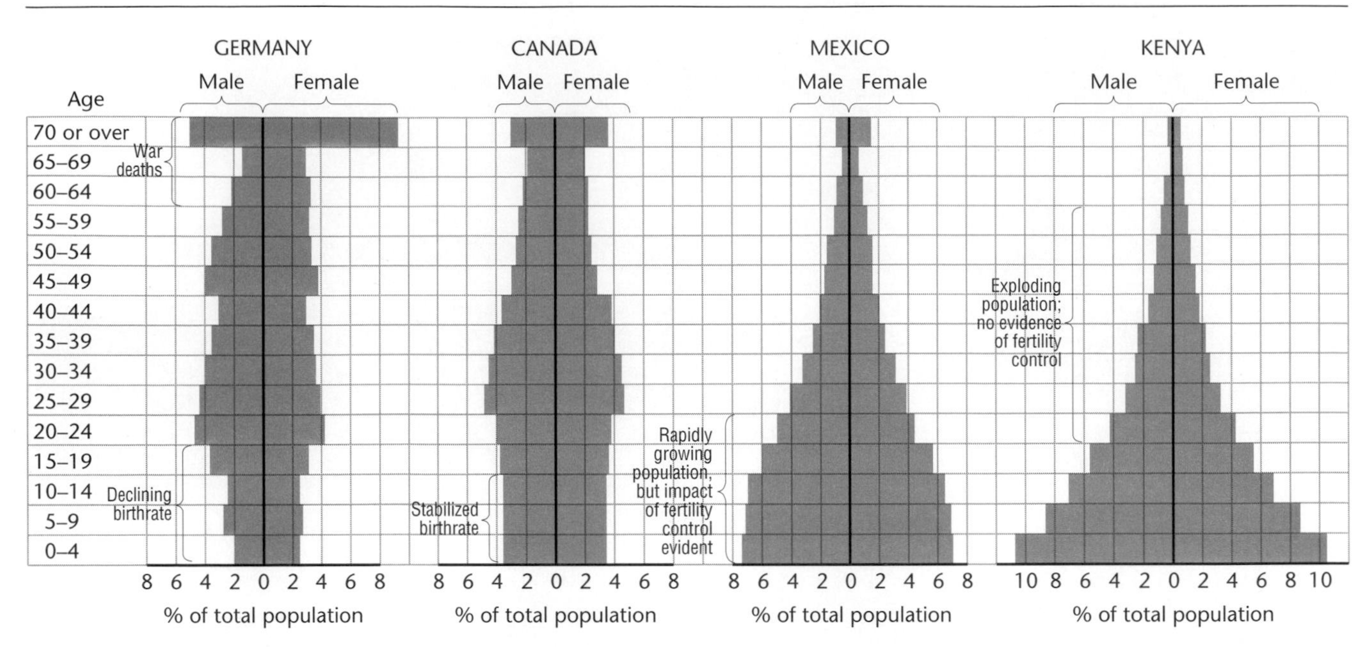

Figure 2.10
Population pyramids for Germany, Canada, Kenya, and Mexico. Germany's "pyramid" looks more like a precariously balanced pillar, an indication that its population is achieving stability. Kenya, by contrast, displays the classic stepped pyramid of an exploding population. Note, too, how population explosion in recent past decades in Mexico would continue to fuel rapid growth in the future, even though birthrates have dropped rapidly, since the number of women in the child-producing age span is so much larger than it was previously. The Canadian pyramid reveals recent sharp declines in the birthrate. Germany is now experiencing actual population decline. (Source: United Nations *Demographic Yearbook*.)

age. Communities such as Sun City near Phoenix, Arizona, legally restrict residence to the elderly. In Great Britain, coastal districts have a much higher proportion of elderly than does the interior, causing the map to resemble a hollow shell and suggesting that the aged often migrate on retirement to seaside locations (Figure 2.11).

Geography of Gender

While the human race is divided almost evenly between females and males, geographical differences in the **sex ratio** occur. Recently settled areas typically have more males than females, as is evident in parts of Alaska, northern Canada, and tropical Australia (Figure 2.12). At the latest census, males comprised 53 percent of Alaska's inhabitants. By contrast, Mississippi's population was 52 percent female, reflecting in part the emigration of young males seeking better economic opportunity elsewhere. Some poverty-stricken parts of South Africa are as much as 59 percent female.

Other causal forces also influence the geography of gender. Prolonged wars reduce the male population, as remains evident in Germany's population pyramid even a half-century after the end of World

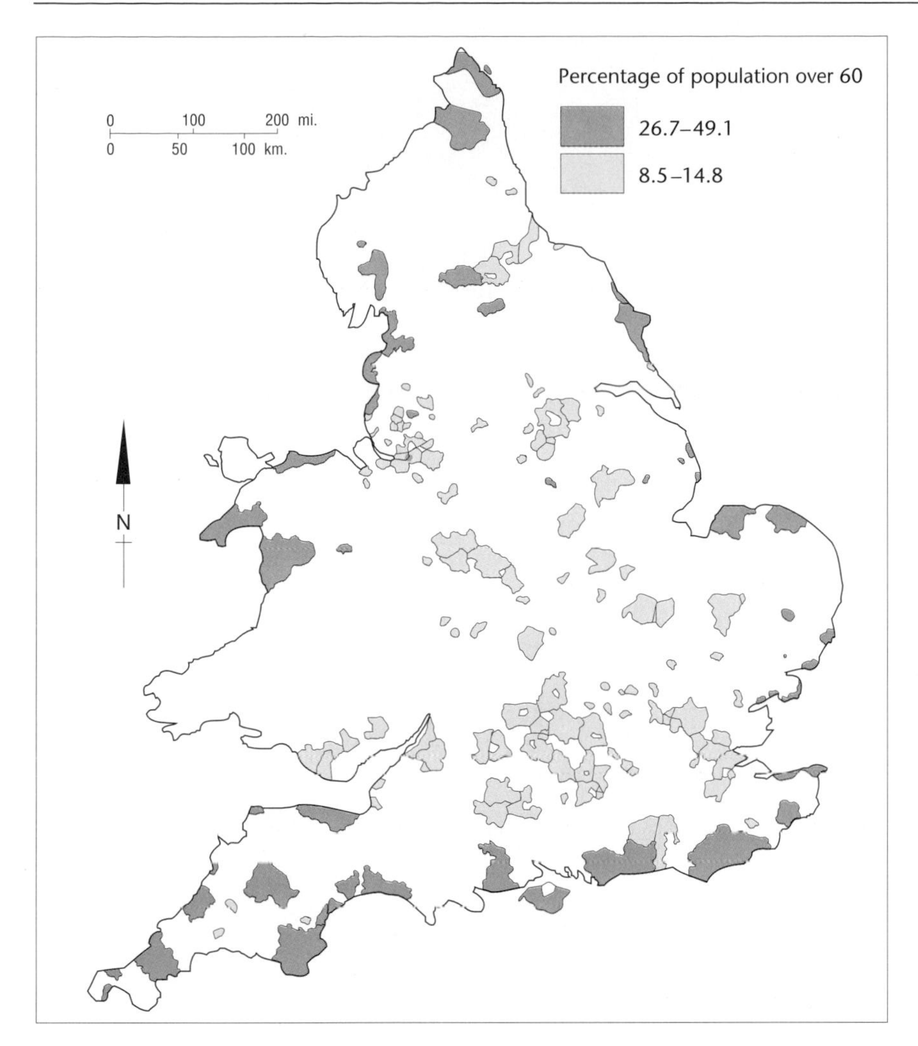

Figure 2.11
Proportion of elderly in the population of England and Wales, 1971. Why did elderly people form a larger part of the population in the coastal regions than in the interior? (After Law, C. M., and A. M. Warnes, "The Changing Geography of the Elderly in England and Wales." *Transactions of the Institute of British Geographers,* 1 (1976): 461.)

War II (Figure 2.10). Even more disturbing is the tendency in certain countries, most notoriously China and India, to engage in female-specific infanticide or abortion, a result of a culturally based preference for male offspring. Ultrasound devices are now available even to rural peasants in China that allow gender identification of fetuses. About 100,000 such devices were in use by 1990 in China. The sex ratio has already been changed, and by the year 2020, China will have 110 males of marriageable age for every 100 females. A profound gender imbalance already exists there, and in India, as well, where today there are only 930 females for each 1000 males.

Daily life also reveals a geography of gender. Daphne Spain refers to *gendered spaces,* which she finds in homes, schools, at work, and elsewhere. In other words, males and females are often spatially segre-

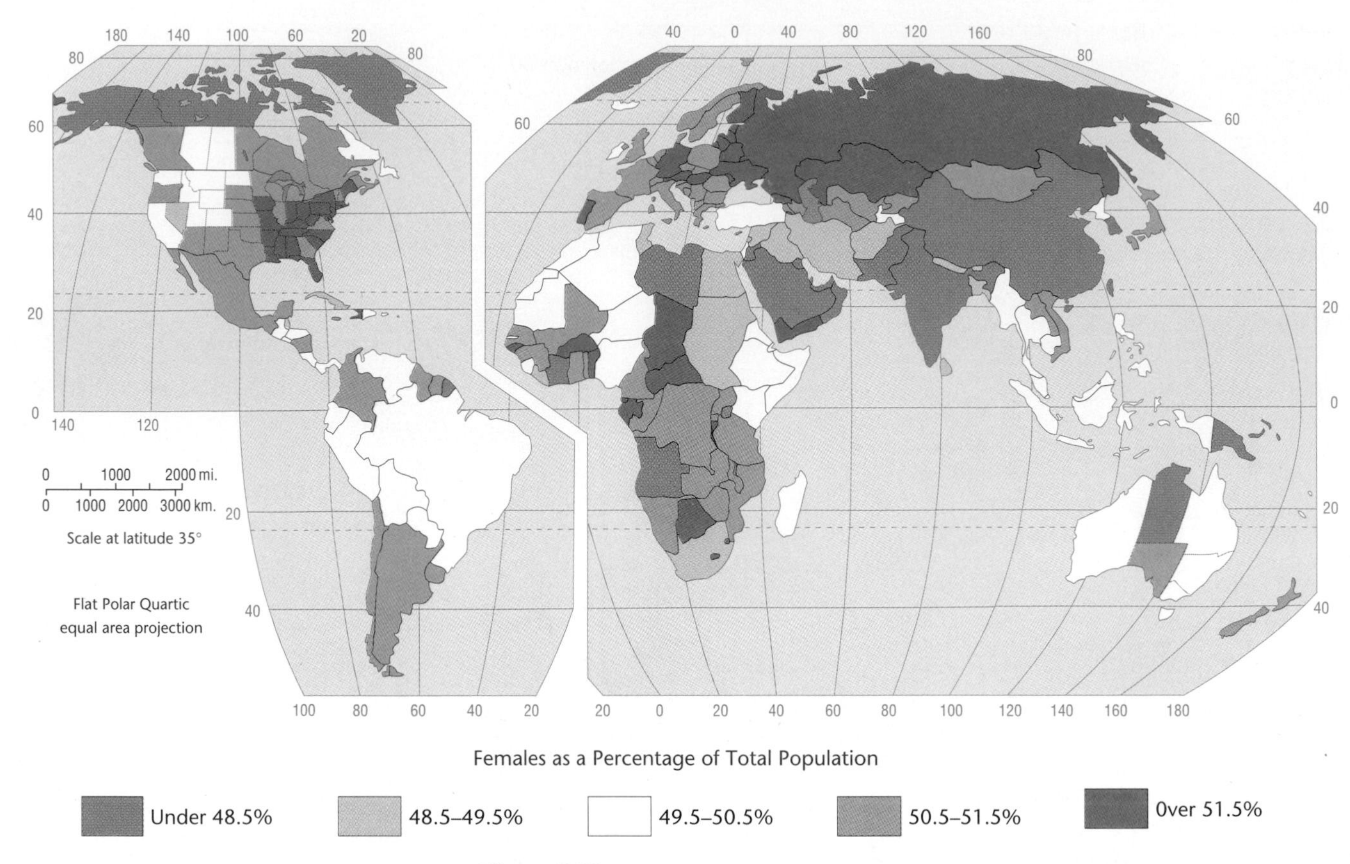

Figure 2.12
Females as a percentage of total population. What cultural practices might explain this curious pattern? (Sources: Same as for Fig. 2.3.)

gated, with attendant inequality of status, access to knowledge, and well-being. Some cultures impose gendered space more vigorously than others, as for example Muslim countries, where women face many restrictions concerning where they may go. Gender-specific place taboos occur in most cultures, as on the Mount Athos peninsula in Greece, where Christian monastic orders bar entry to all women and, indeed, females of any mammal species.

Standard of Living

By combining various demographic traits, we can assess *standard of living* and look at it geographically. Figure 2.13 represents one attempt to measure and map living standards. It is based on an index combining a measure of natural resources, industrial output, education, wealth, health conditions, and level of political rights. Nowadays, we often hear of "north versus south" in terms of prosperous, developed, mid-latitude countries versus poor, underdeveloped, tropical nations. While Figure 2.13 reveals a modicum of truth in that generalization, the spatial pattern also has an east versus west component, brought on by the collapse of the Soviet empire. The great spatial variation in living standards is one of the most fundamental geographical facts of our time and one of the most troubling. It could be the basis of future mass migrations or conflicts, particularly in those areas where the rich border the poor.

Diffusion in Population Geography

The theme of cultural diffusion can be applied to demography in various ways. *Migration,* for example, constitutes cultural diffusion. In fact, the migration of people represents the most basic aspect of relocation diffusion.

Migration

Humankind is not tied to one locale. Although our species apparently evolved in tropical Africa, we have proved remarkably adaptable to new and different physical environments. We have made ourselves at home in all but the most inhospitable climates, shunning only such places as ice-sheathed Antarctica and the shifting sands of Arabia's "Empty Quarter." Our permanent habitat extends from the edge of the ice sheets to the seashores, from desert valleys a thousand feet (300 meters) below sea level to mountain slopes 16,000 feet (5,000 meters) or more high. This far-flung distribution is the product of migration.

For those human beings who migrate, the process generally ranks as one of the greatest events of their lives. Even prehistoric migrations often remain embedded in folklore for centuries or millennia (Figure 2.14). Recognizing the fundamental importance of migration, geographers have long devoted much attention to it, and you will find several books on this aspect of population geography listed in the readings at the end of the chapter.

Migration can be either *voluntary*—by far the most common type—or *forced.* Voluntary migration takes place when people decide moving is preferable to staying, when the difficulties of moving seem more than offset by the expected rewards. Although migration is relocation diffusion, the decision to migrate can spread by means of expansion diffusion. For more detail on these processes, see Chapter 9. Every migration, from the ancient dispersal of our species out of Africa to the present-day movement toward urban areas, is governed by a host of **push-and-pull factors.** These act to make the old home unattractive or unlivable and the new land attractive. Generally, the push factors are the key ones, since a basic dissatisfaction with the homeland is prerequisite to voluntary migration. Perhaps the most important factor prompting migration throughout the thousands of years of human existence is economic. More often than not, migrating people seek greater prosperity through better access to resources, especially land.

Some cultural ecologists see migration in a different light, as a biological species seeking to fill every possible environmental niche. Ecologically, migration is a trial-and-error process that, more often than not, leads to grief rather than success. In other words, certain individuals among us may be preconditioned genetically to strike out into new lands and places, a compulsion not grounded in any rational consideration of push-and-pull factors.

In the nineteenth century, more than 50 million European emigrants, seeking better lives outside their native lands, changed the racial and ethnic character of much of the Earth. By 1970, about one-half of all Caucasians did not live in the European homelands of their ances-

Overall Human Welfare Status

4–5	Highest
6–8	Second highest
9–12	Middle
13–15	Next to lowest
16–17	Lowest

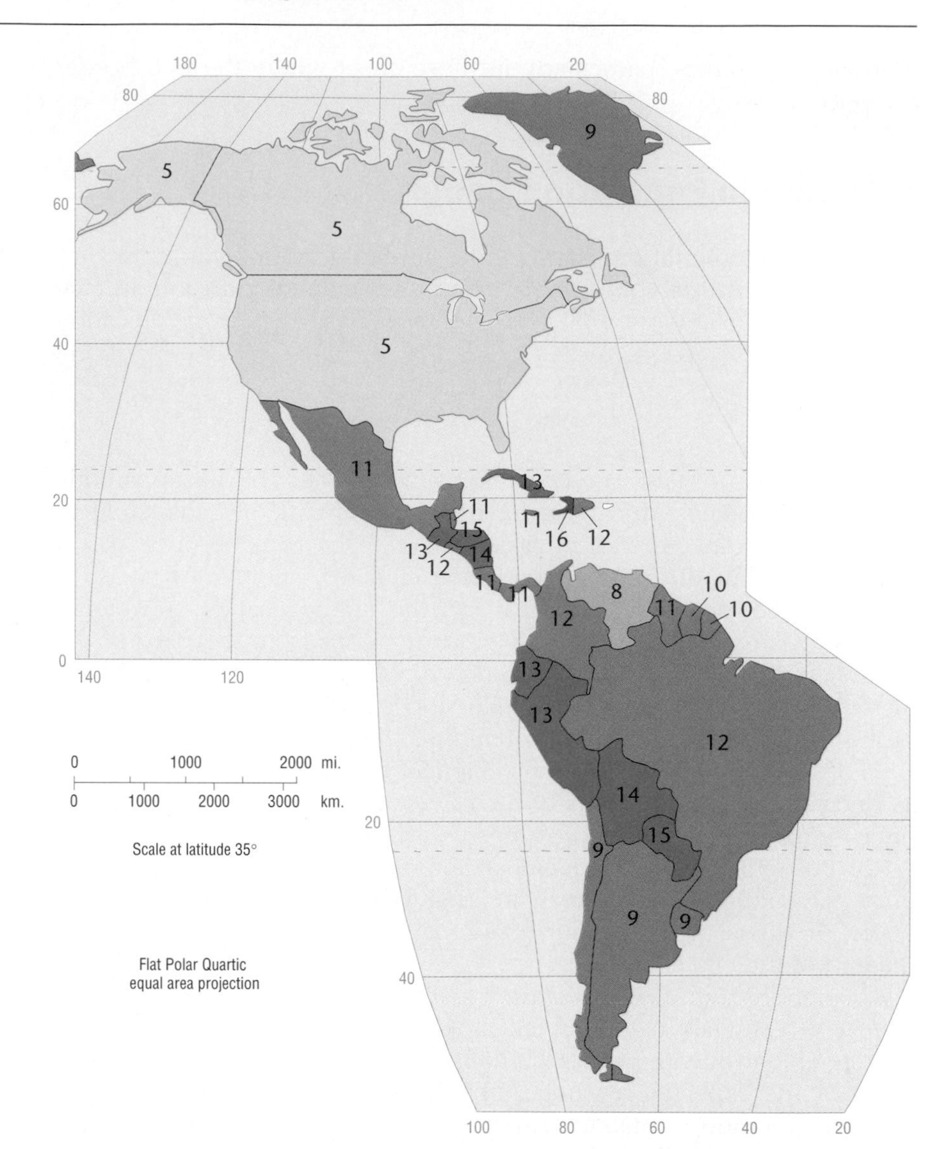

Figure 2.13

Variation in human welfare, by country, mid-1990s. The index employed measures natural resources, economic output, health, education, wealth, and degree of political freedom. More specifically, it is based on gross national product per capita, manufacturing value added per capita, primary industrial output per capita, arable land available per capita, infant mortality rate, percent of rural population, percent obtaining higher education, access to mass media, government expenditures per capita, and access to political rights. (Derived, with substantial updating and modification, from Tata, Robert J., and Ronald R. Schultz. "World Variation in Human Welfare: A New Index of Development Status." *Annals of the Association of American Geographers,* 78 (1988, 586–588.)

tors. International migration often occurs because a country has a negative image in the minds of some of its people. Foreign lands seem more attractive to them. Great Britain, for many years a destination of emigrants, especially from Ireland, loses almost a quarter of a million of its people per year. Many British emigrants are attracted to Australia and New Zealand, in part because these countries are British in culture, yet lack many of the economic and social problems that plague Great Britain. Whether deserved or not, Australia and New Zealand are perceived as something of an earthly paradise by much of the British middle class, an image promoted by publicity offices throughout Britain.

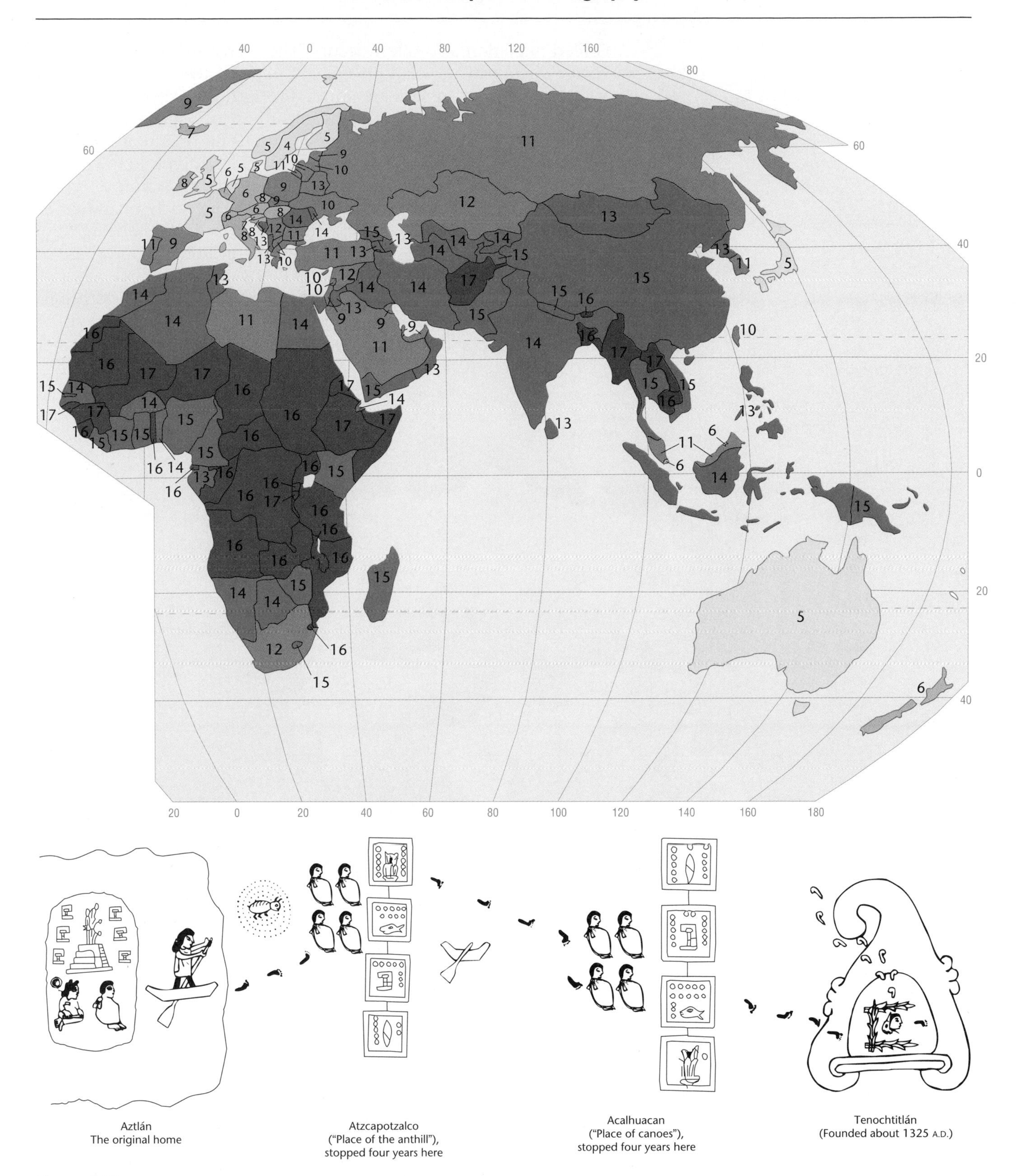

Figure 2.14
Redrawn segments of an Aztec codex. These pictograph maps depict the prehistoric migration of the Aztecs from an island, possibly in northwestern Mexico, to another island in a lake at the site of present-day Mexico City, where they founded their capital, Tenochtitlán. Clearly, the epic migration was a central event in their collective memory. (Source: Modified from de Macgregor, María Teresa de Gutiérrez. "Population Geography in Mexico," in John J. Clarke, *Geography and Population,* Oxford: Pergamon, 1984, 217.)

Forced migration also often occurs. The westward displacement of the Native American population of the United States, the dispersal of the Jews from Israel in Roman times, the terrible export of African slaves to the Americas, and the brutal "clearings" of Scottish farmers by landlords to make way for large-scale sheep raising provide depressing examples. Today, refugee movements are all too common in the world, prompted mainly by despotism, war, ethnic hatreds, and famine. Recent decades have witnessed a flood of refugees from such countries as Ethiopia, the Sudan, and Somalia in Africa; Haiti in the Caribbean; Iraqi Kurdistan and Israel in the Middle East; Bosnia in Europe; and Cambodia in Southeast Asia. In the middle 1990s, 18 million people lived as refugees outside their native lands, with the greatest such dislocations occurring in southern Asia and Africa (Figure 2.15). An additional 21 million displaced persons resided in their own countries, often after failing to cross international boundaries.

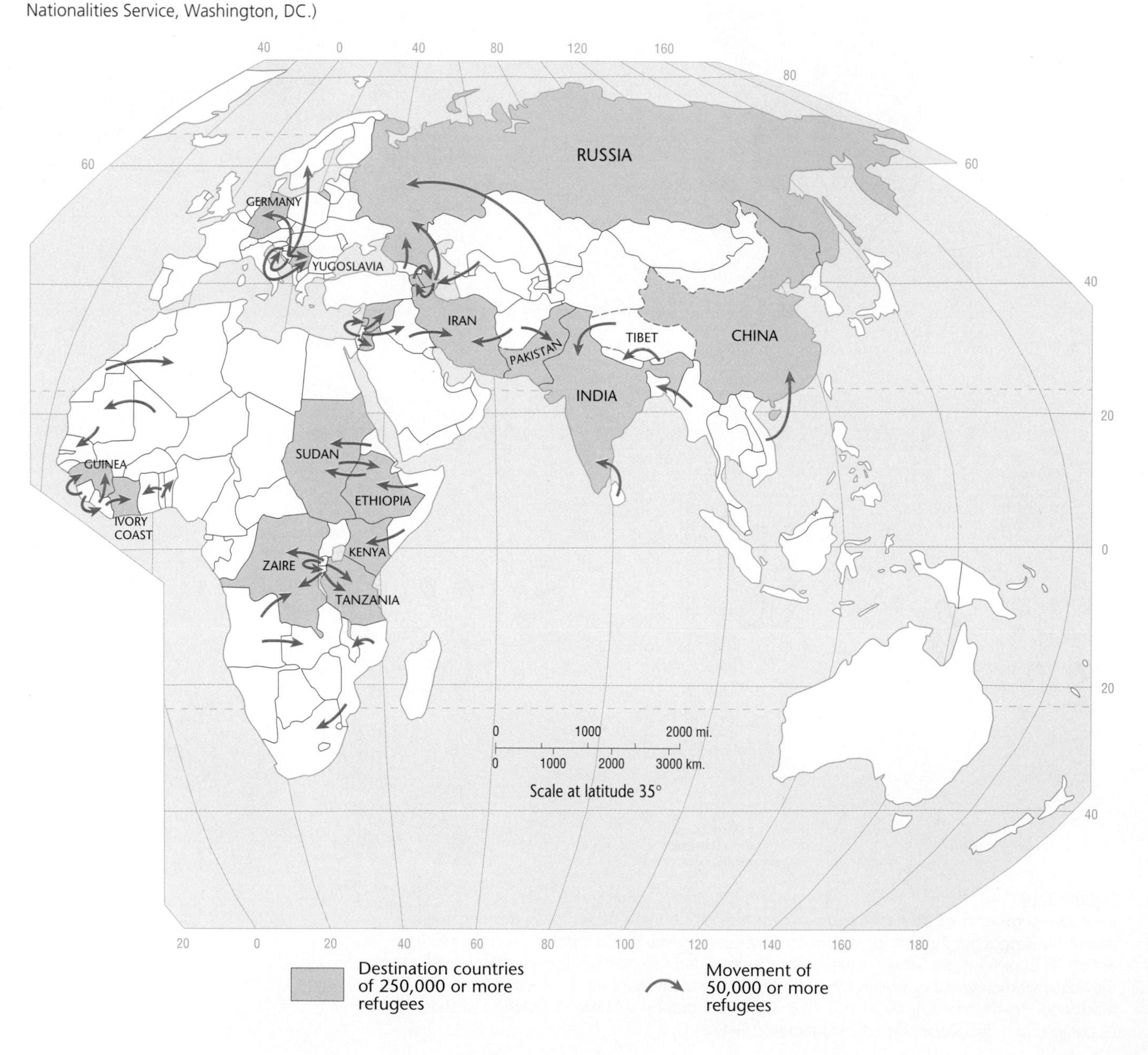

Figure 2.15
International refugees, 1995. No such significant migrations occurred from or to countries in the Americas. Some such movements occurred decades ago, while others are recent. (Source: US Committee for Refugees of the American Council for Nationalities Service, Washington, DC.)

Diffusion of Fertility Control

The final two stages of the demographic transformation depend on the successful cultural diffusion of effective methods of birth control and, in addition, acceptance of the notion that small families are preferable to large ones. Sustained fertility decline arose as an innovation in Europe in the first half of the 1800s. France was the place of origin (Figure 2.16). The idea spread slowly at first, but eventually diffused through

Figure 2.16
Onset of sustained fertility decline in Europe. The movement began in France and slowly diffused through the various other European countries. (Source: Adapted from Coale, Ansley J., and Susan C. Watkins. *The Decline of Fertility in Europe*. Princeton, NJ: Princeton University Press, 1986, following 484.)

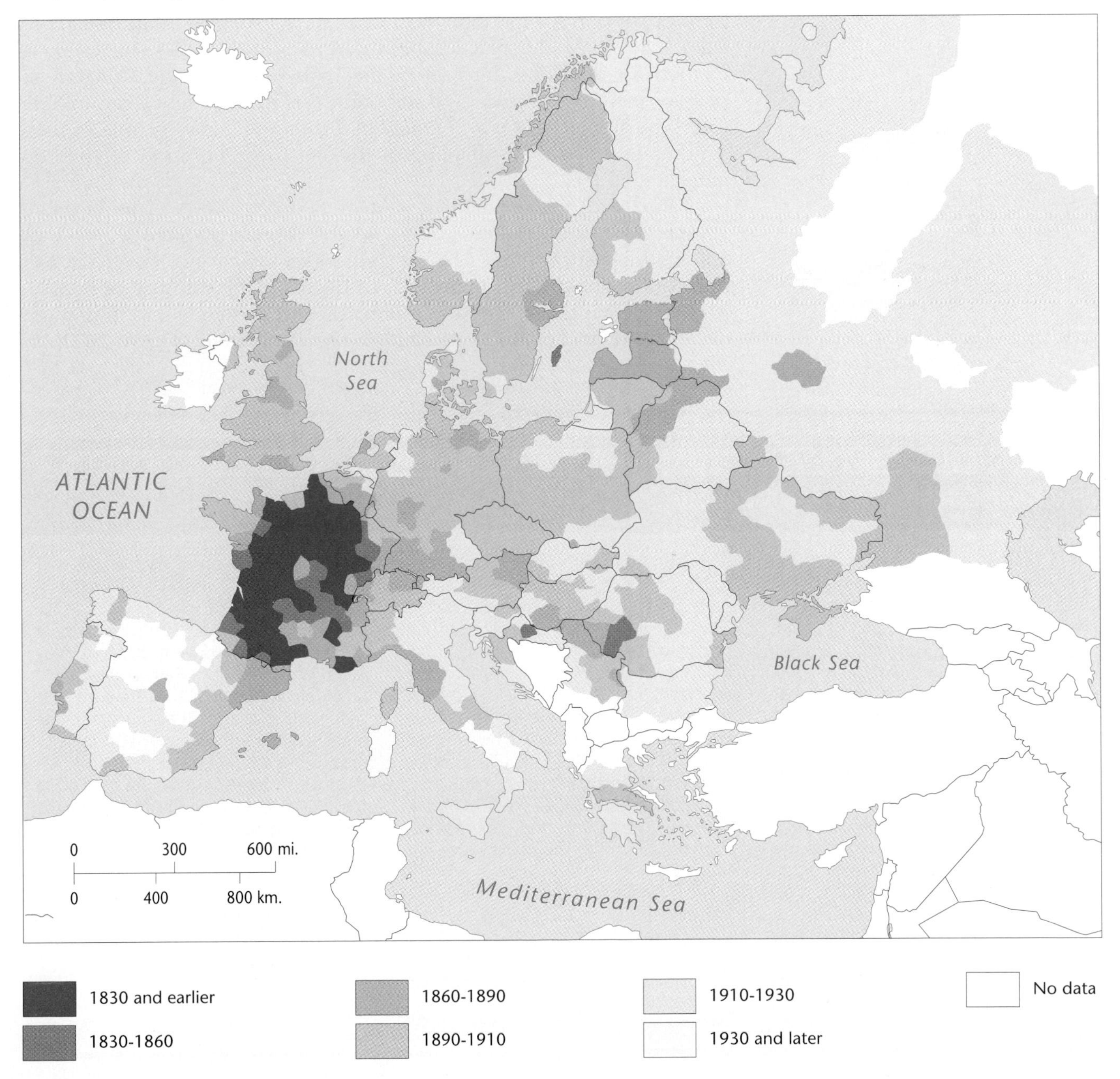

most of Europe. As a rule, fertility decline became accepted as countries industrialized and became prosperous.

The population explosion, at root, is caused by the failure of the European idea of fertility control to spread to less developed countries. What barriers to diffusion might be at work? Put yourself in the place of the people in such poor lands and try to think as they do.

For a farmer in India, children may offer the only way out of a life of poverty and an old age of solitary begging. An urban society invests large sums of money into the formal education of its children and forbids child labor, making children a financial burden (as any parent who has financed a college education for a son or daughter knows all too well). In a rural society, the costs of raising and educating a child are minimal and grow smaller with every child added to the family. The advantages are enormous. The children can work from an early age, replace otherwise expensive hired laborers in the fields, and provide a form of support for the parents in old age. To suggest to an Indian villager that he or she practice birth control without also suggesting a method for attacking the root of the high birthrate—the structure of peasant poverty, tenancy, and insecurity—is to offer less than nothing (see box, *Why Birth Control Failed in Manupur*). Many people in such cultures fear that their offspring might die. Large numbers of children mitigate that fear.

Faced with the unwillingness of its people to reduce the birthrate voluntarily, a few countries, most notably China, adopted a policy of enforced fertility control. Chinese authorities sought not merely to halt population growth but, ultimately, to decrease the number of people. All over China today one sees billboards and posters admonishing the citizens that "one couple, one child" is the ideal family (Figure 2.17). Vi-

Why Birth Control Failed in Manupur

"'They were trying to convince me in 1960 that I shouldn't have any more sons,' commented Thaman Singh, water carrier in Manupur village, part of India's Punjab state. 'Now, you see, I have six sons and two daughters and I sit at home in leisure. They are grown up and they bring me money. One even works outside the village as a laborer. They told me I was a poor man and couldn't support a large family. Now, you see, because of my large family, I am a rich man. . . . Time has proven me right.'

"Thaman Singh, along with the rest of Manupur's villagers, was the subject of a multiyear birth control project that attempted to get them to adopt modern birth control methods and voluntarily limit family size. Often, the villagers politely accepted the birth control tablets offered by the study's field workers. 'But they were so nice,' commented one villager. 'And they came from distant lands to be with us. Couldn't we even do this much for them? Just take a few tablets?' However, many never actually used the foam tablets. In fact, the villagers considered the whole project bizarre, and were constantly looking for 'the clue' to what the project workers were *really* doing. In the end, the project failed to dent the area's birth rate. Project workers attributed this to peasant illiteracy, ignorance, or prejudice. The villagers, particularly the poor, who resisted the project most strongly, looked on the matter quite differently.

"'A rich man invests in his machines. We must invest in our children. It's that simple,' said blacksmith Hakika Singh. The arithmetic of land and labor makes this easy to understand. With a tractor, three people can work about fifty acres. Without a tractor, the same land would take fourteen people year around and twenty at sowing, weeding, and harvesting time. Hakika Singh, like other Manupur villagers, is aware that people are not stuck in poverty because they have large families. Rather they have large families because they are poor, and desperate to change that situation. Sons and daughters in Manupur cost little to raise, replace far more expensive hired laborers in a farmer's fields, can emigrate to other areas or even the city to get jobs augmenting the family's overall income, and support the parents in old age."

From Mamdani, Mahmood. *The Myth of Population Control, Family, Caste, and Class in an Indian Village.* New York: Monthly Review Press, 1972.

Figure 2.17
Population control in the People's Republic of China. China has aggressively promoted a policy of "one couple, one child," in an attempt to relieve the pressures of overpopulation. These billboards convey the government's message. Violators—those with more than one child—are subject to fines, loss of job and old-age benefits, loss of access to better housing, and other penalties.

olators face huge monetary fines, cannot request new housing, lose the rather generous old-age benefits provided by the government, forfeit their children's access to higher education, and may even lose their jobs. Late marriages are encouraged. In response, between 1970 and 1980, the fertility rate in China plummeted from 5.9 births per woman to only 2.7, then to 2.2 by 1990 and 2.0 by 1994. China achieved one of the greatest short-term reduction of birthrates ever recorded, and stringent enforcement of the policy continues. Cultural diffusion, then, can be coerced.

Disease Diffusion

A new depth of meaning is given to the term "contagious" diffusion when we consider the spread of diseases, a topic often addressed by cultural geographers. The previously mentioned AIDS epidemic provides an example (Figure 2.5).

The most widely accepted theory now holds that AIDS began in east-central Africa and probably also the upper Niger River country in the Guinea highlands of West Africa. The former region is linked to the variety of the virus labeled HIV-1, and the latter region is linked with HIV-2 (Figure 2.18). Apparently the disease originally occurred among the local monkey population and passed to their fellow primates through the local cultural practice of injecting monkey blood as an aphrodisiac. Oddly, the HIV-2 variety, most similar to the simian type, is less profound in its impact on the population of its source region and has not spread as effectively beyond Africa as HIV-1. The disease, having diffused from monkeys to people, then apparently moved throughout central and western Africa, following transport routes and greatly benefiting from rapid urbanization of the region. Among those infected, it seems, were Haitians who came from the West Indies to Zaire to fill civil service posts in the early 1960s. They probably took AIDS back to their Caribbean nation, and Europeans visiting central Africa also dif-

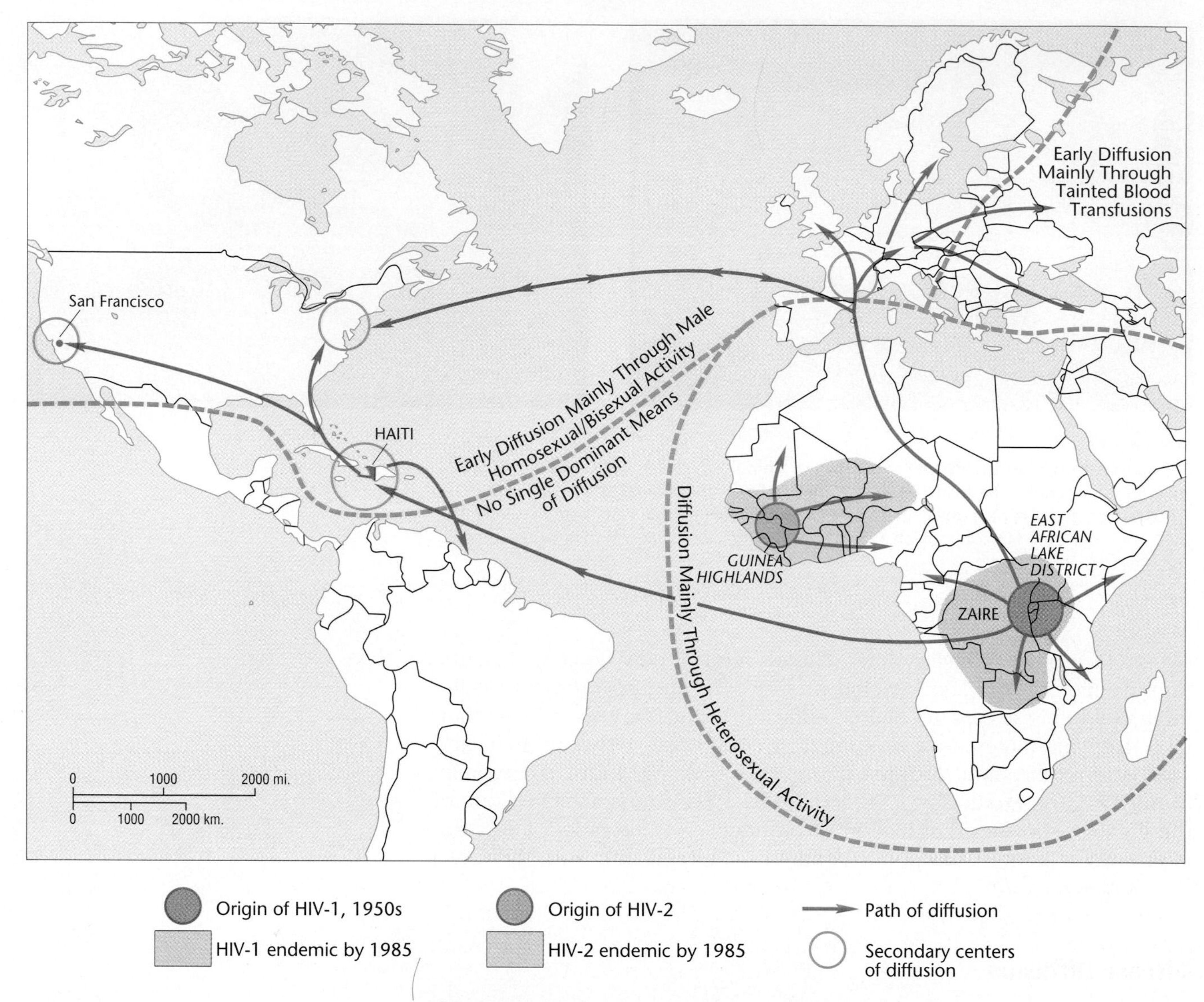

Figure 2.18
Probable sequence of early diffusion of the virus that causes AIDS, assuming African origin or origins. Note the different methods of diffusion. This diffusionary scheme remains far from proved, but some experts now support it. (Source: Shannon et al. *Geography of AIDS:* 49, 68, 73, with substantial modifications.)

fused the disease to their homeland. American male homosexuals vacationing in Haiti likely contracted the virus and spread it through the gay community in the United States, leading many Americans to conclude, falsely, that AIDS was a disease linked exclusively to homosexual behavior. Similarly, western Europe became a secondary diffusion area.

While one might expect all diseases to spread exclusively by contagious diffusion, in fact they spread through all types. Relocation diffusion, in the forms of tourism, long-distance truck transportation in Africa, and the temporary migration of Haitian civil servants to Zaire all apparently played roles. Hierarchical diffusion is implicit in the tendency of AIDS to gain footholds in urban areas and to be spread by persons affluent enough to participate in international tourism.

Population Ecology

The theme of cultural ecology is quite relevant to the study of population geography. At the most basic level, a successful adaptive strategy permits a people to exist and reproduce in a given ecosystem. Population size and growth offer an index to successful adaptation, cultural ecologists believe. Maladaptive strategies can lead to a dwindling of numbers, or even extinction for a people. Similarly, when groups migrate to new places as settlers, their success or failure will depend in part on **preadaptation.** To what extent did the groups' ways of life, their adaptive strategies in the old home, precondition them for success in the new land? Preadaptation is often a matter of chance, particularly when prior knowledge of the new land is sketchy or when migrants have little control over their destinations.

Even successful cultural adaptation may lead to demographic catastrophe. The key is **sustainability**. If practiced over many decades or generations, does the strategy cause such significant environmental alteration and destruction as to undermine livelihood? If so, sustainability is not achieved. To be sustainable, the adaptive strategy must allow generation after generation to use the land in more or less the same manner. This consideration introduces the "humans as modifiers" issue into population ecology. In other ways, too, the theme of cultural ecology bears on demography, as we will see.

Environmental Influence

Regardless of its adaptive strategy, population is influenced in a possibilistic manner by the local availability of resources. Densities, in the middle latitudes, tend to be greatest where terrain is level, the climate mild and humid, the soil fertile, mineral resources abundant, and the sea accessible. Conversely, population tends to thin out with excessive elevation, aridity, coldness, ruggedness of terrain, and distance from the coast (Figure 2.19).

Climatic factors affect where people settle. Most of the sparsely populated zones in the world have, in some respect, "defective" climates, from the human viewpoint (Figure 2.1). The thinly populated northern edges of Eurasia and North America are excessively cold, and the belt from North Africa into the heart of Eurasia matches the major desert zones of the Old World. Humans remain creatures of the humid and subhumid tropics, subtropics, or mid-latitudes and have not fared well in excessively cold or dry areas. Small populations of Inuit (Eskimo), Sami (Lapps), and other peoples live in some of the undesirable areas of the Earth, but these regions do not support large populations. Humans have proved remarkably adaptable in the biological sense, and our cultures contain adaptive strategies that allow us to live in many different physical environments, but perhaps, as a species, we never fully forgot the climatic features of sub-Saharan Africa, where we began. In avoiding cold places, we may reveal even today the tropical origin of our species.

Humankind's preference for lower elevations holds especially true for the middle and higher latitudes. Indeed, most mountain ranges in those latitudes stand out as regions of sparse population. By contrast, inhabitants of the tropics often prefer to live at higher elevations, concentrating in dense clusters in mountain valleys and basins (Figure 2.1). By doing so, they escape the humid, hot climate of the tropical lowlands. For example, in tropical portions of South America, more people

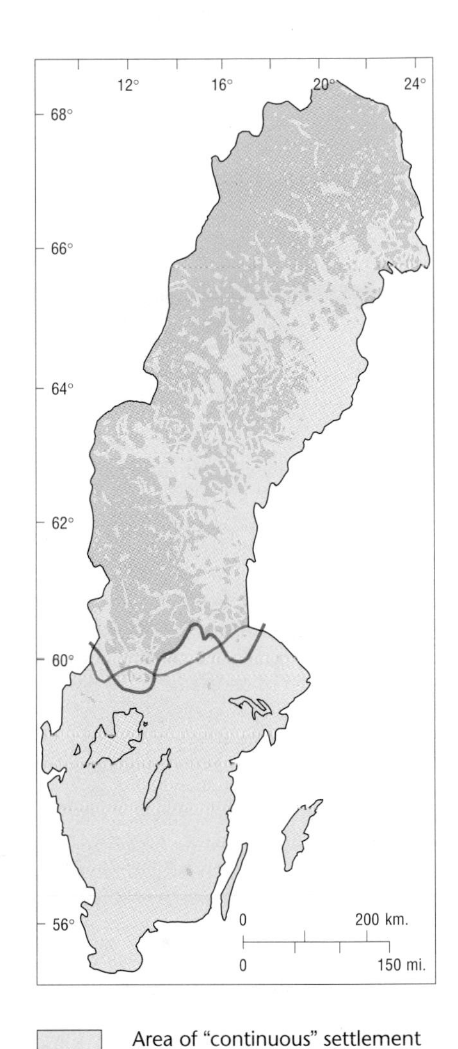

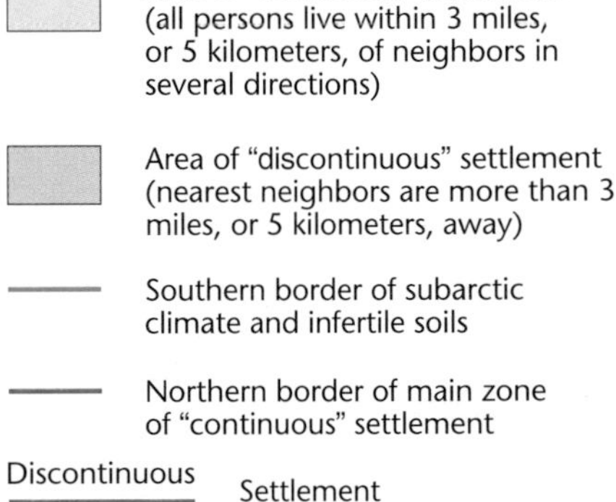

Figure 2.19
Environment and population distribution in Sweden. The northern boundary of the thickly settled area corresponds closely to the southern limit of the bitterly cold subarctic climate and the infertile, acidic soils of the coniferous forests. (Adapted from Stone, Kirk H. "Swedish Fringes of Settlement." *Annals of the Association of American Geographers,* 52 (1962): 379.)

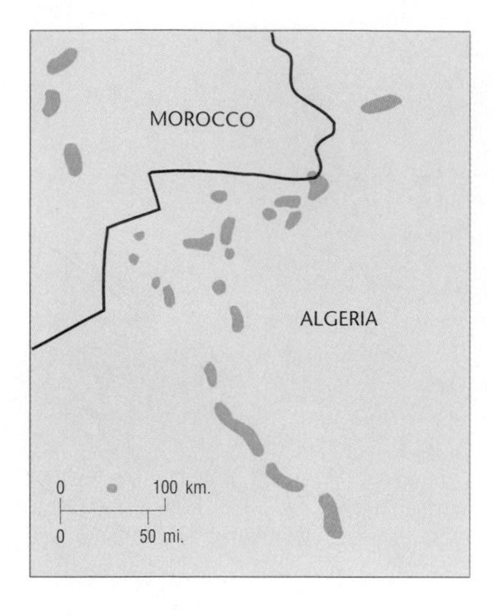

Figure 2.20
Population distribution reveals the availability of water in a desert. These scattered clusters of people lie in the Sahara Desert of North Africa, and the pattern is typical of many arid regions. Dot clusters indicate the presence of oases, while lines reveal stream courses. (After Mattingly, Paul F., and Elsa Schmidt. "The Maghreb: Population Density." Map Supplement 15, *Annals of the Association of American Geographers*, 61 [1971].)

live in the Andes Mountains than in the nearby Amazon lowlands. The capital cities of many tropical and subtropical nations lie in mountain areas above about 3000 feet (900 meters) in elevation.

Our tendency to live on or near the seacoast is also quite striking. The continents of Eurasia, Australia, and South America resemble hollow shells, with the majority of the population clustered around the rim of each continent (Figure 2.1). In Australia, half the total population lives in just five port cities, and most of the remainder is spread out over nearby coastal areas. This preference for living by the sea partly stems from the trade and fishing opportunities the sea offers. At the same time, continental interiors tend to be regions of climatic extremes. For example, Australians speak of the "dead heart" of their continent, an interior land of excessive dryness and heat. People also seek places where fresh water is available. In desert regions, population clusters reflect the locations of scattered oases and occasional rivers, such as the Nile, that rise from sources outside the desert (Figure 2.20).

Still another environmental factor that affects population distribution is disease. In the Mediterranean region, especially in Italy, thickly settled, agriculturally productive coastal lands became virtually depopulated by the spread of malaria after Roman times. Only in recent times, as malaria was eradicated by modern scientific methods, did people reclaim and repopulate these districts. Other diseases attack valuable domestic animals, depriving people of food and clothing resources. Such diseases have an indirect effect on population density. For example, in parts of East Africa, livestock are attacked by a form of sleeping sickness. This particular disease is almost invariably fatal to cattle but not to humans. The people in this part of East Africa depend heavily on cattle, which provide food, represent wealth, and serve a religious function in some tribes. The spread of a disease fatal to cattle has caused entire tribes to migrate away from infested areas, leaving them unpopulated (Figure 2.21).

Environmental Perception and Population Distribution

Perception of the physical environment plays a role when a group of people choose where to settle and live. Different cultural groups often "see" the same physical environment in different ways. These varied responses to a single environment influence the distribution of people. A good example appears in a part of the European Alps shared by German- and Italian-speaking people. The mountain ridges in that area—near the point where Switzerland, Italy, and Austria join—run in an east-west direction, so that each ridge has a sunny, south-facing slope and a shady, north-facing side. German-speaking people, who rely on dairy farming, long ago established permanent settlements some 650 feet (200 meters) higher on the *shady* slopes than the settlements of Italians, who are culturally tied to warmth-loving crops, on the *sunny* slopes. This example demonstrates contrasting cultural attitudes toward land use and different perceptions of the best use for one type of physical environment.

Sometimes, the same cultural group changes its perception of an environment through time, with a resulting redistribution of its population. The coal fields of western Europe provide a good case in point. Before the industrial age, many coal-rich areas—such as southern Wales, the lands between the headwaters of the Oder and Vistula rivers in Poland, and the Midlands of England—were only sparsely or moderately settled. Then the development of steam-powered engines and the

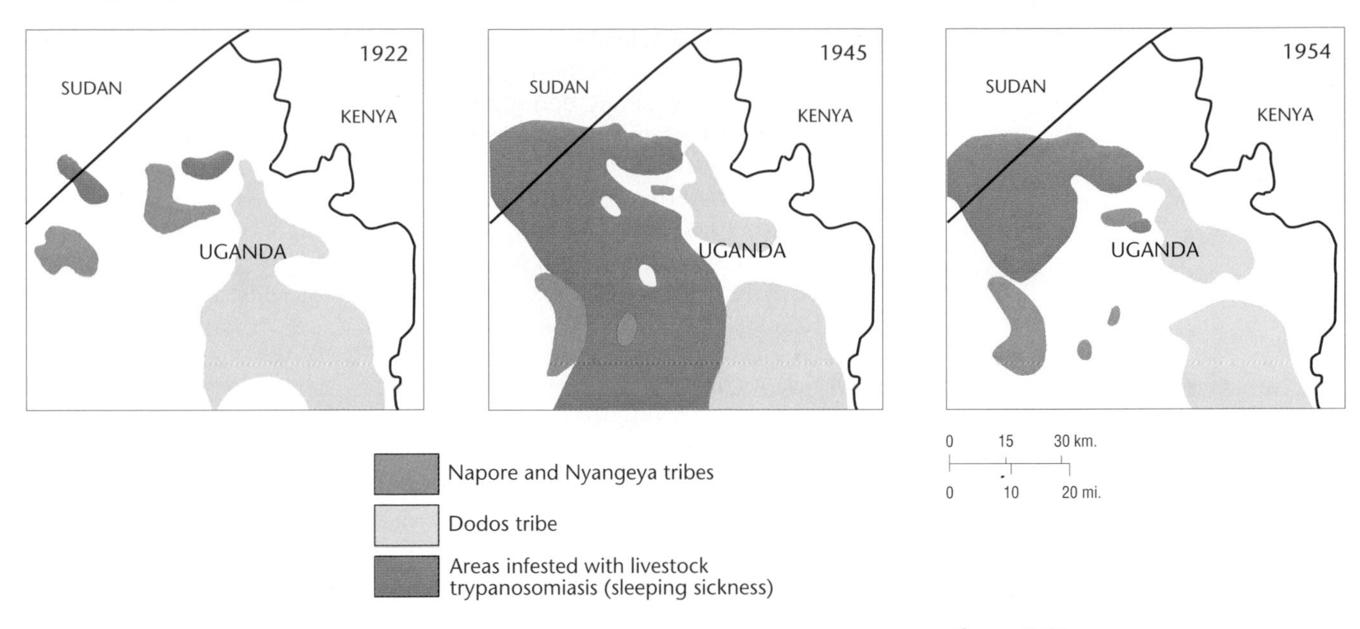

Figure 2.21
Disease can influence settlement. The effect is apparent in this example in northeastern Uganda, East Africa. Note in particular the changing distribution of the Napore and Nyangeya groups based on the spread and eradication of sleeping sickness. (Adapted from Deshler, Walter. "Livestock Trypanosomiasis and Human Settlement in Northeastern Uganda." *Geographical Review,* 50 (1960): 549.)

increased use of coal in the iron-smelting process created a tremendous demand. Industries grew up near the European coal fields, and people flocked to these areas to take advantage of the new jobs. In other words, once a technological development gave a new cultural value to coal, many sparsely populated areas containing that resource acquired large concentrations of people.

Recent studies indicate that much of the interregional migration in the United States today is prompted by a desire for pleasant climate and other desirable physical environmental traits, such as beautiful scenery. Surveys of immigrants to Arizona revealed that its sunny, warm climate is a major reason for migration. Attractive environment provided the dominant factor in the growth of the population and economy of Florida. Desirable environmental traits in the following order as stimulants for American migration include: (1) mild winter climate and mountainous terrain, (2) a diverse natural vegetation that includes forests and a mild summer climate with low humidity, (3) the presence of lakes and rivers, and (4) nearness to the seacoast. Different age and cultural groups often express different preferences, but all are influenced by their perceptions of the physical environment in making decisions about migration. Misinformation is at least as important as accurate impressions, because a person will often form strong images of an area without ever visiting it.

Population Density and Environmental Alteration

Through their adaptive strategies, people modify their habitats. Particularly in areas where population density is high, radical alterations often occur. This can happen in fragile environments even at relatively low densities, since the carrying capacity of the Earth varies greatly from one place to another.

We face a worldwide ecological crisis in part because, at present densities, many of our adaptive strategies are not sustainable. The population explosion and the ecological crisis are closely related. For example, in Haiti, where rural population pressures have become particularly severe, most available biomass is now being collected into small, intensively cultivated kitchen gardens, leaving the surrounding fields and pastures increasingly denuded and humus-deficient. In short, overpopulation can precipitate environmental destruction, which, in turn, yields a downward cycle of worsening poverty, with an eventual catastrophe that is both ecological and demographic. Thus many cultural ecologists believe that attempts to restore the balance of nature will not succeed until we halt or even reverse population growth, although they recognize that other causes are at work in ecological crises. Adaptive strategy is as crucial as density and, in some cases, population pressure leads to more conservational techniques of land use. Rural China offers supportive evidence.

The changes in the vegetation of western and central Europe since medieval times demonstrate how a region's population density and adaptive strategy can have a long-term effect on the environment. During the Middle Ages, farmers cleared vast forests from the plains and valleys of western and central Europe. In time, these fertile agricultural districts became densely populated. Whenever population declined, particularly in times of warfare and plague, the forests expanded again. The spread of the forests during the Hundred Years' War, a conflict between England and France lasting from 1337 to 1453, caused surviving peasants to coin the saying that "the forests came back to France with the English."

The worldwide ecological crisis is not strictly a function of overpopulation. A relatively small percentage of the earth's population controls much of the industrial technology and absorbs a gargantuan percentage of the world's resources each year. Americans, who make up less than 5 percent of humankind, account for about 40 percent of the resources consumed each year. Thus a child born in the United States has more of an impact on the global environment than one born in India or China.

Cultural Integration and Population Patterns

Population patterns are also closely tied to numerous facets of culture. The theme of cultural integration allows us to look at some of these relationships among culture, population density, migration, and population growth. Inheritance laws, food preferences, politics, differing attitudes toward migration, and many other cultural features all can influence demography.

Cultural Factors

Many of the forces that influence the distribution of people are basic characteristics of a group's culture (see box, *Culture and Population*). For example, we must understand the rice preference of people living in Southeast Asia before we can try to interpret the dense concentrations of people in Southeast Asian rural areas. The population in the humid lands of tropical and subtropical Asia expanded as this highly prolific grain was domesticated and widely adopted. Environmentally similar rural zones elsewhere in the world, where rice is not the staple of the inhabitants' diet, never developed such great population densities. Similarly, the introduction of the potato into Ireland in the 1700s allowed a great increase in rural population, because it yielded much more food per acre than did traditional Irish crops. Failure of the potato

Culture and Population

A study of the Tenetehara and the Tapirapé, two Indian tribes of central Brazil, shows the range of population choices available to different cultures within the same physical and material environment. Before European contact, both tribes inhabited similar tropical forest areas, had the same level of technology, and were horticulturists who depended on hunting, fishing, and wild fruits to supplement their diets. Yet the Tapirapé population was, by choice, relatively small and stable, whereas the Tenetehara population of perhaps 2000 was at least twice as large and probably expanding.

Among the Tenetehara, there was little effort to limit family size. Men took pride in the number of children they fathered. Women, eager to bear children, would leave a husband whom they considered sterile. There seem to have been few cultural values in the tribe that would discourage large families.

The Tapirapé, however, had an explicit idea of maximum family size. When asked why their families were no larger, they would say, "The children would be hungry." In Tapirapé society, this meant "hungry for meat," which was sometimes scarce—but no scarcer than for the more numerous Teneteharas. In other words, Tapirapé population controls were based not on possible starvation levels, but on a specific desire for a larger quantity of meat in their diets. Other cultural factors also played a role in the Tapirapé decision. As a result, the tribe set limits on how many children a woman should have (no more than three living and no more than two of the same sex). To keep their society within its desired limits, they practiced infanticide.

Adapted from Wagley, Charles. "Cultural Influences on Population: A Comparison of Two Tupi Tribes," in Daniel R. Gross (ed.), *Peoples and Cultures of Native South America*. Garden City, NY: Doubleday, 1973, 145–156.

harvests in the 1840s greatly reduced the Irish population, through both starvation and emigration.

Geographers have found major cultural contrasts in attitudes toward population growth. France, where, as we have seen, sustained fertility decline first took root in the world, suffered demographically as a result. When the birthrate in nineteenth-century France declined rapidly, neighboring countries, such as Germany, Italy, and the United Kingdom, did not experience the same decline. Consequently, the French population did not keep pace numerically with that in nearby lands (Table 2.3) (Figure 2.22). France, the most populous of these four countries in 1800, became the least populous shortly after 1930 and retains that status today. During this same period, millions of Germans, Britishers, and Italians emigrated overseas, whereas relatively few French left their homeland. At the same time, the French Canadians of the province of Québec, whose ancestors had left France long before, still favored large families. Consequently, the 10,000 people who settled in Québec between 1608 and 1750 multiplied into today's population of about 7 million (Table 2.3). This number does not include many French Canadians who migrated from Canada to New England and the other areas. Clearly, some factor in the culture of France worked to produce their demographic decline.

TABLE 2.3
Population Growth In France, Québec, Germany, Italy, and the United Kingdom (Population in Millions), 1720–1930

Country	1720	1800	1850	1900	1930	Increase from 1720 to 1930
France	19	27	36	38	42	2.2 times
Québec	0.02	0.2	0.9	1.7	2.8	140 times
Germany	14	25	35	56	64	4.6 times
Italy	13	18	23	32	41	3.2 times
United Kingdom	7	11	27	37	46	6.8 times

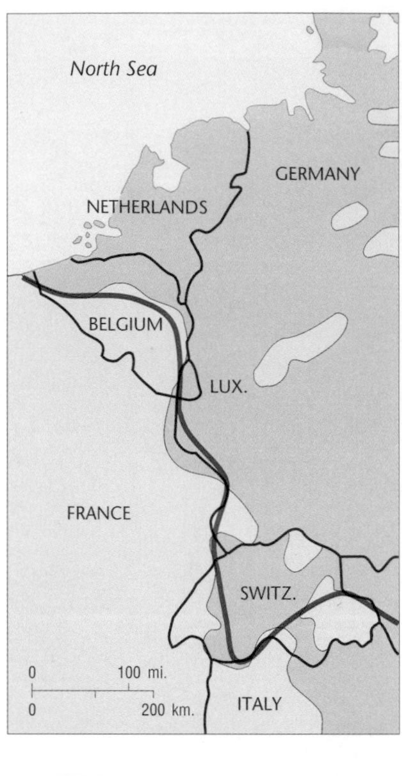

Figure 2.22
Birthrate pattern in western Europe, 1910. Notice how the birthrate border paralleled the linguistic rather than the political boundary. French-speaking people in France, southern Belgium, western Switzerland, and northwestern Italy, together with their Romance-language kinsmen, the Romansh-speaking people of eastern Switzerland, were reproducing at a lower rate than their German-speaking neighbors. What cultural factors might have helped produce this contrast? In later decades this contrast disappeared altogether. (Adapted from Jordan, Terry G. *The European Culture Area: A Systematic Geography,* 2d ed. New York: HarperCollins, 1988, 159.)

Cultural groups also differ in their tendency to migrate. Religious ties bind some groups to their traditional homelands. Sometimes travel outside the sanctified bounds of the motherland is considered immoral, and religious duties, in particular the responsibilities to tend ancestral graves and perform rites at parental death, kept many Chinese in their native land. The Navajo Indians of the American Southwest practice the custom of burying the umbilical cord in the floor of the *hogan* (house) at birth. Psychologically, this seems to strengthen the Navajo attachment to the home and retard migration. Other religious cultures place no stigma on emigration. In fact, some groups consider migration a way of life. The Irish, unwilling to accept the poverty of their native land, proved so prone to migration that the population of Ireland today is only about half the total of 1840.

Migration tendencies can also differ along gender lines, for cultural reasons. In some parts of rural India, particularly the north and west, marriage typically takes place between persons from different villages. Since it is traditional in those parts of India for the woman to move into the household of her husband, females are much more likely to migrate than are males. A fifth or fewer of all married women in northern and western India live in the village of their birth; and in many districts their marriage migration has taken them 18 miles (29 kilometers) or more from their original home (Figure 2.23). By contrast, in south and east India and in Kashmir in the far north, females are much less likely to marry outside their village. Cultural differences lie at the root of these contrasts. In some parts of south India, for example, matrilineal societies, those that trace lineage through the mother, encourage females to remain close to their place of birth. Even in patrilineal south Indian communities, a preference for marriage within the village prevails, so marriage migration is uncommon.

Culture can also condition a people to accept or reject crowding. **Personal space,** the amount individuals feel "belongs" to them as they move about their everyday business, varies from one cultural group to another. When Americans talk with each other, they typically stand farther apart than, say, Italians do. The large personal space demanded by the American may well come from a heritage of sparse settlement. Early pioneers felt uncomfortable when they first saw smoke from the chimneys of neighboring cabins. As a result, American cities sprawl across large areas, with huge suburbs dominated by separate houses surrounded by private yards. Most European cities are compact, and their residential areas consist largely of row houses or apartments.

Political Factors

The political mosaic of the world (see Chapter 4) is linked to population geography in many ways. Governmental policies often influence the birth and death rate, as we have seen in China, and forced migration is usually the result of political forces.

Governments can also restrict voluntary migration. Two independent countries, Haiti and the Dominican Republic, share the tropical Caribbean island of Hispaniola in the West Indies. Haiti, which supports 672 persons per square mile (259 per square kilometer), is far more densely settled than the Dominican Republic, which has only 417 persons per square mile (161 per square kilometer) (Figure 2.24). Government restrictions make migration from Haiti to the Dominican Republic difficult and help maintain the different population densities. If Hispan-

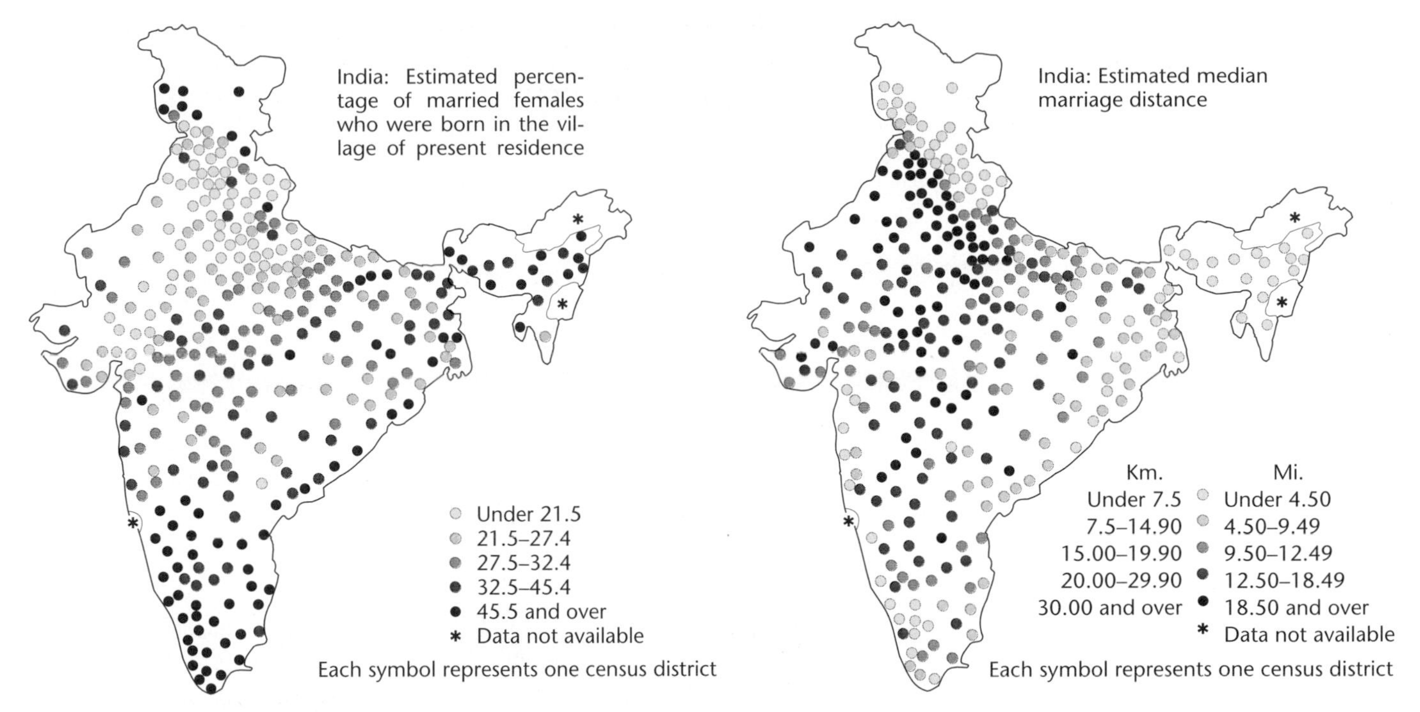

Figure 2.23
Female marriage migration in rural India. Major differences in the tendency of women to migrate for the purpose of marriage and in the distance of migration can be seen from one part of India to another. What might some of the cultural causes of this spatial pattern be? (Source: Adapted from Libbee, M. J., and D. E. Sopher. "Marriage Migration in Rural India," in L. A. Kosinski and R. M. Prothero [eds.], *People on the Move*. Harlow, England: Longman, 1970, 352, 354.)

iola were one country, its population would probably be more evenly distributed over the island.

Every culture has a set of laws based in the political system to maintain order within the society, and these legal codes can affect population density, especially regulations concerning inheritance. In Europe, the code derived from Roman law requires that all heirs divide land and other property equally among themselves. Germanic law, on the other hand, favors the custom of primogeniture, or inheritance of all land by the firstborn son. In areas where divided inheritance is the tradition, farms fragment as the generations pass, causing rural population density to increase. Where primogeniture is the rule, on the other hand, emigration by landless sons retards the growth of population. The most severe rural overpopulation in Germany during the mid-nineteenth century was in the southern lands along the Rhine River and its tributaries, where the practice of divided inheritance implanted by the Romans 2000 years earlier survived (Figure 2.25).

Economic Factors

Economic conditions often influence population density in profound ways. The process of industrialization over the past 200 years has caused the greatest voluntary relocation of people in world history. Within industrial nations, people moved from rural areas to cluster in manufacturing regions. Agricultural changes can have a similar, if less dramatic, impact on population distribution. For example, the Indone-

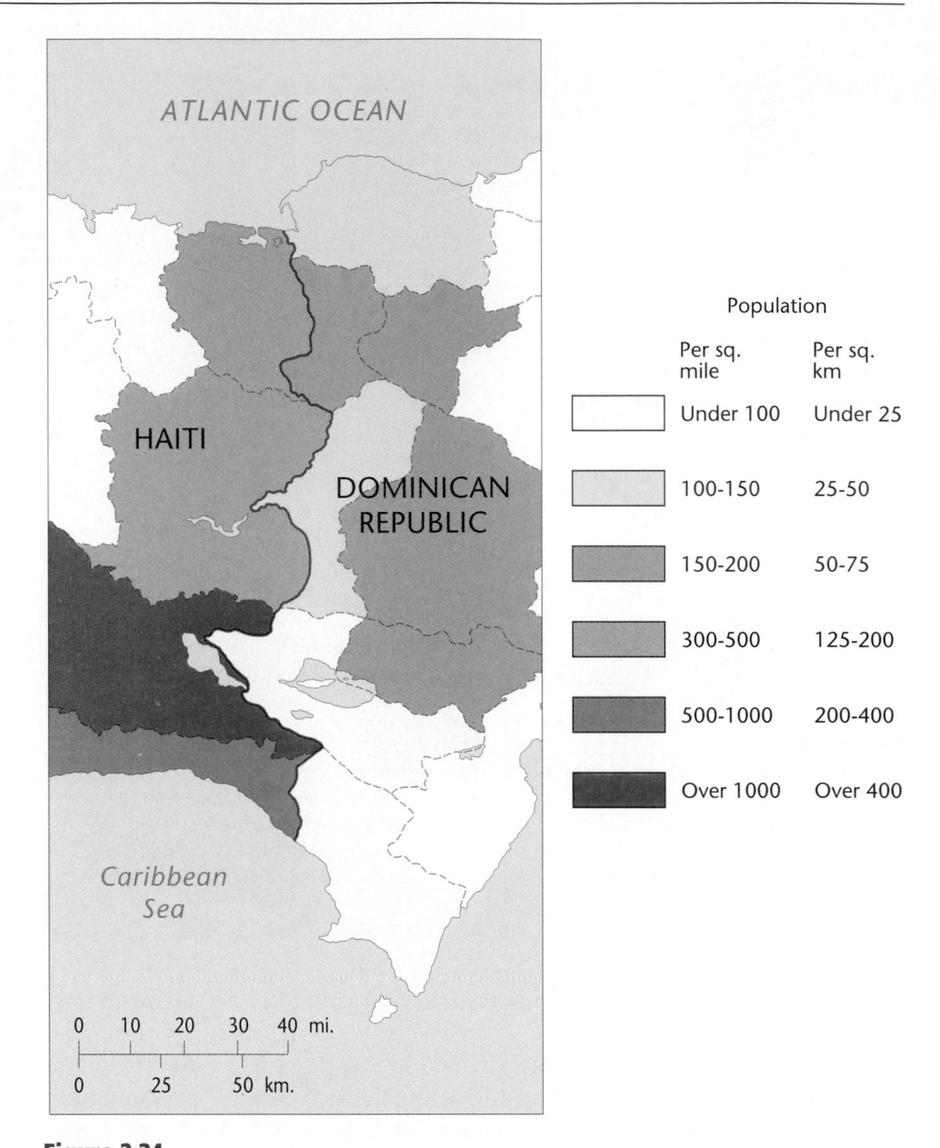

Figure 2.24
Population density contrast along the Haiti–Dominican Republic boundary. Migration across this political frontier on the island of Hispaniola in the Caribbean has been restricted, causing the boundary to become a demographic border as well. (Sources: Most recent national censuses.)

sian island of Java is one of the most densely settled rural areas in the world, with a population density greater than that of other islands nearby. This concentration of people on Java results partly from the efforts of the Dutch, who ruled Indonesia until 1949, to concentrate tropical plantations there. Employment opportunities offered by these plantations drew people from the surrounding islands to Java, causing its population to expand.

Application of the theme of cultural integration by geographers in their demographic research often produces negative results that are as enlightening as positive correlations. For example, many experts had long assumed that vegetarianism in India, based in Hindu religious belief, led to protein deficiency, malnutrition, and resultant health problems in many rural areas of that country. A study by Aninda Chakravarti, a cultural geographer, revealed no spatial correlation be-

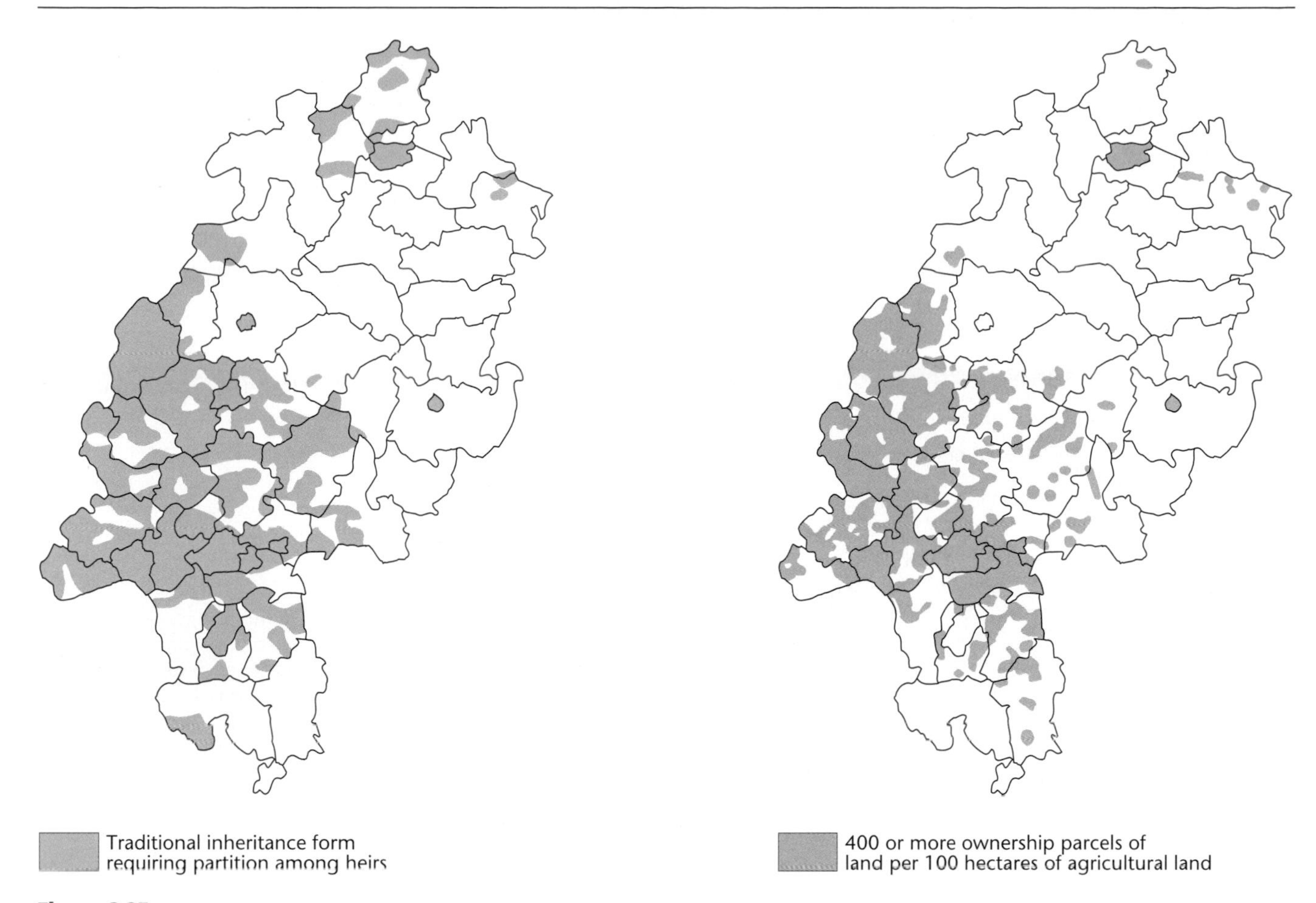

Figure 2.25
Inheritance systems and land fragmentation in the German province of Hessen. In the southern and western parts of Hessen, the tradition, dating to Roman times, was to divide the farms among the various heirs. As a result, the farms there became ever smaller over the centuries, with excessive fragmentation of the holdings. What impact would this have on population density and agricultural prosperity? Northern and eastern Hessen, by contrast, clung to the ancient Germanic custom of primogeniture, by which the farm passes intact to the eldest son. (Adapted from Ehlers, E. "Land Consolidation and Farm Resettlement in the Federal Republic of Germany," in Robert C. Eidt, et al. [eds.], *Man, Culture and Settlement: Festschrift to Prof. R. L. Singh.* New Delhi, India: Kalyani Publishers, 1977, 124.)

tween vegetarians and the consumption of animal protein (Figure 2.26). That is, nonvegetarians also eat little or no meat. Instead, the greatest protein deficiency occurs in areas where rice, rather than wheaten bread, accounts for the greater part of the cereal consumption.

The Settlement Landscape

The distribution of people is clearly reflected in the cultural landscape. Differing densities and arrangements of population are revealed, at the largest scale, by maps showing the distribution of dwellings. We can illustrate these cultural landscape contrasts by using the example of *rural* settlement types. Farm people differ greatly from one culture to another, one place to another, in how they situate their dwellings. The range from tightly clustered villages on the one extreme to fully dispersed farmsteads on the other is shown in Figure 2.27.

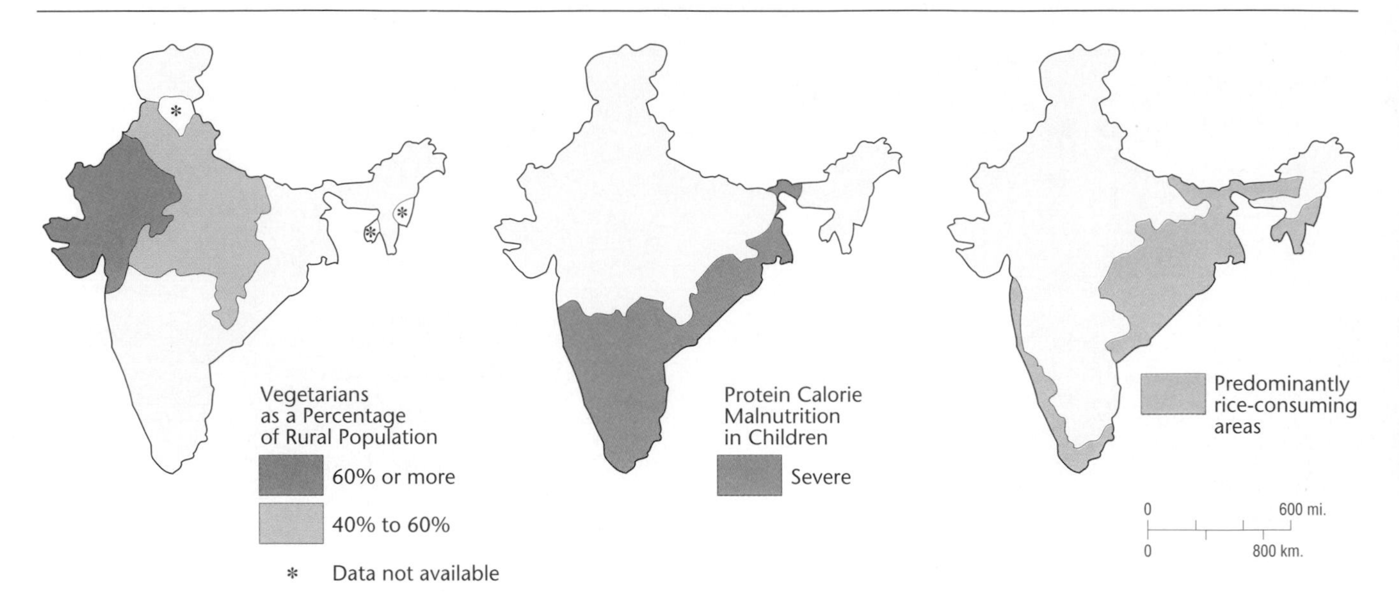

Figure 2.26
Protein malnutrition, vegetarianism, and rice consumption in India. In studying cultural integration, the geographer sometimes finds that the obvious answers are wrong. The disease and death that can result from protein deficiency are apparently unrelated to vegetarianism; instead, a link to rice consumption is suggested. (After Chakravarti, Aninda K. "Diet and Disease: Some Cultural Aspects of Food Use in India," in Allen G. Noble and Ashok K. Dutt [eds.], *India: Cultural Patterns and Processes*. Boulder, CO: Westview Press, 1982, 301–323.)

Farm Villages

In many parts of the world, farming people group themselves together in clustered settlements called **farm villages.** These nucleated settlements vary in size from a few dozen inhabitants to several thousand. Contained in the village **farmstead** are the house, barn, sheds, pens, and garden. The fields, pastures, and meadows lie out in the country beyond the limits of the village, and farmers must journey out from the village each day to work the land.

Farm villages are the most common form of settlement in much of Europe; in many parts of Latin America; in the densely settled farming regions of Asia, including much of India, China, and Japan; and among the sedentary farming peoples of Africa and the Middle East (see box, *Overlooking a Village in India*). These compact villages come in many forms. Most are irregular clusterings—a maze of winding, narrow streets and a jumble of farmsteads (Figures 2.27a and 2.28). Such *irregular clustered* farm villages developed spontaneously over the centuries, without any orderly plan to direct their growth. Other types of farm villages are very regular in their layout and reveal the imprint of planned design. The *street village*, the simplest of these planned types, consists of farmsteads grouped along both sides of a single, central street, producing an elongated settlement (Figures 2.27b and 2.29). Street villages are particularly common in eastern Europe, including much of Russia. Another type, the *green village,* consists of farmsteads grouped around a central open place, or green, which forms a commons (Figure 2.27c). Green villages occur through most of the plains areas of northern and northwestern Europe, and English immigrants

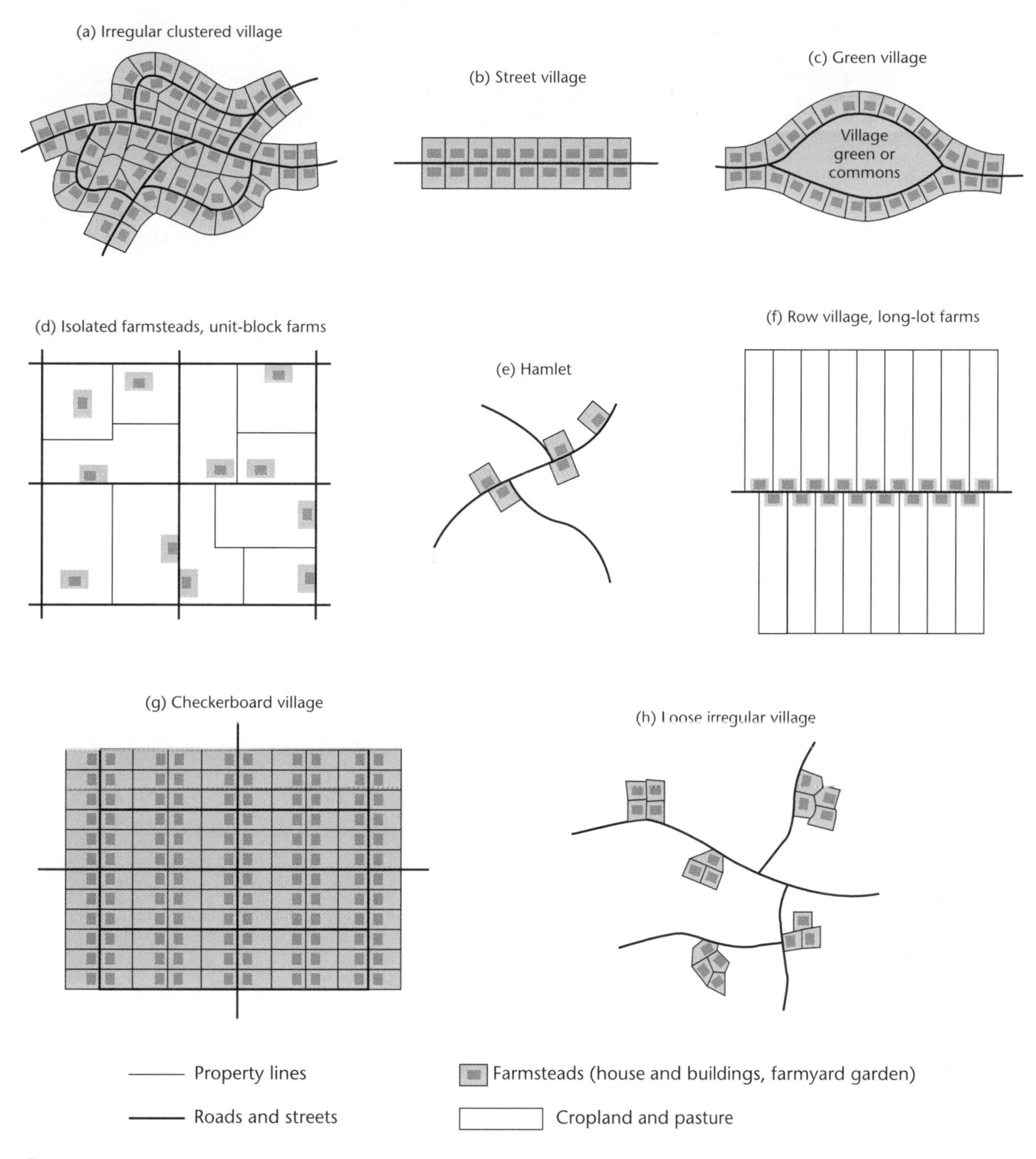

Figure 2.27
Rural settlement landscapes. The way individual farmers choose to locate their farmsteads leads to a general settlement pattern on the land. In some areas, farmsteads are scattered and isolated. In areas where farmsteads are grouped, there are several possible patterns of clustering.

laid out some such settlements in colonial New England. Also regular in layout is the *checkerboard village,* based on a gridiron pattern of streets meeting at right angles (Figure 2.27g). Mormon farm villages in Utah are of this type, and checkerboard villages also dominate most of rural Latin America and northeastern China.

Why do so many farm people huddle together in villages? Traditionally, the countryside was unsafe, threatened by roving bands of out-

Overlooking a Village in India

"On the steep ascent of the first range of hills bordering the southern edge of the great Ganges Valley in the Indian state of Madhya Pradesh, we ask our hired driver to stop the car, overlooking a tightly clustered farm village in the plain below. The village, tucked up against the foot of the hill, is open to our view from above. We look down on a disorderly jumble of tile-roofed, mud-walled farmsteads, each consisting of single-story buildings grouped protectively around a central courtyard. So compact is the settlement that it is difficult to tell where one farmstead leaves off and the neighboring ones begin. Rounded mounds of threshed rice straw rise from many courtyards, and an occasional shade tree conceals parts of the village from our view. From the narrow dusty lanes and tiny courtyards, a rich variety of village noises drifts up to us on our godlike perch—the noises of animals and people going about their daily routines, noises unchanged for thousands of years. Off into the hazy distance stretch tan fields, another reminder that it is December, a month of gathering. Near the village are bright green rectangles of vegetables, irrigated and lush in the subtropical winter sun. Here is simplicity, continuity, attachment to place.

"The twentieth century returns abruptly and disagreeably with the noise of a loaded truck rumbling along the narrow asphalt highway skirting one side of the village, gearing down for the steep slope ahead. Like proper citizens of the new age, we return to the hired automobile and continue our journey."

From the travel journal of T. G. J., 1975.

laws and raiders. Farmers could better defend themselves against such dangers by grouping together in villages. In many parts of the world, the populations of villages have grown larger during periods of insecurity and shrunk again when peace returned. Many farm villages occupy the most easily defended sites in their vicinity, and geographers call these *strong-point* settlements.

In addition to defense, the quality of the environment helps determine whether people settle in villages. In deserts and in limestone areas where the ground absorbs moisture quickly, farmsteads huddle together at the few sources of water. Such *wet-point* villages cluster

Figure 2.28
An irregular clustered farm village. This village with adjacent irrigated grain fields is near Gonggar in southeastern Tibet. The village nestles against a hill, and much of it is built on land unfit for cultivation. Much of the world's rural population lives in such villages.

around oases or deep wells. Conversely, a superabundance of water—in marshes, swamps, and areas subject to floods—prompts people to settle in villages on available *dry points* of higher elevation.

Various communal ties strongly bind villagers together. Groups of farmers linked to one another by blood relationships, religious customs, communal landownership, or other similar bonds usually form clustered villages. Mormon farm villages in the United States provide an excellent example of the clustering force of religion. Communal or state ownership of the land—as in China and parts of Israel—encouraged the formation of farm villages. The people who settle in these tightly knit villages generally depend on crops for their livelihood. Tillage requires less land than raising livestock does. Thus a farming economy permits villagers to live close together without having to travel an undue distance from farmstead to field.

Figure 2.29
Street village in Barbados. In Barbados, an island nation in the West Indies, farmsteads lie mainly along a single street, creating an elongated settlement.

Isolated Farmsteads

In many other parts of the world, the rural population lives in dispersed, isolated farmsteads, often some distance from their nearest neighbors (Figure 2.27d). These dispersed rural settlements grew up mainly in Anglo-America, Australia, New Zealand, and South Africa—that is, in the lands colonized by emigrating Europeans. But even in areas dominated by village settlements—such as Japan, Europe, and parts of India—some isolated farmsteads appear (Figure 2.30).

The conditions encouraging dispersed settlement are precisely the opposite of those favoring village development. These include peace and security in the countryside, removing the need for defense; colonization by individual pioneer families rather than by socially cohesive groups; agricultural private enterprise, as opposed to some form of communalism; rural economies dominated by livestock raising; and well-drained land where water is readily available. Most dispersed farmsteads originated rather recently and date primarily from the colonization of new farmland in the last two or three centuries.

Figure 2.30
An isolated farmstead in southeastern Iceland. Such rural settlement is most common in lands colonized by Europeans migrating overseas. Iceland was settled by Vikings from Norway a thousand years ago.

Semiclustered Rural Settlement

Some forms of rural settlement share characteristics of both clustered and dispersed types and may best be referred to as *semiclustered.* The most common type of semiclustered settlement, the *hamlet,* consists of a small number of farmsteads grouped loosely together (Figure 2.27e). As in villages, the hamlet farmsteads lie in a settlement nucleus separate from the cropland, but the hamlet is smaller and less compact, containing as few as three or four houses. Hamlets appear most frequently in poorer hill districts, especially in parts of western Europe, China, India, the Philippines, and Vietnam.

Occasionally, several hamlets lie close to one another, sharing a common name. These constitute a *loose irregular village* (Figure 2.27h). The individual clusters in such a group are often linked to various clans or religious groups. These loose villages occur most commonly in southeastern Europe, Malaya, Bangladesh, southern Japan, and India. Loose irregular villages involve a deliberate segregation of inhabitants, either voluntary or involuntary. In India, farmers of the "untouchable" caste are occasionally segregated from other people in this manner.

The *row village,* a third common type of semiclustered settlement, consists of a loose chain of farmsteads spaced at intervals along a road, river, or canal, often extending for many miles (Figure 2.27f). The individual farmsteads lie farther apart than those in a street village and do not abut one another. Row villages appear in the hills and marshlands of central and northwestern Europe; along the waterways in French-settled portions of North America, especially Québec and Louisiana; and in southern Brazil and adjacent parts of Argentina. In the extensive French Cajun row villages along Bayou Lafourche in Louisiana, dwellings lie sufficiently close to one another that "a baseball could be thrown from house to house for more than a hundred miles."

Reading the Cultural Landscape

The rural settlement forms described above provide a chance to "read" the cultural landscape. In so doing, we must always be cautious, looking for the subtle as well as the overt and not jumping to conclusions too quickly.

For example, the Maya Indians of the Yucatán peninsula in Mexico reside in checkerboard villages, a rural settlement landscape that is both revealing and potentially misleading (Figure 2.31). Before the Spanish conquest, Mayas lived in templed wet-point villages of the irregular clustered type, situated alongside *cenotes,* natural sinkholes that provided water in a land with no surface streams. The Spaniards destroyed these settlements, replacing them with checkerboard villages. Wide, straight streets accommodated the wheeled vehicles of the European conquerors.

Superficially, the checkerboard landscape suggests a cultural victory by the Spaniards. But if you look more closely, you will see that, in fact, Mayan culture prevailed. Even today many Mayas make little use of wheeled vehicles in village life, and many of the Spaniards' "streets" serve merely as rights-of-way for Indian footpaths that wind among boulders and outcroppings of bedrock. Irregularities in the checkerboard, coupled with a casual distribution of dwellings, suggest Mayan resistance to the new geometry. Spanish-influenced architecture—flat-roofed houses of stone, the town hall, a church, and a hacienda man-

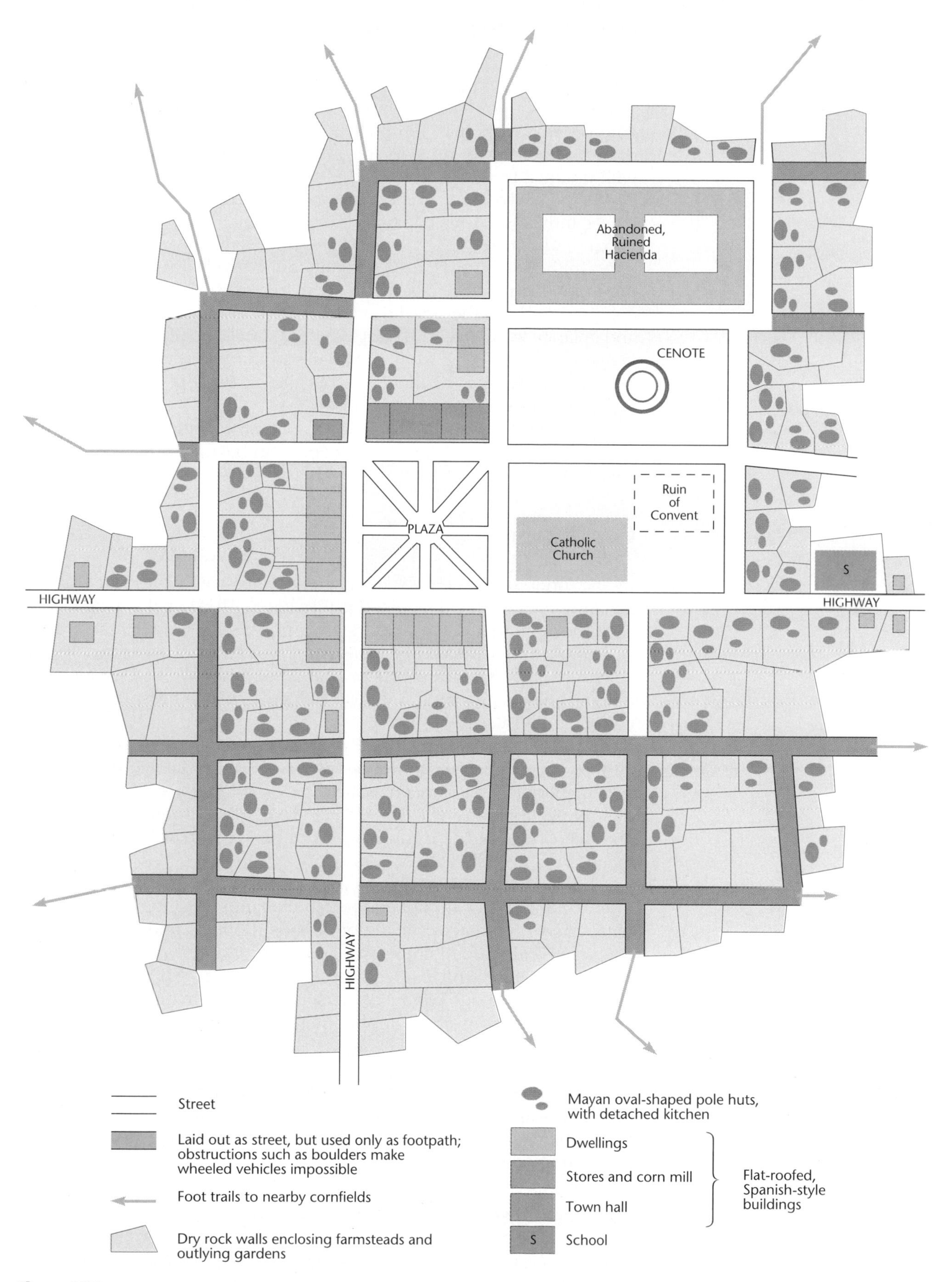

Figure 2.31

A hypothetical modern Mayan checkerboard farm village in Yucatán province, Mexico. Spanish influence, seen in the grid pattern, plaza, church, hacienda, and flat-roofed buildings, weakens with distance from the center, and the rigid checkerboard masks a certain irregularity of farmstead layout. A *cenote* is a large, deep sinkhole filled with water, and these natural pools served a major religious function among the Mayas before Christianity came. (Source: Composite of 1987 field observations by T. G. J. in some 15 villages east and southeast of Mérida.)

sion—remain confined to the area near the central plaza, with newer examples along highway entrances to the village. A block away, the traditional Maya pole huts with thatched, hipped roofs prevail, echoed by cook houses of the same design. Indian influence increases markedly with distance from the plaza.

In the dooryard gardens surrounding each hut, traditional Indian plants thrive, such as papayas, bananas, chile peppers, ramon nuts, yucca, and maize, with only a few citrus trees to reveal Spanish influence. In the same yards, each carefully ringed with dry rock walls, as in pre-Columbian times, pigs descended from those introduced by the conquerors share the ground with the traditional turkeys of the Maya and apiaries for indigenous stingless bees. Occasionally, the Mayan language is heard drifting from hammocks in the pole huts, though Spanish prevails. So does Catholicism, but the absence of huts around the *cenote* suggests a lingering pagan sanctity.

Sometimes, then, the overt aspects of cultural landscape are merely a facade. We should always look deeper and become sensitive to subtle visual clues.

Conclusion

In our brief study of population geography, we have seen that humankind is unevenly distributed across the Earth. Spatial variations also exist for birthrates, death rates, rates of population growth, age groups, sex ratios, and standards of living, and we depicted these patterns as culture regions. The principles of cultural diffusion proved useful in analyzing human migration and also helped explain the spread of birth control and diseases.

By adopting the viewpoint of cultural ecology, we saw how the environment and the perception people have of it influence the distribution of people and sometimes help guide migrations. We also found that population density is linked to the level of environmental alteration and that overpopulation can have a destructive impact on the environment.

We used cultural integration as the device to suggest how demography and mobility are linked to such elements of culture as legal systems, food preferences, migration taboos, politics, and economic opportunity. Cultural attitudes can encourage people to be mobile or to stay in one place, and can lead them to accept crowding or to feel uncomfortable without plenty of personal space. In many ways, then, spatial variations in demographic traits are enmeshed in the fabric of culture.

How people distribute themselves across the Earth's surface finds a vivid expression in the cultural landscape. Using the example of the farm landscape, we have seen how different cultures developed distinctive settlement forms, each of which reflects a unique distribution of population on the local level.

Sources and Suggested Readings

Beaujeu-Garnier, Jacqueline. *Geography of Population,* 2d ed. Beaver, S. H. (trans.). London: Longman, 1978.

Black, Richard, and Vaughan Robinson (eds.). *Geography and Refugees: Patterns and Processes of Change.* New York: John Wiley, 1993.

Burton, Ian, and Robert W. Kates. "The Floodplain and the Seashore: A Comparative Analysis of Hazard-Zone Occupance." *Geographical Review,* 54 (1964): 366–385.

Cater, John, and Trevor Jones. *Social Geography: An Introduction to Contemporary Issues.* London: Edward Arnold, 1989.

Chakravarti, Aninda K. "Diet and Disease: Some Cultural Aspects of Food Use in India," in Allen G. Noble and Ashok K. Dutt (eds.), *India: Cultural Patterns and Processes.* Boulder, CO: Westview Press, 1982, 301–323.

Clark, W. A. V. *Human Migration.* (Volume 7 in the Scientific Geography Series). Newbury Park, CA: Sage Publications, 1986.

Clarke, John I., Peter Curson, S. L. Kayastha, and Prithvish Nag (eds.). *Population and Disaster.* Institute of British Geographers, Special Publication 22. Oxford: Basil Blackwell, 1989.

Coleman, David, and Roger Schofield (eds.). *The State of Population Theory: Forward from Malthus.* New York: Basil Blackwell, 1986.

Compton, P. A. "Religious Affiliation and Demographic Variability in Northern Ireland." *Transactions of the Institute of British Geographers,* 1 (1976): 433–452.

Corbridge, Stuart. "The Economic Value of Children: A Case Study from Rural India." *Applied Geography: An International Journal,* 5 (1985): 273–295.

Currey, Bruce, and Graeme Hugo (eds.). *Famine as a Geographical Phenomenon.* Dordrecht, Netherlands: D. Reidel, 1984.

Doenges, Catherine E., and James L. Newman. "Impaired Fertility in Tropical Africa." *Geographical Review,* 79 (1989): 99–111.

Dupâquier, J., and A. Fauve-Chamoux (eds.). *Malthus Past and Present.* New York: Academic Press, 1983.

Evans, David J., and David T. Herbert. *The Geography of Crime.* New York: Routledge, Chapman and Hall, 1989.

Garnett, Alice. "Insolation, Topography, and Settlement in the Alps." *Geographical Review,* 25 (1935): 601–617.

Gender, Place and Culture: A Journal of Feminist Geography. Published by the Carfax Publishing Co., PO Box 2025, Dunnellon, FL 34430. Volume 1 appeared in 1994.

Gesler, Wilbert M. *The Cultural Geography of Health Care.* Pittsburgh: University of Pittsburgh Press, 1991.

Gober, Patricia. "The Retirement Community as a Geographical Phenomenon: The Case of Sun City, Arizona." *Journal of Geography,* 84 (1985): 189–198.

Gober, Patricia. "Why Abortion Rates Vary: A Geography of the Supply of and Demand for Abortion Services in the United States in 1988." *Annals of the Association of American Geographers,* 84 (1994): 230–250.

Gould, Peter. *The Slow Plague: A Geography of the AIDS Pandemic.* Oxford, UK: Blackwell, 1993.

Graff, Thomas O., and Robert F. Wiseman. "Changing Patterns of Retirement Counties Since 1965." *Geographical Review,* 80 (1990): 239–251.

Harries, Keith D. *Serious Violence: Patterns of Homicide and Assault in America.* Springfield, MA: Charles C. Thomas, 1990.

Holdsworth, Deryck W., and Glenda Laws. "Landscapes of Old Age in Coastal British Columbia." *Canadian Geographer,* 38 (1994): 174–181.

Hooson, David J. M. "The Distribution of Population as the Essential Geographical Expression." *Canadian Geographer,* 4,17 (1960): 10–20.

Howe, G. Melvyn (ed.). *Global Geocancerology: A World Geography of Human Cancers.* Edinburgh: Churchill Livingstone, 1986.

Howe, G. Melvyn (ed.). *A World Geography of Human Diseases.* London: Academic Press, 1977.

Hsu, Mei-Ling. "Growth and Control of Population in China: The Urban-Rural Contrast." *Annals of the Association of American Geographers,* 75 (1985): 241–257.

Hugo, Graeme. *Third World Populations.* New York: Basil Blackwell, 1989.

Hunter, John M. "The Social Roots of Dispersed Settlement in Northern Ghana." *Annals of the Association of American Geographers,* 57 (1967): 338–349.

Johnston, R. J. "Population Distributions and the Essentials of Human Geography." *South African Geographical Journal,* 58 (1976): 93–106.

Jones, Huw. *Population Geography,* 2d ed. New York: Guilford, 1990.

Jones, Kelvyn, and Graham Moon. *Medical Geography: An Introduction.* London: Routledge & Kegan Paul, 1987.

Knapp, Ronald G. (ed.). *Chinese Landscapes: The Village as Place.* Honolulu: University of Hawaii Press, 1992.

Knight, C. Gregory. "The Ecology of African Sleeping Sickness." *Annals of the Association of American Geographers,* 61 (1971): 23–44.

Laws, Glenda. "The Land of Old Age: Society's Changing Attitudes Toward Built Environments for Elderly People." *Annals of the Association of American Geographers,* 83 (1993): 672–693

Learmonth, Andrew. *Disease Ecology.* New York: Basil Blackwell, 1988.

Mackay, Judith. *The State of Health Atlas.* New York: Simon & Schuster, 1993.

Malthus, Thomas R. *An Essay on the Principles of Population.* James, Patricia (ed.). Cambridge: Cambridge University Press, 1989.

Massey, Doreen. *Space, Place, and Gender.* Minneapolis: University of Minnesota Press, 1994.

McColl, Robert W., and Youguan Kou. "Feeding China's Millions." *Geographical Review,* 80 (1990): 434–443.

Meade, Melinda, John Florin, and Wilbert Gesler. *Medical Geography.* New York: Guilford, 1988.

Monk, Janice, and Cindi Katz (eds.). *Full Circles: Geographies of Women over the Life Course.* New York: Routledge, 1993.

Morrill, Richard L. "Regional Demographic Structure of the United States." *Professional Geographer,* 42 (1990): 38–53.

Newman, James L. *The Peopling of Africa: A Geographic Interpretation.* New Haven, CT: Yale University Press, 1995.

Ogden, P. E. *Migration and Geographical Change.* New York: Cambridge University Press, 1984.

Plane, David A., and Peter A. Rogerson. *The Geographical Analysis of Population.* New York: Wiley, 1994.

Rogers, Andrei (ed.). *Elderly Migration and Population Redistribution.* London: Belhaven, 1992.

Seager, Joni, and Ann Olson. *Women in the World: An International Atlas.* New York: Simon & Schuster, 1986.

Shannon, Gary W., and Gerald F. Pyle. *Disease and Medical Care in the United States: A Medical Atlas of the Twentieth Century.* New York: Macmillan, 1992.

Shannon, Gary W., Gerald F. Pyle, and Rashid L. Bashshur. *The Geography of AIDS: Origins and Course of an Epidemic.* New York: Guilford, 1991.

Siddiqi, Mohamed I., "Population Growth and Food Supply Margin in Pakistan." *GeoJournal,* 10 (1985): 83–90.

Slater, Paul B. *Migration Regions of the United States: Two County-Level 1965–70 Analyses.* Santa Barbara: Community and Organization Research Institute, University of California at Santa Barbara, 1983.

Spain, Daphne. *Gendered Spaces.* Chapel Hill: University of North Carolina Press, 1992.

Svart, Larry M. "Environmental Preference Migration: A Review." *Geographical Review,* 66 (1976): 314–330.

Thorpe, Harry. "The Green Village as a Distinctive Form of Settlement on the North European Plain." *Bulletin de la Société Belge d'Études Géographiques,* 30 (1961): 93–134.

Watts, Michael J. "Conjunctures and Crisis: Food, Ecology and Population, and the Internationalization of Capital." *Journal of Geography,* 86 (1987): 292–299.

White, Paul E., and Robert Woods (eds.). *Geographical Impact of Migration.* New York: Longman, 1980.

Whitmore, Thomas M. "A Simulation of the Sixteenth-Century Population Collapse in the Basin of Mexico." *Annals of the Association of American Geographers,* 81 (1991): 464–487.

Wilbanks, Thomas J. "Sustainable Development in Geographic Perspective." *Annals of the Association of American Geographers*, 84 (1994): 541–556.
Wood, William B. "Forced Migration: Local Conflicts and International Dilemmas." *Annals of the Association of American Geographers*, 84 (1994): 607–634.
Woods, Robert, and Philip Rees (eds.). *Population Structures and Models: Developments in Spatial Demography*. London: Allen & Unwin, 1986.

CHAPTER 3

The Agricultural World

The world's huge population seeks its livelihood in various ways, but all of us depend, either directly or indirectly, on agriculture for the daily food that permits our survival. We can too easily forget that the entire urban-industrial society rests, none too securely, on the base of the food surplus generated by farmers and herders, and that without agriculture there could be no cities or universities, no factories or offices.

Agriculture, the tilling of crops and rearing of domesticated animals to produce food, feed, drink, and fiber, has been the principal enterprise of humankind through most of recorded history. Even today, agriculture remains by far the most important economic activity in the world, occupying the greater part of the land area and employing 45 percent of the working population. In some parts of Asia and Africa, over 80 percent of the labor force is devoted to agriculture. We North Americans are unusual, living in an urban society in which less than 2 percent work as agriculturists. As recently as 1880, 44 percent of all Americans were farmers, but in the past century we have relied on an ever-smaller segment of our population to produce the food and fiber we need. Since 1910, the number of Americans residing on farms has fallen from 32 million to fewer than 5 million. Europe's population is as thoroughly nonagricultural as North America's. Most of the rest of the world, however, remains a land of farm villages, like those described at the end of chapter 2.

Over thousands of years, agricultural pursuits became highly diverse regionally, and cultivators and herders altered the environment on a massive scale. The cultural landscape over much of the Earth's surface is largely agricultural. The geographical themes of culture region, diffusion, ecology, integration, and landscape are highly relevant to the study of agriculture.

Agricultural Regions

The practice of raising plants and animals has spread to most parts of the world. Peoples living in differing environments developed new farming methods, creating numerous spatial variations. Geographers

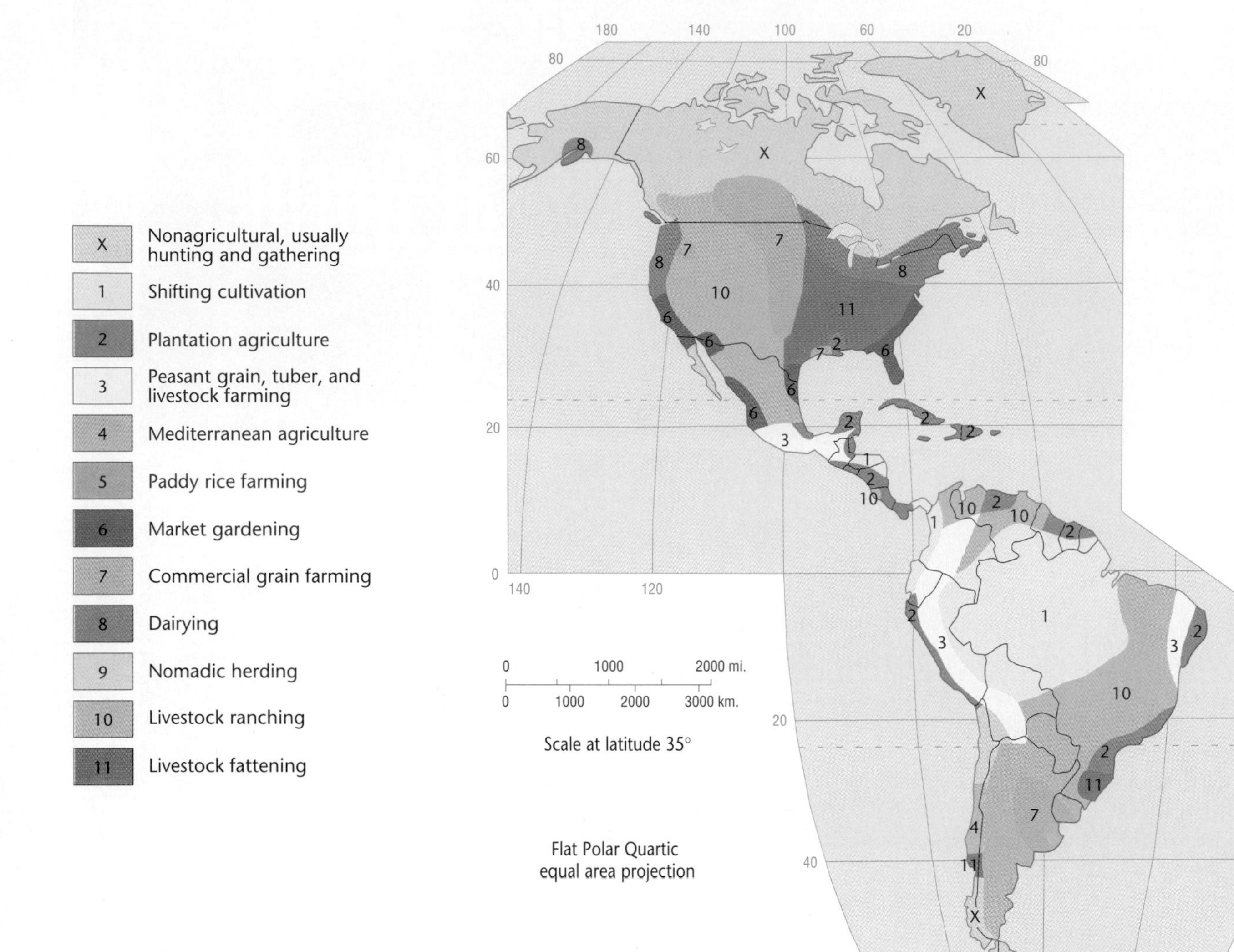

Figure 3.1
Agricultural regions of the world. (Based on Grigg and Whittlesey, with modifications.)

capture these regional contrasts by using the culture region concept, in particular, formal **agricultural regions.** Figure 3.1, showing a classification of agricultural regions, should be referred to as we discuss each type.

Shifting Cultivation

The native peoples of tropical lowlands and hills in the Americas, Africa, Southeast Asia, and Indonesia practice an agricultural system known as **shifting cultivation.** Essentially, this is a land-rotation system.

Using machetes or other bladed instruments, shifting cultivators chop away the undergrowth from small patches of land and kill the trees by removing a strip of bark completely around the trunk. After the dead vegetation dries out, the farmers set it on fire to clear the land. These clearing techniques give shifting cultivation the name of "slash-and-burn" agriculture. Working with digging sticks or hoes, the farmers

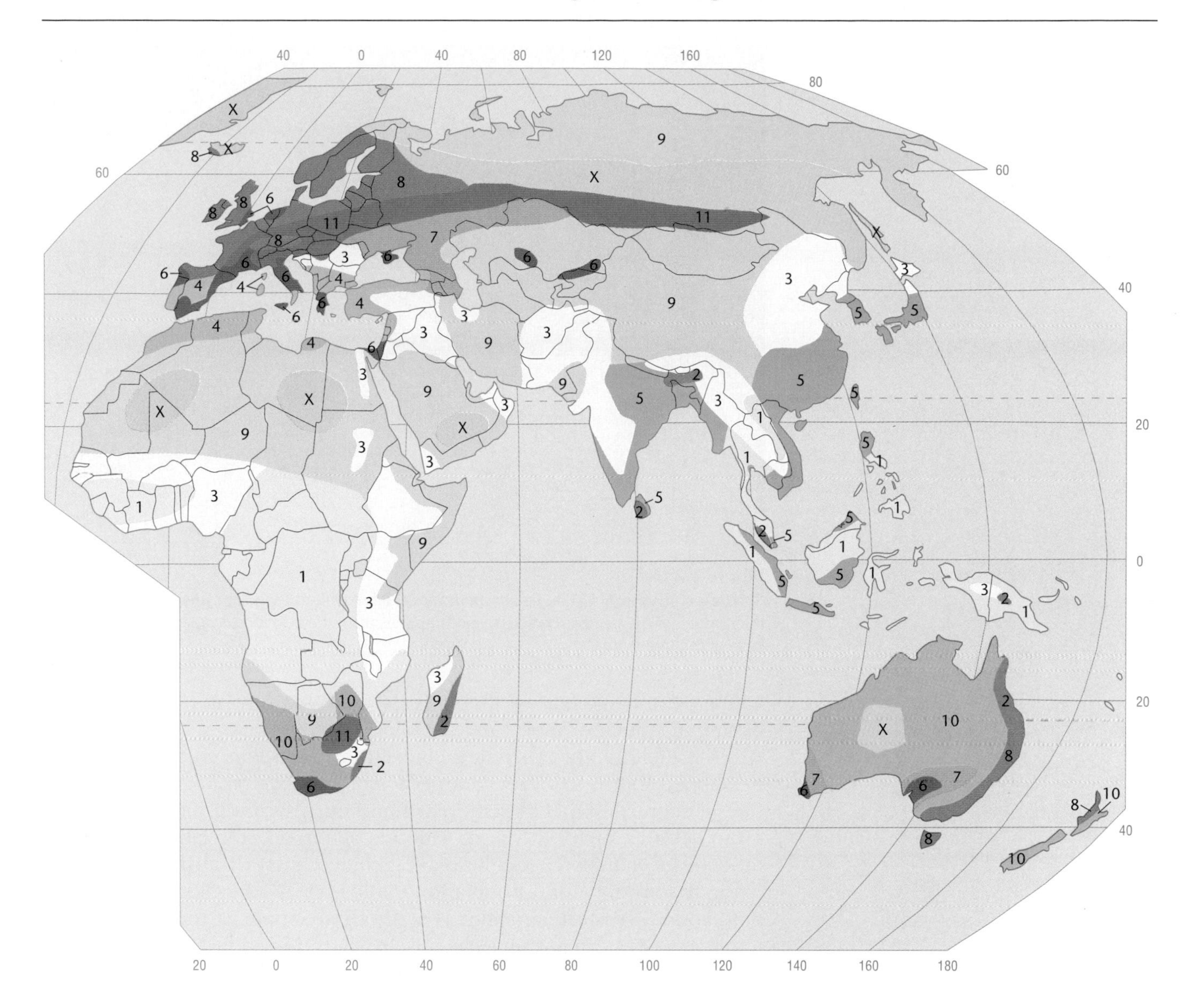

then plant a variety of crops in the clearings, varying from the maize (corn), beans, bananas, and manioc of American Indians to the yams and nonirrigated rice grown by hill tribes in Southeast Asia (Figure 3.2). Different crops typically share the same clearing, a practice called **intertillage.** This allows taller, stronger crops to shelter lower, more fragile ones from the tropical downpours and reveals the rich lore and learning acquired by shifting cultivators over many centuries. Relatively little tending of the plants is necessary until harvesttime, and no fertilizer is applied to the fields.

Farmers repeat the planting and harvesting cycle in the same clearings for perhaps four or five years, until the soil loses much of its fertility. Then these fields are abandoned, and the farmers prepare new clearings to replace them. The abandoned cropland lies unused and recuperates for 10 to 20 years before farmers clear and cultivate it again. Shifting cultivation represents one form of **subsistence agriculture**—involving food production mainly for the family and local community rather than for market. Farm animals play a small role in shifting culti-

Figure 3.2
Shifting cultivation. This Indian in the Amazon Basin of Brazil tends a typical field. Note the intertillage, which includes bananas, and the ashes from the burning of the clearing at the base of the tree stump.

vation. Farmers keep few if any livestock, often relying on hunting and fishing for much of their food supply.

The technology of shifting cultivation may seem crude and poorly developed, but it has proved an efficient adaptive strategy for the people who practice this system. Slash-and-burn farming may well return more calories of food for the calories spent on cultivation than docs modern mechanized agriculture and achieves **sustainability** for millennia in the absence of a population explosion. We should never assume that modern Western agricultural methods are superior to those of traditional non-Western farming systems. Slash-and-burn farming, unlike our modern systems, has endured for millennia. In spite of this, shifting cultivators are continuously under attack from Western agricultural "experts." In many regions, they are being forced off the land by rural development schemes of one kind or another or by nonindigenous immigrants. Improved health conditions have also caused their populations to grow beyond the size that can be supported by this traditional farming system. They passed from the first to the second stage of the demographic transition. As a result, the shifting cultivators must shorten the fallow period, causing environmental deterioration. For these reasons, an ecologically rather benign type of agriculture declines.

Paddy Rice Farming

Peasant farmers in the humid tropical and subtropical parts of Asia practice a highly distinctive type of subsistence agriculture called **paddy rice farming**. From the monsoon coasts of India through the hills of southeastern China and on to the warmer parts of Japan stretches a broad region of tiny, mud-diked, flooded rice fields, or paddies, many of which perch on terraced hillsides. The paddy must be drained and rebuilt each year. The terraced paddy fields form a striking cultural landscape, the hallmark of this type of agriculture (Figure 1.17 in Chapter 1).

Rice, the dominant paddy crop, forms the basis of "vegetable civilizations" in which almost all the caloric intake is of plant origin. Many paddy farmers also raise a cash crop for market, such as tea, sugar cane, mulberry bushes for silkworm production, or the fiber crop jute. Asian farmers also raise pigs, cattle, and poultry and maintain fish in the irrigation reservoirs, though they remain basically vegetarians. Farmers in India use draft animals such as the water buffalo to a greater extent than do other paddy farmers, and the Japanese have mechanized paddy rice farming.

Most paddy rice farms outside the Communist area of Asia are tiny. A 3-acre (about 1 hectare) landholding is considered adequate to support a farm family. Asian farmers can survive on such a small scale of operation partly because irrigated rice provides a very large output of food per unit of land. Still, the paddy farmers must till their small patches most intensively in order to harvest enough food. This means they must carefully transplant by hand the small rice sprouts from seed beds to the paddy. Persons from Western cultures can scarcely imagine the magnitude of tedious hand labor involved. They also plant and harvest the same parcel of land two or three times each year—a practice known as **double-cropping**—while applying large amounts of organic fertilizer to the land. So productive is this system that per-acre yields exceed those of American agriculture (Figure 3.3). The **green revolution** of the last half of the twentieth century, achieved by introducing hybrid rice, chemical fertilizers, and pesticides, further heightened productivity.

Peasant Grain, Root, and Livestock Farming

In colder, drier Asiatic farming regions, climatically unsuited to paddy rice farming, as well as in the river valleys of the Middle East, parts of Europe, Africa, and the mountain highlands of Latin America and New Guinea, farmers practice a system of semisubsistence agriculture based on bread grains, root crops, and herd livestock (Figures 3.4 and 3.5).

Figure 3.3
Hand threshing of rice on the island of Bali, Indonesia. Paddy rice farming entails enormous amounts of human labor and yields very high productivity per unit of land.

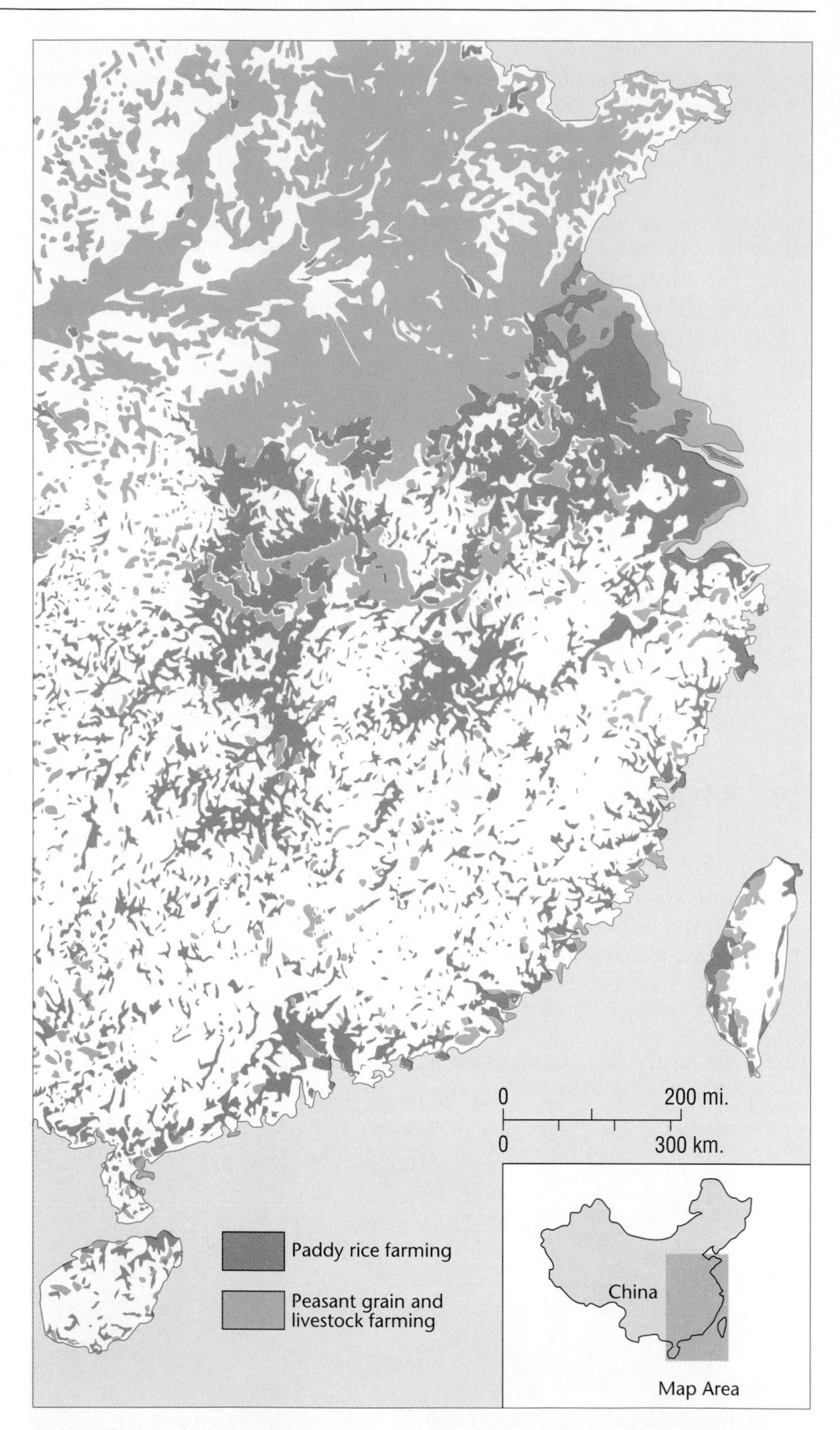

Figure 3.4

Two agricultural regions in China. The intricacies of culture regional boundaries are suggested by the distribution of two types of agriculture in Taiwan and the eastern part of China. What might account for the more fragmented distribution of paddy rice farming, as contrasted with peasant grain, root, and livestock farming? Where would you draw the cultural boundary between the two types of agriculture? All such cultural geographical borders are difficult to draw. (Source: "China Land Utilization," a map in Chinese edited by Wu Chuan-jun and published in 1979 by the Institute of Geography, Academica Sinica, Beijing.)

The dominant grain crops in these regions are, variously, wheat, barley, sorghum, millet, oats, and maize. Many farmers in these areas also raise a cash crop, such as cotton, flax, hemp, coffee, or tobacco.

These farmers also raise herds of cattle, pigs, sheep, and, in South America, llamas and alpacas. The livestock pull the plow; provide milk, meat, and wool; serve as beasts of burden; and produce manure for the fields. They also consume a portion of the grain harvest. In some areas, such as the Middle Eastern river valleys, the use of irrigation helps support this peasant system.

Figure 3.5
Semisubsistence agriculture in New Guinea. Distinctive "raised fields" with sweet potato mounds are found among the farmers of highland New Guinea, an area where peasant grain, root, and livestock agriculture occurs. These people raise diverse crops but give the greatest importance to sweet potatoes, together with pigs.

Mediterranean Agriculture

In the lands bordering the Mediterranean Sea, a truly distinctive type of peasant subsistence agriculture took shape in ancient times, and in a few areas this system survives intact today. Traditional Mediterranean agriculture is based on wheat and barley cultivation in the rainy winter season; raising drought-resistant vine and tree crops like the grape, olive, and fig; and livestock herding, particularly of sheep and goats (Figure 3.6). In recent times, many farmers began using irrigation in a major way, leading to the expansion of crops such as citrus fruits.

Traditional Mediterranean farmers do not integrate stock raising with crop cultivation. They rarely raise feed, collect animal manure, or keep draft animals. Instead, they pasture their livestock in communal herds on rocky mountain slopes, while they plant the valleys and gentler slopes below with vineyards, orchards, and grain fields. Because Mediterranean farmers do not fertilize their land, grain fields must lie fallow every other year to regain their fertility.

Figure 3.6
Traditional Mediterranean agriculture. Farming in Mediterranean lands combines grain cultivation with vine and tree crops, in addition to herding. Often the grain is raised in the orchards, as in this scene of intertillage from the Greek island of Crete, where newly harvested wheat lies in sheaves amid the olive trees. The mountains in the distance provide range for the farmers' sheep and goats.

Figure 3.7
Nomadic herding. South Turkana nomadic herders in Kenya, East Africa.

All three of these basic enterprises—grain raising, vine and tree cultivation, and livestock herding—are combined on each small farm. From this diverse, unspecialized trinity, the Mediterranean farmer can reap nearly all of life's necessities, including wool and leather for clothing, and bread, beverages, fruit, milk, cheese, and meat. Since about 1850, many Mediterranean agricultural areas changed as commercialization and specialization of farming replaced the traditional diversified system. In such areas, the present-day agriculture is better described as market gardening (see later section).

Nomadic Herding

In the dry or cold lands of the Eastern Hemisphere, particularly in the deserts, steppes, and savannas of Africa, Arabia, and the interior of Eurasia, nomadic livestock herders graze cattle, sheep, goats, and camels (Figure 3.7) (see box, *The Wandering Life of the Tatars*). The cold tundra north of the tree line in Eurasia forms another zone of no-

The Wandering Life of the Tatars

"The Tatars never remain fixed, but as the winter approaches remove to the plains of a warmer region, in order to find sufficient pasture for their cattle; and in summer they frequent cold situations in the mountains, where there is water and verdure, and their cattle are free from the annoyance of horseflies and other biting insects. During two or three months they progressively ascend higher ground, and seek fresh pasture, the grass not being adequate in any one place to feed the multitudes of which their herds and flocks consist. Their huts or tents, formed of rods covered with felt, exactly round, and nicely put together, can be gathered into one bundle, and made up as packages. . . . They eat flesh of every description, horses, camels, and even dogs, provided they are fat. They drink mare's milk, which they prepare in such a manner that it has the qualities and flavor of white wine."

From *The Adventures of Marco Polo, as Dictated in Prison to a Scribe in the Year 1298; What He Experienced and Heard during his Twenty-Four Years Spent in Travel through Asia and at the Court of Kublai-Khan.*

madic herders. The main characteristic of nomadic herding is the continued movement of people with their livestock in search of forage for the animals. Some nomads migrate from lowlands in winter to mountains in summer, while others shift from desert areas in winter to adjacent semiarid plains in summer, or from tundra in summer to nearby forests in winter. Many place a high value on the horse, which has traditionally been kept for use in warfare, or the camel. Nomads in sub-Saharan Africa are the only ones who depend mainly on cattle, while those in the tundras of northern Eurasia raise reindeer.

Necessity dictates that the few material possessions the nomads have be portable, including the tents they use for housing. Normally, the nomads obtain nearly all of life's necessities from livestock products, or by bartering with the sedentary farmers of adjacent river valleys and oases. Until almost the modern age, nomads presented a periodic military threat to even the greatest farming civilizations.

Today, nomadic herding is almost everywhere in decline. A number of national governments have established policies encouraging nomads to practice **sedentary cultivation** of the land. A practice begun in the nineteenth century by British and French colonial administrators in North Africa, the settling of nomadic tribes allows greater control by the central governments. Russia adopted such a policy and pursued it with considerable success. Moreover, many nomads are voluntarily abandoning their traditional life in order to seek jobs in urban areas or in the Middle Eastern oil fields. Further impetus to abandon nomadic life recently came from severe drought in sub-Saharan Africa, which decimated livestock herds. Nomadism survives mainly in remote areas, and this traditional way of life may soon vanish altogether.

Plantation Agriculture

In certain tropical and subtropical areas, Europeans and Americans imposed a commercial agricultural system on the native types of subsistence agriculture. This system is called **plantation** agriculture. A plantation is a huge landholding devoted to the efficient, large-scale, specialized production of one tropical or subtropical crop for market. Such a system relies on large amounts of hand labor. The plantation system originated in the 1400s on Portuguese-owned islands off the coast of tropical West Africa, but the greatest concentration is now in the American tropics. Most plantations lie on or near the seacoast, in order to be close to the shipping lanes that carry their produce to non-tropical lands such as Europe, the United States, and Japan.

Most workers live right on the plantation, where a rigid social and economic segregation of labor and management produces a two-class society of the wealthy and the poor. Traditionally, as in the antebellum southern United States, many plantation owners relied on slaves to provide the needed labor. Today, because of the capital investment necessary, corporations or governments are usually the owners of plantations. Tension between labor and management is not uncommon, and the societal ills of the plantation system remain far from cured (Figure 3.8).

The plantation provided the base for European and American economic expansion into tropical Asia, Africa, and Latin America. It maximizes the production of luxury crops for Europeans and Americans: sugarcane, bananas, coffee, coconuts, spices, tea, cacao, and tobacco (Figure 3.9). Similarly, Western textile factories required cotton, sisal, jute, hemp, and other fiber crops from the plantation areas. Profits from

Figure 3.8
Plantation agriculture. This sign was erected by the management at the entrance to a banana plantation in Costa Rica. "Welcome to Freehold Plantation; a workplace where labor harmony reigns; in mutual respect and understanding, we united workers produce and export quality goods in peace and harmony." Such a message suggests that, in fact, not all is harmonious here, that the tension of the two-class plantation system simmers below the surface.

Figure 3.9
Tea plantation in the highlands of Papua New Guinea. While profitable for the owners and providing employment for a small labor force, the plantation displaced a much larger population of peasant grain, root, and livestock farmers.

these plantations were usually exported along with the crops themselves to Europe and North America, impoverishing the colonial lands where plantations developed.

Each plantation district in the tropical and subtropical zones tends to specialize in one particular crop. Coffee and tea, for instance, grow in the tropical highlands, with coffee dominating the upland plantations of tropical America and tea confined mainly to the hill slopes of India and Sri Lanka. Today, coffee is the economic lifeblood of about 40 underdeveloped countries, while sugarcane and bananas are the major lowland plantation crops of tropical America. In most cases, plantation workers at least partially process the crop before sending it to the distant market. For example, sugar is generally milled and cotton ginned on the plantation. This combination of raising and partially processing the crop is a major distinguishing trait of the plantation system.

Since many plantations are now mechanized—a type referred to as the *neo-plantation*—less labor is required, causing underemployment and displacement of the local people. They leave the land and flock to urban centers, contributing to the massive growth of Third-World cities.

Market Gardening

The growth of urban markets in the last few centuries also gave rise to other commercial forms of agriculture, including **market gardening,** also known as truck farming. Unlike plantations, these farms are located in developed countries and specialize in intensively cultivated nontropical fruits, vegetables, and vines. They raise no livestock. Each district concentrates on a single product such as wine, table grapes, raisins, oranges, apples, lettuce, or potatoes, and the entire farm output is raised for sale rather than for consumption on the farm. Many truck farmers participate in cooperative marketing arrangements and depend on migratory seasonal farm laborers to harvest their crops. Market garden districts appear in most industrialized countries and often lie near major urban centers. In the United States, a broken belt of market gardens extends from California eastward through the Gulf and Atlantic coast states, with scattered districts in other parts of the country.

Commercial Livestock Fattening

In commercial livestock fattening, farmers raise and fatten cattle and hogs for slaughter. One of the most highly developed fattening areas is the famous Corn Belt of the midwestern United States, where farmers raise maize and soybeans to feed cattle and hogs. A similar system prevails over much of western and central Europe, though the feed crops there are more commonly oats and potatoes. Smaller zones of commercial livestock fattening appear in overseas European settlement zones such as southern Brazil and South Africa.

One of the main characteristics of commercial livestock fattening is the combination of crop and animal raising on the same farm. This led some geographers to refer to this type of agriculture as *mixed crop and livestock farming*. Farmers breed many of the animals they fatten, especially the hogs. About 1950, commercial livestock fatteners began to specialize their activities; some concentrated on breeding animals, others on preparing them for market. In the factory-like **feedlot,** farmers raise imported cattle and hogs on purchased feed (Figure 3.10). Such feedlots are most common in the western and southern United States, in part because winters are less severe there.

Although commercial livestock fattening is often organized with assembly-line precision and has proved profitable, the specter of famine in recent years has brought its nutritional efficiency into question. In the 1900s world grain production rose significantly faster than world population growth, and cereals provide most of the protein intake of the world's people. But in the same century, meat eating soared in the Western world, particularly in the United States, wiping out most of these gains. At least one-half of America's harvested agricultural land is planted with feed crops for livestock, and over 70 percent of the grain raised in the United States goes for livestock fattening. Livestock are not an efficient method of protein production. A cow, for instance, must eat 21 pounds (9.5 kilograms) of protein to produce 1 pound (0.5 kilogram) of edible protein. Plants are far more efficient protein converters. The protein lost through conversion from plant to meat could make up almost all of the world's present protein deficiencies. The food that today feeds Americans alone would feed 1.5 billion at the

Figure 3.10
Cattle feedlot for beef production. This feedlot, in Colorado, is reputedly the world's largest.

Figure 3.11
Mechanized rice harvest in a commercial grain farming region. North American farmers operate in a capital-intensive manner, investing in machines, chemical fertilizers, and pesticides. Such machines compact the soil, causing long-term problems. Compare this scene to Figure 3.3, which shows rice threshing in a paddy farming area of Asia.

consumption level of China. This basic inefficiency has spread to some poorer nations, such as Costa Rica and Brazil, where rain forest is being destroyed and shifting cultivators displaced to make way for cattle pasture to fatten beef for America's fast-food restaurants.

Commercial Grain Farming

Commercial grain farming represents another market-oriented type of agriculture in which farmers specialize in growing wheat or, less frequently, rice or corn. Wheat belts stretch through Australia, the Great Plains of interior North America, the steppes of Ukraine, and the pampas of Argentina. Together, the United States, Canada, Argentina, Kazakstan, Russia, and Ukraine produce 35 percent of the world's wheat. Farms in these areas are generally very large. They range from family-run wheat farms of 1000 acres (400 hectares) or more in the American Great Plains to giant collective farms. Extensive rice farms, operated under the same commercial system (Figure 3.11), cover large areas of the Texas-Louisiana coastal plain and lowlands in Arkansas and California.

Widespread use of machinery, chemical fertilizers, pesticides, and improved seed varieties enables commercial grain farmers to operate on this large scale. Indeed, planting and harvesting grain is more completely mechanized than any other form of agriculture. Commercial rice farmers employ such techniques as sowing grain from airplanes. Perhaps the ultimate development is the **suitcase farm,** a post–World War II innovation in the Wheat Belt of the northern Great Plains of the United States. The people who own and operate these farms do not live on the land. Most of them own several suitcase farms, lined up in a south-to-north row through the Plains states. They keep fleets of farm machinery, which they send north with crews of laborers along the string of suitcase farms to plant, fertilize, and harvest the wheat. The progressively later ripening of the grain toward the north allows these farmers to maintain crops on all their farms with the same crew and the same machinery. Except for visits by migratory crews, the suitcase farms are uninhabited.

Such highly mechanized, absentee-owned, large-scale operations, or **agribusinesses,** are rapidly replacing the traditional American family farm, an important part of our rural heritage. Geographer Ingolf Vogeler documented the decline of family farms in the American countryside and argued that United States governmental policies have consistently favored agribusiness interests, hastening the decline. We have now reached the point where the American family farm, though perpetuated as a myth and icon, is no longer of much consequence, particularly in the grain lands.

Commercial Dairying

In many ways, the specialized production of dairy goods closely resembles commercial livestock fattening (see box, *Thomas Hardy on the Geography of Dairying*). In the large dairy belts of the northern United States, from New England to the upper Midwest, western and northern Europe, southeastern Australia, and northern New Zealand, the keeping of dairy cows depends on the large-scale use of pastures. In colder areas, some acreage must be devoted to winter feed crops, especially hay. Dairy products vary from region to region, depending in part on how close the farmers are to their markets. Dairy belts near large urban centers usually produce fluid milk, which is more perishable, while

Thomas Hardy on the Geography of Dairying

Farming culture regions are readily observable, and you need not be a professional geographer to observe them. Some of the finest "geography" has been written by regional novelists. Among these writers, none surpasses Thomas Hardy, who penned beautiful descriptions of the countryside of his native southern England. Here is his word picture of a late nineteenth-century commercial dairy region, the Vale of Frome:

> *She found herself on a summit commanding the . . . Valley of the Great Dairies, the valley in which milk and butter grew to rankness. . . . It was intrinsically different from the Vale of Little Dairies, Blackmoor Vale, which . . . she had exclusively known till now. The world was drawn to a larger pattern here. The enclosures numbered fifty acres instead of ten, the farmsteads were more extended, the groups of cattle formed tribes hereabout; there only families. These myriads of cows stretching under her eyes from the far east to the far west outnumbered any she had ever seen at one glance before. The green lea was speckled as thickly with them as a canvas by Van Alsloot or Sallaert with burghers. . . .*
>
> *Suddenly there arose from all parts of the lowland a prolonged and repeated call—Waow waow waow. It was . . . the ordinary announcement of milking-time—half-past four o-clock, when the dairymen set about getting in the cows. The red and white herd nearest at hand, which had been phlegmatically waiting for the call, now trooped towards the steading in the background, their great bags of milk swinging under them as they walked. . . .*
>
> *Long thatched sheds stretched round the enclosure, . . . their eaves supported by wooden posts rubbed to a glossy smoothness by the flanks of infinite cows and calves of bygone years. . . . Between the posts were ranged the milchers. . . . The dairy-maids and men had flocked down from their cottages and out of the dairyhouse with the arrival of the cows from the meads. . . . Each girl sat down on her three-legged stool, her face sideways, her right cheek resting against the cow. . . .*

From Hardy, Thomas. *Tess of the d'Urbervilles.* New York: Harper & Brothers, 1891.

those farther away specialize in butter, cheese, or processed milk. New Zealanders, remote from world markets, produce much butter, which can more easily be exported than milk.

As with livestock fattening, in recent decades a rapidly increasing number of dairy farmers have adopted the feedlot system and now raise their cattle on feed purchased from other sources. Feedlots are especially common in the southern United States. Often situated on the suburban fringes of large cities in order to have quick access to market, the dairy feedlots are essentially factory farms. Farmers buy feed and livestock replacements, instead of breeding and raising them on the farm. In these large-scale automated operations, the number of cows is far greater than on family-operated dairy farms. Like industrial factory owners, feedlot dairy owners rely on hired laborers to help maintain their herds. While less pleasing to the eye and nose than traditional dairy farms, the feedlots are highly profitable establishments, representing still another stage in the rise of agribusiness and the decline of the American family farm.

Livestock Ranching

Superficially, **ranching** might seem similar to nomadic herding, but in reality it is a fundamentally different livestock-raising system. Although both the nomadic herders and the livestock ranchers specialize in animal husbandry to the exclusion of crop raising, and even though both live in arid or semiarid regions, livestock ranchers have fixed places of residence and operate as individuals rather than within a tribal organization. In addition, ranchers raise livestock for market on a large scale, not for their own subsistence, and they are typically of European ancestry rather than being an indigenous people.

Livestock ranchers, faced with the advance of farmers, have usually fallen back into areas climatically too harsh for crop production. There they raise only two kinds of animals in large numbers: cattle and sheep.

Ranchers in the United States and Canada, tropical and subtropical Latin America, and the warmer parts of Australia specialize in cattle raising. Mid-latitude ranchers in the Southern Hemisphere specialize in sheep, to the extent that Australia, New Zealand, South Africa, and Argentina produce 70 percent of the world's export wool. Sheep outnumber people 8 to 1 in Australia, and 16 to 1 in New Zealand.

Nonagricultural Areas

Some lands do not support any form of agriculture. These typically lie in areas of extreme climate, in particular deserts and subarctic forests, as in much of Canada and Siberia. Often such areas are inhabited by **hunting and gathering** groups of native peoples, such as the Inuit and Australian aborigine, who gain a livelihood by hunting game, fishing where possible, and gathering edible and medicinal wild plants. Once, before agriculture began, all humans lived as hunters and gatherers, the ancestral occupation of our species. Today, fewer than 1 percent of all humans are so employed, preserving the ancient ways. Even fewer depend entirely on such a food-producing system, given the various inroads of the modern world. In most hunting and gathering societies, a division of labor by gender occurs. Males perform most of the hunting and fishing, while females carry out the equally important task of gathering harvests from wild plants. Hunters and gatherers can either be specialized, depending on only a few sources for their food, or, much more commonly, unspecialized and reliant on a great variety of animals and plants.

Agricultural Diffusion

The various agricultural regions discussed above result from cultural diffusion. Agriculture and its many components are inventions; they arose as innovations in certain source areas and diffused to other parts of the world.

The Origin and Diffusion of Plant Domestication

The beginnings of agriculture apparently occurred with plant rather than animal domestication. A **domesticated plant** is one deliberately planted, protected, and cared for by humans. Genetically distinct from their wild ancestors because of deliberate improvement through selective breeding by agriculturists, domesticated plants tend to be bigger than wild species, bearing larger, more abundant fruit or grain. For example, the original wild Indian maize grew on a cob only 0.75 inch (2 centimeters) long—that is, one-tenth to one-twentieth the size of the cobs of domesticated maize.

Plant domestication and improvement constituted a process, not an event. It began as the gradual culmination of hundreds, or even thousands, of years of close association between humans and the natural vegetation. The first step in domestication was the perception that a certain plant had usefulness for people, a usefulness leading initially to protection of the wild plant and eventually to deliberate planting.

Cultural geographer Carl Johannessen suggests that the domestication process can still be observed today. He believes that by studying current techniques used by native subsistence farmers in places such as Central America, we can gain insight into the methods of the first farmers of prehistoric antiquity. Johannessen points out that two steps are normally required to develop and improve plant varieties: (1) selection of seeds or shoots only from superior plants; and (2) genetic isolation from other, inferior plants to prevent cross-pollination. Johannessen's study of the present-day cultivation of the pejibaye palm tree in Costa Rica revealed that native cultivators actively engage in seed selection. All choose the seed of fresh fruit from superior trees, those which bear particularly desirable fruit, as determined by size, flavor, texture, and color. Such trees are often given personal names, an indication of the value placed on them. Superior seed stocks are built up gradually over the years, with the result that elderly farmers generally have the best selections. Seeds are shared freely within family and clan groups, allowing speedy diffusion of desirable traits.

Johannessen also reported that some American Indian groups clearly knew of the need for genetic isolation to reduce contamination from cross-pollination in maize plants. In Panama, for example, one Indian tribe of shifting cultivators raised 14 varieties of maize, each in a field separated from all the others by intervening forest.

When, where, and how did these processes of plant domestication develop? Cultural geographers have been among those who have done research on this problem. Early leaders were the German scholar Eduard Hahn and the famous American cultural geographer Carl Sauer (see biographical sketch). Most experts now believe that the process of domestication occurred at many different times and locations, involving repeated independent invention.

Sauer believed domestication probably did not develop in response to hunger. He maintained that necessity was not the mother of agricultural invention, because starving people must spend every waking hour searching for food and have no time to devote to the centuries of leisurely experimentation required to domesticate plants. Instead, it was accomplished by peoples who had enough food to remain settled in one place and devote considerable time to plant care. The first farmers were probably sedentary folk, rather than migratory hunters and gatherers. He reasoned that domestication did not occur in grasslands or large river floodplains. In such areas, primitive cultures would have had difficulty coping with the thick sod and periodic floodwaters. Sauer also believed the hearth areas of domestication must have been in regions where many different kinds of wild plants grew, providing abundant vegetative raw material for experimentation and crossbreeding. Such areas typically appear in hilly districts, where climates change with differing sun exposure and altitude.

Many or most geographers now believe that agriculture arose in at least three such regions of biodiversity (Figure 3.12). Perhaps the oldest among these primary centers is the *Fertile Crescent* in the Middle East, which gave us the great bread grains—wheat, barley, rye, and oats—as well as grapes, apples, olives, and many others. The oldest archaeological evidence of crop domestication comes from that region, suggesting an origin about 10,000 years ago. When diffusion from the Fertile Crescent brought agriculture to Central Africa, a secondary center of domestication developed through stimulus diffusion, adding crops such as sorghum, peanuts, yams, coffee, and okra.

The second great center of agricultural innovation developed in *Southeast Asia*, possibly including some lands now submerged by shallow seas. From it came rice, citrus, taro, bananas, and sugarcane, among other crops. There, too, stimulus diffusion apparently yielded a secondary center, in northeastern China, where millet was domesticated.

Carl O. Sauer
1889–1975

Sauer, a native of the Missouri Ozarks and a graduate of the University of Chicago, was widely regarded as the most prominent American cultural geographer. For over 50 years, he was associated with the University of California at Berkeley. His works were so diverse as to defy simple classification, but important themes in much of his research were (1) humans as modifiers of the Earth, (2) the cultural landscape, and (3) cultural origins and diffusion. As a geographer his work took him on many field trips. He studied by looking at the land and talking to the residents. In his classic book, *Agricultural Origins and Dispersals,* he presented some new and stimulating ideas concerning the domestication of plants and animals, some of which are presented in this chapter. His concern for the environment began when he was a student, and throughout his career he argued for "humane" use of the Earth. Professor Sauer twice served the Association of American Geographers as president and in 1974 received an award from that organization for meritorious contributions to the discipline of geography. (For more information on Sauer, see Kenzer, Martin S. (ed.). *Carl O. Sauer: A Tribute.* Corvallis: Oregon State University Press and the Association of Pacific Coast Geographers, 1987; and Leighly, John. "Ecology as Metaphor: Carl Sauer and Human Ecology." *Professional Geographer,* 39 (1987): 405–412.)

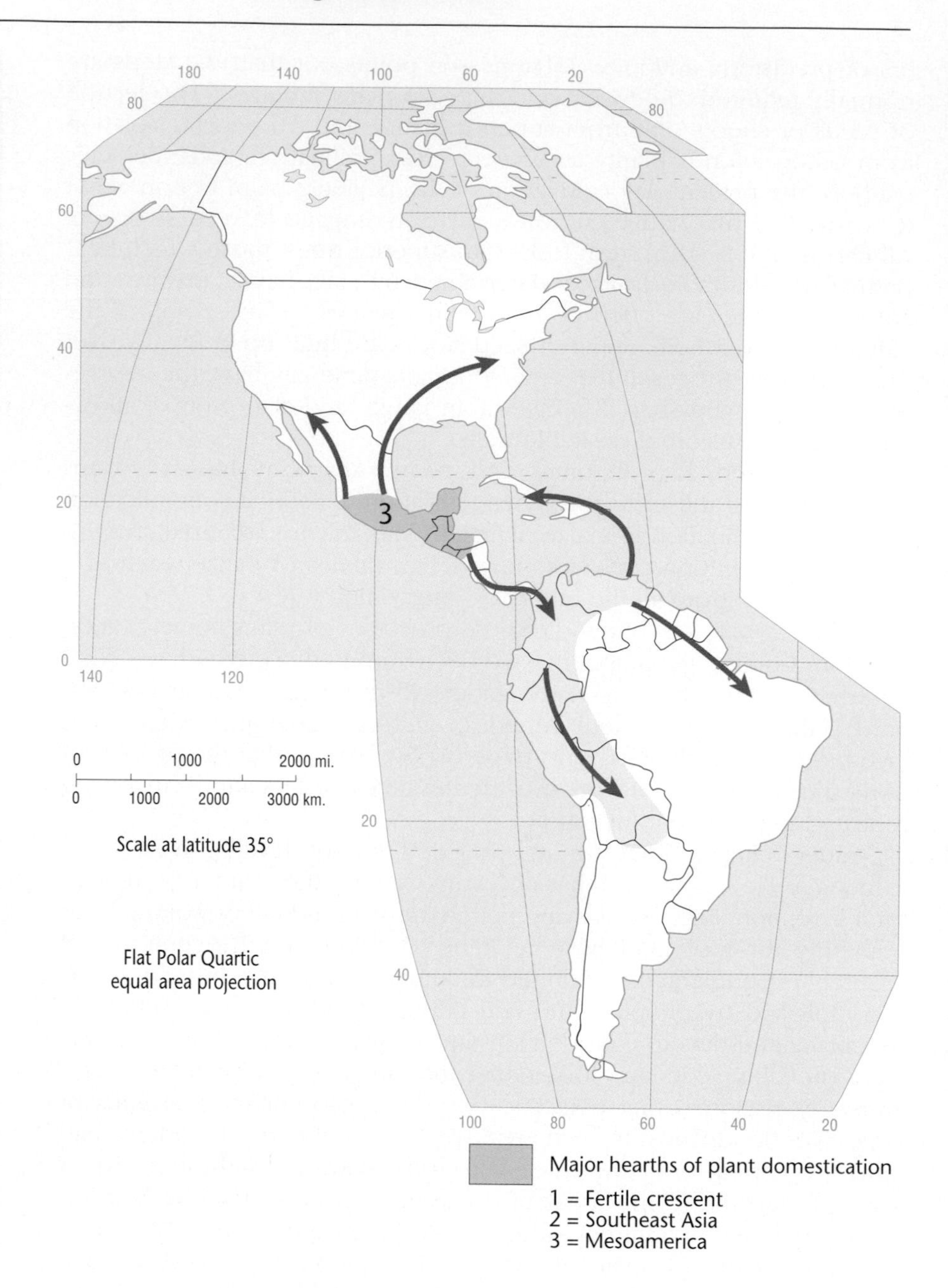

Figure 3.12
The origin and diffusion of agriculture. Because of the antiquity of this cultural diffusion and the paucity of evidence, the map must be regarded as speculative.

Much later, about 5000 years ago, American Indians in *Mesoamerica* achieved the third great independent invention of agriculture, from which came crops such as maize, tomatoes, chile peppers, and squash. Carl Sauer was among the first scholars to argue that American Indians had independently invented agriculture, rather than receiving stimulus diffusion from the Eastern Hemisphere. As the Mesoamerican crop complex spread southward, it, too, produced a secondary center of stimulus diffusion, in northwestern South America, from which came the white potato and manioc.

Overall, the American Indians domesticated an array of crops far superior in nutritional value to those of the two Eastern Hemisphere centers combined. Try excluding all American Indian domesticates from your diet for just a single day. You will have to do without not only those foods listed above, but also pinto beans, pineapples, sunflower

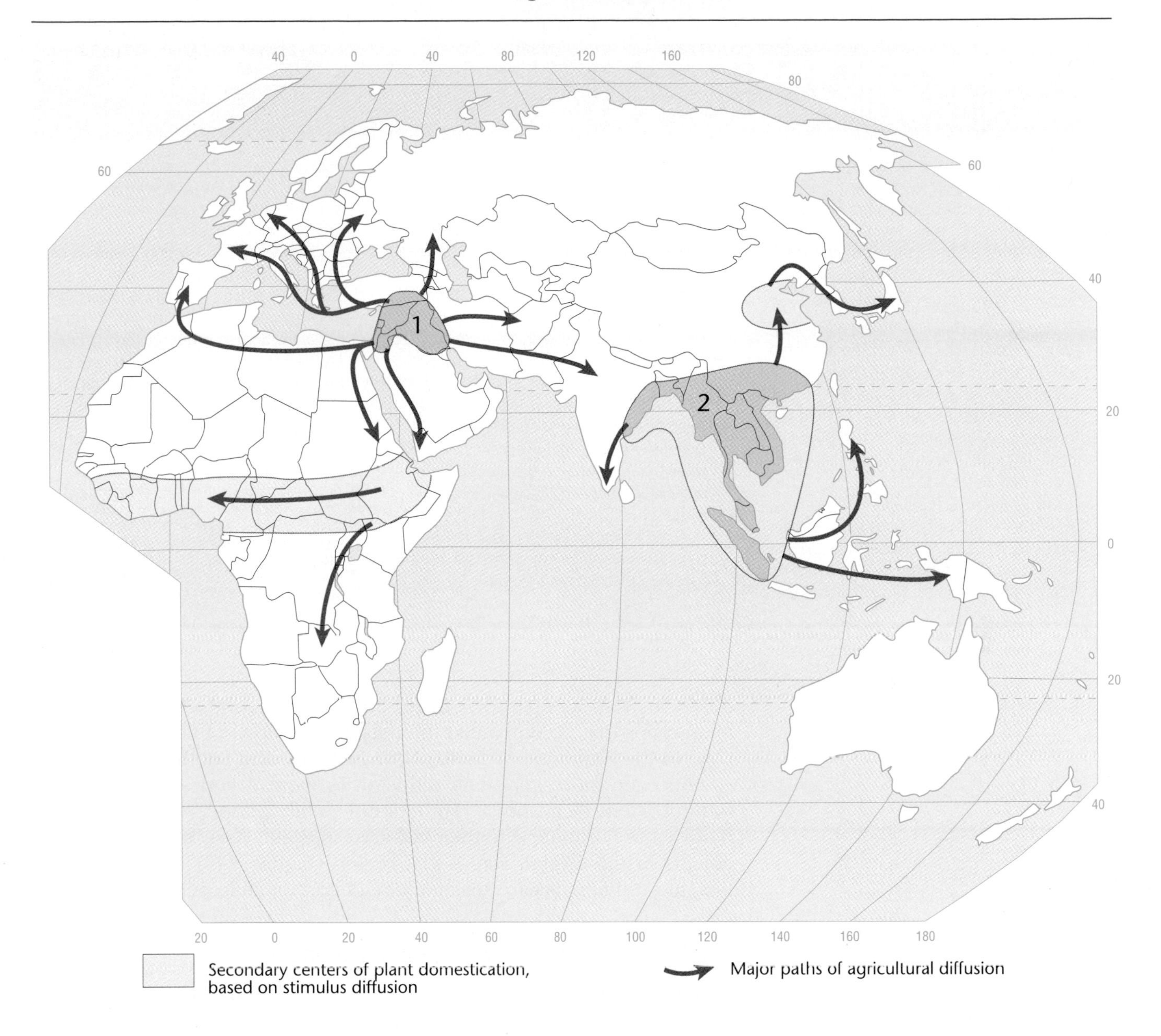

seeds, vanilla, pumpkins, tobacco, Coca Cola (which, as its name suggests, contains a derivative of the coca plant), papayas, and various other foods.

The widespread association of female deities with agriculture suggests that women first worked the land. Recall the almost universal division of labor in hunting-gathering-fishing societies. Since women had day-to-day contact with wild plants and stayed closer to home, they probably initiated plant domestication.

The diffusion of domesticated plants did not end in antiquity (see box, *Cultural Diffusion: The Potato in Germany*). Only within the past century did crop farming reach its present territorial extent, completing the diffusion begun many millennia ago. The introduction of the lemon, orange, grape, and the date palm by Spanish missionaries in eighteenth-century California provides a recent example of relocation

Cultural Diffusion: The Potato In Germany

How does a domestic plant spread into new areas and gain wider acceptance? The progress is often slow and not without resistance, as the following eyewitness account from the province of Pomerania, Kingdom of Prussia, shows:

In 1743, through the goodness of King Frederick the Great, the people of Kolberg district received a present completely unknown to us. A large freight wagon full of potatoes arrived at the market square, and, by a beating of drums, the announcement was made that all farmers and gardeners were to assemble before the town hall. The town councillors then showed the new fruit to the assembled crowd. Detailed instructions were read aloud concerning the planting, cultivation, and cooking of the potato. However, few of the people paid attention to the oral instructions, choosing instead to take the highly-praised tubers in their hands, smelling, licking, and tasting them. Shaking their heads, they passed them around, eventually throwing them to the dogs, who also sniffed and rejected them. "These things,'" they said, "have no smell or taste. What good are they to us?" Hardly anyone understood the instructions for planting. Quite general was the belief that potatoes would grow into trees from which you could gather like fruit in due time. Those who did not throw the potatoes on the rubbish heap, but instead planted them, did so incorrectly.

The town councillors learned that some sceptics had not entrusted their tuberous treasures to the earth. For that reason they instituted a strict potato inspection during the summer months and levied a small monetary fine on those found to be obstinate.

The next year the king renewed his benevolent gift, but this time the authorities sent along a man familiar with raising potatoes, and he helped the people plant and cultivate. In this manner, the new product first came to my district, and ever since has spread rapidly. Now a general famine can never again devastate the province.

Translated and condensed from *Ein Mann: Des Seefahrers und aufrechten Bürgers Joachim Nettelbeck wundersame Lebensgeschichte von ihm selbsterzählt.* Ebenhausen near München: Wilhelm Langewiesche-Brandt, 1910, pp. 8–10.

diffusion. This was part of a larger diffusion—the introduction of European crops that accompanied the mass emigrations of farmers from Europe to the Americas, Australia, New Zealand, and South Africa.

An even more important diffusion brought American Indian crops to the Eastern Hemisphere. For example, chile peppers and maize, carried by the Portuguese to their colonies in South Asia, became basic elements in the diet all across that region (Figure 3.13). One could not imagine southern Asian cuisine today devoid of chile pepper seasoning.

The Origin and Diffusion of Animal Domestication

A **domesticated animal** is one dependent on people for food and shelter, differing also from wild species in physical appearance and behavior, a result of controlled breeding and daily contact with humans. Animal domestication apparently occurred later in prehistory than did the first planting of crops, with the probable exception of the dog, whose companionship with people is seemingly much more ancient. Typically, people value domesticated animals and take care of them for some utilitarian purpose. Yet the original motive for domestication may not have been economic. People perhaps first domesticated cattle, as well as some kinds of birds, for religious reasons. Certain other domesticated animals, such as the pig and dog, probably attached themselves voluntarily to human settlements to feast on garbage. At first, perhaps humans merely tolerated these animals, later adopting them as pets.

Farmers of the ancient crop hearth in southern Asia apparently did not excel as domesticators of animals. The taming of certain kinds of poultry may be attributed to them, but probably little else. Similarly, the American Indian, who made superior contributions to plant domestication, remained rather unsuccessful in taming animals, perhaps in part because suitable wild animals were less numerous. The llama, alpaca, guinea pig, and turkey were among the few American domesticates.

Figure 3.13
Chile peppers and maize in a lowland Nepalese village, South Asia. A Tharu tribal woman prepares a condiment made of chile peppers from her garden. Such peppers originally came from the American Indian and reached her village long ago by cultural diffusion. In the same village, maize—another Mesoamerican domesticate—is also a major crop. To learn how and when this agricultural diffusion occurred, see the article by Andrews cited at the end of the chapter.

Instead, the early farmers of the Middle East in the Fertile Crescent deserve credit for the first great animal domestications, most notably herd animals. The wild ancestors of major herd animals, such as cattle, pigs, sheep, and goats, lived primarily in a belt running from Syria and southeastern Turkey eastward across Iraq and Iran to central Asia. Most animal domestication seems to have taken place in that general region or in adjacent areas. There in the Middle East, farmers first combined domesticated plants and animals into an integrated system, the antecedent of the peasant grain, root, and livestock farming described earlier. These people began using cattle to pull the plow, a revolutionary invention that greatly increased the acreage under cultivation. In turn, the farmers out of necessity began setting aside a portion of the harvest as livestock feed.

As the grain-herd livestock farming system continued to expand, particularly in the Fertile Crescent area, tillers entered marginal lands where crop cultivation proved difficult or impossible. Population pressures forced people into these districts. The herd animals became more important to the occupants of these inferior lands, and they abandoned crop farming. They began wandering with their herds so as not to exhaust local forage. In this manner, nomadic herding probably developed on the margins of the Fertile Crescent.

Modern Innovations in Agriculture

Innovation diffusion in agriculture did not end with the original spread of farming and herding. New ideas arose often during the succeeding millennia and spread through agricultural space as innovation waves. The twentieth century, in particular, witnessed many such farming innovations and diffusions. The spread of hybrid maize through the United States in the present century provides a good example of expansion diffusion (Figure 3.14). Such innovations often gain initial acceptance by wealthier, large-scale farmers, providing a good example of hierarchical diffusion.

One of the major innovation diffusions in twentieth-century American agriculture involved the spread of pump irrigation through many parts of the western Great Plains. A detailed study of this irrigation innovation was made in the Colorado northern High Plains by geographer Leonard Bowden. Farmers there had to decide much more than whether to irrigate, because irrigation brought with it different crops, different markets, and different farming techniques. The Colorado High Plains farmers, in effect, decided whether they wanted an entirely different system of agriculture from the one they had traditionally practiced. The first irrigation well began operation by 1935, but initial diffusion was retarded in part by a shortage of investment capital in the Great Depression years. Beginning in 1948, irrigation spread quite rapidly.

In studying this spread, Bowden observed contagious diffusion from the core area of initial acceptance and time-distance decay. The closer a potential irrigation site lay to an existing irrigated farm, the more likely its owner was to accept the innovation, an example of the neighborhood effect. Some barriers to the diffusion of irrigation weakened through time. Banks and other moneylending institutions proved initially reluctant to lend money to farmers for investment in irrigation. However, once the technique proved to be economically successful, loans were easier to obtain and interest rates fell.

Figure 3.14
The diffusion of hybrid maize in the United States. The spread emanated from a core area of initial acceptance in Iowa and Illinois through expansion diffusion, reaching most of the eastern United States in little over a decade. Can you explain the barriers this innovation encountered in New England, the South, and the Great Plains? (After Griliches, Zvi. "Hybrid Corn and the Economics of Innovation." *Science,* 132 [July 26, 1960].)

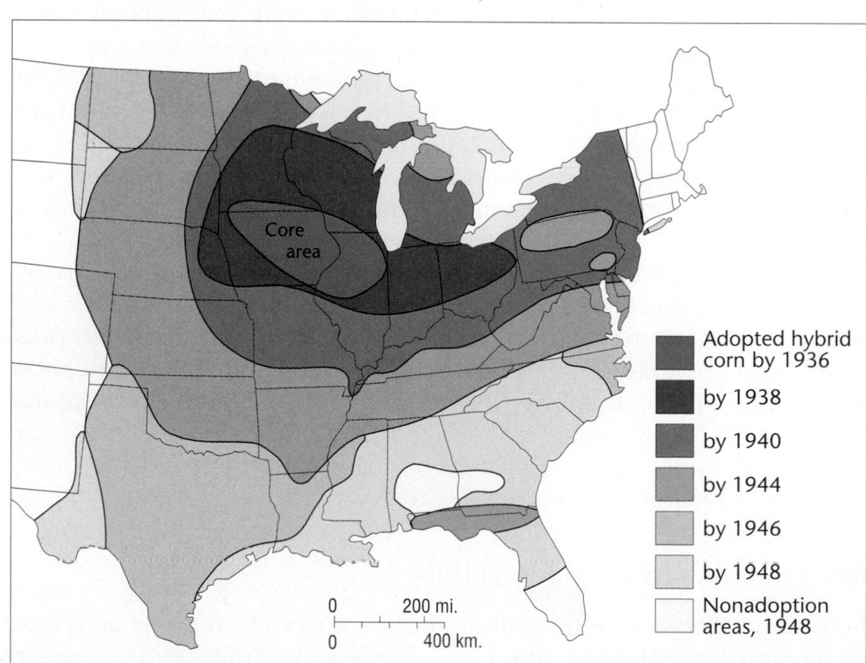

Not all innovations spread wavelike across the land, in the manner of pump irrigation and hybrid maize. More typical is a much less orderly pattern. The previously mentioned green revolution in Asia provides an example. In some countries, most notably parts of India, acceptance of the hybrid seed, chemical fertilizers, and pesticides associated with the green revolution spread widely in a relatively short time span, becoming almost the normal type of farming. By contrast, countries such as Myanmar resisted the revolution, favoring traditional methods. A splotchy pattern of acceptance still characterizes the paddy rice areas today. In the lamentable jargon of Hägerstrandian diffusion studies, nonaccepters are called "laggards" and the inevitability of innovations is assumed, but in reality the green revolution is plagued by problems.

Canadian geographer Aninda Chakravarti made a detailed study of the cultural diffusion of the green revolution in India. The new hybrid rice and wheat seeds first appeared there in 1966. Though requiring chemical fertilizers and protection by pesticides, the new hybrids allowed India's 1970 grain production to double in output from its 1950 level. However, poorer farmers—the great majority of agriculturists—could not afford the capital expenditures for fertilizer and pesticides, and the gap between rich and poor farmers widened. Many of the poor became displaced from the land and flocked to the overcrowded cities of India, greatly aggravating urban problems. To make matters worse, the use of chemicals and poisons on the land heightened environmental damage.

The adoption of hybrid seeds brought yet another problem—the loss of plant diversity or genetic variety. Before hybrid seeds came into widespread use, each farm developed its own distinctive seed types, through the practice of setting aside seeds from the better plants annually at harvesttime for the next season's sowing. Enormous genetic diversity vanished almost instantly when farmers began purchasing hybrids rather than saving seed from the last harvest. "Gene banks" have belatedly been set up to preserve what remains of domesticated plant variety, not just in the areas affected by the green revolution but in the American Corn Belt and many other agricultural regions where hybrids are now dominant. In sum, the green revolution proved at best to be a mixed blessing. Perhaps the "laggards" were correct; in the long run, a Western innovation in plant genetics may have caused more harm than good in India and elsewhere.

Not all diffusion related to agriculture has been intentional. In fact, accidental diffusion accomplished by humans probably occurs more commonly than the purposeful type. Often the results prove quite undesirable. An example is the diffusion of the tropical American "fire ant," so named because of its very painful sting (Figure 3.15). A shipload of plantation-grown bananas from tropical America accidentally brought the fire ant to Mobile, Alabama, in 1949, and a continuing relocation diffusion has since brought the fire ant across most of the American South. These vicious ants now endanger livestock and poultry raising, because swarms of them can attack and kill young animals.

Agricultural Ecology

Agricultural types or systems are **adaptive strategies**, and as a result the theme of cultural ecology is very important to a geographer's study of farming and herding. Because farmers and herders work and live on the land, a very close relationship exists between agriculture and the

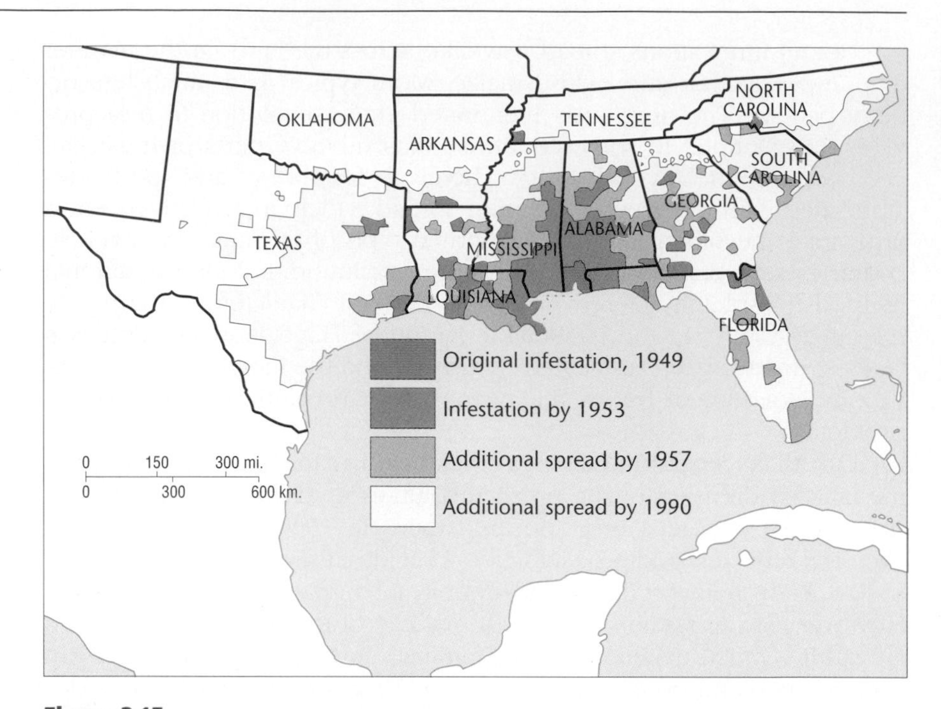

Figure 3.15
Relocation diffusion of the imported fire ant in the American South. Accidentally introduced from tropical Latin America with a boatload of bananas in Mobile, Alabama, the fire ant has since resisted efforts to eradicate it and has continued to spread. How might this relocation diffusion have proceeded, and what barriers would the fire ant encounter? How did outliers develop? Why is this *cultural* diffusion? (Sources: Lofgren, Clifford S., and Robert K. Vander Meer [eds.]. *Fire Ants and Leaf-Cutting Ants.* Boulder, CO: Westview Press, 1986, pp. 38, 39, 44; US Dept. of Agriculture data.)

physical environment. In many ways, the map of agricultural regions reflects adaptation to environmental influences. At the same time, thousands of years of agricultural use of the land have led to massive alterations in our natural environment. This interplay between humankind and the land provides the substance of agricultural ecology.

Cultural Adaptation

Weather and climate exert perhaps the greatest influence on the different forms of agriculture. For example, the cultivation of many crops sensitive to frost becomes prohibitively expensive outside tropical and subtropical areas. This helps explain why plantation agriculture has thrived. Plantation farmers in warm climates can produce cash crops desired by peoples in the middle latitudes, where such crops cannot be grown. Much market gardening in the southern and southwestern United States depends on a similar climatic advantage to produce citrus fruits, winter vegetables, sugarcane, and other crops that will not grow in areas closer to the large urban markets of the Northeast.

In turn, the need for abundant irrigation water to flood the fields confines paddy rice farming to its present limits within Asia. Soils also play an influential role in agricultural decisions. Shifting cultivation reflects in part an adaptation to poor tropical soils, which rapidly lose their fertility when farmed. Groups practicing peasant grain, root, and livestock agriculture often owe their superior farming status to the fertility of local volcanic soils, which are not so quickly exhausted.

Terrain also influences agriculture. As a general rule, farmers tend to practice crop farming in areas of level terrain, leaving the adjacent hills and mountains forested. In the United States, commercial wheat, rice, and corn farming is concentrated in the flattest areas, partly because such farmers depend on heavy machines, and, in the case of rice, on large-scale irrigation (Figure 3.16).

Often environmental influence remains more subtle. For example, in paddy areas near the margins of the Asian wet-rice region, where unreliability of rainfall causes harvests to vary greatly from one year to the next, farmers developed quite complex cultivation strategies to avert periodic famine, including the use of many varieties of rice. Such farmers, like those in parts of Thailand, almost universally rejected the green revolution. The simplistic advice given to them by agricultural experts working for the Thai government and speaking for the green revolution was not appropriate for their marginal lands. In their folk wisdom, the local farmers knew that the traditional diversified adaptive strategy was superior.

A similarly subtle environmental influence can be observed in West Africa, where peasant grain, root, and livestock farmers raise a multiplicity of crops in the more humid lands near the coast. These crops fall away one by one toward the drier interior of the continent, where the careful observer finds instead numerous drought-resistant varieties of only a few basic crops.

Many geographers now believe that we must cease imposing Western technological innovations on farmers in the underdeveloped world. "The methods of traditional agriculture and resource management merit serious consideration," argues geographer Gene Wilken, and we should stop assuming that our scientifically based innovations are necessarily superior to the old ways. For too long, we have behaved arrogantly toward such farmers, and caused irretrievable loss of traditional farming knowledge.

Agriculturists as Modifiers of the Environment

After the domestication of plants and animals, humankind began to alter the environment in a major way, especially natural vegetation (Figure 3.17). To the preagricultural hunter and gatherer, the forest harbored valuable wild plants and animals. To the agriculturist, however, the woodland became less valuable as a source of food and had to be cleared to make fields. Over the millennia, as dependence on agriculture grew and as population increased, humans made ever larger demands on the forests. Farmers expanded small patches of cleared land until these areas merged with other clearings. They used ax and fire in their assault on the woodlands, with devastating effect.

In many parts of China, India, and the Mediterranean lands, forests virtually vanished. In trans-Alpine Europe, the United States, and some other areas, they were greatly reduced. Figure 3.18 illustrates the clearing of the forests in central Europe by farmers over a thousand-year period. Aside from the loss of woodland, burning of dead vegetation pollutes the air. Shifting cultivators in Africa's rain forest produce acid rain levels (see Chapter 12) comparable to those of industrial areas through their slash-and-burn practices.

Grasslands suffered similar modifications. Prairies gave way to the plow or experienced severe damage through overgrazing. Farmers occasionally plow up grasslands too dry for sustainable crop production, and herders frequently allow their herds to overgraze semiarid pastures. The result could be **desertification,** a process perhaps best exemplified by the Sahel, a region just south of the Sahara Desert in Africa. At

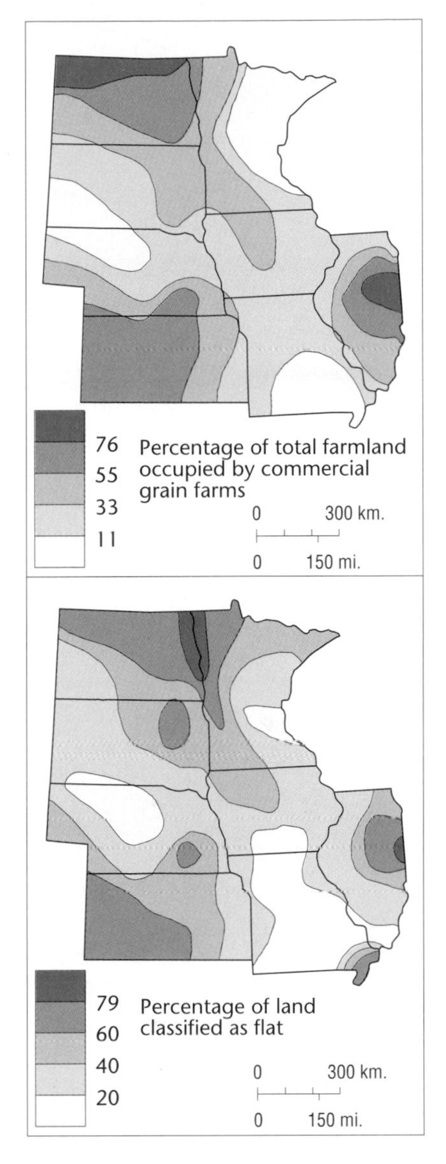

Figure 3.16
The influence of terrain on agriculture. The spatial relationship of commercial grain farming and flat terrain appears in the American Midwest, about 1960. "Flat" land is defined as any with a 3° slope or less. Commercial grain farming is completely mechanized, and flat land permits more efficient machine operation. The result is this striking correlation between a type of agriculture and a type of terrain. What other factors might attract mechanized grain farming to level land? (After Hidore, John J. "Relationship Between Cash Grain Farming and Landforms." *Economic Geography,* 39 [1963]: 86, 87.)

Figure 3.17
Agriculturalists as modifiers of the environment. Millennia of grazing by sheep and goats helped turn parts of the Greek island of Patmos into a rocky wasteland. Four thousand years ago this slope was forested with a scattering of live oaks and covered with a mantle of soil. Cacti and low shrubs now grow in the few remaining patches of thin soil. In this manner, traditional farmers practicing Mediterranean agriculture largely destroyed the land.

some point in the Sahel, the destruction of vegetation could pass a critical threshold, beyond which the plant life cannot regenerate, leading to denudation. This, in turn, would have the effect of reducing rainfall and increasing temperatures. Soon lands that had been covered with pastures and fields could become permanently joined to the dunes of the adjacent Sahara. Large areas of Africa besides the Sahel may now face the risk of desertification. While that continent confronts the great-

Figure 3.18
The agricultural impact on the forest cover of central Europe from AD 900 to 1900. Extensive clearing of the forests, mostly before 1350, was tied largely to expansion of farmland. The forests survived best in hilly and mountainous areas, which proved less attractive to farmers. The distribution of forests for 1900 closely resembles that of hills and mountain ranges. (Redrawn from Darby, H. C. "The Clearing of the Woodland in Europe," in William L. Thomas [ed.], *Man's Role in Changing the Face of the Earth.* Chicago: University of Chicago Press, 1956, pp. 202–203.)

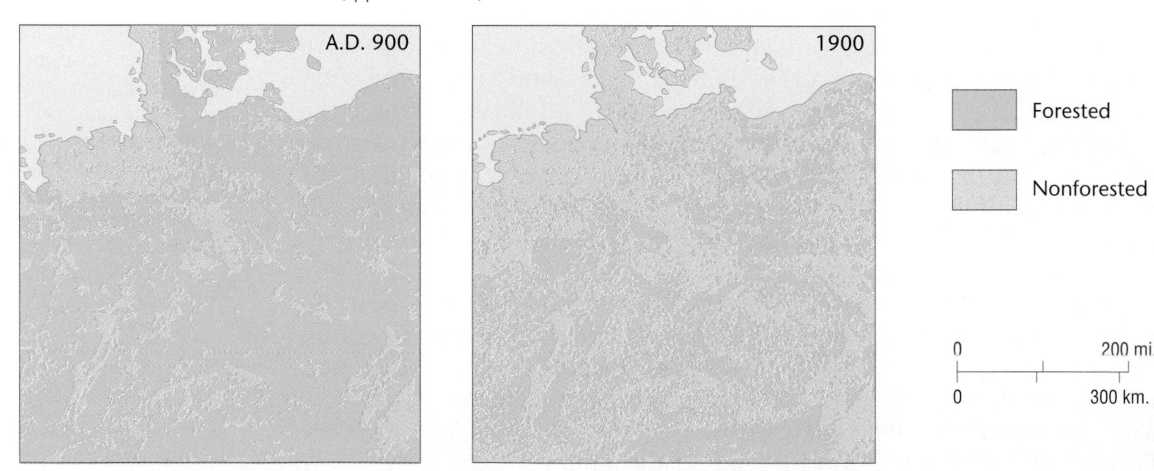

est such problems, Asia, Australia, the Americas, and even Europe may also have endangered districts (see box, *The Dust Bowl*). Desertification could significantly reduce the land area devoted to food production in the decades ahead, with possible dire demographic consequences. Overpopulation leads to overuse of the land, which, in turn, may produce desertification, reduction of food supplies, and mass famine.

Certain other scholars, including David Thomas, challenge the notion that the world's deserts are on the march. Satellite imagery suggests to them that the semiarid lands possess more resiliency than once thought. Since 1960, they claim, the Sahara/Sahel boundary has not migrated steadily south, but instead fluctuated as it always has, responding to wetter and drier years. These natural fluctuations need to be distinguished from actual soil degradation, and if we do so, says Thomas, the actual areal extent of desertification is reduced to a third of the more pessimistic claims.

Those geographers and others who accept the alarmist notions concerning desertification suggest some drastic solutions. In North America, for example, geographer Deborah Epstein Popper and her husband, Frank, proposed that huge areas of the Great Plains be withdrawn from farming and ranching and be replaced by a "buffalo commons," a vast expanse of restored natural grassland grazed by native animals.

You might think that irrigation provides a solution to desertification. However, such artificial watering can have both intentional and unintentional impacts on the land. Obviously, the intended effect is to circumvent deficiencies in precipitation by importing water from another area, using dams and canals, or from another era, using deep wells and pumps to exploit groundwater accumulated over decades and centuries.

Unfortunately, the beneficial effect of irrigation is often offset by unintentional environmental destruction. Ditch and canal irrigation can cause the local subsurface water table to rise, waterlogging the soil, and the mineral content of the water frequently salinizes the ground. In Pakistan, for example, the water table rose 10 to 30 feet (3 to 10 meters), and 800 to 2000 pounds of salt were added per acre of land (900 to 2200 kilograms per hectare), as a result of dam-and-ditch irrigation. Conversely, the water table has been drastically lowered by well and pump irrigation in parts of the American Great Plains, particularly Texas, causing ancient springs to go dry and promising an early end to intensive agriculture there. Irrigation, in other words, had the effect of *spreading* rather than diminishing desertification.

The Dust Bowl

The "Dust Bowl" of the 1930s devastated the American Great Plains, in large part because farmers had plowed up the grasses that originally protected the soil from wind erosion. A nonsustainable adaptive strategy had come to grief. Woody Guthrie, the great folk balladeer, captured the disaster in his song "The Great Dust Storm":

The storm took place at sundown
It lasted through the night.
When we looked out next morning
We saw a terrible sight.
We saw outside our window
Where wheatfields they had grown,
Was now a rippling ocean
Of dust the wind had blown.
It covered up our fences,
It covered up our barns,
It covered up our tractors
In this wild and dusty storm.
We loaded our jalopies
And piled our families in,
We rattled down the high-way
To never come back again

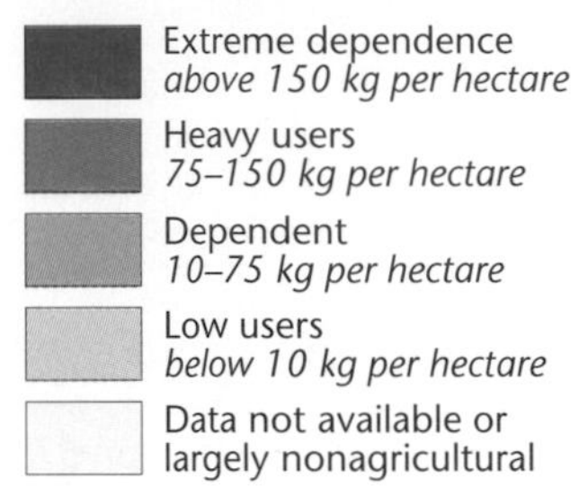

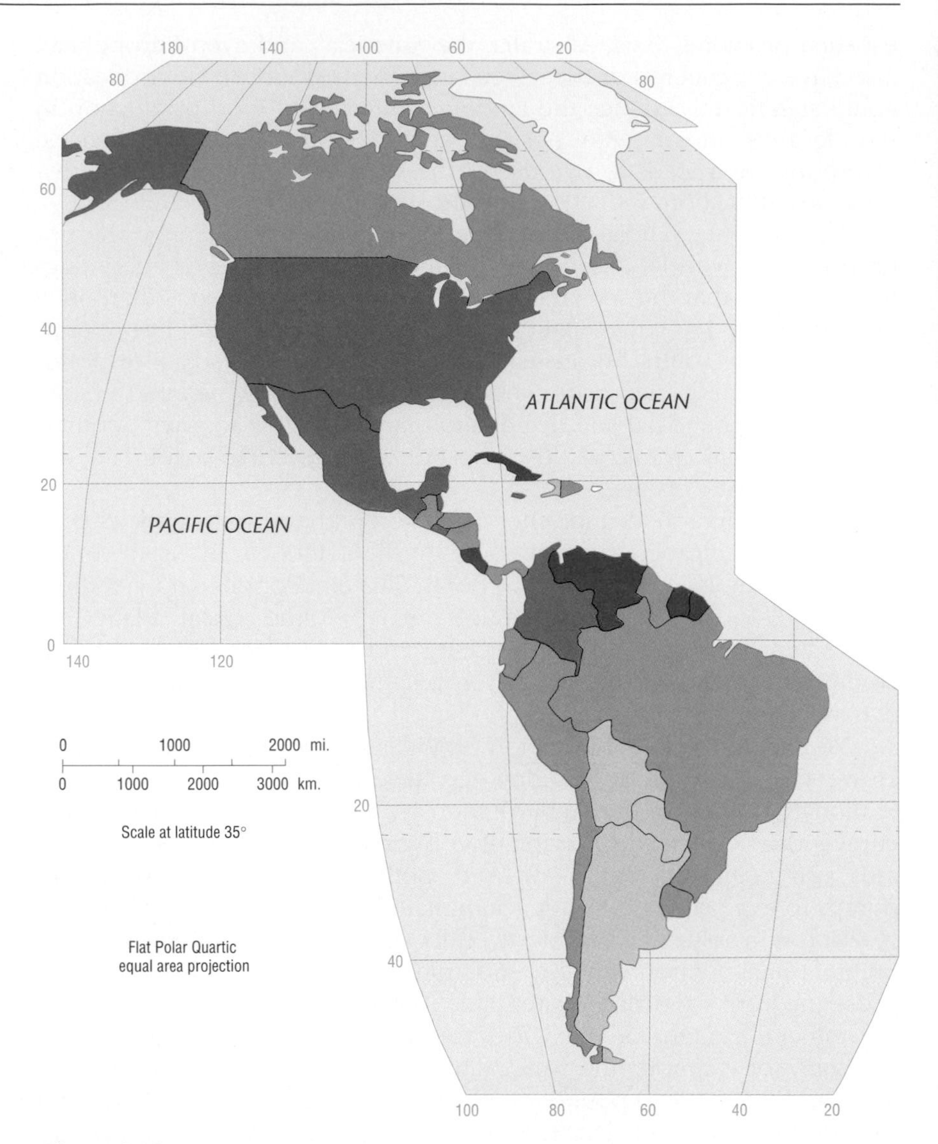

Figure 3.19
Chemical dependence in agriculture, as exemplified by chemical fertilizers. The use of chemical fertilizers began in Germany in the nineteenth century and has diffused widely, especially in the more developed and prosperous countries. It bears potentially serious consequences in the long run. (Based on Seager, Joni. *The State of the Earth Atlas.* New York: Simon & Schuster, 1990, pp. 32–33, with modifications.)

Another area where desertification resulted from irrigation lies on the borderland between Kazakstan and Uzbekistan in central Asia. The once-huge Aral Sea became so diminished by the diversion of irrigation water from the rivers flowing into it that large areas of dry lake bed now lie exposed. Not only was the local fishing industry destroyed, but noxious, chemical-laden dust storms blow from the desiccated lake bed onto nearby settlements, causing assorted health problems. Irrigation destroyed an ecosystem and produced another desert.

Equally as serious as desertification is the increasing chemical contamination of the land through both fertilizers and pesticides, used mainly by commercial farmers in Western cultures. Chemicals first became important as agricultural fertilizers in Germany in the middle 1800s, and central Europeans remain some of the most chemical-dependent farmers to this day. The chemicals diffused widely, spreading in conjunction with the green revolution and neoplantation (Figure

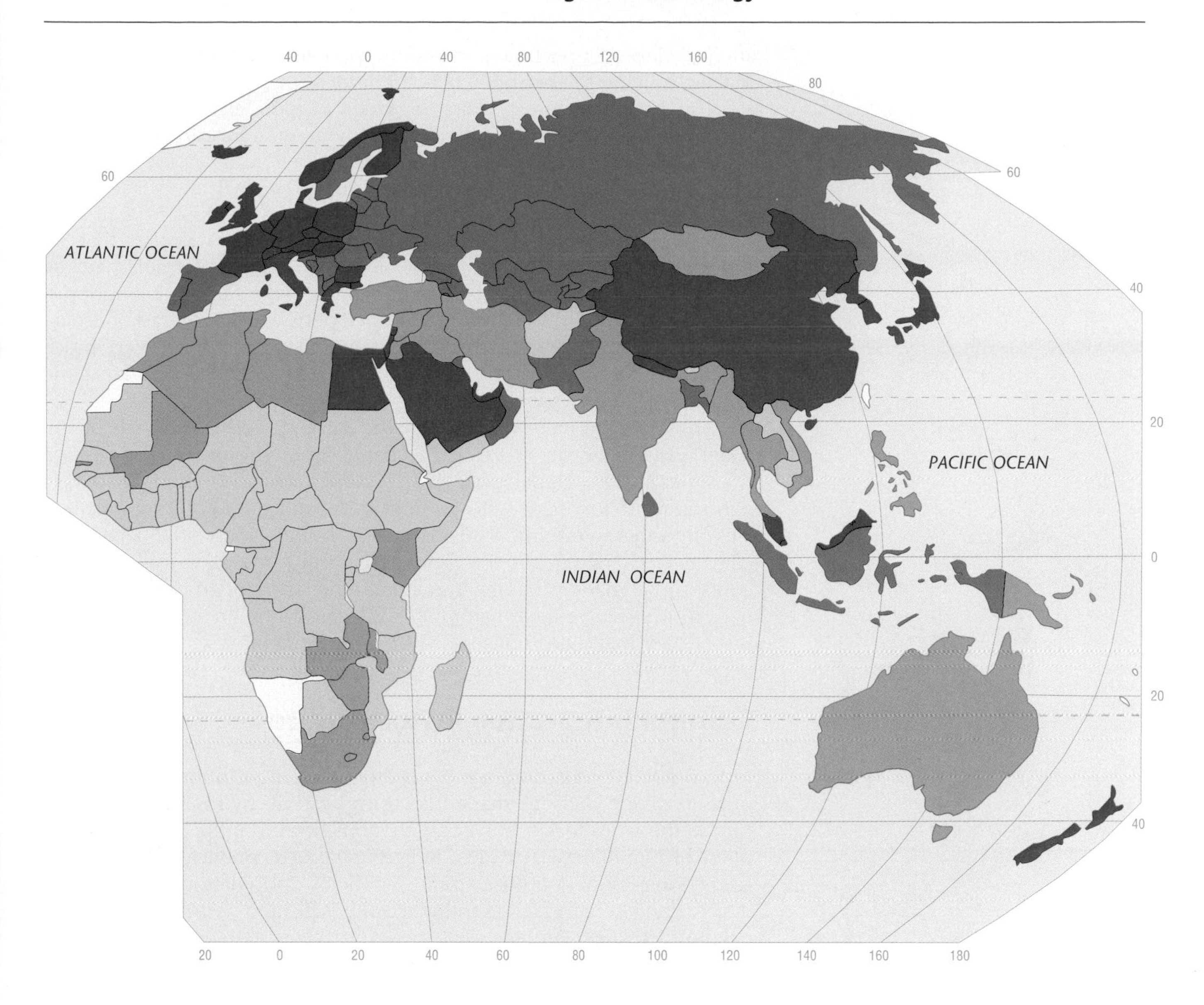

3.19). Together with the use of large machines, chemicals allowed drastic reductions in the amount of labor needed in agriculture. However, the ecological consequences could well be devastating, and in some areas serious contamination problems have appeared. The chemical dependency may be no more sustainable in agricultural systems than in the human body. *Sustainability*—the survival of a land-use system for centuries or millennia without destruction of the environmental base—is the central agricultural ecological issue. Western technological adaptive strategies almost invariably are not sustainable.

Environmental Perception by Agriculturists

People perceive the physical environment through lenses their culture fashions for them. Each person's agricultural heritage can be influential in shaping these perceptions. This is not surprising, because human survival depends on how successfully people can adjust their ways of making a living to environmental conditions.

The American Great Plains provides a good example of how an agricultural experience in one environment influenced farmers' environmental perceptions and subsequent behavior in another environment. Plains farmers came from the humid eastern United States, and they consistently underestimated the problem of drought in their new home. Geographer Thomas Saarinen in the 1960s revealed that although the oldest and most experienced Great Plains farmers had the most accurate perception of drought, almost every farmer still underestimated the actual frequency of such dry periods. By contrast, German immigrants from the steppes of Russia and Ukraine, an area very much like the American Great Plains, accurately perceived the new land and experienced fewer problems.

Above all, farmers rely on climatic stability. A sudden rash of unusual weather events can cause a change in environmental perception by agriculturists. Geographer John Cross recently studied Wisconsin agriculture, following a series of floods, droughts, and other anomalies. He found that two-thirds of all Wisconsin dairy farmers now believe the climate is changing, for the worse, and fully one-third told him that continued climatic variability threatened their continued operation. Perhaps they perceive the environmental hazard to be greater than it really is, but they make decisions based on their perceptions.

Cultural Integration in Agriculture

In the preceding section, we concentrated on how human agricultural pursuits shape and are shaped by the physical environment. Now we turn to the ways that cultural and economic forces influence the distribution of agricultural activities. Religious taboos, politically based tariff restrictions, rural land-use zoning policies, population density, and many other human factors influence the type and distribution of agricultural activities. Among some peoples, the system of crop and livestock raising becomes so firmly enmeshed in the culture that both society and religion are greatly influenced (see box, *Cultural Integration: The Example of Cattle Among the Dasanetch*).

As a result, agricultural borders often parallel other cultural boundaries. In northeastern France, for example, where the French-German

Cultural Integration: The Example of Cattle Among the Dasanetch

The Dasanetch are a herding people living close to Lake Rudolf in East Africa, where the borders of Ethiopia, Kenya, and Sudan meet. For them, cattle are more than mere domestic animals from which they derive milk, meat, blood, and skins. Instead, cattle occupy a central position in their society, serving religious and social roles in addition to their economic function. Dasanetch men identify closely with their cattle and sometimes even assume the personal name of a favorite ox. Cattle themes appear frequently in the song, dance, myth, and ritual of the Dasanetch. Cattle are also an essential aspect of the unmarried woman's dowry and serve as a medium of exchange. "Cattle are therefore central in the organization and functioning of Dasanetch society," bearing utilitarian, subjective, and monetary values. In this way, agriculture, religion, and society are thoroughly integrated.

Derived from data in Carr, Claudia J. *Pastoralism in Crisis: The Dasanetch and Their Ethiopian Lands.* Dept. of Geography, Research Paper No. 180. Chicago: University of Chicago, 1977, pp. 99–100.

language border cuts across French national territory, many elements of agriculture roughly follow the linguistic rather than the political boundary. On the German-speaking side, farms are smaller and more likely to be divided into multiple parcels separated from one another. Efficiency and output are adversely affected, causing the German-speaking farmers to seek second jobs to augment income. They more likely own dairy cows, as opposed to beef cattle, than do their French neighbors across the language border, and they apply more labor in working the land. The cultural geographer, viewing such a spatial correlation, would seek to learn why language and agricultural practices seem to be related. One answer is that language usually identifies separate cultures, which, in turn, have different dietary preferences.

Dietary Preferences

We all have favorite foods, and these preferences often extend through an entire culture. Germanic-speaking peoples, including Anglo-Americans and Anglo-Canadians, exhibit a great fondness for bovine-derived dairy products, including butter, cheese, milk, and ice cream. This helps explain not only the livestock-ownership pattern in northeastern France but also the presence of commercial dairy belts in Germanic parts of Europe, Anglo-America, Australia, and New Zealand. This culturally based preference also accounts for the absence of such agricultural zones in the Mediterranean countries, Japan, and Latin America (Figure 3.1), where people are far less partial to cow's milk.

These dietary preferences extend to drink as well as to food. Coffee, for example, is consumed in enormous quantities by northern Europeans, and Germanic-speaking peoples in general drink far more coffee than tea, producing a vivid spatial pattern (Figure 3.20). Notable in this pattern is the contrast between the preference for coffee in northern Europe and the United States, as opposed to the British fondness for tea. In light of this contrast in beverage preference, it is hardly surprising that tropical highland plantations in the Western Hemisphere, nearer the United States, concentrate on coffee production, while in the Eastern Hemisphere similar hill plantations in the tropical areas in former British colonies such as India produce tea. The Dutch drink more coffee than tea, and during their rule of the East Indies, the name of their tropical island of Java became almost synonymous with coffee. In fact, most dictionaries still list *java* as a slang word for coffee, commemorating the traditional major highland plantation crop of the mountainous, formerly Dutch island.

Intensity of Land Use

A great spatial variation exists in the *intensity* of rural land use. **Intensive agriculture** means that a great deal of human labor or investment capital, or both, is put into each acre or hectare of land, with the goal of obtaining the greatest output in terms of produce. One can calculate intensity either by counting energy inputs or by measuring the level of productivity. In much of the world, especially the paddy rice areas of Asia, high intensity is achieved through prodigious application of human labor, with the result that the local rice output per unit of land is the highest in the world. In the Western countries, high intensity is instead achieved by the massive application of investment capital in machines, fertilizers, and pesticides, resulting in the highest agricultural productivity *per capita* found anywhere.

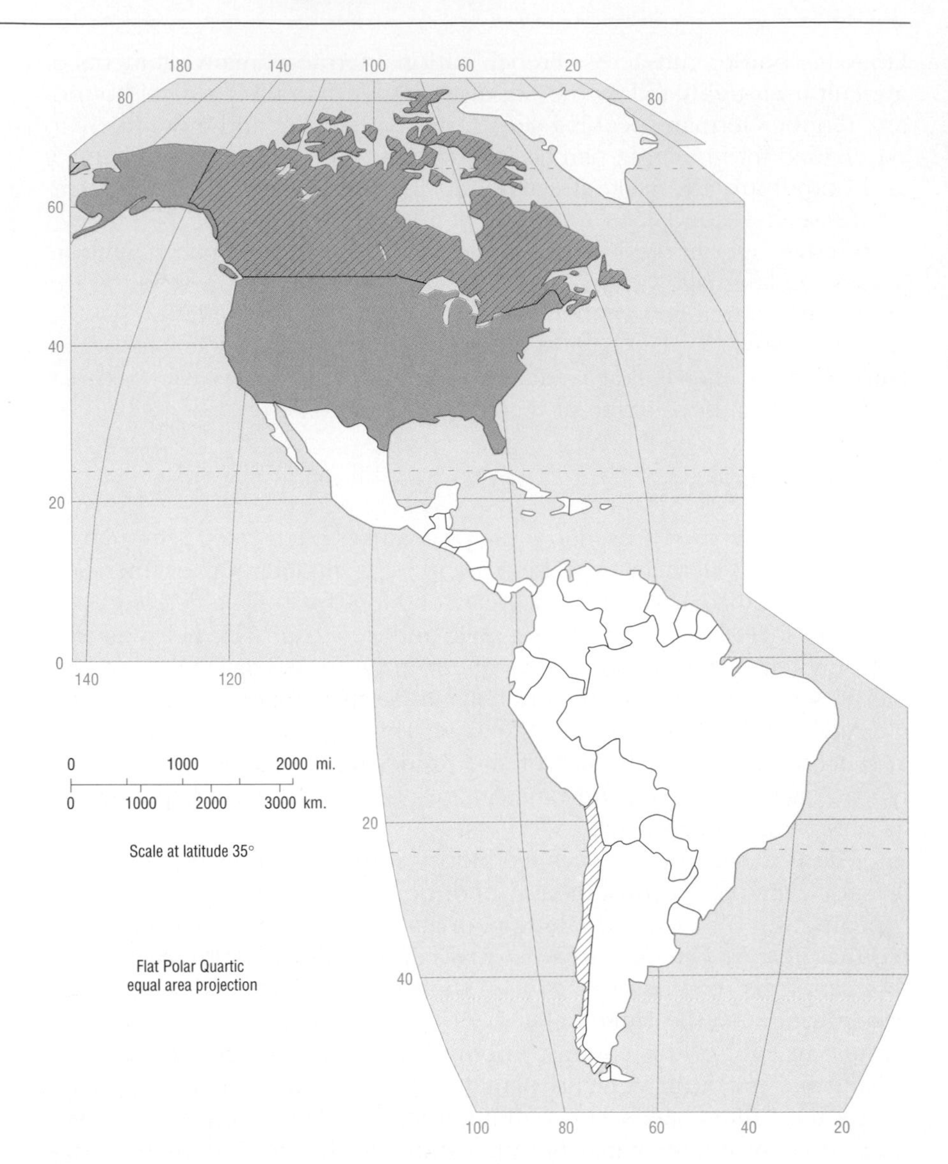

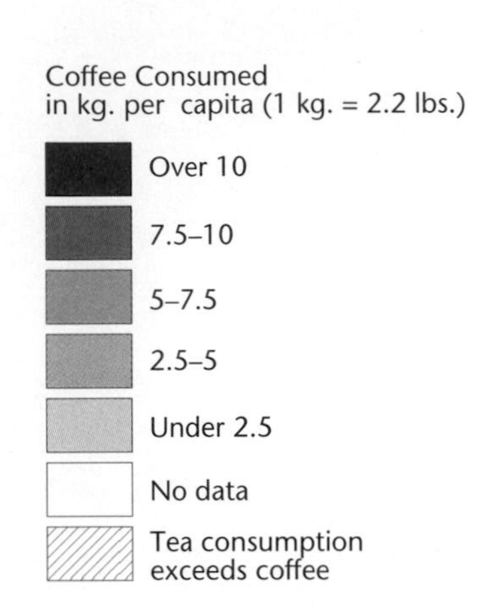

Figure 3.20
Coffee consumption on a per capita basis, for the latest year available. Why are the major coffee-consuming countries so far removed from the tropical production areas, and what might account for the northern European dominance? (Source: *United Nations Statistical Yearbook;* and Berdichevsky, Norman. "A Cultural Geography of Coffee and Tea Preferences." *Proceedings of the Association of American Geographers,* 8 [1976]: 25.)

Geographers employing the social-scientific approach generally support the theory that increased land-use intensity results when population growth forces the need for additional food and reduces the amount of land each farmer can have. As demographic pressure mounts, farmers systematically discard the more extensive adaptive strategies to focus on those that provide greater yield per unit of land. In this manner, the population increase is accommodated. The resultant farming system may be riskier, since it offers fewer options and possesses greater potential for environmental modification, but it does yield more food, at least in the short run. Certain other geographers reject this theory, believing instead that population density increases *following* innovations that lead to greater land-use intensity—that necessity is not the mother of invention.

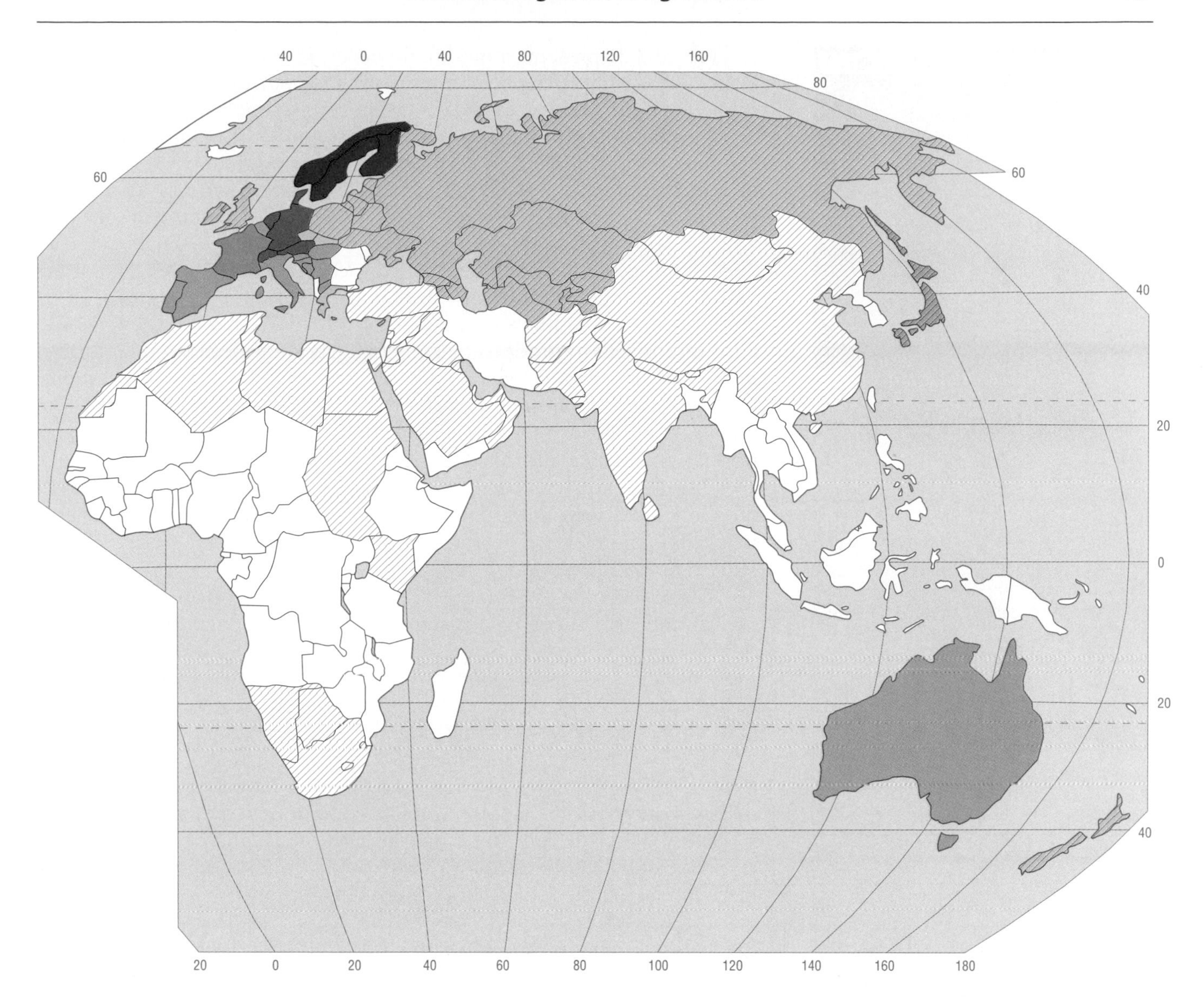

Still other social-scientific geographers, usually economic determinists, look instead to market forces and transportation costs as keys to level of land-use intensity. They use the **core/periphery** model developed in the nineteenth century by the German scholar-farmer, Johann Heinrich von Thünen (see biographical sketch). In his model, von Thünen proposed an "isolated state" that had no trade connections to the outside world; possessed only one market, located centrally in the state; and had uniform soil, climate, and level terrain throughout. He further assumed that all farmers living the same distance from the market had equal access to it and that all farmers sought to maximize their profits and produced solely for market. Von Thünen created this model in order to study the influence of distance from market and transport costs on the type and intensity of agriculture.

Johann Heinrich von Thünen
1783–1850

Von Thünen was not a professional scholar, but rather the landlord of an estate in the German province of Mecklenburg. He did attend several universities in Germany. A contemporary of von Humboldt and Ritter, he apparently never met them, and yet his contribution to geography has been very great. He was concerned with maximizing the agricultural profit from his extensive landholdings. This financial concern and his own curiosity led him to create the "isolated state" model of land use. Modern location theory in agricultural geography is based on von Thünen's model, and he is widely regarded as the originator of spatial models. A Thünen Society was founded in Germany in 1990, and it has branches in North America and elsewhere. He was also honored by having a street named for him in Schwerin, the capital city of his native province in Germany.

Figure 3.21 presents a modified version of von Thünen's model, the isolated state. Improvements in transportation since the 1820s, when he wrote his work, render obsolete certain of his conclusions, such as the finding that bulky products would be produced near the market. The resultant revised model, in common with the original, reveals a series of concentric zones, each occupied by a different type of agriculture, located at progressively greater distances from the central market.

For any given crop, the intensity of cultivation declines with increasing distance from the market. Farmers near the market have minimal transport costs and can invest most of their resources in labor, equipment, and supplies to augment production. Indeed, they *have* to farm intensively in order to make a bigger profit, because their land is more valuable and subject to higher taxes. With increasing distance from the market, farmers invest progressively less in production per unit of land because they have to spend progressively more on transporting produce to market. Moreover, highly perishable products such as milk, fresh fruit, and garden vegetables need to be produced near the market, whereas peripheral farmers have to produce nonperishable products or convert perishable items into a more durable form, such as cheese or dried fruit.

This concentric zone model describes a situation in which highly capital-intensive forms of commercial agriculture, such as market gardening and feedlots, lie nearest to market (Figure 3.21). The increasingly distant, successive, concentric belts are occupied by progressively less intensive types of agriculture, represented by dairying, livestock fattening, commercial grain farming, and ranching.

How well does this modified model describe reality? As we would expect, the real world is far more complicated. Models are not meant to depict reality, but instead to simplify conditions for some specific explanatory purpose. Still, on a world scale, we can see that intensive commercial types of agriculture tend to occur most commonly near the huge urban markets of northwestern Europe and the eastern United States (Figure 3.1). An even closer match can be observed in smaller areas, as in the South American nation of Uruguay (Figure 3.22).

The value of von Thünen's model can also be seen in the underdeveloped countries of the world. Geographer Ronald Horvath made a detailed study of the African region centering on the Ethiopian capital city of Addis Ababa. While noting disruptions caused by ethnic and environmental contrasts, Professor Horvath found "remarkable parallels between von Thünen's crop theory and the agriculture around Addis Ababa." Similarly, German geographer Ursula Ewald applied the model to the farming patterns of colonial Mexico during the period of Spanish rule, and she concluded that even this culturally and environmentally diverse land provided "an excellent illustration of von Thünen's principles on spatial zonation in agriculture."

Amish Agriculture

Perhaps no more striking example of the interplay of culture and agriculture can be found than among the Amish farmers of Pennsylvania and the Midwest. Their religious beliefs instruct them not to depend on nonbelievers for help, leading most to shun modern machines and energy sources (Figure 3.23). As a result, the Amish rely much less on inanimate power and agricultural machines than does the average American farmer.

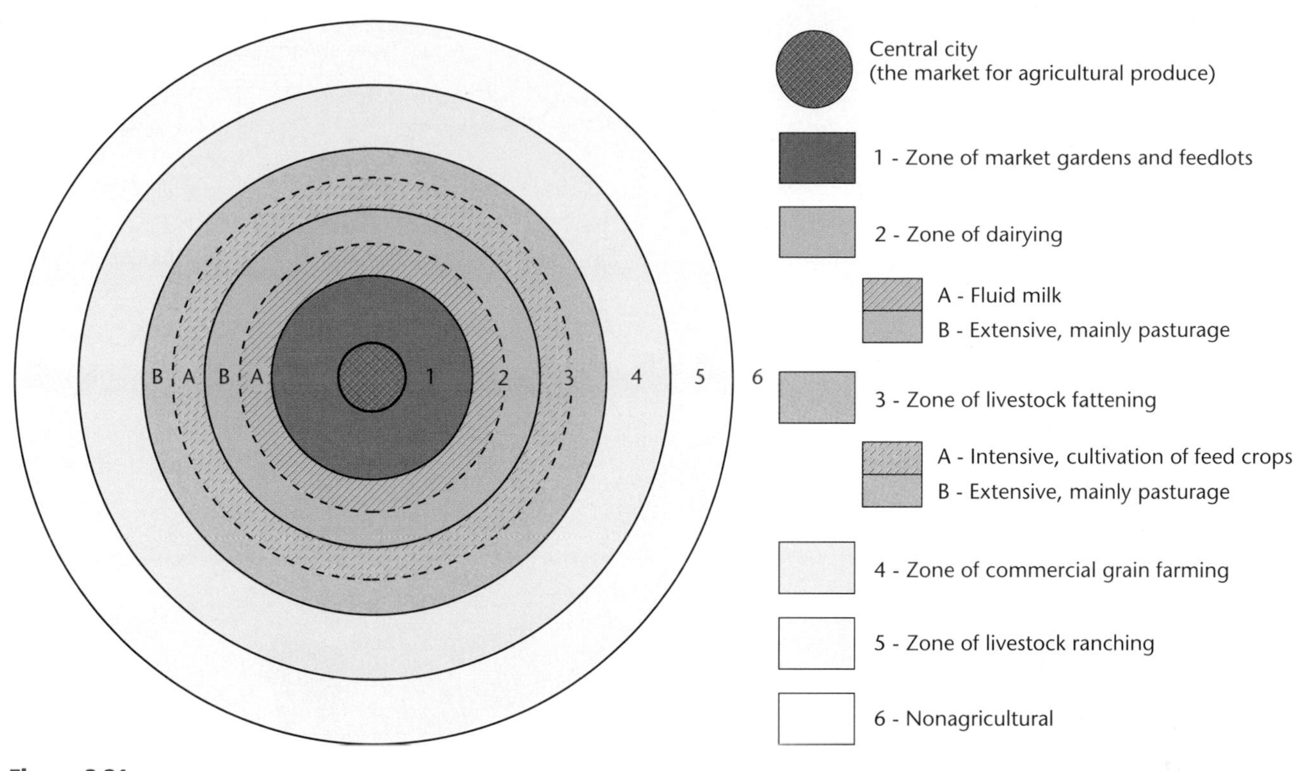

Figure 3.21
Von Thünen's Isolated State model. The model is modified better to fit the modern world, showing the hypothetical distribution of types of commercial agriculture. Other causal factors are held constant to illustrate the effect of *transportation costs* and *differing distances* from the market. The more intensive forms of agriculture, such as market gardening, are located nearest the market, while the least intensive form (livestock ranching) is most remote. Compare this model to the real-world pattern of agricultural types in Uruguay, South America, shown in Figure 3.22.

A study comparing Amish and non-Amish farmers in three states—Pennsylvania, Illinois, and Wisconsin—not only revealed these fundamental differences in farming practices but suggested that, in some regions at least, the Amish surpassed other agriculturists in the amount of food calories produced per unit of energy expended in the production process. Because of their skills in energy conservation, the Amish might eventually be able to instruct a profligate nation on how to live on less electricity, oil, and gas. In the meantime, the Amish will continue to farm differently because of their religion, classically illustrating the workings of cultural integration.

Agricultural Landscapes

A great part of the world's land area is cultivated or pastured. In this huge area, the visible imprint of humankind might best be called the **agricultural landscape** (see biographical sketch of August Meitzen). The agricultural imprint on the land often varies even over short distances, telling us much about local cultures and subcultures. This agricultural landscape also remains in many respects a window on the past. Archaic features abound. For this reason, the rural landscape can teach us a great deal about the cultural heritage of its occupants.

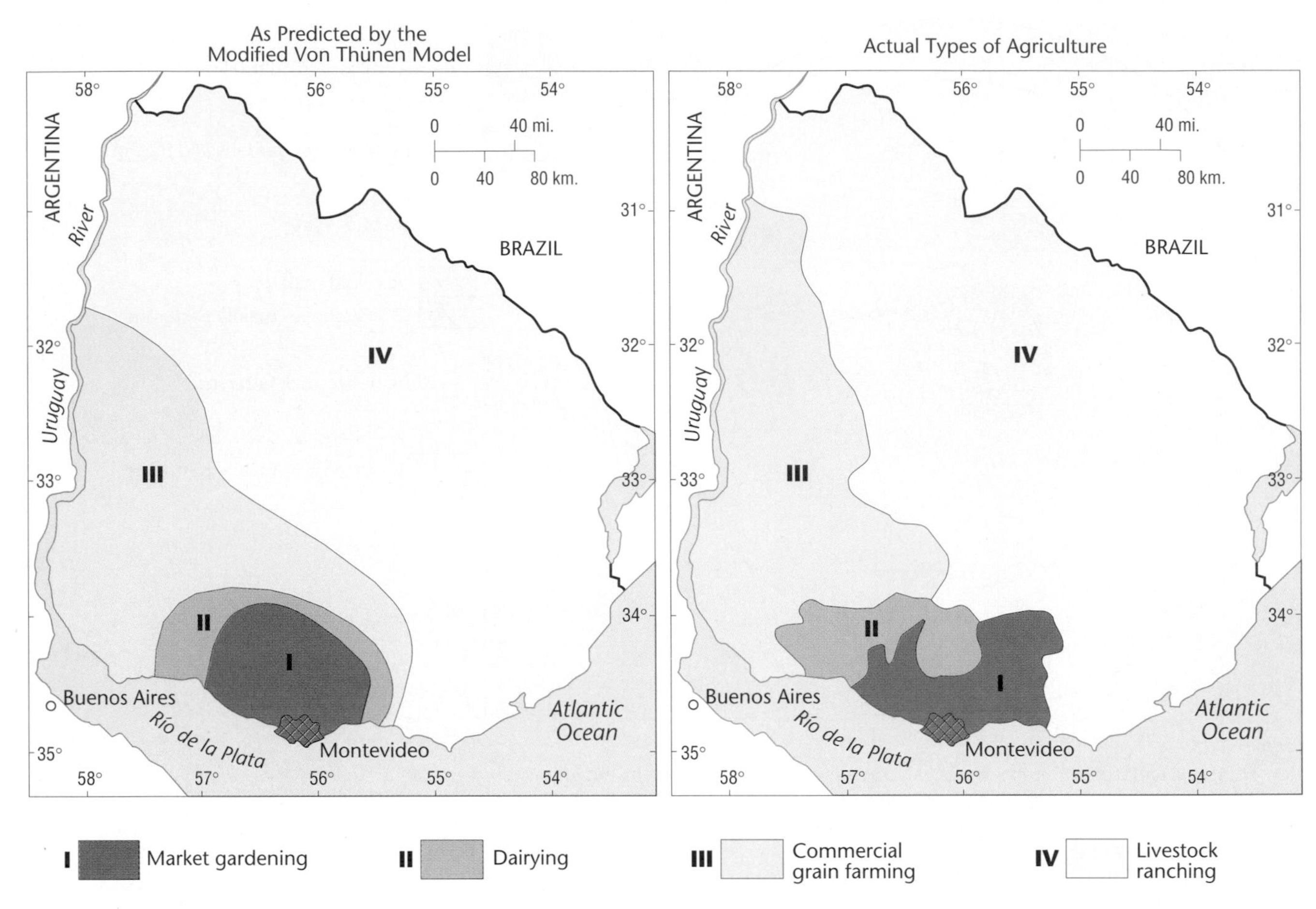

Figure 3.22
Ideal and actual distribution of types of agriculture in Uruguay. This South American country possesses some attributes of von Thünen's isolated state, in that it is largely a plains area dominated by one city. In what ways does the spatial pattern of Uruguayan agriculture conform to von Thünen's model? How is it different? What might cause the anomalies? (For the answers, see Griffin, Ernst. "Testing the von Thünen Theory in Uruguay." *Geographical Review,* 63 [1973]: 500–516; the figure is derived from maps on p. 510.)

Figure 3.23
Amish farmers, Pennsylvania. Because of their religious beliefs, the Amish reject the use of the internal combustion engine and modern farm machinery.

In Chapter 2, we already discussed some aspects of the agricultural landscape, in particular the rural settlement forms. We saw the different ways that farming people situate their dwellings in various cultures. In Chapter 7, which deals with folk geography, we will consider traditional rural architecture, another element in the agricultural landscape. In this chapter, we confine our attention to a third aspect of the rural landscape: the patterns of fields and properties created as people occupy land for the purpose of farming.

Survey, Cadastral, and Field Patterns

A **cadastral pattern** is one describing property-ownership lines, while a *field pattern* reflects the way a farmer subdivides land for agricultural use. Both can be much influenced by **survey patterns,** the lines laid out by surveyors prior to the settlement of an area. Major regional contrasts exist in survey, cadastral, and field patterns, as, for example, *unit-block* versus *fragmented landholding,* and regular, geometric survey versus irregular or unsurveyed property lines.

Fragmented farms are the rule rather than the exception in the Eastern Hemisphere. Under this system, farmers live in farm villages or hamlets. Their small landholdings lie splintered into many separate fields situated at varying distances and directions from the settlement. One farm can consist of a hundred or more separate, tiny parcels of land (Figure 3.24). The individual plots may be roughly rectangular in shape, as in Asia and southern Europe, or they may lie in narrow strips. The latter pattern is most common in western and central Europe, where farmers traditionally worked with a bulky, large plow that was difficult to turn. The origins of the fragmented farm system go back to an early period of peasant communalism. One of its initial justifications was a desire for peasant equality. Each farmer in the village needed land of varying soil composition and terrain. Distance of travel from the village was to be equalized. From the rice paddies of Japan and India to the pastures and fields of western Europe, the fragmented holding remains a prominent feature of the cultural landscape.

Unit-block farms, by contrast, in which all of the farmer's property is contained in a single, contiguous piece of land, occur mainly in the overseas area of European settlement, particularly the Americas, Australia, New Zealand, and South Africa. Most often, they reveal a regular geometric land survey. The checkerboard of farms and fields in the rectangular survey areas of the United States provides a good example of this cadastral pattern (Figures 2.27, 3.25, and 3.29).

The American rectangular survey system first appeared after the Revolutionary War as an orderly method for parceling out federally owned land for sale to pioneers. It imposed a rigid, square, graph-paper pattern on much of the American countryside, geometry triumphant over physical geography. All lines are oriented to the cardinal directions. The basic unit of the system is the "section," a square of land 1 mile (1.6 kilometers) on each side and thus 640 acres (259 hectares) in area. Land was often bought and sold in half-sections or quarter-sections. Larger squares called townships, measuring 6 miles (10 kilometers) on each side, or 36 square miles (93 square kilometers) of land, serve as political administrative subdistricts within counties. Roads follow section and township lines, adding to the checkerboard aspect of the American agricultural landscape. Canada adopted an almost identical rectangular survey system, which is particularly evident in the

August Meitzen
1822–1910

Geographers studying the agricultural landscape owe an enormous debt to the German scholar August Meitzen, widely acknowledged as the founder of rural settlement geography. Meitzen was the Prussian special commissioner for land consolidation, concerned with redrawing property lines so as to reduce farm fragmentation. In this capacity, he traveled over much of the German countryside, becoming intimately familiar with the agrarian landscape. Not content to study only the field and cadastral patterns, he also gave detailed consideration to village types and folk architecture.

Although not a professional geographer, he attended the first annual national meeting of German geographers in 1881 and read a paper on rural house types. Meitzen, not an academician, was nevertheless named honorary professor at the University of Berlin for many years.

His classic work, which provided a scholarly foundation for the study of agricultural landscapes, was published in four volumes in 1895. This work's English title is *Settlement and Agrarian Character of the West and East Germans, of the Celts, Romans, Finns, and Slavs.* Meitzen, more than any other scholar, was responsible for introducing the theme of cultural landscape into geography, and it was he who first proposed that landscape, particularly the relic forms, possessed diagnostic potential.

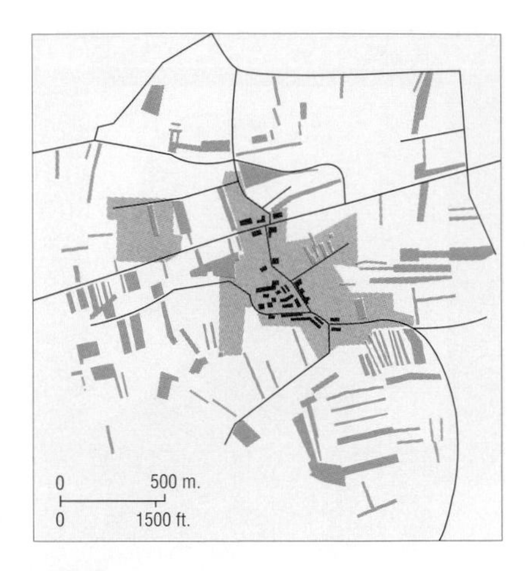

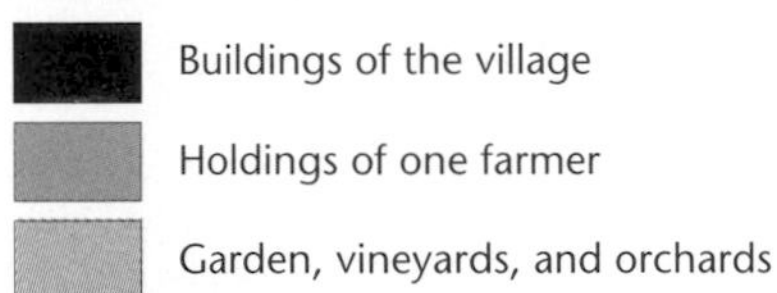

Figure 3.24
Fragmented landholdings surround a French farm village. The numerous fields and plots belonging to one individual farmer are shaded. Such fragmented farms remain common in many parts of Europe and Asia. What advantages and disadvantages does this system have? (After Demangeon, Albert. *La France.* Paris: Armand Colin, 1946.)

Prairie Provinces (Figure 3.26). Traces of more ancient rectangular survey systems can be seen in some European and Asian landscapes.

Equally striking in appearance are *long-lot* farms, where the landholding consists of a long, narrow unit-block stretching back from a road, river, or canal (Figure 3.27). Rather than occurring singly, long-lots lie grouped in rows, allowing this cadastral survey pattern to dominate entire districts. Long-lots occur widely in the hills and marshes of central and western Europe, in parts of Brazil and Argentina, along the rivers of French-settled Québec and southern Louisiana, and in parts of Texas and northern New Mexico (Figure 3.28). The reason for elongating these unit-block farms lay in the desire to provide each farmer with access to transportation facilities, either roads or rivers. In French America, long-lots appear in rows along streams, because water transport provided the chief means of movement in colonial times. In the hill lands of central Europe, a road along the valley floor provides the focus, and long-lots reach back from the road to the adjacent ridgecrests.

Some unit-block farms have irregular shapes rather than the rectangular or long-lot patterns. Most of these result from *metes and bounds surveying,* a type that makes much use of natural features such as trees, boulders, and streams. Parts of the eastern United States were surveyed under the metes and bounds system, with the result that farms there are much more irregular in outline than those where rectangular survey was imposed. The juncture of the two systems of survey is quite appar-

Figure 3.26
Original land survey patterns in the United States and southern Canada. The cadastral patterns still retain the imprint of the various original survey types. What impact on rural life might the different patterns have? The map is necessarily generalized, and numerous local exceptions exist.

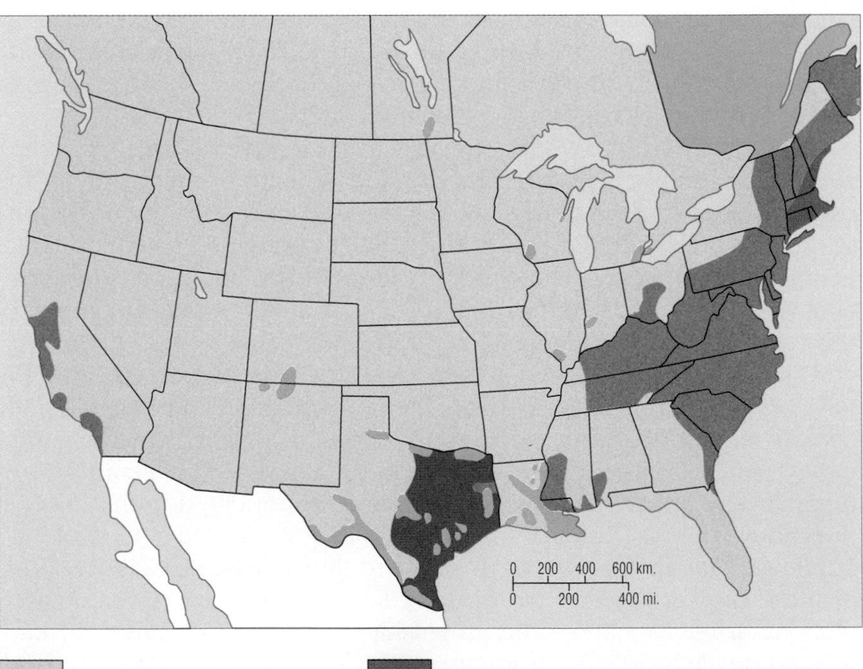

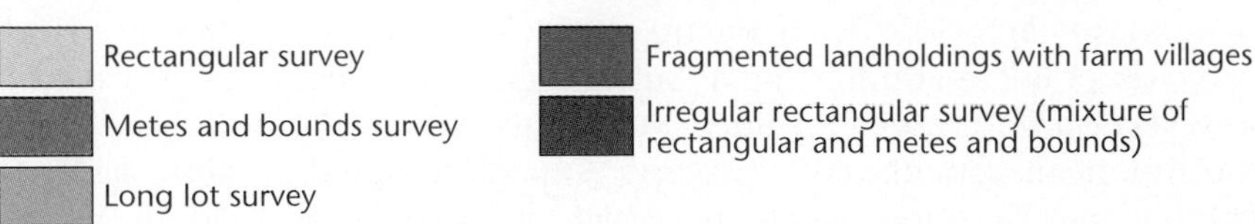

Figure 3.25
American rectangular survey creates a green checkerboard in the Imperial Valley of California, a human mosaic indeed.

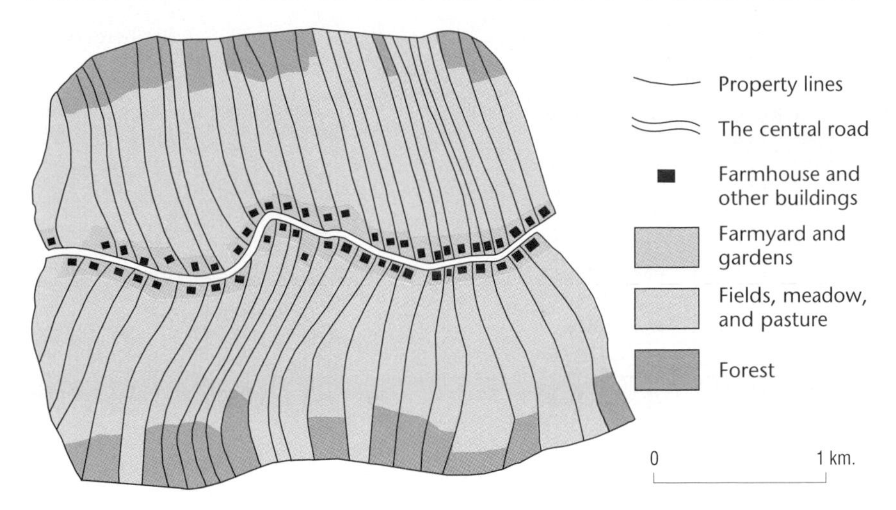

Figure 3.27
A long-lot settlement in the hills of central Germany. Each property consists of an elongated unit-block of land stretching back from the road in the valley to an adjacent ridgecrest, part of which remains wooded.

ent from an airplane (Figure 3.29). In many parts of the world, particularly in Eurasia, major changes in cadastral and field patterns occurred during the last several centuries. Considerable progress has been made in consolidating fragmented holdings into farms that are either unit-blocks or at least less fragmented than they were prior to consolidation (Figure 3.30).

The humanistic geographer seeking to "read" landscapes can learn much even from so apparently passive a feature as these survey and cadastral patterns. For example, in some parts of the Canadian prairie provinces, low, wet places called "sloughs" appear in the terrain, often filled with water to form small lakes. When the section lines of

Figure 3.28
Long-lots near Montréal, Québec. The pattern was created by surveyors centuries ago to provide each farmer access to the river.

Original Survey Lines

U.S. RECTANGULAR SURVEY, HANCOCK AND HARDIN COUNTIES, OHIO

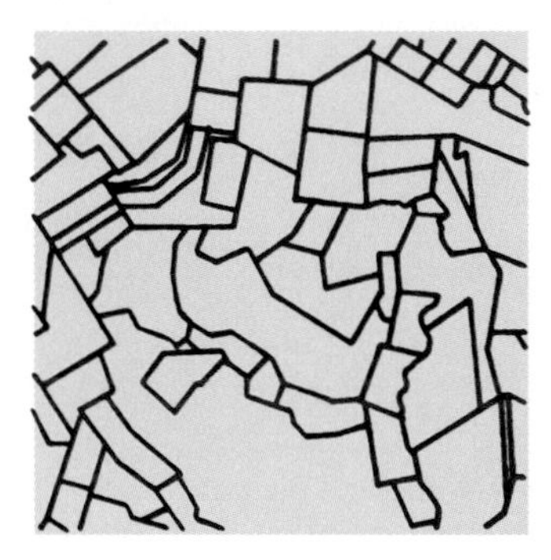

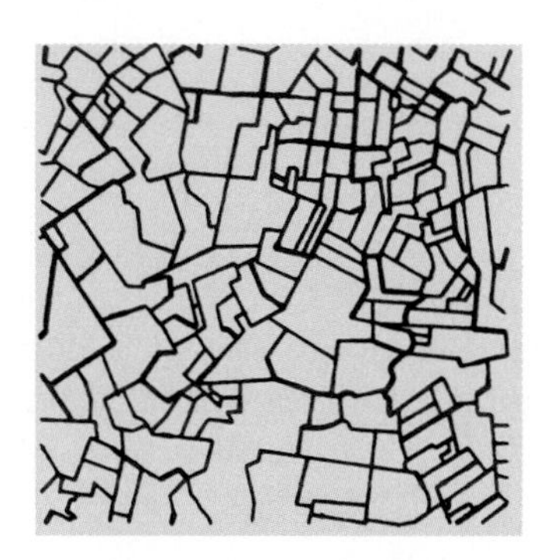

METES AND BOUNDS SURVEY, UNION AND MADISON COUNTIES, OHIO

Figure 3.29
Two contrasting land survey patterns, rectangular and metes and bounds. Both types were used in an area of west-central Ohio. Note the impact these survey patterns had on modern cadastral and field patterns. What other features of the cultural landscape might be influenced by these patterns? (After Thrower, Norman J. W. *Original Survey and Land Subdivision.* Chicago: Rand McNally, 1966, pp. 40, 63, 84.)

Canada's rectangular survey cross one of these sloughs, the roads are generally built right through the lakes, with no attempt to go around. In some cases, two roads intersect in the middle of a lake, built on causeways. What might the humanistic geographer make of this forceful application of the rigid geometric grid, in disregard of the natural habitat? He or she might conclude that North American culture seeks, through technology, to conquer and overwhelm nature rather than live in harmony with it. A cultural determinist might go even further and ask whether people who spend their formative years in one of these checkerboard landscapes differ in any way from those raised in a more chaotic metes and bounds district. Are they less creative or more orderly in their daily lives? Do they tend more toward conservatism?

Fencing and Hedging

Property and field borders are often marked by fences or hedges, heightening the visibility of these lines in the agricultural landscape. *Open-field* areas, where the dominance of crop raising and the careful tending of livestock make fences unnecessary, still prevail in India,

Figure 3.30
Land consolidation in an Irish farm hamlet. The consolidation, carried out in 1909, greatly reduced fragmentation of holdings and produced unit-block farms for some inhabitants. Note that the consolidation caused the breakup of the hamlet and its replacement by isolated farmsteads. What advantages does the new cadastral pattern have over the old one? In what ways might the new be less advantageous than the old? (After Johnson, James H. "Studies of Irish Rural Settlement." *Geographical Review,* 48 [1958]: 564.)

Figure 3.31
Traditional fence in the mountains of Papua New Guinea. The fence is designed to keep pigs out of sweet potato gardens. The modern age has had an impact, as revealed in the use of tin cans to decorate and stabilize the fence. Each culture has its own fence types, adding another distinctive element to the agricultural landscape.

Japan, much of western Europe, and some other Old World areas, but much of the remainder of the world's agricultural lands are enclosed.

Fences and hedges add a distinctive touch to the cultural landscape (Figure 3.31). Different cultures have their own methods and ways of enclosing land, so that types of fences and hedges can be linked to particular groups. Fences in different parts of the world consist of substances as diverse as steel wire, logs, poles, split rails, brush, rock, and earth. Those who visit rural New England, western Ireland, or Yucatán may retain as a visual memory the mile upon mile of stone fence that typify those landscapes. Barbed wire fences swept across the American countryside a century ago, but some remnants of older types can still be seen. In Appalachia, the traditional split-rail zigzag fence of pioneer times survives here and there. Like most visible features of culture, fence types can serve as indicators of cultural diffusion.

The hedge is a living fence. Few who have visited the mazelike hedgerow country of Brittany and Normandy in France or large areas of Great Britain and Ireland fail to perceive these living fences as a major aspect of the rural landscape. To walk or drive the roads of hedgerow country is to experience a unique feeling of confinement quite different from the openness of barbed wire or unenclosed landscapes.

Conclusion

We have seen that the ancient and honored form of livelihood called agriculture varies markedly from place to place, displaying the same tendency for spatial variation that we observed earlier for population. We expressed these patterns as agricultural regions, ranging from traditional subsistence hand-labor farming systems of tropical rain forests to the highly mechanized cash grain operations of mid-latitude wheat belts.

All of these diverse systems are rooted ultimately in the ancient innovations of plant and animal domestication, ideas that diffused from multiple points of origin to occupy their present distributions. Subsequently, countless other agricultural innovations arose, diffused across agricultural space by expansion and relocation, collided with barriers, and reached their present distributions.

Cultural ecology is implicit in the tilling of the soil and grazing of natural vegetation. Humans cannot engage in agriculture, even on the most primitive level, without developing an adaptive strategy and deliberately modifying the physical environment. The results, as we saw, include deforestation, soil erosion, and the possible expansion of deserts. By the same token, and because agriculturists work in such direct contact with the land, they are influenced by the physical environments in which they live and work. We observed the role of climatic advantage and disadvantage and the invitation of level terrain to large-scale mechanized farming as examples of this environmental influence.

Cultural integration taught us to look for cause-and-effect connections between agriculture and other cultural features. In particular, in the von Thünen model we saw the influence of transportation costs and proximity to market on types of farming.

We found the agricultural landscape rich in spatial variations. The ways of dividing land for agricultural use proved to be diverse, ranging from large, unit-block farms to tiny, fragmented ones. These spatial contrasts, added to the differences in rural settlement forms discussed in Chapter 2, reveal a highly varied agricultural landscape.

Sources and Suggested Readings

Allan, Nigel J. R., Gregory W. Knapp, and Christoph Stadel (eds.). *Human Impact on Mountains*. Totowa, NJ: Rowman & Littlefield, 1988.

Andrews, Jean. "Diffusion of Mesoamerican Food Complex to Southeastern Europe." *Geographical Review*, 83 (1993): 194–204.

Bayliss-Smith, T. P. *The Ecology of Agricultural Systems*. New York: Cambridge University Press, 1982.

Binns, T. "Is Desertification a Myth?" *Geography*, 75 (1990): 106–113.

Blume, Helmut. *Geography of Sugar Cane: Environmental, Structural and Economic Aspects of Cane Sugar Production*. Berlin: Albert Bartens, 1985.

Bowden, Leonard W. *Diffusion of the Decision to Irrigate*. Dept. of Geography, Research Paper No. 97. Chicago: University of Chicago, 1965.

Briggs, David, and Frank Courtney. *Agricultural Systems*. New York: John Wiley, 1988.

Briggs, David, and Frank Courtney. *Agriculture and Environment: The Physical Geography of Temperate Agricultural Systems*. London: Longman, 1987.

Chakravarti, A. K. "Green Revolution in India." *Annals of the Association of American Geographers*, 63 (1973): 319–330.

Chisholm, Michael. *Rural Settlement and Land Use: Essay in Location*, 3d ed. London: Methuen, 1979.

Cowan, C. Wesley, and Patty J. Watson (eds.). *The Origins of Agriculture: An International Perspective*. Washington, DC: Smithsonian Institution Press, 1992.

Cross, John A. "Agroclimatic Hazards and Farming in Wisconsin." *Geographical Review*, 84 (1994): 277–289.

Dennett, M. D., J. Elston, and C. B. Speed. "Climate and Cropping Systems in West Africa." *Geoforum*, 12 (1981): 193–202.

Doolittle, William E. "Agricultural Change as an Incremental Process." *Annals of the Association of American Geographers*, 74 (1984): 124–137.

Epstein, D. M., and A. Valmari. "Reindeer Herding and Ecology in Finnish Lapland." *GeoJournal*, 8 (1984): 159–169.

Ewald, Ursula. "The von Thünen Principle and Agricultural Zonation in Colonial Mexico." *Journal of Historical Geography*, 3 (1977): 123–133.

Freestone, Colin S. *The South-East Asian Village: A Geographic, Social and Economic Study*. London: George Philip, 1974.

Galaty, John G., and Douglas L. Johnson (eds.). *The World of Pastoralism: Herding Systems in Comparative Perspective*. New York: Guilford Press, 1990.

Galloway, H. J. *The Sugar Cane Industry: An Historical Geography from Its Origins to 1914*. Cambridge: Cambridge University Press, 1989.

Gregor, Howard F. *Geography of Agriculture: Themes in Research*. Englewood Cliffs, NJ: Prentice-Hall, 1970.

Grigg, David B. "The Agricultural Regions of the World: Review and Reflections." *Economic Geography*, 45 (1969): 95–132.

Grigg, David B. *An Introduction to Agricultural Geography*, 2d ed. London: Routledge, 1995.

Grossman, Lawrence S. *Peasants, Subsistence Ecology, and Development in the Highlands of Papua New Guinea*. Princeton, NJ: Princeton University Press, 1984.

Hale, Gerry A. "The Origin, Nature, and Distribution of Agricultural Terracing." *Pacific Viewpoint*, 3 (1961): 1–40.

Helmfrid, S. (ed.). "Morphogenesis of the Agrarian Cultural Landscape." *Geografiska Annaler*, 43 (1961): 1–328.

Hewes, Lewlie. *The Suitcase Farming Frontier, A Study in the Historical Geography of the Central Great Plains*. Lincoln: University of Nebraska Press, 1973.

Hoggart, Keith, and Henry Buller. *Rural Development: A Geographical Perspective*. New York: Barnes & Noble, 1987.

Horvath, Ronald J. "Von Thünen's Isolated State and the Area Around Addis Ababa, Ethiopia." *Annals of the Association of American Geographers*, 59 (1969): 308–323.

Hudson, John C. *Making the Corn Belt: A Geographical History of Middle-Western Agriculture*. Bloomington: Indiana University Press, 1994.

Ilbery, Brian W. *Agricultural Geography: A Social and Economic Analysis*. New York: Oxford University Press, 1985.

Johannessen, Carl L. "The Domestication Processes in Trees Reproduced by Seed: The Pejibaye Palm in Costa Rica." *Geographical Review,* 56 (1966): 363–376.

Johansen, Harley E. "Diffusion of Strip Cropping in Southwestern Wisconsin." *Annals of the Association of American Geographers,* 61 (1971): 671–683.

Johnson, Hildegard Binder. *Order Upon the Land: The U.S. Rectangular Land Survey and the Upper Mississippi Country*. New York: Oxford University Press, 1976.

Johnson, Warren, Victor Stolzfus, and Peter Craumer. "Energy Conservation in Amish Agriculture." *Science,* 198 (October 28, 1977): 373–378.

Jordan, Terry G. *North American Cattle-Ranching Frontiers: Origins, Diffusion, and Differentiation*. Albuquerque: University of New Mexico Press, 1993.

Kaiser, Harry M., et al. (eds.). *Agricultural Dimensions of Global Climate Change*. Delray Beach, FL: St. Lucie Press, 1993.

Kramer, Fritz L. "Eduard Hahn and the End of the 'Three Stages of Man.'" *Geographical Review,* 57 (1967): 73–89.

Kromm, David E., and Stephen E. White (eds.). *Groundwater Exploitation in the High Plains*. Lawrence: University Press of Kansas, 1992.

Leeds, Anthony, and Andrew P. Vayda (eds.). *Man, Culture, and Animals: The Role of Animals in Human Ecological Adjustments*. Publication No. 78. Washington, DC: American Association for the Advancement of Science, 1965.

Mead, William R. "The Study of Field Boundaries." *Geographische Zeitschrift,* 54 (1966): 101–117.

Overton, Mark. "The Diffusion of Agricultural Innovations in Early Modern England." *Transactions of the Institute of British Geographers,* 10 (1985): 205–221.

Price, Edward T. *Dividing the Land: Early American Beginnings of Our Private Property Mosaic*. Chicago: University of Chicago Press, 1995.

Price, Larry W. "Hedges and Shelterbelts on the Canterbury Plains, New Zealand." *Annals of the Association of American Geographers,* 83 (1993): 119–140.

Rahman, Mushtaqur. "Irrigation and Farm Water Management in Pakistan." *GeoJournal,* 31 (1993): 363–371.

Raup, H. F. "The Fence in the Cultural Landscape." *Western Folklore,* 6 (1947): 1–12.

Reitsma, H. A. "Agricultural Changes in the American-Canadian Border Zone, 1954–1978." *Political Geography Quarterly,* 7 (1988): 23–38.

Rigg, Jonathan D. "The Role of the Environment in Limiting the Adoption of New Rice Technology in Northeastern Thailand." *Transactions of the Institute of British Geographers,* 10 (1985): 481–494.

Rutherford, John. *Rice Dominant Land Settlement in Japan*. Sydney, Australia: Dept. of Geography, University of Sydney, 1984.

Ryu, Je-Hun. "Oral Tradition, Genealogy and Korean Village Morphology." *Journal of Cultural Geography,* 6, No. 1 (1985): 41–50.

Saarinen, Thomas F. *Perception of Drought Hazard on the Great Plains*. Dept. of Geography, Research Paper No. 106. Chicago: University of Chicago, 1966.

Sauer. Carl O. *Agricultural Origins and Dispersals*. New York: American Geographical Society, 1952.

Sauer, Jonathan D. *Historical Geography of Crop Plants*. Boca Raton, FL: CRC Press, 1993.

Seig, Louis. "The Spread of Tobacco: A Study in Cultural Diffusion." *Professional Geographer,* 15 (January 1963): 17–21.

Smil, Vaclav. *Energy, Food, Environment: New Realities, Myths, Options*. New York: Oxford University Press, 1987.

Spencer, Joseph E., and R. J. Horvath. "How Does an Agricultural Region Originate?" *Annals of the Association of American Geographers,* 53 (1963): 74–92.

Suppiah, R. "Four Types of Relationships Between Rainfall and Paddy Production in Sri Lanka." *GeoJournal,* 10 (1985): 109–118.

Thomas, Colin (ed.). *Rural Landscapes and Communities*. Blackrock, Ireland: Irish Academic Press, 1986.

Thomas, David S.G., and Nicholas J. Middleton. *Desertification: Exploding the Myth*. New York: John Wiley, 1994.

Thünen, Johann Heinrich von. *Von Thünen's Isolated State: An English Edition of*

Der Isolierte Staat. Wartenberg, Carla M. (trans.). Elmsford, NY: Pergamon Press, 1966.

Turner, B. L. II, and Stephen B. Brush (eds.). *Comparative Farming Systems.* New York: Guilford, 1987.

Turner, B. L. II, and William E. Doolittle. "The Concept and Measure of Agricultural Intensity." *Professional Geographer,* 30 (1978): 297–301.

Vermeer, Donald E. "Collision of Climate, Cattle, and Culture in Mauritania During the 1970's." *Geographical Review,* 71 (1981): 281–297.

Vogeler, Ingolf. *The Myth of the Family Farm: Agribusiness Dominance of United States Agriculture.* Boulder, CO: Westview Press, 1981.

Wallace, Iain. "Towards a Geography of Agribusiness." *Progress in Human Geography,* 9 (1985): 491–514.

Wallach, Bret. "The Potato Landscape: Aroostook County, Maine." *Landscape,* 23, No. 1 (1979): 15–22.

Whitmore, Thomas M., and B. L. Turner, II. "Landscapes of Cultivation in Mesoamerica on the Eve of the Conquest." *Annals of the Association of American Geographers,* 82 (1992): 402–425.

Whittlesey, Derwent S. "Major Agricultural Regions of the Earth." *Annals of the Association of American Geographers,* 26 (1936): 199–240.

Wilken, Gene C. *Good Farmers: Traditional Agricultural and Resource Management in Mexico and Central America.* Berkeley: University of California Press, 1987.

ОБЪЕДИНЕННЫЙ ФРОНТ ТРУДЯЩИХСЯ
ТРУДОВАЯ КРАСНАЯ ПРЕСНЯ
СОВЕТСКИЙ РАЙОН
ВКПБ
Армия родная! Отечество в опасности!

CHAPTER 4

Political Patterns

From the breakup of empires to regional differences in voting patterns, from the drawing of international boundaries to congressional redistricting in the American democracy, from territorial disputes to separatist violence, human political behavior possesses a geographical aspect. National policies concerning environmental protection, guerrillas seeking a secure base for their operations, or the natural defense provided for an independent country by a surrounding sea all reveal an intertwining of ecology and political phenomena. These spatial and environmental connections provide the basis of the subdiscipline of **political geography** or **geopolitics.** Many geographers pursue such interests, as is suggested by the presence of a designated political geography specialty group within the Association of American Geographers and the publication of a scholarly journal bearing the name *Political Geography* in the United Kingdom.

Political Culture Regions

The theme of culture region is essential to the study of political geography, because an array of both formal and functional political regions exists. Among these the most important and influential is the *independent country.*

Independent Countries

The most outstanding fact of political geography is that the Earth's surface is divided into 190 independent countries, producing a vivid mosaic of functional culture regions (Figure 4.1). Add to those countries the scores of other provinces and districts that enjoy some level of autonomy, without being fully independent, and the pattern becomes even more complex. Closer inspection reveals that some parts of the world are fragmented into many different countries, while others exhibit much greater unity. The United States occupies about the same amount of territory as Europe, which is partitioned among 46 independent countries. Imagine the complexity if every state in the United

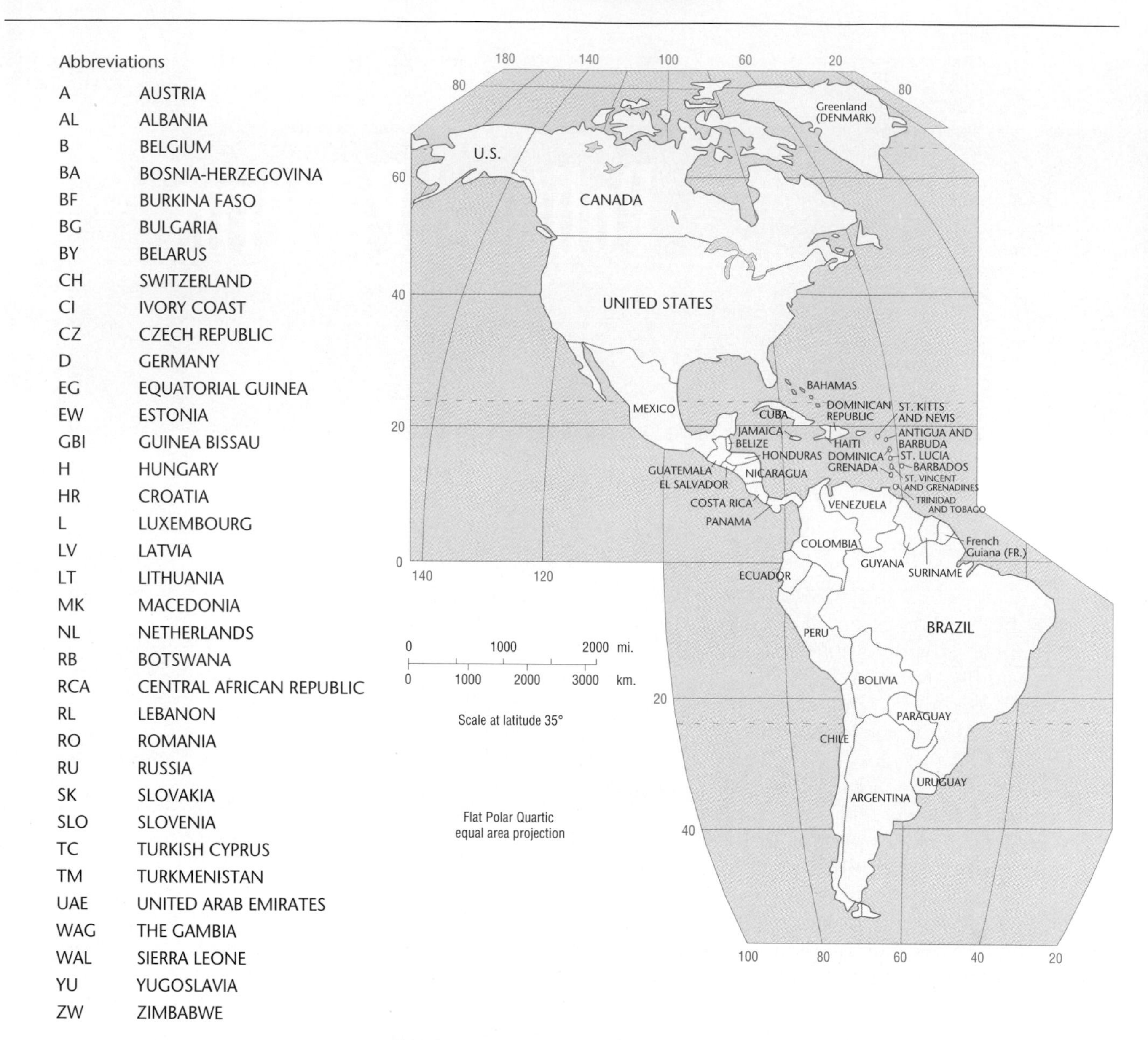

Figure 4.1
The independent countries of the world. In the twentieth century, the map has been in rapid flux, with a proliferation of countries. This process began after World War I with the breakup of such empires as Austria-Hungary and Turkey, then intensified following World War II when the overseas empires of the British, French, Italians, Dutch, Americans, and Belgians collapsed. More recently, the Russian-Soviet empire disintegrated and smaller countries such as Yugoslavia, Czechoslovakia, and Ethiopia fragmented.

States were independent. The continent of Australia is politically united, while South America has 12 and the African mainland 47 independent entities.

The independent country gives tangible geographical expression to one of the most common human characteristics: to belong to a larger group that controls its own piece of the Earth, its own territory. So universally is this trait expressed that scholars coined the term **territoriality** to describe it. Some political geographers believe territoriality is instinctual in humans, as zoologists have demonstrated in the case of certain animal species. They claim that the spatial fragmentation of hu-

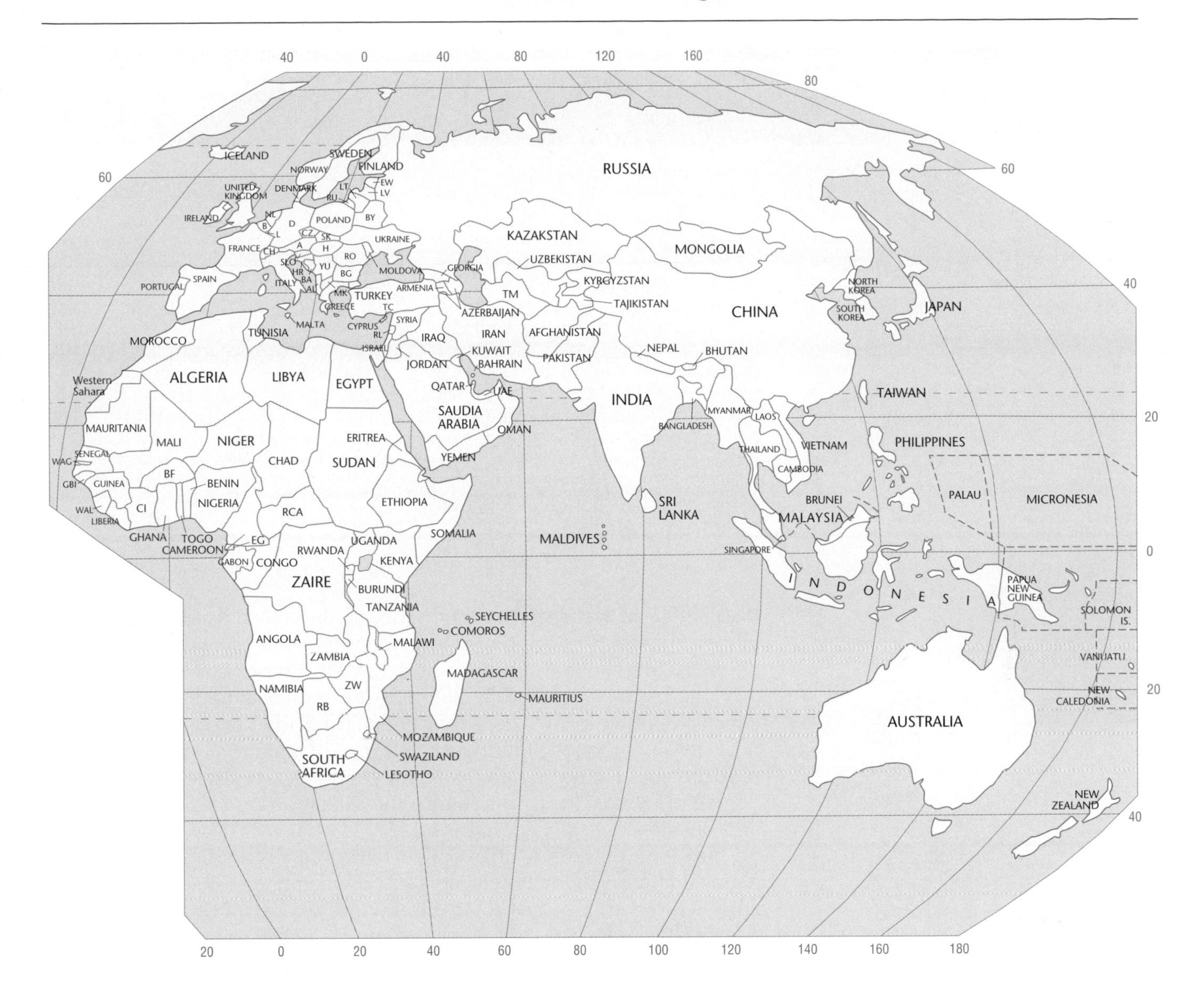

mankind into independent countries is natural and unavoidable, a product of the animal part of our brain, along with nationalism (see box, *The Territorial Imperative*).

Most political geographers disagree. To them, territoriality is *learned.* Robert Sack, for example, regards territoriality as a cultural strategy that uses power to control area and communicate that control, thereby subjugating the inhabitants and acquiring resources. He warns against uncritical borrowing of concepts from students of animal behavior and argues, for example, that the precise marking of borders is a concept originally unique to Western culture. Certain other political geographers suggest a rather recent origin for nationalism, within the past 150 to 500 years, and label it a territorial form of ideology.

Whether learned or instinctual, human territoriality is a thoroughly geographical phenomenon. The implication we should derive from this is that nationalism, the sense of "we," springs from attachment to region and place. Geography and national identity cannot be separated, and it is no accident that territoriality is a spatial word.

The Territorial Imperative

Zoologists have for some time recognized that animal behavior in many species is in part motivated by a territorial instinct, a need to possess and defend a home area as individuals or as members of a group. Territory provides a sense of identity to these animals and satisfies a basic need for belonging. Such an instinct is found in animals as diverse as the mockingbird, lemur, crab, and prairie dog. For these animals and others, the attachment to territory is genetic, a need perhaps even stronger than the sex drive.

Robert Ardrey, in his book *The Territorial Imperative,* says that humans are territorial animals, motivated by the same instinct that affects mockingbirds and prairie dogs. In other words, the political organization of territory into provinces and countries is the product of animal instinct—as are nationalism, patriotism, and the desire to defend territory against invaders. On the smallest scale, the territorial imperative finds human expression in the homestead and family. Then it ranges upward through clan and tribe, through neighborhood, district, and province, to reach humankind's ultimate territorial creation—the independent country. The territory involved may be a family's suburban yard, the domain of a street gang in the ghettos of New York City, the hilly refuge of a Stone Age tribe in New Guinea, or the expanses of an empire. In Ardrey's words, "The dog barking at you from behind his master's fence acts for a motive indistinguishable from that of his master when the fence was built."

Is human territorialism learned or instinctual? Ardrey argues for instinct, but many social scientists do not agree. The question is still being debated.

Based on Ardrey, Robert. *The Territorial Imperative: A Personal Inquiry into the Animal Origins of Property and Nations.* New York: Atheneum, 1966.

Distribution of National Territory. One of the most fundamental geographical aspects of an independent country is the shape and configuration of the national territory. As a rule, the more compact the territory, the better. Theoretically, the most desirable shape for a country is circular or hexagonal. These two geometric forms maximize compactness, allow short communication lines, and minimize the amount of border to be defended. Of course, no countries actually enjoy this ideal degree of compactness, although some—such as France, Poland, Zaïre, and Brazil—come close (Figure 4.2).

Any one of several unfavorable territorial distributions can inhibit national cohesiveness. Potentially most damaging to a country's stability are enclaves and exclaves. An **enclave** is a district surrounded by a country but not ruled by it. Enclaves can be either self-governing or an exclave of another country (Figure 4.2). In either case, its presence can be a problem for the surrounding country. Potentially just as disruptive is the *pene-enclave,* an intrusive piece of territory with only the smallest of outlets free of the surrounding country (Figure 4.2).

Exclaves are pieces of national territory separated from the main body of a country by the territory of another (Figure 4.3). Alaska is an exclave of the United States. Exclaves are particularly undesirable if a hostile power holds the intervening territory, for defense of such an isolated area is always difficult and may stretch national resources to the breaking point. Moreover, an exclave's population, isolated from their fellow countrymen, may develop separatist feelings, causing additional problems. Pakistan provides a good example of the national instability created by exclaves. Pakistan was created in 1947 as two main bodies of territory separated from each other by almost 1000 miles (1600 kilometers) of northern India. West Pakistan had the capital and most of the territory, but East Pakistan housed most of the people. West Pakistan hoarded the country's wealth, exploiting East Pakistan's resources and giving little in return. Ethnic differences between the peoples of the two sectors further complicated matters. In 1973, a quarter of a century after its founding, Pakistan disintegrated. The distant ex-

Figure 4.2
Differences in the distribution of national territory. The map, drawn from Europe, Africa and South America, shows wide contrasts in territorial shape. Poland and, to a lesser extent, Zaïre approach the ideal hexagonal shape, but Russia is both elongated and has an exclave in the Kaliningrad District, while Indonesia is fragmented into a myriad of islands. The Gambia intrudes as a pene-enclave into the heart of Senegal, and South Africa has a foreign enclave, Lesotho. Chile must overcome difficulties associated with extreme elongation. What problems can arise from elongation, enclaves, fragmentation, and exclaves? How might these problems be overcome?

clave seceded to become the independent country of Bangladesh (Figure 4.1).

Even when a national territory lies in one piece, instability can develop if the shape of the state is awkward. Narrow "shoestring" countries, such as Chile, the Gambia, and Norway, can be difficult to administer, as can island nations such as Indonesia, consisting of many separate islands (Figures 4.2 and 4.3). In these situations, transportation and communications become difficult, causing administrative problems. The West Indies Federation, a short-lived union of formerly British islands in the Caribbean, disintegrated in part because the sea encouraged islanders to develop local rather than regional allegiances.

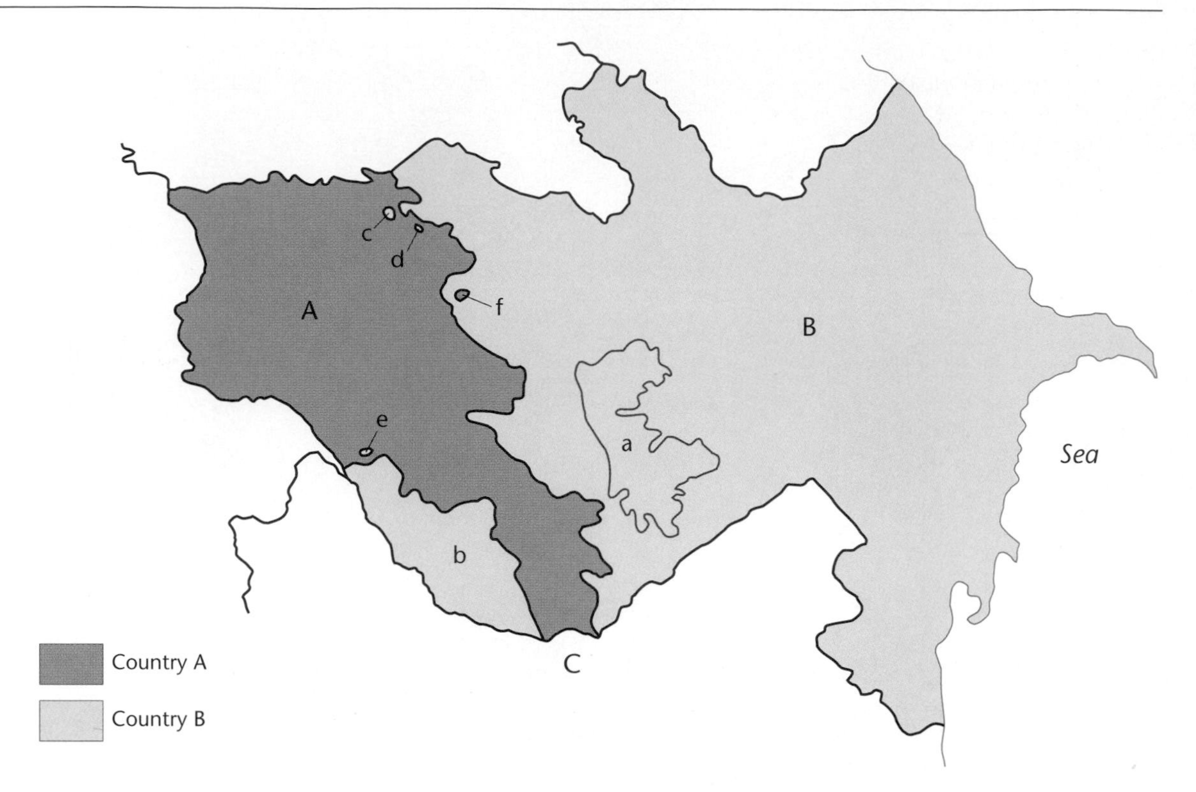

Figure 4.3
Two independent countries, *A* and *B*, engage in a border war. *A* seeks to liberate region *a*, where a population speaking the same language and adhering to the same religion as the people of *A* live as a persecuted minority in *B*. *B*, meanwhile, has an exclave, *b*, on the opposite, western side of *A*, and the people of *b* form another ethnic minority, unrelated to *B*. Many in *b* seek union with country *C*. Country *B* also possesses several much smaller enclaves—*c*, *d*, and *e*, the latter of which is regarded as part of *b* (an exclave of an exclave!). *A* also has a tiny exclave, *f*. In other words, the distribution of national territories is troublesome to both *A* and *B*, particularly given the hostile relations between them. These are real countries. Using an atlas, identify them. If you fail, the answer appears at the end of the Sources and Suggested Readings section. The conditions shown and described are for 1991. What was the territorial outcome of this dispute? (Source: Office of the Geographer, US Department of State.)

Boundaries. The boundaries of political territories are of different types. Until fairly recent times, many boundaries were not sharp, clearly defined lines, but instead zones called **marchlands.** Today, the nearest equivalent to the marchland is the **buffer state,** an independent but small and weak country lying between two powerful, potentially belligerent countries. Mongolia, for example, is a buffer state between Russia and China; Nepal occupies a similar position between India and China (Figure 4.1). If the buffer state falls under the domination of one or the other powerful neighbor, it becomes a **satellite state** and loses much of its independence.

Most modern boundaries are lines rather than zones, and we can distinguish several types. **Natural boundaries** follow some feature of the natural landscape, such as a river or mountain ridge. **Ethnographic boundaries** find their basis in some culture trait, in a particular language or religion; and **geometric boundaries** are regular, often perfectly straight lines drawn without regard for physical or cultural features. The United States–Canada boundary west of the Lake of the Woods is a geometric border. So are most county and state borders in the central and western United States and Canada. Some boundaries are of mixed type, composites of two or more of the types listed.

Relic boundaries no longer exist as international borders, but they often leave behind a trace in the local cultures. With the reunification of Germany in the fall of 1990, the old Iron Curtain border between the former German Democratic Republic in the east and the Federal Republic of Germany to the west was quickly dismantled. In a remarkably short time span, measured in weeks, the Germans reopened severed transport lines and created new ones, knitting the enlarged country together. Even so, remnants and reminders of the old border remained, in the form of memorials, and most of it continued to function as a provincial boundary within Germany and to separate two parts of the country with strikingly different levels of prosperity (Figure 4.4).

The most outstanding geographical aspect of international borders is their divisive character. As Germans knit back together a country long cut in two by an international boundary, other newly independent countries in Europe enforce their borders by severing existing routes. Latvia and Estonia provide an example (Figure 4.5).

Figure 4.4
A boundary disappears. Former barbed-wire barriers on the defunct East-West Germany border had been made into a monument by the spring of 1991, and the once-feared Iron Curtain had been demoted to the status of a provincial border, where a sign greeted travelers to the province of Thuringia. In Berlin, the view toward the Brandenburg Gate changed radically between 1989 and 1991.

Figure 4.5
Newly independent Latvia and Estonia. The two countries demonstrated their status by digging trenches to block old roads that had once connected them and by erecting steel barriers in former city streets. Even this peaceful border now serves to disrupt and channel the movement of people and goods. An earlier, hastily erected barrier on the city street, in the border town Valga/Valka, has apparently been destroyed by an unwary motorist and now rests against the wall on the right.

Spatial Organization of Territory. Independent countries differ greatly in the way their territory is organized for purposes of administration. Political geographers recognize two basic types of spatial organization: *unitary* and *federal.* Unitary governments are characterized by power being concentrated centrally, with little or no provincial authority. All major decisions come from the central government, and policies are applied uniformly throughout the national territory. France and China are unitary in structure, even though one is democratic and the other totalitarian. A federal government, by contrast, is a more geographically expressive political system. It acknowledges the existence of regional cultural differences and provides the mechanism by which the various regions can perpetuate their individual characters. Power is diffused and the central government surrenders much authority to the individual provinces. The United States, Canada, Australia, and Switzerland provide examples, though exhibiting varying degrees of federalism. The trend in the United States, particularly since the defeat of the Confederacy in the Civil War, has been toward a more unitary, less federal government, with fewer states' rights. In Canada, on the other hand, federalism remains vital, representing an effort to counteract French-Canadian demands for Québec's independence. Russia today strives to create a federal state in the place of a deposed unitary one.

Whether federal or unitary, a country functions through some system of political subdivisions, normally on several different levels. In federal systems, these subdivisions sometimes overlap in authority, with confusing results. For example, the Indian reservation in the United States occupies a unique and ambiguous place in the federal system of political subdivisions. These semiautonomous enclaves are legally sanctioned political territories that only indigenous Americans can possess. While not sovereign, they do have certain self-government rights that conflict with other local authority. Reservations do not fit neatly into the American political system of states, counties, townships, precincts, and incorporated municipalities. They add to the confusion that so often typifies federal systems.

Centrifugal and Centripetal Forces. The spatial organization of territory, degree of compactness, and type of boundaries can influence an independent country's stability. However, other forces are also at work, and cultural factors often make or break a country. The most viable independent countries, least troubled by internal discord, have a strong feeling of group solidarity among their population. Group identity is the key.

Political geographers refer to factors that promote national unity and solidarity as **centripetal forces.** Whatever, by contrast, disrupts internal order and encourages destruction of the country is called a **centrifugal force.** Many nations have one principal centripetal force that, more than any other single factor, provides fuel for nationalistic sentiment. Such a unifying force, which stands out above all others in any given country, is referred to as the **raison d'être**—the "reason for being." For example, the Jewish faith is the raison d'être for Israel. We consider an array of centripetal and centrifugal forces later, in the sections on political ecology and politico-cultural integration.

How Many Independent Countries Should There Be? We live in a time that has witnessed a proliferation of independent countries. The former Soviet Union disintegrated into 15 new countries, Yugoslavia into 5, and Czechoslovakia into 2. Canada, Russia, Iraq, Peru, and certain others could also fragment. As political geographer David Knight has pondered, "Should all groups with distinct territorial-based identities have the right to independence?" Would continued proliferation increase the chance for warfare and strife, or lessen such conflict instead? This fundamentally geographical issue remains one of the most important in the modern world, for separatism is widespread. We will return to this issue later in the chapter.

Supranational Political Bodies

The third major type of political functional culture region, in addition to independent countries and their governmental subdivisions, is the *supranational organization* (Figure 4.6). Self-governing countries form international associations of one kind or another for purposes of trade, military assistance, or mutual security. In the twentieth century, supranational organizations grew in number and importance, coincident with and counterbalancing the proliferation of independent countries. Some represent the vestiges of collapsed empires, such as the British Commonwealth, French Community, and Commonwealth of Independent States (CIS)—the latter a shadow of the former Soviet Union. The European Union seeks a widely based confederation, extending even to a single system of currency and passports, while certain other supranationals, such as the Arab League, possess little cohesion. Atop the pyramid of supranationals is the United Nations, with headquarters in New York City, which maintains peacekeeping and charitable functions, while at the same time invoking sanctions against "rogue" countries.

Electoral Geography

When people vote in elections, another vivid mosaic of political culture regions is created. A free vote of the people on some controversial issue provides one of the purest expressions of culture. Revealed in the

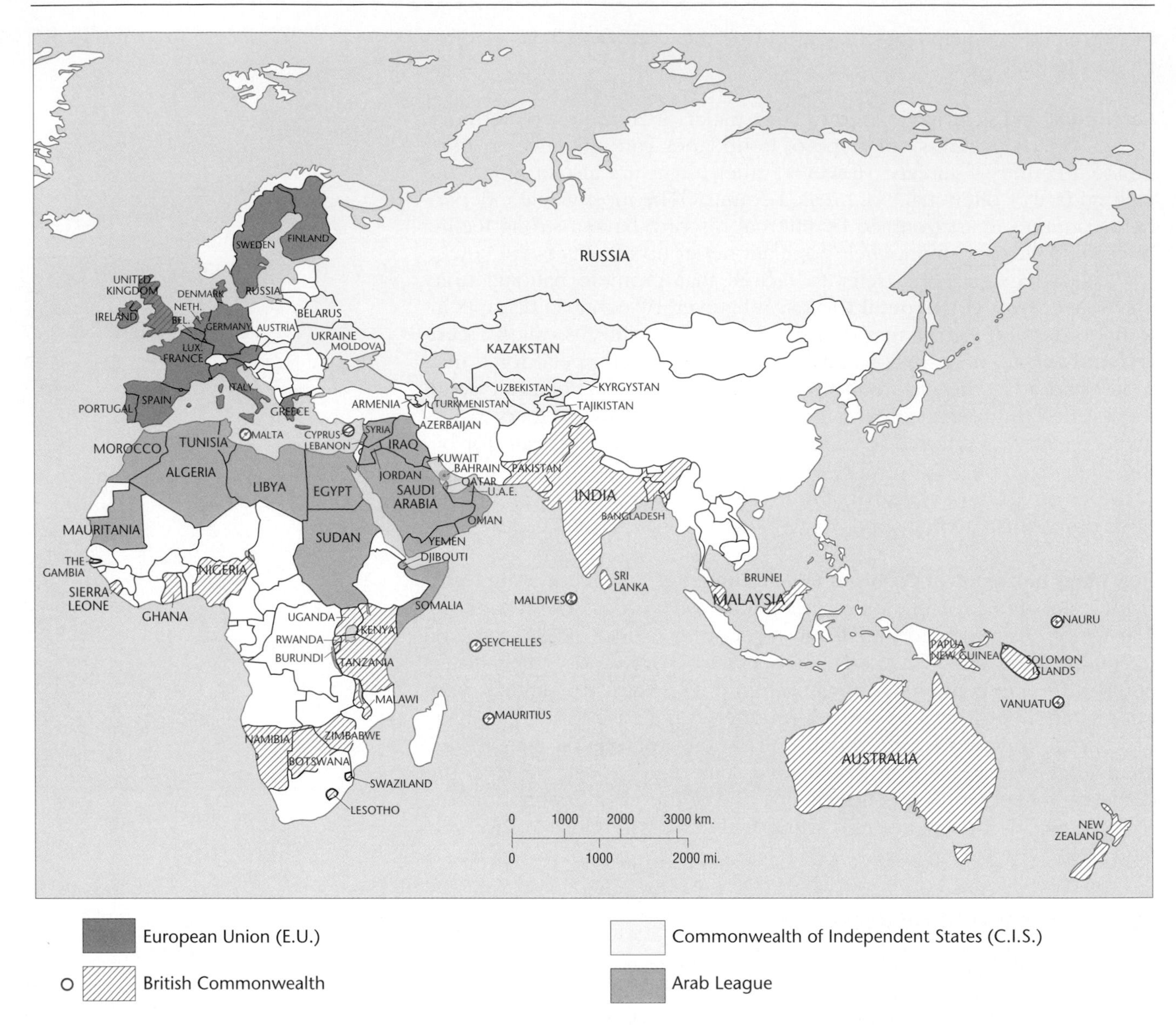

Figure 4.6
Some supranational political organizations in the Eastern Hemisphere. These vary greatly in purpose and cohesion. The British Commonwealth also includes Western Hemisphere members.

process are attitudes reflecting religion, ethnicity, sectionalism, and ideology. Geographers can devise formal culture regions based on voting patterns, giving rise to the subspecialty known as *electoral geography*.

Often voting patterns closely resemble the spatial distribution of other facets of culture. For example, the American culture region earlier identified as the *Lower South* (Figure 1.6) often has an electoral manifestation. In the 1968 presidential election, the areas supporting the independent candidate George Wallace, an avowed segregationist, closely coincided with the Lower Southern culture region. The same pattern occurred four years earlier, when the Lower South supported the conservative Republican presidential candidate, Barry Goldwater, more strongly than did any other part of the United States (Figure 4.7).

Voting tendencies over many decades can also be mapped, revealing deep-rooted electoral behavior regions. Europe provides a vivid example

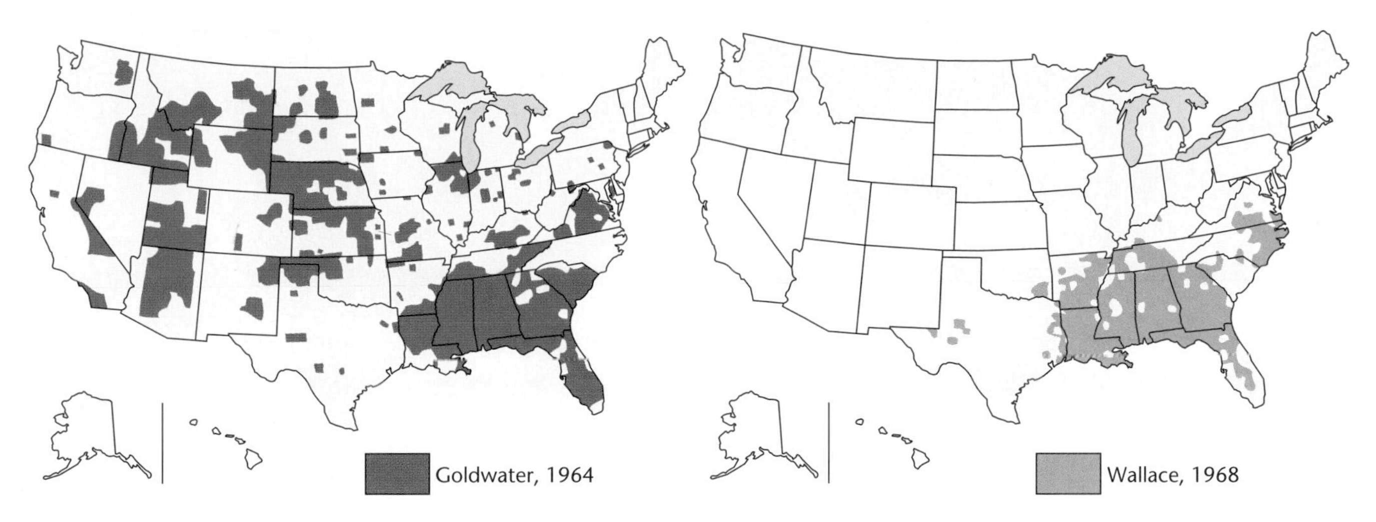

Figure 4.7
Two recent political expressions of the Lower Southern culture region (refer back to Figure 1.6). Goldwater, the conservative Republican presidential candidate in 1964, found his major support in the Lower South, as did independent populist candidate George Wallace in 1968. What might explain the differences between the two maps, as for example in South Carolina? The similarities? (Adapted from Brunn, Stanley D. *Geography and Politics in America.* New York: Harper & Row, 1974, pp. 279, 281.)

(Figure 4.8). Some districts and provinces there have a long record of rightist sentiment, and many of these lie toward the center of Europe. Peripheral areas, especially in the east, are often leftist strongholds. Every country where free elections are permitted has a similarly varied electoral geography. In other words, cumulative voting patterns typically reveal pronounced, sharp sectional contrasts. Electoral geographers refer to these borders as *cleavages*.

Electoral geographers also concern themselves with *functional* culture regions, in this case the voting district or precinct. Their interests are both scholarly and applied. For example, following each United States census, political redistricting takes place in order to establish voting areas of more or less equal population, and these form the electoral basis for the House of Representatives in Washington, DC. State legislatures are based on similar districts. Geographers often assist in the redistricting process. Richard Morrill of the University of Washington directed the redrawing of both congressional and legislative district boundaries in his state following one of the recent censuses.

The pattern of voting precincts or districts can influence election results. If redistricting remains in the hands of legislators, instead of impartial experts such as Morrill, then the majority political group or party will often try to arrange the voting districts geographically in such a way as to maximize and perpetuate their power. Cleavage lines will be crossed to create districts that have a majority of voters favoring the group or party in power and a minority of opposition voters. This practice is called **gerrymandering** (Figure 4.9), and the resultant voting districts often have awkward, elongated shapes.

Political Diffusion

Political ideas, institutions, and countries expand and spread by means of cultural diffusion. Moreover, political boundaries can act as barriers

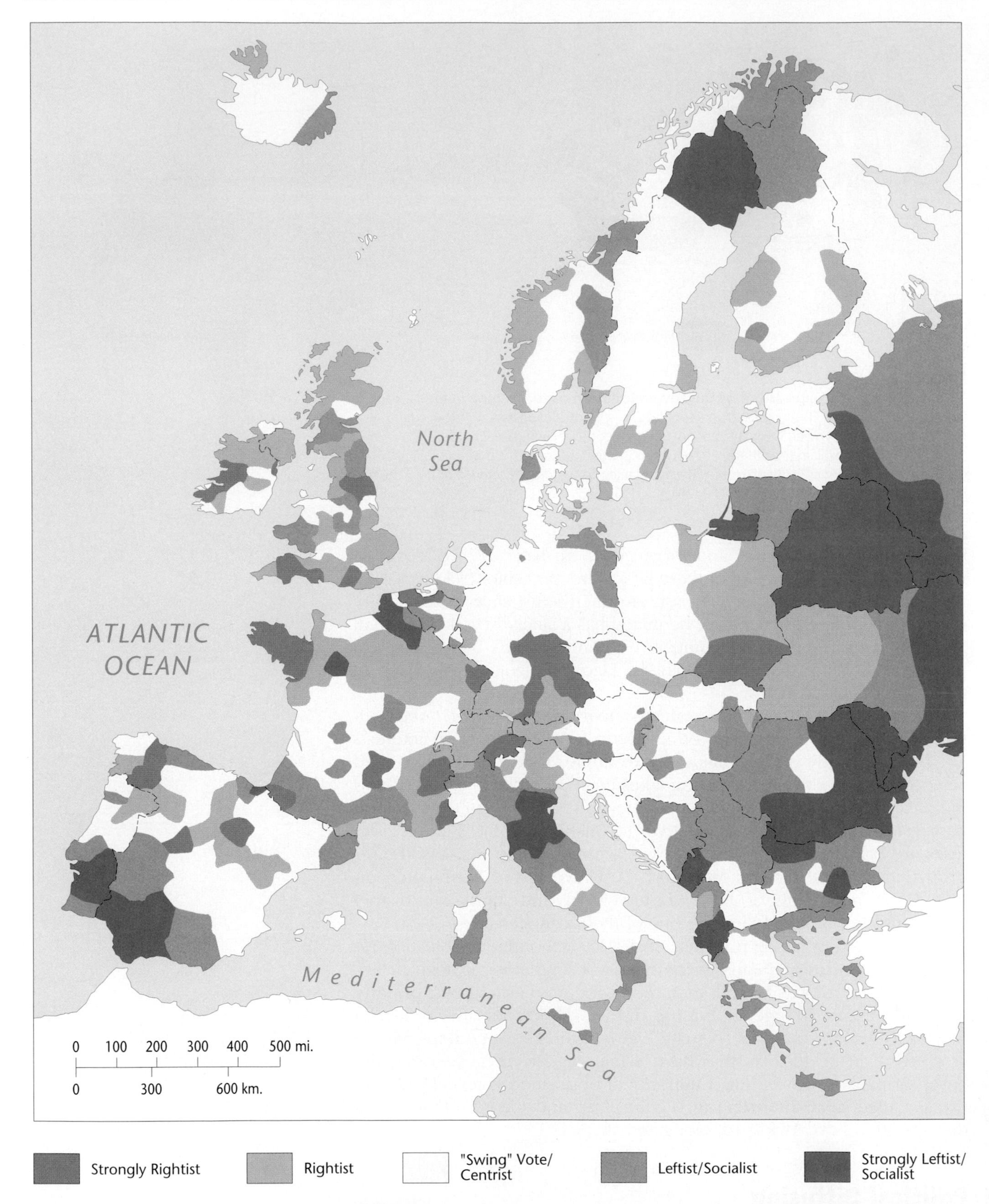

Figure 4.8

The electoral geography of Europe. A conservative/rightist core contrasts with a socialist/leftist periphery. Based on elections held in the period 1950 to 1995. In the formerly Communist countries, the record of free elections began only in 1990. (Source: Jordan, Terry G. *The European Culture Area*, 3d ed. New York: HarperCollins, 1996, p. 226.)

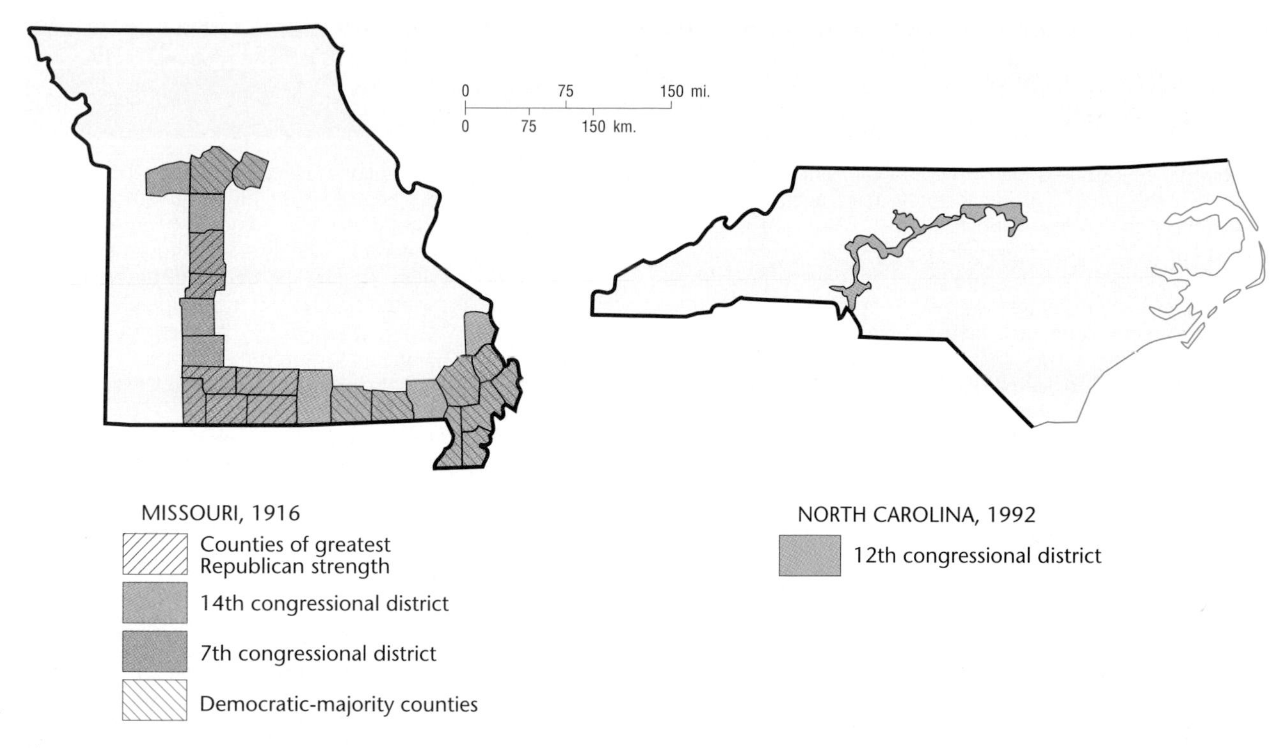

Figure 4.9
Gerrymandering of congressional districts in Missouri and North Carolina. In Missouri's Fourteenth District, the five-county Republican stronghold in the southern Ozark Mountains was linked in 1916 to a larger area of Democratic strength, preventing the election of a Republican to Congress. Geographer Carl Sauer described the Fourteenth District as "atrociously gerrymandered." The Seventh District was more subtly gerrymandered, since it joined several densely populated Democratic counties in the north to two more sparsely settled Republican counties farther south. The North Carolina Twelfth District was created in 1992 to ensure an African-American majority, so that an additional minority candidate could be elected to Congress. Note the awkward shape of these districts, often a sign of gerrymandering. In 1995 the North Carolina district and others gerrymandered for racial purposes were declared unconstitutional. (Source: Sauer, Carl O. "Geography and Gerrymander." *American Political Science Review,* 12 [1918]: 403–426).

to the spread of ideas or knowledge, thereby retarding diffusion (see box, *Political Boundaries as Barriers to Cultural Diffusion*). Clearly, the diffusionary concepts outlined in Chapter 1 can profitably be applied to political geography.

Country Building as Diffusion

Some independent countries sprang full-grown into the world, but most diffused outward from a small nucleus called a **core area,** annexing adjacent lands, often over many centuries. Generally, core areas possess a particularly attractive set of resources for human life and culture. Larger numbers of people cluster there than in surrounding districts, particularly if the area has some measure of natural defense against aggressive neighboring political entities. This denser population, in turn, may produce enough wealth to support a large army, which then provides the base for further expansion and relocation diffusion from the core area.

During this expansion, the core area typically remains the country's single most important district, housing the capital city and the cultural and economic heart of the nation. The core area functions as the node of

Political Boundaries as Barriers to Cultural Diffusion

Political boundaries can strongly affect how we look at the world. For instance, geographers have shown that a political boundary can be a strong barrier against the flow of information from one area to another. A study of schoolchildren in Dals Ed, in Sweden, and Halden, just across the border in Norway, shows that the children can easily recall place-names in their own country but not those of the neighboring country. Although language differences between Sweden and Norway are slight, the border puts a powerful barrier between schoolchildren only miles apart.

When the children of Dals Ed and Halden drew mental maps of both countries, each group showed a marked preference for its own national locations. On the Swedish maps, areas of desirability sloped gently away from Swedish places that the children knew. The nearby Norwegian border looked like a geological fault line. Preference suddenly dropped away.

A partial explanation for this is that the children on each side of the border are open to quite different sources of information. The Swedish geographer T. Lundén has analyzed textbooks on both sides of the border and has demonstrated clearly how the geographical content in them differs, always offering the readers more information about *us* than about *them.*

Adapted from Gould, Peter, and Rodney White. *Mental Maps.* Baltimore: Penguin, 1974, pp. 143–146.

a functional culture region. France expanded to its present size from a small core area around the capital city of Paris. China diffused from a nucleus in the northeast, and Russia originated in the small principality of Moscow, as Figure 4.10 shows. The United States grew westward from a core between Massachusetts and Virginia on the Atlantic coastal plain, an area that still has the national capital and the densest population.

Clearly, the diffusion of independent countries in this manner produces the **core/periphery** configuration, described in Chapter 1 as being typical of both functional and formal culture regions. The core dominates the periphery and a certain amount of friction exists between the two. Peripheral areas generally display pronounced, self-conscious regionalism, and occasionally provide the settings for secession movements.

Even so, countries that diffused from core areas are, as a rule, more stable than those created all at once to fill a political void. The absence of a core area, to which citizens can look as the national heartland, can leave a country's national identity blurred and makes it easier for various provinces to develop strong local or even foreign allegiances. Belgium and Zaïre offer examples of countries without political core areas.

Potentially, countries with multiple, competing core areas are the least stable of all. This situation often develops when two or more independent countries are united. The main threat is that one of the competing cores will form the center of a separatist movement and dissolve the country. In Spain, Castile and Aragon united in 1479, but the union remains shaky—in part because the old core areas of the two former countries, represented by the cities of Madrid and Barcelona, continue to compete for political control and to symbolize two language-based cultures, the Castilian and Catalonian.

Diffusion of Insurgencies and Innovations

The principles of cultural diffusion can also be applied to a great variety of other political phenomena. Insurgencies and guerrilla movements provide an example. The Arab uprising against Israeli rule in the occupied West Bank began late in 1987, and within a year had diffused

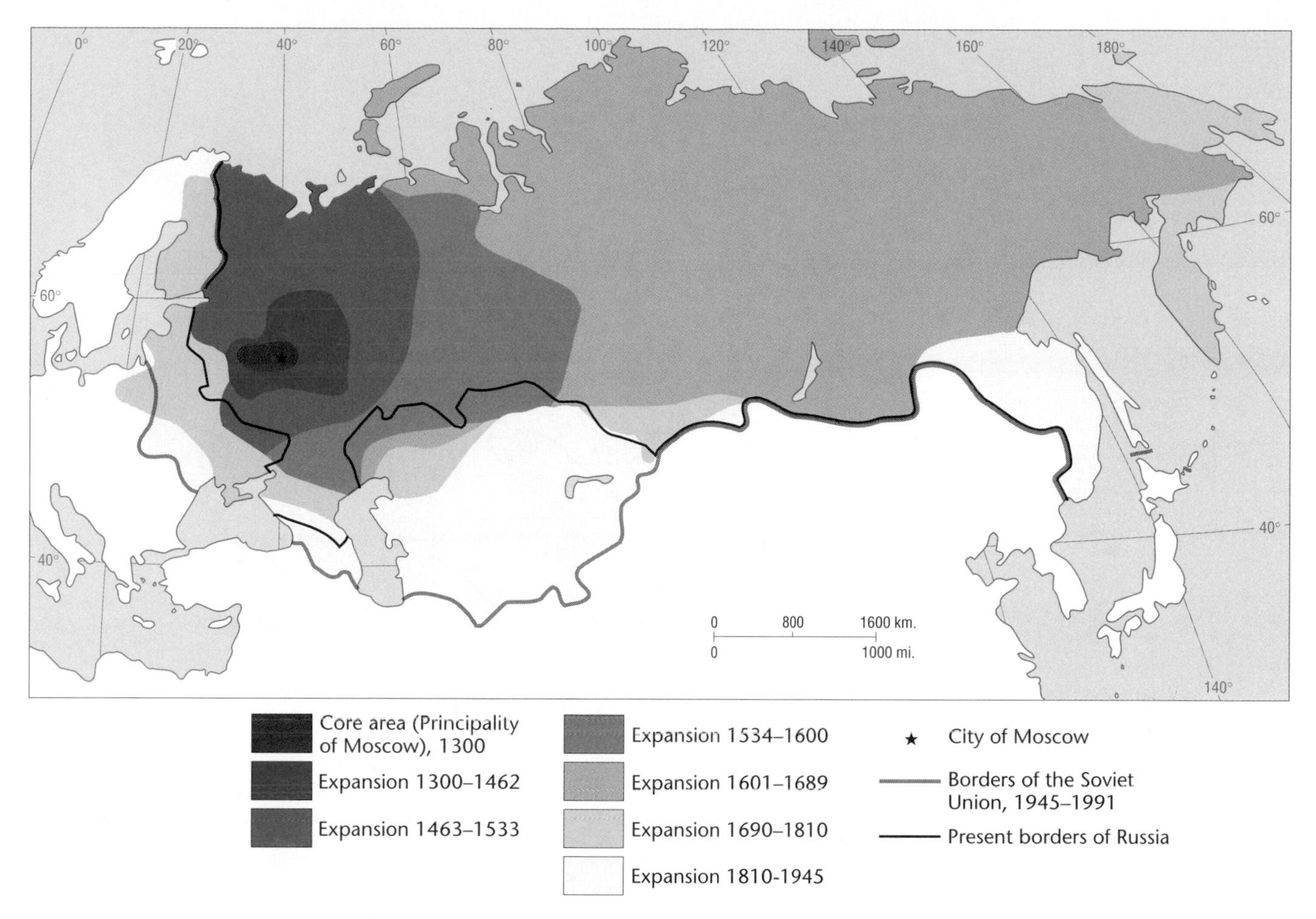

Figure 4.10
Russia developed from a core area. Can you think of reasons why expansion to the east was greater than to the west? What environmental goals might have motivated Russian expansion? What caused the recent contraction of the country?

through most of the area. Figure 4.11 raises interesting questions concerning what types of diffusion occurred and the barriers encountered.

Contagious expansion diffusion frequently operates in the political sphere. It can be seen in the spread of political independence in Africa. In 1914, only two African countries—Liberia and Ethiopia—were fully independent of European colonial or white minority rule. Ethiopia later fell temporarily under Italian control. Influenced by developments in India and Pakistan, the Arabs of North Africa began a movement for independence. Their movement began to gain momentum in the 1950s and swept southward across most of the continent between 1960 and 1965. By 1994, independence had spread into all remaining parts of the continent, even including the Republic of South Africa, formerly under white minority rule (Figure 4.12).

The diffusion of African self-rule occasionally encountered barriers. Spread of independence in the 1950s and 1960s occurred rapidly because most European powers had grown disenchanted with colonialism and viewed their African colonies more as burdens than assets. Portugal, by contrast, clung tenaciously to its African colonies until a change in government in Lisbon reversed a 500-year-old policy and the colonies were quickly freed. Similarly, France sought vainly to hold onto Algeria, since many European colonists had settled there.

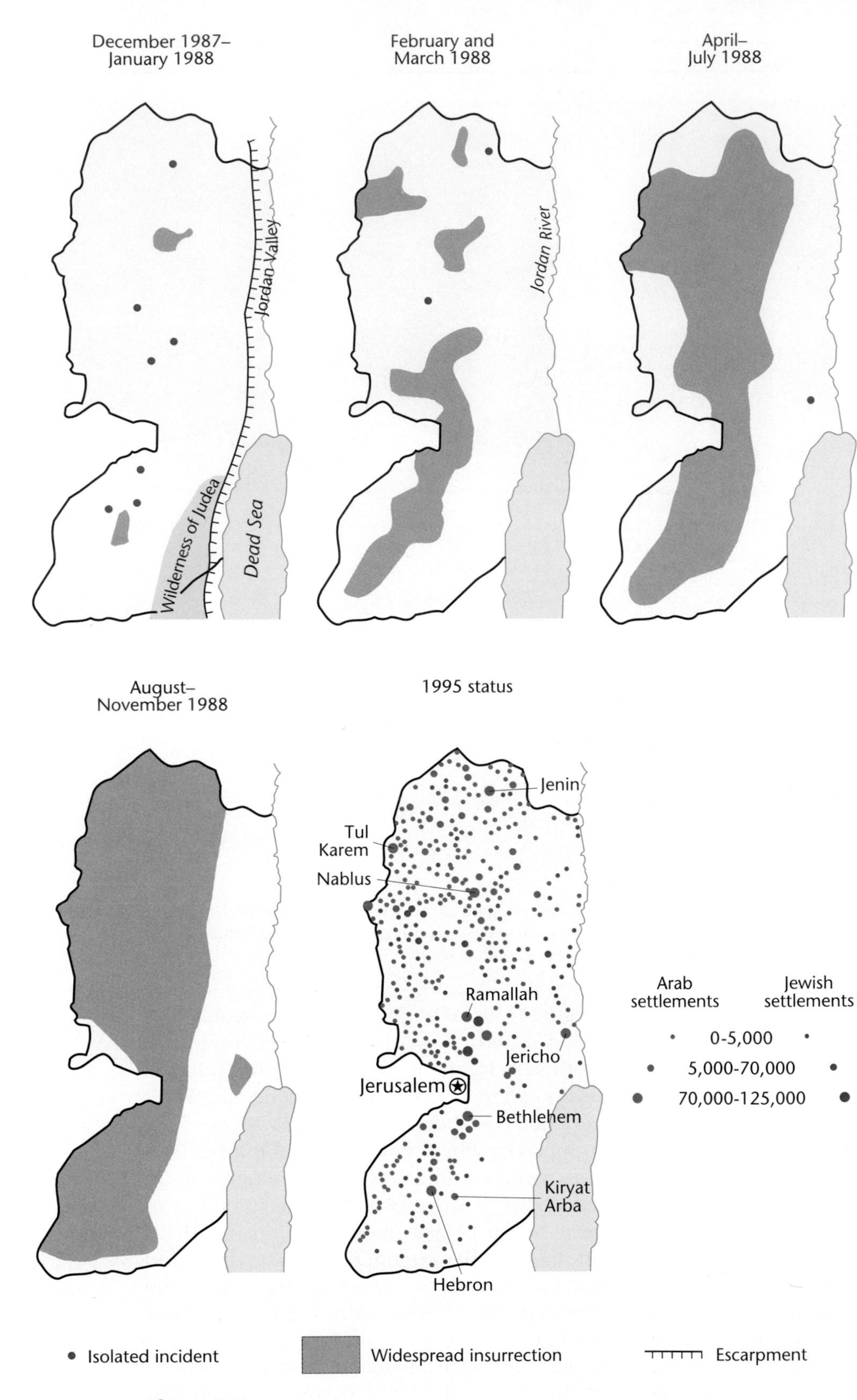

Figure 4.11

Diffusion of the Palestinian Arab uprising, or *intifada,* in the Israeli-ruled West Bank. What specific types of diffusion were seemingly involved? Do the separate nuclei of rebellion in the early stage indicate independent invention, hierarchical diffusion, or very rapid contagious diffusion? What barrier kept the *intifada* from diffusing into the eastern part of the West Bank? The Wilderness of Judea is an uninhabited desert badland, and the Jordan Valley is flat and intensively farmed. (Source: Adapted from Noble, Allen G., and Elisha Efrat. "Geography of the Intifada." *Geographical Review,* 80 [1990]: p. 300.)

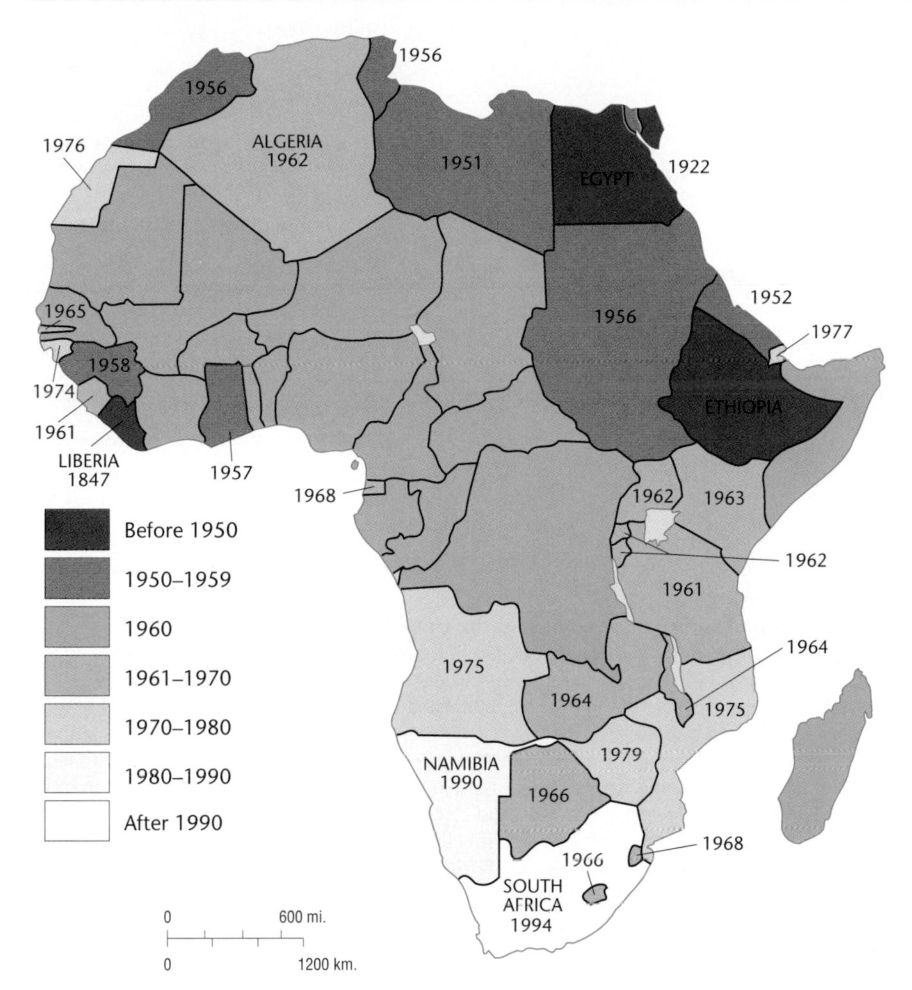

Figure 4.12
Independence from European colonial or white minority rule diffused through Africa. Independence for Africans was an idea first implanted in the northeastern and western reaches of the continent. Between 1959 and 1994, self-rule and independence spread all the way south.

On a quite different scale, political innovations also spread within independent countries. American politics abound with examples of cultural diffusion. A classic case is the spread of suffrage for women, a movement that began in the interior West and culminated in 1920 with the ratification of a constitutional amendment (Figure 4.13). Opposition to women's suffrage was strongest in the Deep South, a region that more recently has exhibited the greatest resistance to ratification of the Equal Rights Amendment and the most reluctance to elect women to public office.

Federal statutes permit, to some degree, laws to be adopted in the individual functional subdivisions. In the United States and Canada, for example, each state and province enjoys broad law-giving powers, vested in the legislative bodies of these subdivisions. The result is often a patchwork legal pattern that reveals the processes of cultural diffusion at work. A good example is provided by the movement to reduce littering by requiring beverage manufacturers to market their products in reusable or deposit containers (Figure 4.14). This innovation encountered barriers and failed to diffuse through the entire country.

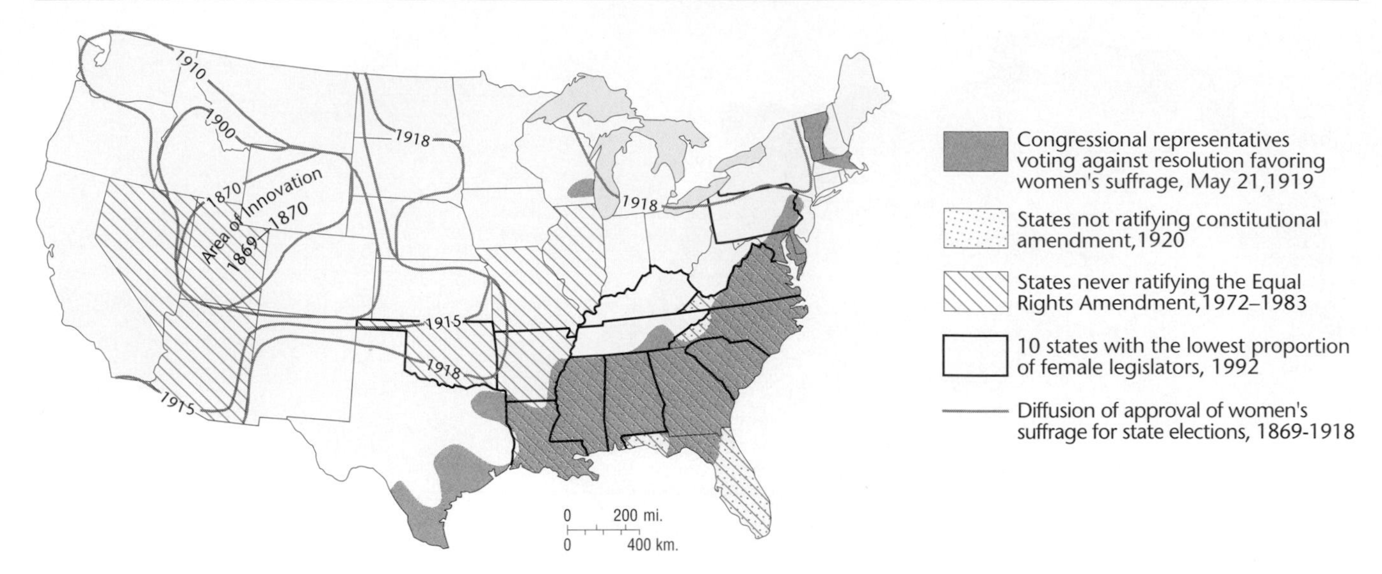

Figure 4.13
The diffusion of suffrage for women in the United States and the Equal Rights Amendment. The suffrage movement began in the West and diffused steadily for five decades, finally gaining national acceptance through a constitutional amendment in 1920. Both the suffrage movement and the campaign for an equal rights amendment (ERA) for women failed to gain approval in the Lower South, an area that also lags behind most of the remainder of the country in the election of women to public office. Compare this map to Figure 1.6. What might be the barriers to diffusion in the Lower South? The states failing to ratify the ERA lay mostly in the same area. Why did certain western states considered centers of suffrage innovation fail, generations later, to ratify the ERA? The ERA movement did not succeed, in contrast to the earlier suffrage movement. (Adapted in part from Paulin, C., and J. K. Wright. *Atlas of the Historical Geography of the United States.* New York: American Geographical Society and the Carnegie Institute, 1932.)

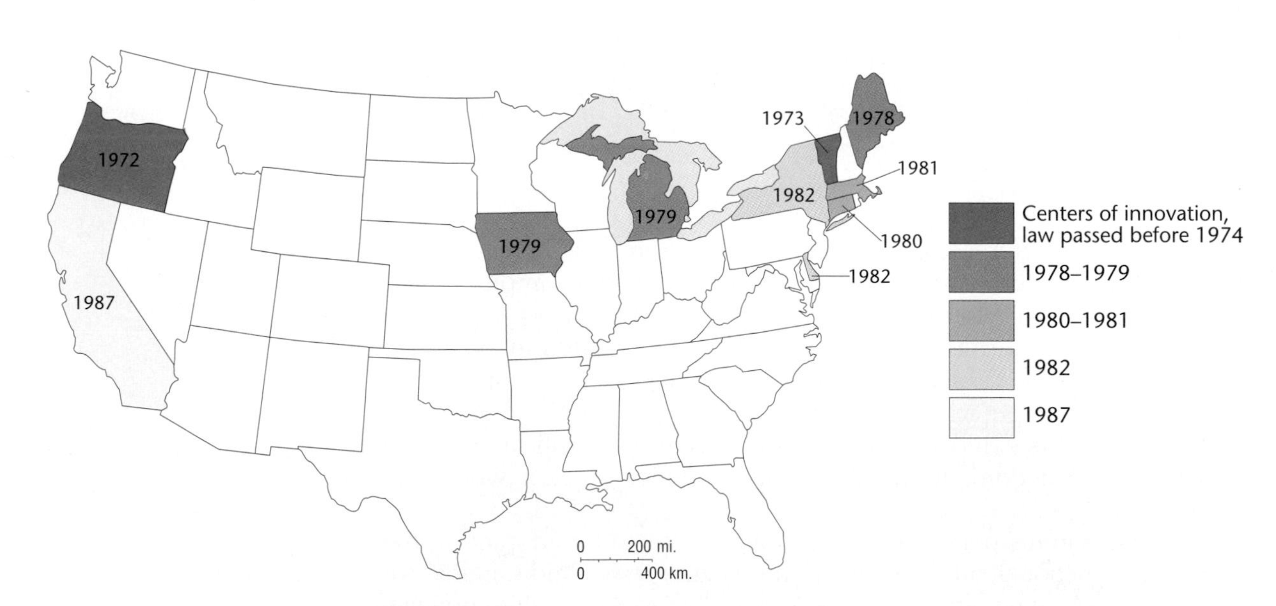

Figure 4.14
The diffusion of state laws requiring deposit or return beverage containers. Two states, one on the Pacific and the other far away in New England, served as the innovation centers. The movement met barriers to further diffusion. The California law of 1987 was far weaker than earlier ones, suggesting a permeable barrier. Beyond apparently lay absorbing barriers, because no additional states have passed such laws. What barriers might lie in the path of diffusion?

Political Ecology

Political culture regions do not exist, nor do political ideas diffuse, in an environmental vacuum. Spatial variations and the spread of political phenomena often can be linked to terrain, soils, climate, vegetation, and other facets of the physical environment. Conversely, established political authority can be a powerful instrument of environmental modification, providing the framework for organized alteration of the landscape and for environmental protection. In these ways, political entities influence and are influenced by the physical surroundings.

Folk Fortresses

Before modern air and missile warfare, a country's survival was enhanced by some sort of natural protection, such as surrounding mountain ranges, deserts, or seas; bordering marshes or dense forests; or outward-facing escarpments. Political geographers call natural strongholds **folk fortresses.** The folk fortress might shield an entire country or only its core area. In either case, a folk fortress was a valuable asset. Surrounding seas sheltered the British Isles from invasion for the last 900 years. In Egypt, desert wastelands on east and west insulated the fertile, well-watered Nile Valley core. In the same way, Russia's core area lay shielded by dense forests, expansive marshes, bitter winters, and vast distances.

Countries without natural defense have often been hard-pressed to maintain their independence. Korea, a land bridge leading from China to Japan, has repeatedly attracted invaders from both directions. Only rarely has Korea achieved unity and full independence. Poland, on the open plains of northern Europe, has been overrun and partitioned many times by hostile neighbors.

Closely related to the concept of the folk fortress is the distribution of terrain. Ideally, a country should have mountains and hills around its edges and plains in the interior (see box, *Terrain and Political Geography*). Such a pattern not only facilitates defense but also provides a natural unit of enclosed plains as the basis for a cohesive country. Few enjoy entirely satisfactory landform patterns, although France—centered on the plains of the Paris basin and flanked by bordering mountains and hills such as the Alps, Pyrenees, Ardennes, and Jura—comes very close to the ideal (Figure 4.15). Mountain-ridge borders are also desirable, because they stand out on the landscape and cross thinly populated country. Rivers, by contrast, prove much less suitable as borders. They often change course and frequently flow through densely settled valleys, creating all sorts of potentially provocative situations for the countries on either bank.

An undesirable arrangement of physical features may disrupt a country's internal unity. A mountain range, a desert, or some other barrier cutting through the middle of the territory forms perhaps the worst pattern imaginable from the perspective of internal unity. Such barriers disrupt communications and often isolate one part of a country from another. Separatist sentiments grow more easily when shielded by environmental barriers. In addition, internal mountain ranges provide excellent potential guerrilla bases where insurgents can live in relative safety. Peru, which straddles the Andes with fringes of territory in the Amazon basin and the Pacific coastal lowlands, faces such a problem. So does

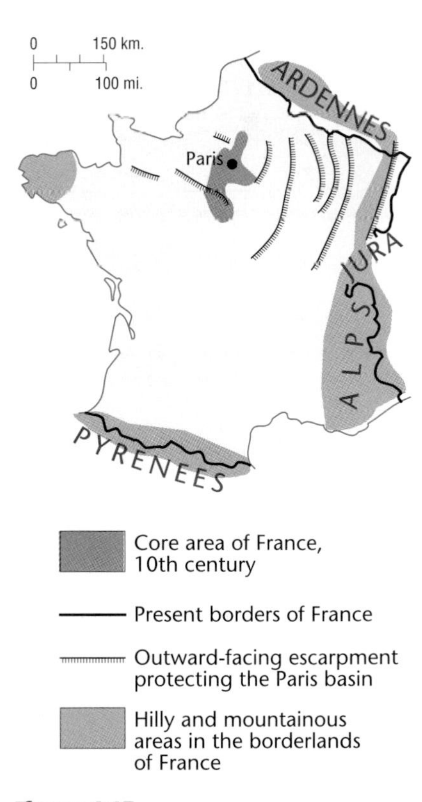

Figure 4.15
The French distribution of landforms. Such terrain features as ridges, hills, and mountains offer protection. Outward-facing escarpments formed a folk fortress protecting the core area and capital of France until as recently as World War I. Hill districts and mountain ranges lent stability to French boundaries in the south and southeast.

Terrain and Political Geography

Berchtesgaden, situated in the Bavarian Alps, lies amid a wreath of high mountains. In the era before modern transportation and communication, these mountains isolated and sheltered the valley, shielding it from both cold winter winds and invading armies.

In this setting, Berchtesgaden developed as an independent principality ruled by a religious order. For six and one-half centuries, from 1156 to 1803, Berchtesgaden maintained its independence, three times as long as the United States. The borders of the principality, which followed the surrounding mountain ridges, scarcely changed at all during this long period. Even after Berchtesgaden lost its independence and was annexed by Bavaria and later Germany, most of its mountain-marked border survived as part of the international boundary between Germany and Austria. In this way, terrain and the political pattern often are linked.

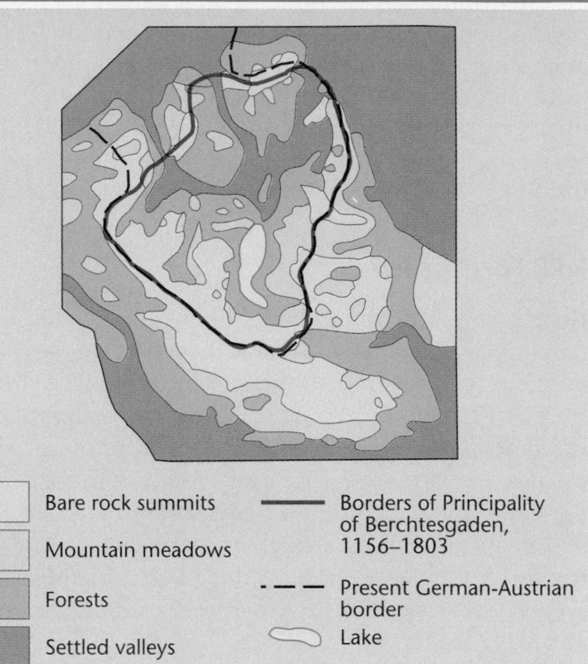

Spain, which consists of a number of plains areas separated by hills and mountains. Both Peru and Spain have problems of internal unity, partly because of their unfavorable physical settings.

Perhaps the best borders of all for independent countries are those marked by seacoasts. Islands and the small continent that hosts Australia provide excellent natural barriers to expansive or acquisitive neighbors. Among others, Iceland, Sri Lanka, and Madagascar have benefited from their island locations. However, island nations are not necessarily free from attacks by neighbors, as the histories of Hawaii, Cuba, and the Philippines show. In addition, disputes still arise among independent countries about the placement of borders in adjacent ocean areas. Peninsular location provides some of the same advantages as islands for such countries as Italy, India, and Turkey, although peninsulas usually prove harder to defend.

Expanding countries often regard coastlines as the logical limits to their territorial growth, even if they belong to other countries. This was true of the United States' drive to the Pacific Ocean in the first half of the nineteenth century, an expansion justified by the doctrine of ***manifest destiny.*** This doctrine was based on the belief that the Pacific shoreline offered the logical and predestined western border for the United States. A somewhat similar doctrine long led Russia to seek expansion in the directions of the Mediterranean and Baltic seas, Pacific and Indian oceans.

The Heartland Theory

Discussions of environmental influence, manifest destiny, and the outward probings of Russia lead naturally to one of the earliest geopolitical theories, the **heartland theory** of Halford Mackinder (see biographical sketch). As early as 1904, Mackinder became concerned with the balance of power in the world and in particular with the possibility of world conquest.

His theory, heavily tinged with environmental determinism, held that the continent of Eurasia would be the most likely base from which a successful campaign for world conquest could be launched. Eurasia dwarfs all other continents in size and natural resources and is home to three-fourths of the human race. In examining this huge landmass, Mackinder discerned two environmental regions. The **heartland,** or interior, of Eurasia lies remote from the sea, except for the frozen ocean of the polar north, which functions more as a continuation of the Eurasian landmass (Figure 4.16).

The densely populated coastal fringes of Eurasia in the east, south, and west (see Chapter 2), called the **rimland,** form the second great physical-strategic region of Eurasia. Remote from the sea, the heartland was invulnerable to the naval power of the former great rimland empires such as Britain and Japan, but the cavalry and infantry of the heartland could spill out through diverse natural gateways and invade the rimland region. In fact, mounted nomadic warriors had done just that from time immemorial, surging outward to conquer and pillage. The Mongol conquest of China and Tatar depredations in Europe provide historical examples. For this reason, in Mackinder's view, a unified heartland power could with impunity probe into the coastlands, eventually conquering the maritime countries and annexing their navies. This sea power could then be turned against the outlying continents and islands until the entire world was subject to the heartland.

Mackinder believed that the unification of the heartland could best be achieved from the East European Plain, the most densely populated and economically productive part of the heartland. Russia had already achieved that unification at the time he proposed the theory. Mackinder, in effect, predicted Russian conquest of the world, a prospect that became more alarming after the Communist revolution there in 1917. The leaders of rimland empires and the United States employed a policy of containment by fortifying the rimland and fighting numerous wars against outward probes by heartland-based Communism. This policy, in no small measure, found its origin in Mackinder's theory.

In this way, a political geographer's theory entered the halls of government and influenced strategic decisions for a half-century or more. Overlooked all the while were the fallacies of the heartland theory. Mackinder had overestimated the power potential of the thinly settled Eurasian interior, which consists largely of frozen tundra, parched desert, and expansive forests. He failed to anticipate the role of airborne warfare and ballistic missiles, as well as the inherent economic weakness of the Marxist system. Russia proved unable to hold together its own heartland empire, much less conquer the rimland and world. In the final analysis, Mackinder's heartland theory, influential as it was, belongs to the discredited doctrine of environmental determinism and serves as yet another warning against such simplistic reasoning.

Halford J. Mackinder
1861–1947

Mackinder developed a fascination for spatial patterns and maps at a young age. At school in England, he was caned by a teacher for drawing maps instead of writing Latin exercises. His interest in geography persisted, and in 1887 he became one of Oxford University's first lecturers in geography.

Much influenced by the scientific geography found in nineteenth-century German universities, Mackinder introduced many of the German concepts into England. Previously, the Royal Geographical Society of London had been interested mainly in exploration rather than in analytical studies and theories. Mackinder's famous heartland theory was first proposed in a scholarly address to the society in 1904 and was later enlarged to book form. He served as a member of Parliament for 12 years, and after World War I he helped redraw the boundaries of Europe. In 1945, he received the Royal Geographical Society's highest honor, the Patron's Medal. His influence on analytical political geography and on the foreign policy decisions of the great powers was very great indeed. (For more on Mackinder and his work, see Parker, W. H. *Mackinder: Geography as an Aid to Statecraft.* Oxford: Clarendon Press, 1982; and Blouet, Brian W. *Halford Mackinder: A Biography.* College Station: Texas A&M University Press, 1987.)

Warfare and Environmental Destruction

Many political actions and decisions have an ecological impact, but perhaps none as devastating as warfare. "Scorched earth," the systematic destruction of resources, has for millennia been a favored practice of

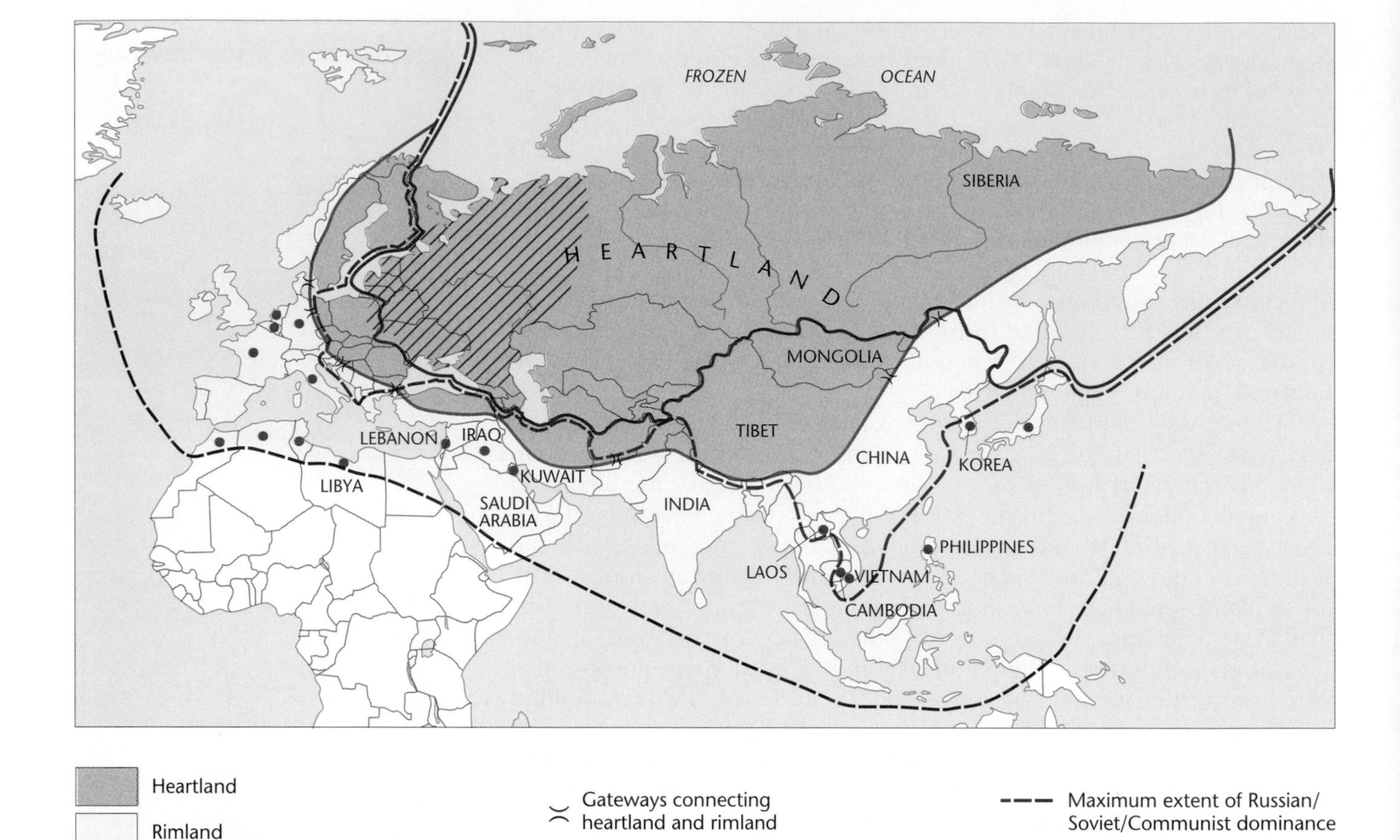

Figure 4.16
Heartland versus rimland in Eurasia. For most of the twentieth century, the heartland, epitomized by the Soviet Union and Communism, was seen as a threat to America and the rest of the world, a notion based originally on the environmental-deterministic theory of the political geographer Halford Mackinder. Control of the East European Plain would permit rule of the entire heartland, which, in turn, would be the territorial base for world conquest. The United States and its rimland allies sought to counter this perceived menace by a policy of containment—resisting every expansionist attempt by the heartland powers. (After Mackinder and Spykman, with liberal modification.)

retreating armies. Even military exercises and tests can be devastating. Certain islands in the Pacific were rendered uninhabitable, perhaps forever, by American hydrogen bomb testing in the 1950s, and, as geographer Susan Cutter pointed out, General Patton's tank exercises in the desert of southern California over 50 years ago damaged the natural vegetation so extensively that only about a third has since recovered.

Cutter went on to catalog the environmental catastrophes associated with the six-week Persian Gulf War of 1991, including an oil spill of 294 million gallons (1.1 billion liters) covering 400 square miles (1000 km^2) in the Gulf waters, with attendant floral and faunal loss; oil fields ablaze; the mass bulldozing of sand by the Iraqis to make defensive berms, with attendant wind erosion and loss of vegetation; and the solid-waste pollution produced by 500,000 Coalition forces in the Arabian desert, including 6 million plastic bags discarded weekly by American forces alone (Figure 4.17).

Clearly, warfare—and especially modern "high-tech" warfare—is environmentally catastrophic. From an ecological standpoint, it does

Figure 4.17
A Kuwaiti oil field ablaze during the Persian Gulf War, 1991. Severe ecological damage almost invariably accompanies warfare.

not matter who started or won a war. The point is, rather, that everyone loses when such destruction occurs, given the worldwide interconnectedness of the life-supporting ecosystem.

Politico-Cultural Integration

Although we learn a great deal from studying how the physical environment and political phenomena interact, we gain an even broader perspective by examining the ties between politics and other facets of culture. The growth of independent countries, voting patterns, and other topics that interest political geographers are largely explained in cultural terms. In addition, political decisions often have far-reaching effects on the distribution of such cultural elements as economy, land use, and migration. Indeed, the political organization of territory, both past and present, is revealed to some degree in almost every facet of culture.

The Nation-State

The link between political pattern and culture finds its epitome in the **nation-state,** a type of independent country that results when a people of common heritage, homeland, and culture, speaking the same language and/or sharing a particular religious faith, possess a desire for nationhood and achieve political independence. In other words, nationality is culturally defined in the nation-state, and the raison d'être lies in that cultural identity. The more the people have in common culturally, the more stable and potent is the resultant nationalism.

While some experts regard the nation-state as a modern aberration, largely a product of the nineteenth and twentieth centuries, such countries, at least on the regional level, have in fact characterized much of human history and might be linked to instinctual territoriality.

Examples of modern nation-states include Germany, Sweden, Japan, Greece, Armenia, and Finland (Figure 4.18). Each of these countries has a culturally homogeneous population, with only small minority groups. Their homogeneity represents a centripetal force. Many other independent countries also function as nation-states because power rests in the hands of a dominant, nationalistic cultural group, but sizable ethnic minorities reside in the national territory as second-class citizens. They present a centrifugal force disrupting the country's unity (Figure 4.18). Israel is such a nation-state, a Jewish country by definition trying to cope with a sizable, restive, underprivileged Arab minority. Similarly, many of the new nation-states carved out of the defunct Soviet Union and Yugoslavia, such as Estonia, Georgia, and Croatia, contain large, territorially compact ethnic minorities, as do some much older nation-states, including France and China. In sum, we can define a nation-state as an independent country that exists as the result of the efforts and desires of a culturally homogeneous and powerful majority.

The Multinational Country

Numerous independent countries—the large majority, in fact—are not nation-states. Instead, they possess some other raison d'être and usually have federal rather than strong central governments. Switzerland, Canada, the United Kingdom, South Africa, and Belgium provide exam-

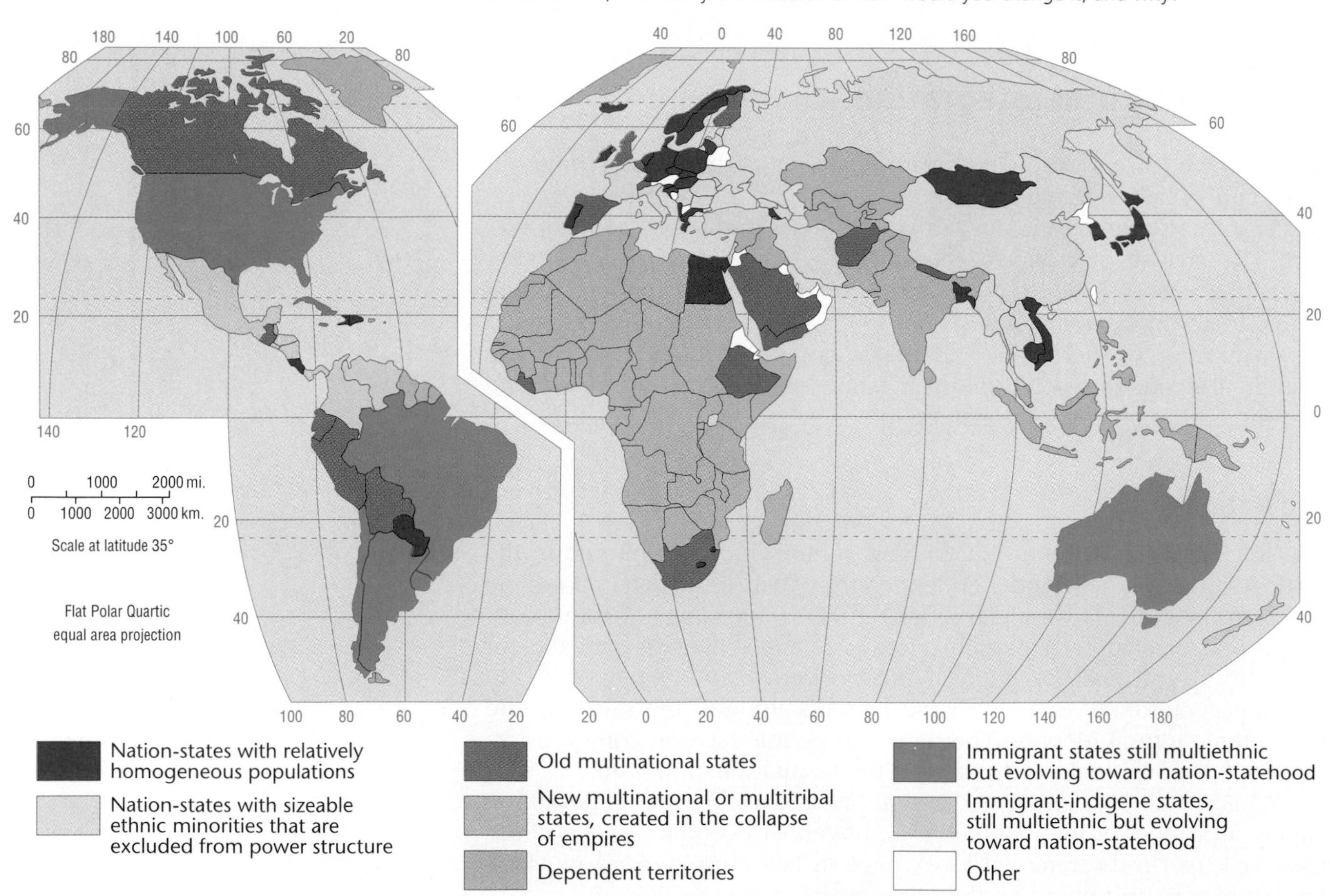

Figure 4.18
Nation-states, multinational countries, and other types. This classification, as is true of all classifications, is arbitrary and debatable. How would you change it, and why?

ples of older multinational countries (Figure 4.19). A much larger number have arisen in recent decades, as a result of the collapse of European-based colonialism, mainly in Africa. Political boundaries drawn in colonial times without regard to the integrity of cultural or tribal groups passed down, unaltered, to the newly independent countries. As a result, their populations are often quite diverse.

Ethnic Separatism

Ethnic groups are cultural minorities living in multinational countries (see Chapter 9 for a full discussion of ethnicity). We live in an age of rising ethnic nationalism, in which numerous such minorities pursue separatism to gain independence. We witness today the continued rise of the nation-state, as one ethnic minority after another demands independence or autonomy (Figure 4.20). This separatist mood has touched multinational countries and nation-states alike. Even some old and traditionally stable multinational countries have felt the effects of this movement, including Canada and the United Kingdom. Some multinational countries collapsed under the pressure, splintering into multiple nation-states. The Soviet Union, Yugoslavia, and Czechoslovakia provide examples. Certain other countries, such as Ethiopia, discarded the unitary form of government and adopted an ethnic-based federalism, in hopes of preserving unity. The impact of ethnic nationalism ranges from simple unrest to insurgencies, forced deportations, attempted genocides, and successful secessions.

Figure 4.19
Languages of the Republic of South Africa, a multinational state. The mixture includes two languages introduced by settlers from Europe and 11 native tribal tongues. (Source: I. van der Merwe, with modifications.)

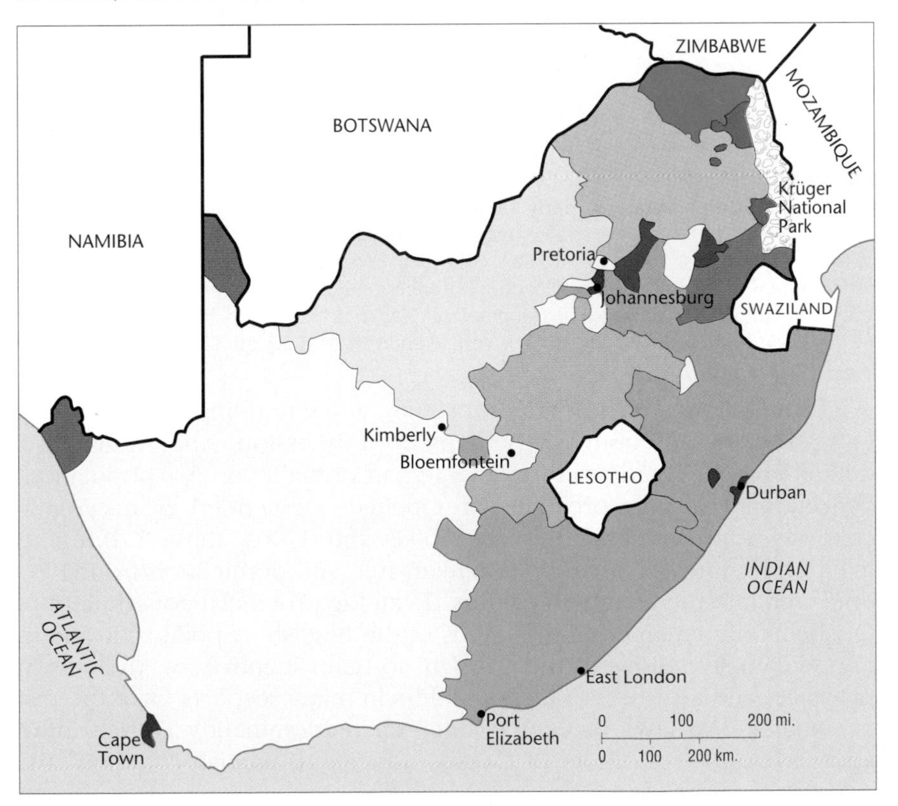

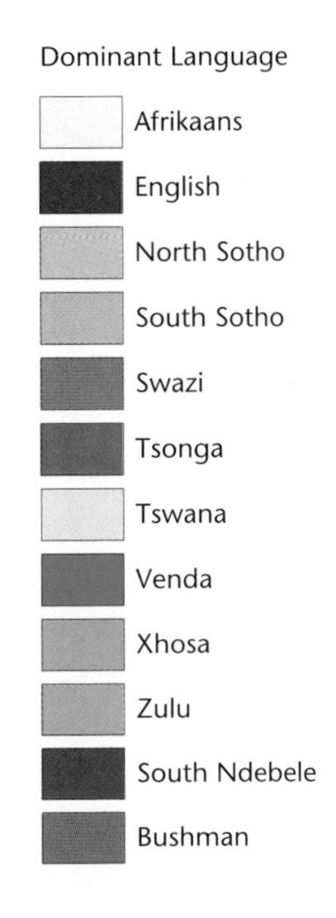

Recent territorial
ethnic problems reflected in:

- Attempted genocide by a ruling group
- Forced removal of ethnic population
- Successful secession of ethnic minority
- Ongoing ethnic separatist strife or civil war
- Largely nonviolent ethnic unrest

Figure 4.20

Ethnic separatism and unrest, early 1990s. Many independent countries now face ethnic problems and some have disintegrated under such pressures. Solutions have ranged from secession to genocide. (Sources: Smith, Dan. "The Sixth Boomerang: Conflict and War," in Susan George, *The Debt Boomerang.* London: Pluto Press, 1992, pp. 140–142; Oldale, John. "Government-Sanctioned Murder." *Geographical Magazine,* 62 [1990]: 20–21; Lean, Geoffrey, et al. *Atlas of the Environment.* New York: Prentice-Hall, 1990, pp. 50–51.)

Francophones in Canada represent a cultural-linguistic minority group seeking autonomy or perhaps even secession. Approximately 7 million French Canadians form a large part of that country's population, concentrated in the province of Québec. Descended from French colonists who immigrated in the 1600s and 1700s, these *Canadiens* lived under English or Anglo-Canadian rule and domination from 1760 until well into the twentieth century. Even the provincial government of Québec long remained in the hands of the English. A political awakening eventually allowed the French to gain control of their own province, and as a result Québec differs in many respects from the rest of Canada. The laws of Québec retain a predominantly French influence, while the remainder of Canada adheres to English common law.

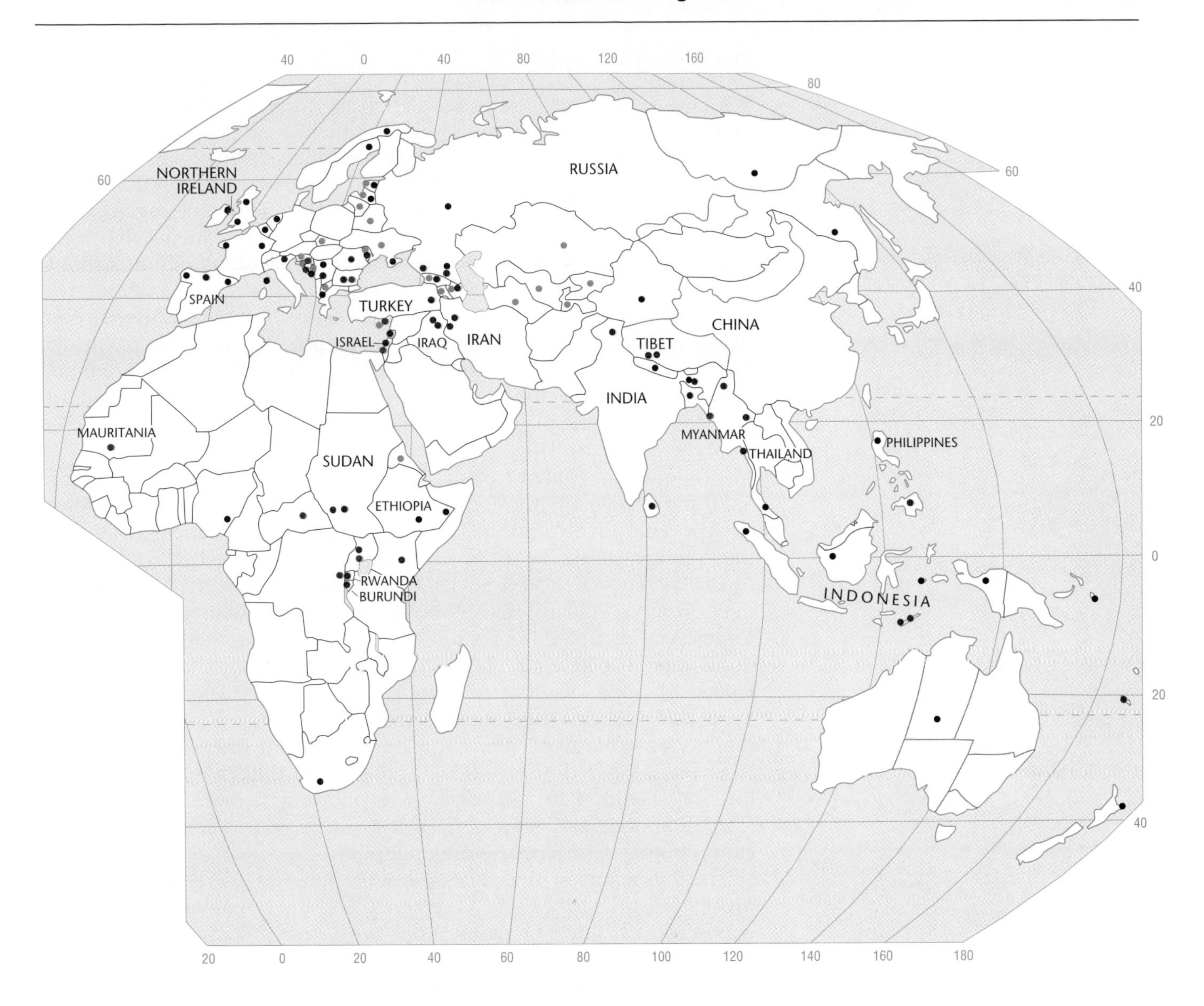

The provincial flag, adopted in 1948, preserves the old fleur-de-lis symbol of the French monarchy. French is the sole legal language of Québec, and visible use of English, illegal until recently, was expunged. In several elections, a sizable minority among the French-speaking population voted for Québec independence, and many Anglo-Canadians emigrated from the province. The issue remains unresolved. In 1995 over half of the French-speaking electorate voted for independence but the non-French minority in the Province tipped the boat narrowly in favor of continued union with Canada.

As a result of such unrest and separatist desires, the number of ethnographic political boundaries has proliferated. Increasingly, the international political map has taken on a linguistic-religious character. Even so, the distribution of cultural groups is so confoundedly complicated and peoples are so confusingly mixed in many regions that ethnographic political boundaries can rarely be drawn to everybody's satisfaction. Border wars and the forced migration of minorities could become alarmingly common in the decades ahead.

The Cleavage Model

Why do so many cultural minorities seek political autonomy or independence? Perhaps a model developed in electoral geography can help explain this phenomenon as well as shed light on regional voting patterns. Called the **cleavage model** and originally proposed by Stein Rokkan and Seymour Lipset, it proposes that persistent regional patterns in voting behavior (which, in extreme cases, can presage separatism) can usually be explained in terms of tensions pitting national core area versus peripheral districts, urban versus rural, capitalists versus workers, and power-group culture versus minority culture. Not infrequently, these tensions coincide geographically, with the result that the core area monopolizes power and wealth, is more urbanized, and links government to the ruling elite culture. Ethnic minorities, then, often live in peripheral, largely rural, and less affluent areas, excluded from the power structure.

The great majority of ethnic separatist movements shown in Figure 4.20, and particularly those that have moved beyond unrest to violence or secession, involve groups living in national peripheries, away from the core area of the country. Every republic that seceded from the defunct, Russian-dominated Soviet Union lay on the borders of that former country. Similarly, the Slovenes and Croats, who withdrew from Yugoslavia, occupied border territories peripheral to Serbia and the national capital at Belgrade. Northern Ireland lies on the periphery of the United Kingdom, as does rebellious Kurdistan in relation to Iraq, Iran, Syria, and Turkey—the countries that currently rule the Kurdish lands (Figure 4.21). Restive Tibet is on the margins of China, and the Arab West Bank–Gaza districts under Israeli rule are likewise peripheral in location (Figure 4.20). Slovakia, long poorer and more rural than the Czech Republic and remote from the center of power at Prague, became another secessionist ethnic periphery.

In a few cases, the secessionist peripheries were actually more prosperous than the political core area, and the separatists resented the confiscation of their taxes to support the less affluent core. Slovenia and Croatia both occupied such a position in the former Yugoslavia.

Federalist government reduces such core versus periphery tensions and decreases the appeal of separatist movements. Switzerland epitomizes such a country, and as a result has been able to join Germans, French, Italians, and speakers of Raeto-Romansh into a single, stable independent country. Canada developed toward a Swiss-type system, extending considerable self-rule privileges even to the Inuit and Indian groups of the north.

Political Imprint on Economic Geography

The core-periphery economic contrasts implicit in the cleavage model clearly reveal that the internal spatial arrangement of the independent country influences economic patterns, presenting a cultural integration of politics and economy. In addition, laws differ from one country to another, and these laws often have an impact on economic land use. As a result, political boundaries can take on an economic character as well.

For example, the United States–Canadian border in the Great Plains crosses an area of environmental and cultural sameness. The land and people on both sides of the boundary are similar. Yet the presence of

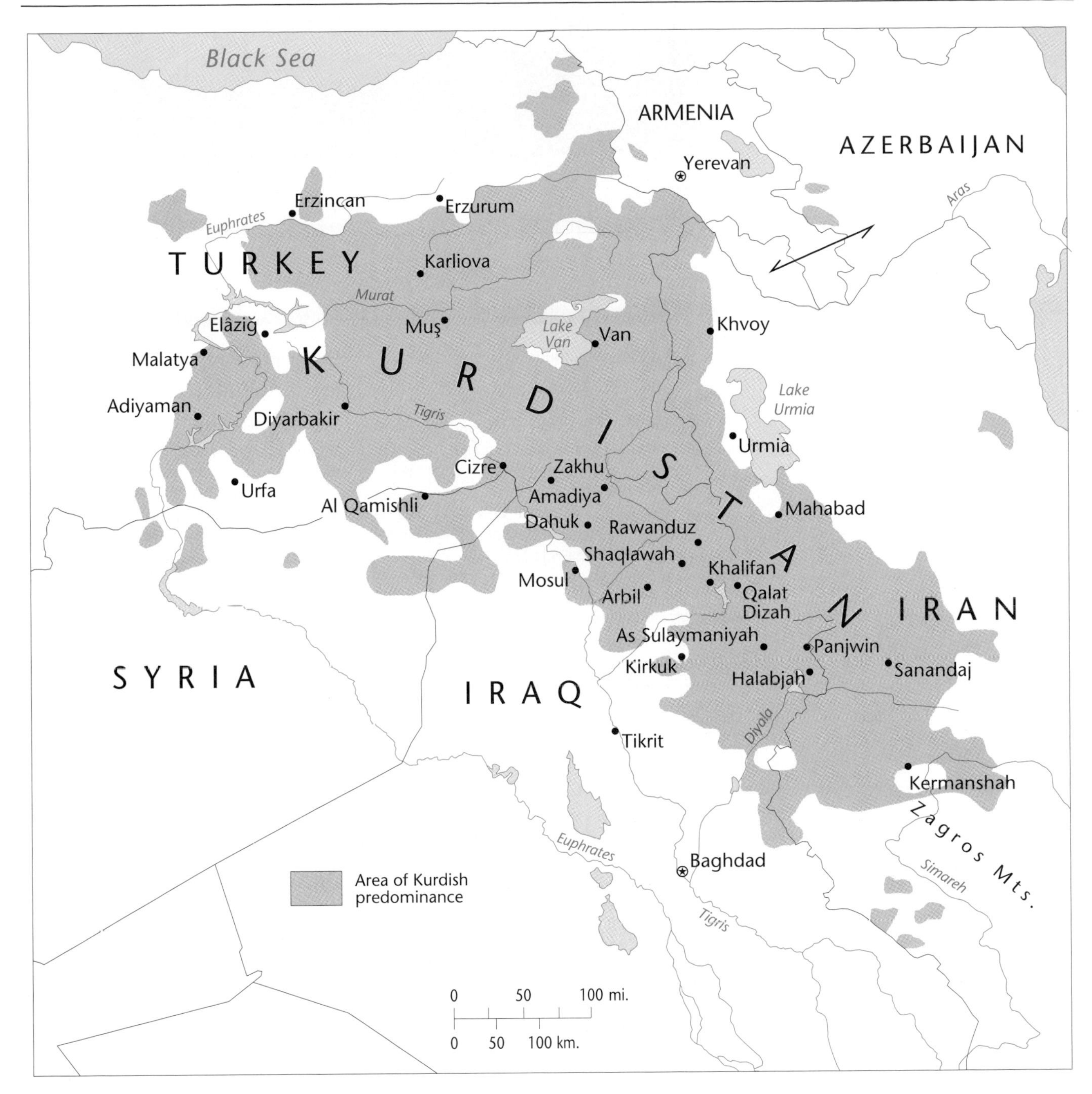

Figure 4.21
Kurdistan. This mountainous homeland of the Kurds now lies divided between several countries. The Kurds, numbering 25 million, have lived in this region for millennia. They seek independence and have waged guerrilla war against Iran, Iraq and Turkey, but so far, independence has eluded them. (Source: US Dept. of State, Office of the Geographer.)

the border, representing two different bodies of law and regulations, fostered differences in agricultural practices. In the United States, an act passed in the 1950s encouraged sheep raising by guaranteeing an incentive price for wool. No such law was passed in Canada. As a result, sheep became far more numerous on the American side of the border, while Canadian farmers devoted more attention to hogs. Figure 4.22 illustrates the difference.

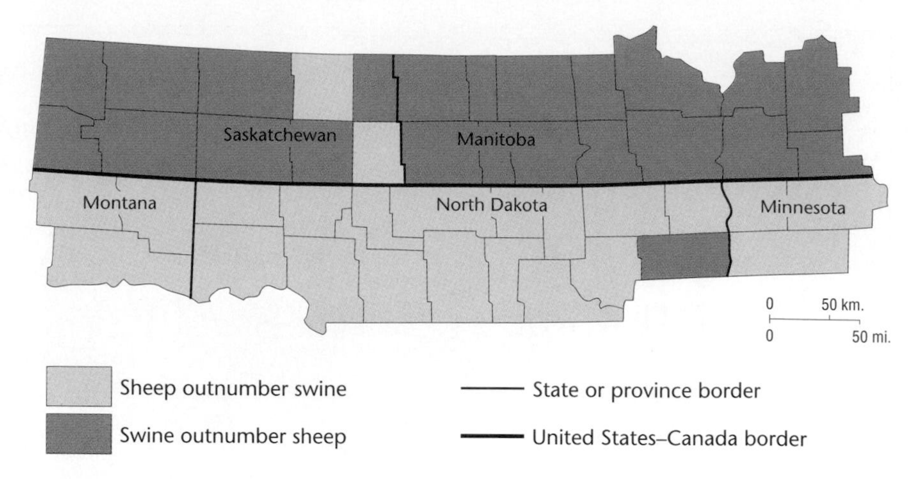

Figure 4.22
The political impact on economy. Government intervention can be seen in the choice of livestock in the border area between the United States and Canada. Sheep are more numerous than swine on the United States side of the boundary, in part because of government-backed price incentives for wool. The map reflects conditions in the 1960s. Since then, the contrast has essentially disappeared. Why might that have happened? (Source: Reitsma, Hendrik J. "Crop and Livestock Production in the Vicinity of the United States–Canada Border." *Professional Geographer,* 23 [1971]: 220–221. See also his sequel article, "Agricultural Changes in the American–Canadian Border Zone, 1954–1978." *Political Geography Quarterly, 7* [1988]: 23–38.)

Borders also usually cause economic disruptions. Highway networks become fragmentary in border zones, due to the need to control crossings from one country to another (Figure 4.23). In extreme cases, borders are closed, causing the flow of goods to cease altogether.

Political Landscapes

Various types of political decision making find a visible expression, and the cultural landscape reveals the imprint of politics in diverse ways. Nationalism, separatism, the legal code, and central authority can all be highly visible, as can the boundaries separating independent countries. All of these, collectively, constitute the political landscape.

Imprint of the Legal Code

Many laws find their way into the cultural landscape. Among the most noticeable are those that regulate the land-surveying system, because the law often requires that land be divided into specific geometric patterns (see Chapter 3). Political boundaries can, as a result, become highly visible (Figure 4.24). In Canada, the laws of the French-speaking province of Québec encourage land survey in long, narrow parcels, but most English-speaking provinces, such as Ontario, adopted a rectangular system. As a result, the political border between Québec and Ontario can be spotted easily from the air.

Legal decisions made long ago by vanished governments can remain imprinted on the landscape. For example, Denmark ruled the provinces of Schleswig and Holstein, now largely held by Germany, until the 1860s. During that period, Danish laws broke up farm villages and dispersed the rural population in isolated farmsteads. At the same time, many fragmented landholdings were combined into unit-block

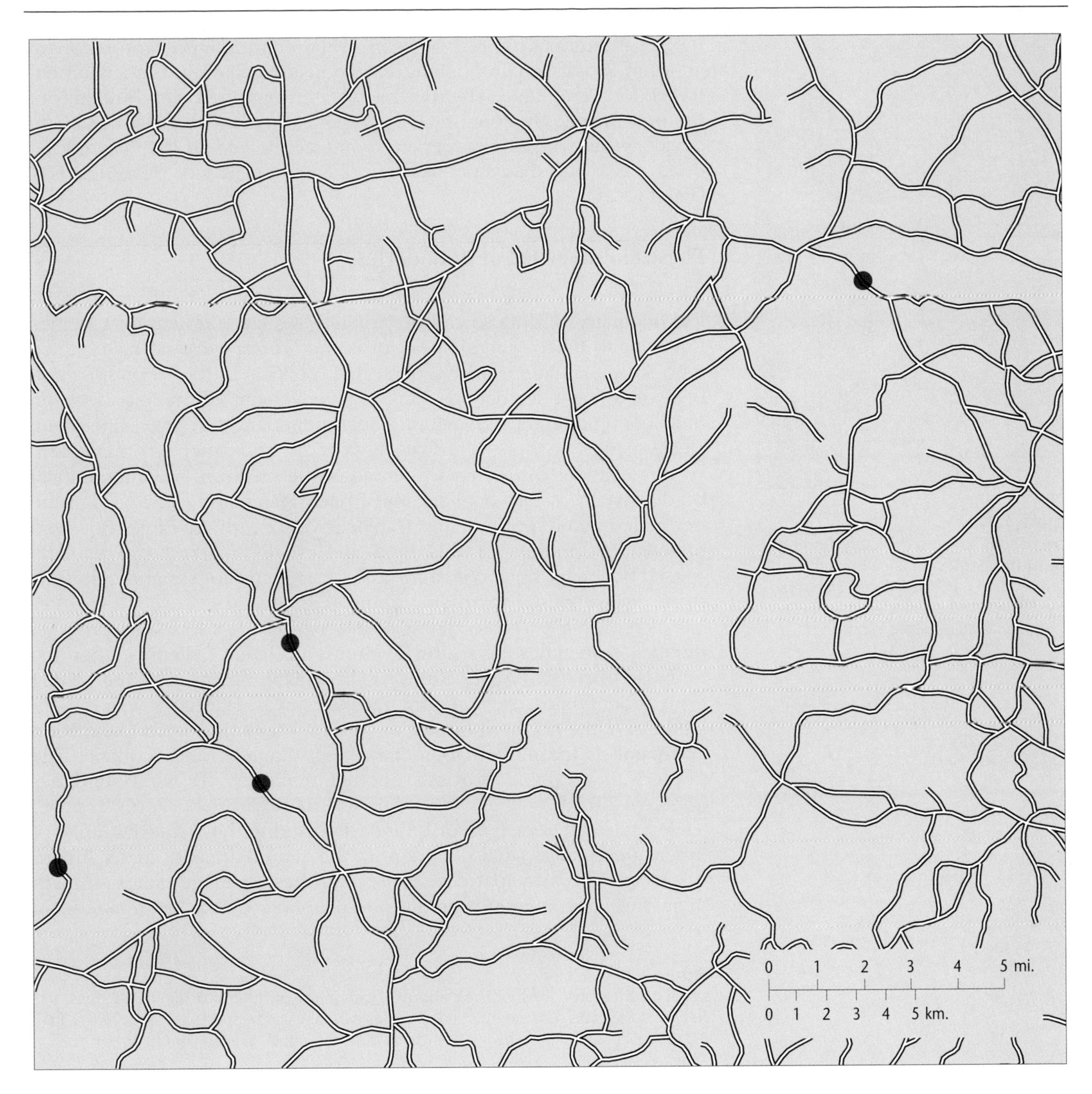

Figure 4.23
International political boundaries can influence transportation networks. This map shows the pattern of motorable roads along a section of the Austrian-Czech border in central Europe. The border is not shown, but disruptions in the road network should let you find it. Draw it with a highlight pen. (Sources: Adapted from *Die General Karte* (Österreich), sheet 3, Mairs Geographischer Verlag and Shell Oil, 1994; and *Auto Atlasz Csehország-Szlovákia*. Prague: Kartografie and Nagy, 1994, pp. 33–34, 48–49; all maps at a 1:200,000 scale.)

farms. In nearby German-ruled provinces, different laws prevailed, and the population and property lines remained unchanged. Today, even though Germany has ruled Schleswig-Holstein for over a century, the old border is still clearly visible in the settlement landscape.

Figure 4.24
You should have no difficulty finding the United States–Mexico border in this picture. Why does the cultural landscape so vividly reveal the political border? The scene is near Mexicali, the capital of Baja California Norte.

Legal imprint can also be seen in the cultural landscape of urban areas. In Rio de Janeiro, height restrictions on buildings have been enforced for a long time. The result is a waterfront lined with buildings of uniform height. By contrast, most American cities have no height restrictions, allowing skyscrapers to dominate the central city. The consequence is a jagged skyline, like that of San Francisco or New York City (Figure 4.25).

Physical Properties of Boundaries

Perhaps no more purely human creation exists than a demarcated political boundary, and these can be strikingly visible. Geographers Dennis Rumley and Julian Minghi speak of *border landscapes* and have edited a book by that name. As a general rule, political borders are most visible where tight restrictions limit the movement of people between neighboring countries. Sometimes such boundaries are even lined with cleared strips, barriers, pillboxes, tank traps, and other obvious defensive installations. At the opposite end of the spectrum are international borders, such as that between the United States and Canada, that are unfortified, thinly policed, and in places very nearly invisible. But even undefended borders of this type are usually marked by regularly spaced boundary pillars or cairns and by customs houses and colorfully striped guardhouses at crossing points (Figure 4.26).

Moreover, the visible aspect of international borders is surprisingly durable, sometimes persisting centuries or even millennia after the boundary becomes relic. Ruins of boundary defenses, some dating from ancient times, are common in certain areas. Hadrian's Wall in England marks the northern border during one stage of Roman occupation and parallels the modern border between England and Scotland. The Great Wall of China provides another reminder of past boundaries (Figure 4.27).

A quite different type of boundary, marking the territorial limits of urban street gangs, is also evident in the central areas of many American cities. The principal device used by these teenage gangs to mark their "turf" is spray-paint graffiti. Geographers David Ley and Roman

Figure 4.25
Legal height restrictions, or their absence, can greatly influence urban landscapes. New York City lacks such controls and its skyline is punctuated by spectacular skyscrapers. In Rio de Janeiro, by contrast, height restrictions allow the natural environment to provide the "high-rises."

Figure 4.26
Even peaceful, unpoliced international borders often appear vividly in the landscape. Sweden and Norway insist on cutting a swath through the forest to mark their common boundary.

Cybriwsky studied this phenomenon in Philadelphia. They found borders marked by externally directed, aggressive epithets, taunts, and obscenities, placed there for the benefit of neighboring gangs. A street gang of white youths, for example, plastered its border with a black gang's neighborhood with slogans like "White Power," "Do Not Enter

Figure 4.27
The Great Wall of China is likely the most spectacular political landscape ever created and one of the few features made by humans that is visible from outer space. Fifteen hundred miles (2400 kilometers) long, the wall was constructed over many centuries by the Chinese in an ultimately unsuccessful attempt to protect their northern boundary from adjacent tribes of nomadic herders.

[District]21-W,—," and similar graffiti painted on walls. The gang's "core area," its "home corner," contains internally supportive graffiti, such as "Fairmount Rules" or a roster of gang members. Thus a perceptive (and courageous) observer can map the gang territories on the basis of these political landscape features.

The Impress of Central Authority

The attempt to impose centralized government appears in many facets of the landscape. Railroad and highway patterns focused on the national core area, and radiating like the spokes of a wheel to reach the hinterlands of the country, provide good indicators of central authority. In Germany, the rail network developed largely before unification of the country in 1871. As a result, no focal point stands out. On the other hand, the superhighway system of autobahns, encouraged by Hitler as a symbol of national unity and power, tied the various parts of the *Reich* to such focal points as Berlin and the Ruhr industrial district.

"Military landscapes" also abound, directly linked to central authority's defense of the country and often concentrated in border districts. The military presence can result in fairly sizable areas being cleared of its permanent inhabitants in order to provide space for defensive installations and maneuvers.

The visibility of provincial borders within a country can reflect the central government's strength and stability. Stable, secure countries, such as the United States, often permit considerable display of provincial borders. Most state boundaries within the United States are marked with signboards or other features announcing the crossing. By contrast, unstable countries, where separatism threatens national unity, often suppress such visible signs of provincial borders.

National Iconography on the Landscape

The cultural landscape is rich in symbolism and visual metaphor, and political messages are often conveyed through such means with an intensity that varies greatly from one country to another. In the United States, flags and eagles convey clear messages to citizen and visitor alike. Statues of national heroes or heroines and of symbolic figures such as the goddess Liberty or Mother Russia form important parts of the political landscape, as do assorted monuments (Figure 4.28). The elaborate use of national colors can be very powerful visually. Landscape symbols such as the Rising Sun flag of Japan, the American eagle or Statue of Liberty in New York Harbor, or the Latvian independence pillar in Riga (which stood unmolested throughout half a century of Russian-Soviet rule) evoke deep patriotic emotions. The sites of heroic (if often futile) resistances against invaders, as at Masada fortress in Israel and the Alamo in Texas, prompt similar feelings of nationalism.

Figure 4.28
Mount Rushmore, in the Black Hills of South Dakota, presents a highly visible expression of American nationalism, an element of the political landscape.

Conclusion

Political spatial variations—from local voting patterns to the spatial arrangement of international power blocs—add yet another dimension to the complex human mosaic. In particular, independent countries function as vital culture regions. They help shape many other facets of culture. Political culture regions constantly change as political innovations ebb and flow across their surfaces. Political phenomena as varied as the nation-state, separatist movements, women's suffrage, and the territorial expansion of countries move along the paths of diffusion.

Cultural ecology helps us understand the links between systems of power and the physical environment. Countries do not exist in an environmental vacuum. The spatial patterns of landforms frequently find reflection in boundaries, core areas, folk fortresses, and global strategies.

The cultural integration approach underscores the relationships between politics and other facets of culture. Harmony and stability within countries often depend on relative cultural homogeneity of the population. The integration of politics and culture is also revealed in the economy, and politics leaves diverse imprints on the cultural landscape.

Sources and Suggested Readings

Agnew, John A. *Place and Politics: The Geographical Mediation of State and Society*. Winchester, MA: Allen & Unwin, 1987.

Archer, J. Clark, and Peter J. Taylor. *Section and Party: A Political Geography of American Presidential Elections, from Andrew Jackson to Ronald Reagan*. New York: Wiley, 1981.

Bateman, Michael, and Raymond Riley (eds.). *The Geography of Defense*. New York: Barnes & Noble, 1987.

Blomley, Nicholas K. *Law, Space, and the Geographies of Power*. New York: Guilford, 1994.

Brunn, Stanley D. "A World of Peace and Military Landscapes." *Journal of Geography*, 86 (1987): 253–262.

Brunn, Stanley D., and Ernie Yanarella. "Towards a Humanistic Political Geography." *Studies in Comparative International Development*, 22 (1987): 3–49.

Burghardt, Andrew. "The Core Concept in Political Geography: A Definition of Terms." *Canadian Geographer*, 13 (1969): 349–353.

Chaliand, Gerard, and Jean-P. Rageau. *Strategic Atlas: A Comparative Geopolitics of the World's Powers*, 3d ed. New York: HarperCollins, 1992.

Cohen, Saul B. "Global Geopolitical Change in the Post-Cold War Era." *Annals of the Association of American Geographers*, 81 (1991): 551–580.

Drake, Christine. "National Integration in China and Indonesia." *Geographical Review*, 82 (1992): 295–312.

Easterly, Ernest S. III. "Global Patterns of Legal Systems." *Geographical Review*, 67 (1977): 209–220.

Elazar, Daniel J. *The American Mosaic: The Impact of Space, Time, and Culture on American Politics*. Boulder, CO: Westview Press, 1994.

Frenkel, Stephen. "Geography, Empire, and Environmental Determinism." *Geographical Review*, 82 (1992): 143–153.

Glassner, Martin I. *Neptune's Domain: A Political Geography of the Sea*. New York: HarperCollins, 1990.

Glassner, Martin I. *Political Geography*. New York: Wiley, 1993.

Gottmann, Jean. *The Significance of Territory*. Charlottesville: University of Virginia Press, 1973.

Gottmann, Jean. (ed.). *Center and Periphery: Spatial Variation in Politics*. Beverly Hills, CA: Sage, 1980.

Gottmann, Jean. "The Basic Problem of Political Geography: The Organization of Space and the Search for Stability." *Tijdschrift voor Economische en Sociale Geografie*, 73 (1982): 340–349.

Holdsworth, Deryck W. "Architectural Expressions of the Canadian National State." *Canadian Geographer*, 30 (1987): 167–171.

Hooson, David. (ed.). *Geography and National Identity*. Oxford, UK: Blackwell, 1994.

House, John W. *Frontier on the Rio Grande: A Political Geography of Development and Social Deprivation.* New York: Oxford University Press, 1982.

Johnston, Ronald J., David B. Knight, and Eleanore Kofman (eds.). *Nationalism, Self-Determination, and Political Geography.* London: Croom Helm, 1988.

Johnston, Ronald J., Fred M. Shelley, and Peter J. Taylor (eds.). *Developments in Electoral Geography.* London: Routledge, 1990.

Kaplan, David H. "Two Nations in Search of State: Canada's Ambivalent Spatial Identities." *Annals of the Association of American Geographers,* 84 (1994): 585–606.

Kent, Robert B. "Geographical Dimensions of the Shining Path Insurgency in Peru." *Geographical Review,* 83 (1993): 441–454.

Kliot, Nurit, and Stanley Waterman (eds.). *Pluralism and Political Geography: People, Territory and the State.* New York: St. Martin's Press, 1983.

Kliot, Nurit, and Stanley Waterman. *The Political Geography of Conflict and Peace.* London: Belhaven Press, 1991.

Knight, David B. "Impress of Authority and Ideology on Landscape: A Review of Some Unanswered Questions." *Tijdschrift voor Economische en Sociale Geografie,* 63 (1971): 383–387.

Knight, David B. "Identity and Territory: Geographical Perspectives on Nationalism and Regionalism." *Annals of the Association of American Geographers,* 72 (1982): 514–531.

Ley, David, and Roman Cybriwsky. "Urban Graffiti as Territorial Markers." *Annals of the Association of American Geographers,* 64 (1974): 491–505.

Lipset, Seymour M., and Stein Rokkan (eds.). *Party Systems and Voter Alignments: Cross-National Perspectives.* New York: Free Press, 1967.

Lutz, J. M. "Diffusion of Nationalist Voting in Scotland and Wales: Emulation, Contagion and Retrenchment." *Political Geography Quarterly,* 9 (1990): 249–266.

Mackinder, Halford J. "The Geographical Pivot of History." *Geographical Journal,* 23 (1904): 421–437.

Martis, Kenneth C. *The Historical Atlas of Political Parties in the United States Congress, 1789–1989.* New York: Macmillan, 1989.

Martis, Kenneth C. "Sectionalism and the United States Congress." *Political Geography Quarterly,* 7 (1988): 99–109.

May, R. J. "Ethnic Separatism in Southeast Asia." *Pacific Viewpoint,* 31 (1990): 28–59.

McColl, Robert W. "The Insurgent State: Territorial Base of Revolution." *Annals of the Association of American Geographers,* 59 (1969): 613–631.

Mikesell, Marvin W. "The Myth of the Nation State." *Journal of Geography,* 82 (1983): 257–260.

Morrill, Richard L. *Political Redistricting and Geographic Theory.* Washington, DC: Association of American Geographers, Resource Publications, 1981.

Murphy, Alexander B. "Territorial Policies in Multiethnic States." *Geographical Review,* 79 (1989): 410–421.

Nijman, Jan (ed.). "The Political Geography of the Post Cold War World." *Professional Geographer,* 44 (1992): 1–29.

O'Loughlin, John (ed.). *Dictionary of Geopolitics.* Westport, CT: Greenwood Press, 1994.

O'Loughlin, John. "The Identification and Evaluation of Racial Gerrymandering." *Annals of the Association of American Geographers,* 72 (1982): 165–184.

O'Sullivan, Patrick. *Geopolitics.* New York: St. Martin's Press, 1986.

O'Sullivan, Patrick, and Jesse W. Miller, Jr. *The Geography of Warfare.* New York: St. Martin's Press, 1983.

Parker, Geoffrey. *Western Geopolitical Thought in the Twentieth Century.* New York: St. Martin's Press, 1985.

Political Geography (formerly *Political Geography Quarterly,* name changed in 1992). The only English-language journal devoted exclusively to political geography. Published in the United Kingdom by Butterworth Scientific Ltd., Sevenoaks, Kent, England. Volume I appeared in 1982.

Poulsen, Thomas M. *Nations and States: A Geographical Background to World Affairs.* Englewood Cliffs, NJ: Prentice-Hall, 1995.

Prescott, J. R. V. *Political Frontiers and Boundaries.* Winchester, MA: Allen & Unwin, 1987.

Rumley, Dennis, and Julian V. Minghi (eds.). *The Geography of Border Landscapes.* London: Routledge, 1991.

Sack, Robert D. *Human Territoriality: Its Theory and History.* Studies in Historical Geography, No. 7. Cambridge, UK: Cambridge University Press, 1986.

Short, John R. *An Introduction to Political Geography,* 2d ed. London: Routledge, 1994.

Siverson, Randolph M., and Harvey Starr. *The Diffusion of War.* Ann Arbor, MI: University of Michigan Press, 1991.

Slowe, Peter M. *Geography and Political Power: The Geography of Nations and States.* London: Routledge, 1990.

Spykman, Nicholas J. *The Geography of the Peace.* New York: Harcourt Brace, 1944.

Studies in Comparative International Development. This international journal devoted all four numbers of Volume 22 (1987–1988) and part of Volume 23 (1988–1989) to "Geography and National & International Issues."

Sutton, Imre. "Sovereign States and the Changing Definition of the Indian Reservation." *Geographical Review,* 66 (1976): 281–295.

Taylor, Peter J. *Political Geography of the Twentieth Century.* London: Longman, 1993.

Wallerstein, Immanuel. *Geopolitics and Geoculture: Essays on the Changing World-System.* Cambridge, UK: Cambridge University Press, 1991.

Whittlesey, Derwent "The Impress of Effective Central Authority Upon the Landscape." *Annals of the Association of American Geographers,* 25 (1935): 85–97.

Williams, Colin H. "Ideology and the Interpretation of Minority Cultures." *Political Geography Quarterly,* 3 (1984): 105–125.

Williams, Colin H. *Linguistic Minorities, Society, and Territory.* Clevedon, UK: Multilingual Matters, 1991.

Zelinsky, Wilbur. *Nation into State: The Shifting Symbolic Foundations of American Nationalism.* Chapel Hill: University of North Carolina Press, 1988.

In Figure 4.3, *A* is Armenia; *B,* Azerbaijan; *C,* Iran; *a,* Nagorno-Karabakh; *b,* the Nakhichevan Autonomous Republic; *c,* the Okhair Eskipara enclave; *d,* Sofulu enclave; *e,* Kyarki enclave; and *f,* Bashkend enclave.

באלט ריגה
אגם הברבורים
בריכת השולטן ירושלים
יום ג' 27.6.89 בשעה 20

CHAPTER 5

The Mosaic of Languages

Language contains the very essence of culture and provides the single most common variable by which different cultural groups are identified. A mutually agreed-upon system of symbolic communication, language offers the main means by which learned customs and skills pass from one generation to the next. Because languages vary spatially and tend to form spatial groupings, they reinforce the sense of region and place. Yi-Fu Tuan even wrote of "the role of human speech in the creation of place." Language also facilitates cultural diffusion of innovations and even helps shape the way we think or how we perceive our environment. For all these reasons and more, cultural geographers study language, employing the five themes of region, diffusion, ecology, integration, and landscape. The terms *linguistic geography* and **geolinguistics** describe this branch of the discipline.

Most cultural groups have their own distinctive form of speech, either a separate language or a dialect. **Languages** can be defined as tongues that cannot be mutually understood. A monolingual speaker of one language cannot comprehend the speaker of another. **Dialects,** by comparison, are variant forms of a language that have not lost mutual comprehension. A speaker of English can generally understand the various dialects of that language, regardless of whether the speaker comes from Australia, Scotland, or Mississippi. But the dialect is still distinctive enough in vocabulary and pronunciation as to label its speaker. Some 6000 languages and many more dialects are spoken today.

Often when different linguistic groups come into contact, a **pidgin** language results. It serves the purposes of commerce and has a small vocabulary derived from the various groups in contact. An example is the largely English-derived pidgin spoken in Papua New Guinea, where it has become the official national language in a nation where many native Papuan tongues are spoken. The New Guinea pidgin includes Spanish, German, and Papuan words in addition to English and is not readily intelligible to a speaker of English. In other situations, one existing language may be elevated to the status of **lingua franca,** or language of communication and commerce, over a wide area where it is not a mother tongue. The Swahili language enjoys this status in much of East Africa.

The logical place to begin our geographical study of languages, dialects, and pidgins is with the theme of culture region. We will find that the spatial variation of speech is remarkably complicated, adding deep hues to the human mosaic.

Linguistic Culture Regions

Many different kinds of formal culture regions can be devised on the basis of speech. They range from those depicting the distribution of individual words to those revealing the broad range of differences in vocabulary, grammar, and pronunciation among separate dialects and languages.

The borders of individual word usages or pronunciations are called **isoglosses.** No two words, phrases, or pronunciations have exactly the same spatial distribution; that is, no two isoglosses are duplicates. Figure 5.1 provides an example of how isoglosses crisscross one another. Geographers commonly devise multitrait formal linguistic culture regions, seeking borders where numerous features of speech change. Isoglosses typically cluster together, and these "bundles" serve as the

Figure 5.1
Isoglosses cluster into "bundles." Many words have been adopted from Spanish into English in the western and southern parts of Texas. Note that the isogloss for each of these representative "loanwords" is slightly different from every other one but that the result is a "bundle" of isoglosses, dividing Texas into two dialect regions. (Source: Atwood, E. B. *The Regional Vocabulary of Texas.* Austin: University of Texas Press, 1962.)

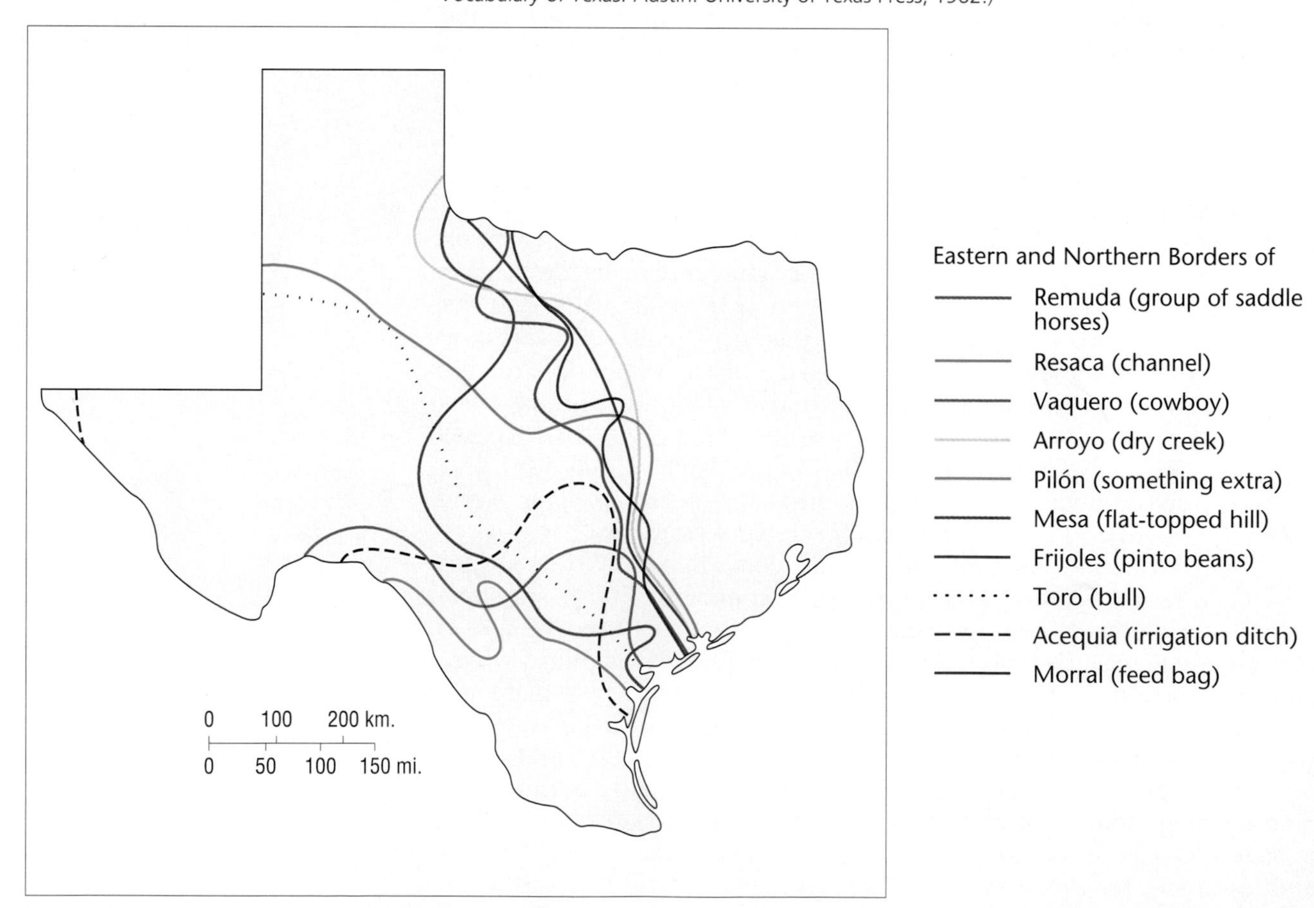

most satisfactory dividing lines among dialects and languages. Another complicating factor in drawing linguistic borders is the overlap of languages that normally occurs. In any given area, more than one tongue may be spoken, as in the mountains of Ecuador (Figure 5.2).

As a result, language boundaries are rarely sharp, in keeping with the general character of cultural borders. Rather than a dividing line, the geographer encounters a **core/periphery** pattern, in which dominance of the language diminishes away from the center of the region, through an outlying zone of bilingualism, or spatial mixing of speakers of two different languages. Linguistic "islands," separated from the main body of a language, often further complicate the drawing of borders (Figure 5.2).

Similarly, dialect terms often overlap considerably, making it difficult to draw isoglosses. Indeed, linguistic geographers often disagree about how many dialects are present in an area and where isoglosses should be drawn. One scholar surveys the speech of the American South and detects two major dialects; another equally qualified linguist surveys the same evidence in the same area and concludes that only one dialect, containing four subdialects, exists. Still another expert asks, in all seriousness, "Do dialect borders exist?" Linguistic borders on maps, like all formal cultural boundaries, are necessarily simplified and, at best, generalizations. Still, the linguistic culture region is a convenient and necessary device to facilitate the spatial study of language.

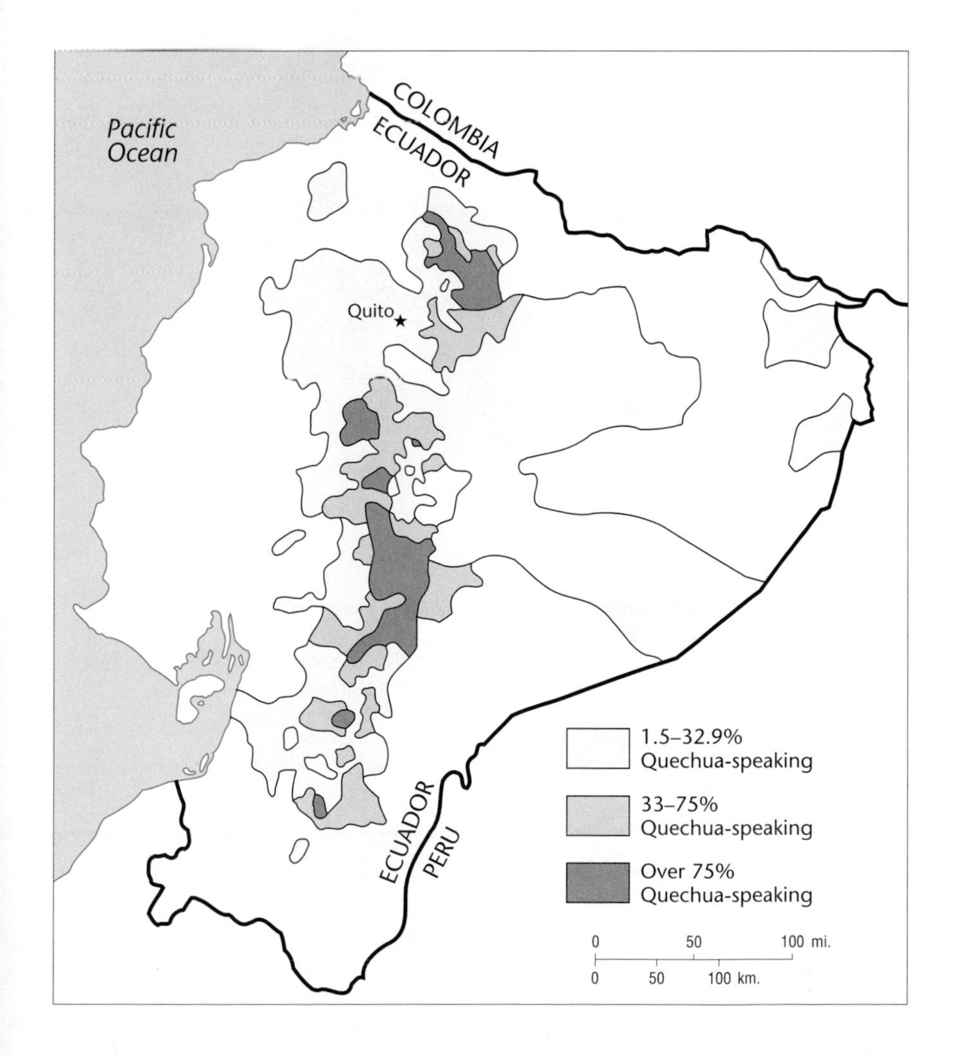

Figure 5.2
The formal culture region of Quechua, the main Indian language of Ecuador, South America, 1950. The core/periphery configuration typical of formal regions is evident. Urban populations are excluded. Does the distribution of Quechua, mapped in this manner, suggest whether the language is advancing or retreating? (Source: Knapp, Gregory. *Geografía Quichua de la Sierra del Ecuador.* Quito: Ediciones Abya Yala, 1987, pp. 53–57.)

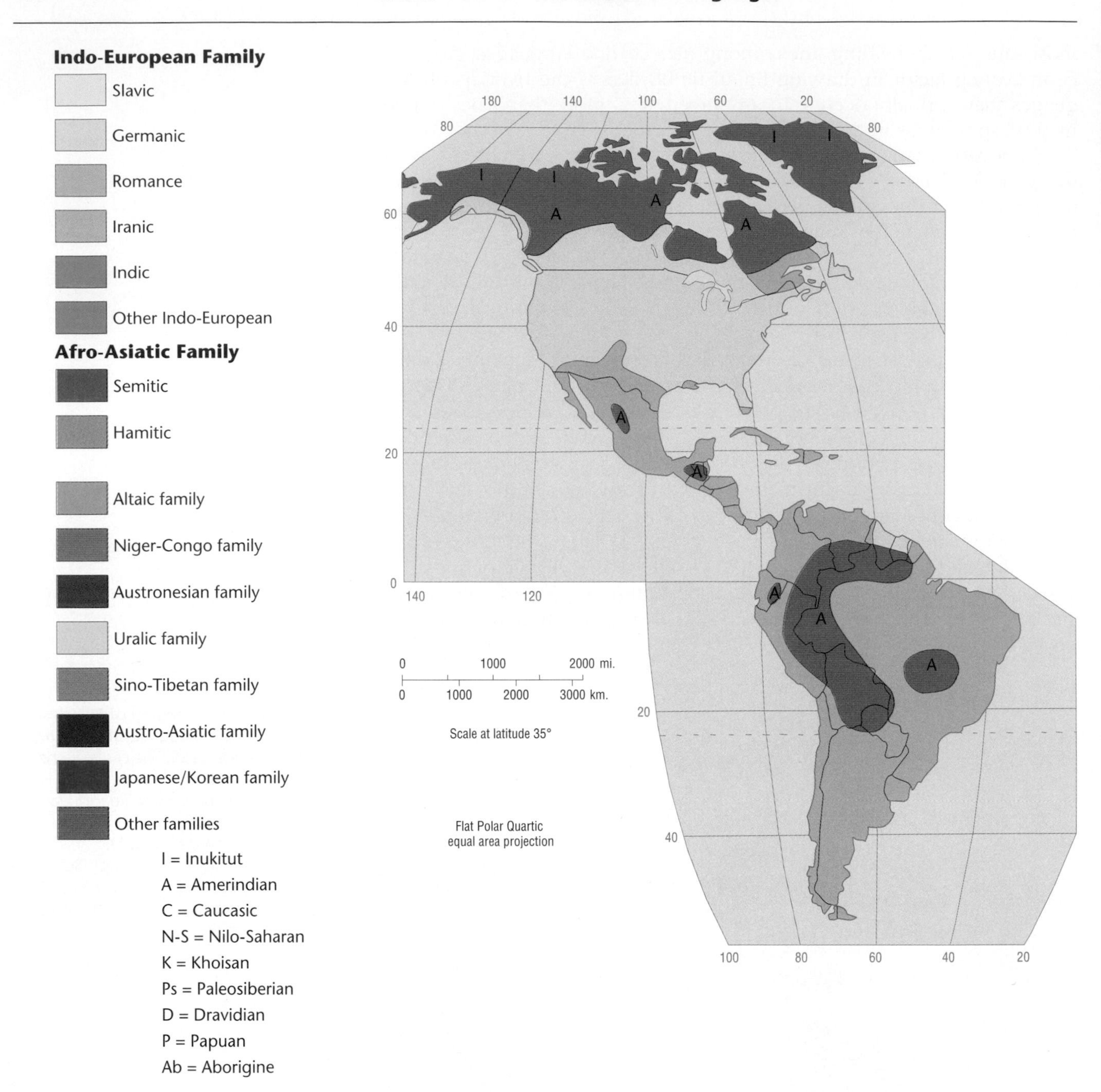

Figure 5.3
The major linguistic culture regions of the world. Although there are thousands of languages and dialects in the world, they can be grouped into a few linguistic families. Note the broad extent of the Indo-European language family. English-speaking North Americans share Indo-European language roots with a wide variety of other cultural groups.

Language Families

At the most inclusive level, formal linguistic culture regions showing **language families** can be mapped (Figure 5.3). The very complicated linguistic mosaic in the world becomes somewhat easier to comprehend if we recognize that most individual languages belong to families, each consisting of related tongues derived from a common ancestral speech.

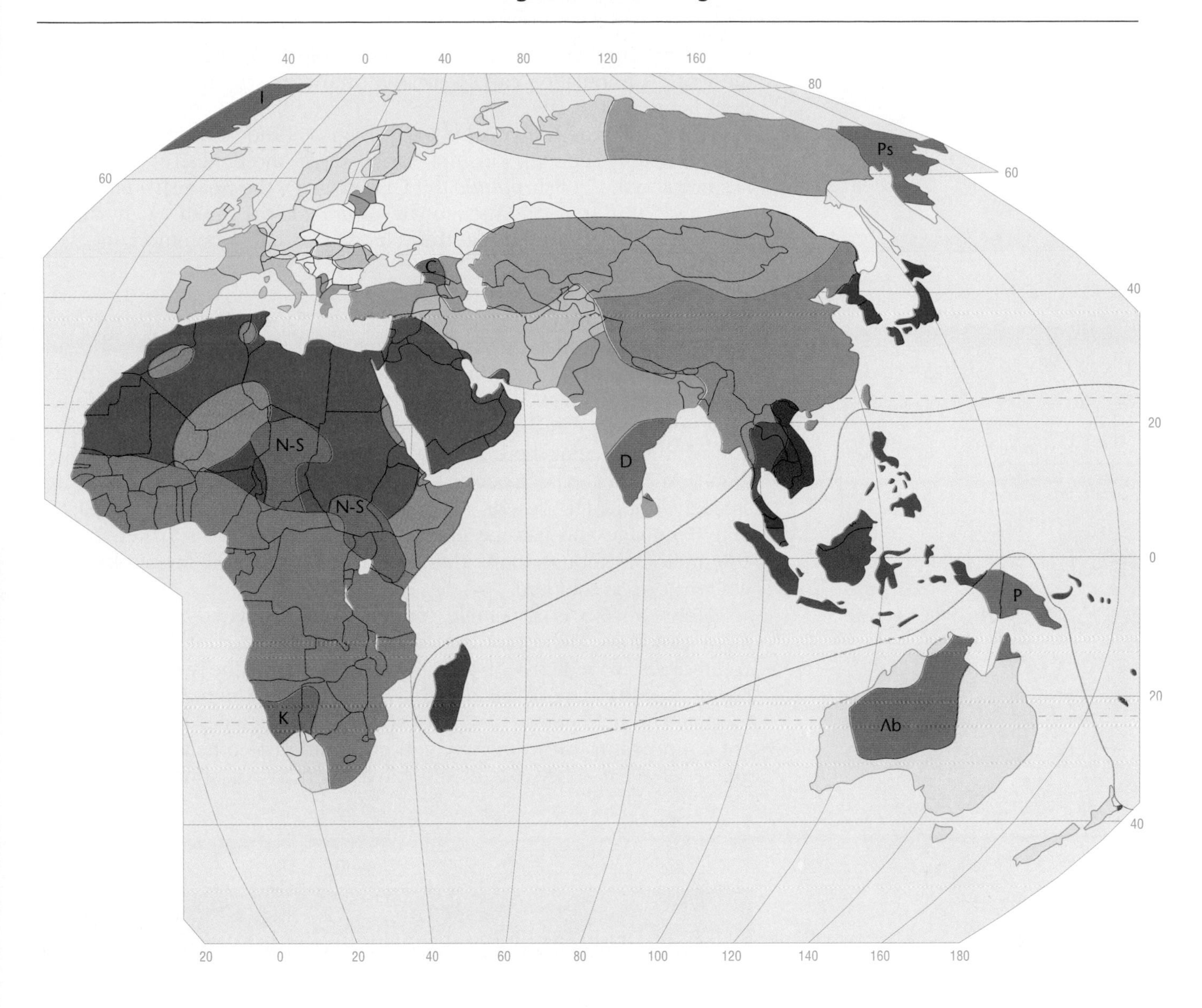

The Indo-European Language Family. The largest and most widespread language family is the *Indo-European,* which is spoken on all the continents and is dominant in Europe, Russia, North and South America, Australia, and parts of southwestern Asia and India. Romance, Slavic, Germanic, Indic, Celtic, and Iranic are all Indo-European subfamilies, and they, in turn, are subdivided into individual languages. For example, English is a Germanic Indo-European language. Seven Indo-European tongues are among the top ten languages in the world, ranked by number of native speakers (Table 5.1), and roughly half of the world's population can speak one or another of these far-flung kindred languages.

If we compare the vocabularies of various Indo-European tongues, we can readily see their kinship. For example, the English word *mother* is similar to the Polish *matka,* the Greek *meter,* the Spanish *madre,* the Farsi *madar* in Iran, and the Sinhalese *mava* in Sri Lanka. Such similarities in vocabulary reveal that these languages had a common ancestral tongue.

The Afro-Asiatic Family. A second language family is the *Afro-Asiatic,* consisting of two major divisions, Semitic and Hamitic. The Semitic languages cover the area from the Arabian peninsula and the Tigris-Euphrates river valley in the Fertile Crescent of Iraq westward through Syria and North Africa to the Atlantic Ocean. Despite the considerable size of this domain, there are fewer speakers of the Semitic languages than you might expect because most of the areas Semites inhabit are sparsely populated deserts. Arabic is by far the most widespread Semitic language and has the greatest number of native speakers, about 186 million. Although many different dialects of Arabic are spoken, the written form is standard.

Hebrew also is a Semitic tongue, closely related to Arabic. For many centuries, Hebrew was a "dead" language, used only in religious ceremonies by millions of Jews scattered around the world. With the creation of the state of Israel in 1947, a common language was needed to unite the immigrant Jews, who spoke the languages of many different countries. Hebrew was revived and made the official national language of what otherwise would have been a **polyglot,** or multilan-

TABLE 5.1
The Ten Leading Languages in Numbers of Native Speakers

Language	Family	Speakers (in millions)	Main Areas Where Spoken
Han Chinese (Mandarin)	Sino-Tibetan	836	China, Taiwan, Singapore
Hindi	Indo-European	333	Northern India
Spanish	Indo-European	332	Spain, Latin America, southwestern United States
English	Indo-European	322	British Isles, Anglo-America, Australia, New Zealand, South Africa, Philippines, former British colonies in tropical Asia and Africa
Arabic	Afro-Asiatic	186	Middle East, North Africa
Bengali	Indo-European	185	Bangladesh, eastern India
Portuguese	Indo-European	170	Portugal, Brazil, southern Africa
Russian	Indo-European	169	Russia, Kazakstan, parts of Ukraine and other former Soviet republics
Japanese	Altaic	125	Japan
German	Indo-European	97	Germany, Austria, Switzerland, Luxembourg, eastern France, northern Italy

Source: *World Almanac and Book of Facts.* "Native speakers" means mother tongue.

guage, state. Amharic, a third major Semitic tongue, today claims 20 million speakers in the mountains of East Africa.

Smaller numbers of linguistically related people who speak Hamitic languages share North and East Africa with the Semites. These tongues originated in Asia but today are spoken almost exclusively in Africa, by the Berbers of Morocco and Algeria, the Tuaregs of the Sahara, and the Cushites of East Africa. The Hamitic culture region was formerly much larger than it is now, but decreased due to the expansion of Arabic over a thousand years ago.

Other Major Language Families. Most of the rest of the world's population speaks languages belonging to one or another of six remaining major families. Africa south of the Sahara Desert is dominated by the *Niger-Congo* language family, also called *Niger-Kordofanian,* spoken by about 200 million people. The greater part of the Niger-Congo culture region belongs to the Bantu subgroup, which includes Swahili, the lingua franca of East Africa. Both Niger-Congo and its Bantu constituent are fragmented into a great many different languages and dialects. Flanking the Slavic Indo-Europeans on north and south in Asia are the speakers of the *Altaic* language family, including Turkic, Mongolic, and several other subgroups. The Altaic homeland lies largely in the inhospitable deserts, tundras, and coniferous forests of northern and central Asia. Also occupying tundra and grassland areas adjacent to the Slavs is the *Uralic* family. Finnish and Hungarian are the two most important Uralic tongues, and both enjoy the status of official legal languages in their respective countries.

One of the most remarkable language families in terms of distribution is the *Austronesian.* Representatives of this group live mainly on tropical islands stretching from Madagascar, off the east coast of Africa, through Indonesia and the Pacific Islands, to Hawaii and Easter Island. This longitudinal span is more than half the distance around the world. The language area also covers a north-south, or latitudinal, range from Hawaii and Taiwan in the north to New Zealand in the south. The largest single language in this family is Indonesian, with 50 million native speakers (Table 5.1), but the most widespread is Polynesian.

Dominated numerically and spatially by Chinese, *Sino-Tibetan* is one of the major language families of the world. The Sino-Tibetan speech area extends throughout most of China and Southeast Asia. Han Chinese is spoken in a variety of dialects as a mother tongue by 836 million people and serves as the official form of speech in China. Among the other Sino-Tibetan languages are Burmese and Tibetan, which border the Chinese speech area on the south and west. Another major Asian family consists of *Japanese* and *Korean,* with nearly 200 million speakers. Japanese/Korean seems to have some kinship to both the Altaic and Austronesian families.

In Southeast Asia, the Vietnamese, Cambodians, Thais, and some tribal peoples of Malaya and parts of India constitute the *Austro-Asiatic* family. They occupy a remnant peripheral domain, and have been encroached on by Sino-Tibetan, Indo-European, and Austronesian.

Minor Language Families. Occupying refuge areas after retreat before rival groups are remnant language families such as *Khoisan,* found in the Kalahari desert of southwestern Africa and characterized by distinctive clicking sounds; *Dravidian,* spoken by the numerous darker-skinned peoples of southern India and adjacent northern Sri Lanka; Australian *Aborigine; Papuan; Caucasic; Nilo-Saharan; Paleosiberian; Inukitut;*

Hans Kurath
1891–1992

Though a native of Austria, Professor Kurath was best known for his pioneer studies of the linguistic geography of the eastern United States, some of which are listed among the readings at the end of this chapter. He immigrated to America in 1907 and was educated at the University of Texas and the University of Chicago. Most of his academic career was spent at Brown University, where he served as professor of Germanics and linguistics, and at the University of Michigan, where he was professor of English until retiring in 1961. Cultural geographers have profited greatly from Kurath's seminal works on American English dialects, works rich in maps of vocabulary and pronunciation usages. His research provided part of the basis for Figure 5.4. Much honored and widely respected, Kurath held honorary doctorates from the universities of Chicago and Wisconsin (see Schneider, Edgar W. "In Memoriam, Hans Kurath." *English World-Wide*, 13 [1992]: 111–113).

and a variety of *American Indian* families. In a few cases, individual minor languages represent the last sole survivors of former families. *Basque,* spoken in the borderland between Spain and France, is such a survivor, unrelated to any other language in the world.

English Dialects in the United States

At the opposite end of the linguistic continuum from language families are dialects, and they, too, reveal a vivid geography. For example, American English is hardly uniform from region to region. At least three major dialects, corresponding to major culture regions, developed in the eastern United States by the time of the American Revolution: the Northern, Midland, and Southern dialects (Figure 5.4) (see biographical sketch of Hans Kurath). As the three subcultures expanded westward, their dialects spread and fragmented. Nevertheless, the dialects retained much of their basic character even beyond the Mississippi River. The three dialects have distinctive vocabularies and pronunciations, as Table 5.2 suggests. Drawing the dialect boundaries is often tricky (Figure 5.5).

Today, many of the regional words are becoming old-fashioned, but new words displaying regional variations are still being coined. For instance, the following terms are all used to describe a controlled-access divided highway: *freeway, turnpike, parkway, thruway, expressway,* and *interstate.* Of these, *parkway* and *turnpike* seem to be mainly northeastern and midwestern words, whereas *freeway* is the California word.

Many African Americans speak their own distinctive form of English. Black English, once dismissed by linguists as no more than inferior substandard English, is in reality a variety of the Southern dialect bearing considerable African influence in pitch, rhythm, and tone. It grew out of a pidgin that developed on the early slave plantations and is today spoken by about 80 percent of African Americans. The structures of Black English, with their African heritage, can be heard in the speech of African American ghetto dwellers who have yet to make all of their compromises with the mainstream culture in America. The use of undifferentiated pronouns ("Me help you?"); the lack of pronoun differentiation between genders ("He a nice little girl"); the "he"/"she" pronoun possessive ("Ray sister she got a new doll baby"); the invariant "be" usage ("I be wash the car"); and many other features of Black English separate it from standard speech. In the American school system, such dialect forms are usually considered mistakes—evidence of the verbal inability or impoverishment of African Americans—rather than, more properly, as part of the legitimate grammar of a separate linguistic group. African Americans have made substantial contributions to speech in the United States, especially to the Southern dialect. At present, this regional dialect is becoming increasingly identified with African Americans, and Caucasians in that section of the country are shifting to Midland speech.

While we are sometimes led to believe that Americans are becoming more alike, as a national culture overwhelms regional ones, the current status of American English dialects suggests otherwise. "Linguistic divergence" is still under way, and dialects continue "to mutate on a regional level," just as they always have, according to Guy Bailey. Local variations in grammar and pronunciation proliferate, confounding the proponents of standardized speech and defying the homogenizing influence of radio, television, and other mass media.

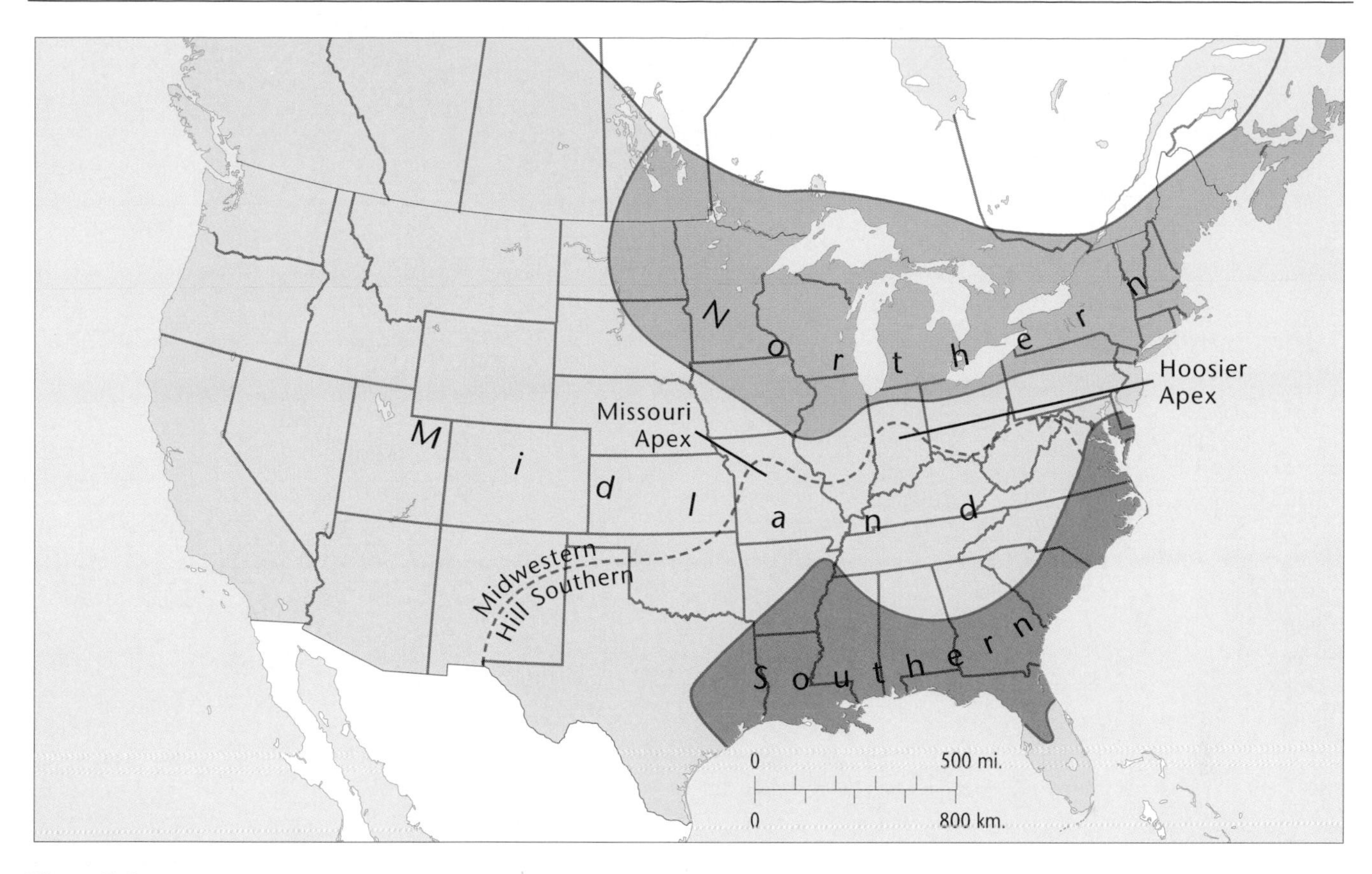

Figure 5.4
Major dialects of North American English, with a few selected subdialects. Compare these with the Anglo-American subcultures shown in Figure 1.6. (After Carver, 1986; Kurath, 1949; and diverse regional word atlases.)

Linguistic Diffusion

Different types of cultural diffusion help interpret the linguistic map. Relocation diffusion has been extremely important, for languages spread when groups, in whole or part, migrated from one area to another. Some individual tongues or entire language families are no longer spoken in the regions where they originated, and in certain

TABLE 5.2
Three Major Dialects of American English, As Indicated by Vocabulary Samples

Meaning	Northern Dialect	Midland Dialect	Southern Dialect
food eaten between meals	bite	piece	snack
dragonfly	darning needle	snake feeder, snake doctor	mosquito hawk, skeeter hawk
fence built of stone	stone wall	stone fence	rock fence
cottage cheese	Dutch cheese, pot cheese	smear cheese	curds, clabber cheese
beans eaten in the pod	string beans	green beans	snap beans
worm in ground	angleworm	fish worm, redworm	earthworm

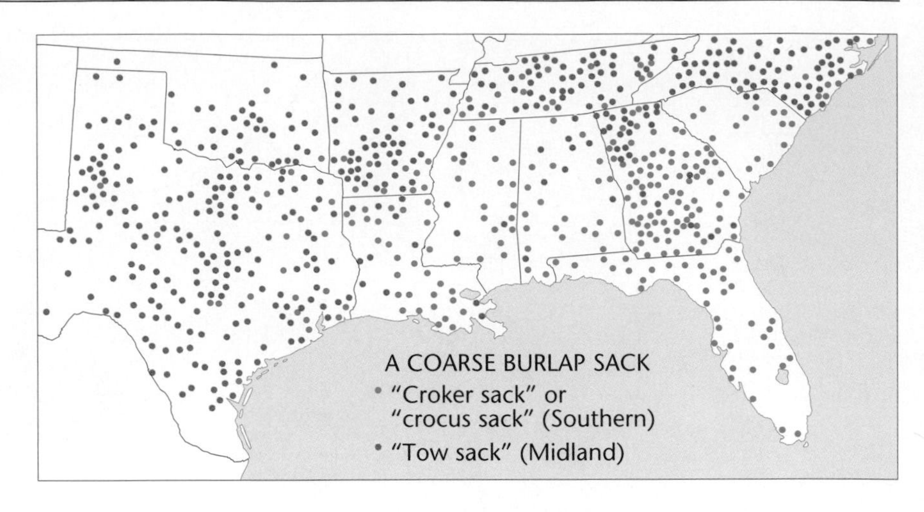

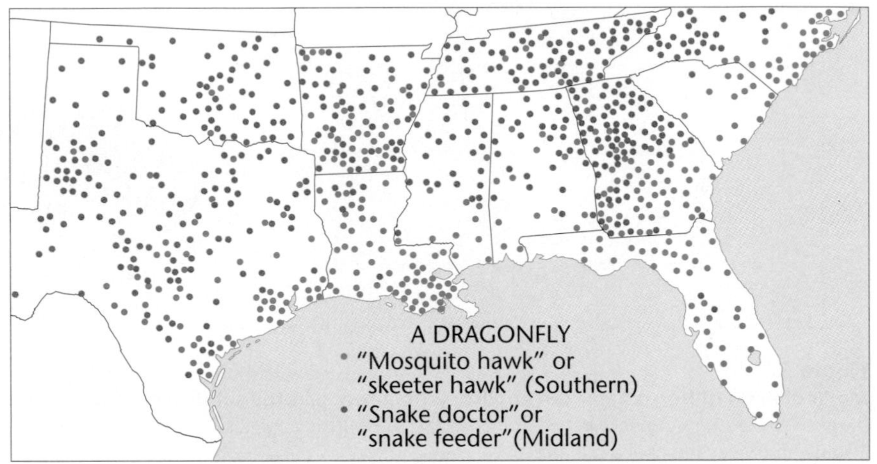

Figure 5.5
Some Midland and Southern words in the South. Each dot represents one person interviewed who gave the response indicated. If you were drawing the isoglosses for these words, where exactly would you place them? If these two maps were your only evidence, where would you draw the Midland-Southern dialect border? These are common problems for the linguistic geographer, and they illustrate how artificial dialect maps and all formal culture regions are. (Sources: Wood, Gordon R. *Vocabulary Change: A Study of Variation in Eight of the Southern States.* Carbondale and Edwardsville: Southern Illinois University Press, 1971, pp. 325, 337–339; Kurath, 1949; Atwood, *Regional Vocabulary of Texas,* pp. 196, 199.)

other cases the linguistic hearth is peripheral to the present distribution (compare Figures 5.3 and 5.6).

Indo-European Diffusion

The earliest speakers of Indo-European apparently lived in southern and southeastern Turkey, a region known as Anatolia, about 9000 years ago (Figure 5.6). They possessed seed-plant agriculture, and their ancient diffusion to the west and north, bringing them into Europe, represented the expansion of a farming people at the expense of hunters and gatherers. Compare Figure 3.12, which shows the diffusion of agriculture, with Figure 5.6. The initial prehistoric advance of the Indo-Europeans, then, hinged on a major innovation—plant and animal domestication—and probably proceeded gradually and peacefully. As these people dispersed and lost contact with one another, different Indo-European groups gradually developed variant forms of the language, causing fragmentation of the family.

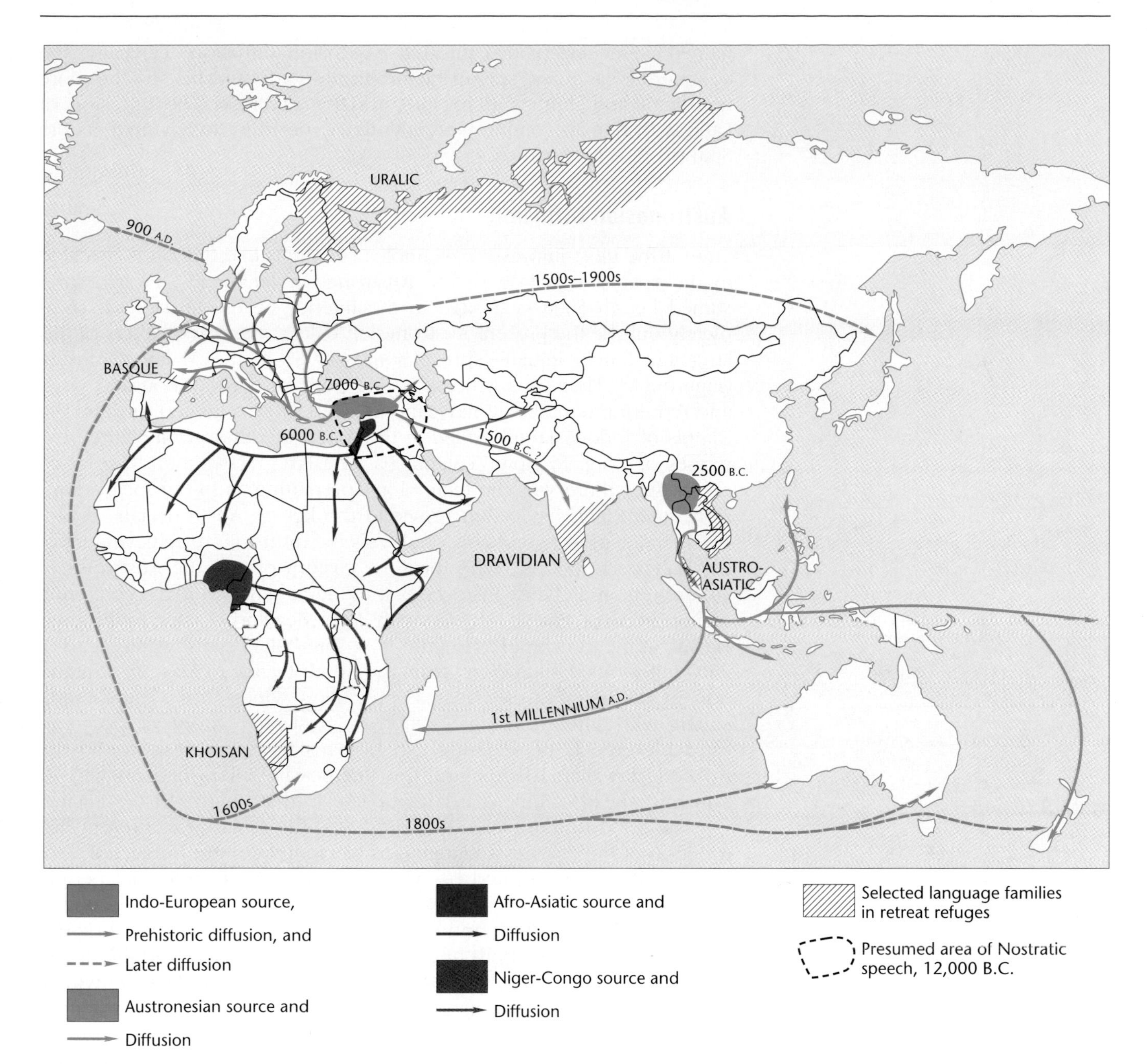

Figure 5.6

Origin and diffusion of four major language families in the Eastern Hemisphere. The prehistoric diffusion of Indo-European speech to the west and north occurred in conjunction with the diffusion of agriculture from the Middle Eastern center (compare with Figure 3.12), as did the early spread of the Afro-Asiatic family. As these and other groups advanced, certain linguistic families retreated to refuges in remote places, where they hold out to the present day. Some sources, dates, and routes are speculative. (Sources: Krantz, 1988; and Renfrew, 1989.)

In later millennia, the diffusion of certain Indo-European languages, in particular Latin, English, and Russian, occurred in conjunction with the territorial spread of great political empires. In such cases of imperial conquest, relocation and expansion diffusion were not mutually exclusive. Relocation diffusion often involved a relatively small number of speakers, a conquering elite who came to rule an alien people. The language of the conqueror, implanted by relocation diffusion, often gained wider acceptance through expansion diffusion. Typically, the conqueror's language spread hierarchically—adopted first by the more important and influential persons and by city folk. The diffusion of Latin with Roman conquests frequently occurred in this manner, as did Spanish in Latin America.

Austronesian Diffusion

One of the most impressive examples of linguistic diffusion is revealed in the spatial evolution of the Austronesian languages. From a presumed hearth 5000 years ago in the interior of Southeast Asia, completely outside the present Austronesian culture region, speakers of this language family initially spread southward into the Malay Peninsula (Figure 5.6). Then, in a process lasting perhaps several thousand years and requiring remarkable navigational skills, they migrated through the islands of Indonesia and sailed in tiny boats across vast, uncharted expanses of water to New Zealand, Easter Island, Hawaii, and Madagascar. If agriculture was the technology permitting Indo-European diffusion, sailing and navigation provided the key to Austronesian spread.

Perhaps most remarkable of all was the diffusionary achievement of the Polynesian people, who form the eastern part of the Austronesian culture region. Polynesians occupy a triangular-shaped realm consisting of hundreds of Pacific islands, with New Zealand, Easter Island, and Hawaii at the three apexes (Figure 5.7). The Polynesians' watery leap of 2500 miles (4000 kilometers) from the South Pacific to Hawaii, a migration in outrigger canoes against prevailing winds into a new hemisphere with different navigational stars, must rank as one of the greatest achievements of seafaring. No humans had previously found the isolated Hawaiian Islands, and the Polynesian sailors had no way of knowing ahead of time that land existed in that quarter of the Pacific.

The relocation diffusion that produced the remarkable present distribution of the Polynesian languages has long been the subject of controversy. How, when, and by what means could a traditional people have achieved the diffusion? What skills were required? Two cultural geographers, John Webb and Gerard Ward, studied this prehistoric diffusion. Their method, both unusual and rewarding, involved the development of a computer model, into which was built data on winds, ocean currents, vessel traits and capabilities, island visibility, duration of voyage, and the like. Both *drift* voyages, in which the boat simply floats with the winds and currents, and *navigated* voyages were considered. Over 100,000 voyage simulations were run through the computer.

The authors concluded, on the basis of these experiments, that the Polynesian triangle had probably been entered from the west, from the direction of the ancient Austronesian hearth area, by way of western insular chains in a process of "island hopping"—that is, migrating from one island to another visible in the distance. The core of eastern Polynesia was likely reached in navigated voyages, but once attained, drift voyages could easily explain much internal diffusion. A peripheral region, an "outer arc from Hawaii through Easter Island to New Zealand," was apparently attainable only by means of "intentionally navigated" voyages—daring feats that must be ranked among the greatest human achievements of all time (Figure 5.7).

Note that in this application of the geographer's spatial skills, Webb and Ward employed the themes of culture region (present distribution of Polynesians) and cultural ecology (currents, winds, visibility of is-

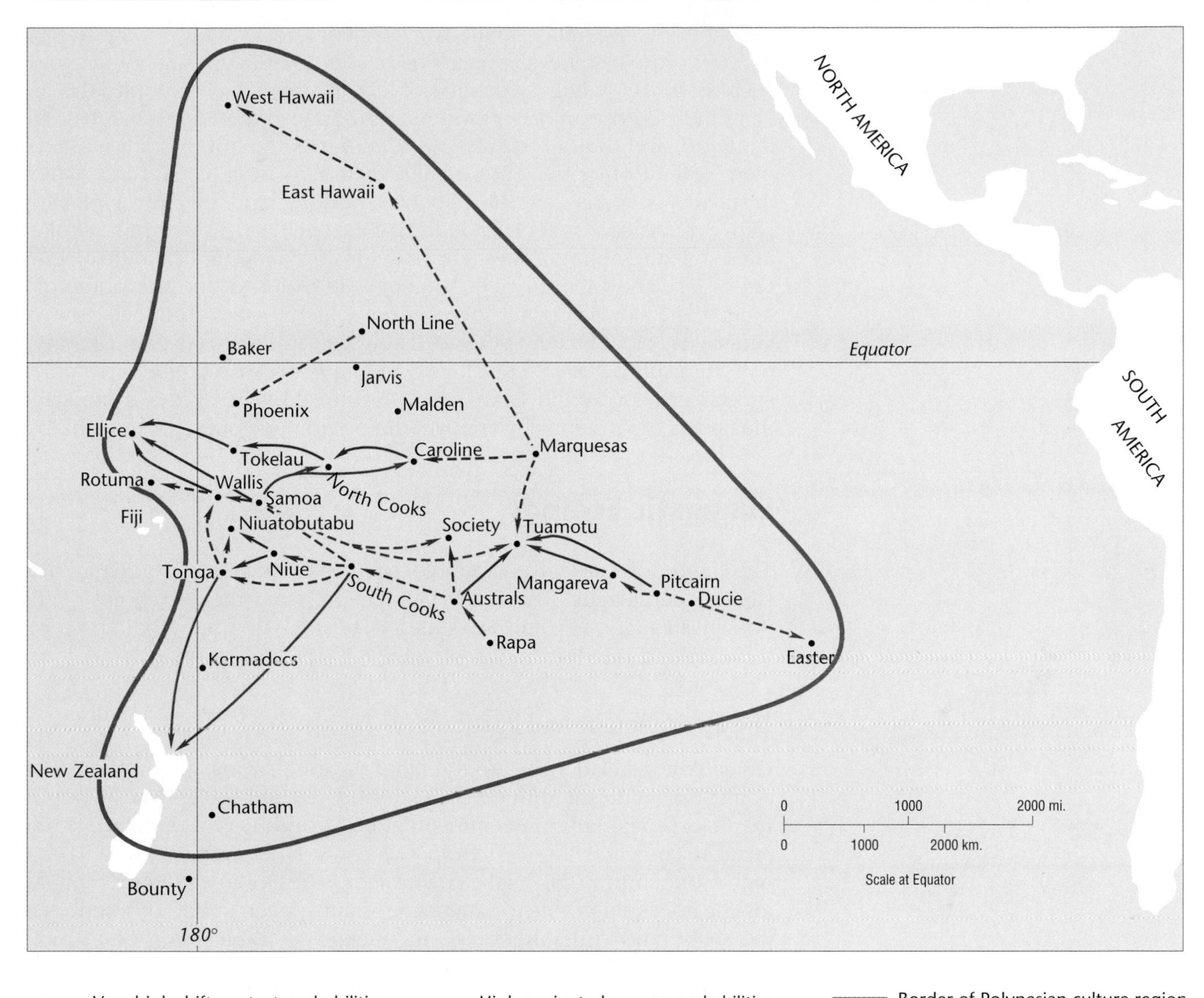

Figure 5.7
Probabilities of selected Polynesian drift and navigation voyages in the Pacific Ocean. According to a computer model, the outer arc of Polynesia, represented by Hawaii, Easter Island, and New Zealand, could have been reached only by navigated voyages. (Adapted from Levison, Michael, R. Gerard Ward, and John W. Webb. *The Settlement of Polynesia: A Computer Simulation.* Minneapolis: University of Minnesota Press, 1973, pp. 5, 33, 35, 43, 61.)

lands) to help describe and explain the workings of a third theme, cultural diffusion. Again, as suggested in Chapter 1, the five themes unite rather than divide cultural geography.

Searching for the Primordial Tongue

Using techniques that remain controversial, linguists are probing even more deeply into the origin and diffusion of languages, seeking still more elusive prehistoric tongues. Evidence is building that an ancestral speech called *Nostratic,* spoken in the Middle East 12,000 to 20,000 years ago, was ancestral to nine modern language families, including

Indo-European, Uralic, Altaic, Afro-Asiatic, and Dravidian (Figure 5.6). A 500-word Nostratic dictionary has been compiled, containing words such as *kuni* ("wife," "woman"), which became, for example, the ancient Indo-European *gwen* (and modern English *queen*), the archaic Altaic *küni,* and the old Afro-Asiatic *KwVn.* Contemporary with Nostratic were several other ancient tongues, including *Dene-Caucasian,* which reputedly gave rise to Sino-Tibetan, Basque, and one form of early Native American speech called *Na-Dene.* These pioneering scholars are now attempting to establish a kinship among Nostratic, Dene-Caucasian, and other ancient languages in order to find the primordial tongue, the single original speech from which they presume all modern languages are ultimately derived. They seek nothing less than the original linguistic hearth area, almost certainly in Africa, where complex speech first arose and from which it diffused. The study of language thus bears the potential to unravel the origin and spread of humankind.

Linguistic Ecology

The theme of cultural ecology contributes greatly to the geographical study of languages. The following section, from the viewpoint of the possibilist, suggests some ways the physical environment influences vocabulary and the distribution of language.

The Environment and Vocabulary

Humankind's relationship to the land played a strong role in the development of linguistic differences (see box, *An English Speaker Walks in the Desert*). The environment even affects vocabulary. For example, the Spanish language, derived from Castile, a land rimmed by hills and high mountains, is especially rich in words describing rough terrain, allowing speakers of this tongue to distinguish even subtle differences in the shape and configuration of mountains, as Table 5.3 reveals. Similarly, Scottish Gaelic possesses a rich vocabulary to describe types of rough terrain—a common attribute of the Celtic languages, spoken by hill peoples. In the Romanian tongue, also born of a rugged terrain, words relating to mountainous features tend to be keyed to use of that terrain for livestock herding. English, by contrast, developed in wet coastal plains, and our language, consequently, is very poor in words describing mountainous terrain (Figure 5.8). By contrast, English abounds with words describing flowing streams. In the rural American South alone, one finds *river, creek, branch, fork, prong, run, bayou,*

An English Speaker Walks in the Desert

Our individual languages evolve in particular physical environmental surroundings. When their speakers try to cope with a very different ecological setting, they find the vocabulary inadequate. Very revealing are the remarks of an American humanist, describing his walk across the desert of Sonora and Arizona:

> *I know no desert language.*
> *I struggle with a tongue forged on another continent, with words*
> *spawned in green forests under*
> *gray, soggy skies.*

Quote from Bowden, Charles. "A Desert Tale: Cherishing the Hidden Waters." *Texas Humanist,* 6 (July–August 1984): 6.

TABLE 5.3
Some Spanish Words Describing Mountains and Hills

Spanish Word	English Meaning
candelas	Literally "candles"; a collection of *peñas*
ceja	Steep-sided breaks or escarpment separating two plains of different elevation
cejita	A low escarpment
cerrillo or *cerrito*	A small *cerro;* a hill
cerro	A single eminence, intermediate in size between English *hill* and *mountain*
chiquito	Literally "small," describing minor secondary fringing elevations at the base of and parallel to a *sierra* or *cordillera*
cordillera	A mass of mountains, as distinguished from a single mountain summit
cuchilla	Literally "knife"; the comblike secondary crests that project at right angles from the sides of a *sierra*
cumbre	The highest elevation or peak within a *sierra* or *cordillera;* a summit
eminencia	A mountainous or hilly protuberance
loma	A hill in the midst of a plain
lomita	A small hill in the midst of a plain
mesa	Literally "table"; a flat-topped eminence
montaña	Equivalent to English *mountain*
pelado	A barren, treeless mountain
pelon	A bare conical eminence
peloncilla	A small *pelon*
peña	A needlelike eminence
picacho	A peaked or pointed eminence
pico	A summit point, English *peak*
sandia	Literally "watermelon"; an oblong, rounded eminence
sierra	An elongated mountain mass with a serrated crest
teta	A solitary, conical mountain in the shape of a woman's breast
tinaja	A solitary, hemispheric mountain shaped like an inverted bowl

Source: Hill, Robert T. "Descriptive Topographic Terms of Spanish America." *National Geographic Magazine*, 7 (1896): 292–297.

and *slough*. This indicates that the area is a well-watered land with a dense network of streams.

Clearly, then, language serves an adaptive strategy, at least in traditional societies. Vocabularies are highly developed for those features of the environment that involve livelihood. Without such detailed vocabularies, it would be difficult to communicate sophisticated information relevant to the adaptive strategy.

The Environment Provides Refuge

One of the most obvious environmental influences on language is the protection and isolation offered by inhospitable environments. Such areas often provide hard-pressed, outnumbered linguistic groups refuge from aggressive neighbors and are, accordingly, referred to as **linguistic refuge areas**. Rugged hill and mountain areas, excessively cold or dry climates, impenetrable forests, remote islands, and extensive marshes and swamps can all offer protection to minority language groups. For one thing, unpleasant environments rarely attract conquerors. Also, mountains tend to isolate the inhabitants of one valley

Figure 5.8
A mountain in the desert of Arizona. Our English language fails us in our attempt to describe this scene. "Mountain," yes, but what *kind* of mountain (see Table 5.3)? "Desert" and "cacti," yes, but can we be more specific? Our English language is not able adequately to describe such a place, because it is the product of a very different cultural ecology. As a result, our environmental perception will be less precise in such places.

from those in adjacent ones, retarding the contacts that might lead to linguistic diffusion.

Examples of these linguistic refuge areas are numerous. The rugged Caucasus Mountains and nearby ranges in central Eurasia are populated by a large variety of peoples (Figure 5.9). Similarly, the Alps, Himalayas, and highlands of Mexico are linguistic **shatter belts**—areas where diverse languages are spoken. The American Indian tongue Quechua clings to a refuge in the Andes Mountains of South America (Figure 5.2), while in the Rocky Mountains of northern New Mexico, an archaic form of Spanish survives, largely as a result of an isolation that ended only in the early 1900s. The Dhofar, a mountain tribe in the back country of Oman in Arabia, preserves Hamitic speech, a family otherwise vanished from Asia. Bitterly cold tundra climates of the far north have sheltered certain Uralic, Altaic, and Inukitut (Eskimo) speakers, and the dry desert has shielded Khoisan speakers from Bantu invaders. On the Sea Islands, off the coast of South Carolina and Georgia, some remnants of an African language, Gullah, can still be heard, protected for centuries by insularity. In short, hostile environments protect linguistic groups that are willing to endure the hardships they offer.

Still, environmental isolation can no longer be the vital linguistic force it once was. It becomes harder and harder to discover spots on the Earth so isolated that they remain little touched by outside influences. Today, inhospitable lands may offer linguistic refuge, but it is no longer certain that they will in the future. Even an island situated in the middle of the vast Pacific Ocean can offer no reliable refuge in an age of airplanes. Similarly, marshes and forests provide refuge only if they are not drained and cleared by farmers who want new farmlands. The reality of the world is no longer isolation but interaction.

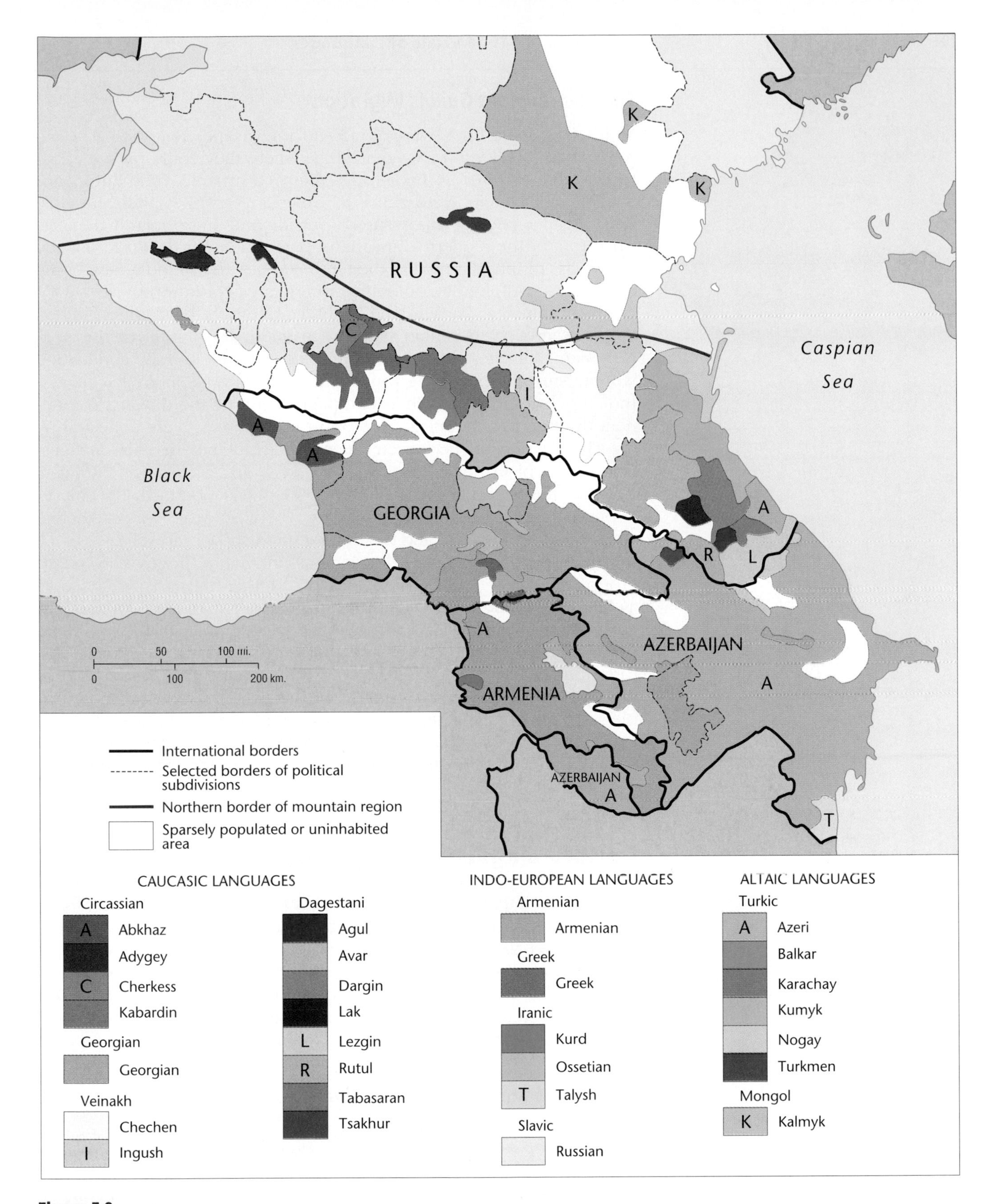

Figure 5.9

The environment is a linguistic refuge in the Caucasus Mountains. The rugged mountainous region between the Black and Caspian seas, including parts of Armenia, Russia, Georgia, and Azerbaijan, is peopled by a great variety of linguistic groups, representing three major language families. Mountain areas are often linguistic shatter belts, because the rough terrain provides refuge and isolation. Compare this map to Figure 4.3.

The Environment Guides Migration

Migrating people often were attracted to new lands that seemed environmentally similar to their homelands, where they could pursue adaptive strategies already known to them. Germanic Indo-Europeans sought familiar temperate zones in America, New Zealand, and Australia. Semitic peoples rarely spread outside arid and semiarid climates. Ancestors of the modern Hungarians, a Uralic linguistic stock, left the grasslands of inner Eurasia in the tenth century and found a new home in the grassy Alföld, one of the few prairie areas of Europe.

Environmental barriers and natural routeways have often guided linguistic groups in certain paths. The wide distribution of the Austronesian language group, as we have seen, cannot be fully understood without studying prevailing winds and water currents in the Pacific and Indian oceans. Migrating Indo-Europeans entering the Indian subcontinent through low mountain passes in the northwest were deflected by the Himalayas and the barren Deccan Plateau into the rich Ganges-Indus river plain. Even today in parts of India, according to Charles Bennett, the Indo-European/Dravidian "language boundary seems to approximate an ecological boundary" between the water-retentive black soils of the plains and the thinner, reddish Deccan soils.

Because such physical barriers as mountain ridges can retard groups from migrating from one area to another, they frequently serve as linguistic borders. In parts of the Alps, speakers of German and Italian live on opposite sides of a major ridge. Portions of the mountain rim along the northern edge of the Fertile Crescent in the Middle East form the border between Semitic and Indo-European tongues. Linguistic borders that follow such physical features generally tend to be stable, and they often endure for thousands of years. Language borders that cross plains and major routes of communication are frequently unstable, as, for example, the Germanic-Slavic boundary on the North European Plain.

Culturo-Linguistic Integration

Language is intertwined with all aspects of culture. The theme of cultural integration permits us to probe some of these complex links between speech and other cultural phenomena. The complicated linguistic map cannot be understood without reference to the comparative social, demographic, political, and technological characteristics of the groups in question. At root, linguistic cultural integration often reflects the dominance of one group over another, a dominance based in culture.

Technology and Linguistic Dominance

One language group can achieve cultural dominance over neighboring groups in a variety of ways, often with profound results for the linguistic map of the world. Technological superiority is usually involved. Earlier, we saw how plant and animal domestication—the technology of the "agricultural revolution"—aided the early diffusion of the Indo-European language family. A similar advantage allowed the prehistoric spread of the Afro-Asiatic peoples from the Middle Eastern agricultural hearth.

The development of alphabets and the resultant rich literary traditions also allowed certain cultures to become more complex and dominant. As a general rule, written languages advanced at the expense of illiterate cultures, a process still under way today. Since alphabets were invariably the invention of agricultural societies, the technological superiority of these groups became even greater. Greek, Latin, and Chinese, among other tongues, enjoyed early advantage because of literacy.

Alphabets also facilitated record keeping, allowing governments and bureaucracies to develop. The result was empire building, and languages tend to spread with imperial expansion. These highly organized, literate empires represent simply another technological advantage for the languages involved. The imperial expansion of European and US power across the globe altered the linguistic patterns among millions of people. The United Kingdom, France, the Netherlands, Belgium, Portugal, Spain, and the United States ruled overseas empires. This empire building superimposed Indo-European tongues on the map of the tropics and subtropics. The areas most affected were Asia, Africa, and the Austronesian island world.

In South America, two expanding empires—Spain and Portugal—clashed in the fifteenth century. Their compromise had far-reaching linguistic consequences. In 1494, Spain and Portugal signed the Treaty of Tordesillas. Under this treaty, Spain received control over all colonial lands west of a certain meridian (Figure 5.10), and Portugal gained control over the lands east of the line. In this way, Brazil eventually became a Portuguese-speaking land, in contrast to most of the rest of South America, where Spanish prevailed.

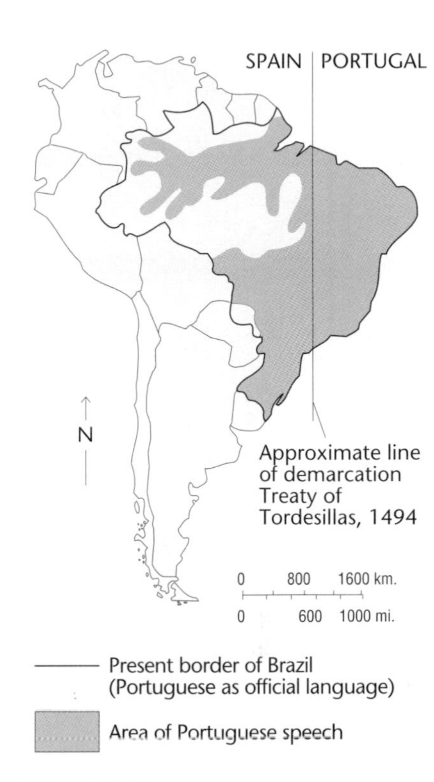

Figure 5.10
The mesh of language and politics in South America. The Treaty of Tordesillas, cosigned by Spain and Portugal in 1494, established the political basis for the present linguistic pattern in South America. Portugal was awarded the eastern part of the continent, and Spain the rest. The Portuguese language was implanted in Portuguese territory, and today it has diffused westward from its source.

Even though the imperial nations have given up part or all of their colonial empires, the languages they transplanted overseas survived. As a result, English still has a foothold in much of Africa, the Indian subcontinent, the Philippines, and certain areas of the Pacific islands. French persists in the former French and Belgian colonies, especially in north, west, and central Africa, Madagascar, and Polynesia. In most of these areas, English and French function as the languages of the educated elite and enjoy a role as languages of government, commerce, and higher education. In fact, they often enjoy official legal status. The colonial tongues function in such settings as link languages, helping hold together states in which the native languages are multiple and divisive.

Transportation technology also profoundly affects the geography of languages. Ships, railroads, and highways usually spread the languages of the cultural groups who build them, sometimes spelling doom for the speech of technologically less advanced peoples whose lands are suddenly opened to outside contacts. The Trans-Siberian Railroad, built around the turn of the century, spread the Russian language eastward to the Pacific Ocean, and the Alaska Highway through Canada carried English into American Indian refuges. At present, the construction of highways into Brazil's remote Amazonian interior threatens the Indian languages of that region.

The Social Morale Model

Once a language diffuses spatially, in conjunction with technological advantage or imperial conquest, the replacement of the indigenous languages can begin. Geographer Charles Withers built a *social morale model* to explain the process by which, over time, the conquered

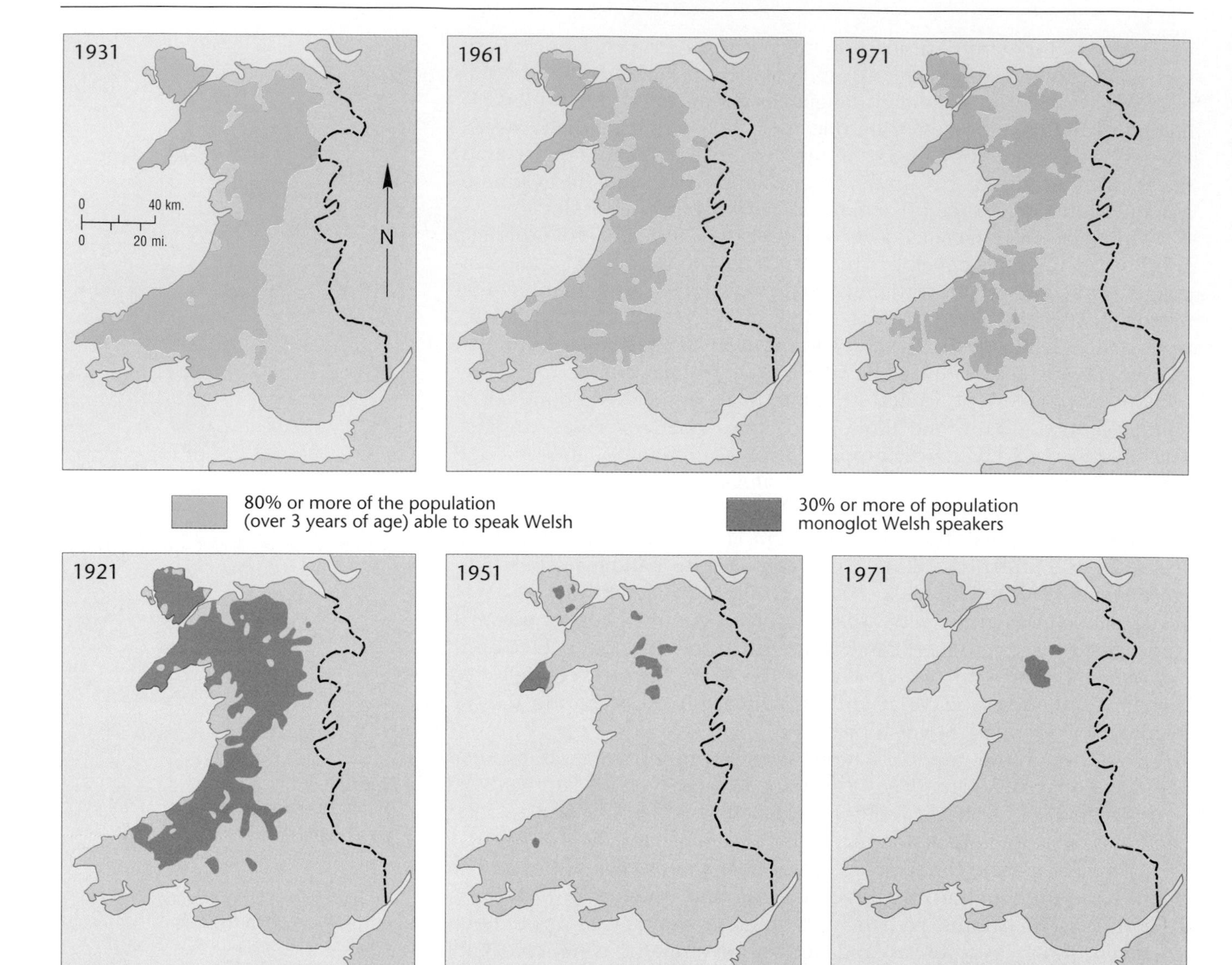

Figure 5.11
Retreat of the Welsh language in the mid-twentieth century. For centuries the Welsh have been dominated by English-speaking people in the United Kingdom. As a result the language has declined. Between 1931 and 1981, the number of Welsh speakers fell from 909,000 to 508,000. Meanwhile, the district known as the *Bro Gymraeg,* where Welsh is spoken, shrank and began to fragment. English penetrates along the coast and valleys, causing Welsh to retreat into the hilliest terrain. *Monoglots* are people who are able to speak only one language, in this case Welsh. Note how their retreat has been far more profound than that of the bilingual Welsh speakers. Bilingualism is often a transitional phase in the extinction of minority languages. (After Williams, Trevor D. "A Linguistic Map of Wales." *Geographical Journal,* 89 [1937]: 146–151; Jones, Emrys, and Ieuan Griffiths. "A Linguistic Map of Wales, 1961." *Geographical Journal,* 129 [1963]: 192–196; Bowen, E. G., and H. Carter. "The Distribution of the Welsh Language in 1971." *Geography,* 60 [1975]: 1–5; and Williams, 1988, p. 191.)

group, placed in a lower social class, loses pride in its language and culture, eventually abandoning both. An educational system based solely on the socially dominant language produces bilingualism, and the number of *monoglots,* or persons able to speak only one tongue, declines (Figure 5.11). If the conquered group had been literate, they usually lapse at this stage into illiteracy in their traditional language. Often, no legal or religious status is accorded to the conquered language, conveying the message of social inferiority—the old way of speech is primitive and its use is socially degrading. One of the first acts of the new republican government of France in 1793 was to mandate the elimination of regional languages and dialects, using the apparatus of government to achieve that goal. In the modern world, where communications media are so pervasive, denying the oppressed language groups access to broadcast facilities can hasten the process of decline.

The linguistic geography of the United States reveals the profound decline of languages other than English, illustrating the social morale model. Almost up to the present day, Native Americans have been subjected to linguistic assaults from the dominant culture (see box, *Conquering the Indian with Words*). Large numbers of Indian children have traditionally been taken from their families and placed in special boarding schools, often hundreds of miles from their homes. In these schools, run by the white-controlled Bureau of Indian Affairs, the Indian children were long forbidden on pain of punishment to speak their own languages.

A similar process led to the abandonment of most immigrant minority languages in the United States. As late as 1910, one out of every four Americans could speak some language other than English with the skill of a native (as compared to 14 percent in 1990). This was a result of the mass immigrations from Germany, Poland, Italy, Russia, China, and many other foreign areas. Much of this linguistic diversity has given way to English, partly because these imported languages lacked legal status. Only the Spanish-speaking population experienced any long-term success in preserving their speech in the United States. They achieved this, however, at the price of discrimination and lower socioeconomic status.

Morale is not always broken by conquest and subsequent discrimination. The Greeks endured lengthy periods of rule by Romans and

Conquering the Indian with Words

An Odawa Indian, born on Manitoulin Island, Ontario, Canada, remembers the problems language caused him when, as a child, he first left the Indian reservation and entered the English-speaking world that surrounded and dominated it:

> *Many of us as children were not even permitted to speak our own language. Of course, we still tried to speak our own language, but we were punished for it. Four or five years ago they were still stripping the kids of their clothes up around Kenora and beating them for speaking their own language. I was punished several times for speaking Indian not only on the school grounds but off the school grounds and on the street, and I lived across from the school. Almost in front of my own door my first language was forbidden me, and yet when I went into the house my parents spoke Indian.*
>
> *Our language is so important to us as a people. Our language and our language structure related to our whole way of life. How beautiful that picture language is where they only tell you the beginning and the end, and you fill in everything, and they allow you to feel how you want to feel. Here we manipulate and twist things around and get you to hate a guy. The Indian doesn't do that. He'll just say that some guy got into an accident, and he won't give you any details. From there on you just explore as far as you want to. You'll say: "What happened?" and he'll tell you a little more. He only answers questions. All of the in-between you fill in for yourself as you see it. We are losing that feeling when we lose our language at school. And that changes our relationship with our parents. All of a sudden we begin saying to our parents "you're stupid." We have begun to equate literacy [in English] with learning, and this is the first step down. The parents know that, but they are unable to do anything about it. And we take on the values, and the history of somebody else.*

From Pelletier, Wilfred. "Childhood in an Indian Village," in Satu Repo (ed.), *This Book Is About Schools,* pp. 23–24.

Turks without succumbing linguistically to either conqueror, and remained convinced their culture was superior to those of their conquerors. The Chinese absorbed Mongol invaders and made Chinese out of them. Sometimes the languages of conquered and conqueror blend, as happened after the Norman-French conquest of England nine centuries ago.

The Economic Development Model

Withers, who developed the social morale model, also proposed an *economic development model.* New technologies and adaptive strategies, particularly industrialization accompanied by urbanization, can break up the social structure needed to perpetuate an indigenous language. The transition from subsistence farming to factory laboring, which accompanies industrialization, is generally destructive to minority tongues, particularly when the language of the factory is not that of the farm. Urban-industrial areas then become the "holes in the Swiss cheese" of minority speech, depriving the minority language of the cultural centers that might allow its survival. Moreover, industrialization tends to draw population out of the rural linguistic refuge areas, leaving far fewer people behind to perpetuate the language. Withers called this process the *clearance model.* By contrast, if the industrial development occurs in the refuge area, it draws in speakers of the dominant language, producing a *changeover model,* in which the native speakers are overwhelmed by an intrusion of foreigners.

The plight of the Welsh language in Great Britain, one of the most thoroughly studied cases of linguistic decline, illustrates Withers's social morale, economic development, clearance, and changeover models (Figure 5.11). The retreat of Welsh, a Celtic Indo-European tongue, before English in the twentieth century was catastrophic, and it now stands near the threshold of extinction. Its speakers were long denigrated, and the British educational system promoted English. Urbanization and industrialization knocked "holes" in the spatial fabric of Welsh, and massive rural emigration followed, directed to the English-speaking towns and factories. Geographer Keith Buchanan referred to the decline of Welsh and other Celtic languages as a "liquidation" carried out by the ruling English in order to produce a loyal, obedient workforce for the mines and factories. In recent decades, the Welsh language has been granted educational and media privileges by the British government, but perhaps too late. The social morale of its speakers is broken and a mere handful of Welsh monoglots, largely aged, survives. The day nears when the inhabitants of Wales may not know what the names of the towns, rivers, and mountains of their native land mean or even be able to understand their very family names.

The ongoing achievement of independence as nation-states by various linguistic minority groups, described in the previous chapter, could well rescue some languages previously endangered by these various assimilative models. Estonian and Latvian in the independent Baltic states offer examples.

Language and Religion

Cultural integration occasionally yields a situation in which a language group is linked to a particular religious faith, a linkage that greatly heightens cultural identity. Perhaps Arabic provides the best example of this cultural link. It spread from a core area on the Arabian peninsula with the Islamic faith. Had it not been for the evangelical fervor of the Muslims, Arabic would not have diffused so widely. The other Semitic languages also correspond to particular religious groups. Hebrew-speaking people are of the Jewish faith, and the Amharic speakers in Ethiopia are Coptic, or Eastern, Christians. Indeed, we can attribute the preservation and revival of Hebrew to the remarkable tenacity of the Jewish faith.

Certain languages even acquired a religious status. Latin survived mainly as the ceremonial language of the Roman Catholic Church and Vatican City. In non-Arabic Muslim lands, such as Iran, Arabic is still used in religious ceremony. Great religious books can shape languages by providing them with a standard form. Luther's translation of the Bible led to the standardization of the German language, and the Koran is the model for written Arabic. The early appearance of a hymnal and the Bible in the Welsh language aided the survival of that Celtic tongue, and Christian missionaries in diverse Third World countries have translated the Bible into local languages, with similar results. In Fiji, the appearance of the Bible in one of the 15 local dialects elevated it to the dominant native language of the islands.

The linkage of language and religion greatly enhances the possibility of nationalistic conflict. Examples include some of the bitterest and most intractable disputes today, such as the Greek/Christian–Turkish/Muslim problem in Cyprus, the Armenian/Christian–Azeri/Muslim war, and the Arab/Muslim battle against Nilo-Saharan/Christian and animist tribal groups in Sudan.

Figure 5.12
Linguistic landscapes can be vividly alien. For those, like Americans, who are visually accustomed to the Latin alphabet, the linguistic landscape of countries such as Israel appears exotic, and we lapse suddenly into illiteracy. Some visitors experience an emotion akin to fright or panic when confronted with alien linguistic landscapes.

Linguistic Landscapes

The cultural landscape, the visible human-made landscape, bears the imprint of language in various ways. Road signs, billboards, graffiti, placards, and other publicly displayed writing not only reveal the locally dominant language, but also can be a visual index to bilingualism, linguistic oppression of minorities, and other facets of linguistic geography. Furthermore, Johanna Drucker points out, "As we observe words in the landscape, they charge and activate the environment, sometimes undermining, sometimes reinforcing our perceptions." Differences in alphabets render many foreign linguistic landscapes vividly alien (Figure 5.12). Messages, both overt and subtle, both friendly and hostile, are sent by language in the landscape.

Toponyms

Most revealing in the cultural sense are the names that people place on the land, the names given to settlements, terrain features, streams, and various other aspects of their surroundings. These place-names, or **toponyms,** often directly reflect the spatial patterns of language, dialect, and ethnicity. Toponyms become part of the cultural landscape when they appear on signs and placards. As you drive through English-speaking portions of North America, you read highway signs such as "Huntsville City Limits," "Harrisburg 25," "Ohio River," "Newfound Gap, Elevation 5048," or "Entering Cape Hatteras National Seashore." For the linguistic geographer such toponyms often provide a visible index to the distribution of other cultural traits.

Many place-names consist of two parts—the *generic* and the *specific*. For example, in the American place-names we listed above—Huntsville, Harrisburg, Ohio River, Newfound Gap, and Cape Hatteras—the specific segments are *Hunts, Harris, Ohio, Newfound,* and *Hatteras*. The generic parts, which tell what *kind* of place is being described, are *ville, burg, river, gap,* and *cape*.

Generic toponyms are of greater potential value to the cultural geographer than specific names since they appear again and again throughout a culture region. There are literally thousands of generic place-names, and every culture or subculture has its own distinctive set of them. They can be particularly valuable in tracing the spread of a culture, and they often aid in the reconstruction of culture regions of the past. Sometimes they provide information about changes people wrought long ago in their physical surroundings. We will look at each of these ways that cultural geographers use generic toponyms.

Generic Toponyms of the United States

The three previously mentioned dialects of the eastern United States (Figure 5.4)—Northern, Midland, and Southern—illustrate the value of generic toponyms in cultural geographical detective work. For example, New Englanders, speakers of the Northern dialect, frequently used the term *center* in the name of the town or hamlet near the center of a township. Outlying settlements frequently bear the prefix *east, west, north,* or *south* with the specific name of the township as the suffix. Thus in Randolph Township, Orange County, Vermont, we find settlements named Randolph Center, South Randolph, East Randolph, and North Randolph.

These generic usages and duplications are peculiar to New England, and we can locate colonies founded by New Englanders as they migrated from their homelands by looking for such place-names in other parts of the country. Westward from New England—through upstate New York, Ontario, and into the upper Midwest—we can observe a trail of "Centers" and name duplications that clearly indicate their path of migration and settlement (Figure 5.13). Thus we can see the toponymic evidence of New England in areas as far afield as Walworth County, Wisconsin, where Troy, Troy Center, and East Troy are clustered; in Dufferin County, Ontario, where one finds places such as Mono Centre; and even in distant Alberta, near Edmonton, where the toponym Michigan Centre doubly suggests a particular cultural diffusion. Other generic place-names identified with the Northern dialect are *brook, notch,* and *corners*. The trace of New England even reaches the Pacific shore, where "Center" and "Corners" suffixes abound in the Seattle area. Similarly, we can identify Midland American areas by such terms as *gap, cove, hollow, knob* (a low, rounded hill), and *burgh,* as in Stone Gap, Cades Cove, Stillhouse Hollow, Bald Knob, and Pittsburgh. We can recognize Southern speech by such names as *bayou, gully,* and *store* (for rural hamlets), as in Cypress Bayou, Gum Gully, and Halls Store.

Toponyms and Cultures of the Past

Place-names often survive long after the culture that produced them vanishes from an area. Such archaic toponyms preserve traces of the past. One need look no further than the numerous Indian place-names of the United States for an example (see box, *American Indian Names*

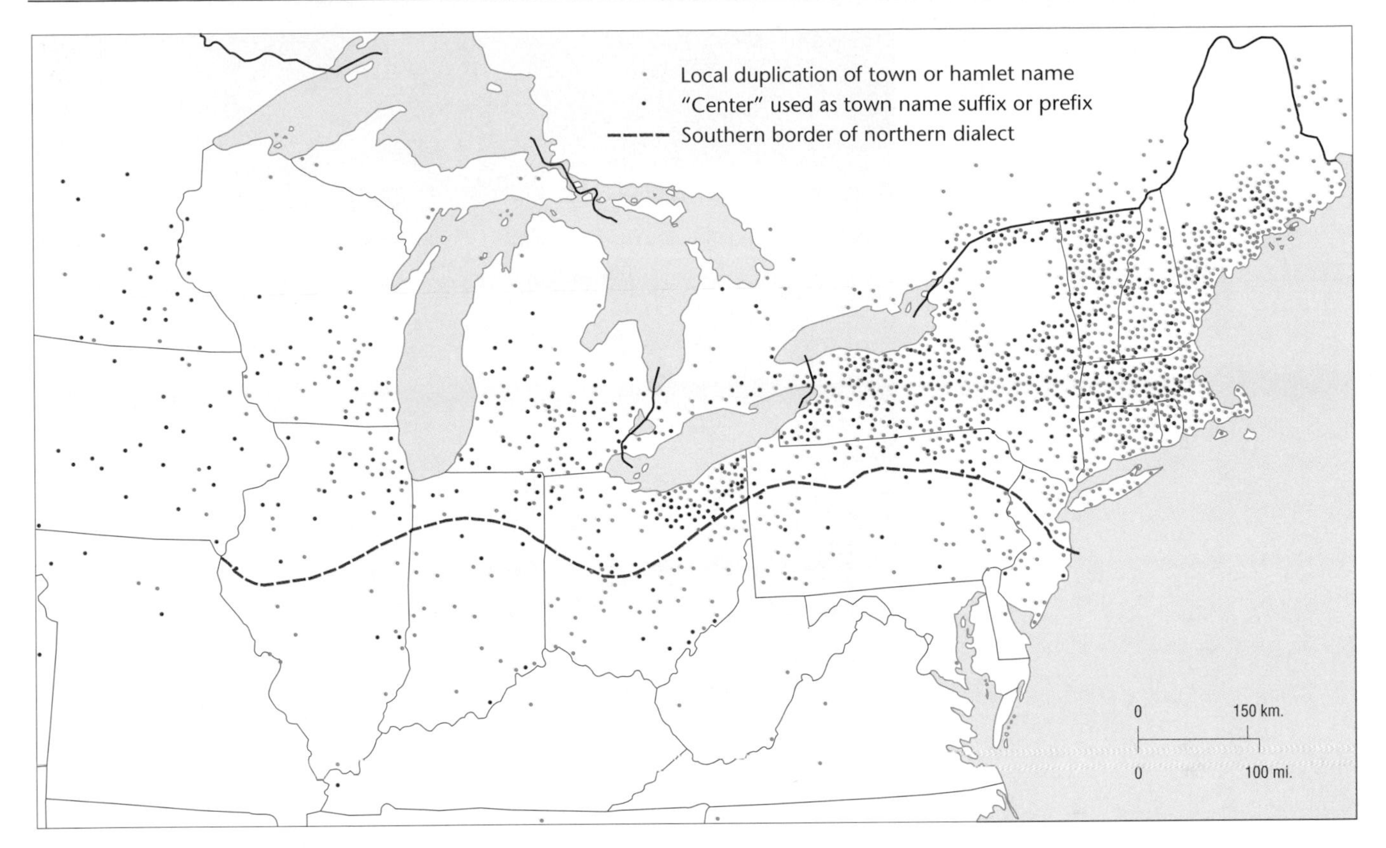

Figure 5.13
Generic place-names reveal the migration of Yankee New Englanders and the spread of the Northern dialect. Two of the most typical place-name characteristics in New England are the use of *Center* in the names of the principal town in a township and the tendency to duplicate the names of settlements within townships by adding the prefixes *East, West, North,* and *South* to the town name. As the concentration of such place-names suggests, Massachusetts, the first New England colony, is where these two Yankee traits originated. Note how these toponyms moved westward with New England settlers, but thinned out rapidly to the south, in areas not colonized by New Englanders.

American Indian Names on the Land

From one part of the country to another, from Walla Walla to Waxahachie, from Kalamazoo to Saskatchewan, North America's map is dotted with all kinds of Indian names. They are on our lips every day. They constitute an integral part of the flavor of modern life and culture. The names of 27 of the 50 states and 4 of the 10 Canadian provinces are Indian in origin.

"These place names represent various types of linguistic treatment. Often the English-speaking settlers merely took over, more or less accurately, the name given to a place by the Indians themselves. Frequently such names were descriptive of the landscape or of the life about it. Mackinac Island [is] a shortening of *Michilimackinac,* 'great turtle.' Mississippi is simply 'big river.' . . . The name *Chicago* has several interpretations, the most likely being 'garlic field,' the final-*o* serving really as a locative suffix.

"Many times in the course of our name giving, the Indian name was translated into its English equivalent. As the survey of place names in South Dakota puts it, 'When a creek is called White Thunder, Blue Dog, or American Horse, the Indian influence is obvious, since these adjectives are not those which a white man would use with these nouns. Four Horns, Greasy Horn, and Dog Ear are other examples.' The survey neglected to mention Stinking Water and Stinking Bear creeks, both of which are further convincing and delightful illustrations of this same process. . . . "

From *American English,* 2d ed., by Albert H. Marckwardt, revised by J. L. Dillard.

Figure 5.14
An Australian Aborigine specific toponym joined to an English generic name, near Omeo in Victoria state, Australia. Such signs give a special, distinctive look to the linguistic landscape and speak of a now-vanished culture region.

on the Land). Similarly, Australia abounds in Aborigine toponyms, even in areas from which the native peoples disappeared long ago (Figure 5.14). No toponyms are more permanently established than those identifying physical geographical features, such as rivers and mountains. Even the most absolute conquest, exterminating an aboriginal people, usually does not entirely destroy such names.

In general, this study of archaic names has greater value in the Eastern Hemisphere where many movements of peoples occurred before history was recorded. East of the Elbe and Saale rivers, in eastern Germany, the suffixes *ow, in,* and *zig* (as in Teterow, Berlin, and Leipzig) are very common in the names of villages, towns, and cities. Each of these suffixes is of Slavic rather than Germanic origin and their distribution accurately reveals the culture region peopled by Slavic tribes as late as AD 800, even though the Slavic languages have since disappeared from most of eastern Germany (Figure 5.15). Similarly, the common occurrence of the suffix *weiler,* as in Eschweiler, in the names of German villages south of the Danube and west of the Rhine, reminds us of former Roman rule and the use of Latin there. *Weiler,* which means "hamlet," derives from the Latin *villare,* meaning "country estates."

Farther south, in Spain and Portugal, seven centuries of Moorish rule left behind a great many Arabic place-names, as Figure 5.16 shows. An example is the prefix *guada* on river names (as in Guadalquivir and Gaudalupejo), a corruption of the Arabic *wadi,* meaning "river" or "stream." Thus Guadalquivir, corrupted from Wadi al Kabir, means "the great river." The frequent occurrence of Arabic names in any particular region or province of Spain suggests a survival of Moorish influence in that area.

New Zealand, too, offers some intriguing examples of the subtle messages that can be conveyed by archaic toponyms. The native Polynesian people of New Zealand, the Maori, are today confined mainly to

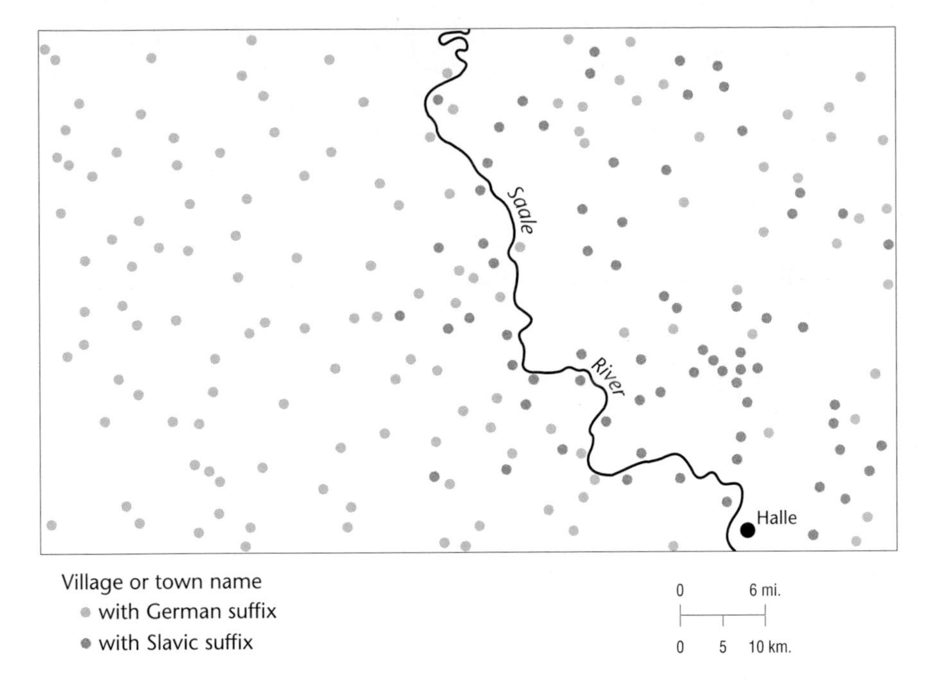

Figure 5.15
A relict language border revealed by toponyms. Twelve hundred years ago, the area along the Saale River near the city of Halle in eastern Germany was a linguistic border zone between Germans on the west and Slavs to the east. For a thousand years German has been spoken throughout the area, and no Slavic people remain. Even so, the ancient language border is still revealed in the landscape by the generic place-names of towns and villages. Names bearing the Slavic generic suffixes *itz, zig,* or *in* remain dominant east of the Saale, while German generic suffixes prevail in the west. If you were drawing the Germanic-Slavic language border of AD 800 on this basis, where would you place it? What other evidence might you seek? (Source: Jordan, Terry G. *The European Culture Area: A Systematic Geography,* 3d ed. New York: HarperCollins, 1996, p. 122.)

refuge areas, not unlike the American Indians. Cultural geographer Hong-key Yoon has observed that the survival rate of Maori names for towns varies according to size. The four largest New Zealand cities all have European names. Next lowest in the urban hierarchy are 20 regional centers, with 10,000 to 100,000 population, and 40 percent of these have Maori names, while almost 60 percent of the small towns, with fewer than 10,000 inhabitants, bear Maori toponyms. Similarly, only 20 percent of New Zealand's provinces have Maori names, but 56 percent of the counties do. What interpretation might the cultural geographer derive from this?

Toponyms and Environmental Modification

Generic place-names also inform us about humankind's alteration of the environment in past times. From about AD 800 to 1300, Germanic peoples cleared forests in lands from England eastward into present-day Poland, an activity well commemorated in toponyms. These names sometimes even indicate how the clearing was accomplished. In Germany, the generic suffixes *roth* and *reuth,* as *Neuroth* and *Bayreuth,* mean "rooted out" or "grubbed out" and refer to the Teutonic practice of digging out roots after cutting down the trees. In England, the suffix *ley* or *leigh,* as in Woodley, means "clearing" or "open place" in the forest. *Brind, brunn,* and *brand,* in European place-names such as Brindley and Branderoda, reveal that clearing was done with fire.

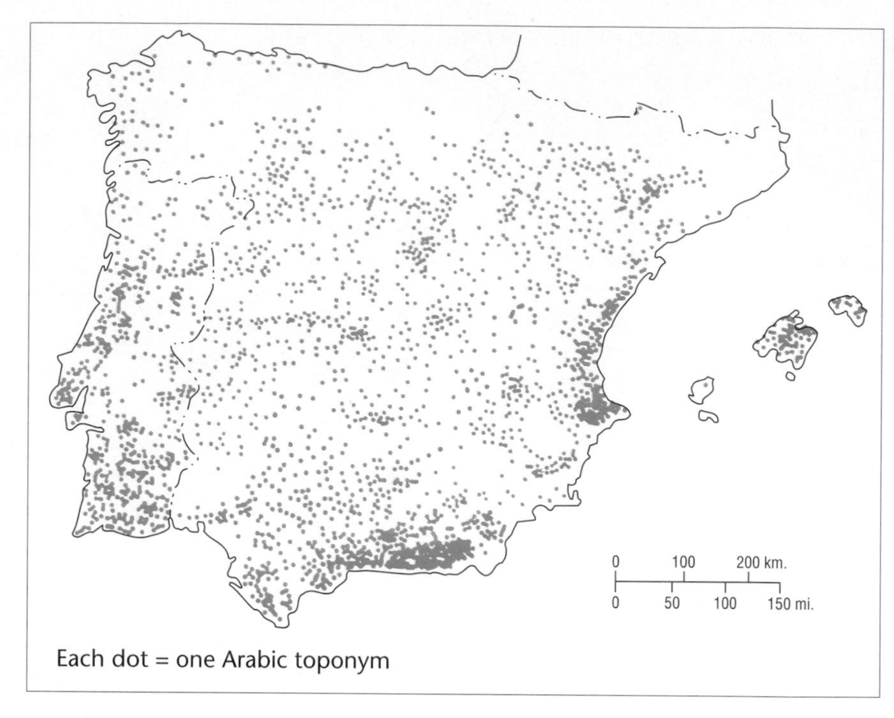

Figure 5.16
Arabic toponyms in Iberia. A Semitic language, Arabic spread into Spain and Portugal with the Moors over a thousand years ago. A reconquest by Romance Indo-European speakers subsequently rooted out Arabic in Iberia, but a reminder of the Semitic language survives still in the toponyms. Using this map, speculate concerning the direction of the Moorish invasion and retreat, the duration of Moorish rule in different parts of Iberia, and the main centers of former Moorish power. (Adapted from Houston, James M. *The Western Mediterranean World.* New York: Praeger, 1967.)

In the eastern woodlands of the United States, agricultural American Indians cleared considerable forest areas before the coming of Columbus. Their abandoned grass-covered fields survived, and white settlers preserved a record of the aboriginal deforestation by placing such generic names on the land as *prairie,* which refers to grassy areas. Over 200 of these generic terms appear in wooded eastern Texas alone, suggesting the wide extent of Native American forest-clearing activities.

Conclusion

Language, then, is an essential part of culture that can be studied using the five themes of cultural geography. Its families, dialects, vocabulary, pronunciation, and toponyms display distinct spatial variations that can be shown on maps of linguistic culture regions. Languages ebb and flow across geographical areas through the processes of diffusion. Relocation and expansion diffusion, both hierarchical and contagious, are apparent in the movement of language, and all the concepts of cultural diffusion can be applied to language.

Language and physical environment interact in a linguistic ecology. The Austronesian people rode the prevailing winds and ocean currents to carry their speech and toponyms across the vast Pacific and Indian oceans. Some linguistic groups found refuge in areas of difficult terrain, such as mountain ranges. Environment helps shape vocabulary, and the secrets of ancient environmental alteration are sometimes revealed in toponyms.

The study of cultural integration shows that language is causally related to other elements of culture. In fact, language is the basis for the expression of all elements of culture, so the geography of languages is closely bound to the geographies of religion, politics, technology, and economy. Certain tongues advanced with empire-building armies; others shared the evangelical diffusion of religious faiths; still others served the purposes of commerce and trade. Language is firmly enmeshed in the cultural whole.

We can see language in the landscapes created by literate societies. The visible alphabet, public signs, and generic toponyms create a linguistic landscape that can accentuate the alien appearance of lands where we cannot understand the speech, comprehend the alphabet, or decipher the toponyms.

Although language allows us to express our culture, religion provides the basis for many of our cultural attitudes. Values and beliefs grow out of religious heritage. The next chapter examines religion from the viewpoint of the cultural geographer.

Sources and Suggested Readings

Aitchison, John, and Harold Carter. *A Geography of the Welsh Language, 1961–1991.* Cardiff, UK: University of Wales Press, 1994.

Bastian, Robert W. "Generic Place-Names and the Northern-Midland Dialect Boundary in the Midwest." *Names,* 25 (1977): 228–236.

Bennett, Charles J. "The Morphology of Language Boundaries: Indo-Aryan and Dravidian in Peninsular India," in David E. Sopher (ed.), *An Exploration of India: Geographical Perspectives on Society and Culture.* Ithaca, NY: Cornell University Press, 1980, pp. 234–251.

Buchanan, Keith. "Economic Growth and Cultural Liquidation: The Case of the Celtic Nations," in Richard Peet (ed.), *Radical Geography: Alternative Viewpoints on Contemporary Social Issues.* Chicago: Maaroufa Press, 1977, pp. 125–143.

Burrill, Meredith F. "Toponymic Generics." *Names,* 4 (1956): 129–137, 226–240.

Cartwright, Donald G. "Linguistic Territorialization: Is Canada Approaching the Belgian Model?" *Journal of Cultural Geography,* 8, No. 2 (1988): 115–134.

Carver, Craig M. *American Regional Dialects: A Word Geography.* Ann Arbor: University of Michigan Press, 1986.

Cassidy, Frederic C. (ed.). *Dictionary of American Regional English.* 2 vols. Cambridge, MA: Harvard University Press, 1985, 1991.

Delgado de Carvalho, C. M. "The Geography of Languages," in Philip L. Wagner and Marvin W. Mikesell (eds.), *Readings in Cultural Geography.* Chicago: University of Chicago Press, 1962, pp. 75–93.

Drucker, Johanna. "Language in the Landscape." *Landscape,* 28: 1 (1984): 7–13.

Dutt, Ashok K., Chandrakanta Khan, and Chandralekha Sangwan. "Spatial Pattern of Languages in India: A Culture-Historical Analysis." *GeoJournal,* 10 (1985): 51–74.

Estaville, Lawrence E. Jr. "The Louisiana French Language in the Nineteenth Century." *Southeastern Geographer,* 30 (1990): 107–120.

Jakle, John A. "Salt-Derived Place Names in the Ohio Valley." *Names,* 16 (1968): 1–5.

Kaplan, David H. "Population and Politics in a Plural Society: The Changing Geography of Canada's Linguistic Groups." *Annals of the Association of American Geographers,* 84 (1994): 46–67.

Kaups, Matti. "Finnish Place Names in Minnesota: A Study in Cultural Transfer." *Geographical Review,* 56 (1966): 377–397.

Kearns, Kevin C. "Resuscitation of the Irish Gaeltacht." *Geographical Review,* 64 (1974): 83–110.

Kirk, John, Stewart F. Sanderson, and John D. A. Widdowson (eds.). *Studies in Linguistic Geography*. London: Croom Helm, 1985.

Krantz, Grover S. *Geographical Development of European Languages*. New York: Peter Lang, 1988.

Kurath, Hans. *Word Geography of the Eastern United States*. Ann Arbor: University of Michigan Press, 1949.

Kurath, Hans, and Raven I. McDavid, Jr. *The Pronunciation of English in the Atlantic States*. Ann Arbor: University of Michigan Press, 1961.

Laponce, J. A. *Languages and Their Territories*. Toronto: University of Toronto Press, 1987.

Leighly, John B. "Town Names of Colonial New England in the West." *Annals of the Association of American Geographers,* 68 (1978): 233–248.

Levitt, Jesse, Leonard R. N. Ashley, and Kenneth H. Rogers (eds.). *Geolinguistic Perspectives*. Lanham, MD: University Press of America, 1987.

Lind, Ivan. "Geography and Place Names," in Philip L. Wagner and Marvin W. Mikesell (eds.), *Readings in Cultural Geography*. Chicago: University of Chicago Press, 1962, pp. 118–128.

Mackey, William F. *Three Concepts for Geolinguistics*. Québec City: International Centre for Research on Bilingualism, 1973.

Matley, Ian. "Perceptions of Mountain Environments as Reflected in the Names of Landforms in the Scottish Highlands, Norway and Romania," in Breandán S. MacAodha (ed.), *Topothesia*. Galway, Ireland: Dept. of Geography, University College, 1982, pp. 25–39.

McDavid, Raven I., Jr. "Linguistic Geography and Toponymic Research." *Names,* 6 (1958): 65–73.

McDavid, Raven I., Jr. *Varieties of American English*. Stanford, CA: Stanford University Press, 1980.

McMullen, E. Wallace. "The Term 'Prairie' in the United States." *Names,* 5 (1957): 27–46.

Moseley, Christopher, and R. E. Asher (eds.). *Atlas of the World's Languages*. London: Routledge, 1994.

Noble, Allen G., and Ramesh C. Dhussa. "The Linguistic Geography of Dumka, Bihar, India." *Journal of Cultural Geography,* 3 (Spring-Summer 1983): 73–81.

Raup, H. F. "Names of Ohio's Streams," *Names,* 5 (1957): 162–168.

Raup, H. F., and W. B. Pounds, Jr. "Northernmost Spanish Frontier in California as Shown by the Distribution of Geographic Names." *California Historical Society Quarterly,* 32 (1953): 43–48.

Renfrew, Colin. "The Origins of Indo-European Languages." *Scientific American* 261, No. 4 (1989): 106–114.

Stewart, George R. *Names on the Land: A Historical Account of Place-Naming in the United States*. Boston: Houghton Mifflin, 1958.

Trudgill, Peter. "Linguistic Change and Diffusion." *Language in Society,* 2 (1974): 215–246.

Trudgill, Peter. *On Dialect: Social and Geographical Perspectives*. Oxford, UK: Basil Blackwell, 1983.

Tuan, Yi-fu. "Language and the Making of Place," *Annals of the Association of American Geographers,* 81 (1991): 684–696.

Wagner, Philip L. "Remarks on the Geography of Language." *Geographical Review,* 48 (1958): 86–97.

Waibel, Leo. "Place Names as an Aid in the Reconstruction of the Original Vegetation of Cuba." *Geographical Review,* 33 (1943): 376–396.

Weightman, Barbara A. "Sign Geography." *Journal of Cultural Geography,* 9 (Fall/Winter 1988): 53–70.

West, Robert C. "The Term 'Bayou' in the United States: A Study in the Geography of Place Names." *Annals of the Association of American Geographers,* 44 (1954): 63–74.

Williams, Colin H. (ed.). *Language in Geographical Context*. Clevedon, UK and Philadelphia: Multilingual Matters, 1988.

Withers, Charles W. J. *Gaelic Scotland: The Transformation of a Culture Region.* London: Routledge, 1988.

Wixman, Ronald. *Language Aspects of Ethnic Patterns and Processes in the North Caucasus.* Research Paper No. 191. University of Chicago, Dept. of Geography 1980.

Wright, John K. "The Study of Place-Names." *Geographical Review,* 19 (1929): 140–144.

Yoon, Hong-key. "Maori and Pakeha Place Names for Cultural Features in New Zealand," in *Maori Mind, Maori Land: Essays on the Cultural Geography of the Maori People from an Outsider's Perspective.* Bern, Switzerland: Peter Lang, 1986, pp. 98–122.

Zelinsky, Wilbur. "Generic Terms in the Place Names of the Northeastern United States." *Annals of the Association of American Geographers,* 45 (1955): 319–349.

Zelinsky, Wilbur. "On the Naming of Places and Kindred Things," in Simon J. Bronner (ed.), *Creativity and Tradition in Folklore.* Logan: Utah State University Press, 1992, pp. 169–184.

Zelinsky, Wilbur, and Colin H. Williams. "The Mapping of Language in North America and the British Isles." *Progress in Human Geography,* 12 (1988): 337–368.

Zelinsky, Wilbur. "On the Superabundance of Signs in Our Landscape." *Landscape,* 31, No. 3 (1992): 30–38.

CHAPTER 6

Religious Realms

As an essential part of culture, religion lends vivid hues to the human mosaic. **Religion** can be defined as a set of beliefs and practices, through which people seek mental and physical harmony with the powers of the universe, through which they attempt to influence and accommodate the awesome forces of nature, life, and death. For some cultural groups, religion is little more than a protective buffer between humans and the mysterious, potentially destructive forces of nature. Others have, over centuries, developed highly articulated systems of belief with elaborate moral codes.

Geographers have long been fascinated by religion, and the Association of American Geographers includes a special-interest group called the Geography of Religions and Belief Systems. The appropriateness of the study of religion in cultural geography will be revealed through our five themes. Religion differs from one place to another, producing variations that can be mapped as culture regions. These spatial variations were produced by cultural diffusion and reflect a complex interplay among religion, the environment, and other aspects of culture. In turn, the spatial pattern of religion is visibly imprinted on the cultural landscape (Figure 6.1). Religion very often lies at the root of conflict between different cultural groups, for people seem less willing to tolerate and to accommodate differences in religious matters than in any other aspect of culture. Having attained some sort of harmony with the cosmos, we do not want to be told that our path is only one of many and possesses no unique attributes of truth. Catholics versus Protestants in Ireland, Hindus versus Muslims in India, Catholics versus Orthodox versus Muslims in the former Yugoslavia, and Jews versus Muslims in the Middle East represent conflicts based largely in religion, as was suggested in Chapter 4. In short, religion is at once a central defining trait of many cultural groups—a label of "we" and "they"—and a highly territorial phenomenon, with strong, often ancient linkages to the spirit of place, ethnicity, and nationality. For these reasons, it represents a key element of cultural geography.

Different types of religion exist in the world. One way to classify them is to distinguish between proselytic and ethnic faiths.

Figure 6.1
Another place, another faith. Muslims at prayer in Pakistan.

Proselytic religions actively seek new members and have as a goal the conversion of all humankind. They instruct their faithful to spread the Word to all the Earth, using one method or another to convert the "heathen." In contrast with proselytic religions are **ethnic religions,** each of which is identified with some particular ethnic or tribal group and does not seek converts. Proselytic religions sometimes grow out of ethnic religions—the evolution of Christianity from its parent Judaism is the primary example. This change usually occurs within an ethnic religion when a charismatic leader or reformer emerges whose revelations are so profound and whose personality is so dynamic that persons beyond the immediate cultural group are attracted. Once the evangelical spirit of such a proselytic religion is spent, a fragmentation and reversion to ethnic status sometimes occurs.

Religious Culture Regions

Because religion, like all of culture, has a strong territorial tie, both functional and formal religious culture regions abound. The functional partitioning of the Earth into networks of parishes and larger church administrative units covers most inhabited areas. The smallest such unit, the congregation, is a functional social unit with spatial dimensions and constraints.

Perhaps the most basic spatial act by religious groups is the functional designation of **sacred space,** including areas and sites recognized as worthy of devotion, loyalty, fear, or esteem. The notion that particular places possess sacredness occurs in many different cultures, past and present, all over the world. James Griffith speaks of "supernaturally sanctioned ties between individual cultures and specific places," a link he calls *spiritual geography.* By virtue of their sacredness, these special places can be avoided by the faithful, sought out by pilgrims, or barred to members of other religions. Often sacred space contains the site of supposed supernatural events or is viewed as the abode of gods. Conflict can result if two religions venerate the same space (see box, *Conflict over Sacred Space*). In Jerusalem, for example, the Muslim

Conflict over Sacred Space

When two or more religions claim the same sacred space, conflict is usually unavoidable. In 1992, at the town of Ayodhya, in Uttar Pradesh state near the Nepal border in northern India, Hindus seized an Islamic mosque and destroyed it. They tore down the 450-year-old mosque in hopes of replacing it with a Hindu temple, claiming that the site is the precise birthplace of the pious god-king Rama, the "perfect Hindu" and protagonist of the epic tale *Ramayana*. Rama, whose very name became a synonym for the divine, is believed to have been an incarnation of the great god Vishnu, the most important solar deity, a preserver and restorer. To Muslims, the destruction of the mosque was an affront to Allah that demanded retribution. Widespread religious violence plagued the country because of this desecration and conflict over sacred space.

Dome of the Rock, the site of Muhammad's ascent to heaven, stands above the Wailing Wall, the remnant of a great Jewish temple (Figure 6.2). Cemeteries are also generally regarded as a type of sacred space.

Related to sacred space are *mystical places*—locations unconnected with established religion where, for whatever reason, some people believe that extraordinary, supernatural things happen. The "Bermuda Triangle" in the western Atlantic, where airplanes and ships supposedly disappear, is such a mystical place and, in effect, a vernacular culture area. Sometimes the sacred space of vanished ancient religions never loses or later regains the functional status of mystical place, which has happened at Stonehenge in England.

We can devise all kinds of formal culture regions based on religion. One might, for instance, define culture regions on the basis of a single religious trait. An example would be a map of all areas where **monotheism,** the worship of a single god, is prevalent. Much of the

Figure 6.2
Conflict over sacred space. Jews pray at the Wailing Wall, the remnant of their great ancient temple in Jerusalem, while one of the holiest sites for Muslims—the mosque called the Dome of the Rock, covering the place from which the Prophet Muhammad ascended to heaven—stands on the site of the vanished Jewish temple. Perhaps no other place on Earth is so heavily charged with religious meaning.

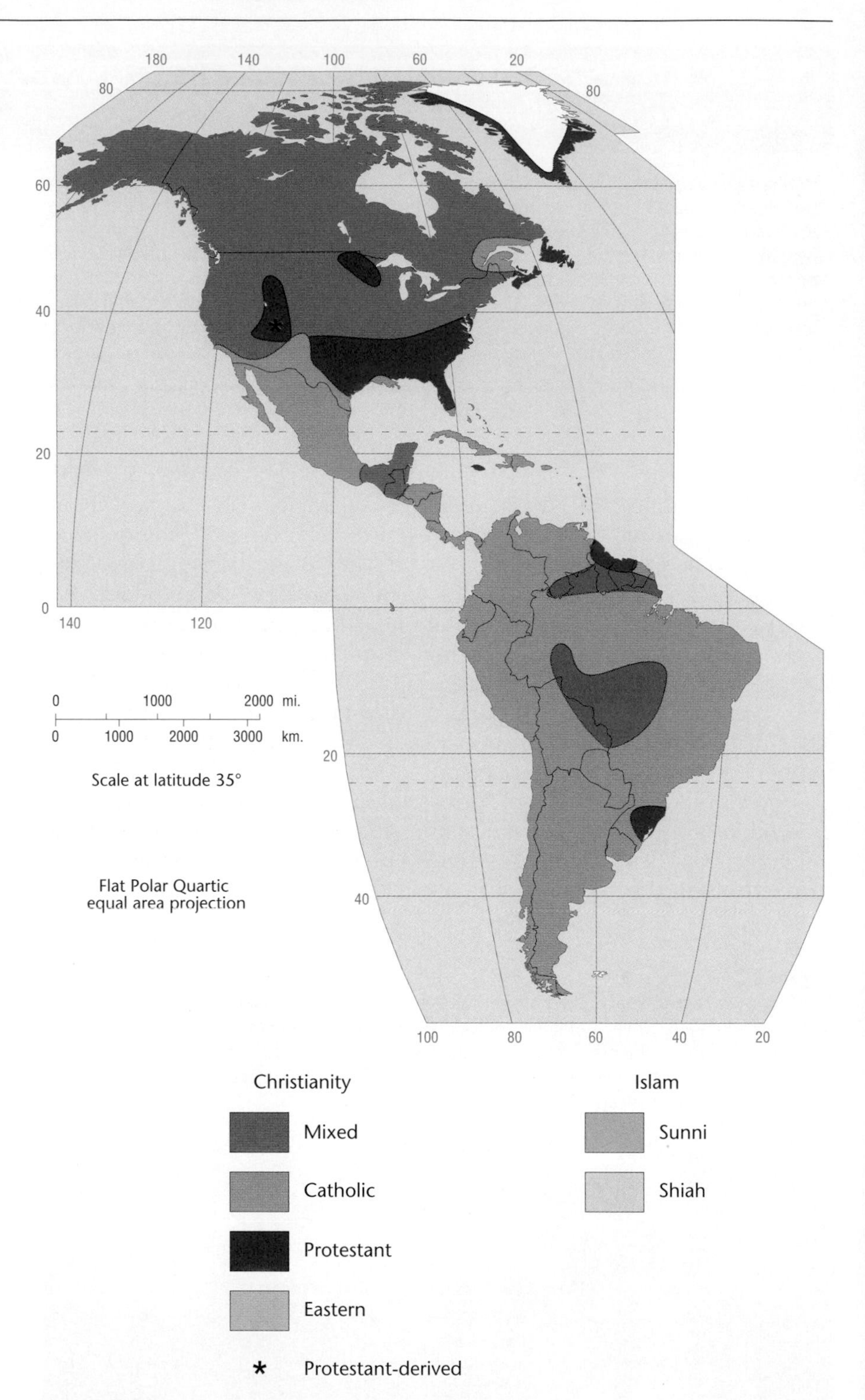

Figure 6.3
The world distribution of major religions. Much overlap exists that cannot be shown on a map of this scale. The attempt is to show which faith is dominant. "Animism" includes a wide array of diverse tribal belief systems.

world is in such a culture region, since monotheism is typical of a number of major religions. We may choose instead to set up religious culture regions based on a combination of traits. The most basic kind of multitrait formal religious culture region depicts the spatial distribution of generally acknowledged religious denominations, such as Christians,

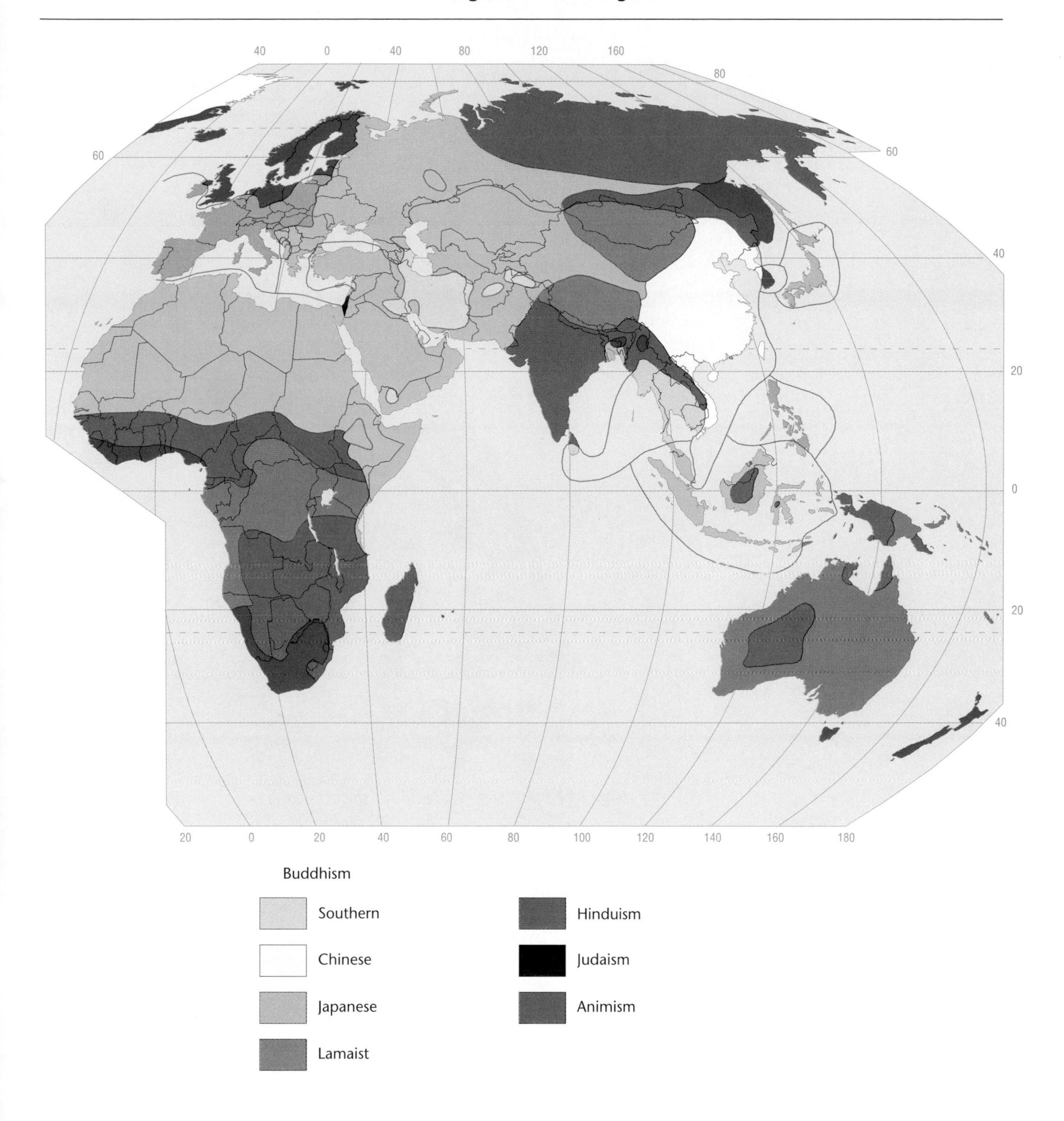

Jews, Muslims, and Hindus (Figure 6.3). Some parts of the world exhibit an exceedingly complicated pattern of religious adherence, and the boundaries of formal religious culture regions, like most cultural borders, are rarely sharp (Figure 6.4). Persons of different faiths often live in the same province or town.

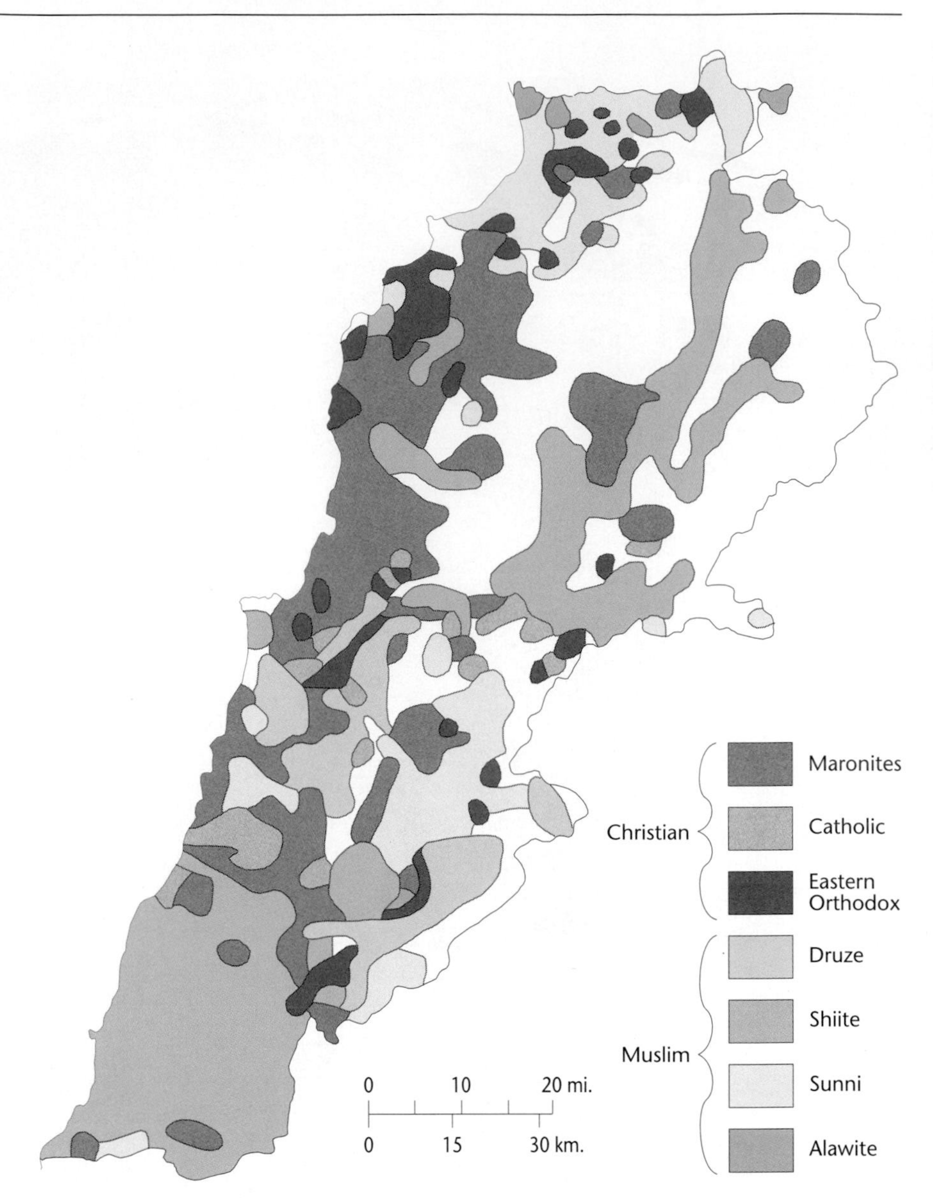

Figure 6.4
Distribution of religious groups in Lebanon. A land torn by sectarian warfare in recent times, Lebanon is one of the most religiously diverse parts of the world. (Derived, with changes, from Klaer, Wendelin, in *Heidelberger Geographische Arbeiten*, Vol. 15, 1966, p. 333.)

Christianity

Christianity, a proselytic faith, is the world's largest religion, both in area and number of adherents, with about 1.9 billion people (a third of humanity). It has long been fragmented into separate churches (Figure 6.3). The single greatest division is between Western and Eastern Christianity, each of which is further subdivided. Western Christianity was initially identified with Rome and the Latin-speaking areas, while the Eastern church dominated the Greek world from Constantinople (now Istanbul). Belonging to the Eastern group are the *Coptic* Church, originally the nationalistic religion of Christian Egyptians and still today a minority faith there, as well as being the dominant church among the highland people of Ethiopia; the *Maronites,* Semitic descendants of seventh-century heretics who retreated to a mountain refuge in

Lebanon (Figure 6.4); the *Nestorians,* who live in the mountains of Kurdistan and in India's Kerala State; and *Eastern Orthodoxy,* originally centered in Greek-speaking areas. After converting many Slavic groups, Eastern Orthodoxy split into a variety of national churches, such as Russian, Greek, Ukrainian, and Serbian Orthodoxy.

Western Christianity splintered also, most notably in the Protestant breakaway of the 1400s and 1500s. Since then, the Roman Catholic Church, which alone accounts for over one-sixth of humanity, has remained unified, but Protestantism, from its beginnings, tended to divide into a rich array of sects. The denominational map of the United States and Canada vividly reflects the fragmented nature of Western Christianity and the resulting complex pattern of religious culture regions (Figure 6.5). Numerous faiths imported from Europe were later augmented by Christian sects developed in America. The American frontier was a

Figure 6.5

Leading Christian denominations in the United States and Canada, shown by counties, or, for Canada, census districts. In the shaded areas, the church or denomination indicated claimed 50 percent or more of the total church membership. The most striking features of the map are the Baptist dominance through the South, a Lutheran zone in the upper Midwest, Mormon dominance in the interior West, and the zone of mixing in the American Heartland. Why are individual denominations less likely to dominate areas in western parts of the continent? (Simplified from Bradley, Martin B., et al. *Churches and Church Membership in the United States.* Atlanta: Glenmary Research Center, 1992; and the *National Atlas of Canada.*)

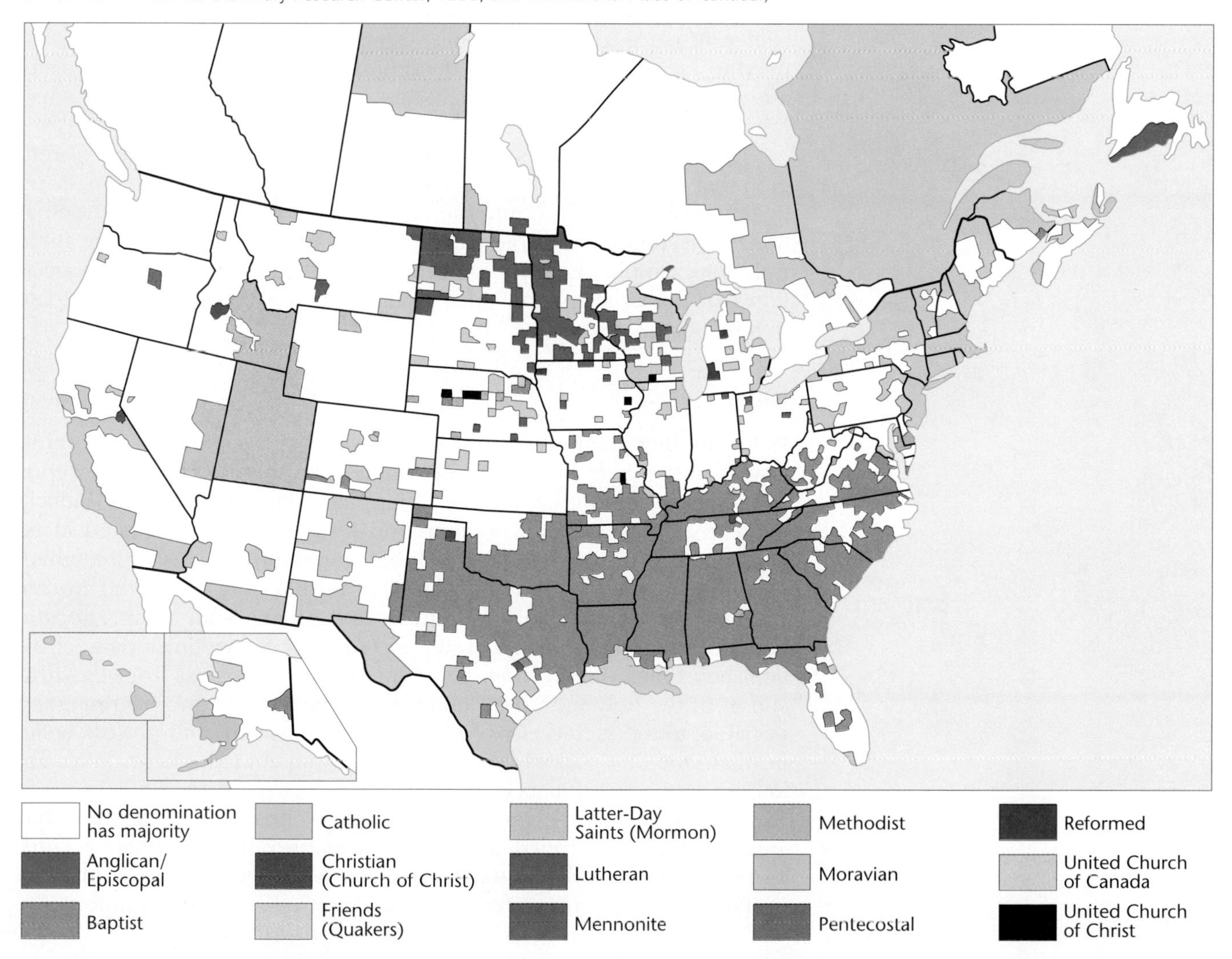

breeding ground for new religious groups, as individualistic pioneer sentiment found expression in splinter Protestant denominations. In numerous parts of the country, a relatively small community may contain the churches of half a dozen religious groups, with individual families sometimes split along religious lines.

As a result of this local fragmentation and mixing, the religious map of the United States displays less regionalization of faiths than is found in much of the rest of Christendom. Still, we can find some patterns in Figure 6.5. In a broad "Bible Belt" across the South, Baptist and other conservative fundamentalist denominations dominate, and Utah is at the core of a Mormon realm. A Lutheran belt stretches from Wisconsin westward through Minnesota and the Dakotas, and Roman Catholicism dominates southern Louisiana, the southwestern borderland, and the heavily industrialized areas of the Northeast. The Midwest is a thoroughly mixed zone, though Methodism is generally the largest single faith.

The geographer Roger Stump points to a twentieth-century trend toward religious regional divergence in the United States. Baptists in the South, Lutherans in the upper Midwest, and Mormons in the West each dominate their respective regions more thoroughly today than at the turn of the century. Each of the three denominations is conservative and has a long-standing, strong infrastructure. In an age when many social scientists proclaim that Americans are becoming homogenized, with a national culture supplanting traditional regional cultures, Stump's findings reassure us that the ancient message of geography, "different place, different people," remains true. At the same time, we need to be aware that certain denominations, in particular Methodism, are very important on a national scale but are dominant in only a small number of counties.

Denominational traits and diversity are not the only aspects of religion that vary spatially. Stump also found that regional variations in religious behavior extend "into the very motivations of religious participation," reflecting the variable cultural importance of religion. In the Bible Belt, for example, the great importance of religion leads to the expectation that higher-status individuals will actively support and participate in religious institutions.

Islam

Islam, another great monotheistic, proselytic faith, claims 1.2 billion followers in the great desert belt of Asia and northern Africa and extends as far east as Indonesia and the Philippines (Figure 6.3). Many biblical figures, such as Moses, Abraham, and Jesus, are also venerated in Islam, but the most important prophet and founder was Muhammad, who lived some 14 centuries ago. The Muslim holy book, the *Koran*, contains a code of morals and ethics, and promises an afterlife for the faithful. Adherents to Islam are expected to pray five times daily at established times (Figure 6.1), give alms to the poor, fast from dawn to sunset in the holy month of Ramadan, make at least one pilgrimage, if possible, to the sacred city of Mecca in Saudi Arabia, and profess belief in Allah, the one god whose apostle was Muhammad. These duties are known as the Five Pillars of the faith.

Although not as severely fragmented as Christianity, Islam, too, has split into separate groups. Two major sects prevail. The *Shiite* Muslims, 11 percent of the Islamic total in diverse subgroups, form the majority in Iran and Iraq. A major fundamentalist revival is occurring among the

Shiites, under Iranian leadership, to throw off Western influences while restoring the purity of the faith. Great political tension, with the potential for severe disruptions, attend the Islamic revival, which has begun spreading beyond the Shiite group.

Sunni Muslims, who represent the Islamic orthodoxy, form the large majority (Figures 6.3 and 6.6). Their strength is greatest in the Arabic-speaking lands, though non-Arabic Indonesia now contains the world's largest Sunni Islamic concentration, and other large clusters occur in western China and in Indo-European Bangladesh and Pakistan. The Shiite group, by contrast, is strongest among Indo-European groups.

Figure 6.6
A Sunni Muslim mosque, near the harbor in Akko (Acre), Israel. The color green is sacred in Islam and appears often on mosques and minarets, the tall circular towers from which the faithful are called to prayer.

Judaism

Judaism, another monotheistic faith, is the parent of Christianity and is closely related to Islam as well. Certain Hebrew prophets and leaders are recognized in all three religions. In contrast to the other monotheistic faiths, Judaism does not actively seek new converts and has remained an ethnic religion through most of its existence. It has split into a variety of subgroups, partly as a result of the forced dispersal of the Jews from Israel in Roman times and the subsequent loss of contact among the various colonies. Jews, scattered to many parts of the Roman Empire, became a minority group wherever they were found. In later times, they spread through much of Europe, North Africa, and Arabia. Those Jews who resided in the Mediterranean lands were called the *Sephardim,* while those in central and eastern Europe were known as the *Ashkenazim.*

The late nineteenth and early twentieth centuries witnessed large-scale Ashkenazic migration from Europe to America. The disaster that befell European Judaism during the Nazi years involved the systematic murder of perhaps a third of the entire Jewish population of the world, mainly Ashkenazim. Europe ceased to be the primary homeland of Judaism and many of the survivors fled overseas, mainly to Israel and America. Judaism has about 18 million adherents throughout the world. At present, nearly 7 million, or about 38 percent, of the world's Jewish population lives in North America; another 19 percent in Europe and western Russia; and 23 percent in Israel.

Hinduism

Hinduism, a religion closely tied to India and its ancient culture, claims about 750 million adherents (Figure 6.3). A decidedly **polytheistic** religion, involving the worship of a myriad of deities, Hinduism is also linked to the *caste system,* a rigid segregation of people according to ancestry and occupation; *ahimsa,* the veneration of all forms of life, involving noninjury to all sentient creatures; and a belief in reincarnation. No standard set of beliefs prevails, and the faith takes many local forms.

Hinduism includes very diverse peoples. The faith straddles a major ethnic/linguistic divide, including both Indo-Europeans and Dravidians (Figure 5.3). The skin color of the Hindu population ranges from dark to light. Hinduism, once a proselytic religion, is today a regional, biethnic (Indo-European/Dravidian) faith. Suggestive of its former missionary activity is an outlier of Hinduism on the distant Indonesian island of Bali.

Hinduism has splintered into diverse religious groups, some of which are so distinctive as to be regarded as separate religions. *Jainism* is an ancient outgrowth of Hinduism, claiming perhaps 4 million adherents, almost all in India, and tracing its roots back over 25 centuries. While rejecting Hindu scriptures, rituals, and priesthood, the Jains share the Hindu belief in ahimsa and reincarnation. Jains adhere to a stern asceticism. *Sikhism,* by contrast, arose much later, in the 1500s, as an attempt to unify Hinduism and Islam. Centered in the Punjab state of northwestern India, where the Golden Temple at Amritsar serves as the principal shrine, Sikhism has about 20 million followers. Sikhs practice monotheism and have their own holy book, the *Adi Granth.*

Buddhism

Buddhism, also derived from Hinduism, began 25 centuries ago as a reform movement based in the teachings of Prince Siddhartha, the Buddha. He promoted the four "noble truths": life is full of suffering; desire is the cause of this suffering; cessation of suffering comes with the quelling of desire; and an "Eight-Fold Path" of proper personal conduct and meditation permits the individual to overcome desire. The resultant state of escape and peace, achieved by very few, is known as *nirvana.*

Today, Buddhism is the most widespread religion in Asia, dominating a culture region stretching from Sri Lanka to Japan and from Mongolia to Vietnam. In the process of its proselytic spread, particularly in China and Japan, Buddhism fused with native ethnic religions such as Confucianism, Taoism, and Shintoism to form composite faiths. Southern Buddhism, dominant in Sri Lanka and mainland Southeast Asia, retains the greatest similarity to the religion's original form, while a special variation known as *Lamaism* prevails in Tibet and Mongolia (Figure 6.3). Buddhism's tendency to merge with native religions, particularly in China, makes it difficult to determine the number of its adherents. Estimates range from 334 million to over 900 million people. While Buddhism in China has become enmeshed with local faiths to become part of an ethnic religion, elsewhere it remains one of the three great proselytic religions in the world.

Animism

Tribal peoples in diverse parts of the world often retain ethnic religions and are usually referred to collectively as **animists.** Currently numbering at least 100 million, animists believe that certain inanimate objects possess spirits or souls. These spirits live in rocks and rivers, mountain peaks and heavenly bodies, forests and swamps. Each tribe has its own characteristic form of animism and has vested a particular set of objects with spirits. A tribal religious figure, or *shaman,* usually serves as an intermediary between the people and the spirits. To some other animists, the objects in question do not actually possess spirits, but rather are valued because they have a particular potency to serve as a link between a person and the omnipresent god. We should not classify such systems of belief as primitive or simple, because they can be extraordinarily complex.

Sub-Saharan Africa is the greatest surviving stronghold of animism, both in terms of numbers of adherents and in percentage of total population (Figure 6.7). Along the northern edge of the animist region, Islam is rapidly winning converts, and Christian missionaries are very active

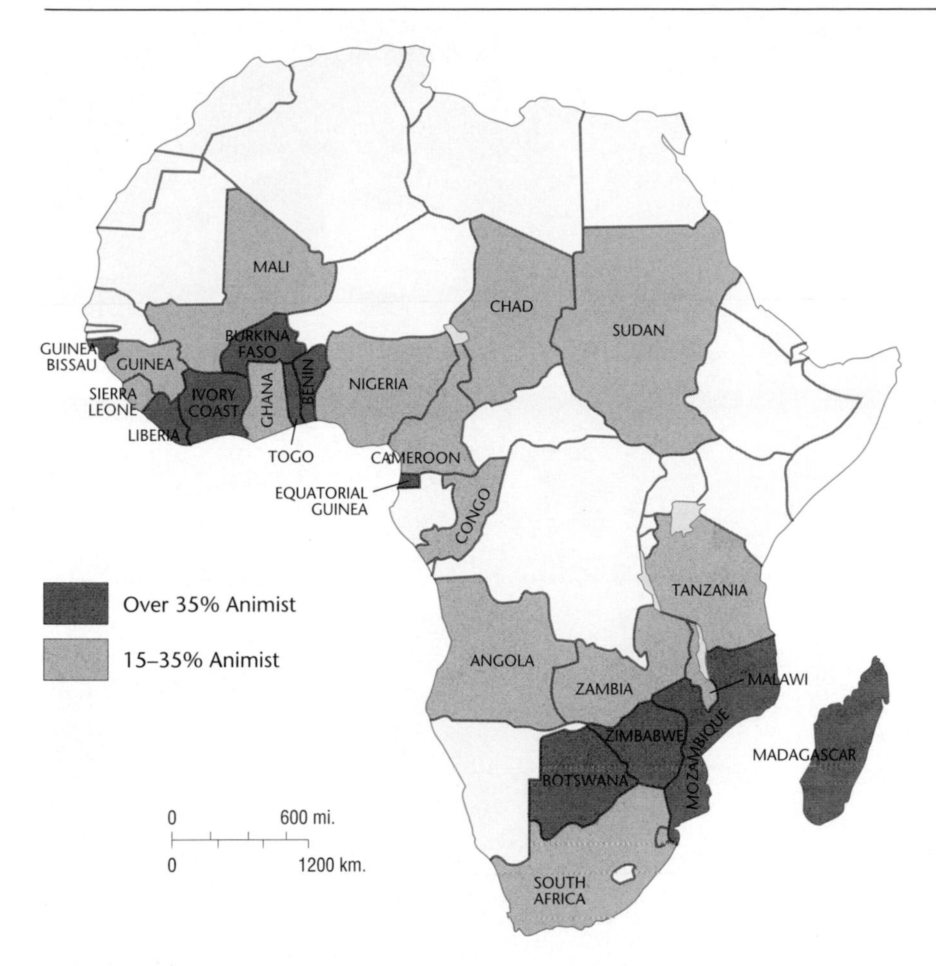

Figure 6.7
Africa is the last major stronghold of animists. Christian and Islamic missionaries are active in the remaining animist regions, but these tribal religions may survive in the long run. (Derived from Johnstone, Patrick. *Operation World,* 4th ed. N.p.: S.T.L. Books, 1986, p. 25.)

throughout the area, but animism seems likely to survive in Africa. Descendants of African slaves in the Americas have kept alive such animistic faiths as *Umbanda,* which claims perhaps 30 million followers in Brazil, and *Santeria,* found mainly in Cuba. These survive beneath a facade of nominal Roman Catholicism.

Secularization

In some parts of the world, especially in much of Europe, religion has declined, giving way to *secularization* (Figure 6.8). The number of nonreligious and atheistic persons in the world is reputedly about 1 billion at present. Typically, secularization displays a vivid regionalization on a variety of scales. Areas of surviving religious vitality lie alongside secularized districts, in a disorderly jumble. Such patterns once again reveal the inherent spatial variety of humankind and invite analysis by the cultural geographer. In some instances, the retreat from organized religion has resulted from a government's active hostility toward a particular faith or religion in general. In other cases, we can attribute the decline to the failure of religions oriented to the needs of rural folk to adapt to the urban scene.

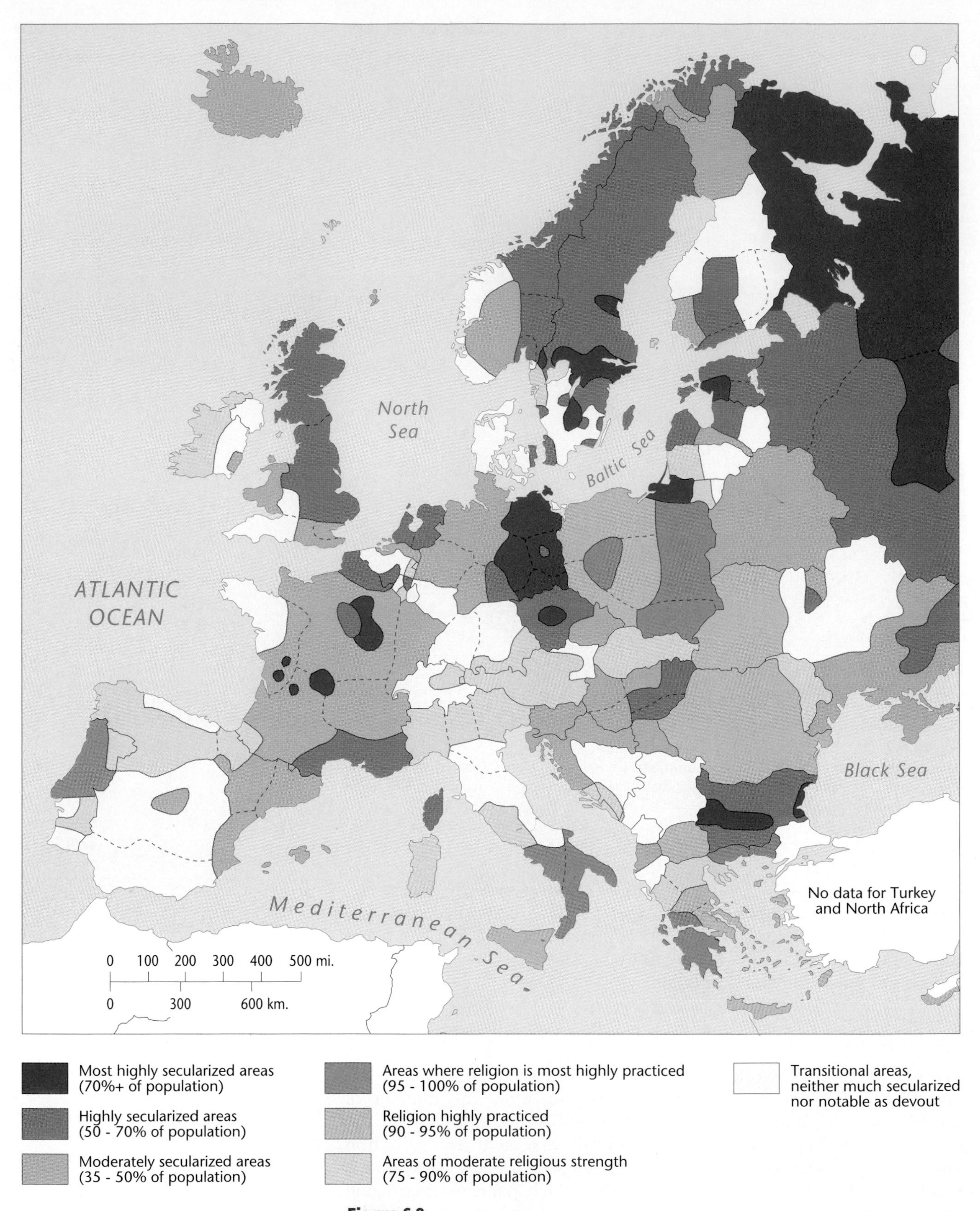

Figure 6.8
Secularized areas in Europe. These areas, in which Christianity has ceased to be of much importance, occur in a complicated pattern. What causal forces might have been at work? In all of Europe, some 190 million persons reported no religious faith, amounting to 27 percent of the population. (Source: Jordan, Terry G. *The European Culture Area: A Systematic Geography,* 3d ed. New York: HarperCollins, 1996, p. 102.)

Religious Diffusion

The distribution of religions, denominations, and secularism is the product of innovation and cultural diffusion. To a remarkable degree, the origin of the major religions was concentrated spatially, occurring in two principal Asian hearth areas.

The Semitic Religious Hearth

All three of the great monotheistic faiths—Christianity, Judaism, and Islam—arose among Semitic-speaking peoples in or on the margins of the deserts of southwestern Asia, in the Middle East (Figure 6.9). Judaism, the oldest of the three, originated some 4000 years ago, proba-

Figure 6.9
The origin and diffusion of four major religions in Eurasia. Christianity and Islam, the two great proselytic monotheistic faiths, arose in Semitic southwestern Asia and spread widely through the Old World. Hinduism and Buddhism both originated in the northern reaches of the Indian subcontinent and spread through southeastern Eurasia.

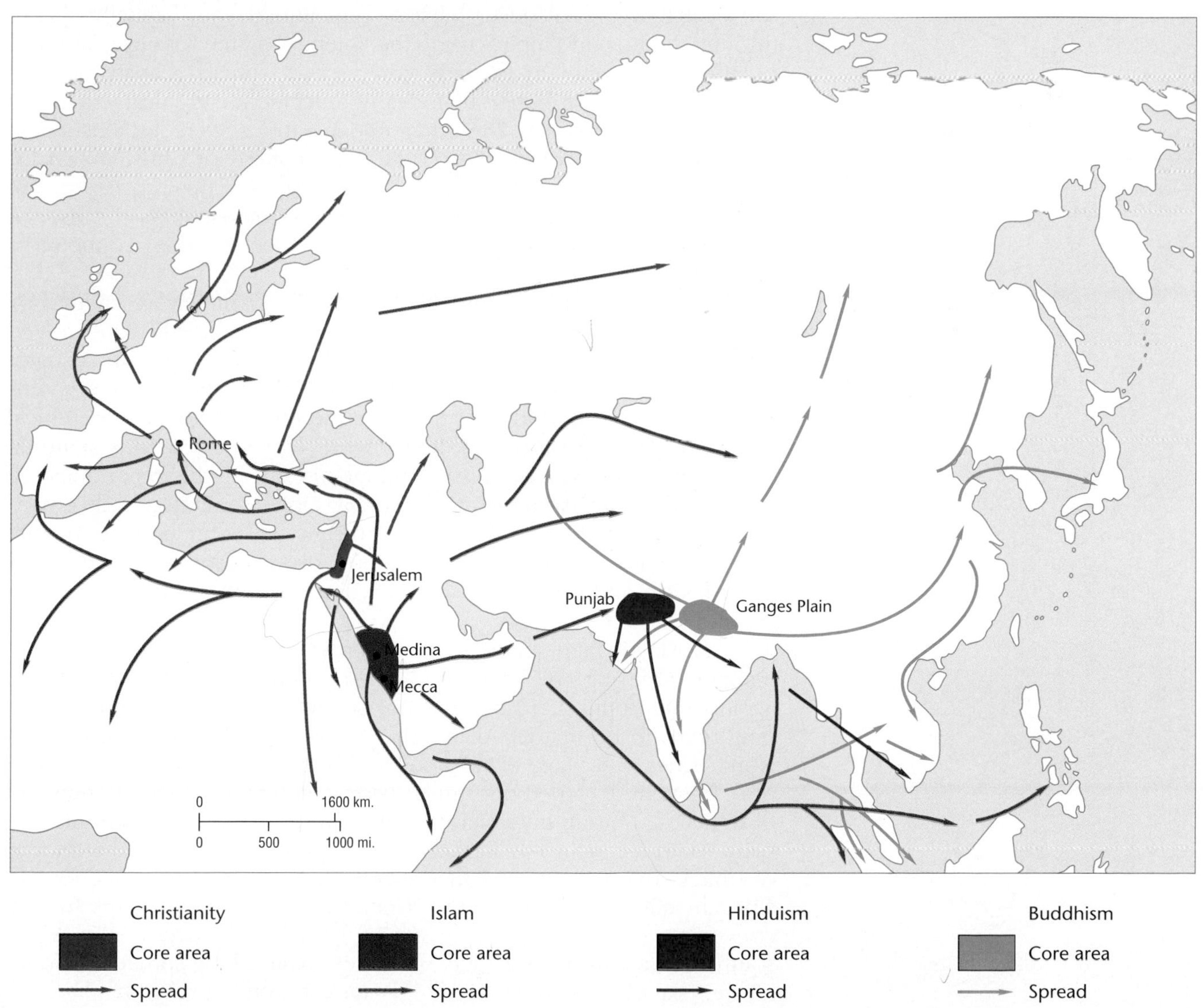

bly along the southern edge of the Fertile Crescent. Only later did its followers acquire dominion over the lands between the Mediterranean and the Jordan River—the territorial base of modern Israel. Christianity, child of Judaism, originated in this "Promised Land" about halfway through the temporal existence of Judaism. Seven centuries later, the Semitic hearth once again gave birth to a major faith when Islam arose in western Arabia, partly from Jewish and Christian roots.

Religions spread by both relocation and expansion diffusion. As you recall (Figure 1.10), the latter can be divided into hierarchical and contagious subtypes. In hierarchical diffusion, ideas become implanted at the top of a society, leapfrogging across the map to take root in cities, bypassing smaller villages and rural areas. The use of missionaries, by contrast, involves relocation diffusion. Obviously, proselytic faiths are more likely to diffuse than ethnic religions, and it is not surprising that the spread of monotheism was accomplished largely by Christianity and Islam, rather than Judaism. From Semitic southwestern Asia, both of the proselytic monotheistic faiths diffused widely.

Christians, observing the admonition in the Gospel of Matthew, "Go ye therefore and teach all nations, baptizing them in the name of the Father, and of the Son, and of the Holy Ghost, teaching them to observe all things whatsoever I have commanded you," initially spread through the Roman Empire, using the splendid system of imperial roads to diffuse the faith. In its early centuries of spread, Christianity displayed a spatial distribution that clearly reflected hierarchical expansion diffusion (Figure 6.10). The early congregations were established in cities and towns, temporarily producing a pattern of Christianized urban centers and pagan rural areas. Indeed, traces of this process remain in our language. The Latin word *pagus,* "countryside," is the root of both *pagan* and *peasant,* suggesting the ancient heathen connotation of rurality.

The scattered urban clusters of early Christianity were created by relocation diffusion, as missionaries such as the apostle Paul moved from town to town bearing the news of the emerging faith. In later centuries, Christian missionaries often used the technique of converting kings or tribal leaders, setting in motion additional hierarchical diffusion. The Russians and Poles were converted in this manner. Some Christian expansion was militaristic, as in the reconquest of Iberia and the invasion of Latin America. Once implanted in this manner, Christianity spread farther by means of contagious diffusion. When applied to religion, this method of spread is called **contact conversion** and is the result of everyday association between believers and nonbelievers.

The Islamic faith spread from its Semitic hearth area in a militaristic manner. Obeying the command in the *Koran* that they "do battle against them until there be no more seduction from the truth and the only worship be that of Allah," the Arabs exploded westward across North Africa in a wave of religious and linguistic conquest. The Turks, once converted, carried out similar Islamic conquests. In a different sort of diffusion, Muslim missionaries followed trade routes eastward to implant Islam hierarchically in the Philippines, Indonesia, and the interior of China. Tropical Africa is the current major scene of Islamic expansion, an effort that has produced competition with Christians for the conversion of animists. As a result of diffusionary successes in Africa south of the Sahara and high birthrates in its older sphere of dominance, Islam has become the world's fastest-growing religion.

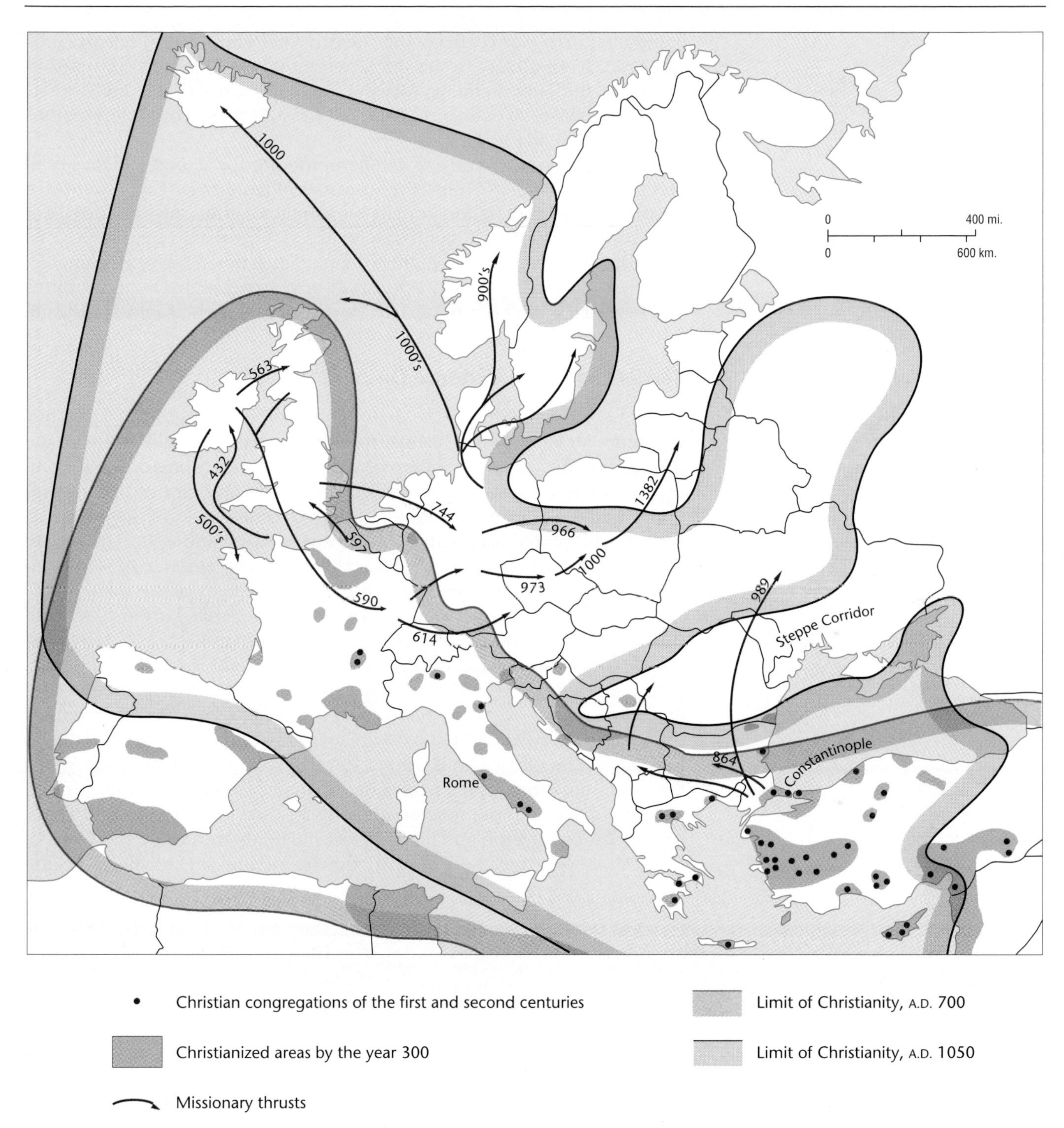

Figure 6.10
The diffusion of Christianity in Europe, first to eleventh centuries. In what way do the patterns for the first and second centuries and for the year 300 suggest hierarchical expansion diffusion? Compare with Figure 1.10. Who were the "knowers" (converts) and who were the laggards at this stage? What barriers to diffusion might account for the uneven advance by the year 1050? Why did retreat occur in some areas?

The Indus-Ganges Hearth

The second great religious hearth area lay in the plains fringing the northern edge of the Indian subcontinent. This lowland, drained by the Ganges and Indus rivers, gave birth to Hinduism and Buddhism. The earliest faith to derive from this hearth was Hinduism, at least 4000 years old. Its origin lay in the Punjab, from where Hinduism diffused to dominate the subcontinent. Missionaries later carried the faith, in its proselytic phase, to overseas areas, but most of these converted regions were subsequently lost.

Buddhism began in the foothills bordering the Ganges Plain about 500 BC, branching off from Hinduism (see Figure 6.9). For centuries it remained confined to the Indian subcontinent, but missionaries later carried Buddhism to China (100 BC to AD 200), Korea and Japan (AD 300 to 500), Southeast Asia (AD 400 to 600), Tibet (AD 700), and Mongolia (AD 1500). Like Christianity, Buddhism developed many regional forms and eventually died out in its area of origin, reabsorbed into Hinduism.

Barriers and Time-Distance Decay

Religious ideas move in the manner of all innovation waves. They weaken with increasing distance from their places of origin and with the passage of time. Barriers often retard or halt their spread. Most commonly, barriers are of the permeable type, allowing part of the innovation wave to diffuse through it, but weakening it and retarding its spread. The partial acceptance of Christianity by various Indian groups in Latin America and the western United States, serving in some instances as a camouflage beneath which many aspects of the tribal ethnic religions survive, is an example. In fact, permeable barriers are *normally* present in the expansion diffusion of religious faiths. Most religions become modified by older local beliefs as they diffuse spatially. Rarely do new ideas, whether religious or not, gain unqualified acceptance in a region (see box, *Passing a Permeable Barrier to Diffusion*).

Absorbing barriers also exist in religious diffusion. The attempt to introduce Christianity into China provides a good example. When Catholic and Protestant missionaries reached China from Europe and the United States in the nineteenth century, they expected to find fertile ground for conversion—millions of people ready to receive the word of God. However, they had crossed the boundaries of a culture region

Passing a Permeable Barrier to Diffusion

The diffusion of Buddhism into China profoundly changed society and culture. Yet China also fundamentally modified Buddhism. In short, Chinese culture presented a permeable barrier to the diffusion of Buddhism.

A few examples illustrate what happened. Early Chinese translations quickly changed the relatively high position Buddhism had granted women. "The husband supports his wife" became, in Chinese, "The husband controls his wife." "The wife comforts her husband" became "The wife reveres her husband." In addition, the Chinese cult of the family was soon interwoven with Buddhist observances. A typical inscription from a Buddhist temple of the fourth century might read: "We respectfully make and present this holy image in honor of the Buddhas, Bodhisattvas, and pray that all living creatures may attain salvation, and particularly that the souls of our ancestors and relatives may find repose and release."

Among the Chinese masses, Buddhism fused with other popular cults. The Buddhist heavens and hells of India, for instance, were retained, but given a Chinese bureaucratic structure. Over time, Chinese artists transformed the Indian sculptural ideal, the half-naked ascetic, into the pot-bellied, earthy "happy Buddha" that can be bought in gift shops today.

Such merging of religions is a common occurrence when adherents of one faith attempt to supplant a traditional religion. In this way, spatial variation develops even within the same religious faith, and each culture or subculture places its own distinctive mark on the belief system.

From Wright, Arthur F. *Buddhism in Chinese History*. Palo Alto, CA: Stanford University Press, 1959.

thousands of years old, in which some basic social ideas left little opening for Christianity and its doctrine of original sin. Long ago the Chinese had settled to their own satisfaction the question of what is basic human nature. As they saw the matter, humans were inherently good. Evil desires represented merely a deviation from that natural state. People only had to shrug them off and they would return to the basic nature that they share with heaven. Consequently, the idea of original sin left the Chinese baffled. The Christian image of humankind as flawed, of a gap between creator and created, of the Fall and the impossibility of returning to godhood, was culturally incomprehensible to the Chinese.

Other aspects of Christianity added to the cultural gap. How could the fall from grace come from too much knowledge, a commodity highly prized in China? What was wrong with a giant snake in the garden of Eden to a people whose art was filled with reptilian dragons, the imperial symbol? In short, many concepts of Christianity fell on rocky soil in China. Only in the early twentieth century, as China's social structure crumbled under Western assault, did a significant, though still small, number of Chinese convert to Christianity. Many of these were "rice Christians," poor Chinese willing to become Christians in exchange for the rice that missionaries gave them.

In addition, religion itself can act as a barrier to the spread of nonreligious innovations. Religious taboos can even function as absorbing barriers, preventing diffusion of foods, drinks, and practices that violate the taboo. Mormons, who are forbidden to consume products containing caffeine, have as a result not taken part in the American fascination with coffee and Coca-Cola. Sometimes these barriers are permeable. Certain Pennsylvania Dutch churches, for example, prohibit cigarette smoking but do not object to member farmers raising tobacco for sale on the commercial market.

Religious Ecology

One of the main functions of many religions is the maintenance of a harmonious relationship between a people and their physical environment. That is, religion is at least perceived by its adherents to be part of the adaptive strategy, and for that reason physical environmental factors, particularly natural hazards and disasters, exert a powerful influence on the development of religions. Environmental influence is most readily apparent in the tribal animistic faiths. In fact, an animistic religion's principal goal is to mediate between its people and the spirit-infested forces of nature. Animistic ceremonies and even the rites of great religions often are intended to bring rain, quiet earthquakes, end plagues, or in some other way manipulate environmental forces by placating the spirits believed responsible for these events (see box, *Interceding with the Cloud People*).

Sometimes the link between religion and natural hazard is visual. The great pre-Columbian temple pyramid at Cholula, near Puebla in central Mexico, strikingly mimics the shape of the awesome nearby volcano Popocatépetl, towering to the menacing height of nearly 18,000 feet (5500 meters). Catholic missionaries retained the sacred status of the Cholula pyramid, though not its volcano-appeasing attribute, by erecting a church atop it.

While the physical environment's influence on the major religions is less pronounced than in animistic faiths, it is still evident. Animistic

Interceding with the Cloud People

The following songs or prayers derived from animistic groups are typical pleas aimed at influencing environmental conditions. From the Pueblo Indians of the Sia Pueblo, near Bernalillo, New Mexico, a plea for rain:

White floating clouds
Clouds like the plains
Come and water the earth.
Sun embrace the earth
That she may be fruitful.
Moon, lion of the north,
Bear of the west,
Badger of the south,
Wolf of the east,
Eagle of the heavens,
Shrew of the earth,
Elder war hero,
Warriors of the six mountains of the world,
Intercede with the cloud people for us.

From the Haida Indians of coastal British Columbia, Canada, a plea for fair weather:

O good Sun,
Look thou down upon us;
Shine, shine on us, O Sun,
Gather up the clouds, wet, black, under thy arms—
That the rains may cease to fall.
Because thy friends are all here on the beach
Ready to go fishing—
Ready for the hunt.
Therefore look kindly on us, O Good Sun.

nature-spirits lie behind certain practices found in the great religions, such as the **geomancy,** or *feng-shui,* of Chinese and Korean Buddhism, by which environmentally auspicious sites are chosen for houses, villages, temples, and graves. The homes of the living and the resting places of the dead must be aligned with the cosmic forces of the world. Chinese Buddhists originally invented the magnetic compass to serve such geomantic needs. For a burial site, the ideal terrain should be neither featureless and flat, nor steep and rugged. The active and passive forces of Chinese cosmology, *yin* and *yang,* should correctly surround the site. As Chuen-yan David Lai, a Canadian geographer, has written: "The *yang* energy is expressed as a lofty mountain range, symbolically called the 'Azure Dragon,' and the *yin* energy as a lower ridge called the 'White Tiger.' The most auspicious model of *feng-shui* topography is a secluded spot where these two energies converge, interact vigorously, and are kept together in harmony by surrounding mountains and streams" (Figure 6.11).

Similarly, rivers, mountains, trees, forests, and rocks often achieve the status of sacred space, even in the great religions. The river Ganges and certain lesser streams such as the Bagmati in Nepal are holy to the Hindus (Figure 6.12), while the Jordan River has special meaning for Christians, who often transport its waters in containers to other continents for use in baptism. Most holy rivers are believed to possess soul-cleansing abilities. Hindu geographer Rana Singh speaks of the "liquid divine energy" of the Ganges, "nourishing the inhabitants and purifying them." Mountains and other high places, likewise, often achieve sacred status among both animists and adherents of the great religions (Figure 6.13). Mount Fuji is sacred in Japanese Shintoism, and many high places are venerated in Christianity, including the Mount of Olives. Some mountains tower so impressively as to inspire sects devoted to them exclusively. Mount Shasta, a massive snowcapped volcano in northern California, near the Oregon border, serves as the focus of no fewer than 30 "new age" cults, the largest of which is the "I Am" religion, founded in the 1930s (Figure 6.13). Geographer Claude Curran, who studied the Shasta cults, found that, while few of the adherents live near the mountain, pilgrimages and festivals held during the sum-

Figure 6.11
The model shows an ideal tomb site according to the Chinese principles of *feng-shui.* The tall mountain range represents the spirit of the "Azure Dragon," a figure of active yang energy. The lower hills symbolize the "White Tiger," a figure of the complementary passive yin energy. The winding stream represents wealth. (After Lai, Chuen-yan David. "A Feng Shui Model as a Location Index." *Annals of the Association of American Geographers,* 64 [1974]: 506–513.)

mer swell the population of nearby towns and contribute to the local economy. Geographer Stephen Jett, an expert on the Navajo Indians of the American Southwest, speaks of their *mythical topography,* produced when tribal legends become linked to certain topographical features, lending these special mythic places a sanctified quality.

Plants, too, often serve a religious role or acquire veneration. Certain types of trees, as well as remnant forests, have an honored position in some major religions. For example, evergreens symbolize eternal life for certain Christian groups. Similarly, geographer Kit Anderson tells us, the *ceiba* (or silk-cotton) tree was to the pre-Columbian Maya Indians of Guatemala the sacred tree standing at the center of the world. Its

Figure 6.12
Some rivers are sacred. The Bagmati in Nepal, at the pilgrimage town of Pashupatinath, near Katmandu is shown. Here ritual bathing and cremations are practiced by Hindus, and the god Shiva is worshipped.

Figure 6.13
Two high places that have evolved into sacred space. The reddish sandstone Uluru, or Ayers Rock, in central Australia, is sacred in Aboriginal animism and inspires awe both from near and afar. Snowy Mount Shasta in California is venerated by some 30 "new age" cults, including the "I Am" religion.

veneration partially survived their Christianization, and in modern Guatemala, the ceiba is the national tree and often stands beside churches.

Even today, environmental stress can evoke a religious response not so different from that of animistic cults. Some adherents to the Judeo-Christian tradition feel that God uses environmental disasters or degradation to punish sinners and that nature is benevolent to the devout, just as it had been in Eden. Stress can prompt attempts at mitigation. Local ministers and priests often attempt to alter unfavorable weather conditions with special services, and there are few churchgoing people in the Great Plains of the United States who have not prayed for rain in dry years. In northeastern China, repeated plagues of crop-destroying locusts gave rise over the centuries to a number of "locust cults," complete with temples. Almost 900 such temples were built, providing a place of worship for the locust and locust-gods (Figure 6.14). Suitable sacrifices and rituals were developed in an effort to avert the periodic infestations.

The Environment and Monotheism

On a grander scale, some geographers sought to explain the origins of monotheism by environmental factors. The three major monotheistic faiths—Christianity, Islam, and Judaism—all have their roots among the desert dwellers of the Middle East. Lamaism, the most nearly monotheistic form of Buddhism, flourishes in the deserts of Tibet and Mongolia. In all of these cases, the people involved (Hebrews, Arabs, Tibetans, and Mongols) were once nomadic herders (refer to Chapter 3), wandering from place to place in the desert with flocks and herds of livestock. The geographer Ellen Semple suggested that such desert-dwelling peoples "receive from the immense monotony of their environment the im-

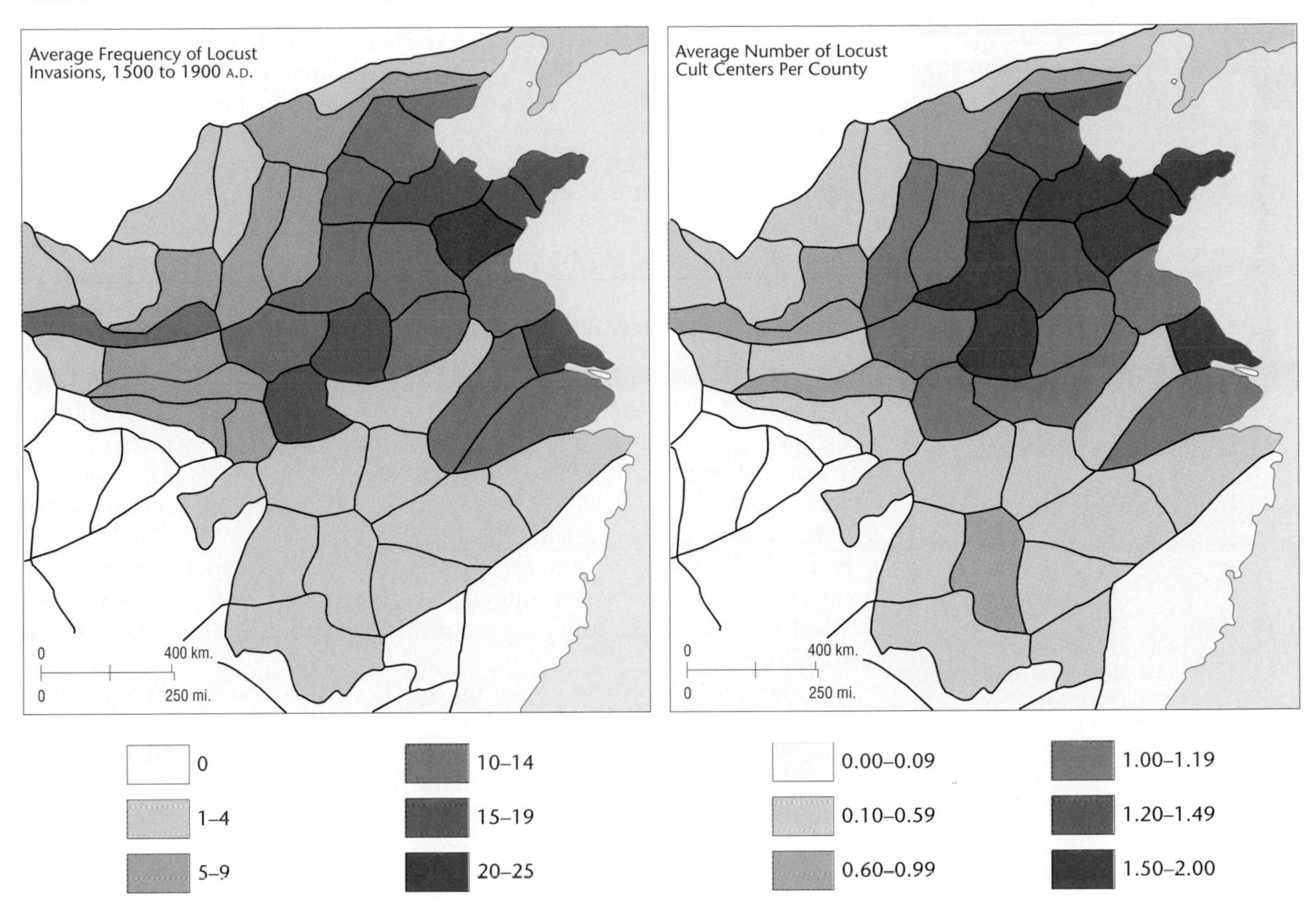

Figure 6.14
The frequency of locust infestations and the number of "locust cults" in China. These cults arose as an adaptive strategy in response to an environmental hazard. The worship of locusts was grafted onto the Buddhist-Confucianist-Taoist composite religion of China. (Redrawn with permission from Hsu, Shin-Yi. "The Cultural Ecology of the Locust Cult in Traditional China." *Annals of the Association of American Geographers,* 59 [1969]: 734, 745.)

pression of unity" (see biographical sketch). Semple believed that the unobstructed view of the stars and planets provided by the clear desert skies allowed the herders to see that the heavenly bodies moved across the sky in an orderly, repeated progression. This revelation supposedly suggested to the desert stargazers that a single guiding hand was responsible for the orderly system. Semple, in the classic style of environmental determinism, concluded that desert dwellers "gravitate inevitably into monotheism."

Other possibilistic rather than deterministic explanations have been proposed for the origins of monotheism. Some cultural geographers feel that we should look at the social structure of nomadic herding people for answers. Desert nomads are organized into tribes and clans ruled by a male chieftain who has dictatorial powers over the members of the group. It is possible that the all-powerful male deity of Middle Eastern monotheism is simply a theological reflection of the all-powerful, secular, male chieftain. Significantly, female deities are usually associated with farming societies, probably because women represent fertility and are the original domesticators of plants, while male deities are linked with herding or hunting peoples.

Ellen Churchill Semple
1863–1932

Born in Louisville, Kentucky, of a well-to-do family, Semple received a master's degree in history from Vassar and then went to Germany to study. At that time, few women attended universities in Germany, and some claim she had to listen to geography lectures from outside the classroom door. When she returned to America, she brought some of the ideas of German geography and subsequently developed many of her own theories. She wrote eloquently and voluminously on environmental determinism. Best known, perhaps, is her book *Influences of Geographical Environment,* published in 1911. Among the ideas presented in her works is the theory that religions are largely the product of the physical environment. Her books gained a very wide readership, both among professional geographers and educated laypersons. She was on the geography faculties at the University of Chicago and Clark University for many years and was a well-known personality in geography. In selecting Semple as president in 1921, the Association of American Geographers became the first national professional academic organization in the United States to place a woman in its highest honorific position.

Other geographers have noted that these monotheistic nomads lived on the edges of larger, more established culture regions. New ideas, these scholars feel, tend to develop at the borders, not at the core of regions where older structures and ideas are firmly entrenched. The fact is, however, that we do not know enough about early monotheism to say with certainty why or even where it arose. We are not even sure that the first monotheists were desert nomads, and we do know that some desert dwellers were polytheistic.

Religion and Environmental Modification

Just as the physical environment can influence religious belief and practice, so the religious outlook of a people can help determine the extent to which they modify their environment. In the words of Lynn White, "Human ecology is deeply conditioned by beliefs about our nature and destiny—that is, by religion." In some faiths, human power over natural forces is assumed. The Maori people of New Zealand, for example, believe that humans represent one of six aspects of creation, the others being forest/animals, crops, wild food, sea/fish, and wind/storms. People rule over all of these except the latter, in the Maori world view.

The Judeo-Christian religious tradition also teaches that humans have dominion over nature, but goes further to promote a teleological view. **Teleology** is the doctrine that the Earth was created especially for human beings, who are separate from and superior to the natural world (Figure 6.15). This view is implicit in God's message to Noah after the Flood, promising that "every moving thing that lives shall be food for you, and as I gave you the green plants, I give you everything." The same theme is repeated in the Psalms, where Jews and Christians are told that "the heavens are the Lord's heavens, but the earth he has given to the sons of men." Humans are not part of nature, but separate, forming one member of a God-nature-human trinity.

Believing that the Earth was given to humans for their use, early Christian thinkers adopted the view that humans were God's helpers in finishing the task of creation, that human modifications of the environment were God's work. Small wonder that the medieval period in Europe witnessed an unprecedented expansion of agricultural acreage, involving the large-scale destruction of woodlands and drainage of marshes. Nor is it surprising that Christian monastic orders, such as the Cistercian and Benedictine fathers, supervised many of these projects, directing the clearing of forests and the establishment of new agricultural colonies.

Christianity, according to White's view, destroyed classical antiquity's feeling for the holiness of natural things. Subsequently, he argues, scientific advances permitted the Judeo-Christian West to modify the environment at an unprecedented rate and on a massive scale. This marriage of technology and teleology is, White proposes, the root of our modern ecological crisis. By contrast, the great religions of Asia and many animistic tribal faiths contain teachings and beliefs that protect nature (see box, *The Yanoama World View*). In Hinduism, for example, geographer Deryck Lodrick found that the doctrine of ahimsa had resulted in the establishment of numerous animal homes, refuges, and hospitals, particularly in the northwestern part of India. The hospitals, or *pinjrapoles,* are also closely linked to the Jains. In this view of the world, people are part of and at harmony with nature. Such religions would presumably not threaten the ecological balance.

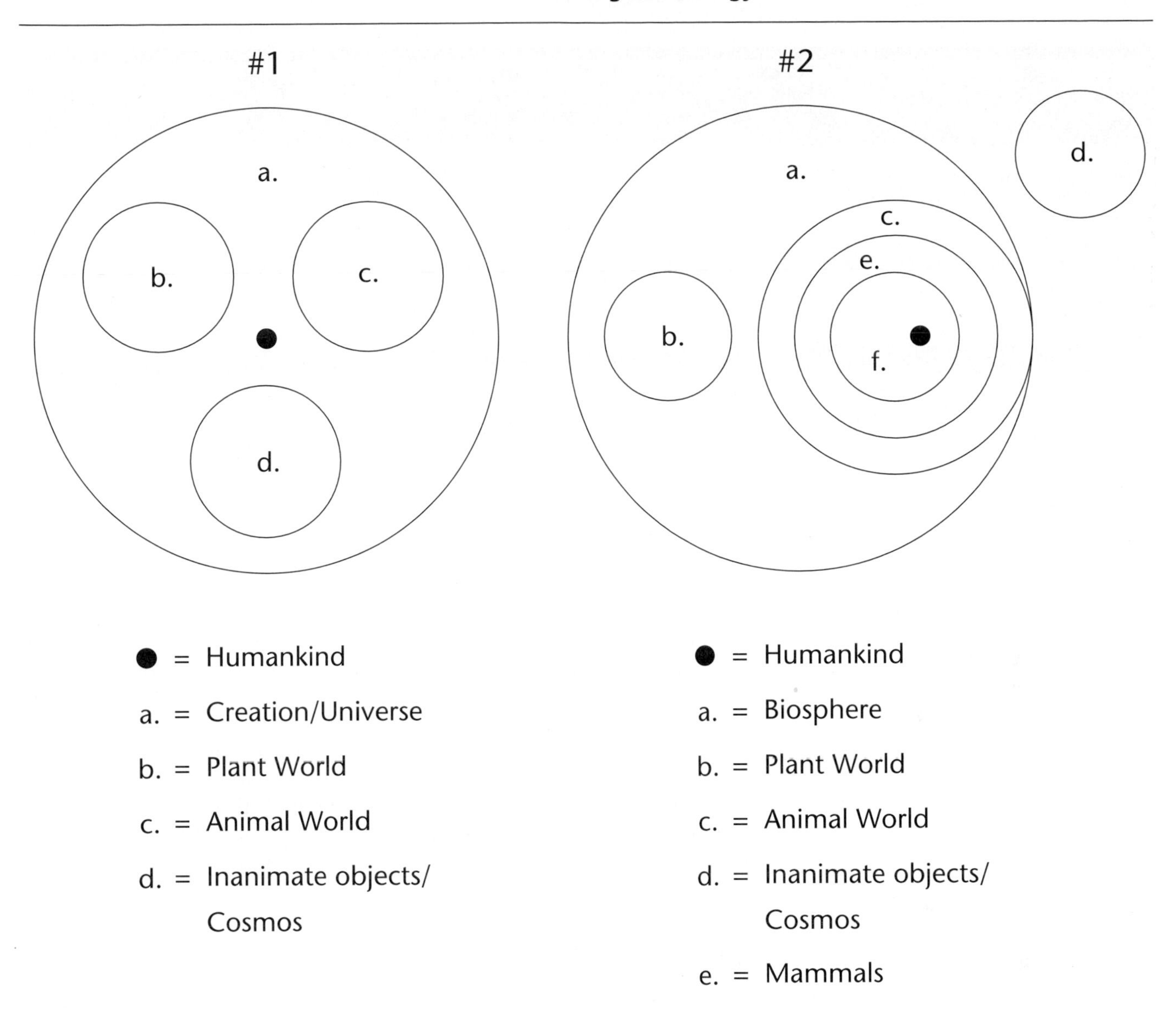

Figure 6.15
Models of the universe. Model 1 represents the traditional, Judeo-Christian, Biblical/scriptural, teleological view, in which humankind is central to creation and autonomous from the natural world. Model 2 describes the modern scientific/elitist view, which rests on the findings of Darwin and others. Proponents of these two views will likely develop unique outlooks concerning environmental modification.

Geographer Yi-Fu Tuan disagrees. He points to a discrepancy between the stated ideals of religions and reality. Even though China enjoys an "old tradition of forest care" based on its composite religion, the Chinese woodlands have been systematically destroyed through the millennia. Nor are the Asian and tribal religions consistently protective of the environment. Buddhism, like Hinduism, protects temple trees but demands huge quantities of wood for cremations (Figure 6.16). Animistic shifting cultivators sometimes make offerings to appease the woodland spirits before destroying huge acreages of forest with machete and fire. Civilization itself, argues Tuan, is the exercise of human power over nature. Religion can resist but not overcome that exercise. Also, if people are assumed to be part of nature, then one might con-

The Yanoama World View

Persons of Judeo-Christian religious heritage need to be reminded that most other cultures do not perceive humans, God, and nature as a trinity of distinct entities. The world view of the Yanoama, an animistic Indian tribe of the Brazilian-Venezuelan borderland, is instructive.

> *Religion impinges on all aspects of life, without the conceptual distinction between man, nature, and the divine that characterizes Judeo-Christianity. No omnipotent God exists. There is no material world surrounding the Yanoama and existing independently of them, no world that they view as capable of being dominated and turned to satisfy their own needs. . . . Mysteriously, man can share a common life with an animal, or even with some natural phenomenon, such as the wind or thunder. People not only live now in intimate association with the monkeys, tapirs, deer, and birds of the forest, but also have been—or might be—these very creatures.*
>
> *There is an easy transmutability among the Yanoama between what [we] commonly define as different realms: the human, natural, and divine. . . . Thus, adult males share spirits, or souls, with other creatures. Among these, the harpy eagle and the jaguar are particularly prevalent. The alter egos of females are associated spiritually with totally different creatures, such as butterflies.*

From Smole, William J. *The Yanoama Indians: A Cultural Geography.* Austin: University of Texas Press, 1976, p. 23.

clude that no stewardship of the land by humankind seems logical, since we and all our works are "natural."

Other ecologists point out, too, that the Judeo-Christian tradition is not lacking in concern for environmental protection. In the Book of Leviticus, for example, farmers are instructed by God to let the land lie fallow one year in seven and not to gather food from wild plants in that "sabbath of the land." Robin Doughty, a humanistic cultural geographer, suggests that "Western Christian thought is too rich and complex to be characterized as hostile toward nature," though he feels that Protestantism, "in which worldly success symbolizes individual predestination," may be more conducive to "ecological intemperance." More-

Figure 6.16
Wood gathered for Hindu cremations at Pashupatinath, on the sacred river Bagmati, in Nepal. These cremations contribute significantly to the ongoing deforestation of Nepal and reveal the underlying internal contradiction in Hinduism between conservation as reflected in the doctrine of *ahimsa,* and sanctioned ecologically destructive practices.

over, some fundamentalist Protestant sects view the ecological crisis and environmental deterioration as a gauge to predict Christ's return and the end of the present age, according to geographer Janel Curry-Roper. They thus welcome ecological collapse and, obviously, are unlikely to be of much help in solving the related problems.

But some conservative, fundamentalist Protestants have adopted conservationist views, citing Biblical admonitions. The Flood story from the Old Testament, in which Noah saves diverse animals by bringing them onto the ark, is now viewed by many fundamentalists as a call to protect endangered species. An ecotheological focus underlies the multidenominational National Religious Partnership for the Environment, which includes many evangelical Protestant members. The hope is to mobilize the Christian Right against wanton environmental destruction in the same manner they oppose abortion. At best, White's pronouncements now seem simplistic.

Religion and Environmental Perception

Religion can also influence the way people perceive their physical environment. Nowhere is this more evident than in the perception of environmental hazards such as floods, storms, and droughts. Hinduism and Buddhism teach followers to accept such hazards without struggle, to regard them as natural and unavoidable. Christians are more likely to view storm, flood, or drought as unusual and preventable. As a result, they will generally take steps to overcome the hazard. Sometimes, however, Christians see natural disasters as divine punishment for their sins, in which case worshipers feel they can prevent future disasters by repenting.

Within a single major religion, people's relationship with the land can vary from one sect to another. We have already discussed the overall Judeo-Christian view of the God-nature-human trinity. A study conducted in several adjacent southwestern settlements in the United States by Florence Kluckhohn suggests that individual religious groups see this trinity differently. The large majority (72 percent) of Spanish-American Catholics interviewed felt that humans are subject to nature. Most Mormons (55 percent) saw humans in harmony with nature, a relationship preserved by proper living and hard work. The most common response from Protestant Anglo-Texans (48 percent) held that humans control nature and can overcome environmental hazards.

Similarly, a study by John Sims and Duane Baumann revealed that residents of Alabama, where intense, conservative Protestantism prevails, were more likely to react to a tornado threat fatalistically, relying on God to see them through, while Illinoisans, as adherents of a liberal, low-intensity Protestantism, felt in control of their own destinies and took more measures to protect themselves. Perhaps partly as a result, the mortality rate per tornado is markedly lower in the Midwest than in the South.

Cultural Integration in Religion

While the interaction between religious belief and the environment can shape both religions and the land, religious faith is similarly intertwined with other aspects of culture. Spatial variations in religious belief influence and are influenced by social, economic, demographic, and political patterns in countless ways.

Religion and Economy: The Cargo Cults of Melanesia

Cultural integration is perhaps nowhere more startlingly revealed than in the so-called cargo cults of the western Pacific tropical islands, the area known as Melanesia. There, a religion has arisen based on the hoped-for arrival of Western material goods delivered in American cargo-laden ships. Savior-like Americans will bring the cargo to the islands. Kal Muller tells of one such cult on the New Hebridean island of Tanna:

> *On the volcano's rim looms a blood-red cross. Nearby, men with "U.S.A." daubed on their bodies shoulder make-believe rifles of bamboo. Soldiers of Christ? Hardly. On the New Hebridean island of Tanna, both cross and marchers herald a hoped-for messiah of material riches—a savior cryptically called John Frum.*
>
> *Some followers of the mythical Frum consider him a beneficent spirit; others see him as a god come to earth, or as the "king of America." All believe he will someday usher in a prosperous, work-free millennium of unlimited "cargo"—pidgin English for Western material goods. . . .*
>
> *In 1942, World War II reached Tanna's shores. U.S. troops landed on nearby islands, bringing food, arms, prefabricated houses, jobs, and legions of jeeps. . . . But with the war's end, the cargo disappeared, and islanders . . . turned to mock military drills in the hope of luring GIs—and cargo-laden Liberty ships—back to Tanna. . . .*
>
> *Although Frum fails to materialize—as has been the case for [a half-century]—his followers remain devout, often attributing his absence to their own shortcomings or to governmental intervention.*

From Muller, Kal. "Tanna Awaits the Coming of John Frum." *National Geographic Magazine,* 145 (1974): 707, 714.

Religion and Economy

In the economic sphere, religion can guide commerce; determine which crops and livestock are raised by farmers, and what foods and beverages people consume; and even help decide the type of employment a person has and in what neighborhood they reside (see box, *Religion and Economy*). Within some religions, certain plants and livestock, as well as the products derived from them, are in great demand because of their roles in religious ceremonies and traditions. When this is the case, the plants or animals tend to spread with the faith.

For example, in some Christian sects in Europe and the United States, celebrants drink from a cup of wine that symbolizes the blood of Christ during the sacrament of Holy Communion. The demand for wine created by this ritual aided the diffusion of grape growing from the sunny lands of the Mediterranean to newly Christianized districts beyond the Alps in late Roman and early medieval times. The vineyards of the German Rhine were the creation of monks who arrived from the south between the sixth and ninth centuries (see box, *Wine and Religion in Germany*). For the same reason, Catholic missionaries introduced the cultivated grape to California. In fact, wine was associated with religious worship even before Christianity arose. Vineyard keeping and wine making spread westward across the Mediterranean lands in prehistoric times in association with worship of the god Dionysus.

Religion also can often explain the absence of individual crops or domestic animals in an area. The environmentally similar lands of Spain and Morocco, separated only by the Strait of Gibraltar, show the agricultural impact of food taboos. On the Spanish, Roman Catholic side of the strait, pigs are common and pork a delicacy, but in Muslim Morocco on the African side only about 12,000 swine can be found throughout the entire country. The Islamic avoidance of pork underlies this contrast. Figure 6.17 maps the pork taboo. Judaism also imposes restrictions against pork and other meats, as is stated in the following passage from the Book of Leviticus:

> *These shall ye not eat, of them that chew the cud, or of them that divide the hoof: as the camel, because he cheweth the cud, but*

Wine and Religion in Germany

Even back into prehistoric times in Europe, wine has been linked to religion. In early Christian times, vineyards were introduced into southwestern Germany by Roman monks, who desired ceremonial wine for the holy sacrament. This close attachment of church to wine in Germany left vestiges discernible even today. Among these vestiges are the religious names given to many individual vineyards, names that in turn appear on the wine bottle labels. Some are listed below. Certain generic wine names also reveal the link to religion. One of the most famous of these is *Liebfraumilch,* a mild, semisweet blend from German Rheinhessen. The name means "milk of the Holy Virgin."

German Wine District	*Town or Village*	*Name of Vineyard*	*(Translation)*
Rheingau	Rüdesheim	Mönchspfad	("Monks' Path")
Rheingau	Rüdesheim	Magdalenenkreuz	("Cross of Mary Magdalen")
Rheingau	Oestrich	Gottesthal	("God's Valley")
Rheinpfalz	Forst	Jesuitengarten	("Jesuits' Garden")
Rheinpfalz	Forst	Mariengarten	("Virgin Mary's Garden")
Rheinpfalz	Deidesheim	Paradiesgarten	("Garden of Paradise")
Rheinpfalz	Deidesheim	Herrgottsacker	("Lord God's Field")
Mosel	Graach	Himmelreich	("Heaven")
Mosel	Klüsserath	Bruderschaft	([Monastic] "Brotherhood")
Nahe	Bad Kreuznach	Mönchberg	("Monks' Hill")
Nahe	Niederhausen	Pfaffenstein	("Priest's Rock")
Nahe	Bad Kreuznach	Kapellenpfad	("Chapel Path")
Saar	Wiltingen	Klosterberg	("Monastery Hill")

Source: Adapted from Johnson, Hugh. *The World Atlas of Wine*. New York: Simon & Schuster, 1971.

divideth not the hoof; he is unclean unto you. And the coney, because he cheweth the cud, but divideth not the hoof; he is unclean unto you. And the hare, because he cheweth the cud, but divideth not the hoof; he is unclean unto you. And the swine, though he divide the hoof, and be cloven-footed, yet he cheweth not the cud, he is unclean unto you.

Scholars explain the Islamic and Judaic pork taboos in various ways. Some suggest that these two cultures were primarily concerned with the danger of intestinal parasites (trichinosis), or that they considered pigs unclean. However, it is unlikely that the cause-and-effect relationship between poorly cooked pork and intestinal parasites could have been detected prior to the days of modern medical technology.

Other scholars have suggested a theory based on economy and ecology, after observing that pork avoidance is characteristic of the monotheistic faiths that arose among desert nomads. The proponents of this view believe that nomadic herding originated on the borders of the great farming areas of the ancient Middle East, near the Tigris, Euphrates, Nile, and other rivers. Population pressures forced people to settle farther and farther from the river banks, so that eventually some groups lost access to irrigation waters. As we saw in Chapter 3, these people were forced to abandon most crop farming and turn to animal husbandry. The poor quality of the range required them to wander from place to place in the desert, in nomadic fashion, seeking forage for their livestock. Pigs, valuable animals to the sedentary farmers of the river valleys, require shade, are poor travelers, and found little to eat in the desert. As a result, the nomad relied instead on sheep, goats, horses, camels, and, in some areas, cattle. Because environmental conditions prevented the nomads from owning pigs, they declared pork undesirable in a "sour grapes" reaction. In time, this declaration found religious expression as a taboo. Ages later, as a final "revenge" Muslim

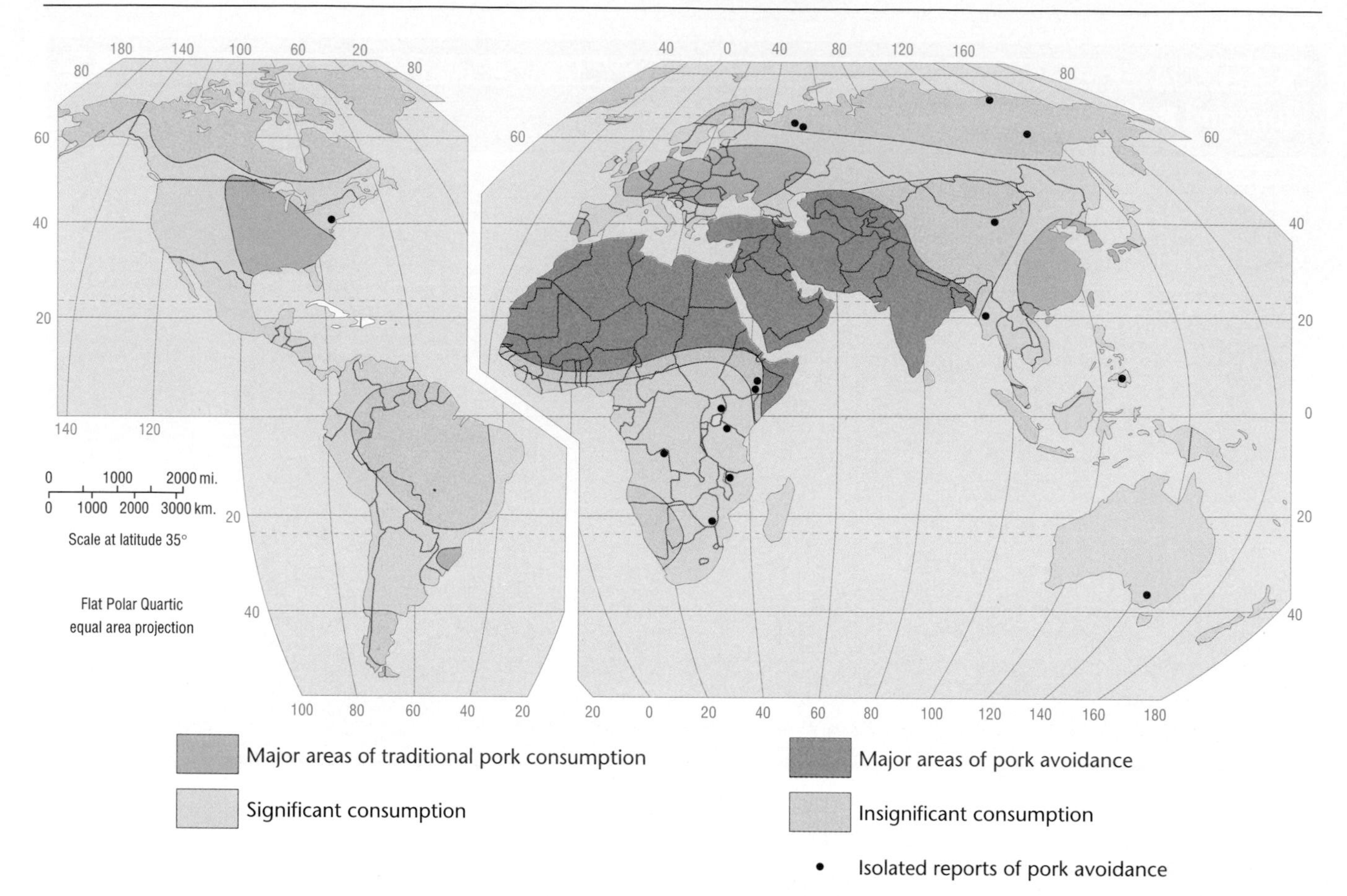

Figure 6.17

Consumption and avoidance of pork are influenced by religion. Some religions and churches—such as Islam, Judaism, and Seventh-Day Adventism—prohibit the eating of pork. Cultural groups with a traditional fondness for pork include central Europeans, Chinese, and Polynesians. Can you explain the pattern in North America? (Based in part on Simoons.)

nomads imposed their religion, complete with the pork taboo, on the farming people of the river valleys.

Muslims are also not permitted any alcoholic beverages. The Koran states: "O ye who have believed, wine, games of chance, idols, and divining arrows are nothing but an infamy of Satan's handiwork. Avoid them so that ye may succeed." Christians failed to reach a consensus on this taboo. Some Christian denominations prohibit all consumption of alcohol, in the belief that it is detrimental to health, welfare, and behavior, while others, as described above, even use wine in religious ceremonies. In the United States, such groups as the Baptists, Mormons, and Seventh-Day Adventists support prohibition, while Roman Catholics, Lutherans, and several other denominations tolerate alcohol. The economic imprint of these different attitudes can be seen in a map of "wet" and "dry" areas in the United States. Texas provides an excellent example, since it is religiously diverse and by law allows each community to decide in local-option elections whether alcohol may be sold or served (Figure 6.18). Almost without exception, Catholic and Lutheran areas in Texas are "wet," while Baptist and Methodist counties vote "dry."

Food taboos also strongly affect the fishing industry. Practices such as the traditional Roman Catholic avoidance of meat on Friday greatly

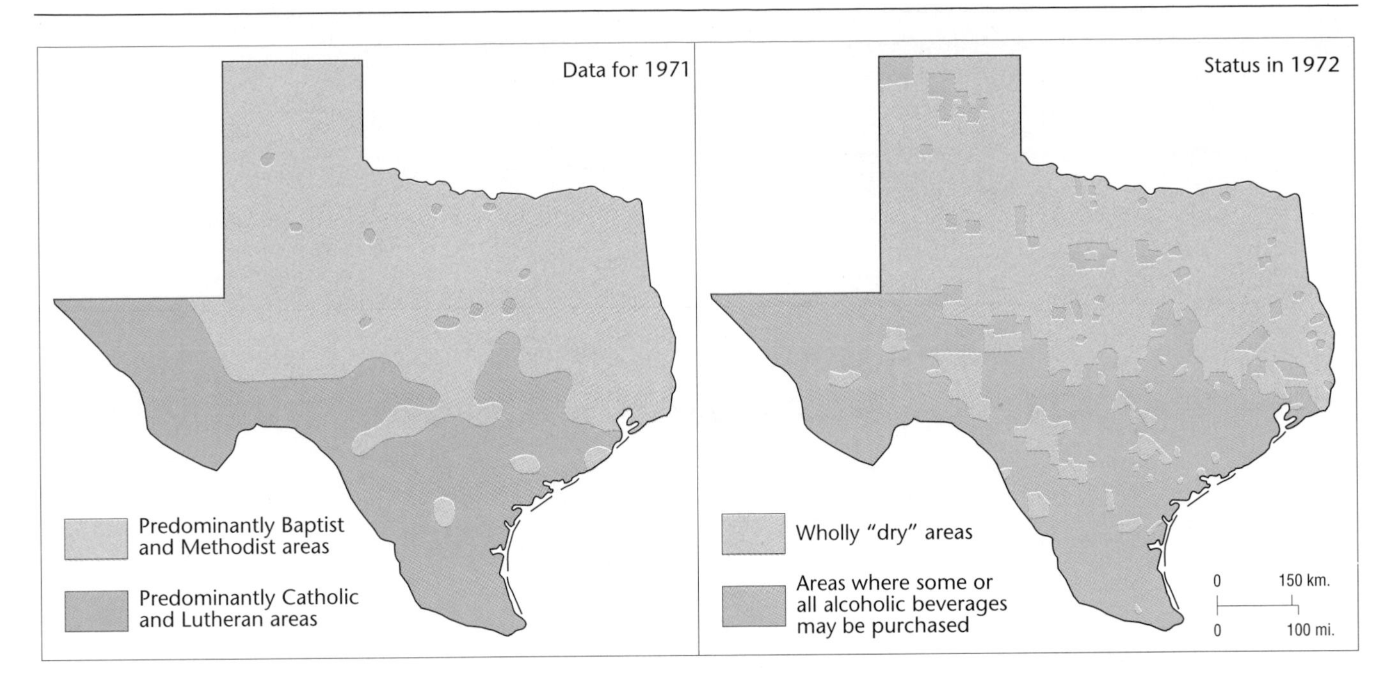

Figure 6.18
The distributions of religion and alcohol sales in Texas. Catholics and Lutherans generally choose to be "wet," while Baptists and Methodists favor prohibition. (Source: Jordan, Terry G., et al. *Texas: A Geography*. Boulder, CO: Westview Press, 1984, pp. 116, 148.)

stimulated fishing, since fish became the standard Friday fare in Catholic areas. Indeed, Christian tradition has always honored fishermen. We can perhaps trace this back to the apostle Peter, a fisherman by profession. The fish was an early symbol of Christianity, initially exceeding the cross in importance. Use of this symbol stimulated the fishing industry, particularly in Catholic countries, and a lively trade in shipping preserved fish from coast to interior developed.

Other cultures place religious taboos on fish consumption and produce an opposite economic result. Most Hindus will not eat fish. India regularly suffers food shortages and dietary deficiencies while the nearby ocean teems with protein-rich fish. Among Christians, the Seventh-Day Adventists have a finless fish taboo and also will not eat pork. When missionaries of this church converted the population of Pitcairn Island in the South Pacific to their faith, the island's economic self-sufficiency collapsed, because the people had previously depended heavily on pork and finless fish in their diet.

Religious Pilgrimage

For many religious groups, journeys to sacred places, or **pilgrimages,** play an important role in the faith (Figure 6.19). Pilgrimages are typical of both ethnic and proselytic religions. They are particularly significant to followers of Islam, Hinduism, Shintoism, and Roman Catholicism.

The sacred places vary in character. Some have been the setting for miracles; a few are the source regions of religions or areas where the founders of the faith lived and worked; others contain holy physical features such as rivers, caves, springs, and mountain peaks; and still others are believed to house gods or are religious administrative centers where leaders of the church reside. Examples include the Arabian cities of Mecca and Medina in Islam; Rome and the French town of Lourdes

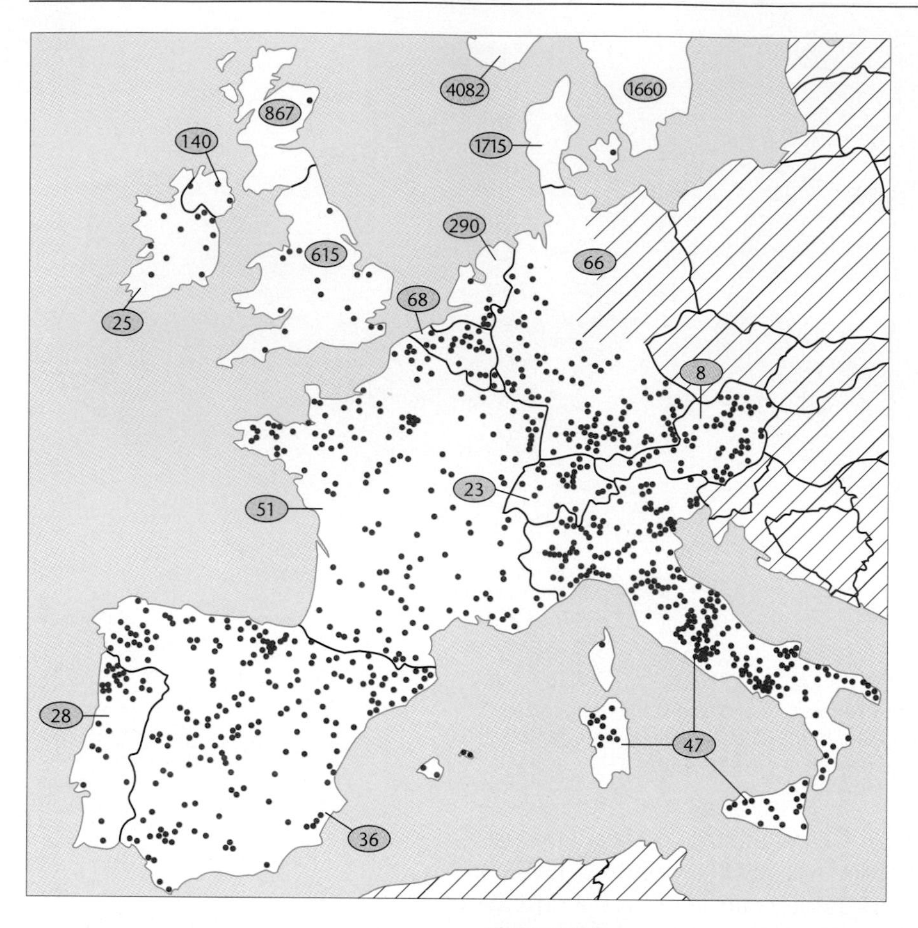

• One major pilgrimage shrine, 1990

Each circled number represents Thousands of inhabitants per religious pilgrimage shrine (major and minor).
For example: 

No data

Figure 6.19
Distribution of major religious pilgrimage shrines in western Europe. These are most numerous in Roman Catholic areas and in regions of surviving religious vitality (compare with Figure 6.8). Nineteen of these shrines attract more than a million pilgrims each year, massively affecting the local economies. (Adapted from Nolan, Mary Lee, and Sidney Nolan. *Christian Pilgrimage in Modern Western Europe*. Chapel Hill: University of North Carolina Press, 1989, p. 31.)

in Roman Catholicism; the Indian city of Varanasi on the holy Ganges River, a destination of Hindu pilgrims; and Ise, the hearth of Shintoism in Japan.

Religion provides the stimulus for pilgrimage by offering those who participate the reward of soul purification or the attainment of some desired objective in their lives. Pilgrims often journey great distances to see major shrines. Other sites, of lesser significance, draw pilgrims only from local districts or provinces. Pilgrimages can have tremendous economic impact, since the movement of pilgrims amounts to a form of tourism.

In some favored localities, the pilgrim trade provides the only significant source of revenue for the community. Lourdes, a town of 16,300, attracts between 4 and 5 million pilgrims each year, many seeking miraculous cures at the famous grotto where the Virgin Mary supposedly appeared. Not surprisingly, among French cities, Lourdes ranks second only to Paris in number of hotels, although most of these are small. Mecca, a small city, annually attracts hundreds of thousands of Muslim pilgrims from every corner of the Islamic culture region, as is

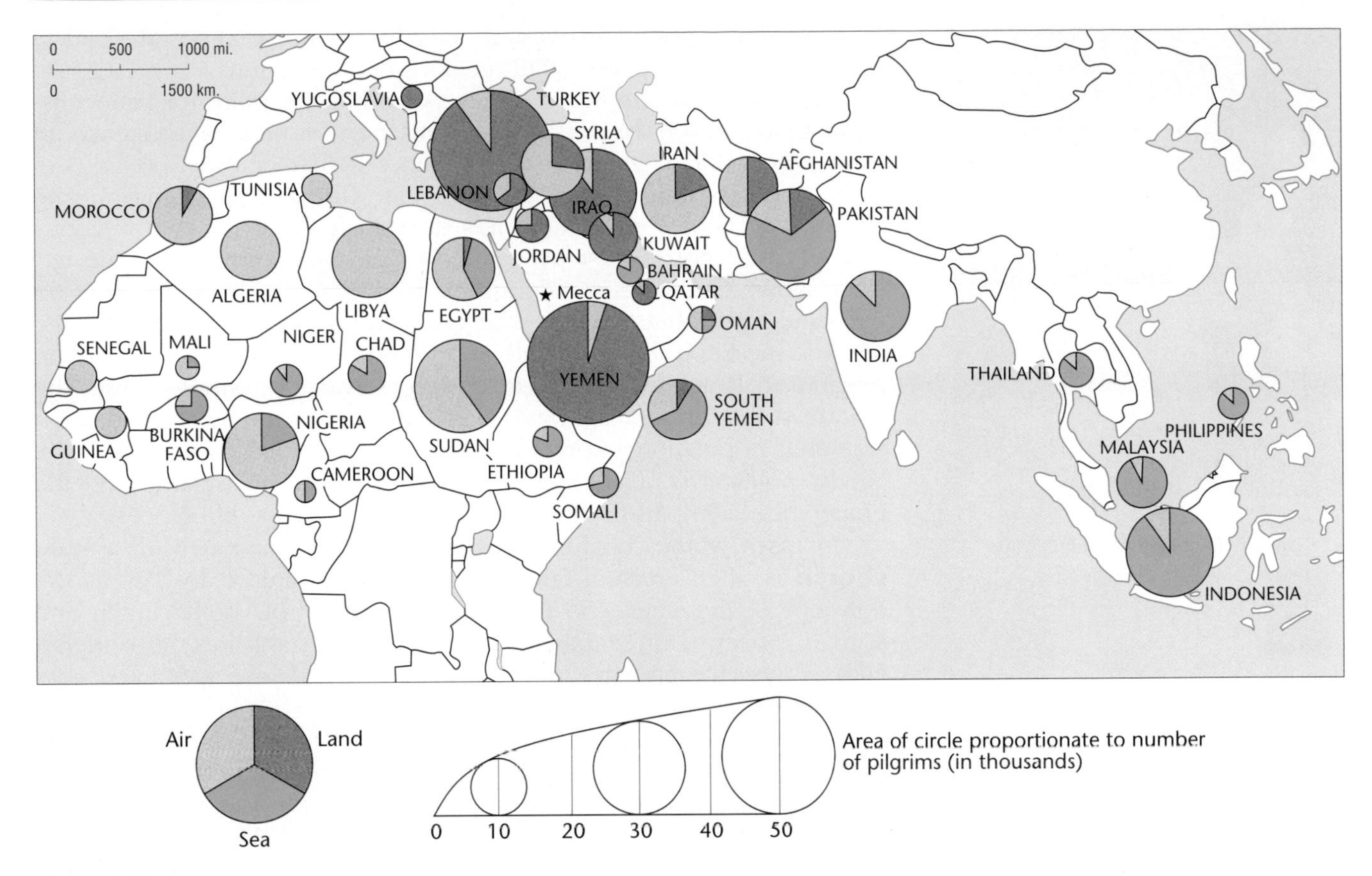

Figure 6.20
The pilgrimage of foreign Muslims to Mecca. In 1968, 375,000 Muslim pilgrims converged on the holy city of Mecca, in spite of the blockage of the Suez Canal that resulted from the Arab-Israeli war of the previous year. Saudi Arabians, in whose nation Mecca is situated, are not shown. (After King, Russell. "The Pilgrimage to Mecca: Some Historical and Geographical Aspects." *Erdkunde,* 26 [1972]: 70.)

shown in Figure 6.20. By land, sea, and air, the faithful come to this hearth of Islam, a city closed to all non-Muslims. Such mass pilgrimages obviously have a major impact on the development of transportation routes and carriers. To facilitate the pilgrimage to Mecca and Medina, steamships connect the Arabian port of Jidda with overseas Muslim areas in Africa, Indonesia, Malaysia, and other lands. Chartered and scheduled airline service is also available to Mecca pilgrims.

In medieval Europe, many roads and bridges were built to accommodate pilgrims. Monks often helped maintain these routes and established shelters at regular intervals as way stations. Some of these hospices still survive, as at the summit of St. Gotthard Pass in the Swiss Alps.

Religion and Political Geography

Accustomed by their heritage to the doctrine of separation of church and state, Americans are usually unaware of how closely religion and politics are intertwined in much of the world. Religious practices and traits often change abruptly at political boundaries, as along parts of the

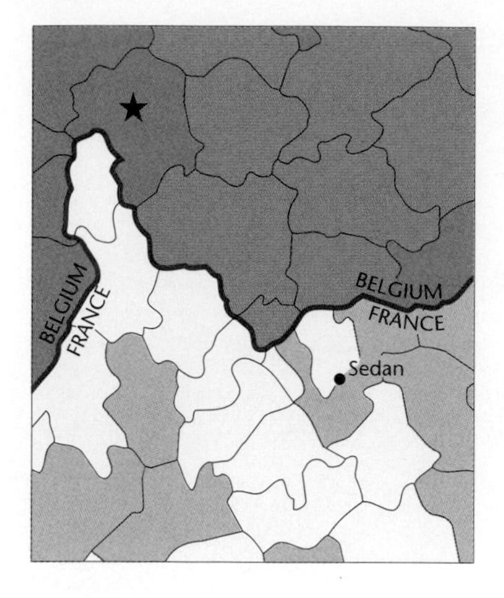

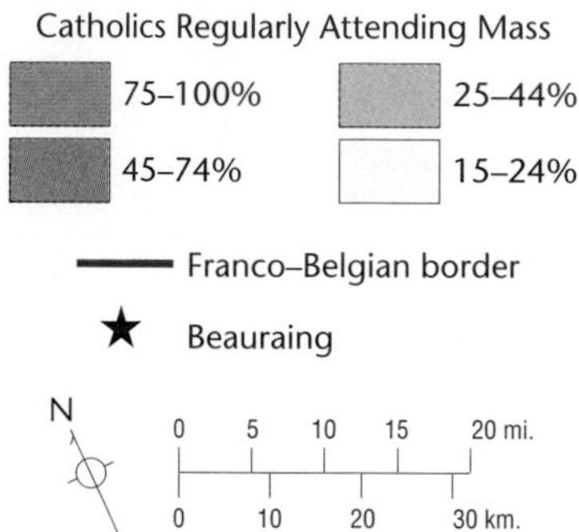

Figure 6.21
Attendance at mass along the Franco-Belgian border, about 1950. The people on both sides of the boundary speak French and share many other cultural traits; yet Catholicism remains a vital force only on the Belgian side. The political border has become a religious border. Beauraing is a major Catholic pilgrimage site, lying on the Belgian side of the border. What developments in the respective countries might help explain this striking pattern? (Adapted from Boulard, Fernand. *An Introduction to Religious Sociology*. M. J. Jackson (trans.). London: Darton, Longman and Todd, 1960.)

Franco-Belgian border in western Europe (Figure 6.21), and political parties are often identified with religious denominations.

In some nations, religion serves as the rallying point for nationalistic sentiment and even provides a justification for national existence. In 1947, when Britain granted independence to her colonial holdings in India, the area split to form a Hindu state (India) and a Muslim state (Pakistan). Those who created this division felt that the two religious groups could not coexist peacefully within the same state. Time has since shown that Hindus and Muslims have difficulty living together on the same subcontinent, even when concentrated in separate states. Israel and the Republic of Ireland are two other nations based largely on religion. In Israel, automatic citizenship is available only to Jews. The demise of the former Yugoslavia derived in part from the religious division of its population among Catholics, Eastern Orthodox, and Muslims. Similar political conflicts in Cyprus, Israel, Lebanon, Ireland, and the Philippines have part or all of their bases in religious differences.

In cases where religion provides a basis for nationalism, a **state church** is often created. Such a church is recognized by law as the only one in the state, and the government controls both church and state. In Norway, for example, the constitution establishes the Lutheran faith as the state church, and pastors and officials are appointed government employees. In still other cases, the church is actively involved in governing countries. Such a government is known as a **theocracy** (see box, *The Mormon Region*). The head of the church is often also the head of state. Vatican City, ruled by the Pope, is a fully independent state.

In some nations, political parties are linked to particular church groups. As a result, voting returns often duplicate the religious map. Such ties are particularly common in Europe, where political parties have names like Catholic People's Party or Christian Democrats. It is common in these countries for churchgoers to be advised from the pulpit on how they should vote. Even in countries like the United States, where legal separation of church and state is maintained, voting patterns often reflect denominational patterns.

On a broader political geographical scale, the division of the world into increasingly hostile economic power blocs is taking on religious overtones. The prosperous First World, with preponderantly Judeo-Christian roots and affiliations, is pitted against an Islamic Third World. In this view, Islam becomes the ideology and consolation of the impoverished, standing against rich infidels, with the potential for widespread conflict. All along the Christian/Muslim borderland in Eurasia and Africa, conflicts erupt. The First World militarily attacks or institutes sanctions against such Islamic states as Iraq, Iran, and Libya, receiving a dose of terrorism in response. Will the next world war be a religious conflict?

Religious Landscapes

Because religion is so vital an aspect of culture, its visible impress, reflecting the role played by religious motives in the human transformation of the landscape, can be quite striking. In some regions, the religious aspect offers the dominant visible evidence of culture, producing *sacred landscapes*. At the opposite extreme are areas almost purely secular in appearance. Religions differ greatly in visibility, but even those

The Mormon Region: A Case Study in Cultural Integration

An excellent example of the interworkings of religion, politics, economy, and population is provided by the Mormon culture region in the Great Basin of the American West. Established by members of the Church of Jesus Christ of Latter-day Saints in 1847, the Mormon culture region spread from the Salt Lake City area to encompass Utah and parts of all bordering states. The population was ancestrally derived from New York and New England, but later immigrants came from Europe and other areas.

Initially, and through most of the nineteenth century, a theocratic government ruled in the Mormon culture region, giving a political expression to the faith. The church leader, Brigham Young, was also the territorial governor of Utah. Repeated efforts were made to create the state of Deseret, to be part of the United States but still under church administration. While the power of the United States government was finally employed to destroy the Mormon theocracy, the tie between church and government remained strong for many years.

In the economic sphere, the church leadership exerted an immense influence on development of the Great Basin area. A goal of economic self-sufficiency was proclaimed. Everything needed in Deseret was to be produced there. Artisans possessing necessary craft skills were actively recruited in Europe and elsewhere. Agricultural colonies were established in southern Utah, the "Mormon Dixie," to produce cotton and other warm-climate crops that did not grow in the colder Salt Lake area. Most facets of the economy were directly or indirectly controlled by the church, even to the point of ownership in some cases. To a remarkable degree, the plan of economic self-sufficiency succeeded, and through organized hard labor the desert of the Great Basin was made to produce abundantly.

The church also profoundly influenced the population geography of the Great Basin. Indeed, the very settlement of the area was undertaken as a result of a decision by church leaders to migrate from Illinois. After colonization of the Salt Lake area, new colonies were founded, also under church direction. Sites for the new colonies were chosen by the church, and even the selection of colonists was made by the religious leaders. From a very early time, the Mormon church has encouraged large families, thereby further influencing the population distribution of the Great Basin.

In this way, an integration of religion, politics, economy, and demography developed in the Great Basin. To this day, the Mormon culture region retains the distinctive imprints of this interplay.

least apparent to the eye normally leave some subtle mark on the countryside. The content of religious landscapes is varied, ranging from houses of worship to cemeteries, wayside shrines, and place-names. Moreover, religion can help shape landscape features such as settlement patterns.

Religious Structures

The most obvious religious contributions to the landscape are the buildings erected to house divinities or to shelter worshipers. These structures vary greatly in size, function, style of architecture, construction material, and degree of ornateness (Figure 6.22). To Roman Catholics, for example, the church building is literally the house of God, and the altar is the focus of vital ritual. Partly for these reasons, Catholic churches are typically large, elaborately decorated, and visually imposing. In many towns and villages, the Catholic house of worship is the focal point of the settlement, exceeding all other structures in size and grandeur.

To many Protestants, particularly the traditional Calvinistic "chapel-goers" of British background, including Methodists and Baptists, the church building is, by contrast, simply a place to assemble for worship. The result is an unsanctified, smaller, less ornate structure. The simpler church buildings of these Protestants appeal less to the senses and more to the personal faith. For this reason, their traditional structures are typically not designed for comfort, beauty, or high visibility, but instead appear deliberately humble (Figure 6.22). Similarly, the religious landscape of the Amish and Mennonites in rural North America, the "plain folk," is very subdued, since they reject ostentation in any form.

Figure 6.22
Traditional religious architecture takes varied forms. St. Basil's Church on Red Square in Moscow reflects a highly ornate Russian landscape presence, while the plain board chapel in the American South demonstrates an opposite tendency favoring visual simplicity on the part of British-derived Protestants. The ornate Hindu temple in Varanasi, India, offers still another sacred landscape.

Some of their adherents meet in houses or barns, and the churches that do exist are very modest in appearance, like those of the southern Calvinists.

In Islam, mosques are normally the most imposing items in the landscape (Figure 6.1), while the visibility of Jewish synagogues varies greatly. Hinduism has produced large numbers of visually striking temples for its multiplicity of gods, but much worship is practiced in private households (Figure 6.22).

The building materials chosen for a religious structure often demonstrate the value that a religion places on its visibility in the landscape. Sects that wish to call attention to their sacred structures typically build them of different materials than those used in the construction of houses and other nonreligious buildings. In some parts of Europe, for example, churches are built of stone, while secular structures in the same communities are made of brick or wood.

Paralleling this contrast in church styles are attitudes toward wayside shrines and similar manifestations of faith. Catholic culture regions typically abound with shrines, crucifixes, crosses, and assorted visual reminders of religion (Figure 6.23), as do some Eastern Orthodox Christian areas. One of the writers of this textbook vividly recalls driving along a mountain road in Bavaria on a summer night many years ago, when suddenly the headlights illuminated a realistic, life-sized crucifix in a shrine bordering the pavement. Instinctively, his foot went to the brake, and it was several seconds before he could adjust to the reality of this Catholic sacred landscape. Protestant areas, by contrast, are bare of such symbols and do not startle the night driver. Their landscapes, instead, display such features as signboards advising the traveler to "Get Right With God," a common sight in the southern United States.

The distinction between sacred and profane in the cultural landscape is not always easy for the outsider to discern. Along the Ganges River in Varanasi, India, steps—or *ghats*—lead down to the stream at many places (Figure 6.24). To the uninitiated, these may seem intended for the convenience of fishers, swimmers, and people doing laundry. The more important role of the ghats, however, is to facilitate ritual bathing in the holy Ganges—the main goal of pilgrims coming to the city. Also, the ghats provide a place for funeral pyres in the cremation of the dead.

Most tribal ethnic religions do not stand out in the cultural landscape. Animistic groups regard many objects as sacred, but these items are commonplace and would not reveal their religious significance to the eyes of an outsider. Tribal religions often do not have separate houses of worship.

Landscapes of the Dead

Religions differ greatly in the type of tribute they award to the dead. This variation appears in the cultural landscape. Hindus and Buddhists cremate their dead. Having no cemeteries, their dead leave no obvious mark on the land. In the same way, the few remaining Zoroastrians, called Parsees, who preserve a once-widespread Middle Eastern faith now confined to parts of India, have traditionally left their dead exposed to be devoured by vultures.

In Egypt, on the other hand, spectacular pyramids and other tombs were built to house dead leaders. These monuments, as well as the modern graves and tombs of the rural Islamic folk of Egypt, lie on desert land not suitable for farming (Figure 6.25). Muslim cemeteries are usually modest in appearance, but spectacular tombs are sometimes erected for aristocratic persons, giving us such sacred structures as the Taj Mahal in India (Figure 6.26), one of the architectural wonders of the world.

Figure 6.25
Landscape of the dead, landscape of the living. The Beni Hassan Islamic necropolis in central Egypt lies in the desert, just beyond the irrigable land, while the living make intensive use of every parcel watered by the Nile River. The mud brick structures are all tombs. Thus the doubly dead landscape is sacred, while the realm of living plants and people is profane.

Figure 6.23
A wayside shrine in southern Poland. Such shrines are a highly visible part of the religious landscape in some Christian areas.

Figure 6.24
A ghat in the pilgrimage city of Varanasi, India. Part of the sacred landscape on the banks of the holy Ganges River, the steps serve ritual bathers and provide a place for cremation, both of which are important in Hinduism.

Figure 6.26
The Taj Mahal in Agra, India. Built as a Muslim tomb, it is perhaps the most impressive religious structure in the world.

Chinese who practice the composite Confucianist-Buddhist religion typically bury their dead, setting aside land for that purpose and erecting monuments to the deceased kin. In parts of pre-Communist China, as much as 10 percent of the land in some districts was covered by cemeteries and ancestral shrines, greatly reducing the acreage available for agriculture.

Christians, of course, also typically bury their dead in sacred places set aside for that purpose. These vary significantly from one Christian denomination to another. Some graveyards, particularly those of southern Calvinists and Mennonites, are very modest in appearance, reflecting the reluctance of these groups to use any symbolism that might be construed as idolatrous (see also Figure 7.3). Among certain other Christian groups, cemeteries are places of color and elaborate decoration (Figure 6.27).

Figure 6.27
Two different Christian landscapes of the dead. In highland Mexico (photo on the right), the indigenous Indian love of color is vividly expressed, while in Sydney, Australia, a Germanic preference for order prevails.

Cemeteries often preserve truly ancient cultural traits, for people as a rule are reluctant to change practices relating to the dead. The traditional rural cemetery of the southern United States provides a case in point. Freshwater mussel shells are placed atop many of the elongated grave mounds. Rose bushes and cedars are planted throughout the cemetery. Recent research suggests that the use of roses may derive from the worship of an ancient, pre-Christian mother goddess of the Mediterranean lands. The rose was a symbol of this great goddess, who could restore life to the dead. Similarly, the cedar evergreen is an age-old pagan symbol of death and eternal life, and the use of shell decoration derives from an animistic custom in West Africa, the source of southern slaves. While the present Christian population of the South is unaware of the origins of their cemetery symbolism, it seems likely that their landscape of the dead contains animistic elements thousands of years old, revealing truly ancient beliefs and cultural diffusions.

Religious Names on the Land

"St.-Jean," "St.-Aubert," "St.-Damase-des-Aulnaies," "Ste. Perpétue de L'Islet," "St.-Pamphile," "St.-Adalbert,"—so read the placards of the town names as one drives from the St. Lawrence River south on Highway 24 in Québec, paralleling the Maine border. All this saintliness is merely a part of the French Canadian religious landscape, as Figure 6.28 shows. The point is that religion often inspires the names that people place on the land. Within Christianity, the use of saints' names for settlements is very common in Roman Catholic and Greek Orthodox areas, especially in overseas colonial lands settled by Catholics, such as Latin America and French Canada. In areas of the Old World that were settled long before the advent of Christianity, saints' names were often

Figure 6.28
Religious place-names dot the map of French Canada. In the French Canadian province of Québec, the dominant Roman Catholic religion finds an expression in the names given to towns and villages. Saintly names are dominant in the areas of purest French settlement. Nearer the United States–Canadian border, in townships settled by English-speaking people, religious place-names are rare. On this basis, where exactly would you draw the French Catholic/English Protestant border at the time of initial settlement? Is that border still in the same location today?

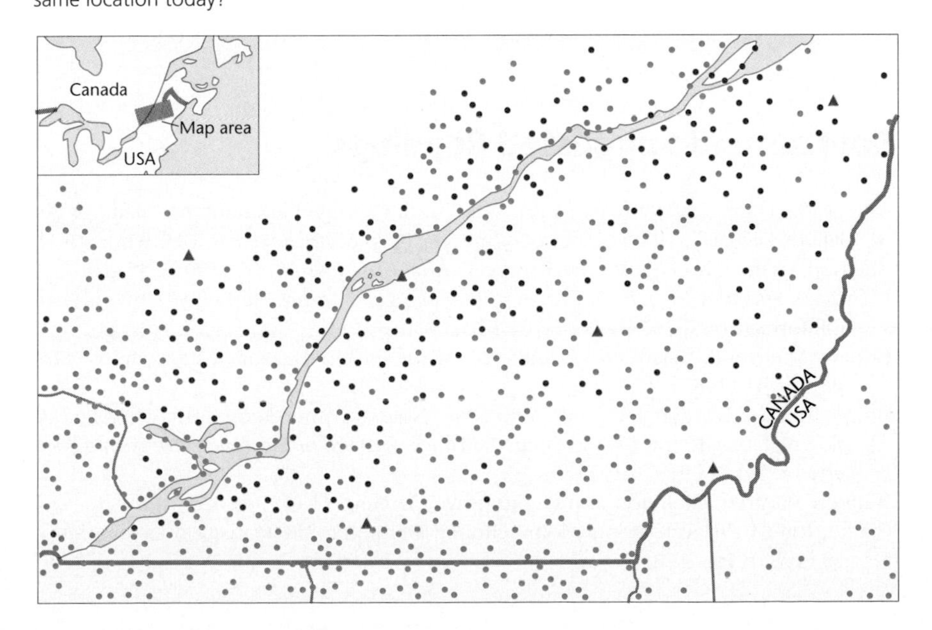

▲ Names beginning with Notre Dame

• Names beginning with Saint or Sainte

• Other names

grafted onto pre-Christian names, as in Alcazar de San Juan, in Spain, which combines Arabic and Christian elements.

Toponyms in Protestant regions display less religious influence, but some imprint can usually be found. In the southern United States, for example, the word *chapel* as a prefix or suffix, as in Chapel Hill and Ward's Chapel, is very common in the names of rural hamlets. Names like this accurately convey the image of the humble, rural Protestant churches that are so common in the South.

Conclusion

Religion is firmly interwoven in the fabric of culture, a bright hue in the human mosaic, for religions vary greatly from one area to another, a regional diversity so profound as to give special significance to James Griffith's admonition that we should all "learn, respect, and walk softly." This religious spatial variation led us to ask how these distributions came to be, a question best answered through the methods of cultural diffusion. Some religions, proselytic denominations, actively encourage their own diffusion. Other religions erect barriers to expansion diffusion by restricting membership to one particular ethnic group.

The theme of cultural ecology reveals some fundamental ties between religion and the physical environment. One major function of many religious systems, particularly the animistic faiths, is to appease and placate the forces of nature and to achieve harmony between the people and the physical environment. Religions differ in their outlook on environmental modification by humans.

Religion is culturally integrated—that is, systemically related to economy and politics, among other things. Everything from tourism to nationalism can have a religious component.

The cultural landscape abounds with expressions of religious belief. Places of worship—temples, churches, and shrines—differ in appearance, distinctiveness, prominence, and frequency of occurrence from one religious culture region to another. These buildings provide a visual index to the various faiths. Cemeteries and religious place-names also add a special effect to the landscape that tells us about the religious character of the population. In all these ways, and more, the five themes of cultural geography are relevant to the study of the world's religions.

Sources and Suggested Readings

Ainsley, W. Frank, and John W. Florin. "The North Carolina Piedmont: An Island of Religious Diversity." *West Georgia College Studies in Social Sciences,* 12 (1973): 30–34.

Atkisson, Alan. "Thou Shalt Care for the Earth." *Utne Reader,* 68 (1995): 15–16.

Bhardwaj, Surinder M. *Hindu Places of Pilgrimage in India.* Berkeley: University of California Press, 1973.

Bonine, Michael E. "Islam and Commerce: Waqf and the Bazaar of Yazd, Iran." *Erdkunde,* 41 (1987): 182–196.

Brunn, Stanley D., and James O. Wheeler. "Notes on the Geography of Religious Town Names in the United States." *Names: Journal of the American Name Society,* 14, No. 4 (1966): 197–202.

Büttner, Manfred. "Religion and Geography." *Numen,* 21 (1974): 163–196.

Clarke, John I. "Islamic Populations: Limited Demographic Transition." *Geography,* 70 (1985): 118–128.

Clawson, David L. "Religion and Change in a Mexican Village." *Journal of Cultural Geography,* 9, No. 2 (1989): 61–76.

Crowley, William K. "Old Order Amish Settlement: Diffusion and Growth." *Annals of the Association of American Geographers,* 68 (1978): 249–264.

Curran, Claude W. "Mt. Shasta, California, and the I Am Religion," in *Abstracts, The Association of American Geographers 1991 Annual Meeting, April 13–17, Miami, Florida.* Washington, DC: Association of American Geographers, 1991, p. 42.

Curry-Roper, Janel M. "Contemporary Christian Eschatologies and their Relation to Environmental Stewardship." *Professional Geographer,* 42 (1990): 157–169.

Doherty, Paul. "Ethnic Segregation Levels in the Belfast Urban Area." *Area,* 21 (1989): 151–159.

Doughty, Robin W. "Environmental Theology: Trends and Prospects in Christian Thought." *Progress in Human Geography,* 5 (1981): 234–248.

Dutt, A. K., and S. Devgun. "Diffusion of Sikhism and Recent Migration Patterns in India." *GeoJournal,* 1, No. 5 (1977): 81–90.

Eyre, L. Alan. "Biblical Symbolism and the Role of Fantasy Geography Among the Rastafarians of Jamaica." *Journal of Geography,* 84 (1985): 144–148.

Al-Fārūqi, Isma'il R., and David E. Sopher. *Historical Atlas of the Religions of the World.* New York: Macmillan, 1974.

Fleure, H. J. "The Geographical Distribution of the Major Religions." *Bulletin de la Société Royale de Géographie d'Egypte,* 24 (1951): 1–18.

Francaviglia, Richard V. *The Mormon Landscape.* New York: AMS Press, 1978.

Fuson, Robert H. "The Orientation of Mayan Ceremonial Centers." *Annals of the Association of American Geographers,* 59 (1969): 494–511.

Glacken, Clarence J. *Traces on the Rhodian Shore.* Berkeley: University of California Press, 1967.

Griffith, James S. *Beliefs and Holy Places: A Spiritual Geography of the Pimeria Alta.* Tucson: University of Arizona Press.

Gutschow, Niels "Varanasi/Benares: The Center of Hinduism." *Erdkunde,* 48 (1994): 194–209.

Halvorson, Peter L., and William M. Newman. *Atlas of Religious Change in America, 1952–1990.* Atlanta: Glenmary Research Center, 1994.

Hannemann, Manfred. *The Diffusion of the Reformation in Southwestern Germany, 1518–1534.* Research Paper 167. Chicago: University of Chicago, Dept. of Geography, 1975.

Hardwick, Susan. *Russian Refuge: Religion, Migration, and Settlement on the North American Pacific Rim.* Chicago: University of Chicago Press, 1993.

Harpur, James. *The Atlas of Sacred Places.* New York: Henry Holt, 1994.

Heatwole, Charles A. "Sectarian Ideology and Church Architecture." *Geographical Review,* 79 (1989): 63–78.

Henderson, Martha L. "What is Spiritual Geography?" *Geographical Review,* 83 (1993): 469–472.

Henzel, Cynthia. "Cruces in the Roadside Landscape of Northeastern Mexico." *Journal of Cultural Geography,* 11, No. 2 (1991): 93–106.

Hershkowitz, Sara. "Residential Segregation by Religion: A Conceptual Framework." *Tijdschrift voor Economische en Sociale Geografie,* 78 (1987): 44–52.

Hobbs, Joseph J. "Sacred Space and Touristic Development at Jebel Husa (Mt. Sinai), Egypt." *Journal of Cultural Geography,* 12, No. 2 (1992): 99–113

Jackson, Richard H. "Religion and Landscape in the Mormon Cultural Region," in K. W. Butzer (ed.), *Dimensions of Human Geography.* Research Paper No. 186. Chicago: University of Chicago, Dept. of Geography, 1978, pp. 100–127.

Jackson, Richard H., and Roger Henrie. "Perception of Sacred Space." *Journal of Cultural Geography,* 3, No. 2 (1983): 94–107.

Jordan, Terry G. *Texas Graveyards: A Cultural Legacy.* Austin: University of Texas Press, 1982.

Kay, Jeanne. "Human Dominion over Nature in the Hebrew Bible." *Annals of the Association of American Geographers,* 79 (1989): 214–232.

Kay, Jeanne, and Craig J. Brown. "Mormon Beliefs About Land and Natural Resources, 1847–1877." *Journal of Historical Geography,* 11 (1985): 253–267.

Kluckhohn, Florence R., et al. *Variations in Value Orientations*. Evanston, IL: Row, Peterson, 1961.

Lehr, John C. "The Ukrainian Sacred Landscape: A Metaphor of Survival and Acculturation." *Material History Bulletin,* 29 (1989): 3–11.

Levine, Gregory J. "On the Geography of Religion." *Transactions of the Institute of British Geographers,* 11 (1986): 428–440.

Lodrick, Deryck O. *Sacred Cows, Sacred Places: Origins and Survivals of Animal Homes in India*. Berkeley: University of California Press, 1981.

Maier, Emanuel. "Torah as Movable Territory." *Annals of the Association of American Geographers,* 65 (1975): 18–23.

Manyo, Joseph T. "Italian-American Yard Shrines." *Journal of Cultural Geography,* 4 (1983): 119–125.

Meinig, Donald W. "The Mormon Culture Region: Strategies and Patterns in the Geography of the American West, 1847–1964." *Annals of the Association of American Geographers,* 55 (1965): 191–220.

Milbauer, John T. "Rural Churches in Northeastern Oklahoma." *North American Culture,* 4 (1988): 41–52.

Noble, Allen G. "Landscape of Piety, Landscape of Profit: The Amish-Mennonite and Derived Landscapes of Northeastern Ohio." *East Lakes Geographer,* 21 (1986): 34–48.

Nolan, Mary Lee, and Sidney Nolan. *Religious Pilgrimage in Modern Western Europe*. Chapel Hill: University of North Carolina Press, 1989.

Norris, Kathleen. *Dakota: A Spiritual Geography*. New York: Ticknor & Fields, 1993.

O'Brien, Joanne, and Martin Palmer. *The State of Religion Atlas*. New York: Simon & Schuster, 1993.

Park, Chris. *Sacred Worlds: An Introduction to Geography and Religion*. London: Routledge, 1994

Pui-lan, Kwok. *Ecotheology: Voices from South and North*. New York: World Council of Churches Publications, 1994.

Rinschede, Gisbert, and Surinder M. Bhardwaj. *Pilgrimage in the United States*. Berlin: Dietrich Reimer, 1990.

Rodrigue, Christine M. "Can Religion Account for Early Animal Domestication?" *Professional Geographer,* 44 (1992): 417–430.

Scott, Jamie, and Paul Simpson-Housley (eds.). *Sacred Places and Profane Spaces: Essays in the Geographics of Judaism, Christianity, and Islam*. New York: Greenwood Press, 1991.

Semple, Ellen Churchill. *Influences of Geographical Environment*. New York: Henry Holt, 1911.

Shortridge, James R. "Patterns of Religion in the United States." *Geographical Review,* 66 (1976): 420–434.

Simoons, Frederick J. *Eat Not This Flesh: Food Avoidances in the Old World,* 2d ed. Madison: University of Wisconsin Press, 1994.

Simpson-Housley, Paul. "Hutterian Religious Ideology, Environmental Perception, and Attitudes Toward Agriculture." *Journal of Geography,* 77 (1978): 145–148.

Sims, John H., and Duane D. Baumann. "The Tornado Threat: Coping Styles of the North and South." *Science,* 176 (1972): 1386–1392.

Singh, Rana P. B. "Water Symbolism and Sacred Landscape in Hinduism." *Erdkunde,* 48 (1994): 210–227.

Smith, George A. *The Historical Geography of the Holy Land*. London: Hodder and Stoughton, 1894. (The 25th edition of this volume was published in 1931.)

Sopher, David E. *The Geography of Religions*. Englewood Cliffs, NJ: Prentice-Hall, 1967.

Stanislawski, Dan. "Dionysus Westward: Early Religion and the Economic Geography of Wine." *Geographical Review,* 65 (1975): 427–444.

Stump, Roger W. (ed.). "The Geography of Religion." Special issue, *Journal of Cultural Geography,* 7, No. 1 (1986): 1–140.

Stump, Roger W. "Regional Migration and Religious Commitment in the United States." *Journal for the Scientific Study of Religion,* 23 (1984): 292–303.

Tanaka, H. "Geographical Expression of Buddhist Pilgrim Places on Shikoku Island, Japan." *Canadian Geographer,* 21 (1977): 111–133.

Tuan, Yi-Fu. "Discrepancies Between Environmental Attitude and Behavior: Examples from Europe and China." *Canadian Geographer,* 12 (1968): 176–191.

Tweedie, Stephen W. "Viewing the Bible Belt." *Journal of Popular Culture,* 11 (1978): 865–876.

Voeks, Robert. "Sacred Leaves of Brazilian Candomblé." *Geographical Review,* 80 (1990): 118–131.

Vogeler, Ingolf. "The Roman Catholic Culture Region of Central Minnesota." *Pioneer America,* 8 (1976): 71–83.

Weightman, Barbara A. "Changing Religious Landscapes in Los Angeles." *Journal of Cultural Geography,* 14, No. 1 (1993): 1–20.

Whitbeck, R. H. "The Influence of Geographical Environment upon Religious Beliefs." *Geographical Review,* 5 (1918): 316–324.

White, Lynn, Jr. "The Historical Roots of our Ecologic Crisis." *Science,* 155, (March 10, 1967): 1203–1207.

Yoon, Hong-key. "The Image of Nature in Geomancy." *GeoJournal,* 4 (1980): 341–348.

Zelinsky, Wilbur. "An Approach to the Religious Geography of the United States: Patterns of Church Membership in 1952." *Annals of the Association of American Geographers,* 51 (1961): 139–167.

Zelinsky, Wilbur. "Gathering Places for America's Dead." *Professional Geographer,* 46 (1994): 29–38.

CHAPTER 7

Folk Geography

Geographers recognize two major classes of culture: **popular,** consisting of large masses of people who conform to and prescribe ever-changing norms, and **folk,** made up of people who retain the traditional. The word *folk* describes a rural people who live in an old-fashioned way—a people holding to a simpler lifestyle less influenced by modern technology. A **folk culture** is a rural, cohesive, conservative, largely self-sufficient group that is homogeneous in custom and race, with a strong family or clan structure and highly developed rituals. Order is maintained through sanctions based in the religion or family, and interpersonal relationships are strong. Tradition is paramount, and change comes infrequently and slowly. Relatively little division of labor into specialized duties exists. Rather, each person performs a variety of tasks, though duties may differ between the genders. Most goods are handmade, and a subsistence economy prevails. Individualism is generally weakly developed in folk cultures, as are social classes.

In parts of the underdeveloped or Third World, folk cultures remain common, in contrast to industrialized countries such as the United States and Canada, where unaltered folk cultures no longer exist. Perhaps the nearest modern equivalent in Anglo-America is the Amish, a German-American farming sect that largely renounces the products and labor-saving devices of the industrial age. In Amish areas, horse-drawn buggies still serve as a local transportation device, and the faithful own no automobiles or appliances. The Amish central religious concept of *demut,* "humility," clearly reflects the weakness of individualism and social class so typical of folk cultures, and a corresponding strength of Amish group identity is evident. Rarely do the Amish marry outside their sect. The religion, a variety of the Mennonite faith, provides the principal mechanism for maintaining order.

By contrast, a **popular culture** (the subject of Chapter 8) is a large, heterogeneous group, often highly individualistic and constantly changing. Relationships among people tend to be numerous but largely impersonal, and a pronounced division of labor exists, leading to the establishment of many specialized professions. Secular institutions of control such as the police and army take the place of religion and family in maintaining order, and a money-based economy prevails. The popular is replacing the folk in industrialized countries and in many developing nations. Folk-made objects give way to their popular equivalent, usually because the popular item is more quickly or cheaply produced, is easier or time-saving to use, or lends more prestige to the owner.

Typically, bearers of folk culture combine folk and nonfolk elements in their lives. The proportion of folk to nonfolk characteristics in an individual's cultural makeup varies from one person to another, but most of us display at least some residual folk traits. Are children's games such as "London Bridge" part of your heritage? Have you ever chanted the ancient count-out phrase "eenie, meenie, miney, moe"? Have you consulted an astrologer or placed a horseshoe over a door for good luck? If so, then you retain some folk elements in your cultural makeup.

Folk culture includes both material and nonmaterial elements. **Material culture** includes all objects or "things" made and used by members of a cultural group: tools, utensils, food, buildings, furniture, clothing, artwork, musical instruments, vehicles, and other physical objects. Material elements are visible. By contrast, **nonmaterial culture,** including **folklore,** can be defined as oral, including the wide range of tales, songs, lore, beliefs, superstitions, and customs that passes from generation to generation as part of an oral or written tradition. Folk dialects, religions, and world views can be regarded as aspects of nonmaterial culture. **Folk geography,** a term coined by Eugene Wilhelm, may be defined as the study of the spatial patterns and ecology of folklife. Folk geography is an integral branch of cultural geography, and our five themes serve it well.

Folk Culture Regions

As a rule, elements of folk culture exhibit major variations from place to place and minor variations through time, while popular culture displays less difference from region to region but changes rapidly through time. For this reason, the theme of culture region is well suited to the study of folk culture. Formal folk regions can be delimited on the basis of material or nonmaterial elements. Cultural geographers have tended to emphasize material culture in most of their studies, but some focus on nonmaterial topics.

Material Folk Culture Regions

In many parts of the world, material folk culture remains abundant. While folk culture is largely anachronistic in the United States and Canada, vestiges remain in various areas of both countries. Figure 7.1 shows culture regions in which the material artifacts of 15 different North American folk cultures survive in some abundance, although generally in decline. Each region possesses many distinctive items of material culture.

For example, the heavily Germanized Pennsylvanian folk culture region features an unusual Swiss-German type of barn, distinguished

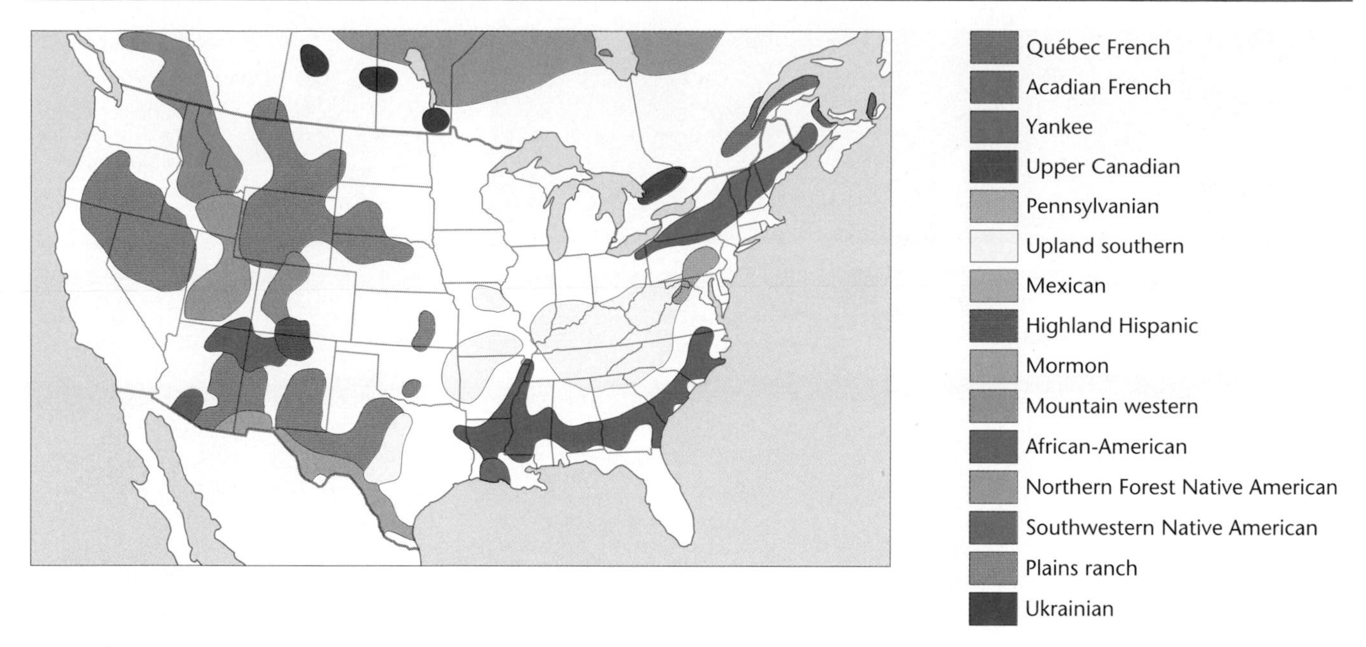

Figure 7.1
Folk cultural survival regions of the United States and southern Canada. All are now in decay and retreat, and no true folk cultures survive in Anglo-America.

by an overhanging upper-level "forebay" on one eave side (Figure 7.2). The Yankee folk region boasts an elaborate traditional gravestone art, featuring "winged death heads," and the attachment of barns to the rear of houses. The Upland South is noted for the abundant survival of notched-log construction, used in building a variety of distinctive house types such as the "dogtrot" (see Figure 7.28). The African American folk region displays such features as the scraped-earth cemetery, from which all grass is laboriously removed to expose the bare ground (Figure 7.3); the banjo, an African instrument by origin; and head kerchiefs worn by women. The Québec French folk region is revealed in grist windmills with sturdy stone towers and *pétanque,* a bowling game played with small metal balls. The Mormon folk culture can be identified by distinctive hay derricks and gridiron farm villages. The western plains ranching folk culture produced such material items as the "beef wheel," a windlass used during butchering (Figure 7.4). These provide only a few of the many examples of material artifacts that survive from different folk regions.

Figure 7.2
A multilevel barn with projecting "forebay," central Pennsylvania. Of Swiss origin, the forebay barn is one of the main identifying material traits of the Pennsylvania folk culture region.

Folk Food Regions

Perhaps no other aspect of folk culture endures as abundantly as traditional foods. In Latin America, for example, folk cultures remain vivid and vital in many regions, with diverse culinary traditions (Figure 7.5). Each displays distinctive choices of food and methods of preparation. For example, Mexican cuisine features abundant use of chile peppers in cooking and maize tortillas; the Caribbean areas offer combined rice-bean dishes and various rum drinks; in the Amazonian region, monkey and caiman are favored foods; Brazilian fare is distinguished by *cuscuz* (cooked grain) and sugarcane brandy; Pampas style features *carne*

Figure 7.3
A "scraped" earth folk graveyard in East Texas. The laborious removal of all grass from such cemeteries is an African-derived custom. Long ago this practice diffused from African Americans to Caucasians and Indians in the southern coastal plain of the United States.

Figure 7.4
"Beef wheel" in the ranching country of the Harney Basin in central Oregon. This windlass device hoists the carcass of a slaughtered animal to facilitate butchering. Derived, as was much of the local ranching culture, from Hispanic Californians, the beef wheel represents the folk material culture of ranching.

Figure 7.5
Folk food regions of Latin America. At least ten different culinary traditions, each confined to a region, can be found. (Sources: Knapp, Gregory. Personal communication; Leonard, J. *Latin American Cooking,* New York: Time-Life Books, 1968; with modifications.)

asada (roasted beef), wine, and *yerba maté* (a type of herbal tea); and Pacific-coastal Creole cooking includes such items as *manjar blanco* (a pudding). These and other Latin American foods derive from American Indians, Africans, Spaniards, and Portuguese. The ten culinary regions are not homogeneous, however, and the pattern of Latin American folk foods is by no means as simple as Figure 7.5 suggests.

Folklore Regions

Nonmaterial folk culture displays regional contrasts in much the same manner as material folk culture does. Folk geographers consider diverse nonmaterial phenomena, such as folktales, dance, music, myths, legends, and proverbs. Nowhere has folklore been more thoroughly studied than in Europe, where some of the first research in folk geography appeared early in the nineteenth century. Even as these folk cultures were collapsing, they underwent detailed cataloging and analysis. The irony is that today we know more about this vanished or moribund lore than we do about most surviving folk cultures in the world. An excellent example comes from Switzerland, where a rich folklore of German, French, Italian, and Raeto-Romanic peoples was gathered and published in perhaps the finest of all works in folk geography—the great multivolume *Atlas der Schweizerischen Volkskunde (Atlas of Swiss Folklore)*. Figure 7.6 shows an example from that atlas, revealing the profound spatial variation of nonmaterial folk culture.

Figure 7.6

Switzerland: Where do newborn children come from? When you were little and asked your parents where babies come from, did you get the old runaround about storks or some other equally absurd answer? If so, don't judge them too harshly, for they were only perpetuating an old folk custom of deception. Different Swiss provinces and districts are characterized by distinctive evasive answers to this age-old question. Nonmaterial folk culture can thus provide an index to culture regions. Where exactly would you draw the boundaries of the culture regions on this map? How many culture regions would you designate? Cultural geographers always face the same difficult decisions in delimiting culture regions. (After Liebl, Elsbeth. "Herkunft der Kinder," in Paul Geiger, et al., *Atlas der Schweizerischen Volkskunde,* Basel: Schweizerische Gesellschaft für Volkskunde, 1950, vol. 2, part 4, plates 202–205.)

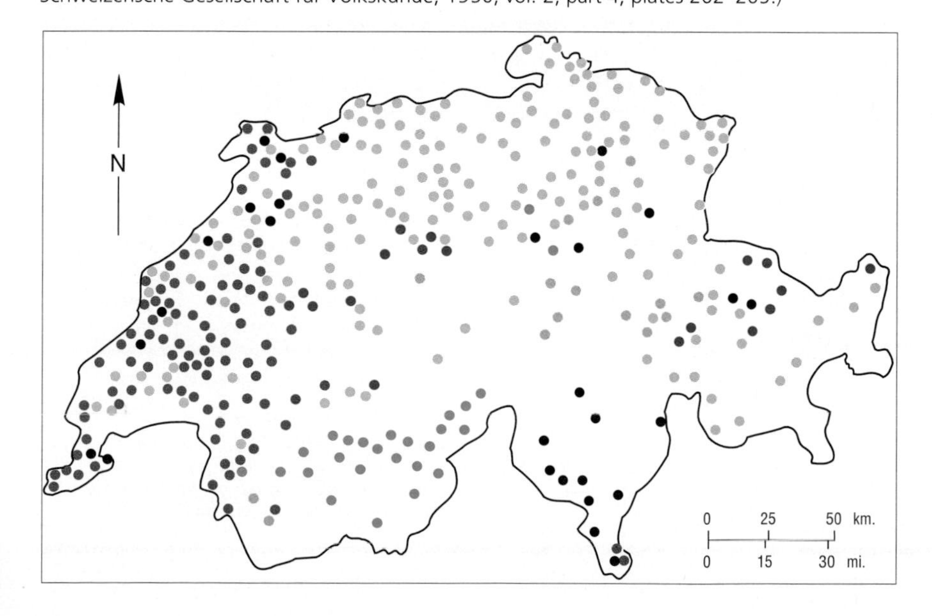

Folk music is another nonmaterial aspect of culture that reveals a highly regionalized character. Alan Lomax, an expert on the English-language folk songs of North America, recognized four folk-song culture regions in the United States: the Northern, Southern, Western, and African American song families. As he said, "the map sings."

The Northern folk-song tradition, characterized by unaccompanied solo singing in hard, open-voiced, clear tones with unison on the refrains, is based largely in British ballads and has not deviated greatly from the English prototype. In the Southern folk-song tradition, by contrast, unison singing is rare and the solo is high-pitched and nasal. Combining English and Scotch-Irish elements, the Southern style features ballads that are more guilt-ridden and violent than those of the North. The Western style, according to Lomax, is simply a blend of the Southern and Northern traditions. The African American folk-song family contains both African and British elements, featuring polyrhythmic songs of labor and worship with instrumental accompaniment, chorus group singing, clapping, swaying of the body, and a strong, surging beat. African American and white Southern styles coexist across much of the coastal plain South, each still closely linked to its respective racial group. Each tradition displays distinctive melodies, instrumentation, and motifs.

Folk Cultural Diffusion

Folk culture, both material and nonmaterial, spreads by the same processes of diffusion as do other types and elements of culture (see box, *A Transatlantic Fish Story*). However, diffusion operates more slowly within a folk setting. The weakly developed social stratification within folk cultures tends to retard hierarchical diffusion, and the inherent conservatism of such cultures produces a resistance to change. Certainly, an essential difference between folk and popular culture (see Chapter 8) is the speed by which expansion diffusion occurs.

A Transatlantic Fish Story

Cultural diffusion is often revealed by comparing folktales in different regions. The following tale, presented in a much-abridged form, occurs both in Celtic Wales on the island of Great Britain and among people of British extraction in the Ozark Mountains of Missouri and Arkansas. It apparently spread by relocation diffusion to America and halfway across the continent, changing somewhat in the process.

Ozark Mountain Version

A man living up the Meramec River caught a yellow catfish using only his hands;
he took it home and put it in a rain barrel;
the fish turned into a woman;
she became a fish again;
he put it back in the barrel and took it back to the river.

Welsh Version

A man living on the River Towey caught a salmon from a small boat with a rod;
the fish spoke Welsh and English, and turned into a naked girl with a fish-hook in her lip;
she became the man's wife.

Adapted from Miller, E. Joan Wilson. "The Ozark Culture Region as Revealed by Traditional Materials." *Annals of the Association of American Geographers,* 58 (1968): 59.

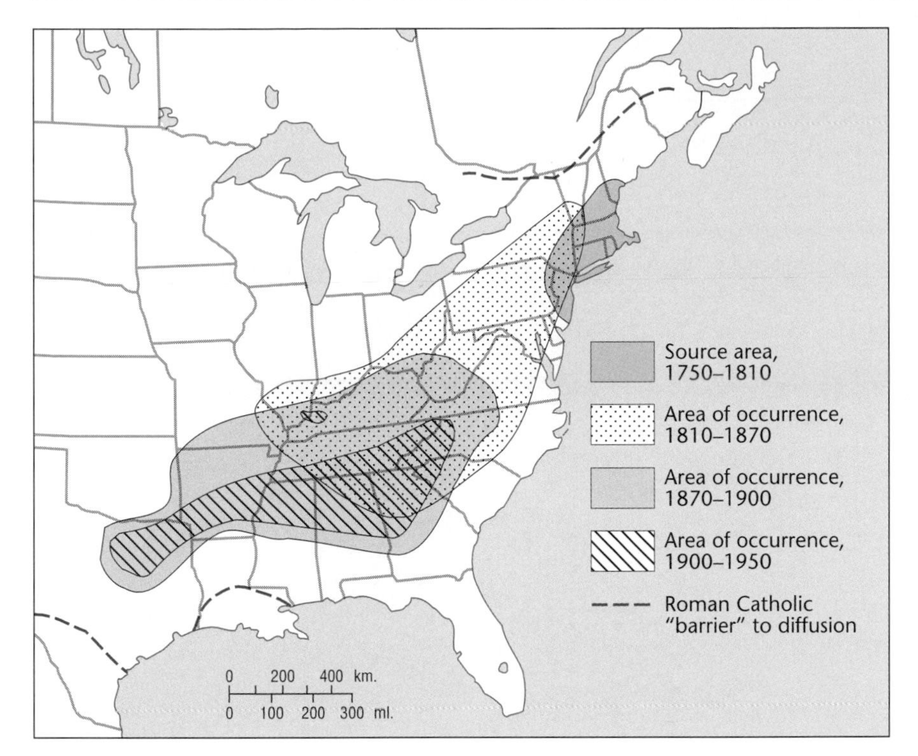

Figure 7.7
Spatial diffusion of Anglo-American religious folk songs, 1750–1950. These songs, white spirituals, spread by expansion diffusion from New England to the South, eventually disappearing from the source region. (After Jackson, George P. "Some Factors in the Diffusion of American Religious Folksongs." *Journal of American Folklore,* 65 [1952]: 365–369.)

Folk Songs

An example of the slow progress of expansion diffusion in a folk setting can be seen in the spread of Anglo-American religious folk songs in the United States (Figure 7.7). From an eighteenth-century core area based mainly in the Yankee Puritan folk culture, these white spiritual songs spread southwest into the Upland South, where such songs retain their greatest acceptance today. In the meantime, religious folk songs largely disappeared from the northern source region, possibly because of the rapid urbanization and popularization of culture in that area. Simple folk melodies remain the main musical device of the spirituals. They diffused by means of outdoor "revivals" and "camp meetings." Non-English-speaking peoples and non-Protestants were little influenced by the spiritual movement, for language and religion proved absorbing barriers to diffusion. For this reason, French Canadians and Louisiana French were not affected by the movement.

Agricultural Fairs

Another element of folk culture that originated in the Yankee region and spread west and southwest by expansion diffusion was the American agricultural fair, a custom rooted in medieval European folk tradition. According to geographer Fred Kniffen (see biographical sketch), the first American agricultural fair was held in Pittsfield, Massachusetts, in 1810, and the idea then gained favor throughout western New England and the adjacent Hudson Valley (Figure 7.8). From that source re-

Fred B. Kniffen
1900–1993

A native of Michigan, Fred Kniffen spent much of his boyhood in the transplanted New England folk culture of the upper Midwest. At UC–Berkeley, Kniffen studied under cultural geographer Carl Sauer and anthropologist Alfred Kroeber. This combination of geography and anthropology in his doctoral degree work provided the basis of Kniffen's interest and expertise in folk geography. He is acknowledged as the founder of American folk geography.

Beginning in 1929, Kniffen worked in the Department of Geography and Anthropology at Louisiana State University, Baton Rouge, where he was professor emeritus in his later years. He wrote some 125 articles and books, and his range of interest was great. In his list of publications are works on folk houses, covered bridges, outdoor folk ovens, log construction, and other items of traditional material culture. Kniffen received many honors and tributes, most notably the honorary presidency of the Association of American Geographers, an Honors Award from the same group in 1978, and membership in Phi Beta Kappa. (For more information, see Walker, H. Jesse, and Miles E. Richardson. "Fred Bowerman Kniffen, 1900–1993." *Annals of the Association of American Geographers,* 84 [1994]: 732–743.)

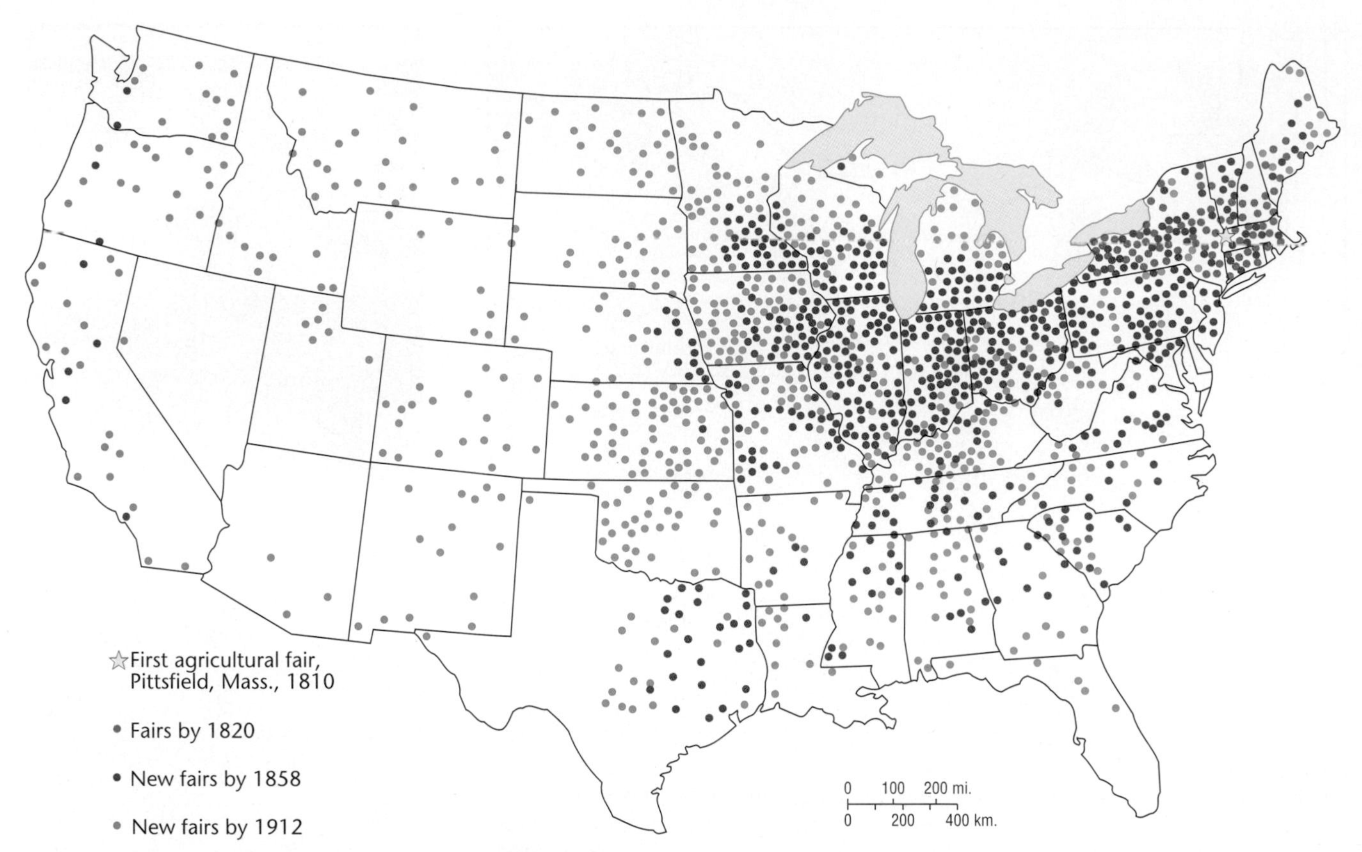

Figure 7.8
Diffusion of the American agricultural fair, 1810–1910. Both the agricultural fair and the white spiritual (Figure 7.7) arose in the same general area. Compare the diffusion of the fair and the spiritual. What differences can you detect in the routes of diffusion? Why might these differences have developed? (After Kniffen, Fred B. "The American Agricultural Fair." *Annals of the Association of American Geographers,* 41 [1951]: 45, 47, 51.)

gion it diffused westward into the American heartland, the Midwest, where it gained its widest acceptance. Normally promoted by agricultural societies, the fairs were originally educational in purpose, and farmers could learn about improved methods and breeds. Soon an entertainment function was added, represented by a racetrack and midway, and competition for prizes for superior agricultural products became common.

By the early twentieth century, the agricultural fair had diffused through most of the United States, though farmers in culture regions such as the Upland South did not accept it as readily or fully as did the Midwesterners. The spread of the agricultural fair followed a more northerly route than that of white spiritual songs, although the source areas of the two were almost identical.

Hay Stackers

The Mountain Western American folk culture also produced innovations. A good example is the *beaverslide hay stacker,* an item of traditional material culture studied by geographers John Alwin and Jon Kilpinen. Because of the relatively recent origin of the device, we know more about its diffusion than is typical of folk culture. The stacker is a

30-odd foot (10 meters) tall, wooden ramp structure, used to raise hay to the top of a stack, employing horsepower to pull a basket up an inclined surface (Figure 7.9). The beaverslide originated in 1907 in Montana's Big Hole Valley and its use subsequently spread to at least eight nearby states and across the international border into three Canadian provinces (Figure 7.10). The map suggests the manner in which items of folk culture diffuse.

Figure 7.9
Beaverslide hay stacker. This device stands in the broad meadows of the Big Hole Valley in southwestern Montana, the place of its origin. The stacker is portable and can be disassembled for easy moving to the next meadow during haying season. Haymaking is essential in the ranching adaptive strategy of the high mountain valleys of the American West, where winters are long and bitter.

Blowguns

Often the past diffusion of an item of folk culture is not clearly known or understood, presenting folk geographers with a problem of interpretation. An example is provided by the blowgun, a long, hollow tube through which a projectile is blown by the force of the breath. The geographer Stephen Jett mapped the distribution of this hunting weapon and found it among folk societies in both the Eastern and Western Hemispheres, all the way from the island of Madagascar off the African coast to the Amazonian jungles of South America, over halfway around the world (Figure 7.11).

Apparently the blowgun was first invented by Indonesian peoples, probably on the island of Borneo. It became the principal hunting weapon of this folk society and diffused with the Austronesian linguistic group through much of the equatorial island belt of the Eastern Hemisphere. How do we account for its presence among American Indian groups in the Western Hemisphere? Was it independently invented by the American Indians? Was it brought by relocation diffusion in pre-Columbian times to the Americas? Or did it spread to the New World only after the European discovery of America? The answers to these questions are not known, but the problem presented is one common to

Figure 7.10
Past and present distribution of the beaverslide hay stacker. Why was the diffusion greatest in an eastward direction? What barriers might have prevented dispersal into Utah and to the Pacific shore? Why did the international boundary not serve as a barrier? Take an atlas showing natural routeways and draw arrows on this figure showing the most likely paths of diffusion from the place of origin. Then refer to Alwin's article and read how the diffusion actually occurred. (From Alwin, John A. "Montana's Beaverslide Hay Stacker." *Journal of Cultural Geography,* 3, No. 1 [1982]: 47; Kilpinen, J. "Material Folk Culture," 35–37; data provided by Charles F. Gritzner.)

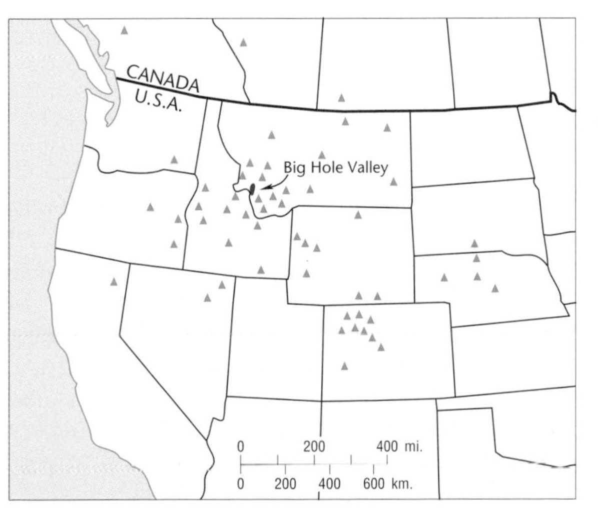

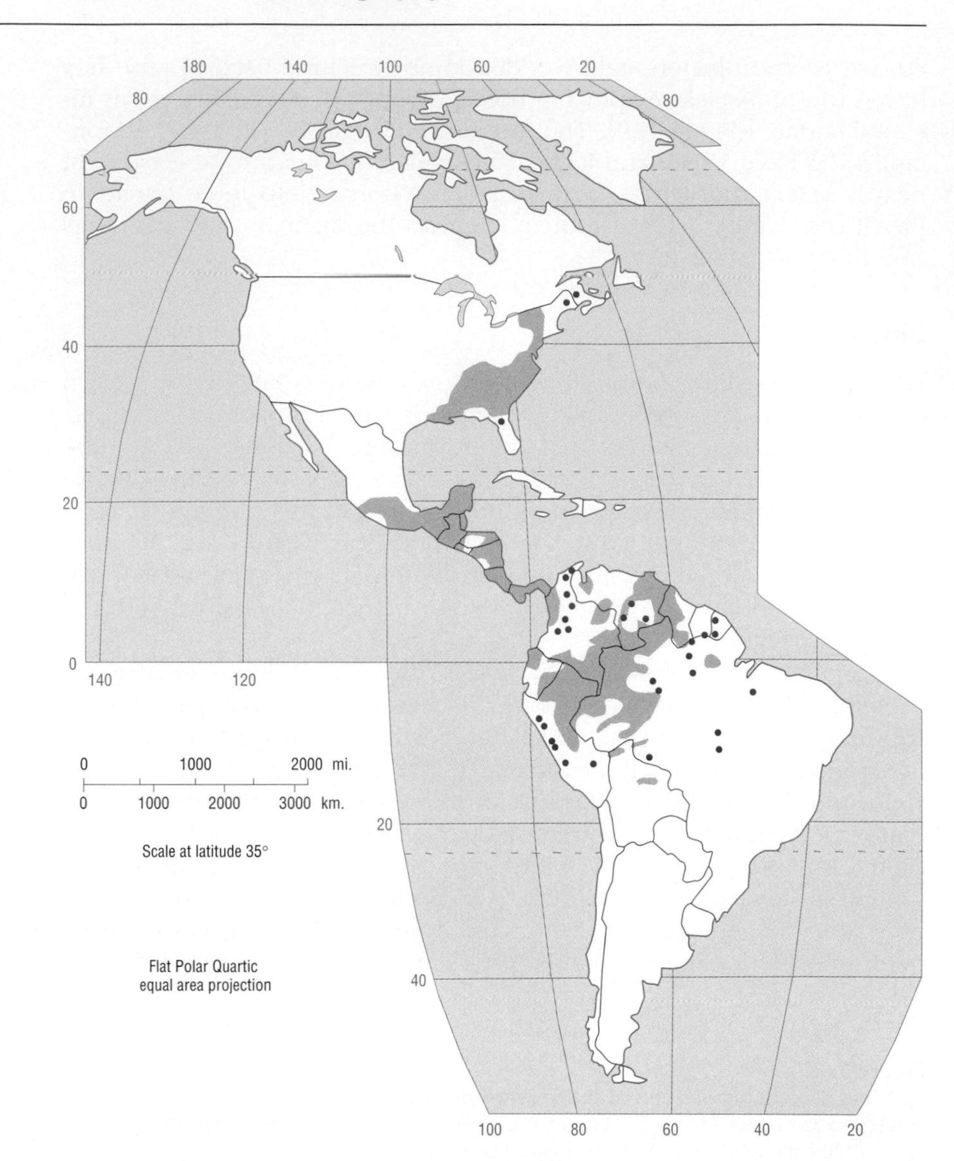

Continuous occurrence

• Isolated occurrence

Figure 7.11
Former distribution of the blowgun among American Indians, South Asians, Africans, and Pacific Islanders. The blowgun occurred among folk cultures in two widely separated areas of the world. Was this the result of independent invention or cultural diffusion? What kinds of data might one seek to answer this question? Compare and contrast the occurrence in the Indian and Pacific ocean lands to the distribution of the Austronesian languages (Figure 5.4). (Source: Jett, Stephen C. "Further Information on the Geography of the Blowgun and Its Implications for Early Transoceanic Contacts." *Annals of the Association of American Geographers,* 81 [1991]: 92–93.)

cultural geography, and particularly to folk geography, since the nonliterate condition of many folk cultures precludes written records that might reveal diffusion.

Jett favors trans-Pacific diffusion from Indonesia before the time of Columbus. If you agree with him, then you must explain the wide gaps where it is not found in the South Pacific island world and Africa, which lie between the two zones of occurrence. If you choose instead to support the independent-invention theory, then you have to accept the proposition that an identical device was invented two times, in very

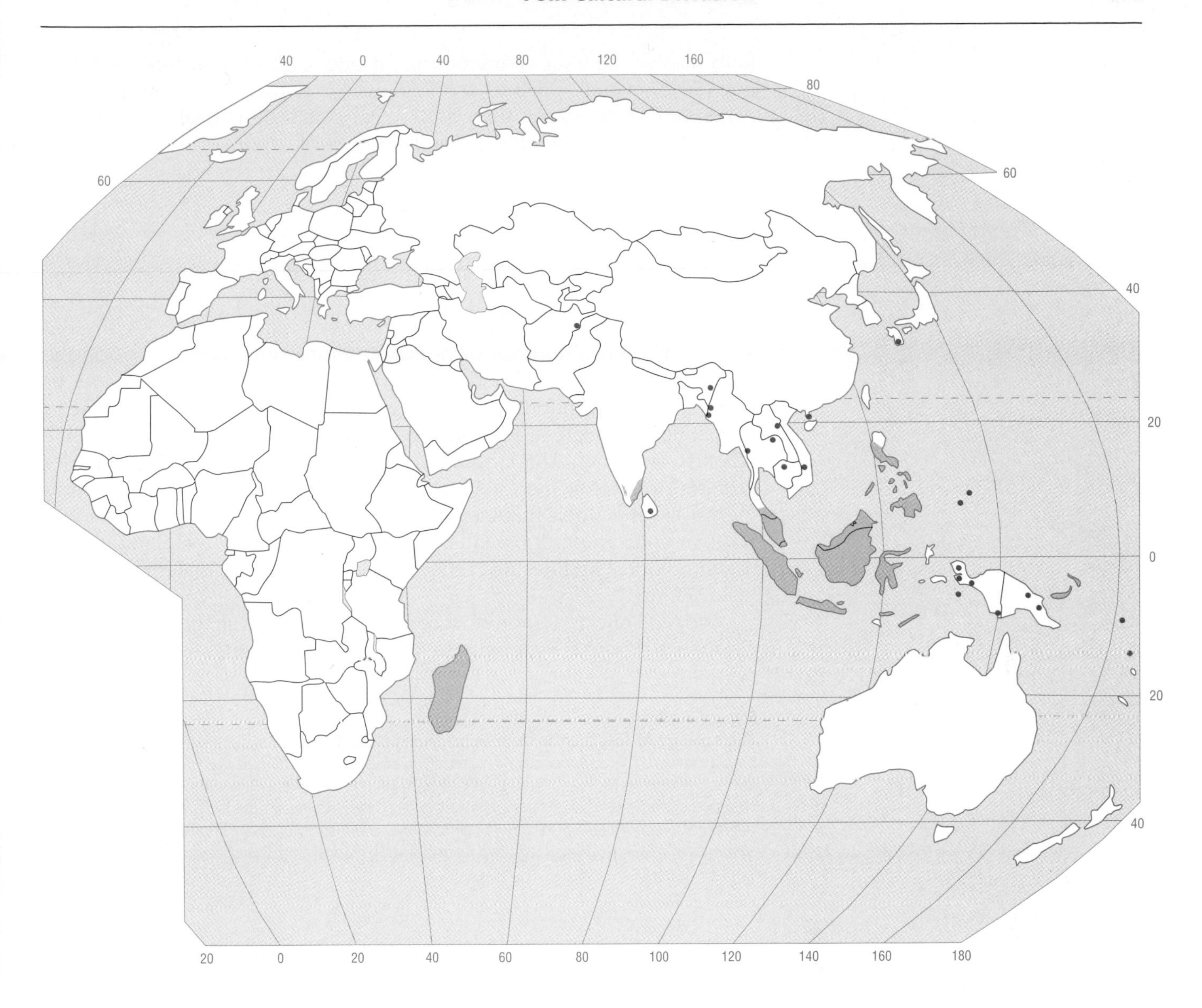

different folk cultures. The study of cultural diffusion often presents such problems.

Indeed, the issue of independent invention versus diffusion has been one of the most perplexing for cultural geographers. Clearly, independent invention is always possible. Carl Sauer's proposal that the domestication of plants occurred independently in the two hemispheres (see Chapter 3) helped free cultural geographers from their traditional cultural-deterministic view that each invention had a single origin. Certain rules of thumb can be employed in any given situation to help resolve the issue. For example, if one or more *nonfunctional* features of blowguns, such as a decorative motif, occurred both in South America and Indonesia, then the logical conclusion would be that cultural diffusion explained the distribution of blowguns.

Folk Ecology

Cultural ecology is an especially appropriate theme in folk geography, because folk groups enjoy a very close relationship with the physical environment. In most cases, their adaptive strategies possess sustainability, in contrast to those of popular culture. Such people live on the land, gaining their livelihood directly through such primary activities as farming, herding, hunting, gathering, and fishing. A great many facets of folk culture relate at least indirectly to the local ecology and involve adaptive strategies. The languages of folk groups bear the vocabularies required to exploit the habitat, their religions act to mitigate environmental hazards, their folktales honor great hunters, their proverbs offer wisdom concerning the weather and the proper time for planting, and their traditional architecture reflects the local building materials and climate (Figure 7.12).

Indeed, one is tempted, when dealing with folk groups, to conclude that culture is synonymous with adaptation—that folkways all ex-

Figure 7.12
The ecology of folk architecture in northern New Mexico. Buildings erected by people belonging to folk groups consist of materials available. So it is among the Highland Hispano and southwestern Native American folk of northern New Mexico, where the type of wall construction changes with elevation above sea level, reflecting in part the progression of microenvironments encountered at different heights. (Adapted from Gritzner, Charles F. "Construction Materials in a Folk Housing Tradition: Considerations Governing Their Selection in New Mexico." *Pioneer America,* 6, No. 1 [1974]: 26.)

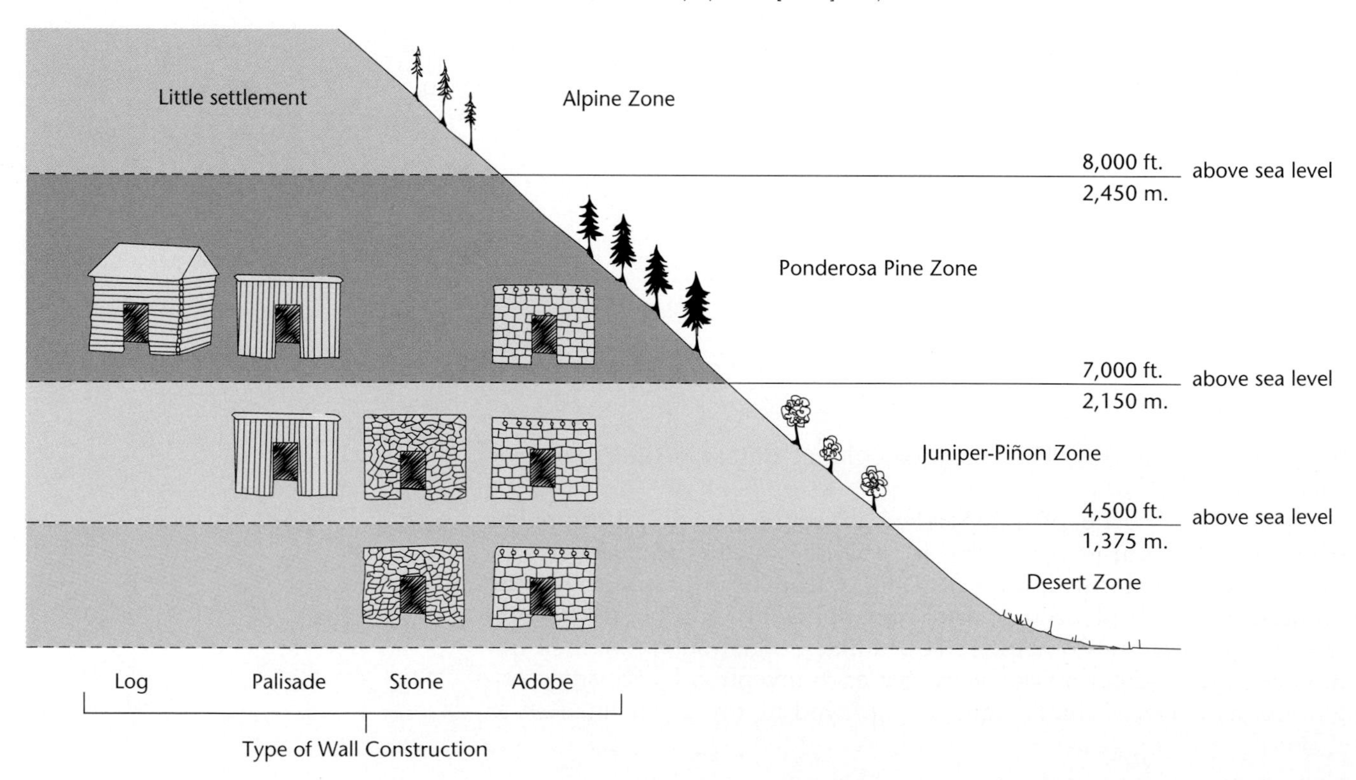

ist to facilitate the adjustment to physical environment. Equally easy is the path of environmental determinism, believing that folk cultures will inevitably be guided along similar courses in similar ecological settings. But folkways involve more than merely cultural adaptation, and a variety of folk cultures can exist in any particular ecosystem. While folk cultures may be more sensitive than popular cultures to the qualities of the soil, climate, and terrain, it does not follow that they are enslaved and wholly shaped by their physical surroundings, nor is it necessarily true that folk groups live in close harmony with their environment, for often soil erosion, deforestation, and overkill of wild animals can be attributed to traditional rural folk. Even so, we must always keep the cultural ecological context in mind when seeking to interpret folk culture, for otherwise we overlook a quite fundamental possibilistic explanatory mainspring.

Geophagy

Most folk groups consume natural foods derived directly from the land either through husbandry of domesticated plants and animals or through hunting and gathering of wild species. The large majority of people in such societies are directly involved in food production and come intimately in contact with the land. Each folk group has its own distinctive selection of foods and means of food preparation.

Perhaps no food habit intertwines environment and culture more closely than **geophagy,** the deliberate eating of earth. While found among many different cultures, dirt eating is most common in parts of Africa and in the South among Americans of African ancestry. Certain kinds of clay provide the preferred earth material for geophagy. In the African source regions of this folk custom, clays are consumed for a variety of reasons (Figure 7.13). Some African earth eaters feel that the clay is an effective treatment for certain diseases and parasites, while others believe it provides needed nutrients for pregnant women and growing children. Some consume clay as part of religious ceremonies.

In the African American folk culture region of the coastal plain South, a study made by cultural geographer Donald Vermeer found geophagy confined mainly to pregnant black women and to black children under the age of 5. By way of comparison, 28 percent of pregnant black women and 7 percent of pregnant whites consume clay. The average intake amounts to about 50 grams per day. The preferred clays, obtained from digs or highway cuts, are fine-textured and grit-free, light gray or whitish in color, and sour in taste. The clay is heated in a pan on a stove for several hours; some add salt and vinegar before baking. Geophagy appears unrelated to dietary deficiencies or intestinal parasites. Rather, we might best regard it as a folk custom that persists for cultural reasons.

Geophagy is deeply rooted in African American folk culture and has survived in spite of persistent attempts to abolish it. In slavery times, some white masters put mouthlocks on their slaves to prevent geophagy, and local health officials today generally oppose it. In Alabama, the consumption level became so great that the Highway Department posted signs forbidding digging at road cuts because of the damage it causes. Pre-examination forms at many southern clinics ask the question: "Do you eat dirt?" Often southern rural people send packages of geophagical clays to kinfolk in northern or western cities.

The barrier preventing a wider diffusion of geophagy in America

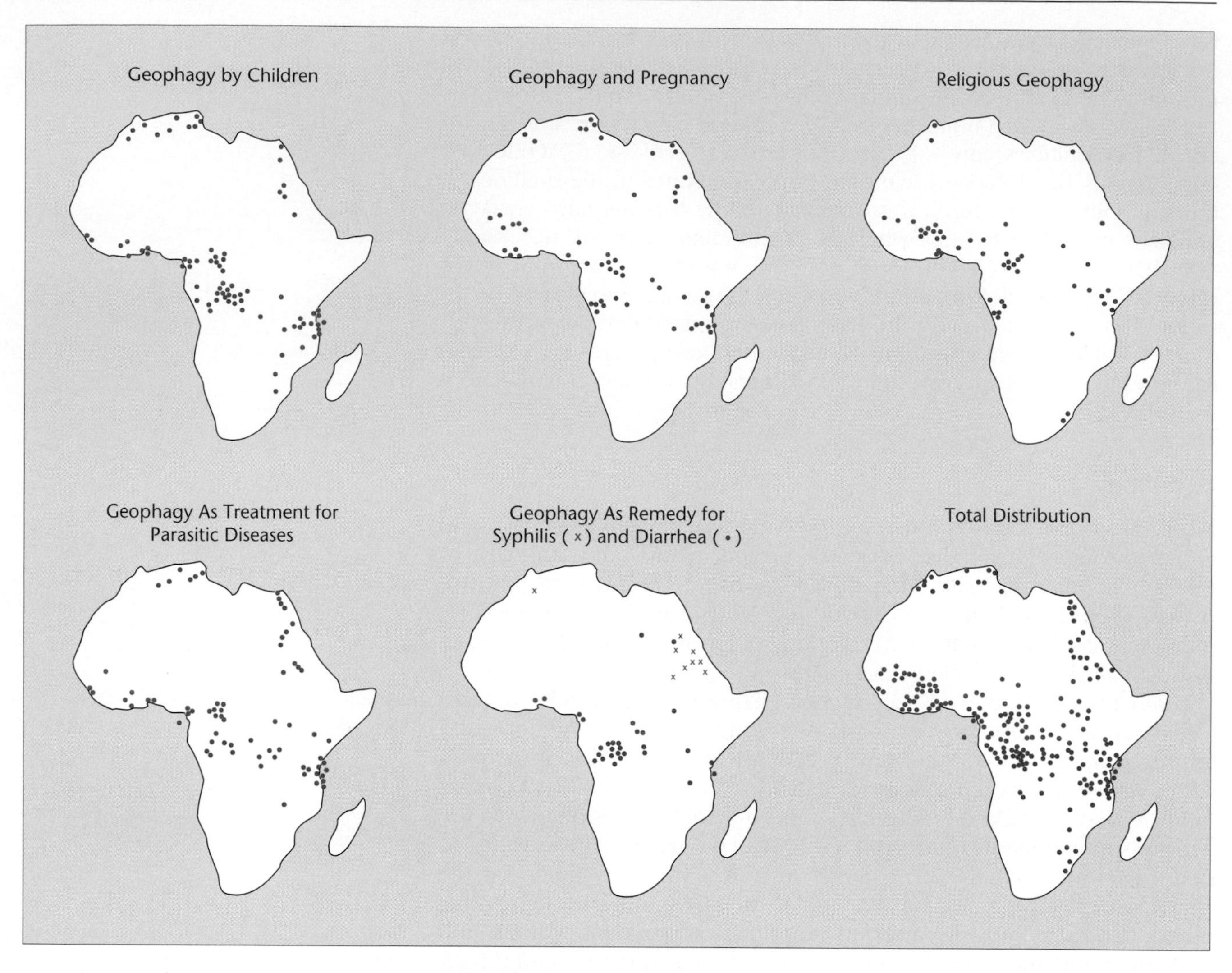

Figure 7.13
Geophagy in Africa. Clay eating is a widespread folk custom in Africa, especially in the West African region where many of the slaves brought to America originated. African geophagy is associated by its practitioners with both health and religion. (After Hunter, John M. "Geophagy in Africa and in the United States: A Culture-Nutrition Hypothesis." *Geographical Review,* 63 [1973]: 172; and Lagercrantz, Sture, and B. Anell. "Geophagical Customs." *Studia Ethnographica Upsalensia,* 17 [1958]: 24–84.)

seems to be the social stigma attached to the practice. Yet it is a permeable barrier: Many persons who did not eat clay consumed commercial, store-bought starch, perceived as a more respectable substitute. In addition to the pregnant black women in the study who consumed clay, another 19 percent ate box starch, as did an additional 10 percent of the pregnant whites. A more recent study by Klaus Meyer-Arendt indicates that geophagy is becoming less common in the American South.

Folk Medicine

In geophagy we find an intimate tie between folk culture and the environment, but close links are also typical of folk medicine. It is common in folk societies to treat diseases and disorders with drugs and medicines derived from the root, bark, blossom, or fruit of plants. In the

United States, folk medicine is best preserved in the Upland South, particularly southern Appalachia; on some Indian reservations; and in the Mexican borderland. Many of the folk cures have proven effectiveness.

The outlook of the Upland Southerner toward cures is well expressed in the comments of an eastern Tennessee mountaineer root digger who, in an interview with cultural geographer Edward Price, said that "the good Lord has put these yerbs here for man to make hisself well with. They is a yerb, could we but find it, to cure every illness." Root digging has been popularized to the extent that much of the produce of the Appalachians is now funneled to dealers, who serve a larger market outside the folk culture (Figure 7.14), but root digging remains at heart a folk enterprise, carried on in the old ways and requiring the traditionally thorough knowledge of the plant environment.

In the Mexican folk culture region along the southern border of Texas, folk medicine is still widely practiced by *curanderos,* or "curers." Over four hundred medicines are derived from both wild and domestic plants growing in the border region, perpetuating a tradition rooted in sixteenth-century Indian and Spanish sources. The local folk medicine is based on the belief that health and welfare depend on harmony between the natural and supernatural; disease and misfortune are thought to involve some disharmony. Through the use of counseling and botanical medicines, the *curandero* strives to restore harmony. In recent years, fewer border folk have sought herbal remedies for infections, sprains, or broken bones, choosing instead to go to doctors and hospitals, but *curanderos* now treat more cancer, diabetes, and hypertension

Figure 7.14
A ginseng root digger. This digger is practicing an Upland Southern folk custom.

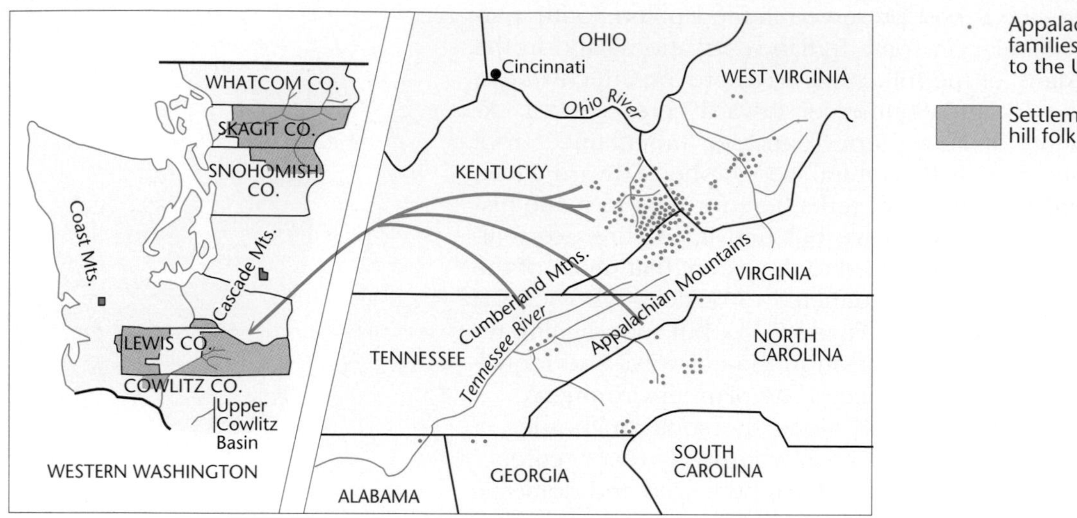

Figure 7.15
The relocation diffusion of Upland Southern hill folk from Appalachia to western Washington. Each dot represents the former home of an individual or family that migrated to the upper Cowlitz River basin in the Cascade Mountains of Washington State between 1884 and 1937. Some 3000 descendants of these migrants lived in the Cowlitz area by 1940. What does the high degree of clustering of the sources of the migrants and subsequent clustering in Washington suggest about the processes of folk migrations? How should we interpret their choices of familiar terrain and vegetation for a new home? Why might members of a folk society choose a similar land? (After Clevinger, Woodrow R. "The Appalachian Mountaineers in the Upper Cowlitz Basin." *Pacific Northwest Quarterly,* 29 [1938]: 120; and "Southern Appalachian Highlanders in Western Washington." *Pacific Northwest Quarterly,* 33 [1942]: 4, with modifications.)

than previously. The thriving *curandero* business along the Rio Grande is best viewed as a persistent folk element in a culture undergoing considerable change and popularization. Some *curanderos* have responded to change by becoming virtual paramedics and employing antibiotics in some cures.

Environmental Perception

An intimate knowledge of the environment, then, provides food and medicines for people in a folk culture. We should not be surprised, in view of this close association with the land, that members of such groups, when migrating, seek lands similar to those they leave behind (Figure 7.15). They function best in environments like those their ancestors have occupied for centuries, because the lore of the land passed down to them relates to one particular ecosystem.

When overpopulation or some other "push" factor causes folk groups to seek a new homeland, they are often "pulled" to places similar in terrain, soils, vegetation, and wildlife. A good example can be seen in the migrations of Upland Southerners from the mountains of Appalachia in the century between 1830 and 1930. As the Appalachians filled up, many highlanders began looking elsewhere for similar areas to settle. In their migrations, they normally moved in clan or extended-family groups. Initially they found an environmental twin of the Appalachians in the Ozark-Ouachita Mountains of Missouri and Arkansas. Somewhat later, others sought out the hollows, coves, and gaps of the central Texas Hill Country. The final migration of Appalachian hill folk brought some 15,000 members of this folk culture to the Cascade and coastal mountain ranges of Washington State between 1880 and 1930 (Figure 7.15). The role of environmental perception and clan ties in directing these migrations can be seen in the following remarks by a Kentucky mountaineer, recorded by W. R. Clevinger in 1937: "I've been figurin' fer a right smart time about leavin' fer Warshin'ton. I hear there's a good mountin country out thar where a man can still hunt, git work in mills and loggin', and git a piece of land right cheap. Some of my kin out thar have writ back, wantin' me to jine 'em."

People so close to nature also remain sensitive to very subtle environmental qualities. Nowhere is this sensitivity more evident than in the practice of "planting by the signs," found among folk farmers in the United States and elsewhere (see box, *Planting by the Signs of the Zodiac*). Reliance on the movement and appearance of planets, stars, and the moon might seem absurd to the managers of huge, corporation-owned farms, but these beliefs and practices are still widespread among the members of folk cultures.

All in all, folk groups are much more observant of their ecosystems than are most people in the popular culture. They strive for harmony with nature, though they do not always achieve it, and often ascribe animistic religious sanctity to the forces of the environment and to particular parts of their habitat. Some members of the popular culture, from Henry David Thoreau to disenchanted American youth of the 1960s and 1970s, lamented the loss of closeness to nature that accompanied the rise of nonfolk culture, and they sought to recapture that intimacy by withdrawing to rural retreats. To reestablish the close ties, they, like folk groups, would have had to depend on nature for their day-to-day livelihood, a risk and sacrifice that relatively few were able or willing to take or make. Such intimacy is the product of centuries of trial and error and, once lost, is scarcely possible to regain.

Planting by the Signs of the Zodiac

Each day of a month is said to be dominated by one of the signs of the zodiac. Every sign appears at least once a month, holding sway for two or three days at a time. The signs were long ago assigned traits, such as masculine or feminine; fiery, airy, earthy, or watery; barren or fruitful.

Many rural folk in America, and elsewhere as well, use the signs as indicators of the proper planting time. The following are some "rules" for farming "by the signs," collected from interviews in rural north Georgia, part of the Upland South, and from various other sources. They illustrate the intimate ties between people and the physical environment so typical in folk cultures:

Planting is best done in the fruitful signs of Scorpio, Pisces, Taurus, or Cancer.

Plow, till, and cultivate in Aries.

Always set plants out in a water or earth sign [Taurus, Cancer, Virgo, Scorpio, Capricorn, or Pisces].

Graft just before the sap starts to flow, while the moon is in its first or second quarter, and while it is passing through fruitful, watery sign, or Capricorn. Never graft or plant on Sunday as this is a barren, hot day.

Plant flowers in Libra, which is an airy sign that also represents beauty.

Corn planted in Leo will have a hard, round stalk and small ears.

Crops planted in Taurus and Cancer will stand drought.

Don't plant potatoes in the feet [Pisces]. If you do, they will develop little nubs like toes all over the main potato.

Plant all things which yield above ground during the increase or growing of the moon, and all things which yield below the ground (root crops) when the moon is decreasing or darkening.

Never plant on the first day of the new moon, or on a day when the moon changes quarters.

Cultural Integration in Folk Geography

In reading the discussion of culture regions, diffusion, and ecology, you perhaps got the impression that folk groups are completely segregated from the popular culture. Rarely is that true. Few folk cultures escape altogether from interaction with the larger world. The theme of cultural integration allows us to see how groups can retain their folk character and yet be in almost daily contact with popular cultures—that is, how folk groups are integrated into the nonfolk world. A lively exchange is constantly under way between the folk and the popular cultures. Perhaps most commonly, the folk absorb ideas filtering down from the popular culture, altering their way of life, but occasionally elements of the folk culture instead penetrate the popular society.

Traditional folk handicrafts and arts often fetch high prices among modern city dwellers, perhaps because they exhibit the quality, attention to detail, and uniqueness generally absent in factory-made goods. Sometimes these folk goods are revised in ways to make them even more marketable. Among the folk items that have successfully penetrated the popular culture are Irish "fisherman sweaters," Shaker furniture, and Panamanian Indian *molas*—decorative cutout and stitched textiles originally worn as blouses.

Mountain Moonshine

An additional example, drawn from the traditional culture of the Upland South, further illustrates the integration of folk and popular culture—the home manufacture of whisky. Corn whisky has been manufactured since the earliest days of Anglo-American pioneering in the Upland South in the eighteenth century. Very likely its origins lie still further back, in the Scottish folk tradition of making whisky from barley. The word *whisky* itself has a Celtic origin, probably from the Scottish Gaelic *uisge beatha* ("water of life"), and the techniques of making the beverage likely diffused to America and to the Appalachians with the previously-mentioned Scotch-Irish, a people of Scottish origin who came from Northern Ireland. Home manufacture of whisky has prevailed in many Appalachian hill settlements for 200 years and is a deep-rooted folk custom (Figure 7.16). Whisky making withstood the prohibitionist attitudes of the great nineteenth-century religious revival, and even though many mountaineers are devout Baptists or Methodists, they continue to defy the antiliquor teachings of these and other Protestant churches. The mountain folk proved more than willing to vote their areas legally "dry," but they were not prepared to give up distilling and drinking hard liquor. Much like the geophagy of southern black people, corn whisky among the Applachian highlanders is very persistent in the folk diet.

Traditionally, corn liquor was intended mainly for consumption within the family, not for market. In other words, the manufacture of "white lightning" remained purely in the folk tradition. Gradually over the years, however, some Appalachian moonshine began finding its way to market. Whisky provided the best opportunity for the hill folk to participate in the money economy of the country, since its manufacture converted a bulky grain crop of low cash value into a beverage that was compact and of high value per unit of weight. As early as 1791, the United States federal government began taxing manufacturers of whisky, but from the beginning the mountaineers found ways to avoid

Figure 7.16
An Appalachian whisky still, an element of Upland Southern folk culture that now serves the popular culture.

the tax. Stills lay concealed in remote coves and hollows to escape detection by the federal revenue collectors; if the stills were discovered and destroyed, new ones in different locations soon replaced them (Figure 7.17). The revenuers proved no more successful in abolishing the making of whisky than the churches had been. In effect, the mountain folk accepted the markets offered by the popular culture but rejected its legal and political institutions.

The Upland Southern people proved more than capable of evading the law. By the 1950s, some 25,000 gallons of white lightning were reaching the market each week from the counties of eastern Tennessee alone. In spite of numerous raids by the federal authorities, production continued unabated. Even today, a substantial amount of illicit whisky reaches market from southern Appalachia. This production, coupled with that of the legal, taxpaying whisky manufacturers of Kentucky and Tennessee, represents an impressive survival of a folk industry to serve a market in the popular society.

Interaction with the popular culture in the production of illegal whisky led to other kinds of contact, providing still more examples of cultural integration. To market the produce, after about 1930 at least, fast vehicles were required in order to outrun the law. The result was a "folk automobile," a souped-up jalopy quite humble in appearance but capable of high speeds. Some claim that the mountaineer's whisky-running automobile provided the forerunner of the basic American stock car and that stock-car racing is simply a recreational form of the traditional flight from revenuers (Figure 7.18). The Ford of the 1930s and

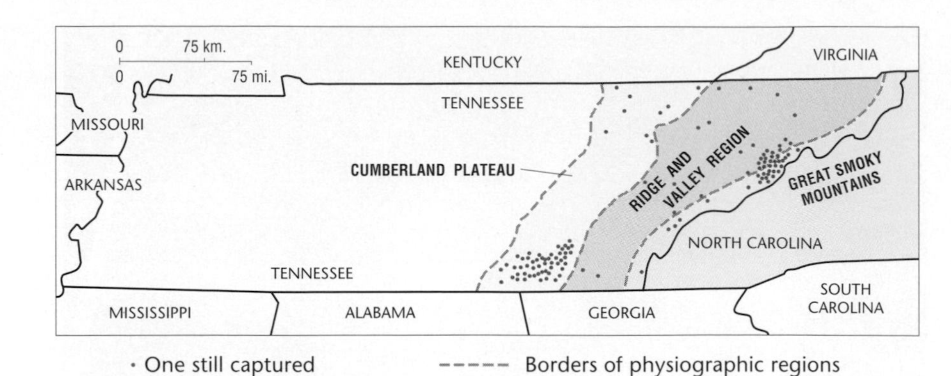

Figure 7.17
Approximate number and location of illegal stills captured monthly in eastern Tennessee in the mid-1950s. The rugged Smoky Mountains and Cumberland Plateau offer more abundant hiding places for stills than does the ridge and valley region. What might account for the clustering in two main areas? (After Durand, Loyal. "Mountain Moonshining in East Tennessee." *Geographical Review,* 46 [1956]: 171.)

1940s owed much of its commercial success in the South to the fact that it had the best and most easily modified engine for these purposes. Thus, stock-car racing is another result of the interplay between folk and popular cultures.

Country and Western Music

Upland Southern folk music made an even more impressive impact on American popular culture. Country and Western music is derived, to a great degree, from the folk ballads of the English and Scotch-Irish who settled the Upland South in colonial times. Some experts have even hypothesized that the use of the fiddle (violin) to produce the shrill sounds so typical of mountain music is an effort to recapture the sound

Figure 7.18
Winston Cup stock car race, Bristol, Tennessee. Such cars probably developed to serve whisky runners, who delivered the illegal product to market from Appalachian folk distilleries.

of the Celtic Scottish bagpipe. Gradually, Upland Southern folk music absorbed influences of the American social experience, becoming a composite of Old World and New World folk traditions. Like whisky making, Appalachian music long remained confined to the traditional society that had developed it. As folk music, it gave expression to a unique lifestyle and a particular land, while dealing with such universal themes as love and hate, happiness and sorrow, comedy and tragedy.

Entry of country music into the popular culture began about the time of World War I and was facilitated by the invention and diffusion of the radio. Popularization brought changes to country music. The number of tunes and songs, which had been relatively small and slow to increase in the folk society, exploded in a few decades into tens of thousands. Performers in crowded, noisy night spots soon resorted to electrical amplification to achieve the needed volume, producing such curious folk-popular mixtures as the electric guitar. The themes of lyrics increasingly addressed life in the popular rather than the folk culture. But at its core, country music remained folk.

Bluegrass, one of many styles of country music, emerged in the 1930s during the process of popularization of Appalachian folk music. Developed by Bill Monroe, a Kentuckian, the unique bluegrass sound is achieved by the joining of a lead banjo with a fiddle, guitar, mandolin, and string bass. In many ways, bluegrass remains faithful to its folk origins. Only nonelectric instruments are used, and the high pitched, emotional vocal sound clearly reveals derivation from Scottish church singing. The acceptance of bluegrass music remains greatest in its Upland Southern core area in Kentucky, Tennessee, Virginia, and North Carolina (Figure 7.19). Most bluegrass performers come from this

Figure 7.19
The geography of bluegrass country music. The Upland Southern core area of bluegrass music is clearly revealed by the residences of major performers; the distribution of festivals indicates both the popularization of this style of country music and the migration of Upland Southern people to other states. How many of the festival sites are in hill or mountain areas? What barriers, if any, might prevent the continued diffusion of bluegrass? (After Carney, George O. "Bluegrass Grows All Around: The Spatial Dimensions of a Country Music Style." *Journal of Geography,* 73 [1974]: 37, 46.)

core area, and the music retains a strong identification with Appalachian places, both in the titles and lyrics of songs and in the names of performing groups. Thus we find such songs as "Hills of Roane County" (Tennessee) performed by such groups as the Clinch Mountain Boys.

The nineteenth-century migration of Upland Southern folk to Missouri, Arkansas, Texas, and Oklahoma, coupled with the Depression-era movement of "Okies" and "Arkies" to the Central Valley of California, provided natural areas for bluegrass expansion in the mid-twentieth century. The distribution of bluegrass music festivals, mapped by cultural geographer George Carney, reflects these migrations (Figure 7.19).

Thus music of the folk tradition has been modified, popularized, and spread by means of technology that is part of the popular culture. Such music provides yet another example of the interaction of cultural forces that underlies the cultural integration theme.

Folk Landscapes

Every folk culture produces, through its greater artifacts, a highly distinctive landscape. One of the most visible aspects of these landscapes is **folk architecture,** and we will use such traditional buildings to illustrate the theme of cultural landscape in folk geography.

Folk architecture springs not from the drafting tables of professional architects, but from the collective memory of a traditional people. These buildings, whether dwellings, barns, churches, mills, or inns, are not based on blueprints, but on mental images that change little from one generation to the next. In this sense, it is an "architecture without architects." Folk buildings are extensions of a people and their region. They help provide the unique character of each district or province and offer a highly visible aspect of the human mosaic. Do not look to folk architecture for refined artistic genius or spectacular, revolutionary design. Seek in it instead the traditional, the conservative, and the functional (see box, *The Cultural Ecology of a Folk House*). Expect from it a simple beauty, a harmony with the physical environment, a visible expression of folk culture.

The house, or dwelling, is the most basic structure erected by people, regardless of culture. For most persons in nearly all folk cultures, a house is the single most important thing they ever build. Folk cultures as a rule are rural and agricultural. For these reasons, it seems appropriate to focus on traditional farmstead architecture, and particularly on the folk house, in this treatment of the cultural landscape.

Building Materials

One way we can classify folk houses and farmsteads is by the type of building material used in construction (see Figure 7.12). A hallmark of folk building is the use of locally available raw materials, causing the structures to blend nicely with the natural landscape. Farm dwellings range from massive houses of stone, endowed with as much permanency as humans can give to a structure, to temporary brush and thatch huts. Figure 7.20 maps the traditional building materials used in rural folk architecture in different parts of the world. Environmental condi-

The Cultural Ecology of a Folk House

Folk houses, as a rule, are beautifully suited to their physical environment. Centuries of trial and error taught their builders how to construct dwellings that provide comfort and protection from the extremes and hazards of the local weather. Nowhere are these attributes of folk architecture better displayed than on Lan Yü (Orchid Island), located in the Pacific Ocean 40 miles off the coast of Taiwan.

The Austronesian inhabitants of Lan Yü, the Yami, build their folk houses mostly below ground level, in stone-lined pits, for protection from hurricanes. The sketch shows a cross section of a Yami house. A strongly reinforced, streamlined roof projects partly above ground level, exposing a section of an elongated slope to the brunt of the hurricane winds. The force of the storm wind presses down on the roof and slides by, keeping it in place. To escape the midday heat when no storms are blowing, each Yami builds a "cool tower" above ground level. These are easily replaced when hurricanes blow them away.

Adapted with permission from Shuhua, Chang. "The Gentle Yamis of Orchid Island." *National Geographic Magazine,* 151 (January 1977): 107. Sketch, National Geographic Art Division, © National Geographic Society.

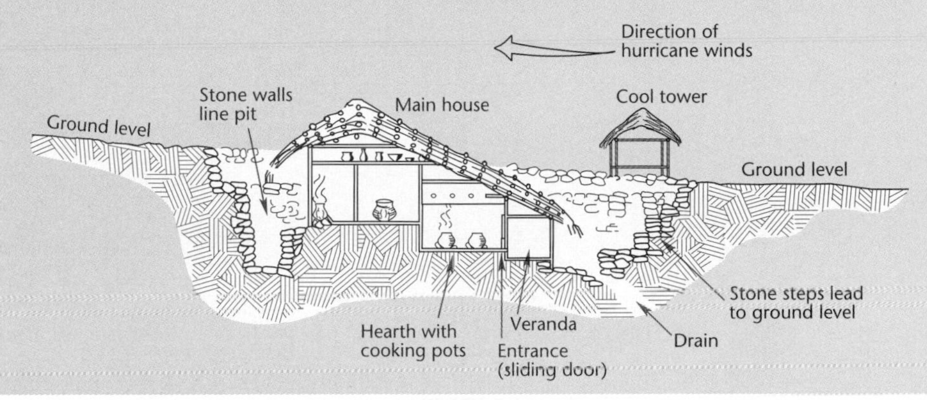

tions, particularly climate, vegetation, and geomorphology, strongly influence the choice of construction materials (Figure 7.21).

Shifting cultivators of the tropical rain forests typically build houses of poles and leaves, while sedentary subsistence farming peoples of the adjacent highlands and the oases and river valleys of the Old World desert zone rely principally on earthen construction, in the form of sun-dried (adobe) bricks or pounded earth. In some more prosperous regions, kiln-baked bricks are available. Peoples of the tropical grasslands, particularly in Africa, construct thatched houses from coarse grasses and thorn bushes. Mediterranean farmers, most of whom live in rocky, deforested lands, use stones as their principal building material, as do some rural residents of interior India and the Andean highlands of South America. Entire landscapes of stone, including walls, roofs, terraces, streets, and fences, lend an air of permanence to the cultural landscapes of these regions.

In middle and higher latitudes, in areas where timber remains abundant, farm folk traditionally built their houses of wood. The log cabin of the United States and its frame successors fit in this category, as do the folk houses of northern Europe and the mountains of eastern Australia (Figure 7.22). In some partially deforested temperate regions, including lands as diverse as central Europe and parts of China, farmers once built half-timbered houses, raising a framework of hardwood beams and filling the interstices with some other material. Sod or turf houses typify prairie and tundra areas, such as the Russian steppes and, in pioneer times, the American Great Plains. Nomadic herders often live in portable tents made of skins or wool.

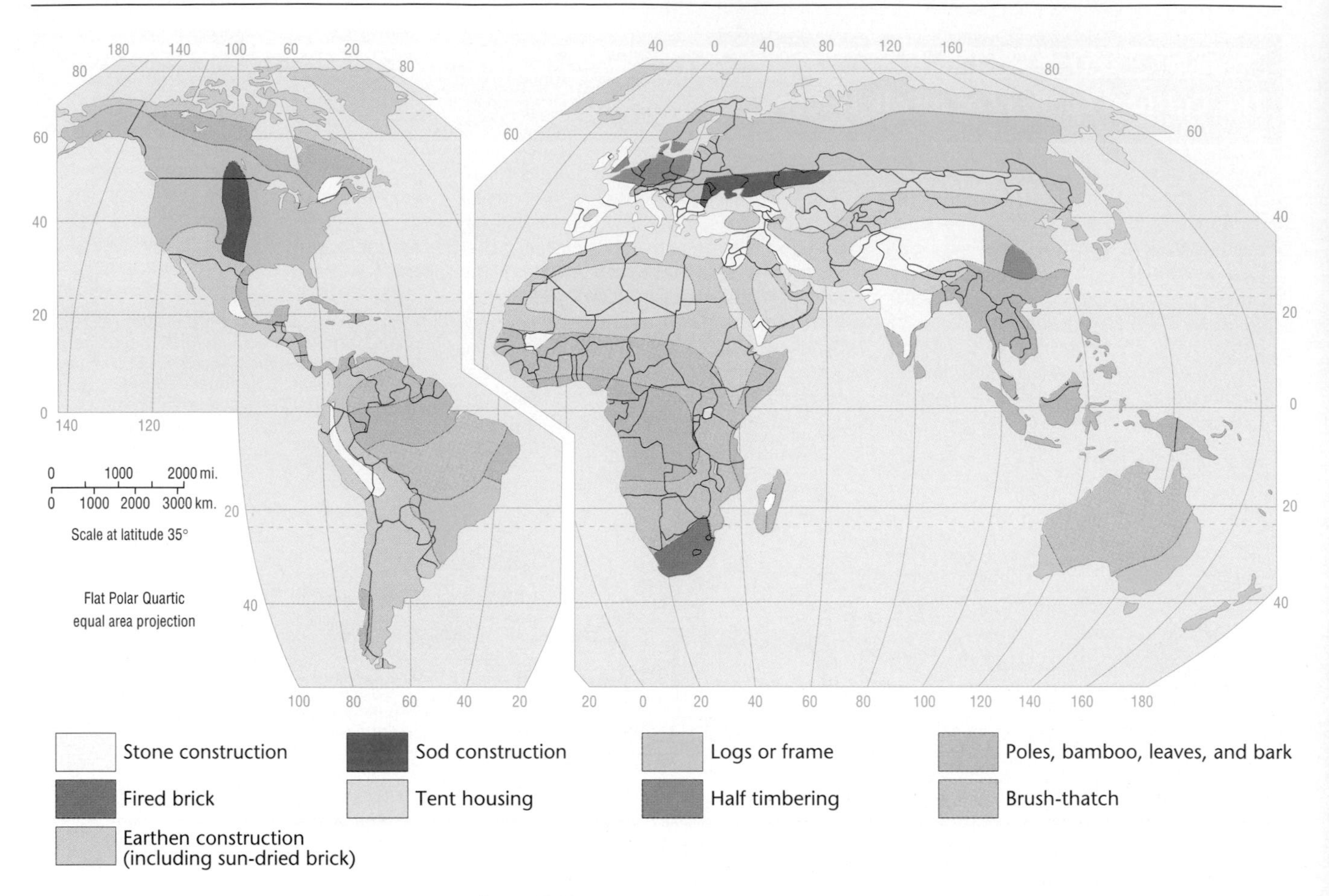

Figure 7.20
Traditional building materials in folk architecture. These materials vary from the relative permanence of stone to cloth tents. What factors might explain this pattern? In some areas, such as the North American Great Plains zone of sod construction, few if any structures built of traditional materials survive.

Figure 7.21
The building materials employed in folk architecture vary from the poles, thatch, and wall mats of highland Papua New Guinea to the half-timbering of central China and the earthen-walled dwellings of northern India. (See also Dunham, Paul. "House Types of Papua New Guinea's Kasakana." *Journal of Cultural Geography,* 8, No. 1 [1987]: 15–23.)

Figure 7.22
A wooden hut made of vertical timbers, or "slab" construction. This type is common in the Australian outback among British pioneers and cattle ranchers, who used the native eucalyptus trees to build their houses.

Floor Plan

Another way to classify traditional farmsteads is on the basis of the floor plan and layout. One style is the *unit farmstead,* in which the family, farm animals, and storage facilities share space under one roof in a single structure (Figure 7.23). Such houses, in their simplest form, are rectangular and single-storied. People and livestock occupy different ends of the structure. Often not even a dividing wall separates hu-

Figure 7.23
Two examples of folk *unit farmsteads.* The half-timbered structure is a single-story "Saxon" farmstead, in which the barn is at the front and the living quarters at the rear. The fortress-like multistory unit farmstead is typical of southern Tibet, in which the lower level houses livestock while the people live above.

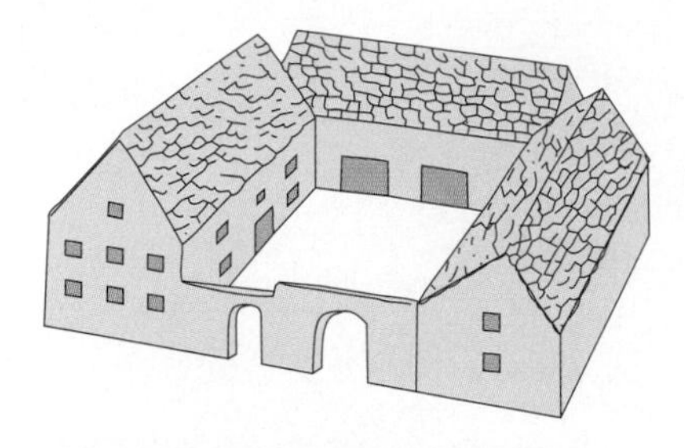

German Frankish farmstead, Central Europe (half-timbering, multistory house)

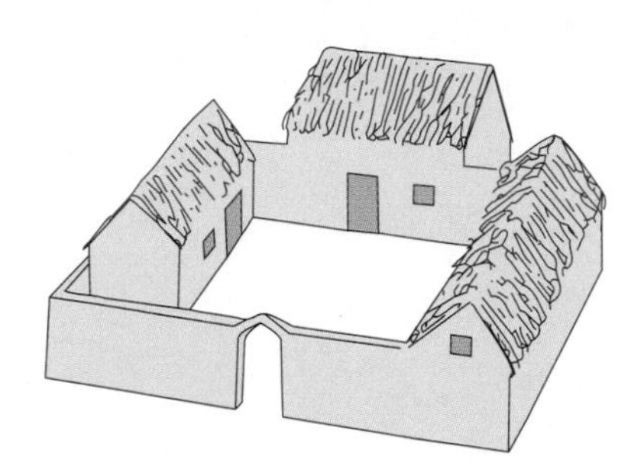

Inca *Marca* farmstead, Peru and Bolivia (stone construction, single story)

Chinese farmstead, Szechwan province (adobe brick, thatched roof, single story)

Figure 7.24
Three multistructure courtyard farmsteads from widely divergent cultures. What could account for the similarity? Is it a case of cultural diffusion? Or did the obvious advantages of the courtyard farmstead for defense and privacy lead to its independent invention by folk societies in Germany, South America, and China?

man and animal quarters. More complex unit farmsteads are multistoried and arranged so that people and livestock live on different levels. Unit farmsteads of both types are widely distributed in Europe.

In some parts of the tropical world, among shifting cultivators, communal unit housing prevails. Multiple families live under the same roof, sleeping and cooking in separate alcoves and sharing living space. An example is the Sarawak *longhouse*, found in the Malaysian portion of the island of Borneo, which accommodates between five and eight nuclear families in an elongated dwelling raised above the forest floor on stilts. Such folk housing reflects a clan or tribal social organization.

Most common are farmsteads in which the house, barn, and stalls occupy separate buildings. The *courtyard farmstead* provides an example (see Figure 7.24). The various structures of the courtyard farmstead cluster around an enclosed yard. This type appears in several seemingly unrelated culture regions, such as the Inca-settled portions of the Andes Mountains, the hills of central Germany, and eastern China. Courtyard farmsteads have a wide distribution in part because they offer both privacy and protection.

In most countries where Germanic Europeans immigrated and settled, including Anglo-America, Australia, and New Zealand, the *strewn farmstead* prevails. The various farm buildings, instead of being linked together around a central courtyard, lie spaced apart from one another in no consistent pattern. Strewn farmsteads are especially common in zones of wooden construction, where the danger of fire is greatest. Spacing the buildings apart reduces the danger that fire will spread from one building to another. Poorly suited to defense, strewn farmsteads are often associated with rural regions of greater than average tranquility.

Irish Folk Houses

Material composition, floor plan, and layout are important ingredients of folk architecture, but numerous other characteristics help to classify farmsteads and dwellings. The form or shape of the roof, the placement of the chimney, and even such details as the number and location of doors and windows can be important classifying criteria. Professor Estyn Evans (see biographical sketch), the noted expert on Irish folk geography, considered roof form and chimney placement, among other traits, in devising an informal classification of Irish folk houses. He discerned three major folk-housing culture regions, as determined by chimney and roof, on the small island of Ireland. If floor plan and material composition had been included, additional culture regions would have been identified, based on local architectural features such as the bed outshot of far north Ireland, the mud wall constructions of the interior counties, and the off-center door found in several districts (Figure 7.25).

Folk Housing in North America

In the United States and Canada, folk architecture today represents a relict form in the cultural landscape. Popular culture, with its mass-produced, commercially built houses, has so overwhelmed the folk

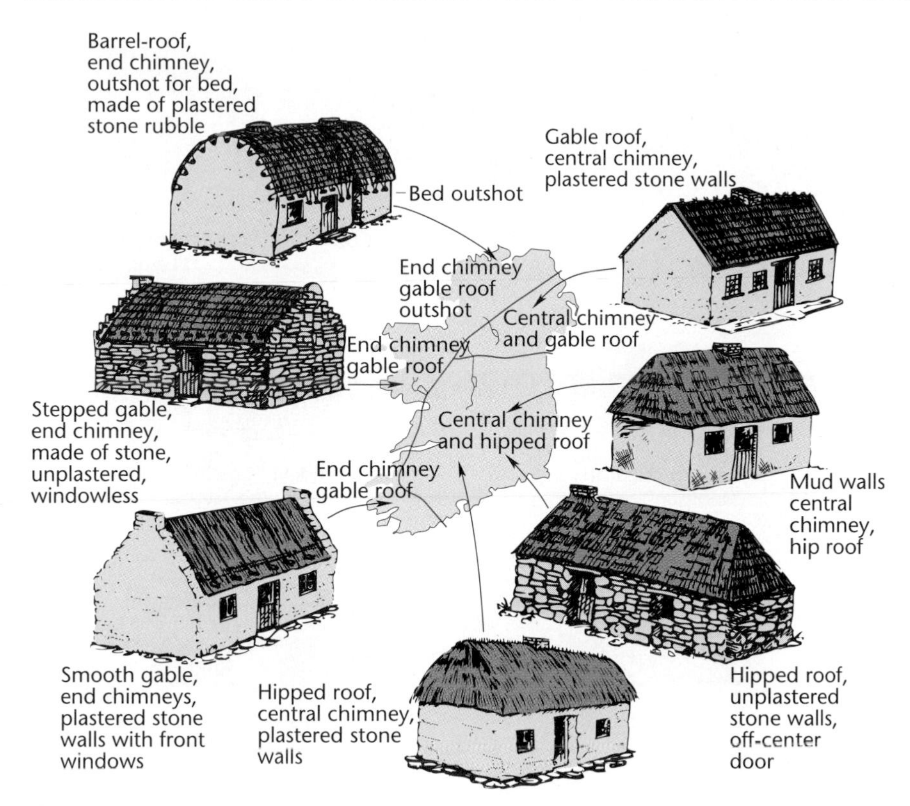

Figure 7.25
Some folk houses of Ireland. The Irish houses, while basically similar, differ in roof form, chimney placement, location of windows, material composition, and floor plan. Some are unit farmsteads, such as the barrel-roofed type, in which people lived in one end and the livestock in the other. What architectural features do all these houses have in common? The western coastal fringe of Ireland is the windiest part of the country. What effect might wind have had on roof form? (After various publications of E. Estyn Evans.)

tradition that few folk houses are being built today, but many survive in the refuge regions of American and Canadian folk culture (Figures 7.1, 7.26).

Yankee, or New England, folk houses are of wooden frame construction, and shingle siding often covers the exterior walls. They appear in a variety of floor plans, including the *New England large* house, a huge two-and-a-half story house built around a central chimney and two rooms deep. As the Yankee folk migrated westward, they developed the *upright and wing* dwelling. These Yankee houses are often massive in part because of the cold winters, which require most work to be done indoors (Figure 7.27).

By contrast, Upland Southern folk houses are smaller and built of notched logs, a technique introduced to North America by early colonial Scandinavian settlers on the lower Delaware River. Many houses in this folk tradition consist of two log rooms, with either a double fireplace between, forming the *saddlebag* house, or an open, roofed breezeway separating the two rooms, a plan known as the *dogtrot* house (Figures 7.26, 7.28). An example of an African American folk dwelling is the *shotgun* house, a narrow structure only one room in width but two, three, or even four rooms in depth. Acadiana, a French-derived folk region in Louisiana, is characterized by the half-timbered

E. Estyn Evans
1905–1989

Evans studied under H. J. Fleure in geography and anthropology at Aberystwyth, Wales. At the young age of 23, he was invited to establish a department of geography at Queen's University in Belfast, Northern Ireland, where he remained throughout his 44-year career.

The marriage of geography and anthropology in his training led him to specialize in the field of folk geography, and he was one of the first geographers in the English-speaking world to pursue the study of material folk culture. Evans developed a deep attachment for Ireland, his adopted home. He is best known to cultural geographers for numerous books and articles about the folk material culture of Ireland, in particular *Irish Heritage* (1943), *Mourne Country* (1951), *Irish Folk Ways* (1957), and *The Personality of Ireland* (1973). Evans was president of the Ulster Folk Life Society and trustee of the Ulster Folk and Transport Museum, of which he was the founder-father. In 1970, he was honored by being appointed Commander of the Order of the British Empire, and in 1973 he received the Victoria Medal of the Royal Geographical Society and in 1979 an Honors Award from the Association of American Geographers. He received honorary doctorates from five universities. (See Glasscock, Robin E. "E. Estyn Evans, 1905–1989." *Journal of Historical Geography,* 17 [1991]: 87–91.)

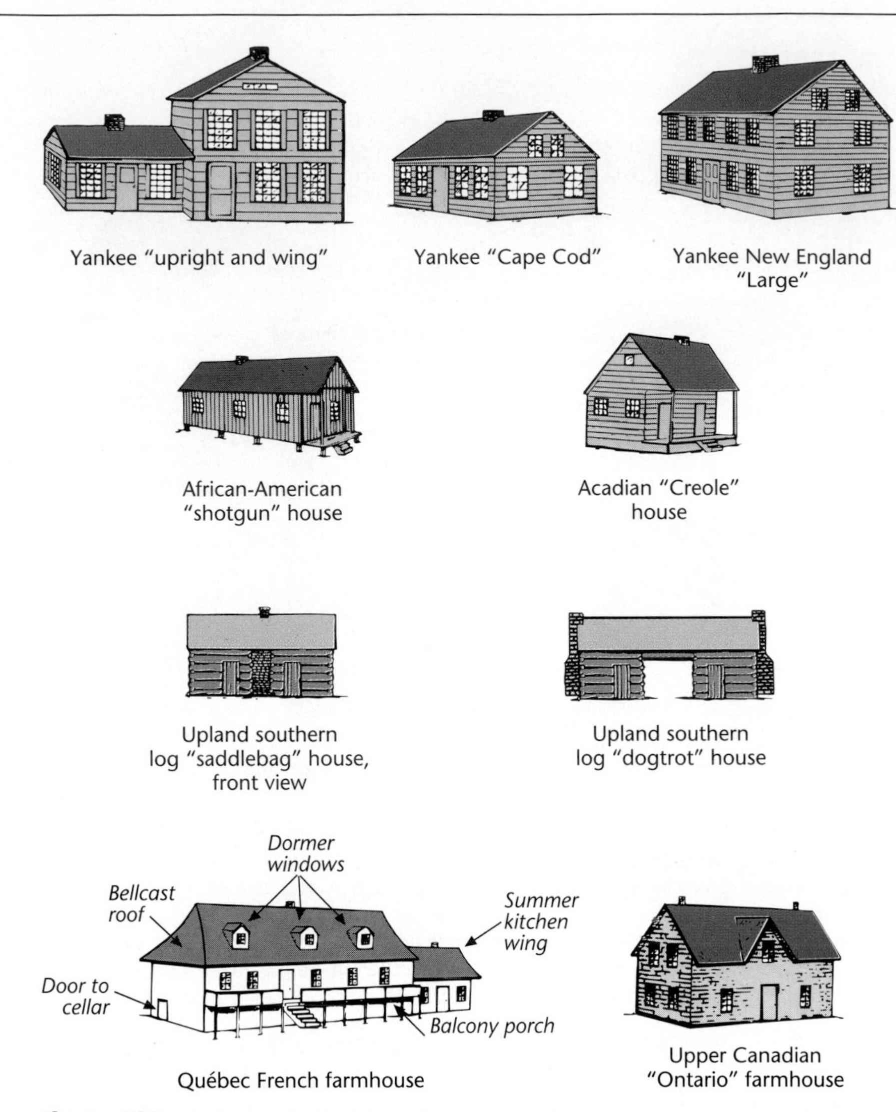

Figure 7.26
Selected folk houses. Six of the 15 folk culture regions of North America are represented (see Figure 7.1). (After Kniffen and Glassie, in part.)

Creole cottage, which has a central chimney and built-in porch. Scores of other folk house types survive in the American landscape, though most such dwellings now stand abandoned and derelict.

Canada also offers a variety of traditional folk houses (Figure 7.26). In French-speaking Québec, one of the common types consists of a main story atop a cellar, with attic rooms beneath a curved, bell-shaped (or *bell-cast)* roof. A balcony-porch with railing extends across the front, sheltered by the overhanging eaves. Attached to one side of this French-Canadian folk house is a summer kitchen that is sealed off during the long, cold winter. Often the folk houses of Québec are built of stone. To the west, in the Upper Canadian folk region, one type of folk house occurs so frequently that it is known as the *Ontario farmhouse.* One-and-a-half stories in height, the Ontario farmhouse is usually built of brick and has a distinctive gabled front dormer window. Now, using

Figure 7.27
A Yankee folk house and Northern dialect generic place-name, in the Western Reserve area of northeastern Ohio. The cultural landscape of this section of Ohio bears the unmistakable imprint of Yankee folk culture. The folk house is a "New England large" (Figure 7.26). The "Center" suffix is also a good indicator of Yankee influence, as is the "Classical Revival" Mediterranean toponym prefix, Mantua, derived from Mantova, Italy. See Figures 5.13 and 8.16.

Figure 7.28
A dogtrot house, typical of the Midland region. The distinguishing feature is the open-air passageway, or dogtrot, between the two main rooms. This house is located in central Texas.

(a)

(b)

(c)

(d)

Figure 7.29
Four folk houses in North America. Using the sketches in Figure 7.26 and the related section of the text, determine the regional affiliation and type of each. The answers are provided at the end of the "Sources and Suggested Readings" section in this chapter.

Figure 7.30
The *sawtooth cottage* folk house type. The red one is in the West Indian island nation of Barbados and the white one is halfway around the world in Victoria state, Australia. Is diffusion or independent invention responsible? How might a folk geographer go about finding the answer?

these sketches (Figure 7.26) and descriptions of eastern North American folk houses, identify the four illustrated in Figure 7.29.

The interpretation of folk architecture is by no means a simple process. Folk geographers often work for years trying to "read" such structures, seeking clues to diffusion and traditional adaptive strategies. The old problem of independent invention versus diffusion is raised repeatedly in the folk landscape, as Figure 7.30 illustrates. But precisely because interpretation is often difficult, geographers find these old structures challenging and well worth studying. Folk cultures rarely leave behind much in the way of written records, making their landscape artifacts all the more important in seeking explanations.

Conclusion

Folk geographers study traditional cultures and are interested in both material and nonmaterial aspects of folklife. Because folk culture displays major variations from one place to another, the device of culture region is a useful starting point for the study of traditional lifestyles. We saw how, by employing the theme of culture region, we could bring spatial order to the myriad of folk traits that survive, in vestige at least, in the United States and Canada.

The study of cultural diffusion allowed us to see how, even in conservative, change-resistant folk societies, innovations and traits spread across geographical space, how a Welsh folktale reaches Missouri or a New England agricultural fair reaches the Pacific Coast. Our study of the blowgun presented us with the kind of spatial problem that leads to speculation concerning diffusion versus independent invention.

By using the theme of cultural ecology, we explored the fundamental, almost religious tie that binds folk groups to the land. We glimpsed the intimate knowledge, far surpassing that of the popular culture, that folk groups have of their physical surroundings.

The study of cultural integration revealed the many connections and causal relationships that exist between folk and popular cultures. We saw how elements of folk culture can penetrate and influence the popular realm and the kinds of changes they undergo in the process.

Through our study of folk architecture, we saw an example of the visible imprint of folk groups on the cultural landscape. The folk house, perhaps the most basic type of structure ever built, served as our guide to the highly varied landscapes created by folk groups.

Sources and Suggested Readings

Bastian. Robert W. "Indiana Folk Architecture: A Lower Midwestern Index." *Pioneer America,* 9, No. 2 (1977): 115–136.

Buchanan, Ronald H. "Geography and Folk Life." *Folk Life,* 1 (1963): 5–15.

Carney, George O. *The Sounds of People and Places: A Geography of American Folk and Popular Music,* 3d ed. Lanham, MD: Rowman & Littlefield, 1994.

Ennals, Peter M. "Nineteenth-Century Barns in Southern Ontario." *Canadian Geographer,* 16 (1972): 256–270.

Ensminger, Robert F. *The Pennsylvania Barn: Its Origin, Evolution, and Distribution in North America.* Baltimore: Johns Hopkins University Press, 1992.

Evans, E. Estyn. "The Cultural Geographer and Folklife Research," in Richard M. Dorson (ed.), *Folklore and Folklife: An Introduction.* Chicago: University of Chicago Press, 1972, pp. 517–532.

Evans, E. Estyn. "The Ecology of Peasant Life in Western Europe," in William L. Thomas (ed.), *Man's Role in Changing the Face of the Earth.* Chicago: University of Chicago Press, 1956, pp. 217–239.

Evans, E. Estyn. *Irish Folk Ways.* London: Routledge & Kegan Paul, 1957.

Glass, Joseph W. *The Pennsylvania Culture Region: A View from the Barn.* Ann Arbor, MI: UMI Research Press, 1986.

Glassie, Henry. *Pattern in the Material Folk Culture of the Eastern United States.* Philadelphia: University of Pennsylvania Press, 1968.

Gritzner, Charles F. "Log Barns of Hispanic New Mexico." *Journal of Cultural Geography,* 10, No. 2 (1990): 21–34.

Gritzner, Charles F. "Log Housing in New Mexico." *Pioneer America,* 3, No. 2 (1971): 54–62.

Jakle, John A., Robert W. Bastian, and Douglas K. Meyer. *Common Houses in America's Small Towns: The Atlantic Seaboard to the Mississippi Valley.* Athens: University of Georgia Press, 1989.

Jordan, Terry G. *American Log Buildings: An Old World Heritage.* Chapel Hill: University of North Carolina Press, 1985.

Jordan, Terry G. "The Saddlebag House Type and Pennsylvania Extended." *Pennsylvania Folklife,* 44, No. 1 (1994): 36–48.

Jordan, Terry G. "The Texan Appalachia." *Annals of the Association of American Geographers,* 60 (1970): 409–427.

Jordan, Terry G., and Matti Kaups. *The American Backwoods Frontier: An Ethnic and Ecological Interpretation.* Baltimore: Johns Hopkins University Press, 1989.

Jordan, Terry G., and Matti Kaups. "Folk Architecture in Cultural and Ecological Context." *Geographical Review,* 77 (1987): 52–75.

Kilpinen, Jon T. "Material Folk Culture of the Rocky Mountain High Valleys." *Material Culture,* 23, No. 2 (1991): 25–41.

Kimber, Clarissa T. "Plants in the Folk Medicine of the Texas-Mexico Borderlands." *Proceedings, Association of American Geographers,* 5 (1973): 130–133.

Knapp, Ronald G. *China's Traditional Rural Architecture: A Cultural Geography of the Common House.* Honolulu: University of Hawaii Press, 1986.

Kniffen, Fred B. "American Cultural Geography and Folklife," in Don Yoder (ed.), *American Folklife*. Austin: University of Texas Press, 1976, pp. 51–70.

Kniffen, Fred B. "Folk-Housing: Key to Diffusion." *Annals of the Association of American Geographers,* 55 (1965): 549–577.

Konrad, Victor A., and Michael Chaney. "Madawaska Twin Barn." *Journal of Cultural Geography,* 3, No. 1 (1982): 64–75.

Lewis, Thomas R. "To Planters of Moderate Means: The Cottage as a Dominant Folk House in Connecticut before 1900." *Proceedings, New England–St. Lawrence Valley Geographical Society,* 10 (1980): 23–27.

Lornell, Christopher, and W. Theodore Mealor, Jr. "Traditions and Research Opportunities in Folk Geography." *Professional Geographer,* 35 (1983): 51–56.

Material Culture: Journal of the Pioneer America Society. Published three times annually, this leading periodical specializes in the subject of traditional American material culture. Volume 1 was published in 1969, and prior to 1984 the journal was called *Pioneer America*.

Mather, E. Cotton, and Pradyumna P. Karan. "Geography of Folk Art in India," in Allen G. Noble and Ashok K. Dutt (eds.), *India: Cultural Patterns and Processes*. Boulder, CO: Westview Press, 1982, pp. 165–194.

Morgan, John. *The Log House in East Tennessee*. Knoxville: University of Tennessee Press, 1990.

Newton, Milton. "Cultural Preadaptation and the Upland South." *Geoscience and Man,* 5 (1974): 143–154.

Nishi, Midori. "Regional Variations in Japanese Farmhouses." *Annals of the Association of American Geographers,* 57 (1967): 239–266.

Noble, Allen G. *Wood, Brick, and Stone: The North American Settlement Landscape*. 2 vols. Amherst: University of Massachusetts Press, 1984.

Otto, John S., and Nain E. Anderson. "The Diffusion of Upland South Folk Culture, 1790–1840." *Southeastern Geographer,* 22 (1982): 89–98.

Pennington, Campbell W. *The Tarahumar of Mexico: Their Environment and Material Culture*. Salt Lake City: University of Utah Press, 1963.

Pillsbury, Richard. "Pattern in the Folk and Vernacular House Forms of the Pennsylvania Culture Region." *Pioneer America,* 9 (1977). 12–31.

Pillsbury, Richard. "The Pennsylvania Culture Area: A Reappraisal." *North American Culture,* 3, No. 2 (1987): 37–54.

Price, Edward T. "Root Digging in the Appalachians: The Geography of Botanical Drugs." *Geographical Review,* 50 (1960): 1–20.

Semple, Ellen Churchill. "The Anglo-Saxons of the Kentucky Mountains: A Study in Anthropogeography." *Geographical Journal,* 17 (1901): 588–623.

Sinnhuber, Karl A. "On the Relations of Folklore and Geography." *Folk-lore,* 68 (1957): 385–404.

Trindell, Roger T. "American Folklore Studies and Geography." *Southern Folklore Quarterly,* 34 (1970): 1–11.

Vermeer, Donald E., and Dennis A. Frate. "Geophagy in a Mississippi County." *Annals of the Association of American Geographers,* 65 (1975): 414–424.

Wacker, Peter O. "Folk Architecture as an Indicator of Culture Areas and Culture Diffusion: Dutch Barns and Barracks in New Jersey." *Pioneer America,* 5, No. 2 (1973): 37–47.

Wacker, Peter O. "Traditional House and Barn Types in New Jersey: Keys to Acculturation, Past Cultureographic Regions, and Settlement History." *Geoscience and Man,* 5 (1974): 163–176.

Wagstaff, John M. "Traditional Houses in Modern Greece." *Geography,* 50 (1965): 58–64.

Wilhelm, Eugene J., Jr. "Field Work in Folklife: Meeting Ground of Geography and Folklore." *Keystone Folklore Quarterly,* 13 (1968): 241–247.

Wilhelm, Eugene J., Jr. "The Mullein: Plant Piscicide of the Mountain Folk Culture." *Geographical Review,* 64 (1974): 235–252.

Wilhelm, Hubert G. H. "The Pennsylvania-Dutch Barn in Southeastern Ohio." *Geoscience and Man,* 5 (1974): 155–162.
Winberry, John J. "The Log House in Mexico." *Annals of the Association of American Geographers,* 64 (1974): 54–69.

Key to Figure 7.29: (a) French-Canadian farmhouse, Port Joli, Québec; (b) New England "large" house, near Fredericton, New Brunswick; (c) Yankee upright and wing house, northeastern Ohio; (d) Shotgun house, Alleyton, Texas.

Denny's
NAME BRAND CLOTHING
KELLOGG
WILLIAMSBU
INN
WICHITA INN
BIG CHEESE
VALUE RATED
USED CARS
DAVIS-MOORE
WE BUY CARS
SPEED LIMIT 45
STOP

CHAPTER 8

Popular Culture

What do Big Macs, symphony orchestras, personal computers, collegiate basketball games, and the latest clothing fads have in common? How are they, in turn, linked to Frisbee tossing, VCRs, a can of beer from a Milwaukee brewery, "gangsta" rap music, or a cruise on the "Loveboat"? The answer is that all are aspects of the **popular culture** (Figure 8.1).

The preceding chapter dealt with folk culture. We suggested there that folk and popular could be regarded as contrasting cultural alternatives, describing popular culture as constantly changing, based in large, heterogeneous groups of people concentrated mainly in urban areas. Popular material goods are mass-produced by machines in factories, and a money economy prevails. Relationships between individuals are more numerous but less personal than in folk cultures, and the family structure is weaker. People are more mobile, less attached to place and environment. A distinct division of labor, reflected in myriad, highly specialized professions and jobs, characterizes the earning of a livelihood, and considerable leisure time is available to most people. Secular institutions of control, such as the police, army, and courts, take the place of family and church in maintaining order.

If a single hallmark of popular culture exists, it is *change.* Words such as *growth, progress, fad,* and *trend* crop up frequently in newspapers and conversations. So pervasive is change that some persons prove unable to cope with it, leading them to an insecurity expressed in the term *future shock.* In a humorous debunking of popular culture and his own inability to change quickly enough, newspaper columnist John Anders recalled not all that long ago that he "danced the Twist when others had moved on to the Swim, wore Old Spice after the rest of the guys had graduated to English Leather, donned corduroy during the burlap frenzy, and ate Big Boy Hamburgers while my peers moved into Quiche Lorraine. . . . " As you can tell, the whole bunch of them is now way out of date.

If all these characteristics seem rather commonplace and "normal" it should not be surprising. You are, after all, firmly enmeshed in the popular culture, or else you would not be attending college or reading a

Figure 8.1
Popular culture is reflected in every aspect of life, from the fast foods we eat to the clothes we wear and the recreational activities that occupy our leisure time.

book. The large majority of people in Europe, the United States, Canada, and other "developed" countries now belong to the popular rather than the folk culture. Industrialization, urbanization, the rise of formal education, and the resultant increase in leisure time all contributed to the spread of popular culture and the consequent retreat of folklife. We and our recent ancestors abandoned the hidebound, secure, stable, traditional folk culture to embrace with enthusiasm the free, open, dynamic lifestyle offered by popular culture. Tradition and superstition gave way to change and knowledge; science challenged religion for dominance in our daily lives. We profited greatly in material terms through this transition.

In reality, all of culture presents a continuum, on which folk and popular represent extreme forms. Many gradations between the two are possible. Disadvantages, as well as the previously mentioned benefits, become apparent as one moves toward the popular end of the continuum. We forfeited much in discarding folkways, as Chapter 7 suggested. Certainly, it would not be proper to regard popular culture as somehow superior to folk culture. With popularization, we weakened both family structure and interpersonal relationships. One prominent cultural geographer, Fred Kniffen (see biographical sketch in Chapter 7), who lived in both folk and popular settings, felt that of all the elements of popular culture and the age of technology, "only two would I dislike to give up: inside plumbing and medical advances."

Popular Culture Regions

Cultural geographers can hardly ignore the ascendant position of popular culture in the world. The first question a geographer asks about popular culture concerns its spatial attributes, a question best answered through the theme of culture region.

Placelessness or Clustering?

Superficially, at least, popular culture appears to vary less areally than does folk culture. In fact, Canadian geographer Edward Relph goes so far as to propose that popular culture produces a profound **placelessness,** a spatial standardization that diminishes cultural variety and demeans the human spirit, while James Kunstler speaks of the "geography of nowhere" to describe modern America. One place becomes pretty much like another, robbed of its geographical essence by the pervasive influence of a continental or even worldwide popular culture (Figure 8.2). When compared to places produced by folk culture, rich in their uniqueness, the geographical face of popular culture often seems expressionless (Figure 8.3). The greater mobility of people in popular culture weakens attachment to place and compounds the problem.

Unquestionably, Relph's and Kunstler's observations bear some truth, but to assume that popular culture lacks regional expression would be a mistake. Indeed, in his book *The Clustering of America,* Michael Weiss argues that "American society has become increasingly fragmented" and, drawing on the work of Jonathan Robbin, identifies 40 "lifestyle clusters" based on postal ZIP codes. "Those five digits can indicate the kinds of magazines you read, the meals you serve at dinner," and what political party you support. "Tell me someone's ZIP code," boasts Robbin, "and I can predict what they eat, drink, drive—even think." The lifestyle clusters, each of which is a formal culture region, bear colorful names such as "Gray Power" (upper-middle-class retirement areas), "Old Yankee Rows" (blue- and white-collar older ethnic neighborhoods of the Northeast), and "Norma Rae-Ville" (lower- and middle-class Southern mill towns named for the Sally Field movie about the tribulations of a union organizer in a textile manufacturing town) (Figure 8.4). For example, Old Yankee Rowers typically have a high school education, like bowling and ice hockey, and are three times as likely to live in rowhouses or duplexes. Residents of Norma Rae-Ville are mostly nonunion factory workers, have trouble making ends meet, and consume twice as much canned stew as the national average. In short, a whole panoply of popular subcultures exists in America and the world at large, each possessing its own belief system, spokespeople, dress code, and lifestyle.

In addition, the popular culture creates new places. Geographer Paul Adams, for example, speaks of "television as a gathering place," as "social space," where members of a household and their friends now assemble. Television, as a sort of miniature functional culture region, has become to the popular culture, worldwide, what the fire and hearth were to folk culture. We must always remember that region and place

Figure 8.2
Placelessness exemplified: scenes almost Anywhere, developed world. Guess where these pictures were taken (answers follow the "Sources and Suggested Readings" section at the end of the chapter). Compare these views to Figure 8.3. See also Curtis, James R. "McDonald's Abroad: Outposts of American Culture." *Journal of Geography,* 81 (1982): 14–20.

exist from micro to macro scales. Popular culture may diminish some of these in the direction of placelessness while enhancing others.

Cyberspace

Perhaps the personal computer and Internet access have created another new type of place. Certainly the words and phrases we use to describe the Internet imply that it possesses a geography—"cyberspace," the "information highway," the "virtual community," "net surfing," "cyberhood," and "cyberbia," to mention a few. The information superhighway, we hear, connects not two points, but *all* points, creating in the process a new sort of place.

But, in fact, "is there a *there* in cyberspace?" as John Barlow asks in *Utne Reader*? Does the Internet contain a geography at all? Certainly, *places*, at least as understood by cultural geographers, cannot be created on the net. What is missing, geographically, in cyberspace? Well, for starters, these "virtual places" lack a cultural landscape and a

Figure 8.3
Retaining a sense of place: a Portuguese hill town. Produced by a folk culture, this town exhibits individuality and charm.

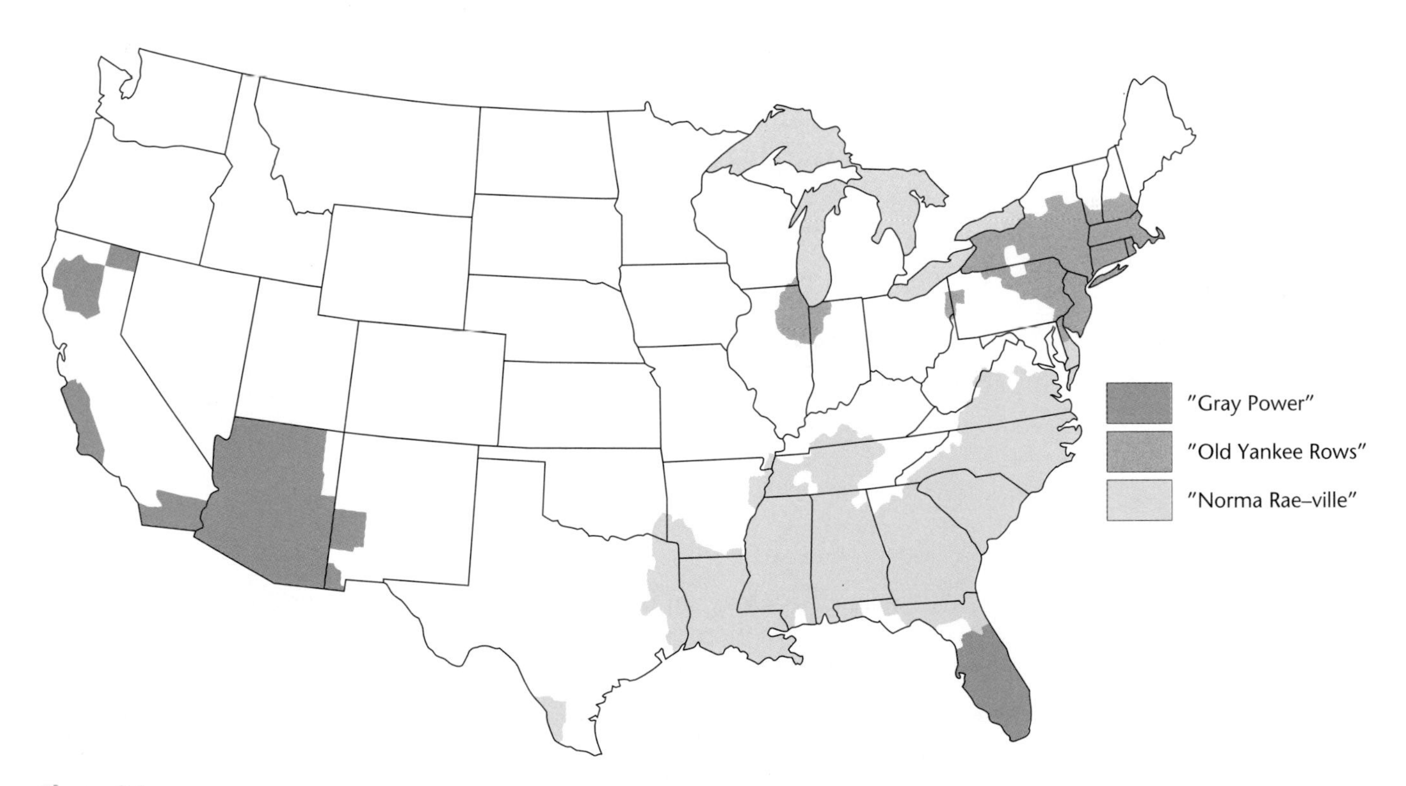

Figure 8.4
Three examples of the 40 "lifestyle clusters" in US popular culture. Any of the 200 television market areas that contained individual ZIP code areas with above-average occurrence of the lifestyle indicated are shaded in their entirety, even though only a portion of the market area was so characterized. For a description of each lifestyle, see the text. (Adapted from Weiss, *Clustering of America,* pp. 307, 335, 362. Weiss drew in part on the work of Jonathan Robbin.)

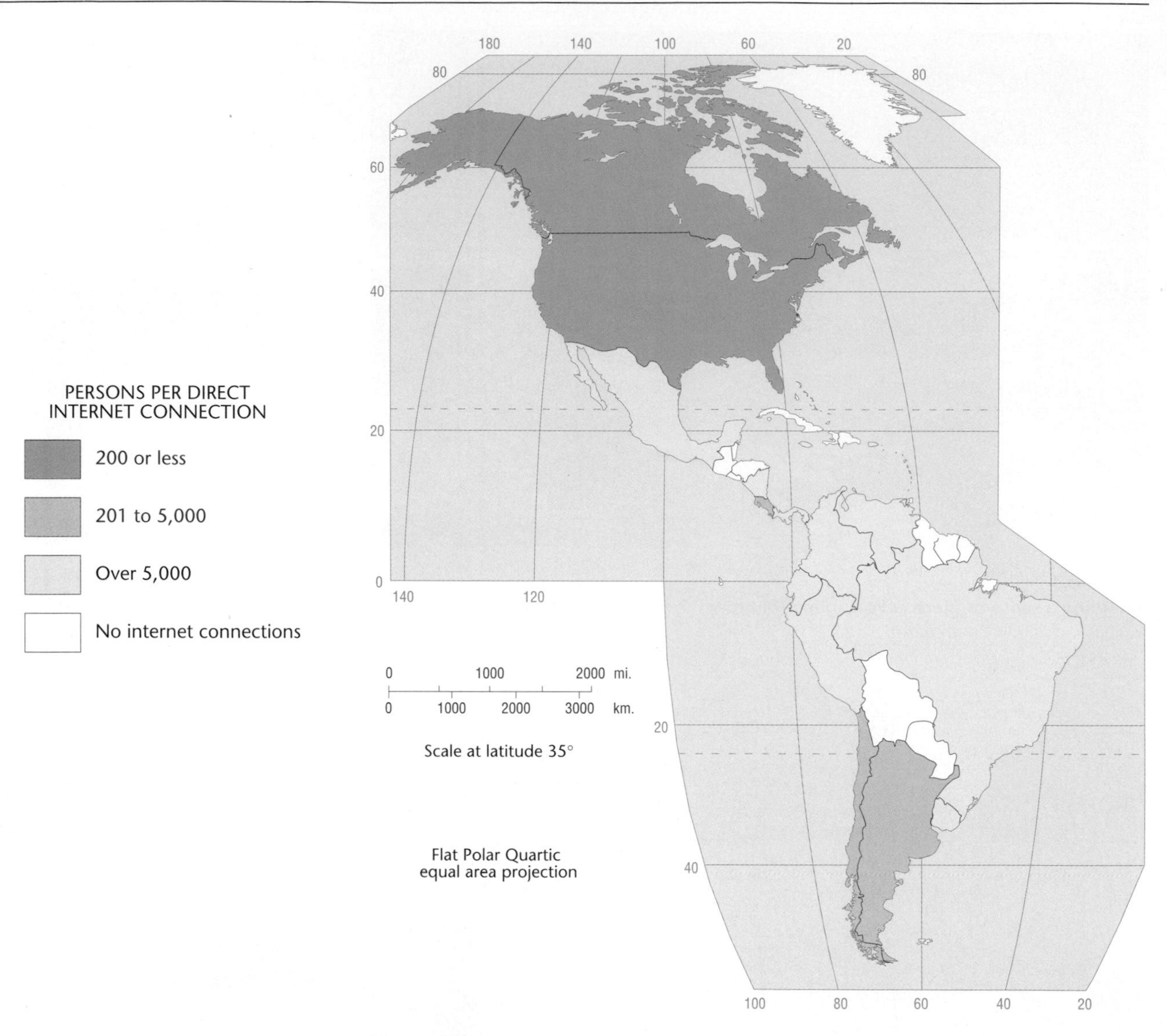

Figure 8.5

Connections to the Internet, shown on a per capita basis. Profound geographical contrasts have developed in access to the "information superhighway," and these will undoubtedly have some shaping influence spatially in the coming new century. (Based on data provided by the Internet Society.)

cultural ecology. In the broader context, on a worldwide scale, human diversity is poorly portrayed in cyberspace. "Old people, poor people, the illiterate, and the continent of Africa" seem not to be "there," as Barlow notes (Figure 8.5). Users end up "meeting" mainly people pretty much like themselves on the net. More essentially, the breath and spirit of place cannot exist in cyberspace. Barlow, resorting to a Hindu term, calls this missing essence *prana.* These are not real places, nor can they ever be.

Still, we should acknowledge that cyberspace possesses some geographical qualities. It enhances the opportunities for communication over long distances and into rare data banks, an attribute that surely encourages and speeds cultural diffusion. Indeed, cyberspace is merely

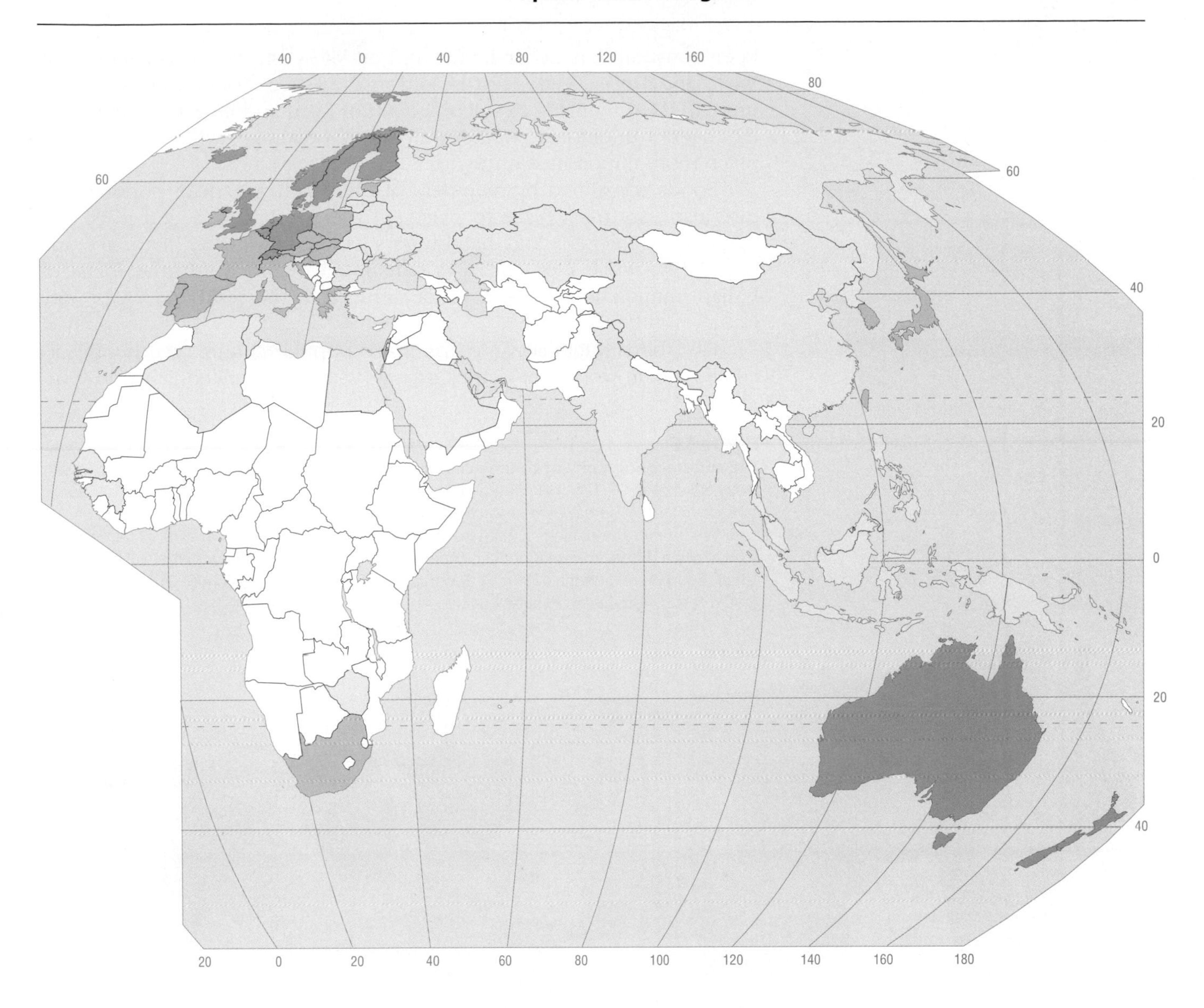

another facilitator of diffusion. The Internet also helps heighten regional contrasts. The very uneven spatial distribution of Internet connections creates a new way in which people differ (Figure 8.5). This provides the principal geographical content and role of cyberspace. Let us now turn to less ethereal aspects of popular culture—food, drink, music, and sport.

Food and Drink

The persistent formal regionalization of popular culture is vividly revealed by what we eat and drink, which differs markedly from one part of the country and world to another. The highest per capita levels of US beer consumption occur in the upper Midwest, Northeast, mountain West, and Texas, while least is sold in the Lower South and Utah (Figure 8.6). Whisky made from corn, both of legal and illegal manufacture, has been a traditional Southern alcoholic beverage, while Californians place more importance on wine.

Foods consumed by members of the North American popular culture also vary from place to place. In the South, barbecued pork and beef, fried chicken, and hamburgers enjoy far greater than average popularity, while more pizza is consumed in the North, the focus of Italian immigration. Indeed, pizza diffused to the southern states only in the mid–1950s.

Fast foods might seem to epitomize popular culture, yet the importance of such restaurants varies greatly within the United States, reveal-

Figure 8.6

The cultural geography of commercial beer consumption. Looking at Figures 6.5 and 9.4 may help explain the regional pattern displayed on this map. About one-quarter of all Americans claim at least partial German ancestry, and their distribution could help explain the pattern. What other causal factors might be at work? The regional pattern of wine or hard liquor consumption differs from that of beer. (Adapted from Rooney, John F., Jr., and Paul L. Butt. "Beer, Bourbon and Boone's Farm: A Geographical Examination of Alcoholic Drink in the United States." *Journal of Popular Culture,* 11 [1978]: 832–856.)

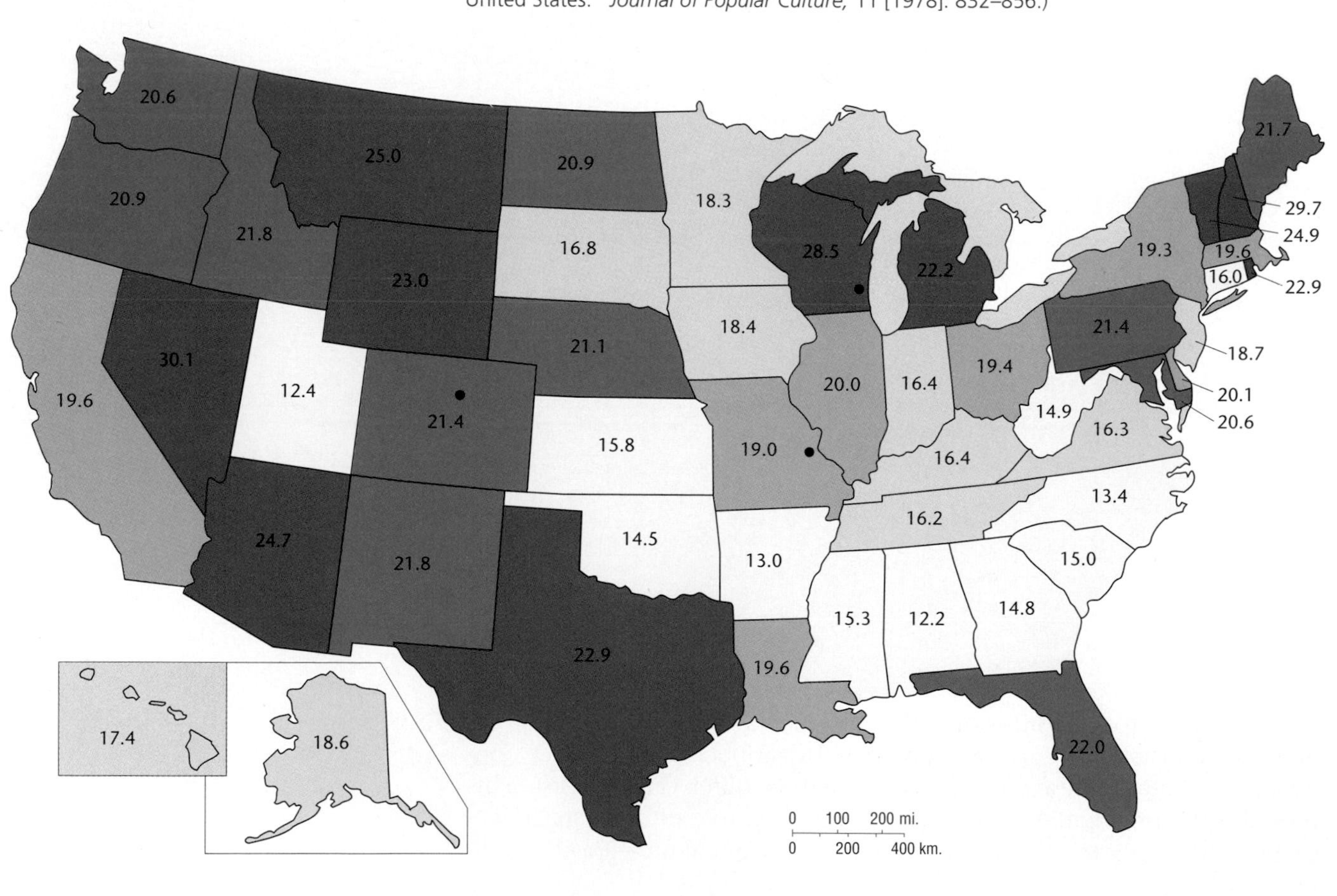

ing a pattern apparently related to that for beer consumption (Figure 8.7). In general, states where fast-food sales form a larger-than-average proportion of total restaurant business also have below-average beer sales. How might these two traits be related? The answer may be in regional cultural differences between North and South rooted in national origins (see Chapter 9) and religion (refer to Figure 6.5).

Popular Music

Many different styles of music have been spawned by the popular culture, and all reveal geographical patterning in levels of acceptance. Pop musicians often receive adulation of a magnitude reserved for deities in folk culture. Elvis Presley epitomized both popular music and the associated cult of personality. Even today, a generation after his death, he retains an important place in American popular culture.

Elvis also illustrates the vivid geography of that same culture (Figure 8.8). In the sale of Presley memorabilia, the nation reveals a split personality. The main hotbeds of Elvis worship lie in the eastern states, while the king of rock and roll is largely forgotten out West. While raising more questions than it answers, Figure 8.8 leaves no doubt that popular culture varies geographically.

Figure 8.7
Fast-food sales as a share of total restaurant sales, by state. What might account for the spatial variation in this aspect of popular culture? Does the pattern bear any similarity to the map of traditional and folk cultures shown in Figures 1.6 and 7.1? What does this suggest about the *convergence hypothesis,* which holds that regional cultures in America are collapsing into a national culture? Compare this map to Figure 8.6. (From "Annual Restaurant Growth Index." *Restaurant Business,* 93, No. 14 [1994]: 70. See also Roark, Michael. "Fast Foods: American Food Regions." *North American Culture,* 2, No. 1 [1985]: 24–36.)

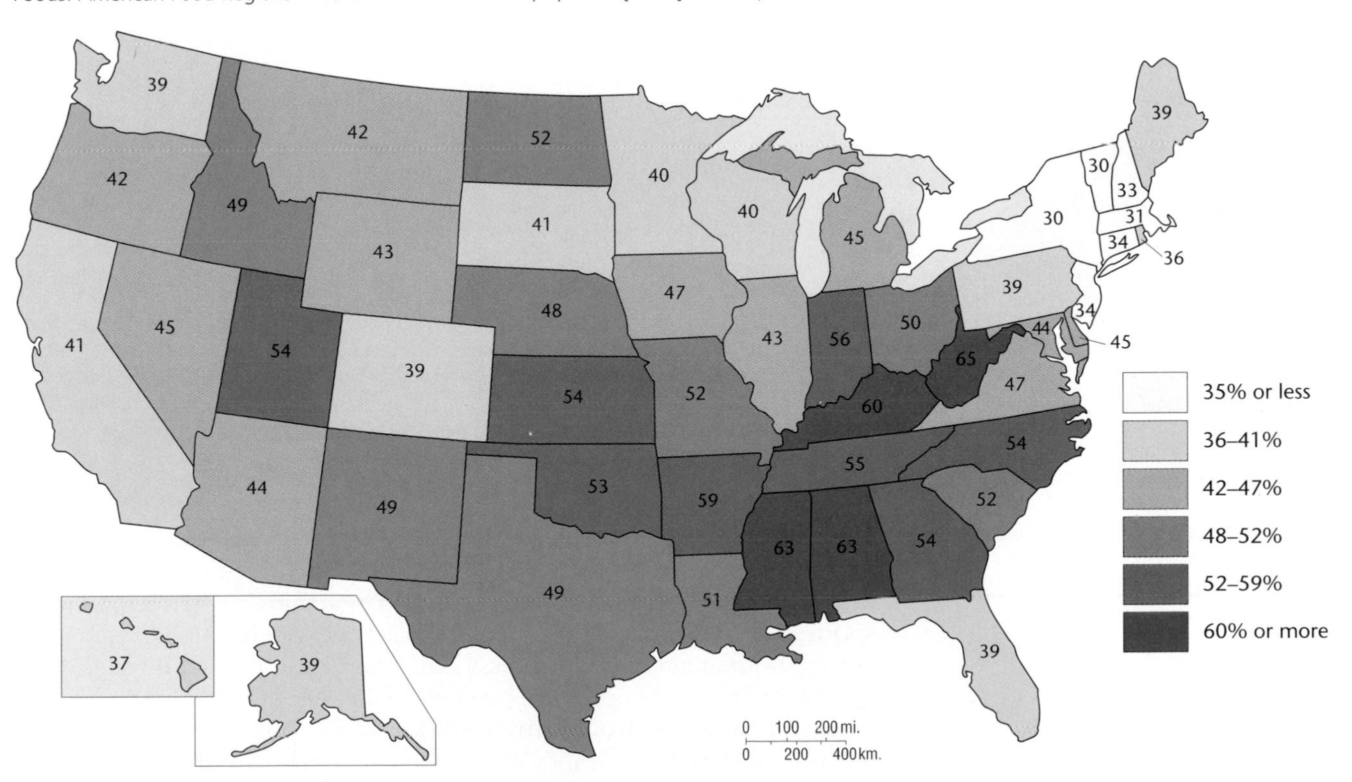

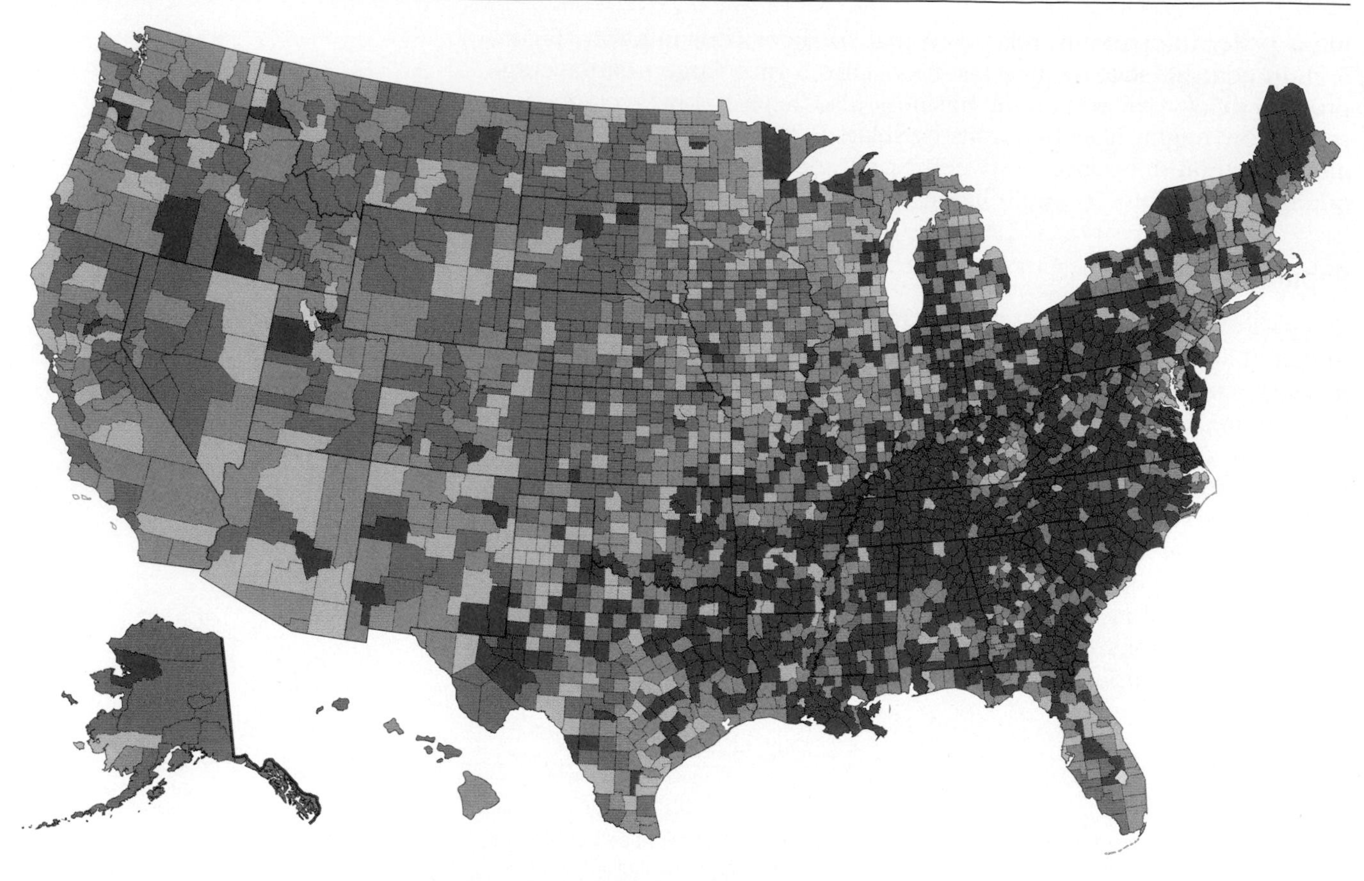

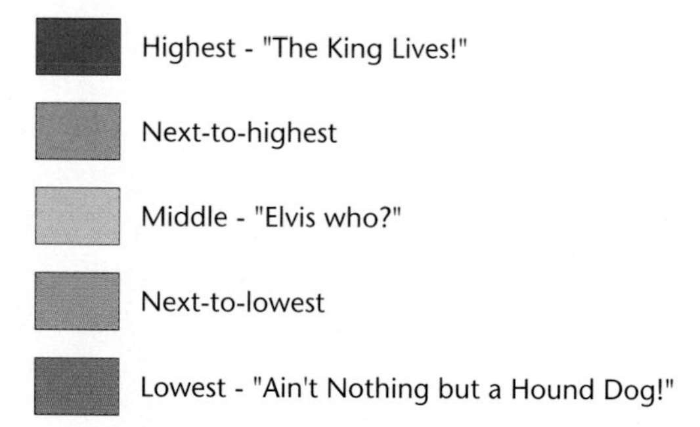

Figure 8.8
Purchases of Elvis Presley memorabilia, 1990s. The hotbeds of Elvis adoration lie mainly in the eastern United States, while most Westerners can take him or leave him. What cultural factors might underlie this "fault line" in the geography of popular culture? (Redrawn, based on data collected by Bob Lunn of DICI, Bellaire, TX, and published by Brad Edmonson and Linda Jacobsen in *American Demographics*, 15, No. 8 [1993]: 64.)

Sports

Abundant leisure is another hallmark of popular culture, and North Americans devote much of that time to watching or participating in sports. Few aspects of popular culture are as widely publicized as our games, both amateur and professional. From Little League through high school, college, Olympic, and professional contests, athletics receive almost daily attention from many members of the popular culture. In fact, the rise of competitive spectator sports parallels closely the development of popular culture in North America and Europe. The further we withdrew from our folk tradition, the more important organized games became for us. The nineteenth century, which witnessed the industrialization and resultant popularization of our culture, also gave us football, ice hockey, baseball, soccer, and basketball—our major spectator sports. While our folk ancestors played a variety of games, these were limited mainly to children or helped hone skills needed in everyday life; relatively little time or attention was devoted to them. Certainly, the concept of professional athletes and admission-paying spectators is unique to the popular culture and is not to be found in folk cultures. Our folk ancestors knew nothing even remotely like our Super Bowl, World Series, Stanley Cup, or NCAA tournaments.

As commercial spectator sports diffused through North America, distinct regional contrasts developed. "Hotbeds" of football arose in some regions, basketball became a winter mania in certain areas, baseball came to rule supreme in some states, and ice hockey ascended to reign in still other provinces. Participant sports reveal similar regionalization. Skiing, tennis, bowling, and golf also vary greatly in popularity from one region to another. Some of these strong regional differences are summarized in Figure 8.9. John Rooney, who initiated the geographical study of sports in the popular culture back in the 1960s, and Richard Pillsbury sum up these and other regional contrasts in American athletics by designating ten "sports regions," each with its own special character (Figure 8.10). These provide a more definitive identity to regions formerly revealed mainly through intuition, as for example by the sports writer who described football in the East as a cultural exercise, in the West as tourism, in the North as cannibalism, and in the South as religion.

Beauty Pageants

In popular culture, contests are by no means limited to the sports arenas. Nearly all of us participate in one or another less strenuous competition, from bingo to contract bridge. Beauty pageants, like it or not, provide a typical expression of American popular culture and provide a good example of these nonathletic contests. They began in earnest at Atlantic City, New Jersey, in the early 1920s with the first Miss America competitions and have since proliferated.

As with all facets of popular culture, beauty pageants reveal pronounced areal contrasts (Figure 8.11). Whether presented on a per capita basis or as simple totals, the winners of such nationwide pageants tend to come preponderantly from certain parts of the country. A "beauty queen belt" stretches from Mississippi to Utah, while directly north of this belt is a sizable block of states that have never produced a major contest winner. As is invariably true of culture regions, this pattern immediately raises questions concerning cause and effect.

Vernacular Culture Regions

A quite different application of the culture region theme is seen in the concept of **vernacular regions**—those perceived to exist by their inhabitants. Rather than being the intellectual creation of the professional geographer, a vernacular region is the product of the spatial perception of the population at large. Rather than being a formal region based on carefully chosen criteria, a vernacular region is a composite of the

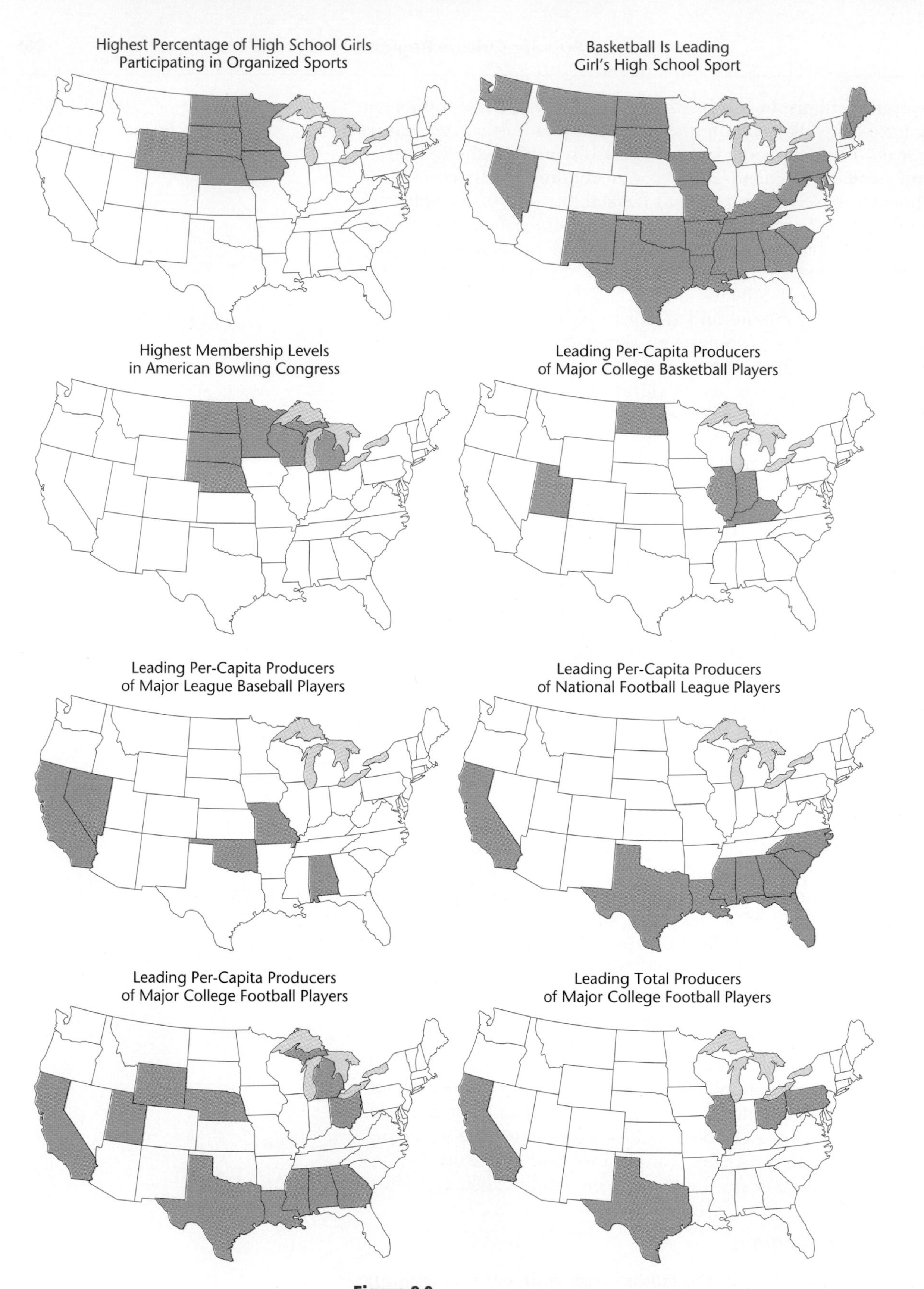

Figure 8.9
Selected geographical variations in American sports. What factors might help explain these patterns? (Sources: Pillsbury, Richard. "Striking to Success." *Sport Place,* 4, No. 1 [1990]: 16, 35; Rooney, John F., Jr. *A Geography of American Sport.* Reading, MA: Addison-Wesley, 1974, pp. 118, 152, 179; Shortridge, Barbara G. *Atlas of American Women.* New York: Macmillan, 1987, pp. 70, 71; Rooney, John F., Jr. "Where They Come From." *Sport Place,* 2, No. 3 [1988]: 17.)

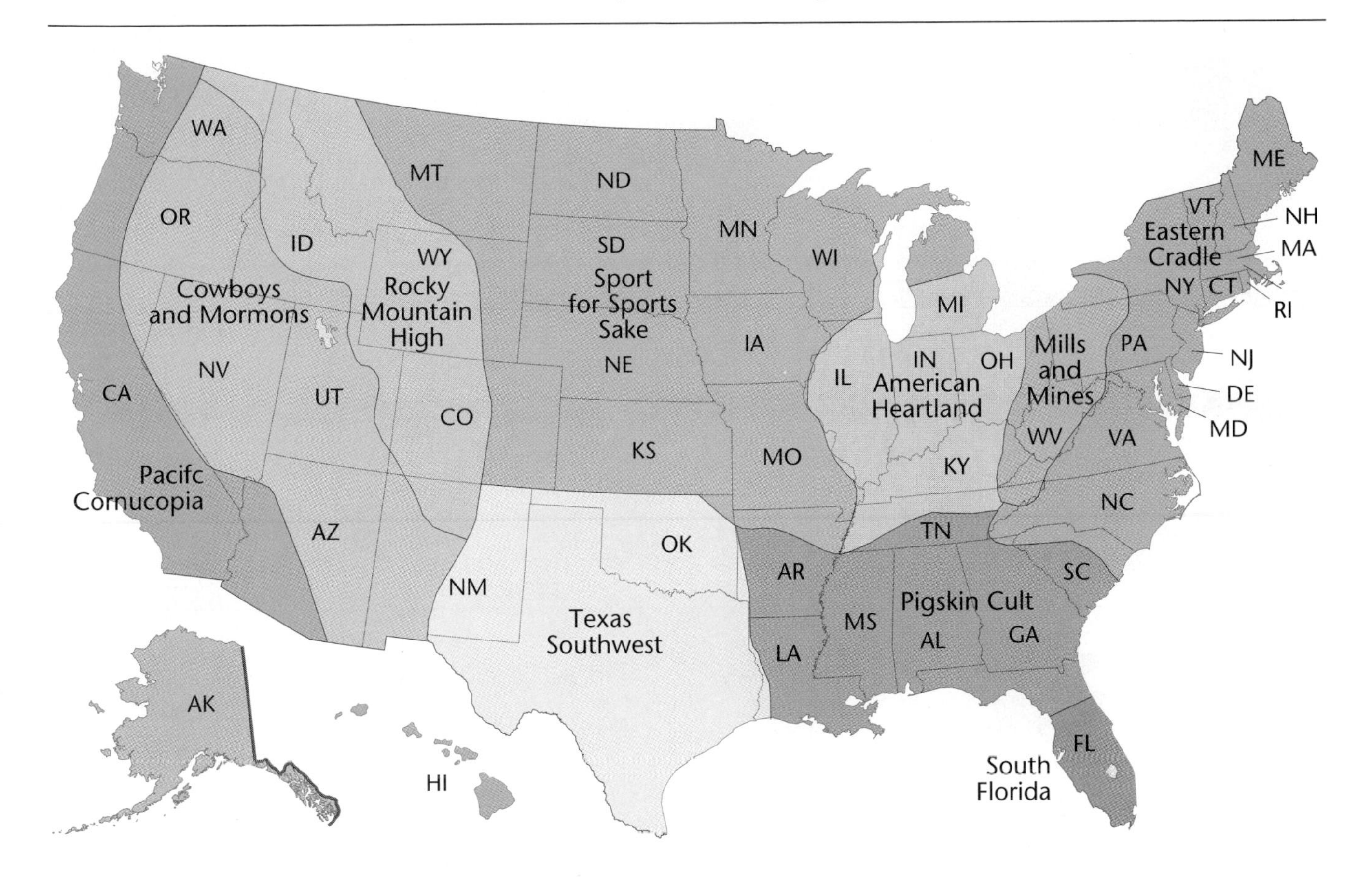

REGION	SPORTS PARTICIPATION RATE: High school "trinity" sports	Other high schools sports	Adults	Women	PER CAPITA PRODUCTION OF ELITE ATHLETES	INNOVATION TENDENCY
Pigskin cult	HIGH	VERY LOW	LOW	VERY LOW	VERY HIGH	LOW
Sports for Sport's Sake	HIGH	VERY HIGH	VERY HIGH	VERY HIGH	LOW	AVG.
Eastern Cradle	LOW	HIGH	AVG.	AVG.	AVG.	HIGH
Pacific Cornucopia	AVG.	HIGH	HIGH	HIGH	HIGH	VERY HIGH
Texas Southwest	HIGH	AVG.	AVG.	HIGH	HIGH	LOW
Cowboys and Mormons	AVG.	VERY LOW	AVG.	LOW	AVG.	VERY LOW
American Heartland	HIGH	AVG.	AVG.	AVG.	HIGH	AVG.
Mills and Mines	HIGH	AVG.	AVG.	AVG.	HIGH	LOW
Rocky Mountain High	AVG.	HIGH	HIGH	HIGH	LOW	AVG.
South Florida	AVG.	HIGH	HIGH	HIGH	HIGH	AVG.

Figure 8.10
Sports regions of the United States. "Trinity" sports are baseball, basketball, and football. "Innovation" refers to the willingness to try new, nontraditional sports. For a fuller description of each region, see the sources listed below. (Redrawn from Rooney, John F., Jr. and Richard Pillsbury. "Sports Regions of America." *American Demographics*, 14, No. 11 [1992]: 33, 38. Stephen W. Tweedie provided data analysis. The map also appeared in Rooney, J., and Pillsbury, R. *Atlas of American Sport*. New York: Macmillan, 1992.)

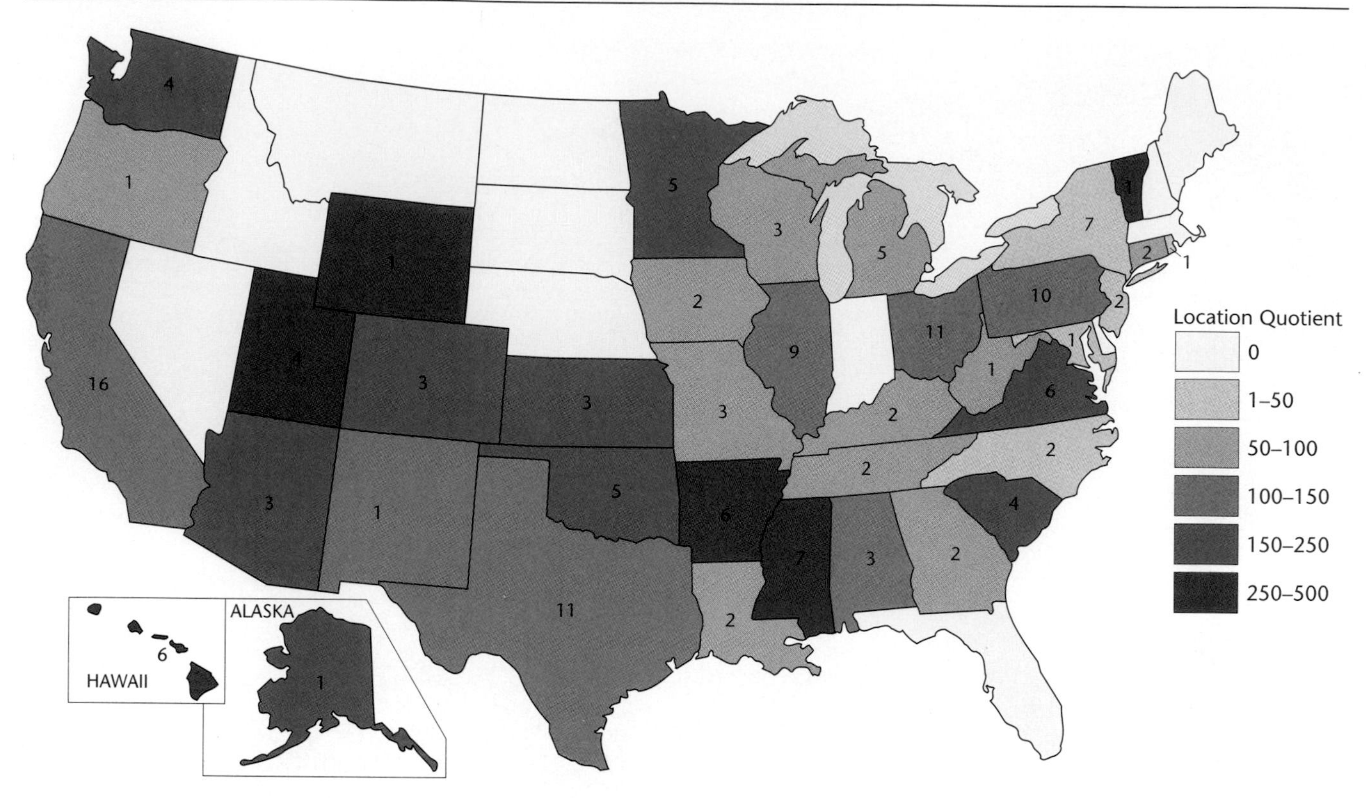

Figure 8.11

Major United States beauty pageant winners, 1921–1988, in proportion to state population. The contests considered were Miss America, Miss USA, Junior Miss, Miss Teenage America, and Miss Teen USA. The location quotient was calculated by multiplying each state's percentage of winners by 100, then dividing by the state's percentage of national population. The figures show the actual number of winners per state. (Source: Walasek, Richard A. "Will Miss Montana Ever Be Chosen?" *North American Culture*, 5, No. 1 [1989]: 62.)

mental maps of the people. Such regions vary greatly in size, from small districts covering only part of a city or town to huge, multistate areas. Like most other geographical regions, they often overlap and usually have poorly defined borders.

An example of a vernacular region—one of hundreds—is "Green Country" in northeastern Oklahoma (Figure 8.12). "Exciting Green Country," proclaims a brochure published by Green Country, Inc., and the Oklahoma Tourism and Recreation Commission, "where a blend of natural beauty, ideal climate and frontier heritage offers visitors a memorable vacation experience." News media based in Tulsa repeatedly drum "Green Country" into the minds of local Oklahomans; billboard advertisements and businesses with "Green Country" as part of their name spread the same message: Northeastern Oklahoma *is* Green Country.

Almost every part of the industrialized Western world offers examples of vernacular regions based in the popular culture. Figure 8.13 shows some province-size popular regions in North America. Geographer Wilbur Zelinsky (see biographical sketch) compiled these regions by determining the most common provincial name appearing in the white pages of urban telephone directories. One curious feature of the map is the sizable, populous district in New York, Ontario, eastern Ohio, and western Pennsylvania where no affiliation to province is perceived. Using a quite different source of information, geographer

Figure 8.12
"Green Country." This popular culture vernacular region includes all of northeastern Oklahoma and manifests itself in state tourism brochures and business names in the town of Tahlequah. Once the proud capital of the Cherokee Indian Nation, Tahlequah is today merely a small town in Green Country. Promotional regions such as this are becoming increasingly common in America. For more detail, see Zdorkowski, R. Todd, and George O. Carney. "This Land Is My Land: Oklahoma's Changing Vernacular Regions." *Journal of Cultural Geography,* 5, No. 2 (1985): 97–106.

Joseph Brownell in 1960 sought to delimit the popular "Midwest" (Figure 8.14). Brownell, in this pioneering study, sent out questionnaires to postal employees in the midsection of the United States, from the Appalachians to the Rockies. He asked each employee whether, in his or her opinion, the community lay in the "Midwest." The results revealed a core area in which the residents looked on themselves as Midwesterners. A similar survey done 20 years later, using student respondents, yielded an almost identical result (Figure 8.14).

Figure 8.13
Some vernacular regions in North America. Cultural geographer Wilbur Zelinsky mapped these regions on the basis of business names in the white pages of metropolitan telephone directories. Why are "West" names more widespread than those containing "East"? What might account for the areas where no region name is perceived? (Adapted with permission from Zelinsky, Wilbur. "North America's Vernacular Regions." *Annals of the Association of American Geographers,* 70 [1980]: 14.)

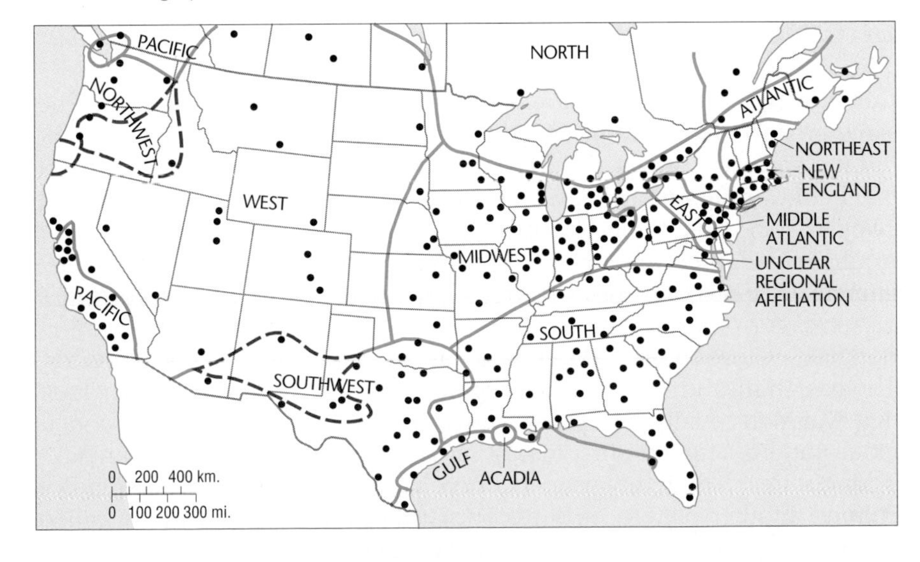

Regional boundary
Regional boundary is uncertain
Telephone directory used in the study

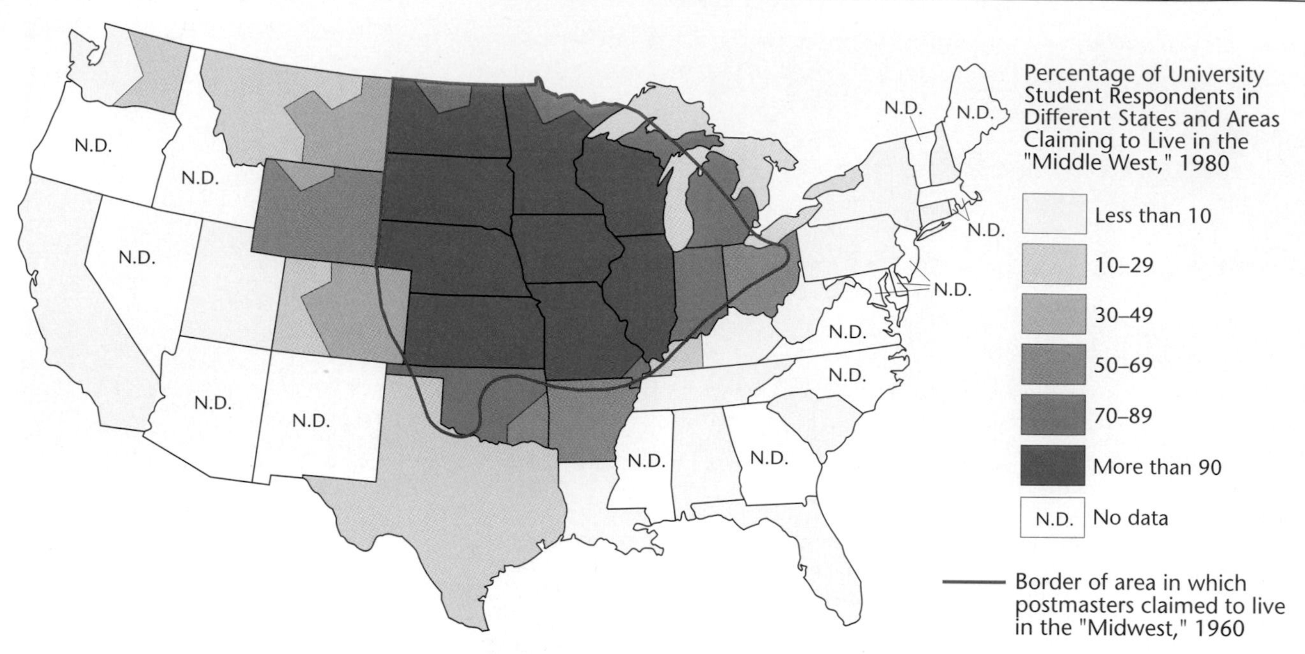

Figure 8.14
The vernacular "Middle West" or "Midwest." Two surveys, taken a generation apart and using two different groups of respondents, yielded similar results. What might account for the differences between this map and Figure 8.13, which utilized still another data base? (Source: Brownell, Joseph W. "The Cultural Midwest." *Journal of Geography,* 59 [1960]: 83; Shortridge, James R. *The Middle West: Its Meaning in American Culture.* Lawrence: University Press of Kansas, 1989.)

Vernacular regions exist on many different scales. A resident of Alabama's "Black Belt," for example, might also claim to reside in "Dixie" and "the South" (see Figure 1.9 in Chapter 1). Regardless of size or origin, vernacular regions of America are perceptual in character. They exist because members of the popular or folk culture perceive them. As befits an element of popular culture, the vernacular region is often perpetuated by the mass media, especially radio and television. In fact, many are initially diffused through the media.

Diffusion in Popular Culture

Culture regions, as you know by now, imply cultural diffusion. The same processes of cultural diffusion described in previous chapters permit the spread of items and ideas of popular culture. We might expect hierarchical diffusion to play a greater role in popular culture, because popular society is highly stratified into classes, unlike folk culture. For example, the spread of McDonald's restaurants in the United States, beginning in 1955, occurred hierarchically for the most part, revealing a bias in favor of larger urban markets. Sometimes, however, diffusion in popular culture works differently, as a study of Wal-Mart reveals. Thomas Graff and Dub Ashton, together with R. Laulajainen, conclude that Wal-Mart intially diffused from its Arkansas base in a largely contagious pattern, reaching first into other parts of Arkansas and into neighboring states. Simultaneously, as often happens in the spatial spread of culture, another pattern of diffusion was at work, a pattern they called *reverse* hierarchical diffusion. Wal-Mart initially chose smaller towns and markets for locations, spreading only later into cities—the precise reverse of the way hierarchical diffusion normally works. This combination of contagious and reverse hierarchical diffusion led Wal-Mart within 30 years to become the nation's largest retailer.

This speed suggests another characteristic of popular cultural diffusion—it progresses far more rapidly than occurs in folk culture, and time-distance decay is considerably weaker. In ancient times, innovations normally required thousands of years to complete their areal spread, and even as recently as the early nineteenth century, the time span was still measured in decades. In the popular culture, modern transportation and communications networks now permit cultural diffusion to occur within weeks or even days. The propensity for change makes diffusion extremely important in the popular culture. The availability of devices permitting rapid diffusion enhances the chance for change in the popular culture.

Wilbur Zelinsky described a personal experience with the lightning-like expansion diffusion of a classic item of popular material culture, the hula hoop. "In August, 1958," he wrote, "I drove from Santa Monica, California, to Detroit at an average rate of about 400 miles per day; and display windows in almost every drugstore and variety store along the way were being hastily stocked with hula hoops just off the delivery trucks from Southern California. A national television program the week before had roused instant cravings. It was an eerie sensation, surfing along a pseudo-innovation wave."

Wilbur Zelinsky
1921–

Wilbur Zelinsky, professor emeritus at Pennsylvania State University, is one of America's most prominent cultural geographers. An Illinoisan by birth, but a "northeasterner by choice and conviction," Zelinsky received his education at the University of California at Berkeley, where he was a student of the famous geographer Carl Sauer. He received his doctorate in 1953.

As the frequent references in this chapter to his work attest, Zelinsky has made numerous important geographical studies of American popular culture, ranging from the diffusion of classical place-names to the spatial patterns of personal given names. One of his most ambitious and imaginative projects was a provocative assessment of the impact of increasingly powerful personal preference on the spatial character of American society. In 1973, Professor Zelinsky published his widely acclaimed book *The Cultural Geography of the United States.* In addition to his research in popular culture, Zelinsky has made substantial contributions in the fields of population and folk geography.

In 1966, Zelinsky received the Award for Meritorious Contributions to the Field of Geography, presented by the Association of American Geographers. He served as president of the association from 1972 to 1973.

Advertising

The most effective device for diffusion in the popular culture, as Zelinsky suggests, confronts us almost every day of our lives. Commercial advertising of retail products and services bombards us visually and orally, with great effect. Using the techniques of social science, especially psychology, advertisers have even learned to sell us products we do not need. The skill with which "Madison Avenue" advertising firms prepare commercials often determines the success or failure of a product. In short, the popular culture is equipped with the most potent devices and techniques of diffusion ever perfected. Grouped under the concept of market advertising, these devices have speeded the diffusionary process and relegated time-distance decay and the neighborhood effect to less important positions.

At the same time, modern advertising is very place-conscious, particularly as messages became less textual, increasingly visual, and dependent on images. As geographers Douglas Fleming and Richard Roth noted recently, images of place now provide a vital component in many ads, and are used to market products and services by linking them to popular, admired places. The "Marlboro Man" cigarette ads provide an excellent example, and even in countries as distant geographically and culturally as Egypt, the romanticized American West is used effectively to sell cigarettes. Is it not remarkable that Egyptian Muslim Arabs should respond favorably to a symbol-laden place image of a land most have never seen or ever hope to see? Such is the power and process of diffusion in the popular culture.

Diffusion of Classical Place-Names

Popular culture is not entirely a new phenomenon. Some of its roots go back to the very beginning of the United States, to the time we were

Figure 8.15
The influence of the Classic Revival. This early manifestation of American popular culture can be seen in classical toponyms that conjure up images of the ancient Roman and Greek world.

naming our towns and cities. An example is the use of classical place-names. If you have traveled much in the United States, particularly in the North and Midwest, you have no doubt encountered town, county, and township names such as Rome, Athens, Syracuse, Troy, Corinth, Arcadia, Euclid, or Homer (Figures 8.15 and 7.27 in Chapter 7). If you live in the United States, these may not seem unusual to you, but is it not strange that in a country with no direct ties to ancient Greece and Rome, so many names of this type appear? They are a product of the so-called Classic Revival, based in the view that America is the latter-day successor to the glories of the Greco-Roman world. This view, which arose with the independence of the United States, persisted through the nineteenth century. Because of it, Americans adopted a neoclassical architecture for public buildings, Latin mottoes and inscriptions (for example, *E Pluribus Unum*), and even Latin and Greek personal names such as Horace, Virgil, and Ulysses. American popular culture took on a decidedly Greco-Roman flavor. The use of place-names derived from Greece and Rome merely represents one aspect of this Classic Revival.

Central New York State served as the hearth area where the innovation of classical town-names first appeared in the 1780s. The cities of that region bear witness to the innovation—Syracuse, Ithaca, Utica, Troy, and Rome. In the decades that followed, on through the nineteenth century, classical names diffused over much of the United States, most commonly in a "classical belt" stretching westward from New York State to central Nebraska and Kansas (Figure 8.16). Some 1500 such names are still in use.

Figure 8.16
Diffusion of classical town-names in the United States, 1780–1910. From a hearth area in upstate New York in the 1780s, classical names diffused across much of America. What might explain the uneven distribution of such names? Do classical town-names occur in your home area? If so, who implanted them there? (After Zelinsky, Wilbur. "Classical Town Names in the United States: The Historical Geography of an American Idea." *Geographical Review*, 57 [1967]: 480, 490, 491.)

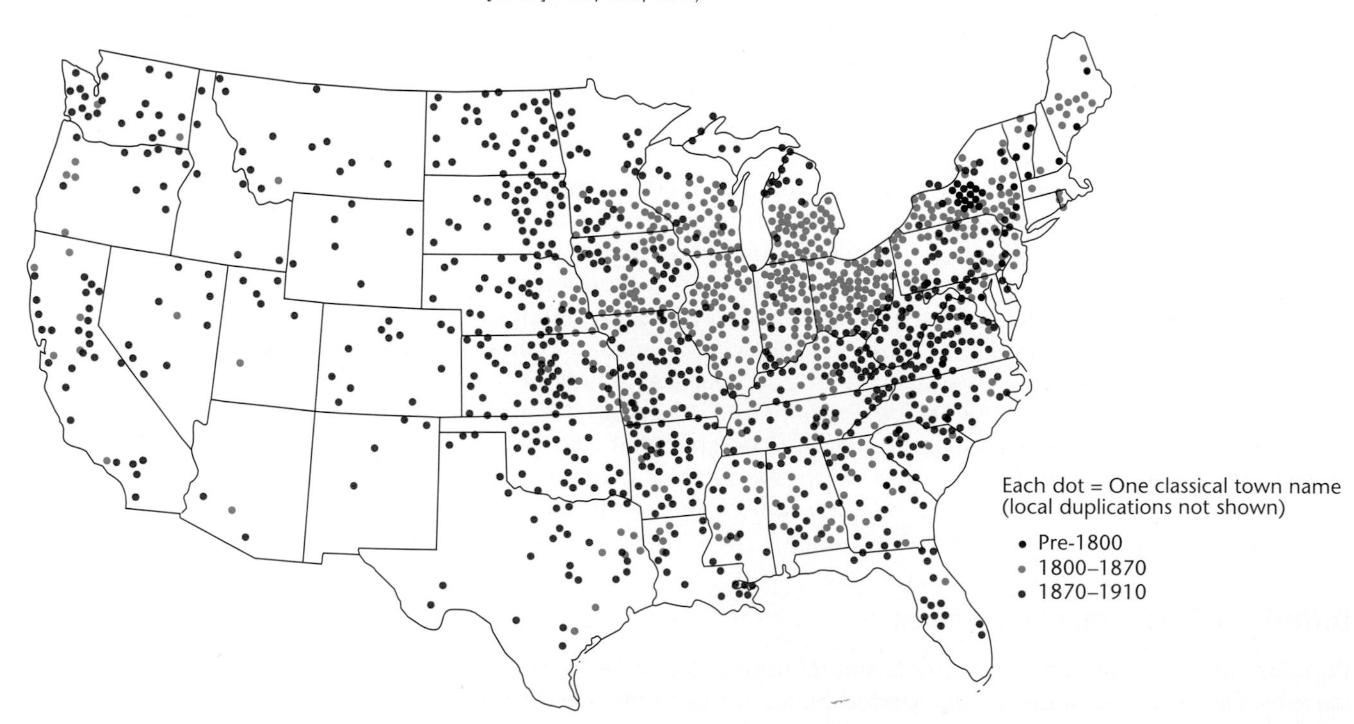

More important, the spread of classical place-names illustrates many of the types and principles of cultural diffusion. Contagious expansion diffusion is suggested by the compact clusters of classical names that occur here and there, as in southern Iowa. The implantation of one or several classical names apparently influenced founders of nearby communities to adopt similar names for their settlements. Relocation diffusion is also apparent, for it is no accident that the density of classical names is greatest along the pathway leading from central New York, the route of thousands of westward-moving settlers. Utica, New York, for example, has namesakes in Ohio, Indiana, Michigan, Illinois, Kansas, and Nebraska—all perpetuating the name of an ancient Phoenician-Roman city in North Africa.

The spread of classical names also suggests hierarchical expansion diffusion. For example, some such names appeared in southern Maine after 1800, east of the core area in central New York. Relocation diffusion is not likely in this instance, since the flow of migrants was westward, and Maine is too remote from central New York to have been affected by contagious diffusion. In all probability, the idea reached Maine through written communications between elite, educated individuals—a perfect example of hierarchical diffusion.

The Canadian–United States boundary between New York and Ontario acted as an absorbing barrier to the diffusion of classical townnames. Canadians, still under British rule as late as 1867, did not envision their country as a latter-day Greece or Rome and found little appeal in classical place-names. To cross into Canada at Niagara or Detroit is to leave "Greece" and "Rome" behind.

Diffusion of the Rodeo

From the Classic Revival to the rodeo may seem a quantum jump, yet popular culture is so diverse as to include both. The American commercial rodeo provides another good example of cultural diffusion (Figure 8.17). Like so many elements of popular culture, the modern rodeo had its origins in folk tradition. Rodeos began simply as roundups of cattle in the Spanish livestock ranching system in northern Mexico and the American Southwest. In fact, the word *rodeo* is derived from the Spanish *rodear,* "to surround" or "to round up."

Figure 8.17
The American rodeo. Commercial rodeos, such as this one in Wyoming, developed from informal cowboy contests, a folk tradition in the American West.

When Anglo-Americans adopted certain Mexican cowboy skills in the nineteenth century, the foundation for riding and roping contests was laid. Cowboys from adjacent ranches began holding contests at roundup time. These competitions initially remained informal displays of the folk skills used in Western cattle ranching. After the Civil War, some cowboy contests on the Great Plains became formalized, with prizes awarded (Figure 8.18).

The transition to commercial rodeo, with admission tickets and grandstands, came quickly as an outgrowth of the formal cowboy contests. One such affair, at North Platte, Nebraska, in 1882, led to the inclusion of some rodeo events in a "Wild West Show" at Omaha in 1883. These shows, which moved by railroad from town to town in the manner of circuses, probably provided the most potent agent of early rodeo diffusion. Within a decade of the Omaha affair, commercial rodeos were being held independently of Wild West shows at several towns, apparently first at Prescott, Arizona, in 1888. The spread moved rapidly, as is typical of cultural diffusion in the popular culture. By the turn of the century, commercial rodeos appeared throughout much of the West. At Cheyenne, Wyoming, the famous Frontier Days rodeo was first

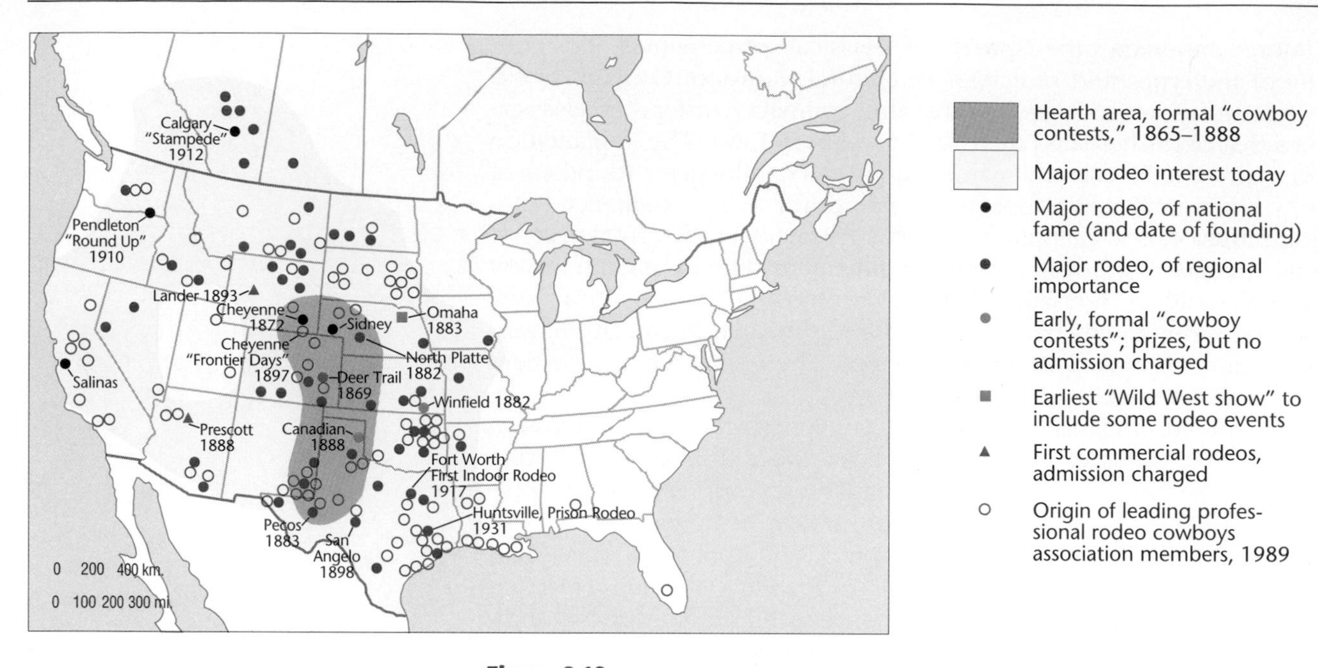

Figure 8.18
Origin and diffusion of the American commercial rodeo. Derived originally from folk culture, rodeos evolved through formal "cowboy contests" and "Wild West shows" to emerge, in the late 1880s and 1890s, in their present popular culture form. The border between the United States and Canada proved no barrier to the diffusion, though Canadian rodeo, like Canadian football, differs in some respects from the US type. (Sources: Pillsbury, Richard. "Ride 'm Cowboy." *Sport Place,* 4 [Fall 1990]: 26–32; Fredriksson, Kristine. *American Rodeo from Buffalo Bill to Big Business.* College Station: Texas A&M University Press, 1984.)

held in 1897. By World War I, the rodeo had also become an institution in provinces of western Canada, where the Calgary Stampede began in 1912.

Today, rodeos are held in almost every community of any size in the western United States. For example, the state of Oklahoma's calendar of events for the period April through September 1977 listed no fewer than 98 scheduled rodeos. Racial and gender lines have been crossed by the rodeo in culturally diverse Oklahoma, producing such events as the Creek Nation All Indian Rodeo at Okmulgee, the All Girls Rodeo at Duncan, and the All Black Rodeo at Wewoka. In Texas and some other states, rodeo competition has become an official high school sport. Professional rodeos are now held in 36 states and three Canadian provinces. Its major acceptance in the popular culture is found west of the Mississippi and Missouri rivers (Figure 8.18).

Absorbing and permeable barriers to the diffusion of commercial rodeo were encountered at the border of Mexico, south of which bullfighting occupies a dominant position, and in the Mormon culture region centered in Utah. A uniquely Mexican form of rodeo, the *charreada,* is popular in central Mexico. Only in California did rodeo popularity penetrate the Cascade and coastal mountain ranges to reach the Pacific shore. As we might expect, the greatest strength of commercial rodeo in the United States lies in the cattle ranching areas.

International Diffusion

Cultural diffusion, even among folk cultures, has never respected international borders, but in popular culture, innovations are diffused between countries and continents as rapidly as jet airplanes and satellite-beamed television programs. As a result, the popular cultures of North America, Europe, and Australia have become rather similar and are constantly in contact with one another.

Country and western music is now heard in Northern Ireland's pubs; Levi-clad Romanians in small towns flock to American-made movies; Americans wait in line to hear touring British rock musicians; Rocky Mountain ski resorts are built in Alpine-Swiss architecture; and the latest Paris clothes fashions appear in American department stores. Fast-food franchises of McDonald's and Kentucky Fried Chicken diffused to Russia, while motel chains such as Holiday Inn took root in Tibet and other countries. Even in many underdeveloped countries, acceptance of Western popular culture occurs among a socioeconomic elite, so that the visitor to a provincial town in India may find a thriving local Lions Club. The international diffusion of popular culture has been so successful that many people now share aspects of a global culture.

Communications Barriers

While the communications media have the potential to allow almost instant diffusion over very large areas, spread can be greatly retarded if access to the media is denied (see box, *The Geography of Rock and Roll*). *Billboard,* a magazine devoted largely to popular music, described such a barrier to diffusion. In a 1977 issue, record company executive Seymour Stein complained that radio stations and disk jockeys refused to play "punk rock" records, denying the style an equal opportunity for exposure. Stein claimed that punk devotees were concentrated in New York City, Los Angeles, Boston, and London, where many young people had found the style reflective of their feelings and frustrations. Without access to radio stations, punk rock could diffuse from these centers only through live concerts and the record sales they

The Geography of Rock and Roll

Diffusion occurs rapidly in popular culture. A style of music, rock and roll, arose in the early 1950s, achieved its maximum diffusion within a decade, then gave way to other music forms. Its chief personality, Elvis Presley, was only 42 years old at the time of his death in 1977, yet the heyday of rock and roll had ended a decade and a half before he died.

The hearth of rock and roll, about 1952 or 1953, was the "Upper Delta" country along the Mississippi River, centered on Memphis, Tennessee. Elvis, Little Richard, Fats Domino, Chuck Berry, and Jerry Lee Lewis, the chief practitioners of rock and roll, all worked in the Upper Delta. The style developed as a blending of African American "rhythm and blues" and Hill Southern white "rockabilly," a fast-tempo country and western style. Diffusion was achieved both through the radio and from sales of inexpensive 45 rpm records, coupled with live concerts. The spread occurred most rapidly between 1955 and 1958; after 1963, rock and roll was in decline, although it influenced many subsequent music styles.

Barriers were encountered in the diffusion. Parental opposition to the music and lyrics as "degraded" led to the banning of rock and roll on radio stations in some cities. The barriers proved to be permeable—explicit sexual references, so common in rhythm and blues and vintage rock and roll, were softened. "Roll with me, Henry" became the less suggestive "Dance with me, Henry."

Hierarchical diffusion was clearly evident. Early adopters were inquisitive, gregarious young people, trendsetters in their generation. From them acceptance spread down through lower hierarchies until the hard core of nonaccepters remained. Similar trendsetters abandoned rock and roll for other rock styles after about 1963, and the major musical phenomenon of the 1950s went into decline.

Adapted from Francaviglia, Richard V. "Diffusion and Popular Culture: Comments on the Spatial Aspects of Rock Music," in David A. Lanegran and Risa Palm (eds.), *An Invitation to Geography.* New York: McGraw-Hill, 1973, pp. 87–96; and from research by Larry Ford.

generated. The publishers of *Billboard* noted that "punk rock is but one of a number of musical forms which initially had problems breaking through nationally out of regional footholds," for *pachanga, ska,* pop/gospel, *"women's music," reggae,* and "gangsta rap" experienced similar difficulties. Similarly, Time Warner Inc., a major distributor of gangsta rap music, had to endure scathing criticism in the United States Congress in 1995, eventually causing them to sell the subsidiary label involved in recording this form of rap. To control the programming of radio and television is to control much of the diffusionary apparatus in popular culture. The diffusion of innovations ultimately depends on the flow of information.

Government censorship can also provide barriers to diffusion, of varying degrees of effectiveness. In 1995 the Islamic fundamentalist regime in Iran, long opposed to what it perceives as the corrupting influences of Western popular culture, outlawed television satellite dishes in an attempt to prevent citizens from watching programs broadcast in foreign countries. Control of the media can approach control of the mind in popular culture, revealing a great deal about diffusion. Even so, repressive regimes must cope with a proliferation of communication methods, including the fax and Internet. The status of inward-looking "hermit" nations is probably no longer attainable, even in totalitarian conditions, so pervasive has cultural diffusion become.

Though potent agents of diffusion in popular culture, newspapers also act as selective barriers, often reinforcing the effect of political boundaries. For example, between 21 and 48 percent of all news published in Canadian newspapers is of foreign origin, mainly involving the flow northward of United States news, while only about 12 percent of all news appearing in papers in the United States comes from foreign areas. One might conclude from this discrepancy that Americans are a more provincial people than Canadians.

The Ecology of Popular Culture

Because popular culture is largely the product of industrialization and the rise of technology, it might seem less directly tied to the physical environment than is folk culture. Gone is the intimate association between people and land known by our folk ancestors. Gone, too, is our direct vulnerability to many environmental forces, though our security is more apparent than real. The adaptive strategies pursued by people functioning within popular cultures have enormous potential for producing ecological disasters, as the concern over atmospheric ozone depletion suggests. Also, because popular culture encourages little intimate contact with and knowledge of the physical world, our environmental perceptions can become quite distorted. Such considerations indicate that the theme of cultural ecology is relevant to the study of popular culture.

Environmental Influence

Even though technology removed the members of popular culture from close touch with nature and reduced many environmental hazards, the physical surroundings can still exert an influence. Indeed, some natural hazards are actually intensified in popular culture. For example, our urbanized society chose to locate many millions of city dwellers astride the major earthquake zone in California, producing the potential for a catastrophe of much greater proportion than a folk culture would face in that area. Similarly, our popular demand for seaside residence greatly increased the number of dwellings susceptible to hurricane destruction along the Gulf Coast, magnifying the inevitable destruction and damage. Also, epidemic diseases can spread more rapidly along our modern transportation networks.

The environmental influence on popular culture can be seen in more frivolous ways as well. Our previous example of American sports provides some suggestion, at least, of environmental influence. Is the greater popularity of basketball and the higher per capita production of players in the North partly a result of colder winters there (Figure 8.19)? Presumably the cold weather might make basketball, a traditional indoor sport, more desirable for spectators. Does cold weather likewise favor bowling and ice hockey, perhaps explaining their greater popularity in northern states and Canada? Surely it is not mere chance that the major college football bowl games are all played in Sun Belt states on the southern border of the United States, or that over 80 percent of the winners of the College Baseball World Series in the past half-century have been teams from the Sun Belt.

Figure 8.19
Basketball is preponderantly a cold climate and cold season game, suggesting some residual environmental influence in popular culture that, increasingly, creates artificial conditions of climate.

Even so, climatic influence on sport is waning. Huge covered stadiums now make it possible to play football and baseball indoors, and artificial wave-making machines permit surfboarding in the Arizona desert (Figure 8.20). Japan tops even this. At Seagaia Ocean Dome at Miyazaki on the island of Kyushu, a huge three-story structure offers indoor surfing thanks to a computer-controlled wave-making machine. The temperature remains at a tropical 84°F (29°C) all year round in the controlled environment at Seagaia, though the world's largest retractable roof permits fresh air in times of perfect weather. Seagaia also boasts palm trees, spotless sandy beaches, an enormous waterslide, 17 restaurants, and no sharks. Nearer to Tokyo, La Laporte Ski Dome, standing 25 stories high, provides year-round indoor skiing for 2000

Figure 8.20
Surfing, once tied to beach locations, can now be practiced in places like the desert, where artificial wave-making machines have been installed. This one is Big Surf of Tempe, in Arizona.

customers at a time, with runs the length of five football fields. Popular culture seems to be moving indoors.

As a result, the popular way of life has become a high-energy-consuming culture. Even the devices of diffusion in the popular culture require large amounts of electricity and gasoline, and countless labor-saving machines add to the seemingly insatiable need for fossil fuels and other energy supplies. Should energy costs rise, we might conceivably reach a point where many aspects of the popular culture could no longer be maintained.

Impact on the Environment

Popular culture makes heavy demands on ecosystems. This is true even in the realm of recreation. Since World War II, leisure time and related recreational activities have increased greatly in the United States, Canada, Europe, and other developed countries. Much leisure time is now spent by members of the popular culture in some space-consuming activity in areas outside the cities. The demand for "wilderness" recreation zones has risen sharply in the last quarter-century, and no end to the increase seems at hand (Figure 8.21).

Hikers, campers, hunters, fishers, bikers, dune buggy and snowmobile enthusiasts, weekend cottagers, surfers, spelunkers, mountain climbers, boaters, sightseers, and others are making unprecedented demands on the open country. Such a massive presence of people in our recreational areas inevitably results in damage to the physical environment. National parks now suffer from traffic jams, residential congestion, litter, and noise pollution—very much like the urban areas (Figure 8.22). A study by geographer Jeanne Kay and her students in Utah revealed substantial environmental damage by off-road recreational vehicles, including "soil loss and long-term soil deterioration." In less congested wilderness districts, as few as several hundred hikers a month can beat down trails to the extent that vegetation is altered, erosion en-

Figure 8.21
Popular culture impacts the environment. Our leisure activities are space-consuming and make heavy demands on the physical environment.

Figure 8.22
Popular culture might be better called "litter culture," as this urban scene suggests.

couraged, and wildlife diminished. Even the best-intentioned, "green"-minded visitors do some damage. One of the paradoxes of the modern age and popular culture seems to be that the more we cluster in cities and suburbs, the greater our impact on open areas. We carry our popular culture with us when we vacation in such regions.

Some countries have reacted to the recreational tourist boom merely by making natural areas ever more accessible, ever more crowded and damaged. Others, including the United States, have now drawn a distinction between national park tourism and wilderness areas. Access to many wild districts is now greatly restricted, in hopes that they can be saved from the damage that necessarily accompanies recreational activity. In some national parks, access by private automobile and camper pickup is restricted, but for the greater part of the countryside, the recreational assault on the environment continues.

Added to the impact of recreational land use on the countryside is the enormous demand for refuse dumps generated by cities. Whether disposed of properly, in landfills, or merely dumped as junk, the refuse of the popular culture is altering the ecology of many rural areas, even in some remote places (Figure 8.23).

Cultural Integration in Popular Culture

The interaction of popular culture and physical environment, while significant, is overshadowed in importance by the internal workings of the culture. The most potent forces shaping any element of popular culture are other elements of the same popular culture. Thus we turn to the theme of cultural integration to increase our understanding of cause-and-effect relationships.

The Convergence Hypothesis

What is the result, geographically, of the interworkings of popular culture? Increased leisure time, instant communications, greater affluence

Figure 8.23
Circle Hot Springs, Alaska. At this very remote place literally at the outermost limit of the North American highway system, the discards of popular culture pile up in a junkyard. Improbably, a hotel appears in the background!

for many, heightened mobility, and weakened attachment to family and place—all attributes of the popular culture—have the potential, in interacting, to cause massive spatial restructuring.

Most social scientists long assumed that the result of such causal forces, especially mobility and the electronic media, would be to homogenize culture, reducing the differences among places. This assumption is called the **convergence hypothesis.** That is, we are supposedly converging in our cultural makeup, becoming more alike. In the geographical sense, this would yield *placelessness,* a concept discussed earlier in the chapter.

Impressive geographical evidence can be marshaled to support this hypothesis. Wilbur Zelinsky, for example, found by comparing the given names of persons in various parts of the United States for the years 1790 and 1968 that a more pronounced regionalization existed in the eighteenth century than today. The personal names bestowed on children by the present generation of parents vary less from place to place than did those of our ancestors two centuries ago.

Mapping Personal Preference

Working against the convergence hypothesis is the greater personal individualism characteristic of the popular culture. Gone is the conformity of folk cultures. What is the geographical result of heightened individualism and personal preference?

Geographer Ronald Abler concluded that individualism, coupled with increasingly rapid communications media, abundant leisure, and widespread wealth, had the ability to create a new regionalism in the popular culture, giving us the will and means to diverge rather than converge. Free exercise of individual preferences, with each person "doing his own thing," could create a new spatial order. Zelinsky concurred, asking "what things will how many persons do, and *where* will they do them?" If we decide to pursue our chosen lifestyles in geographical proximity to others who share our preferences and orientations, then a spatial restructuring will certainly occur. Hints of this trend are seen in certain segregated communities where only the elderly live, as in Sun City, Arizona, and in the residential concentration of gay people in certain districts within cities such as San Francisco (Figure 8.24).

The media cater to and help promote such a restructuring. Special-interest media "narrowcasting," to use Professor Abler's term, can help produce and nurture a spatially diverse popular culture. For example, 163 radio stations in the United States and Canada are oriented to African Americans. In Zelinsky's words, "The increasingly free exercise of individual preferences as to values, pleasures, self-improvement, social and physical habitat, and general lifestyle in an individualistic, affluent national community may have begun to alter the spatial attributes of society and culture."

Place Images

The same media that serve and reflect the rise of personal preference—movies, television, photography, music, advertising, art, and others—often produce *place images,* a subject studied by geographers Jacquelin Burgess and Leo Zonn, among others. Place, portrayer, and medium interact to produce the image, which, in turn, colors our perception and cognition of places and regions we have never visited.

Figure 8.24

Evolution of gay residential and social space in San Francisco in the last half of the twentieth century. Such lifestyle segregation is a typical feature of popular culture. The Castro remains the area most associated with gay culture, where this lifestyle is most openly practiced. (Sources: Adapted and updated from Jackson, Peter. *Maps of Meaning.* London: Unwin Hyman, 1989, p. 126; Jordan, Sonya. Personal communication.)

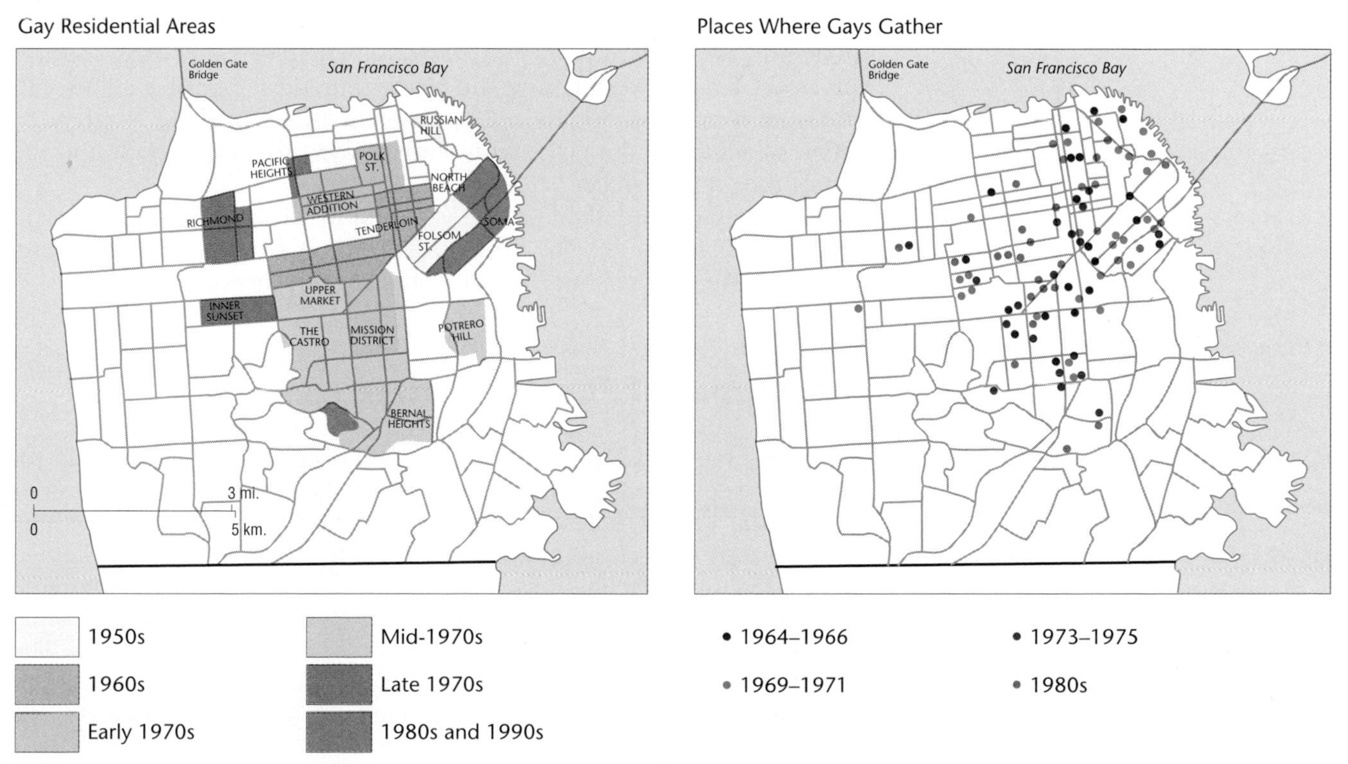

The images, created by the written word, photographs, and movies, may be inaccurate or misleading, but they nevertheless create a world in our minds that has an array of unique places and place-meanings. Our decisions concerning tourism and migration can be influenced by these images. For example, through the media Hawaii has become in the American mind a sort of earthly paradise peopled by scantily clad, eternally happy, invariably good-looking, swarthy natives who live in a setting of unparalleled natural beauty and idyllic climate. People have always formed images of faraway places. Through the interworkings of popular culture, these images proliferate and become more vivid, if not more accurate.

Social Spatialization

British geographer Rob Shields sees the geographical mosaic produced by popular cultural integration from a somewhat different, core/periphery perspective, though he agrees with Abler and Zelinsky that we need to begin "remapping the universalized and homogeneous spatialization of Western Modernity," or popular culture, "to reveal heterogeneous places." He also concurs with Zonn that place images are very powerful. In his book, *Places on the Margin,* Shields devotes particular attention to peripheral areas and locales "left behind in the modern race for progress," either because of remoteness, allowing survival of archaic, even folk lifestyles, or—more central to his main concern—because they are sites of illicit or disdained activities. In either case, a "social spatialization" is produced, and the "*margins* become signifiers of everything *centers* deny or repress." Legalized prostitution in the state of Nevada and gambling casinos in Atlantic City, New Jersey, provide examples. Shields devotes one chapter to the south-coast English resort town of Brighton, which has long had a reputation as a place on the margin where those proper Londoners who are so inclined can spend a "dirty weekend." Another chapter deals with the Canadian North—the Arctic and Subarctic regions of that country where native folk cultures survive at least in vestige and the North American popular culture intrudes more weakly. Southern Canadians mythologized the North as "a counter-balance to the civilized world" of the urbanized South and the seat of the "real" Canada.

Planetary culture, then, is almost certainly illusory in the ascendant age of popular culture. The very interworkings of the popular culture, its integration, work as much against homogenization as for it.

Landscapes of Popular Culture

Landscape mirrors culture. We are what we see and what we build for others to see. Popular culture permeates the landscape of countries such as the United States, Canada, and Australia, including everything from mass-produced suburban houses to golf courses and neon-lighted "strips." So overwhelming is the presence of the popular culture in most American settlement landscapes that an observer must often search diligently to find visual fragments of the older folk cultures. The popular landscape is in continual flux, for change is a hallmark of popular culture.

Elitist Landscapes

A distinctive aspect of popular, as opposed to folk, culture is the development of social classes. A small elite group consisting of persons of wealth, education, and taste occupies the top position in popular cultures. The important geographical fact about such people is that because of their wealth, desire to be around similar people, distinctive tastes, and hedonistic lifestyles, they can and do create distinctive cultural landscapes, often over fairly large areas.

Daniel Gade, a cultural geographer, coined the term *elitist space* to describe such landscapes, using the French Riviera as an example (Figure 8.25). In that district of stunning natural beauty and idyllic climate, he noted, the French elite applied "refined taste to create an aesthetically pleasing cultural landscape" characterized by preservation of old buildings and town cores, a sense of proportion, and respect for scale. Building codes and height restrictions are rigorously enforced. Land values, in response, have risen, making the Riviera ever more elitist, far removed from the folk culture and poverty that prevailed there before 1850. Farmers and fishermen have almost disappeared from the region, though one need but drive a short distance, to Toulon, to find a "scruffy and proletarian port." It seems, then, that the different social classes generated within popular culture become geographically segregated, each producing a distinctive cultural landscape.

America, too, offers elitist landscapes. Exclusive suburbs with rigidly enforced architectural themes are common, as in Santa Fe, where the favored style is pseudo-Pueblo Indian (Figure 8.26). Another excellent example is the *gentleman farm,* an agricultural unit operated

Figure 8.25
The distribution of elitist or hedonistic cultural landscape on the French Riviera. What forces in the popular culture generate such landscapes? (Adapted from Gade, Daniel W. "The French Riviera as Elitist Space." *Journal of Cultural Geography,* 3 [Fall-Winter 1982]: 22.)

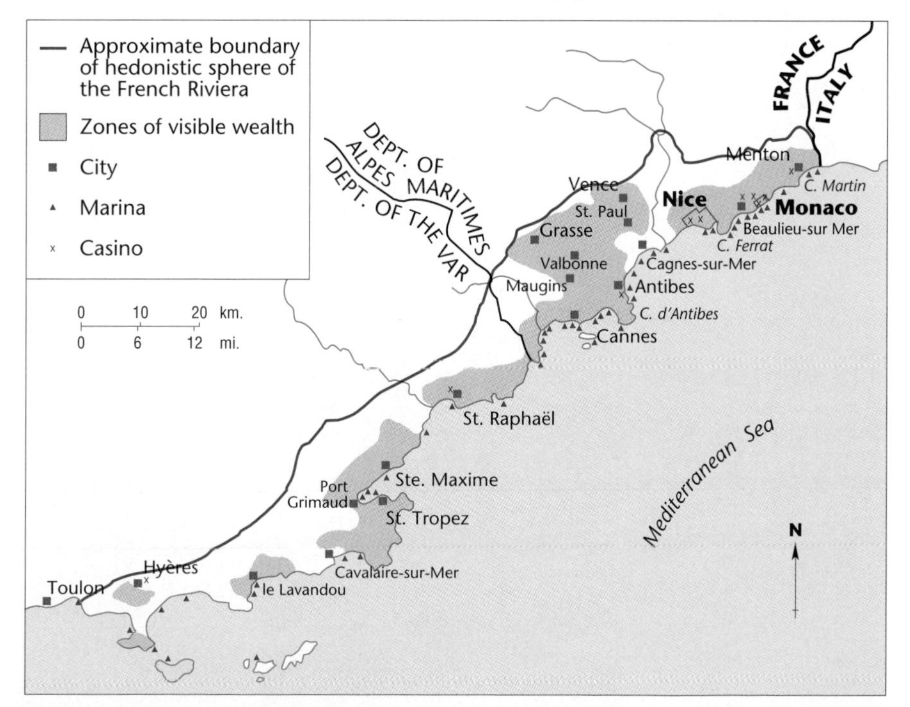

Figure 8.26
An upscale suburb of Santa Fe, New Mexico. Here architectural influences derived from the folk culture of the Pueblo Indians are required by law, producing a striking if ironic elitist landscape. The design, of course, is merely pseudo-Puebloan, since most of these houses are built in typical suburban balloon-frame construction and disguised with plaster and paint to look like adobe walls. A perplexing lack of genuineness, so typical of popular cultural landscapes, is the result.

for pleasure rather than profit (Figure 8.27). Typically, gentleman farms are owned by affluent city people as an avocation, and such farms help to create or maintain a high social standing for those who own them. Some rural landscapes in America now contain many such gentleman farms; perhaps most notable among these areas are the inner Bluegrass Basin of north-central Kentucky, the Virginia Piedmont west of Washington, DC, eastern Long Island in New York, and parts of southeastern Pennsylvania. Gentleman farmers engage in such activities as breeding fine cattle, racing horses, or hunting foxes.

Figure 8.27
Gentleman farm in the Kentucky Bluegrass region near Lexington. Here is "real" rural America as it should be (but never was).

Geographer Karl Raitz made a study of gentleman farms in the Kentucky Bluegrass Basin, where the concentration is so great that they constitute a dominant feature of the cultural landscape (Figure 8.28). The result is an idyllic scene, a rural landscape created more for appearance than for function. Professor Raitz provided a list of visual indicators of Kentucky gentleman farms: wooden fences, either painted white or creosoted black; an elaborate entrance gate; a fine hand-painted sign giving the name of the farm and owner; a network of surfaced, well-maintained driveways and pasture roads; and a large, elegant house, visible in the distance from the public highway through a lawnlike parkland dotted with clumps of trees and perhaps a pond or two. So attractive are these estates to the eye that tourists cruise the

Figure 8.28
The gentleman farm is an elitist landscape feature in central Kentucky. Why might a concentration have developed there? How does such a landscape differ from one that might be produced by a folk culture? (After Raitz, 44.)

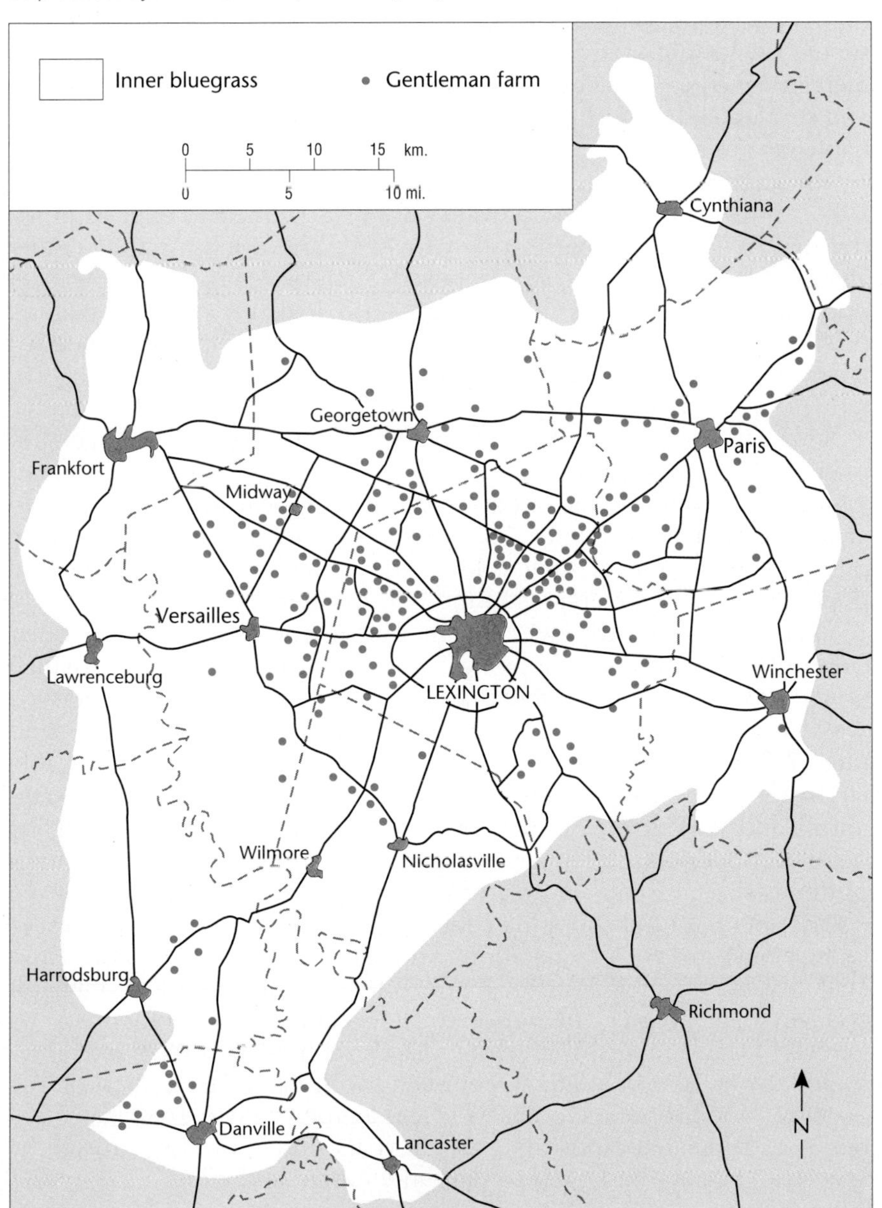

rural lanes to view them, convinced they are seeing the "real" rural America, or at least rural America as it ought to be.

Landscapes of Consumption

Not all popular landscapes are elitist of course. The eye-catching, ubiquitous commercial "strips" along urban arterial streets provide a case in point (Figure 8.2). Geographer Robert Sack has used the term "landscape of consumption," very appropriate for such places.

In an Illinois college town, two other cultural geographers, John Jakle and Richard Mattson, made a study of the evolution of such a strip, covering the period 1919 to 1979. During that 60-year span, the street under study changed from single-family residential to a commercial focus (Figure 8.29). The researchers suggested a five-stage model of strip evolution, beginning with the single-family residential period. In stage 2, the introduction of gasoline stations forms the vanguard of commercialization, while in stage 3 other businesses join the growing number of filling stations, multiunit housing becomes common, and absentee ownership increases. Stage 4 is clearly dominated by the commercial function; businesses catering to the drive-in trade proliferate and residential use declines sharply. Income levels of the remaining inhabitants are low.

In stage 5, the residential function of the street disappears and a totally commercial landscape prevails. Business properties expand in order that off-street parking can be provided, and often a public outcry against the ugliness of the strip is raised. Such places not only represent popular aesthetic values, but perhaps also reveal social and cultural problems that need redress. On the other hand, they may be a needed antidote to the plastic artificiality of elitist landscapes. Moreover, we must be aware that the people who create the landscape likely perceive it differently, in a less elitist way, than do visitors. For example, geographer Yi-Fu Tuan suggests that a commercial strip of stores, hamburger joints, filling stations, and used-car lots may appear as visual blight to an outsider, but the owners or operators of the businesses are very proud of them and of their role in the community. Hard work and hopes color their perceptions of the popular landscape.

Perhaps no landscape of consumption is more reflective of popular culture than the indoor shopping mall, numerous examples of which now dot both urban and suburban landscapes. Of these, the grandest is West Edmonton Mall in the Canadian province of Alberta, and geographer Jeffrey Hopkins recently published a study of this remarkable landscape. Enclosing some 5.2 million square feet (483,000 square miles) and completed in 1986, West Edmonton Mall employs 18,000 people in over 600 stores and services, accounts for nearly one-fourth of the total retail space in greater Edmonton, earned 42 percent of the dollars spent in local shopping centers, and experienced 2800 crimes in its first nine months of operation. And there is more. West Edmonton Mall boasts a water park, sea aquarium, ice skating rink, minigolf course, roller coaster, 19 movie theaters, and a 360-room hotel. Its "streets" feature motifs from exotic places such as New Orleans, represented by a Bourbon Street complete with fiberglass ladies of the evening. Hopkins refers to this as a "landscape of myth and elsewhereness," a "simulated landscape" that reveals the "growing intrusion of spectacle, fantasy, and escapism into the urban landscape."

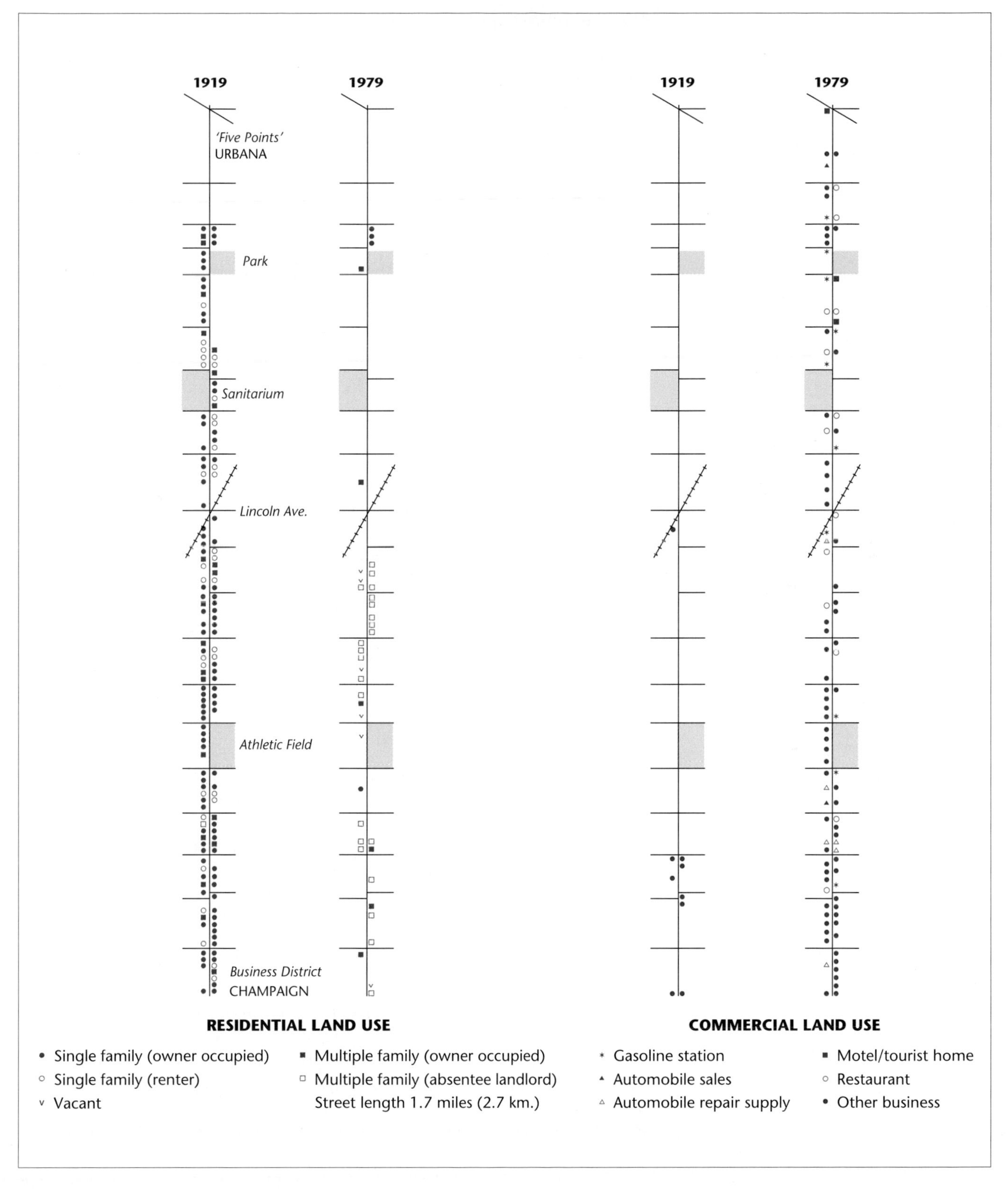

Figure 8.29
The evolution of a commercial strip in Champaign-Urbana, Illinois, 1919–1979. In this way, popular culture reshaped a landscape. (Adapted from Jakle and Mattson, pp. 14, 20.)

Leisure Landscapes

Clearly, West Edmonton Mall represents more than a mere landscape of consumption, for it is designed as much or more for leisure as for shopping. Karl Raitz uses the term *leisure landscapes* to describe such features. Given the fact that increased leisure is one of the hallmarks of popular culture, the spread of related landscapes comes as no surprise.

Leisure landscapes take many forms, and many are related to tourism. For example, geographers Robert Mings and Kevin McHugh describe the "RV resort landscape" of greater Phoenix, where "recreational nomads" spend the winter months. Arnold Holder refers to the "golfscape" created by that popular sport, and you should know that in the United States alone golf courses occupy an area twice the size of the state of Delaware. Still another geographer, Richard Hecock, dealt with kindred *amenity landscapes,* such as in the Minnesota North Woods lake country, where, in one area he sampled, fully 40 percent of all dwellings were not permanent residences but instead weekend cottages or vacation homes. These are often rustic or even humble in appearance.

The past, reflected in relict buildings, also has been drawn into the leisure landscape. Most often, collections of old structures are relocated to "historylands," often enclosed by imposing wire-link fences and open only during certain seasons or hours. If the desired bit of visual history has perished, Americans and Canadians do not hesitate to rebuild it from scratch, undisturbed by the lack of authenticity, as for example at Jamestown, Virginia, or Louisbourg on Cape Breton Island. Normally the history parks are segregated and sanitized to the extent that people no longer live in them. Role-playing actors sometimes prowl these parks, pretending to live in some past era, adding "elsewhen" to "elsewhereness."

The American Scene

Leisure, elitism, and consumption provide only several features of the popular landscape. One perceptive and sensitive cultural geographer, David Lowenthal, attempted a broader analysis, an overall evaluation of the visible impact of popular culture in the American countryside. In an article entitled "The American Scene," Lowenthal lists the main characteristics of popular landscape in the United States. Among these are the "cult of bigness"; the tolerance of present ugliness to achieve a supposedly glorious future; emphasis on individual features at the expense of aggregates, producing a "casual chaos"; and the preeminence of function over form.

The fondness for massive structures is reflected in edifices such as the Empire State Building, the Pentagon, the San Francisco–Oakland Bay Bridge, or Salt Lake City's Mormon Temple. Americans have dotted their cultural landscape with the world's largest of this or that, perhaps in an effort to match the grand scale of the physical environment, which offers such superlatives as the Grand Canyon, the redwoods, and the Yellowstone geysers.

Americans, says Lowenthal, tend to regard their cultural landscape as unfinished. Because of this, they are "predisposed to accept present structures that are makeshift, flimsy, and transient," resembling "throwaway stage sets." Similarly, the hardships of pioneer life perhaps preconditioned Americans to value function more highly than beauty. The state capitol grounds in Oklahoma City are adorned with little more

Figure 8.30
Oil derrick on the Oklahoma state capitol grounds. The landscape of American popular culture is characterized by such functionality. The public and private sectors of the economy are increasingly linked in the popular culture.

than oil derricks, standing above busy pumps drawing wealth from the Sooner soil—an extreme but revealing view of the American landscape (Figure 8.30).

Individual landscape features, says Lowenthal, take precedence over groupings. Five buildings or houses in a row may display five different architectural styles, and rarely is an attempt made to erect assemblages of structures that "belong" together. "Places are only collections of heterogeneous buildings." To be worthy, each structure must be unique and eye-catching, and architects in the popular culture vie with one another in producing attention-grabbing edifices. Each fast-food chain seems to require its own outlandish style of structure to facilitate instant visual recognition by potential customers. Australians share this fondness for unique designs, a predilection that is well reflected in the famous opera house at Sydney (Figure 8.31).

Perhaps no aspect of the American scene is more revealing than residential front yards (Figure 8.32). A dwelling set back from the street, with the nonfunctional intervening space covered by an expanse of grassy lawn, has since the early 1800s been one of the most pervasive symbols of the suburban Anglo-American popular landscape. In the United States, manicured lawns, well-doused with fertilizers, herbicides, and insecticides, now occupy an area equal to the size of Pennsylvania! Homeowners who neglect to tend these lawns properly, or who put the space into some functional use such as vegetable gardening, invite the animosity and contempt of their neighbors, not to mention the lowering of property value or violation of building codes. For most of us, the grass-covered front yard is so universally accepted that we assume it to be a part of the natural order of things in suburbia.

Anglos migrating west in the nineteenth century brought the front lawn with them, even into the desert areas of the American Southwest, where irrigation was necessary to maintain the grass. The desert became dotted with green suburban oases. In cities such as Tucson, the Anglo dwellings flanked by lawns stood in marked contrast to the older Hispano houses, which either lacked yards altogether or had bare-earth areas.

Geographer Melvin Hecht documented the subsequent decline of

Figure 8.31
The Australian scene. The opera house at Sydney, designed by a Dane, is a fine example of public architecture in the popular culture—unique, eye-catching, and a departure from tradition.

the grass lawn tradition. Increasingly, Anglo Southwesterners turned to "desert front" yards, where grass gave way to gravel, crushed rock, desert plants, paving, or undisturbed desert (Figure 8.32). A few innovators among the Anglos adopted such yards even in the early part of this century, but the rapid rise of the desert front yard began in the 1950s, spurred by a new wave of urban immigrants who found the desert beautiful rather than repulsive. In the manner of typical hierarchical diffusion, acceptance occurred earliest in the higher-priced subdivisions and spread gradually to the middle-class districts. Professor Hecht found that fully one-half of all houses built in Tucson between 1965 and 1975 had desert front yards. Some of these are covered with gravel dyed green, a simulation of the lawn and a classic example of a permeable barrier in cultural diffusion, but most represent complete departures from the older custom. Hecht concluded that the decline of the lawn tradition heralded the emergence of a new, distinct popular culture region, one that reflected an appreciation of Arizona's natural set-

Figure 8.32
A suburban grass lawn in Detroit contrasts with the Phoenix "desert front" yard. The landscape of popular culture, then, also reveals contrasts and "places," not merely placelessness.

ting and Hispanic heritage. Desert fronts have since diffused to become part of the popular cultural landscape in neighboring states and even beyond. It is perhaps symptomatic of the visual excesses of popular culture that desert fronts are now appearing in high-rainfall states such as Florida, where plastic sheets have to be installed under the gravel layer to prevent grass and weeds from emerging.

Conclusion

Popular culture, then, possesses a vivid, if at times amusing, depressing, or simply absurd geography. Through the theme of culture region, we revealed the counteracting popular trends toward placelessness and lifestyle spatial clustering. Diffusion of the popular culture, as we saw, occurs more rapidly than in folk times because of the technologies of communication and transportation, as well as the medium of advertising, a child of the popular culture. Ecologically, the influence of the physical environment on daily life has diminished, perhaps merely concealing our continued vulnerability at the very time when our ability to modify the habitat has reached unprecedented heights. The theme of cultural integration allowed us to look at the contradictory forces of individualism versus convergence. The interplay between these opposed forces underlies and helps explain the tension between clustering and placelessness noted in the section on culture region. Finally, an analysis of certain types of popular landscapes—elitist, consumptive, and leisure—allowed us to grasp the variety and magnitude of visual change being wrought by the popular culture.

One form of human diversity that has survived and even thrived in the popular culture is ethnicity. In Chapter 9 we will turn our attention to ethnic geography.

Sources and Suggested Readings

Abler, Ronald F. "Monoculture or Miniculture? The Impact of Communication Media on Culture in Space," in David A. Lanegran and Risa Palm (eds.), *An Invitation to Geography*. New York: McGraw-Hill, 1973, pp. 186–195.

Adams, Paul C. "Television as Gathering Place." *Annals of the Association of American Geographers*, 82 (1992): 117–135.

Aitken, Stuart C., and Leo E. Zonn (eds.). *Place, Power, Situation, and Spectacle: A Geography of Film*. Savage, MD: Rowman & Littlefield, 1993.

Bale, John. *Sports Geography*. New York: Spon, 1989.

Ballas, Donald J., and Margaret J. King. "Cultural Geography and Popular Culture: Proposal for a Creative Merger." *Journal of Cultural Geography*, 2 (1981): 154–163.

Bastian, Robert W. "The Prairie Style House: Spatial Diffusion of a Minor Design." *Journal of Cultural Geography*, 1 (1980): 50–65.

Blake, Peter. *God's Own Junkyard: The Planned Deterioration of America's Landscape*, 2d ed. New York: Holt, Rinehart and Winston, 1979.

Bloomfield, A. Victoria. "Tim Hortons: Growth of a Canadian Coffee and Doughnut Chain." *Journal of Cultural Geography*, 14, No. 2 (1994): 1–16.

Bunce, Michael. *The Countryside Ideal: Anglo-American Landscape*. New York: Routledge, 1994.

Burgess, Jacquelin A., and John R. Gold (eds.). *Geography, the Media, and Popular Culture*. New York: St. Martin's Press, 1985.

Butler, R. W. "The Geography of Rock: 1954–1970." *Ontario Geography*, 24 (1984): 1–33.

Carlson, Alvar W. "The Contributions of Cultural Geographers to the Study of Popular Culture." *Journal of Popular Culture*, 11 (1978): 830–831.

Carney, George O. (ed.). *Fast Food, Stock Cars, and Rock 'n' Roll: Place and Space in American Pop Culture.* Lanham, MD: Rowman & Littlefield, 1995.

Carney, George O. (ed.). *The Sounds of People and Places: Readings in the Geography of American Folk and Popular Music,* 3d ed. Lanham, MD: Rowman & Littlefield, 1994.

Carstensen, Laurence W., Jr. "The Burger Kingdom: Growth and Diffusion of McDonald's Restaurants in the United States, 1955–1978." *Geographical Perspectives,* 58 (1986): 1–8.

Curtis, James R. "The Boutiquing of Cannery Row." *Landscape,* 25 (1981): 44–48.

Curtis, James R., and Daniel D. Arreola. "Through Gringo Eyes: Tourist Districts in the Mexican Border Cities as Other-Directed Places." *North American Culture,* 5 (1989): 19–32.

Curtis, James R., and Richard F. Rose. "The 'Miami Sound': A Contemporary Latin Form of Place-Specific Music." *Journal of Cultural Geography,* 4, No. 1 (1983): 110–118.

Eckbo, Garrett. "The Landscape of Tourism." *Landscape,* 18 (1969): 29–31.

Fleming, Douglas K., and Richard Roth. "Place in Advertising." *Geographical Review,* 81 (1991): 281–291.

Ford, Larry R., and Floyd M. Henderson. "The Image of Place in American Popular Music: 1890–1970." *Places,* 1 (1974): 31–37.

Francaviglia, Richard V. "Diffusion and Popular Culture: Comments on the Spatial Aspects of Rock Music," in David A. Lanegran and Risa Palm (eds.), *An Invitation to Geography*. New York: McGraw-Hill, 1973, pp. 87–96.

Gade, Daniel W. "The French Riviera as Elitist Space." *Journal of Cultural Geography,* 3 (1982): 19–28.

Godfrey, Brian J. "Regional Depiction in Contemporary Film." *Geographical Review,* 83 (1993): 428–440.

Graff, Thomas O., and Dub Ashton. "Spatial Diffusion of Wal-Mart: Contagious and Reverse Hierarchical Elements." *Professional Geographer,* 46 (1994): 19–29

Griffin, Ernst C., and Larry R. Ford. "Tijuana: Landscape of a Culture Hybrid." *Geographical Review,* 66 (1976): 435–447.

Gritzner, Charles F. "Geomythography (Geographic Myths as Popular Culture)," in Mark Gordon and Jack Nachbar (eds.), *Currents of Warm Life: Popular Culture in American Higher Education*. Bowling Green, OH: Bowling Green University Popular Press, 1980, pp. 118–122.

Hecht, Melvin E. "The Decline of the Grass Lawn Tradition in Tucson." *Landscape,* 19 (June 1975): 3–10.

Hecock, Richard D. "Changes in the Amenity Landscape: The Case of Some Northern Minnesota Townships." *North American Culture,* 3, No. 1 (1987): 53–66.

Higley, Stephen R. *Privilege, Power, and Place: The Geography of the American Upper Class.* Lanham, MD: Rowman & Littlefield, 1995.

Holder, Arnold. "Dublin's Expanding Golfscape." *Irish Geography,* 26 (1993): 151–157.

Hopkins, Jeffrey. "West Edmonton Mall: Landscape of Myths and Elsewhereness." *Canadian Geographer,* 34 (1990): 2–17.

Horwitz, Richard P. *The Strip: An American Place*. Lincoln: University of Nebraska Press, 1985.

Inge, M. Thomas (ed.). *Handbook of American Popular Culture*. 3 vols. Westport, CT: Greenwood Press, 1978–1981.

Jakle, John A. *The Tourist: Travel in Twentieth-Century America*. Lincoln: University of Nebraska Press, 1985.

Jakle, John A., and Richard L. Mattson. "The Evolution of a Commercial Strip." *Journal of Cultural Geography,* 1, No. 2 (1981): 12–25.

Jakle, John A., and David Wilson. *Derelict Landscapes: The Wasting of America's Built Environment*. Savage, MD: Rowman & Littlefield, 1992.

Journal of Popular Culture. An interdisciplinary journal published by the Popular Culture Association and Bowling Green State University. Volume 1 appeared in 1967. See in particular Vol 11, No. 4, 1978, a special issue on cultural geography and popular culture.

Kay, Jeanne, et al. "Evaluating Environmental Impacts of Off-Road Vehicles." *Journal of Geography,* 80 (1981): 10–18.

Kunstler, James H. *The Geography of Nowhere: The Rise and Decline of America's Man-Made Landscape.* New York: Simon & Schuster, 1993.

Lowenthal, David. "The American Scene." *Geographical Review,* 58 (1968): 61–88.

McConnell, Harold. "Baseball Is a Warm-Weather Game." *Sport Place,* 8, No. 1 (1994): 5–37.

McPherson, E. Gregory, and Renee A. Haip. "Emerging Desert Landscape in Tucson." *Geographical Review,* 79 (1989): 435–449.

Mings, Robert C., and Kevin E. McHugh. "The RV Resort Landscape." *Journal of Cultural Geography,* 10 (1989): 35–49.

Ojala, Carl F., and Michael T. Gadwood. "The Geography of Major League Baseball Player Production, 1876–1988." *Sports Place,* 3, No. 3 (1989): 24–35.

Pillsbury, Richard. "Carolina Thunder: A Geography of Southern Stock Car Racing." *Journal of Geography,* 73 (1974): 39–47.

Raitz, Karl B. "Gentleman Farms in Kentucky's Inner Bluegrass." *Southeastern Geographer,* 15 (1975): 33–46.

Raitz, Karl B. "Place, Space and Environment in America's Leisure Landscapes." *Journal of Cultural Geography,* 8, No. 1 (1987): 49–62.

Relph, Edward. *Place and Placelessness.* London: Pion, 1976.

Rooney, John F., Jr. *A Geography of American Sport.* Reading, MA: Addison-Wesley, 1974.

Rooney, John F., Jr. "Up From the Mines and Out From the Prairies: Some Geographical Implications of Football in the United States." *Geographical Review,* 59 (1969): 471–492.

Rooney, John F., Jr., and Richard Pillsbury. *Atlas of American Sport.* New York: Macmillan, 1992.

Sack, Robert D. *Place, Modernity, and the Consumer's World: A Rational Framework for Geographical Analysis.* Baltimore: Johns Hopkins University Press, 1992.

Sculle, Keith A. "The Vernacular Gasoline Station: Examples from Illinois and Wisconsin." *Journal of Cultural Geography,* 1, No. 2 (1981): 56–74.

Shields, Rob. *Places on the Margin: Alternative Geographies of Modernity.* London: Routledge, 1991.

Shortridge, James R. "The Concept of the Place-Defining Novel in American Popular Culture." *Professional Geographer,* 43 (1991): 280–291.

Sport Place: An International Journal of Sports Geography deals with this important aspect of popular culture. Published by Black Oak Press, Stillwater, OK. Volume 1 appeared in 1987.

Utne, Eric (ed.). "Cyberhood Versus Neighborhood," a special section with contributions by John P. Barlow, M. Kadi, and Howard Rheingold. *Utne Reader,* 68, No. 3 (1995): 52–64.

Vale, Thomas R., and Geraldine R. Vale. *Western Images, Western Landscapes: Travels Along U.S. 89.* Tucson: University of Arizona Press, 1989.

Weiss, Michael J. *The Clustering of America.* New York: Harper & Row, 1988.

Weiss, Michael J. *Latitudes and Attitudes: An Atlas of American Tastes, Trends, Politics, and Passions.* New York: Little, Brown, 1994.

Zelinsky, Wilbur. "Classical Town Names in the United States: The Historical Geography of an American Idea." *Geographical Review,* 57 (1967): 463–495.

Zelinsky, Wilbur. *The Cultural Geography of the United States,* 2d ed. Englewood Cliffs, NJ: Prentice-Hall, 1992.

Zelinsky, Wilbur. "Cultural Variation in Personal Name Patterns in the Eastern United States." *Annals of the Association of American Geographers,* 60 (1970): 743–769.

Zelinsky, Wilbur. "North America's Vernacular Regions." *Annals of the Association of American Geographers,* 70 (1980): 1–16.

Zelinsky, Wilbur. "Selfward Bound? Personal Preference Patterns and the Changing Map of American Society." *Economic Geography,* 50 (1974): 144–179.

Zonn, Leo (ed.). *Place Images in Media: Portrayal, Experience, and Meaning.* Savage, MD: Rowman & Littlefield, 1990.

The scenes in Figure 8.2 were taken in the following unplaces: McDonald's in Tokyo, Wendy's in Idaho, and Pampas Grill in Finland.

Self Park
W RANDOLPH ST
150 N
THE LASALLE BANKS CHICAGO MARATHON
OCT 15
W RANDOLPH ST
CHICAGO BAR & GRILL

CHAPTER 9

Ethnic Geography

A statue of the American national hero Paul Revere, mounted on his horse, towers over a pedestrian mall near the Old North Church in Boston. Close by is the Revere home, lovingly preserved. As American as apple pie, you may say, a shrine to national independence. But what language are the elderly women speaking as they sit on benches near the statue and go about their knitting? Certainly it is not good Yankee English, by the sound of it. Closer inspection reveals Italian family names on almost every business establishment in Revere's neighborhood, like Giuffre's Fish Market, Italian pizza parlors, an Italian-dominated outdoor vegetable market, a Sons of Italy lodge hall, and Italian-American women leaning out of upper-story windows on opposite sides of the street to converse, Naples-style. Revere, himself of French ethnic extraction, would be astounded. Boston's North End is Italian! A pilgrimage to the site where the American Revolution began has become a trip to Little Italy.

The midwestern town of Wilber, settled by Bohemian immigrants beginning about 1865, bills itself as "The Czech Capital of Nebraska" and annually invites visitors to attend a "National Czech Festival." Celebrants are promised Czech foods like *koláče, jaternice,* poppyseed cake, and *jelita;* Czech folk dancing; "colored Czech postcards and souvenirs" imported from Europe; and handicraft items made by Nebraska Czechs (bearing an official seal and trademark to prove authenticity). "Czech Foods, Czech Refreshments, Czech Bands," proclaim the festival leaflets, offering "breathtaking pageants of old world history" as well. "Many shops are decorated in the Czech motif and ethnic music can be heard on the streets during most hours of the day. Many items of Czech heritage . . . are sold. Czech baking and meat items are offered daily by local merchants who use authentic recipes." Thousands of visitors attend the festival each year. Without leaving Nebraska, these tourists can move on to "Norwegian Days" at Newman Grove, the "Greek Festival" at Bridgeport, the Danish "Grundlovs Fest" in Dannebrog, "German Heritage Days" at McCook, the "Swedish Festival" at Stromsburg, the "St. Patrick's Day Celebration" at O'Neill, several Indian tribal "powwows," and assorted other ethnic celebrations (Figure 9.1).

Figure 9.1
The town of Stromsburg, Nebraska.
Proud of its Swedish heritage, Stromsburg holds a "Swedish Festival" each year in June.

Obviously, the United States retains, in both urban and rural areas, an ethnic crazy-quilt pattern, and ethnic groups continue to form one of the brightest hues of the human mosaic. The same is true of Canada, Russia, China, and many other countries.

What exactly is an **ethnic group?** A great deal of controversy has surrounded attempts to formulate an accepted definition. The word *ethnic* is derived from the Greek word *ethnos,* meaning a "people" or "nation," but that definition is too broad. For our purposes, "ethnic group" means people of common ancestry and cultural tradition, living as a minority in a larger society, or **host culture.** A strong feeling of group identity, of *belonging,* characterizes ethnicity. Membership in an ethnic group is involuntary, in the sense that a person cannot simply decide to join; instead, he or she must be born into the group. Often, however, individuals choose to discard their ethnicity.

Perhaps the main difficulty encountered in defining *ethnic* is that different groups base their identities on different traits. For some, such as the Jews, ethnicity primarily means religion; for the Amish, it is both folk culture and religion; for African Americans, it is skin color; for Swiss-Americans, it is national origin; for German-Americans, it is ancestral language; for Cuban-Americans, it is perhaps mainly anti-Castro, anti-Marxist sentiment. Race, religion, language, folk culture, place of origin, and politics can all help provide the basis of the we/they dichotomy that underlies ethnicity.

Ethnic groups are the keepers of distinctive cultural traditions and the focal point of various kinds of social interaction. They can provide not only group identity but also friendships, marriage partners, recreational outlets, business success, and a political power base. These groups offer the cultural security and reinforcement so essential for minorities, but they can also give rise to suspicion, friction, distrust, clannishness, and even violence.

This is not to say that ethnic minorities remain unchanged by their host culture. **Acculturation** occurs, meaning that the ethnic group adopts enough of the ways of the host society to be able to function economically and socially. On the other hand, **assimilation** implies a complete blending with the host culture, involving the loss of all distinctive ethnic traits. For example, the American host culture now includes many descendants of Germans, Scots, Irish, French, Swedes, and Welsh. Intermarriage is perhaps the most effective assimilatory device. Many students of American culture have long assumed that all ethnic groups would be assimilated in the American "melting pot," but relatively few have been. In fact, the past quarter-century has witnessed a resurgence of ethnic identity in the United States, Canada, Europe, and elsewhere. Indeed, ethnicity easily made the transition from folk to popular culture, confounding many social scientists who predicted assimilation. As a result, popular culture reveals a vivid ethnic component.

Ethnic geography is the study of the spatial and ecological aspects of ethnicity. Ethnic groups often practice unique adaptive strategies and normally occupy clearly defined areas, whether rural or urban. In other words, the study of ethnicity has built-in geographical dimensions, and ethnic geography is the result (see biographical sketch of Walter Kollmorgen). Not suprisingly, then, an American Ethnic Geography Specialty Group exists within the major professional organization, the Association of American Geographers.

Earlier, in Chapter 4, we considered ethnicity and ethnic separatism in the political geographical context. The concept of ethnic geography also appeared implicitly in the chapters on language and religion, but the heightened ethnic awareness in the modern world makes it imperative that we now devote an entire chapter to this inherently geographical phenomenon.

Ethnic Regions

Our five themes of cultural geography are well suited to the study of ethnic groups. Because such peoples typically occupy compact territories, we can map ethnic formal culture regions. Such ethnic regions exist in most countries, from Brazil to China (Figure 9.2).

Two quite distinct geographical types of ethnic regions exist. The first involves ethnic minorities who reside in ancient home territories, lands where their ancestors lived perhaps even back into prehistoric times. They became ethnic when their territory was annexed into a larger independent state. For these groups, such as the Basques of Spain or the Navajo Indians of the American Southwest, place and region provide a basic element in their ethnic identity. The second type of ethnic culture region results from migration, when people move great distances, often crossing oceans, to establish new homes as a minority in a foreign country. Their emotional attachment to the new land tends to be far weaker than among indigenous ethnic groups. Only after many generations pass do the descendants of immigrant groups develop the same strong bond to region and place.

To map ethnic culture regions, geographers rely on data as diverse as surnames in telephone directories and census totals for mother tongue. Each method produces a slightly different map, given the cultural complexity of the real world (Figure 9.3). Regardless of the mapping method, ethnic culture regions reveal a vivid mosaic of minorities in most countries of the world.

Ethnic Culture Regions in Rural North America

The rural areas of Canada and the United States contain thousands of ethnic farming communities, formed by immigrants from many different European countries. These rural ethnic culture regions fall into two categories: **ethnic homelands** and **ethnic islands.** The difference is size, both in terms of area and population. Ethnic homelands cover large areas, often lapping over state and provincial borders, and have sizable populations. The residents of homelands seek or enjoy some measure of political autonomy or self-rule. By contrast, ethnic islands are small dots in the countryside, usually occupying an area smaller than a county and serving as home to several hundred to, at most, several thousand people. Homeland populations usually exhibit a strong sense of attachment to the region. Most homelands belong to indigenous ethnic groups and possess special, venerated places that serve to symbolize and celebrate the region—shrines to the special identity of the ethnic group. In its fully developed form, the homeland represents that most powerful of geographical entities, one combining the attributes of both formal and functional culture regions. Some regard them as incompletely developed nation-states (see Chapter 4).

North America houses a number of viable ethnic homelands, including *Acadiana,* the Louisiana French homeland now increasingly identified with the Cajun people and also recognized as a perceptual region (Figure 8.13); the *Hispano* or Spanish-American homeland of

Walter M. Kollmorgen
1907–

Dr. Kollmorgen, professor emeritus of geography at the University of Kansas and noted agricultural geographer, made early contributions to the study of American ethnic groups. In the late 1930s, he began research on the farming practices of ethnic minorities in the United States—in particular, the Germans in Alabama and Pennsylvania, the German Swiss in Tennessee, the French in Louisiana, and other ethnic minorities located mainly in the American South. His detailed statistical comparisons of ethnic and nonethnic farmers provided geographers with the first conclusive evidence of ethnic distinctiveness in agriculture and established a model of rigorous scholarship for later ethnic geographical studies.

Like many geographers, Professor Kollmorgen received the inspiration for his research while traveling through the countryside and observing what he saw. In the 1930s, he made many tours through the southern Appalachians. Intrigued by the visual contrasts he saw between the settlement areas of Germans and non-Germans, Kollmorgen decided to make a comparative study.

Kollmorgen was honored for meritorious contributions by the Association of American Geographers in 1953 and 1962, and served as honorary president of that organization in 1968.

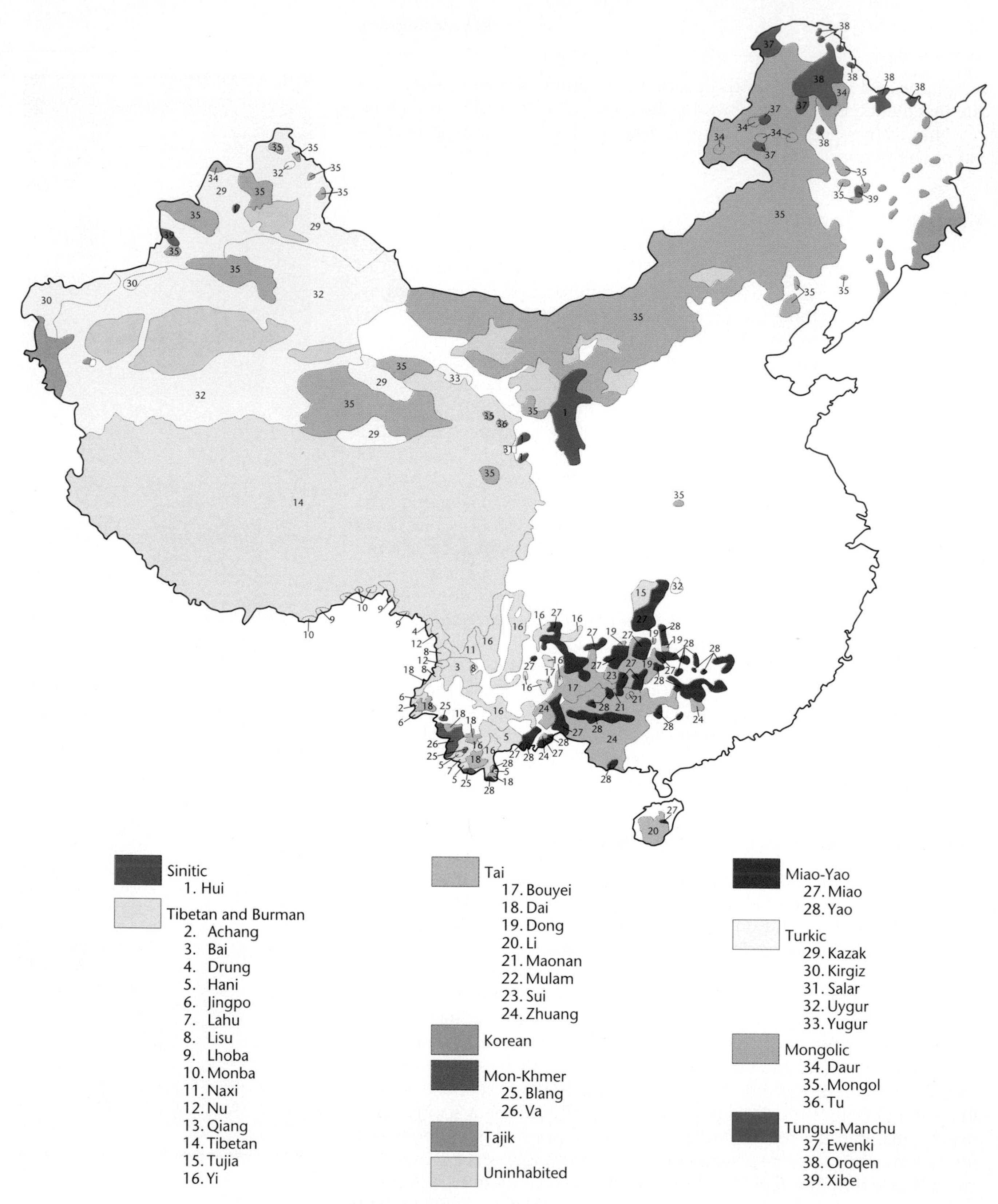

Figure 9.2

Ethnic minorities in China. Most ethnic groups are Turkic, Mongolic, Tai, Tibetan, or Burman in speech, but the rich diversity extends even to the Tajiks of the Indo-European language family. Unshaded areas are Han Chinese, the host culture. Which of these ethnic regions are *homelands* and which *islands?* Why are China's ethnic groups concentrated in sparsely populated peripheries of the country (Figure 2.1)? (Source: Adapted and simplified from Carter, Timothy J., et al. "The Peoples of China," map supplement in *National Geographic Magazine,* 158 [July 1980].)

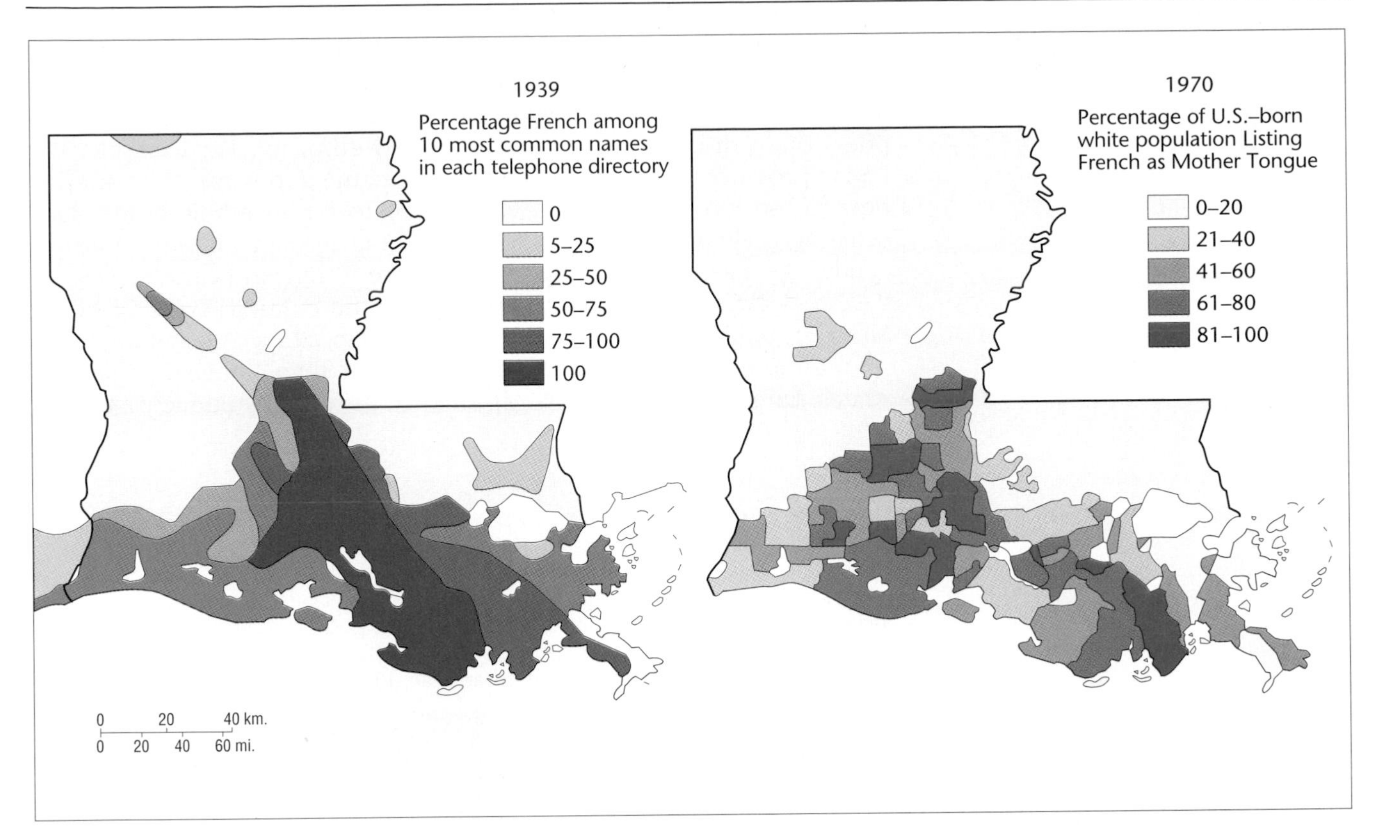

Figure 9.3
Acadiana, the Louisiana French homeland, as mapped by two different methods. The 1939 map was compiled by sampling the surnames in telephone directories. The ten most common names in each directory were determined and the percentage of these ten that was of French origin was recorded. When no telephone directories were available, surnames on mailboxes were used. Look through the telephone directory for your hometown. What are the ten most common family names? What ethnic background do the names reveal? What distortions or inaccuracies might result from using only telephone directories to enumerate ethnic groups? The 1970 map is based on the US census data for the Caucasian population's "mother tongue," defined by the Bureau of the Census as the language spoken in the home during the respondent's childhood. (After Meigs, Peveril, III. "An Ethno-Telephonic Survey of French Louisiana." *Annals of the Association of American Geographers,* 31 [1941]: 245; and a map produced by James P. Allen of the Department of Geography, California State University, Northridge, for distribution at the 1978 meeting of the Association of American Geographers at New Orleans.)

highland New Mexico and Colorado; the South Texas Mexican (or Tex-Mex) homeland; the Navajo Reservation homeland in Arizona and New Mexico; and the French-Canadian homeland centered on the valley of the lower St. Lawrence River in Québec. Some would also include *Deseret,* a Mormon homeland in the Great Basin of the intermontane West. Certain other ethnic homelands have experienced decline and decay. These include the Pennsylvania "Dutch" homeland, weakened to the point of extinction by assimilation, and the southern *Black Belt,* diminished by the collapse of the plantation-sharecrop system and resultant African American outmigration to urban areas. Mormon absorption into the American cultural mainstream has largely negated Mormon ethnic status, while nonethnic immigration has damaged the Hispano homeland. At present, the most vigorous ethnic homelands are those of the French Canadians and South Texas Mexican-Americans.

If ethnic homelands succumb to assimilation, their people absorbed into the host culture, then a geographical residue, or **ethnic substrate,** remains. The resultant culture region, though no longer ethnic, nevertheless retains some distinctiveness. It differs from surrounding regions in a variety of ways. In seeking to explain its distinctiveness, geographers often discover an ancient, vanished ethnicity. For example, the Italian province of Tuscany owes both its name and some of its uniqueness to the Etruscan people, who ceased to be an ethnic group 2000 years ago, absorbed into the Latin-speaking Roman Empire. More recently, the massive German presence in the American heartland (Figure 9.4), now largely nonethnic, helped shape the cultural character of the Midwest, which can be said to have a German ethnic substrate.

Ethnic islands are much more numerous than homelands or substrates. Large areas of rural North America have many ethnic islands, as

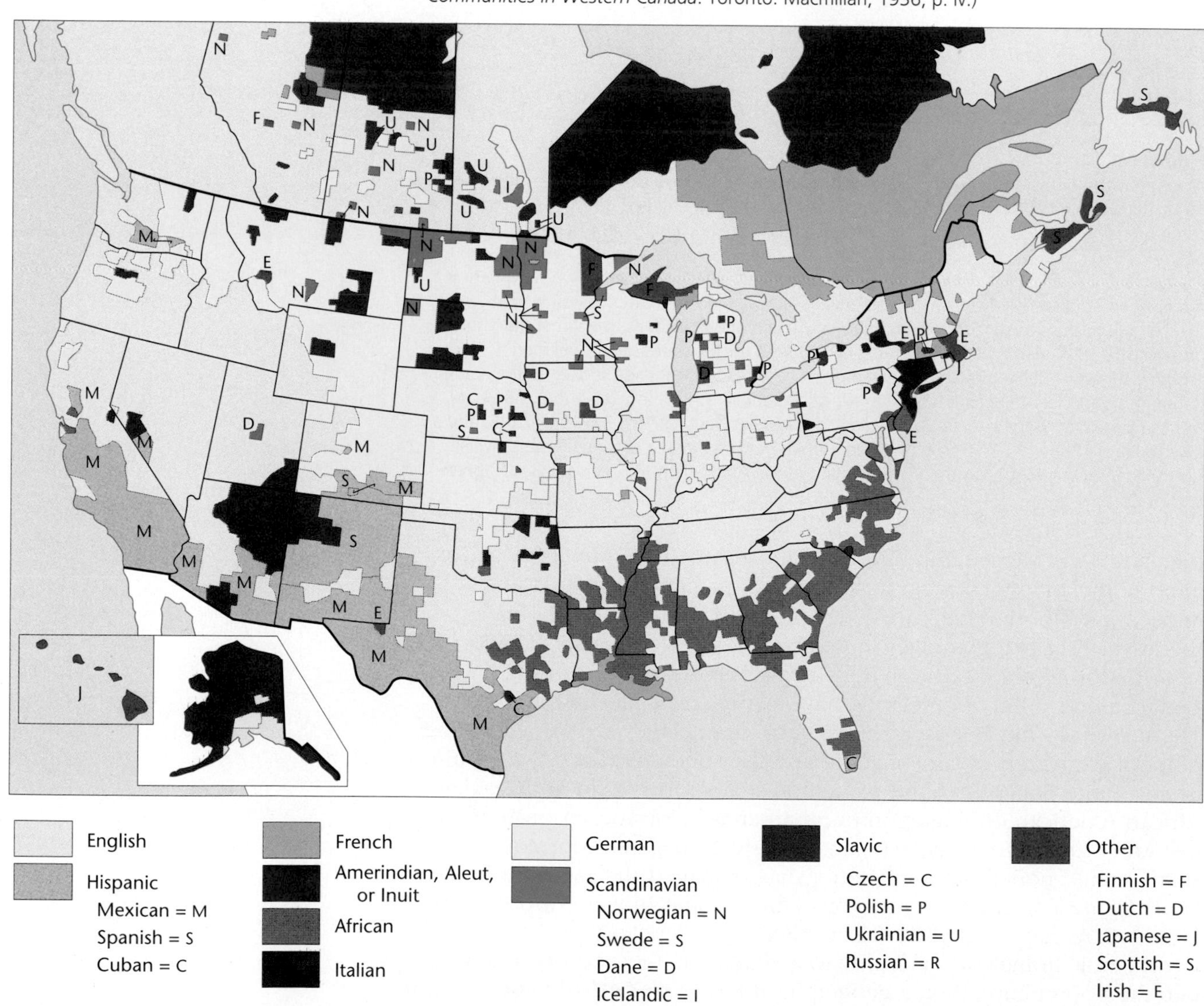

Figure 9.4
Ethnic and national-origin groups in North America. Notice how the Canada–United States border generally also forms a cultural boundary. A striking feature is the German dominance of the northern United States and a Hispanic borderland in the South. Several ethnic homelands appear, as do many ethnic islands. (Sources: US Census, 1990; Allen and Turner, 1987, p. 210; Censuses of Canada, 1981 and 1991; Dawson, C. A. *Group Settlement: Ethnic Communities in Western Canada*. Toronto: Macmillan, 1936, p. iv.)

Figure 9.5 suggests. Figure 9.6 provides some Midwestern examples of ethnic islands, revealing the crazy-quilt pattern typical of much of the American heartland. Germans, the largest single group in American ethnic islands, are clustered principally in southeastern Pennsylvania and in Wisconsin, while Scandinavians, primarily Swedes and Norwegians, came mainly to Minnesota, the eastern Dakotas, and western Wiscon-

Figure 9.5
Selected ethnic homelands in North America, past and present, and concentrations of rural ethnic islands. The Hispano homeland is also referred to as the Spanish-American homeland. (Sources: Carlson, Nostrand, Estaville, Meinig (see Chapter 6 readings), Jett, Arreola, and Rose.)

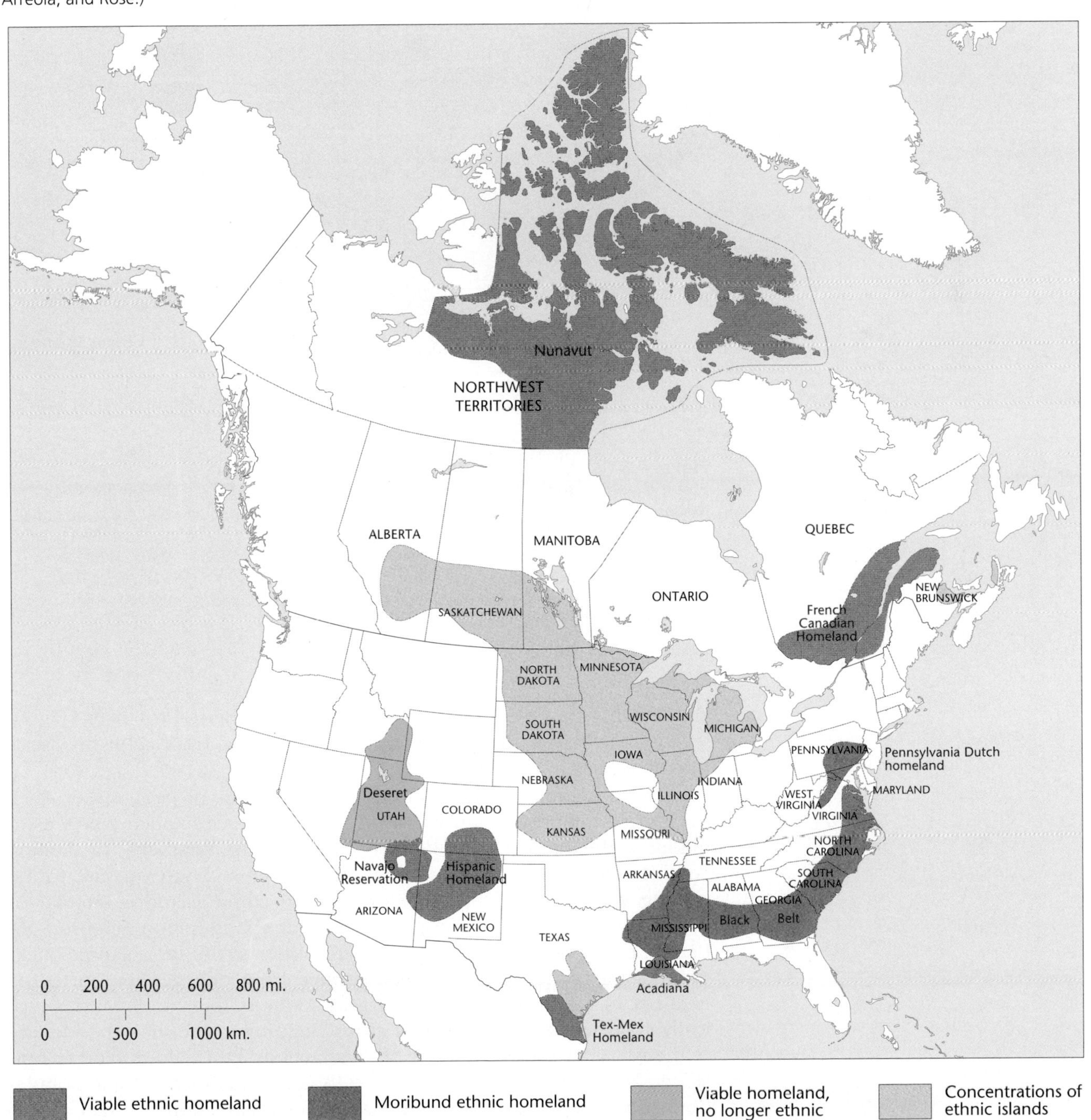

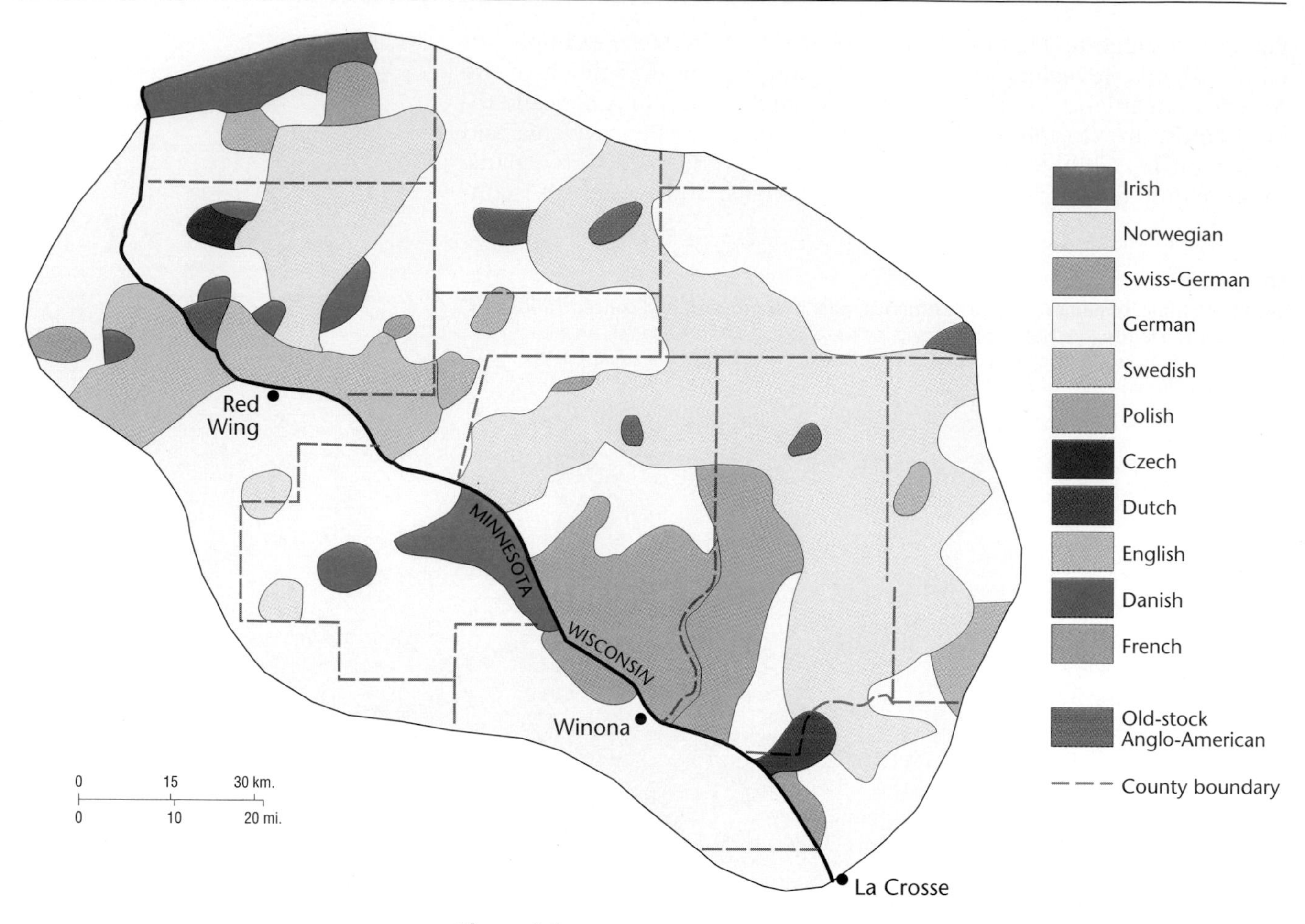

Figure 9.6
Ethnic islands in the rural American heartland. Illustrated is the distribution of ethnic groups in a small portion of western Wisconsin and southeastern Minnesota. Although not all parts of the United States display this many ethnic islands, it is typical of much of the Midwest. (After Hill, G. W. "The People of Wisconsin According to Ethnic Stocks, 1940." *Wisconsin's Changing Population.* Madison: Bulletin of the University of Wisconsin, Serial 2642, 1942; and Marshall, Douglas. "Minnesota's People." *Minneapolis Tribune* [August 28, 1949], Section 4, p. 1.)

sin. Ukrainians settled mainly in the Canadian Prairie Provinces (Figure 9.7). Other Slavic groups, mostly Poles and Czechs, established scattered colonies in the Midwest and Texas.

Ethnic islands develop because, in the words of geographer Alice Rechlin, "a minority group will tend to utilize space in such a way as to minimize the interaction distance between group members," facilitating contacts within the ethnic community and minimizing exposure to the outside world. The ideal shape of such an ethnic island is circular or hexagonal, and many do approximate that configuration (Figure 9.8). People are drawn to rural places where others of the same ethnic background are found. Ethnic islands survive from one generation to the next because most land is inherited. In addition, the sale of land is typically confined within the ethnic group, helping to preserve the identity of the island. A social stigma is often attached to the sale of land to outsiders. Even so, the smaller size of ethnic islands makes their populations more susceptible to acculturation and assimilation.

Urban Ethnic Neighborhoods and Ghettos

Formal ethnic culture regions also occur in cities throughout the world. Minority people tend to create ethnic residential quarters (Figure 9.9). Two types exist. An **ethnic neighborhood** is a voluntary community where people of like origin reside by choice. Such neighborhoods are, in the words of Peter Matwijiw, an Australian geographer, "the results of preferences shown by different ethnic groups . . . toward maintaining group cohesiveness." The benefits of an ethnic neighborhood are many: common use of language, nearby kin, stores and services specially tailored to a certain group's tastes, presence of factories relying on ethnically based division of labor, and institutions important to the group—such as churches and lodges—that remain viable only when a number of people live close enough to participate frequently in their activities.

The **ghetto** is the second type of urban ethnic quarter. The term has traditionally been used to describe an area within the city where a certain ethnic group is *forced* to live. Use of *ghetto* should be reserved for areas of residential segregation where an ethnic group lives because it has very little choice in the matter—options are limited or nonexistent. In other words, a ghetto is an involuntary community and as much a functional culture region as a formal one.

Whether an ethnic group lives in a ghetto or voluntarily forms its own neighborhood usually depends on how discriminatory the host culture is. For example, because American society discriminates more against black people and Asians than Italians, an African American ghetto or Chinatown is more likely to exist than an Italian ghetto. This was revealed in a study of Cleveland, Ohio, by John Kain. In Cleveland African Americans are confined to a ghetto by discriminatory housing practices and are much more highly segregated residentially than are Caucasian ethnic groups. Italians, Poles, Jews, Appalachian folk, and other Caucasian ethnic groups in Cleveland occupy neighborhoods rather than ghettos and disperse to the suburbs more readily than African Americans.

Ethnic residential quarters have long been a part of urban cultural geography. In ancient times, conquerors often forced the vanquished native people to live in ghettos. Religious minorities usually received similar treatment. Sometimes walls built around such ghettos set them off from the rest of the city. Islamic cities had Christian districts, and medieval European cities had Jewish ghettos.

North American cities are perhaps more ethnically diverse than any other urban centers in the world. Ethnic neighborhoods became typical in the northern United States and in Canada after about 1840, coinciding with the urbanization and industrialization of North America. Instead of dispersing through the residential areas of the city, immigrant groups clustered together. The ethnic groups involved, to a degree, came from different parts of Europe than those who went to rural areas. While Germany and Scandinavia supplied most of the rural settlers, the cities drew much more heavily on Ireland and eastern and southern Europe. Catholic Irish, Italians, Poles, and East European Jews became the main urban ethnic groups, though lesser numbers of virtually every nationality in Europe came to the cities of North America (Figure 9.9). These groups were later joined by French Canadians, Southern blacks, Puerto Ricans, Appalachian whites, American Indians, and other groups not of European birth.

Figure 9.7
In a Ukrainian ethnic island near Edmonton, Alberta province, Canada. The church is Uniate (or "Greek Catholic"), an Eastern Orthodox Christian group that acknowledges the supremacy of the Roman pope. About 60 percent of Canadian Ukrainians belong to that denomination. Ukrainians settled particularly in the transition zone between prairie and woodland in western Canada, a setting similar to their European homeland.

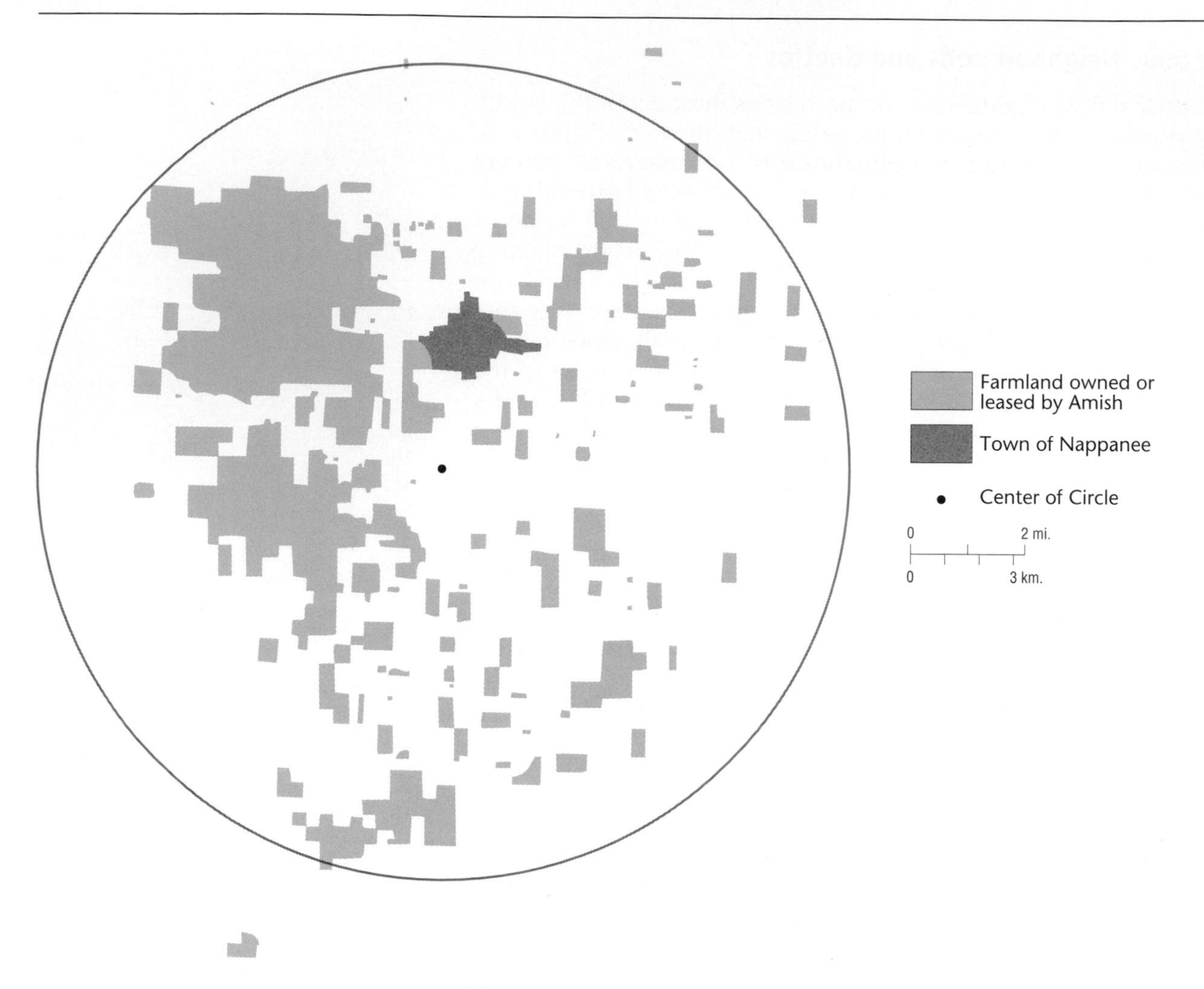

Figure 9.8
The Amish ethnic island at Nappanee, Indiana. A roughly circular configuration is evident, suggesting the ideal shape of such ethnic enclaves. What factors might have acted to prevent the island from attaining a perfectly circular shape? Does this appear to be a pattern reflecting areal growth, stagnation, or retreat? (Derived from Rechlin, Alice. *Spatial Behavior of the Old Order Amish of Nappanee, Indiana.* Michigan Geographical Publication 18, 1976, p. 40.)

Other Ethnic Migrants

In recent decades, as immigration laws changed, the ethnic variety in North American cities grew even greater and the sources of immigration underwent a fundamental change. Asia, rather than Europe, is now the principal contributing continent for both Canada and the United States, with Chinese, Koreans, and Vietnamese comprising the most numerous immigrant groups. Japanese ancestry forms the largest national-origin group in Hawaii, and many West Coast cities, from Vancouver to San Diego, have acquired very sizable Asiatic populations. Already 11 percent Asian by 1981, Vancouver has since absorbed many more such immigrants, particularly from Hong Kong, which became part of China in 1997. According to the latest census, some 7.5 million Asians lived in the United States, representing about 3 percent of the total population. As in Canada, nearly all are concentrated in urban areas, usually in ethnic neighborhoods.

Latin America, including the Caribbean countries, also surpassed Europe as a source of immigrants coming to North America. East Coast cities have absorbed large numbers of immigrants from the West Indies.

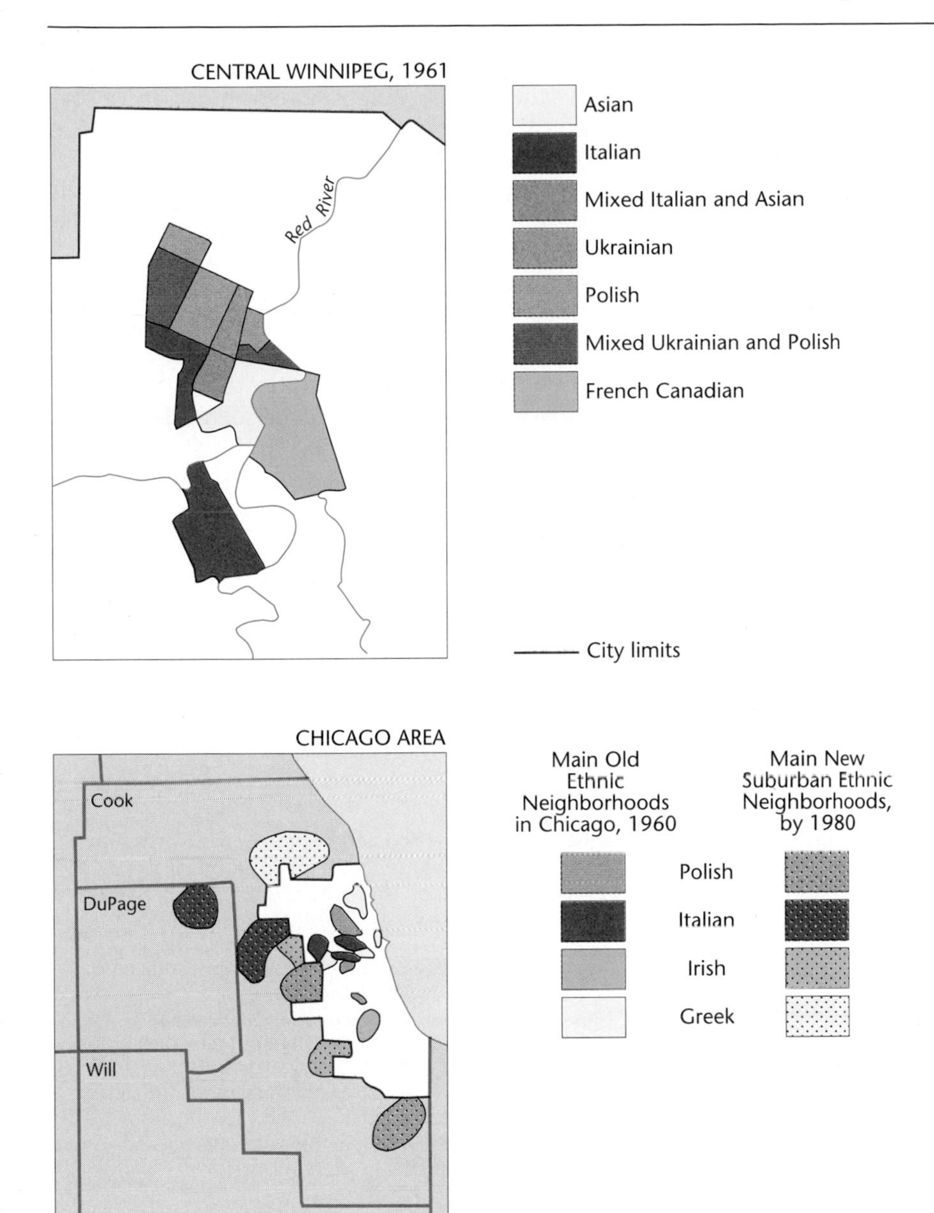

Figure 9.9
Selected ethnic neighborhoods in Winnipeg, Manitoba, and the Chicago area. Central city ethnic neighborhoods are often relocated to the suburbs as acculturation progresses. (Sources: Adapted from Matwijiw, Peter. "Ethnicity and Urban Residence: Winnipeg, 1941–71." *Canadian Geographer,* 23 [1979]: 50; and Winsberg, Morton D. "Ethnic Segregation and Concentration in Chicago Suburbs." *Urban Geography,* 7 [1986]: 142–143.)

In many important cultural respects, Miami has become a West Indies/Caribbean city (Figure 9.10), and the two largest national-origin groups coming to New York City as early as the 1970s were from the Dominican Republic and Jamaica, displacing Italy as the leading source. As a result, the image of both Canada and the United States as predominantly "European" in population may soon change.

Perhaps too often we think of emigrant ethnic groups only in a North American context. We need to be reminded that 28 million ethnic Chinese reside outside China and Taiwan. Most of these overseas Chinese do not live in North America, but instead in Southeast Asian countries. Indonesia has over 7 million, Thailand nearly 6 million, and

Figure 9.10
"Little Havana," or *Pequeña Habana,* the original Cuban ethnic neighborhood in Miami, Florida. Cubans became so numerous in Miami that they now dominate the city culturally, socially, and economically. Little Havana, however, has since become dominated by Central Americans.

Malaysia more than 5 million. Pacific Islanders exhibit a similar pattern. Auckland, New Zealand, has the largest Polynesian population of any city in the world. Immigration-based ethnicity is far from being a phenomenon limited to North America.

Regardless of the source of urban immigrants, the neighborhoods they create tend to be transitory. As a rule, urban ethnic groups remain in neighborhoods while undergoing acculturation. As a result, their central-city ethnic neighborhoods experience a life cycle (Figure 9.11). Often, one group is replaced by another, later-arriving one. We can see this process in action in the succession of groups that dominated certain neighborhoods and then moved on to more desirable areas. Boston's West End was mainly an Irish area in the nineteenth century. As the twentieth century began, Irish were replaced in this deteriorating neighborhood by Jews, who in turn were replaced in the late 1930s by Poles and Italians. In Miami's Little Havana neighborhood, Central Americans replaced Cubans (Figure 9.10). The list of groups that passed through Chicago's Adams area from the nineteenth century to the present provides an almost complete history of American migratory patterns. First came the Germans and Irish, who were succeeded by the Greeks, Poles, French Canadians, Czechs, and Russian Jews, who were soon hard-pressed by the Italians. In turn, they were challenged by Chicanos and a small group of Puerto Ricans. As this succession occurred,

Figure 9.11

A six-stage model of ethnic neighborhood formation and decline in the North American city. (Adapted, with modifications, from a Chinatown model proposed by Lai, David C. *Chinatowns: Towns Within Cities in Canada.* Vancouver: University of British Columbia Press, 1988, p. 6.)

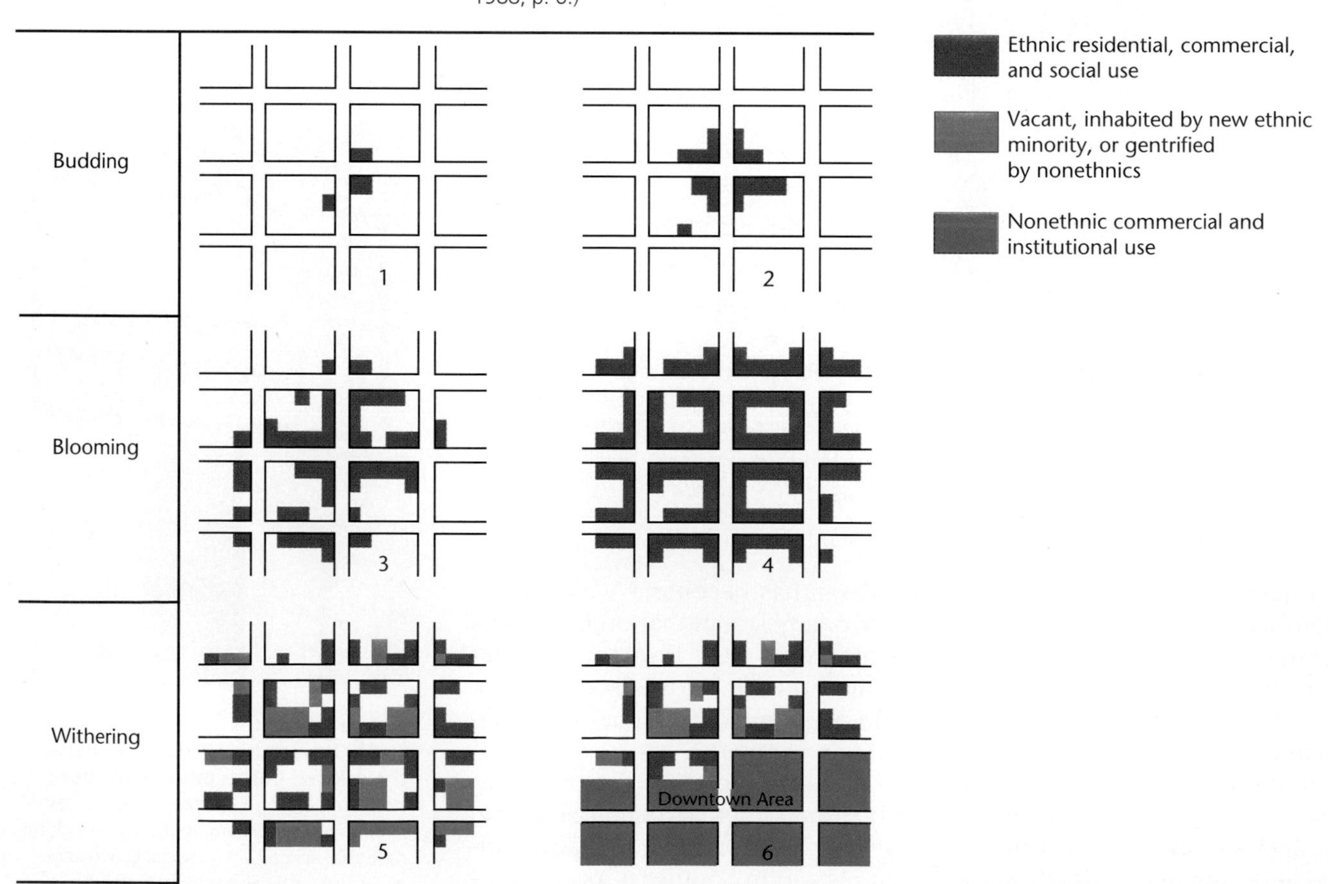

the older groups often established new ethnic neighborhoods in suburban areas.

Ethnic Mix and National Character

Urban ethnic neighborhoods receive additional attention in Chapter 11. For now, we turn to a brief comparison of ethnic culture regions in several of the larger multiethnic countries of the world.

Any country is the sum of its cultural parts. Different countries have their own unique mixes of national origin and ethnic groups, revealed in a mosaic of homelands, islands, neighborhoods, and ghettos that help shape national character. Russia, for example, has less diversity and a largely different array of minorities than the United States (Table 9.1). Canada, too, displays striking differences from the United States, most notably in its far higher proportions of English, French, Scots, and Ukrainians. Germans, Africans, and Hispanics are poorly represented in Canada, adding to the contrast. These differences are vividly revealed in the mosaic of national-origin groups (Figure 9.4). In turn, varied ethnic mixes produce different national characters, even if ethnic assimilation occurs. National origin need not imply ethnicity, and often does not. Most persons in the United States who claim German origin, for example, are not German-Americans. Rather, they have been much acculturated and often assimilated, becoming part of the host culture. The massive absorption of Germans into the mainstream culture of the United States has been a major factor in shaping a national character distinct from that of Canada, as have the other striking differences in the ethnic makeup of the two countries.

TABLE 9.1
The Ten Largest National Origin/Ethnic Groups in Three Multinational Countries

United States, 1990[1]		Canada, 1991[2]		Russia, 1989[3]	
Ancestry Group	% of Total Population	Ancestry Group	% of Total Population Claiming Single Ancestry	Ethno-linguistic Group	% of Total Population
German	23.3%	French	33.8%	Russian	81.5%
English[4]	18.4%	English	26.3%	Tatar	3.8%
Irish	17.8%	German	5.0%	Ukranian	3.0%
African	11.7%	Oriental[5]	4.8%	Chuvash	1.2%
Hispanic	9.0%	Scottish	4.8%	Bashkir	0.9%
Italian	5.9%	Italian	3.9%	Belorussian	0.8%
French	5.3%	Irish	3.9%	Mordva	0.7%
Scottish	4.4%	Ukrainian	2.3%	German	0.6%
Polish	3.8%	Native American[6]	2.1%	Chechen	0.6%
Oriental[5]	2.9%	Jewish	1.4%	Udmurt	0.5%

[1]Includes, for most groups, persons wholly or partially of these ancestries; persons claiming multiple ancestry may appear in more than one category.
[2]Includes only persons claiming single ancestry.
[3]Figures for the Russian Federated Republic, within the now-defunct Soviet Union.
[4]Includes England, "American," and "United States."
[5]Includes South Asian, East Asian, Filipino; excludes Pakistanis.
[6]American Indian, Inuit, and Métis.

Cultural Diffusion and Ethnicity

The complicated mosaic of ethnic homelands, islands, and neighborhoods in different countries around the world might seem to be the result of chance. In reality, orderly processes of relocation, contagious, and hierarchical diffusion worked to produce much of the pattern.

Migration and Ethnicity

Most of the ethnic pattern in many parts of the world, including North America, Australia, and virtually all urban neighborhoods on every continent, is the result of relocation diffusion. In fact, ethnicity is often created by the very migration process, as people leave countries where they belonged to a nonethnic majority and become a minority in a new home. Voluntary migration accounts for the great majority of ethnic groups in the United States and Canada.

In most such cases, **chain migration** is involved. An individual or small group makes the decision to migrate to a foreign country. These "innovators" are natural leaders who influence others to accompany them in the migration, particularly friends and relatives. The word spreads to nearby communities, and soon a sizable migration is under way from a fairly small district, directed to a comparably small area or neighborhood in the destination country (Figures 9.12 and 9.13). In village after village, the first to opt for emigration often rank high in the local social order, so that hierarchical diffusion also comes into play. That is, the *decision* to migrate spreads by a mixture of hierarchical and contagious diffusion, while the actual migration itself represents relocation diffusion.

The process of chain migration continues even after the first emigrants have departed. From their new home, they write letters back to their native place, extolling the virtues of the new life and imploring others to join them. Such letters written from the United States became known as **America letters** (see box, *An America Letter*).

Chain migration caused the movement of people to become *channelized,* linking a specific source region to a particular destination, so that neighbors in the old country became neighbors in the new country as well. It was at work three centuries ago and still operates today. The recent mass migration of Latin Americans to Anglo-America provides an example. Research by geographer Richard Jones revealed that different parts of the southwestern United States draw upon different source regions in Mexico (Figure 9.14).

Involuntary migration also contributes to ethnic diffusion and the formation of ethnic culture regions. Refugees from Cambodia and Vietnam created ethnic minorities in North America, as did Guatemalans and Salvadorans fleeing political repression in Central America. At the same time, such forced migrations often result from policies of "ethnic cleansing," when countries expel minorities to produce cultural homogeneity in their populations. Following forced migration, the relocated group often engages in voluntary migration to concentrate in some new locality. Cuban political refugees, scattered widely through the United States in the 1960s, reassembled in South Florida, while Vietnamese continue to gather in southern California and Texas.

Return migration represents another type of ethnic diffusion and involves the voluntary move of a group back to their ancestral or native country or homeland. One of the most notable movements now under

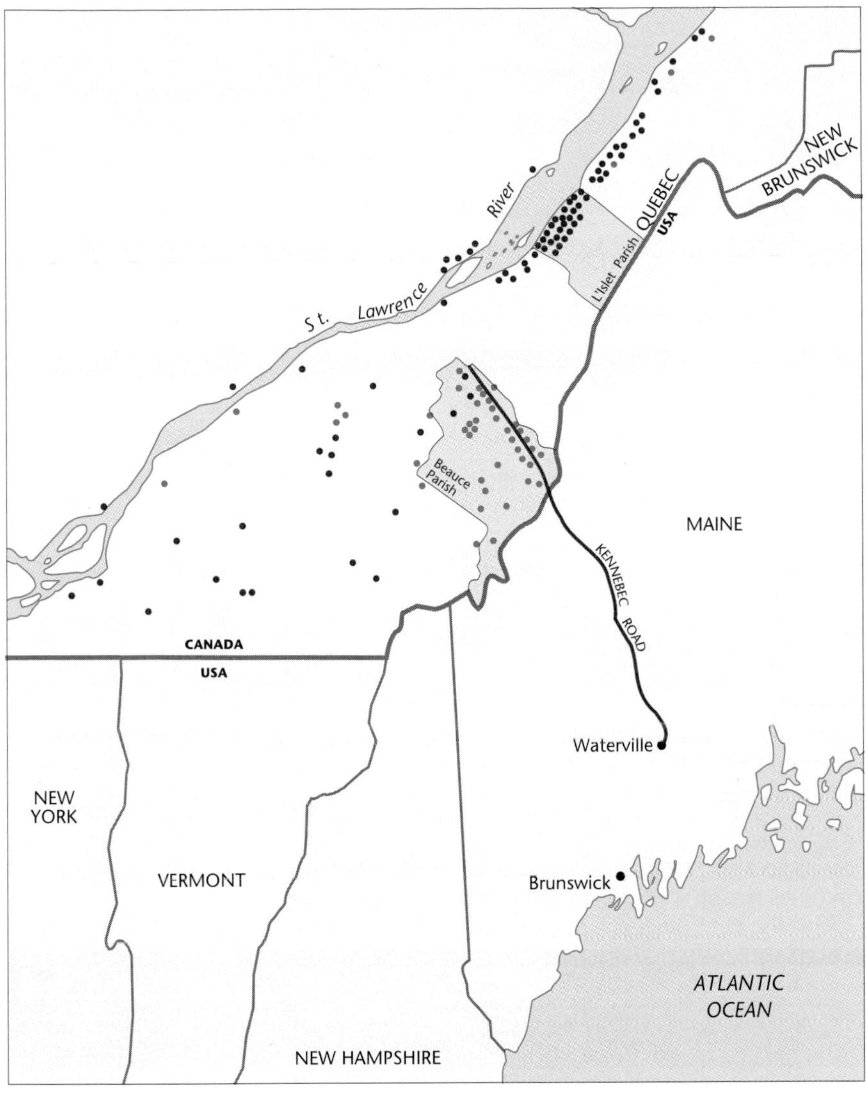

Figure 9.12
Ethnic chain migration from French Canada to the United States. Ethnic islands and urban neighborhoods typically result from chain migration. One of the more significant ethnic migrations of the last century was the movement of French Canadians to the factory towns of New England, a migration accomplished by numerous small clusters of people. This map shows the clustered sources of French Canadians who migrated to the towns of Brunswick and Waterville in Maine in the 1880–1925 period. The parish of Beauce supplied most of the Waterville French, while L'Islet Parish was the leading source of Brunswick French. Try to reconstruct in your own mind the sequence of events that might have led to this clustering of migration source and destination. (After Allen, James P. "Migration Fields of French Canadian Immigrants to Southern Maine." *Geographical Review,* 62 [1972]: 377; see also his "Franco-Americans in Maine: A Geographical Perspective." *Acadiensis,* 4 [1974]: 32–66.)

way is the large-scale return of African Americans from the cities of the northern and western United States to the Black Belt ethnic homeland in the South. This type of ethnic migration is also channelized, for, as geographers John Cromartie and Carol Stack discovered, over two-thirds of the migrants "follow well-worn paths back to homeplaces or other locations where relatives have settled." For example, geographer James Johnson found that 7 percent of African Americans in Los Angeles County, California, moved away between 1985 and 1990, including many who went to the American South. By the year 2000, the once

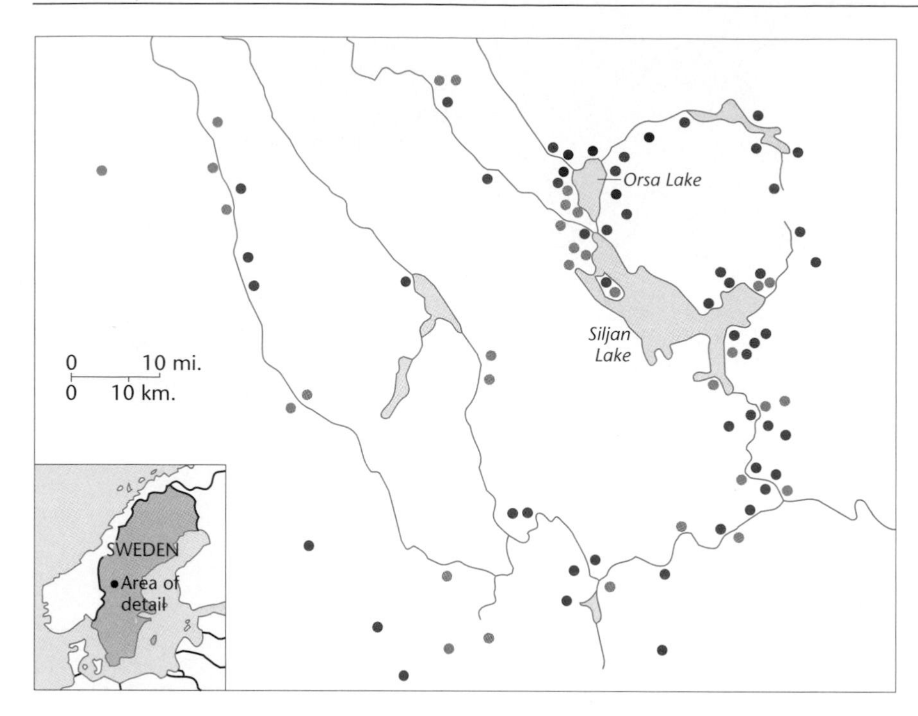

Figure 9.13
Contagious diffusion of the decision to emigrate in a portion of Dalarna Province, Sweden, 1860–1875. Many Swedes left for the American Midwest in the latter half of the nineteenth century, and the decision to leave spread through the countryside, passing from one settlement to the next. This particular emigration peaked during a famine in 1868 to 1870. Draw on the map the most likely paths of diffusion. How might the decision to emigrate have begun? How did it leap so far south, to the two 1864 to 1867 communities at the bottom of the map? (Adapted and simplified from Ostergren, 1988, p. 116.)

An America Letter

The following excerpts are from a letter written in 1832 by the first German settler in Texas to a friend back in Germany. The letter was eventually published in a German newspaper and prompted a large chain migration from northwestern Germany to Texas.

Each married immigrant who wishes to engage in farming receives 4,440 acres of land, including hills and valleys, woods and meadows with creeks flowing through. That is virtually a count's estate, and within a short time the land will be worth $700 to $800. Farmers who own 700 head of cattle are common hereabouts. Europeans are especially welcome in the colony, and I was given excellent land, upon which I built my home.

The land here is hilly, covered partly with forest and partly with natural prairies. There are various types of trees. The climate is similar to that of Sicily. There is no real winter, and the coldest months are almost like March in Germany. Bees, birds, and butterflies stay all through the winter season. The soil requires no fertilizer. The main crops are tobacco, rice, indigo, sweet potatoes, melons of special goodness, wheat, rye, and vegetables of all kinds. Peaches are found in abundance growing wild in the forest, as are mulberries, walnuts, plums, persimmons as sweet as honey, and wine grapes in great quantity. There is much wild game, and hunting and fishing are free. The prairies are filled with the most lovely flowers. The more children you have, the better, for you will need them as field laborers. Mosquitos and gnats are common only near the coast. Formerly there were no taxes at all, and now we have only community taxes. Each year you need work barely three months to make a living.

There is freedom of religion here and English is the prevailing language. Up the river there is much silver to be found, but Indians still live there.

All Germans who come to the colony will be given land at once. When you arrive at San Felipe, ask for Friedrich Ernst of Mill Creek. It is thirty miles from there to my place, and you will find me without any difficulty. For my friends and former countrymen, I have built a shelter on my estate where they can stay while selecting their land.

Your friend,
Fritz Ernst

Translated, adapted, and rearranged from Achenbach, Hermann. *Tagebuch meiner Reise nach den Nordamerikanischen Freistaaten [Diary of My Trip to the North American Free States].* Düsseldorf: Beyer and Wolf, 1835, pp. 132–135; and Dunt, Detlef. *Reise nach Texas, nebst Nachrichten von diesem Lande; für Deutsche, welche nach Amerika zu gehen beabsichtigen [A Trip to Texas, Together with News of That Country, for Germans Who Plan to Come to America].* Bremen: Wiehe, 1834, pp. 4–16.

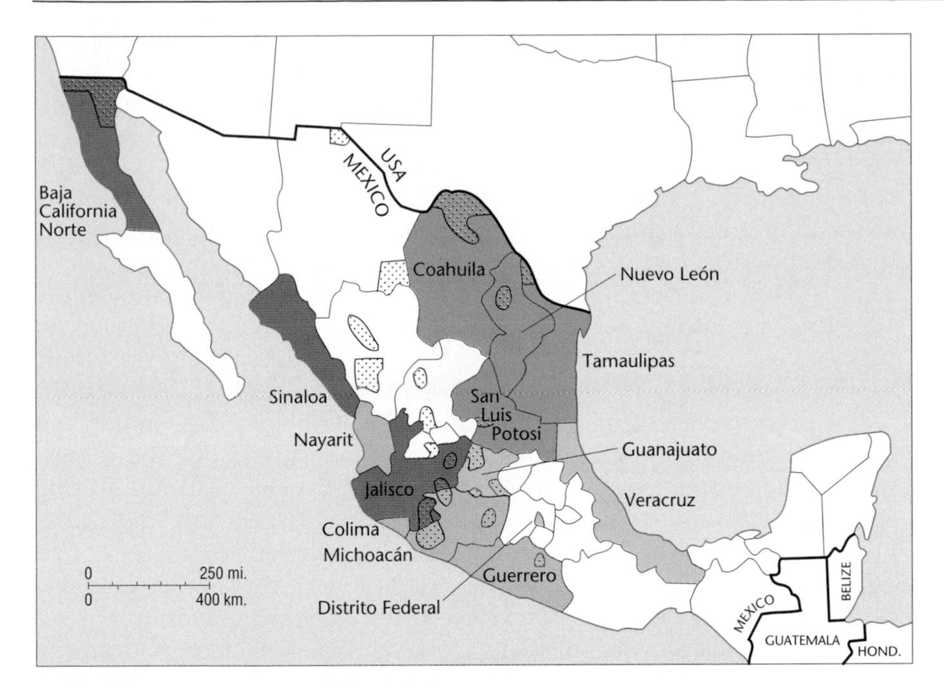

Figure 9.14
Sources by state and county of undocumented Mexican nationals apprehended by the Immigration and Naturalization Service in South Texas and southern California. A weighted index was employed to assign values to the different Mexican states. Why are certain areas greater contributors than others? How might such clustered or channelized migration sources influence the ethnic cultures in the two extremities of the Hispanic borderland? Might it help explain Hispanic cultural contrasts between southern California and South Texas? For answers, see the sources listed below. (Derived from Jones, Richard C. "Channelization of Undocumented Mexican Migrants to the U.S." *Economic Geography,* 58 [1982]: 165–166; and "Micro Source Regions of Mexican Undocumented Migration." *National Geographic Research,* 4 [1988]: 17.)

dominantly African American South-Central district of Los Angeles will become largely Hispanic in population. Similarly, many of the 200,000 or so expatriate Estonians, Latvians, and Lithuanians left Russia and other former Soviet republics to return to their newly independent Baltic home countries in the 1990s, losing their ethnic status in the process. Clearly, migration of all kinds turns the ethnic mosaic into an ever-changing kaleidoscope.

Simplification and Isolation

When groups migrate and become ethnic in a new land, they have, in theory at least, the potential to introduce, by relocation diffusion, the totality of their culture. Conceivably, they could reestablish every facet of their traditional way of life in the new country. If they were to do so, then a visit to an ethnic homeland, island, or neighborhood in, say, North America would be akin to a visit to Europe, Asia, Africa, or Latin America.

Instead, however, ethnic immigrants never successfully introduce their culture in totality overseas. A profound cultural **simplification** occurs. As geographer Cole Harris noted, "Europeans establish overseas drastically simplified versions of European society." This happens, in part, because of chain migration: Only areal fragments of a culture diffuse overseas, borne by groups from particular places migrating in particular eras. In other words, some simplification occurs at the point of departure. Still, more cultural diversity is implanted in the new home than survives. Only selected traits are successfully introduced, and others undergo considerable modification before becoming established in the new homeland. In other words, absorbing barriers prevent the diffusion of many traits, and permeable barriers cause changes in many other traits, greatly simplifying the migrant cultures. In addition, choices that did not exist in the old home become available to immigrant ethnic groups. They can borrow alien ways from groups they encounter in the new land, invent new techniques better suited to the adopted place, or modify traditional or alien ways as they see fit. Most immigrant ethnic groups resort to all these devices, in varying degrees.

The displacement of a group and relocation in a new homeland can have widely differing results. Perhaps most commonly, the relocation weakens tradition and upsets an age-old balance, causing a rapid discarding of traditional traits and accelerated borrowing, invention, and modification—in short, acculturation. The degree of isolation of an ethnic group in the new home helps determine if traditional traits will be retained, modified, or abandoned. If the new settlement area is remote and contacts with outsiders are few, diffusion of traits from the Old World is more likely. Because contacts with alien groups are rare, little borrowing of traits can occur. Isolated ethnic groups often preserve in archaic form cultural elements that disappear from their ancestral country; that is, they may, in some respects, change less than their kinfolk back in the mother country. Language and dialects offer some good examples of this preservation of the archaic. Germans living in ethnic islands in the Balkan region of southeastern Europe preserve archaic South German dialects better than in Germany itself, and some medieval elements survive in the Spanish spoken in the Hispano homeland of New Mexico. Irish Catholic settlers in Newfoundland, whose communities remained rather isolated, retained far more of their traditional Celtic culture than did fellow Irish who colonized Ontario, where contacts with non-Irish occurred frequently.

Ethnic Ecology

Ethnicity is closely linked to cultural ecology and adaptation. The possibilistic interplay between people and physical environment is often evident in the pattern of ethnic culture regions, in ethnic migration, and in ethnic persistence or survival.

Cultural Preadaptation

Earlier in the book, we discussed **cultural adaptation,** involving **adaptive strategy,** the unique way that each culture utilizes a particular physical environment in order to obtain the necessities of life. When migration occurs, creating ethnic minorities in a new land, a related concept, **preadaptation,** must be considered. Preadaptation involves a complex of adaptive traits possessed by a group in advance of migration that gives them the ability to survive and a competitive advantage in colonizing the new environment. Most often, preadaptation results from groups migrating to a place environmentally similar to the one they left behind. The adaptive strategy they had pursued before migration works reasonably well in the new home. As a result, they achieve what geographer Wilbur Zelinsky called the **first effective settlement** and are able to perpetuate much of their culture in the colonization area.

The preadaptation may be accidental, but in most cases the immigrant ethnic group deliberately chooses a colonization area that physically resembles the former home. The state of Wisconsin, dotted with scores of ethnic islands, provides some fine examples of preadapted immigrant groups who sought environments resembling their homelands. Particularly revealing are the choices of settlement site made by Finns, Icelanders, English, and Cornish who came to Wisconsin (Figure 9.15). The Finns, coming from a cold, thin-soiled, glaciated, lake-studded, coniferous forest zone in Europe, settled the North Woods of Wisconsin, a land very similar in almost every respect to the one they departed. Icelanders, from a bleak, remote island in the North Atlantic, located their only Wisconsin colony on Washington Island, an isolated outpost surrounded by the waters of Lake Michigan. The English, accustomed to good farmland, generally founded ethnic islands in the better agricultural districts of southern and southwestern Wisconsin. Cornish miners from the Celtic highlands of western Great Britain sought out the lead-mining communities of southwestern Wisconsin, where they continued their traditional occupation.

Elsewhere in the American heartland, thousands of ethnic Germans from wheat-growing communities on the open steppe grasslands of

Figure 9.15
The ecology of selected ethnic islands in Wisconsin. Notice that Finnish settlements are concentrated in the infertile North Woods section, as are the American Indian reservations. The Finns went there by choice, the Indians survived there because few white people were interested in such land. The English, by contrast, are found more often in the better farmland south of the border of the North Woods. Some of the English were miners from Cornwall, and they were drawn to the lead-mining country of southwestern Wisconsin, where they could practice the profession already known to them. Icelanders, an island people, chose an island as their settlement site in Wisconsin. (After Hill, 1942, cited in caption for Fig. 9.6.)

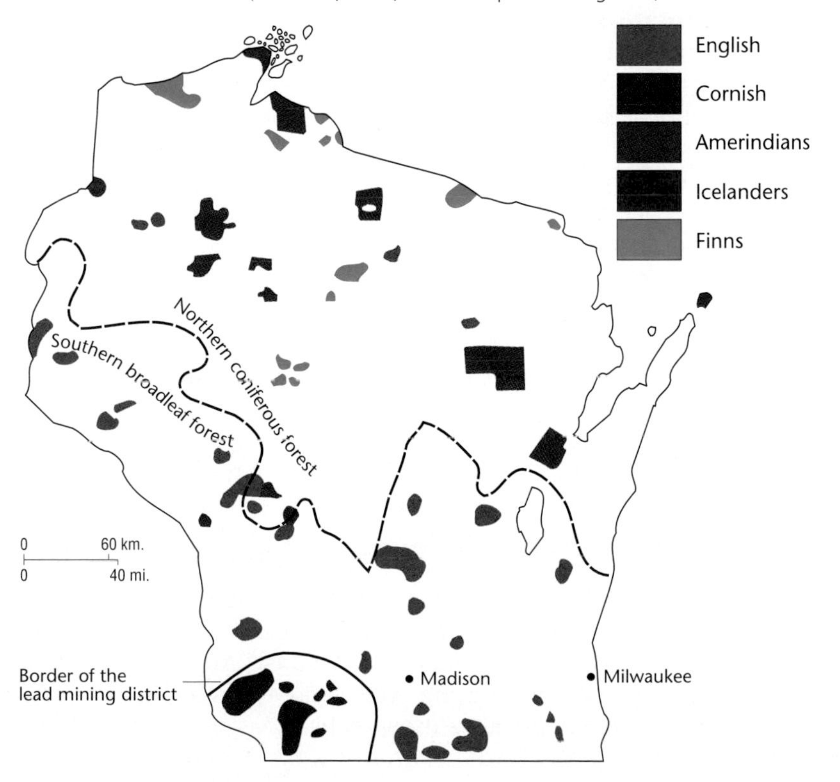

south Russia, the so-called Russian-Germans, settled the prairies of the Great Plains, where they established thriving wheat farms like those of their eastern European source area, using varieties of grain brought from their semiarid homeland. Ukrainians in Canada chose the *aspen belt,* a mixture of prairie, marsh, and scrub forest, as their settlement zone in Manitoba, Saskatchewan, and Alberta, because it resembled their former European home.

Such ethnic niche-filling has continued to the present day. Cubans have clustered in southernmost Florida, the only part of the United States mainland to have a *tropical savanna* climate identical to that in Cuba, and many Vietnamese settled as fishers on the Gulf of Mexico, especially in Texas, where they could continue their traditional livelihood.

Ethnic Environmental Perception

This deliberate site selection by ethnic immigrants represents rather accurate environmental perceptions of the new land. As a rule, however, immigrants perceive the ecosystem of their new home to be more like that of their abandoned native land than is actually the case. Their perceptions of the new country emphasize the similarities and downgrade the differences. Perhaps the search for similarity results from homesickness or an unwillingness to admit that migration had brought them to a largely alien land. Perhaps growing to adulthood in a particular kind of physical environment retards one's ability to perceive a different ecosystem accurately. Whatever the reason, the distorted perception occasionally caused problems for ethnic farming groups. Sometimes crops that thrived in the old homeland proved poorly suited to the particular American setting. A period of trial and error was often necessary to come to terms with the New World environment. In a few instances, the misperception was of such magnitude that economic disaster resulted and the ethnic island had to be abandoned. In such cases, cultural **maladaptation** is said to occur.

Even if the colonization area differed in some important respect from the mother country, ethnic immigrants often used their skills as farmers to choose a settlement site wisely, thereby aiding their economic success and cultural survival. In the colonization of rural North America, for example, Germans and Czechs chose consistently the best farmland, a choice that helped them become prosperous and superior farmers. Geographer Russel Gerlach, researching the German communities of the Ozarks, found that while Appalachian southern settlers in that region chose easy-to-work sandy and bottomland soil, Germans often chose superior soils that were harder to work. In Lawrence County, Missouri, for example, the Germans were relative latecomers but still obtained some of the best land when they selected dark-soiled prairie lands that earlier Anglo-American settlers had avoided. In Gerlach's words, "A map showing the distribution of Germans in the Ozarks can also be a map of the better soils in the region." A similar ability to select choice soils can be detected among the Czechs in Texas, the state containing the largest rural population of that ethnic group in the United States. Figure 9.16 reveals, to a quite remarkable degree, that the Czech farming communities in Texas are concentrated in tallgrass prairie regions underlain by dark, fertile soils. By contrast, Anglo-Texans tended to avoid open prairies as farming sites, and no other group was as drawn to this ecological niche as the Czechs.

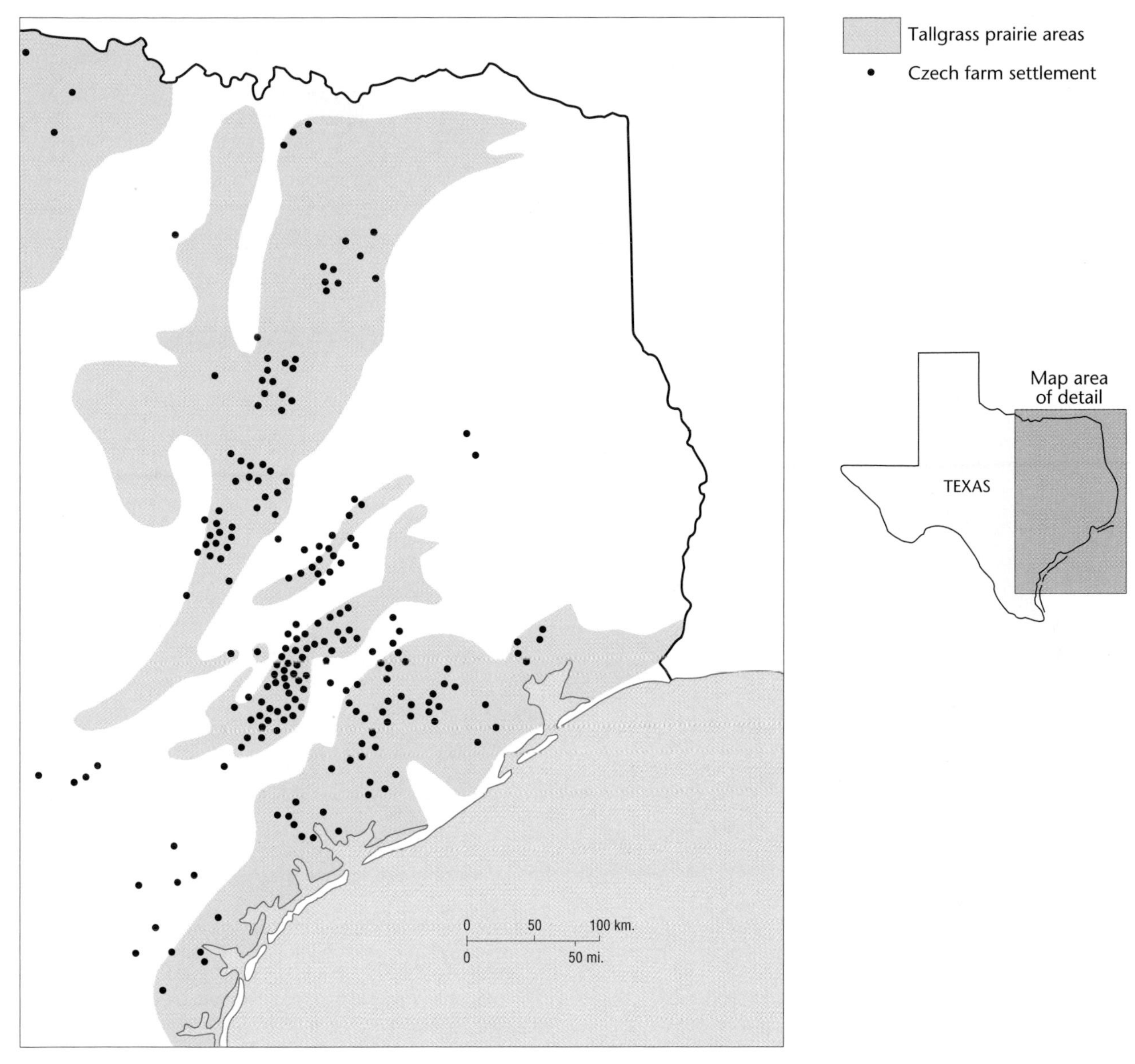

Figure 9.16
The cultural ecology of Czech farm settlements in Texas. Note the tendency of Czechs to settle in tallgrass prairie regions. The prairie grasses were underlain by rich soils that have supported a prosperous Czech farming class for well over a century. (After Maresh, Henry R. "The Czechs in Texas." *Southwestern Historical Quarterly,* 50 [1946–47]: 236–240 and map.)

Ecology of Ethnic Survival

Rather than being the product of migration, many ethnic groups, as we have seen, reside in ancient ancestral home districts and become ethnic only when conquered and surrounded by invading peoples. The American Indians fall into this category, as do the Australian Aborigines and Scandinavian Sami (Lapps). In almost every case, these groups owe their survival to an adaptive strategy that allows occupancy of a difficult physical environment where the invaders proved maladapted.

Consider, for example, the distribution of Indian groups in Latin America (Figure 9.17). If you consult maps of terrain and climate, you will find the Indian population is clustered in mountainous areas, in-

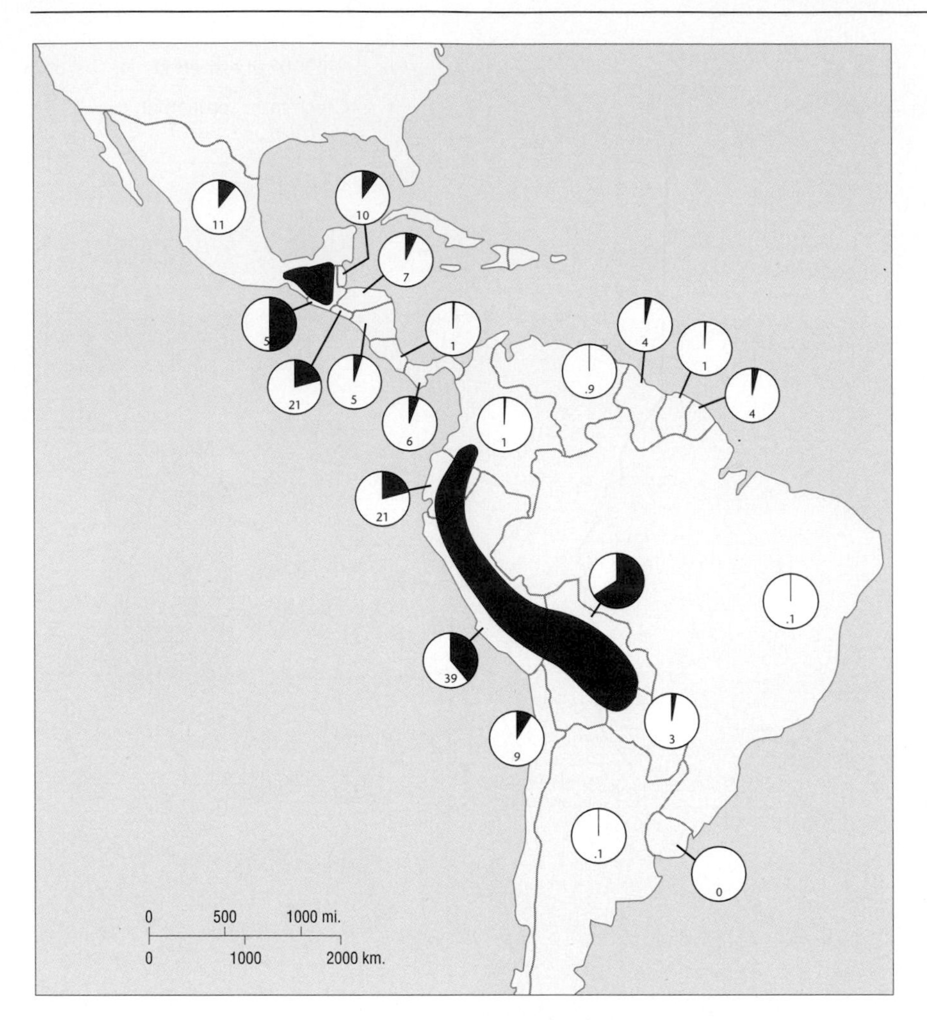

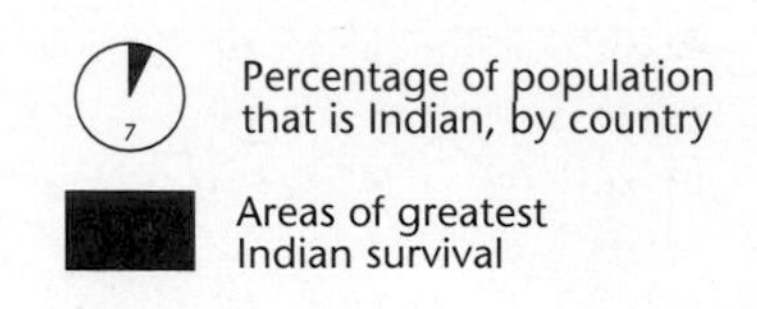

Figure 9.17
Indian (indigenous) population in Latin America, as a percentage of total population by country. The range is from Bolivia, where almost two-thirds of the population is Indian, to Uruguay, where none are found. Mexico has the largest number, with about 8 million, followed by Peru with nearly 7 million. (Source: Adapted and modified from Espinosa, Tina L. "Indigenous Population in Latin America." *The Itinerant Geographer,* University of California at Berkeley [1991]: 17.)

cluding many areas above about 10,000 feet (3000 meters) elevation. The European invaders never adjusted well to these high altitudes. Many other factors are involved in the differential survival of American Indians, but certainly terrain, climate, and indigenous adaptive strategy play a role.

Ethnic Cultural Integration

The complicated spatial pattern of ethnic islands, homelands, ghettos, and neighborhoods resembles the distribution of a variety of other cultural geographical phenomena. Ethnicity can play a role in deciding what people buy, how they vote, how they make a living, where they do their shopping, how they spend their free time, or whom they choose as their marriage partners. In other words, ethnicity is causally related to many other facets of culture, and therefore we can profitably apply the theme of cultural integration to the geographical study of ethnic groups. To illustrate how ethnicity is integrated into the cultural fabric, we will use three economic examples from North America.

Geographer Hansgeorg Schlichtmann speaks of economic *performance,* meaning the level of success "in making a living and accumulating wealth," noting that inter-ethnic differences in performance have frequently been observed. He adds that ethnic groups exhibit contrasts in economic orientation, ranging from those seeking self-sufficiency through a diversified agricultural economy to those specializing in particular products for market, and in economic success. We have chosen both rural and urban examples, involving contrasts in choice of employment, types of business activity, and farming practices to illustrate the integration of ethnicity and economy.

Ethnicity and Business Activity

Differential ethnic preferences give rise to distinct patterns of purchasing goods and services. This in turn is reflected in the types of businesses and services available in different ethnic neighborhoods in a city.

Geographer Keith Harries made a detailed study of businesses in the Los Angeles urban area, comparing Anglo-American, African American, and Mexican-American neighborhoods (Figure 9.18). He found that East Los Angeles Chicano neighborhoods have unusually large numbers of food stores, eating and drinking places, personal services, and repair shops. These Hispanic areas have, in fact, three times as many food stores as Anglo neighborhoods. In large part, this reflects the dominance of small corner grocery stores and the fragmentation of food sales among several kinds of stores, such as *tortillerias*. The large number of eating and drinking places is related to the Mexican custom of gathering in *cantinas* (bars), where much of the social life is centered. Abundant small barbershops provide one reason why personal service establishments rank so high.

African American south Los Angeles ranks highest in personal service businesses, and vacant stores rank second. Eating and drinking places there are the third most numerous. In contrast to the Chicano eastern part of town, the south has relatively few bars but a large number of liquor stores and liquor departments in grocery stores and drugstores. Secondhand shops are very common, but there are no antique or jewelry stores and only one book-stationery shop. A distinctive African American personal service enterprise, the shoeshine parlor, is found only in south Los Angeles.

Anglo neighborhoods rank high in professional and financial service establishments, such as doctors, lawyers, and banks. These services are much less common in the non-Anglo neighborhoods. Furniture, jewelry, antique, and apparel stores are also more numerous among the Anglos, as are full-scale restaurants.

Contrasts similar to those observed by Harries in the urban scene can also be found in rural and small-town areas. An example can be taken from a study by geographer Elaine Bjorklund of an ethnic island in southwestern Michigan settled in the mid-nineteenth century by Dutch Calvinists (Figure 9.19). Their descendants adhered to a strict moral code and tended to regard the non–Dutch Reformed world outside their ethnic island as sinful and inferior. This adherence to the precepts of the Calvinist Reformed Church was clearly the main manifestation of their ethnicity, because the Dutch language had died out in the

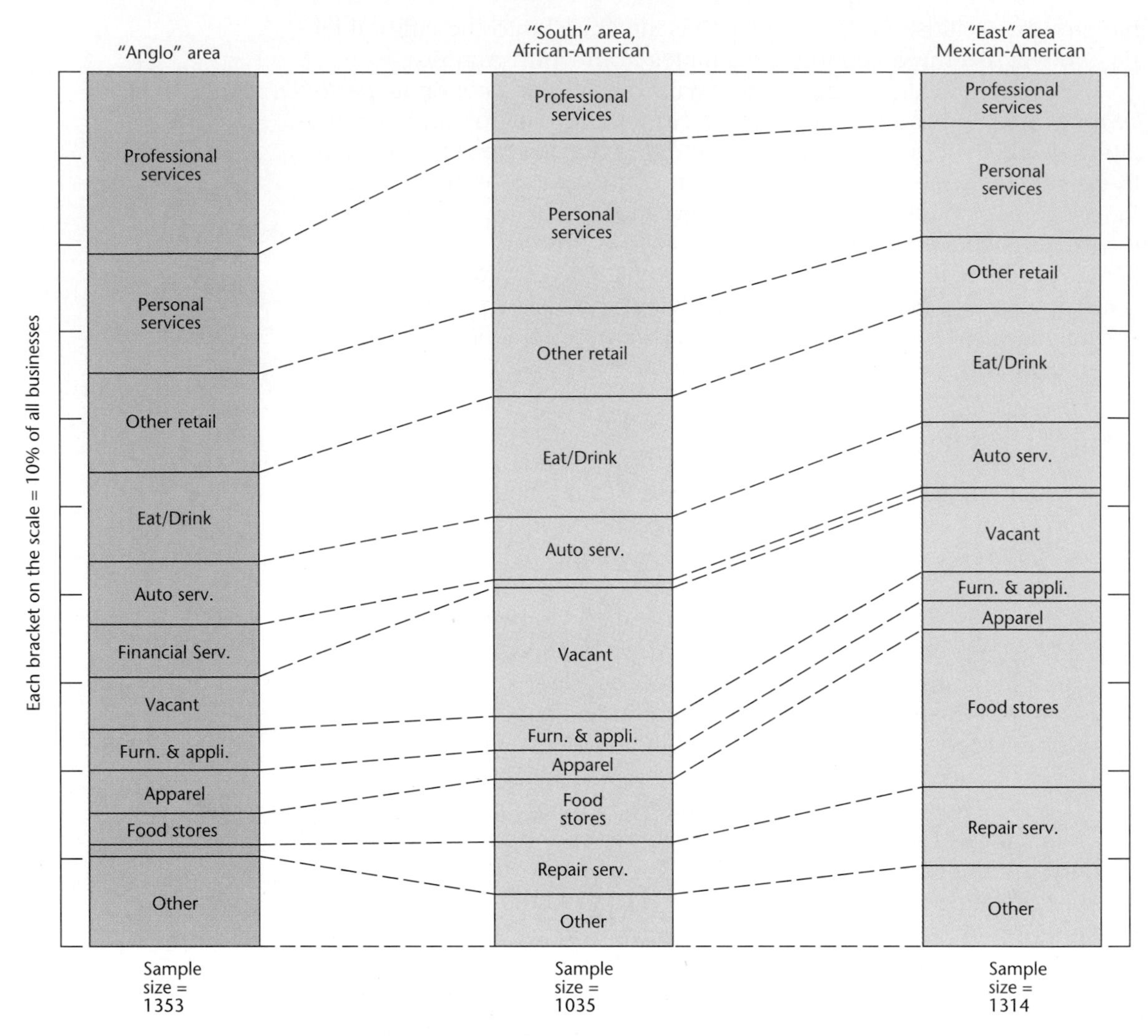

Figure 9.18
Types of businesses found in Anglo-American, African American, and Mexican-American neighborhoods of Los Angeles, California, about 1970. "Professional services" include such persons as doctors and lawyers, while "personal services" are represented by businesses like barbershops and shoeshine parlors. Do such differences exist between ethnic neighborhoods in your city? (After Harries, Keith D. "Ethnic Variations in Los Angeles Business Patterns." *Annals of the Association of American Geographers,* 61 [1971]: 739.)

area. The impact of the Calvinist code of behavior on business activity in this Dutch ethnic island was apparent in various ways. As recently as 1960, no taverns, dance halls, or movie theaters existed there except in the city of Holland, and no business activity was permitted on Sunday. Since traditional Calvinists believe that leisure and idleness are evil, most present-day farmers work at second jobs during slack seasons in the agricultural year.

Ethnicity and Type of Employment

Closely related to type of business is type of employment. In many urban ethnic neighborhoods, individual groups gravitated early to particular kinds of jobs. These job identities, never rigid, were stronger in the decades immediately following immigration than today because of advancing acculturation, but some notable examples can still be found. In

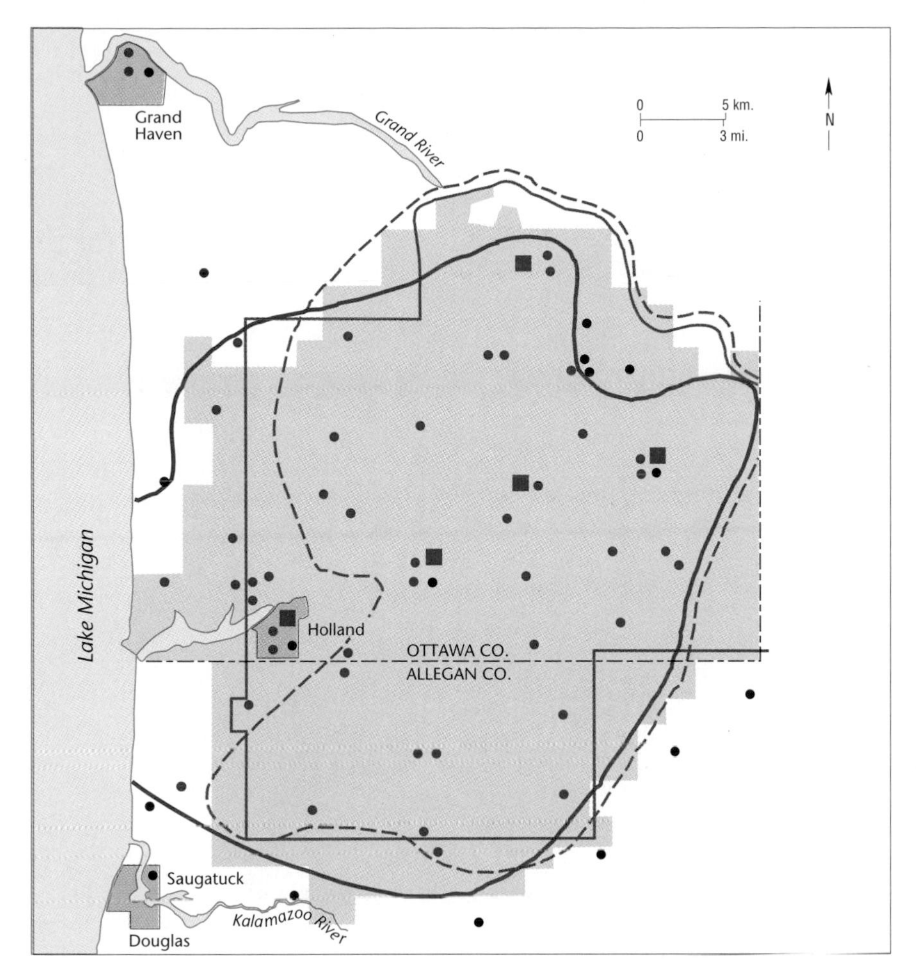

Figure 9.19
The impact of ethnicity in southwestern Michigan, about 1960. An ethnic island of Dutch Reformed (Calvinist) immigrants was established here in the 1840s, and has survived to the present. The Calvinists kept taverns, movie theaters, non-Calvinist churches, and Sunday business activity out of their area. Note, too, that these several traits, though causally related, do not have exactly the same geographical distribution. Look again at Figure 1.5 in Chapter 1. (After Bjorklund, Elaine M. "Ideology and Culture Exemplified in Southwestern Michigan." *Annals of the Association of American Geographers,* 54 [1964]: 235.)

some cases, the identification of ethnic groups and job types is sufficiently strong to produce stereotyped images in the American popular mind, such as Irish police, Chinese launderers, Korean grocers, Italian restaurant owners, and Jewish retailers.

The contrast in ethnic activity in the restaurant trade is striking. Certain groups proved highly successful in marketing versions of their traditional cuisines to the population at large. In particular, the Chinese, Mexicans, and Italians succeeded in this venture (Figure 9.20). Each dominates a restaurant region in North America far larger than their ethnic homelands, islands, or neighborhoods.

In Boston, Irish once provided most of the laborers in the warehouse and terminal facilities near the central business district, Italians dominated the distribution and marketing of fresh foods, Germans gravitated to the sewing machine and port supply trades, and Jews found employment in merchandising and the manufacture of ready-made clothing. Italians in the northeastern United States still control the terrazzo and ceramic tile unions, and Czechs dominate the pearl button

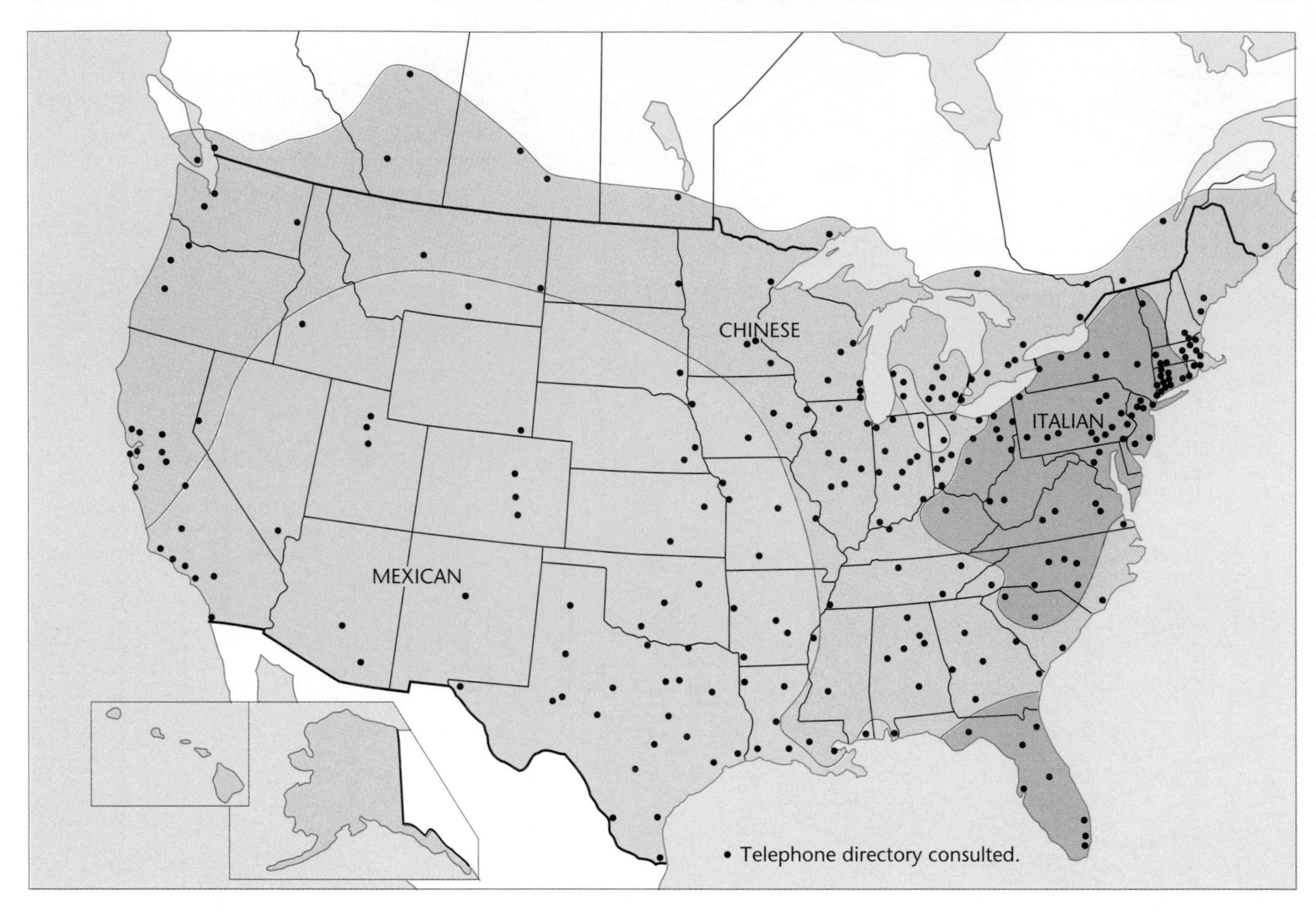

Figure 9.20
Dominant ethnic restaurant cuisine in North America. In each region, the cuisine indicated is the leading type of ethnic restaurant. Why do Mexican foodways balloon northward faster than the main diffusion of these people? Why does Italian cuisine prevail so far south of the major concentration of Italian-Americans? All ethnic cuisines were considered in compiling the map, based on telephone yellow page listings. (After Zelinsky, Wilbur. "The Roving Palate: North America's Ethnic Restaurant Cuisines." *Geoforum,* 16 [1985]: 66.)

industry. In many cases, these ethnic job identities were related to occupational skills developed in the European homeland. A more recent example is the immigration of Basques from Spain to serve as professional *jai alai* players in the cities of southern Florida, where their ancient ethnic ball game has become a major medium of legal gambling. An older example, also provided by Basques, involved their concentration in sheep ranching areas of the American West, where they found employment as herders, a skill well developed in their European homeland.

Ethnicity and Farming Practices

Even within the same occupation, different ethnic groups often retain distinctiveness. For example, a popular belief in the United States holds that farmers of German ethnic origin are superior to Anglo-Americans as tillers of the soil. As early as 1789, Benjamin Rush, describing the Pennsylvania Germans, enumerated 16 ways "in which they differ from most of the other farmers" of that state.

A number of geographers have tested the claim of German agricultural distinctiveness in the United States. One such study focused on the Hill Country of central Texas in the nineteenth century. Germans who settled there farmed the land more intensively, derived more income from their land, and were more likely to be landowners than were the Anglos. German-owned sheep yielded 24 percent more wool per capita, and German poultry laid 15 percent more eggs than their Anglo livestock counterparts because of better feeding and care.

Germans in the South still retained their agricultural superiority in the 1930s, according to a study by Professor Walter Kollmorgen, a pioneer in the field of ethnic geography (see earlier biographical sketch). His research on a German ethnic island in Alabama revealed that German-Americans practiced a more diversified agriculture, had higher incomes, and more often owned land than Anglos. "Agricultural practices in the county," he concluded, "represent to a considerable extent a projection of patterns introduced by the Germans and the non-Germans."

A more recent study by Russel Gerlach revealed that in the 1970s farmers of German descent living in the Missouri Ozarks remained distinct in many respects from non-Germans. They owned larger farms, had more acreage under cultivation, and were less likely to be tenant farmers.

Similar differences along ethnic lines can be detected in present-day Canada. In a study of southern Manitoba, geographers D. Todd and J. S. Brierley compared the rural economies in German Mennonite, Slavic, British, French, and Dutch communities there. After detecting contrasts among these groups in type of agriculture, level of education, and kinds of nonfarm employment, Todd and Brierley concluded that fundamental functional linkages between ethnicity and the regional economic structure exist.

Similarily, some recently arrived Asian immigrant groups introduced intensive gardening techniques to America, as geographer Jennifer Helzer discovered. The Hmong people from Laos, 50,000 of whom now live in California, cultivate their distinctive ethnic gardens in and around cities such as Chico and Redding, utilizing interstate highway easements and other odd parcels of land that Americans would never think of using. A typical Hmong garden includes mustard greens, bitter melon, chile peppers, and other special crops needed in their traditional cuisine. These intensively cultivated Hmong gardens stand in marked contrast to the nearby featureless almond groves of Sacramento Valley agribusiness.

Ethnic Landscapes

Ethnicity is often, or even generally, visible, and we can properly speak of ethnic landscapes. Ethnic groups frequently differ in styles of traditional architecture, in the patterns of surveying the land, in the distribution of houses and other buildings, and in the degree to which they "humanize" the land. In particular, many rural areas bear an ethnic imprint on the cultural landscape. Often the imprint is subtle, discernible only to those who pause and look closely; sometimes it is quite striking, flaunted as an "ethnic flag" and immediately visible, even to the untrained eye (Figure 9.21). Persistence, change, and degree of subtlety in the ethnic landscape can provide valuable evidence of acculturation and the level of group pride (see box, *The Face of the Fox*).

Figure 9.21
An "ethnic flag" in the cultural landscape. This maize granary, called a *cuezcomatl,* is unique to the American Indian population of Tlaxcala state, Mexico. The structure holds shelled maize. In Mexico, even the cultivation of maize long remained an American Indian trait, as the Spaniards preferred wheat.

An "Ethnic Flag"

A good example of ethnicity in the cultural landscape of rural America is provided by the *sauna.* In Finland, these small steam bathhouses, normally built of logs, are seen at almost every farmstead. The Finns find it refreshing in cold weather to take a steam bath in the superheated sauna, often followed by a naked romp in the snow. The sauna is an important element in the cultural landscape of Finland.

When Finns came to America, they brought the sauna with them. Geographers Matti Kaups and Cotton Mather made a study of this Finnish landscape feature in Minnesota and Michigan (Figure 9.22).

"The Face of the Fox": Indian and Non-Indian Landscapes in Iowa

America's Indian reservations have distinctive cultural landscapes. Below is one non-Indian visitor's reaction to the Fox Indian countryside, surrounded by Anglo-American farmland in central Iowa:

> *One fall day I chanced to drive through the Iowa countryside, the landscape wrought by white Iowa farmers: rolling hills stretched out, and impressed upon the hills were rectangular shapes, sharp and precise, each shape its own color. An Iowa farmer looking out upon his handiwork must have sensed, it seemed to me, his enormous power and must have felt great pride. Here and there, along a river or on some steep slope, nature was allowed to hold forth—trees and grass and brush—but not to encroach. Then I drove onto the roads of the Fox community. Immediately nature leapt up: the terrain was formed of hills and bluffs and streams; trees were seen in any direction in small and large clusters and covering whole hills, and some reached high. In the spaces that remained, grass and weeds and brush threatened to reach as high. Growth was beneath me, around me on all sides, and overhead.*
>
> *There, I recognized, was the difference. Passing through the countryside of white Iowa, one senses, as the Iowa farmer must sense, that he stands on top of what he sees, and a relationship is compellingly conveyed: man and his works. Entering the Fox community, one senses, as a Fox must sense, that he is enveloped.*

If a Fox Indian were to provide a similar impression of a nearby Anglo cultural landscape, how might he or she express it? Would the Indian likely have a high opinion of massive transformation of the natural landscape?

Quoted from Gearing, Frederick O. *The Face of the Fox.* Chicago: Aldine, 1970, p. 47.

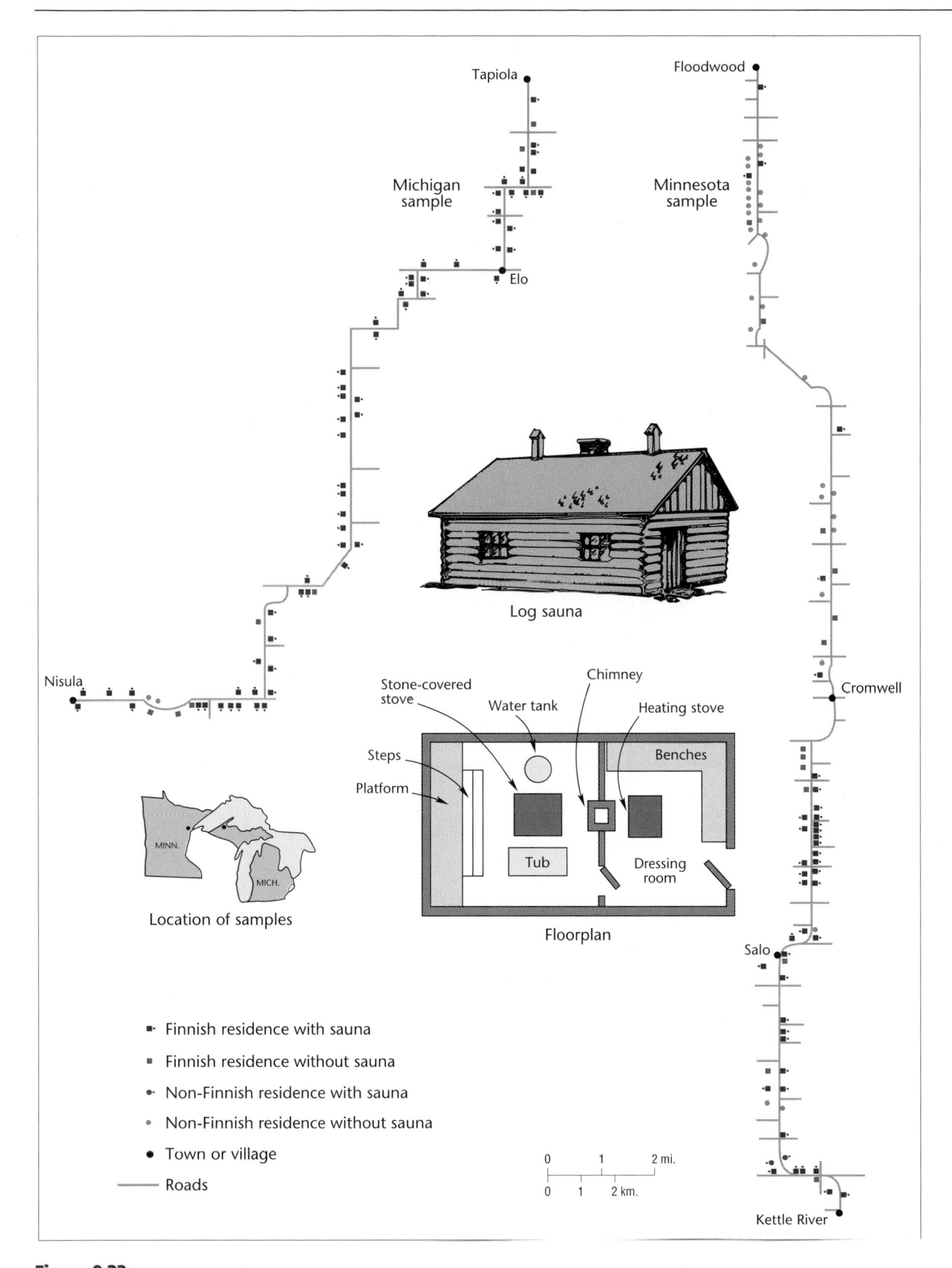

Figure 9.22

A Finnish landscape feature in the upper Midwest. In two traverses through Finnish ethnic islands in northern Minnesota and Michigan, two geographers found that the sauna, a small steam bathhouse, was an almost unfailing visual sign of Finnish settlement. In this way, ethnicity is imprinted on the cultural landscape. (After Mather, Cotton, and Matti Kaups. "The Finnish Sauna: A Cultural Index to Settlement." *Annals of the Association of American Geographers,* 53 [1963]: 495, 499.)

They found the sauna to be an excellent visual indicator of Finnish-American ethnic islands. In one sample area, an almost purely Finnish rural district in the Upper Peninsula of Michigan, 88 percent of all Finnish-American residences had a sauna out behind. In an area of greater ethnic mixture in northern Minnesota, 77 percent of Finnish houses had saunas adjacent, as contrasted with only 6 percent of non-Finnish residences in the same district.

Ethnic Settlement Patterns

Even within the constraints of a governmentally imposed survey system, some ethnic groups created their own distinctive settlement pat-

Figure 9.23
Distribution of farmsteads in German and non-German rural parts of Gasconade County, Missouri, 1970. Both areas have identical survey systems and similar road patterns, yet the German farmers generally situate their houses farther from the public roads than do non-Germans. Can you think of any reasons why the German-Americans are distinctive in this way? (After Gerlach, Russel L. *Immigrants in the Ozarks: A Study in Ethnic Geography.* Columbia: University of Missouri Press, 1976, p. 71.)

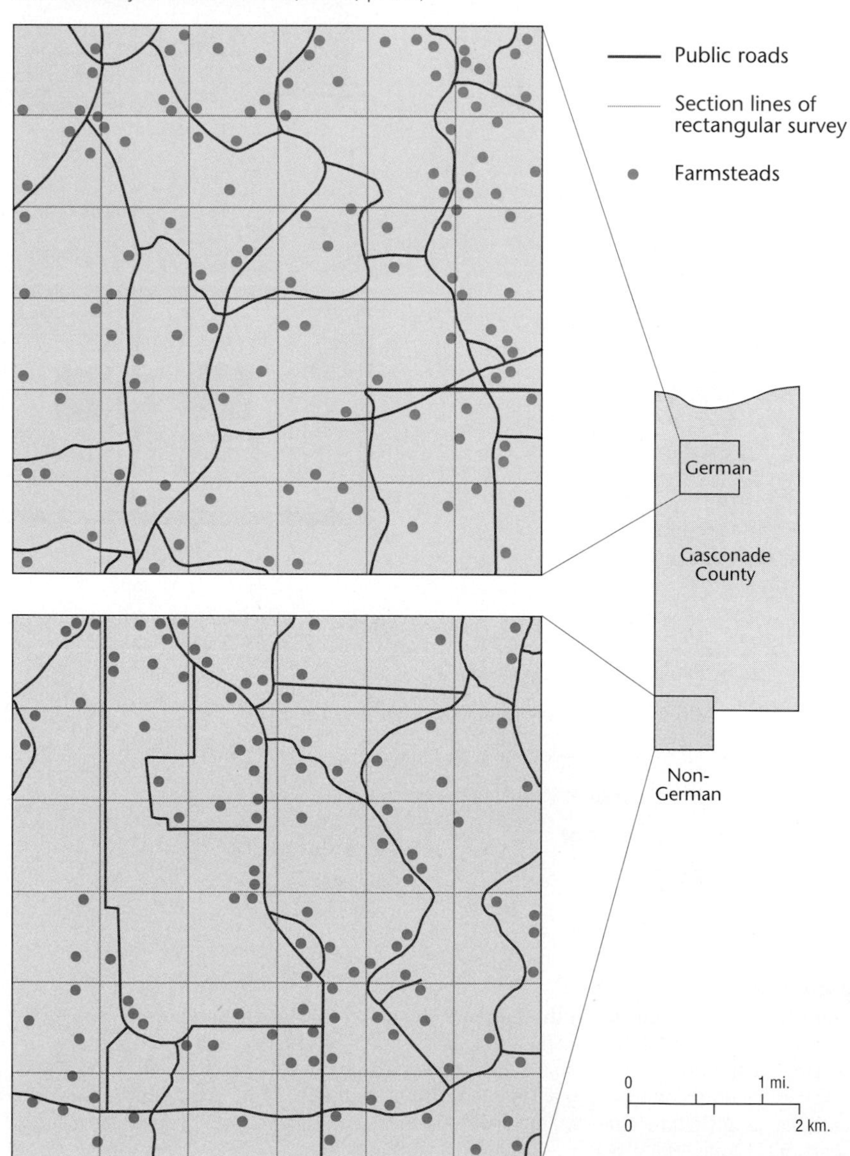

terns. Often this was accomplished even where a rigid checkerboard survey was present.

In the Missouri Ozarks, for example, Germans and non-Germans alike settled a region of rectangular survey. In a close look at present-day settlement maps, we can see that rather different patterns developed. German-American farmsteads much less frequently lie on public roads than do non-German houses (Figure 9.23). In many instances, their farmhouses stand a half-mile from the nearest public road.

Similarly, some Russian-German Mennonite colonists in the prairie provinces of Canada created clustered street villages in a rectangular survey area, in marked contrast to their non-Mennonite neighbors (Figure 9.24). Mennonites duplicated the villages they had known in Russia, while other farmers in the area lived out on their land in dispersed farmsteads. Apparently the cohesive bond of ethnicity encouraged these immigrants to live in clustered communities, where they enjoyed close daily contact with people of their own kind.

The Mescalero Apache Indians of New Mexico also make an ethnic statement in their settlement pattern, as geographer Martha Henderson discovered. Despite a century of federal governmental efforts to disperse these eastern Apaches through their reservation, in the Anglo-American manner, they persist in clustering into villages *matrilocally* (that is, near the maternal clan home). In the process, the Apaches "continue to display vestiges of the precontact heritage" in the landscape.

Figure 9.24

A Mennonite street village in Manitoba province, Canada. The Mennonites, a German-speaking religious sect from Russia, settled this area in 1875. Accustomed to living in such farm villages (see Chapter 2) in Russia, the Mennonites created similar settlements in Canada. The fragmentation of landholdings and communal pasture are also Old World customs. The Mennonites created this village, named Neuhorst, in spite of the Canadian rectangular survey system, which encouraged scattered farmsteads and unit-block holdings. While many such villages later disappeared, some survive as part of the Mennonite ethnic landscape. From a distance, these surviving villages are revealed by long rows of cottonwood trees, which line the central street. What advantages would clustered village settlement offer to an ethnic group? What disadvantages? (After Warkentin, John. "Mennonite Agricultural Settlements of Southern Manitoba." *Geographical Review,* 49 [1959]: 359.)

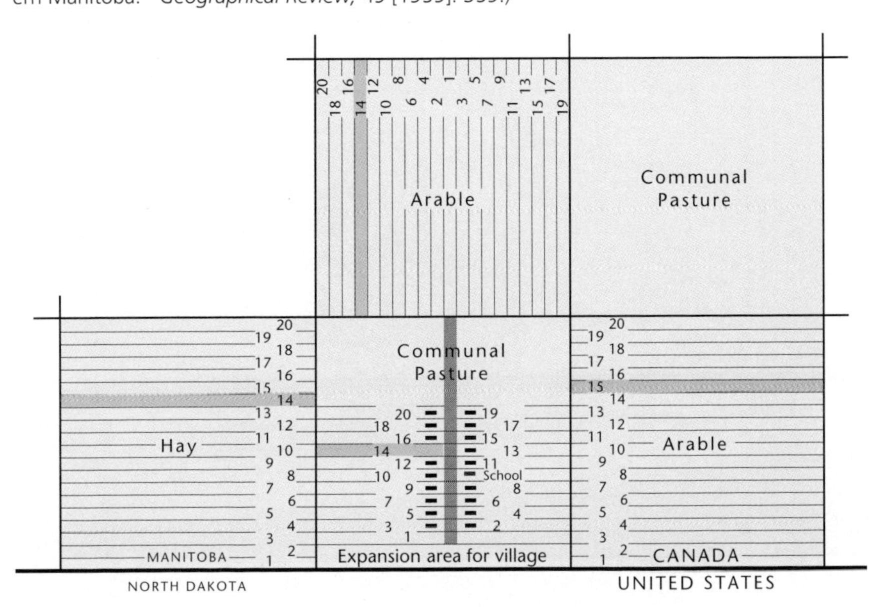

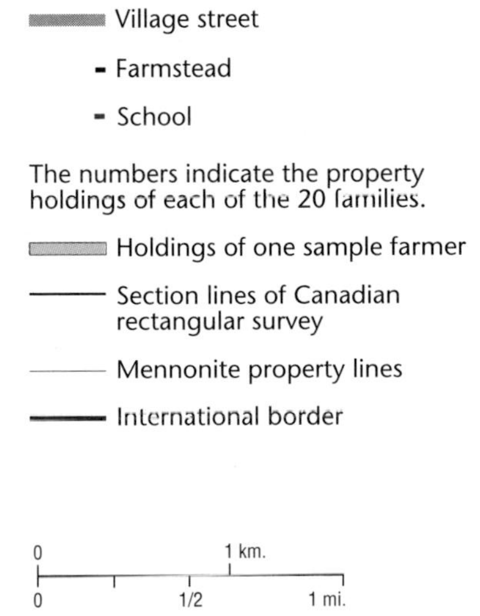

Urban Ethnic Landscapes

Ethnic cultural landscapes also appear in the urban setting, in both neighborhoods and ghettos. A fine example is the brightly colored exterior wall mural typically found in Mexican-American ethnic neighborhoods in the southwestern United States (Figure 9.25). These began to appear in the 1960s in southern California, and they exhibit influences rooted in both Spain and the Indian cultures of Mexico, according to geographer Dan Arreola. A wide variety of wall surfaces offer the opportunity for this ethnic expression, from apartment house and store exteriors to bridge abutments. The subjects also cover a wide range, from religious motifs to political ideology, from statements concerning historical wrongs to urban zoning disputes. Often they are specific to the site, incorporating well-known elements of the local landscape, and thus heightening the sense of place and ethnic "turf." Inscriptions can be in either Spanish or English, but many Mexican murals do not contain a written message, relying instead on the sharpness of image and vividness of color to make an impression.

Usually the visual ethnic expression is more subtle. Color alone can connote and reveal ethnicity to the trained eye. Red, for example, is a venerated and auspicious color to the Chinese, and when they established Chinatowns in Canadian and American cities, red paint proliferated (Figure 9.26). Light blue is a Greek ethnic color, derived from the flag of their ancestral country, and Greeks avoid red, perceived as the color of their ancient enemy, the Turks. Green, an Irish Catholic color, also finds favor in Muslim ethnic neighborhoods in countries as farflung as France and China, because it is the sacred color of Islam.

Conclusion

Through the theme of culture region, we saw how ethnic groups, whether rural or urban, tend to cluster spatially. In fact, we could say that spatial identity is a prerequisite of ethnicity, so that the study of ethnic groups is inherently geographical. Cultural diffusion allowed us

Figure 9.25
Mexican-American wall mural, Barrio Logan, San Diego, California. This mural bears an obvious ideological-political message and helps create a special sense of place in the Mexican *barrio* of the city. Can you identify the persons and events depicted in the mural? See also Arreola, Daniel D. "Mexican American Exterior Murals." *Geographical Review,* 74 (1984): 409–424.

Figure 9.26
Two urban ethnic landscapes. Houses painted red reveal the addition of a Toronto residential block to the local Chinatown. The use of light blue trim, coupled with the planting of a grape arbor at the front door of a dwelling in the Astoria district of Queens, New York City, marks the neighborhood as Greek.

to see the process by which ethnic groups migrated and introduced some of their Old World traits. Cultural ecology taught us that migrating ethnic groups, seeking preadaptive advantage, often look for familiar physical environments in choosing sites for colonization, while ethnic minorities confined to ancient homelands find refuge and survival in difficult environments through their equally venerable adaptive strategies. The imprint of ethnicity on livelihood was revealed through the theme of cultural integration. Examples of the visual aspects of ethnicity, some obvious and some subtle, became evident in our discussion of the cultural landscape. By adopting the viewpoint of the cultural geographer, we have been able to look at many facets of ethnicity, to decipher some of the reasons why the ethnic mosaic has come to be, and to interpret the cultural imprint of ethnic groups.

Sources and Suggested Readings

Aiken, Charles S. "A New Type of Black Ghetto in the Plantation South." *Annals of the Association of American Geographers,* 80 (1990): 223–246.

Airriess, Christopher A., and David L. Clawson. "Vietnamese Market Gardens in New Orleans." *Geographical Review,* 84 (1994): 16–31.

Allen, James P., and Eugene J. Turner. *We the People: An Atlas of America's Ethnic Diversity*. New York: Macmillan, 1987.

Anderson, Kay J. "The Idea of Chinatown: The Power of Place and Institutional Practice in the Making of a Racial Category." *Annals of the Association of American Geographers,* 77 (1987): 580–598.

Arreola, Daniel D. "The Chinese Role in Creating the Early Cultural Landscape of the Sacramento–San Joaquin Delta." *California Geographer,* 15 (1975): 1–15.

Arreola, Daniel D. "Mexican American Housescapes." *Geographical Review,* 78 (1988): 299–315.

Arreola, Daniel D. "Plaza Towns of South Texas." *Geographical Review,* 82 (1992): 56–73.

Asante, Molefi K., and Mark T. Matson. *Historical and Cultural Atlas of African Americans.* New York: Macmillan, 1991.

Baltensperger, Bradley H. "Agricultural Change Among Great Plains Russian Germans." *Annals of the Association of American Geographers,* 73 (1983): 75–88.

Boswell, Thomas D., and Richard C. Jones. "A Regionalization of Mexican-Americans in the United States." *Geographical Review,* 70 (1980): 88–98.

Carlson, Alvar W. *The Spanish American Homeland: Four Centuries in New Mexico's Río Arriba.* Baltimore: Johns Hopkins University Press, 1990.

Cromartie, John, and Carol B. Stack. "Reinterpretation of Black Return and Nonreturn Migration to the South, 1975–1980." *Geographical Review,* 79 (1989): 297–310.

Darlington, James W. "The Ukrainian Impress on the Canadian West," in Lubomyr Luciuk and Stella Hryniuk (eds.). *Canada's Ukrainians: Negotiating an Identity.* Toronto: University of Toronto Press, 1991, pp. 53–80.

Davis, G. A., and O. F. Donaldson. *Blacks in the United States: A Geographic Perspective.* Boston: Houghton Mifflin, 1975.

Desbarats, Jacqueline. "Indochinese Resettlement in the United States." *Annals of the Association of American Geographers,* 75 (1985): 522–538.

Estaville, Lawrence E., Jr. "The Louisiana French Homeland." *Journal of Cultural Geography,* 13, No. 2 (1993): 31–46.

Estaville, Lawrence E., Jr. "Mapping the Louisiana French." *Southeastern Geographer,* 26 (1986): 90–113.

Franklin, Robert L. "Ethnicity and an Emerging Indochinese Commercial District in Orange County." *Yearbook of the Association of Pacific Coast Geographers,* 45 (1983): 85–99.

Hardwick, Susan W. *Russian Refuge: Religion, Migration, and Settlement on the North American Pacific Rim.* Chicago: University of Chicago Press, 1993.

Harris, R. Colebrook. "The Simplification of Europe Overseas." *Annals of the Association of American Geographers,* 67 (1977): 469–483.

Helzer, Jennifer J. "Continuity and Change: Hmong Settlement in California's Sacramento Valley." *Journal of Cultural Geography,* 14, No. 2 (1994): 51–64.

Henderson, Martha L. "Settlement Patterns on the Mescalero Apache Reservation Since 1883." *Geographical Review,* 80 (1990): 226–238.

Jett, Stephen C., and Virginia E. Spencer. *Navajo Architecture: Forms, History, Distributions.* Tucson: University of Arizona Press, 1981.

Johnson, Hildegard Binder. "The Location of German Immigrants in the Middle West." *Annals of the Association of American Geographers,* 41 (1951): 1–41.

Johnson, James H., Jr., and Curtis C. Roseman. "Recent Black Outmigration from Los Angeles: The Role of Household Dynamics and Kinship Systems." *Annals of the Association of American Geographers,* 80 (1990): 205–222.

Jones, Richard C. *Patterns of Undocumented Migration: Mexico and the United States.* Totowa, NJ: Rowman and Allanheld, 1984.

Jordan, Terry G. "New Sweden's Role on the American Frontier: A Study in Cultural Preadaptation." *Geografiska Annaler,* 71B (1989): 71–83.

Jordan, Terry G. "Preadaptation and European Colonization in Rural North America." *Annals of the Association of American Geographers,* 79 (1989): 489–500.

Jordan, Terry G., and Alyson L. Greiner. "Irish Migration to Rural Eastern Australia." *Irish Geography,* 27 (1994): 135–142.

Journal of Cultural Geography. Special issue on ethnic homelands, Vol. 13, No. 2 (1993), 1–148.

Kain, John F. "Race, Ethnicity, and Residential Location." *Discussion Paper No. D75-3, Department of City and Regional Planning.* Cambridge, MA: Harvard University, 1975.

Kilpinen, Jon T. "Finnish Cultural Landscapes in the Pacific Northwest." *Pacific Northwest Quarterly,* 86 (1994–95): 25–34.

Kollmorgen, Walter M. "A Reconnaissance of Some Cultural-Agricultural Islands in the South." *Economic Geography,* 17 (1941): 409–430; 19 (1943): 109–117.

Lehr, John C. "The Landscape of Ukrainian Settlement in the Canadian West." *Great Plains Quarterly,* 2, No. 2 (1982): 94–105.

Lipshitz, Gabriel. "Ethnic Differences in Migration Patterns—Disparities Among Arabs and Jews in the Peripheral Regions of Israel." *Professional Geographer,* 43 (1991): 445–456.

Louder, Dean R., and Eric Waddell (eds.). *French America: Mobility, Identity, and Minority Experience Across the Continent.* Baton Rouge: Louisiana State University Press, 1993.

Luciuk, Lubomyr Y., and Bohdan S. Kordan. *Creating a Landscape: A Geography of Ukrainians in Canada.* Toronto: University of Toronto Press, 1989.

Mannion, John J. *Irish Settlement in Eastern Canada: A Study of Cultural Transfer and Adaptation.* Toronto: University of Toronto Press, 1974.

Marston, Sallie A. "Neighborhood and Politics: Irish Ethnicity in Nineteenth Century Lowell, Massachusetts." *Annals of the Association of American Geographers,* 78 (1988): 414–432.

McHugh, Kevin E. "Hispanic Migration and Population Redistribution in the United States." *Professional Geographer,* 41 (1989): 429–439.

McKee, Jesse O. (ed.). *Ethnicity in Contemporary America: A Geographical Appraisal.* Dubuque, IA: Kendall/Hunt, 1985.

Millward, Hugh. *Regional Patterns of Ethnicity in Nova Scotia: A Geographical Study.* Halifax: International Education Centre, St. Mary's University, 1981.

Noble, Allen G. (ed.). *To Build in a New Land: Ethnic Landscapes in North America.* Baltimore: Johns Hopkins University Press, 1992.

Nostrand, Richard L. "The Hispanic-American Borderland: Delimitation of an American Culture Region." *Annals of the Association of American Geographers,* 60 (1970): 638–661.

Nostrand, Richard L. *The Hispano Homeland.* Norman: University of Oklahoma Press, 1992.

Ostergren, Robert. *A Community Transplanted: The Trans-Atlantic Experience of a Swedish Immigrant Settlement in the Upper Middle West, 1835–1915.* Madison: University of Wisconsin Press, 1988.

Palm, Risa. "Ethnic Segmentation of Real Estate Agent Practice in the Urban Housing Market." *Annals of the Association of American Geographers,* 75 (1985): 58–68.

Price, Edward T. "The Melungeons: A Mixed-Blood Strain of the Southern Appalachians." *Geographical Review,* 41 (1951): 256–271.

Raitz, Karl B. "Themes in the Cultural Geography of European Ethnic Groups in the United States." *Geographical Review,* 69 (1979): 77–94.

Rice, John G., and Robert C. Ostergren. "The Decision to Emigrate: A Study in Diffusion." *Geografiska Annaler,* 60B (1978): 1–15.

Roseman, Curtis C., et al. (eds.). *EthniCity: Ethnic Change in Modern Cities.* Lanham, MD: University Press of America, 1995.

Ross, Thomas E., and Tyrel G. Moore (eds.). *A Cultural Geography of North American Indians.* Boulder, CO: Westview Press, 1987.

Schlichtmann, Hansgeorg. "Ethnic Themes in Geographical Research on Western Canada." *Canadian Ethnic Studies,* 9 (1977): 9–41.

Schreuder, Yda. "Labor Segmentation, Ethnic Division of Labor, and Residential Segregation in American Cities in the Early Twentieth Century." *Professional Geographer,* 41 (1989): 131–142.

Todd, D., and J. S. Brierley. "Ethnicity and the Rural Economy: Illustrations from Southern Manitoba." *Canadian Geographer,* 21 (1977): 237–249.

Trépanier, Cécyle. "The Cajunization of French Louisiana: Forging a Regional Identity." *Geographical Journal,* 157 (1991): 161–171.

Trépanier, Cécyle. "The Catholic Church in French Louisiana: An Ethnic Institution?" *Journal of Cultural Geography,* 7, No. 1 (1986): 59–75.

Vogeler, Ingolf. "Ethnicity, Religion, and Farm Land Transfers in Western Wisconsin." *Ecumene,* 7 (1975): 6–13.

Ward, David. "The Ethnic Ghetto in the United States: Past and Present." *Transactions of the Institute of British Geographers,* 7 (1982): 257–275.

Yoon, Hong-key. *Maori Mind, Maori Land: Essays on the Cultural Geography of the Maori People.* Bern, Switzerland: Peter Lang, 1986.

Zelinsky, Wilbur. "What Do We Mean by Ethnicity? Toward a Definition and Typology." *Geographica Slovenica,* 24 (1993): 115–122.

CHAPTER 10

The City in Time and Space

Imagine the 2 million years that humankind has spent on Earth as a 24-hour day. In this framework, settlements of more than a hundred people came about only in the last half-hour. Towns and cities emerged only a few minutes ago, and large-scale urbanization began less than 60 seconds ago. Yet during these "minutes" we see the rise of "civilization." *Civitas,* the Latin root word for *"civilization,"* was first applied to settled areas of the Roman Empire. Later it came to mean a specific town or city within an area. "To civilize" meant literally "to citify."

Furthermore, urbanization of the last 200 years has strengthened the links among culture, society, and the city. An "urban explosion" has gone hand in hand with the industrial revolution. Recent United Nations estimates demonstrate that the world's urban population more than doubled since 1950 and might well double again by the year 2000. By then, over 50 percent of the Earth's population will live in cities. The cultural geography of the world will change dramatically as we become a predominantly urban people, and the ways of the countryside are increasingly replaced by urban lifestyles.

In this chapter, we consider the overall patterns of urbanization, learn how urbanization began and developed, and discuss the differing forms of cities in the developing and developed worlds. In addition, we examine some of the external factors influencing city location. In the following chapter, we look at the internal aspects of the city, cultural regions, diffusion, ecology, integration, and landscape.

Culture Region

If we were to take a general outline map of the world and shade in each country according to its **urbanized population**—the percentage of the nation's population living in towns and cities—we would see striking differences between countries. Some would have close to 90 percent of their population in cities, others would have less than 20 percent. Consequently, we could speak of culture regions based on varying rates of urbanization; of a world pattern of "urban" versus "rural" countries. Also, if we looked more closely at each country, we could delimit formal and functional culture regions within each nation, separating urban and rural domains.

However, delimiting these regions is often complicated since there is no agreed-upon international definition of what constitutes a city. The criteria used to calculate a country's urbanized population vary from nation to nation. Mapping these data would reinforce a myth of comparability. We can learn more from examining how different countries define their urbanized population. To illustrate, the Indian government defines an urban center as 5000 inhabitants, with an adult male population employed predominantly in nonagricultural work. In contrast, the United States Census Bureau defines a city as a densely populated area of 2500 people or more, and South Africa counts as a city any settlement of 500 or more people. Furthermore, some countries revise their definitions of urban settlements to suit specific purposes. China-watchers were baffled in 1983 when that country's urban population swelled by 13 percent in one year, only to learn that China had simply revised its census definitions for urban settlements with criteria that vary from province to province. In conclusion, an international comparison of urbanized population data can be made only by taking into account the varying definitions of the term *city*.

Nonetheless, several generalizations can be made about the differences in the world's urbanized population. First, there is a close link between urbanized population and the more developed world. Put differently, highly industrialized countries have higher rates of urbanized population than do less developed countries. The second generalization, closely tied to the first, is that developing countries are urbanizing rapidly, and that over the next decade their proportion of urban to rural population will change dramatically. An urban explosion is taking place in the developing world, caused by massive migration away from the country as people flock to cities in search of a better life (Figure 10.1). This urban migration, however, should not be compared to the farm-to-city relocation during Europe or America's industrializing period. City migration in the less developed countries is often driven by desperation, as rural supply systems collapse, and urban migrants today cannot always find employment in the city. Unemployment rates in cities of the developing world are often over 50 percent for newcomers to the city. Consequently, one of the world's ongoing crises will be this radical restructuring of population and culture as people in developing countries move into the cities.

We can also apply the culture region theme within nations to better understand this dynamic urbanization process. This application can be made in various ways. To begin, taking a fairly typical, less developed African country such as Ethiopia, we could conceptualize two distinct culture regions—the urban areas and the rural areas, defined as regions with less than 20 percent of the population living in cities. The cultural patterns of the urbanites in the capital, Addis Ababa, contrast dramatically with the tribal and kinship-based cultural fabric of rural peoples. Furthermore, a map of social and economic indicators—such as income, education, literacy, and fertility—would show striking differences between urban and rural regions.

Urban growth in these countries comes from two sources: first, the migration of people to the cities; and second, the higher natural population growth rates of these recent migrants. Because urban employment is unreliable, many migrants continue having large numbers of

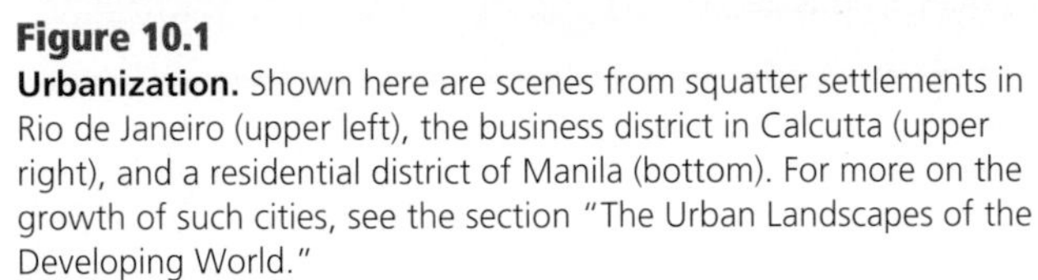

Figure 10.1
Urbanization. Shown here are scenes from squatter settlements in Rio de Janeiro (upper left), the business district in Calcutta (upper right), and a residential district of Manila (bottom). For more on the growth of such cities, see the section "The Urban Landscapes of the Developing World."

children to construct a more extensive family support system. Having a larger family increases the chances of someone getting work. The demographic transition to smaller families seems to come only later, when a certain dimension of security is ensured. Often this results when women enter the workforce (see Chapter 2).

While rural-to-city migration affects nearly all urban centers in the developing world, the most visible cases are the extraordinarily large settlements we call world cities—those having over 5 million in population. Table 10.1 displays the world's 20 largest cities, over half of which are in the developing world. This is a major change from 30 years ago when the list would have been dominated by Western, industrialized cities. Most urbanists agree that by the year 2000, the list will be even more dominated by the developing world because its cities are growing far faster than are Japanese, North American, and European cities. Projections for future growth, however, must be qualified by two considerations. First, cities of the developing world will continue to explode in size only if economic development expands. If it stagnates because of political or resource problems, city growth would probably slow (although urban migration might increase if rural economics deteriorate). For example, Mexico City's growth is linked to that country's economic growth and, more specifically, to Mexico's oil industry, which fluctuates according to the world market for oil. Second, because these world cities are plagued by transportation, housing, and employment

TABLE 10.1
The World's 20 Largest Metropolitan Areas*

Rank	Metropolitan Area	Country	Population (millions)	Average Annual % Change
1	Tokyo/Yokohama	Japan	30.9	0.32
2	Seoul	South Korea	18.5	2.36
3	New York	United States	18.1	0.29
4	Osaka/Kobe/Kyoto	Japan	17.1	0.25
5	Mexico City	Mexico	16.1	1.54
6	São Paulo	Brazil	16.0	1.71
7	Bombay	India	15.2	2.90
8	Calcutta	India	13.7	1.68
9	Los Angeles	United States	13.7	1.25
10	Delhi-New Delhi	India	13.1	4.37
11	Moscow	Russia	12.9	–0.55
12	Jakarta	Indonesia	12.9	3.35
13	Cairo	Egypt	12.8	2.88
14	Buenos Aires	Argentina	12.7	1.15
15	London	United Kingdom	12.1	0.44
16	Manila	Philippines	11.1	3.33
17	Shanghai	China	10.7	1.79
18	Paris	France	10.6	0.72
19	Rio de Janeiro	Brazil	10.4	1.00
20	Beijing	China	9.8	2.08

*Data as of January 1, 1995.

Source: Prepared by Richard L. Forstall. Used by permission.

problems, some countries are trying to control urban migration. The failure or success of these policies will influence city size in the next 10 to 20 years. China, for example, closely regulates urban growth. Accurate population projections, then, are evasive because they depend on variables that range from international economies to national and local policies.

The target for much urban migration is the **primate city**. This is a settlement that dominates the economic, political, and cultural life of a country and, as a result of rapid growth, expands its primacy, or dominance. Once again, Mexico City is an excellent example because that settlement far exceeds Guadalajara, the second-largest city in Mexico, in size and importance. While many developing countries are dominated by a primate city, which was often a former center of colonial power, urban primacy is not unique to these countries: think of the way London and Paris dominate their respective countries.

In summary, we are fast becoming a predominantly urban world, and our cultural geography is increasingly dominated by urban landscapes. Next we investigate the rise and evolution of the earliest settlements to better understand the phenomenon of urbanization.

Origin and Diffusion of the City

As we seek explanations for the origin of cities, we find a relationship between areas of early agriculture, permanent village settlement, the development of new social forms, and urban life. The first cities resulted from a complicated transition that took thousands of years.

Early people were nomadic hunters and gatherers, constantly moving in their search for sustenance. As these hunters and gatherers became increasingly efficient in gathering resources, their campsites became semipermanent, often being occupied for months, seasons, and years at a time. As the quantities of domesticated plants and animals increased (see Chapter 3), settlements became even more permanent. In the Middle East, which is where the first cities appeared, a network of permanent agricultural villages developed about ten thousand years ago. These farming villages were modest in size, rarely with more than 200 people, and were probably organized on a kinship basis. Jarmo, one of the earliest villages, located in present-day Iraq, had 25 permanent dwellings clustered together near grain storage facilities. Although they lacked plows, the inhabitants of Jarmo cultivated local grains, probably wheat and barley. Domestic dogs, goats, and sheep may have been used for meat, and food supplies were augmented by hunting and gathering.

Although small farming villages like Jarmo predate cities in different parts of the world, it is wrong to assume that a simple quantitative change took place whereby villages slowly grew first into towns, then into cities. True cities differed qualitatively from agricultural villages. In agricultural villages, all the inhabitants were involved in some way in food procurement, tending the agricultural fields, harvesting and preparing the products. We can think of the city, however, as more removed, both physically and psychologically, from everyday agricultural activities. Food was supplied to the city, but not all city dwellers were involved in the actual farming. Instead, city dwellers supplied other services, such as technical skills or religious interpretation, considered important to that society. Cities, unlike agricultural villages, contained a class of people who were not directly involved in agricultural activities.

Two elements were crucial to this dramatic social change: the generation of an agricultural surplus and the development of a stratified social system. Surplus food, which is a food supply larger than the everyday needs of the agricultural labor force, is a prerequisite for supporting nonfarmers—people who work at administrative, military, or handicraft tasks. Social stratification, meaning the existence of distinct elite and lower classes, facilitates the collection, storage, and distribution of resources through well-defined channels of authority that can exercise control over goods and people. Without such a hierarchy, the communal surplus could not support city dwellers. A society with these two elements—surplus food, and a means of storing and distributing it—was set for urbanization.

Single-Factor and Multiple-Factor Models for the Rise of Cities

In the search for understanding the transition from village to city life, some scholars prefer to construct models for the development of urban life based on one single factor as the "trigger" behind the change. These scholars ask what activity could be so important to an agricultural society that its people would be willing to give some of their surplus to support a social class that would specialize in that activity. Three answers to this question are discussed next. In addition we will look at the multiple-factor explanation of the rise of cities.

Technical. The **hydraulic civilization** model, developed by Karl Wittfogel, sees the development of large-scale irrigation systems as the prime mover behind urbanization and a class of technical specialists as the first urban dwellers. Higher crop yields resulted from irrigated agriculture, and this food surplus supported the development of a large nonfarming population. A strong, centralized government, backed by an urban-based military, expanded power into the surrounding areas. Those farmers who resisted the new authority were denied water. Continued reinforcement of the power elite came from the need for organizational coordination to ensure continued operation of the irrigation system.

Class distinctions were reinforced by power differences, and labor specialization developed. Some people farmed while some worked on the irrigation system. Others became artisans creating the implements needed to maintain the system, and still others became administrative workers in the direct employ of the power elite's court.

Although the hydraulic model fits several areas where cities first arose—China, Egypt, and Mesopotamia (present-day Iraq)—it cannot be applied to all urban hearths. In parts of Mesoamerica, for example, an urban civilization blossomed without widespread irrigated agriculture, and therefore without a class of technical experts. The hydraulic model also begs the question of how or why a culture might first develop an irrigation system.

Religious. Geographer Paul Wheatley suggests that *religion* was the motivating factor behind urbanization. In early agricultural societies, knowledge concerning such matters as meteorological and climatic conditions was considered to fall within the domain of religion. These societies depended on their religious leaders to interpret the heavenly bodies before deciding when and how to plant their crops. The propagation of this type of knowledge led to more successful harvests, which in turn allowed for the support of more members of this emerging priestly class, as well as the support of people engaged in ancillary activities. This priestly class exercised political and social control that held the city together.

In this scenario, cities are religious spaces, functioning as ceremonial centers for the emerging civilization. The first urban clusters and fortifications are seen as defenses not against human invaders but spiritual ones—demons or the souls of the dead. This religious explanation is applicable in some ways to all the early centers of urbanization, although it seems particularly apt in describing Chinese urbanization (see pages 358–360).

Political. Other scholars suggest that the centralizing authority in urbanization emanated not from the religious order but instead from the political order. Urban historian Lewis Mumford described the agent of change in emerging urban centers as the *institution of kingship*, which involves the centralizing of religious, social, and economic aspects of a civilization around a powerful figure who becomes known as the king. This figure of authority, who in the preurban world is accorded respect by his or her human abilities, ascends to almost superhuman status in early urbanizing societies. By exercising power, the king is able to marshal the labor of others. The resultant social hierarchy enables the society to diversify its endeavors, with different groups specializing in crafts, farming, trading, or religious activity. The institution of kingship provides essential leadership and organization to this emerging complex society, which becomes the city.

Multiple Factors. At the beginning of urbanization, and even much later in some places in the world, the distinctions between economic, religious, and political functions were not always clarified. The king may have also functioned as priest, healer, astronomer, and scribe, thus in some ways fusing secular and spiritual power. Critics of the kingship theory, therefore, point out that this explanation of urbanization may not be different from that based on religion. In other words, attempting to isolate one trigger to urbanization is difficult, if not impossible. A wiser course is to accept the role of *multiple factors* behind the changes leading to urban life. Technical, religious, and political forces were often interlinked, with a change in one leading to changes in the other. Instead of oversimplifying by focusing on one possible development schema, we must appreciate the complexities of the transition period from agricultural village to true city.

Urban Hearth Areas

The first cities appeared in distinct regions, such as Mesopotamia, the Nile valley, Pakistan's Indus River valley, the Yellow River valley (or Huang Ho) of China, and Mesoamerica. These are called the **urban hearth areas** (see box, *Cahokia*). Figure 10.2 gives the general dates for the emergence of urban life in each region.

It is generally agreed that the first cities arose in Mesopotamia, the river valley of the Tigris and Euphrates in what is now Iraq. Mesopotamian cities, small by current standards, covered 1/2 to 2 square miles (1.28 to 5.12 square kilometers) and embraced populations that rarely exceeded 30,000. Nevertheless, with such a population concentrated in such a small area, the densities within these cities could easily reach 10,000 people per square mile (4000 per square kilometer). This is comparable to many contemporary cities.

Cahokia: An Early Urban Center on the Mississippi

Cahokia, a pre-Columbian urban center on the Mississippi, shows that not all early cities were found in the five urban hearth areas mentioned in the text. Instead, Cahokia illustrates the process of independent city origin and can be taken as an example of events duplicated in hundreds of areas around the world.

The Cahokia settlement is an aggregation of mounds and living structures dating from about AD 100, located in the American Bottoms region of the Mississippi River Valley, close to St. Louis. It is the largest of 10 large population centers and some 50 smaller farming villages that flourished between AD 900 and 1500.

How did this city arise? Archaeologists maintain that the city resulted from a complicated feedback process that involved population growth and an increase in agricultural productivity. In the late eighth century, the hoe replaced a less effective digging stick and a new variety of maize diffused into the American Bottoms region better suited to environmental conditions of the warm river valley.

Peak population came centuries later, probably between 1150 and 1250, when Cahokia may have approached a population of 40,000. Archaeological evidence suggests that houses were mainly of pole-and-thatch construction and varied in size according to the status of the occupants. The settlement also contained many ceremonial structures, most notably large earthen mounds similar to the pyramids of Mesoamerican cities. Close to the largest mound was an enclosed area of large public structures that reminds one of the citadel areas of Mesopotamian cities.

Cahokia flourished because it was an ideally located central place, situated on fertile agricultural lands, with access to local and long-distance trade moving through the network of sloughs and rivers. Scholars who have investigated the site believe that Cahokia declined in importance around 1250. Perhaps this was due to exhaustion of local resources, perhaps because its trade hinterland was eclipsed by the growing strength of other Mississippi River cultures. Whatever the reason, further investigation is bound to shed light on the complicated processes that lead to the rise and fall of cities.

Adapted from Melvin Fowler, "A Pre-Columbian Urban Center on the Mississippi." *Scientific American* (August 1975): 93–102.

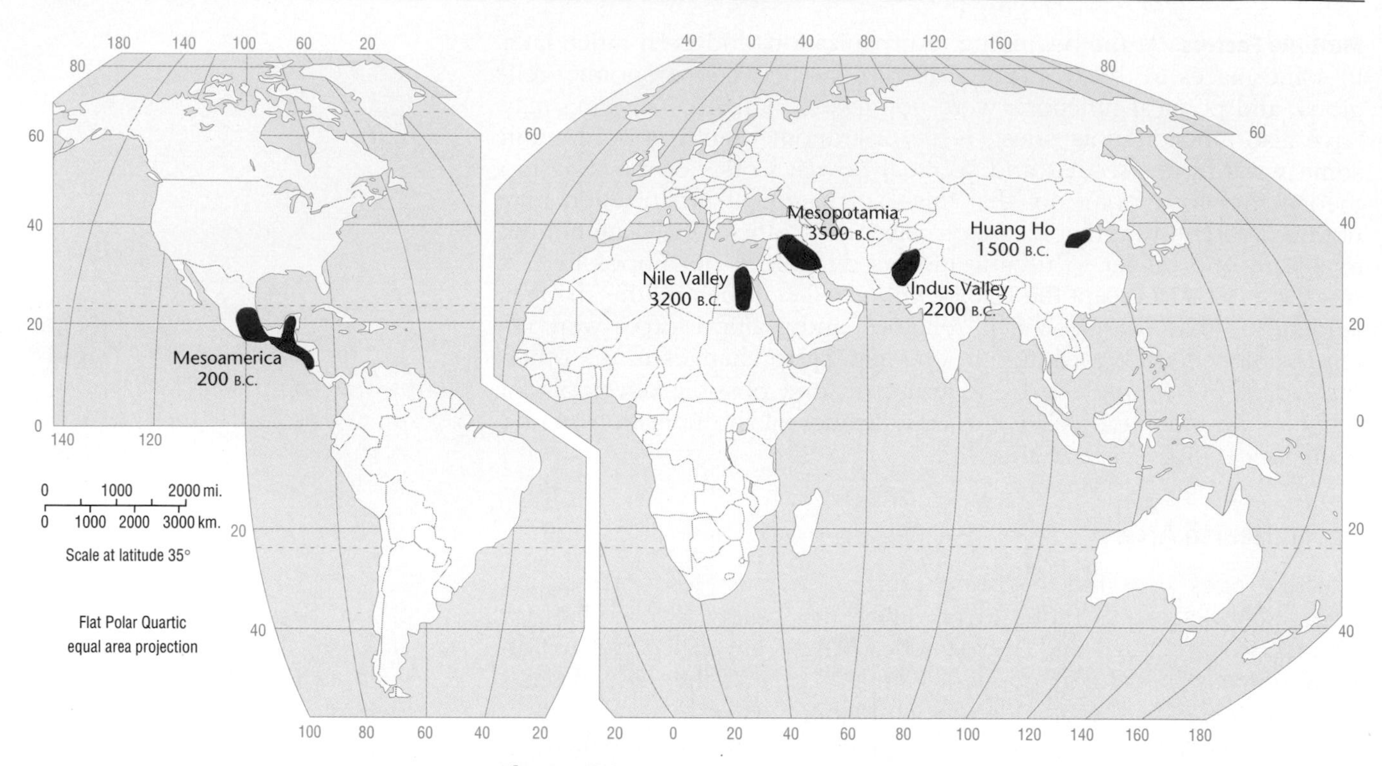

Figure 10.2
The world's first cities arose in five urban hearth areas. The dates are conservative figures for the rise of urban life in each area. Some scholars would, for example, suggest urban life in Mesopotamia existed by 5000 BC. New discoveries are constantly being made suggesting that urban life appeared earlier in each of the hearth areas. Note, however, that the latest date is in Mesoamerica.

The spatial layout of the cities of the urban hearth areas were similar. In particular, these early cities, or what we can call **cosmomagical** cities, exhibited three spatial characteristics (Figure 10.3). The first is that great importance was accorded to the symbolic center of the city, which was thought to be the center not only of the city but also of the known world. It was therefore the most sacred spot, and was often demarcated by a vertical structure of monumental scale that represented the point on Earth closest to the heavens. This symbolic center, or **axis mundi,** took the form of the ziggurat in Mesopotamia, the palace or temple in China, the pyramid in Egypt and Mesoamerica, and the stupa in the Indus Valley.

Often, this elevated structure, usually serving a religious purpose, was close to the palace or seat of political power and to the granary. These structures were walled off from the rest of the city, forming a symbolic center that physically and spiritually dominated the city. This walled inner city reflected the particular significance of certain societal functions. The food surplus was certainly of major importance, and its storage within the inner city suggests that it was often guarded from the general population. The presence of a temple or palace building within this inner city also tells us that power was held by a class of people who were thought of as inhabiting a more sacred world than the other inhabitants of the city. The Forbidden City in Beijing remains one of the best examples of this guarded, fortress-like "city within the city."

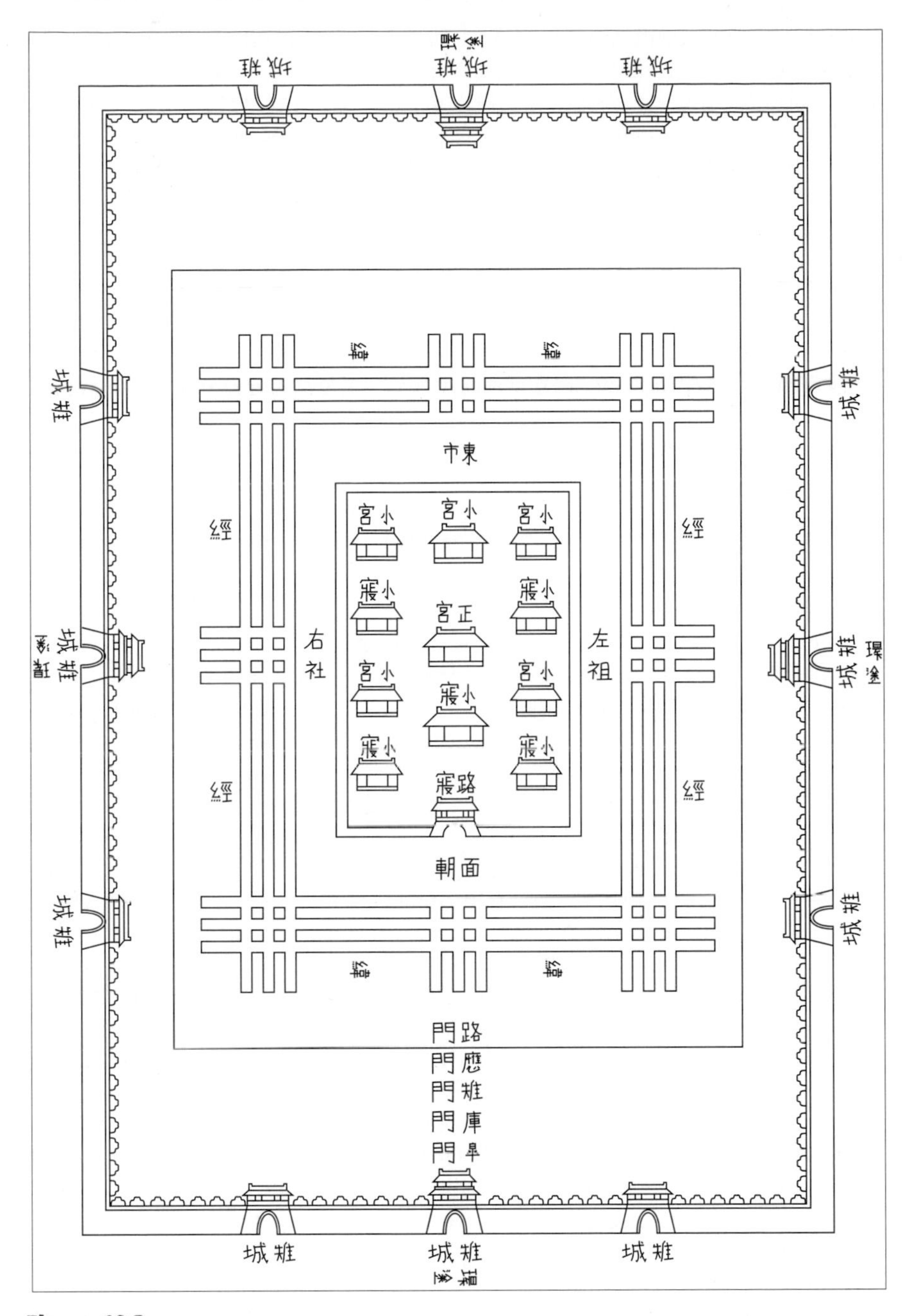

Figure 10.3
Plan of the city of Wang-Ch'eng in China. The city as built did not follow this exact design, but the plan itself is of interest since it suggests the symbolic importance of the three spatial characteristics of the Chinese cosmomagical city. The four walls are aligned to the cardinal directions, and the axis mundi is represented by the walled-off center city containing ceremonial buildings. The physical space of the city (microcosmos) replicates the larger world of the heavens (macrocosmos). For example, each of the four walls represents one of the four seasons, with each gate symbolizing a month. (Source: Wheatley, Paul. *The Pivot of the Four Quarters.* Chicago: Aldine Publishing Co., 1971.)

In Mesopotamia, this area was known as the citadel, and the elite who lived there inhabited a world of relative luxury (Figure 10.4). Before 2000 BC, the streets within the citadels were paved, drains and running water were provided, private sleeping quarters were built, bathtubs and water closets were installed, and spacious villas were constructed. But the privileges of the ruling class did not extend to the city as a whole.

The second spatial characteristic common to the cosmomagical world is that the city was oriented toward the four cardinal directions. By aligning the city in a north-south and east-west direction, the geometric form of the city would reflect the order of the universe. This, it was thought, would ensure harmony and order over the known world. The walls that surrounded these cities delimited the known, and therefore ordered, world from the outside chaos, suggesting that these early rectangular fortifications were serving symbolic as well as functional purposes. In China, for example, when an emperor conquered a city or constructed a new city, he would ceremoniously walk around the square perimeter of the walls, symbolizing his control of, and his ability to bring order to, this new world.

In all these early cities one sees evidence of a third spatial characteristic—an attempt to shape the form of the city according to the form of the universe. The ordering of the space of the city was thought essential to maintain harmony between the human and spiritual worlds. In this way, the world of humans would symbolically replicate the world of the gods. This may have taken a literal form—a city laid out, for example, in a star constellation pattern. Far more common, however, were cities that symbolically approximated mythical conceptions of the universe. Ankor Thom in India presents one of the best examples of this parallelism. An urban cluster that spreads over 6 square miles, Ankor Thom is a representation in stone of a series of Indian myths about the nature of the universe. In this way, the city was a microcosmos, or a re-creation on Earth of an image of the larger universe.

Archaeological evidence from Mesopotamia provides a detailed picture of how people lived their everyday lives in these cosmomagical cities. Most city dwellers lived in dense housing units, within the walls of the city yet outside the citadel. Houses were one or two stories tall, composed of clay brick, and contained three or four rooms. They fronted on narrow streets that were unsurfaced, without drainage, and that served as the community dump. Excavations at Ur, one of the earliest Mesopotamian cities, show that the level of garbage rose so high that new entrances had to be cut into the second stories of the houses. The only open spaces were the small market squares dotting the city. Here artisans clustered to trade their goods, food was distributed, and the military herded the urban population to hear the latest edict from their rulers. The lower classes lived just inside the walls of the city, in huts of mud and reed rather than houses of fired clay.

Yet regional variations of this basic form certainly existed. For example, the early cities of the Nile were not walled, which suggests that a regional power structure kept individual cities from warring with one another. In the Indus Valley, the great city of Mohenjo-daro was laid out in a grid that consisted of 16 large blocks, and the citadel was located within the block that was central but situated toward the extreme western edge.

The most important variations in living conditions within the urban hearth areas occur in Mesoamerica (see box, *City Planning in the New*

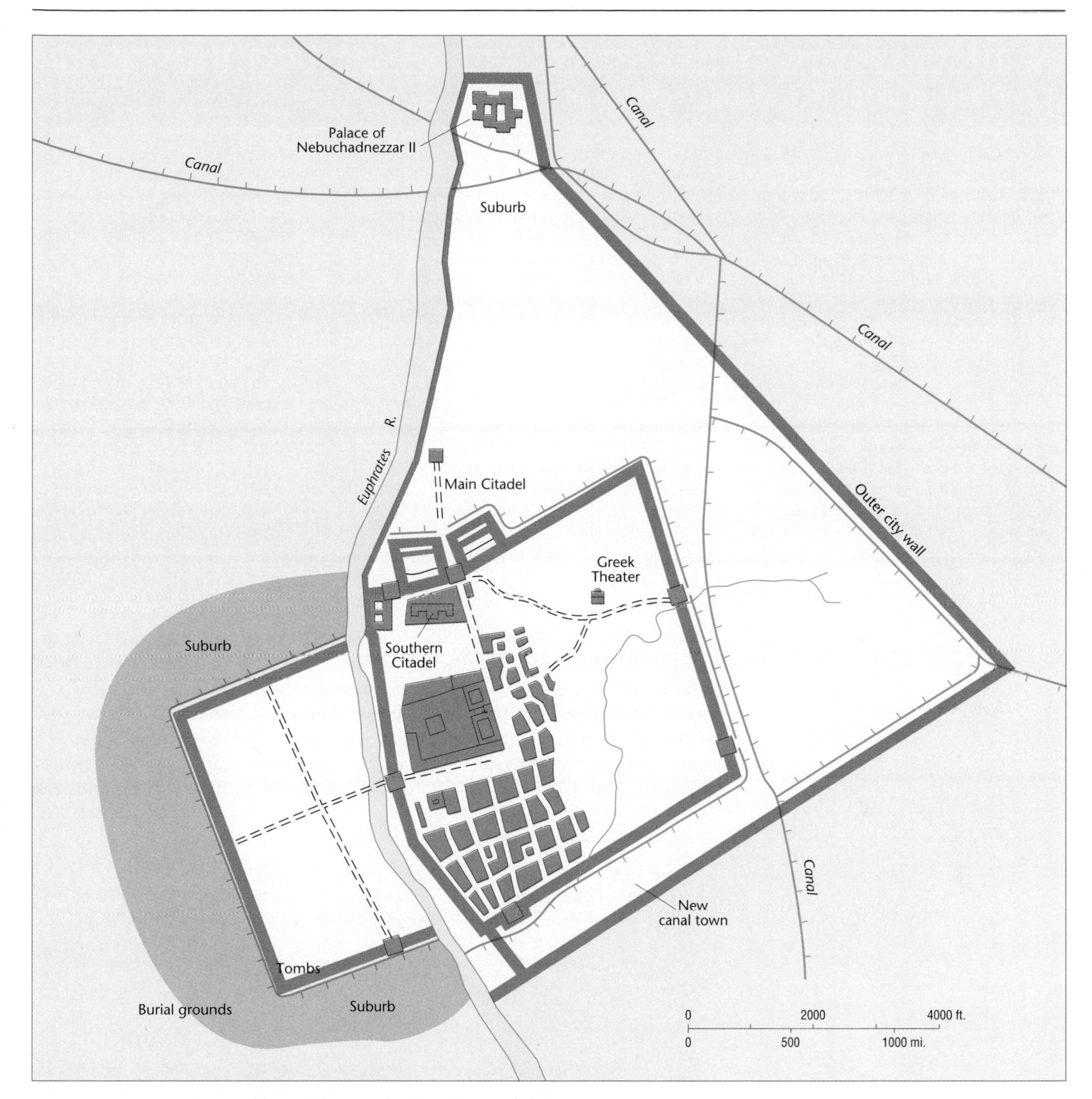

Figure 10.4
Map of Babylon, illustrating the urban morphology of early Mesopotamian cities. The citadel in the inner city is characterized by the ziggurat, main temple, palace, and granary. Beyond that lay the residential areas; we can assume they extended out to the inner walls and occupied both sides of the river. Suburbs grew outside the major gates and were occupied by people not allowed to spend the night in the city, such as traders and noncitizens. (After map in the *New Encyclopaedia Britannica,* vol. 2. Chicago: Encyclopaedia Britannica, Inc., 1984, p. 555.)

City Planning in the New World: Teotihuacán

Teotihuacán was a Mesoamerican city created by a society that had no metal tools, had not invented the wheel, and had no pack animals. At its height, Teotihuacán covered 8 square miles (20 square kilometers), which made it larger than imperial Rome. Its central religious monument, the Temple of the Sun, was as broad at its base as the great pyramid of Cheops in Egypt. Its population may have reached 100,000.

Strategically located astride a valley that was the gateway to the lowlands of Mexico, Teotihuacán flourished for 500 years as a great urban commercial center. Yet it was more than that. It was the Mecca of the New World, a religious and cultural capital that probably housed pilgrims from as far away as Guatemala. Not a trace of fortification has ever been unearthed. Perhaps most startling, Teotihuacán was a totally planned city. Its two great pyramids, its citadel, its hundred lesser religious structures and its 4000 other dwellings were laid out according to a cosmomagical design. Its streets (and many of its buildings) were organized on an exact grid aligned with the city center. Even the shape of the river that divided the city was changed to fit the grid pattern.

Planning for the construction of Teotihuacán's major temples must have been an incredible undertaking. The Temple of the Sun, for instance, rises to a height of 215 feet and has a base of 725 square feet. These dimensions meant that it took about one million tons of sun-baked mud bricks to build the temple. When the Spaniards conquered Mexico in the sixteenth century, they were amazed to find Teotihuacán's ruined temples. Local inhabitants claimed that the temples had been built by giants. They showed the Spaniards the bones of giant elephants (which had lived there in prehistoric times) to prove their point.

But the small as well as the large was cleverly conceived in Teotihuacán. Houses were apparently planned for maximum space and privacy. Apartments were constructed around central patios, and each patio designed to give dwellers light and air, as well as an efficient drainage system. In a Teotihuacán housing complex, a person could indeed have lived in relative comfort.

World: Teotihuacán). Here, cities were less dense and covered large areas (see Figure 10.5). Furthermore, these cities arose without benefit of the technological advances found in the other hearth areas, most notably the wheel, the plow, metallurgy, and draft animals. However, the domestication of maize compensated for these shortcomings. Maize is a grain that yields several crops a year without irrigation in the tropical climate, and it can be cultivated without heavy plows or pack animals.

Figure 10.5
Mayan city of Chichen Itza. Monumental and ceremonial architecture often dominated the morphology and landscape of hearth area cities and reinforced ruling class power.

The Diffusion of the City from Hearth Areas

Although urban life originated at several specific places in the world, cities are now found everywhere—North America, Southeast Asia, Latin America, Australia. How did city life come to these regions? While many of these cities resulted from European colonialism in the last two centuries, let us first discuss the diffusion of cities before this period. There are two possibilities. The first is that cities evolved spontaneously as native peoples created new technologies and social institutions. A second hypothesis is that the preconditions for urban life are too specific for most cultures to invent without contact with other urban areas; therefore, they must have learned these traits through contact with city dwellers. This scenario emphasizes the diffusion of ideas and techniques necessary for city life.

Diffusionists argue that the complicated array of ideas and techniques that gave rise to the first cities in Mesopotamia was shared with other people, in both the Nile and the Indus river valleys, who were on the verge of the urban transformation. Indeed, these three civilizations had contact with one another. Archaeological evidence documents trade ties. Soapstone objects manufactured in Tepe Yahyā, 500 miles (800 kilometers) to the east of Mesopotamia, have been uncovered in the ruins of both Mesopotamian and Indus Valley cities, which are separated by thousands of miles. Indus Valley writing and seals have also been found in Mesopotamian urban sites. Although diffusionists use this artifactual evidence to argue that the idea of the city was spread from hearth to hearth, an alternative view is that trading took place only after these cities were well established. There is also evidence of contacts across the oceans between early urban dwellers of the New World and those of Asia and Africa, although it is unclear if this means urbanization was diffused to Mesoamerica, or simply that some trade routes existed between these peoples.

Nonetheless, there is little doubt that diffusion has been responsible for the dispersal of the city in historical times. This is because the city has commonly been used as the vehicle for imperial expansion. The sociologist Gideon Sjoberg, in *The Preindustrial City,* states: "The extension of the power group's domain, notably through empire-building, is the primary mechanism for introducing city life into generally nonurbanized territories." Typically, urban life is carried outward in waves of conquest as the borders of an empire expand. Initially, the military controls newly won lands and sets up collection points for local resources, which are then shipped back into the heart of the empire and used for its economy. As the surrounding countryside is increasingly pacified, the new collection points lose some of their military atmosphere and begin to show the social diversity of a city. Artisans, merchants, and bureaucrats increase in number. Families appear. The native people are slowly assimilated into the settlement as workers and may eventually control the city. Finally, the process repeats itself as the empire pushes farther outward: first a military camp, then a collection point for resources, then a full-fledged city expressing true division of labor and social diversity.

This process, however, did not always proceed without opposition. The imposition of a foreign civilization on native peoples was often met with resistance, both physical and symbolic. Expanding urban centers relied on the surrounding countryside for support. Their food was supplied from farmers living fairly close to the city walls, and tribute was exacted from these agricultural peoples living on the edges of the urban world. The increasing needs of the city required more and more land from which to draw resources. However, peasants farming that land may not have wanted to change their way of life to accommodate the city. The fierce resistance of many Native American groups to the spread of Western urbanization is testimony to the potential power of folk society to defy the effects of urbanization, although the destructive long-term effects of such resistance suggest that the organized military efforts of urban society were difficult to overcome.

Examples of imperial city building dot history. Alexander the Great, in the course of his conquests, ordered what we would today call architects to establish at least 70 cities. The Roman Empire, a power expanding from a single urban center, built literally thousands of cities, changing the rural faces of Europe, North Africa, and Asia Minor in the process. In other times, the Persians, the Maurya Empire of India, the Han civilization of China, the Greeks, and others performed the same city-spreading task. In more recent times, European empires have used the resources of cities to expand and consolidate their power in colonies in the Americas, Africa, and Asia.

This sort of expansion diffusion has been critical in dispersing urban life over the surface of the Earth. Figure 10.6 shows some of the routes the city took in this diffusion process.

Evolution of Urban Landscapes

Understanding urban landscapes necessitates an appreciation of urban processes both past and present. The patterns we see today in the city, such as building form, architecture, street plans, and land use, are a

Figure 10.6
The diffusion of urban life with the expansion of certain empires.

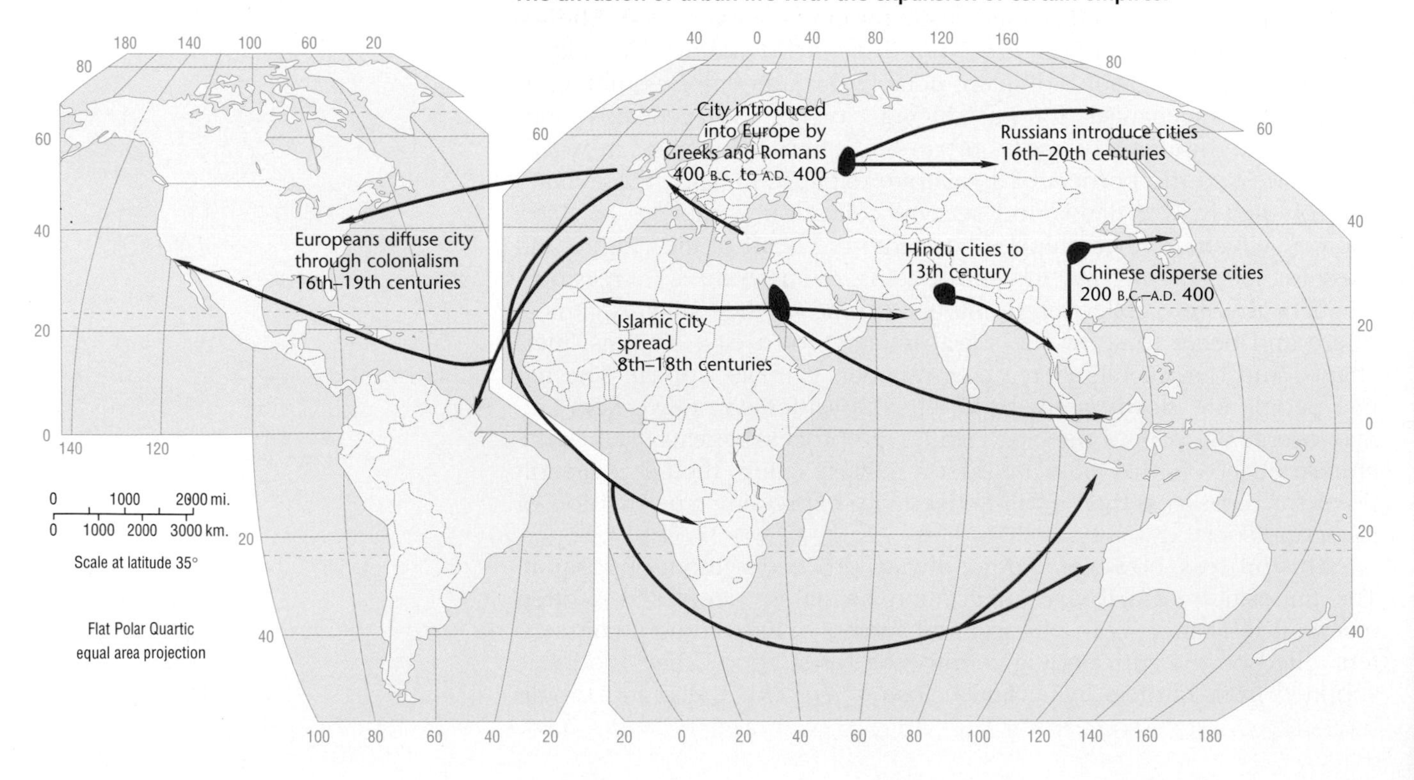

composite of past and present cultures. They reflect the needs, ideas, technology, and institutions of human occupance. This section examines major stages in the evolution of urban landscapes in both the developed and developing worlds.

Two concepts underlie our examination of urban landscapes. The first is **urban morphology,** or the physical form of the city, which consists of street patterns, building sizes and shapes, architecture, and density. The second concept is **functional zonation.** This refers to the pattern of land uses within a city, or the existence of areas with differing functions, such as residential, commercial, or governmental. Functional zonation is also concerned with social patterns—whether an area is occupied by the power elite or by low-status persons, by Jews or by Christians, by high-income persons or by the poor. Both concepts are central to understanding the cultural landscape of cities, because both make statements about how cultures occupy and shape space (Figure 10.7).

We begin our study of urban landscapes by examining the history of our contemporary cities from Greek times to the postindustrial present.

The Greek City

Western civilization and the Western city both trace their immediate roots back to ancient Greece. City life diffused to Greece from Mesopotamia. By 600 BC, there were over 500 towns and cities on the Greek mainland and surrounding islands. As Greek civilization expanded, cities spread with it throughout the Mediterranean—to the north shore of Africa, to Spain, to southern France, and to Italy. These cities were of modest size, rarely containing more than 5000 inhabi-

Figure 10.7
San Francisco. This photo shows how the concepts of urban morphology and functional zonation can be used in examining cities. To the left, close to the shoreline, are older factories, some of which have been converted for the tourist trade associated with the Fisherman's Wharf area. The residential areas exhibit two morphological characteristics: high-rises on the hills to the right, and blocks of low-rise apartments in the middle ground. The skyscrapers of the central business district show up in the background.

tants. Athens, however, may have reached 300,000 in the fifth century BC. (This figure includes perhaps 100,000 slaves, the labor power behind Greek society.)

Greek cities had two distinctive functional zones—the *acropolis* and the *agora*. In many ways, the acropolis was similar to the citadel of Mesopotamian cities. Here were the temples of worship, the storehouse of valuables, and the seat of power. The acropolis also served as a place of retreat in time of siege (Figure 10.8). If the acropolis was the domain of power, the agora was the province of the citizens. As originally conceived, the agora was a place for public meetings, education, social interaction, and judicial matters. In other words, it was the civic center, the hub of democratic life for Greek men (women were excluded from political life). During the classical period, commercial activities were not considered fitting for the agora, but later it became the major marketplace of the city—without losing its atmosphere of a social club.

This physical separation of religious from secular functions, which distinguishes the Greek city from the cosmomagical city, implies that in Greek culture the religious domain was no longer the only source of authority. The agora represented, in some senses, a challenge to the acropolis. The location and architecture of the acropolis itself suggests that the power of the gods and the supernatural was tempered by human aesthetic and reason. Greek temples were located on sacred sites chosen to please the gods, but they were also sited and designed to please the human eye and to harmonize with the natural landscape. This tension between the religious and the secular created what many consider to be one of the greatest achievements of Western architecture.

The earlier Greek cities probably were not planned but rather grew spontaneously, without benefit of formal guidelines. However, some

Figure 10.8

The Acropolis in Athens. The Acropolis dominates the contemporary city and reminds us that many cities throughout the world have been centered on fortified places that eventually became more symbolic than functional. Compare this landscape with other defensive acropolis sites.

scholars think that many ceremonial areas within these cities were designed to be seen according to prescribed lines of vision, and that those lines of vision included not only the buildings but the natural landscape that surrounded it. Again, the human aesthetic was given a degree of authority that it did not have in the cosmomagical city.

More formalized city design and plan are apparent in later Greek cities that were built in areas of colonial expansion. One of the best examples of such planned cities is Miletus, on the eastern shore of the Mediterranean, in Ionia (present-day Turkey). The city was laid out in a rigid grid system, imposing its geometry onto the physical site conditions (Figure 10.9). Although the source of such a plan is debatable, clearly this orderly and coherent layout indicates an abstracted and highly rational notion of urban life, and seems to fit well with the functional needs of a colonial city. The grid system is a creation of the human mind, and its imposition on a highly irregular physical site shows that religious and aesthetic needs had taken a secondary role to the more pressing demands of controlling an empire.

Figure 10.9
The plan of the city of Miletus by Hippodamus, ca. 450 BC. Notice how the strict grid is imposed on the irregular coastline. The central agora area is also regularized, characteristic of this colonial phase of the Greek city. (Source: Vance, James E., Jr. *The Continuing City.* Baltimore: Johns Hopkins University Press, 1990.)

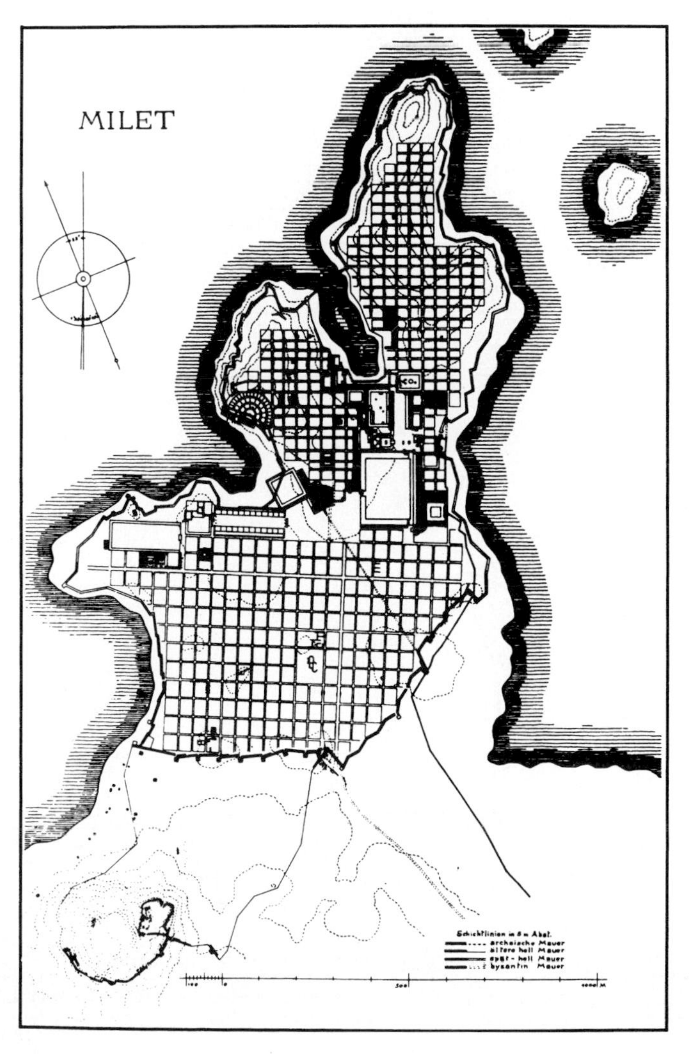

Roman Cities

By 200 BC, the focus for the Western city had shifted from Greece to Rome. The Romans adopted many urban traits from the Greeks, as well as from the Etruscans, a civilization of northern Italy that the Romans had conquered. As the Roman Empire expanded, city life diffused into France, Germany, England, interior Spain, the Alpine countries, and parts of eastern Europe—areas that had not previously experienced urbanization. Most of these cities were military and trading outposts of the Roman Empire. They served as focal points for the collection of products from the agricultural countryside, as supply centers for the military, and as service centers for the long-distance trading network that was controlled from Rome. The military camp, or *castra,* was the basis for many of these new settlements. In England, the Roman trail of city building can be found by looking for the suffixes *-caster* and *-chester*—as in Lancaster or Winchester, cities originally founded as Roman camps. Figure 10.10 shows the diffusion of urban life into Europe as the Greek and Roman frontiers advanced.

The landscape of these Roman cities shared several traits with its Greek predecessors. The gridiron street pattern, used in later Greek cities, was fundamental to Roman cities. This can still be seen in the heart of such Italian cities as Pavia (see Figure 10.11). These straight streets and right-angle intersections make a striking contrast to the curved, wandering lanes of the later medieval quarters or the streets of Rome itself. At the intersection of a city's two major thoroughfares was

Figure 10.10
The diffusion of urbanization in Europe. The early spread of urban development moved in waves across Europe. The nucleus of city life was well established in the Greek lands by 700 BC. In following centuries, urbanization diffused west and north until it reached the British Isles. (Reproduced by permission from an article by Norman J. G. Pounds in the *Annals of the Association of American Geographers,* 59, 1969.)

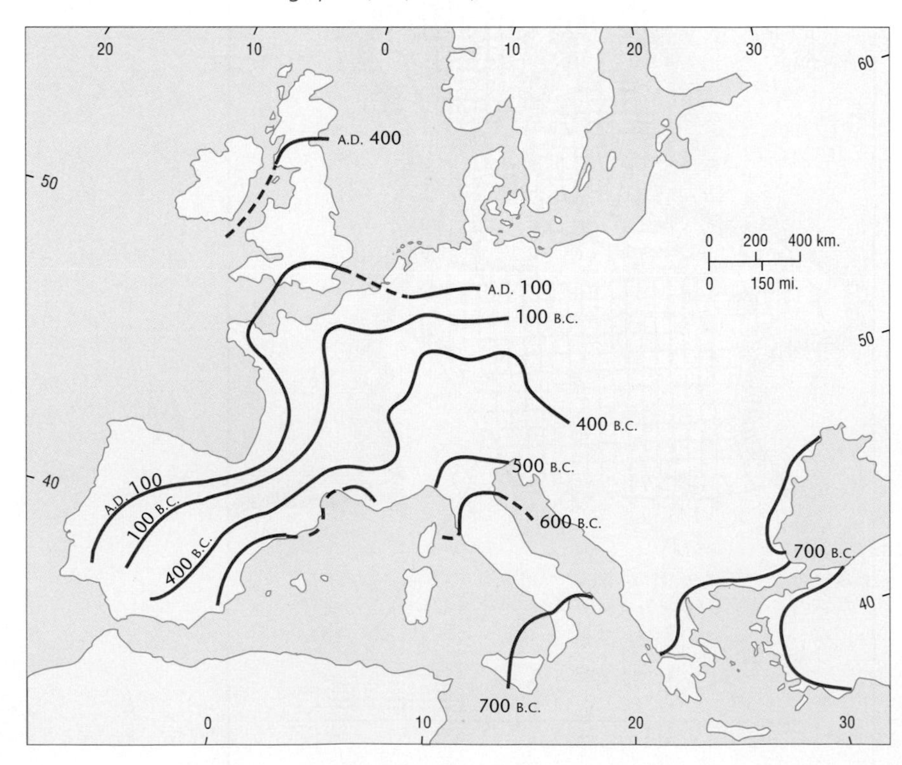

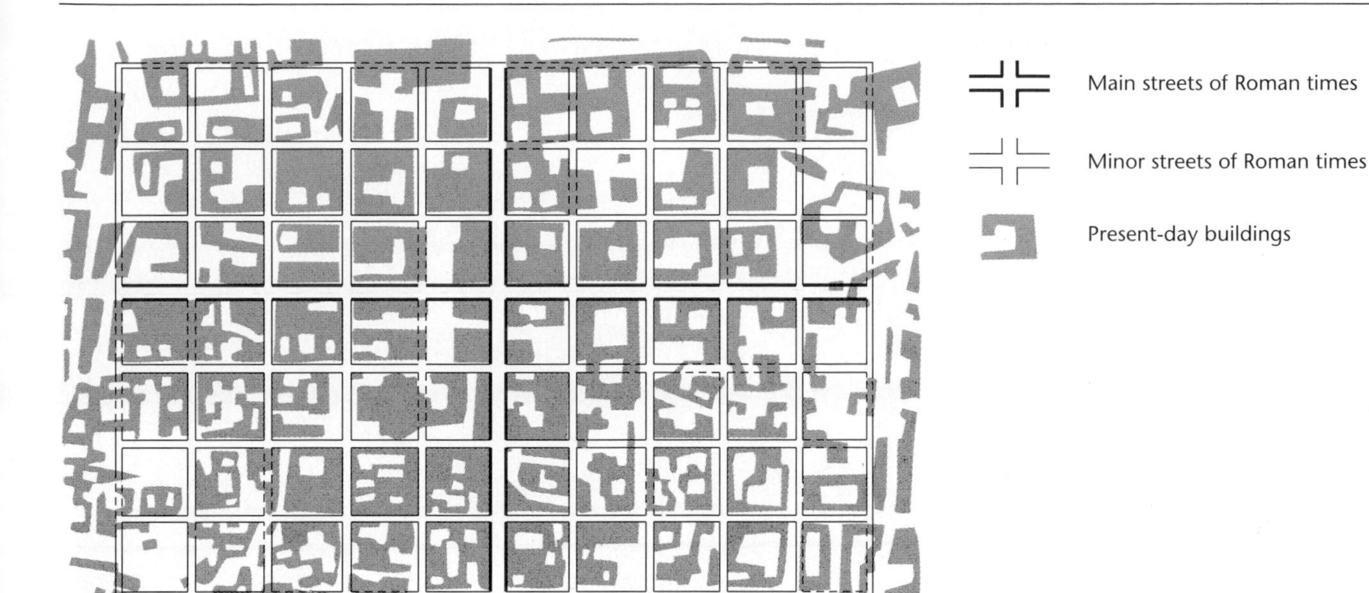

Figure 10.11
The Roman grid street pattern in Pavia, Italy. Many of the straight streets from Roman times remain in use 20 centuries after they were first built. The dotted lines indicate the Roman streets that do not exist today. Beyond the Roman core the streets developed in irregular patterns.

the *forum,* a zone combining elements of the Greek acropolis and agora. Here were not only the temples of worship, administrative buildings, and warehouses, but also the libraries, schools, and marketplaces that served the common people.

Clustered around the forum were the palaces of the power elite. These palaces were sanitary, well heated in winter, and spacious—marvels of domestic architecture. Never again did the West see such luxury until the twentieth century.

Despite the architectural accomplishments of the Roman engineers, the Roman masses lived in squalor. While the homes of the rich spread horizontally across the landscape, the homes of the poor rose vertically. They lived in shoddy apartment houses, often four or five stories high, called *insula*. These tenements seem to be the first Western example of high-density dwellings. With this Roman "invention," two now-common human urban types arrived on the scene—the land speculator and the slum landlord. The elaborate system of aqueducts and underground sewers did not extend to the poor. The result was probably a low in urban sanitation: the garbage of perhaps a million Romans was thrown into open pits around the city. Even in its best days, Rome's population was continually at the mercy of plagues.

Rome's most important legacy probably was not its architectural and engineering feats, although they remain landmarks in European cities to this day (Figure 10.12), but rather the Roman method for choosing the site of a city, which remains applicable today. The Romans consistently chose sites with transportation in mind. The Roman Empire was held together by a complicated system of roads and highways, linking towns and cities. In choosing a site for a new settlement, the Romans made access a major consideration. In contrast, other cultures placed primary emphasis on defensive locations; hence, their set-

Figure 10.12
The Colosseum in Rome. Crowds of 60,000 were entertained in the Colosseum by mock battles, circuses, gladiators fighting, and sports events. Most large Roman cities had similar structures. Today, most cities have stadiums and coliseums that continue the tradition of public spectacles started by the Romans.

tlements might have been located in inaccessible places such as marshes or islands or on hilltops. The significance of Roman location was that even though urban life declined dramatically with the collapse of the empire, numerous old Roman sites—such as Paris, London, and Vienna—were refounded centuries later on the same spots because they offered advantages of access to the surrounding countryside.

With the decline of the Roman Empire by AD 400, urban life also declined. Historians attribute the fall of Rome to internal decay, the invasion of the Germanic peoples, and other factors. Cities were sapped of their vitality. The highway system that linked them fell into disrepair, so that cities could no longer exchange goods and ideas. When Roman cities were invaded by local groups, they could no longer count on outside military support as the administrative structure of the empire collapsed. Isolated from one another, they lost vital functions. As symbols of a conquering empire, Roman outposts were either actively destroyed or, devoid of purpose, simply left to decay. Within 200 years, many of the cities founded by the Romans withered away.

Yet there were exceptions. Some cities of the Mediterranean survived because they established trade with the Byzantine civilization centered in Constantinople. After the eighth century, some cities—particularly those in Spain—were infused with new vigor by the Moorish Empire, which spread across the Mediterranean from northern Africa. But the cities of northern regions were unable to survive. Cities became small villages. Where thousands had formerly thrived, a few hundred eked out a subsistence living from agriculture.

Urban decline occurred only in the areas that had been under Roman rule. Other civilizations continued to thrive throughout this period. The achievements of Chinese civilization, and the great cities of the Incan and Mayan empires remind us that urban decline occurred only in a particular area of Europe.

The Medieval City

The medieval period, lasting roughly from AD 1000 to 1500, was a time of renewed urban expansion in Europe and a period that deeply influenced the future of urban life. Urban life spread beyond the borders of the former Roman Empire, into the north and east of Europe, as the Germanic and Slavic peoples expanded their empires. In only four centuries, 2500 new German "cities" were founded. Most cities of present-day Europe were founded during this period. While many were on old Roman sites, others were new.

Scholars have debated why urban life began to regain vigor in the eleventh century. In essence, the revival of both local and long-distance trade was the result of a combination of factors, including population increase, political stability and unification, and agricultural expansion through new land reclamations and the development of new agricultural technologies. Sustained trading networks required protected markets and supply centers, functions that renewed life in cities. In addition, trading, particularly long-distance, led to the development of a new class of people, a merchant class. Members of this merchant class breathed new life into early medieval cities, providing the impetus and the wealth for sustained city building.

The major functions of the medieval city are depicted in five symbols—the fortress, the charter, the wall, the marketplace, and the cathedral. The *fortress* expresses the importance of defense. Usually the cities were clustered around a fortified place. The importance of this role is reflected in many place-names. This is demonstrated by the names of cities in Germanic lands ending with *-burg,* such as Salzburg or Würzburg; in France with *-bourg,* as in Strasbourg; and in English with *-burgh,* as in Edinburgh. Each suffix has the same meaning—a fortified castle. The terms *burgher* and *bourgeoisie,* which now refer to the middle class, originally referred to a citizen of the medieval city (Figure 10.13).

The *charter* was a governmental decree from a regional power, usually a feudal lord, granting political autonomy to the town. This act had important implications. It freed the population from feudal restrictions, made the city responsible for its own defense and government, and allowed it to coin money. Thus city life became even freer than life on rural feudal estates. These rights and responsibilities contributed to the development of urban social, economic, and intellectual life.

The *wall* served a defensive purpose, but it was also a symbol of the sharp distinction between country and city. Within the wall, most inhabitants were, by charter, free; outside, most were serfs. "City air sets a man free" went the medieval proverb. Indeed, even though the medieval city had feudal characteristics, it generally was a community of citizens able to move about with little restriction, free to buy and sell property and goods. A city of "free" citizens, not based on a vast pool of slave labor, was a first in the history of the Western city.

At the wall's gates the division between city residents and nonresidents was sharpest. Here, goods entering the city were inspected and taxed. Here, nonresidents were issued permits for entry and undesirables were excluded. And here, at sunset, the gates were closed, shutting out the rural world until sunrise. Often nonresidents were required to leave the city at dusk and seek accommodations outside the wall. As a result, suburbs—called *faubourgs,* meaning "beyond the fortress"—sprang up. In time, these communities demanded to be included in the

Figure 10.13
Rothenburg, Germany, typifies the western European medieval city. Houses are built of stone (or, in some cases, are half-timbered), with residences above street-level shops. They are clustered together, with little open space in yards or gardens. This probably resulted from the enclosure of the city by a defensive wall that restricted outward growth. Church towers rise above the city, reminding the residents of the important role played by religion.

true city. If their petition was accepted, the walls would be expanded to encompass the former suburb. By this process, the medieval cities grew, much as modern cities annex their sprawling suburbs.

Another key zone was the *marketplace*. It symbolized the important role of economic activities in the medieval city (see box, *The Greatest City in the World: Hangchow*). The city depended on the countryside for its food and produce, which were traded in the market. The market also was a center for long-distance trade, which linked city to city. Textiles, salt, ore, and other raw materials were bought and sold in the marketplace.

To one end of the marketplace stood the town hall, a fairly tall structure that provided meeting space for the city's political leaders. The town hall often served as a market hall, with many of its rooms used to store and display the finer goods that could not be exposed to the natural elements outside on the market square. Yet, in many of the larger commercial cities, civic and economic functions were located in separate buildings. Brugge, Belgium, an important trading center for northern Europe, had two distinct complexes of buildings at its center (Figure 10.14). Together, the town hall and castle formed an enclosed square. Next to this, forming the edges of a large, open marketplace, was the *wasserhalle,* or waterhall, so named because the building straddled a canal (goods were brought directly into the hall from the barges underneath). On an adjacent edge of the marketplace was the great hall that served as the meeting spot for the merchant class. The tower of the great hall rivaled that of the cathedral. As such, the great hall was a symbol of a world where commerce was beginning to command more attention.

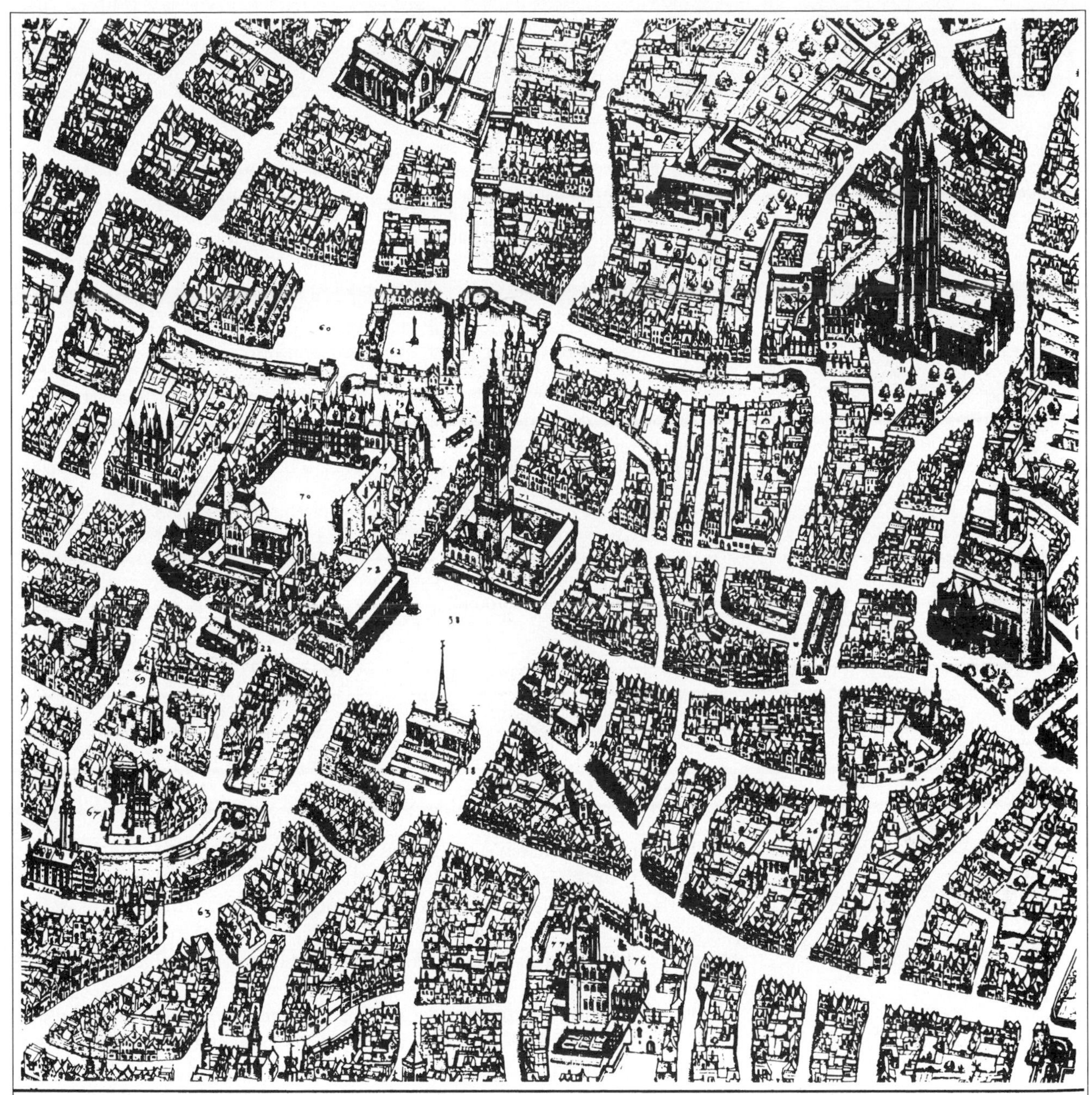

11. Cathedral of Notre Dame.
12. Church of St Sauveur.
18. Chapel of St Christopher.
20. Chapel of St John.
21. Chapel of St Amanda.
22. Chapel of St Peter.
26. Chapel of the Painters.
58. Fish market.
60. Grain market.
62. Leather market.
63. Bourse.
70. Castle, with the Town Hall and Chancellery.
71. Halle.
72. Waterhalle.
75. Prison.
76. Prince's Hall.
77. Mint.
88. So-called 'Castle of the Seven Turrets'.

Figure 10.14

A 1562 panoramic map of the city of Brugge, Belgium, showing the central area. Directly in the center of the image is the great Halle building, the economic heart of the city. Just in front of it and to the left is the waterhall, so named because it straddled the canal, allowing goods to be delivered directly into the building. To the left is the old castle surrounded by guildhalls and the town hall. To the extreme right is the cathedral building. (Source: Benevolo, Leonardo. *The History of the City.* Cambridge, MA: MIT Press, 1980.)

The Greatest City in the World: Hangchow

The Chinese city Hangchow, wrote the Italian Marco Polo, "is the greatest city . . . in the world, where so many pleasures may be found that one fancies himself to be in Paradise." According to a contemporary Chinese account, in the markets of thirteenth-century Hangchow one could buy "beauty products (ointments and perfumes, eyebrow-black, false hair), pet cats and fish for feeding them with, . . . bath wraps, fishing tackle, . . . chessmen, oiled paper for windows, fumigating powder against mosquitoes," and other merchandise unobtainable elsewhere in China (or probably anywhere else on earth). In addition, one could visit any of 15 big specialized markets—including the principal pig market, which was right in the center of town—or the scores of smaller markets for products ranging from flowers and oranges to pearls and precious stones.

Indeed, to the European visitor, Hangchow was a wonder that his medieval city had not prepared him for. As French historian Jacques Gernet comments, "The largest city [sic] of Europe, with a population of several tens of thousands, were nothing but petty market towns in comparison with the 'provisional capital' of China." Its vast ramparts were pierced by five gateways for canals that carried boats loaded with products from all over the country. Its great thoroughfares (the largest 60 yards or 56 meters wide and 3 miles or 5 kilometers long) terminated at the ramparts in 13 monumental gates. It had a population of about 1 million people, which made it "the biggest urban concentration in the world at the time."

Visually, the city had a modern urban look. An unbroken line of dwellings stretched as far as the eye could see. As one of its inhabitants wrote, "The city of Hangchow is large . . . and overpopulated. The houses are high and built close to each other. Their beams touch and their porches are continuous. There is not an inch of unoccupied ground anywhere." Yet almost all the streets of Hangchow were paved, and the level of public cleanliness was probably higher than anywhere in the Western urban world before our own time. The authorities in Hangchow jealously guarded the purity of the water in its giant artificial lake. They realized something that nineteenth-century Europeans had not yet grasped: Polluted water leads to epidemics. "The townspeople who drink no other water but this," wrote a city official, "run the risk of epidemics [if it becomes impure]."

The population was so large (and space so tight) that it spilled beyond the ramparts into giant suburbs. It seems fitting to end this description of thirteenth-century Hangchow with the awestruck words of Oderic de Pordenone, another visitor from medieval Europe, on seeing these suburbs: "At each of [Hangchow's] gates . . . are cities larger than Venice or Padua might be, so that one will go about one of those suburbs for six or eight days and yet will seem to have travelled but a little way."

Adapted from Gernet, Jacques. *Daily Life in China.* New York: Macmillan Publishing Company, 1962. Reprinted with permission of the publisher. Copyright © 1962 by George Allen & Unwin, Ltd.

The medieval town's crowning glory was usually the *cathedral,* a dominating architectural symbol of the important role of the church. Often the cathedral, the marketplace, and the town hall were close together, indicating close ties between religion, commerce, and politics. However, the church was often the prevailing political force in medieval towns.

The morphology and landscape of the medieval city have created problems for contemporary urban life. For example, medieval streets were typically narrow, wandering lanes, rarely more than 15 feet (4 1/2 meters) wide. The narrowness of the streets in these medieval cores constrains twentieth-century automobile use. To illustrate, in 141 German cities, 77 percent of the streets are too narrow for safe and efficient two-way traffic. Similar problems plague other cities. As a result many towns, such as Vienna, Salzburg, and Heidelberg, have excluded auto traffic from the old areas, turning them into pedestrian zones where cars may enter only during certain hours (Figure 10.15).

The functional zonation of the medieval city differed markedly from that of our modern cities. The city was divided into small quarters, or districts, each containing its own center that served as its focal point. Within each of these districts lived people who were engaged in similar occupations. Coopers (people who made and repaired wooden barrels), for example, lived in one particular district, attended the same local church, and belonged to the same guild. Their church and guildhall were located in the small center area of their district. Along the narrow,

Figure 10.15
Heidelberg, Germany, showing the typical narrow, winding street pattern of the medieval period. Besides the pedestrian-scale inner city, we see other typical medieval features, such as residences located above street-level shops and churches.

winding streets surrounding this center area were the houses and workplaces of the coopers. Many worked in the first story of their houses. Their families lived above the shop, and their apprentices lived above them. The more prestigious groups lived in occupational districts close to the main center of the city, while those that were involved in noxious activities, such as butchers and leatherworkers, lived closer to the city walls.

Some of these districts, however, were defined not by occupation but by ethnicity, and these areas have been referred to as ghettos. The origin of the term *ghetto* is somewhat unclear, though one plausible explanation suggests that the word dates from the early sixteenth century when Venetians decided to restrict Jewish settlement in the city to an area already known as *Ghetto Nuovo,* or the "new foundry." This area was physically separated from the rest of the city, and had a single entrance that could be guarded. This practice of spatially segregating the Jewish population was not limited to Venice. In most medieval cities, Jews were forced to live in their own district. In Frankfurt am Main, Jews lived on the *Judengasse,* a street that was formed from the dried-up moat that had run along the old wall to the city. The *Judengasse* was enclosed by walls with only one guarded gate for entrance and exit. Because the area was not allowed to expand beyond those walls, a growing population led to more dense living conditions. In 1462, the population of *Judengasse* was only 110 inhabitants; but by 1610, 3000 people lived in the Jewish ghetto, creating one of the densest districts in the city.

In summary, there are three important points about the role of the medieval period in the evolution of the Western city: (1) This was when most European cities were founded; (2) many of the traditions of Western urban life were begun then; and (3) the medieval landscape is still with us, giving a visible history of the city and a distinctive form into which twentieth-century activities are placed.

Figure 10.16
The townscape of Salzburg, Austria. This illustrates two important periods of urban development. In the foreground is tightly compacted housing of the medieval period, while the middle ground is made up of churches, the cathedral, and the university of the baroque period. In the background is the fortress, built in the medieval period and elaborated in the baroque.

The Renaissance and Baroque Periods

During the Renaissance (1500–1600) and baroque (1600–1800) periods, the form and function of the European city changed significantly. Absolute monarchs arose to preside over a unified nation-state. The burghers, or rising middle class, of the cities slowly gave up their freedoms to join with the king in pursuit of economic gain. City size increased rapidly because the bureaucracies of regional power structures came to dominate cities and because trade patterns expanded with the beginnings of European imperial conquest. A new concern with city planning and military technology also acted to remold and constrain the physical form of the city (Figure 10.16).

Cities and the surrounding countryside began to combine into nation-states, ruled by all-powerful monarchs. One city, the national capital, rose to prominence in most countries. Provincial cities were subjected to its tastes, and power was centralized in its precincts. The first office buildings were built to house a growing new government bureaucracy. Most important, the capital city was restructured to reflect the power of the central government and to ensure its control over the urban masses.

Hand in hand with these developments went a new interest in city planning. This concern grew from a revival of the classical period, including Greek and Roman urban planning; from a new philosophical emphasis on humankind's earthly home; and from new aesthetic concepts that gave urban planners a foundation to work from (see box, *Planning the Ideal City: Humanism and Renaissance Urban Design*).

Planning the Ideal City: Humanism and Renaissance Urban Design

Fifteenth-century humanism, with its stress on the individual as a microcosm of a universe constructed according to fixed mathematical relationships, provided a philosophical framework within which techniques for unitary perspectives could be developed. Many Italian architects and artists combined painting, architecture and social theory to create imaginative plans for ideal cities, all constructed along humanist principles. By stressing supposedly universal values of reason and natural order, these ideal city plans served to mediate between an aristocratic vision of the world where rank and status are regarded as natural and assured by birth, and a bourgeois one where they were economically determined.

All of these plans for ideal cities had certain properties in common. The ideal city is conceived as a unitary space, an architectural totality, a changeless and perfect form. It is delineated by a fortified wall, circular or polygonal in shape. At the center is a large open space surrounded by key administrative buildings: the prince's palace, the justice building, the main church, generally referred to in classical terms as a temple, and often a prison, treasury, and military garrison. Significantly, the market square is rarely discussed in detail and often relegated to a subsidiary open space away from the center. The dimensions of the central piazza and its architecture are rigorously controlled and strictly proportioned. Road patterns are determined by center and periphery, either orthogonally or in gridiron pattern. They are designed to provide visual corridors giving prospects on key urban buildings or monuments. The entire conception is visual, either imagined from above as a visual unity of plan or on the ground as a series of integrated perspectives to and from principal buildings located at the vanishing point. Individual structures are to be designed according to the rules of the classical orders; thus each is rendered a microcosm of the same geometric principles that govern the harmony of the whole city and that are displayed in the physical and intellectual properties of its citizens. The ideal city is designed for the exercise of administration and justice, for the civic life, rather than for production or exchange. It is purely ideological.

The morphological features of ideal cities reveal sharply the integration of proportional theory with its cosmological implications and political ideology. They are social as well as architectural utopias, designed to regulate and determine relationships between classes in an environment where neither merchant nor landed aristocrat dominates, but where a class of noble administrators rules by virtue of its members' superior reason rather than their exercise of economic power or inherited privilege.

Adapted and abridged from Cosgrove, Denis. *Social Formation and Symbolic Landscape.* London: Croom Helm, 1984.

Most planning measures were meant to benefit the privileged classes. Rulers considered the city a stage on which to act out their destinies, and as a stage, the city could be rearranged at will. Typical of the time was the infatuation with wide, grandiose boulevards. The rich could ride along them in carriages, and the army could march along them in an impressive display of power. Other features of the baroque city were large, open squares, palaces, and public buildings. Statues were everywhere.

This environment was strikingly different from the dark, closed world of the medieval quarters, where the middle classes still resided. The spacious, new aristocratic sections often were created at the expense of the middle class, whose homes were demolished to make way for a new palace or boulevard.

Although the height of baroque planning was between 1600 and 1800, this autocratic spirit also carried into the nineteenth century, as is illustrated in Paris (Figure 10.17). There, Napoléon III had Baron Haussmann build a system of boulevards designed to, among other things, control the populace. Cobblestone streets were carefully paved so that no loose ammunition was available for rioting Parisians. Streets were straightened and widened, and cul-de-sacs were broken down to give the army—should the people arise—space to maneuver, with ordered sight lines for its artillery. Whole neighborhoods were torn down to build wide avenues. Thousands were displaced as their apartment buildings were demolished. They had to seek new shelter on their own, and many ended up in the congested working-class sections of east and north Paris. These areas are still overcrowded, and much of the blame can be assigned to the baroque planners.

Figure 10.17
A view of Paris, showing boulevards designed by Baron Haussmann. The boulevard was a favorite of baroque planners. It was a ceremonial street that often led to public buildings and monuments, was lined with upper-income housing and trees, and offered public space for the wealthy. Boulevards were often created at the expense of thousands of those less well off who were displaced as older housing was destroyed by the boulevard builders. Has this happened in your city or one near you as freeways have been built?

Figure 10.18
View of boulevards in Washington, DC. Notice how the wide boulevards and limits on the height of buildings emphasize the importance of our national monuments, such as the Capitol building in the foreground, and the Washington Monument at the opposite end of the Mall.

In these developments, we can see the coming of the modern city. The masses of city dwellers were sacrificed to the traffic pattern. Neighborhoods were overwhelmed by the straight line. In our own times, the highway has replaced the avenue as the yardstick of the urban planner, but the results have been the same—the wholesale destruction of inner-city neighborhoods.

Renaissance and baroque planning influenced many American cities as well as European cities. For example, Washington, DC, was originally designed by a French planner during the height of the baroque period (Figure 10.18). Although the original plan has been compromised somewhat, its intent is still visible in the wide boulevards, open spaces, public buildings, and monuments of the city.

The Capitalist City

Underlying many of the changes in Renaissance and baroque city planning was a sweeping socioeconomic transformation that reshaped western Europe. The transition from a feudal order to a capitalist one involved drastic changes in class structure, economic systems, political allegiances, cultural patterns, and human geographies. These changes occurred over a period of time that stretched from the mid-sixteenth century to the mid-eighteenth century. The countryside was reordered with the introduction of commercialized and specialized agriculture and with the enclosure of individual land units. The city was also reshaped, as the value of two-dimensional location and three-dimensional form in the city acquired economic significance.

Perhaps of greatest significance is how the capitalist mindset introduced a notion of urban land as a source of income. Proximity to the center of the city, and therefore to the most pedestrian traffic, added economic value to land. Other specialized locations, such as areas close to the river or harbor or along the major thoroughfares in and out of the city, also increased land value. This fundamental change in the value accorded to urban land led to the gradual disintegration of the medieval urban pattern.

In the emerging capitalist city, the ability to pay determined where one would live. The city's residential areas thus became segregated by economic class. The wealthy lived in the desirable neighborhoods, while those without much money were forced to live in the more disagreeable parts of the city. In addition, places of work were separated from home, so that a merchant, for example, lived in one part of the city and traveled to another to conduct his business. This spatial separation of work from home, of public space from private space, both reflected and helped to shape the changing social worlds of men and women. In general, men generated economic income from work outside the home and therefore came to be associated with the public space of the city. Women, who were engaged in domestic work, were considered the keepers of the private world of the home. This association of women with private domestic space and men with public work space deepened and became more complex throughout the next few hundred years.

The center of the capitalist city was not the cathedral and guildhalls, but instead consisted of buildings devoted to business enterprises. A downtown defined by economic activity emerged, and, with the coming of industrialization, would eventually expand and subdivide into specialized districts. The new upper classes of the city, whose status was based on their accumulation of economic wealth, not only made money from buying and selling urban land, but also used urban land as a basis for expressing their wealth. With the downtowns devoted to mercantile and emerging industrial uses, the upper classes sought newer land on the edge of the city for their residential enclaves. These new areas often acted as three-dimensional symbols of relatively recent wealth, conferring on their residents the legitimacy of upper-class membership.

One of the first and finest of these new enclaves for the wealthy was London's Covent Garden Piazza, a residential square designed by Inigo Jones in the early 1630s. The square was lined with townhouses that were edged in arcades, with one end of the square dedicated to a church. The inhabitants of Covent Garden included some of London's nobility and wealthier bourgeoisie. The presence of nobility lent an aristocratic aura to the area and provided social legitimacy to the new bourgeoisie who lived there. The economic success of this speculative real estate venture led to many imitations, and similar residential squares cropped up throughout the West End of London (Figure 10.19). These upper-class squares were transplanted to America throughout the seventeenth and eighteenth centuries, arising in such cities as Boston, New York, Philadelphia, and Savannah.

Class, "Race," and Gender in the Industrial City

The function, structure, and landscape of the Western city have changed dramatically since the industrial revolution. In turn, the industrial city has profoundly altered the fabric of society itself.

Up to the industrial period, the rate of urbanization in Western countries was relatively low. For example, in 1600, urban dwellers made up only 2 percent of the German, French, and English populations; in the Netherlands and Italy, 13 percent of the population were urban dwellers. However, as millions of people migrated to the cities during the past 200 years, the rate of urbanization skyrocketed. By 1800, England was 20 percent urbanized, and it became the world's first urban society around 1870. By the 1890 census, 60 percent of its people lived in cities. The United States was 3 percent urbanized in 1800, 40

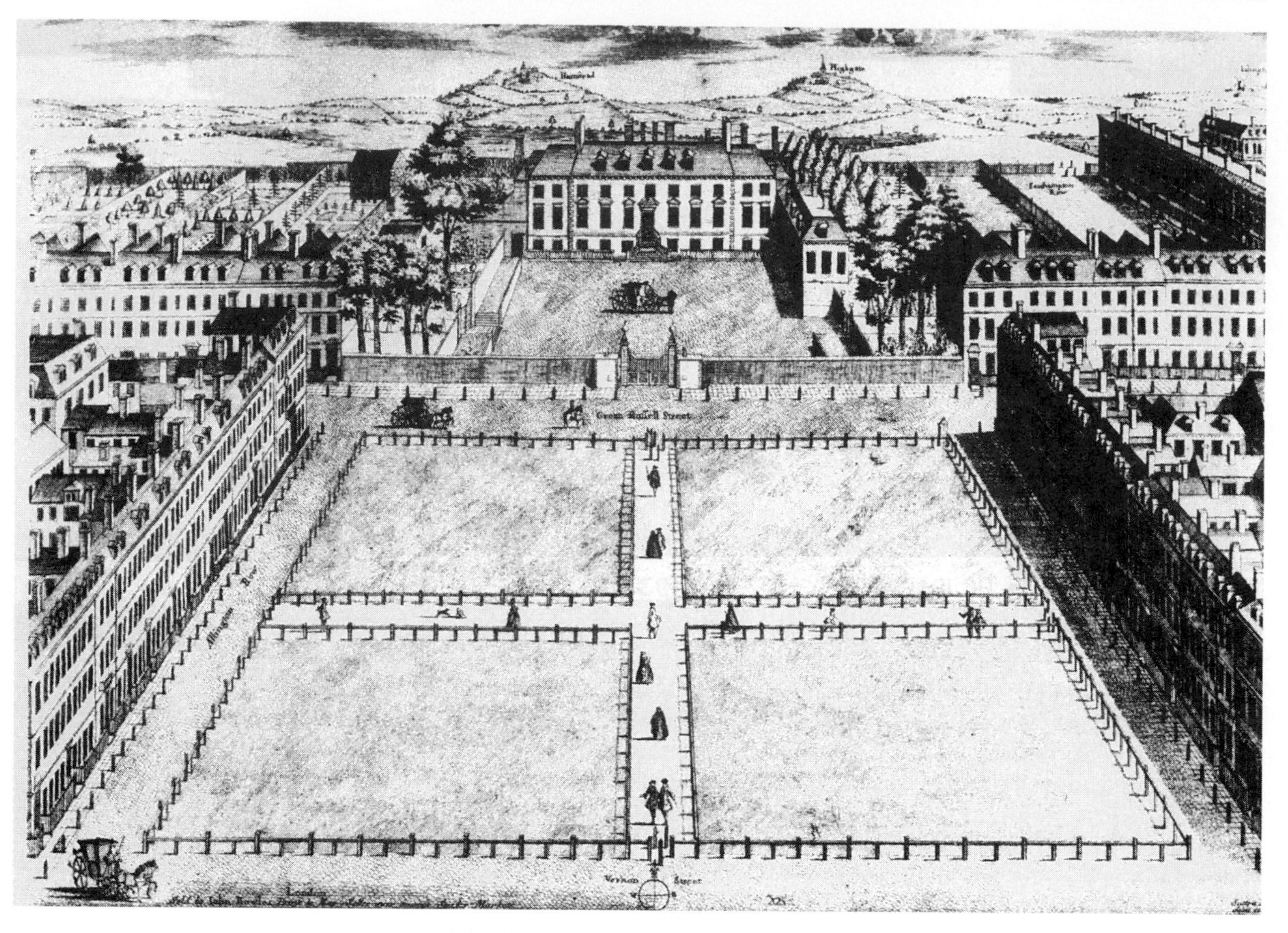

Figure 10.19
A 1730 view of Bloomsbury Square, laid out in 1661 by the Earl of Southampton. Southampton House occupies the far end of the square, lending an aristocratic air to this speculative, mercantile development. Notice the men and women parading in their finery, suggesting the wealthy and leisurely life of the inhabitants. (Source: Hayes, John. *London: A Pictorial History.* New York: Arco Publishing Company, Inc., 1969.)

percent in 1900, 51 percent in 1920 (when it became an urban country), and now about 75 percent of its population lives in towns and cities.

The industrial revolution and the triumph of capitalism turned the city from a public institution into private property—spoils to be divided with an eye to maximum profits. A new philosophy emerged, **laissez-faire utilitarianism.** Lewis Mumford, in *The City in History,* defined this as a belief that divine providence ruled over economic activity and ensured the maximum public good through the unregulated efforts of every private, self-seeking individual. One expression of this new philosophy was a changed attitude toward land and the buildings on that land. Once raw materials such as coal and iron ore could be brought to the city by rail, factories began to cluster together to share the benefits of **agglomeration**—that is, to share labor, transportation costs, and utility costs and to take advantage of financial institutions found in the city. Industry concentrated in the city itself, around labor, the commercial marketplace, and capital. Land use intensified drastically. With the increased competition for land in the industrial period, land transactions and speculation became an everyday part of the city. Land parcels became the property of the owner, who had no obligations toward society in deciding how to use them. The historical urban core was often destroyed, the older city replaced. The result was a mosaic of mixed land uses: factories directly next to housing; slum tenements next to public buildings; open spaces and parks violated by railroad tracks. A planned attempt to bring order to the city came only in the twentieth century with the concept of zoning. Yet even this idea was rooted in some of the same forces—profit, bigotry, and individualism—that had already made the industrial city unresponsive to the needs of most of its inhabitants (see box, *The Origins of Zoning in America: Race and Wealth*).

Class. Laissez-faire industrialism did surprisingly little for the working classes that fueled its shops and plants. If the wholesale distribution of such utilities as gas and water is excluded, the industrial city made no improvements in human living standards beyond what had already been available in the seventeenth-century city. Moreover, the industrial city took environmental necessities from the new working class. In their slum dwellings, direct sunlight was seldom available, and open spaces were nonexistent (Figure 10.20). In Liverpool, England, for instance, one-sixth of the population reportedly lived in "underground cellars." A study from the middle of the nineteenth century in Manchester, England, showed that there was but one toilet for every 212 people. Running water was usually available only on the ground floors of apartment buildings. Disease was pervasive, and mortality rates ran high. In 1893, the life expectancy of a male worker in Manchester was 28 years; his country cousin might live until 52. The death rate in New York City in 1880 was 25 per thousand, whereas it was half that in the rural coun-

The Origins of Zoning in America: Race and Wealth

"The standard zoning ordinance of American cities was originally conceived from a union of two fears—fear of the Chinese and fear of skyscrapers. In California a wave of racial prejudice had swept over the state after Chinese settlers were imported to build the railroads and work in the mines [in the mid-nineteenth century]. Ingenious lawyers in San Francisco found that the old common law of nuisance could be applied for indirect discrimination against the Chinese in situations where the constitution of the state forbade direct discrimination. Chinese laundries of the 1880s had become social centers for Chinese servants who lived outside the Chinatown ghetto. To whites they represented only clusters of 'undesirables' in the residential areas where Chinese were living singly among them as house servants. By declaring the laundries nuisances and fire hazards, San Francisco hoped to exclude Chinese from most sections of the city. . . . Such nuisance-zone statutes spread down the Pacific coast. . . .

"[Meanwhile,] in New York [City] the Fifth Avenue Association, a group composed of men who owned or leased the city's most expensive retail land, demanded that the city protect their luxury blocks from encroachment by the new tall buildings of the garment district. . . . The Fifth Avenue Association feared that the ensuing decades would see the [skyscraper] lofts invading their best properties, bringing with them [lower-class] lunch-hour crowds and a blockade of wagons, trucks, and carts. In short, they feared that skyscraper lofts, low-paid help, and traffic congestion would drive their middle-class and wealthy customers from the Avenue."

The combination of West Coast racism plus the fears of wealthy New York merchants resulted in the New York Zoning Law of 1916, a prototype zoning statute for the nation. These were the roots of the first American attempts to deal coherently with urban growth. Not surprisingly, the zoning law was no sooner passed than it was seized on in the South and elsewhere "as a way to extend [the] laws and practices of racial segregation . . . . A land or structure limitation . . . became a financial, racial, and ethnic limitation by pricing certain groups out of particular suburbs. Italians were held at bay in Boston, Poles in Detroit, blacks in Chicago and St. Louis, Jews in New York."

Abridged and adapted from Warner, Sam Bass, Jr. *Urban Wilderness.* New York: Harper & Row, 1972, pp. 28–32, 117–118.

Figure 10.20
Lower Manhattan, looking north from the Produce Exchange. This view of mid-nineteenth century New York depicts the very crowded living and working conditions as the city's population greatly expanded during industrialization.

ties of the state. The infant mortality rate per thousand live births rose from 180 in 1850 to 240 in 1870. Legislation correcting such ills came only in the latter part of the century.

"Race." And yet industrialization created some of the most vibrant centers of urban activity in modern times. American industrial cities, for example, relied on a diverse labor force, and each social group fought for its place in the urban land market. Despite the harsh living conditions, different groups of laborers carved out identities in the urban landscape.

Industrialization in the United States drew for its workforce not only on European immigrants, but also on African Americans. After the Civil War, many former slaves in the South migrated to northern cities to work in a diverse array of skilled and semiskilled jobs, while industrialization in many southern cities led to a rural-to-urban migration for African Americans. In both northern and southern cities, the African American population lived in segregated neighborhoods, forced by discrimination and often by law to keep their distance from Anglo-American residential districts.

Although for the most part the services provided to these neighborhoods were minimal, many people did find opportunities for cultural expression in the new urban mosaic. A recent study of African Americans in Richmond, Virgina, after the Civil War found that residents effectively used public rituals in the streets and buildings of the city to carve out their own civic representations, as well as to challenge the dominant, Anglo-American order. For example, African American militias were formed that marched through the streets of Richmond on holidays certified by the African American community as their own political calendar: January 1, George Washington's birthday, April 3 (Emancipation Day), and July 4. As urban historians Elsa Barkley Brown and Gregg Kimball state: "White Richmonders watched in horror as former slaves claimed civic holidays white residents believed to be their own historic possession, and as black residents occupied spaces, like Capitol Square, that formerly had been reserved for white citizens." Other spaces, such as churches, schools, and beauty shops, served as community centers and public statements of an African American identity. In this way, the urban landscape acted as one arena for the struggle to control the meanings and uses of an environment often thought to be totally dominated by Anglo-American culture (Figure 10.21).

Gender. Industrialization, then, not only destroyed sections of cities to make way for railroads and factories, but also made possible the creation of new urban identities and neighborhoods. Throughout the nineteenth century, the industrial city became increasingly segregated by function; large areas of the city were dedicated to the production of goods and services, surrounded by working-class neighborhoods. At the same time, the center of the city was remade into an area of consumption and leisure, with large department stores, theaters, clubs, restaurants, and nightclubs. In New York City, one of the foremost displays of such a culture of consumption was located along Broadway between Union and Madison squares. This area was called Ladies' Mile because, as the new class of consumers, middle-class women were the major patrons of the large department stores that architecturally dominated the streets.

Although industrialization led to the creation of separate spheres—the feminine sphere centered on the home and domestic duties, and the male sphere dominated the public spaces and duties—it also created the need for mass consumption to keep the factories running profitably. With men as the class of producers, the duties of consumption fell to the women. And the locational logic of the urban land market meant that retailers were located in the most central parts of the city. This established what some scholars have referred to as a feminized downtown, meaning not only that the downtown was characterized by the presence of middle- and upper-class women, but also that the retailers themselves created spaces considered appropriately "feminine." Interior spaces were well-arranged and orderly, external architectural design was heavily ornamented, and streets were paved and well-lit (Figure 10.22).

Although this type of ornate and "feminine" downtown retailing area is still evident in large cities like New York and San Francisco, the

Figure 10.21
Sketch of an African American congregation in Washington D.C. African American churches often served as centers of community organizations, and as public statements of identity, in the industrializing cities of the North.

Figure 10.22
Stewart's department store. One of the most ornate department stores along Ladies' Mile in New York City was Stewart's store, located on Broadway at 10th Street. Since the store catered to the needs of Victorian women, it can be considered an example of "feminine" space.

decentralizing forces in the twentieth-century city have led to the abandonment of many of these areas, replaced by the suburban shopping mall (see Chapter 11). It would be interesting to speculate in what ways the shopping mall is also a "feminine" space.

Megalopolis

In the nineteenth century, cities grew at unprecedented rates because of the concentration of people and commerce. Movement away from the central city quickened in the last decades of the century. The inner city became increasingly dominated by commerce and the working class. In the twentieth century, particularly since World War II, new forms of transportation and communication have led to the **decentralization** of many urban functions. One metropolitan area blends into another, until supercities are created that stretch for hundreds of miles.

The prototype of this new form is found on the eastern seaboard of the United States, stretching from Boston in the North to Washington, DC, in the South. Some call it the supercity of "Boswash." The geographer Jean Gottmann coined the term **megalopolis** to describe it. This term is now used worldwide in reference to giant metropolitan regions. These urban regions are characterized by high population densities, extending over hundreds of square miles or kilometers; concentrations of numerous older cities; transportation links formed by freeway, railroad, air routes, and rapid transit; and an extremely high proportion of the nation's wealth, commerce, and political power.

The problems of the megalopolis come on a giant scale with such an immense concentration of people and activities. Common problems in these supercities are congestion, high land prices, overcrowding, financial insolvency, deteriorating inner cores, a poor and disenfranchised population in contrast to the affluent in the suburbs, and air and water pollution. Unfortunately, solutions to these problems will not soon be found, for another characteristic of megalopolitan areas is political fragmentation. Because most of the problems are regionwide, they go beyond the legal jurisdiction of the smaller towns and counties. Often they cross state borders. Solutions will come only with increased cooperation among all political units and the formation of regional agencies. Until then, the megalopolis will continue to grow, and its problems will increase.

Edge Cities

The past 20 years have witnessed an explosion in metropolitan growth in areas that had once been peripheral to the central city. Many of the so-called sleeping suburbs of the post–World War II era have been transformed into urban centers, with their own retail, financial, and entertainment districts (Figure 10.23). Author Joel Garreau refers to these new centers of urban activity as *edge cities*, although many other terms have been used in the past, including "suburban downtowns," "galactic cities," and "urban villages" (see box, *Cities on the Edge, Cities of the Future?*). Most Americans now live, work, play, worship, and study in this type of settlement form. What differentiates an **edge city** from the suburbs is that it is a place of work, of productive, economic activity, and therefore is the destination of many commuters. In fact, the conventional work commute from the suburbs to the inner city has been replaced by commuting patterns that completely encircle the inner city. People live in one part of an edge city and commute to their workplace in another part of that city.

Figure 10.23
Edge City. These new centers of economic activity are located on the "edges" of traditional downtowns.

Many scholars are wary of referring to these new nodes of activity as cities because they do not resemble our nineteenth-century vision of a city. Edge cities contain all the functions of old downtowns, but they are spread out and less dense, with clusters along major freeways and off-ramps. This new form is attributable to changes in Americans' lifestyles and to the development of new transportation and communication technologies. The interstate highway system made possible an effective trucking system to transport consumer goods, thereby enabling new industries to locate outside the downtown. Breakthroughs in computer and communication technologies have allowed corporate executives to move company headquarters out of the downtowns and into new, slick glass buildings with parking garages, jogging paths, and picnic tables under the trees. Real-estate speculations in emerging edge cities have fueled their development, resulting in an environment that many people feel is ugly and chaotic. As Garreau points out, however, even a place as revered by designers as Venice, Italy, began as an ad-hoc mercantilist adventure; and the Piazza San Marco was the result not of great urban planning, but of the coincidence of centuries of building and rebuilding by people worried about making money.

Certainly, however, edge cities present a litany of problems for today's planners. These problems range from traffic congestion and planning for mass transit to environmental concerns as these spreading urban areas consume more and more land. Is it possible to provide mass transit in a system that has no center? These problems may be with us for a long time, because these cities on the edge are possibly our cities of the future.

Now that we have examined the evolution of North American and western European cities, let us look at the development of cities in the developing world.

Cities on the Edge, Cities of the Future?

Edge City is any place that:

1. *Has five million square feet or more of leasable office space—the workplace of the Information Age.* Five million square feet is more than downtown Memphis. The Edge City called the Galleria area west of downtown Houston—crowned by the sixty-four-story Transco Tower, the tallest building in the world outside an old downtown—is bigger than downtown Minneapolis.
2. *Has 600,000 square feet or more of leasable retail space.* That is the equivalent of a fair-sized mall. That mall, remember, probably has at least three nationally famous department stores, and eighty to a hundred shops and boutiques full of merchandise that used to be available only on the finest boulevards of Europe. Even in their heyday, there were not many downtowns with that boast.
3. *Has more jobs than bedrooms.* When the workday starts, people head toward this place, not away from it. Like all urban places, the population increases at 9 AM.
4. *Is perceived by the population as one place.* It is a regional end destination for mixed use—not a starting point—that "has it all," from jobs, to shopping, to entertainment.
5. *Was nothing like "city" as recently as thirty years ago.* Then, it was just bedrooms, if not cow pastures. This incarnation is brand new.

An example of the authentic, California-like experience of encountering such an Edge City is peeling off a high thruway, like the Pennsylvania Turnpike, onto an arterial, like 202 at King of Prussia, northwest of downtown Philadelphia. Descending into traffic that is bumper to bumper in *both* directions, one swirls through mosaics of lawn and parking, punctuated by office slabs whose designers have taken the curious vow of never placing windows in anything other than horizontal reflective strips. Detours mark the yellow dust of heavy construction that seems a permanent feature of the landscape.

Tasteful signs mark corporations apparently named after Klingon warriors. Who put Captain Kirk in charge of calling companies Imtrex, Avantor, and Synovus? Before that question can settle, you encounter the spoor of—the mother ship. On King of Prussia's Route 202, the mark of that mind-boggling enormity reads MALL NEXT FOUR LEFTS.

For the stranger who is a connoisseur of such places, this Dante-esque vision brings a physical shiver to the spine and a not entirely ironic murmur of recognition to the lips: "Ah! Home!" For that is precisely the significance of Edge Cities. They are the culmination of a generation of individual American value decisions about the best ways to live, work, and play—about how to create "home." That stuff "out there" is where America is being built. That "stuff" is the delicate balance between unlimited opportunity and rippling chaos that works for us so well. We build more of it every chance we get.

If Edge Cities are still a little ragged at the fringes, well, that just places them in the finest traditions of Walt Whitman's "barbaric yawp over the rooftops of the world"—what the social critic Tom Wolfe calls, affectionately, the "hog-stomping Baroque exuberance of American civilization." Edge Cities, after all, are still works in progress.

They have already proven astoundingly efficient, though, by any urban standard that can be quantified. As places to make one's fame and fortune, their corporate offices generate unprecedentedly low unemployment. In fact, their emblem is the hand-lettered sign taped to plate glass begging people to come to work. As real estate markets, they have made an entire generation of homeowners and speculators rich. As bazaars, they are anchored by some of the most luxurious shopping in the world. Edge City acculturates immigrants, provides child care, and offers safety. It is, on average, an *improvement* in per capita fuel efficiency over the old suburbia-downtown arrangement, since it moves everything closer to the homes of the middle class.

That is why Edge City is the crucible of America's urban future. Having become the place in which the majority of Americans now live, learn, work, shop, play, pray, and die, Edge City will be the forge of the fabled American way of life well into the twenty-first century.

The Urban Landscapes of the Developing World

Most of the world's population lives in the developing world, and in these areas we see the greatest potential for dramatic change in urban patterns. This change is mainly a function of high natural population growth coupled with enormous rates of migration from countryside to cities. Recent growth in these cities has been staggering. In 1950, only 4 of the 15 largest cities of the world were in developing countries; the latest census shows that approximately half of the largest 20 cities are now in these countries (refer to Table 10.1). Accompanying this rapid growth are serious economic, political, and social problems.

It is difficult to generalize about cities of the developing world. More detailed studies use a finer cultural scale so that conclusions take into consideration local and regional influences and explain the similarities—and differences—between cities in one area and those in another. The following is a broad-brush treatment of a complex topic.

The preceding section on the evolving landscape of cities in the developed world was able to delimit specific evolutionary periods, such as medieval and industrial. This is more difficult to do with cities of the developing world because local influences have been so important and city histories are so varied. Instead, we use three models, each one representing an idealized or hypothetical pattern of a city in a developing country.

The Indigenous City

Indigenous cities developed without contact with Western colonial influences. In fact, many of these cities evolved long before there were cities in northern Europe. Most of them predate European colonialism; a very few may have been untouched by the landscape and structure of the later colonial period.

Precolonial indigenous cities in the New World are restricted to Mexico, Central America, and the Andean highlands. In Africa, there are cities in the west associated with the Yoruba civilization (in present-day Nigeria), along the Nile River Valley, a band of Islamic empires in the north, and some more small cities in the eastern highlands, again associated with Islamic empires. Asia has the largest number of precolonial indigenous cities, reaching from the Middle East, across present-day Pakistan and India, to China and Japan.

The basic form of many indigenous cities is derived from what we have referred to as the cosmomagical. Many indigenous cities of Mexico and Central America, China and Japan, and Egypt and India were originally laid out according to religious principles. These principles dictated a fairly rectangular urban form, oriented toward the four cardinal directions and containing a sacred precinct in the symbolic center. Beijing, the core of Imperial China, maintained its basic cosmomagical landscape of rectilinearity, centrality, and axiality until the early twentieth century. Certainly deviations from the strict pattern arose to accommodate the everyday functions of business and culture, and small alleyways and houses were built in an irregular pattern that did not accord with sacred principles. As geographers Marwyn and Carmencita Samuels have pointed out, however, the major force in the design of Imperial Beijing up until the formal abdication of the last emperor in 1912 was the maintenance of the city as the celestial capital of the empire. The power of that force was evident even after 50 years of massive social and political changes had greatly transformed China and Beijing. In 1959, the Socialist government chose to build its symbolic center, Tiananmen Square, exactly on the site of the sacred axis mundi of Imperial Beijing. Sacred principles of urban design in indigenous cities can be very enduring.

Indigenous Cities of the Islamic World. Indigenous cities of the Islamic world exhibit different functional arrangements and landscape forms. In the center of the city is the primary mosque, representing the religious core, and nearby is the bazaar, or marketplace, representing the commercial core. Surrounding this central core are the homes of the elite and government or municipal buildings. Farther away from the core lie areas of decreasing wealth and social status. Groups of recent urban migrants, or unassimilated ethnic groups, might be found on the city's edges.

The city is further divided into occupational districts, similar to the pattern we discussed in the medieval city. In the Islamic city, these trades are arranged in a concentric and hierarchical pattern, with the more noble trades close to the center and the less prestigious trades nearer to the edge. For example, closest to the mosque are located the trades necessary to the religious order, including the selling of candles, incense, and books. Farther out are leather works, tailors, rug shops, and jewelers; then suppliers of foodstuffs; and, at the edges of the city, blacksmiths, basket makers, and potters. Clearly, social status is aligned with proximity to the center. Ethnic groups may dominate certain areas. Sometimes this ethnic pattern is formalized into "quarters" that form semiautonomous villages within the city. For example, Islamic cities commonly reserved one quarter for Jews, another for Christians. Foreign traders and merchants were also usually restricted to certain areas of the city.

Although the overall pattern of the city is fairly well organized by economic function and ethnic ties, an initial impression of the city would suggest anything but order. Islamic cities have a very irregular street plan, with narrow, winding streets, an uneven building pattern, and few open spaces. Residences are usually humble, in keeping with religious dictates. Because Muslim women and men are meant to minimize contact, housing arrangements are often structured around the segregation of the sexes. For example, the typical house of a wealthy Iranian family consists of two sectors organized around separate courtyards. The female half is considered the more private section, and therefore is in the rear of the house; the more public male half is near the entrance of the house (Figure 10.24). However, during daytime hours, when men participate in the public sector outside of the home, the entire home becomes the domain of women.

The Colonial City

A **colonial city** is an administrative, commercial, and often military outpost for an external power. Many colonial cities were established not to serve local populations, but instead to economically or militarily subdue local peoples. This was often expressed in the design of these cities.

When colonial cities were built near indigenous cities, the Europeans would either weld their city onto the existing settlement or, in a few extreme cases, build a totally new city nearby. The British built New Delhi across from original Delhi, and today the two still illustrate the contrast between colonial and indigenous cities. In old Delhi, gross density is 213 persons per acre; in New Delhi, 13 persons per acre. Old Delhi is medieval, with narrow, winding streets, little open space, and cramped residences (Figure 10.25). New Delhi, on the other hand, has wide streets; gardens surround the spacious houses of administrative staff; and parks and squares ring government buildings. All of this reminds one of the baroque period in Western urban development. And well it should. Much European colonialism was coincidental with the baroque era, so it is not surprising that colonial cities express these planning ideas. As the baroque was used in Europe to express the power of the elite, so it was used in colonial cities. Grandiose boulevards were often cut through native residential quarters, large monumental buildings demonstrated the presence of the new power struc-

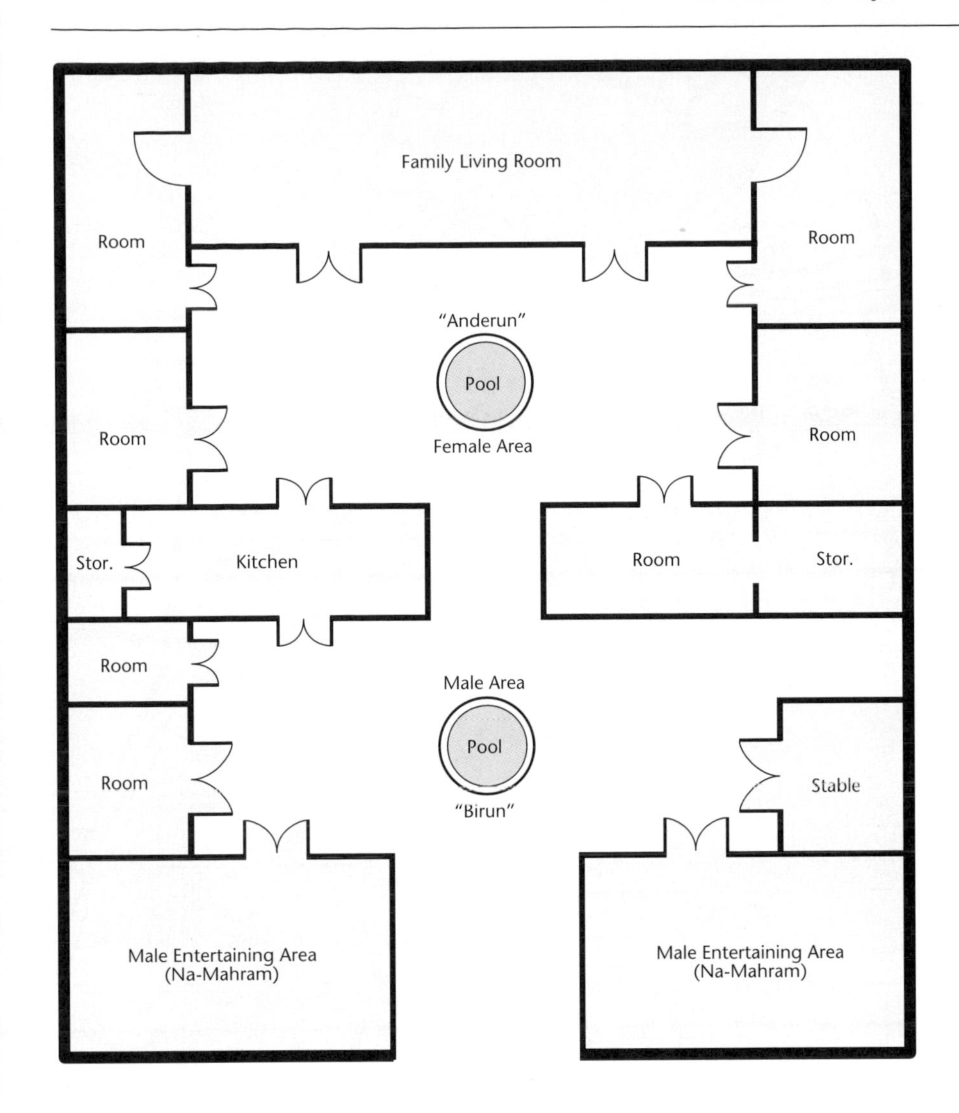

Figure 10.24
Plan of a traditional wealthy Muslim family home. The female area of the house (*anderun*) is located in the more private portions of the house toward the back, while the male area (*birun*) is in the more public, anterior portion of the house. (Source: Spain, Daphne. *Gendered Spaces.* Chapel Hill: University of North Carolina Press, 1992.)

ture, and the Europeans were housed in elaborate residences that constantly reminded locals of their new masters (Figure 10.26).

In his study of the city of Kandy, Sri Lanka, geographer James Duncan shows how British colonial rulers in the nineteenth century consciously manipulated the urban landscape to symbolize and reinforce their claims to legitimate rule. All the symbols of the former kingdom were either replaced by symbols of British rule or allowed to fall into disrepair (see box, *Colonial Rule Symbolized in the Urban Landscape of Kandy, Sri Lanka*). For example, as Duncan states,

> *The king's audience hall located on hallowed ground between the Temple of the Relic and palace became the civic court during the week and the Anglican church on Sundays. In the alcove where the king of Kandy's throne once sat stood the pulpit and behind it hung a picture of the English king. The Malabar palace of the king's relatives became the European hospital and the queen's bath became a European library.*

When new colonial cities were founded, they were often based on a standardized plan. For example, all Spanish cities in the New World were constructed according to the Laws of the Indies, drafted in 1573. The document explicitly outlined how colonial cities were to be con-

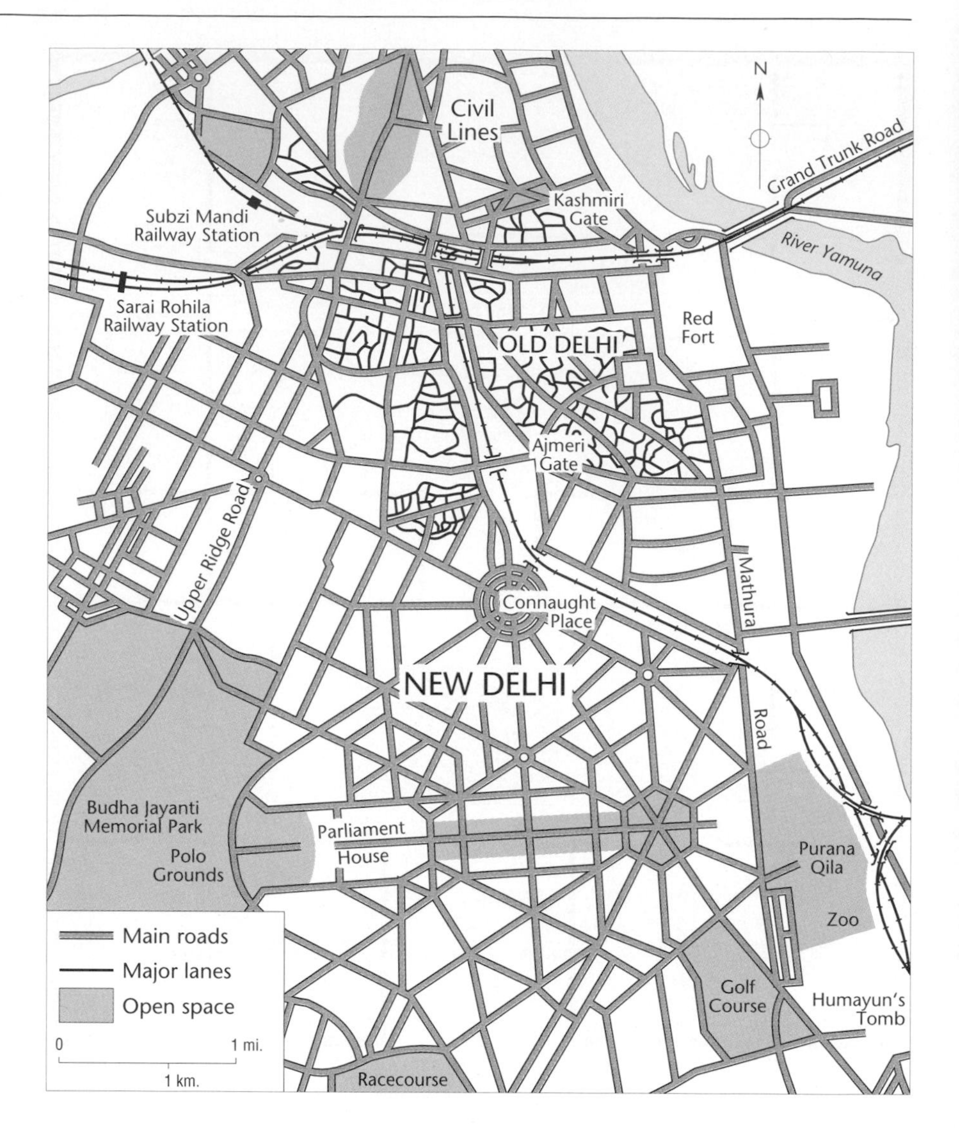

Figure 10.25
Map of Delhi, India. This shows the contrast between the morphology and landscape of the indigenous city, Delhi, and the British colonial addition, New Delhi. Note the straight, symmetrical ceremonial boulevards and open space in the colonial city, expressions of baroque planning in the colonial age. Then compare that with the morphology of Old Delhi. (After Drakakis-Smith, David. *The Third World City.* London: Methuen, 1987: p. 20, with modifications.)

Figure 10.26
A view of La Paz, Bolivia. Monuments, parks, and palaces—often designed by European planners—are found in many former colonial cities, and contrast with the densely populated residential areas that surround the central city.

Colonial Rule Symbolized in the Urban Landscape of Kandy, Sri Lanka

The meaning of Kandy as a place was being changed. A new cultural and political system had been ushered in and the old landscape model which spoke of what had been important under the old system was being transformed or allowed to fall into ruination. Kandy was no longer the city of the god king, for he had been unceremoniously sent into exile. It was becoming a British colonial town and it had to look the part. The British realized that if they were to achieve legitimacy it would have to be largely on their terms. And while they never achieved the degree of legitimacy that they sought, they achieved a degree of cultural hegemony among the Sinhalese elites. This cultural hegemony was achieved in part through a conscious attempt to change the Sinhalese elites, but very largely it was achieved through an attempt to transform Kandy into an outlier of British culture. The assimilation was left to the Sinhalese themselves who were often all too ready to emulate the British. This creation of a bit of British culture in Kandy involved a transformation of the landscape of the place and the natural environment of the Kandyan area lent itself admirably to this task. Because of the elevation and topography of Kandy it was possible to create a facsimile of the landscape of home. One could see in residents' diaries, and official plans the conscious attempt to transform Kandy into a hybrid that was part English and part Sinhalese. Their success in doing so was attested to in the journals and paintings of travelers who visited Kandy throughout the 19th century. Kandy was designed to resemble a romanticized image of a pre-industrial England. The landscape model of the English lake district was superimposed upon the mountains and the Kandy lake to recreate a place where English ladies and gentlemen could somehow escape the tropics and the native culture and symbolically return home.

And how exactly was this done? Promenades, such as Lady Horton's Walk, carriage drives such as Victoria Drive, and riding paths such as The Green Gallop, were created. The dense jungle around Kandy was pruned to reveal the best views of the town, the lake and the surrounding mountains. Travelers and residents alike often wrote about how one might "find enchanting views suddenly opening from the various points where the thick verdure of the trees has been judiciously cut away" (Dougherty 1890, p. 102) and that these openings created an "exquisite framework through which . . . [to] see the distant landscape" (Cave 1912, p. 303). The term sublime was commonly used to describe the Kandyan landscape. English vegetables, fruits and trees were introduced and both formal and informal English gardens and parks were laid out. The Governor's Pavilion was laid out like an English country house situated in a parklike expanse of lawns and shrubbery overlooking the town, the lake and the mountains. Exclusive European residential quarters were located around the lake. English architect–designed bungalows with their gardens full of roses and other English flowers climbed the hills from the lakeside. English style buildings predominated on the main thoroughfares such as Ward Street which contained the European stores like Cargills, Walker and Company, the Merchantile Bank, the Queen's Hotel, the Kandy Club, the Lawn Tennis Club, and the Planters Association of Ceylon.

Source: Agnew, John A., and James S. Duncan (eds.). *The Power of Place: Bringing Together Geographical and Sociological Imaginations.* Boston: Unwin Hyman, 1989, pp. 192–193.

structed. According to the laws a gridiron street plan was to be centered on a church and central plaza and all individual lots were to be walled. Smaller plazas were to dot the neighborhoods, occupied by parish churches or monasteries, so that religious teaching would be evenly spread across the new city. In many ways, the formal guidelines for Spanish colonial cities duplicate the planning rules used by the Romans.

In some instances, the Spanish would superimpose their colonial cities on indigenous cities. For example, Mexico City was constructed on top of Tenochtitlán, the religious and political center of the Aztec culture. As a type of cosmomagical city, Tenochtitlán had been laid out in a rectilinear fashion and could therefore fairly easily accommodate the Spanish colonial grid pattern.

France and England also used the gridiron street plan as the basis for many of their colonial cities. It is found in former colonial towns across both Africa and Asia. Remember also that the United States spread colonial towns across the country during the westward movement. As in other colonial cities, the rectangular gridiron plan was often used, demonstrating that a simple, orderly street plan, fitting for the military, which so often initiated early colonial settlement, could be easily extended and was extremely effective for colonial town planning.

In summary, several themes make up the colonial city model. First, if a colonial city was built close to an existing city, the two would be very different in form and function. This difference is not just physical; the cities would be socially separate as well. Colonialism, after all, involves political control of another culture, so class distinctions are pervasive. Second, most colonial cities contain symbols of the takeover of power by colonial rulers, either through the overall design of the city or by the deliberate subversion of traditional landscape symbols. Last, colonial cities were often built to a standardized plan and frequently used the gridiron street pattern.

The Emerging City

With the end of colonialism and the movement toward political and economic independence, developing countries entered a period of rapid, sometimes tumultuous change. Cities have often been the focal point of this change. Millions of people have migrated to cities in search of a better life. Economic activities clustered in and around cities have often changed their orientation from external to local markets. Political and social unrest has also been centered in the cities. So the emerging city model is a fluid one; the emerging city is in the process of forming, and the results cannot be predicted accurately.

Some scholars think that cities in the developing world will duplicate the changes experienced by cities that underwent industrialization in the nineteenth century. Though there are similarities, the differences are much greater. William Hance has written on the differences between contemporary African urbanization and that experienced earlier in Europe, and most of his conclusions can be extended beyond Africa to include emerging cities in Asia and Latin America.

First, Hance notes that population growth is more rapid in African cities than it was in Europe. This results not only from a high natural increase, but mainly from an extremely high rate of migration to the cities. And although the people flock to the cities in search of jobs, Hance points out that there is less of a correlation between economic growth and urbanization than there was in Europe. Cities increase in size not because there are jobs to lure workers, but rather because conditions in the countryside are so bad. People leave in hope that urban life will offer a slight improvement. This results in high urban unemployment. Often 25 percent of the labor force is without work. In Europe during the nineteenth century, workers could migrate to the New World to find work or land. No such safety valve exists today in the emerging countries; the city is the last hope.

Hance goes on to point out that **emerging cities** have weaker ties with their domestic hinterlands than did European cities. They are dependent on the outside world for raw materials. This means that the local countryside is excluded from the kind of development that could offer employment to rural populations. A vicious circle must be broken: People will leave the countryside for cities until jobs are available in the countryside; yet it will be difficult to develop rural employment as long as economic activities continue to cluster around cities.

Alejandro Portes argues that the large internal migrations that bring impoverished agricultural people into the city are not a new phenomenon but one that can be traced back to colonial times. In colonial Latin America, for example, the city was essentially home to the Spanish elite, and when preconquest agricultural patterns were disrupted, peasants came to the city looking for economic livelihood. These people usually lived on the margins of the city and were completely disenfranchised, because only landowners had the right to hold office. The reaction by the elite to this ongoing pattern of movement of large masses of people into the city was a mixture of tolerance and indifference, with no one taking responsibility to integrate the migrants into the city. This pattern continues today in emerging cities.

The combination of high numbers of immigrants coupled with widespread unemployment leads to overwhelming pressure for low-rent housing. Governments have rarely been able to meet these needs through housing projects, so one of the most common folk solutions has been construction of illegal housing, or squatter settlements. In Lima, Peru, the **barriadas** house fully a quarter of the urban population; in Caracas, Venezuela, about 35 percent. Similar figures are found in emerging cities in Africa and Asia (Figure 10.27).

Squatter settlements usually begin as collections of crude shacks constructed from scrap materials; gradually they become increasingly elaborate and permanent. Paths and walkways link houses, vegetable gardens spring up, and often water and electricity are bootlegged into the area so that a common tap or outlet serves a number of houses. At later stages, economic activities such as handicrafts or small-scale artisan activities take place in the squatter settlements.

Governments treat squatter settlements in various ways. Some bulldoze them down periodically, not simply because they are illegal, but also to discourage migration to the city. The reasoning is that if squatter settlements are destroyed, fewer migrants will come to the city, knowing that any housing solution they find will only be temporary. On the other hand, some city governments turn their backs on the squatter settlements, viewing them as satisfactory solutions to the problem of low-cost urban housing. Zambia has a "site and service" scheme where a settlement is laid out and prospective residents are given about $50 in order to buy basic materials needed for a crude house. Usually this includes concrete for the floor and a corrugated iron roof. After that, the occupants are on their own. The government knows that housing will be improved as the dweller finds work and has a regular paycheck.

Regardless of what the official policy is, squatter settlements are an

Figure 10.27
Squatter settlements in Mexico City (left) and Kuala Lampur (right). Migration to cities has been so rapid that often illegal squatter settlements have been the only solution to housing problems.

important part of the emerging city landscape. They occupy vacant land both on the outskirts and in the city center; downtown parks are often covered by squatters' houses. More frequently they spread over formerly unwanted land, such as steep slopes and river banks.

The outskirts of the growing cities manifest activities other than squatter settlement. This is often where new economic activities are located, so a landscape of factories and warehouses is common. When government money is available, large high-rise apartment houses are built nearby for workers. Middle-class suburbs may also grow up, a function both of jobs in the outlying area for white-collar workers and of "push" forces driving the affluent out of the city center. Traffic noise, air pollution, and congestion make the central city less desirable than before, so those who can afford new housing often relocate. This is similar to the suburbanization of North American cities in the last decades.

Another parallel with the American experience is that the large central-city dwellings vacated by the middle class are often subdivided into smaller apartments for lower-income families. Where previously one middle-class family lived, the dwelling may now house six or seven families. Whether this structural change will eventually lead to the social disparity and ghetto pattern characteristic of North American cities remains to be seen (Figure 10.28).

It is important not to necessarily assume that emerging cities will replicate the pattern of the nineteenth-century industrial city. Although we have noted some similarities with North American cities, the differences must also be kept in mind. As an example, many emerging cities will not undergo the same evolution of transportation systems found in Europe or America. They may evolve directly from foot and cart traffic systems to autos and trucks, skipping the electric streetcar and railroad period so important in molding the industrial urban pattern.

In conclusion, the future of the emerging city is unclear (see box, *Calcutta: Portrait of an Emerging City*). Certainly the urban problems that developing countries face are some of the most important facing the world. Some solutions may come from the American and western European experience; most will not. They will be local solutions, de-

Figure 10.28
The landscape of Ibadan, Nigeria. High-rise office buildings, which are contemporary variants of colonial monuments, contrast with middle-class housing in the foreground. Note also the high amount of pedestrian traffic along the street.

Calcutta: Portrait of an Emerging City

Although all cities are unique in their own ways, Calcutta illustrates many of the problems faced by hundreds of emerging cities around the globe. Thousands of migrants pour into Calcutta each day, leading to overburdened services, scarce housing, and high unemployment—in short, an overcrowded city.

Calcutta is one of India's largest urban centers, with almost 13 million people crowded into an area that sees population densities climbing to 177,000 people per square mile in the city center. This is three times the density of central Manhattan. United Nations estimates forecast that population will easily top 16 million by 2000.

Three-quarters of the city's population live in crowded tenements or *bustees*. These are mostly built of unbaked brick and lack adequate sanitary services. It is reported that generally 30 persons must share one water tap and that 20 share a single latrine. More than half of the city's families share one-room accommodations. But they are the lucky ones: Estimates on the homeless run well over half a million. These are the people who sleep on the city streets.

A recent study shows that 30 percent of the working force is unemployed. However, we can assume the figure to be much higher among the young, new migrants, and certain ethnic groups. As in many Third World cities, scarce economic resources aggravate tensions among ethnic groups, with the result that certain groups monopolize specific sectors of the economy, while others do without. For example, lower-class Muslims have been traditionally employed in soap and leather industries, work regarded by Hindus as polluting and therefore reserved for low-status people. Ethnic and kinship networks are tightly drawn so that group members share resources and exclude nonmembers. This is a typical pattern found in other emerging cities where the social fabric is made up of different ethnic and social groups.

What about Calcutta's future? It is difficult to be optimistic. City planners, working hand in hand with technical agencies of the United Nations, have constructed a two-tier plan. The first phase focuses on the immediate needs of the city, such as sewage, water, housing, and transportation. The second phase looks at the future of the city in the broad context of its hinterland and assumes responsibility for planning over a resource region encompassing some 500,000 square miles of the country. Ideally, such broad planning can control the flow of migrants by offering economic alternatives to city life. If Calcutta's growth can be slowed, then perhaps the city's services can be expanded to serve the existing population.

signed to meet specific needs. A totally unique urban landscape may emerge.

The Ecology of Urban Location

Cultural ecology is useful in understanding how cultures have used and modified the physical environment during urban development. Interaction with the environment is a two-way street: Humans may respond to different physical characteristics yet, equally, humans may modify those characteristics to suit their needs.

Site and Situation

There are two components of urban location: site and situation. **Site** refers to the local setting of a city; the **situation** is the regional setting. As an example of site and situation, think of San Francisco. The original site of the Mexican settlement was on a shallow cove on the eastern or inland shore of a peninsula. The importance of its situation, or regional location, was that it drew upon waterborne traffic coming across the bay from other, smaller settlements. Hence the town could act as a transshipment point.

Both site and situation are dynamic, changing through time. Over time, for example, both the site and situation of San Francisco have changed. During the gold rush period, the small cove was filled to create flatland for warehouses and to facilitate extending wharves into deeper bay waters. The filled-in cove is now occupied by the heart of the central business district (Figure 10.29). The geographical situation has also changed as patterns of trade and transportation technology

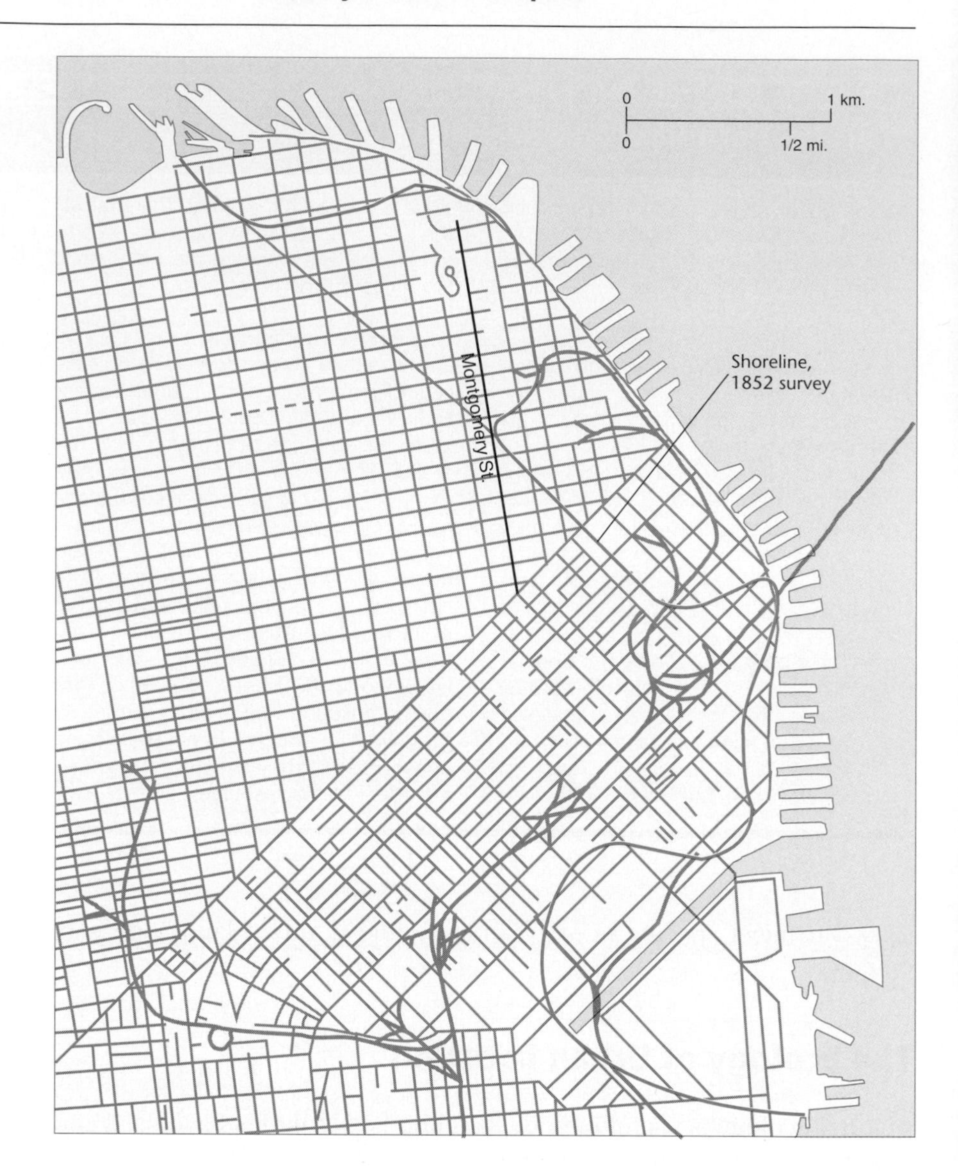

Figure 10.29
Map shows how San Francisco's site has been changed by human activity. During the late 1850s, shallow coves were filled, providing easier access to deeper bay waters as well as flatland near the waterfront for warehouses and industry.

have evolved. The original transbay situation was quickly replaced during the gold rush by a new role, supplying the mines and settlements of the gold country. Access to the two major rivers leading to the mines, plus continued ties to ocean trade routes, were the important components of the city's situation.

San Francisco's situation has changed dramatically in the last decade, for it is no longer the major port of the bay. The change in technology to containerized cargo was adopted more quickly by Oakland, the rival city on the opposite side of the bay, resulting in San Francisco's decline as a port city. One of the reasons that Oakland was able to adjust to containerized cargo was that it filled in huge tracts of shallow baylands, creating a massive area for the loading, unloading, and storage of cargo containers.

Certain attributes of the physical environment have been important in the location of cities. Those cities with distinct functions, such as defense or trade, have sought out specific physical characteristics in their original sitings. The locations of many contemporary cities can be partially explained by decisions made in the past that capitalized on advantages of certain sites. The following classifications examine some of the different location possibilities.

Defensive Sites

There are many types of **defensive sites** for cities (some are diagrammed in Figure 10.30). A defensive site is a location where a city can be easily defended. The river-meander site, with the city located inside a loop where the stream turns back on itself, leaves only a narrow neck of land unprotected by water. Cities such as Bern, Switzerland, and New Orleans are situated inside river meanders. Indeed, the nickname for New Orleans, "Crescent City," refers to the curve of the Mississippi River.

Even more advantageous was the river-island site, which often combined a natural moat with an easier river crossing, because the stream was split into two parts. For example, Montreal is situated on a large island surrounded by the St. Lawrence River and other water channels. Islands lying off the seashore or in lakes offered similar defensive advantages. Mexico City began as an Indian settlement on a lake island. Venice is the classic example of a city built on an offshore island in the sea. New York City began as a Dutch trading outpost on Manhattan Island.

Peninsular sites were almost as advantageous as island sites, because they offered natural water defenses on all but one side (Figure 10.31). Boston was founded on a peninsula for this reason, and a wooden palisade wall was built across the neck of the peninsula.

Danger of attack from the sea often prompted sheltered-harbor urban sites, where a narrow entrance to the harbor could easily be defended. Examples of sheltered-harbor cities include Rio de Janeiro, Tokyo, and San Francisco.

High points also were sought out. These are often referred to as acropolis sites, meaning "high city." Originally the city developed around a fortification on the high ground and then spilled out over the surrounding lowland. Athens is the prototype of acropolis sites, but many other cities are similarly situated.

Trade-Route Sites

In many other instances, defense was not a primary consideration. Instead, urban sites were frequently chosen because they lay at important

Figure 10.30
Types of defensive city sites. Natural protection is afforded by physical features.

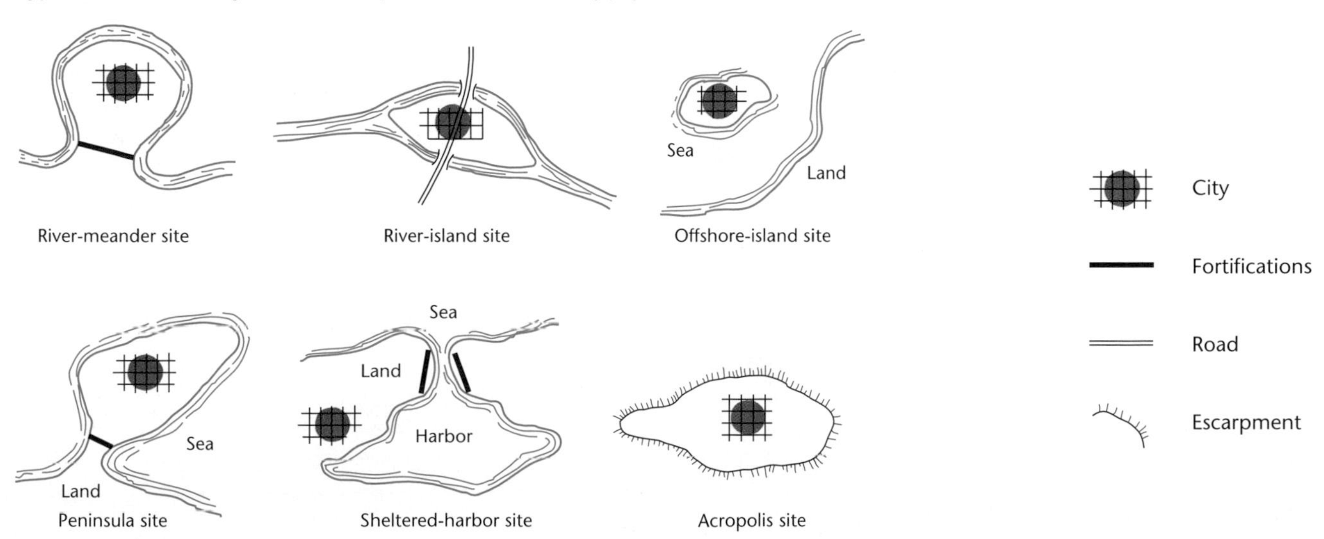

Figure 10.31
The classic defensive site of Mont St. Michel, France. A small town clustered around a medieval abbey, which was originally separated from the mainland during high tides, Mont St. Michel now has a causeway that connects the island to shore, allowing armies of tourists to easily penetrate the town's defenses.

points on trade routes. Here, too, the influence of the physical environment can be detected.

Especially common types of **trade-route sites** (Figure 10.32) are bridge-point and river-ford sites, places where major land routes could easily cross over rivers. Typically, these were sites where streams were narrow and shallow with firm banks. Occasionally, such cities even bear in their names the evidence of their sites, as in Frankfurt ("ford of the Franks"), Germany, and Oxford, England. The site for London was chosen because it is the lowest point on the Thames River where a bridge—the famous London Bridge—could easily be built to serve a trade route running inland from Dover on the sea.

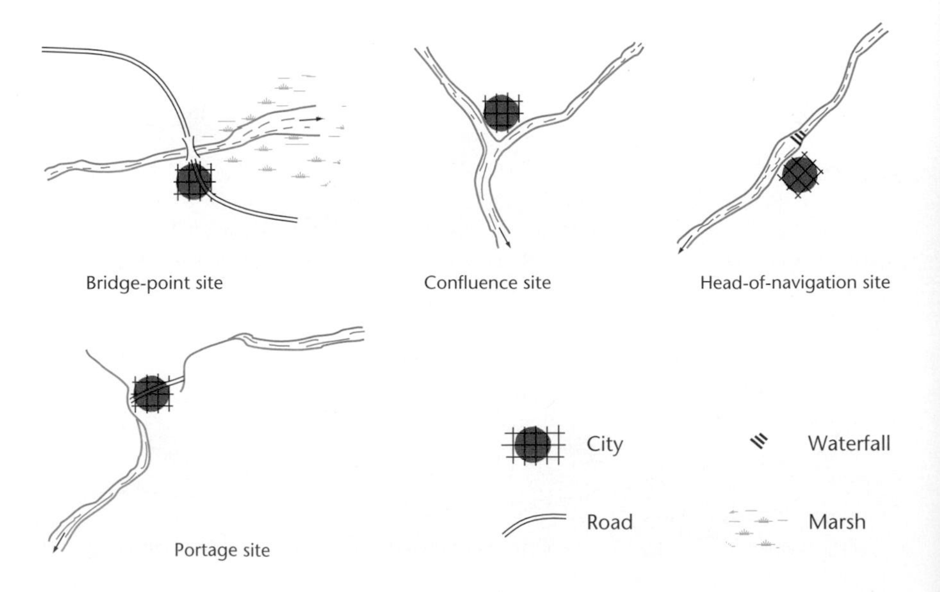

Figure 10.32
Trade-route city sites. These sites are at strategic positions along transportation arteries. Is your city or one near you located on a trade-route site?

Figure 10.33
Pittsburgh's Golden Triangle. At the confluence of the Allegheny and Monongahela rivers, Pittsburgh is a classic example of how an early fortified site has evolved into a commercial center.

Confluence sites are also common. They allow cities to be situated at the point where two navigable streams flow together. Pittsburgh, at the confluence of the Allegheny and Monongahela rivers, is a fine example (Figure 10.33). Head-of-navigation sites, where navigable water routes begin, are even more common, because goods must be transshipped at such points. Minneapolis–St. Paul, at the falls of the Mississippi River, occupies a head-of-navigation site. Louisville, Kentucky, is located at the rapids of the Ohio River. Portage sites are very similar. Here, goods were portaged from one river to another. Chicago is near a short portage between the Great Lakes and the Mississippi River drainage basin.

In these ways and others, an urban site can be influenced by the physical environment. There are, of course, many nonenvironmental factors that can influence the choice of site. Here, it is useful to distinguish between the specific urban site and the general location, or **spatial distribution,** of cities. Spacing implies a broader, overall view of the pattern of urban centers. Site is frequently influenced by the environment, but spacing of cities is less likely to be. The theme of cultural integration will help us understand why cities are spaced as they are.

Cultural Integration in Urban Geography

In recent decades, urban geographers have studied the spatial distribution of towns and cities in order to determine some of the economic and political factors that influence the pattern of cities. In doing so, they have created a number of models that collectively make up "central-place" theory. These models represent examples of cultural integration.

Most urban centers are engaged mainly in the **tertiary industry** stage of production. Primary economic activities are extractive, such as agriculture, forestry, and mining. Construction and manufacturing are secondary activities, those that change the form of products. The tertiary activities of urban centers include transportation, communication and utility services—services that facilitate the movement of goods and that provide the networks for the exchange of ideas about those goods

Walter Christaller
1893–1969

Although Christaller had a precocious beginning as a geographer, spending hours with an atlas as a youth, it was not until he was nearly 40 years of age that he began his study of geography at a university. Christaller became a "maverick" among the geographers in Germany. His ideas on models were too radical for most of his fellow geographers in Nazi Germany to accept. As a result, he was never offered a professorship.

Christaller's classic work, *The Central Places of Southern Germany,* was written in the early 1930s as his doctoral dissertation in geography. In it, he proposed the central-place theory described in this chapter. Acceptance of central-place theory came belatedly, among American and Swedish geographers. Only in his later years did Christaller receive the honors due him.

(see Chapter 12 for a more detailed examination of these different industrial activities). Towns and cities that support such tertiary activities are called **central places.**

In the early 1930s, the German geographer Walter Christaller (see biographical sketch) first formulated **central-place theory,** a series of models designed to explain the spatial distribution of tertiary urban centers. Crucial to his theory is the fact that different goods and services vary both in **threshold,** the size of the population required to make provision of the service economically feasible, and in **range,** the average maximum distance people will travel to purchase a good or service. For example, a larger number of people are required to support a hospital, university, or department store than to support a gasoline station, post office, or grocery store. Similarly, consumers are willing to travel a greater distance to consult a heart specialist, record a land title, or purchase an automobile than to buy a loaf of bread, mail a letter, or visit a movie theater. People will normally spend as little time and effort as possible in making use of services and purchasing goods in a central place, but they will be obliged to travel farther to use those services that require a large market.

Because the range of central goods and services varies, tertiary centers are arranged in an orderly hierarchy. Some central places are small and offer a limited variety of services and goods; others are large and offer an abundance. At the top of this hierarchy are regional metropolises, huge urban centers that offer all services associated with central places and that have very large tributary trade areas, or **hinterlands.** At the opposite extreme are small market villages and roadside hamlets, which may contain nothing more than a post office, service station, or café. Between these two extremes are central places of various degrees of importance. Each higher rank of central place provides all the goods and services available at a lower-rank center, plus one or more additional goods and services. Central places of lower rank greatly outnumber the few at the higher levels of the hierarchy. One regional metropolis may contain thousands of smaller central places in its tributary market area (Figure 10.34). The size of the market area is determined by the distance range of the goods and services it offers.

Figure 10.34
Christaller's hierarchy of central places shows the orderly arrangement of towns of different sizes. This is an idealized presentation of places performing central functions. For each large central place many smaller central places are located within the larger place's hinterland.

With this hierarchy as a background, Christaller then tried to measure the influence of three forces in determining the spacing and distribution of tertiary centers. He accomplished this by creating models. His first model measured the influence of market and range of goods on the spacing of cities. To simplify the model, he assumed that the terrain, soils, and other environmental factors were uniform; that transportation was universally available; and that all regions would be supplied with goods and services from the minimum number of central places. In such a model, the shape of the market area was circular, encompassing the range of goods and services, with the city at the center of the circle. However, when central places of the same rank in the hierarchy were nearby, the circle became a hexagon (Figure 10.35a). If market and range of goods were the only causal forces, the distribution of tertiary towns and cities would produce a pattern of nested hexagons, each with a central place at its center.

Then Christaller created a second model. In this model, he tried to measure the influence of transportation on the spacing of central places. He no longer assumed that transportation was universally and equally available in the hinterland. Instead, Christaller assumed that as many demands for transport as possible would be met with the minimum expenditure for construction and maintenance of transportation facilities. As many high-ranking central places as possible would thus be on straight-line routes between important central places (Figure 10.35b). The transportation factor causes a rather different pattern of central places from the pattern caused by the market factor. This is because direct routes between adjacent regional metropolises do not pass through central places of the next lowest rank. As a result, these second-rank central places are "pulled" from the points of the hexago-

Figure 10.35a
The influence of market area on Christaller's arrangement of central places. If marketing were the only factor controlling the distribution of central places, this diagram would represent the arrangement of towns and cities. Why, in this model, would hexagons be the shape to appear instead of a square, circle, or some other shape?

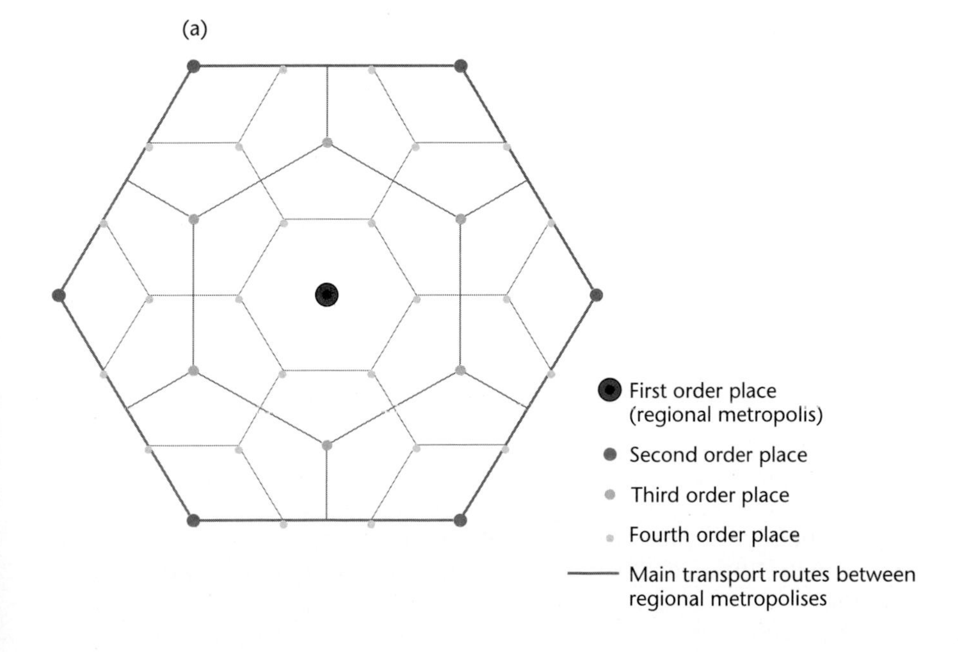

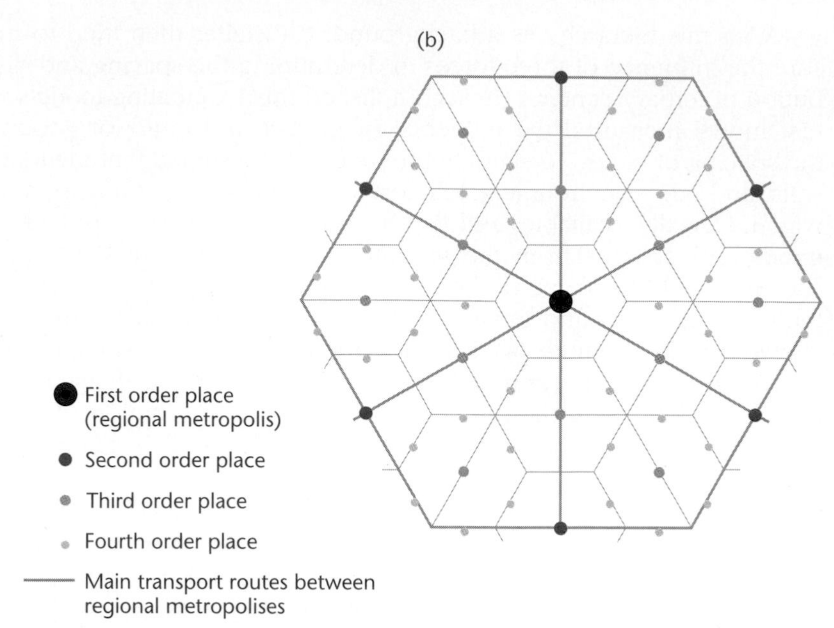

Figure 10.35b
The distribution of central places according to Christaller's model. If the availability of transportation is the determining factor in the location of central places, their distribution will be different than if marketing were the determining factor. Note that the second-order central places are pulled away from the apexes of the hexagon and become located on the main transport routes between regional metropolises. (Both figures after Christaller, 1966, by permission of the publisher.)

nal market area to the midpoints in order to be on the straight-line routes between adjacent regional metropolises.

Christaller thought that the market factor would be the greater force in rural countries, where goods were seldom shipped throughout a region. He also thought that the transportation factor would be stronger in densely settled industrialized countries, where there were greater numbers of central places and more demand for long-distance transportation.

A third model devised by Christaller measured a type of political influence, the effect of political borders on the distribution of central places. Christaller recognized that political boundaries, especially within independent countries, would tend to follow the hexagonal market-area limits of each central place that was a political center. He also recognized that such borders tend to separate people and retard the movement of goods and services. Such borders necessarily cut through the market areas of many central places below the rank of regional metropolis. Central places in such border regions lose rank and size because their market areas are politically cut in two. Border towns are thus "stunted," and important central places are pushed away from the border, which distorts the hexagonal pattern.

Many other forces influence the spatial distribution of central places. Market area, transportation, and political borders are but three. For example, in all three of these models, it is assumed that the physical environment is uniform and that people are evenly distributed. Of course neither of these is true, yet certain assumptions are necessary to construct a theoretical model that integrates different components of culture.

Conclusion

The first cities arose as new technologies, particularly the domestication of plants and animals, facilitated the concentration of people, wealth, and power in a few specific places. This transformation from village to city life was accompanied by new social organizations, a greater division of labor, and increased social stratification. These characteristics still distinguish rural and urban lifestyles. Although the first cities developed in specific places, urban life has now been diffused worldwide, and all indications are that our planet will become increasingly urban in the decades to come.

Many of the problems now plaguing our cities are expressions of uncorrected ills from the past. Traffic and housing problems in Europe, for example, may be understood in the context of the medieval urban landscape. Even though the landscape evolved 500 years ago, the narrow streets and cramped housing conditions of the medieval period still pervade the typical European central city.

This is also true of the North American city. Much of our urban environment evolved only during the last 200 years, when industrialism was the dominant force; yet this has in no way given us immunity against urban ills. Problems of land use, housing, transportation, and social services often trace their origins from the past century.

Many problems of cities in the developing world are products of this century. Cities are bursting at the seams as thousands of new migrants crowd into urban places each day, seeking houses, jobs, and schooling. But jobs are scarce, so unemployment rates are often over 25 percent. Housing is also a problem. In some cities, over a third of the population lives in hastily constructed squatter settlements. Yet many of these same problems have historical roots, as the examination of the political and social history of colonial cities demonstrates. For example, massive rural-to-urban migration is not a new phenomenon. The disruptions of nineteenth-century colonial settlements deprived many people of their land and forced rural inhabitants into the city. This pattern continues today.

The future of the world's cities is unsure. Strong governmental planning measures might alleviate many present-day ills, but the long-range hope lies with decreased population growth and increased economic opportunities. Whether this is possible under contemporary conditions remains to be seen.

This chapter has examined the city at a broad-brush, worldwide level. In the next chapter we look at cultural patterns within the city.

Sources and Suggested Readings

Agnew, John, John Mercer, and David Sopher. *The City in Cultural Context*. Boston: Allen & Unwin, 1984.

Aiken, Robert. "Squatters and Squatter Settlements in Kuala Lumpur." *Geographical Review*, 71 (1981): 460–471.

Al-Mamum Khan, Abdullah. "Rural–Urban Migration and Urbanization in Bangladesh." *Geographical Review*, 72 (1982): 379–394.

Benevolo, Leonardo. *The History of the City*. Cambridge, MA: MIT Press, 1980.

Berry, Brian J. *Comparative Urbanization*. New York: St. Martin's Press, 1982.

Berry, Brian J. *The Human Consequences of Urbanization*. New York: St. Martin's Press, 1973.

Brown, Elsa Barkley, and Gregg D. Kimball. "Mapping the Terrain of Black Richmond." *Journal of Urban History*, 21 (1995): 296–346.

Brunn, Stanley, and Jack Williams. *Cities of the World: World Regional Urban Development*. New York: Harper & Row, 1983.

Buswell, R. J., and M. Barke. "200 Years of Change in a 900-year-old City." *Geographical Magazine,* 2 (1980): 81–83ff.

Carter, Harold. *An Introduction to Urban Historical Geography*. London: Edward Arnold, 1989.

Christaller, Walter. *The Central Places of Southern Germany*. C. W. Baskin (trans.). Englewood Cliffs, NJ: Prentice-Hall, 1966.

Christensen, Terry. *Neighborhood Survival: The Struggle for Covent Garden*. London: Prism, 1979.

Cosgrove, Denis. *Social Formation and Symbolic Landscape*. London: Croom Helm, 1984.

Crow, Ben, and Allan Thomas. *Third World Atlas*. London: Open University Press, 1984.

Davis, Kingsley. *Cities: Their Origin, Growth and Human Impact*. San Francisco: Freeman, 1973.

Detwyler, Thomas, and Melvin Marcus (eds.). *Urbanization and Environment: The Physical Geography of the City*. Belmont, CA: Duxbury Press, 1972.

Dickinson, Robert. *The West European City*. London: Routledge & Kegan Paul, 1961.

Dike, A. A. "Environmental Problems in Third-World Cities: A Nigerian Example." *Current Anthropology,* 26 (1985): 501–505.

Domosh, Mona. "The Feminized Retail Landscape: Gender Ideology and Consumer Culture in Nineteenth Century New York City," in Neil Wrigley and Michelle Lowe (eds.), *Retailing, Consumption and Capital*. Essex: Longman, 1995.

Doxiades, C. A. *Architectural Space in Ancient Greece*. Cambridge, MA: MIT Press, 1972.

Drakakis-Smith, David. *The Third World City*. London: Methuen, 1987.

Duncan, James S. "The Power of Place in Kandy, Sri Lanka: 1780–1980," in John A. Agnew and James S. Duncan (eds.), *The Power of Place*. Boston: Unwin Hyman, 1989, pp. 185–201.

Fawcett, James T., Siew-Ean Khoo, and Peter Smith. *Women in the Cities of Asia: Migration and Urban Adaptation*. Boulder, CO: Westview Press, 1984.

Field, Arthur (ed.). *City and Country in the Third World*. Cambridge, MA: Schenkman, 1970.

Garreau, Joel. *Edge City: Life on the New Frontier*. New York: Doubleday, 1991.

Gilbert, Alan, and Joseph Gugler. *Cities, Poverty, and Development: Urbanization in the Third World*. Oxford: Oxford University Press, 1983.

Gottmann, Jean. *Megalopolis*. Cambridge, MA: MIT Press, 1961.

Gottmann, Jean. "Third-World Cities in Perspective." *Area,* 15 (1983): 311–313.

Griffin, Ernst, and Larry Ford. "A Model of Latin American Urban Structure." *Geographical Review,* 70 (1980): 397–422.

Gutkind, Erwin A. *International History of City Development*. 4 vols. New York: Free Press, 1964–1969.

Hance, William. *Population, Migration, and Urbanization in Africa*. New York: Columbia University Press, 1970.

Hardoy, Jorge (ed.). *Urbanization in Latin America: Approaches and Issues*. Garden City, NY: Doubleday (Anchor Books), 1975.

Hardoy, J. E., and D. Satterthwaite. "Third-World Cities and the Environment of Poverty." *Geoforum,* 15 (1984): 307–333.

Havlik, Spencer. "Third-World Cities at Risk: Building for Calamity." *Environment,* 28 (1986): 6ff.

Hayes, John. *London: A Pictorial History*. New York: Arco Publishing Co., 1969.

Henderson, J. V. "Urbanization in a Developing Country: City Size and Population Composition." *Journal of Development Economics,* 22 (1986): 269–293.

Hottes, Ruth. "Walter Christaller." *Annals of the Association of American Geographers,* 73 (1983): 51–54.

Johnston, R. J. *The American Urban System: A Geographical Perspective*. London: Longman, 1982.

Kahimbaara, J. A. "The Population Density Gradient and the Spatial Structure of a Third-World City: Nairobi, A Case Study." *Urban Studies,* 23 (1986): 307–322.

Keyfitz, Nathan. "Do Cities Grow by Natural Increase or by Migration?" *Geographical Analysis,* 2 (1980): 142–156.

Linsky, Arnold S. "Some Generalizations Concerning Primate Cities." *Annals of the Association of American Geographers,* 55 (1965): 506–513.

Lloyd, William J. "Understanding Late Nineteenth-Century Cities." *Geographical Review,* 71 (1981): 460–471.

Lowder, Stella. *The Geography of Third-World Cities.* Totowa, NJ: Rowman and Littlefield, 1986.

Ma, Laurence, and E. W. Hanten (eds.). *Urban Development in Modern China.* Boulder, CO: Westview Press, 1981.

Mangin, William. "Squatter Settlements." *Scientific American* (1967): 21–29.

Monk, Janice. "Gender in the Landscape: Expressions of Power and Meaning," in Kay Anderson and Fay Gale (eds.), *Inventing Places: Studies in Cultural Geography.* Melbourne: Longman Cheshire, 1992, pp. 123–138.

Mumford, Lewis. *The City in History.* New York: Harcourt Brace Jovanovich, 1961.

Pacione, Michael (ed.). *Problems and Planning in Third World Cities.* London: Croom Helm, 1981.

Pfeiffer, John. *The Emergence of Society.* New York: McGraw-Hill, 1977.

Pirenne, Henri. *Medieval Cities.* Garden City, NY: Doubleday (Anchor Books), 1956.

Planhol, Xavier de. *The World of Islam.* Ithaca, NY: Cornell University Press, 1959.

Portes, Alejandro. "Urban Latin America: The Political Condition from Above and Below," in Janet Abu-Lughod and Richard Hag, Jr. (eds.), *Third World Urbanization.* New York: Methuen, 1977, pp. 59–70.

Redman, Charles. *The Rise of Civilization.* San Francisco: Freeman, 1978.

Rondinelli, D. A. "Towns and Small Cities in Developing Countries." *Geographical Review,* 73 (1983): 379–395.

Rowntree, Lester. "Creating a Sense of Place." *Journal of Urban History,* 8 (1981): 61–76.

Rowntree, Lester, and Margaret Conkey. "Symbolism and the Cultural Landscape." *Annals of the Association of American Geographers,* 70 (1980): 459–474.

Saalman, Howard. *Medieval Cities.* New York: Braziller, 1968.

Salter, Christopher L. "The Paradox of the City." *Journal of Cultural Geography,* 1 (1981): 98–105.

Samuels, Marwyn S., and Carmencita Samuels. "Beijing and the Power of Place in Modern China," in John A. Agnew and James S. Duncan (eds.), *The Power of Place.* Boston: Unwin Hyman, 1989, pp. 202–227.

Simon, D. "Third-World Colonial Cities in Context: Conceptual and Theoretical Approaches with Particular Interest to Africa." *Progress in Human Geography,* 8 (1984): 493–514.

Sjoberg, Gideon. *The Preindustrial City.* New York: Free Press, 1960.

Spain, Daphne. *Gendered Spaces.* Chapel Hill: University of North Carolina Press, 1992.

Summerson, John. *Georgian London.* New York: Charles Scribner's Sons, 1946.

Vance, James E., Jr. *The Continuing City: Urban Morphology in Western Civilization.* Baltimore: The Johns Hopkins University Press, 1990.

Vance, James E., Jr. "Land Assignment in the Pre-Capitalist, Capitalist and Post-Capitalist City." *Economic Geography,* 47 (1971): 101–120.

Warner, Sam Bass, Jr. *The Urban Wilderness: A History of the American City.* New York: Harper & Row, 1972.

Wheatley, Paul. *The Pivot of the Four Quarters.* Chicago: Aldine Publishing Company, 1971.

Häagen-Dazs
巴黎髮廊
79
Paris Salon
JOY LUCK
RESTAURANT
ONE WAY
ONE WAY
GIFT
Häagen-Dazs
ICE CREAM
WINE &
LIQUOR
Marlboro

CHAPTER 11

The Urban Mosaic

Finding patterns in a city can be a difficult matter. As you walk or drive through a city, its intricacy may dazzle, and its form may seem chaotic. It is often hard to imagine why city functions are where they are, why people cluster where they do. Why does one block have high-income housing and another, slum tenements? Why are ethnic neighborhoods next to the central business district? Why does the highway run through one neighborhood and around another? Just when you think you are beginning to understand some patterns in your city, you note that those patterns are swiftly changing. The house you grew up in is now part of the business district. The central city that you roamed as a child looks dead. A suburban shopping center thrives on what was once farmland.

Chapter 10 focused on cities as points in geographical space. The goal of this chapter is geographically different. We try now to orient ourselves within cities to gain some perspective on the patterns in them. In other words, the two chapters differ in scale. Chapter 10 let us see cities from afar, as small dots diffusing across space and interacting with one another and with their environment. In this chapter, we study the city as if we were walking its streets.

Our tour guides in this closeup view of the city are the five familiar themes of cultural geography. Through culture region, we examine spatial differences within cities. Cultural diffusion shows how these internal and regional differences develop. Cultural ecology permits us to see the role of the physical environment within the structure of the city. And through cultural integration, we see what a finely woven fabric the city really is. Of course, the visual impact of these elements is revealed in the urban landscape, a "townscape" perceived in different ways by different people.

Urban Culture Regions

Like society, the city is composed of many different groups. Consequently, the theme of culture regions can be applied to those parts of the city where people live who share similar traits, such as values, income, language, religion, or "race." Most city dwellers are intuitively aware of these urban culture regions. Visual clues—size and condition of housing, dress styles, or kinds of cars—help categorize some areas as high-income, others as low-income, some as Polish neighborhoods, others as Asian.

As we look at these urban regions, different questions concern the cultural geographer: How do ethnic and social regions differ? Why do people of similar social traits cluster together? What subtle patterns might be found within these regions? How does one delimit different kinds of urban districts?

Social Regions

To begin answering these questions, we should try to distinguish between **social culture regions** and **ethnic culture regions.** Although the distinction between the two may seem contrived, there is some usefulness in thinking about the differences that often depend more on the researcher's emphases and interests than on the communities themselves. In studies that focus on social region, the emphasis is usually on socioeconomic traits, such as income, education, age, and family structure. On the other hand, researchers who use the notion of ethnic region highlight traits of ethnicity, such as language and migration history. Obviously the two concepts overlap because there can be social regions within ethnic regions and vice versa. Let us also remember that some researchers choose to look at both social and ethnic regions as functions of the political and economic forces underlying and reinforcing residential segregation and discrimination. (More information on ethnic areas is found in Chapter 9.)

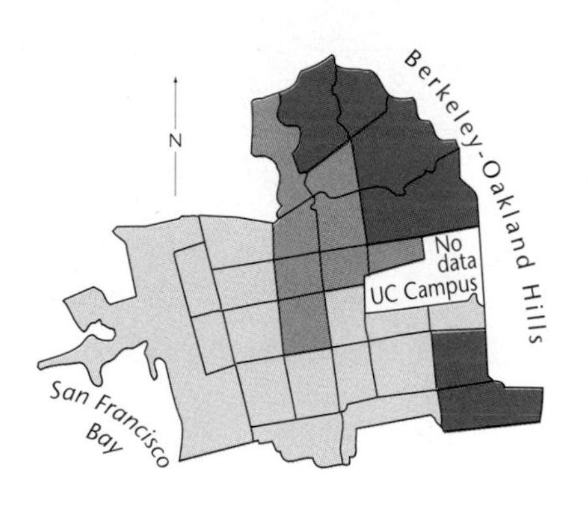

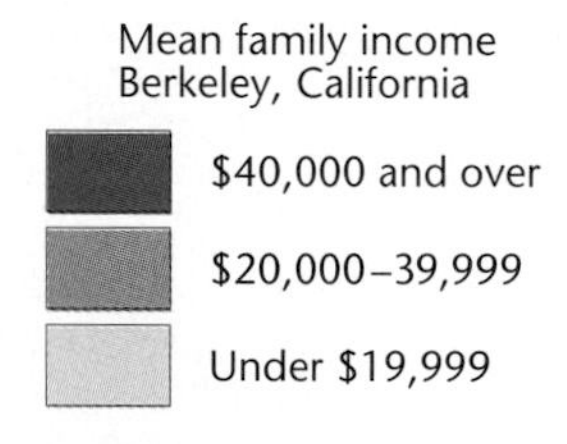

Figure 11.1
The high- and low-income areas of Berkeley, California. The numbers are based on the median family income for each census tract at the 1980 census. The map shows that income can be mapped as cultural regions. The areas of highest income are in the Berkeley-Oakland hills, whereas the areas of lowest income are either directly adjacent to the UC campus on the south or in the flatlands on the west, where low-income housing is mixed with industrial and commercial uses. Students and ethnic minorities dominate the low-income areas and compete for the limited stock of low-rent housing in the city. The upper-income areas are predominantly white families living in better housing.

One way to define social regions is to isolate one social trait and plot its distribution within the city. The United States census is a common source of such information because the districts used to count population, called **census tracts,** are small enough to allow the subtle texture of social regions to show. For example, Figure 11.1 shows the rough distribution of income in Berkeley, California. Census tracts with similar average incomes have been lumped together, showing areas of high, middle, and low income. These areas, in a crude way, correspond to the social stratification of the city. High-income areas are mostly in the hilly area to the east, where white people dominate. Lower-income areas are on the flatlands, closer to the bay-front industrial areas, and are made up of students and minorities. Similar mapping could be done with other social traits taken from the census, such as age, education, or percentage of families below poverty level. A visual field check is often a simple first step in mapping social regions (Figures 11.2 and 11.3).

Another approach is to correlate various social indicators. For example, politicians have long known that districts with certain demographic characteristics (such as age, income, and occupation) tend to vote certain ways. There might be a correlation between, say, Democratic voting and Catholic working-class neighborhoods. What politicians know from experience, urban analysts try to formalize through statistical studies. They look at the degree of correlation among factors such as income, occupation, age, and ethnicity. Their results can then be translated into a pattern of multiple-factor urban social regions.

Figure 11.2
An inner-city neighborhood near the Capitol in Washington, DC. One of the most pressing problems facing the United States is reversing the continued decay of inner cities.

Neighborhoods

Social regions are not merely statistical definitions. They are also areas of shared values and attitudes, of interaction and communication. The concept of a **neighborhood** is often used to describe small social regions where people with shared values and concerns interact daily. For example, if we consider only census figures, we might find that parents between 30 and 45 years of age, with two or three children, and earning between $30,000 and $50,000 a year cover a fairly wide area in any given city. Yet, from our own observations, we know intuitively that this broad social area is probably composed of smaller units of social interaction where people link a sense of community with a specific locale.

A conventional sociological explanation for neighborhoods is that people of similar values cluster together to reduce social conflict.

Figure 11.3
Middle-income neighborhoods in Reston, Virginia. Social areas within the city can be delimited by certain traits taken from the census, such as income, education, or family size. How would the social characteristics of this neighborhood differ from those in Figure 11.2?

Where a social consensus exists regarding such mundane issues as home maintenance, child rearing, everyday behavior, and public order, there is little need to worry about these matters on a day-to-day basis. People who deviate from this consensus will face social coercion that could force them to seek residence elsewhere, thus preserving the values of the neighborhood. Because this definition of neighborhood emphasizes people of like mind and background who choose to live together, it celebrates the social homogeneity or sameness of small spatial communities.

Increasingly, though, we find neighborhoods with more heterogeneity than this traditional definition would allow. Consequently, the current conceptualization of neighborhoods is more flexible and embraces traditional components of locality, such as geographical territoriality, political outlook, and shared economic characteristics. It also emphasizes the consensus that comes from both insiders and outsiders perceiving a certain area as a "neighborhood." For example, a neighborhood might be ethnically and socially diverse, yet also think of itself as a social community sharing similar political concerns, hold neighborhood meetings to address these problems, and achieve recognition with city hall as a legitimate group with political standing. Often this sense of neighborhood develops only when a community coalesces around a specific political issue, and this cohesion may actually erode and wane as the issue passes. Indeed, contemporary urban politics are characteristically caught up in this ever-changing network of neighborhood interest groups.

The concept of neighborhood usually implies that people have access to a permanent or semipermanent place of residence. Increasingly in United States' cities, however, we find that many people are homeless, and divorced from the ties of neighborhood. It is nearly impossible to determine the exact number of homeless people in the United States. Definitions of **homelessness** vary, depending on what criteria are used and the cultural context of the particular situation. For example, does living in a friend's house for more than a month constitute a homeless condition? How permanent does a shelter have to be before it is considered a "home"? To some people, home connotes a suburban middle-class house; to others, it simply refers to a room in a city-owned shelter. Geographer April Veness has studied these various and often contested definitions of home and homelessness, and has concluded that often attempts to house the homeless are bound up with middle-class, suburban definitions of home (see box, *Designer Homeless Shelters in the City*).

In addition, homeless people are often not counted in the census or other population counts. Our estimates of the number of homeless, therefore, are only rough approximations. Recent studies suggest that up to 3 million homeless persons are in the United States, concentrated in the downtown areas of large cities, often in what we call the "zone in transition" (see later section on cultural integration and models of the city).

The causes of homelessness are varied and complex. Many homeless people suffer from some type of disorder or handicap that contributes to their inability to maintain a job and obtain adequate housing. In some way, most have been marginalized by the economic problems that have plagued the United States since the early 1980s, and therefore have been left out of the housing market. Deprived of the social networks that a permanent neighborhood provides, the homeless are left

Designer Homeless Shelters in the City

Transfer of government welfare responsibilities to local, often nonprofit, institutions, growing criticism by a public suspicious of the homeless in general, and local political decisions that increasingly monitor and manage the activities of those organizations that assist the homeless have led to the creation of a group of shelters whose outlook and roles differ from shelters established prior to the 1980s. Designed to do more than provide temporary shelter for homeless people, these designer shelters have been given the role of remaking homeless people to fit a middle-class model of home. While this role, and the practices that must be reproduced in the shelter to make the role successful, is intended to help homeless/poor people, it may not live up to this goal. Under pressure to demonstrate that homeless people are home-worthy and home-ready, designer shelters must select among the homeless group those people whose attitudes and activities conform to normative expectations. People who cannot or will not conform are left to make do in whatever homes they can fashion for themselves. Meanwhile people who do enter the designer shelter may find habits and attitudes that sustained them in a life of economic poverty questioned and devalued.

Personal observations of life in various shelters in Delaware demonstrate how service providers routinely identify residents' habits that do not conform with their ideals of appropriate home life. House rules, which are typed up and distributed to residents at the time they are admitted into the shelter, outline exactly which types of behavior are forbidden and favored. Embedded in these rules are some fairly obvious, and anachronistic, class-based assumptions about what constitutes a good home. Likewise there are many mixed messages and contradictions. In one shelter, for example, it is forbidden for residents to walk around the common rooms without shoes (although slippers in the evening are permissible). Nor are they allowed to lend or borrow items between themselves; to enter one another's rooms or child-sit for one another; to do any personal grooming outside of bath or bedrooms; and to rearrange furniture in their rooms. Favored are "positive, constructive lifestyles," cleanliness and orderliness, and "disciplining children with love."

Women routinely complain that the traditional support systems upon which they rely are not approved of in the shelter. Sharing resources and responsibilities across rather fluid family and, by extension, friendship boundaries are common in lower-income black communities. This strategy of pooling and exchanging resources often enables poor families to seek and retain employment, to avoid evictions, to pay for emergency needs, and to instill in their children a sense of cooperation and confidence in the future. But this trait does not conform to middle-class definitions of the nuclear family and middle-class home life. Thus homeless women are given a model of home life in the shelter that supposedly is intended to enable them, but that may in fact constrain them. For many of these women, marriage, a traditional nuclear family, and the ability to purchase the accoutrements of middle-class home life all at one time are highly unlikely.

Another limitation is that while designer shelters hold open for poor people the expectation that they can enter the middle class, this expectation is by no means guaranteed. In fact it is only a privilege, which means that it cannot be universal. If we actively push a model of home on poor people that fulfills society's version of what home should be, but may do little for the people it is intended to help, what are the consequences? Is it enough to press for shelter and measure our successes by the number of shelters that get sited or the numbers of people who leave the shelter for homes of their own? Embedded in this liberal strategy of social justice are personal injustices that cannot be overlooked.

Designer shelters in the city may well be relying on forms of oppression when they uphold a model of home that is socially constructed. These shelters emerged at a time and in a place when sponsors of the ideal felt that there was much to be gained for the homeless. Because many of the criteria upon which ideal homes, hence designer shelters, were built are arbitrary, elusive, and inherently exclusionary, it seems highly unlikely that the poor will be the benefactors of present-day efforts to rehome them. The designer shelter seems to be an old rehabilitative strategy packaged into a new institutional form. In our efforts to eliminate homelessness we need to take into account the various models of home that exist, as well as the limits of our compassionate responses and social justice strategies.

Source: Veness, April R. "Designer Shelters as Models and Makers of Home: New Responses to Homelessnes in Urban America." *Urban Geography,* 15, No. 2 (1994): 150–167. Reprinted by permission of V.H. Winston & Son, Inc.

to fend for themselves. Most cities have tried to provide temporary shelter facilities, but many homeless people prefer to rely on their own social ties for support in order to maintain some sense of personal pride and privacy. In a study of the Los Angeles skid row district, Stacy Rowe and Jennifer Wolch explored how homeless women formed new types of social networks and established a sense of community in order to cope with the day-to-day needs of physical security and food supply (Figure 11.4). This study points to the importance of social ties in maintaining personal identity, and helps us understand the magnitude of a problem that deprives people of their home and neighborhood.

In summary, the neighborhood concept is central to the cultural geography of cities because it recognizes the sentiment people have for

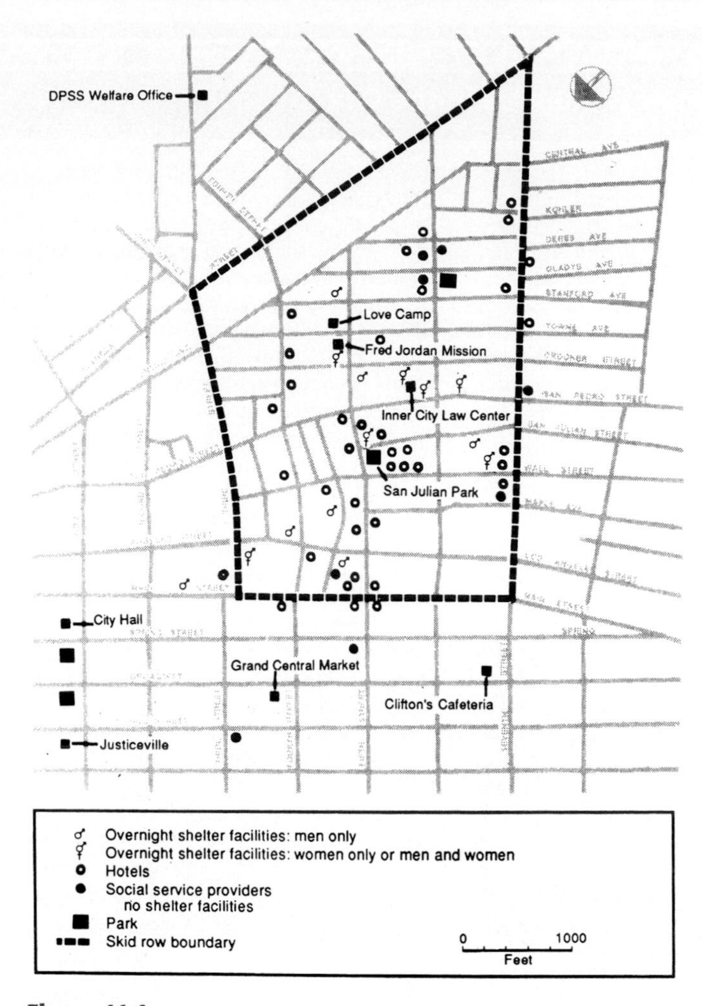

Figure 11.4

The distribution of services for the homeless in the skid row district of Los Angeles. The population of the area is difficult to estimate, ranging from 6000 to 30,000. There are approximately 2000 shelter beds in the area, half of which are available to women. Single-room occupancy hotels provide about 6700 units of longer-term housing. More than 50 social-service programs are run through the agencies, missions, and shelters. Love Camp and Justiceville are the sites of informal street encampments of homeless people. (Source: After Rowe, Stacy, and Jennifer Wolch. "Social Networks in Time and Space: Homeless Women in Skid Row, Los Angeles." *Annals of the Association of American Geographers,* 80, No. 2 [1990]: 184–204.)

places and their attachment to them. It also recognizes how attachment becomes the basis for ongoing social and political action. But we must also appreciate that many—if not most—contemporary urbanites do not share this sense of neighborhood. They live in perceptually undifferentiated residential areas.

Cultural Diffusion in the City

The patterns of activities we see in the city result from thousands of individual decisions made regarding location. Where should we locate our store—in the central city or in the suburbs? Where should we live—downtown or outside the city? The result of such decisions might be expansion at the city's edge or the relocation of activities from one part of the city to another. The cultural geographer looks at such decisions in terms of expansion and relocation diffusion (see Chapter 1).

To understand the role of diffusion, let us divide the city into two major areas—the inner city and the outer city. Those diffusion forces that result in residences, stores, and factories locating in the inner or central city are **centralizing forces.** Those that result in activities locating outside the central city are called **decentralizing forces.** The pattern of homes, neighborhoods, offices, shops, and factories in the city results from the constant interplay of these two forces.

Centralization

We can best examine centralization by breaking it into two categories: economic and social advantages.

Economic Advantages. An important economic advantage to central-city location has always been accessibility. For example, imagine that a department store seeks a new location. Its success depends on whether customers can reach the store easily. If its potential market area is viewed as a full circle, then naturally the best location is in the center. There, customers from all parts of the city can gain access with equal ease. Before the automobile, a central-city location was particularly necessary because public transportation—such as the streetcar—was usually focused there. A central location is also important to those who must deliver their goods to customers. Bakeries and dairies usually were located as close as possible to the center of the city so that their daily deliveries would be most efficient.

Location near regional transportation facilities is another aspect of accessibility. Many a North American city grew up with the railroad at its center. Hence, any activity that needed access to the railroad had to locate in the central city. In many urban areas, giant wholesale and retail manufacturing districts grew up around railroad districts. Thus they became "freight-yard and terminal cities" for the produce of the nation. Today, although many of these areas have been abandoned by their original occupants, a walk by the railroad tracks will give the most casual pedestrian a view of the modern "ruins" of the railroad city.

Another major economic advantage of the inner city is **agglomeration,** or clustering, which results in mutual benefits for businesses. For example, retail stores locate near one another to take advantage of the pedestrian traffic each generates. A large department store generates a good deal of foot traffic, so that any nearby store will also benefit.

Historically, offices clustered together in the central city because of their need for communication. Remember, the telephone was invented only in 1875. Before that, messengers hand-carried the work of banks, insurance firms, lawyers, and many other services. Clustering was essential for rapid communication. Even today, office buildings tend to cluster because face-to-face communication is still important for the business community. In addition, central offices take advantage of the complicated support system that grows up in a central city and aids everyday efficiency. Printers, bars, restaurants, travel agents, and office suppliers must be in easy reach.

Social Advantages. Three social factors have traditionally reinforced central-city location. These are historical momentum, prestige, and the need to locate near work.

The strength of historical momentum should not be underestimated. Many activities remain in the central city simply because they began there long ago. For example, the financial district in San Francisco is located mainly on Montgomery Street. This street originally lay along the waterfront, and San Francisco's first financial institutions were established there in the Gold Rush of 1849 because it was the center of commercial action. In later years, however, land filling extended the shoreline (see Figure 10.29). Today, the financial district is several blocks from the bay; consequently the district that began at wharfhead remained at its original location, even though other activity moved with the changing shoreline.

The prestige associated with the downtown area is also a strong centralizing force. Some activities still necessitate a central-city address. Think how important it is for some advertising firms to be on New York's Madison Avenue or for a stockbroker to be on Wall Street. This extends to many activities in cities of all sizes. The "downtown lawyer" and the "uptown banker" are examples. Residences have often been located in the central city because of the prestige associated with it. Most cities have remnants of high-income neighborhoods close to the downtown area. Although this trend has weakened in North America—downtown areas have become more congested and noisy, and transportation has encouraged suburban residences—it is still important elsewhere. London and Paris have very prestigious neighborhoods directly in the downtown area.

Probably the strongest social force for centralization has been the desire to live near one's employment. Until the development of the electric trolley in the 1880s, most urban dwellers had little alternative other than walking to work. Most people had to live near the central city because most employment was there. Upper-income people had their carriages and cabs, but others had nothing. Even after the introduction of electric streetcar lines in the 1880s, which made possible the exodus of some middle-class residents, many people continued to walk to work, particularly those who could not afford the new housing being constructed in what Sam Bass Warner, Jr. has called "streetcar suburbs."

Decentralization

Decentralizing forces encourage relocation diffusion, such as the movement of a shop or residence from the downtown to the suburbs. Decentralizing forces also promote expansion diffusion, such as the location of a new shop in the suburbs. The forces behind decentralization include the same two general categories (economic and social) that were used to explain centralization and an additional category, public policy. Now, however, people and businesses are moving from the city instead of into it (Figure 11.5).

Economic Advantages. Changes in accessibility have been a major reason for decentralization. The department store that originally located in the central city may now find that its customers have moved to the suburbs. They no longer shop downtown. As a result, the department store may move to a suburban shopping mall. The same process also occurs among industries such as food-processing plants. They must move away to minimize transportation costs. The activities that were located downtown because of the railroad may now find trucking more effective. They relocate closer to a freeway system that skirts the downtown

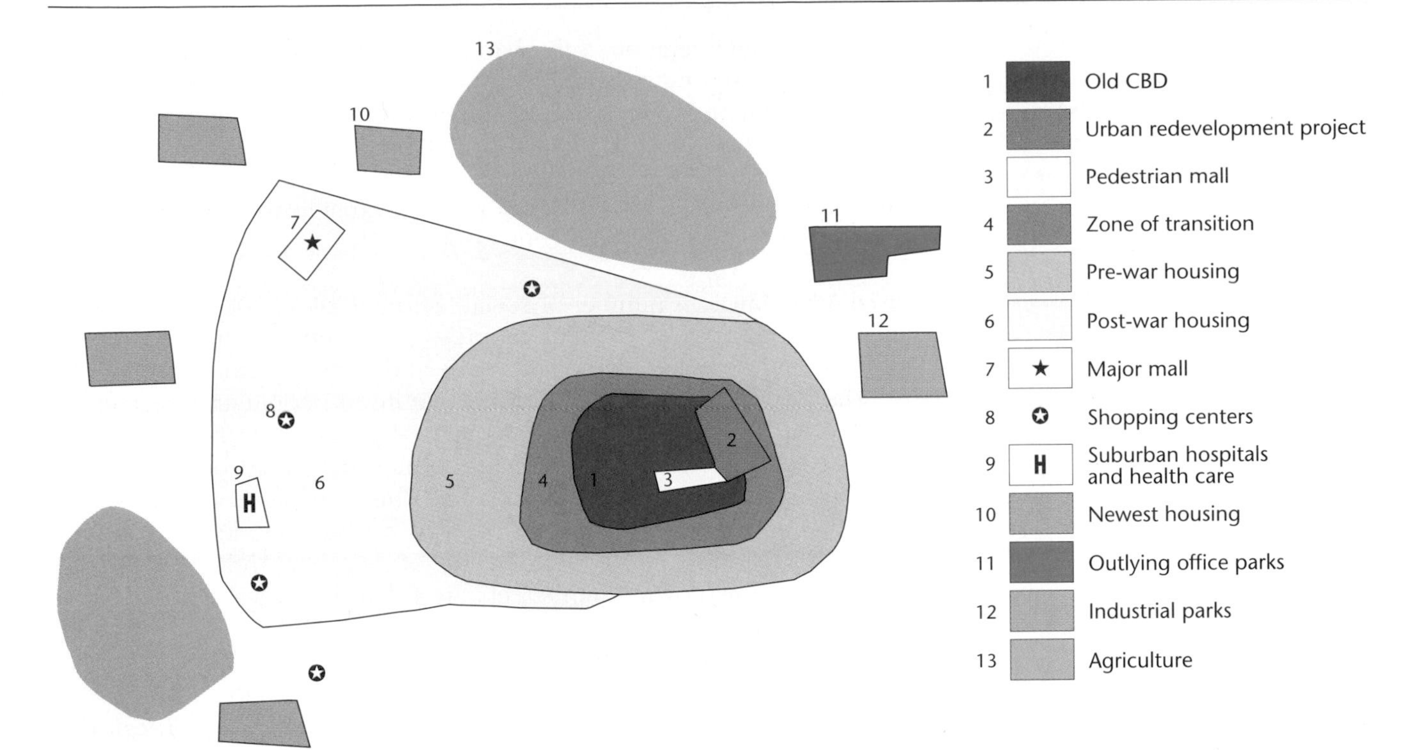

Figure 11.5
A hypothetical decentralized city. While the old CBD struggles (vacant stores and upper floors), newer activities locate either in the Urban Redevelopment Project (offices, convention center, hotel) or in outlying office parks, malls, or shopping centers. However, some new specialty shops might be found around the new downtown pedestrian mall. New industry locates in suburban industrial parks that, along with outlying office areas, form major destinations for daily lateral commuting.

area. And many offices now locate near airports so that their executives and salespeople can fly in and out more easily.

Although agglomeration once served as a centralizing force, its former benefits have now become liabilities in many downtown areas. These disadvantages include increased rents as a result of the high demand for space; congestion in the support system, which means delays in getting supplies or standing in endless lines for lunches; and traffic congestion, which makes delivery to market time-consuming and costly. Some downtown areas are so congested that traffic moves more slowly today than it did at the turn of the century. Traffic studies of midtown New York City show that the average automobile moves at a snail's pace of 6 miles (9.5 kilometers) per hour. According to a 1907 study, horse-drawn vehicles moved through the same area at an average speed of 11.5 miles (18.5 kilometers) per hour, almost twice as fast.

Often dissatisfied with the inconveniences of central-city living, employees may demand higher wages as compensation. This adds to the cost of doing business in the central city, and many firms choose to leave rather than bear such additional costs. Many firms have left New York City, for example, to locate in the suburbs. They claim that it costs less to locate there and that their employees are happier and more productive because they do not have to put up with the turmoil of city life.

There can also be benefits of clustering in new suburban locations, such as industrial parks, where the costs of utilities and transportation links are shared by all the occupants. Similar benefits can come from residential agglomeration. Suburban real estate developments take advantage of clustering by sharing costs of schools, parks, road improvements, and utilities. New residents much prefer moving into a new development when they know that a full range of services is available nearby. Then they will not have to drive miles to find, say, the nearest hardware store. It is to the developer's advantage to encourage construction of nearby shopping centers.

Social Advantages. A number of social factors reinforce decentralization. These include loss of downtown prestige, sentiment attached to the suburbs, and new employment patterns and transportation systems.

The downtown area might once have lured people and businesses into the central city because it was a prestigious location. But once it begins to decay, once shops close and office space goes begging, there may be a certain stigma attached to it. This may drive residents and commercial activities away. Investors will not sink money in a downtown area that they think has no chance of recovery, and shoppers will not venture downtown when streets are filled with vacant stores, transients, pawnshops, and secondhand stores. One of the persistent problems faced by cities is how to reverse this image of the downtown area so that people once again consider it the focus of the city.

Sentiment and prestige attached to the suburbs are significant decentralizing forces. There has been a long-standing preference in the United States and Canada for the single-family dwelling and large lot. These have been most readily obtained where land values are lower, away from the city center. And because the suburbs were originally dominated by upper-income people, socially mobile families have considered a move in that direction a step upward. In addition, families with children often choose affluent suburban locations because many of these communities can support a public educational system that is better than that offered in the city.

The need to be near one's workplace has historically been a great centralizing force, but it can also be a very strong decentralizing force. At first the suburbs were "bedroom communities," from which people commuted to their jobs in the downtown area. This is no longer the case. In most metropolitan areas, most jobs are not in the central city but in outlying districts. Now people work in suburban industrial parks, manufacturing plants, office buildings, and shopping centers. Thus a typical journey to work involves **lateral commuting**—travel from one suburb to another. As a result, most people who live away from the city center actually live closer to their workplaces. A testimony to this is a freeway system at rush hour; traffic is usually heavy in all directions, not just to and from the city center (see discussion of edge cities in Chapter 10).

Public Policy. Many public policy decisions, particularly at the national level, have contributed greatly to the decentralization and abandonment of our cities. Both the Federal Highway Act of 1916 and the Interstate Highway Act of 1956 directed government spending on transportation to the automobile and the truck. Urban expressways, in combination with the emerging trucking industry, led to massive decentralization of industry and housing. In addition, the ability to deduct mortgage interest from income for tax purposes favors individual home ownership, which has tended to support a move to the suburbs.

The federal government in the United States has also intervened more directly in the housing market. In *Crabgrass Frontier,* Kenneth

Jackson outlines the implications of two federal housing policies for the spatial patterning of our metropolitan areas. The first involves the New Deal enactment of the Federal Housing Administration (FHA, established in 1934), and its supplement known as the GI Bill, enacted in 1944. These federal acts were meant to put people back to work in the building trades, and to help house the returning soldiers after World War II. What these policies did was to insure long-term mortgage loans for home construction and sale. Although strictly speaking the FHA legislation contained no explicit antiurban bias, most of the houses it insured were located in new residential developments in the suburbs, thereby neglecting the inner city.

Jackson identifies three reasons for why this happened. First, by setting particular terms for its insurance, the FHA favored the development of single-family over multifamily projects. Secondly, FHA-insured loans for repairs were of short duration and were generally small. Most families, therefore, were better off buying a new home that was probably in the suburbs than updating an older home in the city.

Jackson regards the third factor as the most important in favoring suburban locations for FHA loans. In order to receive an FHA-insured loan, the applicant and the neighborhood of the property were to be rated by an "unbiased professional." This requirement was intended to guarantee that the property value of the house would be greater than the debt. This policy, however, encouraged bias against any neighborhood that was considered a potential risk in terms of property values. The FHA explicitly warned against neighborhoods with a racial mix, assuming that such a social climate would bring property values down, and encouraged the enactment of **restrictive covenants** written in property deeds, which prohibited certain "undesirable" groups from buying property. The agency also prepared extensive maps of metropolitan areas, depicting the locations of African American families and predicting the spread of that population. These maps often served as the basis for **red-lining,** a practice in which banks and mortgage companies commonly demarcated areas (often by drawing a red line around them on these maps) considered to be a high risk for loans.

The effect of these policies was twofold: First, it encouraged construction of single-family homes in the suburban areas while discouraging center-city locations; and second, it intensified the segregation of residential areas and actively promoted homogeneity in the new suburbs.

The second federal housing policy that had a major impact on the patterning of metropolitan areas, the United States Housing Act, was intended to provide public housing for those who could not afford private housing. Originally enacted in 1937, the legislation did encourage the construction of many low-income housing units. Yet most of those units were built in the inner city, thereby contributing to the view of the suburbs as the refuge of the white middle class. This growing pattern of racial and economic segregation arose in part because public housing decisions were left up to local municipalities. Many municipalities did not need federal dollars and therefore did not want public housing. In addition, the legislation required that for every unit of public housing erected, one inferior housing unit had to be eliminated. Thus, only areas with inadequate housing units could receive federal dollars, again ensuring that public housing projects would be constructed in the older, downtown areas, not the newer suburbs. As Jackson claims, "The result, if not the intent, of the public housing program of the United States was to segregate the races, to concentrate the disadvantaged in inner cities, and to reinforce the image of suburbia as a place of refuge for the problems of race, crime, and poverty."

The Costs of Decentralization. Unfortunately, decentralization has taken its toll. Many of the urban problems now burdening North American cities are direct products of the rapid decentralization that has taken place in the last 30 years. Vacant storefronts, empty offices, and deserted factories testify to the movement of commercial functions from central cities to suburbs. Retail sales in North American central cities have steadily declined, losing business to suburban shopping centers. Even offices are finding advantages to suburban location. Like industry, offices capitalize on lower costs and easier access to new transportation networks.

Decentralization has also cost society millions of dollars in problems brought to the suburbs. Where rapid suburbanization has been the case, sprawl has usually resulted. A common pattern is leapfrog or **checkerboard development,** where housing tracts jump over parcels of farmland resulting in a mixture of open lands with built-up areas. This pattern results because developers buy cheaper land farther away from built-up areas, thereby cutting their costs. Furthermore, home buyers often pay premium prices for homes in subdivisions surrounded by farmlands (Figure 11.6).

This form of development is costly because it is more expensive to provide city services, such as police, fire protection, sewers, and electrical lines, to those areas laying beyond open, unbuilt-up parcels. Obviously, the most cost-efficient form of development is adding new housing directly adjacent to built-up areas. That way the costs of providing new services are minimal.

Furthermore, sprawl extracts high costs because of increased use of cars. Public transportation is extremely costly and inefficient when it must serve a low-density checkerboard development pattern—so costly

Figure 11.6
Suburban sprawl. Suburbanization gives us a familiar landscape of look-alike houses and yards, auto-efficient street and transportation patterns, and, in the background, remnants of agriculture, awaiting the day that they are converted into housing tracts.

that many cities and transit firms cannot extend lines into these areas. This means that the automobile is the only form of transportation there. More energy is consumed for fuel, more air pollution is created by exhaust, and more time is spent in commuting and everyday activities in a sprawling urban area than in a centralized city.

We should not overlook the costs of losing valuable agricultural land to urban development. Farmers cultivating the remaining checkerboard parcels have a hard time making ends meet. They are usually taxed at extremely high rates because their land has high potential for development, and few can make a profit when taxes eat up all their resources. Often the only recourse is to sell out to subdividers. So the cycle of leapfrog development goes on.

Many cities are now taking strong measures to curb this kind of sprawling growth. San Jose, California, for example, one of the fastest-growing cities of the 1960s, is now focusing new development on empty parcels of the checkerboard pattern. This is called **in-filling.** New growth takes place not by extending the sprawling outer edge of the city, but by developing the existing urban area, where services are already available and can be provided at lower costs.

Other cities are tying the number of building permits granted each year to the availability of urban services. If schools are already crowded, water supplies inadequate, and sewer plants overburdened, the number of new dwelling units approved for an area will reflect this lower carrying capacity (see box, *Controlling Suburban Growth*).

In summary, the costs of decentralization range from decayed and moribund downtowns to costly and inefficient public transportation. While inner-city poverty and ghettoization can be partially blamed on decentralization, so can the loss of farmland, increased auto air pollution, and higher energy consumption. Though planning measures have alleviated some of these problems, many of these ills will multiply as our cities continue to decentralize.

Gentrification

Beginning in the 1970s, urban scholars began to observe what seemed to be a trend opposite to suburbanization. This trend, called **gentrification,** refers to the movement of middle-class people into deteriorated areas of city centers. Gentrification often begins in an inner-city residential district, with gentrifiers moving into an area that had been run-down and therefore more affordable than suburban housing. The infusion of new capital into the housing market usually results in higher property values, and this, in turn, often displaces residents who cannot afford to stay in the area. This opens up more housing for gentrification, and the gentrified district continues its spatial expansion (Figure 11.7).

Figure 11.7
Commercial gentrification in the center of Society Hill, Philadelphia. This area caters as much to tourists as to local residents. Notice the attempts to appear historical, with brick streets and nineteenth-century storefronts.

Commercial gentrification usually follows residential, as new patterns of consumption are introduced into the inner city by the middle-class gentrifiers. Urban shopping malls and pedestrian shopping corridors bring the conveniences of the suburbs into the city, and bars and restaurants catering to this new urban middle class provide entertainment and nightlife for the gentrifiers.

The speed with which gentrification has proceeded in many of our downtowns, and the scale of landscape changes that it brings with it, are causing dramatic shifts in the urban mosaic. What factors have led to this reshaping of our cities?

Controlling Suburban Growth

Although the first measures to control suburban growth were written more than a decade ago, the controversy continues today, with the issue enmeshed in drawn-out legal battles and bureaucratic red tape.

One of the earliest and precedent-setting growth control plans came from Petaluma, California, a small suburb of 50,000 people within the commuter zone north of San Francisco. Once a sleepy service center for chicken ranches, the town began sprawling with rapid growth in the late 1960s and, a few years later, the city council took strong measures to limit growth by adopting a plan whereby only 500 building permits would be issued yearly. This was roughly half the number granted in the previous years, so the intention was to slow growth by 50 percent. Five hundred permits would be awarded after careful review of all proposed building plans, with the coveted permits going to those structures that met rigorous criteria established by the City Council.

Adverse reaction and opposition to this plan was immediate. Not only did the building industry object because the plan would limit construction and jobs, but they were joined by civil rights groups who saw control of suburban growth as a possible vehicle for racial discrimination. Because some types of suburban zoning, such as large-lot minimums and bans against apartment houses, tend to push up housing prices and discriminate against lower-income people, civil rights organizations saw the Petaluma plan as a threat to minority groups.

Consequently, this Petaluma plan was challenged in court as violating the constitutional "right to travel," a legal right traced to the Magna Carta, and the legal basis for housing without restrictive racial covenants. While a lobby of building industries, trade unions, and civil liberties groups supported a challenge to the Petaluma plan, the city, with financial backing and moral support from other cities interested in establishing a legal precedent for growth control, stood by its plan. Lower court decisions went both for and against the plan until a final decision was made by the Supreme Court in 1978 substantiating the legal basis for this approach to growth control.

However, even if the legal foundation for growth control was established, there are numerous other complexities to be faced by cities and neighborhoods battling unrestricted expansion. First, there is the question of whether growth control restrictions force up housing prices. A recent California study shows that housing prices in areas with growth control are 5 to 8 percent higher than in areas without controls, because of market demand for a scarce supply and because developers tack on additional costs to compensate for the paperwork and delays from a more complicated permit-approval process. A second issue is whether growth control restrictions discourage developers from building low- and moderate-priced homes. If only a limited number of permits are available for building (as in the Petaluma plan), then developers tend to maximize their investment by building higher-priced homes instead of a larger number of middle-income houses. Many cities have addressed this problem by granting incentives to developers who build for lower-income groups. Third, there are problems with how to limit the number of building permits. Some cities use lotteries, granting permits by chance, while others use a complicated point system that rewards plans with the desired attributes. Another common approach is limiting building to those areas of the city where services (such as water and sewers) are already available, thereby restricting leapfrog sprawl.

And, last, some cities link the number of building permits to the carrying capacity of public services, declaring building moratoria when schools, water systems, sewer plants, or roads became overloaded. Because cities prefer to plan their futures and control growth in an orderly manner, building moratoria are the least desirable vehicle for growth control from a city's viewpoint, yet they are often forced on a municipality by citizen movements that place a moratorium on a local ballot by petition and then vote it into effect.

Working out an effective yet equitable way to limit and control suburban growth remains one of the challenges faced by cities and towns in the 1990s.

Economic Factors. Some urban scholars look to broad economic trends in the United States to explain gentrification. Throughout the post–World War II era, most investments in metropolitan land were made in the suburbs; as a result, land in the inner city was devalued. By the 1970s, many home buyers and commercial investors found land in the city much more affordable, and a better economic investment, than the higher-priced suburbs. This brought capital into areas that had been undervalued and spurred on the gentrifying process.

In addition, most Western countries have been experiencing a process known as *deindustrialization,* whereby their economy is shifting from one based on industrialization to one based on the service sector. This shift has led to the abandonment of older industrial districts in the inner city, including waterfront areas. Many of these areas are prime targets of gentrifiers who convert the waterfront from a noisy, commercial port area into an aesthetic asset. The shift to an economy based on the service sector also means that the new productive areas of the city will be dedicated to white-collar activities. These activities often take place in relatively clean and quiet office buildings, contributing to a view of the city as a more "liveable" environment.

Social Factors. Other scholars look to changes in social structure to explain gentrification. The maturing of the baby-boom generation has led to significant modifications of our "traditional" family structure and lifestyle. With a majority of women in the paid labor force, and many young couples choosing not to have children or to delay that decision, a suburban residential location looks less appealing. A gentrified location in the inner city attracts this new class because it is close to their managerial or professional jobs downtown, is usually easier to maintain, and is considered more interesting than the bland suburban areas where they grew up.

Living in a newly gentrified area is also a way of displaying social status. Many suburbs have become less exclusive, while older neighborhoods in the inner city frequently exploit their historical associations as a status symbol. Members of the middle class, often employed in service-sector industries, exhibit their new economic status by living in a gentrified neighborhood.

Political Factors. Many metropolitan governments in the United States, faced with the abandonment of the center city by the middle class and therefore with the erosion of their tax base, have enacted policies to encourage commercial and residential development in downtown areas. Some policies provide tax breaks for companies willing to locate downtown, while others furnish local and state funding to redevelop center-city residential and commercial buildings.

At a more comprehensive level, some larger metropolitan areas have devised long-term planning agendas that target certain neighborhoods for revitalization. Often this is accomplished by first condemning the targeted area, thereby transferring control of the land to an urban-development authority or other planning agency. This area is often an older residential neighborhood that was built originally to house people who worked in nearby factories. In order to reshape the neighborhood for gentrification, the factories are usually torn down or transformed into lofts or office space. The redevelopment authority might locate a new civic or arts center in the neighborhood. Public-sector initiatives often lead to private investment, thereby increasing property values. These higher property values, in turn, lead to more investment and the eventual transformation of the neighborhood into a middle- to upper-class gentrified district.

Sexuality and Gentrification. Gentrified residential districts are often correlated with the presence of a significant gay and lesbian population. It is fairly easy to understand this correlation. First, the typical suburban life tends not to appeal to people whose lifestyle is often regarded as "different," and whose community needs are often different from those in the suburbs. Second, gentrified, inner-city neighborhoods provide access to the diversity of city life, and amenities that often include gay cultural institutions. In fact, the association of urban neighborhoods with gay and lesbian people is long-lived. For example, urban historian George Chauncey has documented gay culture in New York City between 1890 and the Second World War, showing that a gay world occupied and shaped distinctive spaces in the city, such as neighborhood enclaves, gay commercial areas, and public parks and streets.

Yet, unlike this earlier period, when gay cultures were often forced to remain hidden, the gentrification of the post-war period has provided gay and lesbian populations with the opportunity to actively and openly reshape entire neighborhoods. Urban scholar Manuel Castells argues that in cities such as San Francisco, the presence of gay men in institutions directly linked to gentrification, such as the real estate industry, significantly influenced that city's gentrification processes in the 1970s. Geographers Larry Knopp and Mickey Lauria emphasize the community-building aspect of gay males' involvement in gentrification, recognizing that gays "have seized an opportunity to combat oppression by creating neighborhoods over which they have maximum control and which meet long-neglected needs." Similarly, geographer Gill Valentine argues that the limited numbers and types of lesbian spaces in cities also serve as community-building centers for lesbian social networks. According to Tamar Rothenberg, the gentrified neigborhood of Park Slope in Brooklyn is home to the "heaviest concentration of lesbians in the US," and its extensive social networks are marking the neighborhood as a center of lesbian identity and a visible lesbian social space.

The Costs of Gentrification. Gentrification often results in the displacement of lower-income people, who are forced to leave their homes because of rising property values. This displacement can have serious consequences for the city's social fabric. Because many of the displaced people come from disadvantaged groups, gentrification frequently contributes to racial and ethnic tensions. Displaced people are often forced into neighborhoods more peripheral to the city, a trend that serves to disadvantage these people even more. In addition, gentrified neighborhoods usually stand in stark contrast to surrounding neighborhoods where investment has not taken place, thus creating a very visible reminder of the uneven distribution of wealth within our cities.

The success of a gentrification project is usually measured by its appeal to an upper-class clientele. This suggests that gentrified neighborhoods are completely homogeneous in their use of land. Residential areas are consciously planned to be separate from commercial districts, and are themselves sorted by cost and tenure type. Thus, gentrification often draws on the suburban notion of residential homogeneity and eliminates what many consider to be a great asset of urban life—its diversity and heterogeneity. A study of the gentrification process in Society Hill, Philadelphia, highlights these social costs (see box, *The Social Costs of Gentrification*).

The Cultural Ecology of the City

Cities are affected by their physical environments just as urbanization profoundly alters natural environmental processes. Consequently, the theme of cultural ecology is helpful in organizing information about these city-nature relationships. This theme allows us to conceptualize problematic components of the interaction between people and the environment. Although we talk in general terms about these topics in the next pages, we should not lose sight of how the differing cultural fabric within and between cities affects this city-nature relationship. Put differently, urban cultural ecology is a topic that differs vastly from place to place because of different physical environments and, equally important, because of varying cultural patterns.

The Social Costs of Gentrification: The Case of Society Hill, Philadelphia

Society Hill, an old residential area in Philadelphia that dates from the colonial era, represents one of the earliest gentrification projects, and is considered one of the more successful. The following account, however, points out that this first phase (Unit One) of Philadelphia's redevelopment brought many social costs with it.

The physical appearance itself of the redeveloped Society Hill manifests the special difficulty of marketing this inner-city neighborhood in the midst of the suburban age. Previously cited advertisements highlighted stereotypically nonurban attributes of the neighborhood, such as marinas and green pathways. The conscious re-sorting of heterogeneous into homogeneous land-use patterns unlike any of the other older neighborhoods of the city, is, we claim, drawn from a prominent motif in suburban design. The anthropologist Constance Perin, in *Everything in Its Place* (1977), an exploration of cultural and social symbolism in metropolitan land-use patterns, argues that one of the keys to the successful marketing of American suburbia has been the appeal of clearly ordered and discrete land-use units. Prospective homebuyers, who were not only purchasing shelter, but also deeply committing themselves financially, were reassured by the evident presence of neighbors "just like themselves." Thus in the design of Society Hill, residential tracts were separated from most other uses, and also were internally sorted by cost and tenure type. In addition, building design was such as to maximize both privacy and physical security. The inward-facing plans of several new housing clusters, for example, with parking and entrance on the interior of blocks, exemplify one of the earliest applications of "defended space" principles.

Having ensured that "everything was in its place," so too the Society Hill concept carefully saw to it that everybody was in their place; social homogeneity, equally a stereotypically suburban attribute, was relentlessly pursued. Part of the appeal of homogeneity was to snobbery: the advertisements previously cited invited one to come live with Philadelphia's top people: a 1957 advertisement (early in Society Hill's redevelopment) insinuates, "The mayor is, why can't you?" (*Philadelphia Inquirer,* May 19, 1957). Just as important was the need to assuage fears about stereotypical in-city sub-cultures. ("See, you have to understand [that] the fundamental feeling in suburbia is fear [of the impingement of the city], let's face it," a realtor had informed Perin [1977:87].) So, in a suburban age, the advertisements felt they had to stress "nice people . . . coming to live in Society Hill."

It is a commonplace that the Society Hill renewal, so evidently "top-down" in conception and execution, imposed social costs upon pre-existing residents of lower socioeconomic status. The prior residents of Unit One could remain only if the Redevelopment Authority was disposed to resell their property back to them with inevitably expensive contractual stipulations: a timetable for any of a number of specific repairs, mandatory upkeep requirements, plus remodeling to exacting and detailed "historically authentic" standards for facades. Unbending application of these criteria expelled all but a few of the original lower-income residents. Thus, at the public meeting held in conjunction with the unveiling of the Unit One plan (April 28, 1958), the complaint was heard from one resident that it was "a plan for an area of wealthy poodled people," and it was reported that "many [residents] . . . didn't like what they saw, or thought they saw, looming in the future." John P. Robin, president of the Old Philadelphia Development Corporation (the body which had contracted to implement the renewal) responded that "residents would have to compromise their desires with those of others and the city" (*Evening Bulletin,* April 29, 1958). This captures the general tone; in many cases the record documents a degree of insensitivity to or lack of concern with the special needs and claims of pre-existing Society Hill residents.

It was high-income people that were required in Unit One; any possibility of income mix was intendedly minimized.

Abridged from Cybriwsky, Roman A., David Ley, and John Western, "The Political and Social Construction of Revitalized Neighborhoods: Society Hill, Philadelphia, and False Creek, Vancouver," in Neil Smith and Peter Williams, eds., *Gentrification of the City.* Boston: Allen & Unwin, 1986, pp. 92–120.

The Urban Ecosystem

In the first chapter of this book, ecology is defined as the study of the relationship between an organism and its physical environment. To study this relationship, we examine both organism and environment as one unit through which the flow of energy or matter can be traced. This is called the **ecosystem.** We can apply this concept to the city in order to better understand the relationship between urban populations and the physical environment.

There are four important concepts related to the ecosystem approach: *input, storage, output,* and *feedback.* To illustrate, let us examine just one component of the urban ecosystem: water. Obviously, a city needs water to survive, so it imports a given amount each day, either from local sources, such as lakes and reservoirs, or from long distances via canals and aqueducts. This is the **input** of the system.

Through its use in the city, water is transformed and leaves the system in other forms. These are the **outputs.** Some water is consumed by people, temporarily becoming part of their body systems. Other water becomes part of different manufactured products, such as cheese or soft drinks, and may leave the city's system as goods exported to other markets. Still other water is used for industrial cooling and, as it evaporates, returns to the atmosphere as vapor. A small amount of city water is not used, but rather is stored within the system for future use, just the way organisms store energy. But most of the water—about 95 percent—is simply used to convey wastes from one point to another: from home to sewer plant, from factory to river, from sidewalk to gutter. This output is a most troublesome aspect of the urban system.

Feedback is a crucial part of any system. It is the repercussions on a system when an element is returned in modified form by other components of the system. A simplistic example would be a city's use of water from a lake both for its water supply and also as a dumping area for sewage. As more effluent is discharged into the lake, water quality decreases, and the city must expend more energy (measured both in money and activity) to protect its freshwater supply.

A more complicated example—and in no way has this relationship been conclusively proved—is the way that city-produced air pollution may alter weather patterns so that an urban water supply system is strained, either by drought or by flooding. Further examples of the interconnectivity in the urban ecosystem are given in the following discussion of the physical components of the urban environment.

The Urban Geological Environment

In Chapter 10, under the discussion of site and situation, we saw that cities are both affected by—and affect—the physical environment. Let us explore further the relationship between urbanization and the geological environment.

To begin, topography can influence urban development in three ways: the direction of city growth, the patterning of social regions, and the routing of transportation. These potential effects, however, depend on a number of cultural variables. The most important variables are a society's technological level, the amount of energy and capital available for modification of the geological environment, and, lastly, the stage in a city's development. In other words, the geological environment may have a great effect on those cities in early stages of growth, where there are spatial alternatives to expending energy and money on modifying terrain, or where the technology is lacking for bulldozing, landfill, or high-stress building construction. At later stages of growth, in a rich, highly industrialized culture, there will be far more examples of humans modifying the geological environment (Figure 11.8).

Let us look first at the way topography might influence early stages of city growth. Cities usually expand first on those areas where building costs are lowest. This means that flat, well-drained lands that are close to transportation and adjacent to existing urban activities will be built on first. But as topography varies, building costs increase. Areas of hills, marshes, and floodplains may be built on only at later stages of a city's growth when fewer alternatives are available.

The increased costs of site preparation, such as grading hills or draining swamps, can have two very different consequences on the patterning of social regions. On the one hand, the increased cost of building may be passed on to the consumer—meaning that those who

Figure 11.8
Suburban homes built on landfills, Treasure Island, Florida. When land values are high and pressure for housing intense, terrain rarely stands in the way of the developer.

buy the houses pay more, and the area will be occupied by higher-income groups. On the other hand, aspects of construction may be cut in order to compensate for increased site preparation costs. Lots may be smaller, houses undersized, and shortcuts taken in construction methods so that the finished product is of lower quality. This means that lower-income groups will probably occupy the area.

Urban transportation systems also can be affected by topography. And since there is a close link between transportation and urban development, the resulting urban pattern may express these relationships. The first urban transportation system was the horse-drawn streetcar, which was obviously restricted to level parts of the city because horses could not pull car and passengers up or down hills. Slight gradients could be negotiated by smaller horse-drawn carriages; those who could afford such conveyances had access to hilltop building sites. But it was only with the cable car that hills became accessible to the middle class. Starting in San Francisco in 1873, cable cars came into widespread use in American cities. However, cable cars had problems in cold, wet climates because of freezing in the cable conduits, so a better solution to public transportation needs was sought.

Electric trolley systems profoundly altered the pattern of urban development beginning in the 1890s. Like the horse-drawn carriage, they also had limited hill-climbing abilities. Only slight gradients could be negotiated, so trolley lines ascended slopes only when it was possible to follow hillside contours. In the end, it was the automobile that led to widespread building on steep urban slopes. And even this form of development has been influenced by factors such as frequency of heavy snowfalls and ice storms.

Urban Weather and Climate

Cities alter just about all aspects of local weather and climate. Temperatures are higher in cities, rainfall increases, the incidence of fog and cloudiness is greater, and atmospheric pollution is much higher.

The causes behind these alterations are no mystery. Because cities pave over large areas of streets, buildings, parking lots, and rooftops, about 50 percent of the urban area is a hard surface. Rainfall is quickly carried into gutters and sewers, so that little standing water is available for evaporation. Because heat is removed from the air during the normal evaporation process, when moisture is reduced, evaporation is lessened, and air temperatures are higher.

Furthermore, cities generate enormous amounts of heat. This comes not just from the heating systems of buildings, but also from automobiles, industry, and even human bodies. One study showed that on a winter day in Manhattan, the amount of heat produced in the city is 2 1/2 times that reaching the ground from the sun. The result of this heat generation is to produce a large mass of warmer air sitting over the city. This is called the urban **heat island** (Figure 11.9). As a result of the heat island, yearly temperatures average 3.5° Fahrenheit warmer than in the countryside; during the winter, when city-produced heat is higher, the temperature difference can easily be 7° to 10° Fahrenheit.

During the summer, the city center is warmer than the suburbs. There can be a 10° Fahrenheit difference between downtown and outlying residential areas, which is a result of suburban lawns and parks stabilizing temperatures by using up heat through evaporation and releasing heat at night faster than paved areas. Concrete areas tend to store heat longer at night, which leads to a buildup of temperatures over a series of warm days.

Precipitation (rain and snowfall) is also affected by urbanization. Because of higher temperatures within the urban area, snowfall will be about 5 percent less than in the surrounding countryside. However, rainfall can be 5 to 10 percent higher. This is a function of two factors: first, the large number of dust particles in urban air, and, second, the higher city temperatures. Dust particles are a necessary precondition for condensation, offering a focus around which moisture can adhere. If the air has a greater number of dust particles, condensation will take

Figure 11.9
The London heat island forms a dome over the city. Notice the marked contrast in temperature between the built-up central part of the city and the surrounding "Green Belt." (After Chandler.)

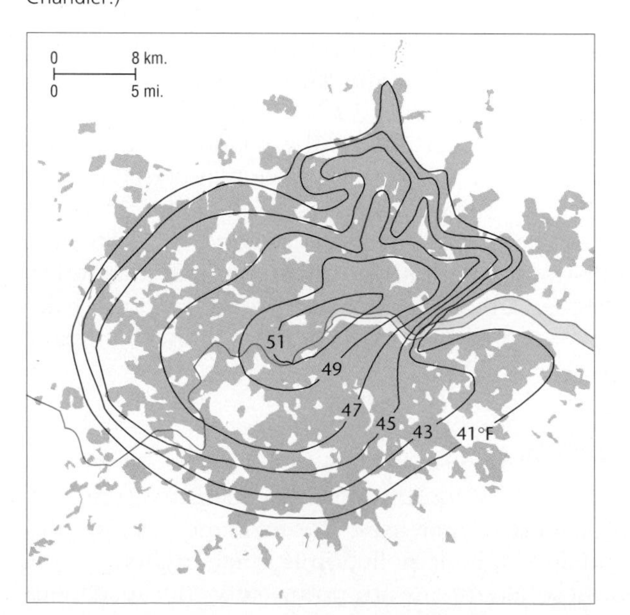

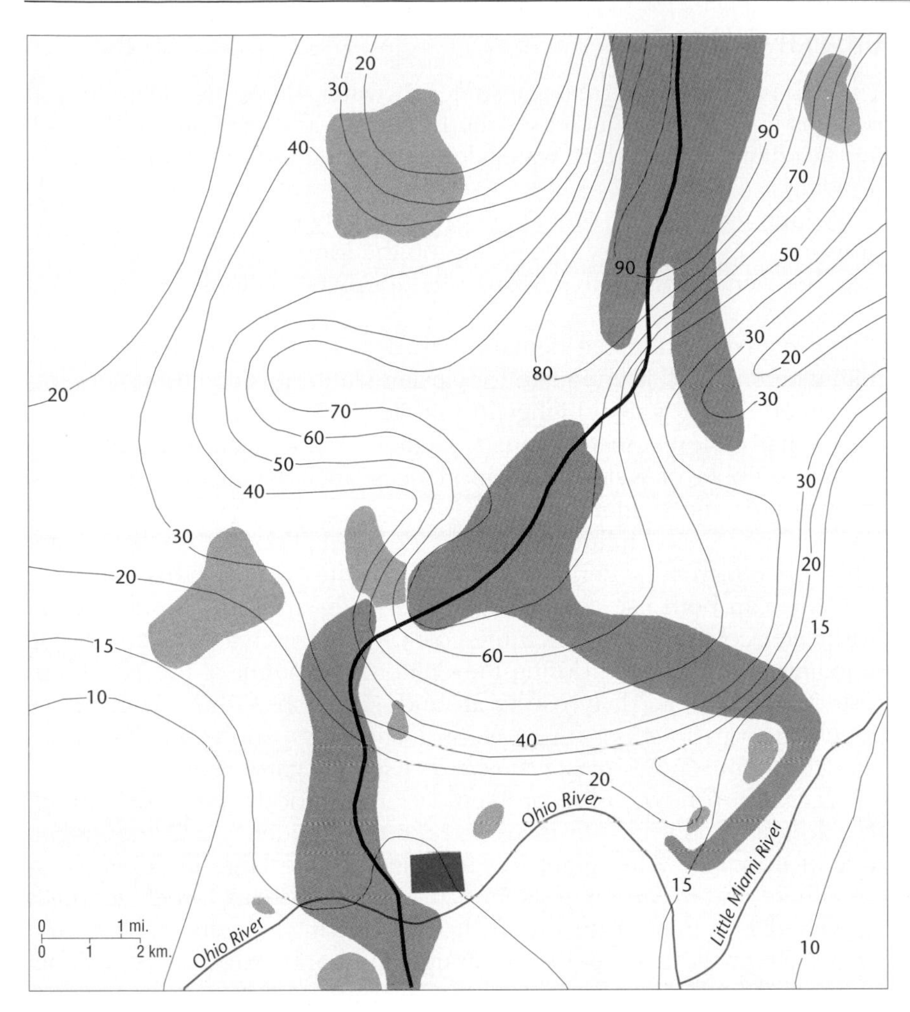

Figure 11.10
The dust dome over Cincinnati, Ohio. Values show the concentration of particulate matter in the air at 3000 feet elevation. The higher the value, the greater the amount of particulate matter. (After Bach and Hagedorn.)

place more easily. That is why fog and clouds (dust domes) are usually more frequent around cities (Figure 11.10).

Once condensation takes place, rainfall is not far behind. Rainfall increases on the order of 10 percent have been documented immediately downwind from cities. For example, thunderstorms in the London area produce 30 percent more rainfall than in the countryside. Some urban climatologists observe a pattern of increase in weekday rainfall: Rainfall is less on weekends because dust particle generation—from autos and industry—is reduced.

City-generated air pollution is one of the most serious problems of our times. No longer is air pollution simply a nuisance; it can cause serious illness, even death. Pollution damages agriculture near cities; and it extracts a high cost from every urban dweller. Unless pollution can be halted, it may actually be the main limiting factor on urban growth. Some suggest that fresh air—not water—will determine the ultimate carrying capacity of the Los Angeles basin. Federal and local air quality agencies are experimenting with regulations limiting further growth and development in those areas suffering from persistent air pollution.

Urban Hydrology

The city not only is a great consumer of water, but it also alters runoff patterns in a way that increases the frequency and magnitude of flooding. We first discuss urban water demands, then the problems of urban flooding.

Within the city, residential areas are usually the greatest consumers of water. This could vary depending on the kind of industry found in a city, but generally, each person uses about 60 gallons per day in a residence.

Of course, residential demand varies. It is higher in drier climates than where rainfall is adequate for garden water; it is greater where lots are larger; and it is also higher in middle- and high-income neighborhoods than in lower-income areas. Higher-income groups usually have a larger number of water-using appliances, such as washing machines, dishwashers, and swimming pools.

However, price influences water demand. People use less water when price increases. Periods of drought in the West demonstrated that residents can both use considerably less water and find alternatives to freshwater consumption when the cost of water increases. Many of the rationing plans adopted during the California drought of the late 1980s restricted per capita daily use to around 40 gallons. Toilets (which use about seven gallons per flush) were flushed less, showers were shortened, and household "gray water" was used for gardens.

Let us turn now to the problem of urban floods. We noted earlier that urbanization seems to increase both the frequency and the magnitude of flooding. Why might this be? Cities create large impervious areas where water cannot soak into the earth. Instead, precipitation is converted into immediate runoff. It is forced into gutters, sewers, and stream channels that have been straightened and bared of vegetation, resulting in more frequent high-water levels than are found in a comparable area of rural land. Furthermore, the time between rainfall and peak runoff is reduced in cities; there is less lag than in the countryside, where water runs across soil and vegetation into stream channels and then into rivers. So, because of hard surfaces and artificial collection channels, runoff is concentrated and immediate.

Several studies show that flooding becomes five or six times more frequent in an urbanized watershed, and because pressures on land from city growth often lead to the development of floodplains, a scenario is set for disaster. Floodplains are, by definition, areas subject to natural flooding, so it should come as no surprise that rivers reclaim their full channels every now and then. And when urbanization increases the frequency of flooding, building on floodplains becomes increasingly hazardous (Figure 11.11).

Urban Vegetation

Until a decade ago, it was commonly thought that the city was made up mostly of artificial surfaces: asphalt, concrete, glass, and steel. Studies, however, show that about two-thirds of a typical North American city is composed of trees and herbaceous plants (mostly cultivated grasses for lawns and weeds in vacant lots). This urban vegetation is usually a mix of natural and introduced species and is a critical component of the urban ecosystem because it affects the city's geology, hydrology, and meteorology (Figure 11.12).

Figure 11.11
A flood resulting from severe weather in Chicago. Often urbanization disturbs the natural hydrology, so that both frequency and magnitude of flooding are increased.

More specifically, urban vegetation affects the quantity and quality of surface water and groundwater; reduces wind velocity and turbulence and temperature extremes; affects the pattern of snow accumulation and melting; absorbs thousands of tons of airborne particulates and atmospheric gases; and offers habitat for mammals, birds, reptiles, and insects, all of which play some useful role in the urban ecosystem. Furthermore, urban vegetation influences the propagation of sound waves by masking out much of the city's noise; affects the distribution of natural and artificial light; and, finally, is an extremely important component in the development of soil profiles, which, in turn, control hillside stability.

Figure 11.12
Vegetation is closely linked to the different components of the urban ecosystem. One of its primary functions in the city is to reduce air temperatures by absorbing ambient heat and solar radiation and transpiring water from the millions of square feet of leaf surfaces. This can result in distinct temperature differences between vegetated and nonplanted areas.

In conclusion, let us remember that our urban settlements are still closely tied to the physical environment. Cities change these natural processes in profound ways, and we must understand these disturbances in order to make better decisions about adjustments and control. Yet the physical environment must not be thought of simply as an adversary to be conquered. This last section on urban vegetation demonstrates that many benefits are to be gained from proper management of the ecosystem. Management, however, is rooted in the cultural context—in the values, ethics, goals, and priorities of a people. This is why the issue is ultimately tied to cultural geography.

Cultural Integration and Models of the City

A number of processes are at work in a city, leading to different social and economic patterns. Six processes are briefly discussed here. The first is *concentration,* which refers to the differential distribution of population and economic activities in a city and the manner in which they have focused on the center of the city. *Decentralization,* defined earlier, refers to the location of activity away from the central city. *Segregation* is the sorting out of population groups according to conscious preferences for associating with one group or another through bias and prejudice. A somewhat similar process operates among economic activities; we call this *specialization*. The process through which a new activity or social group enters an area has traditionally been called *invasion*. And if that new use or social group gradually replaces the former occupants, this illustrates the process of *succession*. These last two terms have been adopted from plant ecology and were originally used to describe changes in vegetation. Because the term *invasion* connotes a hostile, warlike environment, it is used cautiously by social scientists when referring to cultural and ethnic groups.

With these six processes in mind, let us examine how they might influence patterns of economic and social activities in the city. We shall do so by looking at four widely used models of city structure. Let us remember, though, that these models were constructed to examine single cities and do not necessarily apply to the metropolitan coalescences so common in the world today.

Concentric Zone Model

The **concentric zone model** was developed in 1925 by Ernest W. Burgess, a sociologist at the University of Chicago. Although his model closely resembles Chicago (if the east side were not cut off by Lake Michigan), his intent was simply to construct a theoretical model of urban growth.

Figure 11.13 shows the concentric zone model with its five zones. At first glance, you can see the effects of residential decentralization. There is a distinct pattern of income levels from the **CBD** (central business district) out to the commuters' zone. This shows that even at the beginning of the auto age, American cities expressed a clear separation of social groups. The extension of trolley lines into the surrounding countryside had a lot to do with this pattern.

Zone 2, a transitional area between the CBD and residential Zone 3, is characterized by a mixed pattern of industrial and residential land use. Rooming houses, small apartments, and tenements attract the

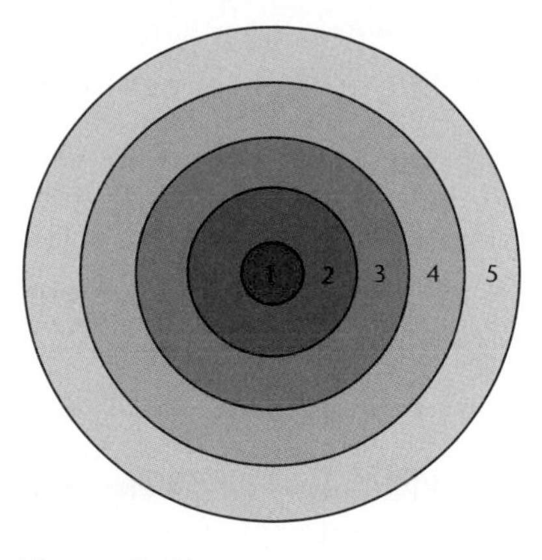

1 CBD (central business district)
2 Transition zone
3 Blue-collar residential
4 Middle-income residential
5 Commuter residential

Figure 11.13
The concentric zone model. Each zone represents a different type of land use in the city. Can you identify examples of each zone in your community?

lowest-income segment of the urban population. Often this zone includes slums and skid rows. Here, also, many ethnic ghettos began. Landowners, while waiting for the CBD to reach their land, erected shoddy tenements to house a massive influx of foreign workers. An aura of uncertainty is characteristic of life in Zone 2, because commercial activities rapidly displaced residents as the CBD expanded. Today, this area is often characterized by physical deterioration (Figure 11.14).

Zone 3, the "workingmen's quarters," is a solid blue-collar arc, located close to the factories of Zones 1 and 2. Yet Zone 3 is more stable than the zone of transition around the CBD. It is often characterized by ethnic neighborhoods: blocks of immigrants who broke free from the ghettos in Zone 2 and moved outward into flats or single-family dwellings. Burgess suggested that this working-class area, like the CBD, was spreading outward, because of pressure from the zone of transition and because blue-collar workers demanded better housing.

Figure 11.14
An abandoned building in the uptown area of Chicago. The transitional zone in the city contains vacant and deteriorated buildings.

Zone 4 is a middle-class area of "better housing." From here, established city dwellers, many of whom moved out of the central city with the first streetcar network, commute to work in the CBD.

Zone 5, the commuters' zone, consists of higher-income families clustered together in older suburbs, either on the farthest extension of the trolley or on commuter railroad lines. This zone of spacious lots and large houses is the growing edge of the city. From here, the rich press outward to avoid the increasing congestion and social heterogeneity brought to their area by an expansion of Zone 4.

Burgess's concentric zone theory represented the American city in a new stage of development. Before the 1870s, an American metropolis, such as New York, was a city of mixed neighborhoods where merchants' stores and sweatshop factories were intermingled with mansions and hovels. Rich and poor, immigrant and native-born rubbed shoulders in the same neighborhoods. However, in Chicago, Burgess's hometown, something else occurred. In 1871, the great Chicago Fire burned out the core of the city, leveling almost one-third of its buildings. As the city was rebuilt, it was influenced by late nineteenth-century market forces: real estate speculation in the suburbs, inner-city industrial development, new streetcar systems, and the need for low-cost working-class housing. The result was a more explicit social patterning than existed in other large cities. Chicago became a segregated city with a concentric pattern working its way out from the downtown in what one scholar called "rings of rising affluence." It was this rebuilt city that Burgess used as the basis for his concentric zone model.

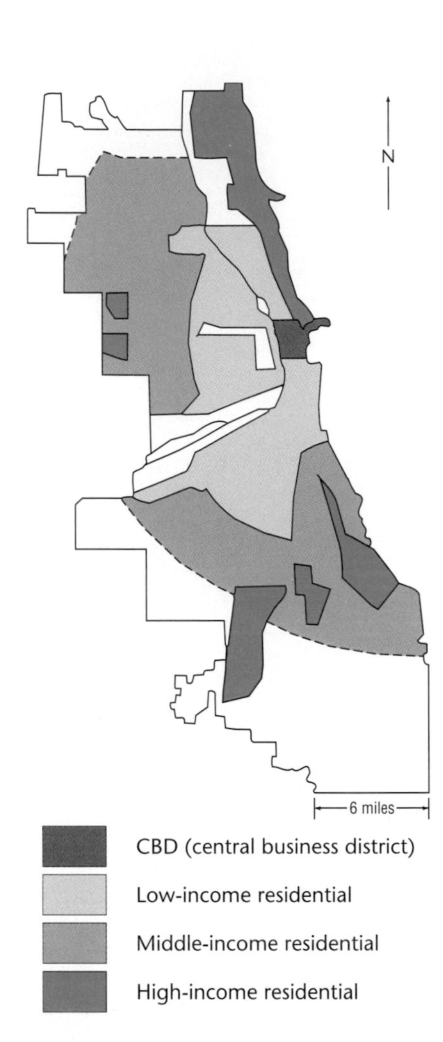

Figure 11.15
Residential areas of Chicago in 1920 were used as the basis for many studies and models of the city. Compare this pattern with the concentric zone and sector models.

However, as you can see from Figure 11.15, the actual residential map of Chicago does not exactly match the simplicity of Burgess's concentric zones. For instance, it is evident that the wealthy continue to monopolize certain high-value sites within the other rings, especially Chicago's "Gold Coast" along Lake Michigan on the north side. According to the concentric zone theory, this area should have been part of the zone of transition. Burgess accounted for certain of these exceptions by noting how the rich tended to monopolize hills, lakes, and shorelines, whether they were close to or far from the CBD. Critics of Burgess's model also were quick to point out that even though portions of each zone did exist in most cities, rarely were they linked in such a way as to totally surround the city. Burgess countered that there were distinct barriers, such as old industrial centers, that prevented the completion of the arc. Still other critics felt that Burgess, as a sociologist, overemphasized residential patterns and did not give proper credit to other land uses—such as industry, manufacturing, and warehouses—in describing the urban mosaic.

Sector Model

Homer Hoyt, an economist who studied housing data for 142 American cities, presented his **sector model** of urban land use in 1939. He maintained that high-rent residential districts ("rent" meaning capital outlay for the occupancy of space, including purchase, lease, or "rent" in the popular sense) were instrumental in shaping the land-use structure of the city. Because these areas were reinforced by transportation routes, the pattern of their development was one of sectors or wedges (Figure 11.16) rather than concentric zones.

Hoyt suggested that the high-rent sector would expand according to four factors. First, a high-rent sector moves from its point of origin near the CBD, along established routes of travel, toward another nu-

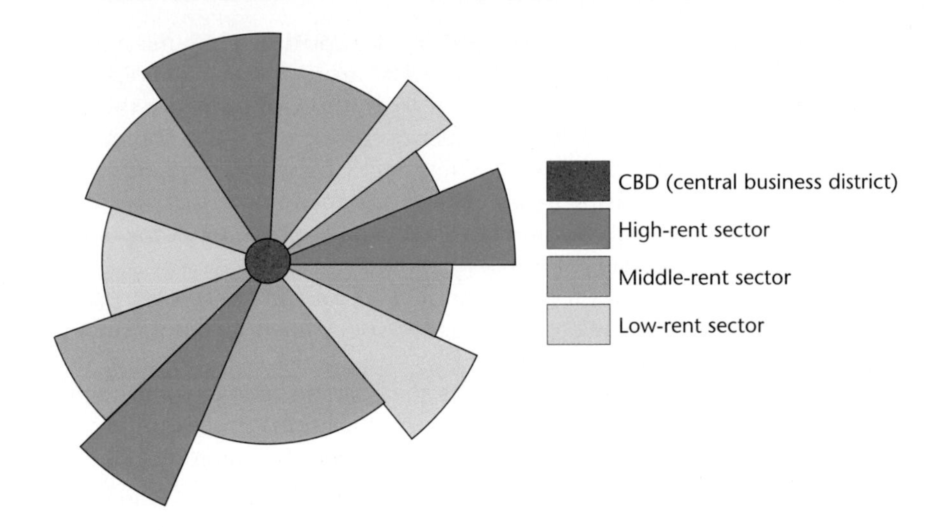

Figure 11.16
The sector model. In this model zones are pie-shaped wedges radiating along main transportation routes.

cleus of high-rent buildings. That is, a high-rent area directly next to the CBD will naturally head in the direction of a high-rent suburb, eventually linking the two in a wedge-shaped sector. Second, a high-rent sector will progress toward high ground or along waterfronts, when these areas are not used for industry. The rich have always preferred such environments for their residences. Third, a high rent sector will move along the route of fastest transportation. Fourth, a high-rent sector will move toward open space. A high-income community rarely moves into an occupied lower-income neighborhood. Instead, the wealthy prefer to build new structures on vacant land where they can control the social environment.

As high-rent sectors develop, the areas between them are filled in. Middle-rent areas move directly next to them, drawing on their prestige. Low-rent areas fill in the remaining areas. Thus, moving away from major routes of travel, rents go from high to low.

There are distinct patterns in today's cities that echo Hoyt's model. He had the advantage over Burgess in that he wrote later in the automobile age and could see the tremendous impact that major thoroughfares were having on cities. However, when we look at today's major transportation arteries—which are generally freeways—we see that the areas surrounding them are often low-rent districts. According to Hoyt's theory, they should be high-rent districts. Freeways are rather recent additions to the city, coming only after World War II. They were imposed on an existing urban pattern. To minimize the economic and political costs of construction, they were often built through low-rent areas, where the costs of land purchase for the rights of way were less and where political opposition was kept to a minimum, since most people living in these low-rent areas had little political clout. This is why so many freeways rip through ethnic ghettos and low-income areas. Economically speaking, this is the least expensive route. This problem will persist until low-income neighborhoods organize effective political resistance against such disturbances.

Multiple Nuclei Model

Both Burgess and Hoyt assumed that a strong central city affected patterns throughout the urban area. However, as the city increasingly decentralized, districts developed that were not directly linked to the CBD. In 1945, two geographers, Chauncey Harris and Edward Ullman, suggested a new model, the **multiple nuclei model.** They maintained that a city developed with equal intensity around various points, or "multiple nuclei" (Figure 11.17). In their eyes, the CBD was not the sole generator of change. Equal weight must be given to an old community on the city outskirts around which new suburban developments clustered; to an industrial district that grew from an original waterfront location; or to a low-income area that began because of some social stigma attached to the site.

Harris and Ullman rooted their model in four geographical principles. First, certain activities require highly specialized facilities, such as accessible transportation for a factory or large areas of open land for a housing tract. The second principle is that certain activities cluster together because they profit from mutual association. For example, car dealers are commonly located near each other because automobiles are very expensive, and people will engage in comparative shopping—moving from one dealer to another until their decisions are made. Third, certain activities repel each other and will not be found in the same area. Examples would be high-rent residences and industrial areas, or slums and expensive retail stores. Fourth, certain activities could not make a profit if they paid the high rent of the most desirable locations. Therefore, they seek lower-rent areas. For example, new-car dealers may like to locate where pedestrian traffic is greatest in order to lure the most people into their showrooms. However, they need great amounts of space for showrooms, storage, service facilities, and used-car lots. Therefore, they cannot afford the high rents that the most accessible locations demand. They compromise by finding an area of lower rent that is still relatively accessible.

The multiple nuclei model, more than the other models, seems to take into account the varied factors of decentralization in the structure of the North American city. Many criticize the concentric zone and sector theories as being rather deterministic, for they emphasize one single factor (residential differentiation in the concentric zone theory or rent in the sector theory) to explain the city. But the multiple nuclei theory encompasses a larger spectrum of economic and social possibilities. Harris and Ullman could probably appreciate the variety of forces working on the city because they did not confine themselves to seeking simply a social or an economic explanation. As geographers, they tried to integrate the disparate elements of culture into a workable model. Most urban scholars agree that they succeeded.

Figure 11.17
The multiple nuclei model. This model was devised to show that the CBD is not the sole force in creating land-use patterns within the city. Rather, land-use districts may evolve for specific reasons at specific points elsewhere in the city, hence the name *multiple nuclei.*

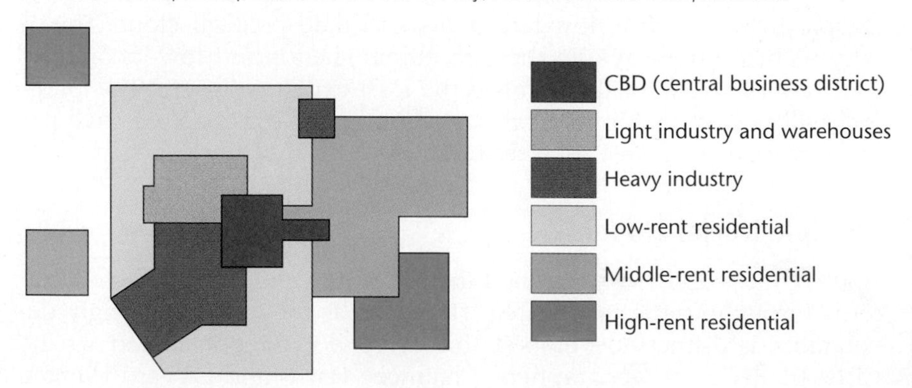

Feminist Critiques

Most of the criticisms of the above models focus on their simplification of reality, or inability to account for all the complexities of urban forms. More recently, feminists in geography have noticed some flaws in the models and in how they were constructed that call into question their descriptive power.

All three of these models assume that urban patterns are shaped by an economic trade-off between, on the one hand, the desire to live in a suburban neighborhood appropriate to one's economic status and, on the other hand, the need to live relatively close to the center city for employment opportunities. These models assume that only one person in the family is a wage worker—the male head. They ignore dual-income families and households headed by single women, who contend with a larger array of factors in making locational decisions, including distances to child care and school facilities and other services important for different members of a family. For many of these households, the traditional urban models that assume a spatial separation of workplace and home are no longer appropriate.

For example, a study of activity patterns of working parents shows that women living in a city have access to a wider array of employment opportunities and are better able to combine domestic and wage labor than are women who live in the suburbs. Many of these middle-class women will choose a gentrified inner-city location to live, hoping that this type of area will offer the amenities of the suburbs (good schools and safety), while also accommodating their activity patterns. Other research has shown that some businesses will locate their offices in the suburbs because they rely on the labor of highly educated, middle class women who are spatially constrained by their domestic work.

When we consider these factors, it becomes apparent that the urban structure described by the traditional models is becoming problematic for most families that now require two real wages to keep pace with the cost of living. The Women and Geography Study Group, a specialty group of the Institute of British Geographers, suggests that these models tend to reflect an urban structure that "results in the isolation of women who do not participate in the urban labour market, and raises problems of timing and organization for those who combine waged and domestic labour." Feminist geographers are currently engaged in rethinking these long-held assumptions about the separation of home from work, and are assessing the implications of such assumptions for urban structure and design.

At a broader level, the traditional models are also criticized for being created by men who shared certain assumptions about how cities operate, and therefore represent a very partial view of urban life. As previously discussed, the concentric zone and sector models were developed by sociologists working in Chicago in the early twentieth century. Geographers David Sibley and Emily Gilbert, however, have brought to our attention the development during the same time of other theories about urban form and structure. These theories incorporated alternative perspectives of female scholars. Drawing on the urban reform work done by Jane Addams at Hull House in Chicago, scholars in the first decades of the twentieth century examined the causes and possible solutions of urban problems. For example, Edith Abbott, Sophonisba Breckinridge, and Helen Rankin Jeter, faculty at the School of Social Service Administration at the University of Chicago, worked with their mostly female students to produce numerous studies about "race," ethnicity, class, and housing in Chicago. These studies differed from those of such theorists as Burgess and Hoyt in several ways. For instance, they emphasized the role of landlords in shaping the housing market, and included an awareness of how racism is related to the allocation of housing and a sensitivity to the different urban experiences of ethnic groups.

The following quote from an essay by Edith Abbott and Mary Zahrobsky highlights their insight into the role of racial discrimination in the housing market:

> *The prejudice among the white people of having Negros living on what they regard jealously as their residence streets and their unwillingness to have Negro children attending schools with white children confines the opportunities for residence open to Negros of all positions of life to relatively small and well-defined areas. Consequently, the demand for houses and apartments within these areas is comparatively steady and, since the landlord is reasonably certain that the house or apartment can be filled at any time, as long as it is in any way tenantable, he takes advantage of his opportunity to raise rents and postpone repairs.*

This summary of why African American communities are faced with limited and often poorly maintained housing is remarkable not only for its intelligent commentary about urban life in the 1920s and 1930s, but also for its application to most urban areas today. For example, a study by urban historian Raymond Mohl chronicles the making of black ghettos in Miami between 1940 and 1960, and his research reveals the role of public policy decisions, landlordism, and discrimination in that process—forces identified by Abbott and others and that continue into the present. It is interesting to consider why the insights gained from the studies of these women have, until recently, been ignored. It is also interesting to speculate on how our knowledge of urban life would have been different if these studies had become part of our accepted urban curriculum.

Latin American Model

The first three models of the city we just discussed were developed out of the North American urban experience. Not to overlook the international component of urban cultural geography, we now turn to models of cities in the developing world.

This is a more complex subject because of the profound influence local cultures have on urban development and form. It is, therefore, difficult to group cities in the developing world into one or two comprehensive models comparable to those formulated from the relatively homogeneous conditions of the United States and Canada. To illustrate cultural integration in cities of the developing world, we draw on a model specific to one region—Latin America—while reminding readers that several other models are applicable to other parts of the developing world.

The Latin American city model is shown in Figure 1.16, in Chapter 1. Refer to the figure as you read this section. This model is a generalized scheme that is both sensitive to local cultures in South America and also articulates the pervasive influence of international forces, both Western and non-Western, as they influence urban structure. This dimension comes through in the description and explanation of each element of the model.

In contrast with contemporary cities in the United States, the CBDs of Latin American cities are vibrant, dynamic, and increasingly specialized. The dominance of the CBD is explained in part by a reliance on public transit that serves the central city and, equally, on the existence of a large and relatively affluent population close to the CBD. Outside of the CBD, the dominant component is a commercial spine surrounded by an elite residential sector. Because these two zones are interrelated, they are referred to as the *spine/sector*. This is essentially an extension of the CBD down a major boulevard, along which are the city's important amenities, such as parks, theaters, restaurants, and even golf courses. Strict zoning and land controls ensure continuation of these activities and protect the elite from incursions by low-income squatters.

Somewhat less prestigious is the inner-city *zone of maturity*, a collection of traditional colonial homes and upgraded self-built homes occupied by people unable to participate in the spine/sector. This is an area of upward mobility. The *zone of accretion* is a diverse collection of housing types, sizes, and quality, which can be thought of as a transition between the zone of maturity and the next zone. It is an area of ongoing construction and change, emblematic of the explosive population growth that characterizes the Latin American city. While some neighborhoods within this zone have city-provided utilities, other blocks must rely on water and butane delivery trucks for essential services.

The most recent migrants to the Latin American city are found in the *zone of peripheral squatter settlements*. This fringe of poor people and inadequate housing contrasts dramatically with the affluent and comfortable suburbs that ring North American cities. Squatter houses are often built from scavenged materials, and the appearance of these areas is that of a refugee camp, surrounded by a landscape bare of vegetation that was cut for fuel and building materials. Streets are unpaved and open trenches carry wastes; residents carry water from long distances, and electricity is often "pirated" by attaching illegal wires to the closest utility pole. If residents have work, their commute is a long one that consumes much of the day. Although this zone's quality of life seems marginal, many squatter settlements are transformed through time by their residents into permanent neighborhoods with minimal amenities.

In concluding this section, we again remind you of both the assets and the liabilities of these models of urban structure. There is a delicate and sometimes dangerous balance between compressing vast and varied information into generalizations, for much information must, by definition, be suppressed. For cultural geographers who celebrate the cultural distinctiveness of places and people, this is often an uncomfortable compromise—and yet, we must start somewhere. These four urban models offer a beginning.

Urban Landscapes

Cities, like all places inhabited by humans, demonstrate an intriguing array of cultural landscapes that give varied insights into the complicated interactions between people and their surroundings. By reading

Figure 11.18
Boston's central city. There are various ways of looking at cityscapes: as indicators of change, as palimpsests, as expressions of visual biases, and as manifestations of symbolic traditions. This photo offers evidence for all approaches. Which clues would you select to illustrate each cityscape theme?

these cityscapes, we gain access to the past, open doors on the future, and better understand the different social forces shaping our settlements. Grady Clay, in his enchanting book on reading American cityscapes, says:

> *No true secrets are lurking in the landscape, but only undisclosed evidence, waiting for us. No true chaos is in the urban scene, but only patterns and clues waiting to be organized.*

We agree. In this section we offer some thoughts on how to view North American urban landscapes. We begin by discussing some themes—geographical reference points, one might say, for investigating cityscapes. This is followed by a brief discussion of the new components in urban landscapes. Much of what we say will strike a familiar chord because our urban scene is the basis of so much of our life. You will find that you have great depths of intuitive knowledge about cityscapes.

Themes in Cityscape Study

Cultural geographers look to cityscapes for many different kinds of information. Here we discuss four interconnected themes that are commonly used as organizational themes for landscape research (Figure 11.18).

Landscape Dynamics. Because North Americans are a restless people with little remorse about incessantly reshaping environments, our settlements are cauldrons of change. Think of some familiar indicators in the cityscape: downtown activities creeping into residential areas; deteriorated farmland on the city's outskirts; older buildings demolished for the new. These are all signs of specific processes effecting urban change; the landscape faithfully reflects this dynamic.

When these visual clues are systematically mapped and analyzed, they offer evidence for the currents of change expressed in our cities. Of equal interest is to note where change is not occurring: those parts of the city where, for different reasons, the city remains relatively static. An unchanging landscape also conveys an important message. Perhaps that part of the city is stagnant because it is removed from those forces effecting change in other parts. Or perhaps there is a conscious attempt by local residents to inhibit change, to preserve open space by resisting suburban development, for example, or by preserving a historic landmark.

In summary, look to the landscape to understand how our cities are changing. Not only is it where change first appears, but documenting landscape changes through time gives valuable insight into the paths of settlement development.

The City as Palimpsest. Because cityscapes change, they offer a rich field for uncovering remnants of the past. A **palimpsest** is an old parchment used over and over for written messages. Before a new missive could be written, the old was erased; yet rarely were all the previous characters and words completely obliterated, so remnants of earlier messages showed through. This mosaic of old and new is called a palimpsest, a word geographers use fondly to describe the visual mixture of old and new in cultural landscapes.

The city is full of palimpsestic offerings, scattered across the contemporary landscape. How often have you noticed an old Victorian farmhouse surrounded by new tract homes, or a historic street pattern obscured by a recent urban redevelopment project, or a brick factory shadowed by new high-rise office buildings? All of these give clues to past settlement patterns, and all are mute testimony to the processes of change in the city.

Our interest in this historical mosaic is more than romantic nostalgia. A systematic collection of these urban remnants provides us with glimpses of the past that might otherwise be hidden. All societies pick and choose what they wish to preserve for future generations and, in this process, a filtering takes place that often excludes and distorts information. But the landscape does not lie.

The urban palimpsest, then, is a way of finding the past in the contemporary landscape, of evaluating these remnants so as to glean a better understanding of historical settlement.

Symbolic Cityscapes. Landscapes contain much more than literal messages about economic function. They are also loaded with figurative or metaphorical meaning, highly subjectivized emotion, memories, and content essential to the social fabric. To some, skyscrapers are more than high-rise office buildings: They are symbols of progress, economic vitality, downtown renewal, or corporate identities. Similarly, historical landscapes, those parts of the city where the past has been preserved, help people define themselves in time, establish social continuity with the past, and codify a forgotten, yet sometimes idealized, past.

D. W. Meinig, a geographer who has given much thought to these landscapes, maintains that there are three highly symbolized townscapes in the United States. They are the New England village, with its white church, commons, and tree-lined neighborhoods (Figure 11.19); Main Street of Middle America, the string street of a small midwestern town, with storefronts, bandstand, and park; and what Meinig calls Cal-

Figure 11.19
A view of Royalton, Vermont. This view of a New England village strikes a familiar chord for most of us because the landscape has become a symbol with diverse meanings. Think of the ways this symbol is used in art, literature, film, and television, and of the messages and emotion conveyed by this landscape.

ifornia Suburbia, suburbs of quarter-acre lots, effusive garden landscaping, swimming pools, and ranch-style homes.

> *Each is based upon an actual landscape of a particular region. Each is an image derived from our national experience . . . simplified . . . and widely advertised so as to become a commonly understood symbol. Each has . . . influenced the shaping of the American scene over broader areas.*

In a more political and problematic sense, the cultural landscape is an important vehicle for constructing and maintaining social and ethnic distinctions. This is often done in subtle and implicit ways that are intertwined with landscape symbols. To illustrate, geographers Jim and Nancy Duncan found that because conspicuous consumption is a major means for conveying social identity in our culture, elite landscapes are created and preserved through large-lot zoning, imitation country estates, and a constellation of detailed ornamental iconography. They see the residential landscapes in upper-income areas as controlled and managed in order to reinforce class and status categories. Their study of elite suburbs near Vancouver and New York sensitizes us to how the cultural landscape can be thought of as a repository of symbols used by our society to differentiate itself and protect vested interests.

Cultural geographers are interested in how townscapes and landmarks take on symbolic significance and whether these idealizations are based on some sort of reality or, instead, are fabricated from diverse predilections. In addition, they are interested in how to assess the impact of these symbolic landscapes. After all, the hidden and shared messages inherent in loaded landscapes usually determine how we treat our environment: how it is managed, changed, or protected.

Perception of the City. During the last 20 years, social scientists have been concerned with measuring people's perceptions of the urban landscape. They assume that if we really know what people see and react to in the city, we can ask architects and urban planners to design and create a more humane urban environment.

Kevin Lynch, an urban designer, pioneered a method for recording people's images of the city. He assumed that all people have a mental map. After all, they must find their way about their cities in the course of daily life. Lynch then figured out ways that people could convey their mental maps to others. With this information, he could discover which parts of the urban landscape are being used as visual clues by which people. What do people react favorably or negatively to? What do they block out?

On the basis of interviews conducted in Boston, Jersey City, and Los Angeles, Lynch suggested five important elements in mental maps of cities:

1. *Pathways* are the routes of frequent travel, such as streets, freeways, and transit corridors. We experience the city from the pathways. Therefore, they become the threads that hold our maps together.
2. *Edges* are boundaries between areas, or the outer limits of our image. Mountains, rivers, shorelines, and even major streets and freeways are commonly used as edges. They tend to define the extremes of our urban vision; then we fill in the details.
3. *Nodes* are strategic junction points, such as breaks in transportation,

traffic circles, or any place where important pathways come together.

4. *Districts* are small areas with a common identity, such as ethnic areas and functional zones (for instance, the CBD or a row of car dealers).
5. *Landmarks* are reference points that stand out because of shape, height, color, or historical importance. The city hall in Los Angeles, the Washington Monument in Washington, DC, or the golden arches of a McDonald's are all landmarks.

Using these concepts, Lynch saw that some parts of the cities were more **legible,** or easy to decipher, than others. Overall, Lynch discovered, legibility comes when the urban landscape offers clear pathways, nodes, districts, edges, and landmarks. The less legible parts of the city do not offer such a precise landscape. Thus it is more difficult for a person to form a mental map of that area. And further, some cities are more legible than other cities. For example, Lynch found that Jersey City is a city of low legibility. Wedged between New York City and Newark, Jersey City is fragmented by railroads and highways. Residents' mental maps of Jersey City have large blank areas in them. When questioned, they can think of few local landmarks. Instead, they tend to point to the New York City skyline just across the river.

There are also distinct ethnic, gender, and age variables to mental maps of cities. These differences often influence everyday behavior. For example, both men and women share a perceived risk of crime that alters their behavior. Women, however, are particularly vulnerable to rape, and studies have documented how such vulnerability results in women engaging in more precautionary behavior than men. Women tend to avoid certain areas of a city at night, and many will even forgo activities that will require them to be out alone at night in their own neighborhoods. Although recent studies have shown that many of the reported cases of violence against women, including rape, occur within the home, the perception that particular areas of the city are dangerous continues to alter women's experiences of the urban environment.

The New Urban Landscape

Within the past 25 to 30 years, our cityscapes have undergone massive transformations. The impact of suburbanization and decentralization has led to an emerging new urban form that we have called the edge city (see Chapter 10). In the older downtown areas, we have seen that gentrification and redevelopment have also created novel urban forms. What we see emerging in our cityscapes, then, is a new urban landscape, composed of distinctive elements that we have not yet discussed.

Shopping Malls. Many people consider the image of the shopping mall, surrounded by mass-produced suburbs, as one of the most distinctive landscape symbols of post–World War II life in North America. Yet, oddly, most malls are not designed to be seen from the outside. As a matter of fact, without appropriate signs, a passerby could proceed past a mall without noticing any visual display. Unlike the retail districts of nineteenth- and early twentieth-century cities, where grand architectural displays along the major boulevards were the norm, shopping malls are enclosed, private worlds that are meant to be seen from the inside. Often located near an off-ramp of a major freeway or beltway of a metropolitan area, and close to the middle- and upper-class residential neighborhoods, shopping malls can be distinguished more by their extensive parking lots than by their architectural design.

Yet shopping malls do have a characteristic form. The early malls of the 1960s tended to be a simple, linear form, with 2 department stores at each end that functioned as "anchors," and 20 to 30 smaller shops connecting the two ends. In the 1970s and 1980s, much larger malls were built, and their form became more complex.

Malls today are often several stories high and may contain 5 or 6 anchor stores, and up to 400 smaller shops. In addition, many malls now serve more than a retail function—they often contain food courts and restaurants, professional offices, movie complexes, hotels, chapels, and amusement arcades and centers (Figure 11.20). The Mall of America in Bloomington, Minnesota, is said to be the largest mall in the world, covering 4.2 million square feet and containing, in addition to retailers, 14 movie screens, 6 supper clubs, and a 7-acre amusement park. Many scholars consider these mega-malls as America's new main streets (see box, *The Shopping Mall as Social Center*, and Chapter 9) because they seem to be the major site for social interaction. After workplace and home, the shopping mall is where most Americans spend their time.

However, unlike the open-air marketplaces of an earlier era, shopping malls are private spaces, not public spaces. The use of the shopping mall as a place for social interaction, therefore, is always of secondary importance to its private, commercial function. If a certain group of people were considered a nuisance to shoppers, the mall owners could prevent them from what Jeffrey Hopkins calls "'mallingering'—the act of lingering about a mall for economic and non-economic social purposes."

Figure 11.20
Food court at the Fashion Mall in Plantation, Florida. A large percentage of the third story of this mall is devoted to fast-food outlets. The fountain and natural lighting are meant to create a garden-like setting for mall dining.

The Shopping Mall as Social Center: "Mallingering" and Consuming at the West Edmonton Mall (WEM)

The role of WEM as a social centre cannot be divorced from the popularity of shopping centres in our consumer society. The popularity of 'mallingering'—the act of lingering about a mall for economic and non-economic social purposes—can be partly attributed to the rapid proliferation of shopping centres during the economic and demographic booms of the post–World War II era and the ensuing rise in consumerism as a way of life. In an age in which consumerism is the dominant lifestyle and material consumption is a popular life objective, shopping malls—the dominant forum for commerce—become the principal forum for consumption and, thus, a popular place to spend money as well as time.

A more tempered explanation of mallingering considers the secondary social and recreational roles associated with retailing. The marketplace has traditionally played the role of communal meeting place. Given the latent social function of the marketplace in general and the congregative and community role of shopping malls in particular, WEM is not merely a mega-shopping mall, nor a mega-recreation centre, but a mega *social* centre, which is claimed to bring together as many as 60,000 people per day from Edmonton and around the world. When placed in the context of the traditional role of the marketplace and the cultural context of consumerism and mallingering, WEM's popularity as a social centre is not surprising. The formal introduction of social activities (e.g., leisure and entertainment facilities) into a shopping centre is more a confirmation of the social role of the marketplace than it is a novel marketing ploy. The socially congregative pull—'the sociopetal' factors—exerted by WEM's size, scale, and leisure facilities, however, renders the mega-mall functionally and socially unique relative to other shopping malls. The fact that social interaction is under the control of a single corporation, like most indoor urban space, makes understanding the freedoms and constraints—the socially divisive or 'sociofugal' factors—imposed upon patrons by WEM's physical design and operation all the more pertinent.

Theatres Of Consumption

To suggest that shopping malls are manipulating wizards able to induce unsuspecting patrons into money-spending frenzies or irrational purchases not only insults the public's intelligence but also pays unwarranted homage to mall designers and management. There is growing recognition, nonetheless, that physical design and atmosphere are important factors influencing customer behaviour. Shopping malls in this latter sense are literally theatres of consumption staged within a carefully contrived set designed to promote retail drama. 'Enclosure, protection and control' is the basic design formula, and organized 'happenings' assist in promoting an exciting, friendly atmosphere. Herein lie factors that may promote and retard social interaction at WEM.

The mega-mall (indeed most shopping malls and indoor space) offers a pleasant alternative to some of the discomforts of the world outside. *Enclosure* provides freedom from climatic extremes, clear signage, ease of mobility, and access to hundreds of stores and services. Pay telephones, plants, statues, fountains, washroom facilities, and benches further contribute to the value of WEM as a social centre. The many and varied sights and objects in the corridors promote 'triangulation,' whereby external stimuli may provide links between people and prompt strangers to talk to one another. A combination of sophisticated electronic security systems and uniformed and plain-clothes personnel ensures, according to the management, 'a safe and secure atmosphere for [the] entire family' (WEM security brochure). No city street can as yet match the 24-hour *protection* provided by 480 computer-monitored security points, 1600 fire detectors, 42 strategically placed 'help phones,' and hidden cameras that 'keep an eye on 38 locations throughout WEM at the same time' (WEM security brochure). *Control* is, therefore, a key ingredient in the success of WEM; its environment can more easily conform to the tastes, needs, and preferences of patrons, as perceived by mall management, than, say, a city street of independent shop-owners.

Taken from Hopkins, Jeffrey S. P. "West Edmonton Mall as a Centre for Social Interaction." *The Canadian Geographer,* 35 (1991): 269–270. Reprinted by permission of The Canadian Association of Geographers.

Office Parks. With major interstates connecting our metropolitan areas, and the development of new communication technologies, office buildings no longer need to be located in the center city. Cheaper rent in suburban locations, combined with the convenience of easy-access parking and the privacy of a separate location, have led to the construction of **office parks** throughout suburban America. Figure 11.21 shows the location of office parks in metropolitan Atlanta in relation to the freeway network. Many of these office parks are occupied by regional and national headquarters of large corporations or by local sales and professional offices. To take advantage of economies of scale, many of these offices will locate together and rent or buy space from a land development company.

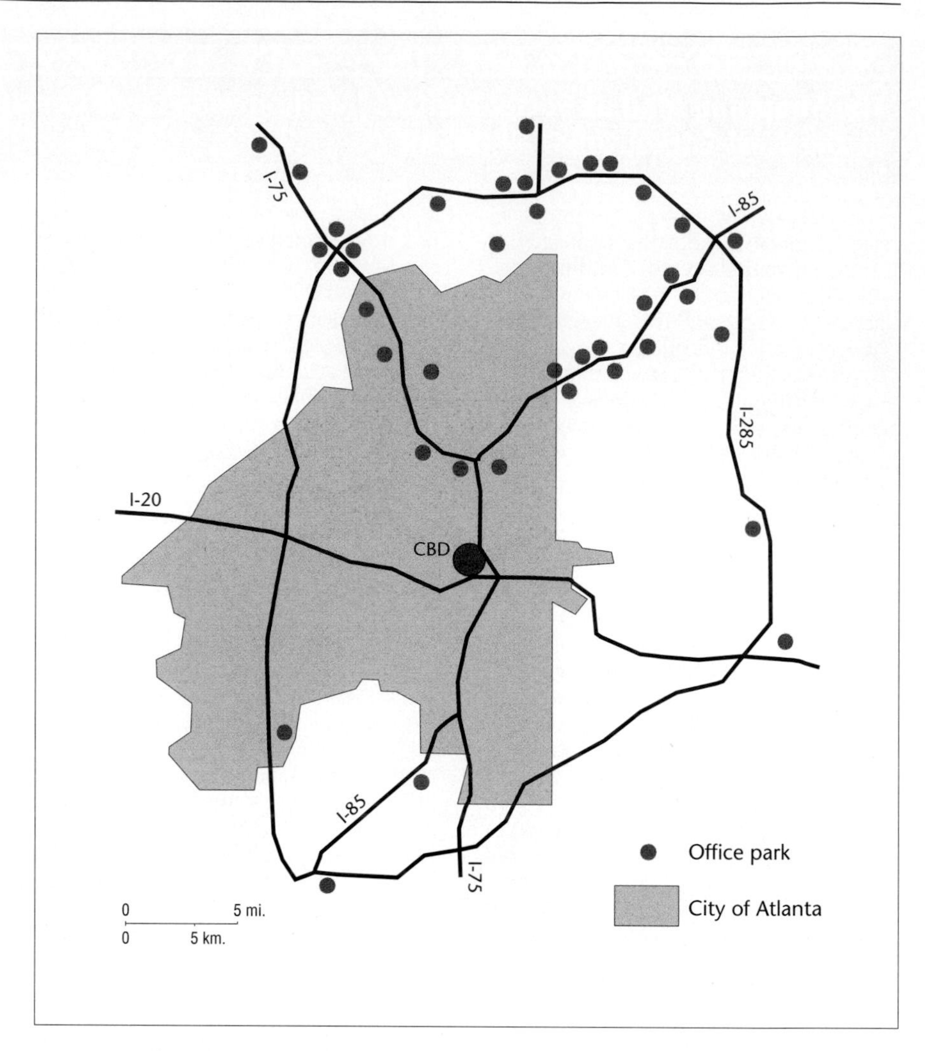

Figure 11.21
Office park locations in Atlanta, Georgia. This map clearly shows their locational ties to major freeways. (Hartshorn, Truman A., and Peter O. Muller. "Suburban Downtowns and the Transformation of Metropolitan Atlanta's Business Landscape." *Urban Geography,* 10 [1989]: 375–395.)

The use of the term *park* to identify this new landscape element points to the conscious antiurban imagery of these complexes. In contrast to downtown skyscrapers, office parks tend to be horizontal in shape, usually three to six stories tall. Many of these developments are surrounded by a well-landscaped outdoor space, often incorporating human-made lakes and waterfalls (see Figure 11.22). Jogging paths, fitness trails, and picnic tables all cater to the new lifestyle of professional and managerial employees.

Although providing numerous conveniences for employees, office parks do remove workers from the social diversity of an urban location. Lunchtime choices are usually limited to the corporate cafeteria, while the inclusion into the office complex of such nonessential functions as fitness centers indicates the often-intrusive role of the corporation in workers' social lives. Many office parks are located along what have been called **high-tech corridors,** areas along limited-access highways that contain offices and other services associated with new high-tech industries. Paul Knox suggests that these corridors differ from the small-

Figure 11.22
Compare this suburban office building in Yonkers, New York, with your image of downtown skyscrapers. Notice the green-space around the building and its horizontal rather than vertical appearance.

scale in-filling that has taken place on many commercial strips. According to Knox, high-tech corridors "are set on a framework of large lots, usually several acres, and include large-scale structures, extensive on-site parking, generous amounts of landscaped parkland (including waterfalls, lagoons, terraces, gazebos, and sculptures), and a variety of services and amenities such as fitness centers, cycling trails, coffee shops, flower shops and day care facilities." As our discussion of edge cities suggests (see Chapter 10), this new type of commercial landscape is gradually replacing our downtowns as the workplace for most Americans.

Master-Planned Communities. Many of our newer residential developments on the suburban fringe are planned and built as complete neighborhoods by a private development company. These **master-planned communities** include not only architecturally compatible housing units but also recreational facilities (such as tennis courts, fitness centers, bike paths, and swimming pools) and security measures (gated or guarded entrances). Paul Knox points out that most of these communities exploit various land-use restrictions and zoning regulations to maintain control over land values, and that homes in these communities maintain their value better than homes elsewhere.

In Weston, a master-planned community that covers approximately 10,000 acres in south Florida, land use is completely regulated not only within the gated residential complexes but also along the road system that connects Weston to the interstate. Shrubbery is planted strategically to shield residents from views of the roadway, the signs are uniform in style, and the road signs are all encased in stylish, weathered-gray wood frame (Figure 11.23). This massive community—Weston developers estimate that the community will be home to 60,000 people when it is completed in 2005—contains different complexes catering to particular lifestyles, ranging from smaller patio homes to equestrian estates.

Figure 11.23
The master-planned community of Weston, Florida. These automated gates keep "undesirables" out of many subdivisions in master-planned communities. The more expensive areas have guardhouses at their entrance, while less expensive ones may have privately installed security systems.

For example, homes in Tequesta Point cost between $250,000 and $300,000, and they come with gated entranceways, split floor plans, and Roman bathtubs. Those in Bermuda Springs, on the other hand, fall in the $115,000 to $120,000 price range, are significantly smaller, and do not offer the same interior features. Typical of master-planned communities, the name of the development itself was chosen to convey a certain image of hometown life. In this instance, developers carried out an extensive marketing survey before they settled on the name Weston.

Festival Settings. In many cities, gentrification efforts focus on a multi-use redevelopment scheme that is built around a particular setting, often one with historical association. Waterfronts are commonly chosen as focal points for these large-scale projects that Knox has referred to as **festival settings.** These complexes integrate retailing, office, and entertainment activities, and incorporate trendy shops, restaurants, bars and nightclubs, and hotels. Knox suggests that these developments are "distinctive as new landscape elements merely because of their scale and their consequent ability to stage—or merely to be—the spectacular." Such festival settings as Faneuil Hall in Boston, Bayside in Miami, and Riverwalk in San Antonio serve as sites for concerts, ethnic festivals and street performances, and also as focal points for the more informal human interactions that we usually associate with urban life (Figure 11.24). In this sense, these festival settings do perform a vital function in the attempt to revitalize our downtowns. Yet, like many other gentrification efforts, these massive displays of wealth and consumption often stand in direct contrast to neighboring areas of the inner city that have received little, if any, monetary or other social benefit from these projects.

"Militarized" Space. Considered together, these new elements in the urban landscape suggest some trends that many scholars find disturbing. Urbanist Mike Davis has called one such trend the "militarization" of ur-

Figure 11.24
Quincy Market, an early-nineteenth century wholesale market near Faneuil Hall in Boston. The market is recreated as a festival setting, complete with upscale shops, restaurants and bars.

ban space, meaning the increasing use of space to set up defenses against elements of the city considered undesirable. This includes landscape developments that range from the lack of street furniture to guard against the homeless living on the streets, to gated and guarded residential communities, to the complete segregation of classes and "races" within the city. This seems particularly true in downtown redevelopment schemes, where the goal of city planners and others is usually to provide safe and homogeneous environments, segregated from the diversity of cultures and lifestyles that often characterizes the central area of most cities. As Davis says, "cities of all sizes are rushing to apply and profit from a formula that links together clustered development, social homogeneity, and a perception of security." Although this "militarization" is not completely new to the late twentieth century, it has taken on epic proportions as whole sections of cities like Los Angeles, Atlanta, Dallas, Houston, and Miami have become "militarized" spaces (Figure 11.25).

Decline of Public Space. Related to the increase in "militarized" space is the decline of public spaces in most of our cities. For example, the change in shopping patterns from the downtown retailing area to the suburban shopping malls that was noted earlier indicates a change of emphasis from the publicness of city streets to the privately controlled and operated shopping malls. Similarly, many city governments, often joined with private developers, have built enclosed walkways, either above or below the city streets. These serve partly to provide climate-controlled conditions and partly to provide pedestrians with a "safe" environment that avoids the possible confrontations on the street. Again, the publicness of the street is being replaced by controlled spaces that do not provide the same access to all members of the urban community. It remains to be seen whether this trend will continue, or

Figure 11.25
The Metro Dade Cultural Center in downtown Miami. Inside this literal fortress is the Dade County's public library and Center for the Fine Arts. The building was designed to be completely removed from the street, with the few entrances heavily monitored with cameras.

whether new public spaces will be formed that will allow for the expression of all groups of people within the urban landscape.

Conclusion

We have examined various components of the intricate urban mosaic. Culture regions are found at a smaller scale than previously explored; in the city, neighborhoods and census units can be thought of as social regions and culture regions.

We also see two major forces at work in the city that can be conceptualized as diffusion processes. One works to centralize activities within the city, the other to decentralize different activities into the suburbs. The latter is the dominant force currently at work in North American cities. But the costs of decentralization run high, not just to the suburbs, where unplanned growth takes its toll, but also to the inner cities, which are left with decayed and stagnant cores.

The cultural ecology of the city is a complicated issue because urbanization has modified natural ecosystems in a profound manner. Feedback from these systems, as in the form of floods, is a significant concern to urban dwellers everywhere. Urban vegetation can mitigate many of these problems if properly managed, yet that becomes an issue of public values, of weighing benefits against costs.

Models of the internal structure of cities describe how social and economic activities sort themselves out in space. The simplification of these models, and their reliance on only one form of urban knowledge, calls into question their usefulness for describing the contemporary city.

As a dense expression of human artifacts, cities offer a fascinating array of cultural landscapes that tell us much about ourselves and our interaction with the environment. These cityscapes tell us about contemporary change, the past, our scenic values, and our symbolic storehouse. New elements in the urban landscape relay information concerning our contemporary social, economic, and political reality, and indicate trends for the future that many scholars find disturbing.

Sources and Suggested Readings

Abbott, Edith, and Mary Zahrobsky. "The Tenement Areas and the People of the Tenements," in E. Abbott (ed.), *The Tenements of Chicago*. Chicago: Chicago Univ. Press, 1936, pp. 72–169.

Adams, John S. (ed.). *Contemporary Metropolitan American*. Cambridge, MA: Ballinger, 1976.

Adams, John S. "The Geography of Riots and Civil Disorders in the 1960's." *Economic Geography*, 67 (January 1972): 24–42.

Agnew, John, John Mercer, and David Sopher (eds.). *The City in Cultural Context*. Boston: Allen & Unwin, 1984.

Anderson, Kay. "The Idea of Chinatown: The Power of Place and Institutional Practice in the Making of a Racial Category." *Annals of the Association of American Geographers*, 77 (1987): 580–598.

Bach, Wilfrid, and Thomas Hagedorn. "Atmospheric Pollution: Its Spatial Distribution over an Urban Area." *Proceedings of the Association of American Geographers*, 3 (1971): 22.

Beauregard, Robert A. *Voices of Decline: The Postwar Fate of US Cities*. Cambridge, MA: Blackwell Publishers, 1993.

Bell, David, and Gill Valentine (eds.). *Mapping Desire: Geographies of Sexualities*. London: Routledge, 1995.

Berry, Brian. *Comparative Urbanization*. New York: St. Martin's Press, 1982.

Berry, Brian J. *The Human Consequences of Urbanization*. New York: St. Martin's Press, 1973.

Brunn, Stanley, and Jack Williams (eds.). *Cities of the World: World Regional Urban Development*. New York: Harper & Row, 1983.

Burnett, Pat. "Social Change, the Status of Women and Models of City Form and Development." *Antipode*, 5 (1973): 57–62.

Castells, Manuel. *The City and Grassroots: A Cross-Cultural Theory of Urban Social Movements*. Berkeley: University of California Press, 1983.

Chandler, T. J. "The Changing Form of London's Heat Island." *Geography*, 46 (1961), pp. 295–307.

Chauncey, George. *Gay New York: Gender, Urban Culture, and the Making of the Gay Male World, 1890–1940*. New York: Basic Books, 1994.

Clay, Grady. *Close-Up: How to Read the American City*. New York: Praeger, 1973.

Conzen, Michael P. "American Cities in Profound Transition: The New City Geography of the 1980s." *Journal of Geography*, 82 (1983): 94–101.

Cybriwsky, Roman. "Social Aspects of Neighborhood Change." *Annals of the Association of American Geographers*, 9 (1983): 99–109.

Cybriwsky, Roman A., David Ley, and John Western. "The Political and Social Construction of Revitalized Neighborhoods: Society Hill, Philadelphia, and False Creek, Vancouver," in Neil Smith and Peter Williams (eds.), *Gentrification of the City*. Boston: Allen & Unwin, 1986, pp. 92–120.

Davis, Mike. *City of Quartz: Excavating the Future in Los Angeles*. New York: Verso, 1990.

Davis, Mike. "Fortress Los Angeles: The Militarization of Urban Space," in Michael Sorkin (ed.), *Variations on a Theme Park: The New American City and the End of Public Space*. New York: Noonday Press, 1992, pp. 154–180.

Detwyler, Thomas, and Melvin Marcus (eds.). *Urbanization and Environment: The Physical Geography of the City*. Belmont, CA: Duxbury Press, 1972.

Drakakis-Smith, David. *The Third World City*. London: Methuen, 1987.

Duncan, James. "Review of Urban Imagery: Urban Semiotics." *Urban Geography*, 8 (1987): 473–483.

Duncan, James, and Nancy Duncan. "A Cultural Analysis of Urban Residential Landscapes in North America: The Case of the Anglophile Élite," in John Agnew, John Mercer, and David Sopher (eds.), *The City in Cultural Context*. Boston: Allen & Unwin, 1984, pp. 255–276.

Fusch, Richard, and Larry Ford. "Architecture and the Geography of the American City." *Geographical Review*, 73 (1983): 460–471.

Gilbert, Emily. "Naturalist Metaphors in the Literatures of Chicago, 1893–1925." *Journal of Historical Geography*, 20 (1994): 283–304.

Godfrey, Brian. *Neighborhoods in Transition: The Making of San Francisco's Ethnic and Nonconformist Communities.* Berkeley: University of California Press, 1988.

Gordon, Margaret T., et al. "Crime, Women, and the Quality of Urban Life," in Catherine R. Stimpson, Elsa Dixler, Martha J. Nelson, and Kathryn B. Yatrakis (eds.), *Women and the American City.* Chicago: University of Chicago Press, 1981, pp. 141–157.

Griffin, Ernst, and Larry Ford. "Cities of Latin America," in Stanley Brunn and Jack Williams (eds.), *Cities of the World: World Regional Urban Development.* New York: Harper & Row, 1983, pp. 199–240.

Hart, John Fraser. "The Bypass Strip as an Ideal Landscape." *Geographical Review,* 72 (1982): 218–222.

Hartshorn, Truman A., and Peter O. Muller. "Suburban Downtowns and the Transformation of Metropolitan Atlanta's Business Landscape." *Urban Geography,* 10 (1989): 375–395.

Hodge, Gerald, and M. A. Qadeer. "The Persistence of Canadian Towns and Villages: Small Is Viable." *Urban Geography,* 1 (1980): 335–349.

Hopkins, George (ed.). *Proceedings of the National Urban Forestry Conference.* Syracuse: State University of New York, 1980.

Hopkins, Jeffrey S. P. "West Edmonton Mall as a Centre for Social Interaction." *The Canadian Geographer,* 35 (1991): 268–279.

Hoyt, Homer. (ed.). *Structure and Growth of Residential Neighborhoods in American Cities.* Washington, DC: Federal Housing Administration, 1939.

Jackson, J. B. *Discovering the Vernacular Landscape.* New Haven, CT: Yale University Press, 1985.

Jackson, J. B. *The Necessity for Ruins and Other Topics.* Amherst: University of Massachusetts Press, 1980.

Jackson, Kenneth T. *Crabgrass Frontier.* New York: Oxford University Press, 1985.

Johnston, James H. (ed.). *Suburban Growth: Geographical Processes at the Edge of the City.* New York: John Wiley, 1974.

Johnston, R. J. *The American Urban System: A Geographical Perspective.* London: Longman, 1982.

Johnston, R. J., and D. T. Herbert. *Social Areas in Cities.* 2 vols. New York: John Wiley, 1976.

Knopp, Lawrence. "Sexuality and Urban Space: A Framework for Analysis," in David Bell and Gill Valentine (eds.), *Mapping Desire.* London: Routledge, 1995, pp. 149–161.

Knox, Paul. "Symbolism, Styles, and Settings." *Architecture and Behavior,* 2 (1984): 107–122.

Knox, Paul L. "The Restless Urban Landscape: Economic and Sociocultural Change and the Transformation of Metropolitan Washington, DC." *Annals of the Association of American Geographers,* 81 (1991): 181–209.

Lanegran, David. "Enhancing and Using a Sense of Place Within Urban Areas: A Role for Applied Cultural Geography." *The Professional Geographer,* 38 (1986): 224–228.

Lauria, Mickey, and Lawrence Knopp. "Toward an Analysis of the Role of Gay Communities in the Urban Renaissance." *Urban Geography,* 6 (1985): 152–169.

Lewis, Peirce. "Learning from Looking: Geographic and Other Writing About the American Cultural Landscape." *American Quarterly,* 35 (1983): 242–261.

Ley, David. *A Social Geography of the City.* New York: Harper & Row, 1983.

Ley, David. "Styles of the Times: Liberal and Neo-Conservative Landscapes in Inner Vancouver, 1968–1986." *Journal of Historical Geography,* 13 (1987): 40–56.

Lloyd, William J. "Understanding Late Nineteenth-Century Cities." *Geographical Review,* 71 (1981): 460–471.

Lynch, Kevin. *The Image of the City.* Cambridge, MA: MIT Press, 1960.

MacDonald, K. "The Commercial Strip: From Main Street to Television Road." *Landscape,* 28 (1985): 12–19.

McCann, L. D. (ed.). *A Geography of Canada: Heartland and Hinterland,* 2nd ed. Englewood Cliffs, NJ: Prentice-Hall, 1987.

McDowell, Linda. "Towards an Understanding of the Gender Division of Urban Space." *Environment and Planning D: Society and Space,* 1 (1983): 59–72.

Meinig, D. W. (ed.). *The Interpretation of Ordinary Landscapes: Geographical Essays*. New York: Oxford University Press, 1979.

Mohl, Raymond A. "Making the Second Ghetto in Metropolitan Miami, 1940–1960." *Journal of Urban History*, 21 (1995): 395–427.

Morrison, Peter A. "Urban Growth and Decline: San Jose and St. Louis in the 1960's." *Science*, 185 (August 1974): 757–762.

Mumford, Lewis. *The City in History*. New York: Harcourt Brace Jovanovich, 1960.

Nelson, Howard. "The Form and Structure of Cities: Urban Growth Patterns." *Journal of Geography*, 68 (1969): 198–207.

Palm, Risa. "Reconsidering Contemporary Neighborhoods." *Landscape*, 26 (1982): 17–20.

Pratt, Geraldine. "Feminist Analyses of the Restructuring of Urban Life." *Urban Geography*, 11 (1990): 594–605.

Relph, Edward. *The Modern Urban Landscape, 1880 to the Present*. Baltimore: Johns Hopkins University Press, 1987.

Rothenberg, Tamar. "'And She Told Two Friends': Lesbians Creating Urban Social Space," in David Bell and Gill Valentine (eds.), *Mapping Desire*. London: Routledge, 1995, pp. 165–181.

Rowe, Stacy, and Jennifer Wolch. "Social Networks in Time and Space: Homeless Women in Skid Row, Los Angeles." *Annals of the Association of American Geographers*, 80 (1990): 184–204.

Rowntree, Lester. "Creating a Sense of Place." *Journal of Urban History*, 8 (1981): 61–76.

Rowntree, Lester, and Margaret W. Conkey. "Symbolism and the Cultural Landscape." *Annals of the Association of American Geographers*, 70 (1980): 459–474.

Salter, Christopher L. "What Geographers See." *Journal of Geography*, 82 (1983): 50–53.

Sibley, David. "Gender, Science, Politics and Geographies of the City." *Gender, Place and Culture: A Journal of Feminist Geography*, 2 (1995): 37–49.

Smith, Neil, and Peter Williams (eds.). *Gentrification of the City*. Boston: Allen & Unwin, 1986.

Sorkin, Michael (ed.). *Variations on a Theme Park*. New York: Hill and Wang, 1992.

Stearns, Forest, and Thomas Montag. *The Urban Ecosystem: A Holistic Approach*. Stroudsburg, PA: Dowden, Hutchinson and Ross, 1974.

Sternlieb, George, and James W. Hughes. "The Changing Demography of the Central City." *Scientific American*, 243 (1980): 48–53.

Stimpson, Catherine, R., Elsa Dixler, Martha J. Nelson, Kathryn B. Yatrakis (eds.). *Women and the American City*. Chicago: University of Chicago Press, 1981.

Suttles, Gerald. *The Social Construction of Communities*. Chicago: University of Chicago Press, 1972.

Tuan, Yi-Fu, *Topophilia: A Study of Environmental Perception, Attitudes and Values*. Englewood Cliffs, NJ: Prentice-Hall, 1974.

US Forest Service. *Proceedings of the Conference on Metropolitan Physical Environment*. Broomall, PA: Northeastern Forest Experiment Station, 1977.

Valentine, Gill. "Desperately Seeking Susan: A Geography of Lesbian Friendships." *Area*, 25 (1993): 109–116.

Veness, April. "Designer Shelters as Models and Makers of Home: New Responses to Homelessness in Urban America." *Urban Geography*, 15 (1994): 150–167.

Ward, David. *Cities and Immigrants*. New York: Oxford University Press, 1971.

Ward, David. "The Ethnic Ghetto in the United States: Past and Present." *Transactions, Institute of British Geographers*, 7 (1982): 258–275.

Warner, Sam Bass, Jr. *The Urban Wilderness: A History of the American City*. New York: Harper & Row, 1972.

Warr, Mark. "Fear of Rape Among Urban Women." *Social Problems*, 32 (1985): 238–250.

Watson, Sophie, with Helen Austerberry. *Housing and Homelessness: A Feminist Perspective*. London: Routledge & Kegan Paul, 1986.

Women and Geography Study Group of the IBG. *Geography and Gender: An Introduction to Feminist Geography*. London: Hutchinson, 1984.

Zelinsky, Wilbur. "Where Every Town Is Above Average: Welcoming Signs Along America's Highways." *Landscape*, 30 (1988): 1–10.

CHAPTER 12

Industrial Geography

Two great economic "revolutions" occurred in human development. The first of these, the domestication of plants and animals, occurred in our dim prehistory. This agricultural revolution, discussed in Chapter 3, ultimately resulted in a huge increase in human population, a greatly accelerated modification of the physical environment, and major cultural readjustments. The second of these upheavals, the **industrial revolution,** is still taking place, and it involves a series of inventions leading to the use of machines and inanimate power in the manufacturing process. We live today at a pivotal point in the destiny of our species, for we are witnesses to this second revolution, with many attendant changes.

The industrial revolution, which began in the eighteenth century, released for the second time undreamed-of human productive powers. Suddenly, whole societies could engage in the seemingly limitless multiplication of goods and services. Rapid bursts of human inventiveness followed, as did gigantic population increases, and a massive, often unsettling remodeling of the environment. Today, the industrial revolution, with its churning of whole populations and its restructuring of ancient cultural traditions into popular forms (see Chapter 8), is still running its course. Few lands remain largely untouched by its machines, factories, transportation devices, and communication techniques. Western nations, where this revolution has been under way the longest, still feel its sometimes painful, sometimes invigorating effects.

On an individual level, no facet of American and Canadian life remains unaffected by the industrial revolution. A Friday night out might involve a drive in a car to a single outlet in a nationwide chain of restaurants, where you order fried chicken raised several states away on special enriched grain, brought by refrigerated truck to a deep freeze, and cooked in an electric oven. Later, at a movie, you buy a candy bar manufactured halfway across the country. Then you enjoy a series of machine-produced pictures flashed in front of your eyes so fast that they seem to be moving. You could just as easily pick almost any other moment in your life, from sleep, with its permanent-press contoured sheets and its mass-manufactured alarm clocks, to your pet cat, with its chemical flea collar, canned food, and distemper shots. Just about every object and every event in your life is affected, if not actually created, by the industrial revolution.

This chapter concentrates on industry and the industrial revolution as the cultural geographer sees it. In Western culture, the majority of the population owe their livelihoods either directly or indirectly to industry and its related products and services. Add to this an uneven spatial distribution of industry and its ecological ramifications, and you can understand the geographer's interest in this subject.

Five types of industrial activity can be distinguished. **Primary industries** are those involved in extracting natural resources from the Earth. Fishing, hunting, lumbering, oil wells, and mining provide examples of primary industries (Figure 12.1). Agriculture, also a primary industry, was treated in Chapter 3. **Secondary industry** is the processing stage, commonly called manufacturing. Secondary industries process the raw materials extracted by primary industries, transforming them into more usable form. Ore is converted into steel; logs are milled into lumber; fish are processed and canned. As a rule, several steps occur in manufacturing. Many factories turn out products that serve as raw materials for other secondary industries. Steel mills provide steel for automobile factories, and lumber mills make building materials for the construction industry, also a secondary industry. The other three types of industrial activity all involve *services* of some sort, rather than the extraction or production of commodities. So wide is the range of services that some geographers find it useful to distinguish three sectors. These three types of industries are referred to as tertiary, quaternary, and quinary.

Because industrialization is closely interwoven with the physical environment and with other facets of culture, because industry is unevenly distributed, because the industrial revolution consists of a series of ideas spreading by means of cultural diffusion, and because entire

Figure 12.1
Oil field in California. Primary industries are involved in extracting natural resources from the Earth.

landscapes have been remolded and often deformed by industrialization, we can profitably apply the five themes of cultural geography to the study of industry.

Industrial Regions

Each of the five types of industrial activity displays unique spatial patterns. Applying the theme of culture region, geographers refer to these as industrial regions, and Figure 12.2 reveals some such patterns on a worldwide scale.

Primary Industry

Primary industries extract both renewable and nonrenewable resources. **Renewable resources** are those that can be used without being permanently depleted, such as forests, water, fishing grounds, and agricultural land. **Nonrenewable resources** are depleted when used, as for example, minerals.

Many regions that lack significant manufacturing activity have major primary industries. Figure 12.2 shows the main formal culture regions of primary and secondary industry. As a rule, however, primary industries more likely develop in conjunction with manufacturing districts. Zones of primary industry distant from manufacturing centers spring up only if the resource is valuable and rare, worth enough to withstand the cost of transporting it long distances as, for example, the gold mines of South Africa. Almost every major area of secondary industry is surrounded by a "halo" of primary activity.

Secondary Industry

Most of the world's industrial activity has traditionally been found in the developed countries of the mid-latitude Northern Hemisphere, especially in parts of Anglo-America, Europe, Russia, and Japan. This is particularly true of manufacturing. In the United States, secondary industries once clustered mainly in the northeastern part of the country, a region referred to as the American Manufacturing Belt (Figure 12.3). On the opposite Atlantic shore, manufacturing occupies the central core of Europe, surrounded by a less industrialized periphery (Figure 12.4). Japan's industrial complex lies around the shore of the Inland Sea and throughout the southern part of the country (Figure 12.5).

Many different types of manufacturing exist within these major regions. Industrial regions usually consist of several zones, each dominated by a particular kind of industry. Figure 12.6 shows this segregation in the Ruhr district of Germany. Iron and steel manufacture is concentrated in one of these zones, coal mining in another, and textiles in a third. This pronounced regional specialization arose with the industrial revolution in the 1700s, causing manufacturing to take on a heightened geographical character.

Core and Periphery. Reflecting the heightened regionalism that accompanied the industrial revolution was the development of the economic **core/periphery** pattern. The evolving industrial core consisted of the developed countries, with their collective manufacturing regions, while the periphery had nonindustrial and weakly industrialized lands, in-

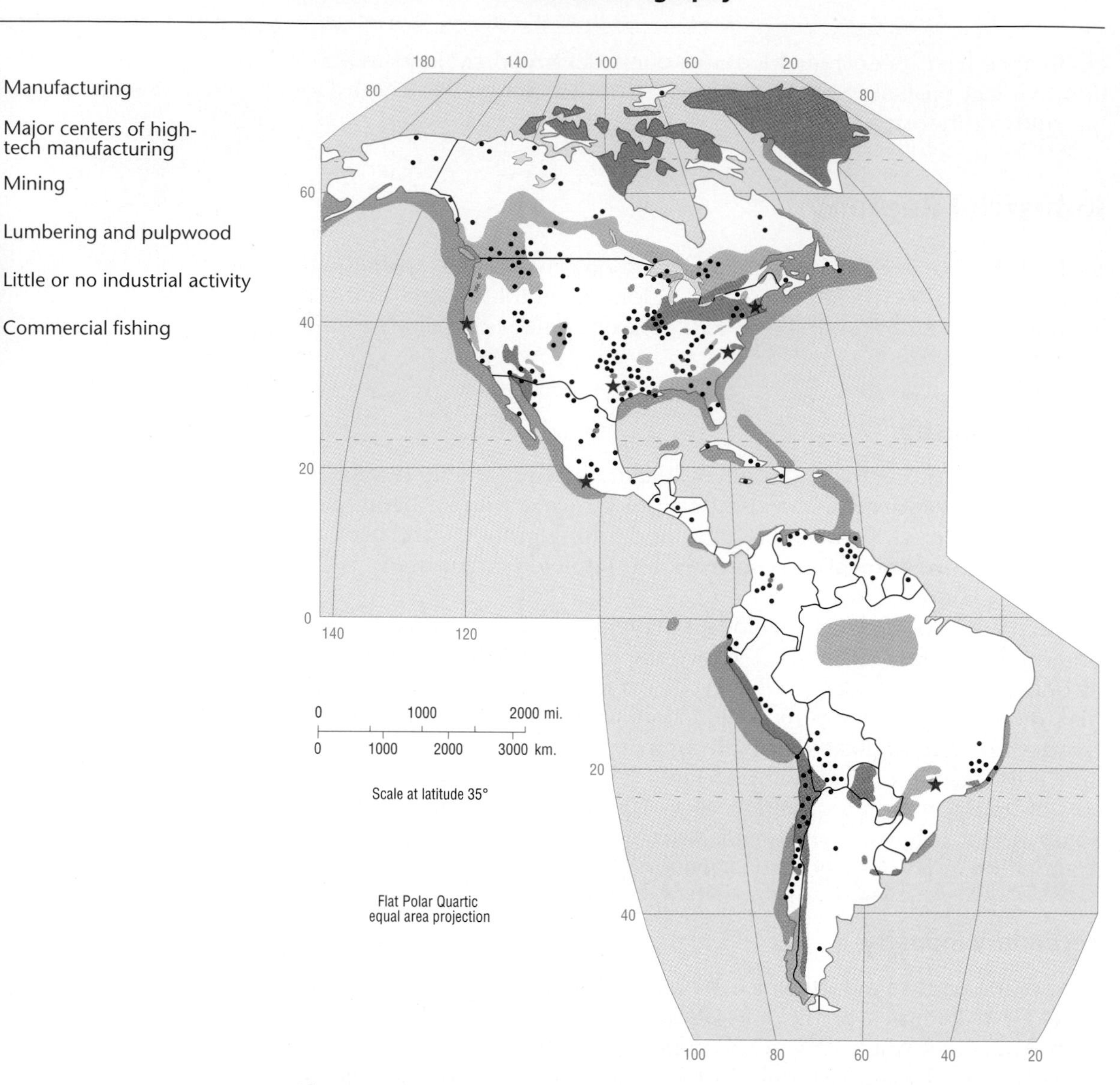

Figure 12.2
Regions of selected primary and secondary industries. Agriculture and hunting are not shown among the primary activities. (After Espenshade, Edward B. (ed.). *Goode's World Atlas.* Chicago: Rand McNally, with modifications and simplification.)

cluding many colonies. Resources extracted from the increasingly impoverished peripheries flowed to the core. The resultant geographical pattern—one of the fundamental realities of our age—is often referred to as **uneven development,** or regional disparity. Opinion differs concerning whether this industrial manifestation of the core/periphery concept is a correctable or inherent geographical feature of the world economy, capitalist and socialist alike. Uneven development has proved to be increasingly and unyieldingly present (Figure 2.13).

Although the manufacturing dominance of the developed countries of the core persists, a major global geographical shift is currently under way in secondary industry. In virtually every core country, much of the secondary sector is in marked decline, especially traditional mass-production industries such as steel making and other types of manufacturing that require a minimally skilled, blue-collar workforce. In such districts, factories are closing, blue-collar unemployment rates stand at

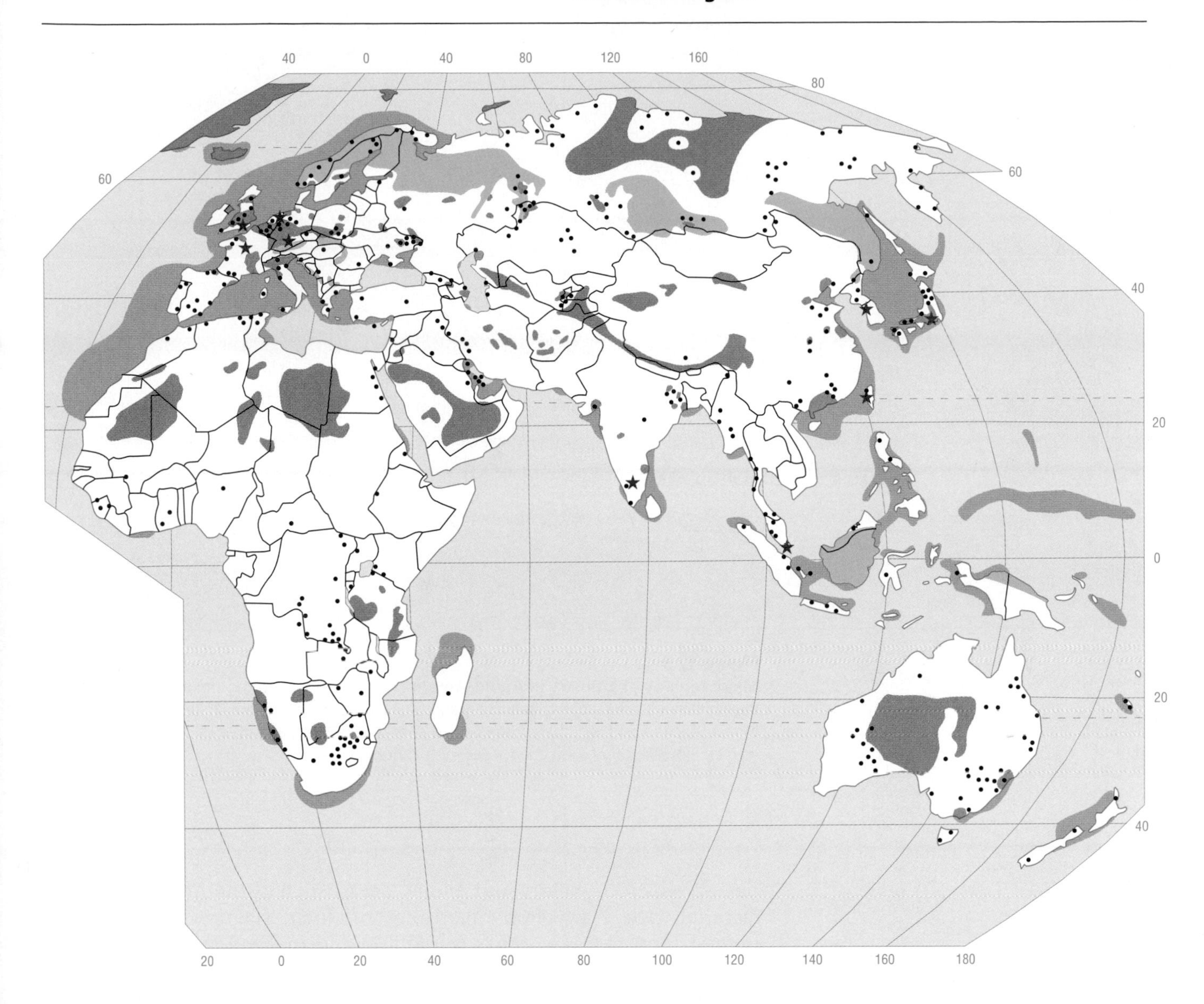

the highest level since the Great Depression of the 1930s, and a "deskilling" of the workforce proceeds. In the United States, for example, where manufacturing employment began a relative decline about 1950, nine out of every ten new jobs in recent years have been unskilled, low-paying service positions. The manufacturing industries surviving and now booming in the core countries are mainly those requiring a highly skilled or artisanal workforce, such as "high-tech" firms and companies producing quality consumer goods. Because the blue-collar workforce has proved largely unable to acquire the new skills needed in such industries, many old manufacturing districts lapse into deep economic depression. Moreover, the high-tech manufacturers employ far fewer workers than the former heavy industries, and they tend to be geographically concentrated in relatively small districts, sometimes called **technopoles** (Figures 12.2 to 12.4).

The word **deindustrialization** describes the decline and fall of

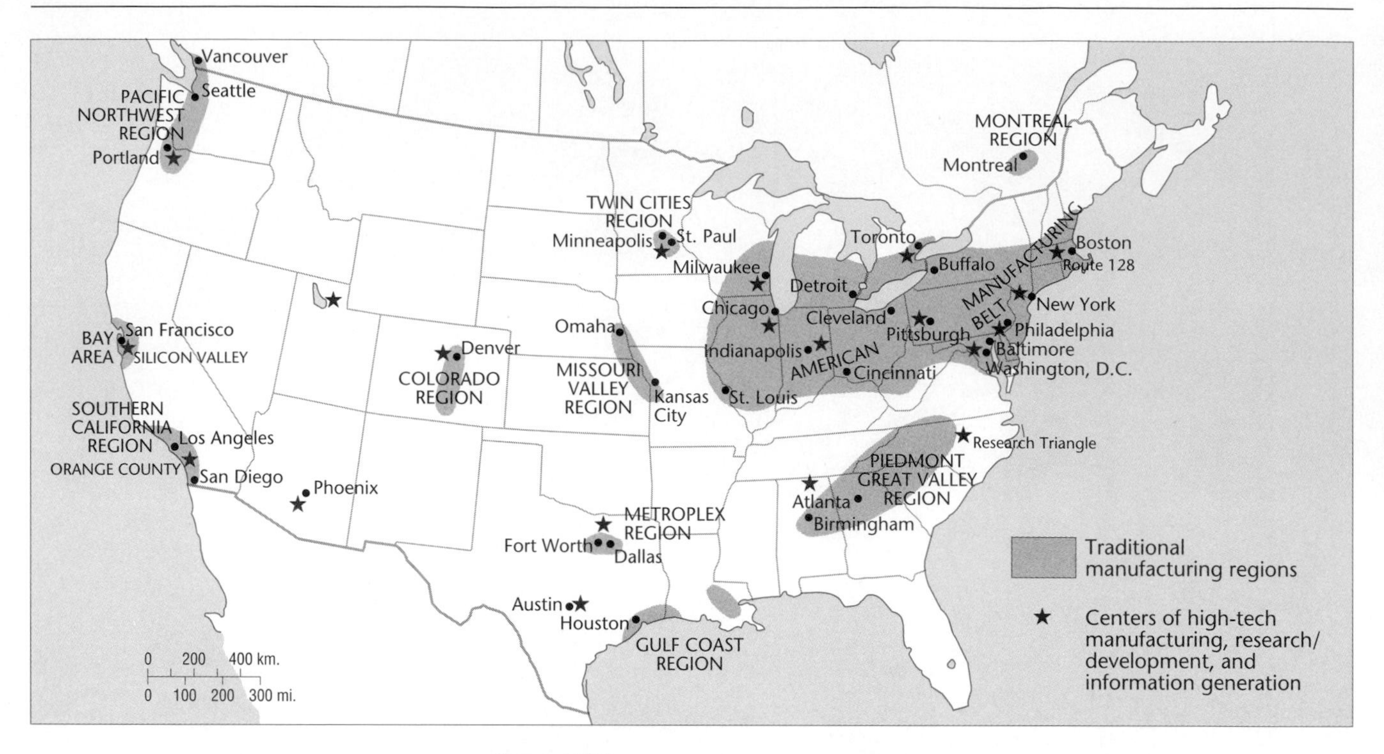

Figure 12.3
Major regions of industry in Anglo-America. The largest and most important region is still the American Manufacturing Belt, the traditional industrial core of the United States. Dispersal of manufacturing to other regions occurred after World War II and now involves mainly high-tech and information-based enterprises, or technopoles.

once-prosperous factory and mining areas, such as the American Manufacturing Belt, now often called the "rust belt" (Figure 12.3). Geographer Shane Davies, who has studied deindustrialization in the coal and steel districts of Wales in Great Britain, speaks of "pauperized belts" and of "a dispirited people who reflect a growing passivity to their plight." Deindustrialization brings demoralization and erosion of the *spirit of place,* as Davies calls it—the vital energy and pride that makes places livable, viable, and renewable.

The affected countries reacted to the problem of deindustrialization in very different ways. The western part of Germany, for example, maintained an unusually high proportion of its workforce in manufacturing by reinvesting for high productivity, offering high wages, specializing in expensive export-oriented products, and protecting the high level of labor skill through a well-developed apprenticeship system. Germany now copes with a very different situation in its eastern regions where the economy was until 1990 dominated by precisely those mass-production manufacturing industries and mines that form the core of decline and deindustrialization.

Manufacturing industries lost by the core countries relocate in newly industrializing lands of the periphery. South Korea, Taiwan, India, Singapore, Brazil, Mexico, Guangdong province in coastal South China, and India have experienced a major expansion of manufacturing, a movement that continues and now involves many other peripheral countries.

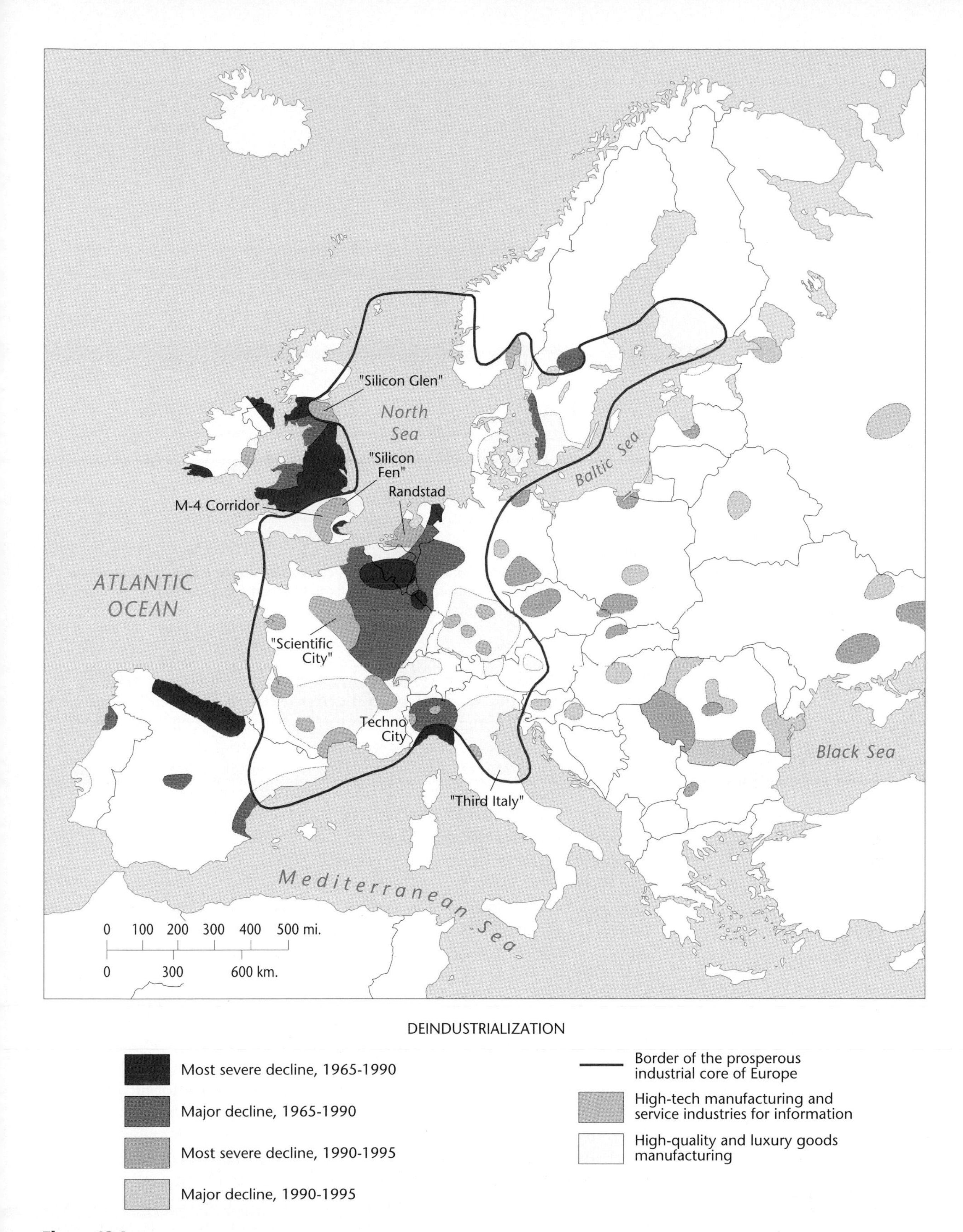

Figure 12.4

Industrial regions and deindustrialization in Europe. New, prosperous centers of industry specializing in high-quality goods, luxury items, and high-tech manufacture have surpassed older centers of heavy industry—both primary and secondary. The regions in decline were earlier centers of the industrial revolution. (Source: Jordan, Terry G. *The European Culture Area*, 3d ed. New York: HarperCollins, 1996.)

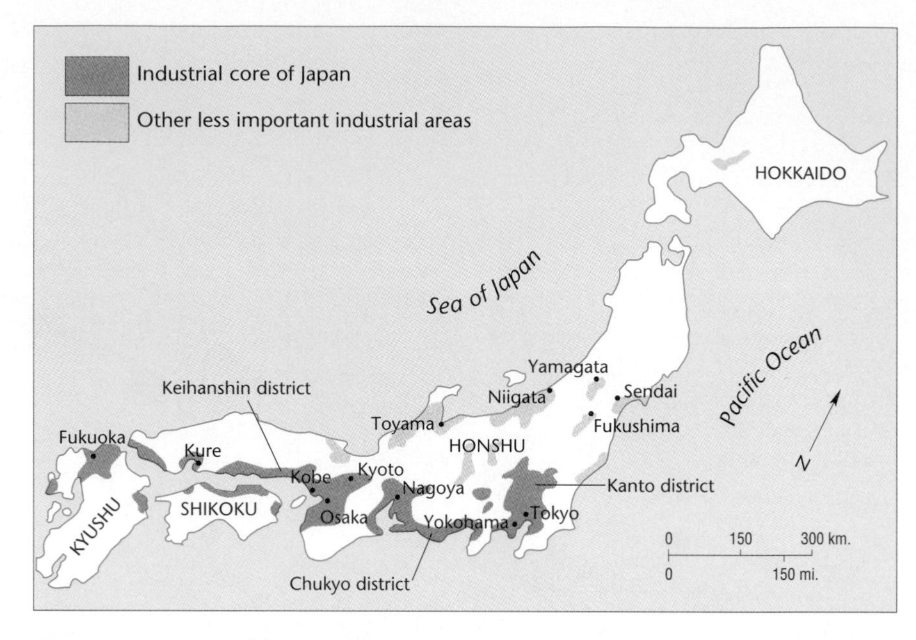

Figure 12.5
Japanese industrial areas manufacture products for the entire world. (In part, after Thompson, John H., and Michihiro Miyazaki. "A Map of Japan's Manufacturing." *Geographical Review,* 49 [1959]: 1–17.)

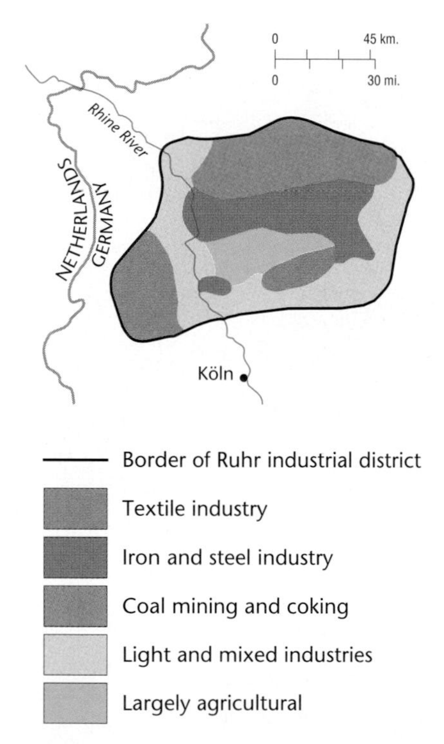

Figure 12.6
The Ruhr industrial district in Germany. The area was long the single most important primary/secondary industrial area in Europe. Note the spatial segregation of different types of industry and the relatively small size of this particular district. (Adapted and updated from Pounds, Norman J. G. *The Ruhr: A Study in Historical and Economic Geography.* London: Faber, 1952.)

Global Corporations. The ongoing locational shift in manufacturing regions is largely the work of **global corporations,** also called multinationals or transnationals**.** We can no longer think of decisions on market location, labor supply, or other aspects of industrial planning within the framework of a single plant controlled by a single owner. Instead, we now deal with a highly complex international corporate structure that plans on a gargantuan scale. Working through great corporations that straddle the Earth, people for the first time utilize world resources with an efficiency more completely dictated by the logic of profit.

Today, the size of corporate conglomeration is breathtaking. The total sales of global corporations are greater than the gross national product of virtually every country. These corporate giants, based mainly in the United States, Europe, and Japan, have sweeping control over international communications networks, the latest advances in modern technology, and large amounts of investment capital. They effectively control the economic structures of many underdeveloped states. Already by 1970, foreign interests controlled 67 percent of the metal-products industry, 84 percent of the tobacco industry, and 100 percent of the rubber, electrical machinery, and automobile industries in Mexico. Global corporations controlled every "top 50" company in Argentina by 1985.

The decline of primary and secondary industries in the older developed core, or *deindustrialization,* has ushered in an era widely referred to as the **postindustrial phase.** The three service sectors—tertiary, quaternary, and quinary—achieve dominance in the postindustrial phase. Both the United States and Canada can now be regarded as having entered the postindustrial era, as has most of Europe and Japan. The aging coal miner of Pennsylvania and veteran auto assembler in Michigan, born into an era of robust primary and secondary industry, now struggle for financial survival in countries that become increasingly deindustrialized.

Tertiary Industry

Tertiary industry, part of both the industrial and postindustrial phases, includes transportation, communication, and utility services. Highways, railroads, airlines, pipelines, telephones, radios, television, and the Internet all belong in the tertiary sector of industry. All facilitate the distribution of goods, services, and information. Modern industries require well-developed transport systems, and every industrial district is served by a network of such facilities. As one measure of this, Figure 12.7 maps the number of persons per motor vehicle by country.

Major regional differences exist in the relative importance of the various modes of transport. In Russia and Ukraine, for example, highways have little industrial significance; railroads, and to a lesser extent waterways, carry most of the transport load. In the United States, on the other hand, highways became most important, while the railroad system declined. Western European nations rely heavily on a greater balance between rail, highway, and waterway transport. Beyond the industrialized regions, transport systems are much less developed. In most of Africa, interior Asia, and other weakly industrialized regions, motorable highways and railroads remain rare, but even there tertiary

Figure 12.7
The number of persons per motor vehicle. The most highly industrialized nations have the largest numbers of cars and trucks per unit of population. (United Nations, *Statistical Yearbook*. See also the annual publication called *World Road Statistics*, published by the International Road Federation.)

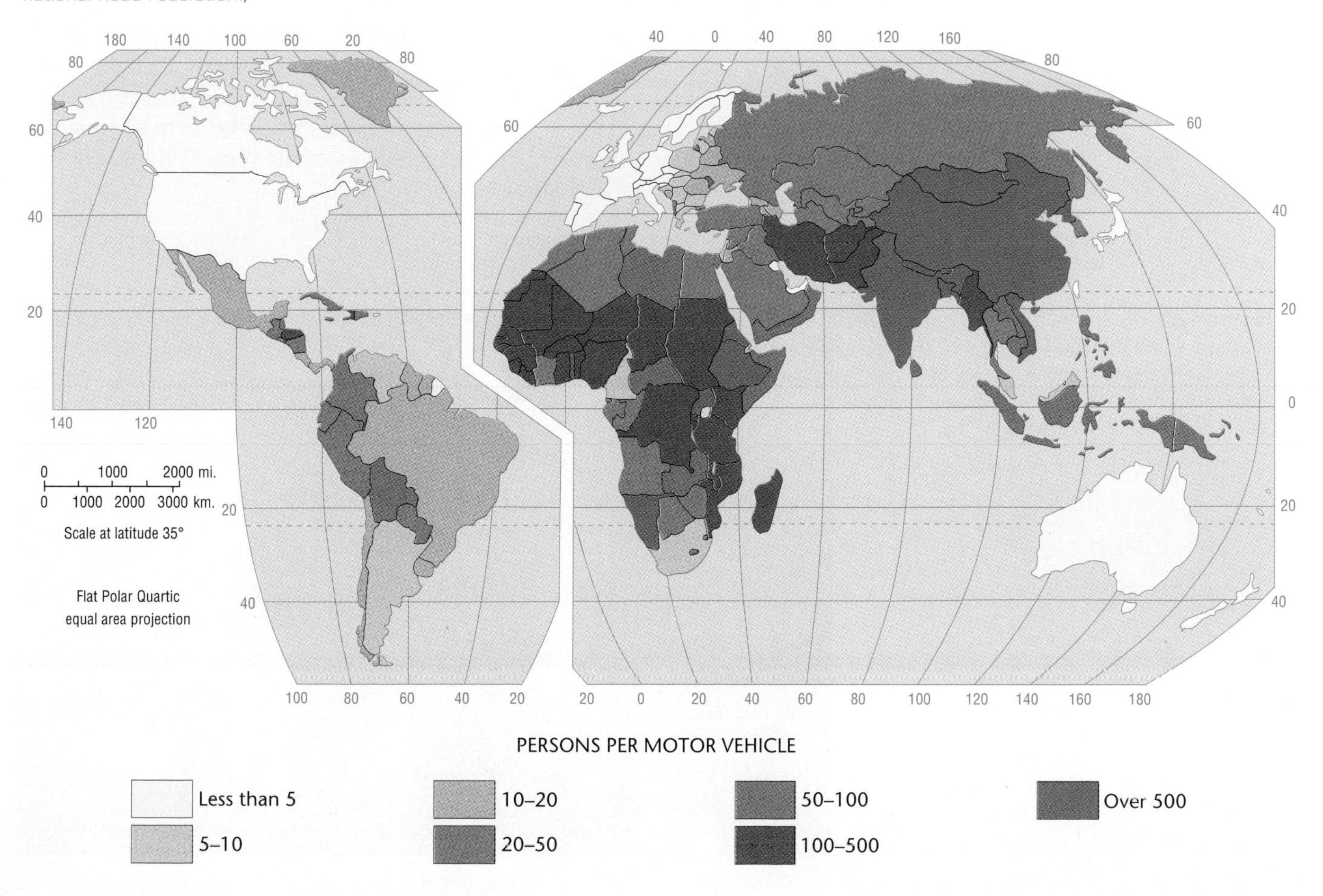

Figure 12.8
A billboard in Beijing, China, promises a motorized future to a nation of bicycle riders.

activity is increasing (Figure 12.8). Meanwhile, in more developed countries such services as electronic transfer of funds and telecommunications between computers continents apart add a new dimension and speed to the transfer of data and ideas. Utilities also belong in the tertiary sector, including the power plants that provide the energy to drive the entire industrial economy.

The transport division of tertiary industry, in particular automobiles, create a special kind of functional culture region sometimes called *machine space.* As automobiles increase, more and more space must be devoted to them, even in congested areas such as the central business districts of cities (Figure 12.9). The result is often visual blight, another unaesthetic type of industrial culture region.

Figure 12.9
Machine space in Atlanta, Georgia. Tertiary industry, represented by the automobile, has created its own functional culture region in the heart of a great city.

Quaternary Industry

Geographers include in **quaternary industry** those services mainly required by producers, such as trade, insurance, legal services, banking, advertising, wholesaling, retailing, consulting, information generation, and real estate transactions. Such activities represent one of the major growth sectors in postindustrial economies, and a geographical segregation seems to be developing, in which manufacturing is increasingly shunted to the peripheries while corporate headquarters, markets, and the producer-related service activities remain in the core. An inherent problem in this spatial arrangement is **multiplier leakage:** global corporations invest in secondary industry in the peripheries, but profits flow back to the core, where the corporate headquarters are located. As early as 1965, American-based corporations took, on the average, about four-fifths of their net profits out of Latin America in this way. As a result of multiplier leakage, the industrialization of less developed countries actually increases the power of the world's established industrial nations. In fact, while industrial technology has spread everywhere, today we face a world in which the basic industrial power of the planet is more centralized than ever. The global corporations are headquartered mainly in quaternary areas where the industrial revolution took root earliest—the mid-latitude countries of the Northern Hemisphere. Similarly, loans for industrial development come from banking institutions in Europe, Japan, and the United States, with the result that interest payments drain away from the poor to the rich countries.

Increasingly important in the quaternary sector is the collection, generation, storage, retrieval, and processing of computerized knowledge and information, including research, publishing, consulting, and forecasting. Postindustrial society is organized around knowledge and innovation, which are used to acquire profits and exert social control. The impact of computers is changing the world dramatically, a process that has accelerated since about 1970, with implications for the spatial organization of all human activities and each of the five industrial sectors. This leads to new ways of doing things and to new products and services.

Many quaternary industries depend on a highly skilled, intelligent, creative, and imaginative labor force, and as such are elitist. While focused geographically in the old industrial core, the distribution of information-generating activity, if viewed on a more local scale, can be seen to coalesce around major universities and research centers. The presence of Stanford and the University of California at Berkeley, for example, helped make the San Francisco Bay area a major center of such industry, and similar foci have developed near Harvard and MIT in New England and the triuniversity Raleigh-Durham-Chapel Hill "Research Triangle" of North Carolina (Figure 12.3). These **high-tech corridors,** or "silicon landscapes," as some have dubbed them, occupy relatively little area. In other words, the information economy is highly focused geographically, contributing to and heightening uneven development spatially. In Europe, for example, the emerging core of quaternary industry is even more confined geographically than the earlier concentration of manufacturing (Figure 12.4).

Quinary Industry

Quinary industry mainly involves consumer related services, such as education, government, recreation/tourism, and health/medicine. Even such mundane activities as housecleaning and lawn service belong in the quinary sector.

One of the most rapidly expanding quinary activities is *tourism*. In 1990, this industry accounted for 5.5 percent of the world's economy, generated $2.5 trillion income, and employed 112 million workers—more than any other single industrial activity and amounting to 1 of every 15 workers in the world. By 1992, the total had risen to $3 trillion and tourism employed 1 of every 14 workers. One advantage of tourism is that it is disproportionately focused in the industrial peripheries rather than the core, somewhat alleviating the problem of uneven development, though multiplier leakage typically drains most of the profits back to the core (Figure 12.10).

The theme of culture region allows a spatial description of industrial regionalization, of uneven development and the core/periphery pattern. By turning now to our second theme, diffusion, we can better see how these distributions came to be.

Diffusion of the Industrial Revolution

The world map of formal industrial regions provides a good measure of how far the industrial revolution has spread, how far the cultural diffusion of constantly evolving technology and ideas has proceeded. As a rule, people strongly resist substantial changes in their basic cultural patterns unless some immediate and great personal benefit is perceived. The enormous appeal and promise of the industrial revolution caused people in a great variety of cultures to discard tradition in order to adopt this new way of life. Until the industrial revolution, the large majority of people were concerned with the most basic of primary economic activities—acquiring from the land the necessities of survival. Society and culture remained overwhelmingly rural and agricultural. To be sure, industry already existed in this setting, since humans are by na-

Figure 12.10
Tourism, often on a primitive level, reaches even into remote areas. Small charter buses now deliver climbers to a thatched tourist hut, which lacks running water, at the foot of Mount Wilhelm in highland Papua New Guinea—an area totally unknown to the outside world as late as 1930. In Australia, a graded road now allows motorists to reach the "Olgas" (aboriginal "Kata Tjuta"), picturesque rock domes in the "Red Centre" of the remote outback country. Increasing numbers of tourists from Europe, North America, and Japan seek out such places.

ture makers of things. For as long as our biological species has existed, we have fashioned tools, weapons, utensils, clothing, and other objects, but traditionally these items were made by hand, laboriously and slowly. Before about 1700, virtually all such manufacture was carried on in two rather distinct systems: cottage industry and guild industry.

Cottage industry, by far the most common, was practiced in farm homes and rural villages, usually as a sideline to agriculture. Objects for family use were made in each household, and most villages had a cobbler, miller, weaver, and smith who worked part time at these trades in their homes. Skills passed from parents to children with little formality.

By contrast, the **guild industry** consisted of professional organizations of highly skilled, specialized artisans engaged full time in their trades and based in towns and cities. Membership in a guild came after a long apprenticeship, during which the apprentice learned the secrets of the profession from a skilled master. The guild was a fraternal organization of artisans skilled in a particular craft, so that guilds existed for weavers, glassblowers, silversmiths, steel makers, potters, and many other trades. While the cottage and guild systems differed in many respects, both depended on hand labor and human power.

Origins of the Industrial Revolution

The industrial revolution arose among back-country English cottage craftspeople in the early 1700s and fundamentally restructured secondary industry. First, human hands were replaced by machines in the fashioning of finished products, rendering the word *manufacturing* ("made by hand") technically obsolete. No longer would the weaver sit at a hand loom and painstakingly produce each piece of cloth. Instead, large mechanical looms were invented to do the job faster and more economically (though not necessarily better). Second, human power gave way to various forms of inanimate power. The machines were driven by water power, the burning of fossil fuels, and later by hydroelectricity and the energy of the atom. Men and women, once the proud producers of fine handmade goods, became tenders of machines.

We know a lot more about the origins and diffusion of the industrial revolution than we do about the beginnings of agriculture. The industrial revolution is a matter of recorded history. Within a century and a half of its beginnings, this economic revolution had greatly altered the first three sectors of industrial activity.

Textiles. The initial breakthrough came in the secondary, or manufacturing, sector. More exactly, it occurred in the British cotton textile cottage industry, centered at that time in the district of Lancashire in western England. At first the changes were modest and on a small scale. Mechanical looms were invented, and flowing water, long used as a source of power by local grain millers, was harnessed to drive the looms. During this stage, manufacturing industries remained largely rural, diffusing hierarchically to sites where rushing streams could be found, especially waterfalls and rapids. Later in the eighteenth century, the invention of the steam engine provided a better source of power, and a shift away from water-powered machines occurred. In the United States, too, the first factories were textile plants.

Metallurgy. Traditionally, metal industries had been small-scale, rural enterprises, carried on in small forges situated near ore deposits. Forests provided charcoal for the smelting process. The chemical changes that occurred in the making of steel remained mysterious even to the craftspeople who used them, and much ritual, superstition, and ceremony were associated with steel making. Techniques had changed little since the beginning of the Iron Age, 2500 years before.

The industrial revolution radically altered all this. In the eighteenth century, a series of inventions by iron makers living in the Coalbrookdale in the English Midlands, allowed the old traditions, techniques, and rituals of steel making to be swept away and replaced with a scientific, large-scale industry. *Coke*, nearly pure carbon and derived from high-grade coal, was substituted for charcoal in the smelting process. Large blast furnaces replaced the forge, and efficient rolling mills took the place of hammer and anvil. Mass production of steel resulted, and the new industrial order was built of steel. Other manufacturing industries made similar transitions, and entirely new types arose, such as machine making.

Mining. Primary industries were also revolutionized. The first to feel the effects of the new technology was coal mining. The adoption of the steam engine necessitated huge amounts of coal to fire the boilers, and the conversion to coke in the smelting process further increased the demand for coal. Fortunately, Britain had large coal deposits. New mining techniques and tools were invented, so that coal mining became a large-scale, mechanized industry. Coal, heavy and bulky, was difficult to transport. As a result, manufacturing industries began flocking to the coalfields in order to be near the supply, in a process of hierarchical diffusion. Similar modernization occurred in the mining of iron ore, copper, and other metals needed by rapidly growing industries.

Railroads. The industrial revolution also affected the tertiary sector, most notably in the form of rapid bulk transportation. The traditional wooden sailing ships gave way to steel vessels driven by steam engines, canals were built, and the British-invented railroad came on the scene. The principal stimulus that led to these transportation breakthroughs was the need to move raw materials and finished products from one place to another, both cheaply and quickly. The impact of the industrial revolution would have been minimized had not the distribution of goods and services also been improved (see box, *Distance in the Preindustrial Age*). It is no accident that the British, creators of the industrial revolution, also invented the railroad and initiated the first large-scale canal construction. Nor is it accidental that the British also revolutionized the shipbuilding industry and dominated it from their Scottish shipyards even into the twentieth century.

The railroads and other innovative modes of transport associated with the industrial revolution, once in place, fostered additional cultural diffusion. Ideas could spread more rapidly and easily after the railroad network came into existence. More exactly, the new industrial-age popular culture could easily penetrate previously untouched areas. Geographer Mark Jefferson, reflecting the cultural arrogance of this age, wrote in the 1920s of the "civilizing rails" as an agent of diffusion.

Diffusion from Britain

For a century, Britain maintained a virtual monopoly on its industrial innovations. Indeed, the British government actively tried to prevent the diffusion of the various inventions and innovations that made up the in-

Distance in the Preindustrial Age

Our lives are a constant adventure in shrinking space. With a car, we're just minutes from a friend miles away. The airplane has put us within jet-lag distance of Paris, Moscow, or Calcutta. In such an age, we can hardly imagine what an obstacle distance often proved to be before the industrial revolution.

A record of 10,000 letters sent to Venice, Italy, in the early sixteenth century shows clearly what a factor distance was in the preindustrial world. Letters from nearby Genoa took an average of 6 days to arrive; London, 27; Constantinople, 37; Lisbon, 46; Damascus, 80. But these average figures hardly tell the whole tale. Changing human and climatic conditions lent a striking elasticity to mail delivery. Deliveries from Paris ranged from a maximum of 34 days to a minimum of 7 days; Barcelona, 77 to 8; and Florence, 13 to 1, to pick three places at random. Zara, which was separated from Venice by only a short stretch of the Adriatic Sea, held the record. Its letters, depending upon sailing conditions, took from a maximum of 25 to a minimum of 1 day to arrive. Compared to other goods, however, letters moved briskly across the map. Sixteenth-century Italians knew that it took even their privileged goods 3 months to reach London.

In fact, before the eighteenth century, distance had been a relatively constant factor for centuries. In terms of travel, the Mediterranean was about the same "size" in the sixteenth century as it had been in Roman times over 1000 years earlier. Traveling times did not change much until the nineteenth century.

From Braudel, Fernand. *The Mediterranean and the Mediterranean World in the Age of Phillip II.* New York: Harper & Row, 1972, Vol. 1, p. 356.

dustrial revolution, because they gave Britain an enormous economic advantage and contributed greatly to the growth and strength of the British Empire. Nevertheless, this technology finally diffused beyond the bounds of the British Isles (Figure 12.11). Continental Europe first received its impact. In the last half of the nineteenth century, the industrial revolution took firm root hierarchically in the coalfields of Germany, Belgium, and other nations of northwestern and central Europe.

Figure 12.11
The diffusion of the industrial revolution. By diffusion from Britain, the industrial revolution has changed cultures in much of the world.

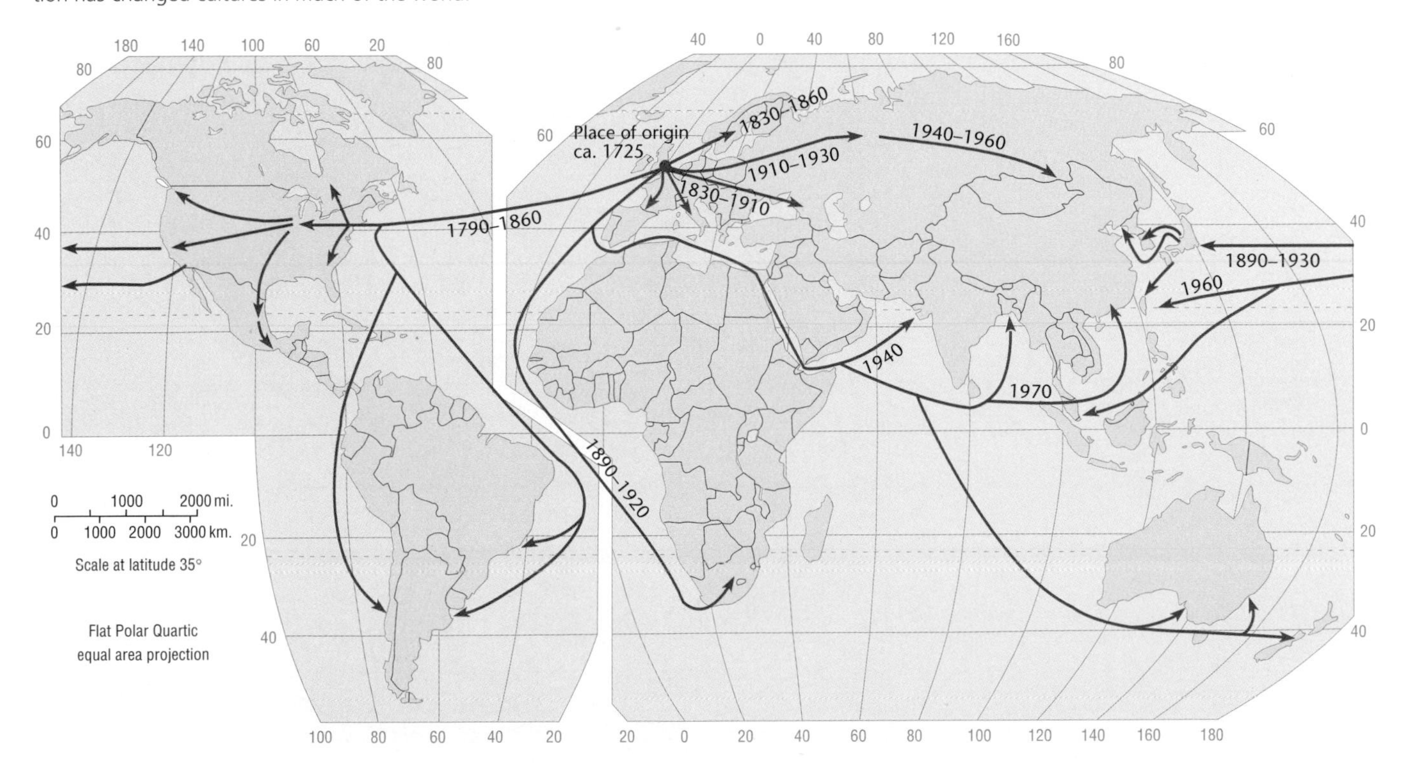

The diffusion of railroads in Europe provides a good index to the spread of the industrial revolution there (Figure 12.12). The United States began rapid adoption of this new technology about 1850, followed a half-century later by Japan, the first major non-Western nation to undergo full industrialization. In the first third of the present century, the diffusion of industry and modern transport spilled over into Russia and Ukraine. More recently, countries such as Taiwan, South Korea, China, India, and Singapore joined the manufacturing age.

Industrial Ecology

The diffusion of the industrial revolution occurred only at enormous environmental expense. By its very nature, the technology of modern industry consumes nonrenewable resources and damages ecosystems. Primary industries gouge huge open-pit mines, destroy large tracts of tropical rain forest (Figure 12.13), and deplete marine life through overfishing. Indeed, a worldwide sea fisheries collapse is apparently occurring today, threatening areas such as Newfoundland that depend heavily on this industry. Secondary industries—even those devoted to "high-tech" products—pollute the air, water, and land with toxic substances (Figure 12.14). Tertiary activities accidentally spill crude oil and chemicals along shipping lanes, railroads, and highways (Figure 12.15). Quaternary and quinary industries, though more ecologically benign,

Figure 12.12
The diffusion of the railroad in Europe. The industrial revolution and the railroad spread together across much of the continent. Can you find evidence of both contagious and hierarchical diffusion?

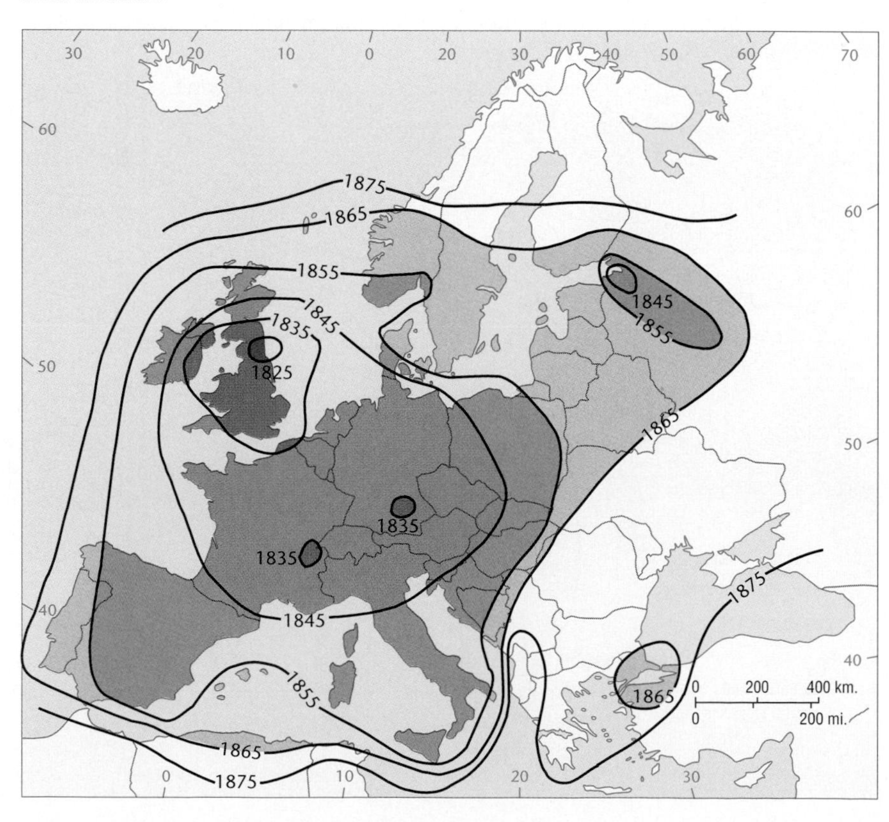

Figure 12.13
Destruction of tropical rain forest near Madang in Papua New Guinea by Japanese lumbering interests. The entire forest is leveled in order to extract a relatively small number of desired trees.

Figure 12.14
Environmental pollution in the United States. The 500 most polluted counties of the United States in amount of toxic chemicals dumped, and the 10 worst states on the *Green Index*, the latter based on 256 environmental indicators. The worst states had inadequate protective legislation and "little public will to correct the problem." Compare this to Figure 12.3. (Sources: US Environmental Protection Agency. *Toxic Release Inventory;* and Hall, Bob, and Mary Lee Kerr. *1991–1992 Green Index: A State-by-State Guide to the Nation's Environmental Health.* Durham, NC: Institute for Southern Studies, 1991.)

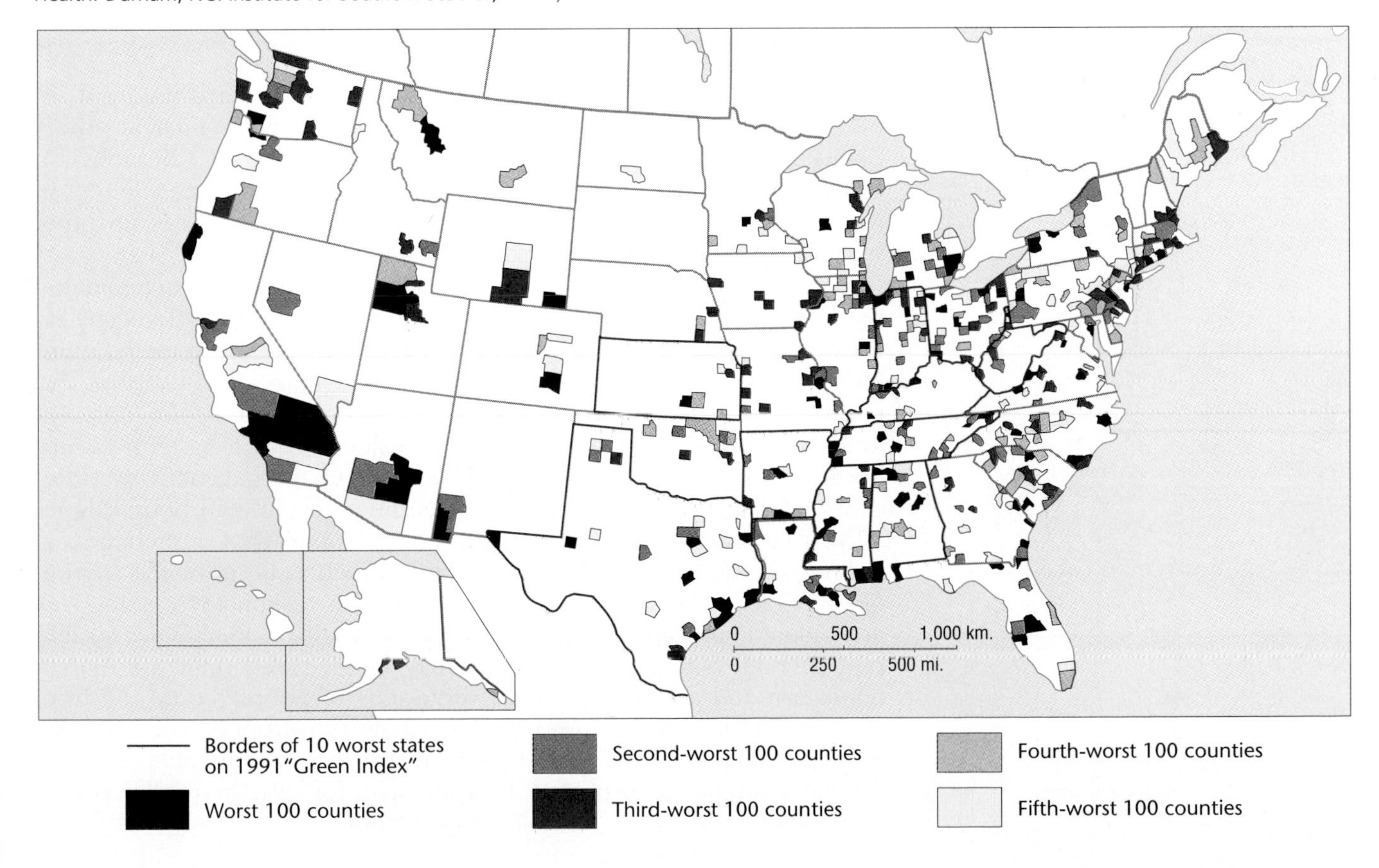

Figure 12.15
Polluted Alaska. The massive Exxon oil spill a few years ago in the waters near Valdez, Alaska, contaminated large stretches of coastline and destroyed much wildlife. Such spills seem to be an unavoidable aspect of industrial activity, given human error.

consume vast amounts of energy that must be generated by the burning of fossil fuels or nuclear reaction, with often dire environmental consequences.

Radioactive Pollution

Industrial pollution takes many forms. Potentially perhaps the most serious, though invisible, is radioactivity from accidents at nuclear power plants and waste storage facilities. The catastrophe at Chernobyl in Ukraine on April 26, 1986, clearly demonstrated the danger inherent in the "Faustian bargain" that has led much of Europe and certain other parts of the world to depend heavily on nuclear power.

A sizable area around Chernobyl became heavily contaminated with deadly radiation, and all land within an 18-mile (30-kilometer) radius of the destroyed reactor had to be evacuated and remains uninhabited today, save for a few elderly people who refused to leave. Beyond, sizable swaths across Europe were bombarded with different kinds of radioactive isotopes, such as cesium-137, a long-term hazard because it has a half-life (the time required for its radioactivity to decrease by half) of 30 years and attacks the entire human body (Figure 12.16). Another major component of the Chernobyl pollution was iodine-131, with a half-life of 8.1 days, which collects in the thyroid gland. Some estimates place the amount of cesium-137 released as equivalent to at least 750 Hiroshima atomic bombs. Ultimately, a sizable part of both Ukraine and Belarus may be declared unfit for human habitation and additional tens of thousands of people could die from exposure to radiation caused by this single catastrophe. The ominous term "national sacrifice area" is now heard in governmental circles in various countries as a potential euphemism for districts rendered permanently uninhabitable by radiation pollution.

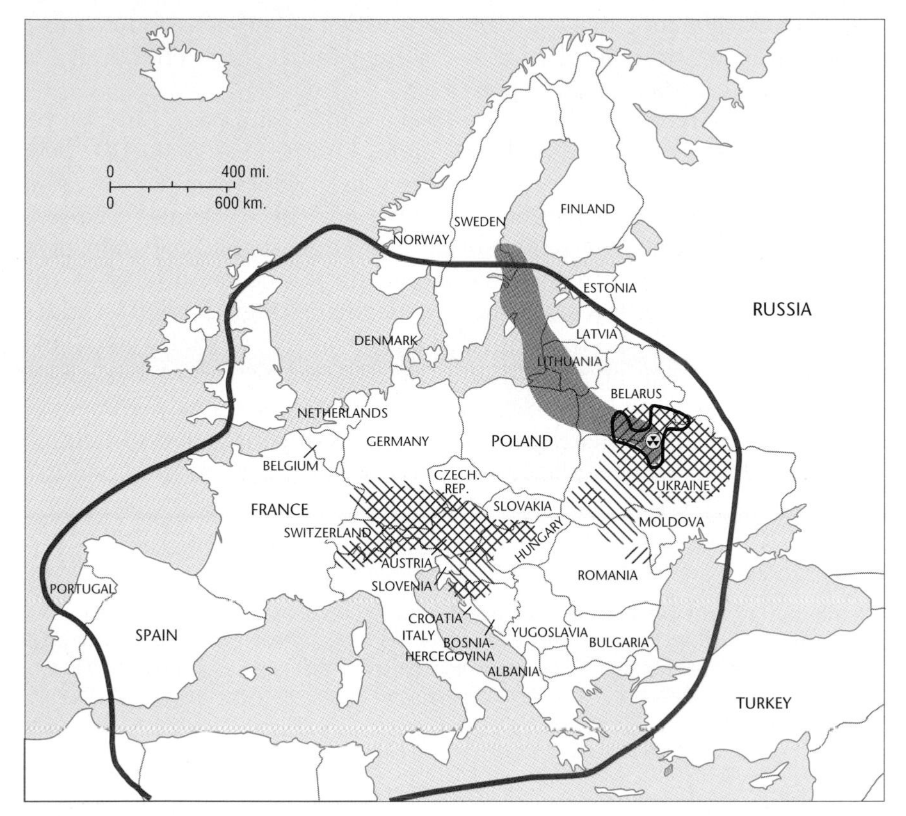

Chernobyl

Worst areas, Iodine-131, April 26–May 1, 1986

Additional worst Iodine-131 areas by May 6, 1986

Worst areas, Cesium-137, by May 6, 1986

Extent of radioactive cloud, May 3, 1986

Area most catastrophically impacted

Figure 12.16
The most severe radioactive contamination from the Chernobyl catastrophe came from two isotopes, cesium-137 and iodine-131. The map is somewhat speculative because of inadequate data. The future of human habitation in the area most catastrophically impacted remains uncertain, but some tracts there have been completely depopulated. (Source: Adapted from Park, Chris C. *Chernobyl: The Long Shadow.* London: Routledge, 1989, pp. 66, 74, 79, 92.)

Acid Rain

Like radiation pollution, **acid rain** is invisible, and its effects can be almost as devastating. Known to researchers for a century and a half, acid rain attained widespread publicity beginning in the early 1980s. The burning of fossil fuels by power plants, factories, and automobiles releases into the air acidic sulfur oxides and nitrogen oxides, which are in turn flushed from the atmosphere by precipitation. The resultant rainfall has a much higher than normal acidity. For example, a shower that fell on the town of Kane, in northern Pennsylvania, on September 19, 1978, had a pH reading equivalent to vinegar. Overall, 84 percent of energy in the world is generated by burning fossil fuels, making acid rain a prevalent phenomenon.

Acid rain is capable of poisoning fish, damaging plants, and diminishing soil fertility. Such problems have been intensively studied in Germany, one of the most completely industrialized nations in the world. German scholars have been impressed by the dramatic suddenness with which the catastrophic effects of acid rain arrived. In 1982, only 8 percent of forests in western Germany showed damage, but by 1990 the proportion had risen to over half. Only a crash program of pollution control and energy conservation can now save the woodlands of Germany. In the words of geographer Wilfrid Bach, "The ongoing forest dieback demands that without any further delay, emission of these pollutants must be controlled at the source much more effectively," if the German forests are not to perish.

In North America the effects of acid rain accumulate, but not yet with the catastrophic speed seen in central Europe (Figure 12.17). Over 90 lakes in the seemingly pristine Adirondack Mountains of New York were "dead," devoid of fish life, by 1980, and 50,000 lakes in eastern Canada face a similar fate. Recent studies suggest that acid rain now causes mass killings of marine life along the northeastern coast of the United States and of forests in the Appalachians (Figure 12.18). Oxides of nitrogen seem to be the principal culprit in the coastal waters, and the impact has been noted in Chesapeake, Delaware, and Narragansett bays, as well as Long Island Sound. For some years, the government of Canada urged United States officials to take stringent action to help alleviate acid-rain damage, since much of the problem on the Canadian

Figure 12.17

Distribution of acid rain in North America. Measurements are taken from the annual sulfate deposition, derived from airborne sulfur oxides (SO_2). Deposition levels of 18 pounds per acre (20 kilograms per hectare) are generally regarded as threatening to some aquatic and terrestrial ecosystems. Nitrate components of acid rain are not shown. (Source: Canadian Embassy, Washington, DC.)

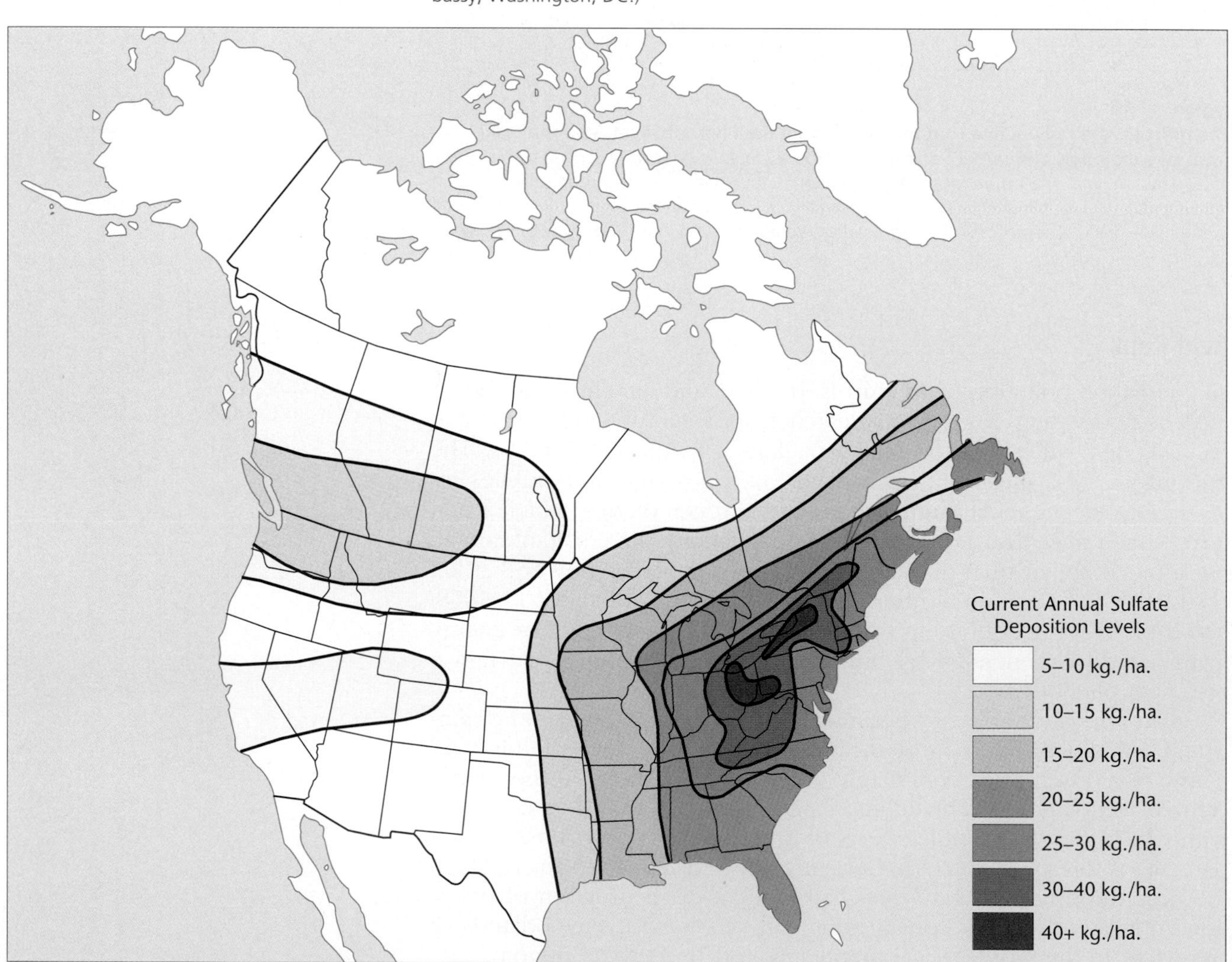

side of the border derives from American pollution, but their pleas were to little avail.

Figure 12.18
Forest death, apparently from acid rain, in North Carolina. Forest death, widespread in central Europe, is now beginning to appear in North America and certain other areas.

The Greenhouse Effect and Ozone Depletion

The world has many pockets of environmental crisis, and on a regional scale some corrective measures can often be successful. Certain other industrially induced environmental changes are global in scale and, as a result, more intractable.

One of these may be the **greenhouse effect.** Also produced by the burning of fossil fuels, this problem brings the possibility of catastrophic change of the Earth's climate. Every year, billions of tons of carbon dioxide (CO_2) are produced worldwide by fossil fuel burning, at a level 50 times that prevalent in 1860. In addition, the ongoing destruction of the world's rain forests adds huge additional amounts of CO_2 to the atmosphere. While CO_2 is a natural component of the Earth's atmosphere, the freeing of this huge additional amount is altering the chemical composition of the air. Carbon dioxide, only one of the absorbing gases involved in the greenhouse effect, permits solar short-wave heat radiation to reach the Earth's surface, but acts to block or trap long-wave outgoing radiation, causing a thermal imbalance and global heating (Figure 12.19).

The result could be, at worst, a runaway buildup of solar heat that would evaporate all water and make any form of life impossible, causing planet Earth to resemble hostile Venus. Less catastrophically, the greenhouse effect could warm the global climate only enough to melt or partially melt the polar icecaps, causing the sea level to rise as much as hundreds of feet and inundate the world's coastlines. The long-term effects of even this lesser change could have disastrous results for humankind. The worst-case scenario for the year 2030 seems to include a climatic warming to the level known 4 million years ago, in the mid-Pliocene Age. Disturbing is the fact that the decade of the 1980s experienced 7 of the 10 warmest years recorded in the last 200 years—the entire span for which reliable meteorological data are available.

Figure 12.19
Global temperature, 1860s–1995. The figure for each year is an average for all the weather stations in the world. Most experts now believe that humans played a role in global warming. (Source: NASA Goddard Institute for Space Studies.)

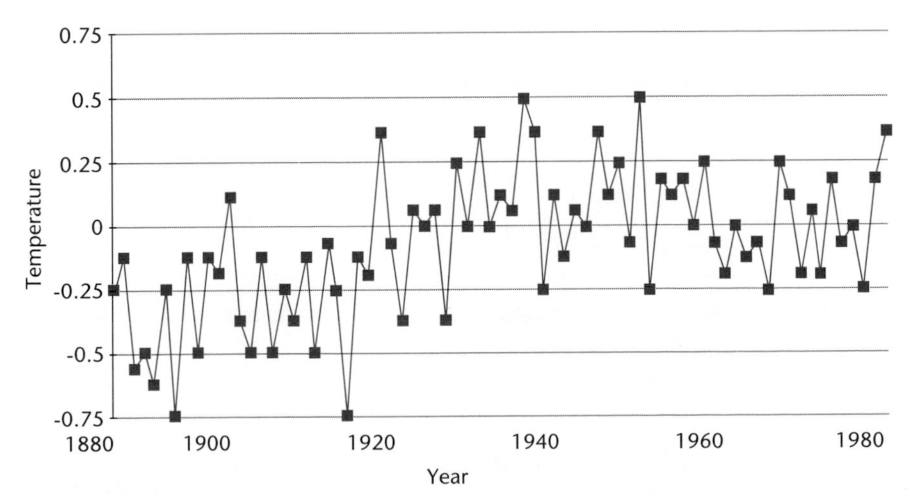

The onset of the greenhouse effect could be sudden, as some critical, unknown threshold is reached in atmospheric CO_2. This doomsday is possibly being delayed by another industrial-related environmental alteration—the addition of huge amounts of **particulate pollutants** to the atmosphere. Such pollution acts to block out solar radiation and cool the climate. The two atmospheric processes, greenhouse effect and particulate pollution, may have acted to neutralize each other, at least so far. If this is the case, the balance achieved is a precarious one.

So poorly understood is this phenomenon that some researchers deny that we are experiencing a global warming of climate. Part of the problem is that we lack good weather records for all but the recent past. Also, even if the climate is becoming warmer, the causes cannot conclusively be determined at this time.

Potentially even more serious is the depletion of the upper-atmosphere *ozone layer,* which acts to shield humans and all other forms of life from the most harmful types of solar radiation (Figure 12.20). Several manufactured chemicals are almost certainly the main culprits, including the freon used in refrigeration and air conditioning. Most of the industrialized countries of the world contribute large amounts of these chemicals, and they signed the Montreal Protocol in 1989 aimed at reducing the ozone-damaging substances. Little progress has been made, however, and recent research suggests that the problem may be far worse than previously believed. In 1995, ozone levels in the Arctic high latitudes fell by one-third, threatening to open an ozone hole in that region comparable to the one first detected in the Antarctic during the 1980s. The activist organization Greenpeace, among others, warns that ozone depletion now threatens the future of all forms of life on Earth. Perhaps in the final analysis we will find that industrialization, which has become so integral a part of our culture in the past two centuries, is simply ecologically untenable and cannot be maintained. In short, our modern industrial way of life may prove a maladaptive strategy in terms of cultural ecology.

Our experience with industrialization as an adaptive strategy has

Figure 12.20
Ozone loss, 1979–1988, at the upper levels of the atmosphere. Destruction of this layer, which protects all life on Earth from excessive solar radiation, could render the planet devoid of life. In the 1990s, the problem worsened, especially in the Northern Hemisphere. (Source: Seager, Joni. *The State of the Earth Atlas,* New York: Simon & Schuster, 1990, pp. 70–71.)

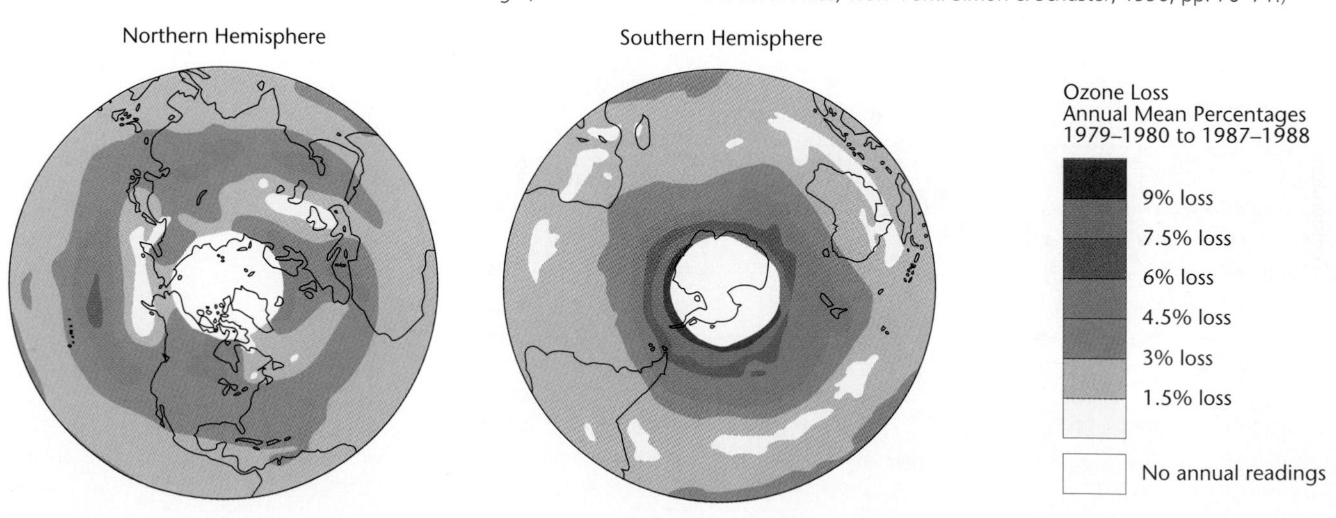

been too short and shallow to permit an adequate perspective on the problem. In the United States, we have lived with the industrial revolution for about 150 years. What would the ecological impact of this system be after 3 centuries, 10 centuries, 20 centuries? We can only guess, but many experts are not optimistic. What we do know is that the technology of the industrial revolution has demanded that we modify our habitat on a previously undreamed-of scale, and at the same time it has provided us with the tools and techniques to carry out that massive modification.

The "Green" Reaction

Around the world, many people have become so distressed by the industrially caused environmental problems that they have become activists, or **greens.** In Europe, "green" political parties now exist in countries such as Germany, where forest death helped build their membership and modest electoral success. The publication of the *Green Index,* some aspects of which are shown in Figure 12.14, is one reflection of increased concern in North America. Organizations such as the Sierra Club operate as political lobbyists for various environmental causes.

Certain other groups prefer direct action in addition to working through political processes. Greenpeace, headquartered in Washington, DC, has carried out scores of spectacular harassments of environmental polluters and despoilers, sometimes in highly controversial ways and occasionally at considerable personal risk to its member participants. It remains to be seen whether such activism can effectively change public attitudes, industrial practices, and governmental policies.

Alfred Weber
1868–1958

Weber was the most influential pioneer theorist of industrial location. In 1909, he published his seminal work, later translated as *Theory of the Location of Industry.* Most subsequent research in industrial location theory represents attempts by others to refine or refute his model. Many aspects of Weber's theory remain viable today and are presented in this chapter.

Weber's wide-ranging intellect defies academic disciplinary boundaries. He dealt at one time or another with sociology, cultural history, economic geography, philosophy, political science, art, poetry, law, and economics; his writings are far too diverse to classify. Born in Erfurt, Germany, Weber earned a doctorate at Berlin in 1897. A decade later he assumed the chair of social science and political economy at Heidelberg University in southwestern Germany, a position he occupied for the remainder of his long career. The Alfred Weber Institute for Social and Political Sciences at Heidelberg commemorates his achievements. He represents yet another of the German founding fathers of modern geography.

Environmental Factors in Industrial Location

While the industrial revolution has brought accelerated and potentially devastating change to the physical environment, it has also been governed in part by the same environment. The spatial distribution of industry in particular has been influenced by environmental considerations.

Industrial location theory, pioneered by Alfred Weber (see biographical sketch), seeks the optimal siting for each firm. The underlying assumption is that the usual goal in locating an industry is cost minimization. Various environmental factors must be figured into cost, including raw materials, energy sources, and restrictions related to climate and terrain.

Raw Materials. In the early stages of the industrial revolution, industries developed near raw materials. The reason was simple. The development of efficient means of mass transportation came a century after the beginning of the revolution. Before about 1830 or 1840, we could not move bulky, heavy raw materials very far. In the last century and a half, the attraction of industry to raw materials steadily decreased, in part because of improved transportation facilities. Alfred Weber's 1909 principle that transport costs for raw materials often possessed great importance in determining factory location in many cases no longer holds true.

Adopting a possibilistic view, we can say that manufacturers, in attempting to minimize the costs of production, will tend to locate near their raw materials if a great loss of weight or bulk occurs in the manufacturing process, or if the finished product is less perishable than the raw materials from which it is made. The refining of minerals, the manufacture of iron, steel, and paper, and the canning of fish provide examples of industries attracted for these reasons to the source of raw materials.

In industrial location, we also need to recognize the phenomenon called **industrial inertia.** This refers to the tendency of industries to remain in their initial locations, even after the forces that attracted them there cease to act. Some industries drawn to the sources of raw materials in the 1700s or early 1800s, before the advent of modern modes of transportation, remain in the same location. This inertia occurs because capital investment in the form of land and structures would have to be sacrificed if the industry were relocated. In addition, the present labor force would be difficult to relocate with the industry. Some industries even remained in the same place after the nonrenewable raw materials that originally attracted them were completely exhausted. Still, the continued improvement of transport facilities caused the locational pull of raw materials to become rather inconsequential in most industries. Moreover, the older mining and manufacturing districts often prove very poorly suited to modern high-tech industries and to the quaternary and quinary sectors, in part because they require a different sort of labor force. Industrial inertia could not save the collapsing coal and steel districts of the United States and Europe.

Energy Supply. The quantity of energy consumed by industries, measured either as a total amount or per unit of goods produced, has increased greatly since the beginning of the industrial revolution. The rapid increase of power use began with the shift from water power to the steam engine and accelerated with the subsequent adoption of other power sources, in particular, electricity.

During the early part of the industrial revolution, long-distance shipment of fossil fuels, from which inanimate power was derived, proved too costly to be economically feasible. As a result, industrial plants requiring large amounts of energy located where water power or coal was available. Later inventions, such as the railroad, pipeline, motorized barges, and seagoing tankers, largely removed this restriction on location. The harnessing of electricity and development of high-tension power lines further reduced the locational pull of power supplies.

A few types of manufacturing remain strongly attracted to the sites of energy production. One of these, the aluminum industry, consumes huge amounts of electricity in the process of converting the raw material bauxite into aluminum. Hydroelectric sites are preferred, since the electricity generated by falling water is renewable and cheaper than electricity produced by nuclear reactors or burning fossil fuels. Since electricity cannot be transmitted great distances without considerable loss of power from the transmission lines, location near the hydroelectric facility is best, though recent developments in superconductivity may alter this situation. Hydroelectric sites attracted aluminum industries to relatively remote places such as Russian Siberia and the Pacific coastal mountains of Canada.

Industrial Cultural Integration

The theme of cultural integration is also relevant to industry. The causal factors influencing industrial location extend beyond the physical environmental elements to include various economic features, and geographers seeking to explain industrial location have more than once succumbed to economic determinism. Industrial location theory seeks to explain the spatial distribution of industry by referring mainly to other aspects of society. From the time of Alfred Weber, location theorists have placed enormous importance on labor supply as a locational factor.

Labor Supply

Labor-intensive industries are those for which labor costs form a large part of total production costs. Examples include industries depending on skilled workers producing small objects of high value, such as computers, cameras, and watches. Manufacturers consider several characteristics of labor in deciding where to locate factories: availability of workers, average wages, necessary skills, and worker productivity. Workers with certain skills tend to live and work in a small number of places, partly as a result of the need for higher education or for person-to-person training in handing down such skills. Consequently, manufacturers often seek locations where these skilled workers live.

In recent decades, the increasing mobility of labor throughout the Western world has lessened the locational influence of labor. Migration of labor accelerated after 1950, especially in Europe and the United States. Large numbers of workers in Europe migrated from south to north, leaving homes in Spain, Italy, Greece, Turkey, and the Balkan States to find employment in the main European manufacturing belt.

The high-tech and "information industries" often locate near major research universities, which offer a source of skilled, innovative laborers as well as an attractive intellectual setting in which to live. For those industries dependent on largely *unskilled* labor, or labor that can be trained quickly and cheaply, relocation to economically depressed rural areas can result in higher profits. The main attraction of such areas is the large supply of cheap labor, a contrast to the high wages typical in established industrial districts. Much industry went to "Norma Rae-Ville" in the American South (Figure 8.4) for this reason. Today, the principal relocations go to Third World countries such as Mexico, where assembly plants now line the border with the United States.

A new global division of labor seems to be in the works. Behind these changes in the international labor market lies the strategic thinking by directors of the global corporations. According to a Department of Commerce study, as early as the mid–1970s, 298 American-based global corporations employed as many as 25 percent of their workers outside the United States. Such factories, despite relocation costs, quickly drive up corporate profit margins. In addition, the ability of these corporations to plan on such an international scale and to shift the production of a given product to faraway lands has a weakening effect on organized labor inside the United States.

Markets

A market, geographically, includes the area in which a product may be sold in volume and at a price profitable to the manufacturer. The size and distribution of markets are generally the most important factors in determining the spatial distribution of industries. Many experts consider the market attraction so great that they regard locating an industry near its market as the norm, revealing in the process their own economic determinism.

Certain industries, they say, *must* locate at the market. That is, some manufacturers have to situate their factories among their customers to minimize costs and maximize profits. Such industries include those manufacturing a **weight-gaining** finished **product,** such as bottled beverages, or a **bulk-gaining** finished **product,** such as metal containers or bottles. In other words, if weight or bulk is added to the raw materials in the manufacturing process, location near the market is economically desirable because of the transport cost factor. Similarly, if the finished product is more perishable than the raw materials, as with bakery goods and local newspapers, a location near market is also required. In addition, if the product is more fragile than the raw materials that go into its manufacture, as in the making of glass, the industry will be attracted to its market. In each of these cases—gain in weight, bulk, perishability, or fragility—transportation costs on the finished product are much higher than on the raw materials.

Obviously, the degree of importance of market as an attractive force increases with the degree of clustering of population. If population is relatively evenly distributed across a country, no single location can be said to be nearest to the market, but the clustering in cities so typical of modern industrial societies pulls manufacturers to the urban centers. Similarly, the type of market being served can affect the location of industries. Some manufacturers supply highly clustered urban markets, while others, such as the makers of farm machinery, cater to a more dispersed body of consumers. Industries selling goods to dispersed markets have greater freedom in their choice of locations. Small-scale service industries dealing in information, as well as specialized high-tech manufacturers, often have one or two principal customers, such as defense contractors, and their tendency is to locate near this market.

As a rule, though, we can say that in Western industrial cultures, the greatest market potential exists where the largest numbers of people live. Once an industry locates in a particular place, it provides additional jobs, attracting laborers into the area. This additional population in turn enlarges the local market, thereby attracting other industries. In the same way, the industries arriving later attract still more people and still more industries, creating an **agglomeration.** Industrial districts develop in this manner, through a snowballing increase in people, infrastructure, and industries. The process is very difficult to control in free-enterprise systems, and if allowed to run its course, agglomeration will produce serious overcrowding and an excessively clustered population. This intense concentration of industries and population is characteristic of most industrialized nations. Consequently, many such countries suffer from associated problems such as congestion, inadequate housing and recreational facilities, and extreme local pollution of the environment.

The Political Element

Political influence on the spatial distribution of industry is common. Governments often intervene directly in decisions concerning industrial location. Such intervention typically results from a desire to establish strategic, militarily important industries that would otherwise not develop; to decrease vulnerability to attack by artificially scattering industry to many parts of the country; to place vital strategic industries in remote locations, far removed from possible war zones; to create national self-sufficiency by diversifying industries; to bring industrial development and a higher standard of living to poverty-stricken provinces; or to halt the agglomeration effect in existing industrial areas. Such governmental influence becomes most pronounced in highly planned economic systems, particularly in certain socialist countries such as China, but it works to some extent in almost every industrial nation.

The scattering of industry in Russia, motivated partly by a desire to lessen the catastrophic effect of a military attack, provides an example. The development of a major industrial complex in the Ural Mountains, deep in the interior of Russia, was partially in response to the German military advance in 1941. For similar strategic reasons, the United States government during World War II encouraged the development of an iron and steel industry in Utah, an economically inefficient location that would not have attracted such industry without government intervention. The American aircraft industry similarly became dispersed as a result of government policy. The Italian government has deliberately caused industries to be established in the impoverished southern part of that country in an effort to improve the standard of living. Similarly, the American government encouraged new industrial development in economically depressed Appalachia. The United Kingdom, with some limited success, has attempted to retard further industrial development in existing population centers, causing many new factories to be situated in rural or small-town areas.

Local and state governments often directly influence industrial locations. Action by such governments sometimes takes the form of tax concessions, such as those granted by a number of states, counties, and cities in the United States. These concessions commonly last for a specified period of time, frequently ten years or less, and are designed to persuade industries to locate in areas under their jurisdiction. Conversely, governments can act to prevent the establishment of industries viewed as undesirable. A brewery, for example, could be kept out of an area where influential local church leaders hold prohibitionist views and brought their influence to bear on government officials. Some American municipalities refused to allow development of particularly pollution-prone industries such as copper smelters, waste disposal, and paper mills.

Another type of government influence comes in the form of tariffs, import-export quotas, political obstacles to the free movement of labor and capital, and various types of hindrance to transportation across borders. Tariffs, in effect, reduce the size of a market area proportional to the amount of tariff imposed, a concept easily illustrated by building a model (Figure 12.21). A similar effect is produced when the number of border crossing points is restricted. In some parts of the world, especially Europe, the impact of tariffs and borders on industrial location has been greatly reduced by the establishment of free-trade blocs, groups of nations that have banded together economically and abolished most tariffs. Of these associations, the European Union (EU) is perhaps the most famous. Composed of 15 nations, the EU has succeeded in abolishing tariffs within its area. The North American Free Trade Agreement (NAFTA), joining the United States, Canada, and Mexico, with future expansion to include other countries, envisions a similar achievement in the Western Hemisphere.

Global corporations, which scatter their holdings across interna-

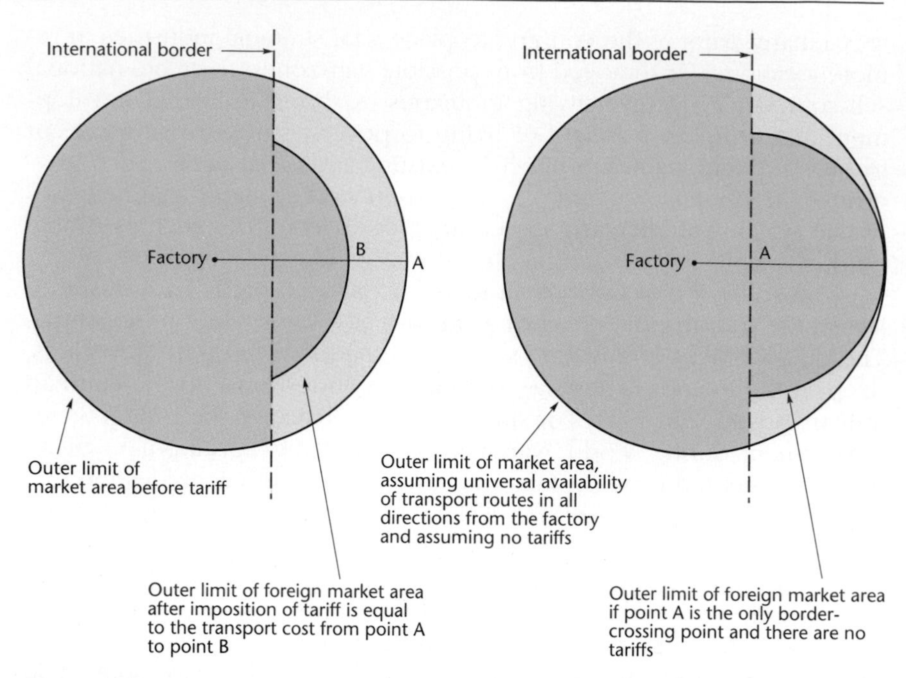

Figure 12.21
Model showing the impact of political borders on market area. The presence of a political border reduces the market area of a factory if a tariff is imposed or if the number of border-crossing points is restricted. As a result, factories tend not to be located in border zones. (After Giersch, Herbert. "Economic Union Between Nations and the Location of Industries." *Review of Economic Studies,* 17 [1949–50]: 87–97.)

tional borders, would seem to diminish the political factor in industrial location. In reality, however, even the multinational enterprises must pay heed to boundaries. Different countries act variously to encourage or discourage foreign investment, creating major spatial discontinuities in opportunities for the global corporations. Even in an era when industrial decisions have worldwide impact, the political locational factor remains viable.

Industrialization and Cultural Change

In these various ways, different aspects of culture are integrated with industrial location, but equally pronounced are the effects of industry on culture. Indeed, industrialization is the most potent and effective agent of cultural change in modern times. Entire cultures have been reshaped as a consequence of the industrial revolution. Traditions thousands of years old have been discarded almost overnight. Much of the replacement of folk culture by popular culture can be attributed at least indirectly to the industrial revolution.

Perhaps the principal cultural change introduced by the industrial revolution, and a subsequent cornerstone of Western civilization, was the concept of technology-based *progress,* a by-product of continual invention and change. By accepting a faith in progress, people looked to a future that would be better than the present. Many discarded the notions of heaven and the afterlife to accept the belief in a better future on Earth, as industrial society became more secularized. In time, says Yi-Fu Tuan, belief in progress led to a Western "arrogance based on the presumed availability of almost unlimited technological power." The optimism bred of faith in progress also allowed industrial cultures to discard, perhaps unwisely, "the ageless fear of the greater power and potency of nature."

On a more prosaic level, the changes wrought by industrialization include increased interregional trade and intercultural contact, basic alterations in employment patterns, a shift from rural to urban residence for vast numbers of people, the release of women from the home, the ultimate disappearance of child labor, an initial increase in the rate of population growth followed by a drop to unprecedented low birthrates, greatly increased individual mobility and mass migrations of people, the decline of the multigeneration family, greatly increased educational opportunities for the nonwealthy, and an increase in government influence and functions. Perhaps the most basic change is the way people make their livings.

Industrial Landscapes

The industrial landscape forms part of daily life, a prominent and often disturbing visible feature of our surroundings. Industry creates a landscape not normally designed for beauty, charm, or aesthetic appeal, but rather for profit and utility. Often by almost anyone's standards ugly, industrial landscapes are poor places for humans to spend their lives.

Each level of industrial activity produces its own distinctive landscape. Primary industries exert perhaps the most drastic impact on the land. The resultant landscapes contain slag heaps, strip-cut commercial forests, massive strip-mining scars, gaping open-pit mines, and "forests" of oil derricks. Some such landscapes take on a bizarre, other-worldly character, at once horrible and fascinating (Figure 12.22). In geographer Richard Francaviglia's words, many "mining communities huddle amid barren piles of waste rock, and mountains of tailings and slag are left in the wake of milling and smelting activity." He calls these "hard places" and feels they accurately reflect much of what we in the Western world value: competition, risk taking, and dominion over nature.

Certain other primary industrial landscapes, in contrast, please the eye and complement the beauty of nature. The fishing villages of Portugal or Newfoundland even attract tourists (Figure 12.23). In still other cases, efforts are made to restore the preindustrial landscape. Examples include the establishment of artificial grasslands in old strip-mine areas of the American Midwest and the creation of recreational ponds in old borrow pits along interstate highways in the same region. A study by geographer Timothy Brothers found the artificial grasslands to be inexpensive for mining companies to establish, poor and potentially toxic for cattle grazing, dominated by exotic Eurasian grasses, and concentrated in areas that bore a forest cover rather than prairie before strip mining.

The landscapes of secondary industry, or manufacturing, contain most obviously factory buildings. Some of these are imaginatively designed and well landscaped, others less appealing and surrounded by gray seas of parking lots. They range from the futuristic, harsh, solid geometry of chemical refineries and formless, stark "brick-pile" factories to award-winning structures designed by famous architects (Figure 12.24).

Manufacturing landscapes initially appeared in Britain, the area first touched by the industrial revolution. British poets and artists of the eighteenth and nineteenth centuries reacted strongly to the emerging manufacturing landscape. Poets and artists are aesthetically sensitive

Figure 12.22
Three primary industrial landscapes. The bizarre color "industrial mosaic" is on the margins of the Great Salt Lake in Utah (upper right), where chemicals and minerals such as metallic magnesium, potassium, and sodium chloride are derived from the water by solar evaporation; the open-pit mine is Bingham Canyon in Utah, the second largest in the world (upper left); and the mind-boggling, artificial "Alp" is the result of potash mining near Kassel in Germany (bottom).

and more perceptive than the average person, so their reactions should interest us. Geographers Gary Peters and Burton Anderson, employing the methods of humanistic geography, studied the works of such writers and painters. They found that after an early period of optimism about industrialization, some poets and artists quickly sensed something amiss in the landscape. Their warnings, in the form of paintings and poems, began appearing in the 1775–1800 period. Typical is the description of an iron foundry written by the poet Robert Burns in his native Scottish dialect:

> *We cam na here to view your warks,*
> *In hopes to be mair wise,*
> *But only, lest we gang to Hell,*
> *It may be nae surprise.*

Some artists of the period left paintings that convey a sinister, forbidding, unpleasant landscape. By the time ordinary people began to

Figure 12.23
A fishing village in Newfoundland. Primary industrial landscapes can be pleasing to the eye.

see with the eyes of poets and artists, the manufacturing landscape was seemingly out of control, and much of the British industrial region was already known, appropriately, as the "Black Country" (see box "*How Green Was My Valley*").

Other humanistic geographers have also addressed the issue of industrial landscapes. Douglas Porteous, writing about the impact of industrialization on his hometown in Yorkshire, England, coined the word **topocide,** meaning the deliberate, planned killing of a place for the benefits of industry. Robert Burns would have understood.

Another British geographer, Shane Davies, a son of the Welsh coalfields, offered a different, even nostalgic view of the industrial landscape. Noting the decline of the coal mining industry in South Wales and the accompanying deindustrialization since 1930, he lamented the deliberate, government-supported obliteration of the defunct mining landscape, a removal prompted, he believed, by the British preference for agrarian scenes. Wales, "its spirit and wealth now broken," is losing

Figure 12.24
The manufacturing and tertiary landscape of Detroit. Other than a graceful suspension bridge, the scene offers little to lift the human spirit and calls to mind the early warnings of the Scottish poet Robert Burns.

"How Green Was My Valley"

Richard Llewellyn, a Welshman, wrote a beautiful novel about growing up in the coal mining district of Wales in the late nineteenth century. He saw the industrial landscape expand across his native valley, and he lamented it:

Bright shone the sun, but brighter shone the Valley's green, for each blade of grass gave back the light and made the meadows full of gold and greens, and yellows and pinks and blues were poking from the hedges where the flowers were hard at work for the bees. May and almond were coming, and further down, early apple was doing splendid in four tidy rows behind Meirddyn Jones' farm. His herd of black cows were all down in the river up to their bellies in the cool quiet water, with their tails making white splashes as they dropped after slapping flies, and up nearer to us, sheep were busy with their noses at the sweet green. When the wind took breath you could hear the crunching of their jaws.

Beautiful was the Valley this afternoon, until you turned your head to the right. Then you saw the two slag heaps. . . .

Below us, the river ran sweet as ever, happy in the sun, but as soon as it met the darkness between the sloping walls of slag it seemed to take fright and go spiritless, smooth, black, without movement. And on the other side it came forth grey, and began to hurry again, as though anxious to get away. But its banks were stained, and the reeds and grasses that dressed it were hanging, and black, and sickly, ashamed of their dirtiness, ready to die of shame, they seemed, and of sorrow for their dear friend, the river. . . .

Big it had grown, and long, and black, without life or sign, lying along the bottom of the Valley on both sides of the river. The green grass, and the reeds and the flowers, all had gone, crushed beneath it. And every minute the burden grew, as cage after cage screeched along the cables from the pit, bumped to a stop at the tipping pier, and emptied dusty loads on to the ridged, black, dirty back.

On our side of the Valley the heap reached to the front garden walls to the bottom row of houses, and children from them were playing up and down the black slopes, screaming and shouting, laughing in fun. On the other side of the river the chimney pots of the first row of houses could only just be seen above the sharp curving back of the far heap, and all the time I was watching, the cable screeched and the cages tipped. . . .

From Llewellyn, Richard. *How Green Was My Valley.* New York: Curtis Brown, 1940, pp. 103, 104, 116.

its coal mining landscape. "So rapid," he wrote, "is the ongoing erasure of the mining scene—the dark, inner landscape of the pit and the more familiar surface features of pithead gear, slag heaps and grey streaked villages—that soon, there will be no palpable evidence of how thousands of ordinary people . . . worked and lived." In this manner, Britain seeks "to sanitize landscapes pillaged while forging an industrial empire."

Service industries, too, produce a cultural landscape. Its visual content includes elements as diverse as high-rise bank buildings, hamburger stands, "silicon landscapes," and the concrete and steel webs of highways and railroads. Some highway interchanges can only be described as a modern art form, but perhaps the aesthetic high point of the tertiary landscape is found in bridges, often graceful and beautiful structures (Figure 12.24). Few sights of the industrial age can match a well-designed rail or highway bridge.

Industrialization has even changed the way we view the landscape. As geographer Yi-Fu Tuan commented, "In the early decades of the twentieth century vehicles began to displace walking as the prevalent form of locomotion, and street scenes were perceived increasingly from the interior of automobiles moving staccato-fashion through regularly spaced traffic lights." Los Angeles, the ultimate automobile city, provides perhaps the best example of the new viewpoints provided by the industrial age. Its freeway system allows individual motorists to observe their surroundings at nonstop speeds. It also allows the driver to look *down* on the world. The pedestrian, on the other hand, is slighted. The view from the street is not encouraged. In some areas of Los Angeles, streets actually have no sidewalks at all, so that the nonautomobile viewpoint is functionally impossible. In other areas, the layout of the main avenues has been planned with the car in mind, and the pedestrian feels ill at ease amid the nonhuman surroundings—noise, traffic jams, drive-in banks, and parking lots. The shopping street is no longer scaled to the pedestrian—Los Angeles's Ventura Boulevard extends for 15 miles (24 kilometers).

Conclusion

One of the most significant events of our age is the spread of industrialization, which has brought a host of far-reaching cultural changes. Already the industrial revolution has modified the cultures and landscapes of some lands so greatly that people who lived there a century ago would be bewildered by the modern setting.

Through the theme of culture region we noted the spatial patterns of five types of industry. We traced the spread of the innovations that made up the industrial revolution, following the routes of diffusion from Britain to the rest of the world. The impact of industrial activity on the environment becomes apparent through the study of cultural ecology, but the relationship between industry and the land is not one-sided. The environment also influences industrial location. Through the approach of cultural integration, we found that industry is related in countless ways to other elements of culture. In particular, industrial location is often governed by economic and political factors. The theme of cultural landscape allowed us some deeper insight into the visible manifestations of the industrial revolution.

Sources and Suggested Readings

Alfrey, Judith, and Catherine Clark. *The Landscape of Industry.* London: Routledge, 1993.

Allen, John. "Service Industries: Uneven Development and Uneven Knowledge." *Area,* 20 (1988): 15–22.

Aspinall, Richard, and Stan Openshaw. "Geographical Aspects of Radiation Monitoring in Britain:" *Area,* (1988): 53–59.

Bach, Wilfrid. "The Acid Rain/Carbon Dioxide Threat—Control Strategies." *GeoJournal,* 10 (1985): 339–352.

Brothers, Timothy S. "Surface-Mine Grasslands." *Geographical Review,* 80 (1990): 209–225.

Brunn, Stanley D., and Thomas R. Leinbach (eds.). *Collapsing Space and Time: Geographical Aspects of Communications and Information.* New York: HarperCollins, 1991.

Castells, Manuel, and Peter Hall. *Technopoles of the World: The Making of 21st Century Industrial Complexes.* London: Routledge, 1994.

Chapman, Keith, and David F. Walker. *Industrial Location: Principles and Policies,* 2d ed. Oxford: Basil Blackwell, 1991.

Clark, David. *Post-Industrial America: A Geographical Perspective.* New York: Methuen, 1985.

Colten, Craig E. "Historical Hazards: The Geography of Relict Industrial Wastes." *Professional Geographer,* 42 (1990). 143–156.

Coombes, Mike. "The Impact of International Boundaries on Labor Market Area Definitions." *Area,* 27 (1995): 46–52.

Cutter, Susan L. *Living with Risk: The Geography of Technological Hazards.* New York: Edward Arnold, 1993.

Daniels, Peter W. *Service Industries: A Geographical Appraisal.* New York: Methuen, 1986.

Davies, C. Shane. "Dark Inner Landscapes: The South Wales Coalfield." *Landscape Journal,* 3 (1984): 36–44.

Davies, C. Shane. "Wales: Industrial Fallibility and Spirit of Place." *Journal of Cultural Geography,* 4, No. 1 (1983): 72–86.

Dicken, Peter. *Global Shift: Industrial Change in a Turbulent World.* London: Harper & Row, 1986.

Feldman, Maryann P., and Richard Florida. "The Geographic Sources of Innovation: Technological Infrastructure and Product Innovation in the United States." *Annals of the Association of American Geographers,* 84 (1994): 210–229.

Forbes, Dean K. *The Geography of Underdevelopment.* Baltimore: Johns Hopkins University Press, 1984.

Forbes, Dean K., and Peter J. Rimmer (eds.). *Uneven Development and the Geographical Transfer of Value.* Human Geography Monograph 16, Research School of Pacific Studies. Canberra: Australian National University, 1984.

Francaviglia, Richard V. *Hard Places: Reading the Landscape of America's Historic Mining Districts.* Iowa City: University of Iowa Press, 1991.

Grotewold, Andreas. "The Growth of Industrial Core Areas and Patterns of World Trade." *Annals of the Association of American Geographers,* 61 (1971): 361–370.

Guyol, Nathaniel B. *Energy in the Perspective of Geography.* Englewood Cliffs, NJ: Prentice-Hall, 1971.

Hall, Peter, and Ann Markusen (eds.). *Silicon Landscapes.* Boston: Allen & Unwin, 1985.

Hanson, Susan (ed.). *The Geography of Urban Transportation.* New York: Guilford Press, 1986.

Hepworth, Mark E. *Geography of the Information Economy.* New York: Guilford Press, 1990.

Hoyle, Brian S., and Richard D. Knowles (eds.). *Modern Transport Geography.* New York: Halstead Press, 1992.

Hussey, Antonia. "Rapid Industrialization in Thailand, 1986–1991." *Geographical Review,* 83 (1993): 14–28.

Jakle, John A. *The Tourist: Travel in Twentieth-Century North America.* Lincoln: University of Nebraska Press, 1987.

Jarrett, H. R. *A Geography of Manufacturing,* 2d ed. Plymouth, England: Macdonald and Evans, 1977.

Jefferson, Mark. "The Civilizing Rails." *Economic Geography,* 4 (1928): 217–231.

Journal of Transport Geography, published by Butterworth-Heinemann in association with the Transport Geography Study Group of the Institute of British Geographers. Volume 1 appeared in 1993.

Kellerman, Aharon. *Telecommunications and Geography.* New York: John Wiley & Sons, 1993.

Kirn, Thomas J. "Growth and Change in the Service Sector of the U.S.: A Spatial Perspective." *Annals of the Association of American Goegraphers,* 77 (1987): 353–372.

Langton, John. *Geographical Change and Industrial Revolution: Coalmining in Southwest Lancashire, 1590–1799.* Cambridge Geographical Studies, No. 11. New York: Cambridge University Press, 1980.

Langton, John. "The Industrial Revolution and the Regional Geography of England." *Transactions of the Institute of British Geographers,* 9 (1984), 145–167.

Markusen, Ann, Peter Hall, and Amy Glasmeier. *High Tech America.* Winchester, MA: Allen & Unwin, 1986.

Marples, David R. "Chernobyl: Five Years Later." *Soviet Geography,* 32 (1991): 291–313.

Martin, Ron, and Bob Rowthorn (eds.). *The Geography of De-Industrialization.* Dobbs Ferry, NY: Sheridan House, 1986.

Massey, Doreen. *Spatial Divisions of Labor: Social Structures and the Geography of Production.* New York: Methuen, 1985.

Massey, Doreen, and Richard Meegan (eds.). *Politics and Method: Contrasting Studies in Industrial Geography.* London: Methuen, 1986.

Meyer, David R. "Emergence of the American Manufacturing Belt: An Interpretation." *Journal of Historical Geography,* 9 (1983): 145–174.

Mounfield, Peter R. *World Nuclear Power: A Geographical Appraisal.* New York: Routledge, 1991.

Pacione, Michael (ed.). *Progress in Industrial Geography.* London: Croom Helm, 1985.

Pearce, Douglas. *Tourism Today: A Geographical Analysis.* New York: Longman, 1987.

Peet, Richard. *International Capitalism and Industrial Restructuring.* Winchester, MA: Allen & Unwin, 1987.

Peters, Gary L., and Burton L. Anderson. "Industrial Landscapes: Past Views and Stages of Recognition." *Professional Geographer,* 28 (1976): 341–348.

Pillsbury, Richard. "From Hamburger Alley to Hedgerose Heights: Toward a Model of Restaurant Location Dynamics." *Professional Geographer,* 39 (1987): 326–344.

Porteous, J. Douglas. *Planned to Death: The Annihilation of a Place Called Howdendyke.* Toronto: University of Toronto Press, 1989.

Rich, D. C., and G. J. R. Linge (eds.). *The State and the Spatial Management of Industrial Change.* New York: Routledge, Chapman & Hall, 1991.

Rubenstein, James M. *The Changing U.S. Auto Industry: A Geographical Analysis.* New York: Routledge, 1992.

Sawyer, Stephen W. *Renewable Energy: Progress, Prospects.* Resource Publication. Washington, DC: Association of American Geographers, 1986.

Scott, Allen J. *New Industrial Spaces.* London: Pion, 1988.

Scott, Allen J., and Michael Storper (eds.). *Production, Work, Territory: The Geographical Anatomy of Industrial Capitalism.* Winchester, MA: Allen & Unwin, 1986.

Seager, Joni. *The State of the Earth Atlas.* New York: Simon & Schuster, 1990. An essential geographical reference for everyone concerned about the deterioration of environments.

Smith, David M. *Industrial Location: An Economic Geographical Analysis,* 2d ed. New York: John Wiley, 1981.

Stafford, Howard A. "Manufacturing Plant Closure Selections Within Firms." *Annals of the Association of American Geographers,* 81 (1991), 51–65.

Sternlieb, George, and James W. Hughes (eds.). *America's New Market Geography: Nation, Region, and Metropolis.* New Brunswick, NJ: Rutgers University Center for Urban Policy Research, 1988.

Storper, Michael, and Richard Walker. *The Capitalist Imperative: Territory, Technology, and Industrial Growth.* New York: Basil Blackwell, 1989.

Taaffe, Edward J., and Howard L. Gauthier, Jr. *Geography of Transportation.* Englewood Cliffs, NJ: Prentice-Hall, 1973.

Taylor, Michael, and Nigel Thrift (eds.). *The Geography of Multinationals.* New York: St. Martin's Press, 1982.

Tolley, Rodney, and Brian Turton. *Transport Systems, Policy and Planning: A Geographical Approach.* London: Longman, 1995.

Trinder, Barrie. *The Making of the Industrial Landscape.* London: J. M. Dent & Sons, 1982.

Tuan, Yi-Fu. "Cultural Pluralism and Technology." *Geographical Review,* 79 (1989): 269–279.

Vance, James E., Jr. *Capturing the Horizon: The Historical Geography of Transportation.* New York: Harper & Row, 1986.

Warren, Kenneth. *The American Steel Industry, 1850–1970: A Geographical Interpretation.* Pittsburgh: University of Pittsburgh Press, 1988.

Warrick, Richard, and Graham Farmer. "The Greenhouse Effect, Climatic Change and Rising Sea Level: Implications for Development." *Transactions of the Institute of British Geographers,* 15 (1990): 5–20.

Watts, Hugh D. *Industrial Geography.* London: Longman Scientific & Industrial Publications, 1987.

Webber, Michael J. *Industrial Location.* Newbury Park, CA: Sage Publications, 1984.

Weber, Alfred. *Theory of the Location of Industries.* Friedrich, Carl J. (trans. and ed.). Chicago: University of Chicago Press, 1929.

Wilhelm, Hubert G. H. "The Borrow Pit Landscape." *Journal of Cultural Geography,* 8 (Fall-Winter 1987): 25–34.

CHAPTER 13

Education and Opportunities in Geography

The purpose of this last chapter is to put cultural geography in its broader context by discussing the contemporary discipline and profession of geography. We look at the national agenda for geographic literacy, what an undergraduate study of geography entails, and what kind of professional opportunities await students with geography degrees. To fully explain where advanced geography study will take you, we also briefly examine the subdisciplines in the field.

It is said that a little knowledge can be a dangerous thing, so we want you to leave this introductory class in cultural geography with an accurate notion of what you know and do not know, as well as how your knowledge fits into a larger picture. Although this chapter repeats some material presented in Chapter 1, its main purpose is to build on the introductory chapter by drawing in new and expanded information.

Toward Geographic Literacy

The public and the press are legitimately concerned today about the study of geography. Perhaps you have seen newspaper or magazine articles with alarming statistics that document "geography illiteracy" in the United States. Some examples from various studies:

Twenty-five percent of the high school seniors in Dallas did not know that Mexico was directly south of Texas.

Of 400 students tested at the University of Tennessee, only half could locate Japan on a map.

Forty percent of the high school students tested in Kansas City could not name three countries in South America.

There are many other indications of ignorance of geography. In a recent Gallup Poll, fewer than half the people questioned knew the population of the United States, and a third could not name a NATO country. Sometimes this ignorance is brought home in a personal way: Once one of the authors was awakened from deep sleep at 5:30 in the morning with a telephone call from the research desk at the National

Geographic Society. The caller from this venerable geographic institution forgot there was a three-hour time difference between Washington, DC, and California!

When compared with other cultures, Americans rank low when quizzed about the world and its countries, people, and natural environment. Furthermore, there is strong evidence that this ignorance is a product of the past few decades; standardized tests show high school and college students scored much higher in the 1950s than students do today. For example, a *New York Times* survey in the 1950s found that 84 percent of the people questioned knew Manila was in the Philippines, but more recently this figure had slipped to 27 percent.

How can this be when we are the so-called global generation, wired across oceans, and continents, with telephones, faxes, e-mail, the Internet, satellites, and cable communications networks—technologies that instantaneously offer us global news and information and the latest fads and styles? Given all the worldly information available, how can we fail to put it all together into some meaningful geographic framework? Though this contradiction is not easily explained, professional educators lay much of the blame on the erosion of systematic geographic study in America's elementary and high schools. In contrast to such countries as Japan, Russia, France, England, and Canada—where geography is prominently featured in high school curricula—in the United States geography is usually buried deep in social studies classes. Is it any wonder students from other countries do better when tested on global knowledge? Beyond the classroom, is it fair to say that businesspeople and politicians from these countries have an advantage in the international arena over those from the United States?

Fortunately there are many positive changes taking place to upgrade geographic education in North America. In 1985, the Geographic Education National Implementation Plan (GENIP) was launched to revitalize the teaching and learning of geography from kindergarten through high school. Major support for this comprehensive program comes from the National Geographic Society, the largest nonprofit, nongovernmental geographic organization in the world. A major facet of this comprehensive program is support for state-based Geographic Alliances, groups that coordinate discussions among classroom teachers, academic geographers, and students on curriculum guidelines, classroom materials, and professional outreach activities. By 1993, every state had its own Geographic Alliance working as a powerful resource to improve geography teaching in grades K to 12.

Then in 1994, *Geography for Life: National Geography Standards* was published. This is an innovative document that gives exhaustive answers to the question, "What should students know and be able to do in geography at the completion of grades 4, 8, and 12?" Eighteen geography standards represent answers to that question and provide guidelines, content, activities, and learning opportunities that will produce geographically literate students.

For example, Standard 1 focuses on the use of maps and other geographic representations, tools, and technologies to acquire, process, and report information from a spatial perspective. Following this goal, standards are then set as to what students should be able to do with maps by the end of their fourth, eighth, and twelfth years of school. Standard 14 illustrates the role cultural geography plays in this new national geography curriculum. That standard addresses the "characteristics, distribution, and complexity of the earth's cultural mosaics" and states that by the end of the twelfth grade, the student knows and understands

1. The impact of culture on the way of life in different regions
2. How cultures shape the character of a region
3. The spatial characteristics of the processes of cultural convergence and divergence

Going further, the standards then require students to demonstrate competency in Standard 14 with specific exercises. They include identifying the cultural factors that have promoted political conflict in a certain region such as Sub-Saharan Africa or eastern Europe.

These recent changes in geographic education underscore the importance our society now places on geographic literacy and global understanding by moving far beyond the mere memorization of place names and esoteric facts about foreign countries (Figure 13.1). Instead two important perspectives are promoted: the spatial perspective, which is the fundamental underpinning of geography, and the ecological, which views Earth as a complex system of interrelated and interactive physical and human forces. These two viewpoints underline the academic discipline of geography; this topic is explored in the next section.

Geography as a Field of Study

As you know by now, geography is fundamentally the study of space on the Earth's surface. In fact, many think of geography as the *spatial science*, or the systematic description and explanation of spatial or *areal* patterns and variation. A simple contrast is useful: compare geography to the study of history, which focuses on time. History can be

Figure 13.1
Hong Kong. While it is important to know the location of a place in the world, geographers are also interested in this city's past and present role in global affairs and how that role may change in the near future.

thought of as the *temporal science* because it systematically describes and explains patterns and variations over time. This contrast, of course, is oversimplified because it is nearly impossible to study space without including time, and vice versa. Therefore the distinction turns on fundamental emphasis. Geographers emphasize the study of space, and historians emphasize the study of time, just as political scientists emphasize the study of government and power, economists stress the flow of goods and services, and so on. Although some aspects of both time and space are usually included in all disciplines, geography is the only field that emphasizes spatial or areal variation on the world's surface.

How does geography accomplish its goals of studying the Earth's space? Most geographers would agree that there are five essential elements to geographic inquiry. These five facets are closely related to, yet not completely synonymous with, the five themes we have used in this cultural geography textbook. Note the similarities—but also note the differences:

1. Geography is the study of *location*. This includes the spatial location or "global address" of people, places, and activities. Where is this place, and why is it there? This textbook has assumed that location is important but we have not placed it in our thematic framework.
2. Geography is the study of *place*. Abstract space is transformed by human action into places, settlements, or locations that have unique characteristics. The study of place is closely related to this book's theme of the cultural landscape because this concept draws out the material and tangible traits of a place.
3. Geography is the study of *regions*. As we have learned, regions are areas of shared characteristics, of similar physical landscapes (such as the tropical rain forest), or, as we have discussed, of shared human traits. When applied to human activities, this theme is very similar to this book's theme of cultural region.
4. Geography is the study of *human-environment interaction*. As we saw in Chapter 1, geographers have always been concerned with the spatial expression of human interaction with the environment. This textbook has used the theme of cultural ecology to capture this important tradition of geographic study.
5. Finally, geography is the study of *movement*. Because people and activities are dynamic, they move through space and across the Earth's surface. Geographers are interested in more than a static world; they are also interested in the fluid and changing world. In this book we put this concern into the framework of cultural diffusion.

These five characteristics of the discipline also form the pedagogical framework for the GENIP, the coordinated plan for how geography will be taught in the late 1990s, which we mentioned earlier. Although you need not be bothered with details of the GENIP, do remember its five aspects of geography because they constitute a concise framework for the discipline. The major difference between the GENIP attributes and the five themes stressed in this book is that *The Human Mosaic*'s themes focus exclusively on cultural geography, and GENIP's five facets encompass the entire discipline, both human and physical. That brings us to the point where we must take a quick look at the entire scope of geography in order to include cultural geography in that broader picture.

The Scope of Geography

Because the spatial study of the Earth's surface encompasses so much information, geography has traditionally been divided into two fields: *physical geography,* which concentrates on the physical environment, and *human, or cultural, geography.* As its name suggests, this second field emphasizes the spatial dimension of human activities. Furthermore, both physical and human geography are broken down into an array of distinct subdisciplines.

Within physical geography, for example, some geographers concentrate on the geological expressions of the Earth's surface, such as landforms, glaciers, earthquakes, and coastal erosion; this study falls under *geomorphology,* or the study of the Earth's form. This subdiscipline is closely related to, but differs from, geology, our close neighbor in the physical sciences. *Biogeographers* study the spatial expressions of vegetation, examining matters such as the effects of acid rain, forest ecology, and wetland dynamics; this subdiscipline draws heavily on biology, botany, and ecology in the natural sciences. *Climatology,* as the name suggests, studies the world's climates—past, present, and future.

Although geography traditionally is divided into physical and human categories, these categories are not mutually exclusive. Clearly, many human activities greatly affect the physical environment. In fact, these effects are so widespread that today some geographers are reluctant to use the conventional term *natural environment* because it no longer describes a world in which most of the planet's areas have not been modified by humans. Because physical geographers now study human-affected environments, classes in human geography are an integral part of their professional education. And the reverse is true as well: Human geographers need to know about the physical environment in order to better understand their subfield. We develop this point later in the chapter, when we discuss a typical undergraduate course of study for a geography major.

Scan this book's table of contents for a quick look at the subdisciplines of cultural geography: they are population dynamics, agriculture, politics, language, and so on. The different subdisciplines of geography emphasize different dimensions of human activity across space, such as economic, political, or historical problems in all parts of the world. What brings together these human activities is the unifying theme of geography: space, spatial patterns, and areal variation. Furthermore, all these subfields organize their questions, methods, and emphases in terms of the five themes of geography—location, movement, place, environment, and region. Though we have emphasized the cultural dimension of human geography, you can see how a class in economic geography would concentrate on different topics, such as the spread of technology or even poverty. Unlike the methods of human geography, where qualitative data and subjective interpretation are legitimate methods, economic geographers instead would emphasize quantitative methods and models.

This brings us to the topic of those specific technical skills needed in professional geography. As you read through the next section, keep in mind that these technical skills are usually a direct pathway to jobs after graduation because they are often much sought after by employers in both the public and private sectors.

The Techniques of Geography

The technical skills geographers use today often draw on modern technology such as satellites and computers to answer age-old questions about the world (see box, *Geography on the Internet*). Where are we? What is the best use of the Earth's resources? How is the environment changing? How should we plan for the future?

Cartography. Cartography, or mapmaking, has long been a part of geography, dating back to the Greeks, Romans, and Muslims of the Classical world. Because maps are one of the best means of graphically depicting spatial patterns on the Earth's surface, geographers must know how to both make maps and read them. Most people can learn to read maps correctly with a little instruction; but making maps is another matter, for the skill combines equal parts of art and science.

Today, good cartography includes both hand-drawn graphic design talent and computer skills. Most maps now are created and produced by a combination of computer graphic programs and old-fashioned pen-and-ink drawings. Though all geographers have the basic map compilation skills necessary to their work, some professionals special-

Geography on the Internet

Good geography lies around the turn of every block: in the rich intercultural mix of vowels and consonants associated with a creolized tongue; in country-western, gypsy, gamelan, or shaped-note music; or in the struggles of aboriginal peoples that are encapsulated in political geography. And all of these themes, to name but a few, have an electronic presence on the Internet, the global constellation of linked computers that forms the well-known "information superhighway."

There is virtually no place on the World Wide Web, the cleanest expression of the Internet, where geography is not full of possibility. A sophisticated Web browser—as an application like Netscape used to "surf" the Web is called—includes helper programs that allow viewing brief movies, listening to digitized sound, downloading images and maps, and pulling up fully-formatted professional papers and publications. With a "helper" like Quicktime VR, a Net surfer can zoom across cities with just the directional click of a mouse. Entirely aside from the immense implications for the geography of information, the Internet offers many means for practicing geographers to gather data from world-wide information servers.

Meanwhile, Web pages proliferate, accessible with the right software simply by typing an URL (pronounced "earl," for Universal Resource Locator). Each URL is in effect the unique call number or address of a web page. Many geographers are turning their skills with graphic representation, computers, and design into work as web page authors, for fun or profit.

Three kinds of "sites" are worth thinking about for the student of cultural geography. First there are the Geography Departments that have been quick to accept this technology. Sophisticated Home Pages are up for a number of Geography Departments—not just in the United States, but around the world. It is in fact much easier to find the names and specialties of geographers abroad through the Internet than through printed sources. Second, there are vast troves of geographical data on the Internet, and these are worth mention, although unsurprisingly the number and usability of these data cores are monthly increasing by leaps and bounds. Finally, there are the Internet Search Engines. These handy tools, already well over a dozen major ones, make it possible to search the World Wide Web with relative ease. Some of the starting points should be soon familiar to you—almost any University or College has someplace where the WWW, as the Web's expression on the Internet is generally known, can be explored.

For all the promise, there is one important warning that needs to be heeded. Getting to this information is all fine and well, and the 1990s, when many people feared the information glut was going to become a reality, is proving to be a time when huge amounts of information are readily accessible, in very user-friendly ways. But, it is up to each student to learn how to analyze, evaluate, and rate what is coming in. Turning in a list of 300 citations, including URLs, isn't worth anything if you have no idea what they mean or how useful these resources are. "Surfing" is not a viable alternative to learning and thinking.

Some of the places you might choose to visit:

Departments

http://www.maxwell.syr.edu/depts/geography/index.html [Syracuse Geography]

http://id-www.ucsb.edu/GEOG/home.html [UC Santa Barbara Geography]

http://www.gis.psu.edu/generalhtml/psginstructions.html [Penn State Geography]

ize in the highly technical aspects of cartography. Cartographic skills are in great demand both within and outside of geography, and increasing numbers of geography departments are emphasizing these mapmaking skills. These classes usually begin with introductory map reading and progress into basic map drawing, then move into computer cartography, where desktop publishing graphics programs or specialized computer-aided design (CAD) packages can produce highly sophisticated maps. Beyond this stage are even more advanced cartography techniques that go beyond the scope of this introduction. You could probably see people at work using cartographic techniques by asking your professor for a tour of the college's geography department and cartography laboratory.

Aerial Photography and Remote Sensing. One of the best ways to gather geographic information is from above, by looking down at the Earth's surface at the varying patterns of landforms, vegetation, and human settlement. Ever since the first aerial photographs were taken from airplanes in the 1930s, geographers and other Earth scientists have used these tools of their trade because aerial photos reveal so much valuable

Geography on the Internet

http://geogweb.berkeley.edu/BerkGeog.html [Berkeley Geography]

http://lorax.geog.scarolina.edu/ [Geography, U of South Carolina]

http://wwwhost.cc.utexas.edu/ftp/pub/grg/main.html [UT Austin Geography]

Some Varied Geographical Resources

http://www.marketingtools.com/ [American Demographics Home Page]

http://riceinfor.rice/edu/projects/RDA/VirtualCity/index.html [The Virtual City]

http://www.esri.com/ [ESRI—Home of the GIS People]

http://elvis.neep.misc.edu/~cdean/index.html [History of Cartography Project]

http://www.delorme.com/ [DeLorme Maps in the News]

http://www.lib.utexas.edu/Libs/PCL/Map_collection/Map_Collection.html [Perry-Castañeda Map Collection]

http://www.si.edu/nmai/ [Smithsonian National Museum of the American Indian]

http://www.census.gov/ [US Bureau of the Census Home Page]

http://www.env.gov.bc.ca/ [Ministry of Environment, Lands, & Parks, British Columbia, Canada]

http://www.clr.toronto.edu/clr.html [Centre for Landscape Research Network]

http://www.lonelyplanet.com/ [Lonely Planet Online]

http://www.infosphere.com/HCN/ [High Country News, Paonia, Colorado]

http://outside.starwave.com/outside/online [Outside Online]

http://www.u-tokyo.ac.jp/ [University of Tokyo]

http://www.ran.org/ran/ [Rainforest Action Network]

http://www.undp.org/ [United Nations Development Programme]

http://www.cris.com/~Psyspy/area51/ [Area51 Research Center]

http://homepage.interaccess.com/~maynard/ [Land Surveying]

http://www.willamette.edu/~tjones/Language-Page.html [The Human Languages Page]

http://www.music.indiana.edu/misc/academic.html [Music Resources on the Internet]

http://www.eit.com/creations/research/share/folkhold/folkhome.html [Folk Music Home Page]

http://www.wchat.on.ca/vic/wwwp.htm [World Wide Punk]

http://www.microstate.com/pub/micros/index.html [Microstate Resources]

Search Engines

http://www.yahoo.com/, *and,* http://www.yahoo.com/Science/Geography/ [Yahoo Subject Searching]

http://www.w3.org/hypertext/DataSources/bySubject/overview.html, *and,* http://hpb1.hwc.ca/WWW_VL_Geography.html [WWW Virtual Library—Geography], *or* http://geog.gmu.edu/gess/jwc/cartogrefs.html [Virtual Library Cartography and Map Sources]; *or* try, http://history.cc.ukans.edu/history/WWW_History_main.html [WWW Virtual Library—History]

http://www.cs.colostate.edu/~dreiling/smartform.html [SavvySearch]

http://www.mckinley.com/ [The McKinley Group]

Source: Prof. Paul Starrs, Dept. of Geography, University of Nevada, Reno. Used with permission. For further discussion, see Starrs, Paul F., and Lynn Huntsinger. "The Matrix, Cyberpunk Literature, and the Apocalyptic Landscapes of Information Technology." *Information Technology and Libraries* [Chicago], 14, No. 4 (December 1995): pp. 251–256.

information that ground-level observation cannot. Land uses such as crop patterns or urban districts, for example, are much clearer from aerial views, as are earthquake traces, river channels, and vegetation gradients. Although much of this information is apparent to the untrained eye, systematic interpretation and translation of the photo details involve special skills. Often, overlapping aerial photographs are used so that the landscape appears three-dimensional when viewed through a tool called a stereoscope. This third dimension facilitates geometric height measurement of landscape features such as a forest, something that would be difficult to measure from ground level. Many other features and patterns can be quantified as well. This technique is called *photogrammetry,* the science of measurement and mapping from aerial photographs.

A refinement from the space age is aerial data taken from satellites that transmit information back to Earth-based computers (Figure 13.2). This is called *remote sensing,* because the device that acquires the data is not in close physical contact with the object it is studying. Images of wider areas can be obtained. In remote sensing a distinction is also made between darkroom-printed photographs and those maps and images produced by computer decoding of information electronically transmitted from satellites. Although remote sensing is fundamental to a geographer's study of the Earth, it is also commonly used in other Earth science fields such as meteorology, which brings the satellite photographs of clouds to the nightly televised weather report or provides images of drought damage to crops that can be used to assess food supplies in Africa. Although the uses of remote sensing have spread beyond the discipline of geography, most geography programs offer classes in this fascinating and useful subject. Again, as is true of cartography, this skill is in great demand by private and public agencies.

Figure 13.2
Remote sensing. Information about the Earth's surface is transmitted from satellites in space, then this data is translated electronically into graphic forms resembling maps or aerial photographs.

Geographic Information Systems (GIS). One of the newest tools and skills of the geographer's trade is GIS (geographic information systems), which, like aerial photographs and remote sensing, is now widely used in all sorts of private, public, and academic pursuits. GIS is an integrated computer package for the input, storage, analysis, and graphic display of spatial information; the computer's ability to quickly display complex information graphically on the screen allows analysis without going to the more conventional output of paper maps. Computer capability allows numerous *what if?* questions to be examined rapidly. For example, one *what if?* problem-solving scenario might be the search for an environmentally sensitive highway route that does not affect endangered habitats, archaeological sites, or expensive agricultural cropland. The first step in the process is feeding the diverse information into the computer; then different possibilities for such a highway can be considered. Finally, because of the integrated nature of GIS, hard-copy output is also relatively easy in the form of detailed computer maps that show the sensitive areas along the new highway route.

Although GIS has been around since the mid-1960s, it remained a cumbersome, mainframe-driven specialized tool until hardware and software costs made GIS more easily accessible in the late 1980s. Today, GIS can be run on personal computers and is now found in just about every planning agency, environmental impact assessment firm, utility district, landscape architect's office, and corporate site location office. In addition, GIS remains a powerful research tool for all kinds of workers in both the social and natural sciences. One of the big advantages of GIS is that it can couple remote sensing data with vast amounts of regional scale data that can be manipulated, analyzed, and displayed.

The fact that GIS is by definition a spatial tool keeps geographers in the foreground of its use. Just about all geography departments now have GIS labs and offer classes in the subject. And, as is the case with the other tools mentioned, students who know GIS have gained important employment skills.

An Undergraduate Education in Geography

Now that you have a broader idea of geography, let us put the pieces together by looking at a typical undergraduate major in the field. The point of this is not to convert you to geography, but rather to give you a sense of how the various emphases and subdisciplines might fit together in the education of a geographer. We start with a word of caution: a geography education can be taken two ways—either as a general liberal arts education or as professional training. Geography can be an excellent liberal arts degree because it brings together so many fascinating aspects of the world. Yet, as interesting as this can be, geography in this sense is a relatively unspecialized education and will probably not lead to a professional job in the field. Consequently, students should decide by their junior year what it is they want from their studies, and, if they expect their major to prepare them for a professional position, they should concentrate on a specific aspect of geography and prepare themselves with the appropriate technical skills.

Geography programs commonly offer two introductory classes, one in physical geography and the other, an overview of human, or cultural, geography. This two-part introductory series reminds us that the foundation for the field lies equally in those two subfields. Often, a third kind of introductory class that combines the two by using a regional approach to the world is offered as well. Instead of organizing material thematically, this regional course explores the physical and human geographies of specific areas of the world. Because such an approach, by virtue of its scope, often results in a broad-brush, general treatment, many world regional classes are taught as service courses for nongeography majors. Students who intend to concentrate or major in geography should spend a full semester on both physical and human geography and use an introductory world regional class only as a way of gaining familiarity with the world.

Geography students are usually required to take classes in other fields that complement their study. Commonly, majors take introductory science classes such as geology, chemistry, and biology, along with social science classes in economics, anthropology, and political science. In addition, to aid quantitative research, statistics and calculus courses are important for advanced geography study.

The real substance of geography starts in the junior year, after students have fulfilled their college breadth requirements and passed the required introductory courses. Upper-division classes are generally grouped into three categories: *topical* or *systematic* classes, such as political geography, climatology, or advanced economic geography; *regional* classes, where a distinct part of the world is the class focus, be it Europe, Latin America, or Asia; and *method* or *technique* classes, such as map reading, cartography, remote sensing, GIS, or quantitative geography.

At this point, geography majors are usually asked to choose an emphasis or concentration in their chosen field. Though some concentrate in physical geography, others may select an aspect of cultural geography. Still others decide to concentrate on methods or techniques, like cartography or GIS. Each one of these special emphases demands advanced classes outside of geography. For physical geography, students should incorporate upper-division courses in geology, meteorology, environmental sciences, or botany. Aspiring cultural geographers need advanced classes in economics, anthropology, urban planning, and statistics; those focusing on methods should add advanced mathematics classes, engineering courses, and computer science and programming courses to their curricula.

Two other kinds of academic experiences are also important. Student internships are an excellent way for juniors and seniors to experience different job situations outside the classroom. An internship is an effective way of making contacts and breaking into professional networks to acquire the personal references and recommendations necessary for building a strong resumé. Commonly, upper-division geography students find internships with planning agencies, cartography firms, environmental consultants, and site location analysts.

Advanced students should also do at least one independent research project in their senior year. This not only gives students an opportunity to investigate a topic in depth, it also gives them a chance to work more closely with a professor. Under such circumstances, a professor can see that a student is indeed highly motivated, skilled, industrious, and capable of independent work. These are the traits that will net the student a strong letter of recommendation that can help cinch a desirable job. In addition, independent studies usually produce a tangible product, such as a research paper or a sophisticated computer map, that can be shown to potential employers as material evidence of technical skills.

Are There Jobs for Geographers?

Yes, very definitely so. Although job opportunities vary from place to place, and you are the one who will have to determine what specific jobs are available in your area, we discuss some general categories of employment for geography majors. Of course, you can always consult your geography professors for their insights on employment in the field.

College graduates with geography degrees usually find employment in one of four areas: teaching, environmental analysis, city and regional planning, and cartography and geographic information systems. Each of these career fields is described briefly below; also consult the "Sources and Suggested Readings" at the end of the chapter for resources that give more information on professional opportunities for geography majors. (Figure 13.3 depicts some geographers at work.

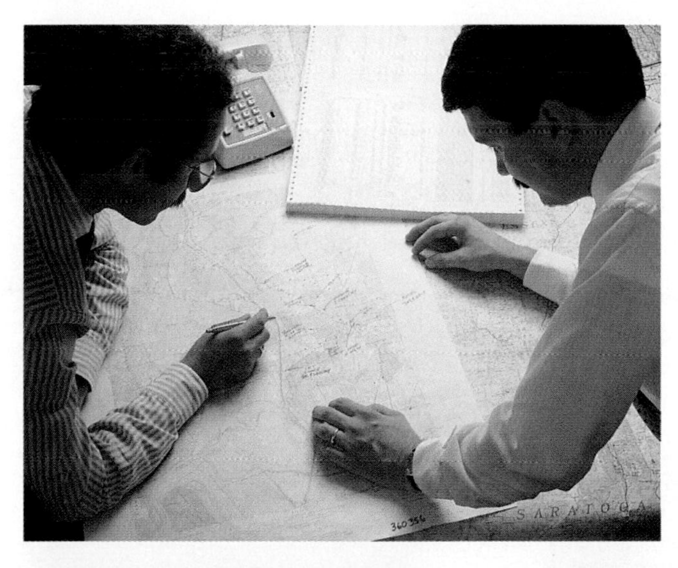

Figure 13.3
Geographers at work. While cartographers actually make maps, other geographers use them in the classroom, for resource planning, and in the field for environmental analysis.

TABLE 13.1
Job Titles of Recent Geography Graduates

Here are some job titles for recent geography graduates from geography programs in various parts of the country. This sample is by no means complete nor comprehensive since it includes only a handful from the hundreds of different geography degree programs in the United States and Canada. This sample was taken in Fall 1995

College or University	Job Title
Arizona State University Tempe, Arizona	Cartographer, county flood control district Forecaster, National Weather Service GIS specialist, State Fish and Game
Brigham Young University Provo, Utah	City planner Image processing specialist County planner GIS technician Public school teacher
California State University Chico, California	Staff planner, regional planning agency Environmental consultant Assistant city planner County planner
Central Washington University Ellensburg, Washington	GIS technician Transportation planner Environmental analyst Planner, regional development agency
University of Colorado Boulder, Colorado	Oceanographer Field scientist, environmental consulting firm
Frostburg State University Frostburg, Maryland	Environmental planner Hydrogeologist Cartographic technician County planner Environmental scientist GIS analyst
University of Nevada Reno, Nevada	City planner GIS specialist Development consultant to Native American groups Regional planner Information specialist, Bureau of Mines and Geology
Northern Arizona University Flagstaff, Arizona	County planner Policy analyst, water resources GIS/Cartographer, highway department Director of public programs, city arboretum
San Jose State University San Jose, California	GIS customer support, software firm Aerial photography editor GIS project manager
University of South Florida Tampa, Florida	Marketing representative, GIS software Geography teacher, community college Environmental consultant Coordinator, state GIS agency

Table 13.1 may also be helpful; it lists the job titles held by recent geography graduates.

Teaching

Although geography has been neglected in schools over the last few decades, this situation is quickly changing. As a result, people with geography backgrounds are—and will be—finding jobs in education.

Why? Because as we mentioned earlier, geography now enjoys equal footing with science, math, English, and history in our national education goals. If this program moves forward as designed, there will be a great demand for geography teachers by the late 1990s.

How does one prepare for the teaching job market? There is no one answer to that question because teaching requirements differ greatly from state to state. Whereas some states require a formal major in geography in order to teach the subject, others require only a certain number of college credits, and instead of a geography degree, they might require a liberal arts, social science, or education degree. If you are interested in teaching, acquaint yourself early in your college career with your state's specific requirements by talking with college advisers in both the geography and education departments.

Environmental Analysis

Because geographers know much about the environment and can think spatially, they are in demand by public and private agencies and firms in the field of environmental analysis. The vitality of this employment sector is often linked to the strength of state and local environmental regulations. That is, there are more of these jobs in those states and municipalities where environmental protection is taken seriously. What skills are important? First, a good understanding of physical geography, including advanced courses in environmental geology, botany, air pollution, and hydrology, is necessary. Second, familiarity with environmental laws and procedures is important. This comes from classes in environmental planning, monitoring, and law; environmental impact assessment; and ecological restoration. Third, geographic methods, like cartography, remote sensing, aerial photo interpretation, GIS, and statistical analysis, are needed. And last, an ability to write reports is essential. Hone your writing skills by taking a technical writing class and producing as many term papers as possible. Save the best ones to show potential employers as examples of your writing skills.

City and Regional Planning

Geographers often work as city, county, and regional planners because—once again—of their spatial and environmental orientation. Since planners work toward an orderly use of land and environmental resources, they must have a comprehensive understanding of the social, economic, political, and environmental factors that make up land-use and resource decisions. That often means bringing together information from maps, air photos, field investigation, GIS and census data, with an understanding of planning regulations and guidelines. A knowledge of environmental and planning law is very important, and this can be gained by classes in urban planning, environmental studies, and political science. Technical classes in GIS, remote sensing, cartography, and statistics are also mandatory. As with many other career pathways, an internship with a city or county planning agency is an extremely valuable experience to learn firsthand about the professional skills needed by planners.

Cartography and GIS

Many geography graduates find jobs in mapmaking at professional organizations ranging in size from large government agencies, such as the

US Geological Survey or US Department of Defense, to small firms specializing in regional and city maps. If you have specialized in geographic methods, you are aware of the cartographic skills these jobs require. Cartographic positions can include both hand-drawn and computer mapmaking. Many firms have summer and part-time jobs, and the learning curve is usually steep with on-the-job training. Try to find one of these positions, not just to learn more professional cartography, but also to acquaint yourself with the daily routine of mapmaking. Some aspects of cartography are creative, artistic, and highly rewarding; others can be tedious or even boring. These highs and lows are commonly part of a cartographer's life, and sampling the job early in your career will tell you whether you have the disposition for this kind of work. If you do not get a chance to try the job beforehand, talk to cartographers about their profession. Not everyone can do cartography because of the detail-oriented design skills and hand-eye coordination that are necessary. Even among those with talent, not everyone is extremely patient or wants to spend all his or her working hours designing and making maps. This job takes a special kind of discipline and disposition.

One of the hottest job markets for geographers is linked to geographic information systems, since just about every planning agency, environmental consultancy, and location analysis firm is turning to GIS to complement their work tasks. Additionally, geographers are getting jobs with private-sector GIS firms to help them develop, market, and support their software and hardware products. The best way to take advantage of this growth area is to take whatever GIS classes are offered in your geography department, do some internship to get real-world experience, then keep on the learning curve with workshops and reading because this area is changing rapidly. Classes in remote sensing, statistics, cartography, and physical geography will complement your career with GIS.

Back to Cultural Geography

Now that you have a better sense of the whole discipline of geography and some of the job possibilities for college graduates, let us revisit cultural geography with a quick look at this subfield in terms of the broader scheme of the entire discipline. First we redefine the topic by elaborating on the concept of culture, then we conclude with a few words about how the study of human geography might be applied to our changing world.

In Chapter 1, we defined cultural geography as "the study of spatial variations among cultural groups and the spatial functioning of society." Although that definition was enough to get us started, we conclude our study by adding some refinements. We start with three points.

First, our initial definition of culture simply added human culture to a basic definition of geography as the spatial science, as the discipline that describes and explains spatial or areal variation.

Second, now that you see the breadth of geography and see that it includes numerous subfields that dissect and emphasize specific aspects of the environment or of human activity, what about culture? Mark Twain once said about the weather, "Everyone talks about it, but no one does anything about it." The same often applies to culture. We all talk about it, but what do we *do* about it? Cultural geographers use the concept of culture *systematically,* by describing and explaining spatial patterns and variation of culture.

Finally, because there is no generally accepted definition of culture, many social scientists (including some geographers) use it in a general, superficial, and uncritical way, and this usually causes more problems than it solves. Culture is a useful and pertinent conceptual tool only when it is used critically and systematically, and when an effort is made to define those aspects of human variety that are under study.

In Chapter 1, we gave you a very general definition of culture. However, now it may be appropriate to elaborate on the concept of culture by introducing additional dimensions to the concept with the intent of laying some groundwork for you to use in the continuing analysis of your world. Culture, as you know, has both material and abstract dimensions. Examples of material culture are artifacts such as tools, dress, buildings, and field patterns; these matters have become familiar to you throughout our study of cultural landscapes. However, we should not overlook the abstract aspects of culture, facets such as speech, behavior, values, and ideology. Although it is understandable that geographers have emphasized the material aspects of culture over the abstract because of the traditional focus on explaining spatial variation on the Earth's surface, the two aspects are intertwined and influence one another.

More to the point is that material culture often reinforces abstract cultural values and ideas. This is important to remember as we look at how people affect their surroundings through the creation of cultural landscapes; those features we often take for granted in the visible world of landscapes can be powerful symbolic statements about a group's culture—what is valued and revered and what is rejected. And, as landscapes change because of complex sociopolitical or economic forces, people must rearrange their cultural values to flow alongside these changes.

Culture, then, should be viewed as dynamic rather than static, and it is best thought of as a process rather than an unchanging state. Furthermore, the process of culture in most of the world is a result of peoples' adjusting or adapting to new, changing conditions: whereas in some aspects people react in conservative ways by preserving traditional behavior, in other dimensions of culture people are trying out these new behaviors, tools, techniques, and values. There is usually an inherent tension within any culture where there is conflict between new impulses and accepted or traditional ways. We spoke of that tension as we discussed the differences among folk, ethnic, and popular culture. Though these three categories were separated for the sake of discussion, in reality all three of these aspects of culture can be merged and found within any given group. Usually this interaction causes tension and sometimes overt conflict.

Some social scientists argue that the concept of culture is relevant today only when it captures the dynamic, ever-changing aspects of a group's life, those facets expressive of the conflicts and tensions resulting from contemporary life. This approach can be summarized in three *C* words: culture is *constructed, contested,* and *contextual.* Without getting caught up in details, we can say that these three terms are useful to human geography because they remind us that culture can be thought of as an ever-changing process of constructing a sense of group identity; that often these needs come from conflict and competition, and finally, that this process should be examined as taking place in a specific social context. Although this advice may seem self-evident, it does shift the analytical emphasis away from the conventional social science view of culture as an abstract, superorganic, and static state governed by its own internal logic. The concept of culture, then, is most meaningful and useful when it is used critically and clearly, and, additionally, when culture is explicitly defined by those using the concept.

Applying Your Skills in Cultural Geography

Whether you know it or not, you now have new skills that are important to understanding our complicated and changing world. Let's take stock of these talents before we end.

First, you have a new understanding of the power of culture and its varied expressions. You see the importance of belief systems in shaping resource exploitation and environmental change, of the cultural framework for economic systems, and of the way cultural elements transform our interaction with the physical environment. You can conceptualize the movement of cultural phenomena geographically using diffusion models, and you can differentiate areas of similarity into cultural regions. You have learned to decipher expressions of human habitation and subsistence through cultural landscapes and assess the different forms of human interaction with the environment through the theme of cultural ecology.

In addition, you can think in different scales, from local to global. This ability can serve you well. One of the intellectual shortcomings of specialization can be a spatial inflexibility that inhibits examining environmental problems at different scales. Complementing these new skills are heightened abilities in reading maps, figures, and graphs.

Because space and time are inseparable in the study of human geography, you have an enhanced temporal perspective about environmental matters and cultural patterns. You have moved beyond *presentism,* which is a sense of life at only this present point in time; often this is a shortsighted, confining view that limits discussion of problems to contemporary evidence. Understanding that global environmental change is one of the more pressing problems facing our world demands a comprehensive spatio-temporal perspective.

Although the emphasis in this book has been on cultural geography, you also have an improved understanding of our physical world and, more specifically, on the ways that humans have modified this world. Finally, think of this book and your introductory geography class as a beginning, not an end. Think of the concepts, skills, and information you learned from this experience not as a complete package but as a foundation for building further understanding of the world, its regions and people, and its growing interconnectedness. Cultural geography has extraordinary power for explaining the complicated human mosaic of our contemporary world. Use your new knowledge often, and use it wisely.

Sources and Suggested Readings

Association of American Geographers. *Geography: Today's Career for Tomorrow.* Washington, DC: Association of American Geographers, 1993.

Association of American Geographers. *Guide to Programs in Geography in the United States and Canada, 1995–96.* Washington, DC: Association of American Geographers, 1995.

Barrows, T. *College Students' Knowledge and Beliefs: A Survey of Global Understanding.* New Rochelle, NY: Change Magazine Press, 1981.

Boehm, Richard. *Careers in Geography*. Washington, DC: National Geographic Society, 1993.

Burrough. P. *Principles of Geographical Information Systems for Land Resources Assessment*. Oxford: Clarendon Press, 1986.

Christopherson, Robert. *Geosystems: An Introduction to Physical Geography*, 2d ed. New York: Macmillan.

Curran, Paul. *Principles of Remote Sensing*. Harlow, UK: Longman, 1985.

Crump, M. *Exploring Your World: The Adventure of Geography*. Washington, DC: National Geography Society, 1989.

Demko, George, Jerome Angel, and Eugene Bee. *Why in the World? Adventures in Geography*. New York: Anchor Books, 1992.

Downs, Roger. "Being and Becoming a Geographer: An Agenda for Geography Education." *Annals of the Association of American Geographers,* 84 (1994): 175–191.

Earle, Carville, Kent Mathewson, and Martin Kenzer (eds.). *Concepts in Human Geography*. Lanham, MD: Rowman and Littlefield, 1995.

Gaile, Gary, and Cort Willmott (eds.). *Geography in America*. Columbus, OH: Merrill Publishing Company, 1989.

Graves, N. "Geography and Recent Trends in Education for International Understanding." *Terra,* 97 (1985): 45–49.

Hardwick, Susan. "Looking Toward the Future: A Concepts, Themes, and Standards Approach to Preservice Teacher Education." *Journal of Geography,* 94 (1995): 508–512.

Hill, A. David (ed.). *International Perspectives on Geographic Education*. Skokie, IL: Rand McNally, 1992.

Hill, A. David. "A Survey of Global Understanding of American College Students." *Professional Geographer*, 33 (1981): 235–237.

Holtgrieve, Donald, and Susan Hardwick. *Geography for Educators: Standards, Themes, and Concepts*. Englewood Cliffs, NJ: Prentice-Hall, 1995.

Kates, Robert. "The Human Environment: The Road Not Taken, The Road Still Beckoning." *Annals of the Association of American Geographers,* 77 (1987): 525–534.

Kenzer, Martin (ed.). *On Becoming a Professional Geographer*. Columbus, OH: Merrill Publishing Company, 1989.

Ludwig, Gail. *Directions in Geography: A Guide for Teachers*. Washington DC: National Geographic Society, 1991.

Marshall, Bruce (ed.). *The Real World: Understanding the Modern World Through the New Geography*. Boston: Hougton Mifflin, 1991.

National Geographic Society. *Geography: An International Gallup Survey*. Princeton, NJ: The Gallup Organization, 1988.

National Geographic Society. *Geography for Life: National Geography Standards, 1994*. Washington, DC: National Geographic Society, 1994.

Salter, Christopher. "What Can I Do With Geography?" *Professional Geographer,* 35 (1983): 266–273.

Taketa, Richard. "Management and the Geographer: The Relevance of Geography in Strategic Thinking." *Professional Geographer,* 45 (1993): 465–470.

APPENDIX

Using and Interpreting Maps

Montine Jordan

Figuratively speaking, the world is smaller than it used to be. Vacations range farther afield, businesses operate on a global rather than a national scale, and even our neighborhoods and schools are multicultural. It takes a map to negotiate the evening news, much less to take a trip or navigate the subway system. As world events swirl at a dizzying pace, maps provide the means to visualize location, assess consequences, and evaluate solutions. Although maps have always been essential tools for geographers, today they have become vital components of our everyday lives.

But as maps become more ubiquitous, they also become more challenging to interpret. First, as more untrained mapmakers enter the fray, the rules, or conventions, by which cartographers have instilled consistency to maps over the decades are losing their impact. Second, a wider variety of maps are available. From nautical charts to stylized street maps to Landsat imagery, hundreds of millions of maps of every shape and description are generated each year. To be comfortable with a simple road atlas is no longer enough. Finally, maps, as graphics, are being influenced by changes in the field of visual communications. Indeed, information graphics (or "infographics"), as eloquently described by Edward Tufte in *The Visual Display of Quantitative Information* (Graphics Press, 1983) and *Envisioning Information* (Graphics Press, 1990), rapidly are becoming standard in everything from newspapers to annual reports to magazines. Clearly, a new form of cartography is emerging. In order to comprehend this growing onslaught of maps, it is necessary to grasp their underlying logic.

Projections

Only a globe can accurately display the properties of area, shape, distance, and direction all at once. As such, through the centuries, the most vexing dilemma for cartographers has been how to depict a spherical globe on a flat page. Projections provided that solution. By projecting light through a globe onto a nearby surface, cartographers were able to transfer maps onto paper. Cartographers found that three surfaces could receive the projected image and be flattened without additional distortion—a cylinder, cone, and plane. To this day, these shapes comprise the three major classes of projections.

Cylindrical Projections

Mercator derived his famous projection in 1569 by projecting a globe onto a cylinder. While it was perfect for plotting compass directions for navigation, it also reflects the Flemish cartographer's Eurocentric view of the world, and reminds us of the power of one cartographer to subtly instill his point of view. In Mercator's image, the Northern Hemisphere fills the upper two-thirds of the map, making both Europe and North America far larger in proportion to their neighbors—notably Africa and South America—than is actually the case. In addition, areas beyond 50° latitude north and south are so distorted that a special scale must be used. The project has been widely adopted for classroom use because of its simple rectilinear grid and realistic depiction of shapes (Figure A.1). Nevertheless, the skewed proportions of Mercator's projection have distorted our collective world view for generations.

Conic Projections

Maps projected onto a cone are identifiable by their evenly spaced meridians that emanate from a pole. They are especially useful for mapping regions in the mid-latitudes. The Lambert conformal conic projection preserves the true shape of geographical features—that is, the outlines of the continents look correct. On the other hand, H. C. Albers's equal-area conic projection (1805) depicts true areal proportions—that is, the continents' relative *sizes* are displayed accurately (Figure A.2). This was Mercator's big shortcoming.

Planar Projections

Planar, or azimuthal , projections are produced by putting a light source at the center of a globe, and are known for showing true directions. The first such map, called Gnomonic, is attributed to Thales, ca. 600 BC and is considered to be the oldest true projection (Figure A.3). Often used to map the polar regions, the Gnomonic is popular among pilots because of its most defining characteristic: Any straight line drawn on this projection represents a great circle. Despite severe distortion away from the center, any line pilots draw between two points indicates their shortest possible route.

Special Projections

Some projections were never actually geometrically projected on a surface, but were mathematically derived (Figure A.4). A cross between planar and cylindrical projections, parallels (lines of latitude) generally tend to remain horizontal while meridians (lines of longitude) converge in a variety of ways.

Four of these projections enjoy especially wide usage: *Goode's homolosine* (Figure A.4), a projection whose distinctive shape appears in everything from textbooks to corporate logos, depicts true proportions as well as relatively realistic shapes by concentrating its distortion in the oceans. *Eckert IV* (Figure A.4), derived in 1906, is a true equal-area projection. Specifically designed for use in world maps, it is a popular choice for atlases because it represents shapes well, without suffering the oceanic interruptions of the homolosine. The *Mollweide* (Figure A.4) projection, also representing area (proportions) faithfully, dates to

Figure A.1

Mercator

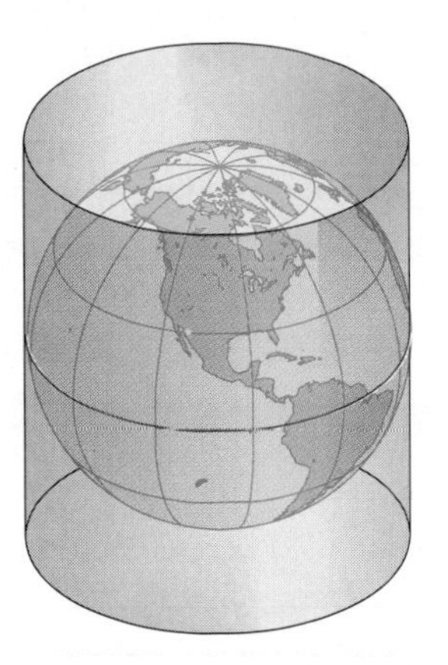

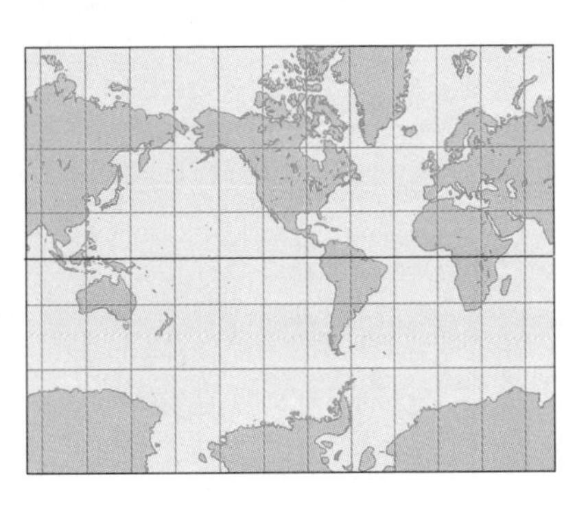

Based upon the projection of a globe onto a cylinder, the familiar Mercator projection is identifiable by its rectilinear grid of latitude and longitude.

Figure A.2

Conic

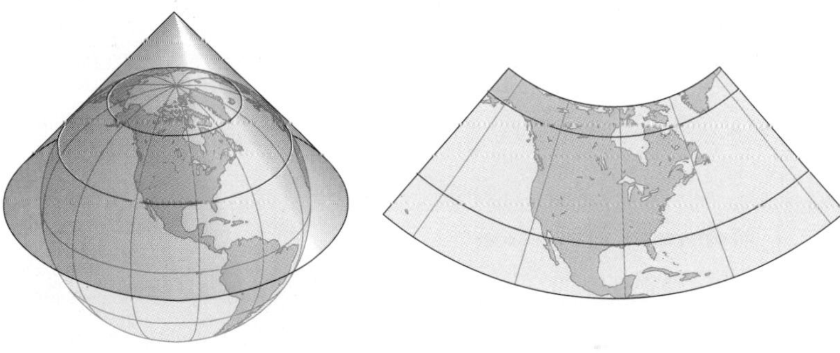

Conic projections are derived by projecting a globe onto a cone. They are most ideally suited for mapping regions in the mid-latitudes (where its distortion is minimal).

Figure A.3

Planar

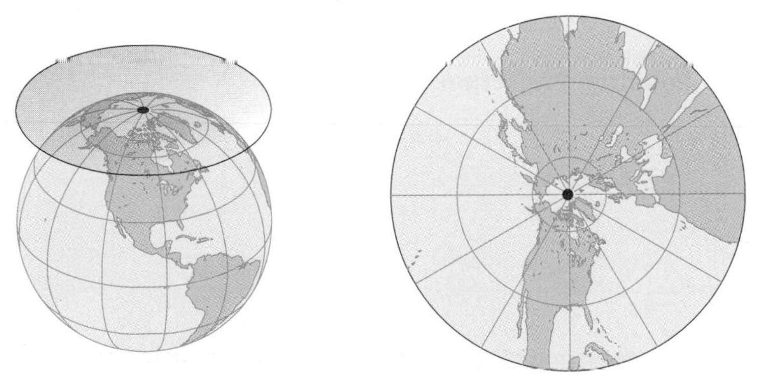

Planar, or Azimuthal, projections are made by projecting a globe onto a flat surface. Because of distortion, they are best for mapping the polar regions.

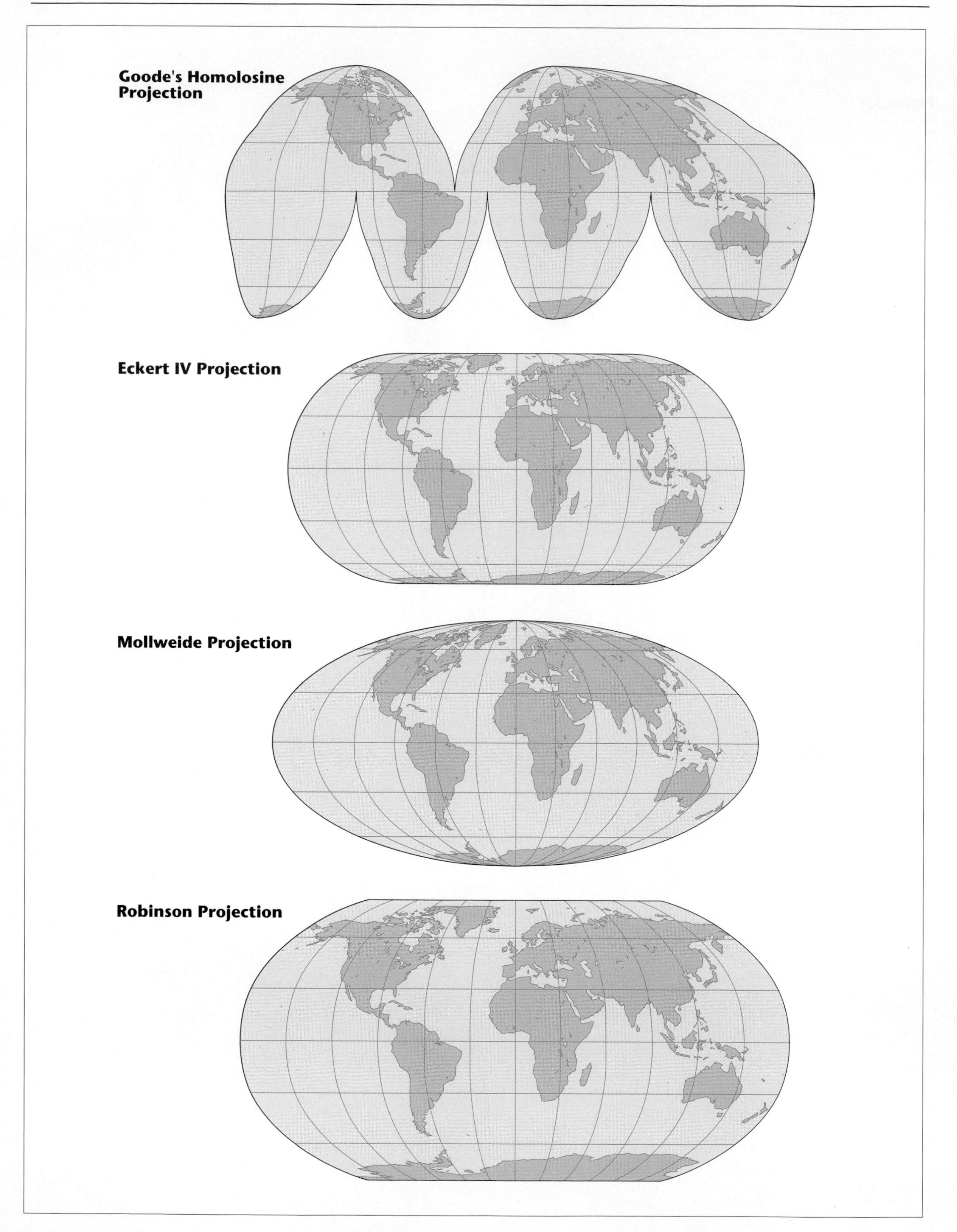
Goode's Homolosine Projection
Eckert IV Projection
Mollweide Projection
Robinson Projection

Figure A.4

1855. Although less popular as a world map, it is nevertheless used by the US Geological Survey for its topographic map series. The *Robinson projection* (Figure A.4), attributed to revered cartographer A. H. Robinson in 1965, is called a compromise projection. Officially adopted by National Geographic for its maps in the late 1980s, this projection preserves neither area nor shape precisely, but strives to approximate both. It is perhaps our most beautiful projection, displaying both proportions and shapes extremely realistically.

This textbook uses the flat polar quartic projection for its world maps (see Figure A.9 on page 516). A true equal-area projection, it depicts the relative sizes of the continents with extreme accuracy, and like Goode's homolosine, it does a respectable job of rendering continental shapes by concentrating its distortion in the oceans.

Projections are only a starting point. To read maps with any confidence, it is necessary to gain a sense of both the language and the process by which cartographers produce maps.

Map Conventions

It is easier to read any language if you understand its basic syntax, and the language of maps is no exception. As graphics, maps adhere to general laws that govern our visual perception: How subtle a contrast can the average person see? How small can text be scaled and still be legible? Moreover, as scientific representations of space and spatial properties, maps follow an equally rigorous set of axioms established over the years by cartographers. An important step in demystifying maps is to recognize that this hidden grammar of mapping exists. Even a passing acquaintance with this unspoken cartographic language will make the most foreign maps easier to use.

Cartographers initially derived conventions to systematize as many aspects of a map as possible. Pragmatically speaking, they make maps easier to produce: Rather than reinvent the wheel for every given task, a cartographer can rely on the collective wisdom of the graphic rules or conventions that have been derived over hundreds of years of mapping. Conceptually, their achievement is more profound. By their very familiarity, they help the reader comprehend a map at a glance—minimizing the tedium of consulting a legend and accelerating the reading process. Conventions apply to all aspects of maps, from how they look to how they reveal their data. Below is a sampling of the guidelines that cartographers use to structure their maps.

Scale and Direction

Some conventions establish the essential orientation of a map. For example, *direction* is indicated by a compass rose or arrow, with north consistently appearing at the top. Conventions also specify a map's essential components—for example, every map contains a *scale,* to ground its cartographic depiction in real-world distances. Scales assume three forms: verbal, linear, or RF (representative fraction) (Figure A.5). Besides letting us calculate relative distances, scales indicate how much a given map has been simplified. Another feature dictated by cartographic rote is *legends,* which form the information hub of a map. Typically, a legend includes the scale, as well as explanations of any symbols and data sets.

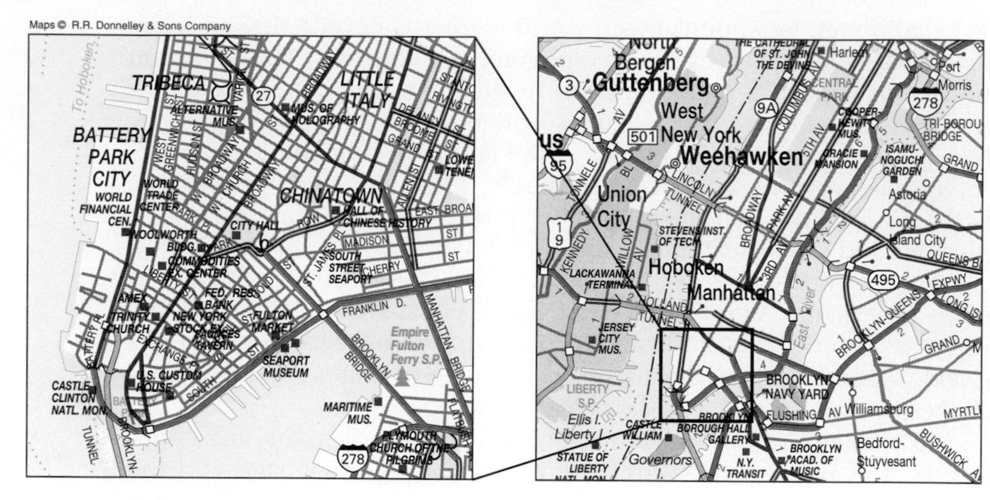

Figure A.5
What a difference a scale makes in these two maps of Manhattan. In general, the smaller the scale (as in the map on the right), the larger the area—but the less detail—that can be shown. Scales assume several forms: A verbal scale literally explains that comparison between distances on the map and those on the Earth ("1 inch equals 10 miles"). The linear scale uses a ruler to visually depict the correlation between units on the map and those on the Earth's surface. A representative fraction (RF) expresses this relationship as a ratio. For example, an RF of 1:50,000 says "1 inch equals 50,000 inches, or approximately 3/4 of a mile." (An RF of 1:50,000 is a common scale used for city street maps.)

Typography

Raised to an art form by German cartographer Eduard Imhof and his American counterpart, Erwin Raisz, *typographic standards* on maps are a code of behavior unto themselves. These conventions are surprisingly universal on a wide variety of maps: Rivers and bodies of water are displayed in italics; names for coastal cities are positioned over the ocean and those for inland cities, over land; typographic labels indicating a large geographical area stretch to approximate that area; the size of type denotes hierarchical importance—the larger the town, river or body of water, the larger the type that labels it; and typographic placement follows a "tilt of the head" logic. With a slight tilt of the head to right or left, any label should be readable. Although cryptic, many of these little conventions have affected the look of maps for centuries.

Symbols

As a shorthand for depicting both natural and cultural phenomena on the Earth's surface, *pictorial symbols* enjoy wide usage among cartographers. Some of the most familiar are those adopted by the U.S. Geological Survey (Figure A.6). While not uniform among mapmakers, these symbols have nevertheless been employed with great consistency for generations.

Symbols provide cartographers the tools for portraying spatial variation, regardless of the type of phenomena. To symbolize data that occur at specific points on a map, graduated circles are a common solution (the circles becoming larger as the value increases). Endless hours

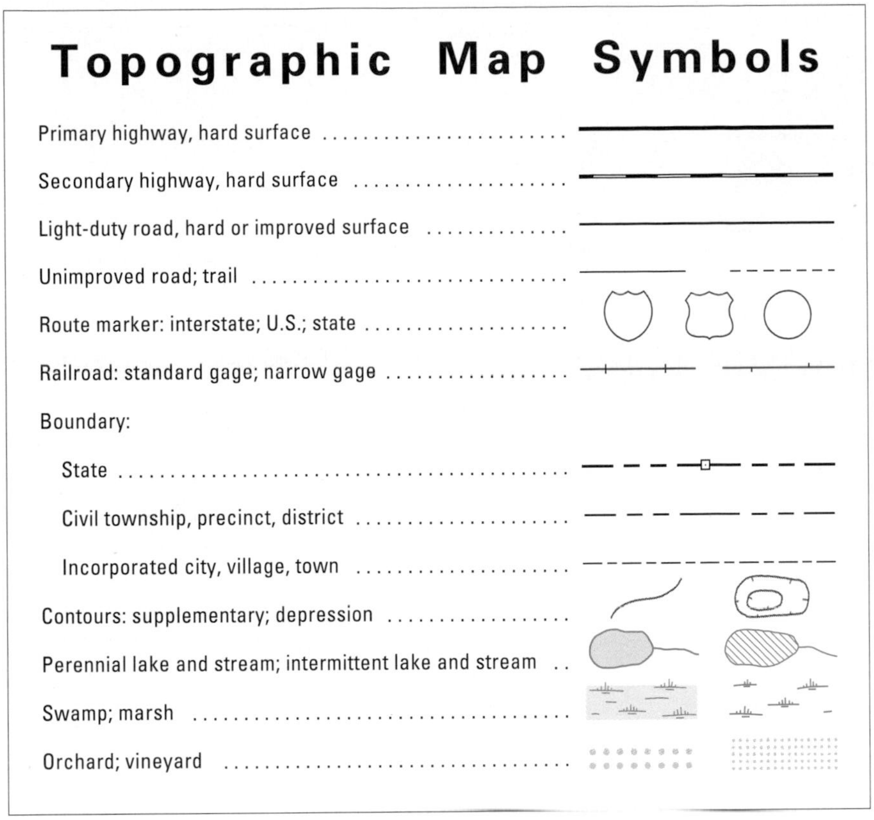

Topographic Map Symbols

Primary highway, hard surface

Secondary highway, hard surface

Light-duty road, hard or improved surface

Unimproved road; trail

Route marker: interstate; U.S.; state

Railroad: standard gage; narrow gage

Boundary:

State

Civil township, precinct, district

Incorporated city, village, town

Contours: supplementary; depression

Perennial lake and stream; intermittent lake and stream

Swamp; marsh

Orchard; vineyard

Figure A.6
While not especially exciting, these symbols nonetheless communicate effectively because of their widespread use in a variety of maps.

of study have been devoted to methods of scaling these circles so they convey the data most clearly. For more complex tasks, cartographers also incorporate such familiar symbols as bar graphs and pie charts into their maps (Figure A.7). What remains a subject of some contention is how effectively such data-intensive maps communicate to the map user.

Cartographers have also standardized how they depict classes of areal phenomena, such as temperatures, population densities, or soils. To show *quantitative change* (differences in volume or amount over an area, like population density or temperature), cartographers have traditionally used graduated tints or shades (that is, white, 20 percent gray, 50 percent gray and black, or similar gradations of a color). Figure A.8 is a classic example of this method of depiction. For *qualitative change* (differences in kind, like varying soil types or religious affiliations), mapmakers turned to patterns. At their very simplest, these are variations of dots, stripes, and checks, but variations of enormous subtlety abound (Figure A.9). True, cartographers have produced many an unreadable map—featuring the most glaring combinations of patterns imaginable—but used with discretion, patterns can be extremely effective. With color becoming more affordable in mapping, cartographers now increasingly employ variations in hue and tint in place of patterns (see Figure A.10) or go further and use the two techniques in combination.

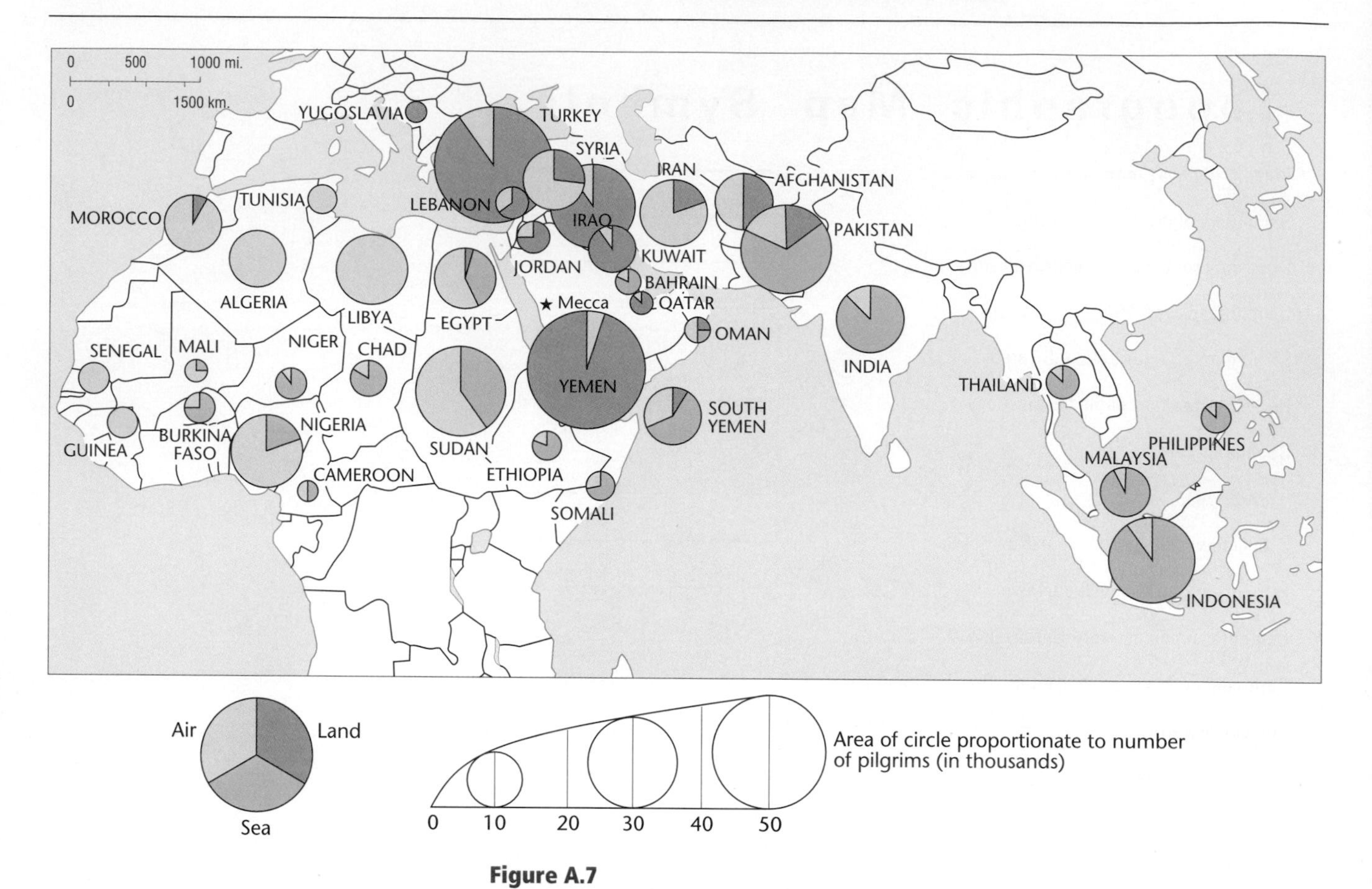

Figure A.7

Elevation

On par with projections as one of the major challenges of cartographers is the depiction of relief or elevation. Dogged in their quest, mapmakers have devised a variety of techniques for representing elevation. Simple *pictorial representations* of terrain (those little hills, hummocks, and peaks in antique maps) are our earliest means of suggesting relief. In addition, cartographers suggested dimension by employing a three-quarter perspective (dubbed a birdseye view), a technique that became especially popular in mapping townscapes. There, they were used to capture, simultaneously, both the plans and built environment of early cities. This perspective is still embraced today, with some remarkable results (Figure A.11).

By the early nineteenth century, *hachures* were commonly used for mapping terrain. These short, parallel strokes run in the direction of the slope and become heavier as hills became steeper. (Hence, the "hairy caterpillar" look of mountains on many smaller-scale maps of the period.) But this form of depiction proved time-consuming as well as inexact. By the late nineteenth century, cartographers developed an extensive vocabulary of *physiographic symbols* for describing different types of terrain. These extremely realistic renderings of everything from sinkholes to badlands to lava-capped plateaus were easy for map readers to understand but, unfortunately, they also lacked precision.

Contour lines (also called *isolines*) are one of the most accurate means of mapping surface variations. First used in 1729 to map water

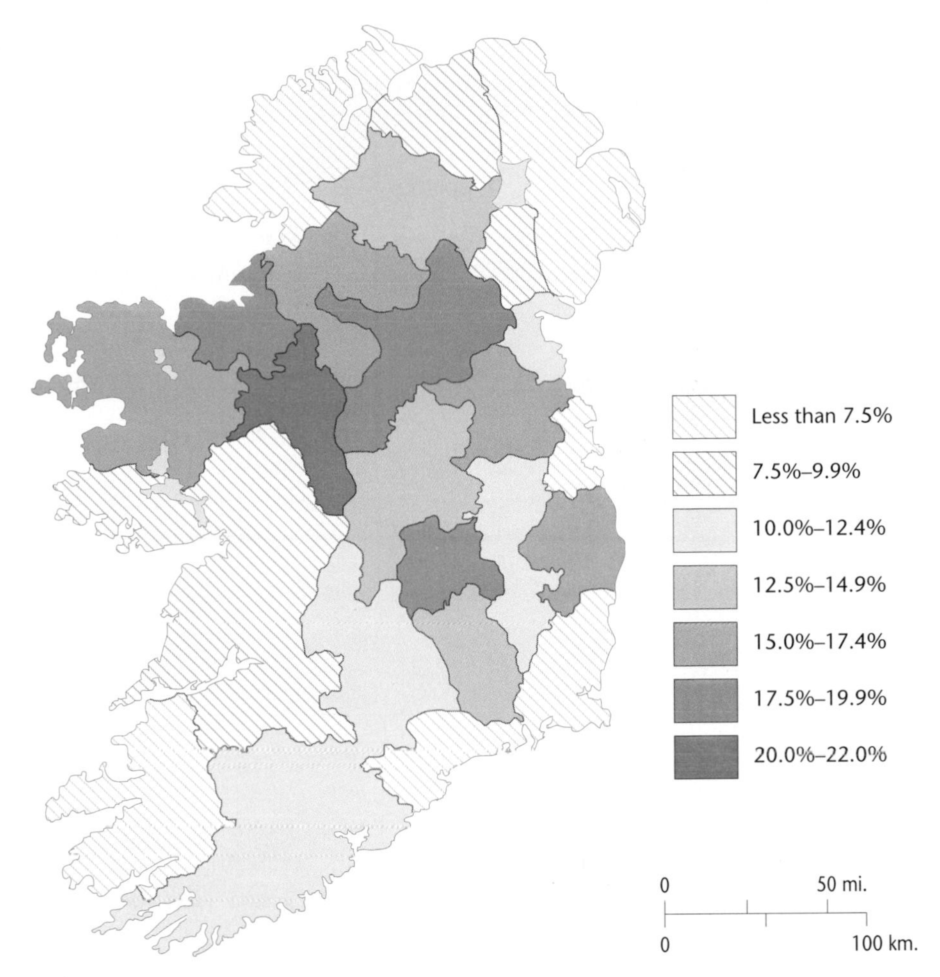

Figure A.8
Emigration from Ireland, 1846–1851, as a percentage of total population. The cartographer, showing quantitative change (in volume/amount), employs a graduated series of tints to make the distribution obvious, even before the reader knows what it being mapped.

depths, contour mapping for land did not find general usage until the late nineteenth century. Perhaps best known for their appearance in US Geological Survey topographic sheets, contours are lines that connect points of identical measurements, be they elevation, temperature, or population density. Theoretically, on a mountainside, by following any given contour, you would always be walking on a level surface and would circle back to where you began (Figure A.12).

Despite the precision of contour lines, many map readers have difficulty visualizing elevation when looking at the lines alone. Thus on many topographic maps, contours rely on other techniques to strengthen their illusion of depth. One such method, *hill-shading* (or *plastic shading*), paints a convincing picture of verticality by simulating shadows from an imagined light source (Figure A.13). *Hypsometric tints* are another alternative. A common choice in atlases, hypsometric tints employ a graduated series of colors to approximate the third dimension. Although precise colors vary, their overall scheme traditionally retains a familiar logic: What begins as bluish-green (suggesting fertile, well-watered, etc.) at sea level gradually becomes paler with elevation (imitating atmospheric conditions) until mountainous areas become

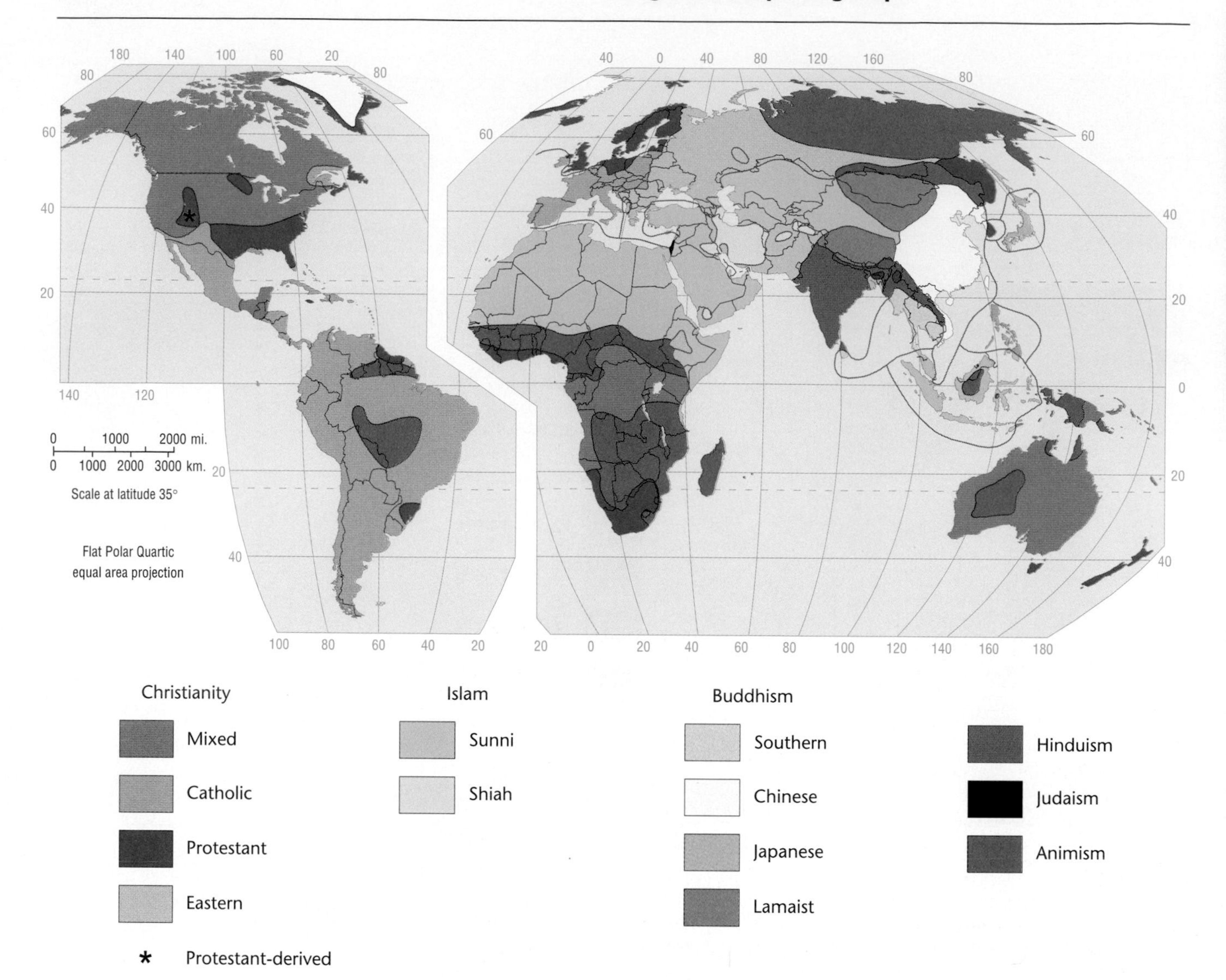

Figure A.9
Mapping the world distribution of major religions, the cartographer uses patterns to show qualitative change (differences in kind) over space. Unless a wide variety of colors were used, it would be extremely difficult to portray this wide an array of categories without resorting to patterns.

ochre to orangish (Figure A.14). Some atlases combine contours, hill-shading, and hypsometric tints simultaneously for especially dramatic illusions of verticality.

Such are some of the axioms that inform and lend consistency to maps. Now, to their accuracy.

The Truthfulness of Maps

Few documents have more power to misinform than maps. Widely considered to have their basis in science, they are regarded by most people simply as fact. "It's on the map; it must be so." In actuality, nothing could be further from the truth. Part of the difficulty lies in the fact that more people are making maps who have no training as cartog-

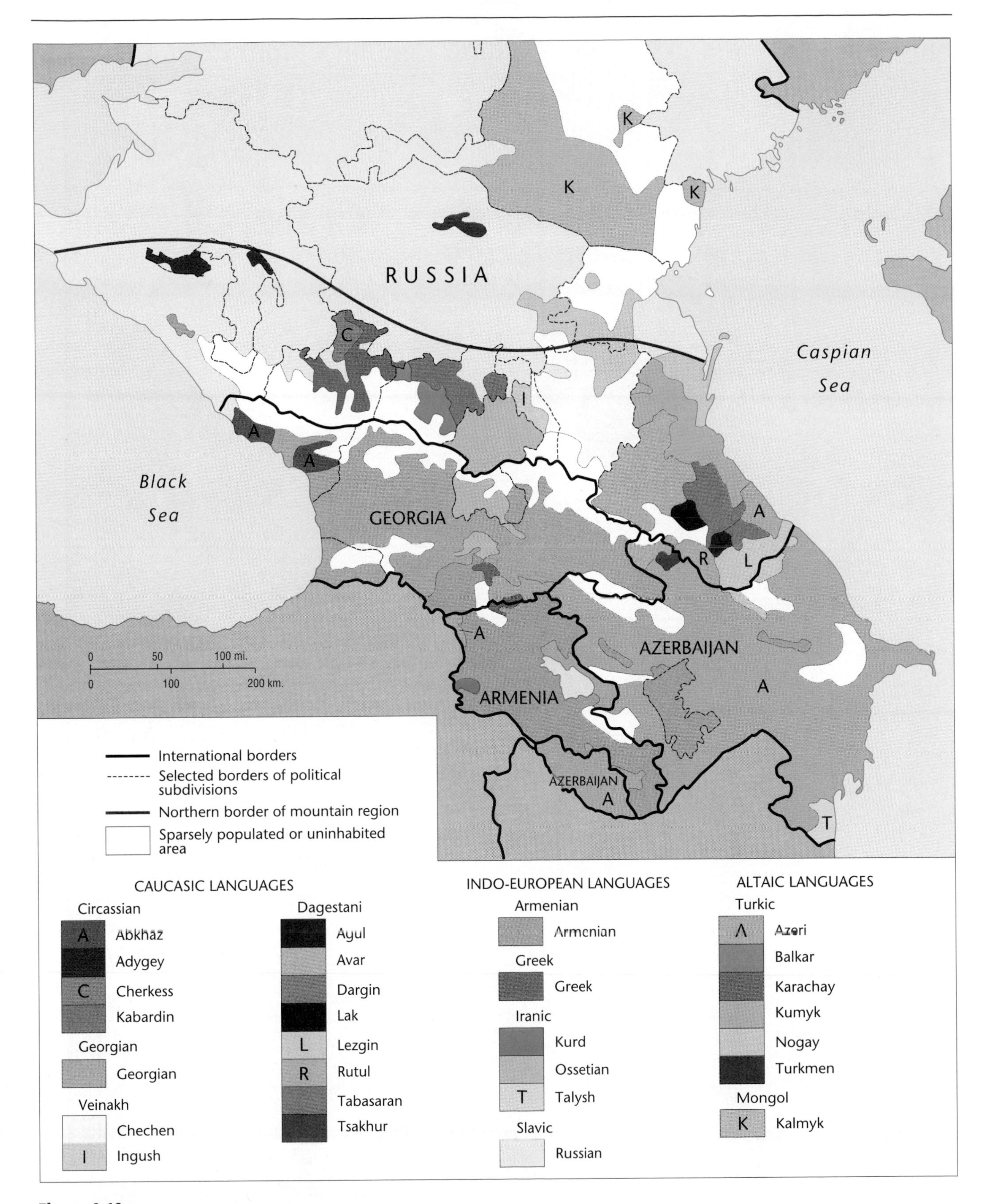

Figure A.10
Here an ample use of color permits the cartographer to effectively depict varying linguistic regions as well as to portray the broader categories into which these dialects belong.

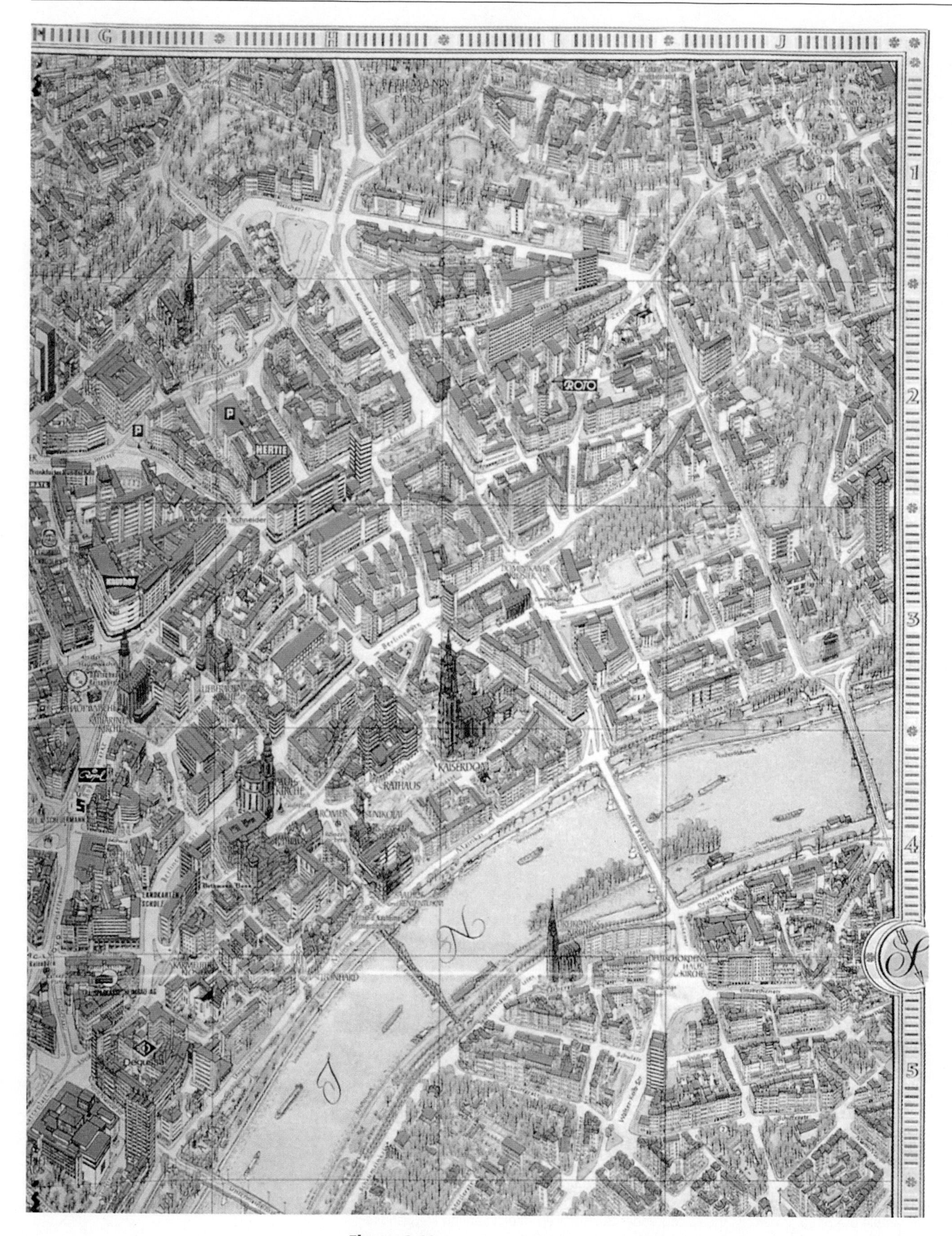
G
H
I
J
1
2
3
4
5
HERTIE
ROTO
KAISERDOM
RATHAUS
PAULS KIRCHE
LANDKARTEN SCHOLZ

Figure A.11

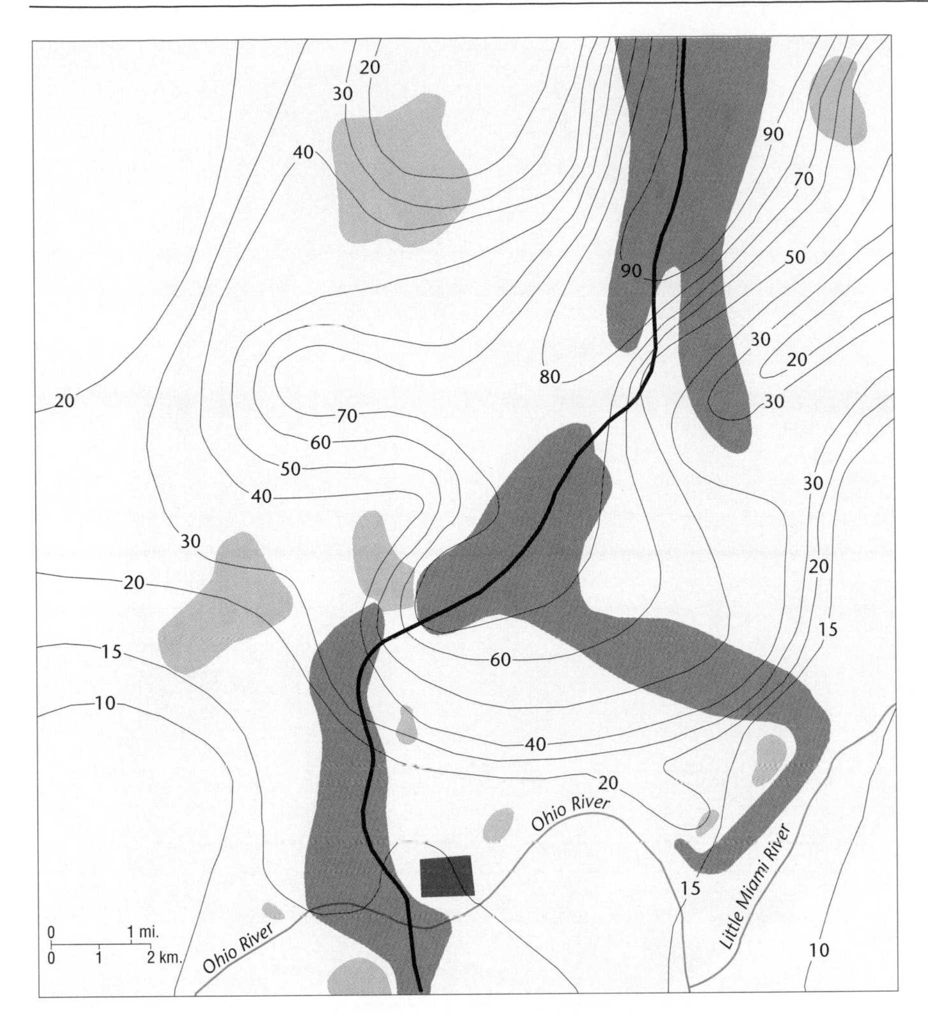

Figure A.12
Although contours represent elevation with extreme accuracy, it is nevertheless difficult to "imagine" the elevational differences in this map. Notice how much longer it takes to get a sense of this area's terrain, versus that in Figure A.13.

raphers. But another part of the problem lies with cartographers themselves. They, too, make mistakes.

Any map is only as reliable as the data on which it is based. A mislabeled city or lake in an atlas may survive several editions before it is ever corrected. In the early nineteenth century, popular notions of a Great American Desert in the central United States (confirmed by maps of the era) are considered to have slowed the pace of westward migration, until by midcentury the error was corrected. Similarly, a great east-west mountain range appeared on many maps of central Africa in the nineteenth century. It took over a century to displace these erroneous mountains from the region's maps.

Read a map as you would the editorial page. For all the accurate information a reader can glean from a map, there is always someone out there with a point of view, poor data, or an overly zealous sense of design that can undermine a map's accuracy. Given this, when consulting a map, ask yourself these questions:

1. *How recently was it printed?* Out-of-date maps, particularly in the case of road maps, can create more problems than they solve.

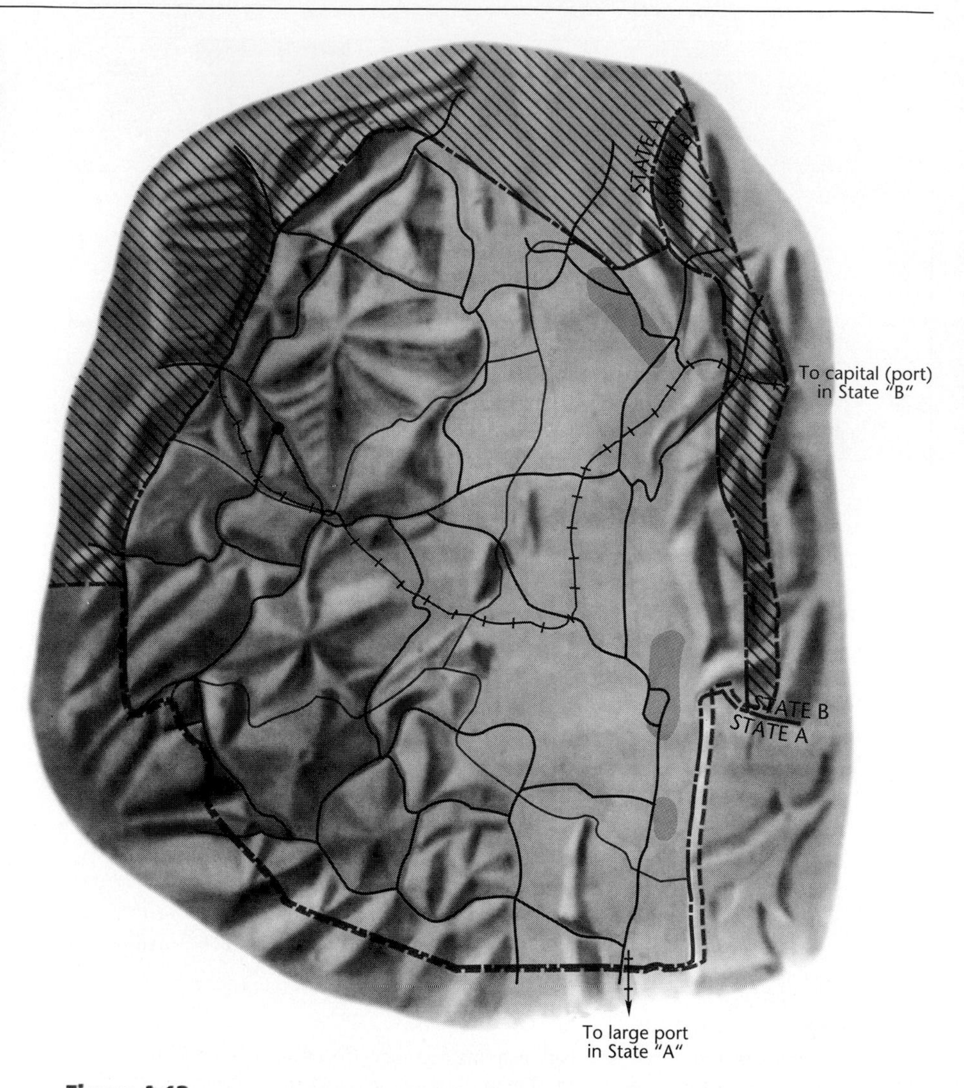

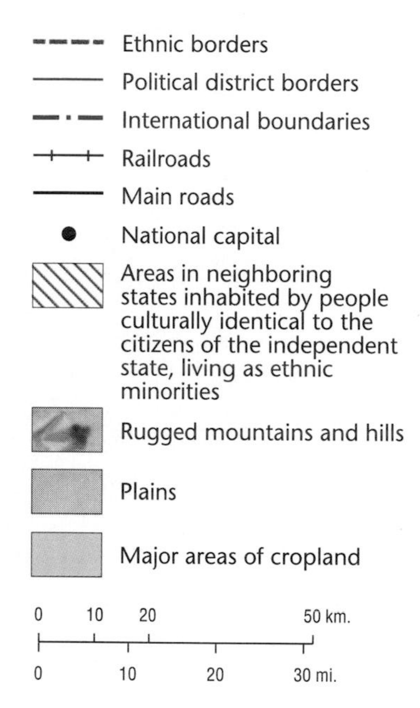

Figure A.13
As convincing as this illustration of relief is, the vertical thrust of mountains off the page is even more dramatic when hill-shading is used in larger-scale maps.

2. *At what scale is it drawn?* Large-scale maps (as of a single locality or state) have undergone far less generalization (simplification) than comparable regional or national maps. For accurate information about a given locality, acquire the most detailed, largest-scale map possible.
3. *Who drew the map?* Authorship is a likely clue to reliability. A National Geographic map of Borneo will, in all probability, offer a far greater degree of accuracy than a map of similar scale produced by Borneo's Bureau of Tourism. The issue is one of expertise and resources, as well as purpose.
4. *What is its purpose?* This can be an easy trap for map readers. Since no one map can hold all the information available about any given locality, it is left to the cartographer to ascertain what is pertinent. Hence, match the map to the function for which it was designed or you may find that critical information is missing or the map is overly generalized. Thus, never navigate by a map from a magazine when a nautical chart is available; never hike into the mountains

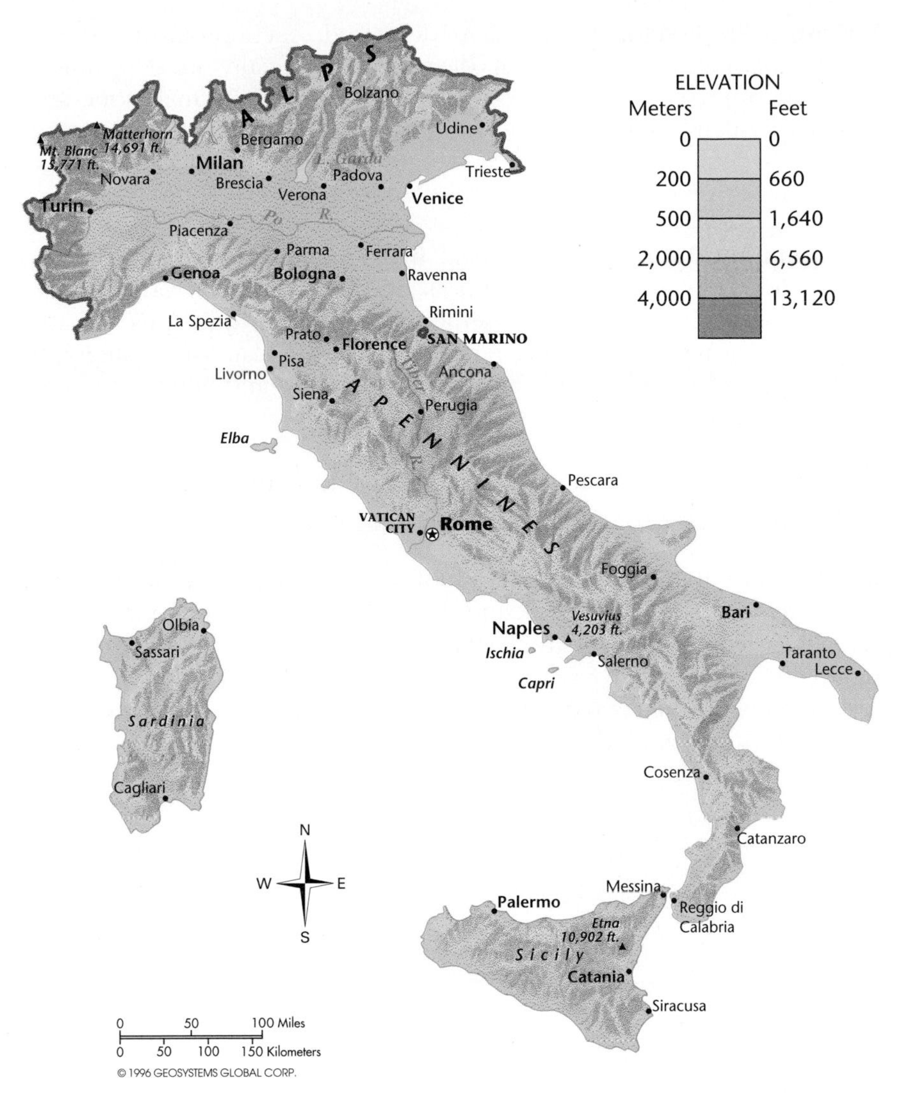

Figure A.14
The addition of color (keyed to elevation above sea level) makes the contour lines far more effective in suggesting relief.

with a picnicking guide when a U.S. Geological Survey topographic map could provide life-saving details. Remember, whatever your objective, use a map the way its author intended it to be used.

The Mapmaking Process

As suggested above, maps are by definition distillations of real world phenomena—selective representations of what is "really out there." Given this, the only way to read a map critically is to understand the many decisions a cartographer makes to produce even the simplest of maps. Although there are countless opportunities in which error can intrude into any map, the three major conceptual stages of mapmaking are as follows.

Picking a Projection. As we have discussed, each projection comes with some measure of built-in distortion. Especially in designing a world map, projections can be selected purposefully to make one area look larger than another (as Mercator did) or to make two regions appear more distant or near than is actually the case. A choice of projection alone can color the impact of the entire map.

Manipulating Data. On a statistical map, a cartographer must group his or her data into sets, or symbols, for representation on the map. This is another step in which a tremendous range of decisions is made. Depending on how the cartographer breaks the data into categories, one set of statistics can yield vastly different maps, and hence send very different messages to the map reader.

Design. Ostensibly the most innocuous task of mapmaking, the design stage is rife with opportunities for errors. Cartographers can omit features that may be significant, but for which there is no room; add features because that part of the map looks empty; or grossly simplify data (roadways, coastlines) for a cleaner look. The unsuspecting map reader often has little inkling of the extent of the cartographer's interpretive hand.

Remember, the importance of noticing who made your map and using it for the purpose for which it was designed.

Glossary

absorbing barrier A barrier that completely halts diffusion of innovations and blocks the spread of cultural elements. (Chapter 1)

acculturation The process by which an ethnic group changes in order to function in the host society. (Chapter 9)

acid rain A result of the burning of fossil fuels, acid rain results when sulfur and nitrogen oxides are flushed from the atmosphere by precipitation, with lethal effects for many plants and animals. (Chapter 12)

adaptive strategy The unique way each culture utilizes its particular physical environment; those aspects of culture that serve to provide the necessities of life—food, clothing, shelter, and defense. (Chapter 1 and throughout)

agglomeration A snowballing geographical process by which secondary through quinary industrial activities become clustered in cities and compact industrial regions in order to share infrastructure and markets. (Chapters 10, 11, and 12)

agribusiness Highly mechanized, large-scale farming usually under corporate ownership. (Chapter 3)

agricultural landscape The cultural landscape of agricultural areas. (Chapter 3)

agricultural region A culture region based on characteristics of agriculture, within which a given type of agriculture occurs. (Chapter 3)

agriculture The cultivation of domesticated crops and the raising of domesticated animals. (Chapter 3)

America letters Written back to friends and relatives in their former homes by early immigrants, the letters describe immigrants' new land in glowing terms, serving to induce others to follow them. (Chapter 9)

animism The belief that inanimate objects, such as trees, rocks, and rivers, possess souls. (Chapter 6)

assimilation The loss of all ethnic traits and complete blending into the host society. (Chapter 9)

axis mundi The symbolic center of cosmomagical cities, often demarcated by a large, vertical structure. (Chapter 10)

barriadas Illegal housing settlements, usually made up of temporary shelters, that surround large cities; often referred to as squatter settlements. (Chapter 10)

birth rate The number of births in one year per thousand persons in the population. (Chapter 2)

buffer state An independent but small and weak country lying between two powerful countries. (Chapter 4)

bulk-gaining product A product in which volume is added to the raw materials in the manufacturing process. (Chapter 12)

cadastral pattern The shapes formed by property borders; the pattern of land ownership. (Chapter 3)

CBD The central business district of a city. (Chapter 11)

census tracts Small districts used by the United States Census Bureau to survey the population. (Chapter 11)

centralizing forces Diffusion forces that encourage people or businesses to locate in the central city. (Chapter 11)

central place A town or city engaged primarily in the service stages of production; a regional center. (Chapter 10)

central-place theory A set of models designed to explain the spatial distribution of service urban centers. (Chapter 10)

centrifugal force Any factor that disrupts the internal order of a country. (Chapter 4)

centripetal force Any factor that supports the internal unity of a country. (Chapter 4)

chain migration The tendency of people to migrate along channels, over a period of time, from specific source areas to specific destinations. (Chapter 9)

checkerboard development A mixture of farmlands and housing tracts. (Chapter 11)

cleavage model Political geographical model suggesting that persistent regional patterns in voting behavior, sometimes leading to separatism, can usually be explained in terms of tensions pitting urban versus rural, core versus periphery, capitalists versus workers, and power-group versus minority culture. (Chapter 4)

colonial city A city founded by colonialism, or an indigenous city whose structure was deeply influenced by Western colonialism. (Chapter 10)

concentric zone model A social model that depicts a city as five areas bounded by concentric rings. (Chapter 11)

contact conversion The spread of religious beliefs by personal contact. (Chapter 6)

contagious diffusion A type of expansion diffusion; the spread of cultural innovation by person-to-person contact, moving wavelike through an area and population without regard to social status. (Chapter 1)

convergence hypothesis A hypothesis holding that cultural differences between places are being reduced by improved transportation and communications systems, leading to a homogenization of popular culture. (Chapter 8)

core area The territorial nucleus from which a country grows in area and through time, often containing the national capital and the main center of commerce, culture, and industry. (Chapter 4)

core/periphery A concept based on the tendency of both formal and functional culture regions to consist of a core or node, in which defining traits are purest or functions are headquartered, and a periphery that is tributary and displays fewer of the defining traits. (Chapters 1, 3, 4, 5, 12)

cosmomagical A type of city that is laid out in accordance with religious principles; characteristic of very early cities, particularly in China. (Chapter 10)

cottage industry A traditional type of manufacturing in the preindustrial revolution era, practiced on a small scale in individual rural households as a part-time occupation and designed to produce handmade goods for local consumption. (Chapter 12)

cultural adaptation The concept, central to cultural ecology, that culture is the uniquely human method of meeting physical environmental challenges—that culture is an adaptive system. (Chapters 1 and 9)

cultural determinism The viewpoint that the immediate causes of all cultural phenomena are other cultural phenomena. (Chapter 1)

cultural diffusion The spread of elements of culture from the point of origin over an area. (Chapter 1)

cultural ecology Broadly defined, the study of the relationships between the physical environment and culture; narrowly (and more commonly) defined, the study of culture as an adaptive system serving to facilitate human adaptation to nature and environmental change. (Chapter 1)

cultural geography The description and explanation of spatial patterns and ecological relationships in human culture. (Chapter 1)

cultural integration The relationship of different elements within a culture. (Chapter 1)

cultural landscape The artificial landscape; the visible human imprint on the land. (Chapter 1)

culture A total way of life held in common by a group of people, including such learned features as speech, ideology, behavior, livelihood, technology, and government. (Chapter 1)

culture region An area occupied by people who have something in common culturally; or a spatial unit that functions politically, socially, or economically as a distinct entity. (Chapter 1)

death rate The number of deaths in one year per thousand persons in the population. (Chapter 2)

decentralization or **decentralizing forces** Diffusion forces that encourage people or businesses and industry to locate outside the central city. (Chapters 10, 11)

defensive site An easily defended place to locate a city. (Chapter 10)

deindustrialization Decline of primary and secondary industry, accompanied by a rise of the service sectors of the industrial economy. (Chapters 11, 12)

demographic region A culture region based on characteristics of demography. (Chapter 2)

demographic transformation A change in population growth that occurs when a nation moves from a rural, agricultural society with high birth and death rates to an urban, industrial society in which death rates decline first and birthrates decline later. (Chapter 2)

demography The statistical study of population size, composition, distribution, and change. (Chapter 2)

desertification A process whereby human actions unintentionally render productive lands into deserts through agricultural and pastoral misuse, destroying vegetation and soil to the point where they cannot regenerate. (Chapter 3)

dialect A distinctive local or regional variant of a language that remains mutually intelligible to speakers of other dialects of that language; a subtype of a language. (Chapter 5)

domesticated animal An animal kept for some utilitarian purpose whose breeding is controlled by humans and whose survival is dependent on humans; differing genetically and behaviorally from wild animals. (Chapter 3)

domesticated plant A plant willfully planted and tended by humans that is genetically distinct from its wild ancestors as a result of selective breeding. (Chapter 3)

double-cropping Harvesting twice a year from the same parcel of land. (Chapter 3)

dust dome A pollution layer over a city that is thickest at the center of the city. (Chapter 11)

ecology The study of the relationship between an organism and its physical environment. (Chapter 1)

economic determinism The social scientific belief that human behavior, including spatial or geographical attributes, is largely or wholly dictated by economic factors and motivation. (Chapter 1)

ecosystem The functioning ecological system in which biological and cultural *Homo sapiens* live and interact with the physical environment (Chapter 1); a unit through which the flow of matter or energy is traced. (Chapter 11)

edge city A term to describe the new urban clusters of economic activity that surround our nineteenth-century downtowns. (Chapter 10)

emerging city A city of a current developing or emerging country. (Chapter 10)

enclave A piece of territory surrounded by, but not part of, a country. (Chapter 4)

environmental determinism The school of thought based on the belief that cultures are, directly or indirectly, shaped by the physical environment, that cultures are molded by physical surroundings. (Chapter 1)

environmental perception The school of thought based on the belief that cultural attitudes shape perception of the environment, causing people of different cultures to perceive their surroundings differently and to make different decisions as a result. (Chapter 1)

ethnic culture region An area shared by people of similar ethnic background, who are of the same race or language. (Chapter 11)

ethnic geography The study of the spatial and ecological aspects of ethnicity. (Chapter 9)

ethnic group A group of people sharing common ancestry and cultural tradition living as a minority in a larger society. (Chapter 9)

ethnic homeland A sizable area inhabited by an ethnic minority exhibiting a strong sense of attachment to the region and often exercising some measure of political and social control over it. (Chapter 9)

ethnic island A small ethnic area in the rural countryside; sometimes called a "folk island." (Chapter 9)

ethnic neighborhood An area within a city containing members of the same ethnic background; a voluntary segregation of urban people along ethnic lines. (Chapter 9)

ethnic religion A religion identified with a particular ethnic or tribal group; does not seek converts. (Chapter 6)

ethnic substrate Regional cultural distinctiveness that remains following the assimilation of an ethnic homeland. (Chapter 9)

ethnographic boundary A political boundary that follows some cultural border, such as a linguistic or religious border. (Chapter 4)

exclave A piece of a country separated from the main body of it by the intervening territory of another country. (Chapter 4)

expansion diffusion The spread of innovations within an area in a snowballing process, so that the total number of knowers becomes greater and the area of occurrence grows. (Chapter 1)

farmstead The center of farm operations, containing the house, barn, sheds, and livestock pens. (Chapter 2)

farm village A clustered rural settlement of moderate size, inhabited by people who are engaged in farming. (Chapter 2)

feedback The output of a system that is returned in modified form and becomes an input. (Chapter 11)

feedlot A factory-like farm, devoted to either livestock fattening or dairying; all feed is imported and no crops are grown on the farm. (Chapter 3)

festival settings Multiuse redevelopment projects that are built around a particular setting, often one with historical association. (Chapter 11)

first effective settlement Occurs when a preadapted immigrant group establishes a viable, self-perpetuating culture in a colonization area. (Chapter 9)

folk Traditional, rural, nonpopular. (Chapter 7)

folk architecture Structures built by members of a folk society or culture in a traditional manner and style, without the assistance of professional architects or blueprints, using locally available raw materials. (Chapter 7)

folk culture A small, cohesive, stable, isolated, nearly self-sufficient group that is homogeneous in custom and race; characterized by a strong family or clan structure; order maintained through sanctions based in the religion or family; little division of labor other than between the sexes; frequent and strong interpersonal relationships; and a material culture consisting mainly of handmade goods. (Chapter 7)

folk fortress A stronghold area with natural defensive qualities, useful in the defense of a country against invaders. (Chapter 4)

folk geography The study of the spatial patterns of elements of folklife; a branch of cultural geography. (Chapter 7)

folklore Nonmaterial folk culture; the teaching and wisdom of a folk group; the traditional tales, sayings, beliefs, and superstitions that are transmitted orally. (Chapter 7)

formal culture region A region inhabited by people who have one or more cultural traits in common. (Chapter 1)

functional culture region An area that functions as a unit politically, socially, or economically. (Chapter 1)

functional zonation The division of the city into different areas for different functions, such as industry and housing. (Chapter 10)

generic toponym The descriptive part of many place-names, often repeated throughout a culture area. (Chapter 5)

gentrification Replacement of lower-income groups by higher-income people as buildings are restored. (Chapter 11)

geography The study of spatial patterns, of differences and similarities from one place to another in environment and culture. (Chapter 1)

geolinguistics The cultural geographical study of languages and dialects. (Chapter 5)

geomancy A traditional East Asian form of environmental perception, also called *feng-shui,* by which particular configurations of terrain, compass directions, soil textures, and watercourse patterns become more auspicious than others, influencing the siting of houses, villages, cities, temples, and graves. (Chapters 1, 6)

geometric boundary A political border drawn in a regular, geometric manner, often a straight line, without regard for environmental or cultural patterns. (Chapter 4)

geophagy The deliberate eating of earth. (Chapter 7)

geopolitics Another name for political geography. (Chapter 4)

gerrymandering Drawing the boundaries of electorial districts in an awkward pattern to enhance the voting impact of one constituency at the expense of another. (Chapter 4)

ghetto A segregated ethnic area within a city, caused by residential discrimination against the will of the people involved. (Chapter 9)

global corporations Also called multinationals or transnationals, these corporations are industries that operate in more than one country, dispersing their factories, headquarters, marketing, and service functions across international boundaries. (Chapter 12)

greenhouse effect The results from the increased addition of carbon dioxide and certain trace gases to the atmosphere through industrial activity and deforestation causing more of the sun's heat to be retained, thus warming the climate of the Earth. (Chapter 12)

green revolution The recent introduction of high-yield hybrid crops and chemical fertilizers and pesticides into traditional Asian agricultural systems, most notably paddy rice farming, with attendant increases in production and ecological damage. (Chapter 3)

greens Organizations, including political parties, whose central concern is addressing environmental deterioration. (Chapter 12)

guild industry A traditional type of manufacturing in the preindustrial revolution era, involving handmade goods of high quality manufactured by highly skilled artisans who resided in towns and cities. (Chapter 12)

heartland The interior of a sizable landmass, removed from maritime connections; in particular, the interior of the Eurasian continent. (Chapter 4)

heartland theory A 1904 proposal by Mackinder that the key to world conquest lay in control of the interior of Eurasia. (Chapter 4)

heat island An area of warmer temperatures at the center of a city, caused by the urban concentration of heat-retaining concrete, brick, and asphalt. (Chapter 10)

hierarchical diffusion A type of expansion diffusion; innovations spread from one important person to another or from one urban center to another, temporarily bypassing persons of lesser importance and rural areas. (Chapter 1)

high-tech corridors Areas along limited-access highways that house offices and other services associated with high-tech industries. (Chapters 11, 12)

hinterland The area surrounding a city and influenced by it. (Chapter 10)

homelessness A condition of temporary or permanent nature that describes people who do not have a legal home address. (Chapter 11)

host culture The dominant, majority cultural group within a country or society, which usually occupies a dominant social-economic position. (Chapter 9)

humanistic geography Subfield of geography that stresses the subjectivity and individuality of humans as essential to analysis of spatial variations; deals with the uniqueness of each region and place; rejects the notion that geography is a social science. (Chapter 1)

hunting and gathering The killing of wild game and the harvesting of wild plants to provide food in traditional cultures. (Chapter 3)

hydraulic civilization A civilization based on large-scale irrigation. (Chapter 10)

independent inventions Cultural innovations that are developed in two or more locations by persons or groups working independently. (Chapter 1)

indigenous city A city formed by local forces. (Chapter 10)

industrial inertia The tendency by industries to remain in their original locations, even after the forces that originally attracted them there have disappeared. (Chapter 12)

industrial revolution A series of inventions and innovations, arising in England in the 1700s, which led to the use of machines and inanimate power in the manufacturing process. (Chapter 12)

in-filling New building on empty parcels of land within a checkerboard pattern of development. (Chapter 11)

input A component that is put into a system. (Chapter 11)

intensive agriculture The expenditure of much labor and capital on a piece of land to increase its productivity. In contrast, extensive agriculture involves less labor and capital. (Chapter 3)

intertillage The raising of different crops mixed together in the same field, particularly common in shifting cultivation. (Chapter 3)

isogloss The border of usage of an individual word or pronunciation. (Chapter 5)

labor-intensive industry An industry for which labor costs represent a large proportion of total production costs. (Chapter 12)

laissez-faire utilitarianism The belief that economic competition without government interference produces the most public good. (Chapter 10)

language A distinctive form of speech that is not mutually intelligible to the speakers of other languages. (Chapter 5)

language family A group of related languages derived from a common ancestor. (Chapter 5)

lateral commuting Traveling from one suburb to another in going from home to work. (Chapter 11)

legible city A city that is easy to decipher, with clear pathways, edges, nodes, districts, and landmarks. (Chapter 11)

lingua franca An existing, well-established language used widely where it is not a mother tongue, for the purposes of government, trade, business, and other contacts among persons. (Chapter 5)

linguistic refuge area An area, isolated or protected by environmental conditions, in which a language or dialect has survived. (Chapter 5)

logical positivism The worldly, secular, antitheological view that knowledge derives only from an empirical analysis, employing the scientific method and normally involving quantification, of the properties and relationships of sensed phenomena; strict adherence to the testimony of observation is maintained. (Chapter 1)

maladaptation Occurs when a group pursues an adaptive strategy that, in the short run, fails to provide the necessities of life or, in the long run, destroys the environment that nourishes them. (Chapters 9, 12)

marchland A strip of territory, traditionally one day's march for infantry, that served as a boundary zone for independent countries in premodern times. (Chapter 4)

market gardening A farm devoted to specialized fruit, vegetable, or vine crops for sale rather than consumption. (Chapter 3)

master-planned communities Large-scale residential developments that include, in addition to architecturally compatible housing units, planned recreational facilities, schools, and security measures. (Chapter 11)

material culture All physical, material objects made and used by members of a cultural group, such as clothing, buildings, tools and utensils, instruments, furniture, and artwork; the visible aspect of culture. (Chapter 7)

megalopolis A large urban region formed as several urban areas spread and merge, such as Boswash, the region including Boston, New York, and Washington, DC. (Chapter 10)

model An abstraction, an imaginary situation, proposed by geographers to simulate laboratory conditions so that they may isolate certain causal forces for detailed study. (Chapter 1)

monotheism The worship of only one god. (Chapter 6)

multiple nuclei model A model that depicts a city growing from several separate focal points. (Chapter 11)

multiplier leakage The process by which industrial profits "drain" back to major industrial districts from factories established in outlying provinces or countries. (Chapter 12)

nation-state An independent country dominated by a relatively homogeneous cultural group. (Chapter 4)

natural boundary A political border that follows some feature of the natural environment, such as a river or mountain ridge. (Chapter 4)

neighborhood A small social area within a city where residents share values and concerns and interact with one another on a daily basis. (Chapter 11)

neighborhood effect The rapid acceptance of an innovation in a small area or cluster around an initial adopter. (Chapter 1)

node In a functional culture region, a central point where functions are coordinated and directed. (Chapter 1)

nonmaterial culture Includes the oral aspect of a culture, such as songs, dialect, tales, beliefs, and customs. (Chapter 7)

nonrenewable resources Resources that must be depleted in order to be used, such as minerals. (Chapter 12)

office park A cluster of office buildings usually located along an interstate, often forming the nucleus of an edge city. (Chapter 11)

outputs Elements produced by and flowing out of an ecosystem; for example, water may leave a system in many forms—as sewage, as a component of food or drinks for export, or as vapor produced by industry. (Chapter 11)

paddy rice farming Cultivation of rice on a paddy, or small flooded field enclosed by mud dikes, practiced in the humid areas of the Far East. (Chapter 3)

palimpsest A term used to describe cultural landscapes with various layers and historical "messages." Geographers use this term to reinforce the notion of the landscape as a text that can be read; a landscape palimpsest has elements of both modern and past periods. (Chapter 11)

particulate pollutants Bits of matter spewed into the air by incinerators, car exhausts, tire wear, industrial combustion, and so forth. (Chapters 11, 12)

permeable barrier A barrier that permits some aspects of an innovation to diffuse through but weakens and retards continued spread; an innovation can be modified in passing through a permeable barrier. (Chapter 1)

personal space The amount of space that individuals feel "belongs" to them as they move about their everyday business. (Chapter 2)

physical environment All aspects of the natural physical surroundings, such as climate, terrain, soils, vegetation, and wildlife. (Chapter 1)

pidgin A composite language consisting of a small vocabulary borrowed from the linguistic groups involved in international commerce. (Chapter 5)

pilgrimage A journey to a place of religious importance. (Chapter 6)

place A term used to connote the subjective, idiographic, humanistic, culturally oriented type of geography that seeks to understand the unique character of individual regions and places, rejecting the principles of science as flawed and unknowingly biased. (Chapter 1)

placelessness May result from the spread of popular culture, which can diminish or destroy the uniqueness of place through cultural standardization on a national or even worldwide scale. (Chapter 8)

plantation A large landholding devoted to specialized production of a tropical cash crop. (Chapter 3)

political geography The study of spatial and ecological aspects of political behavior, from nationalism and the independent country to voting patterns, sectionalism, and regional separatism. (Chapter 4)

polyglot Characterized by many different languages. (Chapter 5)

polytheism The worship of many gods. (Chapter 6)

popular culture A dynamic culture based in large, heterogeneous societies permitting considerable individualism, innovation, and change; having a money-based economy, division of labor into professions, secular institutions of control, and weak interpersonal ties; producing and consuming machine-made goods. (Chapters 7 and 8)

population density The number of people in an area of land, usually expressed as people per square mile or people per square kilometer. (Chapter 2)

population explosion The rapid, accelerating increase in world population since about 1650 and especially since 1900. (Chapter 2)

population geography The study of spatial differences in the distribution, density, and demographic types of people. (Chapter 2)

population pyramid A bar graph used to show the age and sex composition of a population. (Chapter 2)

possibilism The school of thought based on the belief that humans, rather than the physical environment, are the primary active force; that any environment offers a number of different possible ways for a culture to develop; and that the choices among these possibilities are guided by cultural heritage. (Chapter 1)

postindustrial phase The way of life produced by dominance of the tertiary, quaternary, and quinary sectors of economic activity. (Chapter 12)

preadaptation A complex of adaptive traits and skills possessed in advance of migration by a group, giving them survival ability and competitive advantage in occupying the new environment. (Chapters 2 and 9)

primary industries Industries engaged in the extraction of natural resources, such as agriculture, lumbering, and mining. (Chapter 12)

primate city A city of large size and dominant power within a country. (Chapter 10)

proselytic religion A religion that actively seeks converts and has the goal of converting all humankind. (Chapter 6)

push-and-pull factors Unfavorable, repelling conditions and favorable, attractive conditions that interact to affect migration and other elements of diffusion. (Chapter 2)

quaternary industry The producer-oriented service sector of industry; includes business services such as trade, insurance, banking, advertising, research, and wholesaling. (Chapter 12)

quinary industry The consumer-oriented service sector of industry; includes services such as health, education, government, retailing, tourism, and recreational facilities. (Chapter 12)

raison d'être In French, literally "reason for being"; the main unifying force within a country, the principle basis of nationalism. (Chapter 4)

ranching Commercial raising of herd livestock, on a large landholding. (Chapter 3)

range In central-place theory, the average maximum distance people will travel to purchase a good or service. (Chapter 10)

red-lining A practice by banks and mortgage companies of demarcating areas considered to be high risk for housing loans. (Chapter 11)

region A grouping of like places or the functional union of places to form a spatial unit; see also *culture region.* (Chapter 1)

relic boundary A former political border, no longer functioning as a boundary. (Chapter 4)

religion A social system involving a set of beliefs and practices through which people seek harmony with the universe and attempt to influence the forces of nature, life, and death. (Chapter 6)

relocation diffusion The spread of an innovation or other element of culture that occurs with the bodily relocation (migration) of an individual or group that has the idea. (Chapter 1)

renewable resources Resources that are not depleted if wisely used, such as forests, water, fishing grounds, and agricultural land. (Chapter 12)

restrictive covenants Statements written into property deeds that in some ways restrict the use of the land; often used to prohibit certain groups of people from buying property. (Chapter 11)

return migration Involves migrants who eventually return to their place or region of origin. (Chapter 9)

rimland The maritime fringe of a country or continent; in particular, the western, southern, and eastern edges of the Eurasian continent. (Chapter 4)

sacred space An area recognized by a religious group as worthy of devotion, loyalty, esteem, or fear, or the extent that it becomes sought out, avoided, inaccessible to the nonbeliever, and/or removed from economic use. (Chapter 6)

satellite state A small, weak country dominated by one powerful neighbor to the extent that some or much of its independence is lost. (Chapter 4)

secondary industries Industries engaged in processing raw materials into finished products; manufacturing. (Chapter 12)

sector model An economic model that depicts a city as a series of pie-shaped wedges. (Chapter 11)

sedentary cultivation Farming in fixed and permanent fields. (Chapter 3)

sex ratio The numerical ratio of males to females in a population. (Chapter 2)

shatter belt A zone of great cultural complexity containing many small cultural groups. (Chapter 5)

shifting cultivation A type of agriculture characterized by land rotation, in which temporary clearings are used for several years and then abandoned to be replaced by new clearings; also known as slash-and-burn agriculture. (Chapter 3)

simplification, cultural The process by which immigrant ethnic groups lose certain aspects of their traditional culture in the process of settling overseas, creating a new culture that is less complex than the old. (Chapter 9)

site, urban The local setting of a city. (Chapter 10)

situation, urban The regional setting of a city. (Chapter 10)

social culture region An area in a city where many of the residents share social traits such as income, education, and stage of life. (Chapter 11)

social science The branch of learning that seeks to apply the scientific method to the study of humankind, seeking universal principles, theories, and laws of behavior, often through the use of mathematics. (Chapter 1)

space A term used to connote the objective, quantitative, nomothetic, theoretical, model-based, economic-oriented type of geography that seeks to understand spatial systems and networks through application of the principles of social science. (Chapter 1)

spatial distribution The arangement of a particular landscape feature or features throughout a unit of space. (Chapter 10)

state church A church designated by the government as the official, legal faith in a country, usually receiving financial support from the government. (Chapter 6)

stimulus diffusion When a specific trait fails to diffuse but the underlying idea or concept is accepted. (Chapter 1)

subsistence agriculture Farming to supply the minimum food and materials necessary to survive. (Chapter 3)

suitcase farm In American commercial grain agriculture, a farm on which no one lives, planting and harvesting is done by hired migratory crews. (Chapter 3)

supranational organization Group of independent countries joined together for purposes of mutual interest. (Chapter 4)

survey pattern A pattern of original land survey in an area. (Chapter 3)

sustainability Achieved when an adaptive strategy of land use does not destroy the habitat, allowing generation after generation to continue to live there. (Chapters 2 and 3)

technopole A center of high-tech manufacturing and information-based quaternary industry. (Chapter 12)

teleology A philosophy proposing that the Earth was created specifically as the abode for humans, that the Earth belongs to humans by divine intention. (Chapter 6)

territoriality The tendency of humans, perhaps instinctual, to seek control of portions of the earth's surface. (Chapter 4)

tertiary industry A service sector of industry; includes transportation, communications, and utilities. (Chapters 10 and 12)

theocracy A government guided by a religion. (Chapter 6)

threshold The population required to make provision of services economically feasible. (Chapter 10)

time-distance decay The decrease in acceptance of a cultural innovation with increasing time and distance from its origin. (Chapter 1)

topical geography The division of geographical subject matter into topics, such as agricultural geography, rather than into regions. (Chapter 1)

topocide The deliberate killing of a place through industrial expansion and change, so that its earlier landscape and character are destroyed. (Chapter 12)

toponym A place-name, usually consisting of two parts, the generic and the specific. (Chapter 5)

topophilia Literally "love of place," a term describing the strong sense of place identity among certain peoples. (Chapter 1)

trade-route site A place for a city that is at a significant point on transportation routes. (Chapter 10)

uneven development The tendency for industry to develop in a core/periphery pattern, enriching industrialized countries of the core and impoverishing the less industrialized periphery. (Chapter 12)

urban hearth areas The five regions—Mesopotamia, the Nile Valley, Pakistan's Indus Valley, China's Yellow River area, and Mesoamerica—where the world's first cities evolved. (Chapter 10)

urbanized population The proportion of a country's population living in cities. (Chapter 10)

urban morphology The form and structure of cities, including street patterns and the size and shape of buildings. (Chapter 10)

vernacular culture region A region perceived to exist by its inhabitants; based in the collective spatial perception of the population at large; bearing a generally accepted name or nickname. (Chapters 1, 8)

weight-gaining product A product in which weight is added to the raw materials in the manufacturing process. (Chapter 12)

zero population growth A stabilized population created when the average of only two children per couple survives to adulthood, so that, eventually, the number of deaths equals the number of births. (Chapter 2)

Credits

Unless otherwise acknowledged, all photographs are the property of Scott, Foresman and Company. Page abbreviations are as follows: (T)top, (C)center, (B)bottom, (L)left, (R)right.

Terry G. Jordan photographs on pages 5(br), 5(bl), 8, 27, 31(l) , 63(l), 63(r), 76, 77, 91, 93, 103, 108, 120, 123, 135, 136, 160(t), 161, 189, 192, 200, 201, 207, 218, 222, 232, 233, 234, 243, 244, 249, 264-267, 269, 270, 278(br), 279, 289, 300, 304, 309, 310(t), 323, 325, 342, 346, 347, 462, 464, 469, 482, 483(t).
Page 2: Randy Wells/Tony Stone Images
Page 5(t): German Information Center
Page 6: German Information Center
Page 15: Stigi Hagerstrand
Page 24: Pete Tarner/Image Bank
Page 26: Grant Heilman/Grant Heilman Photography`
Page 29: Steve Vidler/Leo de Wys, Inc.
Page 31(r): Rafael Marcia/Photo Researchers
Page 36(2): Tom Wagner/Odyssey Productions
Page 40: Porterfield/Chickering/Photo Researchers
Page 48: Culver Pictures Inc.
Page 84: Roger Du Buisson/Stock Market
Page 88: Helene Trembly/Families of the World
Page 89: Carol Purcell/Photo Researchers
Page 92: Simon Wilkinson/Image Bank
Page 95: Stacy Pick/Stock Boston
Page 96: Norm Thomas/Photo Researchers
Page 99: University of California, Berkeley
Page 116: Corbis/Bettmann
Page 118: Harvey Lloyd/Peter Arnold, Inc.
Page 121: Van Phillips/Leo de Wys, Inc.
Page 128: Chuck Nacke/Woodfin Camp & Associates
Page 149: Courtesy Geoffrey J. Martin
Page 151: Abbas/Magnum Photos
Page 160(br): Martin Wendler/Peter Arnold, Inc.
Page 160(bl): Richard Kalvar/Magnum Photos
Page 162: David R. Frazier Photolibrary
Page 166: Philip & Karen Smith/Tony Stone Images
Page 174: University of Michigan
Page 182: Charlie Ott/Photo Researchers
Page 198: Wendy Stone/Odyssey Productions
Page 217(b): Antoinette Jongen
Page 220: Courtesy Geoffrey J. Martin
Page 240: John Elk/Tony Stone Images
Page 247: Greg Walker

Page 255: Martin Rogers/Stock Boston
Page 259: Earl Palmer/Monkmeyer Press Photo Service, Inc.
Page 260: Dean Abramson/Stock Boston
Page 274: Kevin Horan/Tony Stone Images
Page 276(br): Michael Quackenbush/Image Bank
Page 276(tr): Alvis Upitis/Image Bank
Page 276(l): Bill Bachman/Photo Researchers
Page 278(tr): David R. Frazier/Photo Researchers
Page 278(l): Donald Dietz/Stock Boston
Page 292: Van Bucher/Photo Researchers
Page 293: John P. Kelly/Image Bank
Page 297(b): Peter Menzel/Stock Boston
Page 297(t): Focus on Sports, Inc.
Page 298: Jose Carrillo/PhotoEdit
Page 299: A. Nusca/Liaison (Gamma)
Page 310(br): Cameramann International, Ltd.
Page 310(bl): Carroll Seghers/Photo Researchers
Page 314: Cathy Melloan/Tony Stone Images
Page 350: Superstock, Inc.
Page 353(b): Bruno Zehnder/Peter Arnold, Inc.
Page 353(tr): Earl Young/Tony Stone Images
Page 353(l): Najlah Feaney/SABA Press Photos, Inc.
Page 362: Malcolm Kirk/Peter Arnold, Inc.
Page 365: Steve Proeh/Image Bank
Page 366: James Hanley/Photo Researchers
Page 372: Ulrike Welsch/Photo Researchers
Page 375: Porterfield/Chickering/Photo Researchers
Page 376: Photo Researchers
Page 377: Jeff Greenberg/Photo Researchers
Page 378: Don Sparks/Image Bank
Page 382: Corbis/Bettmann
Page 383: Archive Photos
Page 385: Walter Jimenez/TexStock Photo Inc.
Page 390: M. Bertinetti/Photo Researchers
Page 393(r): Cameramann International, Ltd.
Page 393(l): Cameramann International, Ltd.
Page 394: Owen Franken/Stock Boston
Page 398: Photo Researchers
Page 399: Henryk Kaiser/Leo de Wys, Inc.
Page 400: Courtesy Geoffrey J. Martin
Page 406: Peter Peterson/Tony Stone Images
Page 409, 418, 419, 425: Cameramann International, Ltd.
Page 429(b): Lee Snider/Image Works
Page 429(t): The Daily Herald
Page 431: Cameramann International, Ltd.
Page 438: Steve Dunwell/Image Bank
Page 439: Spencer Grant/Monkmeyer Press Photo Service, Inc.
Page 442: Mona Domosh
Page 445: Michael Melford/Image Bank
Page 446: Donna Faranda
Page 447: Ulrike Welsch/Photo Researchers
Page 448: Mona Domosh
Page 452: David R. Frazier Photolibrary
Page 454: Santi Visalli/Image Bank
Page 470: Vanessa Vick/Photo Researchers
Page 473: Judy Canty/Stock Boston
Page 483(b): Farrell Greshan/Photo Researchers
Page 488: E. R. I. M./Tony Stone Images
Page 491: Sylvain Grandadam/Photo Researchers
Page 496: Kay Chernush/Image Bank
Page 499(bl): Peter Beck/Stock Market
Page 499: Fred George/Tony Stone Images

Index

The Independent States of the World

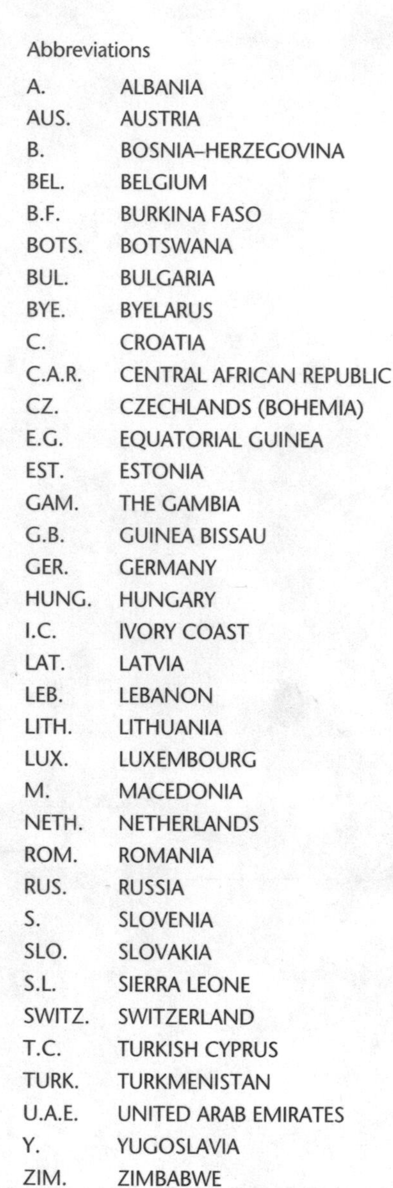

Abbreviations

A. ALBANIA
AUS. AUSTRIA
B. BOSNIA–HERZEGOVINA
BEL. BELGIUM
B.F. BURKINA FASO
BOTS. BOTSWANA
BUL. BULGARIA
BYE. BYELARUS
C. CROATIA
C.A.R. CENTRAL AFRICAN REPUBLIC
CZ. CZECHLANDS (BOHEMIA)
E.G. EQUATORIAL GUINEA
EST. ESTONIA
GAM. THE GAMBIA
G.B. GUINEA BISSAU
GER. GERMANY
HUNG. HUNGARY
I.C. IVORY COAST
LAT. LATVIA
LEB. LEBANON
LITH. LITHUANIA
LUX. LUXEMBOURG
M. MACEDONIA
NETH. NETHERLANDS
ROM. ROMANIA
RUS. RUSSIA
S. SLOVENIA
SLO. SLOVAKIA
S.L. SIERRA LEONE
SWITZ. SWITZERLAND
T.C. TURKISH CYPRUS
TURK. TURKMENISTAN
U.A.E. UNITED ARAB EMIRATES
Y. YUGOSLAVIA
ZIM. ZIMBABWE